MVFO

# I Am Innocent!

# BOOKS BY JAY ROBERT NASH

## FICTION

On All Fronts
A Crime Story
The Dark Fountain
The Mafia Diaries

## NON-FICTION

Dillinger: Dead or Alive?
Citizen Hoover
Bloodletters and Badmen
Hustlers and Conmen
Darkest Hours
Among the Missing
Murder, America
Almanac of World Crime
Look for the Woman
People to See
The True Crime Quiz Book
The Innovators
Zanies: The World's Greatest Eccentrics
The Crime Movie Quiz Book
Murder Among the Mighty
Open Files: The World's Greatest
   Unsolved Crimes
The Toughest Movie Quiz Book Ever

The Dillinger Dossier
Jay Robert Nash's Crime Chronology
Encyclopedia of Organized Crime
Encyclopedia of 20th Century Murder
Encyclopedia of Western Lawmen and
   Outlaws
Crime Dictionary
Spies
Terrorism in the 20th Century

## POETRY

Lost Natives & Expatriates

## THEATER

The Way Back
Outside the Gates
1947 (Last Rites for the Boys)

## MULTI-VOLUME REFERENCE WORKS

The Motion Picture Guide (17 volumes)
Encyclopedia of World Crime (8
   volumes)
The Great Pictorial History of World
   Crime (2 volumes)

# *I Am Innocent!*

A Comprehensive Encyclopedic
History of the World's
Wrongly Convicted Persons

## Jay Robert Nash

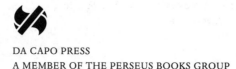

DA CAPO PRESS
A MEMBER OF THE PERSEUS BOOKS GROUP

Set in 10 point Dante by the Perseus Books Group

Cataloging-in-Publication Data for this book is available from the Library
of Congress.

ISBN-13: 978-0-306-81560-7

Published by Da Capo Press
A Member of the Perseus Books Group
http://www.dacapopress.com

Da Capo Press books are available at special discounts for bulk purchase in
the U.S. by corporations, institutions, and other organizations. For more
information, please contact the Special Markets Department at the Perseus
Books Group, 2300 Chestnut Street, Suite 200, Philadelphia, PA 19103, or
call (800) 810-4145, extension 5000, or e-mail
special.markets@perseusbooks.com

1 2 3 4 5 6 7 8 9

*This book is for my son,*
*Jay Robert Nash IV*

# Contents

# Acknowledgments

My deep appreciation goes to my researchers, Cathy Edens and Jay Robert Nash IV, who worked so diligently with me on this work. I am also indebted to the wonderful cooperation of Elizabeth Webster, communications associate of the Innocence Project in New York, as well as directors Barry C. Scheck and Peter J. Neufeld, who allowed me to use many of the illustrations that appear in this work, along with Rob Warden, executive director of the Center on Wrongful Convictions at Northwestern University, his assistant and photographer Jennifer Linzer, and photographer Loren Santow, who also provided many images. All images not otherwise attributed to these sources were provided by History, Inc./Jay Robert Nash Collection. Too numerous to mention here, I am also grateful for the cooperation of several hundred scrupulous police officials and criminal justice attorneys (both prosecutors and defenders) in major metropolitan areas worldwide, who provided documents, correspondence, and interviews, and many news media persons, who shared their views and information with me on scores of wrongful convictions.

# *Introduction*

IN WHAT I BELIEVE TO BE THE MOST COMPRE-
hensive work ever produced on the subject,
this volume includes more than a thousand
wrongful conviction cases. The celebrated judicial
victims of deep history can be found in the pages
of this book, including Joan of Arc, Thomas More,
and Mary, Queen of Scots. The persecution ma-
nias of the Inquisition and the Salem witchcraft
trials are depicted in detail, as are cause célèbre
cases dealing with the Haymarket Riot in Chicago,
Alfred Dreyfus of France, Leo Max Frank of Georgia, and the Scottsboro Boys of Alabama. All manner of wrongful convictions are portrayed,
including the framing of labor leaders Tom
Mooney and Warren Billings in 1916, the railroading of bootlegger Roger "The Terrible" Touhy in
1934, and the flagrant setup convictions of Peter
Limone and three others in 1968, who went to
prison for Boston murders committed by the
Mafia and condoned by the FBI.

To be sure, hundreds of cases included represent the most obscure and unknown defendants,
as should be expected from judicial systems that
randomly and irresponsibly convict and imprison
the innocent with the guilty. In the annals of
recorded history, the numbers of wrongly convicted constitute countless legions. Over centuries, the oppressive regimes of dictators
routinely produced wrongful convictions. Little
or no recourse was left to the accused of those
dark eras, other than the whimsical mercy of
tyrants. With the coming of open and democratic
societies and the establishment of police and judicial systems came the concept of justice under the
law. Pioneers of these systems defined the law,
which saw constant refinement and reform over
the centuries, but ever present inside the core of
these systems human error lurked and corruption
loomed.

Justice, like the coveted Holy Grail, is an elusive
and fragile goal, compromised in endless betrayals
by the venal and the vindictive, where one
wrongly convicted person after another has been
sent to prison, even to execution. In the modern
era, with its burgeoning population, police and judicial systems have been swamped with increasing
crime and subsequent trials. In the nineteenth century England was so overwhelmed by this problem that it shipped thousands of miscreants en
masse to its new territory, Australia, an entire continent that served as a penal colony.

By the twentieth century, meting out justice became an industry—a production line made up of
massive police forces in major metropolitan areas,
constituting tens of thousands of officers in London, Paris, New York, Chicago, Los Angeles, Mexico City, and Tokyo to confront and combat the
burgeoning crime rates of those cities. The judicial process responded by creating armies of prosecutors and defenders.

Injustice for the wrongly convicted has always begun at the front end of the system—the police. Although every police department, large or small, has its criteria of ethical conduct, many of its rank-and-file members abandoned those ethics early for the sake of salary raises, promotions, and favored positions. The police departments of most major cities in nineteenth-century America were flush with corruption, beginning with the ambitious beat cop, who viewed the indigent, the immigrant, the disenfranchised, the impoverished, the mentally retarded, and racial minorities as his exclusive victims. (For graphic examples of police coercion of mentally retarded suspects, see Chapter V, "Conviction by Coercion," for the 1975 murder case of Robert Wilkinson in Philadelphia, the 1986 murder case of Johnny Lee Wilson in Aurora, Missouri, and the 1994 rape case of Christopher Prince in Culpeper, Virginia.)

Then as today, the police officer selected the most vulnerable of suspects in bringing about an easy arrest, assisted by equally ambitious prosecutors seeking convictions to achieve status and power. To be sure, there were and are scrupulous police officers and prosecutors, but they are woefully in the minority. Serpico proved that.

Almost all prosecutors in the United States are graduates of law schools that require courses in ethics, usually in the second year of a three-year course of study. By any dictionary's definition, the word "ethic" means "the discipline of dealing with what is good and bad and with moral duty and obligation." The intellectual applications of the law, however, are thus less defined, allowing for ambiguity in cases, where, in the eyes of many officers of the court, truth is not as significant as effective convictions, and honesty becomes the lickspittle to expeditious imprisonments.

Police are initially responsible for most wrongful convictions, as they have used fabricated evidence, perjury, and every manner of coercion, from beatings to threats of death, to bring about misidentifications and false confessions, which have largely contributed to wrongful convictions.

Chicago police, with a long recorded history of brutality when interrogating suspects, exacted a confession from Earl Heywood Pugh in 1936 after using him as target practice at a police firing range (see Chapter II). Officers have routinely threatened to jail loved ones if a suspect does not confess. For instance, police interrogating Stanford Fewell, after holding him fourteen days without counsel in 1952, for a Birmingham, Alabama, murder in 1949, threatened to charge his ailing mother with the crime and jail her unless he confessed, which he did, in order to save his mother's life. He thought she would die behind bars without medical attention (see Chapter V). Often enough, police have the aid of polygraph (lie detector) operators, who frame their questions in such a way as to prompt admissions of guilt from respondents. Psychiatrists and psychologists working with police have used subtle coercion through autosuggestion and other psychological methods to extract confessions. One psychiatrist promised a suspect, Camilo Weston Leyra Jr., charged with a 1950 New York murder, that his sinus problems would go away if he confessed (see Chapter V).

In 1996, Richard Bingham confessed to raping and murdering seventeen-year-old Jessica Baggen in Sitka, Alaska, but, at his trial, he was acquitted after DNA positively excluded him from being a donor of the spermatozoa found on the victim. Forensic experts also stated that the hair found on the victim had not come from him nor did the lone fingerprint found on a package of cigarettes found at the crime scene match those of Bingham. Jurors viewing the tape of Bingham's "confession" easily determined that he was being coached and prodded into admissions by police since he had to be fed details about the location of the body, unusual properties of the physical scene where the body had been discovered and the unusual modus operandi employed to silence the victim.

In their obsessive ambition to achieve arrests and convictions, police have routinely preyed upon gullible and impressionable children. Typical was the Crowe case. On the night of January 20,

1998, Michael Crowe, who lived with his parents and twelve-year-old sister in an upscale Escondido, California home, accompanied by another friend, reportedly crept into his sister's room and stabbed her nine times in the chest and neck with a ten-inch hunting knife. The reason for the killing was later attributed to sibling rivalry. Stephanie Crowe was an exceptional student and had been named volunteer of the year at the local library.

Stephanie Crowe was the center of attention in the family, and it was theorized that her brother, Michael, who kept to himself in his room reading about medieval torture and O.J. Simpson (stacks of articles about the Simpson murders were later found in his room), nursed a "pure hatred" for his sister, one so deep and passionate that he decided to murder her. The words "kill, kill," were later found written in pencil on the window sill of Stephanie's room. The handwriting was thought to be that of Michael Crowe.

Fatally stabbed about midnight, Stephanie nevertheless had the strength to slip from her bed and crawl to the open door of her bedroom, where she was found the next morning. When police arrived, they questioned Michael, who did not appear to be distraught over the death of his sister. He claimed he knew nothing about the murder, although he admitted waking up about 4:30 A.M. to go into the kitchen, which would have taken him past the body of his sister.

Fourteen-year-old Michael and two of his friends, Joshua Treadway and Aaron Houser, were charged with the murder. One of the friends told interrogators that Michael said, on the night of the murder, "I'd love to kill my sister." The friend reportedly replied, "Well, if you're serious about that, I'd be happy to help you." While one of the boys stood lookout, Michael and his other friend crept into Stephanie's room and Michael stabbed his sister to death, according to a police conclusion.

A probation officer later told Superior Court Judge Laura Palmer that Michael had told her, "There's a chance that I didn't do this, but it's pos-

sible I did do it. I guess I'm almost sure that I didn't do it, almost 100 percent sure."

Michael's parents and those of the other two boys stood by the defendants while they were detained in a juvenile center, none of them willing to believe that the boys enacted the heinous crime. The slaying was part of a rare occurrence in family-related homicides, according to a 1994 Department of Justice report, *Murder in Families*. The department reported that only 1.5 percent of the 20,000 annual family killings in the United States involve sibling murders. That percentage was maintained in subsequent reports from the department.

During the trial proceedings against Michael Crowe and Treadway, who both confessed to the killing, all charges were dropped, the court ruling that the confessions from the boys had been coerced by police officers. It was determined that the police had repeatedly lied to the boys in order to entrap them into confessing, an acceptable legal tactic, but they had illegally promised both leniency if they confessed, and this was outright coercion. Defense attorney Mary Ellen Attridge had relentlessly claimed that the police had illegally obtained confessions from both boys, stating, "They're not confessions. They're false. They're lies and they were manufactured out of whole and coercive cloth by the police department." After six months behind bars, the two boys were released.

Moreover, a new suspect had been found—Richard Tuite, whose shirt bore the blood of Stephanie Crowe, according to prosecutors. Tuite had been a suspect almost immediately after the murder. Neighbors had reported that he had been knocking on doors and asking for the whereabouts of a girl named Tracy Nelson. Police questioned Tuite at the time but dismissed the notion that he might be the killer. He was a drug-taking drifter and a decided schizophrenic, according to analysts, and was incapable of committing the brutal murder.

A month after the Crowe killing, Tuite was arrested for following two young girls off a bus. He was released but arrested again in March 1998, caught while trying to break into a trailer home in Oceanside, California. He was convicted and sent to prison for three years. In 2000, Tuite escaped from a halfway house in Ontario but was recaptured and sent back to prison, his sentence extended after he was caught with a knife. A short time before his scheduled prison release in 2002, Tuite was arrested and charged with the Crowe murder.

Tuite stood trial for more than three months in San Diego before Judge Fredric Link. Prosecutors convinced a jury that its DNA evidence proved that three drops of blood from Stephanie Crowe was on one of the defendant's shirts. In his summation, special assistant attorney general David Druliner told the jury that Tuite was on a "relentless and persistent" search for a girl named Tracy, and that he crept into the darkened Crowe home where he mistakenly and repeatedly stabbed the Crowe girl through a thin comforter covering her, believing he was murdering a girl named Tracy.

The thirty-two-year-old Tuite was convicted on May 26, 2004, of voluntary manslaughter, instead of first-degree or second-degree murder. The jury was convinced that he killed the girl without premeditation or malice. Tuite was sentenced to the maximum term of thirteen years in prison. Meanwhile, Crowe, Treadway, and Houser, the three teenagers from whom police had extracted ironclad "confessions" in the murder, had been set free.

When suspects prove too truculent to confess, prosecutors often rely on jailhouse snitches to provide manufactured confessions. Usually convicted felons seeking reduced sentences, these informants provide perjured testimony against the accused, claiming to have heard a confession while occupying jail or prison cells with the defendant then awaiting trial. Codefendants or actual perpetrators have been routinely given minor sentences in plea bargain arrangements with prosecutors if they turn state's evidence, and inform on their fellow perpetrator, who, in many instances, was innocent of committing the crime. Others

responsible for a crime have simply framed an innocent person by claiming that person to be the chief offender in order to receive a lighter sentence. In many such cases, the innocent person has been sentenced to death, while the actual perpetrator was given a lighter sentence that would see eventual parole.

The rationale of too many prosecutors was mirrored in the career of Robert H. Macy, who was the district attorney for Oklahoma County for twenty-one years, sending seventy-three persons to death row—more than any other prosecutor in the United States. Twenty of them were executed. Macy said publicly that executing an innocent person is a sacrifice worth making in order to keep capital punishment in the United States (see Curtis McCarty case, Chronology, 1986).

Prosecutors, assistant district attorneys, and district attorneys have emulated Macy's wrongheaded perspectives and policies, later becoming judges, in numbers too high to itemize. Many of those judges, as former prosecutors, reached their end goal—the security and the authority of the bench—on the backs of wrongly convicted persons. Most show no remorse for the wrongful convictions they brought about, and a few, when confronted with their wrongful convictions, blame others—the police, eyewitnesses, their own aides—anyone but their black-robed selves.

Many of these same arbiters of justice continue to aid in such wrongful convictions by disallowing evidence and logical arguments from the defense, refusing adequate time and defense money for defense investigations and expert testimony, improperly instructing juries, and allowing all sorts of prejudicial statements, questionable evidence, or suspicious testimony to send an innocent person behind bars. Some have worked in collusion with prosecutors to provide perjured statements from jailhouse informants. Many are ignorant of the law itself and some are illiterate, mendacious, and, out of sloth, indifference or arrogance, as culpable as the actual perpetrator in allowing that perpetrator to frame or railroad an innocent defendant.

As one criminal judge (thankfully deceased) told the author, "Don't try my patience with your lofty ideas about justice. My only concern is to put as many of these people as possible in prison. If some felon can help seal a verdict through his testimony, so be it. The public wants convictions and the harsher the sentences the better. If a national referendum on capital punishment was held today, you'd see more than 75 percent of the public demanding that we put people convicted of murder to death. We give the lady what she wants."

Aiding and abetting the unscrupulous police officer, the unethical prosecutor, and the self-aggrandizing jurist is the public itself, which has brought about the most wrongful number of convictions through eyewitness testimony. Mistaken identity, more than any other factor, has sent innocent persons to prison. In countless capital cases, witnesses have insisted that their identification of a suspect was "positive," yet many changed their testimony later when confronted with another suspect, or when overwhelming evidence, such as DNA, challenged their identifications.

Where most eyewitness misidentifications are made in honest error, many wrongful eyewitness identifications have been intentionally false (see Joseph Majczek, Chapter I) and made for ulterior reasons, while many other identifications have been viciously frivolous. In 1935, two girls identified Arthur O'Connell as having sexually attacked one of them in Boston but later stated that they had made up the accusations "for fun" (see Chronology, 1935). In 1976, Stefan Ivan Kiszko was sent to prison for life for murder on the testimony of three teenage girls who later recanted, saying that they had identified Kiszko as "a joke." (See Chronology, 1976.)

No identification system is infallible, including DNA, which can be intentionally or unintentionally corrupted, misinterpreted, or misrepresented. Forensic "experts" such as Joyce Gilchrist, Pamela Fish, and Fred Zain (see Chapter XV), to name a few, have been exposed as presenting false or incomplete forensic evidence in many capital cases

where scores of innocent persons went to prison, some sentenced to death.

Fingerprints, since their universal adoption as the chief identification system in the early part of the twentieth century, have proven reliable. But they can be planted or forged, or they can exist at a crime scene because they've been left by a suspect before the crime occurs. Such was the case for Anibal Jaramillo-Restrepo, who had left his fingerprints at a murder scene in Miami, Florida, because he had been doing odd jobs at that location before a 1980 killing (see Chronology, 1981). Fingerprints may also be inadvertently left after a crime has occurred; in 1977, Anthony Ray Peek entered a murdered victim's car in Winter Haven, Florida, the day after the victim had been killed, leaving his fingerprints behind (see Chronology, 1978).

Other forensic sciences—pathology, serology, ballistics, hair and fiber analysis—have established the guilt of many a true malefactor, but, to a lesser and still important degree, have wrongly sent innocent persons to prison through technical mistakes, human error, and even purposeful false analyses. (See Chapter VIII, "Forensic Science to the Rescue.") As this book shows chapter by chapter, many other wrongful procedures and methods have sent myriad innocent persons to prison—suppression of evidence, insufficient evidence, coercion, false confessions, perjured testimony, imaginary crimes, prejudicial publicity, and rampant misconduct by police, prosecutors, and forensic professionals. Just how many innocent persons are sent to prison each year in the United States alone can only be estimated through rough figures.

Of the more than 2 million people incarcerated in state and federal prisons in the United States at this writing, almost all claim to be innocent. Given the recent increase of released persons convicted of capital crimes and officially pardoned (not paroled) for those crimes—chiefly as a result of DNA evidence, which has brought about dozens of exonerations in the last decade—it is reasonable to believe that many more prison inmates may also be the victims of wrongful convictions. Philadelphia attorney Herbert L. Maris, who specialized in wrongful convictions in the mid-twentieth century and brought about the exonerations of more than five hundred persons during his spectacular fifty-year career, believed that, in his time, 20 percent of all prison inmates were innocent persons who had, for one reason or another, been wrongfully convicted.

By comparing Maris's standard to the present prison population, more than 400,000 innocent persons are presently behind bars. The most conservative estimates by some contemporary sources claim that between 1 and 2 percent of the present prison population consists of innocent persons, which still yields a staggering number of wrongly convicted persons—between 20,000 and 40,000 victims—equaling a population of any midsize town in America or the total number of effectives in a small army during the American Civil War.

This work also describes convictions that were reversed on technical grounds having to do with judicial misconduct by the judge or the prosecutors, which brought about acquittals. The prison releases resulting from subsequent retrials seeking acquittals of such persons do not necessarily prove the actual innocence of the accused, only that they were officially recognized as being wrongly convicted in a faulty judicial system.

The system can be corrected in many ways. For instance, to improve accuracy in cases where convictions through eyewitness identification is the main evidence, this being the largest contributor to wrongful convictions, police officers conducting photo array and live lineup identifications should be neutral. Such officers should not know the identification of the suspect in order to avoid the police misconduct of coaching, guiding, or directing witnesses in making any kind of identification.

Beyond the appeals process, what is also needed is the establishment of a federal organization that constitutes a severe and exacting monitoring system, not dissimilar to the internal affairs divisions of any police department, to regularly review and question each and every conviction of a capital crime. That organization would verify all testimony—and this means significantly interviewing all witnesses once again—and closely reexamine all evidence originally presented in any case.

Without such authoritative review, the cries, pleas, and prayers for the reform of a police and judicial system that ignores honest and upright police criteria and ethical prosecution procedures are hollow and ineffective. Such an organization would greatly improve the system, if not create a perfect one, and bring about a more precise method of protecting the innocent. Beyond that, at the last gate, still stands the same sentinel—the vigilant and conscientious individual and private organization (such as the courageous Innocence Project), the only watch that ends the night for every wrongly convicted person.

—Jay Robert Nash
Chicago, 2008

# *Fighting for Justice*

## The Press

THE SEARCH FOR TRUTH AND THE ESTAB-lishment of justice are nurtured and best achieved in a country with a free press. The ability to access government documents and information has resulted in countless victims of wrongful imprisonment being set free, but only through the tireless efforts of crusading members of that free press. Getting information, even in a free country, is invariably fraught with obstacles and obfuscation. The uncloaking of that information, usually hidden for political or personal reasons, has exposed the rot of collusion, conspiracy, and corruption at the core of most wrongful convictions.

The inherent problem with the press investigating such cases is that reporters deal with the same people from whom they acquire routine information—police and government officials. Such relationships have always been tenuous and sensitive to injury and even permanent damage. When these relationships are disrupted through investigative searches, the normal flow of information from those officials is often severed. Hostility replaces cordiality and cooperation. They become adversaries, one struggling to reveal the facts in any given case, the other using the law, or the misuse of the law, to prevent the exposure of those facts. To acquire those facts, the press has often had to overcome and impeach the authority of self-serving officials, even though jealously guarded careers and reputations may be ruined in the process.

In turn, officials often retaliate, condemning the press as irresponsible and reckless in attacking the "good name" of a politician or police officer. Advertisers may be pressured to stop doing business with a crusading newspaper or periodical. Government may probe the financial or business operations of such publications. Police harassment, including imprisonment, bodily harm, or death threats, against members of the press—from publisher to lowly reporter—may ensue. These are the hazards faced by any member of the press attempting to prove the innocence of any imprisoned person. In any age and in any country, when a member of the press crusades for the freedom of an innocent person, there exists a bit of sacred earth on which truth and justice rest. It is the home of the brave.

## Alfred Dreyfus and Emile Zola

In the nineteenth century, a Frenchman resided there. He was a successful novelist who, in his declining years, lived with his family in comfort and ease. Gifted with an inspired imagination, this writer was the toast of France and every literary lion gave way before him. He was disinclined to participate in the political strife and turmoil of his country, but was content to pen romantic novels and enjoy the fruits of his labor. He was not an activist, a troublemaker, or a malcontent. However, in 1894, an obscure French officer was tried and convicted of treason and then sent to Devil's Island for life. This event altered the life of the writer forever, for he came to see the Dreyfus case as one of the world's greatest travesties of justice. It stirred in his old age the idealistic fires of his youth, embers that burst into white heat when he put pen to paper in a crusade to free a man he never met. The officer was Alfred Dreyfus and the writer was Emile Zola.

The Dreyfus affair involved a horrendous miscarriage of justice and brought shame and disgrace to the government of France. It was fraught with spies, counterspies, and political corruption so vast and venal that it took France's greatest men to expose France's greatest villains before the victim was grudgingly exonerated. The victim was Alfred Dreyfus, a French Jew born on October 9, 1859, in Mulhouse, Alsace, to a wealthy textile manufacturer. When Germany annexed Alsace in 1870 following the Franco-Prussian War, the Dreyfus family, preferring to remain French, moved to Paris. Two older brothers, Jacques and Mathieu, remained in Alsace to continue operating the lucrative family business.

Captain Alfred Dreyfus at the time he was wrongly convicted of treason in 1894, framed by members of the French general staff. *History Inc./Jay Robert Nash Collection.*

While his brothers operated their father's manufacturing plant, Alfred dreamed of becoming a soldier. A patriot devoted to France, he entered the Ecole polytechnique and became an artillery expert, graduating with the rank of lieutenant. Dreyfus was assigned to the Fourteenth Regiment of Artillery in 1880. He was promoted to first lieutenant and married Lucie Hadomard in 1889. The marriage produced two children.

Dreyfus proved to be a conscientious officer. He lived better than most army officers by supplementing his pay with income from his father's business. Promoted to the rank of captain, Dreyfus underwent rigorous training, after being nominated to the staff college, l'Ecole supérieure de guerre. He finished the challenging two-year course with honors, graduating third in his class. But his dossier included an anti-Semitic remark made by a racist French general, who expressed concern over the presence of a Jew on the French general staff.

The biased remark was ignored and Dreyfus was appointed to the general staff on January 1, 1893. He served a year of probation and was deemed a model officer. At this time, members of the general staff learned that information on certain French fortifications and newly created French weapons had fallen into the hands of the Germans.

This information was supplied by a French spy, Madame Bastian, who worked as a maid at the German embassy in Paris. She had reportedly taken a document from the wastebasket next to the desk of Lieutenant Colonel Maximilian von Schwartzkoppen, military attaché at the German embassy in Paris. This memorandum, or *bordereau*, found its way into the hands of Major Hubert Henry of the statistical section of the Deuxieme, the French intelligence bureau. Henry took the *bordereau*, which was unsigned and had been torn into four pieces, to the general staff.

Officers studying the document concluded that, since it contained information on French artillery emplacements, the *bordereau* had been written by someone on the general staff who was an artillery expert. Suspicion quickly focused on Captain Dreyfus, not out of any logical conviction or evidence but out of envy, peevishness, and bigotry. Officers came forward to denounce Dreyfus as a traitor and a spy for Germany. These officers disliked the accused because they found him to be humorless or distant, because he socialized only with his family or a few friends, or, mostly, because he was a Jew.

So-called handwriting experts then stated that Dreyfus had written the *bordereau*. When it was pointed out that Dreyfus's handwriting differed completely from that of the memorandum, the experts nodded yes, exactly. Dreyfus, the experts insisted, knew he was writing a document that might later prove him to be a German spy and therefore disguised his handwriting.

Dreyfus, utterly confused, was arrested on October 15, 1894. He was imprisoned and an order signed by General Auguste Mercier charged him with high treason. His court-martial occurred on December 19–22, 1894. The proceedings constituted nothing more than a kangaroo court; Dreyfus's guilt had been predetermined by a cabal of French officers who hated Jews, the worst of these being the head of the court, General Mercier. Major Henry testified that a "person of integrity," whom he would not name because of national security, had told him that Dreyfus was the traitor and the author of the infamous *bordereau*.

Contrary to French law, attorneys for Dreyfus were denied the right to examine the so-called evidence against their client, again under the flimsy excuse of protecting national security. The "evidence" that convicted Dreyfus was sealed in a envelope, which Major Armand du Paty de Clam turned over to the court. The court refused to disclose its contents. (Du Paty de Clam had dictated the contents of the memorandum to Dreyfus, had him write out the document and then used the wholly dissimilar writing of the two documents to claim that Dreyfus was the spy.) Dreyfus was sentenced to life imprisonment in "a fortified place" and was ordered to be publicly humiliated for betraying his country.

Thousands of anti-Semites paraded before government buildings and public places, encouraged by equally anti-Semitic French newspapers en-

The infamous "bordereau" or secret message Esterhazy wrote to his German spymasters, which was stolen by a French spy in the German Embassy in Paris, and which was attributed to Dreyfus. *History Inc./Jay Robert Nash Collection.*

raged over the fact that Dreyfus was not to be executed. For weeks, the anti-Semites paraded through the streets of Paris by torchlight, demanding that Dreyfus be killed. January 5, 1895, was the date scheduled for Dreyfus's public degradation.

Emaciated and sickly from sleepless nights in prison, Dreyfus was marched into a military square, where General Darras raised his sword to signal the beginning of the public humiliation: "Dreyfus—you are unworthy to wear the uniform! In the name of the French people, we deprive you of your rank!"

With that, a towering sergeant stepped before the convicted man and ripped away the gold braid epaulets from his uniform and the stripes from his trousers. Then he snatched away the hard-earned medals and decorations pinned on his coat. His kepi hat was snatched and the stripes on it torn away, as were the

Dreyfus, standing at right, hears the charges against him at his 1894 trial. *History Inc./Jay Robert Nash Collection.*

Following conviction, Dreyfus was publicly disgraced, insignias on his uniform stripped away and his sword broken. *History Inc./Jay Robert Nash Collection*

numbers on his high collar which signified his military unit. Even the brass buttons from his coat were pulled off. The final degradation came when the sergeant took away Dreyfus's sword, broke it over his knee, and threw it to the ground.

Dreyfus was then marched about the square. He finally found his voice and shouted, "In the name of my wife and my children, I swear that I am innocent! I swear it! Long live France! You are degrading an innocent man!" Dreyfus halted briefly before a group of newsmen, imploring, "You will say to the whole of France that I am innocent!"

Crowds hissing their hatred pressed against the high iron fence surrounding the courtyard. "Kill him!" came the shout. "Death to the traitor!" Shoulders bent, Dreyfus was ushered into a police van. On January 17, 1895, the cashiered Dreyfus was sent to Devil's Island off the coast of French Guiana, a barren rock that had once housed lepers.

Dreyfus lived in a small stone cottage with barred windows, a stockade fence about the small enclosure. Watched day and night, he was permitted to walk about a treeless half acre in the afternoons. The harsh climate and bad food made him ill; he suffered

The one-room stone cottage (shown surrounded by a barricade) in which Dreyfus was imprisoned on Devil's Island. *History Inc./Jay Robert Nash Collection.*

from fever, indigestion and dysentery. He had to live in silence, without visitors. Even his guards were not permitted to talk to him. This lonely, hapless man confined himself to writing long, passionate love letters to his wife. Even these simple expressions of affection for his wife and family were censored. To the French army, Alfred Dreyfus was a vile traitor not worthy of human consideration or kindness. He was to be ignored and forgotten, as if he were a corpse buried in an unmarked grave.

Only Dreyfus's family and a few close friends refused to forget him. They continued to believe him innocent. So did an officer who proved to be one of the bravest Frenchmen of them all. He was Lieutenant Colonel Georges Piquart (1854–1914), a member of the general staff who had been troubled by the entire Dreyfus affair. Since there were persistent rumors that Dreyfus had been railroaded, the general staff ordered Piquart to reopen the case, with an understanding that the investigation would affirm the conviction. The purpose of the investigation was to pacify protestors and quell growing suspicions that certain aspects of the Dreyfus case were questionable.

Piquart was a diligent, conscientious officer who took his duties seriously. Defying orders not to inspect certain documents too closely, Piquart examined the *bordereau* again and again, comparing it to the handwriting of several French officers. He determined with certainty that the author of the memorandum and the real traitor was Major Ferdinand Walsin Esterhazy (1847–1923). Piquart went to the general staff to report that Major Henry had instantly recognized the handwriting of the *bordereau* as that of Esterhazy, his close friend; to save Esterhazy, he had accused and helped frame the innocent Dreyfus.

Moreover, Piquart pointed out, long after Dreyfus had been sent to Devil's Island, French secrets had continued to flow to the Germans, which Piquart also proved. He offered in evidence handwriting samples of Esterhazy, which he had obtained in August 1896. Esterhazy's writing and that of the memorandum or *bordereau* were clearly identical.

Piquart's statements were like thunderbolts to his superiors, General R. C. F. de Boisdeffre, chief of staff; General Baptiste Billot, war minister; and General Charles-Arthur Gonse, deputy chief of staff. They refused to accept Piquart's evidence, branding it "inadmissible." Piquart was told that he had conducted "the wrong investigation." The general staff was not interested in evidence that did not confirm

Lt.-Col. Georges Picquart, an honorable French officer in the high command, who re-investigated Dreyfus's case, discovering him to be innocent and waging a long battle for his release. *History Inc./Jay Robert Nash Collection.*]

Major Ferdinand Walsin Esterhazy, the actual traitor in the French high command, who was shielded by his fellow officers. *History Inc./Jay Robert Nash Collection.*

the man's conviction. Dreyfus had been identified by the general staff to the world as the French traitor and German spy. Any new evidence to the contrary would compromise the integrity of the general staff.

When Piquart was ordered to cease his investigation, he stubbornly warned his superiors that, if the general staff did not reverse its decision concerning Dreyfus, it risked exposure by others, who might discover that the French high command had known all along that Dreyfus was innocent and that it had criminally protected the real traitor and spy, Esterhazy.

The high command refused to alter its decision and Piquart was directed to return to his duties or face "serious consequences." Meanwhile, Esterhazy was secretly confronted by officers of the general staff, who collusively decided to send him out of the country to perform useless missions. His friend, Major Henry, then created more crude forgeries in a haphazard attempt to disprove Piquart's evidence.

Throughout these covert activities, Mathieu Dreyfus battled to have his brother exonerated.

He publicized Piquart's discoveries, naming Esterhazy as the spy. The general staff, trapped by its blundering machinations, court-martialed Esterhazy on January 10–11, 1898. The hearing was a farce. Esterhazy was asked a few vague questions to which he gave vague answers. He was then cleared of all charges. This flagrant cover-up prompted Emile Zola (1840–1902), the leading French writer of the day, to publicly denounce a military caste system that protected its corrupt members and the government that backed the general staff.

In a momentous publishing event, on January 13, 1898, Zola's celebrated article, *J'accuse*, addressed to Felix Faure, president of the French Republic, was published on the front page of the powerful newspaper *L'aurore*. Zola was fearless. He knew that he was risking criminal charges and possible imprisonment should his indictment of the general staff prove baseless. He nevertheless accused the government and several generals of committing criminal acts when they covered up for Esterhazy in an effort to save their own reputations, of illegally convicting Dreyfus, and of compounding their offenses through lies, forgeries,

Writer Emile Zola, who, in 1898, accused (article in background) the French high command of railroading Dreyfus, which led to a crusade to free him. *History Inc./Jay Robert Nash Collection.*

A cartoon shows the suicide of Major Hubert Henry, who cut his throat in a prison cell while awaiting his own trial for forging documents in an effort to support Dreyfus's wrongful conviction. *History Inc./Jay Robert Nash Collection.*

and the outright destruction of evidence. The great French author Anatole France called Zola's valiant and masterful attack "a moment in the conscience of mankind."

Zola's denunciation exposed the scandal to the world, and France reeled over accusations of corruption at the core of its government. Zola's sensational attack, however, did not bring down the villains. The general staff answered by charging Zola with libel. He was tried and convicted, and his name was struck from the ranks of the Légion d'honneur (Legion of Honor). The militarists attempted to degrade him as they had degraded Dreyfus. To protect his family from persecution, Zola fled to England, where he lived in exile for a year.

France's greatest writers rallied around Zola's cause. Jean Jaurés, Leon Blum, Georges Clemenceau, Anatole France, and others incessantly pressured the government through the press, until Dreyfus was recalled from Devil's Island and retried. Only when Dreyfus was exonerated, his supporters knew, would Zola also be exonerated.

Meanwhile, Major Henry, realizing that he was about to be exposed as the protector of the real traitor, Esterhazy, committed suicide by cutting

A pro-Dreyfus demonstrator is attacked by an anti-Semitic crowd in a Paris street in 1898. *History Inc./Jay Robert Nash Collection.*

his throat (a senior officer reportedly provided the razor to Henry while he was imprisoned and awaiting his own trial, demanding that he "save the honor of the army" by taking his own miserable life). The most radical of Dreyfus's supporters claimed that Henry had been murdered to prevent him from giving testimony exposing the high command as a cabal of conspirators. His gory death inspired Dreyfus's second trial at Rennes, lasting from August 7 to September 9, 1899. It was a sensation. More than three thousand journalists from throughout the world attended. Thousands of citizens choked the streets surrounding the

Dreyfus, sitting at right, went on trial a second time in 1899, at Rennes, France, with about the same results—conviction. *History Inc./Jay Robert Nash Collection.*

Dreyfus is shown, standing, center, objecting to false remarks being stated by a member of the high command during his 1899 trial. *History Inc./Jay Robert Nash Collection.*

Dreyfus supporters demonstrating with placards stating "Long Live Picquart. Down with the Army," "Down with France," and "Long Live Anarchy." *History Inc./Jay Robert Nash Collection.*

Dreyfus in 1906, when he was officially exonerated by a French appeals court. *History Inc./Jay Robert Nash Collection.*

Dreyfus, standing second from right, was restored to the army, promoted to the rank of lieutenant-colonel and awarded the Legion of Honor; he died in 1935. *History Inc./Jay Robert Nash Collection.*

courthouse, arguing the case with each other. Fights and near riots broke out. Throughout the French empire, anti-Semitic crowds destroyed Jewish shops and defaced synagogues.

The general staff was ramrod stubborn. Senior officers refused to admit any guilt in wrongly convicting Dreyfus and covering up blatant fraud and collusion in the case. Dreyfus was again convicted by a military tribunal but "with extenuating circumstances," some of its members voting for acquittal. The world was in shock, as most had come to believe that Dreyfus was innocent. To mollify critics, French President Emile Loubet issued a hedging decree that pardoned Dreyfus.

Dreyfus, however, insisted on complete vindication and continued a long, expensive legal campaign. In 1906 the French court of appeals announced that Dreyfus was completely innocent of treason and espionage. He was ceremoniously restored to the French army and promoted to the rank of major. Further, he was awarded the Chevalier (Knight) of the Legion of Honor. The man who had championed his freedom, Emile Zola, had died four years earlier, but Dreyfus publicly honored the dead writer for the crusade he had waged on his behalf.

After serving with distinction in World War I, Dreyfus was promoted to lieutenant colonel and named an Officer of the Legion of Honor. After a long illness, he died on July 12, 1935, having outlived the real culprit, Estahazy, by thirteen years. Estahazy, after being exposed at the turn of the century, fled to England, where he later admitted spying for the Germans. He died penniless and friendless on May 21, 1923.

The courageous Picquart also triumphed, but not without enduring oppression and privation. After exposing the corruption of the general staff, he was accused of creating the forgeries of Major Henry. He was imprisoned and later cashiered out of the French army. After Dreyfus was vindicated, Piquart was restored to the army and made a brigadier

Emile Zola, a short time before his death in 1902; he did not live long enough to see Dreyfus exonerated, although he is best remembered for chiefly bringing about Dreyfus's freedom. *History Inc./Jay Robert Nash Collection.*

general in 1906. He then joined Georges Clemenceau's cabinet as minister of war (1906–1909). He died on January 18, 1914, seven months before France went to war with Germany. Piquart, like Zola, sacrificed everything for the sake of integrity and ethics.

## Arthur Conan Doyle and Oscar Slater

Like Zola before him, Sir Arthur Conan Doyle (1859–1930) saw great success with his fictional works, particularly his tales about the unconquerable detective, Sherlock Holmes. Doyle, who was once a practicing physician, was content to enjoy the riches the Holmes stories brought him, without seriously involving himself in social or political issues. An early exception was a nonfiction work that established him as a first-rate historian. After serving as a physician in the Boer War in 1900, Doyle wrote *The War in South Africa: Its Causes and Conduct.* The book, which was critical of the British strategy in the war, sold more than 300,000 copies in less than two months. Because of his humanitarian service in the war, Doyle was knighted in 1902.

It was Holmes, however, that had brought fame and fortune to Doyle. The brilliant Holmes and his loyal Watson took their first bow in *A Study in Scarlet,* which appeared in *Chamber's Journal* on March 8, 1886. In this story Doyle showed his seemingly unbeatable detective with a deep, dark fault that made him more human: Sherlock Holmes was ad-

Writer Arthur Conan Doyle, creator of the indefatigable fictional detective, Sherlock Holmes, who also turned a deft hand in solving real life crimes and defending notable wrongly convicted persons such as Oscar Slater. *History Inc./Jay Robert Nash Collection.*

dicted to cocaine. (Doyle, in this instance, drew from his own father, Charles Doyle, who was epileptic and was compelled to take drugs.) Holmes was inhibited by a wrongful addiction, but that humanizing flaw made his character no less wonderful and worthy.

Though the fictional sleuth eventually made Doyle rich, the writer grew tired of his creation, which had come to dominate his literary ambitions (to write histories and "serious" novels) and consume his lifestyle. Readers the world over wanted only Sherlock Holmes and more and more of him, until Doyle became weary with his fabulous character. Doyle did not consider his detective fiction "serious writing." He wished to be considered a writer on subjects held in greater intellectual esteem.

Having ignored his wife and his personal life in his exhaustive production of Holmes stories, Doyle decided to kill off Holmes in *The Final Problem.* Holmes and his mortal enemy, Professor Moriarty, fight to the finish and fall, ostensibly to their deaths, into the Reichenbach Falls, a "dreadful cauldron of swirling water and seething foam." Doyle's enormous reading public reacted with as much concern and dismay as if Holmes had been a living, breathing person. Thousands of letters poured into the offices of Doyle's publishers, all begging the author to revive the great detective. Doyle, however, adamantly refused to resurrect Holmes. The author did not, as suggested by numerous writers, grow to hate and resent his creation, but he was certainly tired of creating puzzles for Holmes to solve, as well as creating new personality traits that would astound readers.

To a friend Doyle wrote, "I have had such an overdose of him [Sherlock Holmes] that I feel towards him as I do towards *pate de foie gras,* of which I once ate too much so that the name of it gives me a sickly feeling to this day." Doyle's publishers and public, however, hounded him constantly, and Doyle finally brought Holmes back to life in October 1903 in *The Empty House.* When the story went on sale, the bookstores and stalls in

London were mobbed by thousands of purchasers, who literally fought for copies.

One of those avid readers, elated at the resurrection of the indomitable Holmes, was a dapper entrepreneur whose questionable activities and nomadic travels increased through the early years of the 1900s, until they enshrouded him with dark accusations of murder and engulfed him with wrongful imprisonment. He was Oscar Slater, and he would become the subject of another work written by Arthur Conan Doyle, and, in fact, the writer's chief obsession and cause célèbre for more than a decade. Doyle knew that Slater, like Holmes, had a flaw in his character: a penchant for shady dealings. Doyle also knew that character trait made him no less innocent of the crime for which he had been convicted.

Oscar Slater (born Oscar Leschziner; a.k.a. A. Anderson, Otto Sando, 1871–1948), a German Jew, left his homeland to avoid military draft. Slater married May Curtis in 1901 but deserted her in 1905 because she was an alcoholic. He met a prostitute, Andre Antoine, in London, who became his mistress, and they often traveled together. He earned his living by gambling and selling jewelry. May Curtis Slater had badgered him for money, so Slater often used false names in his schemes to obtain more money.

**Wealthy spinster Marion Gilchrist, who was murdered in her apartment in Glasgow, Scotland, on the night of December 21, 1908.** *History Inc./Jay Robert Nash Collection.*

Slater and his mistress were in Glasgow, Scotland, in late 1908. On December 21, 1908, he received two letters. One contained a warning from a London friend that May Slater had been asking him for money. The second was a business invitation from a previous associate to go to San Francisco. That day, Slater let his servants go, contacted a London bank, went to a billiard room between 6:20 and 6:40 P.M., and ate dinner about 7:00 P.M.

Marion Gilchrist, an eighty-two-year-old spinster living in Glasgow, spent that same evening reading a magazine. For more than thirty years, she had lived in a seven-room apartment (called a flat in England and a house in Scotland) at 15 Queens Terrace, Glasgow, which was part of West Princes Street at the well-to-do West End of the city. She had extra locks installed on her apartment door (the only entrance to her apartment) and windows to protect a jewelry collection worth about £3,000. There were three locks and a bolt and chain on Gilchrist's heavy door. At 7:00 P.M., Gilchrist's maid, twenty-one-year-old Helen Lambie, left the apartment to buy a newspaper, as was her custom. In the apartment beneath Gilchrist's, tenant Arthur Adams heard something "heavy fall and then three sharp knocks."

Adams went from his own flat at No. 14, going out the street entrance to reenter No. 15 from the street to check on Gilchrist, finding the street door ajar. He climbed the steps to Gilchrist's apartment and rang her doorbell three times. He heard a noise from within, "as if it was someone chopping sticks [for the fireplace]." Adams assumed that Lambie was chopping sticks or working in the Gilchrist kitchen. When Gilchrist did not answer, Adams went back to his apartment. When his sister persuaded him to check again, he went back upstairs and rang the bell once more. He was startled to see Lambie climbing the stairs at about 7:10 P.M. She explained that she had gone out to buy a newspaper for Gilchrist. Adams told her he had heard strange sounds, "like sticks breaking," and Lambie thought perhaps pulleys for the clothesline had come down in the kitchen.

Adams and Lambie—the maid had to use two keys to unlock the entrance door—entered the apartment, standing in the inner hallway, which was dimly lighted by gas. (Gilchrist, a penny-wise spinster, always kept the gas jets low in her apart-

Oscar Slater, a shady entrepreneur, who was convicted of killing Gilchrist on eyewitness testimony and sentenced to death, that sentence later commuted to life imprisonment. *History Inc./Jay Robert Nash Collection.*

ment.) As Lambie took a few steps toward the kitchen, a man walked out of a bedroom, passing her and Adams, appearing "quite pleasantly," according to Adams's later statements. The man said nothing but, when reaching the outer hallway, broke into a run and disappeared down the stairs "like greased lightning," said Adams. Lambie then inspected the kitchen and found everything in order. She went to the dining room where she had last seen Gilchrist and found her body by the fireplace, fatally beaten about the head. Adams ran to the dining room in answer to Lambie's screams. Gilchrist was lying on her back before the dining room fireplace, with a small rug over her. Blood pooled on the floor next to her body and there were blood splashes on the grate of the fireplace.

Adams immediately turned about and ran outside in pursuit of the man he and Lambie had briefly seen leave the Gilchrist apartment. Lambie removed the rug to see Gilchrist still breathing, but she died before the physician—summoned by Adams—arrived. Police were at the scene a short time later, determining that the murdered woman had been struck in the dining room while she was standing and hit fifty or sixty times with a small, sharp instrument (weapon never found), with the assailant kneeling on her chest, fracturing her breastbone and ribs. This fierce, prolonged attack was not typical of a professional burglar, but more consistent with an enraged killer who knew the victim and savagely assaulted her for several minutes.

The killer, police concluded, had left Gilchrist for dead, covering her body with a small dining room rug, and had then gone into a bedroom and used matches to light the gas jet; the room had been dark when Lambie left to retrieve the newspaper. He took time in looking about and rummaged through a wooden box containing documents and then removed from a glass dish on a table a diamond brooch, valued at about £50, which Lambie reported missing, but inexplicably left behind other jewelry, ignored in panic, perhaps, with the unexpected arrival of Lambie and Adams. Police discovered that the intruder had touched several objects in the apartment and had left a bloody handprint on a chair in the dining room.

Oddly, the Glasgow police had no thought of using fingerprints to identify the killer, for he left his prints in abundance at the murder scene. Fingerprint identification had by then become established at Scotland Yard in England, but had not been adopted by police officials in Scotland, even though they knew that this relatively new identification system was effective in having identified some recent notorious British murderers. Professor John Glaister of the University of Glasgow, who had lectured his students about fingerprinting, arrived at the scene of the Gilchrist murder a few hours later, but he never suggested contacting Scotland Yard with a request to send two of its fingerprint experts to Glasgow, which could have been accomplished in a few hours. (Under Scottish law, two experts were required in corroborating their forensic findings.)

Lambie, Adams, and Mary Barrowman, a teenager who said she saw the man running away outside the apartment, gave police conflicting descriptions of the suspect. These identifications would later convict Oscar Slater, but the manner in which they were acquired would raise suspicions and doubt, haunting the top police inspector in the case and nagging the famous Arthur Conan Doyle to launch his own investigation into the case sometime later.

In the days following the Gilchrist slaying, Slater and his mistress prepared to go to the United States. He pawned a diamond brooch and booked two New York passages on the *Lusitania* under the names of Mr. and Mrs. Otto Sando. Two days after the murder, Detective Inspector John Trench, who was investigating the case, talked with a woman named Birrell. She told him that Lambie had told her the name of Gilchrist's killer.

On December 25, 1908, police learned about the brooch Slater had pawned. They went to question Slater, and found that he and his mistress had left a few hours earlier for Liverpool or London. When they learned he was aboard the *Lusitania*, they cabled New York officials to have Slater arrested when the ship arrived. Lambie, Adams and Barrowman were sent to participate in extradition proceedings in New York, where they identified Slater. At their identification of Slater in New York, Adams, Lambie and Barrowman again gave conflicting, even confusing statements.

Adams said that Slater closely resembled the man he saw leave the Gilchrist apartment, but he seemed reluctant to give a positive identification. Lambie's identification of Slater was based on the way he walked: "It was not the face that I went by but the walk." All three witnesses had been given photos of Slater before they made their identifications when picking him out of lineups. Slater agreed voluntarily to return to Scotland. In the meantime, the brooch Slater had pawned was found to have been his for a long time and did not match Gilchrist's.

When arriving in Scotland, the three witnesses again picked Slater out of a police lineup consisting of eleven other men, nine policemen and two railway officials and none of these men in any way came close to resembling Slater. He was charged with murder and was brought to trial on May 3, 1909. The trial lasted four days. Information about the brooch and Detective Inspector Trench's findings were suppressed. A small hammer was found in Slater's luggage, which had been impounded, but experts ruled out this tool as having been the murder weapon, without stating that a killer packing the murder weapon in his luggage instead of discarding it

embraced the ridiculous. The prosecution, undertaken by Alexander Ure, called Lambie, Adams and Barrowman, who again identified Slater, and twelve others, who named Slater as a man seen around the Gilchrist apartment building at different times, though the twelve had given

The small hammer found in Slater's luggage, which was thought to be the murder weapon. *History Inc./Jay Robert Nash Collection.*

conflicting descriptions. The prosecution also attacked Slater's character and sporadic work record and insinuated that he had fled Scotland to escape prosecution.

The prosecution also charged that Slater had seen his name in the newspapers as a suspect before he left for the United States, and he should have come forward immediately to clear himself. The fact that he had fled, prosecutors argued, indicated his guilt. In truth, Slater's name had not actually been printed until about a week later, when Slater was already aboard the *Lusitania*. (A decade later, this ship would be sunk by a German submarine and become, along with other acts of German aggression, one of the reasons why the United States entered the war on the side of the Allies.)

Slater, defended by Ewing Speirs, did not take the stand in his own defense. By not giving testimony, he planted in the minds of some jury members, it was later claimed, the notion that he had something to hide. Before the jury retired to decide its verdict, the judge, Lord Guthrie, told them with considerable prejudice that "a man of that kind has not the presumption of innocence in his favor." The jury of fifteen was out for one hour and ten minutes. One voted not guilty, five did not think the case had been proven, and nine voted guilty. At the time, the United States and England already required a unanimous vote for a conviction, but in Scotland only a majority was required. Slater was judged guilty and sentenced to death.

His execution by hanging was scheduled for May 27, 1909.

Although Scotland had then no means for legal appeal, 20,000 people signed a petition for a stay of execution. The petition was given to the secretary of state for Scotland on May 17, 1909, and, eight days later, the undersecretary sent a telegram authorizing a stay of execution. Slater's sentence was commuted to life imprisonment and he was sent to Peterhead Prison on July 8, 1909.

Many continued to lobby for Slater's release without success. Coming to his aid, however, was Arthur Conan Doyle, who had taken an interest in Slater's case and had begun to investigate its background. Doyle became obsessed with the Gilchrist murder and looked upon it as a real-life mystery, as challenging and baffling as any tale he had created for his great fictional detective, Sherlock Holmes. Doyle came to believe that Slater had been the victim of mistaken identity and sought to prove his theory. Studying the testimony of witnesses, he challenged the verdict, based upon the discrepancies he found in the testimony of those witnesses. In 1912, Doyle wrote and published *The Case of Oscar Slater,* a short study that criticized the verdict and the authorities in the Gilchrist murder, a sharp and observant analysis not dissimilar to Doyle's dissection of the floundering British strategy of the Boer War in his 1903 book.

Oscar Slater in 1927, released after eighteen years in prison, his freedom largely won through the tireless efforts of Arthur Conan Doyle, whom Slater called "the breaker of my shackles." *History Inc./Jay Robert Nash Collection.*

Armed with or inspired by Doyle's accusatory work, Detective Inspector Trench, an officer with an outstanding record, reentered the case. He told his superiors that Barrowman and Lambie had lied. When these officials took no action, Trench made an open charge against the two witnesses, which brought about an official inquiry on April 23, 1914. The two women emphatically denied Trench's allegations, accusing the inspector of slander. The presiding officials at that inquiry took their side, and Trench lost his job.

The firing of Trench infuriated Doyle. He continued his campaign to free Slater, battling Scottish officials for years. Having been born and educated in Scotland, he knew well the stubborn temperament of these authorities. Slater, who had been in communication with Doyle, was suddenly placed in incommunicado, confined to a solitary cell. He nevertheless found a unique way to contact the writer. In 1925, Slater sent a note to Doyle in a pardoned prisoner's mouth, which reportedly told the writer that Lambie had known the identity of the real killer.

Doyle stirred up so much controversy with this claim that investigators tracked Lambie to the United States, where she had migrated. They found her in Pittsburgh, Pennsylvania. She admitted that she knew the real killer, who was actually an acquaintance of Gilchrist's. She said she had told police what she knew just after the Gilchrist slaying, but that they had persuaded her to change her story. The suspect's identity was never revealed. He was only called "A.B." After Lambie's admission, Barrowman too, at Doyle's behest, was contacted. She said she had been influenced by police and had lied in her identification, knowing that Slater was not the man who had fled from the murder scene more than fifteen years earlier.

These admissions led to Slater's release in 1927 after eighteen years in prison. The government, however, had not officially decreed his innocence. Parliament had established a court of criminal appeal for Scotland in 1926, but, because Slater's conviction had occurred before the existence of that court, he could not file an appeal. Through the lobbying of Doyle and others, a special law was enacted on November 30, 1927, to allow his case to be heard before the appeals court. Slater's case came before Lord Alness, Lord Clyde, and three other appeals judges in June 1928. The court overturned the conviction on the grounds that Justice

Guthrie, who had presided at Slater's 1909 trial, had directed the jury inappropriately in a prejudicial speech before the verdict. Slater was awarded £6,000 compensation and officially pronounced innocent. He later wrote to Doyle to call him the "breaker of my shackles."

## "$5,000 Reward for Killers of Officer Lundy"

Four years after Oscar Slater was acquitted in England, a murder occurred in Chicago, Illinois, for which two men were wrongfully convicted and sent to prison for life. Finally, after more than a decade, the meager life wages of a faithful mother and the tireless efforts of two newsmen brought about the release of these two prisoners. Like Zola and Doyle before them, these two Chicago writers faced almost insurmountable barriers in seeking and finding the truth. Their zeal and dedication, backed by their editor and newspaper publisher, were in the great tradition of a crusading press.

Until his life was shattered by a criminal justice system that faltered, Joseph Majczek (1910–1983) lived quietly with his wife Helen in a grimy flat in the Polish-Lithuanian neighborhood on Chicago's South Side known as Back of the Yards. Majczek worked hard to overcome a troubled past and provide a good life for his wife and infant son. In his younger days, Majczek had joined a gang of older men to rob a warehouse. A judge gave him a suspended sentence and a second chance at life. With the onset of the Great Depression, Majczek accepted whatever meager work he could find. Times were hard, but he was resolved to lead a sober, clean life.

Joe Majczek spent the afternoon of December 9, 1932, shoveling coal into the basement of his home. It was a frigid winter day, with temperatures hovering near 11 degrees below zero. Not far away, a Chicago police officer, William D. Lundy, decided to sneak a drink in one of the speakeasies that dotted the South Side during those last days of Prohibition. Vera Walush's neighborhood "delicatessen" was strictly second-rate by the standards of Chicago's gin joints. The speakeasy could be accessed through the kitchen. A sign outside the window advised guests that liquor was fifty cents a shot, but policemen drank free. Moonshine liquor, the kind Walush received from her supplier, Bessie Barron, was technically illegal, but the police on the beat left Walush, and dozens of others like her, alone in return for her continuing "hospitality."

Officer Lundy had just finished his rounds and was kibitzing with Walush when two men entered the store with guns drawn. Walush mistrusted banks and had hidden $9,000 inside her icebox. The gunmen had not anticipated seeing a uniformed policeman drinking moonshine and hesitated. As Lundy reached for his sidearm, the robbers shot seven bullets into him. They fled as Lundy collapsed to the floor, dying.

The shooting resulted in a massive dragnet ordered by Commissioner James Allman, which commenced that afternoon. Hundreds of suspects were pulled into station houses and interrogated by detectives skilled in the "third degree." There were few substantial leads, but they turned up an unconfirmed rumor that a neighborhood man named Theodore Marcinkiewicz, twenty-five, had talked about "knocking off" the Walush speakeasy. Fearful that the police would try to beat a confession out of him, Marcinkiewicz turned to boyhood chum Joe Majczek. He asked to be allowed to hide out for a few days, and Majczek, who sympathized with his friend's plight, put him up in his small apartment.

A neighborhood informant told police that he had observed Marcinkiewicz entering the Majczek dwelling. The police arrived the next morning, shortly after Marcinkiewicz had gone on his way. Majczek told the officers that he had stayed home from work the day of the murder because of his wife's advanced pregnancy. He said that he had spent the day shelling peas and shoveling coal into his cellar, which was corroborated by Helen

Majczek and her father, as well as a deliveryman. Majczek did not match the description, provided by several eyewitnesses, of either of the two men, who fled from the speakeasy after killing Lundy. The gunmen were both tall, whereas Majczek was a short, wiry man. There was seemingly not enough evidence to warrant Majczek's arrest, let alone conviction.

State's attorney Thomas Courtney, however, and other like-minded politicians, wanted to send a clear message to the underworld that shooting a policeman would not be tolerated in Chicago. The city was less than a year away from hosting the Century of Progress World's Fair, and Anton Cermak had been elected mayor on a law and order platform, and had announced a "war on crime." The attack on Officer Lundy, if it remained unsolved, would sully the reputation of the city just months before the arrival of dignitaries and visitors to the fair, and destroy, in the words of one politician, "the need to feel safe in Chicago."

Vera Walush was asked to "reconsider" her earlier statements to police that Majczek was not one of the gunmen. Officers reminded her how easy it would be for them to close her place down for violations of the Volstead Act. Less than an hour later, police brought Majczek before Walush. "Yes, yes, that's the man," she said, avoiding direct eye contact with the twenty-four-year-old Majczek. She later testified in court that Majczek was the man who shot Lundy, despite the contradicting statements of five eyewitnesses. Tillie Majczek, Joe's mother, hired William W. O'Brien to defend her son. He was a corpulent, alcoholic gangland lawyer, and Tillie had hired him only because she had recently seen his name in the newspapers. Bored and disinterested, O'Brien did not offer much in the way of a concrete defense for his client, and refused Majczek's request to take the stand and speak on his own behalf.

Not surprisingly, the jury returned a verdict of guilty against both defendants, Joe Majczek and Teddy Marcinkiewicz, who was also identified by Walush as the second gunman. (Four witnesses

testified that Marcinkiewicz was at another location at the time Lundy had been shot to death.) Both were sentenced to ninety-nine years in the state penitentiary at Joliet. Judge Charles P. Molthrop, who presided in the case, was not entirely convinced of their guilt. He reportedly consulted with Vera Walush in his private chambers and accused the woman of outright perjury. He allegedly vowed to help Majczek and Marcinkiewicz secure a new trial, but in the meantime he was obligated by law to pass sentence.

Majczek went to Joliet to serve his sentence. The sympathetic judge died, and the Lundy case faded from public consciousness. However, Tillie Majczek believed that if she could post a sizable reward, someone might come forward with information that would free her son from prison. Majczek took a job as a cleaning woman and scrubbed the floors of a large downtown office building in quiet dignity, saving every penny for the reward money.

After raising $3,500, Majczek placed her first ad in a newspaper, but there were no takers. From his cell in Joliet, Majczek heard what his mother was trying to do but never believed any good would come of it. His sense of despair was compounded by Helen Majczek's decision to file for divorce in 1937. "They'll never let you get out of here, Joe," she told her husband on a prison visit. "And our child needs a father. A guy asked me to marry him and . . . well, I'm going to." Majczek accepted the news with weary resignation, but in his heart the family's traditional Catholic views held strong. He considered himself still lawfully married to his wife.

When the war came, Tillie Majczek's other son went off to fight. He sent home his allotment checks from the front and ever so slowly Tillie's reward fund grew. When it reached $5,000, Majczek placed an ad in the Chicago *Daily Times* of October 10, 1944, which read, "$5,000 reward for killers of Officer Lundy on Dec. 9, 1932. Call GRO 1758, 12–7 P.M."

*Times* cub reporter Terry Colangelo noticed the obscure little item and reported it to her boss, city editor Karin Walsh, who sensed a good story. He assigned the story to news reporter and former detective James McGuire. After a preliminary inquiry, McGuire reported back that the ad was placed by Tillie Majczek, mother of a convicted cop killer. "Find out where the woman got the five grand," Walsh said. "Maybe there's a feature story in it."

McGuire again called the phone number listed in the ad, which led to an interview with Tillie Majczek. When he learned that she had been scrubbing floors at the Commonwealth Edison Company building every night for more than a decade to save enough money to post the reward that might bring about her son's prison release, McGuire realized he had the makings of a great human interest story. He gave his notes to rewrite man John J. McPhaul, who wrote the first story, which was published in the *Times* on October 12, 1944. McGuire was not really a news writer, but a "leg man" who tracked down information and assembled research for the rewriters at the paper.

McPhaul originally believed that the story was good for "one press run," according to his statements to this author in 1973. "McGuire and I didn't think this melodramatic tale would ever see a follow-up. After all, Majczek had been convicted and sent to prison as a cop killer and few readers, other than members of the Capone mob, would like to see a guy like that sprung from prison."

McGuire, however, had a nagging thought about the Majczek case and he raised it with McPhaul, telling him that something "was not right about the conviction." He pointed out to the rewrite man that the sentences given to Majczek and Marcinkiewicz were unusual, since anyone who killed a police officer in Chicago, or anywhere else in America, invariably received a death sentence. Why, then, were Majczek and Marcinkiewicz only given ninety-nine years? "That judge spared their lives," McPhaul quoted McGuire to this author, "and I think he did it because he believed these two birds were innocent."

McPhaul agreed and looked further into the case, obtaining a thirty-two-page document that Majczek had written in prison. It included a passage describing how Judge Molthrop had taken him into his chambers and told him that a miscarriage of justice had occurred and promised him a new trial. McPhaul also noted that Majczek had included a passage in his document describing how James Zagata, a truck driver, had been present in Molthrop's chamber at the time the judge made his statements to Majczek and that Zagata had come forward during the trial to state (his testimony had been part of the trial record) that he had just made a coal delivery to Vera Walush's speakeasy at the time of the Lundy killing.

Zagata, according to Majczek's recollections, had told Judge Molthrop that he knew that Majczek and Marcinkiewicz were innocent. He was present at the moment of the shooting, Zagata testified, and was later taken to a police station, where he refused to identify against either Majczek or Marcinkiewicz, saying that he (nor Vera Walush, for that matter) had not gotten a good look at Lundy's killers.

With Karin Walsh's blessing, McGuire and McPhaul went back to the story, but McPhaul had great doubts about Majczek's claims. Why would a judge have a defendant convicted in his court later brought to his chambers? That claim could not be supported. Judge Molthrop could not be interviewed; he had died in 1935. The dogged McGuire, however, tracked down James Zagata, who was still working as a truck driver. He was eager to repeat his statements about the Lundy murder and told McGuire that, a few days after Majczek and Marcinkiewicz had been convicted, he had been summoned to Judge Molthrop's chambers, where he repeated his court testimony and while Majczek was also present. Said Zagata, "I told the judge that I was now sure that neither of the men had been involved in the murder." He added that Judge Molthrop replied at the time, "I am sure that there has been a miscarriage of justice concerning the identification of both boys. I am going to see that they get a new trial."

These statements were incorporated in a story written by McPhaul and published by the *Times*. Many more stories on the case came into print. McGuire and McPhaul spent the next ten and a half months digging through dusty court records and interviewing scores of neighborhood people, many of whom distrusted newspaper reporters. In subsequent stories, they revealed that the sole evidence that had convicted Majczek and Marcinkiewicz was the testimony of Vera Walush, who, the reporters stated, had originally told police after seeing the suspects in a lineup that they were not Lundy's killers. They went on to state that police pressured Walush into identifying the two men as the murderers under the threat of charging her with operating an illegal speakeasy. Further, the reporters stated that Judge Molthrop was also pressured into not ordering a new trial for the defendants, prosecutors telling him that if he did so, his political career would be wrecked.

McGuire made a crucial discovery while rummaging through old police records. He found that Majczek had been arrested on December 22, 1933, and had appeared in two separate lineups on that day. In both lineups, Walush had viewed the suspects and refused to identify any of them, including Majczek, as Officer Lundy's killer. Under pressure from police, Walush made a positive identification of Majczek the next day. To conform to that false identification, police then wrote a new report, falsely stating that Majczek had been first arrested on December 23, 1933. Marcinkiewicz surrendered a month later and Walush identified him as the second gunman at that time.

The *Daily Times* paid for Dr. Leonard Keeler, the inventor of the polygraph machine, to visit Joliet and administer a test to Majczek. Only once did the needle on the machine indicate a lie, and that had to do with Majczek's response to the question of his divorce. He said yes, he had separated from his wife, but the machine said he was lying. As a devout Catholic, he believed himself still married. Keeler concluded that Joseph Majczek was telling the truth all along. Although polygraph tests were

not admissible in court, Keeler's findings went a long way to convince many that Majczek was telling the truth.

After the state's attorney's office refused to reopen the case, the reporters presented the results of the polygraph test, the evidence that the police had filed false reports, and the perjured testimony of Vera Walush to an esteemed trial attorney hired by the *Times*, Walker Butler, who was also a Democratic member of the Illinois state senate. In addition, Butler was a close confident of Governor Dwight H. Green (1941–1949).

Butler focused on Majczek's freewheeling attorney, William W. O'Brien. In examining O'Brien's conduct throughout Majczek's trial, Butler learned that O'Brien had not bothered to challenge the unsupported statements of two witnesses who had incriminated Marcinkiewicz, Bessie Barron, who supplied beer to Vera Walush, and Bruno Uginchus. Both implied that Marcinkiewicz had told them he intended to rob Walush's speakeasy, statements in court that were tied to Majczek because he was Marcinkiewicz's friend but had no bearing on his own case. Moreover, and most importantly, Butler discovered that O'Brien failed to cross-examine Walush in response to Majczek's statements that she had disqualified him as a suspect on December 22, 1933, when she first saw him in two police lineups, and then named him as the killer the following day. None of these vital issues had been incorporated in Majczek's appeal and for a good reason—William W. O'Brien handled that appeal, which failed to win a new trial.

There was an additional factor involved in Butler's examination of O'Brien's conduct. He did not include it in his written report but considered it in evaluating the motivation for O'Brien's shabby courtroom performance. O'Brien had a good track record as a defense attorney and was known to win cases on the minutest detail, particularly when defending organized crime defendants. Yet he was sloppy and indifferent to the most significant aspects of Majczek's trial, and a man of his expertise and skill would certainly have disposed of Vera Walush's shaky testimony.

One could easily speculate that O'Brien did not want to win this case and had ulterior reasons for abandoning his client early on. Had he challenged and exposed Walush as a perjurer, police would have arrested her for violating the Volstead Act, then still in force. Subsequently bootlegger Bessie Barron would have been involved, and, beyond her, the hierarchy of the Capone mob, which controlled the illegal distribution of liquor in the state. Many of O'Brien's clients were part of that mob, and he received large retainers from these underworld figures. Majczek and Marcinkiewicz were therefore expendable pawns to be sacrificed in the protection of a multimillion dollar illegal business.

Butler, accompanied by the *Times* reporters, submitted the investigative evidence they had assembled to the state pardon board, which decided that Majczek was innocent. On August 15, 1945, Governor Dwight H. Green accepted the board's recommendation and had Majczek released. In 1948, the touching story was made into a movie, *Call Northside 777*, starring James Stewart as the hard-bitten newsman, whose character merged Jack McPhaul and Jim McGuire into one person.

Theodore Marcinkiewicz languished behind bars another five years before Chief Justice Thomas Lynch of the Cook County criminal court was forced to review the trial record. Before that time, and before he left office in 1949, Governor Green offered to commute Marcinkiewicz's ninety-nine-year sentence to seventy-five years, making him eligible for parole in 1958. Marcinkiewicz, however, like Majczek before him, insisted that he was innocent and refused Green's offer. It proved to be a wise decision.

A short time later, the U.S. Supreme Court ordered the State of Illinois to speed up its judicial procedures to give Marcinkiewicz a second chance in court. In February 1950, Judge Lynch freed Marcinkiewicz but admonished him about the wages of sin. He returned to his stepmother and four sisters, who still lived in the neighborhood

**Wrongly convicted Joseph Majczek, second from left, opens his arms to embrace his son upon his release from prison in 1945; while Jack McPhaul, left, and Jim McGuire, second from right, the two newsmen who had brought about his freedom, look on.** *History Inc./Jay Robert Nash Collection.*

where the tragedy had first unfolded eighteen years earlier. When asked about the release of Marcinkiewicz and Majczek (five years earlier), Vera Walush snarled at reporters from her North LaSalle Street dive: "I got nothin' to say."

Joseph Majczek eventually remarried Helen, settled in a south suburb of Chicago, and went to work for the Cook County circuit court. Special appropriations to compensate the two wrongfully convicted men were approved by the Illinois legislature, which awarded Majczek $24,000 and Marcinkiewicz $35,000.

Shortly before Majczek died on May 30, 1983, his son James placed a classified ad, similar to the one his grandmother had placed almost four decades earlier, in the Chicago *Sun-Times* (the successor to the *Daily Times*) hoping to come up with a fresh lead on the identity of Lundy's killer. None turned up.

## Erle Stanley Gardner and the Court of Last Resort

Around the time the newsmen at the Chicago *Daily Times* began their crusade to free Joseph Majczek, writer Erle Stanley Gardner (1889–1970) envisioned an organization that combined the use of the press and legal expertise to exonerate wrongly imprisoned persons. Gardner, a practicing attorney, was one of the most popular whodunit writers in American history. Born in Malden, Massachusetts, Gardner moved to California and practiced law in Ventura from 1911 to 1938. He wrote more than one hundred detective and mystery books and created the popular Perry Mason, a lawyer-detective who never seemed to lose a case.

Notable Mason novels include *The Case of the Velvet Claws* (1933) and *The Case of the Amorous Aunt* (1963). Gardner also wrote about a district attorney he named Doug Selby, in such works as *The D.A. Calls It Murder* (1937) and *The D.A. Goes to Trial* (1940). He wrote under many pseudonyms, the most popular being A. A. Fair, featuring detective Bertha Cool and legal aide Donald Lam. Gardner was one of the most prolific and popular detective writers in the United States, rivaling the venerable Arthur Conan Doyle and Agatha Christie in sales. His books and the movies and TV series based on them are still avidly read and viewed, but few remember another Gardner achievement, the Court of Last Resort, an organization he founded in 1948 to aid persons thought to be unjustly imprisoned.

This organization, headed by Gardner and supported by a pool of volunteer lawyers, helped free scores of innocent persons from wrongful imprisonment. Gardner first conceived the idea as a monthly magazine series featuring real-life crimes, not unlike the TV concept for *America's Most Wanted*. The sale of articles for this series, Gardner reasoned, would defray investigative expenses in probing questionable convictions. However, many of the challenging cases Gardner and his legal associates undertook incurred expenses far beyond the money realized from any article; Gardner and his fellow attorneys and some private detectives made up the difference from their own pockets. The first real-life Gardner case featured in *Argosy* magazine was that of Clarence Boggie, an itinerant lumberjack from Portland who seemed to have a penchant for being in the wrong place at the wrong time.

Twice imprisoned for crimes he did not commit, Clarence Gilmore Boggie might have died alone, forgotten and innocent in the state penitentiary in Walla Walla, Washington, if not for the intervention of a team of crack crime writers and a conscientious clergyman. Gardner first heard of Boggie through Reverend W. A. Gilbert, a rector at St. Paul's Episcopal Church in Walla Walla, who volunteered his time at the local prison. Gilbert maintained that Boggie had served thirteen years for a murder he never committed, following an earlier robbery conviction that was eventually was overturned.

Boggie's incredible story began early in the Depression, while he was camping out at one of the many hobo "jungles" near Portland, Oregon. Out of work and penniless, Boggie was sleeping under a bridge when a car sped over it. A team of bank robbers tossed a coat from the window of the speeding car, which held a large amount of stolen cash. Not knowing this, the lumberjack tried on the coat and found it a perfect fit. Police searching the riverbed arrested him when they noticed the familiar coat. Boggie was tried, convicted and sentenced to prison, where he remained for several years before being granted a formal pardon, when new facts about the robbery came to light.

Ironically, another coat got him in trouble a second time. On June 26, 1933, an elderly recluse named Moritz Peterson was murdered in his boardinghouse in Spokane, Washington, by a man believed to have rifled through Peterson's small hut two days earlier in search of valuables. Peterson never mentioned Boggie's name before he died, but the police knew of his presence in Spokane at the time of the murder. Then a convicted Idaho bank robber implicated Boggie in the Peterson murder in return for a promise that he would not be extradited to Washington to face more serious charges.

Several months later, police located an overcoat in a small Oregon town where Boggie had stayed following his first parole. When the daughter of the murder victim identified it as having once belonged to her father, the authorities were convinced they had their man. Boggie was arrested after a long chase by police. By attempting to flee, Boggie inadvertently played into the hands of the prosecution, which contended that he would not have run away if he were innocent.

Boggie was convicted, based on perjured evidence submitted by a deputy prosecutor and a shaky identification of the overcoat made by Peterson's daughter. He received a life sentence, which he began serving in 1935. Gardner opened his investigation into the Boggie case in 1948. He and others on his investigating team closely examined the transcript of Boggie's trial, noting one discrepancy after another. The copy of this transcript was submitted to Ed Lehan, a special deputy attorney general from Washington.

Lehan concluded that the evidence submitted in Boggie's case could not support a conviction. The wheels of justice then slowly turned and a written report submitted to Governor Monrad C. Wallgren (1945–1949) gained Boggie a pardon in December 1948. The actual killer was later identified through eyewitness testimony and a second examination of the murder weapon. This time, though, the state declined to prosecute the suspect.

Louis Gross was another prisoner investigated by Gardner, and, like Boggie, was brought to the attention of the Court of Last Resort by a man of religion. Rabbi Joshua S. Sperka was an honest and benevolent man. Highly respected in Detroit, where he lived, his word was considered wise and fair. In 1945, when he took up the cause of Louis Gross, a man convicted of murder in a Detroit suburb thirteen years earlier, people took notice. Rabbi Sperka asked officials to reopen the case and urged that Gross be retried. When officials balked, the rabbi called on the Court of Last Resort, and told Gardner and his associates Gross's story.

Gross was a peddler in the largely Syrian community of Highland Park in 1932, when a man named Mortado Abraham was killed with a .38-caliber pistol. A highly questionable police investigation came to the conclusion that Gross had killed Abraham out of revenge for an unpaid bill. Gross's trial was a fiasco. Witnesses contradicted each other, and "facts" about the case were found to be dubious. Still, the jury returned a verdict of

guilty, and Louis Gross, who proclaimed his innocence throughout, was handed a mandatory life sentence.

Then a series of amazing events occurred. As Gross worked to appeal the verdict, the court reporter discovered that his trial notes had been removed from his stenographer's notebook. Another court reporter for the pretrial hearing found the same had happened to his books, and the prosecutor discovered that his private files had been looted and all information on the Gross case had been removed. A court decided that without the information, the judge had no information to review and Gross's trial could not be reopened.

The case was closed, despite Gross's continued pleas of innocence, and the peddler was eventually forgotten. When Gross told Rabbi Sperka the story, the rabbi took an immediate interest in the case. Through his pleading, the Court of Last Resort instigated a full-scale investigation in 1948. Gardner and other crime writers found information indicating a major cover-up. Gross was most likely a "fall guy" used to cover someone else's guilt. Upon reading a Gardner article detailing the apparent injustice in the Gross case, Gerald K. O'Brien, Detroit's prosecutor, announced he would conduct his own investigation. When his efforts affirmed Gross's innocence, the prosecutor personally filed for a new trial. No sooner had the motion been accepted than O'Brien asked to have the case dismissed. This, too, was accepted and Gross was acquitted of any involvement in Abraham's murder. Louis Gross spent sixteen years in prison for a crime he did not commit.

Vance Hardy was the subject of another Gardner investigative article, which described him as being identified by a man who was coerced into perjured testimony. On that testimony, Hardy was wrongly convicted of murder; he was released only after his sister struggled for twenty-six years to free him.

On May 3, 1924, Louis Lambert of Detroit, Michigan, who ran a soft drink business that was probably a front for a speakeasy, was leaving his bank when a Studebaker with three men inside pulled up to him. Shots rang out and Lambert was pulled inside the car. Bruno Marcelt was in his kitchen as he looked out to see three men running away and watched Lambert fall out of the car. Rushing outside, Marcelt heard Lambert whisper either that the "river gang" or the "river front gang" had gotten him.

Vance Hardy, a young man on the lookout for a fast dollar, had been spending time in bad company. Police, angry at a gun-running scheme they could not break, hauled Hardy and another man into court and charged them with the Lambert murder. Marcelt, brought in for extensive questioning, at first said he could not identify the men he had seen fleeing. After being coerced by police, as he would admit years later, he reluctantly identified Hardy as one of them. Hardy's sister, Gladys Barrett, testified in court that her brother had been with her at the time of the killing, but Hardy was nevertheless convicted of first-degree murder and given a life sentence.

Insisting on his innocence and embittered at his plight, Hardy escaped from jail but was recaptured and put in solitary confinement for ten years. Barrett continued to champion her brother, eventually attracting crime writer Erle Stanley Gardner to the case. Gardner tracked down Marcelt and interviewed him. Marcelt repudiated his earlier statements, explaining to Gardner that he had been forced into identifying Hardy. Gardner's published article caused officials to act. All charges were dropped at a new trial before Judge Joseph A. Gillis, where Marcelt repeated his statements to Gardner and Hardy was finally released.

In regard to Silas Rogers and Robert Ballard Bailey, Gardner saved the lives of two innocent men who had been condemned to death. On July 18, 1943, in Petersburg, Virginia, two policemen saw a red car they thought had been reported stolen and chased it. When the red car stalled, the driver leaped out and disappeared into a ravine, while two soldiers who had been riding in the back stayed in the car. Policeman Robert B. Hatchell

followed the driver, a black man, into the woods where he was shot and killed. The police never searched the ravine systematically, but later they found twenty-one-year-old Silas Rogers on a lonely road as he was walking into Petersburg.

Rogers said he was on the bum and had illegally hitched a ride on a train. He told police that a man who "looked like a mechanic" had found him stowed away on the train and ordered him to leave it. Hours later Rogers was found by police. The two soldiers who had been riding in the red car chose, for reasons they never explained, to identify Rogers as the man who had driven them from Raleigh in the stolen car. Two days and nights of interrogation by the police, which Rogers later said included beating, could not get Rogers to agree that he had driven the car. When the police did inquire into Rogers's alibi, none of the men from the train could positively identify him, and they did not find the man identified by Rogers as the "mechanic." Rogers was tried, represented by a court-appointed lawyer, and convicted, primarily on the testimony of the two soldiers. He was sentenced to death.

Starting with an article that appeared in the Richmond *News Leader,* some people began to believe Rogers's story and his court-appointed lawyers obtained a stay of execution. Years passed and the condemned man, insisting that he was innocent, continued to receive reprieves. Rogers finally wrote to Gardner at the Court of Last Resort, and the attorney-writer agreed to investigate his case. Gardner and his associates learned that the red sedan, which Rogers had reportedly driven, had been dusted for fingerprints by police, but none belonging to Silas Rogers had been found. Moreover, they learned that Rogers had never driven a car and did not have a license. In addition, at the time of Rogers's arrest, a conscientious police sergeant who had witnessed his fellow police officers beating Rogers had been threatened with loss of his job by his superiors if he reported it.

Finally, after almost a year of pursuing the thinnest leads, Gardner's bloodhounds located the man who "looked like a mechanic." He was a diesel supervisor who went from train to train, and so had never been identified as a crew member on the train Rogers had been riding. On his firm identification of Rogers as the man who left the train after the murder happened, Rogers's sentence was commuted to life in prison shortly before his scheduled execution. Following Gardner's published findings of Rogers's case, the State of Virginia took action. In March 1953, almost ten years after his arrest, Silas Rogers was unconditionally pardoned by Governor John S. Battle (1950–1954). The actual killer of policeman Hatchell was never found.

Like Rogers, Robert Ballard Bailey sat on death row awaiting execution. Though he insisted that he was innocent of the crime for which he had been convicted, his case seemed hopeless. He had been convicted in 1950 for the murder of a West Virginia housewife. After his conviction, Bailey, who had already served two prison terms in a West Virginia penitentiary, appealed the decision all the way to the U.S. Supreme Court.

The high court denied his appeal and he was scheduled to be the first to die in the state's new electric chair. Just two days before Bailey was to be executed, prison warden Orel Skeen granted him a reprieve from death row, as he believed Bailey was innocent.

Skeen, an avid reader of Gardner's Court of Last Resort articles, contacted the writer-lawyer and detailed Bailey's case. Gardner and his team went to Charleston, West Virginia, where they dug through the police records, learning that, at the very moment the housewife was being murdered, local police were chasing Bailey, who was drunk at the wheel and driving recklessly. Statements from witnesses who saw Bailey being apprehended for drunk driving at that time were not admitted in his trial.

Further, the witnesses identifying Bailey as being near the residence of the slain woman on the night of the murder later admitted that they did not know Bailey and could not identify him with certainty. After Gardner exposed this miscarriage of justice in print, Skeen won a pardon for the convicted man, who was freed after serving ten years for a crime he did not commit. In 1960, Cecil H. Underwood (1957–1961), the governor of West Virginia, granted Bailey a pardon after he was ruled innocent, a victim of "eyewitness error."

## Gene Miller of the Miami Herald

A thin man with unkempt hair, a raspy voice, and the energy of a whirling dervish, Gene Miller, a reporter and later an editor of the *Miami Herald*, was another crusader for unjustly convicted persons in the journalistic tradition of Erle Stanley Gardner. Miller was part terrier, part bloodhound, and all reporter. He had the instincts and inclinations of an old-fashioned detective who loved productive legwork and was obsessed with getting useful information. Equally, he loved the actual hunt for that information, for he was a born ferret and a thorn in the side of any politician or police officer evading his incessant questions.

This author met Miller in 1975 and came away with the impression of having been grilled so intensely that only the maiden name of my great second aunt had been overlooked. He was a reporter who checked and double-checked everything and anybody having to do with a potential story. He embraced and advocated the dictates of A. A. Dornfeld, the night editor of Chicago's old City News Bureau: "If your mother tells you she loves you, check it out!"

Miller was chronically nagged by suspicion and doubt, and yet he was affable, optimistic, and openminded. He likely believed

Crusading newspaperman Gene Miller, whose investigative articles for the Miami Herald brought about the exonerations of several wrongly convicted persons and for which he was awarded two Pulitzer Prizes. *Miami Herald.*

that Ernest Hemingway was not being sarcastic when he wrote that "the world is a fine place and worth fighting for." There was a childlike innocence in the man and he unabashedly shared that innocence with strangers, believing that innocence resides in the hearts of many thought to be guilty of the most heinous crimes. His great gift was an ability to distinguish the victim and the perpetrator, expertly exercising through the exhausting facts he assembled a mental mechanism that one might call a "built-in guilt detector."

Born in Evansville, Indiana, on September 16, 1928, Miller graduated from Indiana University. He went to work for the *Miami Herald* and stayed there for forty-eight years, until his retirement in 2001. Before he died in 2005 of cancer (he wrote his own obituary that included the jocular line: "Excellent health, except for a fatal disease"), Miller had effected the release of many wrongly convicted persons through his investigative reporting, and he won two Pulitzer Prizes in the process. Humans living ten generations from now may owe their existence to Gene Miller, who saved the lives of their antecedents, innocent people who might otherwise have died childless behind bars or walked that last mile to Florida's electric chair.

One of these persons was an enlisted man in the U.S. Air Force. Strange circumstances and his own inexplicable admissions sent him to prison for life. His story began three miles from Miami International Airport, where the bullet-ridden body of twenty-three-year-old Mary Meslener was found on February 25, 1959, along the bank of the Miami River. The National Airlines reservations employee had last been seen two nights before as she headed toward her car at the airport. The bloodstained car was found two weeks later, 250 miles northwest, in Tampa. Not one clue was discovered on the body or car, and it was not until more than a month later that police were informed of a possible suspect.

Joseph Francis Shea, twenty-one, an airman stationed at the West Palm Beach Air Force Base, told colleagues that he had recently harmed a baby but could not remember what he had done. It was later discovered that a woman he was seeing in the Philippines had refused to marry him and run off with their child. A bloodstained shirt found in his possession also could not be explained. Officials at the base notified police of the shirt and of Shea's statements.

No children had been reported injured or killed, but the Dade County Homicide Bureau was nonetheless interested. After Detective Philip Thibedeau interviewed Shea, however, he determined that he was not Meslener's killer. A week later, two other detectives returned to the base. The stains on one of Shea's shirts had been identified as human blood. Detectives questioned Shea a second time, but, once again, he did not impress them as a suspect in the Meslener slaying. After this interview, the detectives stopped to talk with two military police officers just outside the room where Shea was being held.

Shea heard their detailed conversation of the Meslener murder, and, when the detectives stepped back into the consultation room, Shea repeated their conversation in what the detectives interpreted as a confession. Prior to this "confession," Shea had been examined by a psychiatrist, who determined that he was "agitated, depressed, and anxious." Two days after his arrest, Shea denied committing the murder.

Shea made a second confession within a week. This came after police told him that his fingerprints had been found on Meslener's car, which was not true, and that he had failed a lie detector test. He had actually passed the lie detector test, which reported his innocence. Police also stated that eyewitnesses had identified him, although there were no such witnesses. Further, police said that the blood on his shirt matched Meslener's, when in fact it matched his own. In 1959, this confession was used to convict Shea. He was sentenced to life in prison.

Disgruntled by his department's handling of the investigation, Thibedeau quit the police department. Warren D. Holmes, head of the Miami police polygraph department, felt his superiors' claim that his findings were inaccurate—supporting Shea's innocence instead of indicating guilt—and that their misrepresentation of his tests on Shea had tarnished his record. He also resigned. The two men soon contacted *Miami Herald* reporter Gene Miller, asking him to work with them in clearing Shea's name.

Miller listened to what they had to say, and he and his editor agreed to look into the case. Miller launched a full-scale investigation into the Shea case, which showed that Shea had been coerced into a confession through misrepresentations by police, who claimed to have incontrovertible evidence to prove his guilt, when they had none. Most importantly, Miller discovered that Shea had been on duty eighty miles from the murder scene an hour before the murder, making it impossible for him to have slain Meslener.

Miller's hard-hitting articles about the Shea case and its attendant corruption prompted Shea's attorney, Harry W. Prebish, to seek a new trial. Subsequently, based on the findings of Miller and the statements of Thibedeau and Holmes, Shea was acquitted. In 1967, the Florida state legislature awarded Shea $45,000 in compensation. That same year, Miller won a Pulitzer Prize for his work on the acquittal of Shea and that of a Louisiana woman wrongly convicted of murder, whom Holmes had also worked to clear. That woman was Mary Kathryn Hampton.

In 1959, at the age of seventeen, Mary Hampton left Sandy Hook, Kentucky, to live with boyfriend Emmitt Monroe Spencer. Hampton lived with Spencer for eleven months and gave birth to a son. In April 1960, Spencer was arrested and convicted of murdering a thirty-six-year-old pipe fitter in Key West, Florida. It was Hampton's testimony that helped send Spencer to Florida's death row. In retaliation, the killer concocted a story implicating Mary in two of his many serial killings (claims of almost fifty murders). He told Louisiana authorities that she had participated in the murders of Benjamin Yount and Hermine

Fiedler near Patterson, Louisiana, on December 31, 1959.

Mary Hampton was arrested in Kentucky, where she returned after testifying against Spencer. She confessed on April 11, 1961, after the police threatened her with the electric chair. The confession was accepted, and she forfeited the presumption of innocence. There was no evidence linking her to the murders other than the faulty testimony of an unreliable witness. She was convicted on two counts of first-degree murder and received a life sentence, which she began serving at the women's state prison in San Gabriel, Louisiana, on April 24, 1961.

After studying the Hampton case, reporter Gene Miller began a one-man investigation in the pages of the *Miami Herald* to exonerate Mary Hampton. He spent three years investigating the case and interviewing witnesses before Hampton got a second chance in court on the strength of the stories he had written. By that time, famed criminal defense attorney F. Lee Bailey had become interested in Miller's crusade (at Miller's request) and agreed to waive his fees and represent her. At Hampton's second trial, Bailey destroyed Spencer's testimony, which claimed Mary had participated in forty-seven of forty-eight murders committed in a ten-year period. Hampton's original conviction was upheld in court, but in a special hearing conducted in November 1966, Hampton's sentence was commuted by Louisiana Governor John J. McKeithen (1964–1972) and the state pardons board ordered her release.

In the same year Hampton was released, Miller heard through his extensive grapevine that a prison inmate had confessed to a murder for which two others had been convicted and were awaiting execution. He immediately went after the truth, first learning that, on August 1, 1963, a group of people drove into a service station in Port St. Joe, Florida. Two men, Wilbert Lee, a twenty-year-old army private, and Freddie Pitts, a twenty-eight-year-old pulp cutter, were denied the use of rest rooms because they were black. They quarreled with the attendants, Grover Floyd Jr. and Jesse Burkett, and, three days later, the two white attendants were found dead.

An eyewitness, Willie Mae Lee, blamed Pitts and another soldier for the shootings. When the other soldier provided a solid alibi, she told authorities that Wilbert Lee was responsible. Lee and Pitts were arrested and confessed to the murders after they were beaten by police. They pleaded guilty as advised by their public defender, and on August 28, 1963, both men were sentenced to death.

Shortly thereafter, Curtis Adams Jr. also black, was convicted for the murder of another Florida service station attendant. In 1966, he admitted to his cell mate that he had killed the Port St. Joe attendants. *Miami Herald* reporter Gene Miller learned of Adams's confession and launched a probe into the Lee-Pitts case. His articles detailed the police coercion and the bad advice given by their legal counsel. Two new attorneys took the case. In 1968, Willie Mae Lee rescinded her statement, claiming that police forced her to identify Pitts and Lee as the murderers. Her retraction, however, was not disclosed to the defense until four years later. In 1969, the convictions were overturned and a retrial was granted, but, in 1970, a state appeals court reaffirmed the convictions and death penalties.

Goaded by Miller's many newspaper articles on the case—the *Miami Herald* ran 130 articles about Lee and Pitts, most of which were written by Miller, which later appeared in Miller's book, *Invitation to a Lynching*—state officials began to act. In 1971, the Florida attorney general said the state had illegally concealed evidence and another trial was scheduled. Pitts and Lee were tried again in 1972, this time pleading not guilty, but Adams would not give legal testimony unless the state granted him immunity. Prosecutors sought the death penalty. Again, Pitts and Lee were convicted by an all-white jury and sentenced to death. An appeals court upheld the convictions.

In the same year, Arthur Kennedy, the legal adviser to Governor Reubin Askew (1971–1979),

read a draft of reporter Miller's new book, which detailed how Lee and Pitts had been wrongly convicted and condemned to death for a crime they did not commit. Kennedy convinced the governor to call for an inquiry, one that supported Miller's research and exonerated Lee and Pitts. The governor granted both men full pardons. On September 19, 1975, after twelve years in jail for crimes they did not commit, Wilbert Lee, then thirty-two, and Freddie Pitts, then forty, walked out of the Florida state prison in Starke, Florida. The man who had brought about their freedom was awarded his second Pulitzer Prize in 1976. Lee became a counselor to prison inmates and Pitts went to work as a truck driver. Each man was awarded $500,000 compensation by the state in 1998 as compensation for wrongful imprisonment.

Gene Miller, however, was not a person to rest on laurels or be contented with the accomplishments of the past. His always churning mill found great new grist in the coming decades and new forlorn persons to champion. One of his last crusades involved a ne'er-do-well biker with a reputation so bad that it seemed impossible to prove that he had been wrongly convicted and sentenced to death for a murder he did not commit.

In May 1995, attorney Michael Mello made a phone call to Miller, who was then an editor at the *Miami Herald*. Mello did not know Miller other than through his reputation as a crusading journalist. Mello, who was a law professor at the University of Vermont, had undertaken the case of Joseph Robert "Crazy Joe" Spaziano. He explained to Miller that this was the first such phone call he had ever made. But he had exhausted all appeals for his client, and Spaziano's date of execution was nearing. He needed help and he needed it now.

Over the years Miller had been inundated with requests to crusade for imprisoned or condemned persons, but he had always believed that only a rare few were truly innocent. "Everyone behind bars claims to be innocent," he told this author on one occasion. "Almost all those claims are baseless. Clerical errors in transcripts or any kind of document also doesn't make them innocent. But, if you're looking closely at one of those documents and you find a statement or pinpoint an identity, or identify an event that might solidly contradict the official record as false, you have to look at it, you have to follow the lead, you have to pursue."

Miller told Mello that he would look at his documentation on the case, but he felt, at that time, that he would most probably dismiss the Spaziano case as having no foundation for an appeal. When reviewing Mello's documents, however, Miller saw the name of Joseph B. McCawley, a hypnotist whom he had discredited years before when writing the protracted newspaper series that eventually brought about the exoneration of Lee and Pitts.

The comprehensive documentation in the Spaziano case showed that he had been convicted and sentenced to death for the mutilation murder of eighteen-year-old Laura Lynn Harberts, who disappeared on August 5, 1973. Her remains, and those of another woman never identified, were found in a Seminole County garbage dump on August 21, 1973, but her body was so badly decomposed that police could not determine cause of death. Harberts worked at a local hospital and reportedly had a penchant for hitchhiking.

Initially, police believed that Lynwood Tate, a native of Athens, Georgia, who had a police record, was responsible for murdering Harberts and the unidentified woman. Tate, who had been accused of raping an Orlando woman, had once applied for a job at the hospital where Harberts worked. He was arrested and given a polygraph test, which he reportedly failed. He was then hypnotized, but police did not charge him in the two murders.

In 1974 police learned that a naïve seventeen-year-old boy, Anthony DiLisio, might know something about Harberts. He gave them nothing but vague statements until police summoned hypnotist McCawley. Under hypnosis DiLisio reportedly told McCawley that Spaziano had taken him to the dump and showed him the body, telling him that he not only killed the girl but savagely mutilated her genitals with a knife before he murdered her. He later, again after being hypnotized by McCawley, stated that Spaziano had also raped and murdered Vanessa Dale Croft, who was killed on February 9, 1974.

In August 1975, Spaziano was convicted of murdering and raping Croft, and in January 1976, he was tried and convicted of brutally killing Harberts. DiLisio testified in both trials, but the fact that his statements were obtained through hypnosis was not revealed to jurors. In the 1976 trial, DiLisio provided inconsistent testimony. He had originally told police that he had been taking LSD when he first saw the bodies at the dump, but, at his trial, he said he had not been using any LSD at that time. He made other statements that conflicted with his original statements to police.

Yet these inconsistencies were not challenged by defense attorney Ed Kirkland. The jury at the 1976 trial recommended a life term, but Judge Robert McGregor gave Spaziano a death sentence. His lawyers filed one frantic appeal after another to stave off execution, three by the time Mello (assigned as a public defender in the case in 1983) contacted Miller, and two more reaffirmed death sentences after Miller went to work on the case, five reaffirmed death sentences in all.

Mello stressed to Miller that three key issues had convinced him that his client had been wrongly convicted, the first being that it violated the federal constitution to permit judges to override a jury recommendation of life imprisonment, as Judge McGregor had done. Further, the key witness in Spaziano's trial, DiLisio, had revealed information only under hypnosis, and the jury had never been informed that the witness's testimony had been "enhanced" by hypnosis.

Further, Mello pointed out, Harberts had been talking to a man she knew, Juan Suarez, a coworker and known sex offender, shortly before she disappeared, not Spaziano. The attorney stated to Miller that Suarez had denied seeing Harberts on the eve of her disappearance, but, in an undisclosed documented interview, it was established that police concluded that Suarez had been lying and had indeed talked with the victim shortly before she disappeared. Suarez was not charged in the case.

After reviewing Mello's documentation, Miller concluded that Spaziano might be innocent, particularly since he had been convicted of murdering Harberts only through McCawley's hypnotic evidence from DiLisio, and was shocked to learn that every appeals court in the land had upheld that conviction. (Hypnotism has since been determined unreliable and has been barred from trials.) The first thing Miller did was to contact a friend, former police polygraph expert Warren D. Holmes, who had worked with him to free wrongly convicted Joseph Francis Shea almost three decades earlier. Over the years Holmes had aided Miller on many other miscarriage of justice stories.

Miller gave Holmes all the documentation he had received from Mello. Holmes, whom Miller had once described as "a man with a ruthlessly logical mind," quickly concluded that DiLisio had lied, discrediting the idea of exclusively using hypnosis to convict a man and send him to his death. Miller agreed and subsequently organized a campaign that would involve the whole of Florida's journalistic community, intent on lobbying high officials to stay Spaziano's execution and getting more legal aid in bringing about an exoneration.

In so doing, Gene Miller had abandoned the concept of journalistic "neutrality," where only the facts must speak. The fictional detective Joe Friday of *Dragnet* fame and his "just the facts" philosophy in solving a case would not do in this instance. There were no facts, only the unsupported statements of a teenager who had allegedly been put into a hypnotic trance. But the entire court system had relied on these statements in sending a man to the electric chair. This so-called legal procedure was so ambiguous—ludicrous to many—as to be laughable, if it had not involved a man's impending death.

Miller began by having Mello write a lengthy opinion piece that was sent to almost every newspaper in the state, including the *Herald*. It ran not only in the *Herald* but in the *St. Petersburg Times* and the Orlando *Sentinel*, which competed with the *Herald* for this story.

When criticized for his tactics, Miller replied, "A man's life is at stake. I think I am doing the right thing." In the ensuing campaign, headed by Miller, the *Herald* was lambasted by one of its top competitors, the Orlando *Sentinel*, which eventually took the opposite view—if Spaziano was spared a cold-blooded murderer would escape justice. Harberts had been murdered in the Orlando area and the *Sentinel* took a proprietary view of covering the case. Yet the *Herald* scooped the *Sentinel* in its own backyard. That was the doing of Gene Miller, who brought about the assignment of reporter Lori Rosza to the Spaziano case.

Rosza, thirty-five, worked in the *Herald*'s Palm Beach bureau and chiefly wrote on environmental issues. She was asked if she had any qualms in covering Spaziano's execution, which was scheduled for June 27, 1995. She said she had none, adding that the Ted Bundys of the world deserved to die. She was sent Mello's records and Miller's notes and concluded, like her superiors, that something was terribly wrong with the Spaziano case.

Flying to Pensacola, Florida, Rosza attempted to interview Anthony DiLisio. (She had been given his address by attorney Mello.) At first, DiLisio slammed the front door in her face. When she returned, he did it again, this time threatening to call the police if she came back again. She returned a third time and was ordered away, and then a fourth and fifth time. DiLisio agreed to talk to her on that fifth visit. He told a strange, eerie tale.

DiLisio said that his family had been dominated by his strong-willed father, Ralph DiLisio. He always tried to please his father but always seemed to fail in his father's eyes. He stated that his father had an affair with an employee of his, Keppy, who later became his stepmother, with whom Anthony also had an affair. (In 1974 it was Keppy, or Keppie, DiLisio who told police that Spaziano had raped and murdered Vanessa Dale Croft.) According to DiLisio, at the same time Keppy was separately sexually trysting with Ralph and Anthony DiLisio, she was having an affair with another DiLisio employee—Joseph Spaziano, a biker who had belonged to an outlaw motorcycle gang.

Ralph DiLisio discovered the affair between Keppy and Spaziano and vented his rage against Spaziano, asking his son if Spaziano had ever mentioned mutilating women. Anthony DiLisio replied that he had never heard Spaziano make such statements, but the idea that Spaziano was capable of such barbarous conduct was planted in the teenager's mind.

As a teenager, DiLisio had several brushes with the law involving alcohol and drugs. While he was in juvenile detention, detectives approached DiLisio, asking him to help them solve the Harberts murder. (It is unclear if these investigators were directed to DiLisio by his father, who had a decided animosity toward Spaziano, or by Keppy DiLisio.) The investigators told DiLisio that present charges against him would be dropped and he could go home if he cooperated. His father urged him to do so.

Police then introduced McCawley, the hypnotist, to DiLisio, and he agreed to be placed in a hypnotic trance, but only after police had provided him with details about the remains of Vanessa Harberts. During her interview with DiLisio, Rosza asked him what he thought of hypnotism. DiLisio called it "witchcraft." He recanted everything he had reportedly stated under hypnosis. He said that Spaziano never took him to the garbage dump to show him any body and that he had only made the injurious statements about Spaziano to please his father and the police. He told Rosza that Spaziano's execution should be halted and that he was innocent of murdering Harberts.

On June 11, 1995, only sixteen days before Spaziano was scheduled to die in the electric chair, Rosza's story about DiLisio ran on the front page of the *Miami Herald*. The shock of recognition in this case jarred government officials, incensed an alerted public and forced the Orlando *Sentinel* to immediately dispatch its own reporter to belatedly interview DiLisio.

*Sentinel* bosses were angry at Miller's ploy to use his competitors to support his campaign to save Spaziano's life. They felt that they had been set up by publishing Mello's legal opinion on the case—which they did in an effort to appear fair to Spaziano—and had then been compelled to answer the *Herald's* hard-hitting exposé, written by Rosza, in which DiLisio recanted his statements, an act that essentially collapsed the government's case in the Harberts slaying.

Michael Griffin, the *Sentinel's* bureau chief in Tallahassee, then went to DiLisio and conducted his own interview. DiLisio told Griffin that he had become a Christian and had been clean of drugs for years. He nevertheless repeated almost word for word the recantation he had given Rosza earlier. Where Rosza believed DiLisio's statements, Griffin was convinced that he was not telling the truth. "I caught the guy in the first fifteen minutes in a half dozen lies," Griffin was later quoted.

Griffin and other *Sentinel* reporters wrote a barrage of stories that discredited DiLisio's recantation, demeaned his character and generally profiled DiLisio as an unreliable witness, claiming that he was lying at this time but had told the truth twenty years earlier when he was under hypnosis, a contradictory track of reasoning that actually supported Gene Miller's crusade.

Attorney Mello took heart when he saw the Rosza story and believed that he had a chance to save his client's life. He wrote to Spaziano, stating, "With the help of God and the *Miami Herald*, we'll cross the finish line together... The *Sentinel* will write whatever it wants, and if another [death] warrant comes, your blood will be on their hands."

The State of Florida, like the Orlando *Sentinel*, could not ignore the Rosza story. On June 14, 1995, it dispatched several top officers from the Florida Department of Law Enforcement (FDLE) to interview DiLisio. He repeated his recantation to them and stated that he had not told the truth when McCawley supposedly hypnotized him, implying that he had only pretended to be in a hypnotic state. This police interrogation of DiLisio was videotaped. The following day, Governor Lawton M. Chiles Jr. (1991–1998) issued a stay of execution for Spaziano. Chiles, at the same time, ordered the FDLE to conduct a secret investigation into the credibility of DiLisio's recantation.

On August 17, 1995, FDLE officers submitted a report to Governor Chiles, stating that DiLisio's recantation was not credible. On August 24, 1995, Chiles signed a fifth death warrant calling for Spaziano's execution at 7:00 A.M. on September 21, 1995, stating that FDLE officers had discovered new evidence that supported Spaziano's guilt. On September 7, 1995, oral arguments before the Florida Supreme Court were made on Spaziano's behalf for a stay of execution. On the following day, the court denied a stay and ordered evidentiary hearings to be held within ninety-six hours. Attorney Mello refused to attend these hearings, believing that his client was being railroaded by the government. The Florida Supreme Court fired him from the case and assigned a public defender to handle Spaziano's case. It issued an indefinite stay of execution at that time.

Spaziano's case, despite the heroic efforts of Miller, Mello and the reporters of the *Miami Herald*, seemed hopeless. The *Herald*, however, would not give up on this "lost cause." It brought Hanlon and Holland and Knight, the largest legal firm in Florida with 475 attorneys, into the case. The firm dedicated some of its top people—partner Greg Thomas of its Tampa office, aided by Orlando criminal attorney Jim Russ—to focus on DiLisio's recantation. They brought forth two experts on repressed memory who examined the statements DiLisio made while reportedly under hypnosis and discounted them as fabricated. They also had DiLisio repeat his recantation, which was evaluated by experts to be genuine. These findings

were then presented at another hearing on January 22, 1996. Subsequently circuit court Judge O. H. Eaton Jr. threw out Spaziano's conviction and death sentence in the Harberts case and ordered a new trial.

In an eight-page decision Eaton wrote, "In the United States of America every person, no matter how unsavory, is entitled to due process of law and a fair trial. The defendant received neither. The validity of the verdict in this case rests upon the testimony of an admitted perjurer, who had every reason to fabricate a story, which he hoped would be believed." Eaton's decision, however, only strengthened the resolve of the State to continue proceedings against Spaziano. On June 3, 1997, a grand jury again indicted Spaziano for the murder of Harberts. Further, prosecutors had a new witness against him, Chris Moore, who claimed that Spaziano had admitted murdering Harberts and Croft to him, while they were in prison together. Even though the testimony of such a witness was suspect (Moore was trying to negotiate his own release through such testimony), this new threat to Spaziano was real and might be effective in bringing about another conviction.

Fearing that another wrongful conviction would again put him on death row, Spaziano entered a no-contest plea to second-degree murder in the Harberts slaying. Through plea bargaining, his lawyers negotiated a sentence of time served plus two years. At this writing, Spaziano remains in prison, serving a life term for the rape-murder of sixteen-year-old Vanessa Croft in Orlando, Florida, in 1974, a crime he insists he did not commit. He has continued filing appeals.

Gene Miller could not help him in this case, having died on June 17, 2005, after a long bout with cancer. Yet Joseph Robert Spaziano is still alive. So are many others, who might have died in prison or the electric chair had not this wonderful, enterprising, and inspired newspaperman walked the face of the earth.

# II
# *Fighting for Justice*

## The Citizen

THROUGHOUT HISTORY, FROM THE RANKS of the poor and the rich, the obscure and the famous, brave souls have championed the rights of those they felt were wrongly convicted. Whether prompted by conscience, idealism, or their obligations as officials or citizens, these intrepid defenders of human rights faced and battled the establishment, overcoming judicial decisions and convictions that seemed to be ironclad.

In attempting to free the wrongly convicted, these advocates of justice were often challenged by venal and corrupt officials, conniving police officers, or the actual criminals who had escaped conviction at the expense of another. Many of these champions suffered ridicule and humiliation. Many lost their fortunes and careers in their crusade to exonerate an innocent person. Some lost their health and even their lives.

The dedication of these warriors for justice is indefatigable. In their search for the truth, these fighters battled against seemingly overwhelming evidence. They had to overcome rigged, planted, or suppressed documentation, the false, mistaken, or perjured statements of witnesses. They had to confront corrupt authorities capable of doing them great harm. They had to challenge the unchallengeable—forensic science itself. Their triumphs proved that you *can* fight city hall, you *can* tell it to the judge; the "truth will out," but not

without the vigorous pursuit of justice. In that dogged pursuit, dangers and hazards have always lurked. Those following that path, however, bore powerful weapons—integrity and courage.

One such heroic battler was Herbert L. Maris (1880–1960), a celebrated Philadelphia attorney. He was so successful in clearing wrongly convicted persons that a television series entitled *Lock-Up* (1959–1961) profiled his life and career, with actor Macdonald Carey portraying the intrepid attorney. Maris eventually became known as the "lifer's last hope." In one appeals case, a young man had been convicted of murdering his girlfriend by hitting her on the back of the neck with a beer bottle. He testified that he had been rubbing the girl's neck when she went into convulsions, blood spurted from her mouth, and she collapsed. Three witnesses said they saw the defendant strike the woman, and he was convicted and sentenced to life. On questioning from Maris, none of the witnesses held up. When Maris reintroduced the coroner's report showing that the girl had died of an aortal aneurysm, the conviction was overturned and the supposed killer freed.

Maris was credited with clearing as many as five hundred unjustly convicted persons during his fifty-year career. He once cleared a Pennsylvania farmer convicted of murder and sentenced to death. When Maris took the man's case, his sentence had been commuted to life imprisonment and he had already served ten years. Maris discovered that the farmer had been the victim of a prank by two constables and two civilians. The four had decided to "arrest" the farmer, take him miles from his home, and make him walk back. The farmer, however, thought he was being kidnapped, and shot and killed one of the constables. The other three claimed the farmer was under arrest for stealing a calf when the shooting occurred. Maris showed that the warrant had not been signed until three months after the abduction. Maris believed the guilt of 20 percent of people in prisons was questionable, and he continued trying to free the innocent well into his seventies, often without a fee.

Typical of Maris's cases was the plight of Frank Harris and Wilbert MacQueen, who were stopped by two Philadelphia policemen on March 4, 1926. When shots were fired, MacQueen was killed and Harris was wounded. Convicted of first-degree murder in a quarter sessions court in September 1926, the twenty-eight-year-old Harris was sentenced to life in prison.

Prior to his conviction, Harris had served two short terms for minor offenses. In 1946, Maris visited the penitentiary to talk to prisoners who felt they were eligible for parole. He became convinced of Harris's innocence and spent months finding evidence to prove that the bullet which killed MacQueen could not have come from Harris's gun. Maris presented his evidence, including new ballistics reports that supported Harris's innocence, to state officials. In 1947, Pennsylvania Governor James Henderson Duff (1947–1951) commuted Harris's sentence. At the age of forty-nine, after twenty-one years in jail, the wrongly convicted Harris was released.

## Taking the Extra Step

The justice-seeking Herbert Maris was not alone. Conscientious citizens, officers of the law, and officials of all stripes have given their time, effort, and even money to secure justice for persons they barely knew. The alertness and attention to detail of these good neighbors, as well as nagging curiosity and the satisfaction of correcting a wrong, brought freedom to countless persons and, in many instances, saved the lives of innocent people slated for execution. These benevolent saviors, many of whom are lost in obscurity by their own insistence, quietly accomplished their self-assigned missions by taking the extra step to help their fellow man.

Such was the case involving Cornelius Usher of Lynn, Massachusetts, in 1902. A police officer walked out of a local pawn shop and saw Usher walk in with a large bundle. The recent robbery of a shoe factory made the officer suspicious of what Usher was pawning, which turned out to be a stolen pair of lasting pincers. Usher was arrested and charged with burglary, although he told police that he was innocent and did not know the tool had been stolen. Usher said he met a man named Coughlin in a bar and he was given the tools after Coughlin was unable to pawn them. Despite his pleas of innocence, Usher was convicted of burglary and sentenced to from three to five years in prison.

Nearly two years later, John H. Coughlin was arrested in Salem, Massachusetts. When news of the arrest was made public, a man read the newspaper account, which also mentioned Usher's arrest and his claim that he had been given tools by Coughlin. This citizen stepped forward and told police that he was present when Coughlin gave the tools to Usher, but asked that his name not be made public. He signed a statement that endorsed Usher's claim, and this prompted Judge John W. Berry to recall Usher from prison and initiate proceedings to secure a pardon for the wrongly convicted man. On May 20, 1904, Coughlin pleaded guilty to robbing the shoe factory and was sentenced to eighteen months in prison. Five days later, Governor John L. Bates (1903–1905) granted Usher a pardon, and he later received $1,000 in restitution for his wrongful imprisonment.

Another citizen, George E. Bunting of Virginia, conducted a desperate search for a missing person or the person's body in an effort to free an imprisoned friend. Bunting belonged to a congregation at Reid's Ferry, Virginia, which in 1908 faced a dilemma. Members could not agree on whether to keep Reverend James Smith or replace him with the younger Reverend Ernest Lyons, who had helped Smith conduct services. This situation alone would have caused enough friction between the two clergymen, but their problems intensified when Lyons became suspicious that Smith was having an affair with Lyons's sister-in-law.

Lyons became the preacher after Smith mysteriously disappeared on July 31, 1908, one day before he was to join the congregation at a regional church conference in nearby Suffolk. That day, witnesses saw Lyons and Smith arguing about the conference, and Lyons reportedly threatening to kill his rival. Smith was carrying his church's $45 conference fund when he disappeared.

Smith's supporters were mystified but thought they learned the reverend's fate when a badly decomposed body was found near the church in the Nansemond River. The unidentified body was buried by the county, only to be exhumed following a tip concerning its identity. Unearthed was a ring with a purple setting that matched a description of a ring Smith wore. The body was then closely examined, and cause of death was determined to be a blow to the head with a blunt object.

Lyons was accused of murdering Smith, and his trial began on January 13, 1909, in the Nansemond County circuit court, Judge James L. McLemore presiding. Commonwealth attorney James U. Burgess said the ring proved that the body was Smith's, and that because Lyons kept changing his story about the last time he had seen Smith, he must be guilty of murdering him. Lyons was found guilty and, on January 16, 1909, was sentenced to eighteen years in prison. Lyons's attorney, Robert W. Withers, remained convinced, however, of his innocence.

Then during an interview, Lyons confessed to the murder and accused the congregants who testified against him of being accomplices to the crime. The church members were arrested, but Lyons abandoned his accusations, stating that he could not lie in the Lord's name about their complicity. The congregants were released, and Lyons was sent to the penitentiary.

The case seemed settled, except that Reverend Smith was found living in North Carolina by George E. Bunting, a friend of Lyons's who had conducted his own investigation. Through friends and relatives, Bunting spent more than two years tracking Smith through several states. He eventually located Smith and convinced him to return to Virginia. Smith explained to Judge McLemore that he knew Lyons had been wrongly convicted of murder, but did nothing because he had stolen the $45 church fund. The judge noted that Smith, at the time of his reappearance, was wearing a ring with a purple setting, the same kind of ring found on the corpse. Lyons was pardoned by Governor William H. Mann (1910–1914) on April 3, 1912, three years after the alleged murder.

Unlike the dogged Bunting, Boston police officer Joseph M. Balk never thought of himself as a hero. He was a beat cop supporting a large family and working toward a pension in the hopes that his duties would not leave him crippled or dead in the process. On the night of February 8, 1911, Balk observed two men running along the street, one chasing the other with a gun. Balk entered the chase and caught up to the men after one had fallen down.

John McManus, twenty-nine, knelt on the ground, while John Shorey held a revolver over him. Both men were arrested. Shorey, a deputy sheriff in Conway, New Hampshire, claimed that McManus had stolen his watch and chain, and that he was merely stopping the thief. He was released and fined $50 for carrying a concealed weapon. His story, however, was not in any way similar to the version McManus told.

McManus stated that on that night he had been seeking employment. A heavy snowfall that day convinced a Mr. Coleman that the Boston Elevated Company might need men to shovel snow.

McManus applied but was not hired. While returning home, he said, he ran into Shorey. The officer had just had a fight with his girlfriend, who had ordered him from her house. Shorey decided to take his anger out on McManus and shoved him. When McManus returned the shove, Shorey pulled out his revolver and fired at him. He then chased the fleeing McManus down the street until he fell. When Balk arrived on the scene, Shorey, said McManus, made up the robbery story to avoid further trouble.

The jury, however, believed the tale Shorey told and found McManus guilty of robbing Shorey. McManus was sentenced to three years in prison on March 15, 1911. If not for the curiosity of Balk, McManus would have remained in prison for a crime that never occurred. In January 1912, Balk read a newspaper account of a deputy sheriff who had been arrested for assault and battery and for illegally carrying a revolver after attacking a newspaper boy. The case sounded familiar, and Balk discovered that the offender was Shorey, who had received three months imprisonment for each offense.

Balk conducted his own investigation on his own time, and, after assembling a criminal profile on Shorey, he notified the district attorney and convinced him that McManus was innocent, pointing out that Shorey's criminal conduct supported McManus's claims at his trial. The district attorney recommended on February 27, 1912, that McManus be pardoned, and the next day Governor Eugene Noble Foss (1911–1914) ordered his release.

McManus sought out Balk and found him on his beat. He rushed up to the cop and embraced him, thanking him for proving his innocence. "I was just doing my job," Balk said.

Eight months after McManus was released in Massachusetts, British police were confronted with a letter writer as malicious as John Shorey. They, like Balk, took extra pains to identify the true culprit. In October 1912, Mrs. Mary Johnson, a shop owner in Earlswood, England, whose husband was a traveling salesman, was accused of sending threatening letters to her neighbors, Mr.

and Mrs. Woodman. The letters, inspected by police, threatened murder. Since March 1912, the Woodmans had received the letters almost daily. The letters had been delivered in various ways, including one wrapped around a rock and flung in the direction of Mrs. Woodman. Mrs. Johnson denied these acts but was nevertheless convicted of making murder threats and sentenced to six months imprisonment.

Mrs. Johnson was released in March 1913, but six months later was again accused of sending threatening letters to the Woodmans, as well as other neighbors. She was again convicted, and this time sentenced to twelve months of hard labor. When she was released in June 1914, the letters started again. This time, a jury found her not guilty. The police began to suspect Mrs. Woodman.

Without her knowledge, police marked Mrs. Woodman's stationery. The threats recurred on this paper. Eliza Ellen Woodman was then charged and convicted of criminal slander and wrongful accusations. She was sentenced to eighteen months of hard labor. Mary Johnson received £500 in compensation, but her business had collapsed during her two imprisonments.

An almost identical case occurred in May 1920, when thirty-year-old Edith Emily Swan, a well-bred woman from Littlehampton, England, said Rose Emma Gooding, twenty-nine, her next-door neighbor and a woman of a lower class, had sent her obscene written material. Gooding denied it. The court decided that she was guilty (on the strength of the statements from the esteemed Edith Swan) and sent Gooding to prison twice. Not until Inspector Nicholls of Scotland Yard investigated was it discovered that Gooding had been wrongly accused, and had been a victim of Britain's rigid class system.

According to Swan, Gooding had abused and threatened her and had pushed the obscene writings under her door. Nicholls, however, realized that the paper in Gooding's house in no way resembled the paper on which the obscenities had been written. Further, the writing he found in

Swan's house was similar to that of the notes, and the notes continued arriving even with Gooding in prison.

The inspector pointed out that Gooding could not possibly have written the notes, and he wanted to know why no attorney or investigator had bothered to notice this in either of the woman's two previous trials. On the strength of Nichols's investigation and findings, Gooding was released from prison and given £250 in compensation. Edith Swan was not prosecuted.

## The Stielow Case and George H. Bond

In 1915, Charles B. Phelps, who was in his seventies, and his housekeeper, Margaret Wolcott, lived in western New York State, about one mile south of West Shelby in Orleans County. During the night of March 21, 1915, Erwin King and Clarence O'Connell broke into the farmhouse, shooting the housekeeper and Phelps, and looting the house. The dying housekeeper struggled to a tenant's house and collapsed on the doorstep in the snow.

Several hours later, at 5:00 A.M., a thirty-seven-year-old farmhand, Charles F. Stielow, rose to begin his chores and found the dead housekeeper outside his house. Investigating, he discovered the unconscious Phelps on the kitchen floor. Phelps was rushed to the hospital, where he later died from three bullet wounds.

During the police investigation, officials brought a dog to track the killer and it followed a scent to a stream. Police also found that money had been taken, and that the victims had both been killed with a .22-caliber revolver. Though Stielow had a .22-caliber revolver that had not been fired in years and a rifle in the house, his wife and mother-in-law urged him to move them. He took them to the barn and then gave them to his brother-in-law, Raymond Green. Authorities later found the guns in Green's possession and determined that the bullets that killed Phelps and

the housekeeper had been fired from Stielow's handgun.

On April 21, 1915, Stielow and nineteen-year-old Nelson Green, another brother-in-law, were arrested on murder charges and, on April 23, 1915, officials procured an alleged confession from Stielow, which he steadfastly refused to sign. Stielow's trial at Albion began on July 11, 1915, and he was convicted, primarily on the strength of the unsigned testimony, which Judge Cuthbert W. Pound allowed, saying that both sides could testify regarding the methods used to secure the admission. The officials, two private detectives and the sheriff and a deputy sheriff of Orleans County, insisted that they did not use force to obtain Stielow's confession (and later insisted that they followed proper methods in obtaining Green's confession, when Green's trial followed). Lawyers for Stielow and Green claimed in their separate trials that third degree methods had been used to acquire those statements.

Pound believed the officials and sentenced Stielow to be executed in early September. (Executions in these days were scheduled quickly, allowing little time for the convicted person to make appeals, let alone prove his or her innocence.) Green was then tried, and, after seeing the judicial fate of his brother-in-law, pleaded guilty to save his life. He was convicted and sentenced to twenty years to life in prison at Auburn Penitentiary.

Stielow's execution was put off while he filed frantic appeals. On February 22, 1916, however, Stielow's conviction was affirmed. Appealing to prison officials, Stielow continued to claim his innocence and a New York lawyer, Grace Humiston, as well as the Humanitarian Cult, became active in trying to win his release. A motion for a new trial was refused on July 16, 1916. Stielow received his second stay of execution a mere forty minutes before he was to be sent to the electric chair on July 29, 1916.

Stielow became more hopeful a month later, when a peddler, Erwin King, who had been arrested on another charge, confessed on August 11,

1916, to the two killings at the Phelps farm. Two days later, when King was transported back to Albion, he was accompanied by Detective George Newton, the same officer who had acquired Stielow's so-called confession.

King withdrew his confession and another motion for a new Stielow trial was struck down. Then the case was presented to New York Governor Charles Seymour Whitman (1915–1918), who agreed to hear it on November 28, 1916. On December 4, 1916, the governor commuted Stielow's sentence to a life term, stating that he thought the prisoner was guilty. But evidence existed, he said, that made his guilt questionable.

After another month, King began writing letters from a Buffalo jail to friends that were published by a newspaper, and the governor had King questioned. Satisfied that King was more probably the culprit, the governor secured $25,000 for additional investigation. George H. Bond, a former district attorney, conducted the new inquiry. At first assuming Stielow to be guilty, the tireless Bond later found evidence to the contrary.

Bond discovered recordings of Stielow's conversations that contained no comments implicating him in the crime. Bond then hired ballistics experts, whose tests proved conclusively that the bullets which killed Phelps and Wolcott had not been fired from Stielow's gun and that the prisoner's gun had not been used in years. Bond further reasoned that the housekeeper, Wolcott, would not have run for protection to Stielow's home if he were the actual killer. This report was strengthened when King made another voluntary confession in December 1917.

Charles F. Stielow as a young man; he was wrongly convicted of murder through a manufactured confession and sentenced to death in 1915, but was proven innocent by a crusading citizen, George H. Bond, and released in 1918. *History Inc./Jay Robert Nash Collection.*

That month, Bond presented his findings to a grand jury. However, an indictment was not returned against King, possibly because popular opinion and the newspapers continued to denounce Stielow. When Governor Whitman read Bond's report, and because Bond had changed his opinion about the case, the governor believed both Stielow, then forty, and Nelson Green, then twenty-two, were innocent. He commuted Stielow's sentence and on April 16, 1918, directed that he be freed. Green's sentence also was commuted and he, too, was freed. Neither received financial restitution for three years of wrongful imprisonment. Detective George Newton, who had apparently manufactured Stielow's "confession" out of thin air, and who most likely persuaded King to recant his own original confession, was not prosecuted. Newton's reputation thereafter was that of a detective who would frame an innocent person by falsifying a ballistic report and a confession in order to add another conviction to his police record.

Newton's actions were blatantly repeated in 1921 by a detective who not only arrested an innocent man but forced him to commit a crime at gunpoint. As a switchman for the Terminal Railroad Association of St. Louis, Edward L. Hicks was walking across the railroad yard when he was met by Joseph Fitzgerald, a railroad detective who arrested Hicks for stealing a package of shirts. At Hicks's trial in May 1921, at the Federal Eastern District Court of Missouri, the question rested on the testimony of Fitzgerald and Hicks. The jury believed Fitzgerald, and on May 9, 1921, Judge C. B. Faris sentenced an innocent man to two years of imprisonment at the federal penitentiary in Leavenworth, Kansas, for possessing stolen items from an interstate freight shipment.

During the trial, and earlier at the grand jury proceedings, Fitzgerald testified that he had noticed the stolen merchandise on a freight car and waited for the criminal to return for the loot. He claimed that Hicks picked up the package and he then arrested Hicks. Hicks denied the accusation.

He said his foreman had ordered him to cross the yard, where he ran into Fitzgerald.

Apparently he and Fitzgerald had argued earlier and Fitzgerald had threatened to get even. According to Hicks, Fitzgerald forced him at gunpoint to pick up the package of shirts and then arrested him. The district court granted Hicks the right to file a writ of error on May 13, 1921, but the court of appeals dismissed the writ on March 8, 1924.

Meanwhile, Fitzgerald boasted to a St. Louis attorney, Wayne Ely, of his success in getting even with Hicks "for talking back to me." Fitzgerald laughed, while speculating for the attorney how defiant Hicks might be behind bars. Ely did not respond to the detective. Instead, he conducted his own private investigation into Hicks's case and concluded that Hicks had been framed by the vindictive Fitzgerald.

Ely notified the Department of Justice in Washington, urging the department to probe the case. U.S. Attorney Allen Curry, along with Justice Department agents, conducted the investigation, which agreed with Wayne Ely's conclusions. Curry filed a report with the Department of Justice which showed that Hicks was innocent, urging his release from prison. President Calvin Coolidge (1923–1929) granted the wrongly convicted man a full and unconditional pardon on August 11, 1924. Fitzgerald was later sent to prison on charges of false arrest.

## All Sorts of Saviors

Professional journalists, lawyers, lawmen, and even judges have joined relatives and friends to rescue scores of wrongly convicted people. Their high and low positions in life did not deter them from pursuing the truth, nor did they allow themselves to be thwarted in their sleuthing chores by authorities, governments, or time. Nothing mattered but the exoneration of the person they unswervingly believed to be innocent. One such person was Della Lowery, whose brother was sent

to prison for life for robbing a bank and killing three people.

On December 16, 1932, the Third Northwestern Bank of Minneapolis was robbed by six bandits, one armed with a submachine gun. Two policemen and a bystander were killed as the robbers escaped. Several days later, police followed a tip to look for the gang at a rooming house. Leonard Hankins was arrested when he walked into the house. At his trial, one witness swore Hankins was not the man stationed outside the bank, while several others noted a resemblance between the accused and the man they had seen at the crime scene.

A codefendant who pleaded guilty to the crime said he had never seen Hankins until sometime after the robbery. Several other members of the gang also denied knowing Hankins. Although a barber confirmed Hankins's alibi that he was getting a haircut at the time of the robbery, Hankins was found guilty and sentenced to life in prison.

In 1935, the FBI arrested Jess Doyle, a wanted criminal who confessed to his involvement with the robbery, masterminded by the infamous Barker-Karpis mob. He named all of his companions, saying that Hankins was not with them. The FBI notified the authorities in Minneapolis, but, because the FBI would not release its files, Hankins remained in jail for another thirteen years.

Hankins's sister, Della Lowery, kept struggling to interest reporters, governors, attorney generals, and anyone she thought might help her brother. The attorney who had prosecuted Hankins apparently opposed reopening the case, to avoid exposure of procedural or prosecutorial mistakes.

Lowery finally managed to involve an Associated Press reporter and a Minneapolis detective, who uncovered some of the same evidence that had earlier been gleaned by the FBI, particularly the statements of Doyle and others. A new trial was ordered and Hankins was declared not guilty. It was not until 1951 that a pardons board ordered the wrongly convicted man freed in November, and it was another four years before the state legislature passed a bill granting him $300 monthly for life for his unjust imprisonment. In 1953, the man who had spent sixteen years in jail was given a "final unconditional release." Lowery received $10,000 from the state to cover her expenses in the long fight to free her brother. Hankins was never actually pardoned, only released.

Two years after Hankins went behind bars, Clifford Shephard, forty-nine, was arrested in New Brunswick, New Jersey, on suspicion of being the "phantom forger" who had written bad checks throughout New Jersey in 1935. He was soon identified by a number of merchants, and he and girlfriend Betty Lester were tried for forgery. Although sixteen witnesses testified on their behalf, Shephard and Lester were convicted on the testimony of a liquor dealer, who was positive Shephard was the forger. They were sentenced to nine months imprisonment in the county workhouse. (Lester was released early on the belief that she had nothing to do with the forgeries.)

Following Shephard's release, he was arrested by Newark police for further forgeries committed during the same period as the first conviction. He was found guilty a second time and sentenced to eighteen months in prison. After serving this sentence, Shephard was once again accused of forgery. However, a grand jury did not indict him for this crime since the forgeries were committed while he was in prison. Months went by before the real "phantom forger," Edward Sullivan, was arrested. Sullivan was convicted and sentenced to a prison term in Wisconsin.

Freed after serving two sentences for crimes he did not commit, Shephard had to salvage his reputation. He resolved to clear his own record by traveling to Wisconsin, where the real criminal wrote a confession stating he had forged the checks Shephard was convicted of writing. Even with this signed confession from Sullivan, the New Jersey court of pardons refused twice to pardon Shephard, who could not find worthwhile employment because of his criminal record. Finally, in June 1950, Shephard's persistence was rewarded. He re-

ceived a full pardon from New Jersey Governor Alfred E. Driscoll (1947–1954).

Shephard's quest for exoneration was mirrored by a black youth in Chicago, whose alleged crime was more serious than forged checks. He had gotten mixed up in a murder and became a brutalized victim of the kind of savage police coercion that was rampant during the Depression era. In spring 1936, Earl Heywood Pugh, nineteen, left his home in Tennessee and arrived in Chicago. Several months later, in September 1936, the nineteen-year-old and a friend, Walter Fowler, were walking on the South Side, when they met a drunk who wanted to fight. Pugh was playfully swinging at the man, not hitting him, when police arrived. The drunk began saying the two men tried to rob him. Pugh and Fowler, both black, were arrested and taken to a police station, where they were charged with a killing that had occurred two weeks earlier, when a white man was robbed and stabbed to death in a park.

Fowler, who had previous convictions in Michigan and Ohio, soon confessed to the slaying. Pugh, however, held out for five days, professing his innocence. The teenager was not permitted to talk with a lawyer or friends. His arm was broken during a third degree interrogation, and food and water were withheld from him. Additionally, some police officers placed him at the end of a target range and fired bullets around his head, while demanding that he confess to being Fowler's accomplice in the murder.

On the sixth day, Fowler urged Pugh to sign a confession, reportedly saying, "You'll never live to see trial, unless you give them what they want." Pugh finally confessed. During their trial in 1936, though police offered no evidence that tied the two to the murder and both withdrew their confessions, Fowler and Pugh were convicted. The two were sentenced to life terms and, in January 1937, were sent to Joliet prison, where Fowler died in 1949.

Pugh continued to fight his case, and seventeen years later lawyer George Leighton agreed to help him. The lawyer discovered that the prosecution had suppressed the testimony of two witnesses to the killing, who said a white man was the killer. He also learned of the blatant police coercion and physical torture that had been applied against Pugh. Leighton presented this information at a hearing in 1955, and Pugh's conviction was struck down. The prosecutor dismissed the charges. Pugh was awarded $51,000 in compensation and released.

Where Pugh had waited seventeen years to be vindicated, another man in Texas waited more than two decades to see the light of freedom. The persistence of the foreman of the jury that had convicted him saved Gordon Morris from execution, and the same man eventually brought about his release from prison twenty-three years after he was wrongly convicted of murder.

In 1953, a Houston prostitute was beaten to death, and thirty-three-year-old Morris, who had hired her for the evening, was arrested and charged with the woman's murder. Prosecutors at his trial based their case on circumstantial evidence. In a twenty-four-hour period, Morris was tried, convicted, and sentenced to die. He admitted that on the night of the murder, he had been drinking at a gathering in a waterfront rooming house, but he insisted that he was innocent of murdering the woman.

While awaiting execution, Morris wrote a letter to the foreman of the jury, H. E. Walker, who was an accountant with a law degree. The conscientious Walker decided to conduct his own investigation. He went to the crime scene with the dead woman's brother, who showed him that, contrary to the testimony of the landlord of the rooming house, there was no door through which the landlord could have seen Morris kill the victim and lift the woman onto a bed. Yet this testimony had sealed Morris's fate.

Walker brought his discovery to Morris's cell at Huntsville, where he learned that Morris's left arm had been rendered useless in an accident before the murder charge was filed. Walker presented his findings to state officials in 1955, three

days before Morris was scheduled to be executed. Morris's sentence was commuted to life imprisonment. Walker, however, refused to settle for commutation. He headed a letter campaign that bombarded the parole board for twenty-one years, while regularly visiting Morris, encouraging him and promising him that he would not give up the fight. Gordon Morris was finally paroled in 1976.

Where a jury foreman saved the life of Gordon Morris, an employer and a relative made it their business to see that justice was done in England and that three innocent men were set free. On the night of October 16, 1953, London constable Cecil Pye was nearly beaten to death when he tried to investigate some suspicious activity on Marlow High Street. As he ran to a telephone booth to call for help, Pye was chased by two men with golf clubs. From across the street in her third-floor apartment, Mrs. M. Brown watched as the two assailants battered the officer.

A few days after the incident, two men, James Edmund Powers, twenty-two, and Arthur Joseph Thompson, twenty-five, who had been questioned on the morning of the attempted murder, were arrested. One month later Leonard Richard Emery, twenty-seven, was arrested. The three men were charged with causing grievous bodily harm to a police officer. Pye survived the attack but took thirty-seven stitches in the head.

Throughout the trial, which began on January 25, 1954, the three men maintained their innocence. They had spent the evening in question drinking tea at a friend's house, they said. During the trial, Mrs. Brown identified Emery as one

Leonard Richard Emery and James Edmund Powers were two of three wrongly convicted blue collar workers, who went to prison in 1954 for assaulting a London police officer, but who were released a year later after two citizens proved their innocence. *History Inc./Jay Robert Nash Collection.*

of Pye's attackers and the officer said that Thompson and Emery were both responsible for the attack. The defense argued that there was no evidence to link the three men to the crime, but the jury found the trio guilty. Emery, a baker and ex-convict, was sentenced to ten years in prison. Thompson, a molder, was sentenced to seven years, and Powers, a truck driver, was sentenced to four years for the attack and an additional year for protecting the other two men.

It was only because of the untiring work of Thompson's employer, Lewis Williams, and Thompson's brother-in-law, Leslie Mitchell, that justice was finally served in this case. The two men spent countless hours tracking down leads to locate more witnesses, who supported the claim that all three men were elsewhere when Pyre was assaulted. There was now uncertainty in the minds of those who had given witness against the three men, and Williams and Mitchell succeeded in getting the case reopened. About this time, in November 1955, two prisoners, Geoffrey Joseph, thirty-eight, and William Purdy, thirty-three, confessed to the attack on Pye. After officials reviewed the case, Emery, Thompson and Powers were pardoned, and released from prison. Each was given a small stipend for the time spent in prison.

Where the three men in England spent less than two years behind bars for a crime they did not commit, Lee Dell Walker languished behind bars for eighteen years before seeing exoneration. His freedom came about through the considerable efforts of a Detroit journalist. On the night of February 17, 1954, two gunmen entered a small grocery store in Detroit owned by John Drousiotis. The gunmen brandished pistols and demanded the cash in the till. The outraged owner lunged at the first robber and wrestled him to the floor. However, the bandit broke free and fired two shots, killing Drousiotis.

Six days later, a petty thief named Lee Dell Walker, forty-one, was arrested by Detroit police in connection with an unrelated mugging attempt. According to Walker, he was detained by police for four days and tortured into confessing to a murder he knew nothing about. At one point, police officers reportedly placed a gun in his mouth and threatened to fire unless he admitted to killing Drousiotis.

At the same time, Bill Johnson, Walker's alleged partner in the robbery attempt, was killed by police in a second stickup. Johnson and Walker were linked by virtue of a gun that was later found in an abandoned automobile. The police theorized that Walker had hidden the gun under the hood.

The suspect denied the charge, maintaining that his car had been stolen by the probable murderer, and, through an unfortunate set of circumstances, he had been wrongfully implicated. Walker said he was visiting a girlfriend in Inkster at the time of the shooting.

Walker's murder trial began on June 21, 1954. It lasted one week and a guilty verdict was returned. Walker had renounced his earlier confession, but the court concluded that it had been given voluntarily. The defendant was sentenced to life imprisonment and his appeals were denied. In February 1965, Recorder's Court Judge John Ricca ruled that the original confession was voluntary.

By 1971, Walker had become a model prisoner who assisted fellow convicts in their legal work. A reporter named Howard Kohn from the Detroit *Free Press* became interested in Walker's plight, and initiated an investigation into the case late in 1971. After interviewing police officials and studying the record of Walker's arrest, he concluded that the system had wrongly convicted Lee Walker. Through Kohn's efforts, a new trial was granted. The prosecution entered a motion of nolle prosequi (unwilling to pursue), and Walker was set free after eighteen years in prison. An indemnity bill that would have granted him a $25,000 judgment failed to clear the state senate.

It was evident that the Detroit police had coerced a confession from Walker. In contrast, a South Carolina law enforcement officer not only saved the life of a condemned man but brought about his release from prison. That man was

James Foster, who spent two years on death row for a murder he did not commit.

Foster, thirty-eight, a house painter in Gainesville, Georgia, had lived a reckless life. He had served eighteen months for the armed robbery of a convenience store. He had affairs with other women from the time he got married and drove without benefit of a driver's license. When prominent citizen Charles Drake of Jefferson, Georgia, fifty-seven, was brutally murdered on June 19, 1956, Mrs. Drake swore to the jury that Foster was the guilty man.

Foster's trial was the first case heard by newly elected Judge Julian Bennett. Foster clutched the Bible as he presented his alibi in persuasive detail. He repeated Drake's description of her husband's assailant and then removed his shirt to show the jury he was not the large, muscular man who overcame Drake. After he led the courtroom in an emotional prayer, the jury declared him guilty. Foster cried as he was sentenced to death.

Foster's case went to the Georgia Supreme Court, which affirmed the conviction. The U.S. Supreme Court refused to review the case. When it looked as though nothing more could be done, the head of the South Carolina law enforcement division, J. Preston Strom, stepped in. A year after Foster's conviction, Strom had learned from an ex-convict, since deceased, that Foster was innocent. This lead prompted Strom to conduct an intensive investigation that turned up the real killer, Charles Paul "Rocky" Rothschild, an ex-cop from Cairo, Illinois.

Strom was able to prove that Rothschild had borrowed a car belonging to William Patterson, and, with A. D. Allen, a bootlegger, robbed and killed the wealthy Drake. When Rothschild returned Patterson's car, he told him about the killing. Patterson was later arrested and convicted for a robbery in Spartanburg, South Carolina, and told Strom about Rothschild's secret. On August 14, 1958, Allen and Rothschild were found guilty and sentenced to life for murdering Drake. Foster was finally set free.

In the case of three black youths condemned to death for the abduction and rape of a young girl, a group of Maryland citizens headed by a dedicated scientist came to the rescue. That case began on the night of July 20, 1961, when James Giles, twenty, his brother John Giles, twenty-one, and Joseph Johnson Jr. twenty-two, went fishing and swimming in Towson, Maryland.

In the early hours of the next day, police found a sixteen-year-old white girl engaging in sexual relations with one of the black men on the banks of the Patuxent River. All three blacks were arrested and charged with rape, based on the testimony of the girl's date, Stewart Lee Foster. The boyfriend claimed that the three youths had smashed his car windows, taken twenty-five cents, and abducted the girl.

The Giles brothers were convicted in December 1961 and sentenced to death by Montgomery circuit court Judge James H. Pugh Jr.; Johnson was convicted and sentenced to death in 1962. Rancor immediately arose among a number of citizens, notably Germantown scientist Harold Knapp, who took on the task of righting the wrong he felt had been done to the defendants.

Knapp, with the support and aid of several citizens, discovered that Montgomery state's attorney Leonard T. Kardy had withheld vital evidence from the defense, evidence that would have backed up the defendants' claim that the girl willingly consented to sexual intercourse. Knapp learned that Kardy had suppressed the girl's criminal record and the fact that she was highly promiscuous. In fact, she was on probation for sexual misconduct at the time the Giles brothers and Johnson had been arrested. She apparently informed the younger Giles that she had had sexual relations with sixteen or seventeen men that week.

Knapp and the citizens supporting the defendants convinced Governor John Millard Tawes (1959–1967) to commute the death sentences for the Giles brothers and Johnson on October 24, 1963. The sentences were commuted to life in prison, while the lawyer the defendants had retained,

Joseph Forer, sought their release. In November 1964, Judge Walter H. Moorman ruled that a new trial should be conducted because suppression of evidence had interfered with due process. Kardy appealed and on July 13, 1965, the Maryland court of appeals overruled Moorman's decision.

Nevertheless, the fight was not over. Forer appealed to the U.S. Supreme Court, and the court reviewed the case in March 1966. The case was then remanded by the Supreme Court to the appellate court in February 1967. Once again, the case came before Moorman, this time sent by the court of appeals for another postconviction hearing.

At the hearing on May 15, 1967, Moorman ordered a retrial, to which the new state's attorney, William A. Linthicum, agreed. On October 30, 1967, the charges against the Giles brothers were dismissed by Baltimore County Judge W. Albert Menchine, when the state's two witnesses to the alleged rape failed to appear at the trial. A full pardon was issued in 1968 for Johnson by Governor Spiro T. Agnew (1967–1969).

In the instance of forty-year-old Miguel Arroyo, the judge presiding over his case came to his aid. Arroyo owned a small grocery in the tough Bedford-Stuyvesant neighborhood of Brooklyn, an area plagued by gang warfare between rival Puerto Ricans and blacks, who fought for control of the turf. Edward Davis, a fifteen-year-old, was killed outside Arroyo's store during a street fight on September 19, 1964. Based on shaky eyewitness reports and the fact that his store had recently been burglarized by young hooligans, Arroyo was arrested the next day. He was indicted for manslaughter in December and convicted by a jury on May 12, 1965.

Arroyo was never sentenced. Presiding Judge Harry Gittleson put the verdict aside after Arroyo's defense attorney produced a series of eyewitnesses who swore that another boy had killed Davis. It took almost two years, however, before enough facts were gathered to absolve Arroyo. During that period, Judge Gittleson asked the district attorney's office to conduct an investigation.

The defense witnesses were reexamined, and they were unanimous in their opinion that the killer was twenty-five-year-old Jose Velasquez, who had recently been picked up for narcotics possession.

On July 21, 1966, the stocky young Velasquez, who listed his residence as 85th Street, New York, was arrested in the Manhattan criminal court building after a drug charge against him had been dropped. He was then indicted for the murder of Davis.

Based on the Velasquez indictment and the recantation of those who had borne witness against Arroyo, Judge Gittleson approved an application for a new trial. Arroyo was released on parole without having to post bail, and he was formally cleared on July 25, 1966. Stated Gittleson, "I was persuaded that there was a sharp doubt whether this man was properly convicted and I sent word to district attorney Aaron Koota asking that a further investigation be made. I couldn't escape the conclusion that three young women testifying for Mr. Arroyo were telling the truth."

Small stores owned by people like Arroyo in bad neighborhoods are frequently robbed, with shootings and killings. Just such a killing occurred in September 1970 in Dorchester, Massachusetts, where shopkeeper Levi Whiteside was slain during a robbery at his Talbot Avenue store. Within ninety minutes of the killing, police had picked up Bobby Joe Leaster, whose clothes matched those reportedly worn by the killer. After a positive identification of Leaster by Whiteside's widow and a customer who was in the shop at the time of the shooting, Leaster, whose alibi did not hold up, was tried, quickly convicted of first-degree murder and sentenced to life imprisonment.

In 1977, two attorneys, the father and son team of Robert Muse and Christopher Muse, became interested in Leaster's case and worked for the next nine years on uncovering evidence, logging about $400,000 worth of volunteered time. In 1986, Mark Johnson, a schoolteacher who was thirteen at the time of the murder, came forward to report that he had seen two men fleeing from the scene of the crime, and that neither man was Leaster.

The Muses had discovered that the murder weapon had been used in a robbery that occurred two weeks after Leaster had been arrested. At a new trial in December 1986, the assistant district attorney, Francis O'Meara, said, "We can't say if Bobby Joe Leaster did it or Bobby Joe Leaster didn't do it. He served fifteen years and it's time to let it go." Leaster was released and the state dismissed charges.

In Leaster's case, two attorneys who believed he was innocent brought about his freedom. In the case of a Latino teenager given a life sentence for murder, a local politician initiated proceedings that vindicated the boy. This was all the more startling in that politicians are less inclined to lead crusades, preferring to remain with mainstream beliefs, lest they alienate constituents.

The boy was Gordon Robert Castillo Hall, a sixteen-year-old Hispanic youth from Duarte, California, who was accused of murdering Jessie Ortiz, twenty-seven, on February 25, 1978, based on the eyewitness testimony of the victim's nephews, Victor Lara and Daniel Lara. Hall was sentenced to prison for life for a crime he did not commit.

Some of Hall's relatives and friends contacted state senator H. L. Richardson, who took a deep interest in the case. After reviewing documents, he concluded that there existed enough discrepancies to prove that Hall might be innocent. Richardson urged the Los Angeles County sheriff's office to begin a new investigation. The two detectives, who first worked on the case, became convinced that Hall was innocent. Deputy district attorney David Disco interviewed the two principal witnesses a second time. Under cross-examination, they said Hall was not the person they saw shoot their uncle.

On December 17, 1981, the California Supreme Court overturned Hall's conviction. Murder charges were officially dismissed on February 18, 1982, after Hall had spent nearly three years behind bars. His plight had been shared by Anthony Porter, who lived on Illinois death row for sixteen years and came within forty-eight hours of execution at one point, receiving a stay two days before his scheduled execution on September 23, 1998. Porter found his salvation in a group of students from Northwestern University. A law professor, David Protess, gave a study assignment to these students, but the assignment ballooned into a full-scale investigation of Porter's case, after the students found some discrepancies in the records.

Anthony Porter, convicted of a 1982 murder, with an IQ of 51, was exonerated in 1999 and released from prison after a college professor, his students and a private detective identified the real killer. *Center on Wrongful Convictions/Northwestern University/Loren Santow.*

The students probed the condemned man's background. Porter, at the age of twenty-seven, had been convicted and sentenced to death for killing eighteen-year-old Jerry Hilliard and his nineteen-year-old girlfriend, Marilyn Green, in a South Side Chicago park in August 1982, while they were sitting on bleachers overlooking a swimming pool. A number of inconsistencies had long nagged investigators about the Porter case, including a shaky nighttime identification of the killer and one witness's statement that the shooter used his left hand when firing at the victims (Porter was right-handed). A volunteer Chicago attorney, Daniel R. Sanders, had Porter's IQ tested, which measured 51, indicating that he was mentally retarded. A pro bono lawyer, Larry Marshall, along with three other attorneys, then argued that Porter had no mental comprehension regarding the nature of his punishment, which brought about the 1998 stay. Paul Ciolino, a private detective, then worked on the case with the students, and their investigation led them to interview William Taylor, an eyewitness to the murder, who, in recanting his original testimony, admitted that he had not seen Porter kill Hilliard and Green. They then interviewed another suspect in the case, Alstory Simon, a forty-eight-year-old laborer who lived in Milwaukee, Wisconsin. During the videotaped interview, Simon, incredibly, confessed to the double murder, but claimed that he had shot Hilliard in self-defense over a drug dispute, and Green by accident. Simon's statements had been prompted by his wife, Inez Jackson, who had also been present at the shootings, and told Ciolino and the students that her husband was the assailant.

The tape and other evidence unearthed by the private investigator and the students prompted Judge Thomas Fitzgerald to grant Porter a new trial based on "significant evidentiary developments." Porter was released on bond pending the outcome of his new trial. Simon's wife then testified that she had witnessed her husband committing the murders and Porter was officially released on February 5, 1999. In September 1999, Simon pleaded guilty to two counts of second-degree murder and was sentenced to 37.5 years in prison.

Almost a decade after Porter had seemingly gone behind bars for life, a New York teenager was convicted and sent to prison for murdering another youth in a gang fight. That youth might have languished into old age behind bars had it not been for an elderly, feisty female attorney who refused to believe he was guilty. Her fight to free this boy is, as they say, "one for the books."

That story began when two groups of teenagers got into a shoving match on lower Broadway, near Waverly Place, in Manhattan, New York, at 2:00 A.M. on November 18, 1990. A teenager wearing a DayGlo orange jacket pulled a gun and fired it into the air. The other group of teenagers began to run off as this youth handed the gun to a friend wearing a green jacket. The youth wearing the green jacket fired at the fleeing teenagers and his fire wounded seventeen-year-old Rudy Quesada in the leg. Another bullet slammed into the neck of nineteen-year-old Javier Bueno, who died three weeks later.

The shooter in the green jacket was never found, but the boy wearing an orange DayGlo jacket was located and arrested. He was eighteen-year-old Luis Kevin Rojas, who was convicted in 1991 of second-degree murder and given a fifteen-year to life sentence. The conviction was achieved primarily through the testimony of several of the teenagers who had fled the scene, all saying that Rojas had been the man in the DayGlo jacket, who had handed off the gun to the shooter.

Police officers also testified that they picked up Rojas, a native of Union City, New Jersey, a few minutes after the shooting at a PATH station (a rapid transit rail system running between New York and New Jersey) at West Ninth Street. He was wearing a DayGlo jacket, but the orange side had been reversed. Rojas, when police questioned him, said that he had reversed his jacket and was wearing the burgundy side out so that he would not get the jacket dirty.

Rojas insisted that he was innocent and was eating dinner with a friend at the time of the shooting. His attorney, David Fronefield, put up a weak defense and was later criticized for ineptitude by an appellate court. A New Jersey paper interviewed one of Rojas's teachers, who said that Rojas's involvement with a murder was utterly "impossible" and went on to describe a gentle and good student, who had no criminal background and had never been involved in any violence.

Reading this article, Priscilla Read Chenoweth, a sixty-eight-year-old widow and retired lawyer, came to believe that Rojas had been wrongly convicted. She began to investigate the case, asking lawyers and retired detectives to help her prove that Rojas was innocent. Their long, arduous crusade took several years. Meanwhile, she met Rojas in prison and became his surrogate mother when his own mother died. He sent her cards on Mother's Day and she told him to cut his hair and carried a sport coat in her briefcase for him to wear in court.

Chenoweth contacted a retired Manhattan detective, Dennis O'Sullivan, who specialized in unsolved cases. O'Sullivan became so involved with the Rojas case that he put up his own house to provide bail for Rojas when he was awarded a new trial. Before that happened, Chenoweth and O'Sullivan enlisted the aid of another retired police officer, Mike O'Connor, who later tracked down John Apel, a PATH police sergeant. Apel recalled with certainty that he watched Rojas just miss a train as it left the station; research later determined that the train departed the station at 2:03 A.M. The shooting in Greenwich Village occurred a half mile away at 2:07 A.M., evidence which proved that Rojas could not have been at the site of the shooting.

Tina Mazza, at Chenoweth's urging, served as Rojas's appeals lawyer and presented the evidence unearthed by Chenoweth's investigators to the Appellate Division in 1995. It overturned Rojas's conviction, and he was freed on bail. Prosecutors, however, insisted on retrying him, believing they would win a second conviction on the testimony of the teenagers who had stood witness against Rojas at his 1991 trial.

Criminal attorney Jethro M. Eisenstein, who had donated his services at the urging of Chenoweth, went to court and provided not only policeman Apel to testify but another witness, William Davis, who was present at the 1990 shooting, and described the man in the DayGlo jacket as having a ponytail and the body of a weight lifter. Further, Davis stated that he had earlier told police that Rojas, an undersize youth of 125 pounds, was the wrong man.

A jury agreed and Rojas, after spending more than four years in prison for a crime he did not commit, was found not guilty on all counts. His acquittal was brought about by many selfless persons, investigators, researchers and attorneys, and chiefly a little gray-haired lady named Priscilla Read Chenoweth, a woman of dogged persistence and iron faith.

# III

# Suppression and Fabrication of Evidence

I N ALL AGES AND IN ALL COUNTRIES POLICE
and prosecutors have been expected to present evidence in a convincing manner in
bringing about a conviction. In all too many instances, however, in the course of such police activity and prosecutorial proceedings, evidence found
damaging to the prosecution's case was suppressed
or evidence too weak or almost nonexistent to
bring about a conviction was illegally padded, enhanced, embellished, or even fabricated.

These official offenses are most often committed
by zealous police offers eager to enhance their careers with substantial "collars" (arrests) that hold
up in court as convictions. Prosecutors eyeing
loftier government posts with larger salaries and
more self-satisfying power have taken the same illegal actions, suppressing evidence that otherwise
honest police officers have provided. These prosecutors know from the start that processed evidence
from many sources—the arresting officer, records
officers, and forensic science officials—leaves a de-
tectable paper trail for any future investigator.

Many officials have nevertheless suppressed
such findable evidence in their blind ambition to
advance their careers, despite the likely exposure
of such illegal actions. Such knowledge should
caution any police officer or prosecutor, but, for
some such law enforcement officers and officers of
the court, the hazards and risks of tampering, suppressing, and fabricating evidence means little or

nothing in comparison to securing a promotion, a
pay raise, or a higher seat of authority, all at the
expense of another human being they know to be
innocent. Sometimes, however, the motive for
such misconduct stems from bigotry and racism.

## Bigotry at the Root of Evidence Suppression

The London police in 1864 displayed a bigoted attitude when they discovered a body following a
pub brawl involving Italian immigrants, who were
disliked or even hated by many Londoners of the
period, including some members of its police
force. Certain investigating officers of the London
police force knew that Serafino Pellizioni was
most probably innocent of murdering a pub patron, but several officers suppressed evidence that
would have brought about his release. Instead, he
was convicted and sentenced to death. Pellizioni's
arrest, trial, conviction, and death sentence were
widely publicized in the press, and when the true
facts of the case came to light, police and prosecutors alike were enmeshed in a national scandal of
their own making.

Pellizioni's problems began in late December
1864, when a group of Italians in the Saffron Hill
section of London came into conflict with the patrons of the Golden Anchor Pub. Frederick Shaw,

the owner of the pub, threw out a group of drunken Italians on Christmas Eve. The day after Christmas, Gregorio Mogni arrived at the Golden Anchor and slapped Shaw. The potboy, Alfred Rebbeck, warned some Englishmen in another room that trouble was brewing, and soon a free-for-all started, Italians against English. When the dust cleared, Rebbeck was wounded and a man named Michael Harrington was dying of a severe abdominal wound. Serafino Pellizioni, who was lying atop Harrington, was arrested for his murder.

Pellizioni's own knife was found to be clean (most Italians customarily carried a knife as a defensive weapon because many were attacked by bigoted mobs). Officers found another knife outside the pub window, where it would have been impossible for Pellizioni to have thrown it. The police, eager for a conviction, did not present in evidence the bloodstained knife found outside the pub. Further, they never established that Pellizioni was in the pub when the fray started. He claimed that he had heard the commotion and entered after the brawl had ensued, and was then pushed until he fell over Harrington. The police also failed to mention that Harrington's fatal knife wound was made by a left-handed person. Pellizioni was right-handed. Nevertheless, on February 3, 1865, the twenty-six-year-old Pellizioni was found guilty of murder and sentenced to death.

A man named Negretti, sure that Pellizioni was innocent, started to investigate. He became convinced that Gregorio Mogni was the killer. He persuaded Mogni, who had gone to Birmingham, to return and keep an innocent man from hanging. Mogni admitted to authorities that, indeed, he was responsible for the knife thrust that took Harrington's life, but he insisted that he had been acting in self-defense. On March 2, 1865, a grand jury reduced the murder charge against Mogni to manslaughter and he was found guilty and sentenced to five years in prison.

To save face, the authorities decided to try Pellizioni for wounding Rebbeck, though there was no evidence that two knives were used that day at the fray in the Golden Anchor pub. Pellizioni's new trial started on April 12, 1865. Eminent lawyer Sergeant Ballantyne defended him, stating, "This unparalleled series of trials, which has presented the same machinery of justice apparently hard at work to prevent, and not to attain, the discovery of the truth, has shaken severely public confidence." Pellizioni was acquitted and soon returned to his native Italy.

Just as xenophobic hatred had spurred the wrongful conviction of the Italian Pellizioni in London in 1864–1865, Isidore Zimmerman (1917–1983) of New York was wrongly convicted and sentenced to death when anti-Semitic officials suppressed evidence. In 1937, twenty-year-old Isidore Zimmerman was arrested and charged, along with six other young men, in the robbery of a Manhattan restaurant, in which a police detective was killed. Although Zimmerman was not present at the crime, police contended that he supplied the guns which killed the detective.

Despite his claim of innocence, Zimmerman was convicted and sentenced to die in the electric chair. He spent nine months on death row, receiving a commutation of his sentence to life in prison only two hours before his scheduled execution. For the next twenty-four years, Zimmerman tried to prove his innocence. Finally an attorney volunteered to reinvestigate the case and the conviction was overturned, when it was shown that the prosecutor knew Zimmerman was innocent, suppressed evidence, and intimidated witnesses into perjuring themselves.

After his release in 1961, Zimmerman spent seventeen years lobbying for legislation that would permit him to sue the state for damages. In 1981, New York Governor Hugh L. Carey (1975–1982) signed the necessary legislation. Zimmerman received a $1 million settlement, one-tenth of the figure named in his suit, in June 1983. He died four months later on October 12, 1983.

Racism against blacks and black racism against whites brought about the murder of a New Jersey policeman and the wrongful imprisonment of a black resident of Plainfield. Tension reached the breaking point during the 1960s as riots broke out in urban areas throughout the United States. The predominantly black west end of Plainfield, New Jersey, saw more than three hundred residents take to the streets on July 16, 1967. The mobs smashed windows, looted stores and fire-bombed businesses.

During the melee, a thirty-nine-year-old police officer, John V. Gleason Jr., was killed after he attacked a young black rioter. The white officer was beaten, bludgeoned with either a meat cleaver or a butcher knife, shot with his own revolver, and stomped to death. Twelve people were charged in connection with the murder. Their trial began in September of 1968 and, at the end of fifteen weeks of litigation and fifty-three hours of deliberation, the jury rendered its verdict.

On December 23, 1968, twenty-four-year-old George Merritt (born in 1944) and twenty-two-year-old Gail Madden were found guilty of first-degree murder and sentenced to life imprisonment. A witness identified Merritt as the man who had beaten Gleason with the kitchen utensil and identified Madden as the 250-pound woman who had jumped up and down on the officer's body stomping him to death. Acquitted of the murder were twenty-three-year-old Donald Jones and twenty-year-old Howard Brandon. Six other defendants were acquitted prior to the jury's final decision. Attorneys for Merritt appealed the decision and the New Jersey Supreme Court ordered a retrial. In 1974, Merritt was reconvicted and lawyers again appealed. Merritt's third trial, in 1977, upheld the lower court ruling, but his lawyers were granted a hearing by a federal judge.

New evidence disclosed at the 1980 hearing severely undermined the prosecutor's original case. Defense attorneys introduced a 1967 police report, concealed since the incident, that contradicted the single witness whose testimony had originally convicted Merritt. The judge set aside his conviction and after ten years of incarceration for a murder he did not commit, Merrit was set free.

Racism reared its ugly head in an Iowa murder case involving a black football star, James Hall (born in 1954), who claimed, at the time of the murder, that he was in his dormitory room in Iowa City and had nothing to do with the strangulation death of nursing student Sarah Ann Ottens in March 1973. Hall, a football star at the University of Iowa, was eventually found guilty of second-degree murder and sentenced to a fifty-year term.

Appeals were brought to the U.S. Supreme Court, but the conviction was upheld, and Hall went to prison. After serving nearly ten years for a crime he did not commit, a state district court judge overturned Hall's original conviction in November 1983, declaring that he had not received a fair trial. The ruling resulted from the determined efforts of Hall's lawyer to secure the release of the previously withheld testimony from the county attorney's office.

In May 1984, Judge L. Vern Robinson ruled that the grand jury indictment was not valid because of misconduct on the part of the prosecutor. The judge cited various racial slurs made against Hall, who was black. Evidence that implicated other suspects in the case had been withheld by an assistant Iowa attorney general, Garry D. Woodward, who had prosecuted the case, according to Robinson. On September 1, 1984, a grand jury in Johnson County, Iowa, refused to return an indictment against Hall. After ten years in prison, he was at last a free man. Upon his release, Hall stated, "Ten years of hell doesn't just go away."

## Suppression of Evidence in New York

Throughout the twentieth century, New York City produced an alarming number of wrongful convictions. Suffering from a burgeoning police force of more than 32,000 members in all five boroughs and a labyrinthine court system, this city sent many persons to prison through suppressed evidence, when one would have been one too many. Typical was the case of William Fisher, where suppressed evidence brought about his wrongful conviction of first-degree manslaughter. Fisher, born in 1911, spent eleven years in prison and another forty years trying to clear his name and get compensation for an unjust sentence.

In 1933, Fisher was at Belden's, a Harlem speakeasy and dance hall, when a brawl broke out. In the foray, he was gashed in the leg, hit in the head, and carried out the backdoor before two men were killed by gunshots, one of the victims being an acquaintance of his. An assistant district attorney, Miles O'Brien, linked Fisher with the gun that the prosecutor said was the murder weapon. Fisher was convicted of manslaughter and sentenced to fifteen to thirty years. However, he made good use of his time at Sing Sing Prison and the Comstock Correctional Facility, studying law, filing appeals, and finding new evidence in his case. In 1944, after eleven years in prison, Fisher was paroled as a result of his determination to expose the suppression of evidence in his case by prosecutor Miles O'Brien.

At legal proceedings in 1936 and in 1958, it was established that O'Brien knew there was no connection between Fisher and the gun and that he suppressed evidence, including ballistics findings and police testimony, which proved Fisher was innocent. Years later, the wrongly convicted man explained O'Brien's behavior: "He was a highly ambitious person, who wanted to become a judge. And, in the process, he was willing to send someone like me, a working stiff with no funds, no connections, and no knowledge of legal matters to prison." O'Brien never achieved his desire to become a judge.

Fisher, who married and fathered two children, spent most of his working years driving moving vans and coal trucks before retiring in 1976. Six bills before the New York state legislature requesting permission to sue the state for his wrongful imprisonment were vetoed by Governors Nelson A. Rockefeller (1959–1973), Hugh Carey (1975–1982), and Mario M. Cuomo (1983–1995). In 1983, the seventy-two-year-old man told a reporter, "I'm not the type to walk away. When you pick a fight with me there's got to be a winner or a loser." In 1984, the state waived its immunity in a bill signed by

Governor Cuomo. In 1986, the courts awarded Fisher $750,000 for his wrongful imprisonment.

Seven years after Fisher was victimized through the suppression of evidence, Louis Hoffner (born 1913) was wrongly convicted of the murder of bartender Peter Trifon, killed during a New York City holdup on August 8, 1940. Hoffner, who, like Fisher before him was poorly represented in court, nevertheless knew that a death sentence meant an automatic appeal. "I am not guilty," he told his sentencing judge, "and I have the right to have the higher court review this case." The judge refused to "play with Hoffner's life" and sentenced him to life in prison.

That might have been the end of the story, except that in 1947 a law school professor mentioned the case to newspaper reporter Edward Mowery as an example of a miscarriage of justice. Hoffner had been indicted, the professor told Mowery, on the flimsy identification of one witness, after two other witnesses had said Hoffner clearly was not the murderer. Mowery spent several years putting together witness accounts that corroborated Hoffner's alibi. He presented this new information to the prosecutor's office.

In November 1952, after Hoffner had served almost twelve years in prison, his conviction was thrown out and he was released. Almost three years later, Judge Fred A. Young, of the New York court of claims, found that the district attorney's office had suppressed information provided by two witnesses which had supported Hoffner's claims in the 1940 shooting and had falsely imprisoned Hoffner. Judge Young awarded Hoffner $112,291, stating that "any [financial] reward is bound to be a mere token" of redress for the wrongs done to Hoffner, "but it should compensate as well as the medium allows."

In the case of Robert McLaughlin (born in 1960), suppression of evidence was widespread among police and prosecuting attorneys. On December 29, 1979, three men robbed approximately fifteen people at gunpoint in Brooklyn's Marine Park. During the robbery nineteen-year-old Robert Halstead resisted and was shot to death.

While looking through police photos, fifteen-year-old witness Robert Tobin identified William Ferro as one of the assailants. On the back of Ferro's picture, a notation said Ferro had once been arrested with a man named Robert McLaughlin. Detective John D'Elia produced a picture of McLaughlin, but it was not the McLaughlin associated with Ferro. Then D'Elia violated police procedure and showed McLaughlin's photo to Tobin, pointing out that he had previously been arrested with the man already identified. As a result, the teenager identified the wrong man.

At the trial, the only evidence against McLaughlin was Tobin's testimony. McLaughlin was never linked to the murder weapon or to his codefendant. He had four witnesses testify that he was with them drinking when the murder took place. Of the victims, seven could not identify McLaughlin as one of the robbers. Prosecutor Kathy Plaszner reportedly withheld vital information from the court and defense counsel, who failed to object to Plaszner's overly prejudicial summation. Before addressing the jury, the presiding judge remarked on the record that she thought an acquittal would be forthcoming. The jury disagreed and found McLaughlin guilty of second-degree felony murder. He was sentenced to fifteen years to life in prison.

McLaughlin's conviction was upheld on appeal, but a New York appellate judge requested a reinvestigation into the case. The new investigation was taken up most vigorously by McLaughlin's foster father, Harold Hohne, New York Civil Liberties Union lawyer Richard Emery, who was assisted by Barry Scheck of the Cardozo Law Clinic, New York homicide detective Tom Duffy, and a reporter for the *Village Voice*, Jack Newfield. In August 1985, two weeks after an article by Newfield claimed the prosecution had suppressed the truth, Tobin recanted his original statements in an affidavit presented to district attorney Elizabeth Holtzman.

Holtzman did not order a new trial after new evidence was turned up within a month of Tobin's retraction. Four witnesses, including two police officers, informed Holtzman that McLaughlin's identification was tainted, information she did not reveal to Emery. On April 22, 1986, while Holtzman continued to oppose McLaughlin's request for a retrial, she nevertheless publicly urged Governor Mario Cuomo to grant McLaughlin clemency, and said on network television, "We think Bobby McLaughlin should be set free."

Holtzman's private fight against the wrongly convicted man did not end there, for she opposed the choice of judge for the retrial. In June, Holtzman asked New York Supreme Court Chief Justice Joseph Bellacosa to disqualify acting justice Anne G. Feldman or any judge from the Second Judicial Department because Justice Milton Mollen had stated in public that McLaughlin's case should be reopened. Bellacosa harshly refused the request.

On June 20, 1986, Emery was given for the first time a copy of Detective Richard Wright's notes from the night of the murder. Tom Dell'Osso, a victim who had come face-to-face with the killer during a struggle, had described to Wright a man that in no way resembled McLaughlin. Three days later, for the first time, Emery was allowed to speak to Tobin. Emery pleaded with Tobin to tell the truth. The next day he did. On July 1, 1986, Holtzman's office administered a lie detector test to Tobin, who told how he had been persuaded by police to identify McLaughlin. Tobin, to that time, had told police that he was unsure if McLaughlin was the robber. He passed the test. Two days later, an assistant to Holtzman, Mark Feldman, dropped any opposition to McLaughlin's release. Judge Feldman dismissed the charges and freed McLaughlin.

## Suppression of Evidence in America's Heartland

In the turbulent 1930s, an almost unceasing crime wave in the Midwest and the Southwest saw scores of bank-robbing bandits repeat the nineteenth-century criminal acts of Jesse James, the Younger Brothers, and the Daltons. John Dillinger and the Barker Brothers robbed banks in the Midwest with the alacrity of daily mail deliveries and, in Oklahoma, Charles "Pretty Boy" Floyd looted so many banks that the local press and police pinned every crime in the state on him, until he was shot to death by FBI agents in Ohio in 1934.

Police and prosecutors in Oklahoma, as in many neighboring states, operated in a way much like their criminal adversaries and adopted illegal procedures in their rabid ambition to put criminals behind bars. Much of this was in response to the public outcry for effective law enforcement and unyielding prosecution. Inside a judicial cauldron that mixed the innocent indiscriminately with the guilty, particularly when a police officer was murdered, swirled the fate of Paul Goodwin.

Chris Whitson, a police officer in Seminole, Oklahoma, was shot to death in 1936. Paul Goodwin, twenty (born in 1916), and Horace "Buster" Lindsey were arrested and charged with the murder. Both Goodwin and Lindsey were rough customers with police records and were treated as if they were as notorious as "Pretty Boy" Floyd, which they were not. Officials decided early on that Goodwin killed Whitson, despite the fact that Goodwin's partner told them otherwise.

Goodwin was denied access to counsel for seventy-nine days. During the trial, the prosecution presented a statement from Lindsey accusing Goodwin of shooting the officer, but did not tell the jury that Lindsey, before blaming Goodwin, had twice confessed to the shooting. Additionally, the prosecution suppressed testimony by a witness who testified to police that he heard Goodwin say, "Don't do that, Buster, don't do that," when the officer was shot.

Lindsey was sentenced to life in prison, and on October 17, 1936, Goodwin also received a life sentence. Goodwin was paroled on July 7, 1961, but in 1962 he was convicted of armed robbery in Kingfisher County and received another five-year term. Then, on March 6, 1969, a federal district court ordered Goodwin's release on the grounds of the suppressed testimony, prejudicial pretrial publicity and denial of legal counsel in the 1936 murder trial. Goodwin was released from the penitentiary at McAlester, Oklahoma, on March 7, 1969, having served his time for the robbery offense. Paul Goodwin was not an upstanding citizen and had a verifiable police record, but, in the instance of the 1936 murder, he stood innocent, spending twenty-five years behind bars for a crime he did not commit.

Where Goodwin was wrongfully convicted of murdering an officer in Oklahoma, a hard-working Michigan resident was sent to prison for killing his wife on the basis of suppressed evidence. Eleanor Pecho of Michigan threatened to kill herself several times, once by setting her clothes on fire and once by ingesting pills. She also shut herself in a garage with a running car and another time jumped from a moving car. Family members saved her life each time. Just after midnight on June 9, 1954, her husband, Walter A. Pecho (born in 1919), came home from his factory job in Lansing, and the couple began arguing. They continued the dispute through the night, Eleanor holding her shotgun and threatening to commit suicide.

About 6:00 A.M., sitting on a chair, the woman put the gun to her chest and pulled the trigger. Pecho immediately called police, who found the body and a suicide note in her handwriting. After an autopsy, however, a pathologist determined that because of the angle of the bullet, and because the woman fell backward, Pecho had been murdered.

Walter Pecho was tried, convicted of second-degree murder, and sentenced to fifteen to twenty years in prison. Later, his lawyer found that police had discovered a distinct fingerprint on the back of the shotgun's trigger guard from a finger on Eleanor Pecho's right hand. Pecho's attorney filed a motion for a new trial on the grounds that evidence had been suppressed by the prosecution, but the motion was refused. Several years later, Pecho's sister hired experts to reexamine the evidence.

Lawyer Robert Warner reasoned that if Pecho killed his wife, his fingerprint would have marked over his wife's and, if he cleaned the gun, he would have cleaned off both prints. Well-known pathologist Dr. Richard E. Olsen conducted an independent investigation and came to the same conclusion after conducting extensive forensic tests. Olsen announced that the woman had committed suicide.

Another hearing was held on March 4, 1960, to request another trial, but the judge struck down the motion. Pecho then submitted an application to Governor G. Mennen Williams (1949–1961), who ordered an inquiry by the state parole board. The board's investigation, which encompassed the research of Warner and Olsen, supported Pecho's claim. The governor granted a pardon to Pecho on June 10, 1960.

Where Pecho was convicted on the suppression of fingerprint evidence and other factors that would have absolved him, including the fact that the shotgun blast administered to his wife by herself had propelled her backward from her chair—an impact wrongly described by a pathologist testifying for the prosecution—an honest cab driver in Illinois was convicted on a wrongfully obtained confession and the suppression of evidence that would have proved the prosecution's chief exhibit against him was not at all incriminating.

This case began in Hancock, Illinois, in 1955, when the body of eight-year-old Janice Elizabeth May was found battered to death in an abandoned rail car on the Burlington Railroad tracks close to her home in Canton. Police arrested Lloyd Eldon Miller Jr., twenty-nine, a cab driver with no prior criminal record, and charged him with the murder. The following year, Miller, who had confessed to the killing, was convicted and sentenced to death. He incredibly survived seven execution dates—one stay arriving only eight hours before he was to be executed in the electric chair—and saw his exoneration and release fifteen years later.

The appellate pleas of Miller's attorneys, who managed the seven stays of execution, simply involved the normal appeal procedures to save a client from execution. However, throughout these pleading years, the same lawyers inadvertently discovered just how deceiving the police and prosecution had been in this case, finding one serious legal discrepancy after another. When examining Miller's confession, his appeal lawyers noted several inconsistencies with the known facts of the case. Upon checking the original trial transcript, the same attorneys realized that Miller's trial lawyer had failed to point out those inconsistencies in the 1956 trial.

Miller's landlady, who could have provided an alibi for her tenant, was not called by Miller's attorney to testify at his trial. But years later she testified to Miller's appeal attorney that Miller was asleep at home at the time of May's killing. The appellate attorneys then began a close reexamination of the case, discovering that the prosecution's chief exhibit, a pair of Jockey shorts, were too small for Miller to have worn. These shorts, with red stains on them, were shown to a jury by prosecutors.

Prosecutors did not say that the stains represented blood but referred to Miller's confession, which implied that the stains were from blood. The attorneys had the exhibit retested and the stains were reported to be from paint. Moreover, original police laboratory records confirmed these paint stains at Miller's original trial. The police and prosecutors at Miller's trial had suppressed those lab reports and therefore knew that paint, not blood, was on those shorts.

Miller's confession was then closely examined. At Miller's 1956 murder trial, prosecutors had convinced the trial judge that Miller's confession was voluntary. Miller had all along insisted that he had signed the confession, which had been typed by a police officer, only after he was told that he would receive the death penalty if he refused to sign it. Naive and lacking counsel, he signed it, believing it was the only way he could save his life. In that police-written confession, Miller admitted that the shorts used in evidence against him were his.

After the appellate attorneys introduced this new evidence, Miller was released on a writ of habeas corpus in March 1967, having spent eleven years behind bars for a murder he did not commit. It was not until 1971, however, that prosecutors dropped all charges against him. The Illinois Bar Association investigated the prosecutors' conduct but found no grounds for action, pointing out that the prosecutors had never actually referred to the stains on the shorts as blood, but merely allowed the jury to presume they were, based on Miller's questionable confession.

In taking no action against the deceptive prosecutors, the association's disciplinary committee stated, "The presence or absence of blood on the shorts was not a material question in the case." In this, the association appeared to be whitewashing the prosecutors, who knowingly allowed a jury to come to a false conclusion in sending an innocent man to prison.

Shifty tactics by prosecutors are often matched and overmatched by police in bringing about wrongful convictions. Suppression of evidence by police in Columbus, Ohio, ensnared Thomas H. Broady Jr. (born in 1950), and these omissions largely contributed to his conviction on charges of robbery and murder. On June 12, 1973, restaurateur John Georgeff was murdered during a robbery. Later that year, Thomas H. Broady Jr. was found guilty of the crime and sentenced to ten to twenty-five years in prison. His conviction was overturned when it was discovered that police knew the identity of the real killer.

According to Richard Clark, a suspect in the robbery of Georgeff's restaurant in Columbus, Ohio, Donald Boyd, who had since been killed in a police shootout, had shot Georgeff, and Broady was in no way involved. Broady's attorney, David Long, also learned that police detective Tom Jones had known this information but suppressed it. Broady was subsequently acquitted at his retrial, but he was found guilty of another robbery in the area.

During Broady's second trial, Judge Clifford Rader did not allow witnesses to testify in corrob-

orating Broady's alibi, since an Ohio criminal procedure law permitted the judge to deny all alibis not properly filed with the court a week in advance. This same judge, however, helped Broady obtain his parole in 1978 after he had served five of his ten- to twenty-five-year sentence.

Where Broady had been victimized by police, evidence that might have kept Gary L. Beeman (born in 1951) from a wrongful conviction was indirectly suppressed through a shoddy defense and court restrictions that prohibited him from viewing "discriminatory" materials in the case. A thief who was arrested, tried, and convicted for murder, Beeman adamantly maintained that he was innocent before winning a retrial and acquittal through his own defense. The case began on November 16, 1975, when Robert Perrin, fifty-two, was savagely beaten and murdered in his home in Geneva, Ohio, shot once through the head.

A Geneva policeman, Dennis Brown, testified that he saw a man matching the description of twenty-five-year-old Gary Beeman leaving Perrin's home at 5:20 A.M. Beeman was arrested and tried for aggravated murder at the Ashtabula County Court of Common Pleas. His defense counsel, Thomas Shaughnessy, a court-appointed lawyer, maintained that Beeman's companion for part of that evening, Claire Robin Liuzzo, who had recently escaped from an Ohio penitentiary, had murdered the older man when Liuzzo became angry over Beeman's failure to carry out their mutual plot to rob Perrin.

Prosecuting attorney Ronald Vettel maintained there was no evidence that anyone but Beeman had been in Perrin's house that night. On June 4, 1976, Beeman, who had served a three-year term for armed robbery, was convicted on circumstantial evidence of murder, and sentenced to death by Judge Roland Pontius.

Arguing for a retrial, Beeman cited the court's decision not to let one witness testify since the defense had not laid the necessary groundwork during cross-examination. He said that he had also told his lawyer prior to the trial that he wanted to be involved in the questioning and the cross-examination. Beeman further argued that Pontius denied his request to have legal materials made available for him, which he claimed was "discriminatory" since, had he been released on bond or financially well off, he could have had access to the materials.

Judge Pontius called Beeman's bond argument "presumptuous." Shaughnessy, asking to be excluded from the appeal case, noted that a question of competency came up between himself and his client: "It's my opinion it's a vain attempt to go back to court and rehash and haggle everything. I instructed Beeman that it was a vain act." Facing death, Beeman did not consider any legal measure to be "vain" in attempting to save his life. He continued to lobby until he was granted a retrial in 1978, on the grounds that his right to cross-examine Liuzzo, the prosecutor's main witness, had been unfairly restricted.

At a 1979 retrial, Beeman initially handled his own defense, based on legal studies he had done in prison, but handed his case over to attorney Albert Purola on the tenth day of the twenty-three-day trial. Throughout the proceeding Beeman and Liuzzo continued to accuse each other of the murder. Five witnesses, however, including Robert Westfall, a former cell mate of Liuzzo's, testified that they had heard Liuzzo admit to the murder. Westfall said that, in January 1976, Liuzzo told him he tried to rob a homosexual, scuffled with him, and shot him in the head. Beeman was acquitted of all charges. Judge Robert L. Ford, however, told Beeman the acquittal did not implicate Liuzzo in the killing.

In the case of Adolph Honel Munson, prosecutors in his 1985 case were later identified as having suppressed hundreds of reports and photographs that would have most likely set Munson free. Munson was convicted and sentenced to death for the kidnap-murder of Alma Hall, a store clerk at Love's Convenience Store in Clinton, Custer County, Oklahoma. Hall's body was found on July 4, 1985, in a remote area outside Shamrock, Texas.

The woman had been abducted from the convenience store at approximately 2:00 A.M. on June 28, 1985 ($330 was discovered missing from one of the store's cash registers). To identify the body, Dr. Ralph Erdmann, a medical examiner, cut off the hands to obtain the fingerprints. He reported that the victim had been shot twice in the head and that he had recovered from the body an earring, a watch, and several rings. He was unsure as to whether or not a .22-caliber weapon had caused the fatal wounds.

Shortly before Hall's kidnap-murder, Munson had escaped from the Jess Dunn Correctional Center, where he was on work release after serving time for a 1964 murder. He fled to California and was later apprehended. Returned to Oklahoma, he was again imprisoned and charged with Hall's kidnapping and murder. Munson was brought to trial almost solely on the statements of Donald Bruner, a fellow prisoner and an informant, who claimed that Munson had admitted to him that he had, during his escape, "gone to a little town," where he abducted a convenience store clerk, and later dumped her body in some woods after killing her.

Bruner, who was serving a fifteen-year sentence for murder, said that he had not been promised a deal for his testimony against Munson, but the prosecutor in Munson's case later wrote a letter to the pardon and parole board on behalf of that informant. Two other witnesses testified against Munson, including a so-called eyewitness who claimed that that there was a car in the parking lot at the time of the crime that was "similar" to the one Munson had used in his escape. A forensic expert claimed that a single hair found in the car Munson had been driving when found in California was consistent with the hair of the victim.

The prosecution claimed that Munson had stayed in Room 103 at the Glancy Motel in Clinton a night before the Hall abduction and murder, but Munson, who was black, was only vaguely identified as having stayed at the motel, one witness saying that he saw a black man standing by a car in the motel parking lot. Room 103 was found to contain bloodstained sheets and towels, a .22-caliber spent shell, and a broken earring that prosecutors said matched the single earring found on Hall's body. A witness who had stayed at the motel claimed that at 2:30 A.M., on the morning of June 28, 1985, he heard a scream and then a loud thud coming from Room 103. A towel and tag bearing the name "Dundee" were later found near Hall's body, and both, prosecutors said, were consistent with a towel missing from the Glancy Motel. No one, however, ever claimed to have seen Munson at the motel, and none of the fingerprints recovered in Room 103 matched those of Munson or Hall. Gerald Klemke, manager of the motel, however, identified Munson's car as having been in the motel's parking lot on the night of the murder.

Munson's conviction was affirmed on appeal. However, a postconviction proceeding resulted in the trial court granting a new trial based on findings which showed that the prosecution had suppressed evidence in Munson's case, withholding from the defense 165 exculpatory photographs and reports. Many of the reports from several witnesses held that the crime had been committed by a white man; Munson was black. One of those reports positively identified a white male with a history of abducting and robbing convenience store clerks. Even more revealing were the suppressed photographs showing the tire tracks of the car driven by the actual culprit. These tire tracks did not match those of the car Munson was driving when apprehended. (This kind of evidence is detailed in the entertaining 1992 courtroom comedy-drama *My Cousin Vinny*.)

Moreover, it was discovered that Klemke, the motel manager, had taped his comments under hypnosis and none of this information had been provided to the defense. The testimony of Dr. Ralph Erdmann, who was later convicted on seven charges of fabricating evidence and misrepresenting evidence in several other cases (his license was revoked), was shown to be riddled with errors. The single hair found in Munson's car in Califor-

nia, which had been linked to Hall, was later determined as not belonging to the victim.

Even though prosecutors appealed the new trial order, the Oklahoma court of criminal appeals affirmed the decision. Prosecutors then retried Munson, but, after the suppression of evidence in his first trial was exposed, Munson was acquitted in April 1995 by a Custer County jury. The jury came to its conclusion to free Munson upon the revelation of the gross suppression of evidence in his case. The state was proven to have withheld from three hundred to five hundred pages of police and Oklahoma State Bureau of Investigation reports, including detailed information on a prime suspect in the Hall kidnapping-murder, Ralph Yeary, who police believed had committed several other convenience store robberies and abductions.

A witness had stated that Yeary was in the convenience store shortly before Hall was abducted, but this and other information was withheld from defense counsel. During the trial that attorney noticed Yeary's name on an OSBI report and asked for more information on him. Prosecutors told the attorney that Yeary had been in prison at the time of the Hall murder. This was a lie; prosecutors knew that Yeary was in Oklahoma at the time of the killing and was not apprehended for other related crimes until June 29, 1985, when he was captured in Corpus Christi, Texas—one day after Hall had been kidnapped and murdered.

## Suppression of Evidence in the Deep South

Early in the morning on October 25, 1967, James Richardson, then a thirty-two-year-old Arcadia, Florida, fruit picker, left home with his wife to begin his day's work. His seven children and stepchildren were left in the care of a baby-sitter, Bessie Reese. Later that day the children were found dead, victims of parathion poisoning. The lunch of beans, grits, and rice, allegedly prepared by Richardson and his wife prior to their departure and served to the children by Reese, had been laced with the lethal insecticide.

Richardson was tried in May 1968, charged with first-degree murder of the eldest child, Betty Bryant. After a four-day trial, he was convicted and sentenced to death. The sentence was later commuted to life imprisonment. The prosecution maintained that Richardson's motive for the murders was to collect the $1,000 life insurance policy he had taken out on each child the day before the murders. This motive was substantiated by witnesses who had allegedly heard Richardson talking prior to the deaths about an insurance windfall he expected. Richardson, however, had never paid the first premium on the policies.

Richardson had served twenty-one years of his sentence before statements from two nursing home aides, who attended to Reese, encouraged Richardson's attorneys to request a retrial. The two workers signed statements that, on more than one hundred occasions, Reese said, "I killed those children." Betsy Reese died of Alzheimer's disease in 1992. This development in Richardson's case spurred efforts to gain Richardson a clemency hearing. During the investigation prior to the clemency hearing, Dade County, Florida, state attorney Janet Reno heard that Richardson's original trial had been flawed because prosecutors withheld evidence that might have proven him innocent.

A clemency hearing scheduled for April 6, 1989, was cancelled in anticipation of a new trial. A dispute concerning where the case should be retried held up the process until April 25, 1989, when circuit court Judge Clifton Kelly overturned the conviction and ordered Richardson freed. "The enormity of the crime," Judge Kelly stated, "is matched only by the enormity of the injustice to this man."

On May 6, 1989, the state dropped all charges against Richardson and set him free. In August, he filed a $35 million lawsuit against the state, county, and law enforcement officials who had wrongly convicted him. An out-of-court settlement with DeSoto County brought Richardson $150,000, most of which went to the attorneys who worked to set him free. He sold the film rights to his life for $20,000, but that was gone in about four years. His wife, who had remained loyal to him throughout his imprisonment, later divorced him and Richardson, who spent too much of his life in prison to be entitled to Social Security benefits, developed a heart condition, which he attributed to the poor diet and medical neglect he suffered behind bars.

At this writing, Richardson lives on a ranch owned by his cardiologist, doing light work to offset his room and board. He continues to have nightmares and anxiety attacks about prison and the death sentence that was held over his head for years, particularly his acute memory of death row, which he attaches to the sound of rattling keys. "When I hear a bunch of keys shaking, I think they are coming to get me and put me in the electric chair," he stated. "I'm trying to get over it, but it's something a man can never forget."

The same terrible memories are lodged in the minds of James Creamer and six other defendants convicted in 1973 of a 1971 murder in Marietta, Georgia. Creamer, along with George Emmett, Larry Hacker, Hoyt Powell, Billy Jenkins, Charles Roberts, and Wayne Ruff, were convicted of murdering two Georgia pathologists, Warren Matthews and his wife Rosina, during a home invasion on May 7, 1971. A year after the murders, Cobb County authorities received word from South Carolina state police officials that they had a suspect in custody with intimate knowledge of the crime.

District Attorney Ben Smith replied that he would guarantee Debbie Ann Kidd immunity from prosecution if she agreed to turn state's evidence. During the murder trial held in Cobb County in 1973, Kidd testified that she had taken part in the robbery and had shot Rosina Matthews through the head. She implicated a second woman—Carol Sue Boling Johnson—in the crime, but further investigation showed that Johnson was in Ohio the day of the shootings.

Debra Kidd proved to be an unreliable witness. Just before the trial began, she underwent hypnosis to help regain her memory. Defense attorneys argued that she should have been declared incompetent because of the strong possibility that her memory was "altered" during these sessions. Kidd eventually admitted that she had lied on the witness stand. In 1974, however, the Georgia Supreme Court upheld the convictions and sentences of Creamer and his codefendants.

On August 26, 1975, following an investigation into the true facts of the case by the Atlanta *Constitution*, Cobb County superior court Judge Luther Hames ordered new trials for Roberts, Jenkins, Emmett, and Powell on the grounds that the prosecution had suppressed evidence that would have discredited the star witness, Debra Kidd. Evidence showed that Kidd had made numerous contradictory statements about the defendants, even stating that she herself had shot the two victims. Many of these statements were taped, which prosecutors withheld from defense attorneys. The newspaper's investigative reporters also learned that Kidd was having a romance with one of the detectives involved in the case. The two other convicted men, Creamer and Ruff, were also guaranteed new trials, but were ordered detained in prison on various unrelated charges.

The police had obtained confessions in the Matthews murders from three other men, who did not know the original defendants: Billy Sunday Birt, Billy Wayne Davis, and Willie Hester. On September 2, 1975, charges against Creamer and the other six codefendants were dropped in the wake of this new evidence. Judge Charles A. Moye, who charged prosecutors with the willful destruction of Kidd's testimony—the tapes had allegedly disappeared—ordered all seven convictions reversed. The long, expensive trial cost Cobb County taxpayers $750,000.

Five years after the Matthews murders in Georgia, a police officer in Dallas, Texas, was shot to death and his killer was allegedly convicted and sentenced to death, except that a prosecutor in

that case suppressed evidence which would have freed the convicted man and sent the guilty party to the death chamber. It took a curious moviemaker to bring the real culprit to justice and effect the release of the wrongly convicted Randall Dale Adams.

For Adams (born in 1949), a movie not only changed his life but saved it as well. On November 28, 1976, Adams, a twenty-seven-year-old drifter from Ohio, hitched a ride with David Ray Harris, sixteen, a teenage sociopath with a criminal record of assault and theft. The two spent the day smoking marijuana and drinking beer together, later taking in a drive-in movie. Then, according to Adams, Harris dropped him off at the Comfort Motel in Dallas, angry at the older man for not putting him up in a separate room at the motel. Harris, however, would later testify that the two continued to drive around the Dallas streets.

At 12:30 A.M. police officer Robert Wood, twenty-seven, and his partner, Teresa Turko, twenty-four, stopped a blue car to tell the driver to turn on his headlights. Turko stayed in the police car, sipping a milkshake. Wood walked up to the car and was killed by five bullets shot at point-blank range from a .22-caliber revolver. His murderer escaped, and the slaying remained unsolved for more than a month. Finally clues led police to Harris, who was living in the small town of Vidor, Texas, where he had reportedly bragged to friends that he had "offed that pig in Dallas." Harris admitted that the murder weapon was a gun he had stolen from his father and that he had been in the blue car, which he had stolen in Vidor, but he claimed that it was Adams who murdered Wood.

Five months later, Adams, who had no criminal record, was convicted on the testimony of Harris and three eyewitnesses. Sentenced to die, he spent four years on death row and escaped execution by only ten days in 1979, when Supreme Court Justice Lewis Powell intervened. In 1980, his sentence was commuted to life imprisonment on a technicality and he was transferred to the Eastham Unit Prison.

In 1985, Errol Morris, a documentary film-maker who sometimes worked as a private detective, began research for a Public Broadcasting System film on Dallas psychiatrist Dr. James Grigson, popularly known as "Doctor Death," for his frequent diagnoses of murder suspects in death penalty cases. One of Grigson's clients was Adams, a patient the psychiatrist felt was innocent.

Morris became intrigued with the profile Grigson gave him on Adams, and he began a three-year investigation into Adams's case, logging over two hundred interviews, including several with Harris and with three surprise witnesses, making a movie, *The Thin Blue Line,* in the process. In Morris's first interview with Harris, the twenty-five-year-old told the filmmaker that he would never forget the look in the police officer's eyes as he walked up to the car.

According to his testimony in court, Harris claimed he had been slumped down in the backseat when the shooting occurred. Other witnesses, particularly Emily Miller, gave testimony that conflicted with earlier statements. She said she had picked Adams out of a lineup, but, at a 1987 federal hearing, admitted she had picked out someone else and that a police officer had pointed Adams out to her later.

Harris told the filmmaker on tape, "I know for a fact that Adams didn't do it. I'm the one that was there, so I should know." In September 1988, as Adams served a life sentence and waited for the case to be reopened, Harris said in a television interview that he had been alone in the car and had fired five shots. Because he was on death row for a subsequent murder at that time, his testimony would have meant little in court.

In November 1988, Harris, called as a witness at a hearing to reopen the case, admitted that his finger was on the trigger when the policeman was shot. The death row convict also explained that former assistant district attorney Doug Mulder, prosecutor at the 1976 trial, had promised him that he would "take care of" other criminal charges pending against Harris at that time in ex-

change for his testimony. In *The Thin Blue Line,* Harris went into detail, explaining how he rehearsed his testimony extensively with lawyers.

Appellate judges decided that prosecutor Mulder suppressed evidence and knowingly allowed perjured testimony at the trial. Following the December hearing, District Judge Larry Baraka said Adams did not receive a fair trial and wrote a letter supporting parole and recommending that the conviction be set aside. On March 1, 1989, the Texas court of criminal appeals overturned Adams's conviction. When Adams was finally released, the wrongly convicted man, asked if he was bitter, replied, "I've had thirteen years taken from my life. Can the state replace that?" On April 6, 1989, assistant Dallas County prosecutor Winfield Scott, who assisted in prosecuting Adams, was fired by district attorney John Vance over "disagreements about the case."

Three years after Adams was released, a woman in Virginia found herself accused of murdering her lover, her conviction brought about through the same kind of suppressed evidence that had sent Adams behind bars. In her case, her self-admitted guilt was planted in her mind by a police officer, while other likely suspects were ignored. Finally, the testimony of a questionable witness was used to send her to prison.

## The Ordeal of Beverly Anne Monroe

In the morning of March 5, 1992, Beverly Anne Monroe, an organic chemist and mother of three, arrived at Windsor, a 220-acre estate outside of Richmond, Virginia. She had come to see her lover, millionaire tobacco research scientist and real estate speculator Roger de la Burde, a sixty-year-old émigré who collected rare art works and claimed to be a member of the French aristocracy, a count no less. Monroe, who had abandoned her marriage eleven years earlier for the sake of the flamboyant de la Burde, entered the tycoon's library with the estate's groundskeeper to find him dead on a sofa, a bullet through his forehead, just above the right eye, a .38-caliber Smith & Wesson in his right hand. When the groundskeeper checked the pulse, he later told police, he probably dislodged the gun, which fell to the floor.

As determined by the coroner, de la Burde died about an hour after Monroe reportedly left his estate, at about 10:30 P.M., on the night of March 4, 1992. Monroe had left at 9:30 P.M., stopping for gas before arriving home that night at 10:00 P.M., when she talked with her son, Gavin. She then went to a Safeway store. She claimed that she tried to call de la Burde later that night, but there was no answer.

David M. Riley, a senior special agent of the Virginia State Police, took over the case. Monroe told him that the night before de la Burde died, she had dinner with him and then worked on a manuscript he was writing for an art book. Later she kissed him good-bye and returned home. It was Monroe's belief that her lover had become depressed over his supposed failing health and he took his own life in despair. Though there were other suspects Riley might have closely investigated—an ex-wife, a biochemist allegedly carrying de la Burde's child, and her disapproving husband—the officer focused on Monroe.

After Monroe failed a polygraph test three weeks following de la Burde's death, Riley became convinced that she had committed the murder and then somehow blotted out all memory of the crime. Riley had suggested the lie detector test and Monroe waived her rights to a lawyer. "I know I was naive and stupid," she later stated, but, she added, she felt that she had nothing to hide and had always been taught to cooperate with the police.

As Riley interrogated Monroe, he planted the idea in her mind that she had indeed been present when de la Burde died, but that her crime was so offensive to her that she had subconsciously blocked it from her conscious recollections. Monroe repeatedly told Riley that she was not present when de la Burde died, but Riley's manipulative suggestions were so powerful that the vulnerable

and gullible Monroe accepted his theory that she had fallen asleep on the couch and, when waking, shot her lover over past infidelities. Monroe, after a grueling eight-hour interrogation, began to believe Riley and agree with him. Although police witnesses were present when Riley interviewed Monroe, little of what she said—mostly in response to Riley's suggestions relative to her being present at the crime scene—was recorded. When Riley attempted to restart his recorder, it did not restart and failed to record most of the statements later attributed to Monroe.

Riley met again with Monroe on June 3, 1992. He did not at that time record her answers to his questions, but she signed a rather confused and hypothetical statement that seemed to admit she was present at the time of her lover's death. Prosecutors felt they had enough evidence to convict Monroe and charged her with the first-degree murder of de la Burde, despite the fact that there was no forensic evidence linking her with the crime and she had a strong alibi.

In November 1992, Monroe was brought to trial, prosecutors relying chiefly on Riley's statements and a so-called eyewitness, Zelma Smith, who claimed that Monroe posed as a "Mrs. Nelson," and asked her to obtain an untraceable pistol a few months before de la Burde's death. Prosecutors argued that Monroe murdered de la Burde out of jealousy for his many sexual transgressions. It was disclosed that the millionaire had a strange career which mixed business with romance. De la Burde had come to the United States in the 1950s, fleeing communist Poland, he said, after marrying a West German pediatrician and having two daughters with her. He claimed to be the descendant of French aristocrats, and when he arrived in Richmond, Virginia, he claimed to be an organic chemist.

De la Burde had gone to work for the tobacco firm Philip Morris in 1961, staying with the firm until 1987. In 1979, Beverly Anne Monroe, also an organic chemist, went to work in the patent office of Philip Morris, and there she met and fell in love with de la Burde. Her affair with him caused her separation from her husband, Stuart Monroe, in 1981 and also caused the dissolution of de la Burde's marriage to Brigette. Monroe, who had been raised on a South Carolina farm, had been married to a scientist and had had three children from that marriage, two daughters and a son.

During his tenure at Philip Morris, de la Burde developed a carbon dioxide process to expand tobacco, an application that the firm later acknowledged as saving Philip Morris $300 million between 1979 and 1985. The enterprising chemist, though well paid, quit Philip Morris and sued the firm, claiming that he had been cheated out of the profits promised to him for his process. The firm countersued, claiming that de la Burde was holding company documents he had threatened to disclose. A large undisclosed settlement was made, the payment going to de la Burde's estate, and the chemist turned over the documents to Philip Morris. Meanwhile, de la Burde occupied himself with works of art that he donated to several institutions. When they proved to be fakes, chiefly African paintings and sculptures, de la Burde came under FBI investigation (dropped after his death).

During Monroe's trial, it was disclosed that de la Burde had many affairs during his relationship with Monroe, most with his coworkers at Philip Morris. Obsessed at lacking a male child to inherit his fortune, he contracted with a biochemist, Krystyna Drewnowska, to have his child, and it was this infidelity, prosecutors claimed, that motivated Monroe to shoot and kill her lover. Prosecutors Jack Lewis and Warren B. Von Schuch pointed out the fact that Monroe, upon learning of de la Burde's arrangement with Drewnowska, informed her husband, Wojtek Drewnowska, that his wife had engaged in sexual relations with de la Burde. Mrs. Drewnowska later gave birth to a daughter. Further, prosecutors produced a letter written in 1990 by Monroe in which she severely criticized de la Burde for his unfaithfulness and sexual profligacy.

Moreover, prosecutors said Mrs. Monroe felt she had been shortchanged in de la Burde's will.

Riley testified that, even though no fingerprints or any other kind of forensic evidence was present at the murder scene, he believed that Mrs. Monroe shot and killed de la Burde, wiped her prints from the gun and then planted it in the victim's hand before leaving the Windsor estate. Prosecutors then pointed out that she was incensed by the recent news that her lover was planning a ménage à trois within a few days. All of this, prosecutors insisted, proved that she was jealous enough to murder her lover.

Defense attorneys pointed out Monroe's statements that she had reconciled her differences with de la Burde over his relationship with Drewnowska, and had made plans to marry him shortly before he killed himself. She understood that de la Burde had made arrangements to financially support the child produced by Drewnowska. Her attorneys made a strong case that de la Burde committed suicide, but, against the weight of the evidence shown by the prosecutors, a jury, after deliberating only fifty-five minutes, decided that Monroe was guilty of first-degree murder and using a firearm in the commission of a felony. Posting bail while appealing the verdict, Monroe remained free. That appeal failed and, in March 1996, she began serving a twenty-two-year prison sentence at the Pocahontas Correctional Center in Chesterfield, Virginia.

Throughout her trial and following her imprisonment, Monroe insisted that she was innocent. "I did not kill Roger," she often stated. "I loved Roger." Her daughter Katie, an attorney working for the U.S. Commission on Civil Rights, also believed her mother innocent and, from the moment of her mother's conviction, began to assemble a team of new lawyers and criminologists to review the case and hopefully bring about her mother's exoneration. One of those joining the new defense team was Richard A. Leo, a professor of criminology and psychology at the University of California–Irvine, a specialist in police interrogations, confessions, and wrongful convictions.

Leo was quoted by the New York *Times* as stating, "It is the most outrageous case I've ever seen," while stating that Riley had crossed the line from permissible police deception to illegal intimidation. He typified the impressionable Monroe as a person who could have easily imagined she "could have done it."

Attorneys for Monroe filed a writ of habeas corpus, arguing that prosecutors had illegally suppressed evidence in her case, which had resulted in an unfair trial and a wrongful conviction. Among the many pieces of evidence withheld by the prosecution, the Monroe petition cited the fact that prosecutors had struck a deal with Zelma Smith, in exchange for her testimony that Monroe had asked her to obtain an untraceable gun. Smith, defense attorneys pointed out, had a history of testifying on behalf of prosecutors in an effort to escape her own criminal problems. They also pointed out suppressed evidence from witnesses who stated that they had seen a car other than Monroe's driving away from the de la Burde residence late on the night of the murder.

A statement from the victim's groundskeeper that he, not Monroe, had dislodged the gun in de la Burde's hand when checking the body had also been suppressed. In addition, the petition cited the suppression of medical documents that determined the victim's death as a suicide and notes from two women, present during Riley's eight-hour examination of Monroe, which supported Monroe's claim that she had been manipulated by Riley into a confession. It was also stated that Riley offered Monroe a fake plea bargain deal and told her that if she did not accept it, she would most likely be found guilty and would never see anyone again, including her three children. (The same kind of threat was made by police to Mary Kathryn Hampton in a 1961 investigation into several Florida serial murders, for which she was falsely accused by her former boyfriend, a convicted murderer who, ironically, possessed the middle name of Monroe; see Chapter I.)

On March 28, 2002, federal district Judge Richard L. Williams set aside Monroe's 1992 murder conviction, overruling a recommendation by U.S. Magistrate David G. Lowe, who had upheld the conviction in 2001 following a December 2000 hearing. Lowe had concluded that forensic evidence showed conclusively that de la Burde had been murdered, but Judge Williams rejected that conclusion, stating that "the physical evidence necessary to show whether [de la Burde's] death was a murder or suicide was. . . either tainted or lost." He went on to state that "the tactics engaged in by Riley were deceitful, manipulative and inappropriate." He agreed with Judge Lowe that Monroe's original defense counsel, Murray J. Janus, had not been effective since he failed to challenge the credibility of three statements Monroe had made to Riley.

At Judge Williams's order, Beverly Anne Monroe was released from prison on April 5, 2002, to the embrace of family members, including her daughter Katie, who, along with attorney Stephen A. Northrup and many others, had fought for years to set her mother free. After serving almost seven years for a crime she did not commit, Monroe wanted to hug her children, play her piano and "read [my grandson] a bedtime story." Although prosecutors stated they would seek a new trial, they dropped the case after the Fourth U.S. Circuit Court of Appeals affirmed Williams's ruling on March 26, 2003.

## Suppression of Evidence in Canada

The law enforcement policies and prosecutorial procedures of Canadian justice are not dissimilar from those of the United States. In that vast but less populous country, many have met with the same wrongful convictions stemming from the suppression of evidence endured by their neighbors to the south. Gary Staples was one such victim, as justice failed in sending him to prison for a crime he did not commit.

On the night of April 26, 1970, Staples was dragged from his bed by police. Officers trained guns on him while they charged him with the murder of cabdriver Gerald Burke, who had been shot in the front seat of his cab. His body was found in the cab behind an industrial plant on Dunbar Avenue in Hamilton, Ontario in December 1969. The officers had been led to Staples's door by his jilted lover, who provided police with information in exchange for leniency in her own ongoing robbery case. The woman stated that Staples, her former boyfriend, had killed Burke for the $40 he was carrying.

While struggling into his clothes, Staples, then twenty-five, said to arresting officers, "This must be some kind of sick joke." It was no joke, one of the officers replied and showed him an arrest warrant with his name on it. "If this isn't a joke, it's some kind of mistake," Staples added. But he would see in coming months just how seriously that mistake would impact his life. Based on the questionable statements of Staples's former lover, and very little else, on January 23, 1971, Staples was convicted and sentenced to life imprisonment. As his second wife, Marie Staples, wept openly, her husband turned to her and the rest of the court and shouted, "I haven't killed anyone!"

Staples was sent to Kingston Penitentiary, where a guard asked him if he would like to work in the kitchen. Staples told the guard he knew nothing about cooking. The guard told him that he might as well take that job since he had "the rest of your life to learn." He remained behind bars for almost two years until he won an acquittal in 1972, when an appeals court determined that there was insufficient evidence to convict him. By that time, Staples's life was in shambles and, though acquitted, he had not been fully exonerated in his eyes since the Hamilton, Ontario, police had not admitted its error in arresting him and building a faulty case against him.

Many believed that the Hamilton police had suppressed evidence in the Staples case, and the Innocence Project at Osgoode Hall Law School in North York, Ontario, undertook to find evidence of that contention. Working under the direction of Osgoode faculty member Paul Burstein, two law students, Colleen Robertson and Dean Ring,

closely examined Hamilton police documents and, on June 5, 2001, unearthed an incriminating police memo written at the time of Staples's 1971 trial. The memo stated that two witnesses had seen three youths fleeing the scene where Gerald Burke had been killed. All of the police information about these witnesses had been purposely withheld from Staples's defense attorneys during his murder trial. The memo stated that this information had not been passed along by police because it might confuse the jury and bring about Staples's acquittal.

Armed with this evidence, Staples's attorneys filed a lawsuit against Hamilton officials, seeking $6 million in damages. On December 5, 2002, Staples, then fifty-eight, received a written apology from the Hamilton, Ontario, police department for his wrongful arrest and imprisonment. He also received an undisclosed amount of money as a settlement. It took thirty years for Gary Staples to see his full exoneration, and, over that time, he believed that his neighbors thought him guilty of murdering Burke. He continued to be plagued by nightmares of his wrongful imprisonment, remembering how, while behind bars, "I worked in an environment where I was afraid for my own life. I worked with twenty-four men who had committed murder."

Where Gary Staples was a reserved and low-profile person, a fellow Canadian who also experienced wrongful conviction was a flamboyant and controversial figure, an easy target for police in Toronto, Canada. Michael McTaggart, born in 1954 in Etobicoke, Ontario, was obsessed with singer Elvis Presley and, bearing some resemblance to the rock and roll star, became one of his many imitators. He began performing in Toronto's subways in 1970, making the Yonge/Bloor subway station as his public platform and singing à la Elvis for tips. He was dubbed "Subway Elvis."

On February 17, 1986, McTaggart was arrested by police as he was about to board a train in Toronto's Kipling Station, charging him with seven armed bank robberies, three in Kitchener and four in Burlington. He spent ten months in jail awaiting his trial, which began in 1988. After two trials, McTaggart was convicted in the second trial for two of the robberies and sentenced to five years in prison. He was released on bail, pending appeal. At this time, an armed robber committed a holdup in Woodbridge and, two days later, McTaggart was arrested at his mother's home and charged with the Woodbridge holdup. He spent almost nine months in jail awaiting trial for that robbery.

McTaggart was acquitted in the Woodbridge robbery case, and a newly appointed police investigator probing into other robberies for which McTaggart was convicted took special notice that similar robberies by someone resembling McTaggart had continued while McTaggart was imprisoned. Based on the investigator's observations and other evidence, McTaggart won a second trial in June 1990, and was acquitted of the two robberies that had originally sent him to prison. In 1991, he filed a lawsuit, seeking $4.24 million in damages for malicious prosecution.

During a civil trial in 2000, evidence was provided to the court that two bank employees had identified to police a man other than McTaggart as the one who had held up their banks, robberies for which McTaggart had been convicted. This telling evidence was found in a hidden, second set of Halton police notebooks that were withheld from prosecutors and McTaggart's defense attorneys. On December 15, 2000, a judge exonerated McTaggart, stating that he had not received a fair trial when Halton police purposely withheld evidence that would have acquitted him. On July 3, 2001, McTaggart signed a settlement with officials that awarded him $380,000 in compensation.

In the case of Felix Michaud, it was not only the local police in the province of New Brunswick who suppressed evidence to bring about his wrongful conviction, but also the vaunted Royal Canadian Mounted Police (RCMP), who had also hidden evidence that would certainly have acquitted him of a rape-murder he never committed. Michaud's nightmarish odyssey began on the night of December 3, 1991, when the home of seventy-three-year-old Rose Gagne burned to the ground in the village of Connors, nestled beside the St. John River in northwestern New Brunswick.

At first, firefighters and police concluded that the fire had been an accident and that Gagne had met death by mishap. Michaud and his family grieved over this death, as the elderly woman was a second cousin of Mrs. Michaud and grandmother to their adopted children. On May 2, 1992, RCMP officers learned from a man named Luc Bonenfant that Marco Albert, a petty criminal who lived next door to Michaud in the village of Claire, which was close to the village of Connors, had told him that the Gagne death was not an accident. An arson investigator then determined that the Gagne home had been deliberately set on fire and police found that the telephone wires to the Gagne residence had been intentionally severed. The victim's body was exhumed and a pathologist reported that the woman had died before the fire began, although he could determine the exact cause of her death.

Marco Albert was interviewed at length by police and gave interrogators several stories about his participation in the Gagne murder. In his third and final statement, he admitted that he had robbed the Gagne resident, but his friend, Felix Michaud, had raped and strangled Gagne to death and then set fire to the house. For his "cooperation," charges against Albert were reduced to robbery, to which he pleaded guilty, receiving a two-year prison sentence. On July 7, 1992, RCMP officers arrested and charged Michaud with the murder of Rose Gagne. He went to trial in 1993. Albert testified against him, repeating the statements he had made to officers earlier. Michaud was convicted of first-degree murder and sent to prison for life.

In 1995, Michaud's lawyers successfully appealed his conviction, which was overturned by the New Brunswick court of appeals and also the Supreme Court of Canada, chiefly based on the judicial errors committed at Michaud's 1993 trial by presiding Justice Joseph Z. Daigle. A second trial was ordered for Michaud, and his attorney, Kim Jensen, recruited veteran criminal lawyer Gilles Lemieux to aid her, since Lemieux spoke fluent French and would cross-examine witnesses who spoke French, including the star prosecution witness, Marco Albert. Lemieux, however, would never put a single question to Albert. Three weeks before Michaud's second trial began, Marco Albert, on August 17, 1996, walked down the stairs to the basement of his parents' house, scribbled a note, and then shot himself to death. In his suicide note, Albert stated, "Forgive me for all my sins," but he said nothing about framing his casual acquaintance, Michaud.

At Michaud's second trial, his attorneys offered new evidence, chiefly the testimony of three prison inmates who stated that Albert, while he was behind bars with them, had told them that he had lied about Michaud's involvement with the Gagne murder. This testimony, however, coming from convicted felons, had little effect on the court and Michaud was again convicted and sent back to prison.

Lemieux and other attorneys made another appeal, based on inflammatory remarks made by the prosecution in Michaud's second trial, and secured another trial. In the third trial, Lemieux asked the prosecution to turn over all of the documents from Michaud's 1993 and 1996 trials, stating that he feared some of the documents and exhibits might have been misplaced during the long legal wrangling in the case. Lemieux was staggered to receive not only the original 250 documents that had been present in the 1993 and 1996 trials, but another 2,500 documents that had never been shown to Michaud's defense attorneys.

Among these suppressed documents, Lemieux discovered an RCMP report dated November 13,

1992, which stated that officers had reviewed transcripts of wiretaps indicating "inconsistencies" in Marco Albert's testimony. Lemieux found a tape recorded by Luc Bonenfant with Marco Albert (Bonenfant had secreted the recorder in a backpack when talking to Albert), a conversation in French that took place before Michaud was charged and one that Lemieux, an expert translator, understood. On that tape, Albert stated to Bonenfant that Michaud was innocent and was not the kind of man who would kill Gagne.

At Michaud's third trial in 2001, Lemieux shrewdly asked the trial judge to exclude all of Marco Albert's testimony since crucial evidence, which would have been used during cross-examination in Michaud's first and second trials (the tape recorded between Bonenfant and Albert), had been suppressed by the RCMP. Faced with no other choice, the judge threw out Albert's damning testimony and the case against Michaud collapsed. The defendant was acquitted. On May 30, 2001, after spending almost nine years in prison as an innocent man, Felix Michaud, thirty-five, was freed.

Michaud had suffered much, losing his wife and daughter, who was twelve at the time of his release. He was nevertheless grateful for his freedom. "It was rough," he said, "always thinking 'I'm innocent and I'm in jail, I'm innocent and I'm in jail.' I'm happy I'm out. I was angry when I was locked up. Now I feel relieved. The justice system failed me twice, but this time it didn't. This time I feel that there is still justice."

The first thing Felix Michaud did when leaving prison was to drive through the woods around his hometown, smelling the forest. On the first night of his release, he stayed awake so that he could watch the sunrise for the first time since 1992.

# *Insufficient Evidence*

IN THE PAST THREE CENTURIES, COURT RECORDS show an alarming number of persons who were wrongly convicted for capital offenses based on insufficient evidence, or "incompetent" evidence. Often a conviction was brought about by a thread of claimed evidence that consisted of no more than a bit of gossip or a snippet of hearsay. Circumstantial evidence, from a puzzling unsigned note to a cryptic remark uttered by a suspect, too readily became the foundation in a case that sent an innocent person to prison. Sometimes, particularly in the early days of unrefined forensic science, accused persons were convicted on shoddy scientific findings from experts having very little expertise.

Suspicion and not facts inspired police and prosecutors to bring flimsy circumstantial evidence against defendants. In such cases, the police seized upon the most improbable clue or the prosecution clung to the thinnest thread of possible evidence to bring about a conviction. In all of the foregoing cases, naive or gullible juries were overawed and convinced of a defendant's guilt through clever innuendo and dazzling theories that had no basis in fact.

Insufficient evidence can also stem from eyewitness accounts, particularly when identification by witnesses is contradictory and ambiguous. Many cases involve only a few or even a single eyewitness whose testimony hinges on conviction or ac-

quittal. Convictions have been brought about by the sole statements of a lone witness, whose credibility went unchallenged by defense attorneys. Such was the classic case involving Joseph Majczek (see Chapter I). In many other cases the mental capacity of the lone eyewitness was not investigated or revealed, and eyewitness statements are accepted carte blanche by either a jury or a judge (see this chapter, Joseph Nahume Green).

At bench trials, judges have accepted outlandish scenarios from prosecutors that had little or nothing to do with the reality of a given case, or such jurists conveniently ignored facts that would mitigate against a defendant's guilt. Insufficient, incompetent, or faulty evidence was often exposed as such in appeals. Even if a defendant is ultimately released through the exposure of shoddy evidence, that person's life and career has been tainted forever.

## *Faulty Evidence in the Nineteenth Century*

Dr. Thomas Smethurst was a young physician practicing medicine in England. In 1827, he married a wealthy patient twenty years his senior, and for the next fifteen years Thomas and Mary Smethurst enjoyed the fruits of his practice and her wealth.

Dr. Thomas Smethurst of England was convicted of murdering his wife in 1859, but later set free after a court ruled that his conviction was based on insufficient evidence, although his conviction for bigamy was retained. *History Inc./Jay Robert Nash Collection.*

At the time Smethurst retired, he met Isabella Bankes, a forty-three-year-old single woman who moved into the boarding-house where the Smethursts were living. A romantic involvement between the doctor and the new lodger soon became apparent, and she was asked to move. The doctor followed shortly thereafter, and he and Bankes were married bigamously.

In 1859, Bankes became ill with dysentery. After treating her for a while, Smethurst called in several other doctors. Although agreeing originally with the diagnosis of dysentery (the doctors did not know that Bankes was two months pregnant), they finally diagnosed that she was suffering from poisoning. They reported their finding to a magistrate and learned that Smethurst was the beneficiary of her recently drawn will. The suspicious authorities were already watching Smethurst when his "wife" died on May 3, 1859.

Smethurst was arrested and a lengthy, controversial trial took place. The autopsy revealed no poison in the body, but the jury still found Smethurst guilty of murder and put him behind bars. However, the Home Secretary took an interest in the case, and a prominent physician, Sir Benjamin Brodie, was called in to examine the case. Based on his findings, it was determined that no poison was present in the remains of Isabella Bankes. Authorities stated that Smethurst had been wrongly convicted on insufficient evidence, and he was released on the murder charge. Smethurst was nevertheless sentenced to a year in prison for bigamy. He successfully claimed his bigamous wife's estate following his release.

Like the enterprising Dr. Smethurst, Dr. Paul Schoeppe had money on his mind. In the late 1860s, Schoeppe, a young German-born physician, was practicing general medicine in Carlisle, Pennsylvania. One of his patients, a wealthy woman named Maria Stennecke, had a romantic interest in the doctor and offered him a great deal of money to marry her. But on the evening of January 27, 1869, Stennecke died shortly after taking medicine prescribed by Dr. Schoeppe.

The doctor then produced a will that bequeathed Stennecke's entire fortune to him. But her relatives balked, and the document was discovered to be a forgery, written in the doctor's hand. Stennecke's body was exhumed and medical experts concluded that prussic acid was present in the corpse. Schoeppe was brought to trial for murder. Found guilty on the medical claims that he had poisoned Stennecke, Schoeppe was sentenced to death.

While Schoeppe awaited the gallows, several other doctors reexamined the case. They determined that Dr. Schoeppe had been convicted by faulty test results, stating that any evidence of acid found in Stennecke's remains was due to "a reaction with the atmosphere, not to internal consumption."

There was still the question of the forged document, but Schoeppe appeared to be an opportunist rather than a murderer. The court ordered a retrial, and on September 8, 1872, in the courtroom of Judge Junkin, Schoeppe was found wrongly convicted on insufficient evidence. He was acquitted of all charges in regard to the death of Maria Stennecke, and was released from death row. Before getting into the buggy that took him home, Dr. Schoeppe was seen to "do a little jig of joy."

Where faulty forensic science provided insufficient evidence in the Smethurst and Schoeppe cases, the young and willful member of one of Kentucky's most illustrious families was wrongly convicted of manslaughter, based on third-party hearsay. Thomas Crittenden came from a prestigious Kentucky family, with members who had served as U.S. marshals, senators, congressmen, and governors. With every advantage of education, wealth, and position, Crittendon was known as a reckless man prone to fighting. While living with his father, R. H. Crittenden, a U.S. marshal in Anchorage, Kentucky, Thomas Crittenden went to the railroad station drunk on December 8, 1882, and got into a fight with Philip Young, a black porter, slapping him across the face and striking him several times with his fists.

On December 9, 1882, a warrant against Crittenden was issued and the trial took place on December 13, 1882. The key witness against the defendant was Rose Mosby, a young black man who worked as a dining room servant in the Crittenden home. He gave testimony that helped find Crittenden guilty of assault, with a ruling of a one-cent fine and court costs. On his way out of the courtroom, Crittenden reportedly told Mosby he would "see you later about this."

That evening Mosby and a friend, William Butler, returned to their place of work and the cook warned Mosby to leave, since Crittenden had appeared three times looking for him. Butler and Mosby walked to the railroad station. Crittenden showed up shortly after and asked Mosby, "Aren't you going up to the house and clean up the dishes?" Mosby replied, "No, I don't think I'll go back there anymore," and Crittenden left only to return with a double-barreled shotgun. A later report held that Crittenden called Mosby a name and said that he had lied in court against him. Crittenden shot Mosby twice, killing the youth instantly, then briefly chased Butler as he fled.

At the inquest, it was decided that Mosby died of wounds inflicted by Crittenden, who caused them with malice aforethought, and the marshal's son was held without bail. In January 1883, he was indicted for willful murder and tried on that charge in April. A hung jury ended in Crittenden's release on a $2,000 bail. In February 1884, the case was tried a second time, with Asher G. Caruth as the prosecuting attorney while the attorneys defending Crittenden included Judge P. B. Muir, Isaac Caldwell, Major W. R. Kinney, and Marc Mundy.

Brumbley Crittenden testified that Mosby had a large rock in his hand, but other witnesses said they saw no rock on the platform or in Mosby's hand before or after he fell, and that no rock was found anywhere on the platform. The defense presented the theory that several young black men, members of a secret order, were at the depot to assist Mosby, who planned to assault Crittenden, and that the servant had been shot when he lifted a large rock to throw at his employer's son. The jury found the defendant guilty of voluntary manslaughter and Crittenden was sentenced to eight years imprisonment.

Attorneys for the imprisoned Crittenden then filed an appeal. In reviewing the case, Judge W. L. Jackson reversed Crittenden's conviction, citing incompetent evidence, in that the cook who had warned Mosby to stay away had said at first, "I did not think he would be killed; I did not know." She later responded to a similar question about whether she had told someone else that Mosby might be killed: "I don't know whether I told Henry that or not." The court judged this testimony to be illegal because it showed that the witness had stated, out of court, facts that she failed to prove while in court, thereby transforming hearsay testimony into substantive evidence.

The case then moved to Spencer County, where at a retrial prosecuting attorney James Morris fought to convict Crittenden, but the jury acquitted the defendant. Soon after this final trial, the Spencer County courthouse, including all the records of the case, burned down. Crittenden was released.

Where hearsay evidence had been at the core of the prosecution's case against Crittenden, hearsay from a private detective sent two railroad workers to prison for a robbery they most likely did not commit. This case began on the night of March 12, 1886, when Kellogg Nichols boarded a Rock Island Express train in Chicago. A messenger for the United States Express Company in Chicago, Nichols carried $22,500 in cash and negotiable securities bound for an office in Davenport, Iowa.

Between Joliet and Morris, Illinois, Newton Watt, a railroad employee, reported to his superior that unknown persons had broken into the baggage car and looted the safe. Watt, brakeman Harry

Schwartz, and conductor Fred Wagner discovered the body of Nichols, who had been beaten and shot to death. An examination of the body indicated Nichols had put up a fight. His hands were bloody and there were bits of skin under his fingernails.

After notifying local authorities of the robbery and murder, Wagner questioned coworker Watt. Watt said that a masked gunman had held a revolver to the back of his head, but later statements revealed inconsistencies in the story that puzzled the veteran trainman. When Detective William A. Pinkerton arrived, he immediately suspected brakeman Schwartz, whose badly scratched hands suggested a recent struggle. Pinkerton called in fellow detective Frank Watt to help solve the case.

Watt posed as a Rock Island employee to learn more about Newton Watt (no relation) and Schwartz. He reported that they were close friends and that Watt was planning to move to Philadelphia. In one of their conversations, Schwartz warned Watt to be careful once in Philadelphia. Schwartz suspected the railroad had put extra detectives on the case and cautioned, "Be careful how you spend your money, Harry. I think they're still onto us and you want to be careful." This statement was overheard by Frank Watt and repeated later at the trial of Schwartz and Newton Watt.

The investigation zeroed in on Schwartz when he began flashing a large bankroll around Philadelphia. Pinkerton detectives at this time reported that Schwartz was a bigamist who had a wife in Chicago and another in Philadelphia. Schwartz was arrested for bigamy and later, on December 3, 1886, was charged with the train robbery.

Conversations between Pinkerton and Mrs. Schwartz revealed that her husband had recently come into a large sum of money. He told his wife he had found a brown envelope containing $5,000 under a seat in one of the train cars. In March, the case came to trial. The evidence against Schwartz and his close friend Watt was purely circumstantial—and was chiefly based on the unfounded statements of Pinkerton detective Frank Watt. But this "evidence" nevertheless convicted Schwartz and Newton Watt of robbery and murder, and both were sentenced to life imprisonment. Watt died in the Joliet Penitentiary in March 1889, swearing innocence until his death. Nine years later, Illinois Governor John Peter Altgeld (1893–1897) pardoned Schwartz amid a continuing debate about his innocence or guilt. Altgeld, who had meticulously reviewed the case, concluded that Schwartz and Watt had been sent to prison on insufficient evidence.

In a sensational San Francisco case, a physician with a notorious reputation was convicted of murdering one his patients. The conviction was achieved through the same flimsy "evidence" that sent Schwartz and Watt to prison. Though he lacked a motive for this crime, Dr. Eugene West went to prison based on circumstantial evidence, which later proved to be insufficient. In this case, a bad reputation and the questionable conduct of the defendant largely contributed to that wrongful conviction.

Dr. West's troubles began when Addie Gilmour, a Colusa milliner, traveled to San Francisco in August 1893 to purchase hats. To acquaint herself with the latest fashions, she took a job at the F. Toplitz Millinery on Market Street. She lived in rooms at the Elmer House on Bush Street. When her partner, Laura Allen, arrived in San Francisco on September 1, 1893, she was told that Gilmour had left both her job and her lodgings without notice. Allen returned immediately to Colusa but did not find Gilmour there.

Gilmour's twin sister received a letter from Addie dated September 4, 1893, explaining that she was about to undergo surgery performed by Dr. Eugene West. With this information, investigators learned that Gilmour had moved to Dr. West's address on Turk Street on September 1, 1893. West later told police that he performed the operation on September 4, 1893, but Gilmour died on September 9, 1893. Stating that he had no knowledge of the whereabouts or the existence of her relatives, he gave the unclaimed body over to other physicians for postmortem examination and dissection, a routine practice at that time.

Several days later, on September 12, 1893, fishermen found Gilmour's head floating in the San Francisco Bay. After that, her torso and several other body parts were also found. On September 28, 1893, an oilcan floating in an Oakland creek was found to contain two arms, a foot, and Gilmour's purse. Dr. West was arrested, which came as no surprise to the medical community, which held him in very low esteem. Annie Staley, his assistant, was thought to know damaging information about West, but she kept silent, and even married West on September 28, 1893. Investigators theorized that Staley had married her employer so that she could not be called to testify against him and would be able to visit him in prison.

A coworker of Gilmour's went to Dr. West's office after hearing about Addie Gilmour's letter and found May Howard there. She claimed to have met Gilmour three times, twice in West's office and once on the Oakland ferry, where Gilmour was reportedly despondent and considering suicide. Howard told of Gilmour entering the ladies room of the ferry and never coming out, and of finding the window there open. Before West's trial began, however, Howard recanted, saying that the story about the ferry was a fiction that Dr. West had persuaded her to tell.

West's trial began on February 5, 1894, before Judge Wallace. On February 16, 1894, he was found guilty of second-degree murder, chiefly on the hearsay evidence of Laura Allen and May Howard. Several days later, West was sentenced to twenty-five years in prison. On appeal to the Supreme Court, he won a second trial, which began in December 1895. This time, West claimed that he inherited Gilmour's case from a colleague, Dr. W. A. Harvey, whose previous malpractice had already doomed her. West said he gave Gilmour's body to a Dr. Tuchler for postmortem examination, and that he had refrained from identifying the two men in his previous trial because they

were friends he wished to protect. When this was corroborated, the jury, after an hour's deliberation, acquitted Dr. Eugene West. The manner in which the remains of Addie Gilmour had been savagely disseminated brought censor and criticism to Dr. Tuchler, who claimed to have ordered the remains buried in a pauper's grave. However, mortician workers simply dumped the body parts into San Francisco Bay. The mortician was convicted and fined for littering.

## The Snare of Inconsistency

During the reckless 1920s, an age of social upheaval and fashionable loose living, courts around the world tended to admit fragile evidence in cases involving major crimes. As old morals and traditions were abandoned, so too were the studied and careful criminal investigations of yesteryear. This was the age of tabloid news, where scandal was popularized and rumor and whimsy were twisted into facts (a rebirth of this kind of irresponsible media occurred in the 1990s–2000s, with the coming of the babbling Internet).

Prosecutors often employed irresponsible statements and uncorroborated allegations in their cases, which intimidated and influenced the authority of the courts. Motiveless crimes were given credibility by outlandish claims. Inconsistent circumstantial evidence was employed with alacrity to convict the innocent. Such was the case of J. Adelard Delorme, wrongly convicted of murdering his own brother because he seemed too tranquil to his neighbors and officials.

On January 7, 1922, Raul Delorme was found dead on a Montreal street with his hands tied, pieces of bed quilt wrapped around his head, and six bullet wounds in his skull and neck. The victim was last seen the night before at the house he lived in with his half-brother, J. Adelard Delorme, a Roman Catholic priest. The dead man shared a considerable interest with his brother in his late father's estate. When the priest went to identify the body, onlookers were surprised at his casual attitude. In Quebec at that time, a clergyman was considered above suspicion, and in many ways Delorme retained this status throughout the subsequent two years of legal proceedings. The coroner examining his brother's corpse was so appalled at the idea of Delorme being a suspect that he refused to consider the possibility.

Delorme was certainly not indifferent to his brother's brutal murder. He offered a $10,000 reward for the capture of the killer. He nevertheless continued to seem unconcerned about the death in the eyes of some. When his nerveless conduct was pointed out to him, he referred to his vocation, possibly as a way of explaining his unusual calm. Nevertheless, Delorme was held on the charge of murder following the final inquest.

The evidence against Delorme at first appeared substantial. Although the body had been discovered in the snow in the Montreal suburb of Notre Dame de Grace, also known as Snowdon Junction, the doctors who examined the corpse did not believe he had been killed at that location. The boots were clean and dry and, though one bullet had penetrated the victim's chest, it had not made a hole in his coat. The deceased had almost certainly been slain elsewhere, the physicians concluded, and then driven to the place where it was discovered. The dead man was last seen alive at the home he shared with his brother.

Neighbors had heard several gunshots on the night of the murder. Fresh car tracks proved that the family car had been driven at a late hour, which coincided with the time the body could have been moved. There were bloodstains in the car. The quilt wrapped around the corpse's head matched fragments found in the Delorme home. Ten nights before the killing, the priest had purchased a .25-caliber revolver, and a week before he had taken out an $88,000 life insurance policy on Raul, a twenty-four-year-old student at the time of his death. Delorme's only defense was to suggest that his brother had been killed by strangers. The priest's two sisters adamantly insisted that Raul

had called the house a few hours after the supposed time of his death, but these statements were discredited when the sisters stated that their living brother had told them these calls were made to the house.

In June 1922, Delorme's defense moved that the priest was unfit to be tried by reason of insanity, but Delorme objected to the implication that there was insanity in his family. He remained unconcerned throughout the legal proceedings, feeling confident that, as a priest, he would not be convicted of murder. Over Delorme's objections to an insanity defense, the jury, ignoring the inconsistencies and contradictory statements made by witnesses, accepted his attorney's plea of insanity after ten minutes of deliberation. Delorme was convicted of murder and sent to an asylum.

Discovering that he would not be able to administer his family's estate, which he felt might not be judiciously distributed while he was legally insane, the priest insisted on being released and tried again. In June 1923, he was brought into court, this time before Sir Francis Lemeiux, Quebec's chief justice, who was called to preside because of the widespread controversy surrounding the case. The trial lasted for more than a month, during which 170 witnesses were called. Because two of the six jurors stood firm for acquittal and a unanimous conviction was required, the case was tried a third time.

The jury in the third trial reversed the previous verdict, based on insufficient evidence, determining that Delorme was sane, as new court-appointed analysts confirmed, and that he had no motive to murder his brother for financial reasons since Delorme had taken vows of poverty and distributed his family's wealth to other members of that family, as well as charitable organizations. Delorme was freed on October 30, 1924, coming into an inheritance of $250,000, with an additional $88,000 from the insurance money. As the executor of the family estate, he divided the funds equally among the family heirs. Delorme died of a brain hemorrhage on January 19, 1942.

Inconsistency was at the rotten core of the De-lorme case and inconsistent statements by a rape victim resulted in a death sentence for a mentally retarded black youth in an unenlightened South. A jury found seventeen-year-old Alvin Mansell (born in 1908) guilty of a 1925 North Carolina rape, but several of its members were not convinced of his guilt and said so to presiding Buncombe County Judge A. M. Stack. Judge Stack nevertheless sentenced Mansell to death. If all the evidence that supported him had been included in the trial, Mansell would not have been convicted at all. Five years of horror on death row ended when the truth became known and Mansell was pardoned.

Shortly after the attack on her, a Mrs. Cartee described her rape assailant to C. P. Ryman, J. R. Brooks, and Deputy Sheriff Merrill, saying he "was about thirty-five years old, was a rather large yellow Negro with a blue shirt, yellow trousers, and a felt hat." Mansell was seventeen years old, 5 feet 4, weighing about one hundred pounds with a very dark complexion. He was convicted because, due to tight time constraints, the defending attorney was unable to collect and present most of the pertinent information and he relied on the inconsistent statements from the victim.

The jury, it was later determined, would not have found Mansell guilty if it had heard testimony from Ryman, Brooks, and Merrill that the description Cartee gave of her assailant at the trial contradicted the one she gave to the three men immediately following the ordeal. The jury never learned that the doctors who examined Cartee after the attack doubted Mansell's guilt. The jury did not know that seven patients at the sanatorium where Mansell worked and where Cartee had been on the day the crime was committed contradicted her statements as to the time she said she left and supported Mansell's alibi.

The Mansell case remained a thorn in the side of the black community, which organized to save the boy's life. Approximately four thousand citizens, including some whites, of nearby Asheville and Buncombe County either signed a petition or wrote letters to North Carolina Governor Angus Wilton McLean (1925–1929) asking for a commutation of the prisoner's sentence because they doubted his guilt.

The verdict, however, had already been upheld by a state appeals court. On July 8, 1926, Governor McLean commuted Mansell's sentence to life imprisonment, reasoning that evidence might later be discovered to prove Mansell innocent and the punishment reversed. In 1929, Democrat Oliver Max Gardner was elected governor of North Carolina (1929–1933). He was an enlightened man, having taught chemistry before becoming a lawyer. Gardner not only reformed the state's agrarian system, including crop diversification, but doubled the allotments to schools and established a secret ballot.

Gardner was particularly interested in reforming the penal system in North Carolina and, to that end, abolished the hateful chain gang system. As he improved the state's prison conditions, the conscientious Gardner began reviewing questionable convictions, including that of Mansell. He and his researchers discovered the discrepancies in the Mansell case and noted the rape victim's inconsistent statements, which had not been wholly exhibited in Mansell's trial.

Based on these discoveries and despite opposition from the Ku Klux Klan and other racial hate groups, Governor Gardner ordered Mansell freed in 1930, declaring that he was "absolutely convinced" of the defendant's innocence. Another southern governor, John Slaton of Georgia (1911–1912; 1913–1915), made the same courageous stand for the wrongly convicted Leo Max Frank fifteen years earlier, a decision that ruined his political career and exiled him from the state. (See Chapter XI, "Railroading and Framing.")

A year after Mansell was wrongly convicted, inconsistent statements from the husband of a murder victim sent three innocent persons to prison for life in Florida. On August 1, 1926, sixty-seven-year-old Mary McMillan was brutally axed to death in her rural Florida home. Her husband, sixty-eight-year-old Malcolm McMillan, said he and his wife had been attacked by three men who hit him over the head and chopped at him, before he managed to escape by hiding under the house.

At the crime scene, McMillan told Officer E. L. Waldron that his assailants had been foreigners. The men, who were eventually arrested, were not foreigners but local residents. Later at the hospital, McMillan told Dr. W. W. Hartman that the men who attacked him wore masks, a statement that he later denied in court. Within a week, Howard Shaffer, Charles Stevens, and William Troop were arrested and charged with the murderous attack.

During this time, McMillan, while still in the hospital, informed three detectives that he had no idea who committed the crime, statements he later denied in court. No other witnesses saw the men who attacked McMillan. One witness claimed to have seen Shaffer a few blocks away at the time of the crime, while another heard Troop mention that Mrs. McMillan deserved a good beating because of her meddling ways.

Other than that, there was only McMillan's inconsistent words and denials against Shaffer, Stevens, and Troop. McMillan identified the trio in court, despite the fact that he had earlier stated that the invaders had worn masks and that he had no idea who murdered his wife. The evidence, which favored the defendants at their trial in early 1927, was the well-substantiated testimony of witnesses who had seen or heard McMillan abusing and striking his wife in drunken rages. He had also threatened to kill her with an ax, according to one account. Despite the lack of evidence and motive, as well as McMillan's rampant inconsistency, the jury found all three men guilty of first-degree murder.

Judge Daniel T. Simmons immediately threw out the decision and ordered a retrial. Shaffer, Stevens, and Troop once again were found guilty and sentenced to death in 1928. This decision was appealed to the Florida Supreme Court, which overturned the trial decision because of the inconsistency in McMillan's testimony and the lack of a motive. A new trial was ordered, and on April 30, 1930, after the three men had spent three years and eight months on death row, Judge DeWitt T. Gray dropped the charges and Shaffer, Stevens, and Troop were released from custody.

Two years later, three men in England were sent to prison for life in a case that paralleled the Florida murder—a conviction that was obtained on meager circumstantial evidence that might have been overturned had the murder victim's dying statement been made available. George Donovan, thirty-one, Percival Taylor, twenty-four, and James Weaver, twenty-one, were all found guilty of the 1928 murder of chemist Ernest Friend-Smith, who died after being struck repeatedly by a large object in Brighton, England.

Friend-Smith's gold watch, chain, and £15 in treasury notes had been stolen. In the court of criminal appeal, Lord Chief Justice Heward expressed surprise that the victim did not provide a statement concerning his assailants before he died, since he had lingered for a month following the attack. In actuality Friend-Smith had provided a statement, but the prosecution did not deem it important enough to be read in court.

The three accused men were subsequently found guilty based only on circumstantial evidence. Tacky green and white fluff was found sticking to the victim's pants, and a car eventually traced back to Donovan, Taylor, and Weaver had worn upholstery and frayed floor mats of the same color. A barmaid at the St. James Hotel believed she saw the three accused men and a man fitting Friend-Smith's description leaving the hotel together on the night of the murder. Further, a Hastings woman said Donovan had told her he was in trouble with the police for hitting an old man in the jaw and would leave Brighton as soon as possible.

The jury concluded that Donovan, Taylor, and Weaver must be guilty and Justice Avory handed down a harsh condemnation, sending the three men to prison for life. The decision made to convict the three unfortunates was based on circumstantial evidence, which, at the time, was all the evidence the jury thought existed. Twenty-seven years after the trial, when Donovan had died and Weaver and Taylor had been released from prison, William Teeling, conservative Member of Parliament for the Pavilion Division of Brighton, revealed that Sir Ernley Blackwell had been shown a statement made by Friend-Smith before his death concerning his assailants. Blackwell showed the statement to his counselors and asked them what they would have done if they had known about it at the time. The overwhelming, tragic response was that they would not have found the men guilty. Yet David Lloyd George, Home Secretary, maintained he did not consider the statement admissible in court because it was not done in the form of a proper dying declaration.

## Circumstantial Evidence in the Wallace and McDermott Cases

One of the most baffling murder cases in the history of England involved William Herbert Wallace (1878–1933), a mild-mannered man with a staid personality. He spoke quietly, selecting his words with precision. There was no flair or flamboyance in his character and anyone meeting him would likely find him instantly forgettable. However, his innocuous demeanor was the reason why he was accused and tried for murdering his spouse. Wallace, an insurance salesman and amateur chess player, was scheduled to play in the second-class championship at the Liverpool Central Chess Club on January 19, 1931, the night before his wife was murdered. Julia Wallace, like her husband, was mild-mannered and refined.

The couple first met in Manchester in 1911 after Wallace had returned from the Orient, where he had done bureaucratic work in China and India while studying Stoic philosophy. The two shared an interest in music and philosophy and were married in 1913. Wallace recorded eighteen years of peaceful, happy married life in his diary.

On the night of the chess championship, club manager Samuel Beattie took a telephone message for Wallace. A man who identified himself only as R. M. Qualtrough requested that Wallace meet him at 7:30 P.M. the next night at 25 Menlove Gardens East. Although the name Qualtrough was fairly common in Liverpool, the caller spelled out his name for Beattie to make sure he got it correctly. When Wallace, fifty-two, arrived late at the club and received the message, he remarked that he did not know anyone by that name.

Assuming the matter concerned insurance, Wallace went to meet Qualtrough, but the address proved to be fictitious. Wallace returned to his Liverpool home on January 20, 1931, at about 8:45 P.M. He was apparently unable to gain entrance. The front and back doors were bolted from the inside and his wife did not answer. His neighbors, John and Florence Johnston, were leaving their house at that moment, and Wallace spoke to them about his house being locked. Then he tried the door again and was able to open it.

Upstairs, Wallace found fifty-year-old Julia Wallace dead. She had been bludgeoned eleven times, although the police pathologist later testified that

William Herbert Wallace, the central figure in one of England's most baffling murder cases, and for which he was wrongly convicted and sentenced to death. *History Inc./Jay Robert Nash Collection.*

Julia Wallace, attractive, refined and without enemies, mysteriously murdered on the night of January 20, 1931. *History Inc./Jay Robert Nash Collection.*

the first blow almost certainly killed her and that all the additional blows were "gratuitous." Wallace ran back downstairs, calling out to the Johnstons, "Come and see. She has been killed."

When interviewed by police, Wallace mentioned that he had been out that night to meet a customer he had never met, a man named Qualtrough (who was never found). Wallace also told police that he had been home between "about 6:05 and 6:45" on the night of the murder. A fourteen-year-old milk delivery boy said he saw Julia Wallace take in the milk at 6:30 P.M., and the evening paper had been delivered at 6:35 P.M. The paper was found spread out on the kitchen table. The pathologist, Professor John Edward MacFall, set the time of death at 6:10 P.M. When a locksmith was asked to check the locks on the doors, he found them inadequate. The strongest evidence against William Wallace was his normal stoicism. Police thought he was behaving too calmly. Arrested on February 2, 1931, Wallace went to trial on April 22, 1931.

Prosecutors stated that Wallace invented "Qualtrough" out of thin air, and had made the "Qualtrough" call himself to place suspicion on this fictional character, instead of himself. Beattie testified that the voice on the phone was "gruff but ordinary." He did not identify the voice as being that of Wallace. The defense surmised that surely Beattie would have recognized Wallace's voice as he was well-known to Beattie. Defense attorneys also pointed out that Wallace had no apparent motive for killing his wife and emphasized that no murder weapon was ever found. Justice Wright

The Wallace residence in Liverpool, England; William Herbert Wallace returned home to find all doors and windows locked, but then found a door open and discovered the body of his slain wife. *History Inc./Jay Robert Nash Collection.*

instructed the jurors that all the evidence against Wallace was circumstantial, strongly suggesting that he considered the case not proven. The jury nevertheless found Wallace guilty of murder. Wright reluctantly sentenced Wallace to death.

The court of criminal appeal decided that Wallace's conviction was not supported by the circumstantial evidence offered by the prosecution, and it overturned his conviction four weeks later. Wallace, who believed in those four weeks he was going to the hangman, was set free. A bizarre backlash of public opinion occurred following Wallace's release. During the trial, Liverpool residents seemed to believe that Wallace had been horribly wronged, but, after his release, he was harassed by people who believed he had gotten away with murder. His insurance company considerately transferred him out of the field to a desk job, his former chess-playing partners refused to associate with him, and children followed him in the streets and taunted him by chanting rhymes they made up about the murder.

Wallace had had recurring stomach troubles and they returned full force in December 1932. By February 9, 1933, the pain was so severe he needed to be hospitalized, and he died of kidney disease on February 26, 1933. To this day, many believe Wallace killed the wife he ostensibly loved and supported for most of his adult life.

Where the Wallace case was haunted by uncommon circumstantial evidence—an unidentified stranger, real or mythical, and the unflappable personality of the defendant—the case of Frederick McDermott was also rife with circumstantial evidence that brought about a wrongful conviction, in this case an offhand remark that sent the defendant to the death house. In spring 1936, a New South Wales general store owner was reportedly murdered at Old Glenelg. Though William Henry Lavers's body was never found, evidence of blood and tissue samples on the handle of his gas pump indicated that he had been slain by one or more men who had driven to his station, gotten gas they didn't pay for, smashed in his skull with an old pump handle, and driven off with the body.

Detective sergeants Allmond and Calman investigated the case, coming up with a lead when a traveling sideshow artist, Essie May King, told of seeing an older model car with two men in it that matched the description of the one that left tire tracks at Lavers's gas station. Several years passed with no other clues. Then, on December 13, 1944, Calman, Allmond, and another detective named Humphries questioned Frederick Lincoln McDermott, whose description loosely fit that given by King eight years earlier. An uneducated shearer, McDermott said he thought the two men in the car might have been sheep shearers, believing that one of the men, Fred Munro, who had not shown up for work, might have been involved with the Lavers slaying. The police informed McDermott that some of his friends claimed to have heard him say he and another man had killed Lavers and gotten rid of the body.

McDermott treated that allegation as a joke. He laughed and then replied, "I told Florrie that I had been questioned by the police at Bathurst and since then she has told people that I killed Lavers for a drop of petrol." McDermott gave a written testimony to what he suspected and was then released, only to be picked up again in October 1946. He was questioned again, and this time charged with murder. The main testimony against him was that of his estranged live-in lover, Florrie Hamp-

Wallace shown in a contemporary Liverpool newspaper; most believed him innocent before his trial, but, following his release after an appeals court ruled that he had been convicted on insufficient evidence, most believed him guilty. *History Inc./Jay Robert Nash Collection.*

ton, a drunk who took a facetious remark McDermott made about the murders for the truth.

The murder trial began on February 17, 1947, before Justice L. J. Herron in the Bathurst circuit court, with Tom Crawford prosecuting and Fred Vizzard for the defense. After five days of testimony that included forty-three witnesses, including Hampton, who was suspected of being in an alcoholic state when giving testimony, McDermott was found guilty and sentenced to death. Six months later, the death sentence was abolished in New South Wales, and McDermott was removed to Goulburn Jail to serve a life sentence.

Maintaining his innocence throughout, McDermott, who had never made a confession, filed several appeals, including one to the High Court of Australia in 1948. In 1951, McDermott again appealed, and his plea was examined by Governor Sir John Northcott, who realized that McDermott had been convicted on evidence so thin as to be almost inadmissible, and that the chief witness against him had been a vengeful drunk. Appalled, Northcott ordered a commission to make an extensive investigation into the case. The subsequent report proved that McDermott had been sent to prison for life on insufficient evidence. On January 11, 1952, justice minister R. R. Downing recommended McDermott's release. The wrongly convicted man was released from the Long Bay Penitentiary less than one hour later. He was given no compensation for spending five years behind bars for a crime he did not commit.

## Insufficient Evidence in Two Virginia Spouse Murders

Two murder cases occurring in Virginia in the 1940s involved allegations of extramarital affairs which provided the thin circumstantial evidence that wrongly sent two persons to prison. The first of these two cases began on February 20, 1945, when the lifeless body of Frank Smith, a World War II veteran, was found in his Harrisonburg,

Virginia, home, suspended from a rope. Bloodstains were found in the house, but investigators found no sign of a struggle. From all appearances, Smith had committed suicide, yet the court found his wife, Grace M. Smith, and her alleged lover, Ralph H. Garner, guilty of murder. Grace Smith was sentenced to twenty years in prison. A year and a half later, however, her case was brought back on appeal.

The Virginia Supreme Court determined that Grace Smith's original conviction was based on speculation and was not supported by any substantial evidence. Grace Smith and her husband were said to have fought over her alleged affairs with other men during Frank Smith's absence while serving in the army. Eventually the Commonwealth of Virginia admitted that Grace Smith was physically incapable of killing her husband, that she could not have dragged him to the basement and hoisted his heavy body onto the footstool where it was discovered.

The Virginia Supreme Court found that she and Garner together might have committed a murder, but that the evidence against the pair was in no way conclusive. Furthermore, the court ruled that the lower court had failed to prove that a fight occurred in which Frank Smith was subdued before being carried to the basement. In fact, the shaky circumstantial evidence only proved that Grace Smith was in the house when her husband died. After she had served more than one year of her sentence, her conviction was reversed on November 25, 1946. Garner was also released.

Three years later, an almost identical murder case occurred in the same state. Kenneth Raymond Holland, a former Norfolk County, Virginia, police officer, was convicted and later acquitted of murdering Everett Utt on June 17, 1948. Utt, who had known Holland for five years, was found bludgeoned to death in his car. Holland was convicted of the murder and sentenced to twenty years in prison in November 1949. The conviction was overturned for lack of sufficient evidence, and Holland was retried several months later.

Holland was originally linked to the crime by a photograph of the dead man's wife, Mary Lee Utt, which he kept in his apartment. Officers questioning Holland about the photo noticed bloodstained clothes in the man's laundry room. Holland had told detectives that he had been in a fight with a neighbor, Vaden Tomblin, and had broken Tomblin's nose. The fight was substantiated through a lawsuit Tomblin filed against Holland for assault.

This evidence was presented by defense attorneys at both of Holland's trials. Mary Lee Utt testified that she had given Holland her photograph and had dated the defendant, with her husband's consent, while he was serving in the navy. Nell Duke, one of Utt's neighbors, testified that she had seen Holland driving Utt's car the night before the murder, but, under cross-examination, revealed that she had never seen the defendant at close range before the trial. After less than one hour of deliberation, a jury acquitted Holland on April 14, 1950.

## Insufficient Evidence That Ruined Lives

In many capital crime cases, insufficient evidence has not only brought about wrongful convictions but has permanently ruined the lives of defendants and brought untold suffering to their family members. When Edward F. Kanieski (1919–1975), thirty-three, went to the state prison in Waupun, Wisconsin, in 1952, he was a healthy, robust construction worker. Twenty years later, he was frail with a serious heart condition. During the intervening years, his family lived a hand-to-mouth existence. His wife was committed to an asylum, and Kanieski's eldest son lost his sight as a result of a brawl with another boy, who had teased him about having a "jailbird" father. During his incarceration, Kanieski maintained his innocence.

Kanieski's troubles began on June 29, 1952, after he stopped for a drink at a Wisconsin Rapids tavern owned and operated by Clara (Cad) Bates, seventy. She was later found strangled and beaten to death on the premises. Based on circumstantial evidence, chiefly the fact that he had been present in the tavern on the night of the murder, Kanieski was convicted and sentenced to life. In 1964, his parole was turned down after he refused to admit his guilt.

The tireless efforts of one of his sons finally convinced the Wisconsin Supreme Court to issue an order freeing Kanieski in March 1972. The court ruled that there had been insufficient evidence to convict him. The little evidence that existed pointed to Mrs. Bates's former lover, a man never brought to trial. Kanieski filed a $250,000 claim against the state, which he later reduced to $75,000. The state claims board denied him the money, citing his failure to "prove his innocence beyond reasonable doubt." Edward Kanieski died three years later, penniless.

Kanieski's fate was shared by Delbert Lee Tibbs in a notorious case involving rape and murder. In 1974, Tibbs, thirty-four, a black divinity student and aspiring writer, was hitchhiking through the South gathering material for a novel. Police in Daytona Beach, Florida, picked Tibbs up for hitchhiking and photographed him. When police in Fort Myers began searching for a black man who had raped a sixteen-year-old white girl, Cynthea Nadeau, and murdered her white male companion, Terry Milroy, the Daytona police sent Tibbs's picture to the Fort Myers police department. Milroy had been en route to a job waiting for him in the Florida Keys, and Nadeau was on her way to nowhere. They received a ride from a black man driving a green pickup truck on February 3, 1974, but he stopped the truck in a vacant lot and asked Milroy to step out and help him with something, according to Nadeau's later testimony. She said that the driver then produced a gun and shot and killed Milroy, ordering her to undress before he raped her.

The Fort Myers police improperly showed the rape victim pictures of Tibbs before having her at-

tempt to identify her attacker in a lineup. Cynthia Nadeau, a runaway from Rhode Island who later admitted to being high on marijuana at the time of the crime, identified Tibbs as her assailant from the subsequent police lineup, after Tibbs had been located hitchhiking in Mississippi and returned to Fort Meyers. Although Tibbs did not fit the original description of the killer Nadeau gave to police, she nevertheless picked him out of the police lineup, causing Tibbs to be charged with murder and rape.

Tibbs claimed he was never in Fort Myers, and only Nadeau's testimony placed him within two hundred miles of the crime, other than a jailhouse informer, who claimed that Tibbs had confessed to him in the cell they both occupied. The green truck Tibbs supposedly drove was never located, and no one ever asked why, if indeed Tibbs had been driving a truck, would he be found on a Mississippi road hitchhiking? An all-white jury, however, found Tibbs guilty of rape and first-degree murder after only ninety minutes of deliberation.

Tibbs was subsequently given a life sentence for the rape conviction and sentenced to die in the electric chair for the murder of Milroy. He spent two years on death row before the Florida Supreme Court reversed his conviction on the grounds that it was not supported by "weight of the evidence." Prior of that time, the jailhouse informer, a convicted rapist, recanted his testimony, saying that he had perjured himself in testifying against Tibbs in order to get a more lenient prison term.

Released on bail in 1977, Tibbs later discovered that despite semantic similarities, "weight of evidence" does not mean "insufficient evidence." In 1982, the U.S. Supreme Court ruled that Tibbs could be retried for the crimes on the same evidence used in the first trial because a reversal on "weight of evidence" does not mean that acquittal is the only proper verdict. Joseph D'Alessandro, Lee County state's attorney, announced plans to exercise the newly elucidated option to retry Tibbs, but he had no case at all when it was discovered that Nadeau was by then a confirmed drug addict. When James Long, who had prosecuted Tibbs in 1974, announced that the Tibbs trial had been "tainted from the beginning" and that he would testify on Tibbs's behalf, D'Alessandro decided not to reopen the case.

Many notable persons supported Tibbs during his trials, including activist Angela Davis and singer Joan Baez. Pete Seeger wrote a ballad about him, "Ode to Delbert Tibbs." Upon his release, Tibbs moved to Chicago and found work in a packaging warehouse. He stated that employment was difficult to find for anyone with a prison record, let alone a person with a death row conviction for murder. Tibbs was resigned to oblivion: "The jobs I've gotten have been out of the benevolence of friends. Jobs in mainstream America I don't even try for anymore."

Tibbs was an innocent man who had fought the good fight in the 1960s during the civil rights crusades in the South. He had planned to return to Chicago to study for a degree at the Chicago Theological Seminary, after he hitchhiked through the South "to experience firsthand the woes and wonders of the world," according to one journalist covering his case. What he experienced was an American judicial system so imperfect that it nearly put him to death wrongfully.

Four years after Tibbs was wrongly arrested, another man in Florida was sent to death row on insufficient evidence. At 3:45 P.M., on the Thursday afternoon of October 12, 1978, twelve-year-old Linda Pirkuritz left her home in Port Charlotte, Florida, riding her bike. When she failed to return home by 9:00 P.M., her sister, Deborah Bianchi, filed a missing persons report with the Charlotte County sheriff's department. At 11:57 P.M., local police, responding to a report of a brush fire, found Pirkuritz's body.

There was no evidence of sexual assault and it was determined that she had died from smoke inhalation. There was no evidence of trauma or injuries not caused by the fire. Her bicycle was found the next day in some bushes next to the Li'l General Store, a local convenience store where Linda and many other children bought candy (an unopened package of bubblegum was found next to the girl's body, along with a shell necklace, a leather visor, a pair of underpants, and a red-and-white tennis shoe).

Bradley Scott became a suspect after some children said that they often saw him near the convenience store, talking to them and to Linda Pirkuritz. Further, a few months after the Pirkuritz girl was found, Scott was investigated as a suspect in the assault of a teenage girl. He supplied a strong alibi at the time, however, showing receipts for purchases he and his wife had made at a shopping mall some distance away from the crime scene. He also willingly took a lie detector test, which he believed he had passed with flying colors. He was released without any further comment from the police. In 1986, however, seven years and seven months after the murder, local authorities charged Scott with the murder of Pirkuritz.

The so-called eyewitnesses clung to their claims that they had seen Scott talking with Pirkuritz at the store on the day of her death. Two teenage girls, friends of the victim, stated that Scott had often met with them near the convenience store shortly before Pirkuritz vanished, and bought them beer and smoked marijuana with them.

At Scott's trial in 1988, forensic experts testified that they had examined two hairs belonging to Scott that had been found in his car, four months after he sold the car and more than a year after Pirkuritz's death. They said they had matched those hairs to a wool cap belonging to the girl. Another expert insisted that the hair samples were so old and so small a sample that they were impossible to match to those found on the cap, stating that "fifteen or twenty hairs" were necessary for as an ideal sampling. The victim's mother had provided to the police a wool ski cap worn by her daughter, but not worn by her at the time of the girl's death. Prosecutors also provided a small shell they said had been found in Scott's car, which might have matched the shells of the necklace the girl had worn. Scott's mother testified that she had often used her son's car to transport seashells, as one of her hobbies was collecting and working with shells.

On this flimsy evidence Scott was convicted of murdering Pirkuritz and was sentenced to death. His attorneys appealed, pointing out that some of the witnesses had been interviewed and taped after undergoing hypnosis and that the tape had subsequently been lost. They also pointed out that several other officers had taken over the case since the original 1978 investigation and many records were not available to them during the 1988 trial.

In 1991, the Florida Supreme Court, its panel voting unanimously, vacated Scott's conviction and ordered an acquittal, based on an "unjustified" delay in bringing the defendant to trial, as well as insufficient evidence presented at that trial. The court stated, "We find that the circumstantial evidence presented by the prosecution could only create a suspicion that Scott committed this murder. Suspicions cannot be a basis for a criminal conviction. Our law requires proof beyond a reasonable doubt and a fair trial for a defendant."

## Insufficient Evidence in the Chamberlain Case

Michael and Alice Lynne "Lindy" Chamberlain (both born in 1948), a young couple with three children living in Mount Isa in western Queensland, took a camping trip in August 1980. They traveled to scenic Ayers Rock in Australia's Northern Territory near Alice Springs. Along with other tourists, the family pitched a tent in the shadow of the towering, dome-shaped Ayers Rock. On the night of August 17, 1980, Lindy Chamberlain put four-year-old Reagan and nine-week-year-old Azaria to sleep in the tent and then, with her husband and seven-year-old Aidan, went outside to help prepare supper at the campfire.

At about 7:00 P.M., Michael Chamberlain turned to his wife and said he thought he heard the baby crying in the tent. As Lindy approached the tent, she later stated, she saw a dingo, a breed of Australian wild dog that populated the outback, running from the tent, its head down, shaking something in its jaws. "I dashed into the tent, but the carry-cot was empty," Lindy later testified. "I looked around, but there was no sign of Azaria." She then realized what had happened, and Lindy turned and ran back to her husband screaming, "My God! My God! The dingo's got my baby!"

Chamberlain then ran frantically through the camp asking campers to join him in a search for his child. More than three hundred campers with blazing torches began scouring the rocky, brushy area. Not a trace of the baby could be found. Lindy told her story to the local police, who conducted an official search. A week later, some of the baby's bloodstained clothing was found near a dingo's lair. The case caused such a sensation that the inquest was televised in 1981. Coroner Dennis Barritt of Alice Springs determined that a dingo had indeed killed the child and that both Chamberlains were innocent of any wrongdoing.

A short time later, however, Paul Everingham, chief minister of the Northern Territory, ordered police to continue the investigation, and forensic experts were asked to examine the child's clothing. Dr. Kenneth Brown of Adelaide reported that the holes found in the child's jumpsuit were not caused by bite marks. An esteemed London

Alice Lynne "Lindy" Chamberlain, who was sent to prison for life in Australia for murdering her infant child in the outback; she was released in 1986 due to insufficient evidence, claiming, as later evidence indicated, that a dingo had snatched her child from a tent. *History Inc./Jay Robert Nash Collection.*

pathologist, James Cameron, then examined the jumpsuit and agreed with Brown, further adding that the holes in the jumpsuit had been made by a scissors. Joy Kuhl, an Australian biologist, added that there were bloodstains on the front seat of the Chamberlain car and on a pair of scissors owned by the Chamberlains and that these bloodstains were from an infant less than six months old.

There were other factors that seemed to point suspicion at the couple. The parents announced their child's death long before the official search for the baby was called off, and Michael allegedly tried to sell family photographs to an Adelaide publication. Moreover, gossip and rumors abounded about the Chamberlains belonging to a weird cult or sect. Chamberlain was a Seventh-Day Adventist, which led some to believe that he might be associated with a killer cult, and that the baby's name, Azaria, meant "sacrifice in the wilderness," a name linked to biblical sacrifice. Coupled to that was an ancient aboriginal legend of a giant dingo that lived in the vicinity of Ayers Rock. In ancient times their tribes supposedly sacrificed children to this eternal, ravenous beast. After Professor Cameron's statements about the jumpsuit, many came to believe that the Chamberlains were baby killers. The couple received death and bomb threats.

The coroner's original verdict was abandoned, and in February 1982 a second coroner's inquest ordered a trial. On September 13, 1982, Lindy Chamberlain was charged with murdering her infant Azaria, and Michael Chamberlain was charged as an accessory after the fact. Prosecutor Ian Barker maintained that Lindy had cut her child's throat with a pair of scissors in the front seat of the family car and then hid the body in her husband's camera bag and buried the tiny corpse near Ayers Rock. To that claim, the reserved, almost unimpassioned Lindy Chamberlain sobbed loudly and shouted, "That's not true!" This was exceptional. Lindy Chamberlain showed very little emotion in court, she being a person of extraordinary composure. This conduct was interpreted by many to mean indifference; some believed it indicated guilt.

Barker made some telling forensic points, saying that examination of the child's jumpsuit showed that not only did it have scissor cuts instead of bite marks, but no trace of saliva was found and saliva would certainly be evident if a dingo carried the child in its jaws for three miles, the distance from the site of the tent to where the jumpsuit was later found. Moreover, Barker stated, so little blood was found in the tent area that Lindy must have sprinkled this blood in the tent after murdering her baby to create the appearance of a dingo attack. Barker finished his summation: "It was murder. It was her mother, and there is no room for any other reasonable hypothesis." The defense brought in its own forensic experts to undo the evidence provided by the prosecution, but these experts proved to be confusing and contradictory. At the end of a seven-week trial, the jury deliberated for six and a half hours and returned a verdict of guilty.

Lindy Chamberlain was sentenced to life imprisonment and was led to a cell in Darwin's Berrimah Jail. Her husband was found guilty of being an accessory after the fact. Michael Chamberlain's counsel pleaded for him with a good deal of passion, saying that his two sons would be bereft without one of their parents to take care of them. Judge Muirhead rendered a surprising sentence in light of having sent Lindy Chamberlain to prison for life. He gave Chamberlain a suspended sentence of eighteen months at hard labor. Chamberlain was ordered to pay a bond of £500. A short time after Lindy Chamberlain went to prison, she gave birth to a baby girl, Kahlia. Lindy was released on bail three weeks after giving birth, pending her appeal of the trial conviction. Three federal judges dismissed the appeal on April 29, 1983, and she was returned to prison to serve out her life sentence.

In the next few years, support for Lindy Chamberlain grew. More than 130,000 names were gathered in petitions by the Save Lindy Campaign headquartered in Melbourne, and these petitions demanded that Chamberlain be given a new trial.

Moreover, other forensic scientists quarreled with the conclusions of the experts during Lindy's trial. Then, in February 1986, searchers looking for a lost tourist near Ayers Rock found Azaria's jacket about one hundred yards from where her jumpsuit had been located, which appeared to support Lindy Chamberlain's claims. A new inquiry was ordered, and Lindy Chamberlain would be released and remain free. By then Hollywood actress Meryl Streep had already begun a film production based on the Chamberlain case, a sympathetic account that aroused popular support for Chamberlain. A Darwin court later declared Lindy Chamberlain innocent, having been convicted on insufficient evidence.

The Chamberlains moved to Cooranbong, eighty miles north of Sydney, where they filed a $3 million suit against the Australian government in compensation for damages and legal fees, claiming that Lindy was wrongfully imprisoned. Lindy Chamberlain admitted to newsmen that "some people will die believing we did it. I can live with it quite easily because I know they are wrong. The hardest person to live with is yourself and I know I didn't do it." In 1994, Lindy Chamberlain was awarded $900,000 for having wrongly spent three years in jail. Michael Chamberlain, who spent no time in prison, was awarded $400,000.

## Reams of Unreliable Evidence

On June 10, 1977, Linda Jo Edwards, an attractive twenty-one-year-old secretary in Tyler, Texas, was brutally raped and murdered. On August 5, 1977, Kerry Max Cook (born in 1957) was arrested and tried for the fatal attack. The key witness against him was Robert Hoehn, a jailhouse informant who claimed that Cook had confessed to the crime to him while he was behind bars awaiting trial. Other witnesses testified that Cook had sometimes peered through the victim's window to watch her undress. One witness said that Cook, shortly before Edwards's murder, had watched a

film showing the mutilation of a cat, a sadistic film that had allegedly inspired his attack on Edwards.

A Dallas forensic scientist, Dr. James Grigson (who figured prominently in the Randall Dale Adams case; see Chapter III "Suppression and Fabrication of Evidence"), known by defense attorneys as "Dr. Death," stated at Cook's trial that the defendant had an antisocial personality disorder and might murder again. The prosecutor called Cook a "little pervert" and added gratuitously, "I wouldn't be surprised if he didn't eat [the victim's] body parts." Cook was convicted and sentenced to death.

The conviction and death sentence was affirmed by the Texas court of criminal appeals, and in 1988 Cook was scheduled to be executed. Eleven days before that execution, however, the U.S. Supreme Court ordered the Texas court to review the case. In 1991, the court granted Cook a new trial. Following a mistrial, Cook received his second conviction and death sentence in 1994. Two years later, with the help of Centurion Ministries, Cook made another appeal to the Texas court of criminal appeals and this time, the court reversed his conviction, stating that "prosecutorial and police misconduct has tainted this entire matter from the outset."

Texas prosecutors, however, stubbornly refused to dismiss the charges against Cook, despite the fact that their chief informant, Hoehn, had died, and a new DNA test showed that someone other than Cook had murdered and raped Linda Jo Edwards. Prosecutors did not inform Cook about the new DNA results when they threatened a fourth trial, even though David Dobbs, who had prosecuted Cook's last two trials, admitted that the original prosecution against the defendant "was mishandled from the start."

Dobbs knew his case was weak and stated that he would allow Cook to make an Alford plea— plead guilty while still maintaining his innocence (a 1970 U.S. Supreme Court decision, *Carolina v. Alford*, stated that the Constitution allows such a plea). Paul Nugent, who had defended Cook since

1991, later stated that the Texas prosecutors had forced this decision on his client to save face: "They couldn't admit that they had made a mistake, they couldn't admit that perhaps the State of Texas almost executed an innocent man."

Cook, who had been behind bars for twenty-two years, was repeatedly raped and abused and had twice contemplated suicide, and he had enough of the fight. He took the deal and was released on February 16, 1999. Cook, who married and had a son, often regretted taking the Alford plea rather than fighting it out in another trial. He had deep apprehensions of being rearrested for any minor offense and remarked, "So. . . was it worth it [making the Alford plea]? Sometimes when I am holding my son I can say yes. Sometimes when I am by myself, I say no. They won."

Winning cases on the kind of shoddy evidence offered in the Cook trials in Texas was matched by prosecutors in Ohio, who tried Dale Johnston on charges of murdering his stepdaughter and her boyfriend in Hocking County, Ohio. Tried in 1984 for these murders, Johnston was confronted by evidence that could only have been created by Hollywood B film producers. A witness stated that he saw a man angrily order a young couple into a car on a street in Logan, Ohio. Nineteen days after bodies were found in a cornfield, this same witness underwent hypnosis and identified Johnston as a man he had seen in a newspaper photo, the same man he had seen on the Logan street with the young couple.

In addition to this tenuous testimony, prosecutors brought forth a North Carolina anthropologist who claimed that a boot print found near the bodies had been made by one of Johnston's boots. This "expert" was later discredited, but his testimony and that of the hypnotized witness resulted in a death sentence for Johnston.

In 1990, however, the Ohio appeals court threw out the conviction, stating that the "hypnotically induced testimony was admitted without even minimal demonstration on it reliability." Further bolstering the court's decision was the testimony of four other eyewitnesses, who stated that they had seen the victims walking along some railroad tracks at the same time the chief witness against Johnston said he saw the couple in Logan. The court also learned that these witnesses were known to the prosecution during the 1984 trial but their identities had not been disclosed to Johnston's defense attorneys.

Where the evidence in the Johnston case approached the ridiculous, the prosecution's evidence in another Texas case presented one of the most labyrinthine and poorly manufactured scenarios ever shown to a jury. This case involved the slayings of three teenagers by a savage biker, forty-year-old David Spence, and two of his accomplices, brothers Anthony and Gilbert Melendez. On July 13, 1982, Spence and the Melendez brothers went on a murder spree in Waco, Texas, kidnapping and raping seventeen-year-old Jill Montgomery, seventeen-year-old Raylene Rice, and eighteen-year-old Kenneth Franks. They tortured their victims and then stabbed them to death (more than 30 stab wounds pierced the bodies that were found the next day in Lake Waco's Koehne Park).

Apprehended for this crime, Spence and his accomplices told police that the mastermind behind the murders was Muneer Mohammed Deeb, a Jordanian immigrant who owned a Waco convenience store. Spence said that Deeb wanted one of his employees murdered for $20,000 insurance money; after receiving payment, he would pay off the killers.

Deeb was brought to trial and the murder-for-hire story Spence had told was presented to the jury. The prosecution had to admit that the woman Spence said Deeb wanted murdered was not murdered, since he, Spence, mistook Jill Montgomery for the intended victim. He said he and the Melendez brothers killed the other two teenagers simply because they were present when they confronted Montgomery. The three slayings, therefore, according to Spence, and the prosecuting attorneys who used Spence's outlandish conspiracy story, had been brought about by Deeb.

In his defense, the bewildered Deeb, who was the beneficiary of the person he had supposedly marked for murder, stated that he had taken out insurance policies on all of his employees as a hedge against worker compensation claims. The conspiracy theory was weak from the start in that the murders were not professional hits but involved savage rapes and torture. One witness against Deeb, however, stated that Deeb admitted to him that, if one of his employees was murdered, he would indeed receive the insurance payment. The innuendo impacted the jury, even though it appeared as if Deeb had been manipulated into making that admission.

Prosecutors then had a jailhouse informant testify against Deeb. This witness stated that he had shared a cell with one of the killers and that the killer described Deeb's so-called murder-for-hire scheme in detail. When defense attorneys objected, the trial judge overruled the motion, stating that he would permit this testimony because it fell within a conspiracy exception to the rule barring hearsay. Deeb was convicted and sentenced to death. In 1991, the Texas appeals court reversed and remanded the case for a new trial based on the grounds that the testimony from the prison informant was nothing more than hearsay and should not have been admitted into Deeb's case. Since this was the only real foundation for the prosecution's wild-eyed "evidence" against the storeowner, it was no surprise that Deeb was acquitted and released in 1993.

Spence and his cohorts did not escape punishment, even though they had attempted to put the blame for their murder spree on the wrongly convicted Deeb. Spence was sentenced to death and executed by injection on April 3, 1997. This savage murderer insisted up until the time of his death that Deeb was the real culprit: "The truth is, if they execute me, it's not an execution but a cold-blooded murder. I had nothing to do with the crime." The Melendez brothers had pleaded guilty to the murders, Anthony Melendez receiving a ninety-nine-year prison sentence and his brother Gilbert Melendez receiving life.

Insufficient evidence, in many cases stretching into the twenty-first century, was offered in woefully weak presentations by prosecutors using the same kind of unreliable witnesses who testified against the hapless Deeb. One of these cases involved the shooting death of Virdeen Willis Jr., an assistant warden at the Pontiac Correctional Center in Pontiac, Illinois. Willis was drinking in the Shamrock Lounge on the South Side of Chicago during his off hours on June 30, 1985. When he stepped outside, he was shot to death by a fleeing assailant. A short time later, Debrah Caraway identified the killer as Steven Smith, thirty-six.

Police readily accepted this identification after learning that Smith had been convicted of murder twice earlier. In 1964, when he was sixteen, Smith had pled guilty to a robbery on Chicago's South Side. In 1969, he was convicted of killing a rival gang member and received a forty-year sentence, serving about seven years until he was released, after it was determined that the actual killer was Smith's brother, Charles Lee Smith, who was never charged or tried for that killing.

Smith, who had been drinking at the bar that night, was arrested and convicted solely on Caraway's statements, and then sentenced to death.

Steven Smith was twice convicted for the same 1985 Chicago murder and sentenced to death, but the Illinois Supreme Court reversed the convictions and released Smith in 1999, ruling that he had been convicted on insufficient evidence. *Center on Wrongful Convictions/ Northwestern University/Loren Santow.*

Prosecutors insisted that Smith had a strong motive for killing Willis. As a member of the King Cobras Gang, prosecutors said, Smith sought revenge against Willis for the harsh punishment he had meted out to fellow gang members in prison. At Smith's trial, Caraway said she was standing across the street when the killer appeared out of the dark to shoot Willis. Although she had been smoking crack cocaine at the time, she insisted that the victim was standing alone outside the bar when he was murdered. But two other witnesses were standing beside Willis when he was shot and both stated that they could not identify the murderer. Even though Pervis "Pepper" Bell, Caraway's boyfriend, was also a suspect in the case, prosecutors insisted that Smith was the lone killer.

Smith was actually convicted twice. The first conviction was reversed because of misconduct by a prosecutor who described Smith's street gang experience in his summary to the jury, although it had never been proven. In his second trial in 1996, Smith was again convicted and again sentenced to death. While Smith awaited execution, the Illinois Supreme Court reviewed the case and, on February 19, 1999, vacated his conviction and ordered him released. The court stated that Caraway's testimony was no more reliable than the contradictory statements of the other two witnesses. The court did not exonerate Smith but said the state had not proven its case.

In the case of Canadian Jerry Bigelow (born in 1960), a jury believed witnesses on his behalf, but a trial judge ordered the jury to reconsider its innocent verdict, which it did, resulting in a death sentence. Bigelow, because of the flagrant conduct of the judge, was ordered released from California's San Quentin Prison on July 5, 1989, after spending nearly eight years on death row. The California Supreme Court decided not to hear the prosecutor's appeal of Bigelow's acquittal the second time the case went to trial. Bigelow became the second person to walk away from California's death row. (The first was Chol Soo Lee, whose story formed the basis of the movie *True Believer*.)

Bigelow's problems began in August 1980, when he and an acquaintance, Michael Ramadanovic, were hitchhiking along a road south of Sacramento, California. Motorist John Cherry picked them up and offered to give them a ride to Los Angeles, but, as the car approached Merced, California, the two men reportedly ordered Cherry to pull over to the side of the road. They then ordered him at gunpoint to walk into a cornfield where he was shot and killed.

After both were arrested, Bigelow accused Ramadanovic of firing the shot that killed Cherry and Ramadanovic blamed Bigelow. In the first trial, the presiding judge allowed Bigelow to defend himself. He was found guilty and sentenced to death, but the conviction was overturned three years later when State Supreme Court Chief Justice Rose Elizabeth Bird ruled that the trial judge erred in allowing Bigelow to represent himself. According to Justice Bird, the defendant was "totally incompetent as a defense attorney, and this trial of a capital case could rightly be described as a farce or a sham."

A change of venue was ordered for Bigelow's retrial because of the strong feelings the case engendered in Merced County. During the May 1988 proceedings in Monterey County, defense attorney Robert R. Bryan argued that his client had passed out in the car and thus could not have fired the fatal shot. Witnesses testified that Ramadanovic told them in the jail cell they shared that he alone had shot Cherry. The jury deliberated for six days before returning a verdict of not guilty on May 9, 1988. The jury expressed the belief that the shooting had occurred during the kidnapping and robbery of Cherry, which was conducted by Ramadanovic.

Superior court Judge Harkjoon Paik ordered the jury to reconsider its verdict. During the next round of deliberation, one of the jurors changed his vote to guilty. Judge Paik declared a mistrial. The jury's initial decision to acquit was upheld by Justice Harry F. Brauer of the court of appeal on March 20, 1989. "The absolute power of the jury to acquit, for reasons consistent or inconsistent, is beyond dispute in our criminal justice system," Brauer announced in refuting Paik's instructions. By then Bigelow was a free man.

Where Judge Paik ordered a jury to reconsider its verdict of not guilty in the Bigelow case, the judge in the murder trial of Joseph Nahume Green allowed a lone witness with an IQ of 67 to send Green to the death house for the murder of Judy Miscally. On the night of December 8, 1992, Miscally, the society editor for a newspaper in Starke, Florida, was using a public phone when a man confronted her and demanded money. Miscally screamed and the robber fatally shot her and then fled. When police found the dying victim, she told officers that her assailant had been a skinny black man, who was in his mid-twenties and that he had brandished a small, semiautomatic pistol.

Three persons came forward to say that they had witnessed the killing, but two of them said they could not provide a positive identification of the slayer. One person, Lonnie Thompson, stated to police that he could provide an identification. He at first said that the killer was a white man wearing brown pants, but he quickly changed his identification when he was brought to a police lineup, where he was shown only one man— Green, who was black. Thompson nevertheless identified him as Miscally's killer.

Green's attorneys produced three witnesses who stated that Green was with them at the time of the murder. Thompson took the stand and insisted that Green was the killer, and it was his testimony alone, without any other evidence provided by the prosecution, that brought about Green's conviction and subsequent death sentence. Green's attorneys pointed out that Thompson's eyewitness identification was insufficient since he had an IQ of 67, which bordered on retardation, and, most importantly, he had been intoxicated on the night of the murder, and therefore his memory had been impaired.

The Florida Supreme Court, in late 1996, overturned Green's conviction, stating that Thompson's testimony was "inconsistent and contradictory." If

Green was to be retried, the court stated, the new trial had to be moved to a new venue. That new trial occurred in Gainesville, Florida, where a judge ruled that Thompson was an incompetent witness and his testimony unreliable. Prosecutors then dropped the case and Green was released in 1999. The state failed to bring another trial against Green, who was acquitted on March 12, 2000. Of his seven years in prison, Green spent three on death row awaiting execution.

A judge and jury had presumed, without challenge, that Lonnie Thompson's testimony was reliable. The presumption—incredible as it was—in the case of the state prosecuting Tabitha Pollock outlandishly demanded that the defendant had the ability to read the mind of a killer. Prosecutors insisted that Pollock was guilty of abetting the murder of her three-year-old daughter Jami Sue because she should have known that her live-in boyfriend was capable of murder. On the morning of October 10, 1995, Scott English, Pollock's boyfriend, murdered the little girl in Pollock's Kewanee, Illinois, home. English was convicted and sent to prison, but prosecutors brought Pollock to trial in 1996, charging her with first-degree murder on charges that she "should have known" that English posed a dangerous threat to her child's life.

A jury convicted Pollock on this contention and she was given a thirty-six-year sentence. In

Tabitha Pollock, at right, with counsel Jane Raley, went to prison for not reading her boyfriend's mind in the killing of her child. *Center on Wrongful Convictions/Northwestern University/Jennifer Linzer.*

1999 the Appellate Court of Illinois, Third District, reviewed this case, the judge in her initial trial noting that Pollock "did not commit the act of killing, nor did she intend to kill the child, nor was she present in the room when her boyfriend killed the child." The appeal was nevertheless turned down.

Another attorney told Pollock that filing another appeal was hopeless. Having nowhere else to turn, Pollock contacted the Northwestern University School of Law, and Jane Raley agreed to represent Pollock in another appeal. This appeal was heard by the Illinois Supreme Court in October 2002, which reversed Pollock's conviction, stating that Pollock was wrongly held accountable in her first trial on an assumption of what she "should have known."

Actual knowledge of the crime was necessary for such a conviction and the court stated that the prosecution and trial judge wrongly told the jury that it had only to conclude that Pollock should have known, and not that she actually knew, that English was a threat to her child. In fact, the prosecution presented no evidence at all, only a theory that, under the law, was unacceptable. Pollock was released shortly before Christmas 2002, and was reunited with her family.

The prosecutors' case that sent Jason Kindle to prison for seventy years to life for armed robbery was almost as thin as the nonexistent evidence present in the Pollock case. In October 2000, Kindle was put on trial for the 1999 armed robbery of an Office Depot in Los Angeles. Prosecutors showed the jury a robbery "to-do" list police had taken from Kindle's home, as well as videotape of the robbery and an audiotape of the robber that was purported to be Kindle's voice. The videotape indistinctly showed the robber, who prosecutors insisted was Kindle.

Convicted and sent to prison for seventy years to life, Kindle obtained a new Los Angeles attorney through the California Innocence Project, and investigators reexamined the "evidence" that had brought about his conviction. The robbery "to-do" list turned out to be nothing more than notes Kindle had taken during his training course with Cover-all Cleaning, his employer. It was then determined that the audiotape of the robber did not contain Kindle's voice, which had been inaccurately recognized. Further, when reexamining the videotape of the robber at the scene of the crime, investigators were able to fix the height of the actual robber at 6 feet 6 inches, which was six inches taller than Kindle's height. Because of this new evidence, Kindle was released on February 3, 2003, after spending more than two years in prison for a crime he did not commit.

# V

# *Conviction by Coercion*

OUNTLESS INNOCENT VICTIMS HAVE BEEN wrongly charged, convicted, and jailed through the physical coercion of police and the psychological coercion of prosecutors and their aides. Throughout human history police forces have applied physical torture to suspects. The Romans used whips and all sorts of torture devices to wring confessions from suspects, as the Spanish Inquisition did for four centuries. The chief inquisitor, Tomás de Torquemada (1420–1498), is personally credited with the deaths of between three thousand and five thousand people suspected of being heretics who were tortured into admitting their heresy before being executed.

In the modern era, police around the world continued to apply "third degree" (physical torture) methods. The British military police (Black and Tans) occupying Ireland in the early 1920s savagely tortured persons suspected of belonging to the rebellious IRA—dangling suspects from ropes in the basement of their Dublin headquarters, burning them with white-hot pokers, half-drowning them in tubs of water—the same kind of tortures employed by Hitler's Gestapo and Hirohito's secret police, Kempei Tai.

In the nineteenth century, such terror tactics were blatantly practiced in New York City, most victims being naive, gullible immigrants. To obtain quick convictions, police detectives in New York City, who had been organized in 1883 under

the command of a brutal law enforcement officer, Thomas F. Byrnes (1842–1910), coerced suspects into admissions of guilt through physical force. Byrnes, an Irish immigrant from Dublin, began as a lowly fireman in 1862 and then moved to the NYPD the following year as a beat cop, helping to quell the 1863 New York Draft Riots. He became a sergeant in 1869 and a captain in 1870. By 1880, he had become chief of the New York Detective Bureau. He was promoted to that lofty post after he solved the burglary of the Manhattan Savings Bank, with a reported initial loss of $3 million, engineered by the master bank burglar of that day, George Leonidas Leslie.

A personable and charming man to his friends and the politicians who promoted him but displaying a savage character to the average citizen, Byrnes obtained permission to organize all NYPD detectives under his command in 1882–1883, imposing a strict policy of secrecy in regard to police procedures and actions. As chief of detectives, Byrnes created the criminal lineup, where victims viewed suspects in an attempt to identify perpetrators. To his infamy, Byrnes also created the interrogation technique called the third degree (which may have been coined by Byrnes himself), a routine interrogation policy in which suspects were held for days and beaten until they made confessions.

Although he was suspected of being as corrupt as the politicians who supported him (he reportedly

NYPD Inspector Thomas F. Byrnes, standing at left, watches as his officers struggle with a felon about to be photographed in 1893; Byrnes instituted the "third degree" interrogation of intimidation, beating and torture, then acceptable police practices. *History Inc./Jay Robert Nash Collection.*

assembled a portfolio worth between $350,000 and $500,000, an enormous asset for a police administrator in that day, who received a yearly salary of $5,000), Byrnes was never charged with malfeasance. He claimed that his investment portfolio had been provided by grateful bankers who made stock investments on his behalf as a reward for his solving the Leslie bank burglary. His vicious interrogation tactics, however, were well-known, especially to reformer Theodore Roosevelt, who became New York's police commissioner in 1895 and planned to fire Byrnes for his brutal treatment of suspects. But the chief of detectives resigned in June of that year, after appearing before the Lexow Committee, which had been probing police corruption. He later established a detective agency that worked for Wall Street firms, chiefly those he claimed had helped him build his lucrative stock portfolio.

NYPD Inspector Alexander S. "Clubber" Williams, who embraced Byrnes's abusive police procedures with zeal and retired rich from graft. *History Inc./Jay Robert Nash Collection.*

The number of innocent persons victimized by Byrnes and his detectives—beaten into confessions with blackjacks, rubber hoses, nightsticks, phone books, and fists—may have been in the thousands, certainly the hundreds. The 1891 Old Shakespeare case, one of Byrnes's most sensational murder cases, involved an Algerian man, Ameer Ben Ali. Byrnes claimed to have solved the case, but coerced confessions from witnesses and suppressed evidence eventually caused the release of this innocent man. Byrnes was under great pressure in this murder case, which had the earmark style of Jack the Ripper, especially after Byrnes, in 1888–1889, had publicly criticized the London police for not capturing that serial killer.

Byrnes's third degree procedure was embraced and practiced widely by NYPD officers until the early 1930s, when the Wickersham Commission exposed its brutal tactics, which by then included dangling people from high windows, questioning them for days on end with food or sleep, placing them in sweatboxes containing insufferable heat and stench from garbage, or stuffing a suspect's head into a water sink or toilet bowl until the suspect almost drowned. In 1936, the U.S. Supreme Court outlawed the use of physical force in interrogations (*Brown v. Mississippi*).

In Byrnes's savage era, NYPD officers chose pliable suspects from a bottomless well of innocent victims—thousands upon thousands of newly arriving immigrants. Officers routinely preyed on uneducated, gullible immigrants having little or no access to legal representation. NYPD Inspector Alexander S. "Clubber" Williams (1839–1910) looked on these hapless persons not as citizens but as readily available victims. He and his successors epitomized the image of the brutal cop who remorselessly beat the innocent suspect into making a confession.

Williams moved from Nova Scotia to join the police force in 1866. As a towering man of great strength, he quickly made his reputation by picking fights with known hoodlums, beating them and their associates unconscious with his nightstick and then arresting them for assaulting an officer. He had a fight each and every day and quickly won promotion, later stating, "There is more law at the end of a policeman's nightstick than in a decision of the Supreme Court." Although he was admired for taking on some of the most notorious underworld thugs in New York City, Williams indiscriminately attacked and jailed dozens of innocent persons in his climb up the department's hierarchy.

In his brutal law enforcement reign, Williams demanded and received from underworld leaders a percentage of their illegal profits from gambling to smuggled whiskey. In 1894, he was accused of collusion and graft by the reforming Lexow Committee, but he denied everything and was not charged, retiring the following year with more than $1 million in his bank account. One of Williams's protégés was an even more notorious NYPD officer, Charles Becker (1870–1915), who, like Williams, was tall and powerful and used his large fists as well as his nightstick to beat confessions out of suspects.

In 1893, Becker paid an official of the Tammany Hall political machine $250 for his appointment to the police force. He quickly earned back his investment by preying on prostitutes along his beat, forcing them and their pimps to pay him kickbacks and beating them mercilessly when they failed to meet these obligations, before arresting them and then further beating them into confessing to their illegal trade. One of his illegal arrests, on September 15, 1896, was witnessed by author Stephen Crane (1871–1900), who wrote *The Red Badge of Courage.* Crane testified to the girl's innocence in a court hearing, where a scowling Becker lost his case.

NYPD Lt. Charles E. Becker, who beat suspects senseless, savaged street girls for kickbacks, and later controlled all gambling in Manhattan, until he went to the electric chair in 1915 for ordering the murder of a gambler, who refused to pay him off. *History Inc./Jay Robert Nash Collection.*

Five days later, on September 20, 1896, Becker shot and killed a young man at some distance, believing him to be a thief fleeing the robbery of a tobacco shop. He was at first lauded for his police work until it was later discovered that Becker had shot and killed an innocent person who had apparently stepped into Becker's wild line of fire, nineteen-year-old John Fay, a plumber's assistant. Following this wrongful shooting, Becker was suspended for a month before going back to his oppressive ways. He later rose to the rank of lieutenant and became the secret boss of all gambling in Manhattan, arresting and beating a confession out of any gambler failing to turn over a share of gambling proceeds. He went too far, however, when he ordered the murder of gambler Herman "Beansie" Rosenthal on the night of July 16, 1912, committed by four thugs under Becker's direction in front of dozens of people outside the Metropole Hotel. The four killers implicated Becker before they were sent to the electric chair, and Becker also went into the little green room in 1915.

The coercive tactics of Williams and Becker were embraced by most police officers in America in the following decades, especially in the crime-ridden 1920s and 1930s. In the 1940s, a powerful young man named Frank L. Rizzo (1920–1991) joined the Philadelphia police force, and his attitude toward suspects was no less ferocious than that of Williams and Becker. As police chief for eight years, Rizzo shaped a force that many regarded as one of the toughest and most effective crime fighting agencies in the country. Others, including the Justice Department, considered the Philadelphia police the most brutal in the nation. At that time, Rizzo was known as "Cisco Kid," "Big Bambino," and "Super Cop." Frank Rizzo had been a policeman for almost thirty years when he became mayor of Philadelphia (1972–1980).

The son of a policeman and a high school dropout, Rizzo was born in Philadelphia on October 23, 1920. He became a police officer in 1943. He was soon describing himself as the toughest cop in America. Garnering great public popularity

Philadelphia's "super cop" Frank Rizzo, who later became mayor; he encouraged his police officers to beat up suspects and wore a nightstick wherever he went. *History Inc./Jay Robert Nash Collection.*

as a result of his outspoken stance on law and order, Rizzo moved up to become commissioner and then mayor. He was the first incumbent police officer elected to that post.

Although the Philadelphia police department was technically under the leadership of Joseph F. O'Neill, Rizzo maintained tight control. He continued to nurture and protect the police: "Even if they make errors of judgment, nobody will get to them while I'm mayor." Their lapses of judgment included a series of suspect interrogations that wrested confessions from innocent people. Sworn testimony revealed that Philadelphia police interrogators would hold a phone book on a suspect's head and hammer on it. Third degree questioning could continue for twenty-four hours straight, and suspects were allegedly beaten in the kidneys, genitals, back, and ribs.

Commenting on the case of a mentally retarded white man who had been subjected to beatings and intimidation, Rizzo explained that he kept the officers involved on duty because they were "good men who did nothing wrong." After ten policemen broke their nightsticks while beating a prostrate black man, Rizzo mused, "It's easy to break some of these nightsticks nowadays."

Rizzo made a religious pilgrimage to Rome during the Italian student riots and offered to send Philadelphia police to teach the Italian officers "how to eat those guys up," suggesting in Italian that they should "break their heads." Rizzo was reelected in 1975 and in 1978 attempted to amend the city charter to allow him to run for a third term in 1979. His proposal was initially considered

a sure thing, but the issue of police brutality turned public opinion against him and the proposal was defeated 2 to 1. Rizzo died of a heart attack on July 16, 1991, before he could run for mayor again.

Brutal methods of coercing suspects into confessions were embraced and employed by police departments throughout the country. Jon G. Burge became a Chicago police officer in 1970, a detective in 1972, and headed Chicago's violent crime units, Area 2 and Area 3, during the 1980s, which became notorious for police coercion. Burge was later accused by more than a hundred black suspects of having his detectives torture them through electric shocks to their genitals from a hand-cranked device, a technique Burge reportedly learned while serving in Vietnam in 1968–1969.

To wrest confessions from suspects, Burge and his detectives allegedly placed plastic bags and typewriter covers over the heads of suspects and suffocated them into confessions. Cattle prods and a shock wand were also used to obtain confessions.

The coercion practiced by Burge and his detectives was exposed long after Burge was fired from the department. On January 10, 2003, Governor George Ryan (1999–2003), who was later convicted of graft and corruption and sentenced to seven years in prison, issued pardons to four Illinois death row inmates. The first was Aaron Patterson, who confessed to murdering an elderly Chicago couple, Vincent and Rafaela Sanchez, in April 1986. But Patterson never signed his confession and instead scratched with a paper clip on a wooden bench inside the interrogation room: "I lied about murders, police threaten me with violence, slapped and suffocated me with plastic—no phone, no dad signed false statement about murders."

**Aaron Patterson of Chicago, convicted through beatings.** *Center on Wrongful Convictions/Northwestern University/Jennifer Linzer.*

The second was Leroy Orange, who claimed he was tortured into confessing to the 1984 stabbings of four persons. The third was Stanley Howard, who confessed to killing a forty-two-year-old man in 1987 after police kicked and punched him and then placed a plastic typewriter cover over his head, shutting off his air. (He produced medical evidence that supported the torture he had undergone.) The fourth was Madison Hobley, who had been framed for a deadly 1987 fire that claimed seven lives. Investigators later found that a metal can containing the fluid that had ostensibly set the fire, which led to Hobley's death sentence, had been planted at the scene of the crime.

These four wrongly convicted persons were not the only victims of coercion at the hands of Chicago police. Four teenagers—fourteen-year-old Calvin Ollins, sixteen-year-old Larry Ollins, seventeen-year-old Marcellius Bradford, and eighteen-year-old Omar Saunders—were convicted and imprisoned on the coerced confessions of Larry Ollins and Marcellius Bradford. Police beat Ollins and Bradford until they falsely confessed to murdering and raping medical student Lori Roscetti in Chicago on October 18, 1986. All were found innocent and exonerated in 2001 through DNA evidence.

Burge was dismissed from the CPD in 1993 but was never charged with these abuses. Instead, he retired to Florida, where, at this writing, he continues to receive his CPD pension. (The CPD has a notorious history of using the third degree, such as the 1936 case of Earl Heywood Pugh, who confessed out of terror after police used him for target practice at a firing range; see Chapter II.)

Though prosecutors do not employ the same coercive

Leroy Orange, tortured by police into confessing; he is shown flanked by Professor Thomas F. Geraghty and Cathryn Crawford of the Bluhm Legal Clinic, Northwestern School of Law, in January 2003. *Center on Wrongful Convictions/ Northwestern University/Jennifer Linzer.*

tactics used by the police, many resort to more subtle coercion in obtaining convictions of innocent persons. Witnesses, as innocent as those they may testify against, have routinely become the victims of such coercion. Jailhouse snitches or prison informants are most vulnerable to the official pressure that often results in false testimony against innocent defendants. In the present U.S. prison population of more than 2 million as of June 30, 2002. small armies of such informants are readily available to unethical prosecutors.

Madison Hobley of Chicago, convicted on manufactured evidence. *Center on Wrongful Convictions/Northwestern University/Jennifer Linzer.*

The most flagrant coercion employed by prosecutors is compelling a witness into wrongly testifying against a defendant by threatening legal action against such witnesses 'in unrelated cases. Some prosecutors have threatened to make the witness a part of the capital case, causing the witness to commit perjury in self-defense. Bigotry involving racial and national hatreds has been widely employed in coercing witnesses. Even judges have been coerced by prosecutors who threaten to ruin their political career or prevent their reelection, unless they supply jury instructions and judicial decisions that result in convictions. Though not as brutal as police tactics, coercive methods used by unethical prosecutors bring about the same result—an innocent person is sent to prison or, worse, sentenced to death.

## The Old Shakespeare Case

The Jack the Ripper murders that plagued and baffled London police in 1888 (still unsolved to this date) brought sneering criticism from Thomas F. Byrnes, chief of detectives for the NYPD. For three years, Byrnes boasted that if a Jack the Ripper–type killer reared his head in his city, the fiend would be in jail within thirty-six hours. In 1891, Byrnes's arrogant boasting was challenged by just such a killer.

Byrnes captured this killer, he later claimed, sending him to prison and exalting in his law enforcement triumph. However, the man convicted on the flimsy circumstantial evidence Byrnes provided was later proved innocent and was released nine years later, before being transported to his native Algeria. By that time, Byrnes had left the force and was making a fortune running a private detective agency for Wall Street millionaires.

At 9:00 A.M. on April 4, 1891, night clerk Eddie Harrington made his rounds of Manhattan's sleazy East River Hotel on the Lower East Side at the foot of Water Street and Catherine Slip, kicking transient stragglers out of their low-rent rooms. Most of the prostitutes and vagrants had paid their twenty-five cents for the night and moved on, except for the occupant of Room 31. Getting no response when he knocked on the door, Harrington opened it with a master key and entered the dimly lit room, only to reel backward in stark terror. The disemboweled and mutilated remains of a sixty-year-old prostitute named Carrie Brown, better known to the habitués of the waterfront dives as "Old Shakespeare"—she had once been an actress—lay on the floor before the horrified clerk. She had been strangled and slashed with a filed-down cooking knife; the sign of a cross was carved on her thigh.

A regular in the dissolute neighborhood, Brown was the former wife a New England sea captain, and, in her younger days, an actress in the legitimate theater with more than a little talent. She was nevertheless a hopeless alcoholic who had taken to the streets to support her habit. She would recite Shakespeare to the bleary-eyed patrons of the low dives hugging the waterfront, which she routinely visited when soliciting customers. Why anyone would murder and mutilate such a pathetic old woman was a mystery to every New Yorker. The case attracted considerable pub-

lic interest, in part because the sign of the cross was thought to be the mark of London's Jack the Ripper. (No such mutilations were recorded in the Ripper killings.) New York newspapers blared the gruesome story in all of its gory detail and widespread public demand that the case be solved mushroomed onto the desk of chief of detectives Thomas F. Byrnes.

Reminded by newsmen of his earlier boasting about solving the Ripper murders, Byrnes moved quickly to identify and arrest a likely suspect in what the press had now dubbed the "Old Shakespeare Case." Suspicion first fell on a young sailor Brown had picked up, but the police were satisfied with his alibi. He said that he had left the East River Hotel before dawn.

There was also a report that Brown had been seen coming into the hotel at around 11:00 P.M. on the night of April 3, 1891, with a thirty-year-old blond male companion of stocky build, described by witnesses as a seafaring man. This man was never found, but another regular at the hotel, Ameer Ben Ali, a dark-haired man nicknamed "Frenchy," who otherwise matched the description of the killer, was arrested, along with several others for questioning. Ben Ali had spent the night of the murder in Room 33, just across the hall from Room 31 and was known to be an occasional companion of Brown.

Byrnes assumed that Ben Ali had waited across the hall for Brown's last patron to leave before he entered Room 31 and murdered Brown. Based on bloodstains and marks in the hallway between the two rooms and on the door, chair, blanket, and mattress of Room 33, as well on Ben Ali's socks, Byrnes charged Ben Ali with Carrie Brown's murder. While awaiting trial in the Tombs, Ben Ali reportedly had conversations with several other inmates, two of whom later testified at his trial that Frenchy owned a knife much like the one found at the scene of the murder.

Ben Ali was brought to trial on June 24, 1891. An interpreter translated for the accused, who spoke in his native Arabic. Byrnes provided witnesses for the prosecution to prove that Ben Ali had been living a sordid existence and often stayed at the East River Hotel, sometimes wandering from room to room at night. Francis Wellman, who had authored a book entitled *The Art of Cross Examination*, led for the prosecution. Wellman based much of his case on blood analysis and a curious substance scraped from Ben Ali's fingernails and later claimed to be traces of the victim's last meal, acquired by Ben Ali as he savagely disemboweled the victim.

Several experts testified that the bloodstains had come from one body, probably the abdomen of the murdered woman. When, on July 2, the defense directly asked the confused Ben Ali for the first time if he killed Brown, the Algerian became hysterical. Throughout the rest of the trial, he shouted his innocence. Able to speak only limited English, Ben Ali made a poor showing on the witness stand. The excitable Arab implored a higher power to intervene on his behalf. "Allah is Allah!" he screamed. "Allah is great! I am innocent! Oh Allah, save me!" His protestations, translated by an interpreter who mimicked the defendant's high-pitched shrieks, terrorized the jurors and convinced them that Ben Ali was a fanatic, if not a raving lunatic.

Ben Ali was convicted of second-degree murder, indicating a compromise made by the jury. On July 10, 1891, he was sentenced to life imprisonment at Sing Sing. Shortly after he began serving this sentence, he was transferred to the hospital for the criminally insane at Matteawan. The case did not end there, since many believed that Ben Ali had been railroaded into prison by Byrnes. Reports widely circulated that Byrnes had instructed his detectives to "pound the right story" out of the witnesses he brought to court in the Ben Ali murder trial, and that many of the witnesses who testified against the Algerian later privately admitted that their testimony had been coerced by police. "One dick kept hitting me in the face with a wet mop until I agreed to say terrible things in court about Frenchy," claimed one such witness.

Rumors abounded that the real killer had escaped and boarded a boat bound for the Far East, and this tale continued to circulate in New York City during the nine years following Ben Ali's conviction. The difficult and controversial case was later revived in the press by Jacob Riis and Charles E. Russell, who reported that the trail of blood leading to Room 33 had not been there when Harrington made his discovery. During the course of the police investigation, Ben Ali, who had been repeatedly brought back to the scene of the crime at Byrnes's order, had accidentally tracked through the pools of blood and had transferred it to his clothing and socks. At one point during Byrnes's allegedly thorough investigation, detectives ordered Ben Ali to removed his shoes and walk to and from Rooms 31 and 33, obviously having the suspect plant the bloodstains on his own clothes.

In 1900, a pardon application was made on Ben Ali's behalf, based on new evidence that a man answering the killer's description had begun working in Cranford, New Jersey, shortly before the murder and was absent from his home on the night of the killing, disappearing a few days later. In his abandoned room, a brass key with a tag reading "31," which matched the key at the East River Hotel, was found, along with a bloodstained shirt. The key easily slipped into the lock of Room 31, which convinced New York Governor Benjamin Barker Odell (1901–1904) that Ameer Ben Ali was the victim of a miscarriage of justice. Governor Odell and other officials concluded that the bloodstains found leading to and inside Room 31, the prosecution's main evidence, as provided by chief of detectives Byrnes, had been made when the coroner and police visited the scene of the crime.

Governor Odell ordered that Ben Ali be released, judging that the new evidence demolished Byrnes's case against him. He was freed from Sing Sing on April 16, 1902, after serving ten years. Ben Ali, with funds provided by the French government, sailed on the first ship to Algeria, promising never to return to this "crazy country." The real killer vanished, though the police continued to hunt for him for the better part of a decade.

## Police Coercion in the Early Twentieth Century

A former British middleweight boxing champion trying to start a boxing career in Rand, South Africa, Jewey Cooke was a proverbial tough guy. He and restaurant owner Jack Silverstein were thought capable of committing the rape they were charged with, but they were most probably not guilty.

The girl who accused them was the fourteen-year-old daughter of a widow who did Cooke's laundry. The girl often returned the laundry to him, and on one such occasion in 1907, she had sexual intercourse with Cooke and Silverstein, who was visiting Cooke. She later went to the police and filed charges. "You call it rape?" Cooke asked incredulously when arrested. "Why, the kid went with me of her own free will."

The trial was held in February 1907, with Justice Curlewis presiding. Attorney General E. Wingfield Douglass prosecuted, and Henry Harris Morris, King's Counsel, defended Cooke. Morris pointed out many inconsistencies in the girl's story, but she managed to evade his more pointed questions.

The jury sympathized with the youngster from the beginning. After only an hour of deliberation, it returned a verdict of guilty for both men. Silverstein received a seven-year prison sentence and ten lashes. Cooke was given eight years and eight lashes.

After Silverstein and Cooke went to prison, it was revealed that they had paid the girl for her services, giving her a golden "half sovereign" that was, in fact, a gilded sixpence. But Cooke never told his lawyer this, afraid of facing counterfeiting charges. Morris also mentioned years later in his memoirs, *Genius for the Defense* (written by Benjamin Bennett), that the police told him that anyone called to disparage the girl's character would

be arrested. It is not clear why Morris never mentioned this coercion to the judge.

Where police used coercion against potential witnesses in the Cooke-Silverstein case, John A. Johnson was coerced by a police detective into a confession of murder before an angry crowd. A former mental patient, Johnson served more than ten years for a crime he did not commit. On September, 6, 1911, seven-year-old Annie Lemberger disappeared from her bed. Four days later, she was found dead in a nearby rural Wisconsin lake. There was a small wound behind her left ear, but no water in her lungs, proving she did not drown. After pursuing a number of disconnected leads, the police arrested Johnson.

After initially pleading not guilty, Johnson confessed to the murder in a detailed testimony on September 25, 1911. He demanded to be taken immediately from jail to prison, but, once inside his prison cell, he again stated his innocence. Ten years later, on September 27, 1921, in hearings conducted by Rufus B. Smith, Johnson stated that he had been frightened into a confession by Detective Edward L. Boyer. Aware that Johnson was mentally deficient and that he had once witnessed a lynching, Boyer warned him to stay away from the windows of his jail cell, as the angry crowd assembled outside wanted to lynch him. The only way he would be safe, Boyer told Johnson, was if he confessed to murdering the girl so that he could be placed in a secure prison where no lynch mob could reach him.

As the hearing was about to end, Mae Soronson identified Martin Lemberger, the little girl's father, as the real killer. On January 5, 1922, Lemberger was convicted of second-degree murder, but Judge Hoppman was forced to release him because of a ten-year statute of limitations. On February 17, 1922, Governor John J. Blaine (1921–1927) commuted John Johnson's sentence and he was released. (Most states have no statute of limitations for capital crimes, chiefly murder.)

No threat of lynching was used to obtain a forced confession from a student named Wan Zian

Sung. He was simply beaten for hours until, in a half-conscious state, he made the admission a police officer wanted. Five years after narrowly escaping the hangman, Wan was given his final release from custody on June 16, 1926. He had served seven years for the January 29, 1919, murders of Dr. Ben Sen Wu, undersecretary of the Chinese Educational Mission of New York, Dr. T. T. Wong, and Dr. Chang H. Hsie. The murder of the three academics was attributed to a forged check in the amount of $5,000 that Wan's brother, Tsong Ing Van, allegedly tried to cash.

Wan was convicted based solely on a third degree confession taken by a New York City police officer. Found guilty and sentenced to die on the gallows, Wan had his sentence commuted to life imprisonment several days before the execution date. Former Democratic presidential aspirant John W. Davis agreed to act as voluntary counsel for the defendant during his Supreme Court appeal.

The high court granted Wan a new trial, which resulted in two trials, and both subsequent juries refused to convict him after it was graphically shown that the defendant had been beaten senseless by a police officer during his initial interrogation. Prosecuting attorney Peyton Gordon asked that the original judgment against Wan be dropped since the prosecution could uncover no new evidence to support a conviction. Forgery charges against Tsong were not prosecuted at Gordon's request.

## The Ordeal of Stephen Dennison

Stephen Heath Dennison was subjected to great miscarriage of justice not once, but *twice*. Dennison came from a broken home in Salem, New York. His father, George Dennison, beat his mother Mary so severely that she left him in 1917, and moved with Stephen to her father's small farm. Stephen was a good child but a slow learner, flunking several grades. At fifteen, he was still in the seventh grade. He quit school to go to

work to help his mother and elderly grandfather. While looking for work on September 9, 1925, the fifteen-year-old Dennison passed a road stand that was closed.

Dennison intended to buy a hot dog and sat down to wait for the owner, Nellie Hill, to return. When she did not arrive, the hungry youth took out a pocket knife and cut a hole in the canvas covering the stand. He reached inside and from the counter took some candy bars and cigarettes, worth about $5.00. A passerby saw Dennison run from the stand, and the youth was later arrested by A. M. Alexander, deputy sheriff of Salem. He was charged with burglary in the third degree.

With his nervous mother at his side, Dennison later appeared in the Salem court before Judge Erskine C. Rogers. This was his first offense and he pleaded not guilty. Judge Rogers appointed the boy a lawyer, Herbert Van Kirk, from Greenwich, New York, who talked briefly with the youth. Dennison told him that he had left money at the hotdog stand for the items he had taken.

Van Kirk ignored this statement and then coerced the boy into admitting the crime, implying that if he would be given a reprimand and sent home without having a criminal conviction on his record. Dennison's plea was changed to guilty. Rather than send the boy to Elmira Reformatory, Judge Rogers gave him a ten-year suspended sentence, but ordered him to report once a month for a year to Claude Winch, a Methodist minister in town.

Dennison got a job and dutifully reported to the minister. He was later fired for smoking in the men's room of a machinery company. Dennison then failed to report to the minister, missing four appearances. He was picked up while walking along a Salem street, carrying a bucket en route to pick berries. Sheriff N. Austin Baker took him directly to see Judge Rogers, who told him that he had violated his parole. Dennison explained that he had missed his parole appointments because he had been ill.

Judge Rogers disbelieved him and then summarily sentenced the boy to Elmira reformatory

Stephen Heath Dennison, age fifteen, who was sent to prison in 1926 on trumped-up charges and remained behind bars for thirty-four years. *History Inc./Jay Robert Nash Collection.*

for "an indeterminate sentence until discharged by due process of law." Judge Rogers told Dennison that he would probably be released in about thirteen months. This sentence, rendered without compassion for a first offender (when guilt for that first offense was in question) and leaving the time to be served open-ended, might as well have been a life sentence. It was later reported that Judge Rogers had been influenced by Sheriff Baker, who believed, without one shred of evidence, that Dennison had been responsible for a number of petty thefts in Salem and that it was best "to get rid of the boy."

Baker reportedly told Rogers that, if Dennison were later proved to be the thief, and Rogers had "let him off scott free," the judge's political future would be in jeopardy. This not too subtle coercion from Baker certainly prompted Judge Rogers's brutal sentence of Stephen Dennison, which taints the jurist's name to this day and doomed a good-natured boy to the horrors of savage prison life. It was another case of "turning the key and throwing it away." The "thirteen months" confinement turned into thirty-four years of frustration, mental agony, and physical pain.

Dennison entered Elmira reformatory on August 14, 1926. He was not released in thirteen months, but was, because of the ambiguously worded sentence, kept in confinement for the entire ten years Rogers had originally imposed, a ten-year sentence for stealing $5 worth of merchandise, a crime for which he was most probably innocent. He was later transferred to another institution at Napanoch, where, after years of vicious treatment from prisoners and guards alike,

Dennison, in 1936, was judged insane and sent to the cellblock for the criminally insane in the Clinton Correctional Facility at Dannemora.

Dennison's memory weakened, his responses slowed, and his reasoning was impaired by beatings and brutalities. He was sent to Dannemora and forgotten. By then his mother was dead and his impoverished brothers and sisters were unable to finance a legal campaign to free him. Years later, while regaining his lucidity, Dennison wrote to his half brother George, imploring him to "go after a lawyer. I don't know why I am being held as a slave. I don't belong in this place."

George Dennison went to George Wein, a lawyer in Glens Falls, New York, who turned the case over to William Vincent Canale. He investigated and soon learned that Stephen Dennison had been transferred to the mental ward of Dannemora without the benefit of a lawyer or trial, to which he was entitled, or the opportunity to produce witnesses on his own behalf or challenge witnesses testifying against him. The court's action was not related to Dennison's relatives, friends or a lawyer acting on his behalf. Worse, in 1936, Dennison had been committed to the hospital at Dannemora *after his original sentence had expired* and *without his knowledge.* This disgraceful miscarriage of justice was partly set right by attorney Canale, who first battled to have Dennison set free.

On December 12, 1960, Dennison was brought to a courthouse wearing ball-and-chain and handcuffs. Minutes later, Charles H. Lewis, assistant attorney general, admitted that the state had wrongfully detained Dennison in 1936. Judge Robert C. Main asked Dr. Ross E. Herold, assistant superintendent of Dannemora State Hospital, if Dennison would be a danger to himself or to the community if released. Dr. Herold said no, and Judge Main ordered Stephen Dennison released after thirty-four years in prison.

Canale then sued the State of New York, seeking compensation for Dennison's long, illegal ordeal in the New York penal system. Although only fifty-one at the time of his release, Dennison's hair had

Stephen Dennison in 1960, at the time of his release; he was given $115,000 in compensation and apologies from the State of New York. *History Inc./Jay Robert Nash Collection.*

turned completely white and he was bent and stooped from prison hardships. Before being officially released, Dennison was given two pennies taped to a piece of cardboard, all that he had in his pockets when arrested and shipped off to the reformatory in 1926.

After protracted appeals and trials, the dogged Canale triumphed on March 16, 1966, when the New York court of claims awarded Dennison $115,000. In making the award, Judge Richard S. Heller stated that "no sum of money would be adequate to compensate the claimant for the injuries he suffered and the scars he obviously bears. In a sense, society labeled him as a subhuman, placed him in a cage with genuine subhumans, drove him insane, and then used the insanity as an excuse for holding him indefinitely in an institution with few, if any, facilities for genuine treatment and rehabilitation of the mentally ill."

The end of Dennison's story was as bitter as the years New York took from him. Judge Heller's decision was reversed and the claim dismissed by a higher court. Stephen Dennison never received a dime of the $115,000 once awarded to him. Though Canale continued to seek justice for Dennison, his firm financing the cause, all appeals were denied (many of them never even heard). Dennison was last seen alive in 1985 by his lawyer, Canale, in Glens Falls, New York, where Dennison had worked for years as a janitor. His wrongful imprisonment stands as an ugly monument to an indifferent, compassionless bureaucracy. His coerced imprisonment at the hands of his indifferent defense attorney, Herbert Van Kirk, the conviction-seeking Sheriff N. Austin Baker and the politically

goaded Judge Erskine C. Rogers, as well as his continued illegal imprisonment at the hands of other New York officials after he served his original harsh sentence, is a disgrace to the American judicial and penology systems.

## Terrorist Tactics and Police Coercion of the 1930s

In 1919, thirty-three-year-old William E. Potter, a Chicago native, was elected to the city council of Cleveland, Ohio. Potter served on the council for ten years during Prohibition. During his tenure, he was twice investigated and twice cleared for corruption. After a third investigation, Potter was tried on charges that he helped arrange for the city to purchase land for a playground, a deal that gained the seller a $33,000 profit. He was acquitted on December 23, 1929, but his power in the council began to wane. On or about February 3, 1931, he was murdered in an apartment that he had just rented on January 28.

Apparently two assailants, one of them armed with a .32-caliber pistol and one with a .38-caliber pistol, shot at Potter and fled through the kitchen door. The .38-caliber pistol was later discovered on a neighbor's lawn. On February 8, 1931, the custodian's wife found Potter shot in the head with a .38-caliber bullet. Mildred Scribano, also known as Betty Gray, a prostitute who lived downstairs from the apartment, claimed that alleged bootlegger Hyman Martin (a.k.a. Pittsburgh Hymie; born in 1903) had visited the apartment twice on February 1, 1931.

Martin, twenty-eight, was arrested in Pittsburgh and charged with Potter's murder. His trial began on March 25, 1931, and he pleaded not guilty. Martin said he had checked out of a Cleveland hotel about 6:10 P.M. on February 3, 1931, with his mistress, Mary Outland Woodfield, who confirmed his claim. They had left Cleveland about 7:15 P.M. and traveled to Akron, arriving about 8:00 P.M. On January 28, 1931, the day Martin allegedly rented the apartment in Cleveland, Martin was paying a hospital bill in Pittsburgh, which was verified by records. However, he was identified by a sixteen-year-old girl, Queen Esther Morgan, who said she saw Martin enter the apartment at the end of January and the beginning of February.

On April 2, 1931, Martin was convicted of murder and sentenced to life in prison, but an appeals court ordered a new trial after Martin had already served ten months of his sentence because the judge at Martin's first trial, Walter McMahon, had, in effect, directed indecisive jurors: "The majority view on the subject under discussion is safer than the minority opinion."

In early 1932, Mildred Scribano signed an affidavit saying that police had pressured her to identify Martin by threatening to arrest her and her ex-con boyfriend if she did not. She also said she heard noises from the apartment above at about 8:30 P.M., not 7:15 P.M. or 7:20 P.M., as she had earlier claimed. Other witnesses said they had been coerced by police, who had shown them photographs of Martin before they identified him. Martin was acquitted by a second jury on June 16, 1932, and was released. Potter's murder remained unsolved.

In November 1931 an Arkansas sheriff, like William Potter, was killed in a seeming gangster hit, or so police rightly assumed, except that they wrongly selected two men for that killing. Sheriff Manley Jackson had stopped a car in Pocahontas, Arkansas, for a routine license plate check. The driver pointed a .45-caliber pistol at Jackson and forced him to walk to a nearby gravel pit. He shot the sheriff five times in the back before speeding off.

Lige Dame (born in 1888) and Earl Decker of Randolph County, Arkansas, were taken into custody and grilled for eight hours by police in Memphis, Tennessee. Both were mercilessly beaten. Dame confessed to shooting Jackson, whose father was a state senator at the time. He implicated Pocahontas police chief John Slayton in the shooting, but insisted that Decker was actually responsible.

Decker emphatically denied this charge and maintained his innocence even after conviction.

Dame later repudiated his earlier confession, only to make another in the presence of the warden of the Arkansas state penitentiary and a reporter with the Arkansas *Gazette*. He cleared Decker of any responsibility in the death of Sheriff Jackson and stated the he, too, was innocent of the crime and that his confession had been beaten out of him by brutal police. A sanity test was eventually ordered for Dame, which he passed. In 1941, Decker was paroled with the clear understanding that he had been wrongly convicted, but he was not granted a pardon. Dame died in prison, and Chief Slayton spent his remaining years and life savings trying to clear his good name.

The crime was forgotten until 1971, when the Pocahontas *Star-Herald* reprinted excerpts from the *Alvin Karpis Story*. The notorious 1930s bank robber vividly described the murder of a Pocahontas sheriff committed while he was driving through town in the company of one of Ma Barker's sons, Freddie Barker. Karpis claimed that the kill-crazy Barker fired the shots that killed Jackson. The Karpis autobiography was published thirty-five years after the Pocahontas murder.

Where police beatings brought about the wrongful convictions of Hyman Martin in Cleveland and Dame and Decker in Arkansas, four illiterate blacks were terrorized into making false confessions to a 1933 Florida murder. In this instance, police used the same terror tactic that had been employed in getting a confession from John A. Johnson in 1911—the threat of mob lynching, the fate of many blacks accused of serious crimes in the South for more than five decades after the American Civil War. (See "Police Coercion in the Early Twentieth Century," p. 92)

Four black tenant farmers in Florida—Isaiah Chambers, Charlie Davis, Jack Williamson, and Walter Woodward—were tried, convicted, and sentenced to death for a killing they did not commit. When finally acquitted, almost nine years had gone by since the murder. One of the four went insane while on death row and was released to a mental hospital. On May 13, 1933, Pompano, Florida, fish dealer Robert Darcey, a white man, was murdered in a holdup. With intense public indignation about the killing, a police dragnet brought in four young tenant farmers, all black, who were arrested on suspicion, and without warrants, and were held and questioned for almost a week without counsel.

Held at the local jail, the suspects cowered in their cells while white mobs assembled each night outside the jail, demanding that they be lynched. These vigilantes were encouraged to assemble and make such threats, so that police interrogators could demand confessions from the suspects that would bring them to trial and the safety of a well-guarded prison. Terrified of the posed mob violence, three of the accused men, dubbed the "Pompano Boys" by the press, confessed, though Isaiah Chambers maintained his innocence throughout.

Found guilty of the murder on the evidence of their alleged confessions were Charlie Davis, Jack Williamson, and Walter Woodward. Chambers was convicted in a separate trial in the Broward County court after his court-appointed attorney offered a perfunctory defense, and all four of the convicted men were sentenced to be executed in the electric chair. Their case was appealed, but the convictions were affirmed. The issue of whether the confessions had been obtained under duress continued to come up as the case went through several courts, with the four men found guilty three more times.

On February 12, 1940, Chambers, Davis, Williamson, and Woodward won a seven-year struggle to escape execution, when the U.S. Supreme Court overturned their convictions. Justice Hugo Black, who delivered the opinion, condemned the Florida officials' techniques, saying "to permit human lives to be forfeited upon confessions thus obtained would make of the constitutional requirement of due process of law a meaningless symbol."

In March 1942, three of the defendants were tried again before Judge Charles E. Chillingworth. Eight witnesses for the state gave testimony tending to show that sticks and a hammer had been found near the homes of the men, and a pocketbook belonging to the victim was found in a room occupied by one of the accused.

Williamson and Woodward had offered to change their pleas to guilty of second-degree murder "to get it over with." Davis said before the bar, "I've suffered for nine years over this. I still say I'm innocent and I won't say I'm guilty." Judge Chillingworth refused to accept the pleas, and four hours later directed the jury to bring in a verdict of not guilty. Davis, Williamson, and Woodward were acquitted after nine years. The judge in this case, Chillingworth, was abducted and murdered, along with his wife, Marjorie, in 1955, in an unrelated revenge murder orchestrated by a former Florida judge, Joseph Peel Jr.

Chambers went insane on death row at Raiford prison and was transferred to the state mental hospital in Chattahoochee in 1940. With S. D. McGill, the Jacksonville lawyer who defended the men for six years, the acquitted men left for unannounced destinations. They had spent seven years on death row. The case came to be known as "Little Scottsboro" in reference to a similar highly publicized incident in Mississippi in 1931, when nine black youths were unjustly accused of raping two white women (see Chapter XI, "Railroading and Framing").

In another case, police used coercion to solve a murder and cover up their own criminal involvement with parties connected to that case. Not only did Philadelphia police wrongly arrest two men for the murder of a fellow officer, but, after shooting to death the actual killer in a gunfight, they arrested and beat a confession out of a third innocent man. Patrolman James T. Morrow, working in plain clothes and tracking down a suspect involved in a current robbery spree, a man who had reportedly killed John Canham and wounded another victim, May Baxendale, was himself shot in the back three times and killed on November 23, 1936. Joseph Broderick, the first man police tried forcing a confession from in the Morrow shooting, was released, when it was revealed how the police obtained the confession through beatings.

Certain officers were relentless, however, in tracking down Morrow's killer. In May 1937, police arrested twenty-year-old George Bilger, whom Morrow had been tailing. After being beaten by police officers, Bilger confessed, accusing a patrolman of being his accomplice. At his trial in June 1937, he was found guilty, but the decision was set aside because Judge Harry S. McDevitt did not feel Bilger had told the truth. A second trial found the defendant guilty and Bilger was sentenced to life in prison, while the police officer Bilger implicated was exonerated of collusion.

The Philadelphia robbery spree nevertheless continued, even with Bilger behind bars. On September 12, 1938, schoolteacher Edward Tamkin was killed. Police learned that the killer was Jack Batton (real name, Jack Howard), whom they fatally shot in a running gunfight on February 6, 1939. Howard died before he could be questioned, but the guns he possessed were proof enough that he had killed Morrow, Canham, and Tamkin. The police, however, wanted a living killer to stand trial. Bilger had incurred the wrath of many officers when, in stubbornly asserting his innocence, he had blackened an officer's name at his trial. The unwritten police credo that they protect their own at all costs was very much in force, as it unfortunately still is today.

The police were in a quandary, however. The ballistics evidence from Howard's guns might prove him to be the robber and killer, and Bilger might be cleared, leaving the force stained by its own coercive tactics. The Tamkin killing, these officers believed, could be tied to the previous two murders committed by Howard. Subsequently they would need to have another person take responsibility for the Tamkin slaying, and, if necessary, found guilty of the two murders for which Bilger had been sent to prison. There was an addi-

tional and vital reason why the six policemen involved in the Bilger interrogations desperately sought to hide Howard's responsibility for the three murders, and, especially, the robberies he had committed—these officers had been directly involved in Howard's robberies, protecting him and sharing in the profits from those robberies.

To cover the Tamkin murder by Howard, the officers needed a new victim. Unfortunately for twenty-seven-year-old Rudolph Sheeler, he was just what the police wanted for the crimes committed by Howard. By visiting the same hospital Howard had once visited, Sheeler, police said, connected himself with the dead Howard, whom they portrayed as Sheeler's accomplice; Sheeler, not Howard, had actually been responsible for the robbery spree and three murders. Sheeler was promptly arrested. It did not matter that the patient Sheeler had visited in the hospital was his sister or that Sheeler did not know or visit the patient Howard had gone to see. All that mattered was that he confessed to Howard's crimes.

The police booked Sheeler under a false name and proceeded to beat a story to their liking out of him. He was beaten so badly that he had to be kept in solitary confinement for days before police-inflicted welts and bruises disappeared. He finally gave the police what they wanted and blurted a confession. After days of desperate searching, his wife discovered his whereabouts and a lawyer procured a writ of habeas corpus.

Sheeler immediately recanted his confession at his arraignment, but, after further beatings and fearing more beatings to come, he finally pleaded guilty. The details outlined in Sheeler's plea did not match his confession, so the police rewrote it. Three separate trial judges accepted Sheeler's confession without question at his trial on March 29, 1939. Sheeler's confession detailed his responsibility for all of Howard's robberies and his three murders. This confession immediately brought about Bilger's release. He was pardoned, but his wrongful imprisonment had driven him insane and he was placed in a mental hospital.

Twelve years after his trial and sentence to life imprisonment, Sheeler was finally cleared of the charge, when honest Philadelphia officers discovered that Sheeler had been convicted through a forced confession, complete with its numerous inconsistencies with the murders in question. A new investigation was ordered, which proved that Sheeler was in New York at the time of the Tamkin murder. On May 1, 1951, Sheeler was found innocent and released. Some time later, six police officers were suspended for their involvement in the case, but they were never brought to trial.

## Coercion as an Unwritten Rule of Law Enforcement

No police department in the world or any law enforcement officer would ever admit to administering physical punishment and torture to get a confession or coercing a witness into making false statements that would result in a conviction. There was, and is, however, a widely practiced unwritten law enforcement rule that, if all else fails, use the fist, the nightstick, the sap to exact an admission from a suspect, or, in the case of reluctant witnesses, to convince them to identify a suspect at hand as a guilty party, often under the threat of arrest. To be sure, many scrupulous and upstanding police officers refuse to take part in such illegal interrogations, and many such wrongful coercive acts have been disclosed by honest and courageous officers, even at the risk of their jobs, pensions, and reputations. Sadly, too many ethical police officers remain silent in order to avoid censure and retaliation from their fellow police officers and to maintain their careers.

Some conscientious NYPD officers did take that courageous step in helping exonerate a twenty-year-old suspect who had been beaten into a conviction. In the early morning of October 11, 1945, Leo Conlon, thirty, attempted to stop a robbery in a Coney Island bar and was shot and killed by the robber. William Cronholm, eighteen, was found sleeping in a stolen car. He had two revolvers with him in the car; three more were found in a garage he rented near his Brooklyn home. Cronholm confessed to killing Conlon, at first claiming that he tried to rob the bar alone. Later he signed a confession naming three accomplices. At his trial, however, he reverted to his original story. Cronholm was convicted and sentenced to life in prison.

Investigating detectives learned that John Valletutti, twenty, was a friend of Cronholm. Valletutti had been sentenced to jail for stealing a car and he was out on parole the night Conlon was killed. Within a month of the slaying, Valletutti was returned to prison due to a parole violation. Released from Coxsackie Prison on December 7, 1945, he was taken to Brooklyn for questioning about the Conlon killing. About thirty hours after Valletutti was taken into custody, his confession was recorded by a stenographer and an assistant district attorney.

Since no one recognized him from the bar, no one could place him in the vicinity, and no one saw him with Cronholm that night, the confession was the only evidence against him in his trial at King's County court on June 2, 1947. Valletutti protested his innocence, saying he had confessed only after he was beaten for several hours. Witnesses supported his claim that he had been playing shuffleboard several miles away from the bar on the night of the slaying.

A routine physician's report, made when the defendant entered jail, recorded several bruises on Valletutti's lower chest and scalp. Although Cronholm was brought in from jail to testify that Valletutti had not been with him and that he had acted alone, Valletutti was found guilty of first-degree murder by the jury, which recommended mercy, indicating a sentence of life imprisonment.

Assistant district attorney James McGough said that he offered Valletutti a chance to plead guilty to second-degree manslaughter, which had a maximum sentence of fifteen years in prison; Valletutti refused, saying he was innocent. On June 17, 1947, Judge Louis Goldstein disregarded the jury's recommendation. He labeled Valletutti a vicious killer and sentenced him to death in the electric chair.

A mandatory appeal, according to New York law, resulted in a majority opinion reversing the conviction and ordering a new trial, with Judge Desmond pointing out that Valletutti had not been arraigned in court until about forty-eight hours after he was taken into custody, and that he had been held without being allowed to talk to a lawyer, friends or relatives.

Returned to Brooklyn for a new trial, Valletutti was brought before Judge Goldstein again. The prosecution admitted that the defendant's confession was the only evidence against him and agreed to dismiss the case. The judge said he wanted to study the case further. On September 28, 1948, the district attorney dismissed the indictment. Apparently some police officers were willing to testify that Valletutti's confession had been beaten out of him by other officers. Valletutti was released after spending two years in behind bars.

In 1950, George Lettrich of Chicago shared John Valletutti's experience of being convicted and condemned to death for the 1948 murder of a ten-year-girl in McCook, Illinois. Prosecutors had no evidence other than two confessions from Lettrich, which he signed after more than sixty hours of third degree interrogation by police in Lyons, McCook, and Chicago.

At his trial, Lettrich recanted his confessions, saying that police had denied him sleep, food, and drink, and then had coerced him into signing those confessions under the threat of physical punishment. He quoted one police interrogator who told him that "he would knock my head through the wall and go on the other side and make mincemeat out of it." Police denied using coercion to obtain Lettrich's confessions.

The Illinois Supreme Court reversed Lettrich's conviction in 1952 and ordered a second trial, based on new evidence provided by Lettrich's at-

torneys, who argued that their client had not only been coerced into signing false confessions, but that, a few days after Lettrich had been indicted, another man admitted to the director of a county behavioral clinic that he had murdered the girl. Prosecutors in Lettrich's 1950 trial knew of this man's confession but ignored it. The Illinois Supreme Court, in its decision to overthrow Lettrich's original conviction, stated that prosecutors had erred in suppressing the other man's confession and had "made inflammatory and prejudicial remarks to the jury."

The court considered Lettrich's trial testimony in which he accused police of coercing him into making his two confessions. Lettrich equivocated those statements, which had been admitted into the trial as evidence, by saying that his accusations might not be "entirely true." Chicago prosecutors, not wanting to readdress those accusations for fear of casting more doubt on the conduct of the police, dropped all charges against Lettrich in 1953, and he was released.

Where Lettrich was directly coerced in Illinois in 1950, New Orleans police that same year employed coercion to pressure witnesses into making false statements about two black suspects, creating false testimony that sent them to the Louisiana death house. In November 1950, Edgar Labat (born in 1925) and Clifton Alton Poret, two black men from New Orleans, were accused of raping a white woman and robbing her male escort in the downtown section of the city. The racial climate of the times led to hasty convictions and death sentences imposed by the Louisiana court system in March 1953, but the prosecutor offered to let Labat off with a reduced sentence if he pleaded guilty to armed robbery.

Labat refused to confess to a crime he never committed and was placed in solitary confinement. The two men were sentenced to die at the Louisiana state penitentiary, but their case went under appeal a dozen times over the next seven years. In 1955, the U.S. Supreme Court rejected their appeal for a new trial, which discouraged their attorneys from pursuing the matter. In desperation, the two men smuggled an appeal for legal help out of the prison. Their ad was placed in the Los Angeles *Times* and a sympathetic doctor offered to help them.

With a new lawyer, Labat and Poret won their ninth stay of execution in 1960, received by the warden just three hours before the appointed time of execution. The original witnesses were questioned a second time and one recanted previous statements on the grounds that he had lied under pressure from the police. Additional witnesses provided Labat with a sorely needed alibi, and the rape victim's story was found to contain inaccuracies and factual errors.

Despite this new evidence, rife with police coercion, the state refused to grant the men a second trial. Finally, in 1967 the U.S. Supreme Court handed down a ruling that ordered Louisiana officials to schedule a new trial on the grounds that blacks had been excluded from jury selection. Criminal district court Judge Edward A. Haggerty presided at the second Labat-Poret trial but refused to acknowledge that the defendants had suffered from a miscarriage of justice. Instead, he sentenced them to sixteen years, two months, and two days, which was the exact amount of time they had spent on death row. They received credit for "time spent," which freed them from the custody of the state. The two men were released on December 31, 1969.

Where previous cases showed how physical torture produced confessions, the murder confession from a fifty-year-old New Yorker was brought about by a psychiatrist, whose persuasive manner and psychological suggestions produced a confession from a unsophisticated suspect that might not otherwise have been given.

On the afternoon of January 10, 1950, seventy-five-year-old Camilo Weston Leyra Sr. and his eighty-year-old wife, Catherine Leyra, were found bludgeoned to death in their Bedford-Stuyvesant apartment in Brooklyn, New York. Police noted that no robbery had been committed and that

three cups of tea still remained on the kitchen table, which led them to suspect fifty-year-old Camilo Weston Leyra Jr. of the hammer killings.

Leyra, born in 1899, had previously been convicted of bigamy and theft. He was brought in for questioning. Suspicion against him mounted when his alibi was disproved and he was unable to produce the clothes he had been wearing the day of the murders, clothing that police suspected would be covered with blood. Following extensive questioning, Leyra made a number of admissions but failed to confess to murdering his parents. Captain Meenahan of the homicide squad, who was conducting the interrogation, called in a psychiatrist, Dr. Max Helfand.

Helfand probed the suspect's psyche and promised him an end to his emotional stress and sinus trouble, if he confessed to murdering his parents. After an hour and a half, Leyra broke down and confessed to Meenahan. He said he killed his father because of an argument concerning the family business. He killed his mother first so that she would not have to watch her husband die. He repeated this confession to a business associate, William Herrschaft, and two assistant district attorneys.

The first of three trials began in April 1950. All four confessions were introduced in court, and the jury quickly convicted Leyra of first-degree murder; he was sentenced to death. The conviction was overturned by the New York appeals court because the confessions had been coerced psychologically. A second trial ensued, and again Leyra was found guilty and sentenced to death, which the New York appeals court upheld because, it then claimed, Helfand's psychological persuasion had not led to the confessions.

The U.S. Supreme Court intervened and, on June 1, 1954, voted 5–3 to reverse the conviction, arguing that all the confessions had been tainted by Helfand's methods. Once again Leyra was tried, and once again he was found guilty and sentenced to death. This time, however, the New York appeals court, on April 27, 1956, reversed the trial court's decision by a 4–2 vote and ordered Leyra's release. Leyra left Sing Sing Prison on May 2, 1956, after spending four years, nine months, and three days on death row, the longest death row stint at Sing Sing up to that time since the introduction of the electric chair in 1889.

Where Leyra had been psychologically coerced into a confession, a citizen in Alabama confessed to a murder he did not commit when local police used a different tactic—either he confessed or they would arrest his ailing mother. In 1949, the nine-year-old cousin of Stanford Fewell was sexually assaulted and murdered in a town near Birmingham, Alabama. That same day, Stanford Ellis Fewell visited his mother and four other people at the Fewell family farmhouse, thirty miles from the scene of the murder. Three years later, in 1952, two girls accused Fewell of making sexual advances toward them. Police in Jefferson County, Alabama, remembered the 1949 slaying, and, certain they had the killer, questioned Fewell for fourteen days, denying him access to counsel.

On the fifteenth day, having gotten nowhere, police threatened to arrest his mother for collusion in the crime. Fewell then confessed, believing that his sick mother would be jailed. After police posed suggestive questions that detailed the elements of the 1949 murder, Fewell easily gave a statement which parroted all the correct details of the murder. He was tried, convicted, and sentenced to thirty years in prison. The conviction was upheld on appeal.

Skeptical of the ruling, Clancy Lake, the former city editor of the Birmingham *News,* and Fred J. Bodeker, a private detective in Birmingham, reexamined the evidence. They found that the conviction was based solely on police coercion that had produced the defendant's confession; further, they produced four witnesses who corroborated Fewell's alibi. The Alabama parole board freed Fewell, who left Kirby Prison in Montgomery, Alabama, on May 4, 1959, seven years after his wrongful conviction.

In the 1950s, police coercion was practiced from rural Alabama to distant Japan. Even though it emerged from World War II as a democratic society, Japan has mostly kept secret its police activities and judicial rulings involving all serious crimes. It seldom if ever releases information about convictions and sentences and executions, the press and public often learning that a convicted criminal was put to death years after the execution took place. An exception to this covert policy was the case of Akabori Masao (born in 1929), who was arrested in May 1954 for kidnapping and strangling to death six-year-old Sano Hisako in Shimada, 125 miles southwest of Tokyo.

Japanese police reportedly coerced Akabori into confessing through systematic beatings that went on for weeks, but he recanted when the case went to trial in July 1954. Despite the lack of evidence against Akabori, other than his recanted confession, he was convicted in 1958 and sentenced to death. The Supreme Court of Japan upheld the sentence under the first of four appeals two years later.

The prisoner languished on death row for the next twenty-seven years, which has to be a world record, while he exhausted the appeal process. Akabori finally won a new trial in 1987. The final verdict was handed down on January 31, 1989, by Chief Judge Ozaki Toshinobu of the Shizuoka district court, when he ruled that the defendant's confession "lacked full credibility" and ordered Akabori released. It marked the fourth time in six years that an inmate on Japan's death row had won acquittal in a retrial.

The decision handed down in the case of Akabori did not specify police coercion, but the trial judge could not base his judgment about the lack of credibility in the defendant's confession on anything other than police torture. (Japan has never officially admitted to its many atrocities or its sexual enslavement of millions of women in conquered countries during World War II, so it is understandable that it would not admit to wrongdoing by an authority in the case of a lowly defendant.)

## Justice for Rubin "Hurricane" Carter

In a highly publicized and controversial case that spanned more than a decade, former leading middleweight boxing contender Rubin "Hurricane" Carter, born in 1937, became a cause célèbre of civil rights fund-raising efforts. On June 17, 1966, at 2:30 A.M., three people were killed by shotgun blasts at the Lafayette Grill, a tavern in Paterson, New Jersey, during a period of racial tension. The victims were James Oliver, the fifty-two-year-old bartender and part owner of the tavern, Fred Nauykas, a patron, and Hazel Tanis, fifty-one, who died from bullet wounds a month later. Separately arrested and charged with the crime on October 14–15, 1966, were John Artis and Rubin Carter, who claimed he barely knew Artis. The motive was said to be revenge for the killing of a black tavern owner in the same area earlier that evening; all three of the victims at the Lafayette Grill were white.

The police officer who apprehended Carter and later Artis testified that neither man had acted nervous or guilty, and that both had followed him to the scene of the crime with no reservations. A key witness at the initial trial, Alfred P. Bello, said he saw the defendants flee the tavern with guns and escape in a white car. Bello allegedly had been robbing a factory nearby when he was drawn to the scene of the murders after hearing shots. He admitted stealing money from the cash register of the Lafayette Grill soon after the shootings, and was present when police brought Carter and Artis in about half an hour after the attack. Both Bello and Arthur D. Bradley identified Carter and Artis four months after the shootings.

Bello, who had served prison terms for burglary and robbery, recanted his testimony in 1974, claiming that detectives had coerced him into identifying Carter and Artis. He later disavowed his testimony a second time, offering two different versions of

what he had seen. Another witness, Patricia Graham Valentine, who lived above the tavern, identified the two men, although she had seen them only from the back; she also described their escape car. Emil DiRobbio, a homicide detective, testified that he had turned in shotgun shells found at the scene to the police property clerk's office.

In May 1967, Artis and Carter were convicted, found guilty on three counts of first-degree murder, and sentenced to life imprisonment. The case became a liberal cause, with Carter receiving support from the black community as well as the sports and entertainment worlds. In December 1975, the Night of the Hurricane benefit was held at New York City's Madison Square Garden to help raise money for an appeal. By March 1976, the New Jersey state court overturned both convictions, ruling that important evidence had been withheld from the defense. Carter was freed on $20,000 bail, and Artis on $15,000.

Because of prejudicial publicity against the defendants in Passaic County, a second trial was moved from Paterson to Jersey City. This trial began on October 12, 1976, presided over by Judge William J. Marchese. The judge disqualified himself on October 19, 1976, when defense lawyers protested that he might become a witness at the trial since he had sentenced Bello in an unrelated 1974 case.

Marchese was replaced by Judge Bruno L. Leopizzi. Patricia Valentine added to her testimony of ten years earlier that police had shown her a cartridge and shotgun shell they said they had found in the car Carter and Artis were driving when they were arrested. In the 1966 trial, Detective Emil DiRobbio never mentioned showing the shell or cartridge to anyone but the police. The question of whether the shell and cartridge had been found the day of the killings was a key issue in the 1966 trial. An investigation by *New York Times* reporter Selwyn Raab led to the reopening of the case.

Bello, the key prosecution witness, recanted earlier testimony, which claimed that he had been "brainwashed" by police into identifying Artis and Carter as the murderers. Bello then renounced his recantation and declared in court on November 15, 1976, that he had lied consistently throughout the trial and during the 1975 grand jury hearings. Asked about statements he had made in an affidavit to Assemblyman Eldridge Hawkins in 1975, Bello replied, "It's true that I said it, but it's not true." He later added, "Most of the things I said were complete lies to avoid the issue." Bello would later claim that both a television producer and an investigator from the public defender's office had offered him bribes to change his testimony.

On November 22, 1976, Detective Donald La-Conte corroborated Patricia Valentine's testimony when he said that he, too, had seen the bullet and shell when he brought her to police headquarters so she could identify the car driven by Artis and Carter. The defense contended that the bullet and shell were planted by police to frame their clients. LaConte, the officer to whom Bello had first identified Carter and Artis as the men he had seen at the murder scene, said Bello told him later that he was "scared" because friends of Carter's had threatened him. LaConte said Bello told him, "You guys had the right men and you let 'em go," referring to Artis and Carter.

On November 18, 1976, Judge Leopizzi prohibited anyone from contacting the jurors or their families about the case. The defense emphasized that the descriptions of the killers did not match either defendant, except that they were black, and that there was no strong case against the defendants until they were identified by the coerced Bello and Bradley four months after the crime. Vincent DeSimone Jr., who had headed the initial investigation into the shootings, told a 1966 grand jury twelve days after the triple murders that the clothing worn by Carter and Artis did not fit descriptions from witnesses. DeSimone had said, "With the time element, we feel it is almost impossible that these men could have changed clothes." In the four-month interim between the incident and the arrest of Carter and Artis, DeSi-

mone secured a positive identification of the defendants from Bello.

In the 1976 trial, DeSimone, referring to a deal he made with Bello to drop charges on Bello's robbery attempt on the night of the killings, said, "If I could solve a murder by not taking action on a lesser crime, I'd do it every day of the week. I'd do it again tomorrow." William Hardney and Welton Deary, two former friends of Carter's, testified on November 27, 1976, that they had been asked, prior to the 1967 trial, by Carter and his attorney at the time, Raymond Brown, to say that they had been with the former boxer at the time of the slayings. Hardney did not testify at the first trial. Deary now admitted giving false testimony when he said he had been with Carter at the time of the murders.

Artis testified on December 15, 1976, again telling the jury that he was not guilty. Carter declined to testify, just as he had in 1967. In final summations on December 20, 1976, Passaic County prosecutor Burrell I. Humphreys said the evidence built a "rope strong enough to bring two murderers to justice," while defense lawyers Myron Beldock and Lewis Steel, attorneys for Carter and Artis, respectively, challenged the credibility of most of the state's witnesses and focused on the uncertainty of the identifications of the defendants.

On December 26, 1976, Carter and Artis were found guilty for the second time on three counts of first-degree murder. On February 9, 1977, Carter was sentenced to two consecutive life terms and one concurrent life term and would not be eligible for parole until 1996. The Carter case nevertheless continued to generate widespread publicity. When Chicago novelist Nelson Algren died in 1981, he was working on a novel about Rubin Carter.

Artis was released on parole in 1981, but Carter remained behind bars. He insisted that he was innocent and because he thought he had been wrongly imprisoned, he refused to eat prison food, wear prison uniforms, or leave his cell. He spent his time reading. His attorneys, meanwhile, fought long legal wars over their assertion that Carter had been denied a right to a fair trial. On

November 7, 1985, federal district Judge H. Lee Sarokin ordered that Carter be set free, stating that his conviction had been based on racial prejudice and had ignored the true facts. Carter later went to work for a Canadian firm that assists those wrongfully accused of various crimes. He was portrayed by Denzel Washington in the 1999 film *The Hurricane*.

## Coercion and the Lie Detector

The use of lie detectors (polygraphs) in criminal cases has always been controversial. In most states, the results are not admissible in court, but they can influence the perspective of prosecutors and defense attorneys. In the case of two Florida defendants, a lie detector operator allegedly coerced confessions from both men while conducting polygraph tests on them, and these wrongly obtained confessions were used to send them to prison.

This case began on the evening of September 18, 1970, when an off-duty deputy sheriff, Thomas Revels, was gunned down during the robbery of a Quincy, Florida, grocery store. After the shooting, four black youths fled the store in a single car. Five young local men, including John "Johnny" Frederick and David Roby Keaton, were arrested and charged with the robbery-murder.

Frederick, Keaton, and the three others, known as the Quincy Five, were identified by five eyewitnesses and confessed to lie detector operator Joe Townsend in Tallahassee, Florida. One of the defendants was acquitted, one was found incompetent to stand trial, and charges were dropped against another. Frederick was sentenced to life, and Keaton received the death penalty. One year later, defense attorneys representing Frederick and Keaton learned that three Jacksonville men had been arrested for the Revels murder and two of them had confessed.

The Florida Supreme Court retried and cleared Frederick and Keaton. Both were released, following revelations that Townsend coerced false confessions from them while conducting polygraph tests, and threatened them with the death penalty if they did not change their stories.

Frederick and Keaton were wrongly sent to prison on confessions coerced by a lie detector operator. But because Terry Seaton passed a polygraph test, defense attorney Robert Rothstein took up his case and brought got him exonerated from the killing of a baker in New Mexico. The coercion that later surfaced in this case involved several witnesses with shady backgrounds who were pressured by police to bring about Seaton's wrongful conviction.

At 5:45 A.M. on May 19, 1971, Grover Beard stopped at the Davis Bakery in Carlsbad, New Mexico, to visit his friend, William L. Davis. The sixty-five-year-old Davis, a baker, lay on the floor of the frying room, his mutilated corpse castrated and covered with hot grease. Several miles away, the bakery's cash register was found in a ditch.

Eddy County chief deputy LeRoy Payne and district attorney investigator Ray Magness had no clues in the case until twenty-four-year-old James Williams told the sheriff's department that he and Terry Seaton had robbed a clothing store in Clovis the night Davis was murdered. Williams said that they then drove 110 miles south to Roswell, before continuing another seventy-six miles south to Carlsbad.

The time involved in the travels Williams described in his testimony would have given the alleged bandits only ten minutes to travel the last leg of their journey, requiring a speed of 426 miles per hour. Santa Fe public defender Robert Rothstein noted that fact much later, but officials at the time ignored it. It was not until Williams repeated his statement a third time, on May 17, 1972, before Sheriff Tom Granger, that he mentioned the stolen cash register. He repeated his statement to district attorney Pat Hanagan. During this time, another suspect was being investigated by the Carlsbad police.

Officer Ernie White discovered t Workman Jr. had confessed to his s

Marie Workman Cook, and girlfriend, Mattie Tweedy Hillman, of having had a dream in which he killed Davis. White also learned from Workman's estranged wife, Karen Mae Workman, that the suspect had threatened to kill the baker for flirting with his wife. Her mother corroborated Workman's hatred of Davis.

On April 10, 1972, Workman confessed to Officer White and showed the officer where he left the cash register, a spot within fifty yards of where it had been found. But he would not consent to a lie detector test. Not long after Hanagan interviewed Williams, he was killed in a car accident, and with a new district attorney, the case took a new turn.

J. Lee Cathey was appointed district attorney in June 1972, and assistant district attorneys Peter Fleming and Michael McCormick immediately quit. Cathey replaced Magness with Carlsbad police chief Carl Hawkins, and by year's end, three more witnesses were found to testify against Seaton. L. D. Bickford and Jerry Burns, fellow inmates of Seaton while he was briefly held in jail on burglary charges, said Seaton told them he killed Davis. Ted Williams, James Williams's brother, claimed he saw Seaton leaving the bakery with the cash register.

Seaton surrendered to police on December 20, 1972, the day the warrant for his arrest was issued. Attorneys Charles Feezer and Leonard May had no idea that their client, Seaton, was not the only suspect. Cathey claimed he was never aware of the investigation involving Workman, nor did he know of any file regarding Workman's confession.

Rothstein and former Santa Fe public defender director Steven Farber, who joined Rothstein on behalf of Seaton, learned later that information on Workman was in the district attorney's file on Seaton. At the time, McCormick felt Workman was not a viable suspect. On the evidence of prosecution witnesses, Seaton was found guilty after three days of testimony and thirty-five minutes of jury deliberation in May 1973. He was sentenced to life imprisonment.

Rothstein took up Seaton's case in fall 1975, after he learned that the wrongly convicted man had

passed a lie detector test in prison. He also learned that a state police officer, Larry Allen, had investigated Seaton's conviction in 1973 and 1974, and concluded in October 1974 that "there is no reasonable doubt on whether or not Terry Seaton is guilty. . . With the evidence they had, I don't see how they convicted the accused." In February 1976, Burns recanted his statement to Rothstein but then disappeared and did not testify.

In March 1978, Bickford recanted his testimony, too. At the time, Bickford was (and still is) serving a 120-year sentence for two murders, one very similar to the Davis murder, with the body found near where a cash register was found (a crime Bickford denies). Bickford nevertheless admitted that he had fabricated his entire testimony against Seaton. He added that his story had been arranged by police and that he was even given $200 by the district attorney's office. When Bickford had made his statement against Seaton, he was being held on three felony charges.

On July 17, 1972, Cathey allowed Bickford to plead guilty to misdemeanor charges. He was given six months, four of which were suspended, and six months probation. Soon James Williams also recanted. He told Rothstein and Farber that he had been given the file on the Davis murder and, if he agreed to implicate his friend, Seaton, the charges against him would be dropped. Williams claimed that officers even drove him to where the cash register was found, so that he could later pinpoint the location of that stolen item when testifying in court. Cathey, Granger, McCormick and Payne denied the deals that Williams described.

Eight of eleven charges had been dropped, however, and, after Williams pleaded guilty to the remaining three, he was sentenced to one to five years in prison, a sentence that was suspended, after he spent five months in jail, by Judge D. D. Archer. Although Ted Williams never recanted his testimony, he never appeared against Seaton at the second trial, for he suffered a mental breakdown which prevented him from testifying at Seaton's habeas corpus hearing. The court determined that widespread coercion of witnesses had been used by officials in Seaton's case and he was ordered released, after six years in prison. Seaton immediately sued for damages, and in 1983, the courts awarded him $118,000 from Eddy County, the sheriff and deputy. This verdict was not appealed. Attorney fees of $217,500 were also paid by the state.

## Suspect and Witness Coercion and the Mentally Retarded

Police and prosecutors have the legal right to employ reasonable deception in trapping suspects into confessions or acts that will confirm their culpability, but interrogators sometimes abuse that right. The use of deception with a person known to be retarded or simpleminded, as illustrated in the following cases, is a clear violation of that psychological tactic. Such suspects have nevertheless been coerced into making false confessions. When this tactic fails to produce results, physical coercion is often applied by police interrogators—a clear violation of civil rights. Witnesses in many capital cases were shown to have been coerced into false testimony—a flagrant violation of police and prosecutorial procedures. Police or prosecutors have often wrongly claimed to possess information that would involve witnesses in those cases, but promise to bury such evidence in exchange for testimony. In the case of a young man from Colorado, California police secured for prosecutors a first-degree murder conviction and a life sentence based on the coerced testimony of a lone witness.

In December 1971, twenty-one-year-old Juan Venegas left Colorado to visit Lawrence Reyes, a childhood friend in Long Beach, California. Reyes committed a murder in another house, while Venegas was asleep. Both men were arrested and charged with the killing. Although Reyes exonerated Venegas of the murder, a bartender, who later said police ordered him to lie, testified that both men had been in his bar shortly before the slaying. Although he was sent to prison for life, Venegas spent only two and a half years behind bars. In 1974, the California Supreme Court reversed his conviction because the evidence against him was not sufficient to sustain the conviction, and coercion had been employed to obtain the bartender's testimony. Venegas was released and prosecutors made no attempt at a retrial.

In 1980, Venegas won a $1 million suit against the City of Long Beach for false imprisonment on the grounds that his conviction was secured partially through false testimony resulting from police misconduct. Presiding Judge Ronald E. Swearinger, of the Los Angeles County court, explained, "I think the jury was horrified at what happened to this man."

The jurors, in voting unanimously for the judgment, "wanted to show there was no doubt that Mr. Venegas wasn't involved in the murder." Venegas hugged the jurors in the emotional moments following the verdict. The judgment was reversed later on the grounds of governmental immunity, but in 1986 Venegas was awarded more than $2 million for his false conviction. Less than a year after Venegas was falsely charged with murder in California, a young black man was charged with a Boston murder he did not commit, his conviction based on the coerced testimony of a witness.

In 1974, twenty-nine-year-old Frank "Parky" Grace was found guilty by an all-white jury of the 1972 Boston murder of nineteen-year-old Providence, Rhode Island, drug addict, Marvin Morgan, and sent to prison. Grace's conviction was based largely on testimony provided by Eric Baker and Jasper Lassiter, who said they saw Grace shoot Morgan. They named Grace's younger brother, Ross Grace, as an accomplice.

In 1983, information presented in an evidentiary hearing by the New England American Friends Service Committee showed that Frank Grace, a former Black Panther member and political activist, had been targeted by the New Bedford police as a troublemaker. He had been arrested more than twelve times but never convicted.

In 1984, eleven years after Grace's incarceration, Lassiter signed an affidavit saying Ross Grace alone had killed Morgan and that he saw Frank Grace for the first time at his trial. He admitted that police officers coerced his testimony. Officers told him that Frank would be sitting next to Ross in the courtroom and that he should testify that Frank fired the fatal shot. Ross Grace later confessed that he alone had committed the murder and was sent to prison. Finally, in 1985, Frank Grace was freed.

Where one coerced witness had sent Frank "Parky" Grace behind bars, two witnesses were coerced by police in San Jose, California, to send Glen "Buddy" Nickerson to prison for life in 1987. Nickerson, along with two codefendants, Murray Lodge and Dennis Hamilton, were convicted in separate trials for the 1984 murders of John Evans, a crack dealer, and Evans's half brother, and the attempted murder of Michael Osorio. There was no evidence linking the murders to Nickerson, but San Jose police at the time theorized that Nickerson had participated in the killings in revenge for John Evans's earlier shooting of Nickerson's brother.

Shortly after the killings, Osorio, who had been shot in the head execution style by one of three masked men but miraculously survived, told police that the killers were all average size. Nickerson, at that time, weighed more than four hundred pounds. Police spent a great deal of time with Osorio until he came around to identifying Nickerson as one of the assailants who had been shot at by the Evans brothers in an exchange of gunfire, according to a second witness, eighteen-year-old Brian Tripp. Under severe grilling by police, Tripp testified that Nickerson had been shot during the firefight and was lying close to the scene of the crime, bleeding profusely.

In the separate trial of Murray Lodge, however, Tripp recanted his testimony, saying that police had coerced him into pinpointing Nickerson as

one of the killers, who were all persons of average size. His earlier statements about Nickerson being wounded in the firefight was repudiated by forensic police evidence that showed that the trail of blood leading from the murder scene did not match any of the defendants, including Nickerson. Even though the court in Lodge's separate trial determined that investigating officers had manufactured evidence, destroyed exculpatory evidence, and committed perjury, Nickerson was nevertheless sent to prison for life.

Nickerson filed an appeal, claiming that he was innocent and witnesses against him had been coerced by police. While he made his appeals, forensic experts matched the blood in the trail from the crime scene to William Jahn, an original suspect in the case. Jahn was brought to trial and convicted and sent to prison for life, as had been Lodge and Hamilton. All three insisted that Nickerson had not been involved in the killings. The State was then confronted with having convicted four men for a crime committed by three men.

Nickerson's conviction was overturned by Judge Patel, based on the fact that all three of the convicted perpetrators—Lodge, Hamilton, and Jahn—had denied Nickerson's involvement, despite the fact that each had confessed to his own guilt and inculpated one another, and because of the broad police misconduct in the case. Nickerson, after spending sixteen years in prison, was released in 2003.

Authorities in San Jose attributed coercion and other abuses by police in the Nickerson case to "overzealous" efforts to solve a capital crime and bring the perpetrators to quick justice. This kind of lame excuse for inexcusable police misconduct was uttered routinely in Philadelphia during the days of "Super Cop," Frank Rizzo.

To quickly solve a bombing murder, Philadelphia police—who operated without restraint during the Rizzo era—not only used coercion on a witness but used a blackjack to beat a confession from a suspect. On October 5, 1975, a firebomb exploded in the Philadelphia home of Radames Santiago, killing his wife, three of his children, and a guest. A fourteen-year-old witness, Nelson Garcia, stated that a neighbor, Robert Wilkinson, had tossed the flaming bottle through the window. The twenty-five-year-old Wilkinson and his wife were arrested and questioned for twenty hours. Wilkinson, who was mildly retarded, eventually confessed to the crime. He was convicted in 1976 on five counts of murder.

Later that year, a neighbor of Wilkinson's, David McGinnis, confessed to the murders, and the original witness admitted that he had lied, his testimony obtained through coercion. A further investigation by the Philadelphia *Inquirer* revealed that Wilkinson's confession had been forced by two detectives who had assaulted him with a blackjack. The *Inquirer* also found six other incidents of brutality.

On June 2, 1977, all charges against Robert Wilkinson were dropped, and he was awarded $325,000 in damages. In March 1978, McGinnis was sentenced to twenty-two years in prison. On November 10, 1979, six detectives found guilty of maltreating suspects began serving fifteen-month prison sentences at the Eglin Federal Prison Camp in Florida.

A decade after Philadelphia police victimized the retarded Wilkinson, Missouri officers coerced a young retarded man into confessing a crime he did not commit. This case began when the home of seventy-nine-year-old Pauline Martz in Aurora, Missouri, caught fire in 1986. Inside the home, bound and gagged, Martz had been beaten and left to die by a thief, who also set the house on fire. A large crowd assembled before the burning house, and among the onlookers was a retarded twenty-one-year-old janitor named Johnny Lee Wilson. According to another person in the crowd at that time, Wilson made incriminating remarks about the murdered woman.

These statements, along with Wilson's so-called confession to police, served as enough evidence to convict him in 1987 and send him to prison for life. The conviction did not set well with some prose-

cutors, who brought a detailed profile of the case to Governor Melvin Eugene "Mel" Carnahan (1993–2000). For more than a year, Carnahan reviewed the so-called evidence that had convicted Wilson.

During that period, the witness in the crowd had recanted those statements. Moreover, Carnahan came to the conclusion that police interrogators had fed Wilson details about the Martz robbery and murder, and that they had "manipulated a weak mind" into confessing a crime he did not commit.

On September 29, 1995, Governor Carnahan pardoned Wilson: "It is clear that Johnny Lee Wilson's confession is false and inaccurate. Furthermore, there is no evidence to corroborate or substantiate it. Quite to the contrary." Wilson, after eight and a half years behind bars, stepped from the gray walls of Jefferson City Correctional Center with tears in his eyes, saying in a sobbing voice, "I didn't do what they said. I'm glad it's over. I feel wonderful, absolutely wonderful."

A year before Wilson was released, another mildly retarded man in Virginia was wrongly accused and sent to prison on charges of rape. Eighteen-year-old Christopher Prince, a resident of Culpeper, Virginia, had an IQ of 75, which some experts consider borderline retarded. Lacking communication skills, Prince, a black, was slow to object when, at a court hearing, he was identified by two white girls, ages twelve and thirteen, as the man who invaded an apartment and sexually attacked one of them on February 9, 1994.

An attorney representing Prince told his client that the girls' testimony would be strong enough to convict him, whether he was guilty or not, and that his only hope for a light sentence was to seek a plea bargain. Prince entered a plea which admitted there was enough evidence to convict him of breaking and entering with intent to commit a felony. He was sentenced to twelve years in prison.

Prince's parents believed their son to be innocent, and family members hired a private detective, former FBI agent Roger Goldsberry, to investigate the case. Goldsberry interviewed the two girls, who, after several meetings and polygraph tests, admitted that they had lied, claiming that police had forced them to falsely identify Prince. The older girl then formally recanted her courtroom testimony at Prince's trial.

With this evidence in hand, Governor George Allen (1994–1998) issued a full and unconditional pardon on December 21, 1995, first calling Prince's parents to inform them that their son would be immediately released from prison. The Princes went to the correctional center in Staunton, where they were reunited with their smiling son, who had been wrongly imprisoned for fifteen months. His mother, forty-four-year-old Mary Prince, had spoken earlier with Governor Allen: "You have given us the best Christmas present."

Allen told newsmen, "As far as I'm concerned, it's clear that Christopher Prince is innocent of the crime for which he was accused and incarcerated."

He emphasized that such mistakes were rare in the criminal justice system, but "when it does happen, this is the right thing to do." (Unfortunately, Governor Allen was mistaken in his belief that such wrongful convictions were rare occurrences. As case after agonizing case in this volume clearly shows, such wrongful convictions occur with terrible regularity.)

Prosecutors considered charging the girls with perjury, but the oldest girl had since moved to Florida, and the matter was complicated. The girls' allegation that police had coerced them into identifying Prince led to an investigation.

When Christopher Prince arrived at his Culpeper home on December 21, 1995, he was oblivious to any action that might be taken against his lying accusers. He was only concerned with buying Christmas presents for his parents. On the front door of his home was a homemade sign reading, "Welcome home, Chris! God is good!"

# VI

# *The Real Culprit Stands Up*

M ANY WRONGLY CONVICTED PERSONS have been exonerated—some after execution—when the real perpetrators later confess. The actual culprits are motivated to declare their guilt through pangs of conscience, religious conversion, or, as in the many cases involving deathbed confessions, the thought of eternal damnation. Some notorious criminals, such as England's Charles Peace and America's Thomas "Black Jack" Ketchum, confessed just before they were executed. Having no options and having exhausted all possible avenues of escape, these professional criminals confessed to crimes for which others had been wrongly convicted. For the most part, such confessions were made many years, sometimes decades, after the innocent person had gone behind bars or, worse, to the scaffold.

The judicial and fragile destinies of these innocents were not determined by any other source of authority than the actual criminal, many of these furtive malefactors clutching terrible secrets until the last moment of life. Those criminals harbored their guilt through revenge against the innocent person they may have framed or fear of corporal punishment or a psychological inability to accept responsibility for their wrongdoing.

One must wonder which of the two—the innocent person or the guilty person—lived out the more agonizing life. Though the innocent person

in such cases suffered through time behind bars, the guilty person, if having an enlightened conscience, was also imprisoned by his or her own guilt, a guilt that nagged and hectored the hours of each day. For many criminals, releasing the burden of that guilt had nothing to do with a magnanimous desire to free an innocent person but to escape from his or her own prison, one housed in the mind and heart.

## Culprit Confessions of the Nineteenth Century

In 1815, Elizabeth Fenning (1794–1815), twenty-one, was hired as a cook in the London household of Robert Turner. After several weeks with the family, she made yeast dumplings for dinner one night, which were eaten by Turner, his wife, his father, Elizabeth, and an apprentice of Turner's named Thomas King. Within a few minutes of eating the dumpling dish, they all suffered extreme pain and vomiting.

The next morning, suspecting arsenic poisoning, Turner examined the bowl in which the dumplings had been mixed. He discovered a white powder, which he gave to a surgeon, Dr. Marshall, who positively identified it as arsenic. Turner also found that a packet of arsenic for killing mice was missing from a drawer in his office. When the left-

111

over flour and yeast used to make the dumplings were checked, they contained no arsenic. Elizabeth Fenning was arrested for the poisoning.

Fenning swore her innocence and virtually no evidence existed to bring about her conviction, but she was tried in April 1815, convicted, and sentenced to death. Though the public supported her and several people tried to get the sentence commuted, Fenning, clothed in white, was hanged at Newgate on July 26, 1815. Almost twenty years later, in 1834, Robert Turner confessed on his deathbed that he, not Fenning, put arsenic in the dumplings.

Where the hapless Elizabeth Fenning went to her death for a crime she did not commit, a knock-about man in Manchester went behind bars for a crime committed by one of England's archburglars. William Habron, born in 1854, and his two brothers, John and Frank, were local terrors at the Royal Oak Pub in Manchester, England. Police Constable Cock had repeatedly warned William about his penchant for drunken brawls. When he had too much to drink, Habron was prone to violence and would engage anyone who crossed his path in a fight. After the final warning seemingly fell on deaf ears, Cock made good on his threat to bring Will Habron before the magistrate. "I promised you a sorry day if you ever ran afoul of me," Habron scowled in court.

On the evening of August 1, 1876, Constable Cock was shot to death by a gunman lurking in the shadows as he made his rounds. With his dying breath, the policeman identified Habron as a possible assailant. Police Superintendent Bent pieced together a trail of circumstantial evidence that seemed to confirm Cock's accusation.

A pair of muddy boots at Habron's home matched the tracks left behind at the scene of the murder. Two clerks in a small shop that sold weapons and ammunition identified Habron as the man who had examined revolver cartridges the day before the murder. Their testimony, coupled with the ominous threat uttered by Habron in court, was enough to convict him of murder. On Novem-ber 28, 1876, the judge sentenced him to life in prison at Portland after the jury had attached a recommendation for leniency to its verdict.

William Habron served three years for a murder he never committed. The actual killer, Charles Peace, was a career criminal well-known to the Crown as a violent and dangerous man. He had shot and killed Cock while committing one of his burglaries. This was the story he told to police after being arrested on October 10, 1878, near Black-heath for the murder of Albert Dyson. Peace went to the gallows on February 25, 1879. William Habron was pardoned and given £500 compensation.

Charles Peace was a hard-hearted criminal whose confession had nothing to do with a compunction to free a wrongly convicted man. Peace admitted to the killing of Cook because, out of his warped arrogance and ego, he wanted the credit for the murder, another terrible deed he insisted was his to claim, as if arguing for a trophy or a reward, gruesome though it may have been.

Where Peace's confession was motivated out of perverse pride in his criminal acts, the harping conscience of a Massachusetts farmer stirred a confession that released a man the farmer had wrongly sent to prison. In the fall of 1885, John Chesterman, a Polish immigrant also known as John Christman, returned to the farm of his former employer Charles P. Vokes, apparently to ask for money owed him. The result of his visit was a conviction for a crime he never committed.

After Chesterman left the farm, Vokes informed police that the man had attempted to steal jewelry and clothing, but had been stopped in the act by the farmer himself. Chesterman was arrested by Officer Woodward of Hardwick, Massachusetts, as he ran from his boardinghouse. On November 16, 1885, Vokes retold his story before Judge Horace W. Bush, which led to a grand jury indictment for larceny on January 21, 1886. At his trial, which began the same day at the superior court in Worch-ester, Chesterman pleaded innocent and told an entirely different version of the incident.

Chesterman claimed that Vokes had shot at him when he asked the farmer for his back pay of $42, and that he had run from the police because he was afraid that Vokes had turned him in on a lie. The jury did not believe Chesterman, who spoke halting English, and he was found guilty and sentenced to one year in prison.

Not long after Chesterman's conviction, on February 6, 1886, Vokes, suffering from pangs of conscience, came forward and confessed before Justice Clarence Burgess Roote to lying in court to avoid paying Chesterman his wages. Prosecutor W. S. B. Hopkins sought a pardon from Governor George D. Robinson (1884–1887), which was granted on February 12, 1886, and Chesterman was released the following day. Vokes was tried, convicted, and imprisoned for perjury.

In France, five years later, the religious awakening of a murderer brought about the release of an innocent person. When the heir of an eighty-year-old woman found her strangled in her bed, he was accused and convicted of the murder, while the actual sixteen-year-old killer escaped punishment. Madame Montet (or Mottet), an elderly woman living in a villa at La Blancharde, a suburb of Marseilles, disapproved of her relatives and intended to leave her estate to Louis Cauvin, a neighbor she had known for years. Montet lived with a sixteen-year-old maid, Marie Michel, whom she had found at the orphanage of the Sisters of the Hospital of Toulon.

Cauvin called on Montet daily to visit and talk. He had known her since early childhood. Shortly before Christmas in 1891, Montet was found dead in her bed, and a medical examination showed strangulation. The suspects were Cauvin and Michel. Cauvin had reported the death to the police, saying that Michel had awakened him around 1:00 A.M. to tell him she had heard Montet groaning and crying and she seemed to be choking.

The girl said she was so frightened that she ran to find Cauvin at once. Cauvin found Montet dead and then returned to his house. Four hours later, with his wife, mother-in-law, a servant and Michel,

he returned to Montet's villa and then called a doctor. Cauvin told the physician that Montet had died of suffocation.

At first corroborating Cauvin's story, Michel, after several hours of questioning, confessed, saying that Cauvin had approached her on December 16, 1891, saying that he was going to murder Montet to acquire her estate, and that Michel had the choice of either helping him, for which he would give her 3,000 francs and guaranteed lifelong employment, or hindering him, in which case he would soon get rid of her, too. Frightened, she had hidden him in the house, she told police, later holding the old woman's hands out of the way while Cauvin choked her. Cauvin claimed innocence, but he was tried, found guilty, and condemned to a life of penal servitude. Michel was acquitted and sent back to the orphanage.

Five years later, Michel heard a sermon that stirred her conscience. She went to the prosecutor and said she had given false evidence against Chauvin and that she alone had murdered Montet. The case was tried a second time, with Michel confessing that she had killed her mistress because she had "reproached me with eating too much. . . grumbling because I had broken a dish. . . [and] said if I broke anything more she would cut it out of my wages."

Michel told authorities that, on the night of the murder, she had crept up to Mottet's room, knelt on the elderly woman's chest, and stuffed her fingers down her throat, holding her down until she stopped breathing. Michel, following Cauvin's conviction, had moved to Toulon to work for another family. Five years later, she was touched by a sermon of Father Marie Breny and was prompted to tell the truth. Cauvin won an acquittal and the maid was condemned to five years in prison.

About the same time Cauvin was released from prison in France, the days of the Old West in America were coming to an end, where hard-riding train and bank bandits were being tracked down, imprisoned, or killed in large numbers. American justice was swift and often as reckless as the culprits it imprisoned or executed. These bandits were mostly cowboys working large ranches, who would occasionally branch out into robbery, holding up a bank or train and then returning to the ranch where they worked. In those days, if a posse found someone in the vicinity of a recently committed crime, that was enough evidence to bring about a lightning conviction. Often informants, seeking revenge or trying to shield their own criminal activities, gave local sheriffs the names of cowboys suspected of highway robbery. The names of three innocent cowboys working on a large ranch were given to New Mexico officials after a murderous train robbery in late 1897.

Leonard Alverson, David Atkins, and Ed Cullen were cowboys working at Cushey's Ranch in Cochise County, Arizona. All three were arrested by a hard-riding posse on December 13, 1897, and quickly convicted of robbing the SP Sunshine Special train at Stein's Pass, New Mexico, on December 9, 1897. This robbery had been particularly bloody. The express agent of the mail car had been killed. One gang member was also killed, and another wounded during a wild gun battle. Out of five members of the holdup gang, three escaped. Alverson was assumed, without a great deal of evidence, to be the leader of the holdup gang. The three cowboys were convicted and given long sentences at the Santa Fe Prison.

In 1899, the notorious Thomas "Black Jack" Ketchum, who had robbed numerous stagecoaches, trains, and banks, had some noble thoughts while awaiting execution for robbery. He sent a letter from prison to President William McKinley (1897–1901), in which he admitted that he and some others were wholly responsible for the murderous robbery of the Sunshine Special in 1897. Wrote Ketchum, "William Carver, Sam Ketchum, Bronco Bill, and I did the job. I have given my attorney these names and a list of what was taken and where same can be found. I make this statement realizing that my end is fast approaching and I very soon must meet my Maker."

Alverson, Atkins, and Cullen were released with apologies but no compensation. Atkins was particularly grateful in seeing freedom since he had also been convicted and sentenced for the murder of a man in Tom Green County, Texas, which was later proved to be the work of Bill Carver, a member of Butch Cassidy's Wild Bunch.

A year before Black Jack went to his Maker and a half a continent away, a Boston robbery-murder brought about a wrongful conviction that would take more than ten years to set right, even though the real culprit had confessed many times, before an innocent man was set free.

After the shooting of drugstore clerk Charles L. Russell during an attempted robbery on April 4, 1898, a man wearing an overcoat ran from the store, which was inside the U.S. Hotel in Boston. Three weeks after the crime, which no one saw, the police finally discovered the coat and duly arrested its owner, John Henry Chance, thirty-two, as well as Arthur Hagan. The latter had gone to Chicago, where he was apprehended in October. The two men were charged with second-degree murder in the indictment filed on June 11, 1898. Their trial began on February 8, 1899.

Hagan, who was represented by George R. Swasey, was able to provide an alibi for the night of the murder. He accused Chance of robbing a cutlery shop two nights before the murder and taking a revolver that was subsequently used in the drugstore killing. The story he told was corroborated by a prosecution witness, Liz Nagle. Chance, unable to offer a defense, was found guilty on February 22, 1899. Hagan was acquitted. Chance's sentence of life imprisonment began on September 11, 1899, after an appeal failed.

On November 20, 1905, after several appeals for executive clemency, Chance wrote Massachusetts Governor William Lewis Douglas (1905–1906) claiming that Hagan had made a confession to the murder in Chicago and that others knew of his own innocence. This plea was ignored, and it was not until 1911 that Governor Eugene Noble Foss (1911–1914) looked into the matter. He learned that Hagan had indeed confessed and did so again to Boston authorities on the promise of immunity. Finally, on June 7, 1911, John Henry Chance was released with a full pardon.

## Confessions from Fits of Conscience and Remorse

A wealthy farmer, Clyde Showalter, drove into Mount Carmel, Illinois, on October 19, 1905, where he received $1,485 from the sale of some hogs. After banking $1,400, he spent the afternoon purchasing supplies and visiting saloons. The farmer rashly bragged about his substantial sale that day and flashed a wad of bills, buying drinks all around in one saloon. As he left the saloon, someone followed him into the darkness. Before he could drive home, Showalter was attacked by George R. Pond, who struck him on the head with a hammer, took $50, and pushed the body into a river. Later, Pond returned to the river and took the corpse to Patoka Creek, burying it in a sandbar.

On May 26, 1906, two boys paddling on the Patoka Creek spotted Showalter's body, which had been loosened from the sandbar and had floated to the surface after a flash flood the night earlier. Meanwhile, "Curly" Conrad, a prisoner serving time for attacking a thirteen-year-old girl, made an agreement with officials to give evidence to convict the Showalter killer, on the condition that he would be released. He implicated a woman, Oma Johnson, who was confined for several months and threatened until she agreed to testify in the case. On September 30, 1908, Jesse Lucas, a factory worker with a reputation for honesty, was arrested on murder charges along with his mother, Margaret Lucas, who was charged as an accomplice.

Their trial began in April 1909. Conrad and Johnson testified that they had witnessed Lucas strike Showalter with a club and that his mother helped him take Showalter's body to the creek. On the strength of this testimony, Lucas and his mother were convicted and imprisoned for life.

Later, Lucas's conviction was confirmed, but his mother was granted a new trial and the charges against her dismissed.

While Lucas was in prison, neighbors with influence from his hometown urged him to admit to the crime, telling him they would try to win parole for him, but Lucas insisted that he was innocent. Twenty-three years later, Pond was dying of a fatal disease. He had fits of conscience and summoned a priest and officials to his deathbed, where he confessed to the Showalter killing. A short time later, Johnson withdrew her previous testimony, saying that she had been coerced into lying on the stand. Lucas was released from Menard Prison on September 27, 1931. He was given no apologies or compensation from the state.

George Pond held his terrible secret for more than twenty years, keeping an innocent person behind bars, until he confessed with the expectation that his final judgment would be made by Providence. The confession that set an innocent Ohio man free was delivered by a bragging youth with so much money that he had no need to commit a crime, other than the perverse thrill such crimes brought him.

On Valentine's Day, 1922, night patrolmen Henry Adams and Emory McCreight were making their rounds in Wilmington, Ohio, when they heard sounds from the back of a hardware store. Calling out, they heard a man say he was looking for a dog. When the officers flashed their lights, gunfire roared and both were wounded. McCreight died the next day.

A reward and a manhunt turned up testimony from Charles Smalley, a farmhand who had seen two men in a car with a flat tire carrying several gallons of whiskey and telling him to "never say a word you saw us." On February 26, 1922, officers arrested Clarence LeRoy McKinney in Cincinnati, picking up Jim Bill Reno a few days later. Positively identified, first by two men as having been in a drugstore near the scene of the crime the night of the shootings and later by Officer Adams, they were indicted by a grand jury for transporting liquor and for murder. Both men were tried and convicted on the bootlegging charges, then tried separately for the murder.

McKinney's trial began on August 20, 1922, before Judge Frank M. Clevenger of the Clinton County Court of Common Pleas, with S. L. Gregory and Joe T. Doan prosecuting, and J. G. De Fosset and R. L. Neff for the defense. McKinney's alibi did not hold up and, when cross-examined by the prosecution, his record of prior convictions and trouble with the police was revealed. McKinney was found guilty and sentenced to life imprisonment in the Ohio State Penitentiary in Columbus. Reno was held in jail, serving time for the liquor charge.

Several months after McKinney's conviction, some young men approached the sheriff of Clinton County to tell him that nineteen-year-old Louis Vandervoort, the son of a wealthy local family, had been bragging about murdering McCreight. When questioned, Vandervoort not only confessed to the murder but gave police extensive and accurate information about other burglaries he had committed in Greene and Clinton Counties, even leading them to the hidden loot. Walter Bingham, whom Vandervoort named as his accomplice in the McCreight murder, also confessed. Vandervoort confessed in order to capture headlines, as he wanted to be known as a master criminal. He had little or no concern for McKinney. Vandervoort and Bingham pleaded guilty on February 20 and 21, 1923, to charges of second-degree murder and manslaughter, and received prison sentences. Consequently a new trial was ordered for McKinney.

When McKinney was tried a second time on the murder charges on February 24, 1923, before Judge Clevenger, the case was discontinued by the state's attorney and Clevenger ordered that the wrongly convicted man be released immediately. The liquor fines for both McKinney and Reno were suspended as restitution. McKinney had served five months of the life sentence term. He admitted to falsifying his alibi in order to escape conviction on the liquor charge and in the hope that he would not be convicted of murder.

Where Vandervoort's confession was accepted as concrete evidence that McKinney was innocent, the confession of a lowly miscreant was not taken seriously until five years after the killer's execution. On August 5, 1922, Cyrus Jones, a letter carrier who drove a taxicab on the side, was shot on the highway a mile and a half from his hometown of Swansboro, North Carolina. According to Jones, the men who attacked him included "Collins, Williams, and Doves." Arrested for the murder were Willis "Willie" Hardison, George Williams, and brothers Frank and Fred Dove. At their trial, prosecutors proved to the jury that the "Collins" the dying man had referred to was actually Willie Hardison. With the aid of Hardison's testimony—later discovered to be perjured—the jury convicted all four men for Jones's murder and all were sentenced to death.

On April 27, 1923, the morning of his scheduled execution, Hardison admitted that he alone had murdered Jones, and the other three were innocent. He explained that he had perjured his testimony because he was afraid of being lynched, and as soon as he was out of Raleigh, North Carolina, where the lynching threats originated, and when he no longer had a hope of clearing himself or getting his sentence reduced, he admitted everything. Hardison was electrocuted, but the debate over who killed Jones continued, while stays were granted to the Dove brothers and Williams.

In August 1925, Williams and the Doves petitioned North Carolina Governor Cameron Morrison (1921–1925) for a full pardon, stressing the fact that they were convicted solely on Hardison's perjured testimony. The governor also received letters requesting executive clemency for the three imprisoned men from an attorney named Powers who had prosecuted the men in the first place and from H. E. Stacy, his assistant.

More than four hundred people signed a petition demanding the pardon, including leading citizens of Onslow County, four original jurors, the

Swansboro postmaster, an ex-sheriff, the current sheriff, and the clerk of the superior court. Even trial Judge E. H. Cranmer pleaded with the governor: "After thought, reflection, and prayer, I recommend, my dear Governor, that you pardon George Williams, Frank Dove and Fred Dove." Cranmer then commuted the men's sentences to life in prison. Three more years passed before justice was done. On March 1, 1928, Governor Angus W. McLean (1925–1929) granted a pardon. Frank and Fred Dove and George Williams were released after serving six years for a crime they did not commit, five of those years served after the real culprit confessed to the crime.

For Sidney Wood, an Englishman visiting Los Angeles, the confession of a train robber set him free from prison; that confession came from a teenager who had a conscience, unlike his two fellow thieves. On the evening of November 7, 1923, three masked bandits robbed a train running between Los Angeles and Pasadena, California.

After the robbery, the bandits stopped the train, jumped off, and fled in a car driven by a fourth man. Los Angeles police questioned a young Englishman, Sidney Wood, who had no previous criminal record and produced evidence of an exemplary record in the British military, but had a flimsy alibi for the night of the robbery.

On the basis of identifications by the motorman and the conductor, police charged Wood with the crime. The jury was unable to decide the case, but, just before the district attorney was about to drop all charges against Wood, a passenger on the train positively identified Wood as one of the bandits.

A second trial was convened, and several passengers identified Wood as one of the robbers, their identifications based on his physical stature and his facial resemblance to one of the masked bandits, whose features had not been fully covered. The jury returned a verdict of guilty on March 3, 1924, and Wood was sentenced to five years to life at San Quentin Prison.

In January 1925, police received a tip regarding the identities of the men who had actually committed the crime. Three of the four, James Hovermale, Mark Godfrey, and Russell Smith, were arrested in Idaho and extradited to Los Angeles. Charges were filed against them, as well as the fourth man, Roy Smith, whose whereabouts was not known.

Godfrey, who was only seventeen at the time of the robbery, was acquitted because of his age and his cooperation with the police, telling detectives that Wood had nothing to do with the robbery. Hovermale and Smith were tried, found guilty, and sent to prison. Sidney Wood's conviction was reversed and he was released from San Quentin on May 5, 1925.

Four years after Wood was released, a gangster confessed to the crime for which Edward Larkman had been condemned to die. Larkman had been arrested for the August 12, 1925, murder of Ward Pierce, paymaster of the Art Metal Shop in Buffalo, New York. Knowing that the killer had worn sunglasses, the police at the lineup forced Larkman to stand alone, wearing dark glasses, under a bright light. Dorothy Littleworth, an eyewitness to the crime, positively identified him under these rigged circumstances, though she saw his profile for a total of three seconds and his full face for only two seconds during the commission of the crime.

Although the jury at Larkman's trial requested information regarding the means by which the witness had identified Larkman, the police method was not revealed. After debating for forty-three hours, the jury brought in a verdict of guilty, and the judge condemned Larkman to die in the electric chair. A court of appeals affirmed, by a majority, the conviction, but two judges dissented because the identity of the defendant had not been determined beyond a reasonable doubt.

On the night of January 13, 1927, just ten hours before the scheduled execution, with the convicted man's head already shaved, Governor Alfred E. Smith (1919–1920; 1923–1928) commuted the sentence to life imprisonment, following the custom in the case of a dissent. In April 1929 a Buffalo gangster, Anthony Kalkiewicz, arrested for another crime, confessed that he and four other men had murdered Pierce. Larkman applied for a pardon on the basis of Kalkiewicz's confession, and Governor Franklin D. Roosevelt (1929–1932) appointed Carlos C. Alden to investigate the case. On March 24, 1930, Alden recommended that Larkman be granted a new trial, a motion denied because the new evidence had not been submitted within a year of Larkman's conviction.

Not until June 1933 did Larkman renew his application for a pardon. The new governor, Herbert Lehman (1933–1942), again appointed Alden to study the case. After uncovering the information about the means the police had used to secure an identification, Alden this time recommended a pardon. Governor Lehman pardoned Larkman on April 18, 1933. The wrongly convicted man had spent eight years in prison.

In the case of Lonzo Thornton, who made the mistake of visiting an old friend in jail, the crime partner of that friend—a Thornton look-alike—made a full confession that brought about Thornton's prison release. On October 6, 1926, in Middletown, Ohio, a recent immigrant, Louie Parkalab, was accosted on the street by two men who robbed him of $20 and an insurance policy. A police officer observed the incident and apprehended one of the men. James Ivory was locked up and the next morning received a visitor. The police wondered if the second man could be the second assailant, and brought Louie Parkalab to the station, where Ivory's visitor, Lonzo Thornton, had been detained.

Parkalab quickly concurred that Thornton was the man who had attacked him. On February 15, 1927, in the Butler County courtroom of Judge Clarence Murphy, Thornton and Ivory were found guilty and sentenced to the Ohio penitentiary for ten to twenty-five years.

Less than a year after Ivory and Thornton were imprisoned, Simon "Babe Ruth" Williams confessed that he had been the second man who robbed Parkalab. Williams resembled Thornton, and had such convincing information regarding

collateral evidence that Thornton received a pardon. Williams was charged, convicted, and given ten years in prison.

One week after Parkalab had been robbed in Ohio, a bloody mail robbery occurred in a New York City street, which brought about the life conviction of James Sweeney. Like Thornton in the Parkalab case, Sweeney was released from prison when the real culprits confessed. On the morning of October 14, 1926, a mail truck was transporting $300,000 in registered mail from the Federal Reserve Bank in New York to the Elizabethport National Bank. The truck was driven by John Enz, accompanied by Patrick S. Quinn. Police officer Jacob Christman followed on a motorcycle.

Suddenly a sedan rounded a corner and drove toward the truck, causing it to swerve onto a side street and collide with a parked car. Another car hit the police officer and a shotgun blast was fired at him. Meanwhile, Enz was cut down by machine-gun fire. As Quinn jumped from the vehicle, he fired twice before he himself was shot in the arms, hands, and left leg.

A bystander was also wounded. Gang members then forced open the truck door, taking $151,300 in mail and driving off, running over the dead truck driver and his injured helper. Later, the gang members drove to a Newark apartment, where they divided the haul. The robbers included James Cuniffe, William Crowley, Frank Kiekart (alias Charles Miller), William Fanning, Charles Neary, Daniel Grosso, and Benjamin Haas.

The bold and bloody robbery outraged the public, and authorities started an intense investigation, which included giving state troopers and top post office department detectives orders to "shoot on sight and shoot to kill." During the investigation, one of the gang, Haas, was questioned, and police found a business card for James Sweeney, listed as "making books on crap games."

Sweeney was arrested and put on trial on April 11, 1927. Sweeney had two previous convictions, one for attempted grand larceny. He was positively identified by two eyewitnesses to the robbery, and the prosecutor cast doubts on Sweeney's alibi. Sweeney was found guilty and given a life term in prison.

Later, however, Sweeney's lawyer learned that one witness had not even been present at the scene of the crime. Two of the actual gang members, Haas and Kiekart, were arrested and soon confessed, clearing Sweeney. Sweeney was released in November 1928. Of the other six robbers, Cuniffe was murdered in Detroit by "parties unknown," Crowley was killed in Detroit, when he resisted arrest, and Fanning, Neary, and Grosso were convicted of robbery and murder and condemned. Their sentences were later commuted to life terms.

The robbers in the Sweeney case knew they would be convicted and imprisoned, which prompted their confessions clearing Sweeney. A bank robber in Illinois came to the same conclusion, when confessing to a crime for which he and an innocent man had been sent to prison. On January 25, 1930, Everett Howell left the county court in Golden, Illinois, a free man after spending sixteen months in prison trying to clear his name.

Albertus Janssen, cashier of the Exchange State Bank of Golden, was robbed of $4,305 in the early morning on August 20, 1928. He and customer James Garrison were forced at gunpoint to retreat to the bank's vault. Later the two men would testify conclusively that Howell was the robber.

Henry J. Gerdes, Samuel R. Woerman, and Frank F. Winkle, who had sold gasoline to a man driving a car similar to the getaway car, provided descriptions of the driver. Based on these descriptions, Howell was arrested in Peoria, Illinois. Earlier, police had tracked down another suspect in the robbery, Farmer Barnhill, by piecing together scraps of paper found along the path of the getaway car.

On September 20, 1928, just one month after the crime, Barnhill and Howell were indicted. They denied knowing each other, and Howell provided an alibi corroborated by disinterested witnesses. The jury, apparently believing the witnesses from Golden over those from Farmington and Canton,

returned a verdict of guilty against Barnhill and Howell. Each was sentenced to the state penitentiary for terms of from one year to life.

While Howell was preparing an appeal, Barnhill made a full confession to the crime and said Howell had nothing to do with it. Officials would not accept Barnhill's statements about Howell, knowing that he had associates, so the bank robber took one more step, breaking the code of the underworld by naming those associates in his amazing attempt to clear Howell's name. Barnhill named Gilbert Ammerman and Peter McDonald as associates in the robbery. Ammerman and McDonald were arrested and eventually confessed, and were given prison sentences.

On January 25, 1930, Judge Wolfe ordered a new trial. The state's attorney dropped the case against Howell, who was set free. He and Ammerman bore only a slight resemblance to each other, yet five people, including the principal victim, were positive that Howell was guilty.

Where a bank robber in Illinois cleared the name of his accused associate, a man in Mississippi was sent to prison for killing his son-in-law and was freed through the confession of his daughter. The real culprit never served a day behind bars because she and her father, upon his release, vanished from the face of the earth in one of Mississippi's most bizarre murder cases.

Based on the perjured testimony of his daughter and seven-year-old granddaughter, Thomas Gunter was convicted in Mississippi of murdering his sleeping son-in-law. Marlin Drew, his wife Pearl, and their three children lived in the home of Pearl's parents, Mr. and Mrs. Thomas Gunter. During the summer of 1929, Pearl was pregnant and Marlin was unemployed. They argued continually over Marlin's drinking and womanizing, and Marlin claimed that he was not the father of the child. The Gunters supported their daughter.

In July 1929, Marlin Drew's body was found on his bed, shot through the chest. Although investigators initially called it a suicide, they later arrested Thomas Gunter on July 7, 1929. Dorothy Louise

Drew, Gunter's granddaughter, told relatives that, while she was sleeping in the same bed with her father, "granddad" shot "pop."

The trial was held on August 16, 1929. Mrs. Gunter, a witness for the defense, claimed her husband was in a drunken stupor at the time of the killing, an assertion Gunter did not deny. The jury found the defendant guilty based on the convincing testimony of Dorothy Louise and the corroborating testimony of her mother. Judge Thomas E. Pegram sentenced Gunter to five years in prison.

After Pearl Drew recovered from the birth of her fourth child, she wrote to Governor Theodore Gilmore Bilbo (1916–1920; 1928–1932), confessing to the killing of her husband in the form of a variation on the famous folk ballad "A Jealous Lover in Lone Green Valley." Claiming she always intended to confess to the murder of her husband after her baby was born, she asked the governor to pardon her father, then sixty-three, as she had shot her husband in anger when he made insinuations about her unborn child.

On November 19, 1929, Gunter's sentence was suspended for ninety days and he was released from prison, pending a new trial. Three months later, a grand jury indicted Pearl Drew for murder and perjury, to which she pleaded guilty. Judge Pegram suspended Drew's sentence, while Governor Bilbo denied Gunter's application for a pardon.

In a public statement, Governor Bilbo said, "Somebody ought to be in the penitentiary all the time for the murder of a sleeping man. If Judge Pegram does not believe Mrs. Drew is guilty enough to serve her term, then the man convicted of the murder will have to serve his term. Husbands ought to have some protection." Refusing to return to prison, Thomas Gunter fled Mississippi, along with his daughter Pearl, and was never located again.

## The Guilty Out of the Blue

Circumstantial evidence and unfortunate physical likenesses implicated Frank and Norma Howell in a West Virginia filling station holdup in 1929. The charges against the Howells would have meant fifteen years in prison had it not been for a last-minute confession by the true culprits, Irene Crawford Schroeder and Walter Glenn Dague, two notorious bandits awaiting execution for murder.

Frank Howell spent fourteen months in prison for a crime he did not commit. Surprisingly, his wife was acquitted, though she was tried on the same charge and with the same testimony. During Howell's trial, prosecutors made several arguments against Howell. First, they pointed out that Norma had expressed concern that police would think she and her husband were the guilty couple because they fit the physical description of the filling station bandits. C. W. Edgell, the Howells' landlord, reported that they were usually late in paying rent, but, on September 7, 1929, two days after the robbery, Norma Howell paid him $10. Jack Cotts, owner of the gas station, swore to the jury that Howell was the guilty man. "I couldn't be mistaken," he said.

Howell testified that on the day of the crime he had helped George Coburn move, which Coburn corroborated. That evening, Howell and his wife were at home at 9:00 P.M., when their three children returned from the movies. The children corroborated the story. The jury nevertheless turned in a verdict of guilty, and Howell was sentenced to fifteen years in prison. He was saved by the confession on January 5, 1931, of two murderers awaiting execution, Schroeder and Dague. There was a remarkable likeness between the two couples, but that did not explain the discrepancy in evidence presented at the trial. On January 14, 1931, Governor William G. Conley (1929–1933) granted Howell a full pardon, and the State of West Virginia paid him $1,000 in compensation.

Five years later in Italy, an unsavory character, Carlo "Crackshot" Corbisiero, was also convicted of a robbery he did not commit. Although the guilty party confessed, he had to wait almost two decades to be set free. In many respects Corbisiero was a victim of the fascist system of government in Italy that allowed no quarter for poets, dissenters, or, in this case, a free spirit and bootlegger.

In 1934, three holdup men named the twenty-seven-year-old Corbisiero as an accomplice in a robbery in which an innocent person died. At the time, Corbisiero was two miles away loading a consignment of bootleg liquor onto a wagon. "Crackshot," as he was known to his friends in the town of Marzano di Nola, near Naples, maintained his innocence but was sentenced to life in prison. According to Italian law, a suspect is guilty until proven innocent.

After a year in prison, one of the convicted gunmen confessed to a priest that Corbisiero had been framed. After the man died in prison, the priest reported his findings to Rome, but nothing was done until February 1953, long after the fascist government of Benito Mussolini had been toppled.

Corbisiero was granted a new trial, and his innocence was established by famed defense attorney Giacomo Augenti, who produced thirty-five favorable witnesses, in addition to the confession of the real culprit as provided by the priest. Corbisiero was released from prison. For his troubles, Corbisiero received a new suit of clothes and 10,360 lira from the government, the equivalent of $16. He had served nineteen years in prison for a crime he did not commit.

Corbisiero languished behind bars for years until the real culprit's confession convinced authorities to release him. In the case of a hapless black man in North Carolina, however, a rapist's confession came harrowingly close to that innocent man's execution. William Mason Wellman was actually sitting in the electric chair, waiting for the executioner to pull the switch, when the news of that confession arrived.

After an elderly white woman was raped in Iredell County, North Carolina, on February 11, 1941, she identified her attacker as Wellman. At the time of the rape, however, Wellman was working for a construction firm at Fort Belvoir, Virginia, nearly 350 miles from the crime scene. He collected his pay about midday and signed a payroll receipt, which was not available at his trial.

In August 1942, Wellman was convicted and sentenced to death. On the morning that Wellman was scheduled to be executed, North Carolina's governor learned that another man had confessed to the rape and the governor granted a reprieve, which arrived just after Wellman had taken a seat in the electric chair.

Following an investigation by the State Parole Commission, the board found the original payroll records, verified Wellman's signature, and located two witnesses who stated that Wellman was present at work that day. The confession of the actual rapist was upheld. Wellman was granted a full pardon by Governor Joseph Melville Broughton (1941–1945) on April 15, 1943, and freed that afternoon, the first man under the death penalty ever released by the State of North Carolina.

Wellman remembered where he was on the day of the rape of which he was wrongly accused, but John Fry, an alcoholic, had trouble recalling the events of his own wife's murder. That absence of memory, blotted out by booze, sent him to prison, where he would most likely have remained had it not been for the impulsive confession of the real killer.

On the night of August 1, 1958, fifty-one-year-old John Fry drank himself into oblivion. He knew the hangover would wear off eventually, but another side effect would end up getting him in a lot of trouble. He could not remember what happened on that night. It also happened to be the night that Fry's common-law wife, forty-seven-year-old Elvira May Fry, was found brutally beaten and strangled in a bathtub in a San Francisco rooming house. Fry, fifty-one, had a history of beating her, and, when he was found in another rooming house nearby, he was apprehended as the prime suspect in the killing. Traces of blood on his bedsheets and his previous assault arrests did not help his case.

Under interrogation, Fry admitted that his heavy drinking prevented him from remembering anything about the night his wife was murdered. He was eventually charged with murder, but, on advice from his state-appointed counsel, pleaded guilty to manslaughter. He was convicted and handed an indeterminate sentence of one to ten years at San Quentin Prison in California.

That was the end of John Fry's story, until June 4, 1959. On that day, Richard T. Cooper, an unemployed janitor, strolled into a San Francisco police station and admitted to strangling Erlean Mosley, a hotel maid. Cooper told police he was turning himself in because he was afraid he was going to do it again. After all, he told them, he had strangled someone else the previous August—Elvira May Fry.

Before long, the district attorney's office and the police found that Cooper was telling the truth. Fry, who had insisted he was innocent ever since his conviction, consented to a lie detector test, and he was found to be telling the truth. On June 16, 1959, Governor Edmund G. Brown (1959–1967) granted a pardon, and Fry walked free and penniless, except for the $40 standard pay given to every freed convict, and $1.15 for bus fare. Fry sued the State of California for $5,000 compensation, and was finally granted $3,000 in 1960. Unlike the paltry award (by today's standards) to Fry for his wrongful incarceration, there would be no financial compensation for a drug-abusing Boston recidivist, but he also was released from a life prison term for a crime he did not commit.

On July 21, 1967, George Reissfelder (1940–1991) and William G. "Silky" Sullivan were sentenced to life in prison for the fatal shooting of a security guard during a 1966 robbery. Both men had been accused of shooting to death security guard Michael Shaw, following a botched payroll robbery at Boston's South Station and were arrested on October 14, 1966. Boston police reportedly knew that Reissfelder was innocent of the robbery-murder but pursued their case against him, working with prosecutors, in fear of losing the case against Sullivan, a notorious Massachusetts felon.

In July 1972, on his deathbed, Sullivan confessed to Reverend Edward Cowhig that Reissfelder was innocent of the shooting. Reissfelder, who had a ninth-grade education and a long police record for

assault, jailbreak, and bad checks, claimed that had accepted the sentence because he did not understand the law.

Cowhig later went to authorities to restate Sullivan's deathbed confession, and in 1980 a judge reopened the case, assigning Roanne Sragow to represent Reissfelder. After Sragow submitted an affidavit from Cowhig, the court ordered a new trial for Reissfelder and prosecutors declined to bring charges.

In 1982, a special hearing was ordered. Five policemen, an FBI agent, a probation officer, and the prison chaplain, Cowhig, offered testimony that led to Reissfelder's sentence being overturned on June 21, 1982. A concurrent attempted murder sentence in Florida was waived (after John Kerry, then an assistant for Sragow, went to Florida and successfully pleaded Reissfelder's case, which brought a parole from the Florida parole board), as Reissfelder had already served fifteen years.

On August 30, 1982, Reissfelder was released from prison. In 1985, a bill to compensate Reissfelder with $900,000 was defeated in the Massachusetts state legislature, members believing that Reisfelder was innocent of the robbery-murder in Boston. But he continued his criminal career after his exoneration and violated his parole several times by bouncing bad checks and then becoming involved in a Boston cocaine distribution gang. In 1991, Reissfelder died of cocaine poisoning after a lifelong addiction to the drug.

In early December 1967, six months after Reissfelder began serving a life sentence in Massachusetts, twenty-eight-year-old Roger Zane Dedmond began serving an eighteen-year sentence for manslaughter at a Union, South Carolina, county prison camp. Although Dedmond persistently claimed innocence, a Union police officer testified that Dedmond had confessed to killing his wife. Dedmond, like John Fry almost ten years earlier in San Francisco, said he could not remember where he was when his wife was slain. That lack of memory had aided prosecutors in sending Dedmond to prison.

In February 1968, Bill Gibbons, managing editor of the Gaffney *Ledger*, received a call from a man who said he had three stories. The caller explained how he had murdered two women. He gave Gibbons details that led police to the strangled bodies of Nancy Carol Parris, twenty, and Nancy Christine Rinehart, fourteen. He also said that he had been involved in the killing of Annie Lucille Dedmond. A few weeks later, the self-described "psycho killer" called Gibbons again, providing more details: "I killed them with them all begging me not to do it. The only reason I'm telling you this is to get that other boy [Dedmond] out."

When Gibbons tried to convince the man to surrender, he replied, "They'll have to shoot me like the dog I am." A few hours later, fifteen-year-old Opel Diane Buckson was taken, screaming, from a school bus stop and pushed into the trunk of an old black car. Two local men noticed a car parked in the woods twelve miles north of Gaffney. Officers found the stabbed, strangled body of Buckson inside. Lee Roy Martin (1937–1972), thirty-one, a local textile mill worker who owned the car, was arrested at about 12:15 P.M. on February 16, 1968, at the Musgrove cotton mill in Gaffney, where he worked part-time.

Based on Martin's confession, Dedmond, after serving ten months behind bars, was released from prison on April 30, 1968. "They tried to tell me I killed her. I knew in my heart I never did kill her, and I never did confess to it." Martin, the actual killer of Annie Lucille Dedmond, was tried before Judge James B. Morrison of Georgetown, South Carolina. Pleading guilty, Martin was convicted of murdering Buckson and Dedmond and sentenced to two consecutive life sentences. In May 1969, Martin again pleaded guilty, was convicted for the murders of Rhinehart and Parris, and was sentenced to two more consecutive life terms. On May 31, 1972, Martin was killed at the Central Correctional Institution in Columbia, South Carolina, stabbed in the chest and back by another inmate.

Where Roger Dedmond's memory failed to help his defense, Sergeant H. Jackson knew exactly where he was when a California killing was committed. When twenty-one-year-old Jackson was on trial for the murder of a San Diego gas station attendant in February 1974, he swore he was in church when Robert Hoke was killed. Hoke's wife identified a wallet found on Jackson when he was arrested as her husband's killer. After first claiming he received the wallet from relatives, Jackson admitted that two friends had taken it in a burglary. He also denied that he had confessed to a prosecution witness. Jackson was found guilty and sent to a medium security prison in Tracy, California.

Seven months later, Charles R. Blunt confessed to Hoke's murder and named Andrew Donelly as his accomplice. The charges against Jackson were dismissed and he was freed in October. A jury award to Jackson of $280,000 for false imprisonment was overturned by a judge, who said Jackson was eligible for compensation only for the time he was under warrantless arrest. As it turned out, Jackson was first apprehended without a warrant. The City of San Diego ultimately awarded Jackson $17,000.

Just as Blunt's confession brought about Jackson's exoneration, the confession of a mentally disturbed and conscience-stricken killer in a small Arkansas town set an innocent man free from prison, a man believed by almost everyone in his town to be guilty. This story began when a hunter stumbled across the badly decomposed remains of a young woman lying in the thick underbrush in rural Pulaski County, Arkansas, on September 12, 1981. It would take many weeks before a positive identification would be made of the remains. The corpse came to be known as "Jane Doe."

In the small farming town of nearby Bigelow, thirty-four-year-old Ronald Carden was known as a hard-drinking, easy-living ex-Marine, though some would call him the "black sheep" of his family. The woman's death infuriated the townspeople, who demanded the killer be brought to justice immediately. Most residents believed that the womanizing Carden was responsible for the woman's death.

Three eyewitnesses supplied the police with information that pointed to Ron Carden as the likely murderer. First, his uncle, James Johnson, said that he and Carden had picked up two female hitchhikers on Highway 113 outside Bigelow and that later he helped Carden drag a woman's body into the bush. But under cross-examination on the witness stand, Johnson recanted this earlier statement, saying that when he made those remarks to police he was drunk.

James Malott, who owned a nursing home in Little Rock, said that he recalled seeing Carden pick up the two women on September 9, 1981, mimicking Johnson's original remarks. Malott then changed his testimony, saying that only one man picked up the hitchhikers, and he could not identify that man with certainty.

Most damaging of all was the testimony of Berwin Monroe, an analyst for the local crime lab who positively stated that the hairs found on the tank top of the victim matched those from Carden's arm. Two weeks later, however, the FBI lab refuted Monroe by declaring that the hair follicles found on the remains were too small for positive identification.

At the time of Carden's trial, the victim had not yet been positively identified. By order of Judge William Beaumont, the remains were cremated and the ashes spread at a Little Rock cemetery.

Arkansas *Democrat* reporter Mike Masterson became interested in this case. Even after Arkansas law enforcement agencies had given up hope of ever identifying the corpse, Masterson established the dead woman's identity. Through his analysis of the victim's tissue samples, fingerprints, and dental records and from information gathered from an interview with the family of Mildred Kay Honeycutt, of Pocahontas, Arkansas, Masterson correctly identified the dead woman. Honeycutt had recently been reported missing. Further, a handwriting sample of Honeycutt's contained four fingerprints that perfectly matched those of the dead

woman, which police had taken before her remains were cremated.

None of this forensic sleuthing aided Carden, who was convicted on May 28, 1982, of murdering Honeycutt and sent to prison for life. Two weeks later, Reverend Marlin Howe of North Little Rock received a call from William Walter Perry, the thirty-five-year-old boyfriend of the slain woman. "A man named Carden has already been convicted of that crime," he said, "and I do not want him to serve a life sentence for something I have done." He admitted to having an affair with Honeycutt, whose estranged husband was a friend of Perry's. Through the nagging conscience of a killer, the major break in the case had finally come.

Perry said an "inner voice" had commanded him to strangle the woman, which he did on the morning of September 10, 1982. He then took the body to a ditch off Highway 113. The prosecutor's office doubted the story at first, but forensic evidence later confirmed sperm samples as belonging to Perry and tied to the victim before the body was cremated. Perry was tried, convicted, and sent to prison for life.

A new trial for Carden was held, and his conviction was overturned on December 20, 1982. Carden decided to leave his past behind. He settled in New Mexico, where he found work as a truck driver. After having been wrongly imprisoned for seven months, and just before leaving Arkansas, Carden emphatically told court officials, "I have given up drinking for good."

## The Cop and the Killer

Jeffrey Scott Hornoff was a dedicated twenty-seven-year-old police officer serving on the Warwick, Rhode Island, police department in 1989. He was married and had an infant son. He was also a member of the Warwick police scuba and underwater assault team, and, in that capacity had reason to visit Warwick's Alpine and Ski Shop, where he met attractive twenty-nine-year-old Victoria

Cushman, a store clerk. He began an affair with Cushman but broke it off after a few months, saying that he wanted to remain friends but without any further romantic relationship.

Cushman, however, told some fellow workers that Hornoff was going to leave his wife to marry her. Then, on August 9, 1989, Cushman said that Hornoff wanted to have only a platonic relationship with her. Two days later, Cushman failed to appear at work. Several employees went to her home late on August 11, 1989, to find her dead, lying in a pool of blood. A seventeen-pound fire extinguisher found nearby had been used to bludgeon her to death.

In searching Cushman's apartment, police found an unmailed letter addressed to Hornoff in which Cushman stated that she realized she and Hornoff "could no longer have a future, but could continue to have a present." She obviously wanted to continue seeing the handsome young officer. When asked by fellow officers about his relationship with Cushman, Hornoff admitted knowing the woman, but denied having any sexual relationship with her. He later admitted having two sexual encounters with Cushman. There was no evidence that linked Hornoff to the murder of Cushman, and he had a solid alibi—he had been with his wife and several friends at a party on the night of Cushman's murder. Further, he voluntarily took a polygraph test conducted by Warwick police, and the results, according to three experts, indicated that he was telling the truth regarding his whereabouts on the night of the murder.

A grand jury considering all available evidence failed to indict Hornoff. Five years passed without any new clues or evidence in the case, although Hornoff was widely believed by local residents to have murdered Cushman. Carlo Pisturo, a Warwick city councilman, later stated that Hornoff had long been painted with a black brush: "By then it was almost common knowledge that Scott had killed the girl. All indications were that he was guilty and that the cops had covered for him."

This belief was shared by some of the officers of the Rhode Island state police, which took over the case from the Warwick police department. In 1996, a second grand jury, following the case offered by the Rhode Island state police, indicted Hornoff and he was brought to trial, charged with murdering Victoria Cushman. The prosecutor waved aside the alibi Hornoff offered, which was supported by several persons who insisted that he was attending a party on the night of the murder.

Hornoff, the prosecutor said, could have easily slipped away from the party, murdered the girl, and then returned to the party undetected. In this contention, the prosecutor failed to explain why, if that was the case, Hornoff would not have returned to the party coated with the victim's blood. Cushman's unmailed letter was entered as circumstantial evidence. This was the core of the prosecution's case. The flimsy case offered by the prosecution, however, was accepted by a jury that convicted Hornoff. After being sentenced to life in prison, Hornoff declared, "Am I guilty of something? Yes, I am. I broke my sacred wedding vows and for that I will never forgive myself."

In 1999, Hornoff's attorneys filed an appeal, but their arguments were dismissed by the Rhode Island Supreme Court. It appeared that Hornoff would spend the rest of his life behind bars. Then, according to Rhode Island attorney general Sheldon Whitehouse, "a one-in-a-million situation" occurred. On November 1, 2002, accompanied by his attorney, Todd Barry, a forty-five-year-old carpenter, whose brother, Ward Barry, was a retired Narragansett police officer, admitted to murdering Victoria Cushman. While his attorney, William Devereaux, stood by, Barry explained to officials that he had been consumed by guilt over an innocent man spending the rest of his life in prison for a crime he had committed. The guilt, according to Whitehouse, was something "bottled up in within him that appears to have boiled over."

Barry had met Cushman in 1988 and had seen her on and off for more than a year, even during the time Hornoff had a relationship with the woman, and admitted that their relationship had been "primarily sexual." Barry's name and telephone number was near the front of Cushman's Rolodex, which had been seized by police, but he had never been contacted or thought to be a suspect in the murder. He and Hornoff had never met. The attorney general's office spent the weekend checking all of the known facts involved in the Cushman murder with Barry's statements and, on November 4, 2002, concluded that Barry was telling the truth and officially charged him with Cushman's murder the following day. (He would be tried and sentenced to life in prison.)

On November 6, 2002, Jeffrey Scott Hornoff, age forty, was released from prison after spending six years, four months, and eighteen days behind bars for a murder he did not commit. A blizzard was raging at that time, but Hornoff was happy as a child to see it. He had nothing. He had lost his wife, Rhonda, who had divorced him years earlier, his position with the police force, his home, and his possessions. He owned nothing but the clothes on his back. On December 11, 2002, about 150 people attended a fund-raising dinner in Warwick, contributing more than $5,300 for the wrongly convicted Hornoff.

# Mistaken Identity

A COMMON ERROR THAT RESULTS IN END-less trials and wrongful convictions is the testimony of witnesses who wrongly identify a suspect. Such cases of mistaken identity are invariably made through innocent error, especially when a suspect bears a striking resemblance to the actual perpetrator. But such misidentifications have nevertheless brought about myriad wrongful convictions.

Witnesses throughout history have insisted to police and courtrooms that their identifications of suspects were positive. They detailed the appearance of those they identified down to the tiniest scar and the last wart. They described the physical actions of the suspects—a peculiar sideways nodding of the head, gesticulating of the hands and arms, a pigeon-toed or splayfooted walk. They catalogued every physical aspect of a suspect: bandy or bow legs; a flat, bulbous, or aquiline nose; a long, oval, or square face; curly, straight, or wavy hair; the color of hair and eyes, every color in the spectrum, including green and purple.

Exaggeration was traditionally rife in such identifications—a person with a small knot on a shoulder might be described as a hunchback; an undersize person might be described as a dwarf or midget; someone with a small head might be described as a pinhead. Police have traditionally been plagued by such routine descriptions when attempting to assemble a physical profile of a suspect that matches that of a perpetrator.

Mistaken identities are honest errors on the part of credible witnesses and are not to be confused with false identifications, which are purposely made to mislead police and courts. A classic case involving the latter instance was the wrongful conviction of Luigi Zambino in 1906, who was named as an accomplice by a clever, manipulating perpetrator because he knew that witnesses would mistakenly identify Zambino for his real crime partner—his own brother—who looked so much like Zambino as to be his twin. (See below, "Mistaken Identity: Classic and Obscure.")

In many mistaken identity cases, witnesses believe they have seen the suspect/perpetrator, when in fact poor vision, obstructions, or even mirages have limited, obscured, blocked, or misrepresented their ability to identify a suspect. Yet in their eagerness to serve society and their passion to see justice meted out, upstanding citizens have inadvertently harmed their fellow creatures in making mistaken identifications. Scores of innocent persons have gone behind bars for years or decades, some even forfeiting their lives, all because a "positive" eyewitness identification was nothing of the kind.

## Mistaken Identity Cases from History

Because of a slip of the tongue he made while drunk, Richard Coleman of Kingston, Surrey, was executed for a crime he apparently did not commit. In July 1748, while walking home late one night from a festival in Kennington Lane, young Sarah Green was raped and beaten and left for dead. But she survived and crawled home to Southwark.

At St. Thomas Hospital, she told doctors she thought her assailants were connected with Taylor's Brewhouse, a local pub. Two days later, Richard Coleman and Daniel Trotman stopped by the Queen's Head Alehouse in Bandy-Leg Walk for a drink. Already intoxicated, Coleman was asked by a stranger if he was the rogue who assaulted Sarah Green. "If I had, you dog, what then?" he answered, in turn insulting and threatening the stranger.

Suspicious of Coleman, Trotman went to a local magistrate to incriminate him in the assault against Sarah Green. When questioned by the constable, Coleman was sober and composed. He said he had no memory of his behavior at the Queen's Head Alehouse, but if he had said such a thing, it simply was not true. Still suspect, however, Coleman was twice brought before the dying woman. The first time she could not say with certainty whether or not he was the man who had attacked her. At the urging of her lawyer, Mr. Wynne, the suspect was brought back to Sarah and she made a positive identification.

Sarah Green soon died, and Coleman was indicted for murder. Fleeing to Pinner, near Harrow on the Hill, he dispatched a message to the local newspaper: "I, Richard Coleman, seeing myself advertised in the Gazette, as absconding on account of the murder of Sarah Green, knowing myself not any way culpable, do assert that I have not absconded from justice; but will willingly and readily appear at the next [judicial inquest], knowing that my innocence will acquit me."

On November 22, 1748, Coleman was arrested at Pinner and jailed at Southwark until the court convened in Kingston. The prosecution based its case on Sarah Green's shaky identification and Trotman's hearsay. Coleman was nevertheless found guilty and condemned to die at Kennington Common on April 12, 1749. Resigned to his fate, the condemned man bewailed the plight of his wife and children, who would henceforth depend on the charity of the church to survive. Coleman went to the gallows proud and defiant, protesting his guilt to the very last. More than a few people that day in Surrey believed that the courts had hanged an innocent man.

Six months after Coleman was hanged, a London barber went to the gallows, following a conviction based on the same kind of mistaken identity that had ensnared Coleman. Bosavern Penlez (1726–1749) was a hardworking barber in London. On July 1, 1749, three drunken sailors were robbed at a brothel in the Strand, near Penlez's home. When the sailors demanded their money back, they were ushered out. They then rounded up a number of comrades and returned to the establishment. The angry mob turned the women of the house out into the street and proceeded to wreck the place before setting fire to it. The sailors moved on to another brothel, where they duplicated their destruction before police arrived.

The next evening, twenty-three-year-old Penlez was on his way home when he saw a group of people trying to destroy what remained of one house. Penlez and two friends, intoxicated from an evening of revelry, ventured into the house only to be arrested along with the rest of the mob. In the trial at the Old Bailey, the owner of the house, Peter Wood, testified that Penlez and John Wilson were among the men who destroyed his house.

Several witnesses came forward to discredit Wood, claiming that Wood's identification of Penlez was mistaken, but the jury convicted Penlez and Wilson for their involvement in a riot. An acquaintance of the convicts, Benjamin Launder, was acquitted. The parishioners from St. Clement Danes petitioned for both men to be pardoned. The king was agreeable to the acquittal of both men, but Lord Chief Justice Willes said that an example had to be made to discourage further riots.

Wilson was ultimately freed, but Penlez was made to pay for the crime. A last-minute attempt to rescue him failed, and Bosavern Penlez was hanged at Tyburn on October 18, 1749. In honor of his memory, Penlez was given a proper burial in the graveyard at St. Clement Danes.

Where Coleman and Penlez in England were wrongly identified as obscure miscreants, many other innocent persons were mistaken for infamous or notorious criminals. Such was the case of Thomas Berdue. Because the people of San Francisco were enraged at the inability of the criminal laws to reduce the amount of crime that came with the gold rush to their city, and because he bore a remarkable resemblance to a notorious criminal, Berdue almost lost his life.

In 1850, when California had just been admitted to the Union as a state, San Francisco was the hub of gold fever, accompanied by a brutal crime wave of robberies and murder. On February 19, 1851, a shopkeeper, C. J. Jansen, was robbed in his dry goods store of $2,000, severely beaten, and left to die by two assailants. Jansen gave a description of the thieves, one of whom matched James Stuart, a thief and murderer from an Australian group of escaped convicts known as the "Sydney Men."

Within twenty-four hours, police had arrested two Australians. One was Robert Windred, apprehended as the accomplice. The other claimed to be Thomas Berdue, although he matched the description of Stuart. Jansen, still in critical condition, identified Berdue as his attacker. An angry crowd of almost seven thousand people tried to seize the prisoners as they were taken to the police station and attempted it a second time as the mob swelled by another two to three thousand. A popular court was formed, with judge, jury, and counsel, and the prisoners were tried in absentia in the recorder's room at city hall. Several more attempts were made to seize the two men, who barely escaped public execution.

Windred and Berdue were legally tried on March 14, 1851, with Jansen the main witness for the prosecution. A verdict of guilty was delivered by a jury and the convicted pair sentenced to fourteen years in the state prison. Berdue was then sent to Marysville, California, to stand trial for the murder of Charles Moore, a man Stuart had been accused of killing. At that trial, several witnesses positively identified Berdue, down to a scar on his right cheek and a stiff middle finger on one hand. Two defense witnesses, however, including a judge who had once tried Stuart, adamantly denied that the man on trial was the notorious Australian thief and murderer.

On July 4, 1851, the prisoner again was found guilty, and this time sentenced to be hanged. Berdue maintained his innocence throughout the trial. A month earlier, in June, a group of San Francisco businessmen dissatisfied with law enforcement in their city formed a vigilance committee. On July 1, 1851, a shack had been robbed and a party from the vigilance committee picked up a well-dressed, well-spoken man as they searched for the thief. Though he said his name was Willard Stevens, he proved to be James Stuart.

Letters were sent to the Marysville prison where Berdue was waiting to be executed. Stuart signed a full confession, admitting to the assault on Jansen, as well as to several other crimes. Berdue was pardoned by Governor John McDougall (1851–1852), and the vigilance committee, hearing that the wrongly convicted man was penniless, collected a fund of $302. Berdue's petition for reimbursement from the State of California for the $4,000 he had spent in his efforts to prove himself innocent was refused on the grounds that "to grant the prayer of the petitioner would establish a precedent which, if carried out in all cases of this kind, would more than exhaust the entire revenue of the State." This statement blatantly admitted that mistaken identity was as commonplace as wrongful convictions in California at that time.

While San Francisco experienced a crime wave in the early 1850s, a similar outbreak occurred in Ontario, Canada, and it offered the same results when residents believed they had captured the mastermind of a criminal gang behind the crime wave. Late in 1854, a gang of criminals embarked on a spree of burglaries, highway robberies, and murders in the Niagara peninsula of Ontario. Suspicion, in particular for the robbery and murder of John Hamilton Nelles on October 18, 1854, fell upon William Townsend, a resident of the area and the alleged leader of a gang bearing his name.

Townsend, who was noted for his cleverness in the use of disguises and dialects, initially eluded pursuers. His companions, however, John Blowes, William Bryson, and a man named King, were captured and, in spring 1855, were tried for the Nelles murder. Although all three testified that it was Townsend who had shot Nelles, they were found guilty. Blowes and King were later hanged, but Bryson, who had turned Queen's evidence, was sentenced to life imprisonment.

Townsend came out of hiding and resumed his criminal activity as early as November 1854. Crimes ranging from robbery to murder were attributed to him for the period between late 1854 and his arrest in 1857. John Iles, a Cleveland boardinghouse proprietor and former London constable who had known Townsend for eight or nine years, recognized him as he ate dinner in a saloon.

Townsend was arrested and charged with the murder of John Nelles. His trial began on September 27, 1857. Although Townsend did not say who he was, he insisted that he was not William Townsend. Large numbers of witnesses on either side took the stand to either affirm or deny the identity of the man standing trial. The jury, unable to reach a verdict, was discharged.

On March 26, 1858, Townsend was brought to trial again, this time for the murder of a constable, Charles Ritchie. Once again, the question of iden-

tity dominated the trial. The most persuasive piece of evidence presented by the defense was that Townsend was known to have large, misshapen feet, whereas the man standing trial in Ritchie's murder, who by now claimed to be a Scottish immigrant named Robert J. McHenry, was shown to have small, well-formed feet. On April 6, 1858, the jury announced its belief that the defendant was Robert J. McHenry, who bore an amazing resemblance to the wanted Townsend. He was judged not guilty and released.

In a strange burglary case, the mistaken identity made against a reputable dealer of expensive musical instruments had nothing to do with his appearance. The dealer possessed a priceless violin, which was thought to be stolen, leading to a wrongful conviction that wrecked the dealer's life. When an elderly German musician's prized Stradivarius violin was stolen, he lost the will to live. After his death, a dealer in musical instruments was wrongly convicted of stealing the violin and lived with the expense, shame, and guilt of the conviction for eight years.

In 1885, Jean Bott and his wife, Matilda Bott, emigrated from Germany to the United States, settling in New York City, so the elderly man, a former orchestra leader in Saxe-Meiningen, could give lessons and continue to play his beloved "Duke of Cambridge" Stradivarius violin. With a meager income, Bott unhappily decided to put his violin up for sale, and, through Victor S. Flechter, a dealer and friend, offered the Stradivarius to Nicolini, husband of famous opera singer Adelina Patti. But when Nicolini offered Bott a certified check, the financially inexperienced musician insisted on cash, and Nicolini, believing himself insulted, tore up the check and cancelled the deal. Flechter, angry at losing his commission, was later presumed to have stolen the violin in revenge.

On March 31, 1894, not long after the Nicolini incident, Bott returned home to find the Stradivarius gone. A sad and fruitless search ensued, with Flechter giving Mrs. Bott a letter suggesting she offer a $500 reward for the instrument's return.

She did, with no results. Mrs. Bott went to the district attorney, visiting the criminal courts building, and a detective named Colonel Allen became interested in the case, as did his friend, Harry P. Durden, and another detective, Mr. Baird. Sadly, on April 28, 1895, the heartbroken Bott, whose violin had been like a child to him, died at the Botts' Hoboken, New Jersey, boardinghouse, taking his own life.

Matilda Bott told Flechter that she was thinking of going back to Germany. Two days later Flechter wrote to a central office man, offering a genuine Stradivarius. Allen, the detective Matilda Bott had earlier contacted, saw the letter and immediately suspected the dealer. On May 28, 1895, Mrs. Bott received a letter signed "Cave Dweller," telling her that the violin "taken from your house some time ago will be returned if you are willing to abide by agreements that will be made between you and I later on." Mrs. Bott believed the letter to be written in Flechter's hand.

On June 23, 1895, Detectives Durden and Baird came to Flechter's and were shown a Stradivarius by the office clerk. Returning three days later, Flechter himself showed it to the detectives, explaining it had come from a retired merchant named Rossman, and was offered for $5,000. Asking to be allowed to take the violin to a rear room to show to a friend, Durden brought it to Mrs. Bott, who identified it as her late husband's most prized possession.

Flechter was arrested immediately. On August 28, 1895, an indictment against him accused the dealer of receiving stolen goods. His jury trial lasted for three weeks, with Arthur W. Palmer for the defense and James W. Osborne for the prosecution. Widely covered in the press, the case involved the testimony of a number of violin makers, including John J. Eller, and the testimony of several handwriting experts who believed that Flechter had written the "Cave Dweller" letter to Mrs. Bott. Flechter denied any guilt, asserting that his brother-in-law, John D. Abraham, was the author of an earlier letter to Matilda Bott that was used to connect him to the "Cave Dweller" missive. Abraham helped write the earlier note. The key witness for the defense, John J. Eller, claimed that the Stradivarius was his own instrument, which had been stolen by a music teacher, who later sold it to Flechter.

Flechter was found guilty and sentenced on May 22, 1896, to a twelve-month prison term. After serving three weeks in the Tombs, he obtained a certificate of reasonable doubt and was released on bail until his conviction could be reviewed on appeal. Disgraced, his reputation destroyed, and his business ruined, Flechter, after several years, was given another hearing at the appellate division of the Supreme Court. His conviction was sustained. Again, he paid the $5,000 bail and was free pending yet another appeal to the New York Supreme Court.

On August 17, 1900, Flechter found the "Duke of Cambridge" Stradivarius in the possession of the Springer family in Brooklyn. It was initially discovered by a violin maker, Joseph Farr, who had once worked for Flechter and had testified on his behalf at the trial. An investigation by the district attorney's office and the detective bureau uncovered the fact that the violin had been pawned at the shop of Benjamin Fox within an hour of its theft from the Bott home, for the sum of $4. It lay exposed on a shelf until a tailor named James Dooly bought it for $20 in December 1895; he later sold it to the Springers for $30. On July 7, 1902, the elderly Matilda Bott positively identified her late husband's violin, and Flechter was finally proved innocent.

## The Mistaken Identity and "Execution" of Will Purvis

Will Purvis (1872–1943) was a simple, twenty-one-year-old farmer living quietly in Marion County, Mississippi. His ambitions were confined to the daily ritual of plowing his fields and tending his livestock. Unthinkable in the mind of the young farmer in 1893 was that, in the following year, he would stand accused of a murder he did not commit, that he would mount a gallows before thousands of gaping spectators and be sent through a trapdoor only to survive his execution. For many, the strange salvation of Will Purvis was designed in heaven. It proved his innocence and condemned those who had brought about his wrongful conviction and an incomplete execution that convinced thousands of spectators that he had been saved by the "hand of God."

The Ku Klux Klan was a powerful secret society that held sway in the South for several decades following the Civil War. It almost went out of existence in the early 1890s, only to be reborn in 1915 as an underground society of racial terrorists. In Mississippi and other southern states, the KKK was replaced by a group called the White Caps, named for white caps with face masks that were worn by night riders. Full-flowing sheets smeared with red paint to simulate blood were also donned. Members of the White Caps mindlessly and sadistically busied themselves by threatening white farmers who were sympathetic to the workaday plight of black field hands and flogging blacks who defied them.

In early 1893, a black worker left the employ of a widow living in Marion County, going to work for a farmer named Will Buckley who paid him a higher wage. Some White Caps visited Buckley's farm and horsewhipped the worker, in spite of the fact that Buckley himself was a member of the White Caps. When Buckley learned of the beating (he was away from the farm at the time of the flogging), he flew into a rage and went to the grand jury, which, upon Buckley's testimony, indicted three leaders of the White Caps who were reportedly responsible for the flogging. Buckley, his brother Jim, and the black man, all riding horses, then proceeded home after the hearing.

As the trio forded a small stream, two men fired at them from thick bushes. Will Buckley fell dead from his saddle, and his brother Jim and the black man fled in a hail of bullets. Hours later, Jim Buck-ley swore to local lawmen that he recognized one of his brother's killers, Will Purvis, who was thought to be a member of the White Caps. Purvis's home was near the scene of the killing, and one of his neighbors, who had hated the Purvis family for years over a land dispute, immediately seized upon Jim Buckley's identification, stirring up hatred for the youth, urging that he be arrested and hanged. The Purvis family had long resided in Mississippi, the nearby town of Purvis was named after one of Will's ancestors, and Will had never been arrested before. Still, he was taken to the local jail and held for trial.

Many relatives and friends came forward at Purvis's trial to insist that he was at home with his family at the time of the Buckley shooting. It was proved that his shotgun, the kind of weapon used in the murder, had not been fired in a long time. Yet Jim Buckley's identification of Purvis was unshakable and Purvis was convicted and sentenced to be hanged.

On February 7, 1894, Will Purvis, his face pale from his many months of prison confinement, was led to a scaffold in the courthouse square at Columbia, Mississippi. His hands were tied to his sides, and the executioner held the black cap that was to cover Purvis's head. Purvis scanned the vast throng before him, estimated to be more than five thousand people. Indifferent farmers chewed tobacco and swapped jokes. Women passed out sandwiches from picnic baskets. Children frolicked through the throng. Peddlers yawped their wares and vendors hawked their food and drink.

"I can't hardly see a friendly face," Purvis said as he tried to recognize neighbors in the vast unsympathetic crowd. Some men in the throng began to shout for the executioner to "get on with it, get on with it!" Others took up the cry. A shrill-voiced woman screeched, "Confess, boy, for the sake of your immortal soul!" Her cry became a sickening chant: "Confess! Confess! Confess!"

The executioner took a step forward, holding up the black cap in one hand and the strongly knotted rope in the other. He suddenly stopped as

Will Purvis began to speak in a resolute, calm voice: "You are taking the life of an innocent man. There are people here who know who *did* commit the crime and if they will come forward and confess, I will go free. I did not do it. I am innocent!"

The crowd was not stilled by the young man's words, even though many believed him to be innocent as they scanned their neighbors for a response that might save Will Purvis from the noose. One of those in the crowd who thought a great wrong was about to be done was the Reverend J. G. Sibley, pastor of the Columbia Methodist Church.

During the many months Purvis waited in prison while exhausting his appeals, the pastor had visited the condemned man in his cell and Purvis became a convert to his church. Sibley then began to conduct church prayers for Purvis every Wednesday night until hundreds overflowed his little church. On the night before the hanging several hundred parishioners met in Columbia's town square and, at the foot of the gallows, knelt beneath flickering torchlight to pray that God would somehow intervene in the next day's execution. Sibley stood praying on the scaffold next to Purvis as he was positioned on the trapdoor the following morning, his ankles tied, a black cap slipped over his head.

From beneath the cap, Purvis murmured to the executioner, "Tell me when you are ready." The hangman shook his head in the direction of Sibley to indicate that a condemned person was never told when the trapdoor would be flung open so that he could not brace himself.

In the tense stillness, Reverend Sibley's resonant voice could be heard: "Almighty God, if it be Thy will, stay the hand of the executioner."

The sheriff came close to Purvis, placing his hand on the shoulder of the condemned man: "God help you, Will Purvis." He held up a small hand ax over the stay rope that held up the trapdoor. When the rope was chopped through, the door would spring open and Will Purvis would be sent to eternity.

A woman screamed wildly in the crowd as the ax was raised. She fainted, as did other females. A child near the gallows began to cry. The ax fell and the stay rope was spliced. A second later, the trapdoor flung open and Purvis plummeted downward. Many strong men turned their faces away and others merely gaped. Those who looked and expected to see the body suddenly jerk and dangle into death were dumbfounded as they watched Purvis go straight through to the ground. The rope, instead of tightening about the youth's neck like the unfeeling bony fingers of a garrotter, crazily untwisted, spinning away from Purvis's neck like a recoiling whip, burning his flesh but sending him very much alive to the earth beneath the gallows.

Purvis recalled, "I heard the door creak, my body plunged down, and all went black. When I regained consciousness, I heard someone say, 'Well, Will, we've got to do it all over again.'"

As he lay helpless beneath the gallows, Purvis also heard scores of dazed and horrified members of the crowd push forward, shouting, "What's the matter? Did the noose slip? They didn't tie the knot right!" Some would later claim that the hangman's rope was purposely misarranged, but a committee examining the rope and knot only minutes before the execution verified that all had been in order.

Somehow Purvis managed to stagger to his feet. The black cap slipped from his head and he blinked large blue eyes into a reddening sun, then at the crowd, which surged forward, its members aghast at his breathing body. Purvis turned to a deputy who had scrambled from the scaffold to him and bravely said, "Let's get it over with."

Many in the crowd began to shout that Purvis was innocent, that God had made a miracle and had saved him. Others shouted back that his survival was an accident. An official calmly leaned over the railing of the scaffold and shouted down to Dr. W. Ford, who was standing at the foot of the gallows, "Toss that rope up here, will you, doctor?"

Ford, who had publicly condemned the White Caps and had been one of Purvis's chief accusers, denouncing him repeatedly as a member of that group, picked up the rope. The elderly gray-haired physician held the rope in his hands while studying the face of Will Purvis, who calmly stared back at him. Then Ford threw the rope to the ground and shouted up to the official, "I won't do any such damn thing! That boy's been hung one too many times now!"

Spectators broke into pandemonium. Some screamed, "Don't let him hang again!" "He's guilty, hang him!" others roared back. Through this mounting panic, deputies half-carried Purvis back up to the gallows platform like a sack of potatoes. As they edged the youth toward the trapdoor, Sibley leaped forward in front of Purvis, standing on the trapdoor himself. A fire-and-brimstone orator of the most dramatic kind with an impressive appearance, the pastor's eyes flashed as he threw his arms skyward. His voice boomed over the throng, "People of Marion County! The Hand of Providence has slipped the noose! Heaven has heard our prayers! All those who want to see this boy hang a second time hold up their hands!"

The crowd was utterly mesmerized at Sibley's words. No longer were its members casual, anonymous observers at the execution of a fellow human being. They were now asked to signify their individual responsibility for the death of Will Purvis. They were asked, as their neighbors stood by as witnesses, to personally condemn for a second time a man who had survived his own execution. Not a single hand was raised. Reverend Sibley then cried out, "All those who are opposed to hanging Will Purvis a second time hold up your hands!"

As the officials on the gallows stared open-mouthed, they saw a sea of hands flutter upward, seemingly every hand in the huge throng, waving "as if magically raised by a universal lever," one eyewitness explained.

In an instant, public sentiment had swung wholly in Purvis's favor. Crowd members began to sing hymns as they sank row on row to their knees. Here were the steadfast believers in "That Old Time Religion," staunch unswerving defenders of "the Good Book." Men and women shouted hosannas and threw their hats in the air, as they swore Will Purvis should not be hanged. He had been saved by the hand of God. A miracle had happened. They had seen it with their own eyes.

The sheriff, his deputies, and hard-faced jailers shrank back on the scaffold bewildered and frightened. "What are we going do, sheriff?" asked one of his deputies. The sheriff scanned the crowd, which was now roaring that Purvis be released. Turning to Ford, who stood on the steps of the gallows, the sheriff said, "These folks don't want to see Purvis hanged again, doctor, but I am bound in honor to carry out the sentence of the court. Because the rope slipped, I can't see that the situation is altered. What do you think?"

"It's a point of law, I guess," said Ford. "See if you can find a judge or lawyer."

The sheriff shouted to the crowd, calling for any jurist or lawyer to come forward. A young lawyer pushed his way to the gallows steps and there held a conference with the sheriff. Meanwhile, Will Purvis stood mute, his head bent downward as he silently prayed with Sibley at his side.

Finally, the lawyer was heard to say, "The letter of the law must be adhered to. It is my belief that Purvis must be hanged by the neck until dead. That is in accordance with the meaning of his sentence." The sheriff nodded and began to mount the scaffold. He then looked over the crowd, which was chanting with one voice that Purvis be allowed to live. Ford suddenly blurted to the attorney standing next to him, "I don't agree with you." Then the aged doctor turned to the sheriff. "Now, if I go upon that scaffold and ask three hundred men to stand by me and prevent the hanging, what are you going to do about it?"

The sheriff blinked in amazement at the elderly Ford, behind whom a legion of strong young men swelled, inching up the scaffold steps. The sheriff was speechless for moments. He opened his mouth to form words but Ford cut him off, saying in a solemn voice, "I'm ready to do it, too." The sheriff walked to Will Purvis and untied his ankles and hands. The crowd roared its approval with a deafening blast.

"Don't let him go," Ford cautioned. "Take him back to his cell." Purvis was escorted back to jail and placed in his cell. This was not an easy task as hundreds in the crowd jostled the deputies, pulling at Purvis, insisting that he be set free immediately.

At a later hearing, the sheriff defended his actions, explaining that he could not have hanged Purvis again without risking the lives of his men. "The crowd had turned hostile, thousands of people. It might have meant open warfare. And they thought God was on their side. I ain't one to go up against five thousand folks and God, too." (This was not the only time Providence intervened in an official execution, many claimed. Ninety-one years earlier in Sydney, Australia, a convicted murderer, Joseph Samuels, was hanged three times, but the ropes kept breaking. He survived to see the real killer go the gallows. See Chronology, 1803.)

A commission thoroughly examined the rope used on Purvis, but could not explain its failure to hang the man. One of the staff executioners, Henry Banks, later told reporters what he thought might have happened. "The rope was too thick in the first place," Banks announced. "It was made of new grass and very springy. After the first man tied the noose, he let the free end hang out. It was this way when the tests were made, but when it came to placing this knot around Purvis's neck it looked untidy. The hangman did not want to be accredited with this kind of a job so he cut the rope flush with the noose knot. It looked neat but when the weight of Purvis's body was thrown against it, the rope slipped and the knot became untied." Banks's published statement was met with universal disdain by the God-fearing populace of Marion County.

Governor John M. Stone (1890–1896), on the other hand, did not believe in miracles of any kind. Will Purvis had been sentenced to hang, and the governor refused to commute his sentence. Lawyers for Purvis argued that he had already been hanged and that the State of Mississippi could not legally hang him again, basing their appeals on Article 5 of the U.S. Constitution dealing with double jeopardy. Three appeals were denied by the Mississippi Supreme Court, which decreed that Will Purvis would indeed be hanged again, on December 12, 1895, almost two years after he had survived the gallows.

Public opinion, however, had become a tidal wave of support for Purvis, who continued to quietly pray in his cell for deliverance. Jailers, in an extraordinary move, took Purvis from the strong jail in Columbia and put him into a ramshackle box of a jail in his hometown of Purvis, only a few weeks before his scheduled second hanging. When the governor demanded to know why this had been done, the sheriff of Marion County replied that he had approved of the transfer so that Purvis "could be near relatives and friends in the last few weeks of his life."

It came as no surprise to many, including the jailers, that those very relatives and friends, a few days before Purvis was to be hanged, stormed the tiny jail and freed the condemned man, spiriting him away to a remote farm, where he lived in hiding. In 1897, Jim Buckley changed his mind, publicly stating that he was not certain, after all, if Will Purvis had shot and killed his brother. Moreover, a new governor, Anselm J. McLaurin (1896–1900), was elected. He who had stated in campaign speeches that Will Purvis had been saved by the hand of God and that he would commute Purvis's sentence to life imprisonment if the fugitive would turn himself over to lawmen.

Will Purvis rode into Columbia on the back of a farm wagon, while thousands cheered him all the way to the sheriff's office. He went back to prison and began serving his sentence. Then began a statewide campaign to free Purvis. Thousands signed a petition asking that he be released. Even the district attorney who had prosecuted the farm boy signed the petition. On December 19,

1898, Will Purvis was granted a full pardon. Some months later, while farming his homestead, Purvis met the daughter of a local preacher and married her a short time later, a union that produced eleven children.

Yet the only evidence that had freed Purvis was Jim Buckley's recantation of his original identification of Puvis, which he later claimed to be a case of mistaken identity. Beyond the law of Mississippi, there was a different kind of evidence, "an act of God," evidence wholly acceptable to most of the people of that God-fearing state. Equally amazing was the corroboration of that act of God in 1918. In the spring of that year, a dissolute old man named Joe Beard stumbled into a backcounty Holy Rollers meeting in the middle of the night. He sat silent in a rear pew, sickly and sinful. As the congregation swayed and swooned in its religious tremors, Joe Beard stood up, then quaked his way down the aisle to the pulpit, where he knelt before the preacher and cried out a lifetime of offenses.

To the religious zealots surrounding him, Beard shockingly stated that it had been he, not Will Purvis, who had hidden in ambush with one Louis Thornhill, then deceased, and shot the hapless Will Buckley to death. Beard, who had borne an amazing resemblance to Purvis in his youth, then collapsed and was taken to a sickbed, where he again confessed to the murder before stenographers and a host of witnesses, not dying until he had once and for all cleared the name of Will Purvis.

Good people throughout Mississippi knowingly patted their Bibles and nodded, "I told you so." The legislature of Mississippi did much more than that, voting in a special meeting to pay Purvis $5,000 compensation for his years of wrongful imprisonment. Will Purvis, who would die at age seventy-one in 1943, never lost faith that he would be saved from the hangman, even in his darkest hours. "God heard our prayers," he remarked shortly before his death. "He saved my life because I was an innocent man." Purvis also never lost a grim reminder of his nightmare ordeal in 1894—the rope burns around his neck, which he bore to the grave.

## Mistaken Identity: Classic and Obscure

One of England's classic cases of mistaken identity involved Adolph Beck (1841–1909), a sometime clerical worker who led a nomadic life, living at times in Norway, South America, and England. Although he was a drifter, Beck was no criminal. Yet he was so firmly identified as such by a number of witnesses that he was sent to prison for crimes he did not commit, while his double remained at large to go on defrauding and stealing.

In late November 1896, Beck was walking along London's Victoria Street when Ottilie Meisonnier, a language teacher, stared at him as he passed beneath the street lamps. She walked up to Beck and held on to his arm, demanding the return of two wristwatches and some rings. "You stole my jewelry and I want it back!" she insisted.

Beck tried to pull away, but the determined woman clung to him. He managed to yank his arm free and then, spotting a constable, summoned the policeman, and asked him to deal with the woman who was accosting him. Beck told the constable that he thought the woman was drunk. The teacher explained that Beck was a thief, having bilked her out of her jewelry two weeks earlier. The constable took both Beck and Meisonnier to the Rochester Row police station.

There the teacher explained how Beck had approached her in early November,

**Adolph Beck, a sometimes clerk, was convicted twice (1896, 1901) for fraud in London, crimes that had been committed by a startling look-alike.** *History Inc./Jay Robert Nash Collection.*

tipping his hat to her and addressing her as Lady Everton. When realizing his mistake, he had told Meisonnier how much she resembled the beautiful noblewoman, whom he knew well as one of his peer group. Beck, continued the teacher, had mentioned his vast estate in Lincolnshire, his six gardeners, and his friendship with Lord Salisbury, then prime minister of England. The two of them had gone off to a restaurant, where Beck had told the naive teacher that he had been smitten by her, and insisted she tour the Riviera with him on his yacht. Her clothes and jewelry, he had said, would not do, however, as the couple would travel through "high social strata."

Beck had given her a check for £40 and told her to buy some new clothes. He then took her two wristwatches and some rings, saying that he would have them refitted with better mountings. He arranged to meet her later but never arrived at the rendezvous. His check, of course, was worthless, and Meisonnier realized that she had been victimized in one of the oldest confidence games practiced.

Beck was put into a lineup and Meisonnier once again positively identified him as the swindler. In addition, several other women came forward and were equally sure that Beck was the man who had worked a similar fraud on them. Two policemen then identified Beck as a thief and con man named John Smith, whom they had repeatedly arrested in the past. A handwriting expert named Gurrin (who would later offer wrong comparisons and testimony in the case of George Edalji, another wrongly convicted man) testified that he had examined the writing on the bogus check written by the swindler and Beck's handwriting, and found them the same.

Still claiming innocence, Beck was brought before a judge who recognized him as the man named Smith, someone he had sent to prison before. Beck was convicted of defrauding Meisonnier and sent to prison for seven years; he was even given Smith's old prison number. To seal his fate, Beck was *positively* identified as Smith, when his Bertillon measurements were compared with those of Smith. One discrepancy presented itself, but authorities dismissed it as a clerical error. The Smith records showed that Smith had been circumcised, but Beck had not.

After serving five years, Beck was released. Again, while walking along a London street three years later, a young woman ran up to him, calling for the police, telling constables that Beck had swindled her out of her jewelry. Once more, after being *positively* identified by eyewitnesses, Beck was tried and convicted. While he was waiting to be sentenced, Detective Inspector John Kane heard of another swindler who had been using the same methods as Smith and he visited this man in a detention cell.

When Kane took a look at this man, he stepped back in shock. The prisoner, whose real name was Wilhelm Mayer, was the exact double of Adolph Beck, and he had been using the aliases William Thomas and John Smith for years. It was quickly proven that Mayer was the real culprit and had committed all the crimes for which Beck had been accused and for which he had served five years of his life.

Mayer was sent to prison and Beck released with apologies. In compensation for his five years imprisonment, Beck was awarded £5,000 by the government. The embittered Beck, however, had become so dissolute by the time he received the money that he spent it wastefully, dying in the gutter in 1909.

Beck's fate was shared in 1905 by a hardworking mill hand bearing a striking resemblance to a notorious counterfeiter. He too went behind bars after a witness mistook him for his criminal

Wilhelm Mayer, who was Beck's exact double, was identified as the real confidence man by Detective Inspector John Kane; Beck, who had served prison time for Mayer's crimes, was given £5,000 in compensation, but nevertheless died in poverty in 1909. *History Inc./Jay Robert Nash Collection.*

doppelganger. In December 1905, Luigi Zambino, a Massachusetts mill hand, was implicated by Frank Manfra in the passing of counterfeit $5 silver certificates. Manfra was arrested in New York City, where he passed the phony bills and identified Zambino as his accomplice. Zambino was jailed in Trenton, New Jersey, and indicted for counterfeiting and fraud in June 1906 following a grand jury investigation.

Zambino's trial began July 11, 1906, with Manfra already convicted and testifying for the prosecution. Also working against Zambino was the testimony of liquor store owner Charles Wyatt, who positively identified Zambino as the man who had accompanied Manfra when the two attempted to pass the counterfeit bills in his store.

Despite Zambino's claims that he had been at work on the day of the incident, he was found guilty and sentenced to six years at hard labor in the New Jersey state prison and fined $500. After Zambino had been convicted and sent to prison, an attorney in Lawrence, Massachusetts, became interested in the case and discovered that Zambino's alibi was sound. Both Zambino's overseer and the timekeeper confirmed with certainty that Zambino had been at the mill on the days in question.

The overseer and timekeeper were subpoenaed but failed to appear at Zambino's trial. Charles Wyatt's identification was dismissed when it was discovered that Manfra, who by this time had been arrested again for passing the same kind of bad bills, had a brother who closely resembled Zambino, and whose likeness to Zambino convincingly challenged Wyatt's identification. Manfa had recognized Zambino as a near twin to his brother and, to protect that brother from prosecution, named Zambino as his partner in crime.

Massachusetts attorney J. C. Sanborn appealed the conviction, pointing out the fact that Zambino had been a victim of mistaken identity. Zambino was formally released by a full and unconditional pardon granted by President William Howard Taft (1909–1913) on November 24, 1909. At the time of his release, Zambino had served more than three years of his sentence, sent behind bars because he had a face almost identical to the real culprit's.

President Taft had the chilling experience of granting another pardon the next year to a wrongly convicted person who had been sent to prison for the same reason that had incarcerated Zambino—a case of mistaken identity. That victim, a wealthy horse owner named Willard Powell, was able to prove that he was more than a thousand miles away from the elaborate conspiracy for which he was convicted.

In March 1908, a Cabool, Missouri, storeowner, Henry Stogsdill, became unwittingly involved in a complicated scheme to fleece millionaires at the racetrack in Denver. William Scott asked Stogsdill to help him get even with some wealthy employers, who, he said, had cheated his cousin, Frank Maxwell. Stogsdill agreed to take betting money at the racetrack. The race would be fixed, Scott explained, so the millionaires' horse would lose. To prove that he was a man of means and trustworthy, Stogsdill asked his bank to send $10,000, but was only able to get $3,000 by mortgaging his property. Matching the funds, he later loaned $3,000 for the day to Maxwell. Taking $10,000 in bet money, Stogsdill became nervous and apprehensive when a jockey and a horse fell, and the millionaires' horse won.

Stogsdill pulled a gun and started for the jockey, who had thrown the race by faking a fall and using a blood pack in his mouth. Stogsdill left to await his returns, but neither his own $3,000 nor any of the share of the cash fleeced from the millionaires was delivered. J. S. Swenson, a post office investigator, was apprised of the bilking schemes that were going on in Denver and other cities. The massive fraud, known as "The Millionaires Club," was masterminded by John C. Mabray, who was arrested in Arkansas in late spring.

Eighty con artists had participated in the scam, and a federal grand jury in Iowa returned an indictment on September 23, 1909, against Mabray and about eighty codefendants. Willard Powell, known in Denver as "The Waco Kid," owned horses and followed the racing season through several states with them. Powell was accused of being part of the scheme, and Stogsdill positively identified him in court as one of the men who had been in Denver as part of the bilking.

Powell claimed that Stogsdill had mistaken him for someone else, a confidence man who bore a strong resemblance to Powell. Further, Powell insisted that he had been in Havana in March 1908. Fifteen of the defendants went to trial. Powell was among the fourteen found guilty and was sentenced on March 21, 1910, by Judge McPherson to two years in Leavenworth and fined $10,000. Defense counselors, however, canvassed Denver hotels soon after the conviction and learned that Stogsdill had been at Denver's Brown Palace Hotel on March 19, 1908. The race had taken place in Denver on March 28, 1908. Powell, however, proved that he was in Cuba at that time. He was granted a full pardon by President William Howard Taft on July 12, 1910.

Thirty-five years after President Taft pardoned Powell, President Harry S. Truman (1945–1953) pardoned a man who had twice been the victim of mistaken identity. At the age of eighteen, Charles Bernstein, born in 1897, decided to give up a criminal career after spending fourteen months at the Elmira Reformatory for stealing from a New York drugstore. Crime, however, would follow Charles Bernstein, for the conviction remained on his record and eventually led to his conviction for bank robbery and murder, neither of which he committed.

While Bernstein was on a business trip to St. Paul, Minnesota, a bank robbery was committed the same day in Hopkins, a town just west of the state capital. Police looking into hotel guest lists discovered Bernstein, who, upon checking, had a prior conviction. In February 1919, he was arrested in New York and returned to Minnesota for trial. Though many eyewitnesses stated that Bernstein could not have been the robber, others swore that he was bandit, based on their eyewitness identifications. Bernstein was found guilty and sen-

tenced to five to forty years in prison. He served nine years at the state prison in Stillwater before he was paroled in 1928 at the urging of prosecutor Floyd B. Olson, who felt that Bernstein had been the victim of mistaken identity. Olson would later become the state's governor (1931–1936).

Four years later, the unbelievable happened. Bernstein was charged with killing a gambler named Milton W. "Milsie" Henry in Washington, D.C., on April 21, 1932. Henry was shot with five bullets from a sawed-off shotgun while sitting in his car. The man pulling the trigger was observed by government attorney Carroll Rhodes just after the shooting, and the day before by laundry driver James Hughes. Again, though witnesses for the defense outnumbered those for the prosecution, Bernstein lost the trial. Rhodes and Hughes positively identified Bernstein as the killer. He was found guilty on March 24, 1933, and sentenced to death by electrocution on October 7, 1933.

An investigation was reopened when it was learned that the testimony of the prosecution's eyewitnesses was suspect. Rhodes had poor eyesight and would have had to look through a tree and a distance of seventy feet to see the killer, if he had even looked out his window, which he told a coworker he had not. Witness Hughes had apparently made up his story. Eventually President Franklin D. Roosevelt (1933–1945) commuted Bernstein's sentence to life in prison on May 28, 1935, twelve days prior to Bernstein's eighth execution date. On June 13, 1940, Roosevelt commuted the sentence further to time served already, and a full and unconditional pardon was granted by President Harry S. Truman on April 30, 1945.

## Mistaken Identity in the Roaring Twenties

According to Jazz Age chronicler F. Scott Fitzgerald, "all Gods were dead" in the opulent era of the 1920s. For many, the traditional perceptions of law and order were also defunct as shady businesses boomed and Wall Street, vacuous of the actual earnings of its inflated stocks, soared to dizzy heights. Inside this synthetic era of easy living and easy morals, Prohibition nurtured the development of gangsters and the U.S. crime syndicate. Lawlessness became chic and bank robberies and highway stickups were commonplace, embracing the reckless philosophy of "take what you can when you can." Caught in the flotsam and jetsam of this fabulous and uncontrolled decade were many an innocent person, invariably identified for crimes they did not commit. As usual, and has been the case in all ages, the impoverished, the disenfranchised, and minority groups were the most likely victims of such travesties of justice.

Typical were four Mexican migrant fruit pickers in California who happened to be in the vicinity of a recent bank robbery. They were not only available suspects but easy police targets, offering quick convictions that would settle local angst and apprehensions. While on their way through the San Gabriel Valley en route to Los Angeles, where they were to pick oranges, four young Mexicans driving a rented Ford were stopped on the highway and charged with robbery on April 5, 1922. The migrant workers were Broulio Galindo, Jose Hernandez, Salvador Mendival, and Faustino Rivera.

An hour earlier, the First National Bank of Arcadia, California, was robbed of $9,000 in currency, silver, bonds, and American Express Travelers Cheques. The bandits made a clean getaway until the Chevrolet they were driving plunged into a ravine. A farmer named Virgil Barlow who lived south of Arcadia saw the speeding car career off the road and went to investigate. The disabled car had continued on for three-quarters of a mile before the bank robbers abandoned it near a bridge crossing the San Gabriel River. The police later surmised that the men had switched cars.

The four Mexicans were charged with the holdup after a cache of revolvers was found inside the Ford. They were used for rabbit shooting, they said. Several of the bank tellers and customers mistakenly picked out Galindo and Hernandez as the bank robbers. Based on this testimony, three of the Mexicans were convicted of armed robbery on November 6, 1922. Salvador Mendival received a term in San Quentin of one to ten years. Broulio Galindo and Jose Hernandez were taken to Folsom Prison, where they began serving sentences of one year to life.

Just as the bars slammed shut behind them, a man identified only as Jack Thomas requested an interview with the deputy district attorney. He told them that the Mexicans were innocent and that the real robbers were Frank Sullivan, W. F. McMahon, Tom Gray, and Eddie Burns. The four new suspects were arrested in Los Angeles on an unrelated charge. It took nearly two years to assemble a case against them, while all the time the Mexicans languished in prison. Finally, on May 2, 1924, Mendival received a pardon. Hernandez was released on May 26, and Galindo four months later. The fourth member of the party, Faustino Rivera, died in jail before trial. None received any compensation from the state for their time spent behind bars.

Five months after the California bank robbery that had brought about the wrongful imprisonment of the four migrant workers, two union electricians were accused of assaulting two nonunion workers in Washington, D.C. Mistaken identity sent Robert N. Sisson and Maurice J. Sullivan behind bars. Although Sisson and Sullivan had alibis supported by several people that explained their whereabouts on the night of September 20, 1922, they, along with Earle D. Dean, were convicted of assault and battery against two coworkers. Sisson and Dean were sentenced to five years and Sullivan sentenced to seven years at the reformatory in Lorton, Virginia.

A year and a half later, Dean confessed that he and seven other men were guilty of the crime and that Sisson and Sullivan had nothing to do with it. Although seven other men confessed, several were given lighter sentences than either Sisson and Sullivan. The faulty convictions were based on mistaken identification. The victims, James R. Keeton and Judson L. Powers, who were employed as electricians at the Pullman Company in Washington, D.C., were accosted by seven coworkers because they had failed to comply with a union-organized strike. Keeton and Powers had applied for union membership, but the strike had broken out before they were approved.

Of those seven newly convicted, three received three-year sentences, two others were sentenced to two and a half years, and the others each received a year and a half. On July 12, 1924, Sisson and Sullivan were formally pardoned by President Calvin Coolidge.

Whereas the mistaken identity of the two Washington, D.C., electricians involved several guilty persons, Edward A. Kimball, an upstanding citizen, was wrongly identified as a notorious confidence man (shades of Adolph Beck). After one man had mistakenly identified him, another man suddenly appeared at his trial to make the same mistaken identity. Kimball, a mild-mannered man whose primary interests were religion and books, was tried and convicted. When the judge told the jury that he felt the verdict was a mistake, the twelve members requested a meeting with him in his chambers. He said it was unfortunately too late.

On June 10, 1926, Edward A. Kimball, a forty-seven-year-old philosophy student and devoted supporter of the Salvation Army, waited for the train in Baltimore, Maryland, that would take him to the sesquicentennial celebration in New York City. An excited Michael Funicielo suddenly ran up to Kimball and told a policeman to arrest him, claiming Kimball had swindled him out of $15,000 at the Emerson Hotel just hours earlier.

Funicielo had come to Baltimore with a man named Costello, stopping there on June 8, 1926, on their way to Washington, where Costello said they could buy whiskey permits and sell them for a big profit. On the train, Costello had received a telegram explaining that he should stop over in Baltimore for a conference. At dinner in the Joyce

Hotel, Costello found a wallet under the table containing a large amount of cash, notes on what appeared to be stock market investments, and a telegram addressed to a Mr. Moyer at the Emerson Hotel. Funicielo accompanied Costello as he returned the wallet to a grateful Moyer, who offered a reward that Costello refused.

Moyer then offered to give the two men some hot stock market tips. After a long and convoluted process during which Moyer claimed to have invested $60,000 that had grown into $181,000, and had introduced the two men to a "Mr. Rose, manager of the stock exchange," Funicielo ultimately turned over $15,000 of his own money and was left waiting for Costello and Moyer to return. They never did. After several hours, the suspicious Funicielo went to the front desk to inquire about Moyer and saw a man he believed he recognized as "Mr. Rose" getting into a cab. Following the taxi to the train station, Funicielo pointed out Kimball, and police officer William Curd arrested him as the swindler.

Kimball was charged with grand larceny of the $15,000 and indicted on June 28, 1926. On November 10, 1926, Kimball appeared before Judge Eugene O'Dunne. A surprise witness for the prosecution, Joseph Elsie of Canton, Ohio, described a similar swindle in Chicago on April 27, 1925, in which he had lost $17,000 to a man who matched Costello's description. Costello, then calling himself "Madison," had worked that swindle with another man whom Elsie positively identified as Kimball, noting his distinctive glasses. Kimball took the stand in his own defense and testified that he was innocent, and had been elsewhere at the times he was alleged to be bilking Funicielo and Elsie, his testimony corroborated by his wife, son, and an old friend.

Nevertheless, after an hour of deliberation, the jury delivered a verdict of guilty. Judge O'Dunne said he believed the judgment was "a terrible mistake," but that nothing further could be done. At a new trial on January 7, 1927, again before O'Dunne, twenty-five exhibits gave conclusive evidence that

Kimball could not possibly have been in Chicago when the Elsie swindle occurred. Kimball's attorneys also provided evidence that Kimball was not present when Funicielo had been swindled, and he was judged not guilty. Judge O'Dunne apologized to Kimball, explaining that there was no provision of restitution for wrongful conviction in Maryland under present law.

There would be no restitution for the wrongful Illinois murder conviction of Henry Olson, which was based on mistaken identity. Olson, however, regained his freedom through the actions of a young woman who wanted justice served for a man she had never met. Floyd Stotler, a Rockford, Illinois, gas station attendant, was shot to death during a robbery attempt on September 6, 1927. His father, Orville Stotler, also an attendant, witnessed the shooting.

Police apprehended a number of suspects, including twenty-six-year-old mechanic Henry Olson, who generally fit Stotler's description of the killer. Because the robber had covered his face with a handkerchief, and because Olson had an alibi, police released him. Stotler failed to identify his son's murderer after he viewed several suspects. A week later, however, Stotler identified Olson immediately when he was added to the group in a police lineup. Olson was arraigned on October 7, 1927, and brought to trial October 24, 1927, in the Winnebago County courtroom of Judge Arthur E. Fisher.

Many witnesses for the defense described Olson's activities on the night of the murder, none of which put him anywhere near the crime scene. They discredited Stotler's testimony, saying he had changed the description of the bandit since the day of the shooting. The jury deliberated, but the vote was a 6–6 deadlock and a new trial was ordered to begin on February 13, 1928. This time, Olson was found guilty and sentenced to life imprisonment in Joliet Prison.

However, pending appeal, Olson was released on $10,000 bond. Granting bond in this case was an extraordinary measure, given the fact that Olson

had been sentenced to life imprisonment for a capital crime. Authorities, however, believed that his conviction was questionable and they wanted him and his attorneys enough time to not only prepare an appeal but possibly develop new evidence that would exonerated him. Though he was not considered a fugitive risk, Olson nevertheless vanished from Rockford, instigating a nationwide search.

While Olson was a fugitive, the police received a tip that the real killer was eighteen-year-old George Bliss. His partner, Maurice Mahan, bragged to his girlfriend that he and Bliss had committed the crime, and someone who was a Bliss look-alike was going to serve time. The young woman was incensed by the scheme and she went to authorities, repeating Mahan's story. Bliss and Mahan were arrested. They pleaded guilty before Judge Edward D. Shurtleff. Bliss was sentenced to thirty years, while Mahan received fourteen. Exonerated, Henry Olson returned from exile in New Orleans, where he had almost given up any idea that he would be vindicated. In his third trial, however, that is exactly what happened. On March 16, 1928, he was acquitted and set free.

Like Olson before him, Louis Klass went through two trials before he was sent to prison. And, like Olson, Klass had been convicted on the eyewitness testimony of two upstanding citizens who "positively" identified him as the perpetrator of a sensational bank robbery. Klass's ordeal began in spring 1928. Desperate to arrest at least one of four men who robbed the First National Bank of Spring Valley, Minnesota, of $15,000, police arrested Louis Klass and charged him with the crime. As would be proved three years later, Klass had had nothing to do with the robbery, even though he looked like one of the men who participated in that holdup.

Detectives were hot on the trail of the thieves the same day the robbery occurred, May 7, 1928. On that day, bank president Lyle Hamlin and vice president C. A. Gilbert chose Klass from a group of several police photos, which were on record since Klass had a criminal record in Iowa. Before police could arrest him, Klass, knowing he was wanted, surrendered to authorities. He denied participating in the Spring Valley holdup. Regardless of a sound alibi provided by twelve witnesses, Klass was convicted. Because of irregularities in his first trial, Klass was granted a retrial on June 10, 1929. Once again, he was found guilty, chiefly on the strength of his identification by Hamlin and Gilbert. He was sentenced to a maximum thirty-year stay at Stillwater.

Meanwhile, Frank Devers, a convicted criminal, confessed that he had participated in the Minnesota robbery and Klass had not. He later retracted his confession, but because Devers bore a strong resemblance to Klass, the attorney representing Klass decided to follow up on his hunch and, with police assistance, brought Devers to meet Hamlin and Gilbert.

Klass had been convicted almost solely on Hamlin's and Gilbert's identification. The bankers, who had been convinced enough of Klass's identification to allow him to be convicted and sentenced, retracted their identification of Klass upon seeing Devers. On July 16, 1931, after three years of litigation and one year in prison, Klass was granted a full pardon.

Where two bankers in Minnesota made mistaken identities of Louis Klass, five women in Massachusetts in the same year insisted that a dishwasher had stolen their purses in a crime spree that had been plaguing police for three months. In the summer of 1928, a purse snatcher stalked female pedestrians in Somerville, Massachusetts. On September 1, 1928, twenty minutes after one of the robberies, police arrested a hotel dishwasher matching the description of the offender. Once forty-five-year-old Benjamin F. Collins was in custody, several victims identified him as the man who had robbed them.

Somerville police officers, however, were uncomfortable with Collins's arrest, after realizing that he had no prior police record and appeared to be a law-abiding citizen who kept to himself, worked without complaint at his job, and caused

no trouble. Officers repeatedly told assistant district attorney Richard S. McCabe that they believed Collins was not the thief. McCabe retorted, "I've got a bunch of women who have positively identified him and that's good enough for me."

McCabe ignored the officers and charged Collins with seven counts of larceny and two counts of robbery. Based on the eyewitness testimony of Catherine Davis, Carrie M. Decker, Marion P. Jackson, Cecelia Ketter, and Mildred King, five of the purse snatcher's victims, Collins was found guilty and sentenced on October 23, 1928, to serve between two and a half and three and a half years in prison. Four days later, another woman was victimized.

On October 27, 1928, the purse snatcher struck again but was apprehended after being shot and wounded by a police officer. After police searched George Hill's Medford apartment and recovered many of the stolen purses, he gave a full confession. Collins was given a second trial, acquitted of all charges, and released. Hill, who was a striking look-alike to Collins, pleaded guilty and was sent to a state penitentiary, where he later died from an infection in the gunshot wound. The Massachusetts legislature later vetoed payment of reparations to Collins for his wrongful conviction, nor did he receive any apologies from the five women who had mistakenly identified him.

## From the Look-Alike Legions

One victim of mistaken identity swore that he would clear his own name following his prison release. After his good name had been sullied and his lucrative business ruined, this victim did what most in his position do not—he went looking for the real culprit, his twin, in the dark side of the world. In February 1938, police knocked on the door of Bertram Campbell (1886–1946), a securities salesman for several leading New York brokerage houses, and told him that he was going downtown as a suspect in a forgery case.

Five bank tellers picked Campbell out of a lineup as the man who had cashed two checks totaling $4,160 under the name of George Workmaster. Insisting that he was innocent, Campbell was nevertheless convicted of forgery and sentenced to five to ten years at Sing Sing. Late in 1941, Campbell was paroled, but the three years in prison had taken their toll. The man was sick, but determined to clear his name. He worked as a bookkeeper for the next three years, saving his money—an "investigative repository" one might say, while he researched recent forgery cases in the United States. Then, early in 1945, he read a report about a forger whom the FBI had arrested in Kentucky and returned to New York for arraignment.

The description of Alexander Thiel's crimes so perfectly matched the forgery Campbell had been charged with that Campbell hired a lawyer to investigate. That investigation unearthed many photos of Thiel, who bore an astounding resemblance to Campbell. The attorney then knew that Campbell had been the victim of mistaken identity.

When Thiel was brought before the five bank employees whose testimony sent Campbell to prison, they admitted their earlier error and said that Thiel, who looked like Campbell, was the real forger. The FBI learned that Thiel was "Mr. X," a slippery forger and drug addict who had bilked banks of $600,000 for more than forty years. Bert Campbell was pardoned and awarded a $115,000 settlement for lost earnings and personal humiliation. Just eighty-two days after winning the settlement, Campbell died of a stroke.

Campbell was an exceptional man. Most wrongly convicted persons would not have taken the extra steps he employed in clearing their name, let alone seek out the true perpetrator. Such victims gratefully settle for prison release, since most are not in a position to do anything else. In the case of a postman wrongly convicted through mistaken identity, the very man who sent him to prison brought about his release by identifying a look-alike who had committed the actual crimes.

A string of rapes in Tennessee led two victims to point out thirty-one-year-old Douglas Forbes as the man who had assaulted them. Forbes, a postman from Elizabethton, Tennessee, was playing volleyball at a Veterans Administration hospital, where he was being treated for stress, when he was identified in 1973.

After the women picked out the man who taught Sunday school at the church where he was a deacon, Forbes, a father of six, was arrested. The rapes continued during his trial, but prosecutor Louis May was so sure Forbes was the rapist that he vowed to Forbes's family "that if they could prove he was innocent, I would fight to free him." In 1975, Forbes was sentenced to sixty years in prison, but the prosecutor kept his word.

While in prison, Forbes was attacked and almost killed by another inmate who jammed a sharpened broom handle down his throat. On September 9, 1980, however, the end of Forbes's suffering in prison was in sight when police arrested Jerry Williams in Johnson City, Tennessee, less than ten miles from Elizabethton, whom Louis May identified as a dead ringer for Douglas Forbes. When Williams confessed to a number of rapes, May questioned him about the two attacks attributed to Forbes. Williams then admitted that he had committed the two attacks. Williams was convicted and sent to prison, while May conducted a vigorous campaign to legally secure Forbes's innocence. The prosecutor convinced Tennessee Governor Lamar Alexander (1979–1987) to pardon the wrongly convicted man, and Forbes was released from prison on November 25, 1980.

An innocent man in Washington, D.C., was sent to prison in the same year Forbes was wrongly convicted in Tennessee. Like Forbes, this man was a victim of mistaken identity, and, also like Forbes, would be released through the extraordinary efforts of a city official, in this case a diligent and dogged detective who more than earned his right to wear the badge.

On November 2, 1974, Rodney Frazier was shot and killed in his Washington, D.C., home when a man tried to steal drugs. In April 1975, twenty-eight-year-old Bradford Brown was picked up by police on a gun charge and, because he fit the description of Frazier's killer and had been picked up on Frazier's block ten months earlier, he became a suspect in the murder. An eyewitness positively identified Brown as the slayer: "I am sure of this guy's face. I will never forget his face." Brown was convicted on November 28, 1975, and sentenced by Judge Norma Johnson to a prison term of eighteen years to life. The convicted man continued to maintain that he had been at his six-year-old niece's birthday party at the time of the shooting.

In 1979, a police informant told Detective Robert Kanjian that he knew Frazier's killer, naming Richard Harris, a twenty-nine-year-old man with seven convictions, who was serving time at Lorton Reformatory on robbery charges. When Kanjian discovered that Bradford Brown had been convicted of the crime, he began a new investigation and found a phone number written down by the killer in a message to Frazier's father and left in the house. Kanjian tracked the number back to Harris, and the case was reopened.

Harris pleaded guilty to manslaughter because his court-appointed attorney, John Treanor, explained that Harris thought he had shot Frazier in the leg, not the abdomen, and claimed that he did not know Frazier had died. Harris was convicted and given a four- to twelve-year sentence. Because of Detective Kanjian's revealing investigation, Brown was released after serving five years in prison. Kanjian, who had previously supported capital punishment, considered changing his mind: "I kept thinking about what could have happened if Bradford Brown had been in a state with the death penalty."

A prosecutor in Tennessee and a detective in Washington, D.C., had brought about the prison releases of two separate wrongly convicted men, both victims of mistaken identity. In Ohio, a public defender duplicated their efforts in bringing about the release of young carpenter mistakenly identified in the dying words of a murder victim. The carpenter was wrongly convicted of murdering a store owner and spent two years in prison before his name was cleared.

On the evening of March 28, 1978, a masked man armed with a sawed-off shotgun walked into Andy's Carry-Out in Perrysburg, Ohio, where Fred Ery, twenty-six, was working behind the counter. When the armed man announced a robbery, Ery called the man an obscene name, and the gunman shot him in the neck and fled. Before dying four hours later, Ery said, "It looked like Buzz, but it couldn't have been." On March 29, 1978, only one day after the murder, twenty-six-year-old Floyd "Buzz" Fay was arrested. Based on Ery's identification and the misinterpreted results of two lie detector tests, Fay was convicted of aggravated murder on August 11, 1978. His conviction was upheld in the Ohio appeals court on July 5, 1979.

Imprisoned at the London Correctional Institute in London, Ohio, Fay was represented by public defender Adrian Cimerman, twenty-eight. Cimerman felt that his client had been wrongly identified and decided to do something about it, conducting his own investigation into the case. Following tips implicating three teenagers, Cimerman located the driver of the getaway car used in the Ery killing.

The driver was serving in the U.S. Army in West Germany. After Cimerman contacted the driver, the young serviceman, in exchange for immunity, confessed his role in the robbery-murder. He then incriminated Cliff Markland and William Quinn, both nineteen. They were charged with Ery's murder, convicted, and sent to prison. On October 30, 1980, Fay was released and on November 17, all charges were dropped. He returned to his job building bridges and later launched a crusade against lie detector tests.

## Convictions Out of Hand through Mistaken Identities

Though the number of mistaken identities that have led to wrongful convictions are substantial—most such wrongful convictions stem from such mistaken identifications—thousands of similar cases exist where suspects are arrested and charged but are not convicted. Though many of these fortunate persons find acquittal instead of imprisonment, they live miserably under a cloud of suspicion, while they and their family members suffer as they await trial, sometimes years, as the suspect's reputation is destroyed, family relations disintegrate, and employment disappears.

A classic example of such mistaken identity cases was chillingly profiled in Alfred Hitchcock's 1956 film, *The Wrong Man* (see Filmography), which depicts the plight of Christopher Emmanuel "Manny" Balestrero, a bass player from Queens who played in the band at the celebrated Stork Club in Manhattan. Balestrero's ordeal began with his arrest on January 13, 1953, charged with a string of store robberies. He was then identified by several storeowners as the man who robbed their stores at gunpoint—all mistaken identifications that broke up Balestrero's marriage and sent his wife to a mental institution before the real culprit, an amazing look-alike, was arrested.

A similar, celebrated case, which did not result in conviction thanks to the conscience of the real look-alike perpetrator, involved a distinguished Maryland clergyman. For twenty-one years, assistant pastor Bernard T. Pagano attended to the spiritual needs of his congregation at St. Mary's Refuge of Sinner's Church in Cambridge. Parishioners recalled his many acts of kindness, such as the time he took a pack of cigarettes to an aging woman. "He was always there whenever there was a problem," said Marjorie Seebode.

On February 28, 1979, Delaware state police arrested Reverend Pagano, fifty-three, and charged him with robbing five retail stores in the Wilmington area. The police dubbed the lone gunman the "Gentleman Bandit" for his polite airs and distinguished manner. "I wouldn't do this, but I need the money," the robber told one saleswoman.

The money stolen from the five stores amounted to only $701, an inconsequential sum when measured against Pagano's total assets, valued at $25,000. The chain-smoking priest operated a lucrative dog kennel in Maryland with his half

Emmanuel "Manny" Balestrero, a victim of mistaken identity charged with several Manhattan robberies in 1953, was played by actor Henry Fonda, left (his double right) in the riveting 1956 film *The Wrong Man*, directed by Alfred Hitchcock. *History Inc./Jay Robert Nash Collection.*

sister, Doris Doerner. She shared living space on the sprawling two-acre compound with Reverend Pagano.

Pagano's problems were further compounded when he told police that he held a Ph.D. from the University of Pittsburgh and had attended postgraduate courses at Pennsylvania State University and the University of Illinois. A check of the records office at these institutions revealed that no one by that name had ever attended classes there. Parishioners, who refused to believe that their priest was a holdup man, raised $15,000 for his bail and another $12,000 for the defense fund. "People who know him don't think he did it," explained Ed St. Clair of St. Mary's Parish.

On the recommendation of New Castle magistrate John Wilding, Reverend Pagano entered the Delaware State Hospital for examination. For all practical purposes, he was incarcerated while undergoing institutional review. Hearing of his plight, industrial engineer Ronald Closter, on leave from his job with the U.S. Postal Authority in Pennsylvania, confessed to the five robberies.

Closter, whose amazing resemblance to Pagano resulted in mistaken identifications by seven different witnesses, was plagued by a guilty conscience. What prevented him from coming forward sooner was his belief that Pagano, purely on the strength of his status as a priest, would be acquitted. Closter was later convicted for the robberies and sent to prison. In August 1979, Attorney General Richard Gebelain of Delaware apologized to Pagano for the "extreme trauma that he has been put through."

A month before Father Pagano was publicly exonerated in Delaware, a freelance photographer underwent the same kind of harrowing accusations experienced by Pagano. Between July 1979 and November 1980, Robert "Bob" Dillen, twenty-eight in 1979, was arrested thirteen times in Pennsylvania and Indiana, standing trial in five cases on charges of robbery, rape, and kidnapping. In each case, at least one eyewitness "positively" identified Dillen as the criminal.

After a Fotomat shop in Castle Shannon, Pennsylvania, was robbed, the kidnapped clerk led police to a Venango County cabin, where she had been held. There police found Frank Jeziorski, twenty-eight, who confessed to all the crimes for which Dillen had been accused. Police Superintendent Robert Kroner, whose investigators eventually tracked down Dillen's look-alike, said that the fact Dillen was cleared was proof that "our legal system works."

Dillen's career as a freelance photographer, however, was destroyed. His father's $30,000 retirement fund went for legal fees, and his wife left him. Dillen expressed bitterness toward the police: "This thing about being innocent until proven guilty isn't true. Once you're there, you're it. They don't look for anyone else." In fact, he was correct. It was Dillen's lawyer, John Murtagh, who actually helped crack the case. After an October robbery of a Fotomat shop, Murtagh suggested that Dillen leave town. When two more stores were robbed on October 28, 1980, Murtagh proved Dillen was hundreds of miles from the crime scenes. Three days later, Jeziorski was arrested. On July 1, 1981, Jeziorski was sentenced to thirty-five to seventy years in prison for robbery, robbery associated with theft, and kidnapping.

Where Dillen was exonerated through the clever efforts of his attorney, a career criminal in New York, who was arrested and charged with a bloody robbery-murder on the basis of mistaken identity, secured his freedom simply through the measurement of his height. In June 1989, sixty-three-year-old Lawrence Condon was convicted of the 1987 execution-style murders of Jackson Heights, New York, liquor store owners Alfred and Martha Romaniello and a customer, Mohinder Singh. Condon had robbed the store and then forced the owners and the customer into a back room, where he killed each victim with a shot to the head. William Gergel, sixty-one, in a case of mistaken identity, had been held for seventeen months awaiting trial on the same charges. Condon and Gergel were career criminals who had spent much of their adult lives in jail. Condon, who had previously served time for armed robbery, was convicted on three counts of intentional murder, robbery, weapons possession, and felony murder.

Gergel's wrongful arrest was discovered when an eyewitness who survived the shooting, Cathy Maize, insisted that the gunman was more than six feet tall. Later, Maize explained to authorities that Gergel was "a lot shorter than the person I saw [in the store]. He was six foot." Gergel, who was freed in November 1988, testified that he was home alone at his Brooklyn residence when the Romaniellos and Singh were shot to death on June 4, 1987. His alibi was corroborated by prison inmate John Forsyth, who told police that Condon confessed the triple murder to him while they were incarcerated at the Green Haven Correctional Facility. Gergel, who bore a striking resemblance to Condon, was 5 feet 8; Condon, 6 feet 2. Acting through his attorney, Marvyn Kornberg, Gergel subsequently filed a $17 million suit for false arrest—$1 million for each month of his wrongful incarceration.

## More Look-Alike Perpetrators and Their Innocent "Twins"

In July 1983, twenty-five-year-old William Smiddy was shot to death with a .22-caliber pistol outside a Houston, Texas, nightclub, after he chased a man who stole $20 from a waitress's serving tray. He caught and choked the thief and retrieved the stolen money but then was shot to death. His assailant fled with a woman.

At a murder trial for this case before state district Judge George Walker, the assistant district attorney for Harris County, Larry Shreve, produced four witnesses who testified that thirty-two-year-old Everett Baily Malloy killed Smiddy. Malloy claimed he was innocent of the murder and produced witnesses who testified he was not the killer. He was nonetheless found guilty and sentenced by Walker in February 1984 to fifteen years in prison.

Two months later, Malloy was freed. The woman seen with the killer was finally located in April 1984 after an anonymous caller phoned police. The statement she gave police convinced them that she had witnessed firsthand the murder, and Malloy was released on April 13, 1984. Joseph Franklin Shelton, twenty-one, who bore a striking resemblance to Malloy, was charged with Smiddy's murder, convicted, and sent to prison.

Malloy's experience was duplicated by Jeffrey Cox, who was sent to prison in Virginia for a brutal murder he did not commit. That murder occurred in the early hours of August 31, 1990, when sixty-three-year-old Louise Cooper was dragged from her Richmond apartment by two assailants, taken to a car, and driven away. Stabbed to death, her body was found a short time later.

Two of Cooper's neighbors said they had seen two white men abduct the woman. Police initially believed that the two assailants were William Madison and Steven Hood, but the two eyewitnesses failed to identify either man in a photo lineup. They did, however, tentatively identify twenty-two-year-old Jeffrey Cox, a friend of Madison's. Both witnesses asked police to bring Cox in person so that they could be positive. Cox was presented to the witnesses, who both made tentative identifications.

Although he had no criminal record, Cox became the chief suspect in the Cooper murder, particularly when he had difficulty in providing an alibi. He was arrested and charged with the kidnapping and killing of Cooper, and was then placed in a police lineup, where one of the two witnesses failed to identify him; the second witness did not attend the lineup.

Cox was nevertheless brought to trial in 1990, where both eyewitnesses identified him as the perpetrator. Cox insisted that he was innocent and provided several alibi witnesses. Jurors, before reaching their verdict, asked the trial judge several questions. They wanted to know why Cox was a suspect, why forensic evidence—such as the skin and hairs under the victim's nails—had not been tested, and how police conducted their interrogation of Cox. The judge refused to answer any of these questions. The jury then brought in a verdict of guilty and Cox was sentenced to life in prison plus fifty years.

Cox's attorneys filed several appeals, pointing out the inconsistencies of his case and emphasizing that police had withheld from the defense a report containing the eyewitness description of the perpetrator, which did not match Cox's physical description. The eyewitnesses had pinpointed Cox in another case of mistaken identity. Meanwhile, an FBI investigation revealed the existence of considerable evidence implicating Stephen Hood in the Cooper killing. Hood was arrested and then confessed to murdering the woman, naming Madison as his accomplice. On November 13, 2001, Cox's conviction was vacated and he was released from prison the following day, after serving eleven years behind bars as an innocent man. At that time, Cox's mother, who had long crusaded for his son's release, said, "This is the happiest moment of my life. I never gave up hope." The real perpetrator, Stephen Hood, was convicted in 2002 and sent to prison for sixty-five years.

The same sad destiny that had engulfed Cox embraced a hapless young woman in Mississippi, positively identified and sent to prison by a victim who was later amazed to see that the woman had an almost exact double, the real criminal. In December 1993, Darron Terry's house in Jackson, Mississippi, was invaded by a burglar. Terry was later shown a mug shot of Mellissa Gammill, who had been arrested earlier with a group of lawbreakers. Terry positively identified Gammill, a mall food mart worker, as the burglar. His testimony largely contributed to the ten-year prison sentence Gammill received.

Family members and friends of Gammill, however, refused to believe that she was guilty and investigated the case further. In 1995, an investigator turned up another police mug shot, one that startled lawmen, lawyers, and the courts. It portrayed another blond woman, who was almost an identical twin to Mellissa Gammill, twenty-seven-year-old Pamela Meshea Bailey, who was then serving a prison term for another offense.

Terry was shown Bailey's photo and he appeared in court to tell a judge that had identified the wrong person. On April 13, 1995, the judge threw out Gammill's wrongful conviction and ordered her released from prison. She had served ten months behind bars for a crime she did not commit. Jimmy Houston, Jackson's chief of detectives, stated, "It was certainly a case of mistaken identity. These people [Gammill and Bailey] look so much alike it's unbelievable."

# Forensic Science to the Rescue

FORENSIC SCIENCES—BALLISTICS, HAND-writing (graphology), serology, toxicology, fingerprinting, pathology, and crime scene investigations, to name a few—have brought about convictions in countless cases. But these same forensic sciences have also served to establish the innocence of wrongly convicted persons. These forensic sciences are not perfect (including DNA analysis; see Chapter IX), being subject to human error, misjudgment, and miscalculation. Forensic sciences began to be developed in the eighteenth century, when early toxicologists proved through crude experiments the existence of certain poisons used in murder cases.

The nineteenth and twentieth centuries saw the emergence of pathology, ballistics, graphology, and fingerprinting, but law enforcement agencies and courts were slow to recognize these forensic sciences in bringing about credible convictions. Until scientific tests became admissible with evidentiary exhibits, the courts of the world depended on eyewitness testimony in convicting or acquitting defendants. As shown already (Chapter VII, "Mistaken Identity"), such eyewitness identification sent many a wrongly convicted person to prison or, worse, to the executioner, and is still the chief cause of wrongful convictions.

For the most part, experts involved in these forensic sciences are highly trained and knowledgeable. Their work and testing is accepted uni-versally in courts the world over and, coupled to eyewitness identification (always subject to question), myriad convictions have been accomplished. These same experts have repeatedly and consistently come to the rescue of wrongly convicted persons, challenging the prosecutors who originally employed them. The overall view of such scientists does not deal with the morality of right or wrong, but the evidence that their science determines through precise testing. That science is their "religion," and that "religion" has provided the salvation of many innocent persons.

## Ballistics and the Wrongly Convicted

Throughout the history of crime detection, many forensic sciences have identified the perpetrator of a criminal act. One of the earliest was forensic ballistics, which is the scientific study of projectiles in flight and, in criminal law, the study of firearms. Aimed at identifying a gun used in a crime, the science was first successfully applied in England in 1835 and in the United States at the turn of the twentieth century. Criminals were identified from the guns they used in committing crimes.

Ballistics identification is made through an examination of the spent cartridge or the bullet casing. All have distinctive marks made by the rifling

Dr. Calvin R. Goddard, shown inspecting a pistol barrel with an instrument of his own design, was a pioneer in developing the science of ballistics. *History Inc./Jay Robert Nash Collection.*

of a weapon, and all types of weapons vary among models and manufacturers as to number and shape of the grooves, twist rate, and bullet direction. This identification process is known as ballistic fingerprinting, and it has been successfully used in thousands of capital cases to bring about convictions. It has also been used with less frequency to bring about exonerations.

A 1919 ballistics case involved a farmer, Luca Tirpula, who was shot and killed in Detroit, Michigan. Alexander Ripan was charged with the murder, brought to trial, and convicted mainly due to the fact that the bullet that killed Tirpula fit easily into the barrel of Ripan's recently fired revolver. After serving ten years of a life sentence, Ripan escaped and remained at large for six years. In 1935, he was apprehended and returned to prison.

In the intervening years, the prosecutor who had originally brought Ripan to trial began to doubt the correctness of the verdict. In 1939, he obtained a new trial for Ripan at which an expert testified that recent findings in the field of ballistics absolutely reversed the evidence on which Ripan had been convicted: a bullet cannot easily be reinserted into the barrel of the gun that fired it. The judge dismissed the murder conviction against Ripan, who had spent fourteen years in prison.

An almost identical case involved a New York resident who unfortunately owned a type of gun used in a 1924 killing. Trying to protect himself from a lynching, Harry L. Hoffman almost signed his own death warrant. When the police announced they were looking for a man wearing horn-rimmed glasses and a brown hat, who owned a .25-caliber gun, Hoffman figured he would be a leading suspect in the 1924 murder of Mary A. Bauer in Staten Island, New York. He had read a lot about the lynching of Leo Frank, a Jewish pencil manufacturer in Atlanta, Georgia, nine years earlier by an angry mob, and did not want to end up the same way. (See "The Framing of Leo Max Frank" in Chapter XI, "Railroading and Framing.") Hoffman, who was also Jewish, mailed his pistol to his brother. This action and that weapon, however, became the backbone of the prosecution's case against the Staten Island movie projectionist.

The people of New York demanded that someone be punished for the Bauer murder, and Hoffman was convicted of first-degree murder after a ballistics expert testified that Hoffman's handgun was the weapon used to kill the victim, and prosecutors claimed that Hoffman had tried to conceal ownership of the gun by sending it to a relative. A new trial was ordered, however, after it was found that the wording of the original indictment was faulty. At his second trial, Hoffman's lawyer collapsed on the courtroom floor with a heart attack. A mistrial was called. The third trial ended with a hung jury. During the fourth trial, held five years after the crime had been committed, a ballistics test entered as evidence showed that the bullets recovered from Mary Bauer's corpse had not been fired from Hoffman's gun.

Hoffman was acquitted and released in 1929, but the state, for all the trouble it had caused him, claimed to owe him nothing but the six cents it confiscated from him when he went to prison. His car, which was impounded as evidence, was never returned to him. His daughter was placed in an orphanage after his wife left him for another man. His wife returned to him after her lover left. Ironically, Hoffman's attorney asserted when his client was freed that the Hoffmans were "going to begin life afresh, right where they left off five years ago."

One of the most celebrated criminal trials involving ballistics dealt with the heinous murder of a priest, a disillusioned young man, and a doubting prosecutor, whose dramatic demonstration of the science of ballistics made national news. Harold F. Israel, a young itinerant laborer, was picked up by frantic police shortly after a priest, Father Hubert Dahme, had been killed at 7:40 P.M. on February 4, 1924, as he stood on Main Street in Bridgeport, Connecticut, while taking his evening constitutional.

The fifty-six-year-old priest stopped momentarily to look across the street to the front of the Lyric Theater, where enthusiastic theatergoers were lining up to see the resplendent Ethel Barrymore appear in *The Laughing Lady*. Father Dahme, the much liked pastor of St. Joseph's Roman Catholic Church, took a few steps to the corner and paused to light his pipe. Suddenly a figure stood behind him, raising a revolver and firing a bullet into his brain, killing him instantly. The killer, wearing a long overcoat with the collar turned up and a cap pulled low over his face, fled up the street while dozens of shocked citizens stared after him.

Eight days later, on February 11, 1924, South Norwalk, Connecticut, Detective John R. Reynolds eyed a young man who seemed to be walking about in a daze. He identified himself as Harold F. Israel, a native of Bridgeport, and told Reynolds that he was penniless, hungry, and had no place to sleep. The plainclothes cop took Israel to the station house to get him a hot meal and give him a warm cell as an overnight vagrant. The youth was routinely searched and a rather ancient, Spanish-made .32-caliber revolver was found in his pocket. Officers looked the young man over with gathering suspicion.

The South Norwalk officers, well aware of the ruthless murder of Father Dahme, began to grill Israel, who told them he was trying to get to his sister's home in Pennsylvania. Bridgeport police

were contacted and their vague description of the killer seemed to match the vagrant. Israel was taken to Bridgeport police headquarters, where he was grilled endlessly without sleep and given very little food and water. Detectives in Bridgeport were sure they had gotten the priest killer and had already entered the old revolver taken from Israel as Exhibit B in a case that they later felt, despite its surprising outcome, was open-and-shut.

Several passersby who had seen the young man in the shabby overcoat shoot the priest on Main Street came forward and, with goading from officers, halfheartedly identified Israel as the murderer. Moreover, groggy from sleepless nights, Israel confessed to the killing. He was quickly placed on trial, with a speedy conviction expected from the energetic state's attorney, Homer Stille Cummings, a rising political star. Born in Chicago on April 30, 1870, Cummings became a lawyer and entered politics at an early age, becoming mayor of Stamford, Connecticut (1900–1902, 1904–1905). In 1924, Cummings served as the state's attorney for Fairfield County, Connecticut.

Cummings was an exacting and conscientious prosecutor, who, after examining the evidence against Israel, decided to reinvestigate. He learned about the questionable conditions under which police had extracted the confession from Israel and discovered that the so-called confession had been made to one police officer, Captain John H. Regan, head of Bridgeport's detective division. After interviewing Regan, Cummings realized that the detective suggested to Israel that he killed Father Dahme, and the youth, thoroughly exhausted after two days of grilling, blurted, "There ain't no use of my denying it any further or any longer. You got the gun, you got the cartridge, you have the one who knows me there. What is the use of me denying it any further?" A police stenographer took down a confession from Israel, which appeared coached to Cummings.

The murder weapon found on Israel was another matter that troubled Cummings. It was an old, rusty gun that actually belonged to Israel's roommate, Charles Cihal. Both Israel and Cihal had served in the army together in the Canal Zone and, when discharged in the summer of 1923, decided to room together. The young man sometimes took the revolver to the woods and did some practice shooting. The "cartridge" from this gun, which Israel supposedly referred to in his confession, was the cartridge found in Israel's Bridgeport room, which a local ballistics expert matched against the bullet extracted from the victim's brain. Yet according to Israel's landlady, the youths often left empty cartridges in their room after they used the revolver for practice shooting.

The ballistics report on this weapon was probably the most damning to Israel's case, other than his so-called confession. One of the most distinguished experts in that field, Captain Charles J. Van Amburgh, had positively identified the bullet taken from the priest's brain as having been fired by the weapon found in Israel's overcoat pocket. Van Amburgh, a top engineer for the ballistics division of the Remington Arms Company, had taught weaponry to U.S. troops during World War I as an ordnance expert and marksman. He was considered one of the best ballistics experts available and had, for years, testified in important criminal cases as to identifying murder weapons through ballistics analysis, and this included the sensational 1921 Sacco-Vanzetti case. (See Chapter XIV, "Language Barriers and Prejudicial Publicity.") Van Amburgh insisted that the bullet that killed Father Dahme was fired by the .32-caliber revolver found on Harold Israel.

Cummings delved into the procedures employed by Van Amburgh in his comparison with the murder bullet and the revolver, now marked Exhibit B. Six additional ballistics experts were summoned to examine the revolver, and Cummings asked Van Amburgh to walk him through the expert's own examination of the weapon and the murder bullet. Van Amburgh demonstrated a less than exacting procedure, pointing out that he merely compared photographs of the murder bullet and several bullets fired from the gun taken

from Israel. He had slit the photograph of the murder bullet, separated the photo, and then inserted the blowup of a photo of a bullet fired from the Israel weapon.

For some minutes he moved both photos around so that "all the markings coincide," as he informed Cummings. The expert was really manipulating both photographs so that only certain markings seemed to match up. Cummings ordered Van Amburgh to "lift up the flap [of the photo] and see what is under it." When this was done, the markings did not match. Further, Cummings had his own experts from the New York Police Department, the Winchester Operating Arms Company, and Van Amburgh's own firm, Remington, carefully examine the weapon, test-fire it, and compare its spent bullets with the murder bullet in regard to the shape of its groves, twist rate, and direction. The universal report to him from these experts was that "there is no evidence that the mortal bullet came out of the Israel revolver," and that the murder bullet had been fired from "some other unknown weapon." So much for Exhibit B.

Israel's so-called confession nagged at Cummings, so he sent several doctors to interview the young man. The accused was still in an exhausted state when the physicians examined him and reported later to Cummings that Israel had been asked if he had killed the priest, and he admitted and denied the act in almost the same sentence. Cummings took note that, after these examinations, when Israel was no longer under tremendous nervous stress, he denied killing the priest and never deviated from that denial. Moreover, the suspect's competency was in great doubt. Examining psychiatrists concluded that the suspect "was a person of low mentality, of the moron type, quiet and docile in demeanor, totally lacking in any characteristics of brutality or viciousness, of very weak will, and peculiarly subject to the influence of suggestion."

Retracing the police grilling, Cummings realized that investigators walked the suspect through the crime and drove him along the killer's murder and escape route, narrating the action and suggesting that he, Israel, had enacted the murder. It was in *response* to these pointed suggestions that Israel supposedly blurted his confession, an admission that was nowhere in the documented evidence as having been his own idea. In other words, Harold Israel did not *volunteer* his guilt; he merely agreed with the police officers, who detailed the crime step by step and pinned it on him. As Cummings would later point out to the court, "All the admissions of an incriminating character were admissions with reference to facts already known to the police prior to the examination of the accused and presumably related to the accused during the period of his examination."

There was one other significant factor in this case which kept Cummings up endless nights. Harold F. Israel had no motive for killing Father Hubert Dahme. He did not know the priest, nor was there any record that the two men ever exchanged words, let alone glances. When he was being grilled by police in his sleepless state, the accused groggily nodded that he had shot "the man," never referring to the victim as a priest or a clergyman. This "admission" was in light of the statement by Israel that he was unaware of what his supposed victim looked like and that he was wearing a Roman collar when killed.

It was assumed by police, according to Cummings's investigation, that Israel, for no apparent reason, walked up to Father Dahme, picked him out as a random victim, and shot a nameless stranger to death. Of course, it was an easier task for detectives to arrest a drifter with a gun in his pocket than sift through other suspects, who might have had a reason to kill the clergyman. Oddly, none of the priest's parishioners were interviewed to determine if Father Dahme had any enemies who hated him enough to kill him.

Then there was the dubious question concerning the so-called eyewitnesses who had identified Israel in a police lineup as the young man they had seen shoot the priest and then flee up the street and into the darkness. One by one, Cummings painstakingly examined these witnesses. The killer had been wearing a cap and a long overcoat, most of the witnesses agreed (Israel had been wearing a long overcoat when arrested). Edward Flood had first reported seeing the fleeing man run up the street past him but never mentioned his wearing a cap. When Cummings read the same person's testimony at a later inquest, he noticed that Flood had added that the killer had been wearing a cap, a description easily available from newspapers after the killing and before the inquest.

Ralph Esposito, a delivery boy who had been standing on Main Street some twenty feet from where the priest was killed, said the killer wore a gray cap. Cummings noted that Israel's cap was green. Esposito also said that he had gotten a good look at the murder weapon and told the coroner that it was "one of those black pistols that do not shine." Cummings went back to the so-called murder weapon, Israel's .32-caliber revolver, and noted that it was nickel plated and would have certainly glowed somewhat in the light from the nearby street lamp.

Esposito's other remarks describing the killer's escape and his manner of running perplexed the coroner at the inquest. Said Esposito, "When I see the man run, he run like a Jewish man." This stumped the Fairfield County coroner, John G. Phelan, who replied, "I never heard of that before. What kind of a run is that?" Esposito shrugged, as if he had described a commonplace and identifiable gait, and stated, "Did you ever see a Jewish man walk from one side to the other?" Said Phelan, "A kind of a side-wheel movement?" Esposito said yes and added, "I didn't see the man clear in the face." Margaret Morrill, a social worker, said she saw the killer run up the street but could not positively identify him, only his manner of running, "a rather long stride." She thought the murderer was tall. Railroad station ticket agent James H. McKiernan described the killer as a "little fellow" and said he saw only part of the killer's face. Frederick Morris, a carpenter, had been closest to the priest and the killer, and he had identified Israel in a police lineup as the murderer.

Later, however, Cummings took special note that Morris was asked to state at the inquest whether he still felt Israel was the killer. "His side face did look familiar to me the night I was called to identify him, but I couldn't swear to the man because it just didn't look like him at that time." There were others, many of them, who had picked Israel out of the police lineup as the killer after he had been arrested. Later, Hilda Baer, a German immigrant, was unsure. Nellie Trefton, a waitress, who first said Israel walked past the window of the restaurant where she worked only seconds before Father Dahme was killed, was now unsure. Teenager Alfred Berry was positive about Israel, later unsure. One by one, the original identifications from eyewitnesses disintegrated.

Cummings had destroyed his own case, systematically picking apart what had at first amounted to the open-and-shut conviction of an illiterate, confused, and utterly accessible suspect, a conviction that would have won him accolades, not to mention an avalanche of votes, from an anxious and enraged public. Yet he chose to exonerate a man he came to believe innocent, which won for him the heroic image of a prosecutor who sought justice before personal aggrandizement. Dramatically, he demonstrated how anyone could stand wrongly accused when he selected several persons in an open courtroom and asked them into his office, where they were identified as looking very much like the murderer of Father Dahme. Said Cummings later, "It shows how easy it is for similarities in appearance, and especially similarity in clothes, to be made the basis for a mistaken identity."

Going before Judge L. P. Waldon Marvin in the criminal superior court on May 27, 1924, Cummings presented the findings of his independent investigation, which had consumed more than three months, and requested Marvin to dismiss charges against the defendant: "In view of what I have said about every element of the case, I do not think that any doubt of Israel's innocence can re-

main in the mind of a candid person. Therefore, if Your Honor approves, as I trust you will, of my conclusion in this matter, I shall enter a nolle (refusal to prosecute) in the case of State vs. Harold Israel."

Israel went free and moved to Pennsylvania, where he later married and raised two children, working honestly as a miner and becoming a regular churchgoer. Cummings kept in touch with Israel as late as 1938, sending him gifts of money from time to time. He later recalled,

U.S. Attorney General Homer S. Cummings, right, with FBI Director J. Edgar Hoover. Cummings rose to fame in 1924 by proving that Harold Israel, a man that Cummings himself was scheduled to prosecute, had not murdered a priest in Bridgeport, Connecticut in that year. *History Inc./Jay Robert Nash Collection.*

"I went out on a limb for him and I wanted to make sure he never got in trouble again."

Cummings rose to great prominence as U.S. attorney general (1933–1939) during the first two terms of President Franklin D. Roosevelt. He later admitted that he had no logical reason to question the Israel case when it was first put before him. "The case against the accused seemed overwhelming. Upon its face, at least, it seemed like a well-nigh perfect case. . . In fact, it seemed like an *annihilating* case. There did not seem a vestige of reason for suspecting for a moment that the accused was innocent."

Yet everything was too perfect for the prosecution, too convenient. Cummings looked over the evidence and then, for no other reason than an intuitive urge, which he later admitted, decided to challenge that evidence: "There were sufficient circumstances of an unusual character involved to make it highly important that every fact should be scrutinized with the utmost care and in the most impartial manner. It goes without saying that it is just as important for a state's attorney to use the great powers of his office to protect the innocent as it is to convict the guilty."

His widely publicized investigation, which undid Cummings's "airtight" case and certain conviction, did not go unnoticed by Franklin D. Roosevelt. As governor of New York (1929–1932), Roosevelt had been fascinated by the case, after reading about its details in the 1931 report issued by the National Commission on Law Observance and Enforcement (the Wickersham Commission), which praised the ethics and high scruples of Homer Stille Cummings. Roosevelt appointed Cummings as U.S. attorney general after his first choice, Thomas J. Walsh of Montana, died. Cummings was an effective but low-profile attorney general, who fully supported the activities and programs of J. Edgar Hoover, director of the FBI. Cummings sponsored many reforms in the U.S. Department of Justice and federal judicial system, such as new rules of civil procedure.

Cummings created an administrative office for federal courts and sponsored a juvenile delinquency act. Cummings took special pains to expand and improve the federal prison system, establishing Alcatraz as the country's leading maximum security prison. Cummings called for the first National Conference on Crime, and he secured legislation for J. Edgar Hoover's FBI to extend its authority, enlarging the scope of FBI powers concerning kidnapping and interstate crime. President Roosevelt's so-called court-packing plan (1937) was drafted by Cummings. The riveting fact-based 1947 film *Boomerang*, directed by Elia Kazan, profiled the Israel case (see Filmography). Cummings died on September 10, 1956.

## Guilty or Innocent Through Graphology

Graphology is the science of analyzing handwriting, which police use to authenticate handwriting and to analyze character and personality. The individual style of handwriting contains certain hand-

writing patterns, which are compared by experts to other documents written by suspects and to identify the writer in the questioned document. Handwriting is also a title for a branch in most major police departments, where handwriting experts rank and compare handwriting samples involved with criminal cases. Graphologists maintain that handwriting is as unique as fingerprints.

One of the most flagrant misuses of graphology involved the wrongly convicted Alfred Dreyfus a French military officer railroaded on charges of treason in 1894. (See Chapter I, "Fighting for Justice.") The conviction that sent Dreyfus to Devil's Island for life was based chiefly on an infamous *bordereau* (memorandum) penned by the actual traitor, who was shielded by members of the French high command. Moreover, to support its claims that Dreyfus was the traitor, the high command had several false documents created. But when these forgeries, along with the original *bordereau*, were closely examined and exhibited later, the real author of the *bordereau* and the creator of the forged documents supporting it were exposed. In this instance, handwriting analysis largely contributed to Dreyfus's exoneration.

Although graphology supported the innocence of a man accused of robbing a Georgia post office, he was nevertheless wrongly convicted and sent to prison in 1924. In October 1922, Hugh C. Lee stood trial in Tennessee for theft. He was found guilty and sentenced to three to ten years in prison. He escaped in December 1922. On September 15, 1923, the post office of Priors, Georgia, was robbed of blank money order forms, a money order stamp, and a metal cutter. On September 19, 1923, one of the money orders was passed in Nashville, Tennessee, and authorities began looking for Hugh C. Lee, who had been arrested in June 1922 for cashing a money order stolen in Snowden, Virginia.

Lee was recaptured and indicted for the Priors robbery in October 1924 in Emporia, Virginia. He was sent back to Rome, Georgia, for trial in the Priors robbery. Lee pleaded not guilty, saying he was in Detroit, Michigan, at the time of the robbery, and his handwriting did not match the writing on the money order passed on September 19, 1923. However, a fourteen-year-old boy who had been in the post office during the holdup identified Lee as the robber and other residents, including a waiter and a hotel manager, recognized Lee. On November 19, 1924, the thirty-seven-year-old Lee was convicted and sentenced to five years in the Atlanta Penitentiary.

Lee's prospects brightened when Will Barrett was arrested in Nashville, Tennessee, in January 1925 for passing forged checks. He confessed to robbing the village postmaster of Priors, for which Lee had been wrongly convicted. A handwriting comparison convinced detectives that Barrett had signed both sets of forged checks recovered from Nashville and Polk County. Will Barrett, an escapee from the Alabama penitentiary, was brought to trial in the U.S. District Court, northern Georgia, on February 9, 1925. He pleaded guilty and was sentenced to three and a half years in the Atlanta penitentiary.

On March 13, 1925, following Barrett's conviction, President Calvin Coolidge pardoned Lee. Lee was then taken to Lynchburg, Virginia, to stand trial for the Snowden postal robbery. Since the state's primary witness in that case had died, he was given a verdict of nol prosse on January 4, 1926. Lee was nevertheless extradited to Tennessee to complete the prison term he was serving when he had escaped four years earlier.

Five years later, a Detroit man was sent to prison for murdering his wife, but ballistics and graphology findings brought about his exoneration and release nine years later. On October 15, 1931, Lonnie Jenkins, a twenty-nine-year-old Detroit streetcar conductor, notified police that his wife, Edith, had committed suicide. He said he had found his wife lying on her back on the floor of their home in a pool of blood. She had been shot through the head and the automatic pistol still lay on her chest. A suicide note was nearby. Because Mrs. Jenkins had attempted to kill herself

only a few weeks earlier, a coroner deemed her death a suicide.

Detectives investigating the case, however, found Jenkins's description of the body's position unusual. In their experience, suicides by shooting almost always fell forward. They persisted in their investigation despite the coroner jury's finding. They questioned a woman named Betty, a former neighbor of the Jenkins, who had lived with the couple for a time and helped Mrs. Jenkins clean and take care of her daughter, Helen. Betty told police that she wrote the suicide note at Jenkins's urging, that she and Jenkins had been involved in a love affair, and that Jenkins had promised to marry her. On the strength of this statement and other circumstantial evidence, Jenkins was arrested and charged with murdering his wife. Though Jenkins maintained his innocence throughout the trial, the jury found him guilty of first-degree murder and sentenced him to life in prison.

Jenkins's defense attorney, Allen W. Kent, concentrated on the way the body would fall in a suicide of this type. In a freak accident, Kent shot himself in the head while attempting to demonstrate his theory to the deputy chief of detectives. Jenkins's daughter took up the fight in his behalf after Kent died. On December 23, 1940, Jenkins was granted a new trial in which the defense presented ballistics evidence that showed that the position of Mrs. Jenkins's body was not unusual for a suicide. The defense also presented certification from FBI handwriting experts that the suicide note had indeed been written by Mrs. Jenkins. Betty recanted her earlier testimony. On the strength of the new evidence, Lonnie Jenkins's conviction was overturned and he was set free.

In a 1982 Arkansas case, *Carroll v. State*, graphology came into sharp critical focus, as experts on both sides of the case came close to destroying its credibility. Opposing experts called each other charlatans and frauds, displaying a fierce antagonism and raw competitiveness that severely undercut the common ground that the general approaches to handwriting analysis have to each

A nineteenth-century Chinese document showing the use of a thumbprint as a means of identification. *History Inc./Jay Robert Nash Collection.*

other. Some self-styled graphologists have employed the science for occult purposes, claiming that they can provide spiritual guidance or even read the future from someone's handwriting, a practice denounced by the International Graphoanalysis Society, the British Association of Graphology, and other reputable organizations representing this science.

## Bertillonage and the Evolution of Fingerprinting

Before the coming of DNA, fingerprinting was universally believed for more than a century to be near infallible as the most reliable of criminal identifications. As such, it determined the fate of countless defendants involved in major and minor criminal cases. Fingerprinting was an old science in Asia, where the Chinese used thumbprints for identification more than twenty centuries ago. The West, however, did not develop this criminal identification system until the middle of the nineteenth century, and even then it was zealously challenged by Alphonse Bertillon. For decades his Bertillon Anthropometric System, or Bertillonage, was employed by almost every police department in Europe, the United States, and South America.

Alphonse Bertillon (1853–1914) is generally credited with creating forensic science and establishing the first universally used criminal identification system. Bertillon was sickly as a child, and his constitution continued to be frail into adulthood. He also had a sour, pedantic disposition. Bertillon began his career as a junior filing clerk in the Paris prefecture of police, where he began to develop a theory of creating an exact system of measurements, or anthropometry (man measurements). This concept was twin to the ideas advanced by American criminologist Charles Caldwell, who outlined the theory of phrenology as early as 1824.

Charles Caldwell (1772–1853), an American physician from Philadelphia, wroted *Elements of Phrenology* (1824), the first textbook in the country on the subject. Elaborating on the works of Franz Joseph Gall (1758–1828) and Johann Cristoph Spurzheim (1776–1832), Caldwell approached phrenology as a valid science of criminal identification. He believed that criminal tendencies and inclinations can actually be identified through the measurement and study of physical shapes and proportions, chiefly the human head, a belief that was accepted by many forensic specialists, notably French criminologist Alphonse Bertillon.

As late as 1924, when phrenologists examined Richard Loeb and Nathan Leopold, who killed Bobby Franks in Chicago, this "science" still stood in good repute and experts in the field were called to testify in that case. Phrenology, however, fell into disrepute in the late 1920s and has no place in modern criminology.

Taking phrenology concepts to the extreme, many realized, was similar to the ridiculous Nazi propaganda that Jewish blood is demonstrated in the shape of the nose, chin, or ears. The basic concepts of phrenology stemmed from comparing physical attributes (thick lips, long earlobes, various bumps in the skull, the setting of the eyes) to known criminals. Those who physically conformed to the physical dimensions of felons of the past were labeled arbitrarily as having criminal tendencies, thus rendering, on the part of phrenologists, a moral judgment relative to those who stood accused of criminal acts.

Alphonse Bertillon, a French police researcher, who developed the first modern criminal identification system based upon physical measurements. *History Inc./Jay Robert Nash Collection.*

Bertillon photographing a body at a murder scene. *History Inc./Jay Robert Nash Collection.*

In the mid-twentieth century, phrenology focused on the human intellect, localizing the cognitive aspects of the brain as if human intellectual geography could actually be mapped. To some degree, the teaching regimen of certain academies, particularly Jesuit educators over several centuries, focused on a sort of phrenological thought process, or compartmentalized teaching and thinking processes. This intellectual perspective was wholly embraced by modern intelligence agencies when recruiting and training agents and analysts. For that reason, the CIA and other U.S. intelligence agencies have traditionally sought recruits from such Jesuit institutions as Holy Cross College, Marquette University, and Loyola University.

Alphonse Bertillon, however, confined his perspective of phrenology to its physical applications, with a deep-seated belief that any adult could be identified if exact measurements were recorded of that person and later compared with measurements taken of a criminal suspect. In 1879, Bertillon drafted a proposal to adopt this identification system and submitted it to the prefect of police, Louis Andrieux. Bertillon was told to stop daydreaming and pay attention to his filing chores.

The novice forensic scientist persisted, however, and his break came when he used his measurement system to identify a criminal named Martin, who had been using the alias of Dupont. The French police slowly adopted Bertillon's measurement system. In 1892, Bertillon scored a major triumph by identifying one of the most sought-after terrorists on the continent, Claudius Francois Koenigstein, who had been arrested and booked under the name of Ravachol. When it pinpointed these two identities—Koenigstein and Ravachol—as one and

the same, Bertillon's ID system was hailed as foolproof and was adopted by most governments.

Bertillonage had ardent followers in Italy, Germany, Spain, Russia, and Austria. The American police slowly adopted this system into police and prison procedure, while the British were reluctant to embrace it, pointing out that it required endless measuring procedures and paperwork. The British looked more optimistically at the development of fingerprinting for the best ID system, although it was untried at the time.

Despite challenges from police and discrepancies between known felons who often had the same measurements, Bertillon's complete measurement system was hailed as foolproof if all of Bertillon's directives were followed. His fourteen measurements included the circumference of the head and chest, the length of the arms, legs, feet, fingers, nose, ears, and so on. In addition, Bertillon instituted a system of photographing criminals that is employed to this day, in which the suspect is photographed with a complete profile and a full head shot, the same distance from the camera, with the same amount of light, and kept in a fixed position, which would correspond to the computation of Bertillon's measurement requirements. Bertillon made hundreds of thousands of files with specific measurements of all known criminals and an equal number of photographs taken in France and in other countries.

Bertillon's measuring instruments, which he used to detail the specific physical sizes of eyes, ears, noses, faces, hands, feet, bodies of accused persons and convicted felons, assembling files numbering in the hundreds of thousands and which police used for years to identify wanted criminals and to solve crimes committed in future cases. *History Inc./Jay Robert Nash Collection.*

Bertillon being elaborately measured with his own instruments. *History Inc./Jay Robert Nash Collection.*

Bertillon measurements and photograph of the much-wanted terrorist, Ravachol, which identified him in 1892 when he was under arrest as a suspect in a bombing and when using an alias, a case that caused Bertillon's criminal identification system to be accepted by most major European police departments. *History Inc./Jay Robert Nash Collection.*

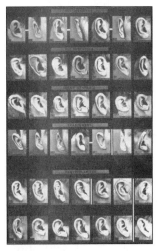

An example of Bertillon's sectional photography of ears from his files, another method by which he identified wanted felons. *History Inc./Jay Robert Nash Collection.*

Having struggled to establish his system, Bertillon was naturally the most severe critic of the newly proposed fingerprint identification system, claiming that it was an inexact science. Of course, he was proven wrong and lived long enough to see fingerprinting replace Bertillonage. He grudgingly admitted that there was some use to fingerprinting: "My measurements are surer than any fingerprint pattern, but the criminal does not leave his measurements at the scene of the crime." Bertillon did not discredit fingerprinting altogether. In 1902, he helped the cause of fingerprinting by identifying a wanted felon, Henri Leon Scheffer, with fingerprints alone.

Bertillon believed himself an expert in all fields of forensic science, including handwriting. When he examined the writings of Alfred Dreyfus, the accused French army captain, he stated that Dreyfus indeed had written a notorious document describing French fortifications and equipment, and delivered this to the German government. Dreyfus was convicted and sent to Devil's Island, wrongly convicted on the so-called evidence provided by Bertillon and the forgeries that supported it that were sponsored by the corrupt French high command. When Dreyfus was later proved innocent, Bertillon was held in disrepute by many of his fellow criminologists.

By the turn of the century, Bertillonage began to lose ground to fingerprinting with Bertillon's early advocates going over to "the other side," so to speak. A leading Italian criminologist, Salvatore Ottolenghi, who once championed Bertillonage, began to endorse the universal use of fingerprinting, embracing the theories and procedures advanced by fingerprinting pioneers Edward Henry, Francis Galton, Henry Faulds, William Herschel, and most notably Juan Vucetich. By early 1913, Bertillon was suffering from incurable pernicious anemia. His doctors told him he would die, and Bertillon feared that his precious identification system would die with him. For almost a year, he was in terrible physical discomfort, feeling cold and covering himself with blankets and keeping a stove at white heat around the clock. Bertillon was in a state of constant exhaustion and was losing his sight.

Bertillon received reports that countries all over the world were abandoning Bertillonage for fingerprinting and became enraged when South American criminologist Juan Vucetich stated, "I can assure you that, in all the years during which we applied the anthropometric system, in spite of all our care, we were unable to prove the identity of a single person by measurements." Vucetich later visited Bertillon

Bertillon photographs of felon Henri-Leon Scheffer, the first person in Europe to be convicted on fingerprint evidence alone, a forensic science that Bertillon contested as a stand-alone criminal identification system. Bertillon actually found and took the prints at a Paris murder scene on October 24, 1902, matching them to Scheffer, which brought about the conviction. *History Inc./Jay Robert Nash Collection.*

A murder-robbery scene photographed in Paris by Bertillon, 1908. *History Inc./Jay Robert Nash Collection.*

Bertillon photographing a convicted felon, 1909. *History Inc./Jay Robert Nash Collection.*

blind and racked with pain. By that time Bertillonage was already a thing of the past.

Among the distinguished supporters of Bertillonage was Cesare Lombroso (1835–1909), who is credited with founding the science of criminology. He began his medical career as an army doctor and later became professor of forensic medicine (1876), psychiatry (1896), and criminal anthropology (1906) at the University of Turin. In 1889, Lombroso published *L'uomo delinquente* (The Delinquent Man), in which he expounded his theory of the criminal personality. Lombroso theorized that a criminal represents a distinct anthropological type and is identifiable by specific physical and mental characteristics. He also held that a criminal is the product of heredity, atavism, and degeneracy.

Another early supporter of Lombroso's theory of anthropological identification was Francis Galton (1822–1911). A cousin of Charles Darwin, Galton was a physician but never practiced medicine. Instead, he devoted his considerable energies to the study of statistics and anthropology. Galton, who entered British civil service, applied statistics to what he termed "the human faculty," as detailed in his work, *Enquiries into Human Faculty* (1883). Galton was influenced by Lombroso, who believed there is a hereditary link to criminals and that criminals can be identified through certain physical characteristics, an early version of the now generally discarded science of phrenology, as well as the

at his home in Paris. Bertillon opened his door and Vucetich put forth his hand. Bertillon said, "Sir, you have tried to do me a great deal of harm" and slammed the door in Vucetich's face. Bertillon continued to drag himself to his office, where he supervised his workers from a couch. He was dying and the French government, which had given him the red ribbon of the Legion of Honor for Bertillonage, now wished to confer on him the rosette that went with it, the additional decoration Bertillon so desired.

A government representative arrived to tell him that France wished to award him the rosette, but there was one small condition. He had to admit his error in judgment regarding the handwriting of Captain Alfred Dreyfus, who had long since been vindicated and had become a hero of the Republic. The obstinate Bertillon shouted from his deathbed, "No! Never! Never!" The rosette was denied him, and Alphonse Bertillon died on February 13, 1914,

A contemporary caricature of Bertillon shows him looking for clues by earnestly examining graffiti on the walls of an outhouse, the first of many such profiles that increasingly criticized his fallible criminal identification system, which was abandoned when fingerprinting replaced *Bertillonage. History Inc./Jay Robert Nash Collection.*

A handprint used in India by British civil servant William James Herschel by which he identified workers contracted for government jobs in 1860. *History Inc./Jay Robert Nash Collection.*

An 1898 Boston police record of a felon with Bertillon measurements, used as a wanted poster for this wanted man in 1905. *History Inc./Jay Robert Nash Collection.*

Henry Faulds, one of the first pioneers in developing fingerprinting, tried unsuccessfully to convince Scotland Yard to adopt his system for criminal identification in the late 1880s. *History Inc./Jay Robert Nash Collection.*

Bertillonage identification system of the 1890s and early 1910s. Galton, using Lombroso's theories as well as his own, founded the science of eugenics.

Galton also developed composite photography in which he attempted to show patterns in the physical makeup of criminals that can be traced to diseases. He became interested in anthropometric photography developed by Alphonse Bertillon and visited Bertillon in Paris, where he studied the French criminologist's techniques.

In 1892, Galton departed from Bertillonage when he advanced the science of fingerprinting through his exhaustive work, *Finger Prints.* It was Galton who advanced the first statistical evidence proving that fingerprints are unique and can be used as a system of identification. The criminologist calculated that the chance of two fingerprints being identical is 64 billion to 1. Galton never created a fingerprint identification system, but Sir Edward Henry, one of his most ardent followers, developed Galton's statistical applications into a practical method of using fingerprints as identification.

Several years before Galton and Henry pioneered fingerprinting as a reliable identification system, criminologist Henry Faulds (1843–1930) began publicizing the use of fingerprint science. After obtaining his medical degree, Faulds spent his later years trying to convince Scotland Yard

that fingerprints left at the scene of a crime can be identified as easily as those taken from the prisoner at the station house. Faulds's interest in fingerprinting dated to 1880, when he published a letter on the subject in *Nature*. Between 1886 and 1888, Faulds offered to demonstrate his findings to Scotland Yard, but officials were not interested. Law enforcement agencies of the period relied on the Bertillon system of body measurements to classify prisoners.

Faulds was not the first to propose the use of fingerprinting in criminal cases. That honor belonged to an Englishman living in India named William James Herschel (1833–1917). Herschel was the grandson of the celebrated British astronomer William Herschel and the son of another famous astronomer, John Herschel. He was a British civil servant working in India who began to experiment with fingerprinting as early as 1858, having Indian merchants sign their contracts with him by imprinting their palm and fingerprints to documents as a form of security.

In 1860, while working as a magistrate in India for the East India Company, Herschel devoted a great deal of time to the exclusive study of fingerprinting, believing that human fingerprints are unique. He used his system as a method of checking the identities of Indian workers. This was the only way he could identify workers, he said, since they all looked alike to him and, he claimed, had been cheating the government by sending relatives and friends to collect salaries repeatedly in the same name. Herschel first collected all the fingerprints of the workers. When they arrived to receive their pay, they had to "sign" for this money by pressing inked fingers to receipts.

Francis Galton, who first embraced Bertillonage, began to advance fingerprinting as a more reliable criminal identification system in 1892. *History Inc./Jay Robert Nash Collection.*

By 1874, Herschel had come to realize that fingerprints do not change over the years and are ineradicable. In that year, Herschel wrote to the inspector general of India, presenting him with his findings and urging him to use fingerprinting as an identification system that offers "the means of verifying the identity of every man in jail." By using his fingerprinting system, Herschel stated, the government could prevent impersonation, such as the fraud committed by his former Indian workers, and the repudiation of contracts. The inspector general, however, rejected the idea and Herschel did not pursue it. In 1880, he read an article by Henry Faulds in the publication *Nature* in which Faulds claimed to have discovered fingerprinting as an identification system for criminals.

Herschel wrote a letter to the publication, claiming that *he*, not Faulds, had invented an identification system using fingerprints *before* Faulds, and thus began a controversy that lasted several decades. In the end, Herschel was credited with making the first practical use of fingerprinting, but it was Faulds who received credit for first establishing the fact that fingerprints are ineradicable and establish identity in a foolproof way.

The first person to use fingerprinting in a large police department was Francis Galton's most devoted protégé, Sir Edward Richard Henry (1859–1931). Henry served as London's police commissioner from 1903 to 1918, and he was best known for his work in developing the fingerprint classification system used by Scotland Yard and the Indian civil service.

Henry, along with Sir Francis Galton and Sir William Herschel, in-

Sir Edward Henry, who supported Galton's fingerprinting theories and put them into actual service as the first reliable criminal identification system used by Scotland Yard and, subsequently, all other police departments around the world. *History Inc./Jay Robert Nash Collection.*

vented the Henry fingerprint system, which replaced the Bertillon method of anthropometry. Henry's system categorized the fingerprints of all known criminals, suspects, and those lifted from crime scenes. He introduced the method in India, where he served as inspector-general of the Bengal police beginning in 1891.

By 1900, the procedure was fully operational in India, replacing the Bertillon method completely in 1914, and was adopted by Scotland Yard in 1901. Henry was named assistant commissioner of the Metropolitan Police force in 1901, and served until 1903, when he became commissioner. For establishing fingerprinting at Scotland Yard, he was presented with the Grand Cross Order of Dannebrog, the Order of St. Sava, and the Order of Villa Vicosa.

Juan Vucetich, who pioneered fingerprinting in Argentina and who brought about the world's first exoneration through this identification system in 1892. He was pilloried by Alphonse Bertillon, who believed Vucetich was out to destroy *Bertillonage*. *History Inc./Jay Robert Nash Collection.*

One man who worked as hard as Henry, Galton, Faulds, and Herschel to bring fingerprinting into worldwide use as a forensic science did not live to see a knighthood or rewards. Instead, he was vilified and sent into oblivion for his pioneering efforts in helping to establish fingerprinting as the world's most reliable identification system. He was Juan Vucetich (1858–1925), and his first use of fingerprinting in a criminal case not only identified a killer but exonerated a wrongly accused man.

Sir Edward Henry and Francis Galton of Great Britain had long been recognized as the forefathers of modern fingerprinting, which, for nearly a century, has been the accepted method of prisoner classification, and still is, even with the advent of DNA identification. Vucetich, a Croatian-born criminologist, is no less important to the field than his illustrious contemporaries. The prevailing attitudes of his own people, however, doomed him to relative obscurity. Shortly before he died in 1925, Vucetich wrote to his friend Edward Lomax, "My work is destroyed and perhaps will be forgotten . . . nobody will ever remember me."

Vucetich was born on the island of Lesina, near the coast of Dalmatia, in 1858. Lesina was then a part of the Austro-Hungarian Empire, but it avoided the political turbulence that swept through the Balkans while Vucetich was growing up. After completing his studies at the university school in Spalato, Vucetich joined the local police force but found the work dull and unrewarding.

A restless young man with intense nationalistic leanings, Vucetich emigrated to Argentina in 1884. Rather than live on an island under the political thumb of the Austrian colonial government, he settled in the bustling city of La Plata, where he quickly assimilated into the local culture, even to the point of changing his name from "John" to the Spanish "Juan."

Vucetich went to work for the central police department, where he greatly impressed his superiors with his energy, enthusiasm, and willingness to take on whatever tasks came his way. By 1891, he was the head of the Statistical Bureau and was given the responsibility of organizing the Department of Identity. Alphonse Bertillon's anthropometric method of prisoner classification, Bertillonage, had recently come into vogue in the police agencies on the European continent and in the United States.

It was up to Vucetich to implement Bertillonage in La Plata. In order to familiarize Vucetich with the Frenchman's work, Chief Nuez of La Plata provided his subordinate with a file folder of articles and instructions. Among the relevant publications contained was a French journal known as the *Revue scientifique*. An article by Henri de Varigny describing the recent work of British criminologists Francis Galton and Edward Henry caught Vucetich's eye.

Juan Vucetich saw that the Galton-Henry fingerprinting system was going to revolutionize police work. Unlike Bertillonage, which allowed for a margin of error, a suspect's fingerprint is unique. Vucetich introduced Bertillonage to the La Plata police force, but he harbored grave doubts about its long-term effectiveness. In the next twelve months, Vucetich closely followed the progress of Henry Faulds and Sir William Herschel of the Indian civil service, who proved that fingerprints rarely, if ever, change over the course of time.

By September 1891, Vucetich had developed his own system of ten-finger classification, in which he identified four common traits: arches, prints with a triangle pattern on the right side, those with a triangle on the left side, and prints with triangles on both sides. Vucetich categorized these under the first four letters of the alphabet. The system incorporated the pattern identifications of whorls and ridges found in a human fingerprint.

The system became known as "dactiloscopia," but it would take several more years to be recognized by major law enforcement agencies as the definitive identification system. Vucetich encountered stiff resistance to his identification system among his reactionary superiors in the La Plata police force. In summer 1892, Vucetich was given his first opportunity to demonstrate the practical usages of dactiloscopia.

A heinous murder had occurred in Necochea, a coastal town two hundred miles south of La Plata. Francisca Rohas, a twenty-five-year-old mother of two, informed the police that a man named Hernando Velasquez from a neighboring village had battered her children to death in a jealous rage. Velasquez admitted that he loved Rohas but categorically denied killing her children. The La Plata police tried to beat a confession out of him, even though he had an indisputable alibi that showed he could not have committed the murders. In the end, it was Vucetich's fingerprint system that established the true identity of the actual killer.

Inspector Carlos Alvarez went back to the murder scene to take a second look. He found a bloody thumbprint on the door of the murder house. Alvarez carefully cut out the piece of wood and brought it back to the station, where, using Vucetich's fingerprinting system, a comparison was made with the right thumb of Francisca Rohas. They were identical. Under questioning, the woman confessed that she had murdered her own children and framed Velasquez in order to please a secret lover, who objected to the presence of two children. She was tried for murder and convicted and imprisoned. Consequently Vucetich gained widespread credibility throughout South America for his work in this case.

In 1894, Vucetich published his classic study of criminal identification methods entitled *Dactiliscopia comparada*. That year, the police chief of Buenos Aires Province adopted the Vucetich system. Thus Argentina became the first nation in the world to discard Bertillonage in favor of fingerprinting. Alphonse Bertillon and his followers did not react well to Vucetich. There was a great enmity and professional rivalry between the two men, which was apparent in Paris in 1913, when Bertillon publicly snubbed Juan Vucetich at the moment of his greatest triumph.

On July 18, 1916, the Argentine parliament passed into law a controversial bill requiring that every man, woman, and child be fingerprinted and catalogued in central police files. Vucetich was appointed to oversee the project, but no one, certainly not the head of the Statistical Bureau himself, foresaw the great public outcry this policy engendered.

There were riots in the streets as young and old alike protested this perceived violation of their civil rights. The General Registry building was stormed and the windows smashed before order was restored. Within days, Juan Vucetich had gone from hero to scapegoat. He was banished from the city, and in May 1917 many of his files were destroyed. Bitter and disillusioned, Vucetich retired to the country estate of his friend Edward Lomax. He lived out his final years in quiet contemplation before passing away from stomach cancer in 1925. Before dying, Vucetich was satisfied that fingerprinting was the standard worldwide criminal

identification system, even though systems other than his own were being used.

One of the first American police officials to adopt that system was Joseph Arthur Faurot (1872–1942). An official of the New York Police Department, Faurot is credited with instituting the use of fingerprinting in New York. He attended the 1904 Louisiana Purchase Exposition in St. Louis and witnessed a demonstration of fingerprinting by Scotland Yard experts. British police had by then adopted this method of identification over the Bertillon system.

Vucetich's 1904 pamphlet (published in La Plata, Argentina), which detailed his fingerprinting identification system, predating almost all other works on the subject used by police departments. *History Inc./Jay Robert Nash Collection.*

The St. Louis Police Department was so impressed by the demonstration that it became the first in the United States to adopt the use of fingerprinting. Faurot returned to New York and attempted to persuade his superiors to adopt the same system. Police Commissioner William McAdoo, however, sent Faurot to England to study the new fingerprinting identification system at Scotland Yard. When he returned, he was able to identify several known criminals through fingerprinting. Faurot also solved a number of murder cases through fingerprints. His successes led the NYPD to adopt fingerprinting as the chief method of criminal identification in 1911. Faurot continued to be its leading exponent until he retired in 1930. He is acknowledged as the founder of fingerprint identification in the United States.

The FBI, however, was not a pioneer user of the system until 1925, a year after a young man named J. Edgar Hoover became the director of that agency. Hoover established the most comprehensive, reliable fingerprinting system in America, one that all state and local agencies consult to this day. At one point, Hoover urged Congress to pass a law that would require all American citizens to be fingerprinted, but Washington politicians declined, mindful of the chaos that erupted in Argentina when a similar law was legislated a decade earlier.

After the FBI adopted fingerprinting as its criminal identification system, most other American police departments followed suit in the same year. That system began to bring about many convictions in capital cases, but shortly after it was adopted by the Huntington, West Virginia, police department, it served to exonerate a man who had been wrongly convicted of murder and sent to prison.

In May 1918, in Modoc, West Virginia, Cleveland Boyd, a miner with a reputation for aggressive behavior, was called before Squire H. E. Cook on vagrancy charges. Boyd had stood before Cook five months earlier on charges of drunken misconduct, and had vowed revenge on Cook at the sentencing. At the May hearing, Cook sentenced Boyd again, this time to thirty days imprisonment, or road work, and a $25 fine.

As Deputy Sheriff A. M. Godfrey and Cook were taking Boyd to the Matoaka Jail, Boyd asked permission to go to his home nearby to change shoes. Cook and Godfrey waited outside Boyd's shack. Seconds later, Boyd reappeared, firing a revolver and killing Cook with two shots. Godfrey ran for his life, and Boyd took off for the hills. Because of Cook's status as a leader in the town, the murder aroused great indignation and a description of the killer was released to the police.

Six years later, in 1924, police in Richmond, Virginia, arrested a man named Payne Boyd of Winston-Salem, North Carolina, for a minor infraction. A routine check of police records discovered that the man matched Cleveland Boyd's description. A photograph of Boyd was mailed to Mercer County authorities, who came to Richmond to positively identify him in a jail lineup as the man who had murdered Cook. Though the prisoner denied that he was Cleveland Boyd and insisted he had never been in Mercer County, he was indicted for the six-year-old murder.

Given a three-day trial on February 5–8, 1925, before Judge George L. Dillard, Boyd was found guilty of first-degree murder, but the verdict was set aside on technical grounds and a second trial took place in late April, when the accused again was found guilty and sentenced to life imprisonment by Dillard. In both trials, the only issue was whether or not the defendant was Cleveland Boyd. Thirty-one witnesses for the defense, including Cleveland Boyd's father-in-law, the judge who married him, neighbors, coworkers, and guests at his wedding, testified with total conviction that the prisoner was not the accused murderer.

Another twenty-four witnesses for the prosecution, however, were positive in identifying Payne as Cleveland Boyd, noting a scar over his left eye and one under his left jaw, which matched markings on the accused. An appellate court set aside Dillard's second verdict and ordered a third trial held in Cabell County in October 1925, in Huntington, before Judge Thomas R. Shepherd. A fingerprint expert, Garfield Rose of the Huntington police department, took the prisoner's fingerprints and found they matched those of Payne Boyd, on record with the War Department in Washington. Payne Boyd had served in the U.S. Army in 1917–1919 and could have not been present in Mercer County at the time Cook was murdered, and he was not Cleveland Boyd. On October 13, 1925, the jury found Payne Boyd not guilty. Boyd was released from jail, having served a year and a half in custody because of his resemblance to Cleveland Boyd.

Also by 1925, the Los Angeles Police Department had established an extensive fingerprint branch that was able to exonerate a wrongly convicted man in a violent robbery and send the real culprit to prison. On the evening of October 18, 1924, Earl M. Carroll, known as "the Weasel," climbed through the first floor of a home in Los

Angeles, leaving his fingerprints on the screen. He startled the wife of Dick R. Parsons and demanded her diamonds. He took her rings, but she was so flustered she could not remember where she put her other jewelry. As she looked in the den, the robber continued to threaten the woman and she tried to run outside. The intruder shot her in the back and escaped.

Several days later, James W. Preston was arrested on a charge of illegally wearing a naval uniform. Mrs. Parsons, recuperating in the hospital, identified Preston as her attacker, and Preston's trial began on March 11, 1925. During the trial, his dubious background was examined, including a vagrancy conviction, desertion from the U.S. Army, a dishonorable discharge from the U.S. Navy, and the arrest for illegally wearing the U.S. Navy uniform.

Preston's fingerprints did not match those on the window screen, but the prosecution suppressed that evidence, and Judge Hardy privately received inaccurate information that led him to believe Preston's fingerprints matched those left by the robber. On March 14, 1925, Preston was convicted of burglary, robbery, and assault with a deadly weapon. The judge sentenced Preston to eleven years and to life in prison, each sentence to be served consecutively, and on March 21, 1925, Preston began serving the time in San Quentin.

Meanwhile, a fingerprint specialist in the Los Angeles Police Department, Sergeant H. L. Barlow, discovered that Preston's fingerprints did not match those found on the screen at the Parson home and methodically compared the fingerprints of suspects as they were arrested with those on the screen. He found a match after Earl Carroll was arrested in May 1926 as a burglary suspect. Carroll refused to confess but was later convicted and imprisoned for the Parsons robbery. On September 2, 1926, after serving eighteen months in prison, Preston was granted a full pardon by Governor Friend William Richardson (1923–1927).

Fingerprinting, for all of its vaunted achievements in identifying perpetrators, is subject to

misapplication or interpretation through human error. In such cases, which are not as numerous as those involved in early forensic pathology or serology, wrongful convictions and imprisonments have resulted. One such case involved Stephan Cowans, a black resident of Boston, Massachusetts.

On May 30, 1997, a Boston police officer responding to a disturbance came upon an unknown black suspect and struggled

The fingerprints of a man named Robert Pitts, arrested in Austin, Texas in 1941, which amazed police experts in that the prints bore no papillary lines on the tips of the fingers and therefore no way by which to identify him. *History Inc./Jay Robert Nash Collection.*

with the man, who managed to wrest the officer's handgun from his control and shoot the officer and then fire another shot at a witness standing in a window nearby before fleeing. The assailant left behind a baseball cap he had been wearing and then forcibly entered a nearby home, where he remained with a family for some time, pausing to take a drink of water and leaving the officer's handgun and a sweatshirt he had been wearing before departing.

The wounded officer later identified Stephan Cowans as his attacker from a police array of photos

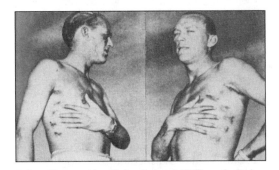

Robert Pitts was identified as Robert J. Phillips, who had a long police record (serving a term at Alcatraz), and whose fingerprints had been obliterated by skin grafts from his chest, as shown in these photos, operations performed by Dr. Leopold William August Brandenburg of Union, New Jersey, and underworld physician; both Pitts-Phillips and Brandenburg went to prison. *History Inc./Jay Robert Nash Collection.*

A misread thumbprint sent Stephan Cowans to prison. *Innocence Project, New York.*

and also identified Cowans on July 2, 1997 at a police lineup. Cowans was also identified by the person the assailant shot at, who was standing in a second-floor window. Members of the family present in the home forcibly entered by the assailant could not identify Cowans as the intruder. Cowans was tried and convicted in 1998 of armed assault with intent to murder, home invasion, and assault and battery with a dangerous weapon and sentenced to thirty to forty-five years in prison.

Prosecutors at his trial relied on the eyewitness testimony of the officer and the witness at the window, as well as a latent thumbprint taken from the mug used by the assailant when he invaded a nearby home. Prosecutors said that the thumbprint matched that of Cowans. In 2003, the mug was released for testing, along with the baseball cap and the sweatshirt. After testing, DNA results said that there were no matches for Cowans. The district attorney retested the thumbprint and a fingerprint expert reported that the original fingerprint analysis at Cowans trial was in error and that the thumbprint did not actually match Cowans's. On January 23, 2004, Cowans was released after being wrongly imprisoned for five and a half years.

## Forensic Pathology: The Corpse and the Clues

Forensic pathology is the scientific study of the human body in a detailed autopsy to determine the cause, time, and method of a homicide or other related crimes. Through this exacting science, which can nevertheless fail through human error, numerous celebrated pathologists, such as the indomitable Sir Bernard Henry Spilsbury

(1877–1947) of England, solved many classic crimes. Spilsbury almost single-handedly brought about the murder convictions of some of Great Britain's most notorious killers—Dr. Hawley Harvey Crippen (1910), George Joseph Smith (1915), and John Norman Thorne (1925). Yet this brilliant forensic pathologist was fallible.

In the celebrated 1932 case of Elvira Barney, a London society woman accused of killing her sweetheart, Michael Scott Stephen, in Knightsbridge, Spilsbury upheld the view of Scotland Yard that Barney had shot the young man to death. On the witness stand, though, defense counsel Sir Patrick Hastings subsequently demonstrated that Stephen's death was, in fact, a suicide. Barney was freed, but a shadow of doubt about Spilsbury's methods and ready acceptance of Scotland Yard's investigative abilities remained.

British crime writer Edgar Lustgarten later wrote, "To the man in the street, he [Spilsbury] stood for pathology as Hobbs stood for cricket or Dempsey for boxing or Capablanca for chess. His pronouncements were invested with the force of dogma and it was blasphemy to hint that he might conceivably be wrong." When Spilsbury died, his files were found to contain some 25,000 entries from every postmortem investigation he had conducted.

Another such star of forensic pathology was Dr. Milton Helpern (1902–1977), who was the chief medical examiner for New York City for twenty years. Helpern was instrumental, along with Dr. Charles Umberger, in bringing about the conviction

The most celebrated pathologist-sleuth of his era, Sir Bernard Spilsbury, shown in his London laboratory in 1921. *History Inc./Jay Robert Nash Collection.*

of Dr. Carl Coppolino for murdering his wife in 1966, although F. Lee Bailey, the defense counsel in that case, charged that Helpern and Umberger had fabricated forensic evidence in that case.

Sir Sydney Alfred Smith (1883–1969), who headed the forensics department as dean of the medical facility at the University of Edinburgh (and was often at odds with the redoubtable Sir Bernard Spilsbury), was another leading pathologist credited with solving many crimes. Smith worked to solve the riddle of what was called the Shark Arm Case in Australia in 1935, after a captured shark disgorged a human arm. Smith, who happened at that time to be attending a forensic science convention in Sydney, Australia (where Bernard Spilsbury was also in attendance), identified the arm as belonging to James Smith, a handyman. He concluded that the arm had not been bitten from Smith's torso, but had been cut away with a saw or another sharp instrument.

Smith explained, following his detailed examination of the arm, that the killer had undoubtedly placed the body of the victim inside a small tin trunk but was unable to get the arm inside as well, and simply chopped it off. Said Smith, "Unable to get this in [the trunk], the murderer cut it off and attached it to the trunk with the rope from the boat, tying one end of it around the wrist. [Smith had determined rope marks around the wrist of the severed arm.] The trunk and its contents and the blood-soaked mattress and mats were then taken out to sea and dumped. The arm worked loose and was swallowed by the shark." Patrick Brady, who had been accused of murdering James Smith, was nevertheless acquitted after his defense attorney argued that a single human arm without the rest of the body being present did not constitute enough evidence to convict his client.

Spilsbury, Helpern, and Smith were giants in the field of forensic pathology, as well as experts in forensic anthropology, the study of the history of a human body, particularly bones, in determining the causes and time of death and the study of forensic medicine (forensic chemistry) to deduce cause or time of death or for other legal purposes. They were not, however, perfect and errors in their sterling careers presented themselves as they have with many another competent forensic pathologist. This was evident in the case of Gerald C. Wentzel, who was wrongly convicted of murdering a Pennsylvania woman, a conviction chiefly based on reports from pathologists.

In December 1946, Miriam Greene, a twenty-seven-year-old divorcée, was strangled with a scarf in her Pottstown, Pennsylvania, apartment. When she did not report for work, her landlady opened the apartment on December 9, 1946, and found her body. During the police investigation, officials questioned her former husband, George Greene, and her married lover, Gerald C. Wentzel.

Renowned Scottish pathologist Sydney Alfred Smith, who unraveled Australia's "Shark-Arm" murder in 1935. *History Inc./Jay Robert Nash Collection.*

Wentzel initially claimed he had only passing knowledge of the murdered woman, but later admitted to having an affair with her and to finding her body on Sunday night, December 8, 1946. He did not notify police, he said, because he was married and did not want to get involved.

Wentzel also gave police an alibi, saying that he was hunting from December 5, 1946, until the evening of December 8, 1946, with fifteen other men several hundred miles away. Each of the hunting partners independently verified his alibi. He was nevertheless charged with Greene's murder and brought to trial.

When Wentzel was brought to trial in 1947, pathology experts gave conflicting testimony about the time of Greene's death. Despite the doubts about the time factor, the jury found Wentzel guilty and he was sentenced to ten to twenty years at the Pennsylvania penitentiary. After Wentzel's conviction, Greene's mother and sister announced that they believed Wentzel was innocent, and offered a substantial reward for information leading to the true killer's arrest.

Following Wentzel's conviction, Dr. LeMoyne Snyder, a medical-legal expert, determined that Greene's death occurred on the evening of December 7, 1946, while Wentzel was still on the hunting trip. This information was sent to the board of pardons and paroles of Pennsylvania, and in 1950 Governor John Sydney Fine (1951–1956) commuted Wentzel's original sentence to a term for the time already served, an action that automatically prevented Wentzel from obtaining compensation.

Dr. Snyder, the pathologist who brought about Wentzel's release, was one of the foremost medical experts in the United States. In May 1944, Dr. Snyder, the medical-legal chief for the Michigan state police, published *Homicide Investigation,* a work that outlines effective methods for conducting murder and suicide investigations. Snyder argues that the first fifteen minutes of an investigation are crucial, that the scene should be thoroughly photographed and sketched, and that distances should be measured and fingerprints taken. Snyder addresses several fallacies concerning murder cases.

These include the belief that quicklime destroys bodies, the victim's expression will remain fixed, the killer always returns to the scene of the crime, and a bullet in the heart is always fatal. In addition, Snyder discusses different types of poisons, including bichloride of mercury, morphine, strychnine (which can kill in as little as fifteen minutes), and arsenic. The latter two are easily traced in the body.

Snyder also details differences between murders and suicides, saying that suicides often hang themselves and try several times to shoot themselves. Snyder evaluates lie detector tests, methods for extracting specks of gunpowder from a victim's hand, and detecting lead by X ray. In addition, he warns against making snap assumptions, such as assuming that a body discovered in water has been drowned.

Forensic sciences do not produce reliable results overnight, as Snyder cautions, but only through exacting and time-consuming testing and retesting. Forensic pathology is no exception, where scientific studies are methodically applied to entry and exit wounds, bloodstains at the scene of the crime, or bloodstains found on a suspect or a suspect's apparel or possessions. Without such studies, Samuel "Sammie" Garrett, Kenneth Marsh, Sabrina Butler, and Nathaniel Walker would likely have remained behind bars for most of their lives after being wrongly convicted of crimes they did not commit.

Garrett's problems began in 1969, when his distraught twenty-eight-year-old girlfriend, Karen Thompson, went to a Chicago motel, wrote a suicide note, and then used a shotgun to end her life. Garrett was not charged with wrongdoing in Thompson's death until a pathologist examining her corpse mistook the exit wound in Thompson's skull for an entrance wound. He decided that Thompson had been murdered, and Garrett was arrested and charged with killing Thompson.

At his 1970 trial, two police officers, based on the pathologist's report, testified that the length of the shotgun and the location of the wound ruled out suicide and any possibility that Thompson could have physically taken her own life. Her suicide note was discounted since Thompson had been, prior to her death, in a "highly emotional state" that may have produced the note without a real intention of taking her own life.

Garrett was sentenced to twenty to forty years in prison by Judge Philip Romiti, who had convicted Garrett at a bench trial, based on the testimony of the two police officers and the statements of the pathologist. On an appeal, Thompson's remains were exhumed and reexamined, but this time a pathologist discovered the real entrance wound at the roof of Thompson's mouth, a wound that had been entirely overlooked by the pathologist in the first trial. This discovery confirmed that Thompson had the ability to use the shotgun to take her own life. Garrett was released in 1975, after spending five years in prison. In 1980, the U.S. District Court for the Northern District of Illinois denied a civil rights claim made by Garrett, who received no compensation for his wrongful conviction and imprisonment.

Kenneth Morgan Marsh received substantial compensation for his wrongful conviction and imprisonment, but he had to wait twenty-one years to receive it. Marsh was convicted of the death of two-year-old Philip Buell, the son of Marsh's girlfriend, Brenda Buell Warter. The boy was found dead on April 27, 1983, in Warter's San Diego home. Marsh, who worked nights at a Coca-Cola bottling plant, looked after the boy and his sister, while Brenda Warter worked at a day job. Police investigating the death originally concluded that the boy had died accidentally after falling off a couch and striking his head on a brick hearth. San Diego prosecutors, however, came to the conclusion that the child had been killed and charged Marsh with the boy's death. At Marsh's trial, six medical experts for the prosecution, including the state pathologist who had conducted an autopsy on the boy, testified that the only way the toddler could have died was through abuse.

Deputy district attorney Jay Coulter, who prosecuted Marsh, claimed that Buell had multiple cuts and a gash on his neck one and a half inches deep. No blood was found on the hearth where Marsh said the boy fell. Marsh's attorneys countered that the boy had been cut when he fell onto the hearth and struck a glass ashtray, breaking it; glass shards caused the cuts and gash. Prosecutors stated that no blood was found on those glass shards. "The cuts were scrapes [that] occurred when Buell fell on the hearth," said defense attorney Donnie Cox.

In November 1983, Marsh was convicted of second-degree murder and sentenced to fifteen years to life in prison. After his appeals failed, the California Innocence Project undertook his case, attorneys Justin Brooks, Tracy Emblem, and Jeff Chin petitioning the state to review the case again in October 2002, with new medical evidence

showing that the Buell child had an undiagnosed blood disorder and that a physician had administered the drug mannitol to him, both contributing to his actual death following his accidental fall. This coincided with the state's original conclusion that the boy had died from brain hemorrhaging.

When this new medical report was reviewed in 2004, Marsh was released and all charges against him dismissed. He was reunited with Brenda Warter, who remained convinced of his innocence throughout his twenty-one years of wrongful confinement. In January 2006, Governor Arnold Schwarzenegger signed into law a bill that awarded the fifty-one-year-old Marsh $765,000 in compensation for his wrongful conviction and imprisonment.

The same kind of human error in an autopsy report occurred in 1989, after Brenda Dalton was found dead in her Newfoundland, Canada, home. Several pathologists determined that she had been strangled to death, based on findings from their detailed autopsy. Her husband, Ronald Dalton, was convicted of the crime and sent to prison for life. He made several appeals and was acquitted in 2000, when two pathologists reexamined the evidence and realized that Brenda Dalton had choked to death on breakfast cereal. Dalton was released with apologies, after serving more than ten years behind bars.

Another pathologist in that same year made a serious misdiagnosis in examining the corpse of a small child in Lowndes County, Mississippi, a mistake that sent the child's mother to death row. Sabrina Butler, an eighteen-year-old mentally retarded woman, rushed her nine-month-old son, Walter Dean Butler, to a hospital on April 12, 1989, saying that she had tried to resuscitate the child but had no success. The boy was pronounced dead and a pathologist examining the remains stated that the boy had suffered fatal external wounds, chiefly a blow to the stomach, which police later claimed had been inflicted by Sabrina Butler.

Butler went on trial in 1990 and was chiefly convicted on the pathologist's autopsy report. She was sentenced to death, but the Mississippi

Supreme Court vacated the conviction in 1992, on the grounds that prosecutors had wrongfully inferred to the jury that Butler was guilty since she had not taken the witness stand on her own behalf. A new trial was ordered and the autopsy was reexamined by the same pathologist, who then admitted that his autopsy research had been inadequate and that the boy most likely died from sudden death syndrome (SIDS) or a cystic kidney disease.

Moreover, a witness at Butler's new trial in 1995 claimed to be present when Butler attempted CPR on her child and stated that no blows were struck. A jury acquitted Butler on December 17, 1995. Where pathology had failed Sabrina Butler, serology wrongly condemned Nathaniel Walker.

Ten years after he went to jail for abducting and raping an Elizabeth, New Jersey, woman, forty-four-year-old Nathaniel Walker was freed by Judge Alfred Wolin when new forensic evidence came to light. The crime for which he was charged occurred on the night of October 19, 1974, when a woman was abducted near her home and forced to drive with her assailant to a parking lot outside a public housing project in Newark. There she was assaulted and raped.

In February 1975, the victim picked Walker out of a police lineup. He was convicted in a jury trial and received a life sentence in June 1976, despite testimony from coworkers that they had driven Walker home shortly after he had completed his shift at 11:30 P.M. at the Phelps Dodge Plant.

In 1978, Walker's conviction was overturned on appeal, and Walker was freed on bail. Then, just a year later, the New Jersey Supreme Court reinstated the conviction. Walker fled to Los Angeles, where he was eventually arrested and returned to New Jersey to finish out his sentence.

In July 1985, James McCloskey, a graduate of Princeton Theological Seminary, became interested in the case. McCloskey became a celebrated attorney for Centurion Ministries in Princeton, New Jersey, bringing about exonerations of wrongly convicted persons. (See Clarence Lee Brandley in Chapter XI, "Railroading and Framing.") McCloskey had serology tests conducted at the laboratory at Elizabeth General Hospital on vaginal fluids taken from the victim a short time after she had been attacked.

Following those serological testes, McCloskey demonstrated to the court that the actual rapist had B antigens in the red blood cells, but Walker and the victim both had A antigens. The case was reopened, and Nathaniel Walker was granted his freedom on November 5, 1986, after nearly a decade in prison.

## Odontology: The Bite Marks of Crime

Forensic odontology, also called forensic dentistry or bite mark evidence expertise, has long been practiced as a criminal identification system. This forensic science involves the identification of an assailant through the comparison of the suspect's dentition (set of teeth) with the record of a bite mark left on the victim. To solve a particular problem, experts employ X rays, models, photography, and microscopy. Such experts are invariably board certified (having observed autopsies, having worked on as many as twenty-five cases, and having accumulated 350 qualification points through attendance at meetings and conferences). Few such qualified forensic odontologists are successfully challenged on the stand in court, since considerable judicial notice has been given to this expertise.

Teeth, which are the most durable remains found in a decomposed body, have long been employed to identify victims. Agrippina, the savage mother of Emperor Nero, ordered the murder of Lollia Paulina in A.D. 66, demanding that the victim's head be shown to her as proof of death. When this grisly, largely decomposed exhibit was brought to her, Agrippina could not be sure of the identity until examining the front teeth, which bore a discolored front tooth the victim was known to have. Paul Revere of the American Revolution, as a young dentist, identified the mangled remains of soldiers from battlefields through their bridgework. In 1945, the charred bodies of Adolf Hitler and his mistress, Eva Braun, were identified by comparing the undamaged teeth of the otherwise indistinguishable remains.

Forensic odontology, however, is a relatively new science in its application to criminal cases, rising to prominence in the twentieth century. Animal bite marks were examined in many criminal cases before that time. Joseph Vacher (1869–1898), known as the French Ripper, went to the guillotine on December 31, 1898, following his conviction for several brutal murders. This serial killer claimed that he had become a werewolf and was thus unwillingly compelled to take the lives of his victims. He insisted that he had been bitten by such a demonizing creature early in life, but the bite marks examined were of human origin.

In the celebrated 1982 case of Lindy Chamberlain (Chapter IV), the defense claimed that her child had been taken and killed by a wild dingo in the Australian outback and not murdered by her and her husband. The prosecution in that case offered forensic dentistry experts, however, who insisted that the "bite marks" found on one of the child's abandoned garments had not been made by a dingo, but a scissors, which brought about a conviction later proved to be wrongful. In 1998, Mario Orantes Najera was wrongfully accused of murdering his employer, activist Bishop Juan Jose Gerardi in Guatemala, prosecutors claiming that he had caused his German shepherd to repeatedly bite the prelate while he crushed Gerardi's head with a concrete block. Bite marks from the dog, however, were not found on the body after it had been exhumed and examined (Chapter XI).

Human bite marks were identified in the remains of four female victims, murdered between 1968 and 1971, by forensic odontologists as belonging to Canadian serial killer Wayne Boden (a.k.a. the Vampire Rapist). Boden savagely bit his victims on the breasts. Forensic dentistry in this

case resulted in Boden receiving four life terms in prison. Odontology experts also sealed the judicial fate of serial killer Theodore "Ted" Bundy (1947–1989). As he did with most of his victims, Bundy had savagely bitten Lisa Levy, one of five female students he attacked in a sorority house on the campus of the University of Florida in Tallahassee on the night of January 15, 1978, killing two of the young women, including Levy.

Bundy was apprehended a short time later, and on April 27, 1979, detectives brought Bundy to an examining room. When he learned that they intended to take a wax impression of his teeth, Bundy went berserk, struggling violently so that a half dozen men had to pin him down and hold his mouth open for the impression to be made. Bundy knew what the detectives were seeking. The impressions of his teeth were later perfectly matched to the bite marks found on the buttocks of Lisa Levy, and it was this piece of evidence that would later, more than anything else, convict and bring about the execution of Ted Bundy for the many murders he had so ruthlessly committed.

Though many capital cases have been solved through odontology, experts in this field are not infallible. This proved evident with devastating results in two cases, one in Louisiana and another in New York. The Louisiana case opened on the night of December 12, 1986, when a female patron left a bar in Marrero, Louisiana. She went to a restaurant where she bought breakfast for her son and took the meal back to her car. She saw a piece of paper on her windshield and put it into her pocket. She was then accosted by a black man who forced her into his car, bit her several times, and then had oral and vaginal sex with her. Finally he drove her to another neighborhood and let her out of the car, telling her not to call police since no one would help her because she was black.

The woman did call the police, who quickly identified the attacker as Willie Jackson, since the piece of paper the victim had found on her windshield and kept was a bank receipt bearing his name. Jackson had moved to Natchez, Mississippi, eight months before the crime, although he periodically visited his mother, who continued to live in Marrero. Police found a car driven by Jackson's mother that the victim identified as the one in which she had been attacked. In searching the Jackson home, police found a sweatshirt emblazoned with the name "Milton," and the victim also identified the shirt as having been worn by her assailant.

Jackson's photo was placed in a photo array, which the victim reviewed, selecting Jackson from several others, and she further identified Jackson in a police lineup. At his 1989 trial, Jackson was again identified by the victim and, most importantly, a forensic odontologist stated that the bite marks on the victim came from Jackson's teeth.

Though a rape kit was collected from the victim, lab experts could find not semen. Jackson was convicted of rape and robbery and sentenced to forty years in prison. Only a few days after his conviction, however, Milton Jackson, Willie's brother, confessed to the crime. A bartender later testified that he saw Milton Jackson in the bar with the victim on the night of the attack, but that Willie Jackson was not present. The victim viewed Milton Jackson in a lineup and said he was not the man who had attacked her.

The legal firm of Regan & Associates of New Orleans then took over Willie Jackson's case. Two of its attorneys, Martin Regan Jr. and Karla Baker, located an independent forensic odontologist who examined the bite marks in the case and reported that they had not come from Willie Jackson, but from Milton Jackson. A handwriting expert provided by Regan and Baker stated that Milton Jackson had written the note on the back of the bank receipt found by the victim, not his brother Willie.

The lawyers secured DNA testing in June 2003, where semen was found on the victim's pantyhose and, following testing by Reliagene, Willie Jackson was excluded from being the donor. The test conclusively proved that the semen had come from his brother, Milton Jackson, who was then serving a life sentence for an unrelated 1998 rape conviction. All charges against Willie Jackson were dis-

missed on May 26, 2006, and he was released from prison after serving seventeen years behind bars.

In the case of thirty-one-year-old Roy Brown, a native of Auburn, New York, an odontologist identified Brown's bite marks with those of a killer. Brown was not an ideal citizen in the eyes of the police, who iden-

**Roy Brown's wrongful murder conviction was based on bite marks.** *Innocence Project, New York.*

tified him as a likely suspect in a murder case. According to police records, he had alcohol and drug problems, patronized prostitutes, and abused his wife and children. His daughter had been placed in a residential care facility by Cayuga County Social Services and Brown repeatedly called and threatened the director of that agency, until he was arrested and given a short jail term. That incident caused police to link him to the murder of Sabina Kulakowski, who was a social worker for Cayuga County.

On the night of May 23, 1991, Kulakowski's body was discovered in a field outside the farmhouse where she was living near Aurelius, New York. Firefighters had responded to a fire in that house and found the victim beaten, strangled, and stabbed to death. Police investigators found a bloody nightshirt at the scene, and, when seeing that the victim had suffered many bite marks all over her body, swabbed these bite marks as evidence. Police shortly arrested Brown, since he had had a police history related to the agency for which the victim worked, although Kulakowski had not been involved in the case dealing with Brown's daughter and there was no evidence that she and Brown knew each other.

Charged with first-degree murder, Brown was brought to trial in 1992. Prosecutors realized that the saliva from the nightshirt worn by the victim, as well as the swabs from the bite marks, had proved inconclusive following analysis. They concentrated on the statements from a forensic odontologist, who said that the seven bite marks on the victim's body were "entirely consistent" with Brown. Defense attorneys claimed through their own expert that six of the bite marks were insufficient to provide any definitive results following analysis and that the seventh bite mark excluded Brown altogether in that that mark bore two more upper teeth than Brown possessed.

Brown was nevertheless convicted and sentenced from twenty-five years to life at the Elmira Correctional Facility. Here, Brown undertook a new investigation with the aim of solving the murder by identifying another man as the culprit. After a fire at his stepfather's home destroyed Brown's court documents, he requested copies of those documents under the Freedom of Information Act.

Brown received much more than he had expected or even seen at his trial, including statements sheriff's deputies had taken during their 1991 investigation. Those statements, which defense attorneys later claimed were not disclosed at Brown's trial, raised suspicions about a man named Barry Bench, who lived near the house where Kulakowski was killed. In fact, Brown learned, Bench was the brother of a man who had dated the victim for some time, until that relationship was broken off by the victim two months before her murder and that the victim leased the farmhouse from the Bench family.

Brown concluded that Barry Bench was the real killer of Sabina Kulakowski and wrote to Bench in 2003, telling him that he intended to request post-conviction DNA analysis of the crime, which would prove Bench guilty. Less than a week after Brown mailed the letter to Bench, he committed suicide by walking in front of a speeding Amtrak train.

The Innocence Project in New York became involved with Brown's case in 2005, requesting more postconviction DNA analysis. In the following year, six saliva stains found on the victim's shirt that had never been tested proved that they had come from Barry Bench.

To be sure of Brown's exoneration, district attorney James B. Vargason ordered Bench's remains exhumed and tested for DNA. The results showed that his DNA was on the shirt of the victim. On January 23, 2007, Brown was released from prison and the prosecution formally dismissed all charges against him on

**Ray Krone went to prison on erroneous bite mark evidence.** *Innocence Project, New York.*

March 5, 2007. He spent fifteen years in prison for a murder he did not commit. In May 2007, Brown filed a $5 million suit against the State of New York, saying, "All the money in the world isn't worth a day [in prison]."

Seven months after Sabine Kulakowski was murdered in New York, an innocent man in Arizona was sent to prison, on the basis of the same evidence that had convicted Roy Brown. In the case of Ray Krone of Phoenix, Arizona, forensic dentistry brought about a conviction that was overturned on the strength of an even more effective identification system, DNA.

On the night of December 29, 1991, the naked body of thirty-six-year-old Kim Ancona was found in the men's restroom of a Phoenix lounge where she worked as a cocktail waitress. Ancona had been fatally stabbed, her assailant leaving behind little physical evidence. Serologists matched the victim's type to the blood left behind, and saliva proved to come from the most common type of blood. Examiners could find no semen present and no DNA tests were made.

Friends of the victim told police that Ancona had told them that a regular patron, Ray Krone, had offered to help her close up the bar the previous night and police soon zeroed in on Krone as a prime suspect. Krone had no criminal record and had been honorably discharged from the U.S. Air Force with the rank of sergeant after having served seven years. He had had a clean record at the local postal service, where he had worked for seven years. Everything about him indicated that he was an upstanding citizen. He had been born and raised in York, Pennsylvania, where he was a Cub Scout, a Boy Scout, sang in a local church choir, and graduated in the top 10 percent of his high school class.

Asked to make a Styrofoam impression of his teeth, Krone agreed, and his teeth marks were matched, according to forensic dentistry experts, with those found on the breasts and neck of the victim. Krone was arrested and charged with Ancona's murder on December 31, 1991. The odontology evidence brought about Krone's conviction of first-degree murder and kidnapping at his 1992 trial, where the press dubbed him the "snaggletooth killer," based on the distinctive dental pattern left on the victim's body. Krone, who was found not guilty on an additional charge of sexual assault, was sentenced to death, plus twenty-years.

Throughout his trial, Krone maintained that he was innocent, claiming to have been asleep at home at the time of the murder. His parents, Carolyn and James Leming, hired a new attorney, Christopher J. Plourd. The lawyer convinced the Arizona Supreme Court to review the case, arguing that DNA had not been employed in the case and that, if it had, the saliva found at the scene of the crime would exonerate his client.

In June 1995, the Supreme Court ordered a new trial for Krone, which took place the following year. The DNA saliva test proved inconclusive and Krone was again convicted on the forensic dentistry evidence. The judge in the case, Maricopa County superior court Judge James McDougall, however, reduced Krone's death sentence to twenty-five years to life imprisonment, expressing doubts about the defendant's guilt, which included "the clear identity of the killer."

Following his second conviction in 1996, Krone realized he would be seventy-five before he became eligible for release, which caused him to lose hope in ever seeing his vindication. "That pretty much ruled out all the faith I had in truth and justice," he said later. Krone's attorneys, however, did not give up. Lawyer Alan Simpson had a new and improved DNA test performed on the saliva and blood found on Ancona's tank top in 2002, a test that excluded Krone and pointed to another man, Kenneth Phillips, who lived a short distance from the scene of the crime but had never been a suspect.

Prosecutors then realized that Krone was innocent and told Maricopa County superior Judge Alfred Fenzel that the chances were 1.3 quadrillion to one that the DNA evidence of the saliva found on Anacona's clothing came from inmate Kenneth Phillips, who was then serving time in a Florence, Arizona, prison for an unrelated crime. Further, odontologists who had testified in Krone's previous trials admitted that Phillips could not be ruled out as the person who had made the bite marks on Ancona's breast. Four days after a police lab confirmed the DNA results, Krone was released on April 8, 2002. The district attorney dismissed all charges against him on April 24, 2002.

Krone spent ten years behind bars as an innocent person. Said Maricopa County prosecuting attorney Rick Romley, "What do we say to him? An injustice was done and we will try to do better. We are sorry." A short time later, Krone stated, "I still find it hard to believe that only a few weeks ago I was sitting in my Arizona jail cell and today I am a free man. I owe my freedom to the extraordinary efforts of my family, friends, and volunteer lawyers, who fought tirelessly for me to obtain the DNA evidence from my case."

Krone was the 100th former death row inmate freed as an innocent person since the reinstatement of capital punishment in the United States in 1976. "True," Krone stated, "I have recently received notoriety—if it can be called that—for being the 100th American exonerated, but the fact is that being 100 or 99 or 98 doesn't really matter. What matters is that our death penalty system is broken. What happened to me can happen to anyone."

# The Near Miracle of DNA

I N THE LATE 1980S, THE REVOLUTIONARY NEW DNA (deoxyribonucleic acid) "fingerprinting" became one of the most reliable (if not tainted or corrupted or improperly processed and analyzed) identification methods in criminal investigation. DNA, the most trusted of identification systems in present-day criminal procedures, is also subject to error through contamination, misidentification through wrong evaluations by inexpert testing, and, in some instances, outright fabrication and falsification. Because of this human condition, prosecutors have challenged even the most sophisticated and updated DNA testing by independent forensic organizations, having the same testing performed by their own DNA experts. In most cases, however, the same testing produces the same results.

Before DNA, fingerprinting (Chapter VIII, "Forensic Science to the Rescue") was the most trusted method of identifying criminals. DNA, however, relies on the basic genetic material found in all human cells. With the exception of identical twins, DNA makeup is reportedly different in every person. DNA had been identified in the 1980s, but the first profiling test was not developed until 1985 by Sir Alec Jeffreys in England (the same country that was first to institutionalize fingerprinting as a definitive system of criminal identification). The following year, the perpetrator of a double murder in the Midlands

was identified, convicted, and imprisoned through DNA.

Genetic testing of this sort analyzes hair roots, blood, semen, and other bodily fluids for DNA. Results are less precise for hair than for fluids, or even spermatozoa in a dried condition. DNA hair testing has the ability to exclude someone, but not to identify an individual with the same degree of accuracy as fluid testing does. This is the chief reason why the FBI will not accept DNA profiles obtained from hair for comparison in its database, a practice also upheld by many databases maintained by state law enforcement agencies.

This exacting science, however, compares the unique genetic profiles of individuals and can discriminate among billions of people to conclusively identify and tie a person to a specific crime. It has been most effective in rape cases, where rape kits have preserved spermatozoa on swabs or on the clothes of a victim, but it can be equally effective in other capital offenses such as murder, robbery, arson, kidnapping, and burglary, where any kind of preserved genetic fluids, from blood to saliva, left behind by a perpetrator can be later analyzed and defined by DNA.

A most recent and classic example was the May 17, 2007, conviction of thirty-three-year-old Juan Luna by a jury in Cook County, Illinois. Fourteen years earlier, and late on the night of January 8, 1993, Luna had entered a Brown's Chicken fast food outlet in Palatine, Illinois, near closing time. He and an alleged accomplice, James Degorski, herded seven employees into a back area walk-in cooler and freezer, and ruthlessly murdered them before robbing the place. (Killed were restaurant owners Richard and Lynn Ehlenfeldt and employees Marcus Nellsen, 31; Michael Castro, 16; Guadalupe Maldonado, 46; Thomas Mennes, 32; and Rico Solis, 17.) The arrogant Luna, then eighteen, paused to help himself to a chicken dinner and enjoyed a leisurely meal before departing. That meal was found by detectives and preserved. Eventually DNA from Luna's saliva determined that he had been one of the last persons alive in the place, which Luna admitted in a taped confession that also brought about his conviction and the jury's recommendation to Judge Vincent Gaughan that this mass murderer should be sent to prison for life.

Luna had been arrested in 2002, along with an alleged accomplice, James Degorski, after a woman, Anne Lockett, contacted officials, telling them that both Luna and Degorski had admitted the slayings to her. Prosecutors stated that Luna and Degorski shot and stabbed the seven victims during a robbery that netted them less than $2,000. Degorski is also charged with the murders and is still awaiting trial at this writing. Luna's defense attorney, Clarence Burch, described Luna as having an IQ of 86 and being nothing more than a follower of the manipulative Degorski, dragged into drugs and a life in crime. That Luna had a deep sadistic streak was evident from testimony by Lockett, who stated that he had once electrocuted a cat with a car battery. Another friend, Eileen Bakalla, stated that Luna once threw a kitten tied to a leash from a speeding car, laughing as it bounced to death.

Widely supported by the scientific community, DNA was responsible for the

Vincent Moto, at left, wrongly convicted of a 1985 Philadelphia rape. *Innocence Project, New York.*

conviction of murderer-rapist Timothy Wilson Spencer in Virginia in 1988, and, in a landmark decision, marked the first time an appeal had been upheld by a higher court solely on the strength of DNA evidence. (See "The Vasquez-Spencer DNA Case" this chapter.) Another early conviction based exclusively on DNA was that of Sell Lee Andreas, who was sent to prison for 115 years in a Florida rape case.

As many convictions as DNA has brought about since these precedent-setting cases, a great number of wrongly convicted prisoners have been set free after DNA proved their innocence. Typical was Vincent Moto, who served more than eight years in a Pennsylvania prison for a rape he did not commit. Moto, while pushing his baby in a stroller on a Philadelphia street in 1986, was identified by a woman who claimed he and an accomplice had raped her on December 2, 1985. He was convicted on her testimony and sent to prison on a sentence of twelve to twenty-four years.

DNA testing by Forensic Science Associates in California eliminated Moto as the source of the spermatozoa found on the victim's underwear, and on November 13, 1995, Judge Joseph Papalini vacated Moto's 1986 conviction and granted him a new trial based on the DNA report. He was released in July 1996. Full exoneration came for Moto when an independent laboratory confirmed the exculpatory DNA test results made by Forensic Science Associates. By the end of 1997, DNA testing led to the release of ten wrongfully convicted men from Illinois prisons. These included death row inmates Alejandro Hernandez, Rolando Cruz, Verneal Jimerson, and Dennis Williams (See Chapter X, "False Confessions").

Many police departments have sought to take DNA fingerprints from all those booked for serious crimes, but individuals and groups have fought against this procedure. In 1996, two Marines refused to contribute blood samples for a DNA registry and received reprimands. The two Marines feared that DNA would provide "genetic dog tags" that might be used against them in the future. In 1998, New York Police Commissioner Howard Safir proposed taking DNA samples from everyone arrested, but this proposal drew a storm of protest from the New York Civil Liberties Union, which stated that an arrest is not sufficient grounds for forced collection of DNA samples. Under Safir's proposal, police would take a swabbing from inside a suspect's cheek, the present standard procedure of collecting DNA evidence.

In many U.S. states, however, police, as well as prosecutors, stubbornly oppose DNA, while the science slowly moves these seemingly immovable persons toward reform. Even though many states now have databases of samples from which "cold cases" can be tested to irrefutably identify the actual perpetrator of a crime, recalcitrant police and prosecutors refuse to submit such samples, or delay and obfuscate such testing in their own databases. Says Robert McCulloch, president of the National District Attorneys Association, which represents more than 2,300 chief prosecutors, "There is absolutely no excuse for not putting the samples into any database to find out who did it. You don't want the wrong guy in prison and the right guy walking the streets."

The fear of submitting those samples, however, is based on the suspicion that testing cases in the thousands, perhaps tens of thousands, not the present hundreds, would prove myriad more people wrongly convicted, irrespective of the amoral decision to allow, without such action, the actual perpetrators to remain free. Such a deluge of overturned cases would result, police and prosecutors know, in pinpointing the shoddy, ineffective police and prosecutorial procedures of the past, not to mention the exposure of official corruption in those cases.

A Chicago-area prosecutor (who understandably insisted on remaining anonymous) said to this author in April 2007, "I believe that if we threw everything we had into the DNA hopper, it would prove to be catastrophic—judges, prosecuting attorneys, high- and low-ranking police officers, as well as armies of forensic scientists outside of DNA—would be exposed as being inept at best and criminally negligent at worst. They might be joining the very persons they wrongly convicted in prison and they know it. Then there is the compensation to more armies of wrongly convicted people such en masse testing would exhibit. Right now, some exonerated persons receive compensation in the many millions of dollars for their wrongful convictions. If all of the wrongly convicted persons were exonerated by DNA—and they may be in the tens of thousands—we would have to pay off in the billions, maybe trillions, and bankrupt most major metropolitan areas. The only way to fix this growing problem is for police officers, prosecutors, and judges to do their job right or apply for a position with the sanitation department."

Police and prosecutors have nevertheless resisted the results of DNA with unreasonably unyielding behavior, not unlike the unwillingness of those resisting the transition from the horse and buggy to the automobile at the turn of the past century. In many rape cases, which is where DNA shines brightly in pinpointing actual perpetrators from biological evidence, prosecutors, judges, and police have defied such results, with lame dog excuses such as "well, the perpetrator did not ejaculate, so the evidence must come from someone else," or, if a person other than the one convicted is shown to be guilty, "how do we know that person did not have consensual sex with the person?"

Such officials simply refuse to believe in the science. In 2002, Bruce Godschalk (Chapter X), convicted of two rapes in Philadelphia, was cleared by DNA testing done by two separate laboratories, and yet prosecutor Bruce Castor Jr., who declined to retry Godschalk, said "that he could not be proven guilty beyond a reasonable doubt" because of the DNA results. But he inexplicably believed in Godschalk's conviction: "There is an equally huge body of evidence" indicating his guilt. That very "huge body of evidence" is what had been utterly refuted by DNA results. Historical cases where all parties involved are dead, gone, or retired are more understandably applied to DNA testing without much resistance since the outcome will not affect the living. In doddering but celebrated cases of the past, DNA is sanctioned by officials not to set the record straight but to satisfy curiosity, similar to an archeologist examining the remains of a dinosaur.

Such was the case of Dr. Sam Sheppard, where DNA helped clear up a nagging murder mystery. Sheppard had for years insisted that an intruder had murdered his wife, Marilyn Sheppard, in 1954. (His case inspired the long-running TV series *The Fugitive.*) In 1997, Sheppard's son had his father's body exhumed and DNA samples taken from the body. Sheppard's DNA did not match the blood and semen found at the murder scene, exonerating Sheppard with scientific fact. (See Chapter XIV, "Language Barriers and Prejudicial Publicity.")

His exoneration, however, came too late for many in the Sheppard family. Sheppard's mother, Ethel, and Marilyn's father, Thomas Reese, had both committed suicide. Sheppard, though winning a prison release through the efforts of criminal attorney F. Lee Bailey, was forever haunted by the murder, taking to drugs and alcohol and choking to death on his own vomit in 1970 at age forty-six.

By the end of 1998, only Louisiana compelled all those under arrest to provide test samples for DNA. Many states (not New York) allow DNA testing of prison inmates. According to the *National Institute of Justice Journal*, in Britain DNA samples are taken from every suspect, and British officials have solved seventeen major cases by employing DNA data since 1995. DNA, however, appears to be a fallible identification system. In summer 2004, two black men with criminal records were reported to have identical DNA patterns, which prevented authorities from charging either with a crime.

The DNA identification system is similar to the fingerprinting system. Since the 1890s, fingerprint technology has been an important tool in solving myriad crimes. Fingerprints left on objects touched by the perpetrator of a crime may be compared to those of persons committing the crime, thereby inculpating them or excluding them as the guilty party. Even where there is no known suspect, fingerprints may be instrumental in bringing the guilty to justice. Matching crime scene prints to fingerprint records available in state and national databases—reflecting the routine collection and maintenance of fingerprints from arrestees and convicts in criminal cases—may identify the perpetrators of crimes that might be unsolvable by other investigative methods.

Beginning in the late 1980s, working groups associated with the FBI laid the groundwork for a comparable system of DNA identification. About the same time, some states began to collect DNA samples routinely from certain categories of convicted offenders. Congress subsequently provided the statutory basis for a nationwide DNA identification system through the DNA Identification Act of 1994. The standards developed for the system included the convention of using thirteen DNA locuses, which do not designate any overt trait or characteristic of an individual but, in the aggregate, identify that person uniquely. The effect was to produce, through the analysis of DNA samples taken from crime scenes and offenders, DNA profiles that amount to genetic fingerprints.

Comparing the DNA profile derived from biological material left by the perpetrator at a crime scene, such as semen in a sexual assault examination kit, to that of a known suspect may confirm or refute the suspect's identity as the perpetrator. In cases where there are no known suspects, matching of crime scene DNA to DNA profiles of convicted offenders maintained in state and national databases can solve crimes that would otherwise be unsolvable. Even where an individual is not specifically identified, common DNA profiles at multiple crime scenes may show a common perpetrator, thereby permitting the pooling of critical investigative information.

At present, all states collect DNA samples from some categories of convicted offenders, and many collect DNA samples from some persons in non-convict categories, such as adjudicated juvenile delinquents. A substantial majority of the states have enacted legislation authorizing the collection of DNA samples from all convicted felons, and the strong trend in state law reform advocates broader sample collection. The states maintain databases that include the profiles derived from the crime scene and offender DNA samples they collect, and the FBI maintains a national DNA identification index that makes the DNA profiles obtained under the state systems available on a nationwide basis for law enforcement identification purposes.

The FBI also maintains the Combined DNA Index System (CODIS), which links the state and national databases and enables experts to communicate with one another. The FBI established this database in 1990, and it became operational nationwide in 1998. By 2003, the FBI database contained profiles from 65,868 unsolved cases and 1,507,278 convicted offenders. Since the bureau's DNA database was established, there have been 8,675 DNA matches at this writing.

Results of this cooperative system have been effective, even though many states are only beginning to use DNA to its full crime-solving potential, and the nation's DNA databases contain only a fraction of the DNA profiles that they will eventually include as the system develops and enlarges in an ever aggregating process. Virginia was the first of the statewide organizations to develop a DNA database and remains a leader in the field. Its director, Paul Ferrara, announced that it had, by 2002, matched its 1000th convicted offender to a genetic profile developed from a crime scene and that it had solved more than 350 murders and rapes through its DNA database.

Professor James Liebman of Columbia University produced a twenty-three-year study of more than 4,500 capital cases in thirty-four states to reveal that the court found serious reversible error in 68 percent of capital cases. Of these, 82 percent were not sentenced to death upon retrial, including 7 percent who were found to be factually inno-

cent of the capital charge. The Innocence Project claims that in a third of the cases it handles, in which DNA evidence is still available, convicted defendants are found to be outright innocent. The President's DNA Initiative, which was announced by the attorney general on March 11, 2003, proposed allocating $232.6 million for DNA-related purposes in 2004 and continuing this level of funding in successive years through 2008. The funding is administered through various components of the Department of Justice, including (in 2004) $177 million through the National Institute of Justice, $13.5 million through existing programs of other Office of Justice programs components, and $42.1 million for activities of the FBI.

When experts compare the DNA profile derived from biological material left by a perpetrator at a crime scene, such as semen in a sexual assault examination kit, to that of a known suspect, the results may confirm or refute the suspect's identity as the perpetrator. In cases where no known suspects are available, matching of crime scene DNA to DNA profiles of convicted offenders accessed through state and national databases can sometimes solve cases that would otherwise remain open. (The same applications have been routinely made for decades when employing fingerprint identification where millions of prints are on file in such databases.) An individual not specifically identified may be shown to be a common perpetrator from common DNA profiles at multiple crime scenes in different locations. This collective DNA profile then permits the pooling of critical investigative data that can be assembled in a case against that individual.

All U.S. states presently collect DNA samples from some categories of convicted offenders. A majority of the states have enacted legislation authorizing the collection of DNA samples from all convicted felons, and the trend in state law reform is for more encompassing sample collection. The states maintain databases that include the profiles derived from the crime scene and offender DNA samples they collect, while the FBI maintains a national DNA identification index that makes the DNA profiles obtained under the state systems available on a nationwide basis for law enforcement identification purposes. The FBI also operates CODIS, which links state and national databases and enables them to communicate with each other.

The results from this system have been impressive, even though many states are only beginning to use DNA's full crime solving potential and the nation's DNA databases contain only a fraction of the DNA profiles they will eventually include as the system expands. One such result occurred in 1983, when a Virginia boy was raped and murdered while walking along a path. Investigators resubmitted the case in 1999 for DNA analysis. In August 1999, DNA experts matched the profile to Willie Butler, who was in the database due to a previous conviction for burglary. Butler was convicted of this crime and imprisoned. In December 1998, a twenty-one-year-old pediatric nursing student was kidnapped, sexually assaulted, and murdered in Broward County, Florida. Three months later, a DNA sample from Lucious Boyd was matched to semen found on the victim's body. Boyd was convicted of sexually assaulting and murdering the nursing student and sentenced to death in June 2002.

An even older case, from 1977, involved a six-year-old girl who disappeared while vacationing with her family in Reno, Nevada. Her remains were found two months later. DNA testing was not available in 1977, and the case remained unsolved for twenty-three years. In 2000, however, renewed investigative probes (police routinely review unsolved major crimes or cold cases) resulted in a DNA test of the victim's clothing and entry of the resulting DNA profile into the Nevada state DNA database. A database search revealed a match to a man who had been paroled in 1976 for a previous sexual assault of a child. The man was charged and pleaded guilty to the 1977 murder in October 2000.

Maintaining a backlog of accumulating DNA samples is an expensive, time-consuming task. The U.S. Congress and the Department of Justice have worked for years to further develop the system. In 2000, Congress enacted the DNA Analysis Backlog Elimination Act, which authorized funding assistance to the states to clear DNA backlogs and provided the initial authorization for collecting DNA samples from convicted federal offenders. The department's activities have included extensive DNA programs at the National Institute of Justice and the FBI. By the end of 2002, the National Institute of Justice had disbursed funds supporting the analysis of more than 470,000 DNA samples collected from convicted offenders by the states, and awarded federal funds to support the analysis of more than 24,000 crime scene DNA samples in state cases having no known suspects.

In many instances, persons arrested for crimes are released before going to trial after DNA tests prove them innocent. On August 25, 1993, Raymond Holder was arrested and charged with raping and sodomizing a twelve-year-old girl who identified him as her assailant. DNA tests, however, exonerated him on April 30, 1994, and he was set free after nine months in jail awaiting trial. In too many cases, DNA testing has taken so much time to complete that suspects have been released only to commit more crimes before tests can prove them guilty of prior offenses. This was the case of Christopher Banks, who was accused of stabbing and raping a woman in Virginia on August 31, 1998.

Experts at the Virginia Division of Forensic Science lab received the victim's rape kit and other physical evidence. A blood sample was received later, on November 13, 1998. Police warned lab experts that unless their testing was quickly concluded, Banks could no longer be held as a suspect in the rape case and, following a scheduled court appearance for another offense, would probably be released. Facing a shoplifting charge, Banks appeared in court on January 6, 1999, and, when no police officer or prosecutor was present, he was released.

The analysis of the DNA evidence in the August 31, 1998, rape case had not yet been completed, the end results of which would have allowed police to charge and detain Banks for trial in that case. On February 3, 1999, the lab announced that the semen in the August rape case matched Banks. However, eleven days after his January 6, 1999, release, he had raped and murdered twenty-two-year-old Jemma Saunders, whose life might have been saved had DNA testing been completed more expeditiously. In its defense, officials for the lab pointed out a lack of funds and manpower to address the extensive backlog evidence on hand in dozens of major cases, which largely contributed to the tardy delivery of the test results in the August 1998 rape case.

Educating, training, and employing tens of thousands of new forensic experts, as well as obtaining the necessary funding, is crucial to providing timely results from crime scene evidence. The new forensic experts join the community of criminal investigators, forensic pathologists and medical investigators, forensic nurses, physicians, first responders, and forensic technicians. These experts address a host of forensic sciences which contribute to state and national databases other than DNA, and include, among many, for fingerprints the FBI's IAFIS (Integrated Automated Fingerprint Identification System); for firearms the ATF's NIBIN (National Integrated Ballistic Information Network); for paints the RCMP's (Royal Canadian Mounted Police) PDQ (paint data query); for footwear a proprietary database, SoleMate, and for tires a database called Tread Assistant.

## The Vasquez-Spencer DNA Case

The landmark DNA case that firmly placed this forensic science in the front rank of criminal identification involved a woman named Carolyn Hamm, a thirty-two-year-old Washington, D.C., lawyer, who was found murdered in her Arlington, Virginia, home on January 25, 1984. She had been assaulted, raped, and hanged with a piece of rope from a water pipe in her garage. Investigations led police to forty-one-year-old David Vasquez, a man who had lived in the Arlington neighborhood for several years and was later described in court as having "borderline retarded/low normal" intelligence. A neighbor had seen Vasquez walking near Hamm's house about the time of the murder, and another had observed him two days later, on the same day police found the body. Vasquez maintained that he was home or with a friend on the night of the killing.

Arrested at the McDonald's restaurant where he worked cleaning tables, Vasquez was taken to the Manassas police station. He was not read the Miranda warning by detectives William Shelton and Robert Carrig. Henry E. Hudson, who prosecuted in the Vasquez case, said the warning was unnecessary because Vasquez was, at the time he was brought in for questioning, considered a potential witness, not a suspect. However, in this first ninety-minute session with the extremely frightened man, who was described as acting like a child by those who knew him, the detectives, according to later testimony, told him that they had found his fingerprints at the scene of the crime, which was not true.

Further, detectives told Vasquez dozens of details about the murder and encouraged him to repeat these facts. Vasquez repeatedly cried for his mother. Later, detectives took him to the Arlington station, where they read him the Miranda warning, which he signed, and then asked him to repeat the crime details. Later in that session, Vasquez went into a sort of trance and told of "a horrible dream," going into a rambling monologue in a deep voice, repeating the details of the case as he had learned them from the detectives. That day, he was arrested and charged with rape, capital murder, burglary, and robbery. Carrig and Shelton questioned him a third time, with Shelton suggesting "think about your dreams." Vasquez again recounted the story he had heard. This version was admitted as evidence and was construed to be a confession. (See Chapter X, "False Confessions.")

Vasquez waited in jail a year to be tried, after a court-appointed psychiatrist judged him competent to stand trial. Although forensic tests proved that the bloodstains found at the scene did not match Vasquez's blood type, his court-appointed attorneys, Richard J. McCue and Martin Bangs, did not know how to explain his "confession." On the advice of his attorneys, Vasquez used the Alford Plea, which allows a defendant to maintain his innocence while recognizing that the evidence probably will result in a guilty verdict.

The Alford plea is essentially a guilty plea. By choosing it, a defendant forfeits his right to a jury trial and to an appeal. In exchange for that plea by Vasquez, prosecutors reduced the capital murder charge to second-degree murder. Prosecutor Hudson said he believed Vasquez had not acted alone. On February 4, 1985, Judge Winston found the defendant guilty and sentenced him to thirty-five years in prison, stipulating that he receive psychological treatment. On August 15, 1985, Vasquez entered the Buckingham Correctional Center in Dillwyn, Virginia, where he was sexually assaulted repeatedly and saw a psychiatrist only infrequently.

In this brutal environment, David Vasquez held no hope of freedom. After Vasquez had languished in prison for two years, however, a series of violent murders occurred that would lead to his freedom. The slayings attributed to Vasquez, DNA would prove, had been committed by a serial killer, Timothy Wilson Spencer (1962–1994), who had grown up in the Arlington area.

With three juvenile and three adult convictions for burglary already behind him, Timothy Spencer was paroled to a Richmond, Virginia, halfway house in September 1987. In the three following months, Spencer raped and murdered four women in Arlington County and Richmond. On September 19, 1987, the young black man, later described by psychiatrists as having a mother fixation, entered the Richmond apartment of Debbie Dudley Davis, thirty-five. Davis was bound, raped, and strangled with a sock. His second victim, Dr. Susan Elizabeth Hellams-Slag, lived only a short distance away from Davis. Hellams-Slag, a neurosurgery resident at the Medical College of Virginia, was strangled with a belt on October 3, 1987. Her body was found stuffed into a closet by her husband Marcel when he returned home later that night.

The third slaying, that of fifteen-year-old Diane Cho on November 22, 1987, established a definite pattern in the minds of police investigators. Cho, like Davis and Hellams, was of medium height and heavily built. The teenage girl was found strangled to death in her family's apartment in Chesterfield County. Duct tape was affixed to Cho's mouth, and, for the third time, the killer attempted to conceal the dead body on the premises. Spencer committed a fourth rape-murder a few days after Thanksgiving 1987. The victim was identified as forty-four-year-old Susan M. Tucker of Arlington. Her body was found on December 2, 1987, in the bedroom of her townhouse.

With a pattern established, Arlington police detective Joseph Horgas went to work on a series of earlier rape cases dating back to 1983, in which the assailant had used a rope and burglary tools to gain admittance to homes. Horgas recalled an arson fire set in the mid-1970s, in which a ten-year-old boy named Timmy had been implicated. His recollection put him on the trail of Timothy Spencer, who was picked up in January 1988.

DNA tests, then commonly called "genetic fingerprinting," conclusively proved that the same man was involved in the Davis, Hellams, and Tucker slayings. Genetic testing of this sort analyzes hair roots, blood, semen, and various other body fluids for DNA. In the case of Spencer, his blood and that found on the victim matched only 13 percent of the population. The scientific odds against such a match in black North Americans were 1 in 705 million, according to DNA experts.

Timothy Spencer, dubbed the "South Side Strangler" by the media, was convicted in July 1988 in Arlington County for the rape-murder of Susan Tucker. The case against Spencer rested primarily on DNA fingerprinting evidence submitted by Dr. Michael Baird, forensics laboratory director at Lifecodes Corporation of Valhalla, New York, who matched semen samples found in Tucker's bedroom.

"This is a major point in the case," explained commonwealth attorney Helen Fahey. "The judge found [DNA testing] reliable and that it is supported by the scientific community." On July 16, 1988, Spencer was sentenced to death by an eight-woman, four-man jury that deliberated for an hour.

On November 2, 1988, Spencer received a second death sentence for the rape-strangulation murder of Debbie Davis. The defendant's conviction resulted from a DNA pattern found in his blood. "This whole case, the identification of Timothy Spencer, relies strictly on that," explained defense counsel Jeffery L. Everhart, who pointed out that Britain's Home Office had stopped using DNA fingerprinting to identify paternity in immigration cases.

Everhart would later take his case before the state Supreme Court, arguing unsuccessfully that DNA evidence "is not now ready to be used in a capital murder case." In passing sentence, Judge James B. Wilkinson noted with sadness, "I can think of no murder case. . . in twenty-eight years in this business, where the facts are as outrageous as the facts are in this case."

Spencer was convicted by a South Richmond jury of murdering Dr. Hellams in January 1989. For the third time the jury recommended the electric chair on the grounds that the defendant posed a serious threat to society. On March 27, 1989, Judge Wilkinson imposed the death sentence and two life terms plus twenty years. After hearing the decision, Spencer accused Detective Horgas and the commonwealth attorneys of "setting him up."

The fourth and final murder trial took place in Chesterfield County in May 1989. Prosecutors Warren Von Schuch and William Davenport pointed to the similarities between the three earlier murders and that of Diane Cho. The evidence they submitted included a more sophisticated genetic typing method called amplified PCR (poly-

merase chain reaction) DNA. The tests matched body fluid stains found at the murder scene with samples taken from Spencer. On May 12, 1989, the jury returned a guilty verdict, sentencing Spencer to death on capital murder charges, life imprisonment for rape, and twenty years for burglary.

On September 22, 1989, the Virginia Supreme Court upheld the murder convictions of Timothy Wilson Spencer. The landmark decision marked the first time an appeal had been upheld by a higher court solely on the strength of DNA evidence. In handing down its decision, the court expressed its confidence in the DNA test results introduced into evidence at two of Spencer's trials. "The record is replete with un-contradicted expert testimony about the reliability of DNA fingerprinting," the court explained.

The conviction of Timothy Spencer had far-reaching implications, not only for future murder trials involving DNA fingerprinting but also for David Vasquez, who had been imprisoned for raping and murdering Washington lawyer Carolyn Hamm. Detective Joseph Horgas came to realize that the four rape-murders committed by Spencer fitted the pattern in the Hamm slaying. Noticing the similarities, Horgas pieced together the circumstantial evidence that implicated Spencer in the Hamm case as well as the others. In reviewing the similarities between the Tucker murder and that of Hamm, Horgas concluded that they were not only striking but indicated that the same man had committed both murders. In each case, the victim had been bound and gagged without apparent signs of struggle.

After Horgas disclosed his findings, Attorney Fahey petitioned the governor to pardon Vasquez, describing his client in that plea as a semiliterate "incapable of understanding his Miranda rights." On December 31, 1988, Governor Gerald L. Baliles (1986–1990) granted Vasquez a full and unconditional pardon. On January 4, 1988, Fahey informed Vasquez that he had received a full pardon. He was released from prison after serving five years for a murder he did not commit.

The man who had committed that murder refused to talk with profilers trying to analyze his murderous behavior. On April 27, 1994, Timothy Wilson Spencer was executed in Virginia's electric chair, without expressing a single word of regret. He had earlier been asked how he felt about allowing an innocent man, David Vasquez, to be imprisoned for a crime Spencer had committed. Spencer only shrugged and said, "I don't know him."

Four years after David Vasquez was wrongly convicted, another Virginia resident met the same fate in regard to a similar crime. Where Vasquez was convicted on a false confession, Troy Lynn Webb (born in 1967) was wrongly convicted and sent to prison through unsophisticated serology testing. After serving seven years of a forty-seven-year prison term, twenty-nine-year-old Troy Lynn Webb was released with apologies from the state of Virginia for his wrongful conviction for a rape and robbery that occurred on the night of January 23, 1988. Webb had been convicted for robbing and raping a waitress in Virginia Beach, Virginia, based on blood samples and the waitress's eyewitness statements. The victim had identified Webb from police photos and again identified him in a police lineup. The identification was questionable in that when the victim first picked Webb's photo from a police photo array, she said that Webb looked "too old" to be her assailant. When police showed her a photo of a younger Webb that had been taken four years before her attack, she then made a "positive" identification.

The blood samples tested through serology examinations showed that the semen found in the victim was type A, but Webb was determined to be a nonsecretor, a man whose blood type could not be determined from his semen. The serologist in Webb's 1989 trial, however, stated that the semen of a second male, such as the victim's boyfriend, might mask the semen of a nonsecretor assailant.

Troy Lynn Webb, wrongly convicted of a 1988 Virginia rape-robbery. *Innocence Project, New York.*

This evidence, more than anything else, seemed to convince the jury in delivering a guilty verdict.

Webb's attorney filed an appeal, stating that two of the jurors in Webb's 1989 trial should have been dismissed in that one female juror worked as a cocktail waitress and had been raped, and the wife of a male juror had also been the victim of a rape. Prosecutors argued before the Virginia Supreme Court that Webb had been convicted on sufficient evidence which proved his guilt beyond a reasonable doubt. The high court denied Webb's appeal.

Insisting that he had been wrongly convicted, Webb, in September 1996, wrote to the Innocence Project at Yeshiva University's Benjamin N. Cardozo School of Law in New York. Lawyer Barry Scheck, a founder of the project who had helped destroy a jury's confidence in the DNA evidence offered in the O.J. Simpson trial, undertook Webb's case.

More sophisticated DNA analysis was applied to Webb's case, new technology that could test and identify factors within the genetic code of organic material. The new test was conducted by the state Division of Forensic Science. Webb had been convicted on a less sophisticated blood serology test conducted from a semen stain on the victim's clothing. The new DNA test proved that the semen could not have come from Webb, and Virginia authorities had to release Webb, despite the fact that the waitress's testimony identified Webb as her assailant. Governor George Allen (1994–1998) granted executive clemency to Webb, who was released in 1996 without compensation.

## Five Virginia DNA Exonerations from One Woman's Conscience

After most U.S. states, as well as Canadian provinces, enacted legislation that would allow postconviction DNA analysis in the 1990s, thousands of imprisoned persons applied for this testing in an effort to prove their innocence and obtain exoneration. Many did, but only with the aid of private attorneys, crusading public defenders, and the many innocence projects that sprang up throughout the country in some of America's most distinguished law schools.

Among the tens of thousands of law enforcement personnel, including forensic scientists and prosecutors, there were many who resisted postconviction DNA testing. Some failed to accept the effectiveness of advanced DNA testing, while others challenged its results by having their own DNA labs redo the same tests (which, in most instances, endorsed the results of tests made by defense experts). The staunch resistance to postconviction DNA testing by some prosecutors was undoubtedly based on their avid ambition to protect a catalog of convictions that might otherwise suggest their own ineffectiveness and credibility in cases they considered closed.

Defense attorneys and innocence projects, however, doggedly demanded any genetic samples that might be used in postconviction DNA testing, and, for the most part, received cooperation from prosecutors, grudgingly or not. Regarding five Virginia men, however, the credit for their exonerations belongs to a woman long gone to her grave, who, either out of peculiar and inexplicable habit or incredibly perceptive foresight far in advance of the birth of DNA, preserved the forensic evidence that would prove their innocence.

Mary Jane Burton was a forensic serologist who worked for the Virginia state crime lab from 1974 to 1988 (she died in 1999). Before DNA was invented, Burton independently did similar research, taking small samples of evidence she tested—cotton swabs and clothing fragments smeared with blood, saliva, and semen—and inserted these samples into the case files of many convicted persons, all of which eventually went into storage. These files were later discovered by Paul Ferrara, director of Virginia's Department of Forensic Science. From Burton's preserved samples (in thirty-one cases), sophisticated postconviction DNA testing was made available, bringing about the exonera-

tion of Willie Davidson, Marvin Lamont Anderson, Arthur Lee Whitfield, Julius Ruffin, and Phillip Leon Thurman.

Marvin Lamont Anderson, a black man who had been a model student and a volunteer fireman, had been selected by police as a suspect rapist simply because he dated a white woman. On July 17, 1982, a young white woman was approached by a young black man riding a bicycle in Hanover, Virginia. He

**Marvin Lamont Anderson, wrongly convicted of a 1982 rape in Virginia.** *Innocence Project, New York.*

threatened her with a gun, while raping and sodomizing her for more than two hours. In the course of this brutal attack, the rapist told the victim that he had a white girlfriend. After police learned this from the victim, they made Anderson a suspect, knowing that he had a white girlfriend.

The victim was shown a photo array of suspects and she picked out Anderson's photo, which stood out from the other photos of the suspects since it was the only color photo shown to her. Since Anderson had no criminal record, there were no police mug shots of him, so officers simply took a color photo of him from his employee identification card and used it in the photo array, where all other photos were in black and white. The victim later identified Anderson in a police lineup, although he did not fit the victim's original description of the assailant.

Another possible suspect in the case, John Otis Lincoln, a young black man, was not investigated by police, even though Lincoln was the more likely suspect. He was also known to have a white girlfriend, and witnesses stated that they had seen Lincoln riding a bicycle toward the crime scene shortly before the attack. Moreover, Lincoln was heard by white female passersby to make statements to them about forcibly compelling them to engage in sex acts. Once the victim had identified Anderson, however, police abandoned any idea of pursuing other suspects, including Lincoln.

The reports about Lincoln were recounted to Anderson's attorney by Anderson and his mother, but the lawyer did not investigate Lincoln or use any information about that suspect at Anderson's trial. That attorney had earlier represented Lincoln in an unrelated case and had advised Lincoln that he could possibly become a suspect in the case against Anderson. The attorney did not disclose his contact with Lincoln to Anderson or his mother.

Prosecutors relied most heavily on witness identification at Anderson's trial. Though DNA had not been established at that time, an expert from the Virginia Bureau of Forensic Sciences testified that Anderson could not be identified as the source of semen samples collected from the rape kit after the expert had performed blood typing on swabs from the victim and Anderson. On December 14, 1982, the eighteen-year-old Anderson was convicted on two counts of rape, forcible sodomy, abduction, and robbery. He was sentenced to 210 years in prison.

In a 1988 appeal, Anderson's conviction was upheld, in spite of the fact that Lincoln by then had admitted the rape for which Anderson had been convicted. At that time, Lincoln provided details of the attack that only the assailant would have known. The judge in that case nevertheless dismissed Lincoln's confession as having no credibility and refused to order a new trial or set Anderson free. Anderson petitioned the governor, but his plea was denied. In 1997, after serving fifteen years behind bars, Anderson was released on parole, compelled under that parole to register as a sex offender while continuing to insist on his innocence and continuing his efforts to obtain exoneration.

In 1993, Anderson's attorneys had sought a retesting of the forensic evidence in his case through DNA, but officials stated that all such evidence had been been destroyed as a matter of police and prosecutorial protocol. The file in that case was later found in storage, along with the forensic evidence that lab technician Mary Jane Burton had preserved, an action that was not in keeping with police procedures or the lab's policy, but one that would exonerate Anderson. The evidence, with the help of the Innocence Project, which had entered Anderson's case, was retested through DNA. The results announced on December 6, 2001, stated that Anderson had not been the rapist and that the crime had been committed by Lincoln (who was later charged and convicted of the crime).

On August 21, 2002, Governor Mark Robert Warner (2002–2006) pardoned Anderson and his conviction was expunged from police and court records. Anderson, who had married, fathered a child, worked as a truck driver, and maintained a clean record since his 1997 parole, was awarded $1.2 million in compensation for his wrongful conviction. Governor Warner was so impressed by the DNA evidence in the case that he came to believe that many others may also been wrongly convicted, in addition to Julius Earl Ruffin, a man he pardoned in 2003, who was exonerated through DNA testing.

Warner believed that Roger Keith Coleman, executed in 1992, might not have been guilty of the stabbing death of Wanda McCoy, his nineteen-year-old sister-in-law. Coleman had insisted that he was innocent of murdering McCoy and his case was profiled by *Time* magazine before his execution. Warner ordered DNA testing in that case, but the results announced on January 12, 2006, confirmed Coleman's guilt. In the Anderson and Coleman cases, therefore, DNA had proved itself impartial in deciding the innocence or guilt of two defendants.

The conscientiousness of serologist Mary Jane Burton in preserving forensic evidence in conviction cases also set free Arthur Lee Whitfield, who had been convicted in 1982 of raping a Norfolk, Virginia, woman on the night of August 14, 1981. A second woman was attacked and raped a short time later that night, and Whitefield would also be convicted of that crime. The first victim was attacked at 2:40 A.M., when she arrived home from work and after parking her car. The attacker, she said, threatened her with a knife and forced her to a secluded area, where he took her money and then raped and sodomized her before fleeing. About an hour later, another woman was also attacked in the same neighborhood. The two victims believed they had been attacked by the same man.

Whitfield became a suspect in the case after police arrested him for a burglary that had occurred on the same night of the two rapes and within two miles of the area of those crimes. The first victim identified Whitfield from a police photo array, saying that she was 95 percent sure Whitfield was the man who had raped her, despite the fact that the woman had initially stated that the assailant had no facial hair and Whitfield at the time (as well as in the photo) had a mustache. She and the second victim, who had known each other before the attacks, drove together to a subsequent police lineup, discussing before their arrival the appearance of the attacker, which both believed to be the same man. Both women had described their assailant to police earlier as a man with light eyes. When they viewed the police lineup, there were six men to view, five with dark eyes and one with light eyes, Whitfield. On the basis of this secluded physical appearance, where police had obviously selected all of the alternate suspects with dark eyes, both women said Whitfield was their assailant.

At his trial in January 1982, which dealt with the first rape victim, Whitfield provided four alibi witnesses, who testified that he had been at a birthday party at the time of the attacks. The two victims, however, testified in court that they were sure Whitfield was the assailant. The prosecution offered no physical evidence at the trial that linked Whitfield to the two rapes. He was convicted and, for the first rape, was sentenced to forty-five years in prison. To avoid a similarly severe sentence in the second rape, Whitfield pleaded guilty to the second attack, hoping to receive a lighter sentence

for which a parole might be possible. He was sentenced to eighteen years for the second attack, to run consecutively, so that Whitfield faced sixty-three years in prison.

Although he had pleaded guilty in the second rape, Whitfield continued to claim he was innocent of both crimes. A court of appeals denied his petition, and, when he later asked for a copy of his trial transcript from Norfolk's circuit court, officials refused to give it, thus prohibiting him from filing a writ of habeas corpus. No other options remained for Whitfield, until the state of Virginia passed new legislation in 2001, which created an exception to its twenty-one-day rule, which specified that prisoners had only twenty-one days following the date of their conviction to provide evidence of innocence. The new legislation was aimed at the possibility of new biological evidence, where DNA testing might establish innocence.

In October 2003, Whitfield filed pro se to have his case reviewed under the 2001 Virginia law. Prosecutors initially told Whitfield that biological evidence in his case no longer existed, but then his old file was found in storage in December 2003, along with biological samples that had been preserved by serologist lab expert Mary Ann Burton. The samples were DNA tested, and the results, announced in August 2004, stated that Whitfield could not have committed the two rapes for which he had been convicted, and in fact indicated that the two rapes had been committed by another man, who was already in prison and serving time for an unrelated rape. The state of Virginia, realizing that Whitfield was by then eligible for parole, gave him that parole and released him from custody on August 23, 2004, after he had served more than twenty-two years in prison as an innocent man. He was not officially exonerated or given compensation.

Another man posthumously exonerated by Mary Ann Burton was Julius Earl Ruffin, who was also accused of raping a woman in Norfolk, Virginia, and also went to prison for a crime he did not commit. The crime occurred on the night of

December 6, 1981, when an intruder awakened a young nurse, a divorced mother of three, in her apartment. Using a knife to threaten the victim, the intruder told her that he only wanted to rape her, not injure her, and he told her not to look at his face. He left and reentered two rooms, her bedroom and living room, several times, pretending to be different people and raping her several times. He then ordered her to take a shower and demanded money. Before leaving, the rapist told her that he would be watching her.

The victim waited for forty-five minutes after the assailant left and then ran to a neighbor's home, where she called police. She was taken to the Norfolk police station, where she looked at more than five hundred police mug shots, stating that only one photo showed a person looking similar to her attacker, but nowhere near identical. She described her assailant to police as a dark-skinned black male, with a height of between 5 feet 6 inches to 5 feet 8 inches.

Some weeks later, the victim thought she saw her assailant as he stepped into an elevator at the school she attended as a nursing student and where the man worked in maintenance. The victim called police and reported the maintenance man, Julius Earl Ruffin, as being her assailant. Ruffin did not match the description the victim had originally given to police. He was a light-skinned black man standing 6 feet 1. He also had two gold teeth and facial hair the victim had not mentioned in her first description.

Ruffin was placed in a police lineup and the victim identified him. He was charged with rape and sodomy, although he denied committing the crimes. He said that he and his brother and their girlfriends had been watching a movie on the night of the attack. Ruffin underwent three trials, the first two ending in mistrials when two juries made up of mixed white and black members could not reach a verdict. In the third trial in 1982, prosecutors employed preemptory strikes to eliminate any black jurors and wound up with an all-white jury.

The victim altered her original testimony at the third trial, saying that her attacker was much taller. The officer to whom Ruffin gave his alibi when arrested had not challenged that alibi, but, when testifying at the third trial, expressed doubts about its validity. Forensic science experts testified that their tests showed that semen found at the scene of the crime was linked to a group that contained only 8 percent of black men. The jury took only seven minutes in deliberating a verdict of guilty. Ruffin was sentenced to life imprisonment.

Ruffin's appeals were denied, and he alienated officials by refusing to participate in parole proceedings since such participation required his admission of guilt. In 1994, Ruffin requested that the forensic samples used in his case be retested with DNA, but officials told him that all such evidence had been routinely destroyed. He was overjoyed to learn in 2002, however, that his old forensic file had been uncovered in storage and that the deceased serologist lab expert on that case, Mary Jane Burton, had attached the forensic samples to his file.

Those samples underwent DNA testing and proved that he was innocent of the crime that had sent him to prison for almost twenty-one years. The test also showed that the real attacker had been Aaron Doxie, who was then serving three life terms for many sexual assaults, including those for which Arthur Lee Whitfield had also been wrongly imprisoned. Ruffin was released on February 13, 2003. Governor Mark Warner granted him a full pardon on March 19, 2003. He later received $1.5 million in compensation from the state of Virginia, more than the amount awarded to Marvin Lamont Anderson, who had been exonerated through DNA in 2002.

Another of the men rescued through Burton's preserved samples was Willie Davidson. He had been convicted in 1981 of rape and sodomy in the case of a sixty-six-year-old widow living in Norfolk, Virginia. The woman was attacked by an intruder on the night of November 27, 1980, Thanksgiving Day. The assailant, she later stated, wore a stocking face mask, cap, gloves, and coat. Six days after the attack, the victim identified Davidson out of a police photo array, stating, "This is Willie. I know him. He visited me on the day before the attack." Davidson was later brought to a police station and a stocking was placed on his head. The victim viewed him in this condition and positively identified him.

In court, the victim testified that she had known Davidson all his life and had good relations with his family until they moved away. Davidson and family members returned to Norfolk on the day of the attack and visited her. Davidson claimed innocence, saying he was at home sleeping on the night of the attack. A jury refused to accept the alibi and convicted Davidson of rape and sodomy. He was sentenced to twenty years in prison.

When the Innocence Project became involved in Davidson's case, its attorneys pointed out to Governor Mark Warner that their client might be among those cases for which Mary Jane Burton had preserved biological evidence. In 2004, Governor Warner ordered that DNA be tested on 10 percent of Burton's old cases, and that included Davidson's. Swabs taken from the victim's body, as well as tissues the assailant used to clean up after the attack, had been preserved by Burton in the Davidson case and these samples were DNA tested, which showed that Davidson was innocent of the crime. Before that time, in 1992, Davidson had been released after serving twelve years in prison. On December 22, 2005, Governor Warner granted Davidson a full pardon. On that same day, the governor also exonerated Phillip Leon Thurman.

Thurman's case began on the night of December 30, 1984, when an assailant dragged a thirty-seven-year-old woman from a bus stop in Alexandria, Virginia. He took her to a secluded area, where he beat and raped her and then attempted to strangle her to death. The victim, who managed to escape, told police later that a tall, thin black man had attacked her. Thurman was arrested a short time later close to the crime scene, while he was walking home.

Explaining that he had just visited some friends, Thurman was identified by the victim as her assailant, and she and another witness testified at Thurman's 1985 trial that he had been that attacker. Also at that trial, serologist Mary Jane Burton testified that biological evidence found at the crime scene matched Thurman's blood type—B—but she was careful to point out that 20 percent of the black men in America shared that blood type. Thurman was convicted of abduction and rape and sentenced to thirty-one years in prison.

DNA testing in this case was conducted after Governor Warner ordered forensic tests made on 10 percent of Burton's preserved samples. The DNA testing of swabs taken in Thurman's case proved that he had not been the 1984 rapist. The state's database, when comparing the evidence in this case, showed that another man in that database had committed the crime. Thurman, like Willie Davidson, was officially exonerated by Governor Warner in 2005.

Anderson, Whitfield, Ruffin, Davidson, and Thurman had been given their freedom through the meticulous efforts of an obscure lab serologist, Mary Jane Burton, a woman who defied a system that summarily destroyed evidence. What motivated Burton to take such measures (certainly at the risk of losing her job) can only be speculated about, but she must have believed these men to be innocent and also believed, as does any forthright scientist, that a developing science may in future bring about their exoneration, which is exactly what happened.

## DNA Exonerations in New England

### Connecticut

Two rapes in Hartford, Connecticut, occurring only two months apart, caused two separate victims to wrongly identify two different innocent men and send them both to prison. The first offense occurred on November 30, 1987, when a woman walking along a dark Hartford street was pushed off the sidewalk by an assailant and dragged to a car. The attacker drove to a deserted area and raped her, then drove her to an area unfamiliar to her, letting her out of the car and warning her not to talk to police or he would find her and kill her.

The victim later identified Ricky Hammond as her attacker, first from a police photo array and then at his 1990 trial in Hartford. She also provided several details about Hammond's car, including its make and model, scratches on the body of the car, a ripped child seat, and a wristwatch hanging on the gearbox. A forensic expert stated that hairs found in Hammond's car matched hairs from the victim. Hammond offered a weak alibi, which he altered several times. He was convicted by a Hartford jury in March 1990 and sentenced to twenty-five years in prison.

The Supreme Court of Connecticut ruled on February 25, 1992, that the court and prosecutors at Hammond's trial had made several errors regarding blood and DNA evidence and ordered a new trial. Prior to this court review and ruling, the FBI lab, in May 1989, had performed DNA tests, with a bureau forensic analyst stating that the semen from the physical evidence could not have come from Hammond. Three more tests were made with the same results and Hammond was acquitted at a second trial.

On January 22, 1988, a woman was warming up her car in a Hartford, Connecticut, parking lot, when an intruder got into her car and drove it to a secluded area, where he robbed and raped the woman. He then drove to a different area, stopped the car, and fled. The victim, a white woman, identified James Calvin Tillman, a black man, as her attacker. Claiming his innocence, Tillman was convicted of sexual assault, kidnapping, robbery, larceny, and assault on September 19, 1989. In addition to the eyewitness identification of the victim, prosecutors offered forensic evidence in the form of serological testing, showing that the semen found on the victim's pantyhose and dress

might have come from Tillman, but admitted that the same evidence could apply to 20 percent of the population. Samples from a rape kit taken at the hospital following the crime had not been tested.

Tillman was sentenced to forty-five years in prison. In 1990, he requested that DNA tests be made on the victim's clothes, but that test, at a time

James Calvin Tillman, wrongly convicted in 1989 in Connecticut. *Innocence Project, New York.*

when DNA was still in its development stages, showed only inconclusive evidence. Tillman wrote to the Innocence Project in 2005, and attorneys Brian Carlow and Karen Goodrow took on his case, requesting new DNA testing. The more sophisticated DNA showed that all of the semen samples came from a single source, excluding the victim's husband as well as Tillman. On June 6, 2006, the superior court vacated Tillman's 1989 conviction and ordered a new trial, its ruling based on the new DNA evidence. Released without bail, Tillman was exonerated after spending more than sixteen years in prison when all charges against him were dropped on July 11, 2006.

Governor M. Jodi Rell (2004–) publicly apologized to Tillman for his wrongful conviction, offering him $500,000 in compensation. Tillman's attorneys refused that amount and demanded and got in May 2007 a $5 million settlement, which Rell endorsed. In exchange for this settlement, Tillman agreed not to sue the state and police for other claims, which included medical malpractice involving a botched prison surgery that left Tillman with a permanently damaged right leg.

### Massachusetts

On May 21, 1980, Katherine (or Katharina) Brow was found dead in bed in her trailer home in Ayer,

Massachusetts, stabbed more than thirty times, her money and jewelry gone. Kenneth Waters was charged with the murder two years later after two former girlfriends, Roseanna Perry and Brenda Marsh, told police that Waters had admitted killing Brow. Waters and Brow had had a long, antagonistic relationship. The woman had turned Waters in to police when he was ten years old, claiming that he had burglarized her home. Waters had been sent to reform school for that offense and police later believed he killed Brow through a long-standing grudge. At his 1983 trial, serologists testified that great quantities of blood had been found at the crime scene and that two types, A and O, had emerged from their tests. Brow was type A and Waters type O. Further, workers at the Park Street Diner, where Waters worked as a chef, stated that a knife similar to the one reportedly used in the attack went missing from the restaurant after the time of the murder.

Defense attorneys pointed out that the serology tests were inconclusive and that 48 percent of the population had type O blood. Hair samples taken from the scene, also used in evidence against Waters, were from neither Brow nor Waters, the defense stated. Waters provided an alibi, stating that he had been working a double shift on the night of Brow's murder. He was nevertheless convicted of murder and robbery and sentenced to life at Walpole State Prison. After Waters lost all appeals, his sister, Betty Anne Waters, a high school dropout, dedicated her life to exonerating her brother, working her way through law school. Kenneth Waters later said, "There was no alternative. We were out of money for lawyers. . . The legal system works if you have the money to make it work. If you don't have the money to make it work, you're going to prison."

While managing a pub, Betty Anne Waters worked tirelessly as an attorney to free her brother. She learned of the New York–based Innocence Project and contacted one of its founders, Barry Scheck, a celebrated attorney long involved with DNA evidence. Betty Anne Waters, when

searching for evidence in her brother's 1983 trial, discovered a box in a courthouse basement containing that evidence, including pieces of cloth with blood samples on them and the knife used in the slaying.

Through the efforts of Scheck and the Innocence Project, Waters was able to secure new DNA testing on the old evidence, which was performed by Forensic Science Associates as well as the Massachusetts State Police Crime Laboratory. Both concluded that Kenneth Waters was excluded as the male donor of the biological material tested. His conviction was vacated in 2001 and prosecutors dropped all charges.

Exonerated, Kenneth Waters was released from prison on March 15, 2001, after spending seventeen years in prison for a murder-robbery he had not committed. Said Waters, "I feel blessed. I was one of the lucky ones." Inspired by his sister's dogged crusade to free him by acquiring her own law degree, Waters said he planned to become a criminal investigator and solve crimes, beginning with the Brow murder: "We will get to the bottom of it if it takes the rest of our days." Waters, unfortunately, died of a fractured skull on September 19, 2001, after falling from a fifteen-foot wall.

Where Betty Anne Waters found a box of evidence in the basement of a courthouse, an identical discovery was made in the basement of a Middlesex courthouse that eventually brought about the exoneration of Dennis Maher, who had been convicted of two rapes in Lowell, Massachusetts, as well as one in Ayer, Massachusetts, where Kenneth Waters's problems had begun in 1980. On November 16, 1983, a twenty-eight-year-old woman in Lowell was sexually attacked by a man when she was walking home from work. The next night, a twenty-three-year-old woman in Lowell was also attacked, but she broke free and contacted the police, telling officers that the assailant had worn a red, hooded sweatshirt and a khaki military-style jacket.

Maher was stopped on the night of the second attack and police found in his car an army field jacket and a knife believed to have used by the assailant. He was wearing a red, hooded sweatshirt when stopped. He was brought to trial in 1984 and convicted chiefly on the eyewitness identification of the victims. A month later, he was convicted of a similar sexual attack that had occurred in Ayer, Massachusetts. Maher was given a life sentence. While maintaining his innocence and having exhausted all appeals, Maher contacted the Innocence Project and its ally, the New England Innocence Project, which undertook his case. In 2001, one of its workers, a law student, found two boxes of evidence dealing with the Lowell attacks in the basement of the Middlesex courthouse.

Forensic Science Associates performed tests on the Lowell evidence, which excluded Maher in its genetic profile. Orchid Cellmark then tested evidence from the Ayer case and also excluded Maher in that genetic profile of March 2003. A new trial was ordered, but prosecutors dropped all charges and Maher was set free on April 3, 2003, after spending nineteen years in prison. He was later awarded $550,000 in compensation.

On August 24, 1986, a woman in Marlborough, Massachusetts, was raped and later gave police a description that was used as a police composite sketch. A Marlborough officer later saw twenty-seven-year-old Eric Sarsfield on the street and thought he recognized him from that composite sketch. He asked Sarsfield if he had a tattoo of a cross on his arm and Sarsfield showed him a bare arm. The officer nevertheless continued interviewing Sarsfield and finally brought him to a police station, where he was told to don a dark blue windbreaker the assailant had left behind after the attack. Wearing that windbreaker, Sarsfield was viewed by the victim, who stood on the other side of a two-way mirror and identified him with some uncertainty as her assailant.

Eric Sarsfield, wrongly convicted in 1987 in Massachusetts. *Innocence Project, New York.*

Sarsfield, always maintaining his innocence, was convicted of rape on July 14, 1987, on the testimony of the victim, as well as acrimonious testimony from an ex-wife. A school dropout who worked as a logger and at other jobs, Sarsfield had been drunk at his show up and slurred his words as the assailant had done. Prosecutors at his trial did not offer any physical evidence, despite the fact that a rape kit in the case possessed biological evidence. Sarsfield, who could not remember where he was on the night of the attack and had no alibi, was sentenced to ten to fifteen years in prison.

In prison, Sarsfield was offered early release if he admitted his guilt. This he refused to do, saying "I am no rapist." He worked to get his high school diploma and paid more knowledgeable inmates to prepare appeals for him. On December 29, 1997, he filed a motion that sought DNA comparison with the rape kit taken from the scene of the crime, but his motion was opposed by prosecutors until a judge allowed DNA testing, which was conducted by an independent organization as well as state experts. In both instances, Sarsfield was excluded from the samples tested from the rape kit. Sarsfield was released on parole in June 1999, and his attorney, George Garfinkle, who had taken his case pro bono, filed a motion for postconviction relief on August 3, 2000. Sarsfield, as had been the case with Maher, received $1.5 million in compensation for having been wrongly convicted and wrongly imprisoned for nine years.

The same compensation paid to Maher and Sarsfield was paid to a third wrongly convicted Massachusetts man, Eduardo Velasquez, who had been convicted on November 23, 1988, under the name Angel Hernandez, for a rape he had not committed. The rape occurred in Chicopee, Massachusetts, at 7:30 P.M., on December 9, 1987, when a woman was forced at knifepoint to perform oral sex by an assailant, who pushed her back into her car after she had parked it on Springfield Avenue. After twenty minutes, the assailant fled and the victim ran to a nearby convent where nuns took her in and called police.

Eduardo Velasquez (AKA: Angel Hernandez), wrongly convicted in 1988 in Massachusetts. *Innocence Project, New York.*

Velasquez/Hernandez was picked up on a nearby street by officers, who thought he fit the general description of the assailant. He was taken to the convent where the victim hesitantly identified him as her attacker. At his 1988 trial, a serologist reported that tests from the samples of a rape kit matched Velasquez/Hernandez's genetic makeup, and that two hairs found on the victim were "within the range" of Velasquez/Hernandez's hair samples. Convicted of rape, he was sentenced to twelve to eighteen years in prison. In February 1998, the Innocence Project, working with the New England Innocence Project, undertook Velasquez/Hernandez's case. After DNA testing on the victim's rape kit was performed by Forensic Science Associates in 2001, Velasquez/Hernandez was excluded as the genetic donor in the rape and he was released on August 15, 2001, after being imprisoned for twelve years.

The compensation paid to wrongly convicted Neil Miller far exceeded that received by Maher, Sarsfield, and Velasquez/Hernandez. In fact, the City of Boston paid Miller $3.2 million for wrongly convicting him and keeping him behind bars for nine years. In 1989, a black man wielding a screwdriver forced his way into a Boston, Massachusetts, apartment, forcing the female occupant, a young Emerson College student, to submit to vaginal sex with him and then commit oral sex before he robbed her and fled.

The victim selected Miller's photo from a police photo array of convicted black offenders (Miller had been convicted of a nonsexual crime), and he was arrested and jailed in 1989. Brought to trial in 1990, he claimed that he was a victim of mistaken identity, insisting that he had never been in the woman's apartment. An expert from the Boston

Police Crime Lab testified that semen stains found at the crime scene did not exclude Miller. The victim again identified Miller in court and he was convicted on December 19, 1990, of aggravated rape and robbery and sentenced to twenty-six to forty-five years in prison.

Supported by the Innocence Project in 1998, Miller was able to have new DNA testing done in his case, which resulted in a report from Forensic Science Associates that Miller had been excluded from being the source of the spermatozoa found at the scene of the crime. He was released and exonerated in 2000, but then sued prosecutors and Boston police in 2003, stating that they had wrongly convinced the victim to identify him as her assailant.

Discovery showed that the victim did not initially identify Miller from among the six hundred photos shown to her, although his photo was among them. After she helped a police artist put together a composite sketch, an officer said that the sketch looked like Miller. The police next put together a dozen new mug shots of offenders, including a photo of Miller, and showed this photo array to the victim. The victim chose two photos, selecting a photo of Miller first and then a photo of another convicted offender. A police officer then told the victim that the best thing to do was to go with her first impression, in other words, telling her to focus on Miller. This she did.

In 2005, Larry Taylor, another black man in Boston with a long criminal record, confessed to committing three rapes, including the one for which Miller had been convicted. In 2006, Miller was given $3.2 million in compensation for his wrongful conviction, a Boston official stating at the time of the settlement that the city recognized

Neil Miller, wrongly convicted in 1990 in Massachusetts. *Innocence Project, New York.*

"the terrible tragedy of an innocent man incarcerated in 1989 for a crime he did not commit."

## DNA Exonerations in New Jersey and New York

### New Jersey

On December 24, 1983, two black men abducted a woman from a Union County, New Jersey, shopping mall. Forcing the woman into the backseat of her car, one man pinned her arms and legs, while the other drove the car to a secluded area. There both men sexually assaulted her. They then forced her from the car, which they later left parked near the Newark airport. Police investigating the case arrested twenty-year-old David Shephard, who worked on planes at the airport.

Tried in 1984, Shephard was identified in court by the victim as one of her attackers. Her purse and other personal items were used in evidence at the trial, prosecutors stating that they had been discarded by the assailants at the airport when they abandoned the car. Biological evidence provided by the prosecutor did not exclude Shephard as one of the attackers. In September 1984, he was convicted of rape, robbery, terrorist threats, and weapons violations and sentenced to thirty years in prison.

In 1992, prosecutors cooperated with Shephard's request that he be given access to the evidence in his case for retesting through DNA. After two rounds of testing, DNA results showed that Shephard was excluded from the biological evidence in his case and, on May 18, 1994, he was released after spending nine years in prison. In Shephard's case, eyewitness misidentification had brought about his conviction, but in a New Jersey case involving Larry Peterson, fabricated confessions and a weak forensic report convicted Peterson of a heinous rape-murder and sent him to prison for life.

On the morning of August 24, 1987, a woman walking her dog along a dirt road in Burlington County, New Jersey, found the partially naked body of a young woman with some of her remaining clothes torn. Police soon discovered the victim was twenty-five-year-old Jacqueline Harrison, a resident of Pemberton Township and the mother of two children. She had been sexually molested and manually strangled. A stick had been forced down her

**Larry Peterson, wrongly convicted in New Jersey in 1989. Innocence Project, New York.**

throat and another into her vagina. A short time later, two callers, the victim's closest friend and a former boyfriend, phoned police to say that the perpetrator was Larry Peterson, a black man, who lived in Pemberton and worked at a lumberyard. The callers explained that Peterson had recently acquired scratches on his arms.

Three of Peterson's coworkers told police that Peterson was with them, driving to work, on the day the body was found. After prolonged interviews with police, however, they stated that Peterson had confessed to them, saying that he strangled Harrison after having oral and vaginal sex with her and then forced sticks into her body. Peterson, who voluntarily went to the police, was jailed a month after the crime. A jailhouse informer with a long criminal record later testified that Peterson confessed to the murder while they were in jail together.

Coupled to this testimony, a forensic expert from the New Jersey State Police Laboratory System testified at Peterson's 1989 trial that she had linked pubic hairs found on the victim to Peterson. She also said that she had found a stick forty feet from where the victim's body had been found and identified some hairs on it that were linked to Peterson. She confirmed that the victim had sex with two consensual partners on the night before the murder and that neither of the two consensual sex partners had contributed to the hairs she had found. Biological evidence from the rape kit proved inconclusive, according to another forensic scientist.

Peterson claimed innocence throughout his trial, testifying on his own behalf. His attorneys showed work records which stated that Peterson did not go to work on the day the three witnesses against him claimed to be on their way to work with him and when he allegedly confessed the crime to them. Alibi witnesses endorsed Peterson's claim of being elsewhere at the time the crime had been committed.

In March 1989, a jury convicted Peterson of felony murder and aggravated sexual assault. He was sentenced to life in prison. In the early 1990s, Peterson sought postconviction DNA analysis, and in 1995 the Innocence Project took his case. A motion for DNA testing was granted in 2003, and tests were conducted by the Serological Research Institute, where STR and mitochondrial DNA testing were performed on the hairs, rape kit, clothing, and fingernail deposits. In 2005, the results stated that Peterson was excluded from all biological evidence tested. In July 2005, Peterson's conviction was vacated and prosecutors declined to retry him. He was released in August 2005.

Burlington County prosecutor Robert D. Bernardi had thought to retry Peterson even without the support of the DNA evidence that showed him innocent, relying on the testimony of the three coworkers. The testimony of those witnesses, however, had eroded over the sixteen years Peterson had spent behind bars. One of the witnesses changed his statements and a second, Robert Elder, recanted, saying that he fabricated Peterson's so-called confession by employing key facts he had been fed by police. "I simply told them what they wanted to hear," he said. The jailhouse informer's testimony was dismissed and Bernardi finally admitted that he had no real evidence by which to convict Peterson at a second trial.

## New York

A Westchester County woman was abducted by an assailant as she walked along a street in the early morning of August 12, 1982. The attacker dragged her to an alley and dropped her down a flight of stairs between a warehouse and another building. She was knocked out, and when she came to, saw three men. One held her legs, another held her arms, and a third man raped her.

The victim later identified the rapist as Charles Dabbs, saying that she recognized him since they were distant cousins and that he had worn a distinctive cap and had a memorable laugh. (The other two assailants were not identified or apprehended.) Beyond this identification, prosecutors at Dabbs's trial presented forensic evidence consisting of ABO typing of a semen stain found on the victim's pants.

The stain, according to a forensic expert, showed the presence of the H and B antigens. Dabb was an O secretor whose body fluids contained the H antigen, the expert testified, and the blood typing showed that Dabbs could not be excluded as a source of the semen. On April 10, 1984, a jury in a Westchester County court convicted Dabbs on charges of first-degree rape. He was sentenced to twelve and a half to twenty years in prison.

Dabbs lost an appeal in June 1988 when an appellate court upheld his conviction, but the Westchester County Supreme Court allowed Dabbs's request for DNA testing on November 21, 1990. The court ordered Lifecodes, Inc., to conduct the testing, and it reported that its RFLP testing on a cutting from the victim's underwear showed that the semen on the panties did not match the DNA from a blood sample provided by Dabbs. On July 31, 1991, the Westchester County Supreme Court announced that the DNA analysis sufficiently indicated that Dabbs was not the perpetrator. Since the victim was reluctant to appear at a new trial, prosecutors dismissed all charges against Dabbs on August 22, 1991, and he was released after serving seven years in prison for a rape he did not commit.

A particularly violent rape and robbery occurred in the Bronx, New York, at 4:00 A.M. on June 23, 1984, when a female victim was dragged backward from a convenience store by a man who placed a box cutter to her throat and then forced her into blue and white Grand Prix car and drove away. He took her to a nearby park where he orally sodomized her, raped her, and took her money and cigarettes. When she attempted to flee, he caught up with her and took her to an abandoned building where he again raped her and, to prevent her from ever identifying him, slashed her eyes in an effort to permanently blind her, telling her that if she called police, he would return and kill her. She was able to see the back of the assailant as he ran away with her one good eye before passing out. When she regained consciousness, she went to police call box and summoned officers.

Police brought more than two hundred mug shots to the victim to review while she was recuperating in the hospital. She selected a photo of Alan Newton. She later identified Newton in a police lineup and at his 1985 trial. A convenience store clerk who witnessed the abduction also identified Newton from a police photo array and later in a lineup. Biological evidence from the rape kit was inconclusive, but in May 1985 prosecutors won a guilty verdict on charges of rape, robbery, and assault in the instance of the second rape in the abandoned building. Newton was sent to prison for between thirteen and a half and forty years.

On August 16, 1994, Newton petitioned the courts for postconviction DNA testing, which was denied by the court on November 3, 1994, on the grounds that the rape kit evidence could not be located. In November 2005, however, the evidence was located in a barrel at a Queens warehouse and was submitted to two separate testing organizations, both finding in March 2006 that the DNA testing excluded Newton from the rape kit's biological evidence. Newton's conviction was vacated and he was released on July 6, 2006.

Like Newton, Anthony Capozzi was wrongly convicted of rape and, like New-

Alan Newton, wrongly convicted in New York in 1985. *Innocence Project, New York.*

ton, had little chance of vindication after officials could not locate the original biological evidence from his 1987 trial that put him behind bars for twenty years. On September 13, 1985, Capozzi was arrested and charged with three rapes in Delaware Park in Buffalo, New York. He was

Anthony Capozzi, wrongly convicted in New York in 1987. *Innocence Project, New York.*

identified by three victims when he appeared in police lineups, as the assailant who had assaulted them while they were running on bike paths. At his 1987 trial, he was convicted of two of the rapes, based on that identification. In their initial descriptions of the attacker, the victims described a white man weighing about 160 pounds. Capozzi at that time weighed between 200 and 220 pounds and he bore a prominent three-inch scar on his face that the eyewitnesses never mentioned.

Sentenced to between eleven and thirty-five years, Capozzi appeared before the parole board five times and each time his parole was denied since he refused to admit guilt for committing the two rapes. Since the evidence in his case, particularly the rape kits, was no longer available, Capozzi would have to serve out his entire thirty-five-year sentence. Then, in August 2007, a forty-eight-year-old machine worker, Altemio Sanchez, confessed to three slayings that had long been on record and were known as the Bike Path Murders: Linda Yalem, Majane Mazur, and Joan Diver. (Capozzi bore a close resemblance to Sanchez, which is why the rape victims were so sure that he was their assailant.)

When Buffalo police probed these killings, which involved sexual molestation, they also investigated the rapes for which Capozzi had been convicted. To obtain evidence in those cases, police found it next to impossible to find the biological evidence, as had Capozzi, when seeking to have postconviction DNA testing done in his case. Police and officials at the Erie County Medical Center, where the original rape kits were tested, ransacked the place for weeks and then found slides for those cases in a seldom used drawer and produced them for testing on March 20, 2007.

The DNA results announced on March 29, 2007, showed that Capozzi, then fifty, was innocent of the two rapes; he was ruled out as a donor of the sperm tested on the slides. Sanchez was identified as the actual perpetrator of those rapes. Although the statute of limitations prohibited prosecutors from bringing Sanchez to trial for those rapes, the DNA evidence brought about Capozzi's exoneration and release after serving twenty years in prison.

On April 2, 2007, Erie County Judge Shirley Troutman signed the order that set aside Capozzi's conviction and dismissed all charges against him. Capozzi's release from the Marcy Correctional Center had really been brought about by several conscientious Buffalo-area detectives—Dennis Delano, Samuel V. De-John, and Eddie Monin—who doggedly went after the forensic evidence, realizing early on in their investigations that Capozzi was innocent. So convinced of Capozzi's innocence was Delano that he said he would testify on his behalf if Capozzi was brought to trial a second time.

That was no longer a prospect after Judge Troutman dismissed all charges against Capozzi, who had been loyally defended by Thomas C. D'Agostino from the time of his 1987 trial. "At last, he's been vindicated," D'Agostino said. "He always said he didn't do it." Capozzi's exoneration so impressed local politicians that they introduced legislation to be known as Anthony's Law, which would expedite compensation cases brought in the court of claims by persons exonerated by DNA evidence.

Like Newton and Capozzi, Leonard Callace, a sometime construction worker and cab driver, was wrongly identified by a rape victim and was sent to prison. Callace always insisted that he was inno-

cent and refused to plea-bargain for a lesser charge that would bring him four months in prison. Instead, he was sent to prison for twenty-five to fifty years for a crime he did not commit.

An eighteen-year-old nursing aide was sexually assaulted by two men, one wielding a knife, at a shopping center in White Plains, New York, in January 1985. One of the men sat in the front seat of a car and watched the other man sexually attack the young woman in the backseat. The victim later identified Callace as the man who attacked her in the car in a police lineup and further identified him as the perpetrator at his 1987 trial. Callace, who had a record as a petty thief, offered little defense, particularly when he could not corroborate his alibi. He was convicted by a jury in one hour of sexual abuse, sodomy, wrongful imprisonment, and possession of a weapon. On March 24, 1987, Callace was sentenced to twenty-five to fifty years in prison.

On June 27, 1991, a Suffolk County court judge permitted Callace to have postconviction DNA testing, which was performed by Lifecodes, Inc. DNA testing determined that the semen found on the victim's jeans at the time of the 1985 attack did not match Callace. He was released from prison on October 5, 1992. When prosecutors reviewed the DNA results and learned that the victim refused to appear at a second trial, all charges against Callace were dismissed. He had served six years in prison. Like many wrongly imprisoned persons before and after him, Callace did not adjust well to his new freedom. His insecurity and fear of reimprisonment, according to sources, drove him to drugs. He died from a heroin overdose in 1996.

Another resident of White Plains, Terry Leon Chalmers, was accused of raping a woman on August 18, 1986. The victim identified Chalmers as her assailant in a police photo array, in two police lineups, and at his trial. On June 9, 1987, Chalmers was convicted by a Westchester County jury of rape, sodomy, robbery, and two counts of grand larceny. Chalmers filed an appeal which claimed that the police lineups in which he had been identified had been improperly conducted. The New York Supreme Court ruled on July 18, 1990 that the lineups had indeed been properly conducted, and, even if they had not, the positive identification by the witness at his trial was sufficient for conviction.

After the Innocent Project undertook Chalmers's case, Forensic Science Associates conducted postconviction DNA testing on the physical evidence in the case (secured by attorneys of the Innocence Project). FSA tested samples of the vaginal and cervical swabs from the rape kit, as well as blood samples from both Chalmers and the victim. In two reports, July 8, 1994, and July 26, 1994, FSA stated that Chalmers was excluded as being the donor of the spermatozoa tested. On January 31, 1995, Chalmers's conviction was vacated and all related charges were dismissed the following April. Chalmers had served eight years behind bars.

Again, mistaken identity sent Michael Mercer of New York City to prison for a rape he never committed. In that regard he suffered the same wrongful identification as had Anthony Capozzi, and, like Capozzi, he bore a close resemblance to another man who was the actual rapist. In May 1991, a seventeen-year-old girl entered a New York City elevator, where she was attacked by a man who took her to the roof of the building, robbed her, and raped her. In July 1991, the victim saw Michael Mercer entering a building to see a friend and the girl screamed for police. An officer came running and she pointed Mercer out. He was arrested and charged with rape, sodomy, and robbery.

A jury in Mercer's first trial could not reach a verdict and he was tried a second time in 1992. The victim resolutely identified him in court as her assailant and he was convicted of rape, robbery, and sodomy and sentenced to prison for between twenty and a half and forty years. His conviction was upheld on appeal in 1995. In the following year, he was denied a request for DNA testing after the court said his plea had no merit.

In March 2000, however, New York City instituted a new procedure where old rape kits were retested and compared with the state DNA database, and this produced amazing results for Michael Mercer. In January 2003, DNA results from his case showed that not only was he innocent of the rape that had sent him to prison, but that another man had been positively identified by DNA testing of the biological material—Arthur Brown, who was serving a life sentence for several rapes and armed robberies.

The victim in Mercer's case was shown Brown's photo and she identified him as the person who had raped and robbed her. Brown, however, because of the statute of limitations in that case, could not be charged with the crime. Mercer was released and all charges against him were dismissed in January 2003, after he had spent ten years in prison.

Mistaken identity also snared James O'Donnell, who was convicted in 1998 of sexually assaulting and sodomizing a woman in a park in Staten Island, New York, in May 1997. The woman noticed a man following her while she taking her morning walk in the park, and when she attempted to elude him, he caught up with her and threw her to the ground, demanding that she go with him. She fought back, scratching the attacker, until he bit her hand and she passed out. A passerby later found the woman, who was rushed to a hospital. There she gave police a description of the attacker, which was made into a police composite. The sketch and a report of the attack were run in a local newspaper.

Someone who read the article called police to say that the sketch resembled a man he knew, James O'Donnell, who had been seen in the park about the time of the attack. O'Donnell was arrested, claiming he was

James O'Donnell, wrongly convicted in New York in 1998. *Innocence Project, New York.*

home with his girlfriend at the time the crime occurred. The victim, however, as well as others who had been in the park, identified him and he was convicted and sent to prison for three and a half to seven years.

Lori Schellenberger, a Legal Aide attorney who was handling O'Donnell's appeal, discovered a police report which stated that biological evidence from a rape kit in O'Donnell's case had been preserved, including a paper towel that had been used to swab the bite wound on the victim's hand. Richmond County's district attorney cooperated in helping Schellenberger locate the biological evidence, which was then sent to the New York medical examiner's office, where it was inspected and catalogued before being sent to Forensic Science Associates for DNA analysis. Fingernail scrapings as well as the swab from the victim's bite mark were tested, excluding O'Donnell as the contributor of the evidence, proving that he had not bitten the victim and had not been scratched by her. O'Donnell was released in April 2000, and, after the medical examiner's office had conducted DNA tests on the same evidence and had come to the same conclusion, O'Donnell's conviction was vacated in December 2000.

## Pennsylvania

Linda Mae Craig, a thirty-two-year-old saleswoman from Boothwyn, Pennsylvania, was abducted in her car from the Tri-State Mall on December 16, 1981. Her husband called police when she failed to arrive at home and investigators soon found her abandoned yellow Chrysler Cordoba on a road in Chichester, Pennsylvania, which bordered northern Delaware, close to where the mall was located. Less than two miles from her car, Craig's snow-covered body was found the next day. She had been beaten, raped, and stabbed to death. The victim had been left fully clothed, but her assailant had cut open her heavy clothing to commit his sexual attack.

Determining that Craig had bled to death from the multiple stab wounds to her chest, forensic police experts collected sperm samples and fingernail scrapings from the victim. Found in the victim's car were gloves police thought the perpetrator had left behind. Four days later, Nicholas James Yarris was stopped for a minor traffic violation on a Pennsylvania road. He got into a heated conversation with the police officer, which escalated into a violent struggle. Yarris was arrested and jailed on charges of attempted murder. In an effort to gain his release, Yarris accused a man of committing the Craig murder and, when that suspect was ruled out, Yarris himself became the primary suspect.

Nicholas James Yarris, wrongly convicted in Pennsylvania in 1982. *Innocence Project, New York.*

Yarris was brought to trial for the Craig slaying in 1982, where serology experts claimed that the rape kit biological evidence tested in the case did not exclude him. A jailhouse informer stated at Yarris's trial that Yarris had implicated himself in the murder, and he was further identified by Craig's coworkers as a man who had been harassing Craig shortly before she was killed. Although he had a credible alibi and no murder weapon had been found, Yarris was convicted and sentenced to death.

On March 20, 1988, Yarris became one of the first death row inmates to request postconviction DNA testing. Many DNA tests were performed but none conclusively proved his innocence. Dr. Edward Blake, head of Forensic Science Associates of Richmond, California, conducted a final round of testing on the gloves, spermatozoa, and fingernail scrapings, employing PCR-enhanced DNA testing, and, on July 2, 2003, Yarris was excluded from the biological evidence. He was exonerated on September 3, 2003, when a court vacated his conviction. He was not released, however, since he continued to serve time for a 1985 conviction for an escape connected with charges in Florida. On January 16, 2004, Yarris was set free from a Pennsylvania prison, after Florida reduced his term for that offense to time served, granting his release. He had been behind bars for twenty-one years for a crime he did not commit.

The Yarris case involved considerable bureaucratic bickering among DNA database officials. Forensic Science Associates is not accredited by the FBI, which says it does not meet the Bureau's criteria. Dr. Blake, head of Forensic Science Associates (FSA), had long refused to conform to those criteria, stating that the FBI or any other DNA database could not be proven more advanced or accurate than his own operation. The FBI came under criticism for not accepting tests from the FSA, and by not doing so, said critics, eliminated the possibility of locating Craig's actual killer in the Bureau's own database. Said Michael Wiseman, one of Yarris's lawyers, "It is an outrage. The real killer might be in some databank. As a citizen who lives in the same county where this crime occurred, I'd like to know who the killer is."

That same question haunted Thomas Doswell for almost nineteen years, while he served a prison sentence for a crime he did not commit. A black resident of Pittsburgh, Pennsylvania, Doswell underwent the same mistaken identification that had engulfed so many others victimized by wrongful convictions, coupled to a tailor-made police photo that singled out Doswell in a less than impartial photo array. In March 1986, a white woman entering Forbes Hospital (now Forbes Nursing Center and Hospice) on Frankstown Avenue in Pittsburgh, Pennsylvania, where she worked, was attacked by a black man who followed her into the deserted cafeteria, locking the doors behind him and threatening to kill her if she struggled while he raped her. Another hospital worker, hearing the commotion, began banging on the locked cafeteria doors, which caused the assailant to flee. He was chased by yet another hospital worker for three blocks but escaped.

Thomas Doswell, wrongly convicted in Pennsylvania in 1986. *Innocence Project, New York.*

The victim was taken to another hospital, where a rape kit was prepared by experts from the Allegheny County crime laboratory, who collected spermatozoa with vaginal swabs. Police at the time showed the victim a photo array of possible suspects, but only one photo, that of Thomas Doswell, was marked with the letter R. During Doswell's 1986 trial, a police office explained that photographs marked with an R represented photographs of persons who had been charged with rape. The Pittsburgh *Post-Gazette* later stated that Doswell claimed that Detective Herman Wolf of the PPD "focused the rape investigation on him just an hour after it was reported because Doswell had been acquitted of a sexual assault charge against his girlfriend just a year before."

The victim and the coworker who had chased the assailant both identified Doswell as the attacker in court. A serologist testified that tests from the rape kit in the case showed A, B, and H antigens on the samples, but because the victim was a type AB secretor, no blood type for the rapist could be determined since the victim's type masked that of the perpetrator. Defense attorneys argued that the initial description of the attacker made by the victim differed from their client's appearance and that the photo of Doswell marked R was the only such photo among many shown to the victim and was therefore discriminatory. Doswell was nevertheless convicted of rape, assault, terrorist threats, and unlawful restraint. He was sentenced to spend between thirteen and twenty-six years in prison.

Doswell continued to challenge the identifications made of him, but all his appeals were denied. He wrote to the Innocence Project in 1996. With help from that organization and defense attorney James DePasquale, he filed a motion to gain access to the evidence in order to have it DNA tested. This was granted in March 2005. The tests conducted by the Allegheny County Crime Laboratory excluded Doswell as the rapist, and his conviction was vacated. He was released on August 1, 2005, on orders of Allegheny County Common Pleas Judge John A. Zottola.

Doswell spent eighteen years in prison, going behind bars at age twenty-five and emerging at age forty-four. He was not embittered, however, and was so overjoyed at gaining his freedom that, when stepping from the prison gates, he began singing "Amazing Grace." Doswell said he forgave the witnesses who had wrongly identified him, Detective Wolf (then retired) who had reportedly singled him out prior to his conviction, and prosecutors who fought against his many appeals. "Having the faith I have in Jesus," Doswell said, "has taught me that I couldn't walk around for twenty years with anger bottled up in me. It would have killed me. It would have done more damage to me than good." He then happily went to a reunion party in his eighty-year-old mother's townhouse in Homewood, Pennsylvania, where barbecued ribs, fried chicken, collard greens, and dumplings awaited him.

Dale Brison of Chester County, Pennsylvania, was another wrongly convicted person, who, like Doswell, was the victim of mistaken identity. On July 14, 1990, a thirty-seven-year-old woman returning home from a convenience store was accosted by a black male who stabbed her in the side and then took her to a secluded area and raped her before fleeing. The victim later identified Dale Brison to police after seeing him in the neighborhood as the man who had attacked her, and she resolutely repeated that identification at his 1990 trial. There was no physical evidence linking him to the crime other than a single hair found at the crime scene, but one, insisted the defense, that could have come from any black male.

Brison's attorneys requested DNA testing during the 1990 trial, but this was denied. Brison offered an alibi that was supported only by his mother. He was convicted of rape, kidnapping, aggravated assault, and carrying a weapon and was sentenced to between eighteen to forty-two years in prison. In 1992, the Pennsylvania superior

court ruled that DNA testing could be performed if the evidence had been maintained and if the semen stain from the victim's underpants had not degraded.

Cell Mark Diagnostics performed the DNA testing, which reported that no result was discernible from the vaginal swab from the rape kit, but testing of the semen stain on the panties yielded results that exculpated Brison as the attacker. The district attorney's office conducted its own test, which produced the same results. Brison was released in 1994, after having served three years in prison for a crime he did not commit.

## DNA Exonerations in the South

### Alabama

In 1983, eighteen-year-old Pamela Pope of Bessemer, Alabama, reported to police that she had been abducted in a shopping mall by two men wearing stocking masks. They drove her to a wooded area, where they forced her to smoke marijuana, she said, and she was then raped four times by one of the men, while the other held her down. The victim said she had gotten a look at both of the men when they briefly lifted their masks.

Six weeks later, Pope identified brothers Ronnie Benjamin Mahan and Dale Mahan in a police photo array. Both men were arrested and charged with rape and kidnapping on January 23, 1984, and were held on $50,000 bond for each offense. The victim testified against both brothers in their 1986 trial. Both were convicted of rape and kidnapping on June 23, 1986, Ronnie Mahan receiving a life sentence as the actual perpetrator and Dale Mahan sentenced to thirty-five years in prison as his accomplice.

In 1998, the Mahan brothers secured DNA testing in their case, the results showing that both had been excluded from the source of the semen recovered after the assault and preserved in the rape kit. Both were granted a new trial. Pamela Pope then changed her story, telling officials that the reason why the semen had not come from either brother was because she had sex earlier that day with her husband, a fact she had not disclosed in 1983.

Prosecutors tailored their new argument to this new version, stating that the assailant had not ejaculated, a traditional tactic employed by prosecutors when confronted with such DNA evidence. DNA evidence, however, also excluded the victim's husband. Pope then added a new wrinkle to her story, saying that she also had sex with a boyfriend on the day of the crime and before the attack. The genetic profile from the boyfriend, who had since died, matched the profile from the evidence, which left prosecutors with no case at all. Still, they stubbornly clung to the Mahan conviction, preparing to retry the Mahan brothers on more DNA evidence, sending a hair recovered from the victim's clothing for further testing. Again, DNA showed that the hair had not come from the husband, the boyfriend (Toby Tyler), or the Mahan brothers. Defense attorneys were then provided with an argument in which they claimed that the hair must have then come from the real rapist and neither of their clients.

After serving thirteen years in prison, Ronnie and Dale Mahan were released from the Jefferson County Jail on December 2, 1998, maintaining that they had been exonerated. Arthur Green, Jefferson County assistant district attorney, did not agree. He wanted to retry the case with the revised theory that the attacker had not ejaculated, but by that time, the victim refused to cooperate. Because she had changed her story so many times, Pamela Pope was no longer a credible witness. The hair found at the crime scene had nothing to do with the attack, Green maintained, and he persisted, despite the overwhelming evidence presented, that the Mahan brothers were involved. "These sons of bitches are guilty as sin," he was quoted by the Chicago *Tribune*, which reviewed the case. "There is no question in my mind. This is not a case of innocence. . . These two bastards are guilty. I just can't prove it."

Justice for Larry Randal Padgett of Marshall County, Alabama, was a fleeting ghost, and the shabby forensic evidence that sent him to death row was also a mocking specter. Prosecutors presented muddled forensic evidence, which they admitted lacked integrity, but were nevertheless able to convince a jury that Padgett was guilty of murder. Padgett had been arrested in October 1990 and charged with raping and stabbing to death his estranged wife. He was brought to trial in 1992, where a DNA expert testified that the semen and blood samples found at the scene of the crime matched Padgett. The defense offered its own DNA expert, who challenged the testimony of the prosecution's DNA expert, saying that the samples did not match Padgett's genetic makeup.

Added to this confusion was the tacit admission by the prosecution that it had serious questions about the integrity of the DNA testing. There was even uncertainty as to the blood samples employed for comparison with the blood found at the scene of the crime and that those blood samples belonged to Padgett. A jury nevertheless convicted Padgett of rape and murder on April 16, 1992, and recommended a life sentence. The presiding judge, however, sentenced Padgett to death and he languished on death row at Atmore State Prison until legitimate DNA retesting could be done.

The Alabama Court of Criminal Appeals reversed Padgett's conviction in August 1995, after the FBI crime lab reported that the blood samples used to convict Padgett were not connected to Padgett and that the prosecution had suppressed that information. A second trial was granted, but again prosecutors withheld a second PGM test differing from the first test used at Padgett's first trial. The defense asked for a mistrial, which was granted. At that time, more evidence surfaced which indicated that the murder had been committed by a woman (not charged).

Padgett was released and exonerated in October 1997 at age forty-eight, after spending five years on death row. Having exhausted his savings and lost his home to pay for defense attorneys, he moved to his mother's chicken farm in Arab, Alabama. He stated at that time, "If there's seventy-five people on death row who have gotten exonerated, I've got to believe that there's a lot more that haven't gotten that chance."

## *Florida*

On April 14, 1985, eight-year-old Shandra White-head was beaten and strangled to death in her Fort Lauderdale, Florida, home, by a burglar. An autopsy disclosed that the girl had been raped and sodomized by the intruder. At the time of the murder, Chiquita Lowe, a neighbor of the Whitehead family, told police that a black male with a full beard, scraggly hair, and droopy eyes had flagged her down. Police focused on a black male with a crime record, Frank Lee Smith. Chiquita Lowe testified that she had seen Smith lurking outside the Whitehead residence, and this was supported by neighbor Gerald Davis, as well as the girl's mother, who was then returning home from work.

Smith had lived a terrible life. His father was fatally shot by a police officer while committing a crime and his mother was an alcoholic. She carried Smith into a raucous bar when he was a small child, and a fight broke out. A flying beer bottle broke his skull and exposed brain tissue, causing him permanent brain damage. As a teenager, he participated with an older brother in a robbery. He had been convicted of two homicides. When released, he went to live with an aunt, vowing never again to commit a crime.

On April 29, 1985, Smith was arrested and charged with the Whitehead rape and murder. Lowe, Davis, and the victim's mother all identified Smith in court as a man leaving the Whitehead residence shortly after the home invasion, and the victim's mother stated that she saw him leaving the residence by a living room window. Prosecutors also used Smith's criminal history to bring about his conviction in 1986. An insanity defense offered the defendant no relief and a jury not only convicted Smith of rape and murder but recommended the death penalty. Governor Robert Mar-

tinez (1987–1991) signed Smith's death warrant on October 16, 1989, but in January 1990, a month before his scheduled execution, Smith got a stay of execution.

In 1998, the Florida Supreme Court ordered a judge to hold an evidentiary hearing, based on new statements made by eyewitness Chiquita Lowe, who had recanted her identification of

Frank Lee Smith, wrongly convicted in Florida in 1986. *Innocence Project, New York.*

Smith, saying that she had been pressured into identifying Smith by police who told her that Smith was a dangerous man. She nevertheless insisted that she did see a man outside the Whitehead residence on the night of the murder. Prosecutors who had earlier offered Lowe to the court as a reliable witness then branded her a liar. During this hearing, defense attorneys requested postconviction DNA tests, which were denied because of a two-year statute of limitations.

That testing was conducted posthumously, the results of which exonerated Frank Lee Smith. By then, however, he was dead. He had developed cancer in prison and gradually lost thirty to forty pounds. Further, according to defense sources, his medical ailment was all but ignored by prison authorities. According to defense investigator Jeff Walsh, who visited Smith a week before he died of cancer on January 20, 2000, he found the unattended fifty-two-year-old Smith writhing in pain and strapped to a prison hospital bed, crying out, "Help me!" The bed was in a solitary confinement cell at the North Florida Reception Center. "He was moaning, begging for water," said Walsh. "He was lying in his own excrement."

A month after Smith died, a sample of his blood was sent to the FBI crime lab, where it underwent DNA testing against a preserved vaginal swab from the victim. The bureau's lab reported eleven months later that, after completing its testing, Frank Lee Smith was excluded as the depositor of the semen. Said Martin McClain, Smith's former attorney, "We knew he was innocent in December 1989. We told the courts, and we told them who was the real killer, but no one cared, and they kept Frank Lee Smith on death row for another ten years until he died." The real killer of Shandra Whitehead was undoubtedly Eddie Lee Mosely, a serial killer who raped at least sixty-two persons and murdered many others in the Fort Lauderdale area from the early 1970s to the mid-1980s. Mosely's conviction was brought about by the 2001 exoneration of Jerry Frank Townsend, who had falsely admitted to eight of Mosely's murders (Chapter X).

In another Florida murder, DNA brought about the conviction and death sentence of Robert Earl Hayes, a black racetrack groom. Based on examination of other evidence, however, Hayes was acquitted. That acquittal did not bring about exoneration and actually spurred a dogged investigator of an earlier case to bring Hayes to justice for a second murder. For years, Hayes had lived a nomadic life, working at racetracks from New York to Florida as a groom. For decades, the seedy world of racetracks had been plagued by crime and violent murders.

Warring Illinois stable owners, brothers Silas and George Jayne, plotted with their employees to kill each other for years until George Jayne was murdered in 1970, with Silas Jayne going to prison for the killing. Kenneth Hansen, one of Silas Jayne's employees, a predatory white homosexual groom who reportedly raped more than a thousand young boys over a forty-year period, was sent to prison in 1995 for between two hundred and three hundred years for abducting and murdering two brothers, thirteen-year-old John Schuessler and eleven-year-old Anton Schuessler, as well as fourteen-year-old Robert Peterson in 1955.

Sexual assaults, beatings, and robberies were rife in the netherworld of racetracks and stables, where Robert Earl Hayes lived. On February 20, 1990, Pamela Albertson, a thirty-two-year-old white woman who worked at the Pompano,

Florida, harness racetrack, where Hayes, then twenty-six, was also an employee, was found dead. She had been raped and strangled to death. A witness told police that he had seen Hayes with Albertson a short time before the murder and that the victim had rejected his advances. Hayes, who was known to have a volatile temper and had many fights with fellow employees, was arrested the following day, February 21, 1990, and charged with Albertson's murder.

In Hayes's 1991 trial, the witness, who said he had seen the defendant with the victim shortly before she was killed, testified for the prosecution, which also provided DNA evidence reporting that Hayes had been identified from semen found in the victim as the rapist and murderer. Defense attorneys claimed that the DNA evidence was tainted and pointed to the fact that the victim had been found clutching several strands of long blond-red hair and that their client was black and his hair was black. Hayes was nevertheless convicted by a Broward County, Florida, jury and sentenced to death.

Fort Lauderdale attorney Barbara Heyer read about Hayes's trial and agreed to represent him pro bono. She succeeded in convincing the Florida Supreme Court to reverse Hayes's conviction in 1995. The court ordered a new trial but noted that "the record contains evidence suggesting that Hayes committed the homicide." However, the evidence "also contains objective physical evidence suggesting that someone else other than Hayes was responsible." The court stated that the semen found on the victim's shirt and used to link Hayes to the crime had been tested by DNA "band-shifting," a less than reliable DNA technique at the time of Hayes's trial, and that that technique had not yet reached the appropriate level of scientific acceptance, which was a Florida state opinion not universally shared.

Hayes was retried in 1997, and his defense attorneys won an acquittal on July 16, 1997, chiefly based on the blond-red hair the victim had clutched, which could not have come from the defendant. Hayes left prison with little more than the clothes on his back, his attorney paying for a bus ticket to his hometown of Canton, Mississippi, where he moved in with his grandmother. He found work as a city truck driver and sewer cleaner but remained bitter about his imprisonment, telling reporters that he blamed and hated whites for his incarceration. He had often used the race card in claiming his innocence in the Albertson murder, saying that he had been railroaded because he was black. His 1997 acquittal, however, did not establish actual innocence, only that there had been reasonable doubt on the part of the jury.

The law was not done with Robert Earl Hayes, however. A murder conviction awaited him in Utica, New York. On August 14, 1987, almost three years before Pamela Albertson was murdered in Pompano, Florida, another female racetrack employee had suffered a mysterious death. On that night, thirty-eight-year-old Leslie Dickenson, a female groom working and living at Vernon Downs, was found hanging in her apartment in the grooms' quarters of the racetrack. Covered in blood, she had multiple stab wounds to her wrists and neck. Her death was ruled a suicide.

Michael Coluzza, Oneida County's first district attorney, disagreed, with his opening remarks in the 2004 murder trial of Robert Earl Hayes: "It is painfully obvious from the photographs [of the original crime scene] that this is no suicide. Evidence wasn't collected. It wasn't preserved. Leslie's killer staged it to look like a suicide and it worked." Before moving to Florida, Hayes had been a groom at Vernon Downs and had worked with the victim. He was extradited from Mississippi to stand trial for killing Dickenson. Two and a half hours into the trial, Hayes asked through his attorneys for a conference with prosecutors. He then made a plea bargain deal, confessing to killing Dickenson and accepting charges of manslaughter in the second degree, burglary in the second degree, and arson in the second degree.

Hayes told prosecutors that he had been smoking crack in his room at the grooms quarters when he decided to go downstairs to Dickenson's room and ask for money. "I seen money on her fridge," he said. "I reached for it and she slapped my hand. Then she called me a nigger. [Again, Hayes played the race card.] I punched her in the face. She hit the floor and I thought she was dead." He said he panicked and, as Coluzza had earlier outlined, he staged the woman's suicide. He cut her wrists and neck and tied an electric cord around her neck and attached it to a shelf on the wall, as if the woman had hanged herself. The photos of the crime scene (which had been entered into evidence at Hayes's 2005 trial) taken by deputy sheriff Kevin Revere clearly showed that it was impossible for the woman to have hanged herself from the low-hanging shelf. This Hayes evidently realized before he decided to make his confession.

Hayes also said that he burglarized the victim's apartment and then poured vodka about and set it afire, hoping that the fire would obliterate clues that might lead to his arrest. Gregory Flynn, a Broward County sheriff's detective who had investigated the Albertson murder, backtracked Hayes's career for more than twenty years, discovering that he had been a groom at many racetracks where rapes of female grooms and horse walkers had occurred in New Jersey, Delaware, and Pocono Downs. When he discovered the "suicide" of Dickenson at Vernon Downs, he probed further into Hayes's connection with that death. He had attempted to introduce the Dickenson death into Hayes's 1991 trial in Florida, but a judge ruled against him. Following Hayes's 1997 acquittal, Flynn contacted New York officials and urged them to indict Hayes for murdering Dickenson. This they did in June 2003.

Barbara Heyer, the attorney who had brought about Hayes's 1997 acquittal, originally denounced the New York indictment: "They don't have any physical evidence tying him [Hayes] to the New York murder. It's outrageous what they are putting him through." She was wrong. There was physical evidence—the crime scene photographs, which dispelled any possibility that Dickenson had committed suicide. Further, witnesses who had been roused by Hayes himself when giving the alarm of a fire in the area—one he had started himself—recalled that Hayes had been wearing his cowboy boots shortly before the fire, but was now without them, running about barefoot. He had left his boots in the victim's room. In November 2004, Hayes was convicted and sentenced to between fifteen and forty-five years in prison.

At the time of Hayes's second conviction, a provocative play called *The Exonerated* was then running in New York (and released as a made-for-TV movie in 2005), one that profiled Hayes, along with five other wrongly convicted persons, as a racial victim of oppressive police and prosecutors, vaunting his 1997 acquittal. In truth, Robert Earl Hayes was a clever, insidious sexual predator and murderer, whose 1997 acquittal had challenged DNA results in the 1991 murder by offering other evidence—the strands of blond-red hair found clutched in the murder victim's hand. Since Hayes admitted to staging his killing of Dickenson in 1987 as a suicide, one could easily conclude that he used the same ploy four years later to throw investigators off his track in the 1991 murder of Pamela Albertson by planting the blond-red hair in the hand of his victim, as he had implanted his semen into her vagina while raping her. If that indeed was the case, then the DNA evidence that had originally convicted him was correct after all.

For Wilton Dedge, DNA produced the opposite result, proving that he did not sexually assault a woman on December 8, 1981, in her Brevard County, Florida, home. The woman was changing her clothes in the afternoon when she turned to see a male home invader holding a blade. He cut off her clothes, raped her, and cut her body several times during the attack. After contacting her boyfriend, she was taken to a hospital where a rape kit collected evidence and police took the clothes the victim was wearing during the assault.

The victim identified a white male in a convenience store the following January and told her sister that she had seen her attacker, except that he

appeared shorter. The sister identified the man as "Walter Hedge," and the victim then reported the sighting to police. Walter Dedge was arrested, but when the victim saw his picture, she said the attacker was Wilton Dedge, not Walter, and she later identified a photo of Wilton Dedge as her assailant. He was arrested and charged with sexual battery, aggravated battery, and burglary.

Wilton Dedge, wrongly convicted in Florida in 1982. *Innocence Project, New York.*

Before and during his 1982 trial, Dedge insisted that he had not been in the area at the time of the crime, an alibi supported by his brother and mother. Defense attorneys pointed out that the victim had initially described her attacker as being 6 feet tall, weighing 160 pounds, and so muscular that he physically manipulated her with ease. Their client stood only 5 feet 5 inches and weighed 125 pounds. The only physical evidence offered by the prosecution was a single pubic hair. A forensic expert testified that a single pubic hair had been found on the victim's bed and that tests of that single hair showed that Dedge could not be excluded as a possible source of that hair.

Clarence Zacke, a jailhouse informer, testified that Dedge had confessed the rape to him while they were both being transported in a prison van. In exchange for this testimony, Zacke received a steep reduction of his sentences. John Preston then offered dog-sniffing evidence. Preston, who had appeared as an expert witness in several cases in many states, said that his dog had sniffed an item belonging to Dedge and was then able to sniff Dedge's presence in the victim's home. Preston was later discredited by prosecutors as providing unreliable evidence.

The rape kit produced no results from a swab of sperm taken from the victim. Other than that, prosecutors chiefly relied on the in-court identification of Dedge by the victim. He was convicted and sentenced to life imprisonment. When all appeals failed, Dedge was one of the first Florida inmates to request postconviction DNA testing in 1996. The testing did not take place until June 2001, when mitochondrial DNA testing excluded the single pubic hair as coming from Dedge. The state, however, refused to grant a new trial, stating that Dedge had won access to DNA too early, before a state law existed that permitted such postconviction DNA testing (that law was not enacted until 2001). For three years, the state opposed a new trial for Dedge on these and other procedural grounds, but in effect said it would oppose Dedge's release, even though prosecutors knew he was actually innocent. These arguments were rejected by Brevard County Judge Silvernail, and, through appeal, by the Fifth District Court of Appeals in April 2004.

At a second trial, a police officer absurdly explained the difference between Dedge's 5 foot 5 inch height and the 6 foot height of the assailant as described by the victim—Dedge had worn boots with higher than normal heels to compensate for that difference. That meant that Dedge had had to be wearing *seven-inch heels*. Further, the DNA swab from the rape kit had by then been tested and excluded Dedge as the donor. He was acquitted and released in 2004, after spending twenty-two years in prison. In December 2005, Dedge was awarded $2 million compensation by the State of Florida.

Height was a problem for another wrongly convicted Floridian, Luis Diaz. From 1977 to 1979, at least twenty-five women were sexually assaulted along the Bird Road area of Coral Gables, Florida. Most of the victims were stopped in their cars by the Bird Road rapist, who would follow a car being driven by a lone female at night and then flash his dim and bright headlights, simulating the flashing lights of a police car. Thinking they were being pulled over for a traffic violation, the women stopped. Brandishing a gun, the attacker would force the victim into her own car and compel her at gunpoint to perform oral sex. He sometimes raped the women vaginally. Most victims described this predator as a Latino male speaking good English, standing 6 feet 0 or 6 feet 2 inches tall, and weighing about two hundred pounds. His speech was laced with vulgarities. He drove a two-door black or green car.

Luis Diaz, wrongly convicted in Florida in 1980. *Innocence Project, New York.*

The first victim, who had been attacked in July 1977, saw a man at a gas station where she worked, believing him to be her assailant of four days earlier. He was Luis Diaz and he was driving a green four-door Chevrolet. Taking down his license plate number, the victim called police. Diaz was located by police through his license plate number and the victim identified him from his driver's license photo and later in a police photo array. Diaz, however, did not fit the description of the Bird Road rapist. He stood a diminutive 5 feet 3 inches and weighed only 134 pounds. He spoke no English and worked as a fry cook. He had no criminal record, was married, and had three children. Police did not file charges against him.

The attacks along Bird Road, however, continued, and, after another victim identified Diaz from a police photo array as the assailant, he was arrested in August 1979. A few days later, fourteen of the rape victims were asked to view a police lineup. Five of the victims identified Diaz, one was unsure, four could make no identification, and four selected other men in the lineup. Days later, police showed a videotape of the lineup again to the victims and four more identified Diaz as their attacker. He was charged in eight cases with kidnapping, sexual battery, and aggravated assault.

Diaz insisted he was innocent, while prosecution consolidated all eight cases against him in one trial in May 1980. There was no physical evidence linking him to the crimes and no evidence found in his home or car, where four of the victims had reportedly been attacked. No weapon or any of the items taken by the attacker were found. Defense attorneys pointed out their client was much smaller than the man described by most of the victims, and that his skin and facial hair differed from their descriptions. Further, none of the victims had reported any distinctive body odor of their assailant, while Diaz consistently smelled of onions because of his fry cook job. The victims, however, were collectively positive in their identification of Diaz and he was convicted of seven of the eight charges. He was given seven life sentences.

Defense investigator Virginia Snyder, however, continued to investigate other suspects and interview victims. Two of those victims recanted their identification of Diaz in 1993, which prompted Diaz to file a motion in 1994 to vacate his conviction. The two cases involving these women were vacated and Diaz was resentenced. In September 2003, postconviction DNA was granted to Diaz. Several DNA tests in 2005 excluded Diaz from one of the cases. Most of the rape kits in the 1977–1979 attacks were no longer available, but DNA testing of samples from a second rape kit also excluded Diaz. He was released on August 3, 2005, after spending twenty-five years in prison for a crime he did not commit, a victim of mistaken identity—the chief cause for most wrongful convictions.

Mistaken identity also sent two other Florida residents, Alan Crotzer and Orlando Boquette, to prison for 130 years and 60 years respectively. Crotzer was accused of being one of three men who broke into a Tampa, Florida, home on the night of July 8, 1981. The home was burglarized, several persons were tied up, and an adult woman and a twelve-year-old girl were abducted and later raped by one of the invaders. Crotzer, along with brothers Douglas and Corlenzo James, were charged with this crime, and all were

Alan Crotzer, wrongly convicted in Florida in 1981. *Innocence Project, New York.*

identified as the invaders, the rape victims identifying Crotzer as the actual rapist. In 1981, Crotzer was convicted by a jury and sentenced to 130 years in prison. Crotzer continued to claim innocence and, in 2003, had access to postconviction DNA testing, which proved that he had not committed either of the rapes for which he had been convicted. Further, the James brothers admitted that Crotzer did not know them, had never met them until going to trial, and had not been with them on the night of the Tampa home invasion; another man had accompanied them. Crotzer's conviction was overturned on January 23, 2006, and he was released after spending twenty-four years behind bars.

A home invasion in Stock Island, Florida, on June 25, 1982, involved two men. One of them broke into an apartment and raped the female occupant, while the other remained outside. The victim later described her attacker as a Latino man with no shirt and no hair. Within twenty minutes of the attack, the victim was accompanying police in a squad car, searching for the attacker. Police saw a group of Cuban men outside a convenience store and one of them, Orlando Boquette, had no shirt or no hair, although he had a thick, dark mustache. The victim identified Boquette as her assailant while standing twenty feet away as police flashlights played on him. She later told police that her assailant had had a mustache like Boquette's.

At his 1983 trial Boquette claimed that he was at home watching TV with family members at the time of the attack and later went with his cousins to the convenience store. The victim, however, insisted that Boquette had attacked her, and he was convicted and sentenced to fifty years in prison. In 2003, Boquette requested postconviction DNA testing on the semen stains found on the victim's pajama top and under-

Orlando Boquette, wrongly convicted in Florida in 1983. *Innocence Project, New York.*

wear, which apparently police had never tested. A judge ordered the evidence sent to a lab for testing in 2004, and in November 2005 Orchid Cellmark, a private lab, conducted the tests pro bono. It found no results from the pajama tops, but tests of the underwear excluded Boquette as the donor. Boquette was not released, however, until August 22, 2006, because he had been detained for twice escaping prison.

### Georgia

Robert Clark was arrested for the July 30, 1981, rape of a woman in East Atlanta, chiefly convicted on May 26, 1982, and sentenced to life imprisonment on the victim's identification of him as the perpetrator and the fact that he had been driving the woman's stolen car. In his defense, Clark said he had gotten the car from a friend, Tony Arnold. The twenty-one-year-old Clark stood 6 feet 2 inches, where the victim initially described her attacker as being 5 feet 7 inches. A forensic expert at Clark's trial admitted that the vaginal swabs from the rape kit in the case had been lost and no physical evidence linked Clark to the crime.

With the help of the Georgia Innocence Project, Clark's attorneys, after overcoming challenges from prosecutors, obtained the right to have postconviction DNA testing. The testing was performed in July 2005 by the Serological Research Institute of California, which reported that Clark could not have contributed the spermatozoa found on a vaginal slide in the case. The district attorney's office then conducted a search for the male profile in this test through CODIS and the state's DNA database of convicted offenders, identifying Tony Arnold as the contributor. Arnold, by that time, had been imprisoned on a 1985 sodomy conviction and a 2003 cruelty to children conviction. Clark, exonerated, was released from prison on December 8, 2005, after spending twenty-three years behind bars. On March 19, 2007, the Georgia House of Representatives awarded Clark $1.2 million compensation for his wrongful conviction and imprisonment.

**Robert Clark, wrongly convicted in Georgia in 1982.** *Innocence Project, New York.*

Another Atlanta resident met Clark's fate three years after Clark went to prison. On April 5, 1985, a woman driving her car from the parking lot of an apartment complex north of Atlanta, Georgia, was stopped at gunpoint by a black man who drove her car to a dead end street and raped her. He then drove her back to the place where he had abducted her, leaving her on foot before he drove away. A second woman was stopped and raped in the same manner from another apartment complex on April 10, 1985, by a black man. In the first instance, the victim was taken to a hospital where a rape kit was assembled. She described her attacker to a police artist, who sketched a composite image of her attacker. When the second victim was shown the same sketch later, she identified the man as being her assailant.

Less than three weeks later, on April 28, 1985, Willie Otis "Pete" Williams was stopped by police for suspicious conduct. In addition, an officer thought Williams matched the police sketch of the rapist. He was identified by both victims in a police photo array and later at his trial, where Williams was convicted in 1985 and sentenced to forty-five years in prison. In the appeals process, his attorney, Michael Schumacher, uncovered evidence that several other similar rapes had occurred after Williams was arrested and while he was incarcerated in the Fulton County Jail, and that another black man, Kenneth Wicker, who lived on the same block as Williams, had pleaded guilty to three of these rapes.

**Willie Otis "Pete" Williams, wrongly convicted in Georgia in 1985.** *Innocence Project, New York.*

Clarence Harrison, wrongly convicted in Georgia in 1987. *Innocence Project, New York.*

Schumacher was able to have postconviction DNA testing done by the Georgia Bureau of Investigation on the rape kit from the first victim. In January 2007, it announced that Williams was not the rapist and he was released on January 23, 2007. On February 13, 2007, Judge Thomas Campbell officially exonerated Williams, wishing him "the best" for the remainder of his life. He had served twenty-one years in prison.

Both Robert Clark and Willie Williams were aided by the Georgia Innocence Project in gaining their freedom from wrongful convictions. Clarence Harrison, a black man, was actually the first person to be exonerated through the considerable efforts of the Georgia Innocence Project. On October 25, 1986, a woman walking in the rain to a bus stop in Savannah, Georgia, was abducted by a black man who dragged her to an embankment and raped her three times before she managed to escape. She reported the attack to police, along with the fact that the assailant had stolen her watch.

Shortly thereafter police received a call from a tipster who said that Clarence Harrison had been attempting to sell a watch. Harrison was arrested and identified as the rapist by the victim as well as the tipster, although the watch Harrison had attempted to sell was not the one belonging to the victim. On the identification of these two witnesses, Harrison was convicted of kidnapping, rape, and sodomy on March 18, 1987, and sentenced to life in prison.

In February 2003, Harrison wrote to the Georgia Innocence Project, asking that it undertake his case. Students from Emory School of Law and the Georgia State University College of Law began to investigate and located slides from the rape kit in the case, which had been thought destroyed. DNA testing proved that Harrison was not the perpetrator. On August 31, 2004, DeKalb superior court Judge Cynthia J. Becker granted Harrison a new trial, requesting the district attorney to release him. All charges were dropped. Harrison had served seventeen years in prison and was later compensated with a $1 million award, paid as an annuity over twenty years.

## *Louisiana*

Calvin Willis, wrongly convicted in Louisiana in 1982. *Innocence Project, New York.*

In June 1981, a black home invader beat and raped a ten-year-old girl in Shreveport, Louisiana. Calvin Willis, who had once lived in the area, was identified by the victim and was brought to trial, where a serologist from the Northeast Louisiana Crime Laboratory testified that tests on the sperm taken from the victim indicated that the attacker had type O blood, which was Willis's type, although type O was very common. Willis said at his trial that he had been at home with his wife on the night of the attack, which was supported by his spouse, but the jury disbelieved him, and he was convicted in February 1982 and sentenced to life. DNA testing proved Willis innocent and he was released on September 19, 2003, after spending twenty-one years in prison.

A forensic expert testifying in another Louisiana rape case was instrumental in sending Gene Bibbins, a black man, to prison for life, along with the victim's identification of Bibbins as the assailant. The attacker invaded a Baton Rouge, Louisiana, home in June 1986, raping a teenage girl and then stealing a radio before fleeing. Less than an hour later, Bibbins was arrested carrying the radio, telling police that he had just found it next to his apartment building, which was in the same complex as that of the victim. The victim identified Bibbins on the spot as he sat in the backseat of a

Gene Bibbins, wrongly convicted in Louisiana in 1987. *Innocence Project, New York.*

patrol car with a flashlight shining in his face.

Bibbins was again identified by the victim at his 1987 trial, despite the fact that the victim had initially described her attacker as a man with long, curly hair, and Bibbins' hair at that time was short-cropped. Another suspect had been brought before the victim shortly after the attack, but the girl rejected this man as her assailant. Further, samples tested from the rape kit showed that Bibbins could not be excluded as the contributor of the spermatozoa. Convicted and sentenced to life, Bibbins maintained his innocence, and was the first inmate to win access to postconviction DNA testing in Louisiana. Both defense and prosecution labs reported from separate DNA testing that Bibbins could not have been the perpetrator, and he was exonerated in March 2003 after spending fifteen years in prison.

In 1981, the same year Calvin Willis was arrested for a Shreveport rape, twenty-seven-year-old Clyde Charles, a black shrimp fisherman, was arrested for sexually attacking a white nurse outside Houma, Louisiana. In 1982, the same year Willis was wrongly convicted, Charles too was found guilty and sentenced to life imprisonment, a mandatory sentence in Louisiana for that crime. "I felt I was going to be convicted," he said years later, "because the jury was all white. . . Everything was set up, from the time they picked me up to the end of this."

Learning that DNA testing had reopened old cases and had set innocent persons free, Charles began writing letters to officials in 1990, requesting postconviction DNA testing. He was ignored and his petitions were either blocked or denied by state officials. The Innocence Project undertook his case and persuaded Louisiana officials to allow

DNA testing in May 1999. The results, announced in November of that year, showed that Charles was innocent. He was released from prison on December 17, 1999, after serving fifteen years in prison. Where DNA had brought about Charles's exoneration, the two-edged sword of this forensic science identified the real perpetrator of the Houma rape—Charles's brother Marlo, who was then convicted and imprisoned.

Clyde Charles, wrongly convicted in Louisiana in 1982. *Innocence Project, New York.*

### North Carolina

Early in the morning of August 10, 1984, twenty-five-year-old Deborah Sykes, a copy editor for a local newspaper in Winston-Salem, North Carolina, was attacked on her way to work. She was raped and stabbed to death, the assailant inflicting sixteen stab wounds. She was found naked from the waist down with semen on her body. A resident called police to tell them that he had seen a black man with Sykes on the day of the murder and he later identified Darryl Hunt as that man. Johnny Gray, who had also called police to report the murder, identified Hunt. Further, Hunt's girlfriend, who had been arrested on larceny charges, said that Hunt had admitted the killing to her.

These same witnesses later testified at Hunt's 1985 trial, saying the he had been with the victim and that he had been at a local hotel where he had left bloody towels behind in a rest room. After three days of deliberation, a jury convicted Hunt, despite the fact that the defendant had insisted that he had never met the victim and was innocent. Hunt was given a life sentence. His conviction was overturned by the North Carolina Supreme Court on the grounds that the prosecu-

Darryl Hunt, wrongly convicted in North Carolina in 1985. *Innocence Project, New York.*

tion had introduced indicting statements from Hunt's girlfriend after she had recanted them.

Prosecutors then offered Hunt a plea bargain deal: he would be released with time served, which was then five years, if he pleaded guilty. Hunt refused, saying he was innocent, but he was nevertheless convicted again in his second 1989 trial by an all-white jury in rural Catawba County, which took only two hours in deliberation. Hunt was sent to prison for life.

Attorneys Mark Rabil, who had worked for twenty years as Hunt's defense lawyer, and Ben Dowling-Sendor requested postconviction DNA testing for their client. In 1994, the DNA testing showed that Hunt's DNA did not match that of the killer-rapist. Despite this overwhelming evidence, North Carolina judges refused to release Hunt, claiming that the tests did not prove Hunt's actual innocence. This stiff judicial resistance to DNA came at a time when it was still under prosecutorial scrutiny as a genuine identification system. However, in 2004, the DNA profile of the crime scene was processed through the state's database, which produced results that stunned officials. The DNA profile excluded Hunt altogether and perfectly matched another man, Willard E. Brown, as the killer of Deborah Sykes. Brown confessed to the murder, and Hunt was released and exonerated in 2005.

Another North Carolina man, Ronald Cotton, became the victim of mistaken identity in two rapes, and, like Darryl Hunt, was sent to prison for life. Cotton's dilemma started with the two rapes in July 1984, when a home intruder entered separate apartments on separate nights in Burlington, North Carolina. In both instances, he cut the phone wires and, using a knife to intimidate his victims, raped each victim and stole money and other items. Both of the victims were taken to hospitals, where rape examination kits were put together.

The first victim, Jennifer Thompson, an attractive young blond who later went public with her story, described her assailant as a tall black man in his early twenties. Police collected photos of men in the area

fitting that description, including twenty-two-year-old Ronald Cotton, who worked at a restaurant near Thompson's apartment. Cotton was a likely suspect, having two prior convictions on his record, one for breaking and entering and one for attempted rape. He was identified by Thompson in a photo array and at a police lineup. He was arrested on August 1, 1984, and brought to trial in January 1985, when Thompson again identified him.

Cotton claimed that he was with friends on the night of Thompson's attack, but he could not get those friends to corroborate his story. He was convicted and sentenced to life plus fifty-four years. The North Carolina Supreme Court overturned the 1985 conviction because the second rape victim had identified another man and her testimony had not been admitted in Cotton's trial. He was tried again in 1987, but this time both Thompson and the second victim testified that Cotton was the assailant in both attacks.

During that second trial, Cotton's attorneys tried to introduce evidence that another man was responsible for the two rapes. Attorneys knew that Robert Poole, a resident of Burlington who had been imprisoned for rape, had bragged to fellow inmates that he had committed the Thompson rape for which Cotton had been convicted. Poole was a tall young black man who bore a strong resemblance to Cotton.

The judge at the 1987 trial, however, refused to admit any evidence about Poole, and Cotton was again convicted and was given a second life sentence. In 1988, a defense attorney filed an appeal but failed to argue that the second suspect's confession had not been admitted in the 1987 trial, and Cotton's conviction was again confirmed. Two new attorneys took over Cotton's defense, and in 1994 they requested postconviction DNA testing, which was granted in October of that year. In 1995, the Burlington police department turned over all rape kit evidence.

The samples in one case had deteriorated and could not be used in testing, but the samples in the second case showed that Cotton was excluded as the culprit. Defense attorneys then asked that the samples be sent to the state's DNA database for comparison to any other convicted person, and the results showed that the samples matched Robert "Bobby" Poole. On June 30, 1995, Cotton was officially exonerated and all charges were dropped against him. He was pardoned by the governor the next month and became eligible for $5,000 compensation for the ten years he had spent in prison.

No one was more surprised at the DNA results in the Cotton conviction than Jennifer Thompson, who later stated (in evaluating her initial identification of Cotton), "I was positive. I couldn't have been more certain of anything in my life." She accepted the DNA results and not only apologized to Cotton but became his friend and went on to publicly lecture about the hazards of mistaken identity.

## South Carolina

Police in Lexington, South Carolina, were stymied by a rape that occurred in a wooded area outside of town on the night of December 29, 1982. The victim was a seventeen-year-old white girl, who said she had been sexually assaulted by a black man. The loose description the victim gave to police left them with no specific suspect. They then concluded that since the attack had occurred close to the home of Perry Mitchell, a black man, that Mitchell was the perpetrator. He roughly resembled the description given by the victim, but most importantly to police, he lived "only yards away from the scene of the crime."

Mitchell claimed that he was not at home at the time of the attack but was attending a party with about fifteen people. The victim was unsure of identifying Mitchell in two police photo arrays but in the third photo array she picked Mitchell's photo. Exclusively on this evidence, Mitchell was convicted by a jury of first-degree criminal sexual conduct on January 23, 1984, and was given a thirty-year prison sentence. A direct appeal was denied, but he was granted postconviction DNA testing in 1996,.

Cellmark Diagnostics tested the semen found on the victim's underwear and announced in June 1998 that Mitchell was excluded as the depositor of the semen. Judge James Johnson Jr. granted Mitchell a new trial, but prosecutors declined to go back to court. On August 4, 1998, after spending fourteen years in prison, Mitchell was released.

## Tennessee

On October 26, 1979, a sixteen-year-old girl and her boyfriend, both white, were abducted by a black man with a deadly weapon in the Overton Park area of Memphis, Tennessee. The attacker robbed the teenagers and took them into some woods, ordered them to undress, and lie prone on the ground. He then raped the girl and cut her several times, telling both to remain on the ground and not dress until he was gone. Unable to find the keys to the car they had driven to the area, the couple flagged down a ride and were taken to the nearby home of a schoolteacher. Police were called and took the girl to a hospital where evidence for a rape kit was collected.

Police learned from physicians that the victim was a virgin prior to the attack. The crotch of her jeans was caked with semen, and examination of the vaginal swabs showed motile spermatozoa, but no tests were made at the time of trial except for presumptive screening of seminal fluid, which showed positive. Based on the description given to police by the victim and her boyfriend, Clark Jerome McMillan was arrested and detained on October 30, 1979. He was identified by the victims in a photo array and later at a police lineup. The victims had not originally described the assailant as walking with a limp. Macmillan wore a leg brace, having been shot in the leg two years earlier. When the rape victim testified in court at McMillan's May 1980 trial, she added the limp to her description.

Clark Jerome McMillan, wrongly convicted in Tennessee in 1980. *Innocence Project, New York.*

In his defense, McMillan insisted that he was innocent and that he had been at his sister's home with his girlfriend at the time of the attack. Both sister and girlfriend supported his alibi, which was not accepted by the jury. The victims' identification was the chief cause of McMillan's conviction, and the twenty-four-year-old McMillan was sentenced to 119 years on charges of aggravated rape and robbery with a deadly weapon. After all of his appeals failed, McMillan contacted the Innocence Project, which undertook his case in 1996.

Law students diligently researched his case for years, attempting to obtain pertinent files and information. With the help of a celebrated criminal attorney, Kemper Durand, the Innocence Project convinced prosecutors to agree to postconviction DNA testing. Examination of the spermatozoa in the rape kit, as announced in April 2002, showed that McMillan could not have been the depositor of the spermatozoa.

Memphis prosecutors vacated McMillan's conviction and dismissed all charges against him on May 2, 2002. McMillan, however, was held in prison on an unrelated 1979 gun possession charge for which he had been sentenced to two years in federal prison. The U.S. Bureau of Prisons then granted him time served and he was released on May 15, 2002, after spending more than twenty-two years in prison on the wrongful rape conviction. Further, the Tennessee Bureau of Investigation DNA tests showed that the actual rapist was David Lloyd Boyd, a suspect in many other rape cases, who was then serving a life sentence in Texas on a conviction of aggravated rape with a deadly weapon.

### Virginia

On June 22, 1984, a young woman and her boyfriend became lost and pulled their car over to the side of the road in Virginia's Blue Ridge Parkway in Nelson County. They decided to sleep in the car for the night but were awakened by someone knocking on the window. The man announced that he was a police officer and ordered the couple from the car, demanding the keys. When they complied, the man, who was white, brandished a gun and then told the boyfriend that if he did not run away he would be shot.

The boyfriend ran away and the man ordered the woman into his own vehicle, a truck, and drove to an abandoned building, where he repeatedly raped and sodomized the victim over a two-hour period. When pausing to smoke a cigarette, the attacker told the victim that he had been in Vietnam and hated an officer who had needlessly sacrificed men in his unit. He later released the victim, telling her how to get back to her car. When she returned to that location, her boyfriend was there, accompanied by police officers.

A police officer made a sketch of the attacker from the descriptions provided by the woman and her boyfriend. Meanwhile, more than one hundred miles distant, a rape victim accused Edward Honaker, who lived near her, of attacking her, but he had a solid alibi and was not charged. A detective then showed a picture of Honaker to the Blue Ridge Parkway victim and she and her boyfriend identified him as the assailant. They also stated that Honaker's truck was similar to the one driven by the assailant. The victim and the boyfriend then identified Honaker in a police lineup and once again at his 1985 trial. At that trial, a forensic expert stated that hairs found on the victim matched Honaker's hair type and that it was "unlikely that the hair would match anyone other than the defendant."

In his defense, Honaker provided an alibi that was supported by several persons. He testified in his own defense, insisting that he was innocent, stating that he had never served in Vietnam. More importantly, he told the jury that he had had a vasectomy and was unable to produce the sperm that had been found on the victim and her clothes. The jury, despite this convincing evi-

**Edward Honaker, wrongly convicted in Virginia in 1985.** *Innocence Project, New York.*

dence, convicted him on two counts of rape, one count of forcible sodomy, one count of aggravated battery, one count of abduction, and two counts of use of a firearm in the commission of a felony. On April 10, 1985, Honaker was sentenced to three life terms, plus thirty-four years.

When all appeals failed, Honaker contacted Centurion Ministries, an organization that represents wrongly convicted persons. When looking into the case, investigators discovered that the two witnesses had been hypnotized before identifying Honaker, and their initial descriptions of the assailant were inconsistent with Honaker's actual appearance. Centurion, working with the Innocence Project, secured postconviction DNA testing in the case in 1993, which showed that neither the victim's boyfriend nor Honaker could have been the rapist. When the victim admitted having a secret lover, that man's DNA was tested, and he was also excluded from being the rapist.

Further, the defense offered another forensic expert who challenged the findings of the expert who had tested the hairs found on the victim, showing that the hairs could have come from any number of males. On October 22, 1994, Honaker was granted executive clemency and was released from prison after serving nine years behind bars. Virginia later awarded him $500,000 in compensation for his wrongful conviction and imprisonment. The perpetrator was never found.

Walter Snyder shared Honaker's nightmare experience after a woman was raped and sodomized in her Alexandria, Virginia, home on October 27, 1985. The intruder burglarized the residence before fleeing. The attacker, the victim later told police, was a black man with smooth hands, who had a strong body odor and smelled of alcohol. He wore red shorts and a gray hooded sweatshirt. She said it was very dark when the attack occurred and she had difficulty seeing her assailant's face.

Police questioned people in the neighborhood, asking if they had seen anyone suspicious in the area at the time of the attack. Two persons said that Walter Snyder, an amateur boxer, was outside his home, directly across the street from where the attack occurred at about the time it occurred. Snyder agreed to have his photograph and fingerprints taken, and, while talking with officers, admitted that he owned a pair of red shorts. Snyder's photo was later shown in a police photo array to the victim, but his photo was discriminatory in that it only showed his face prominently in a head and shoulders photo, while all of the other photos showed full-length shots of other men. The victim picked out four of the men but not Snyder. The victim viewed the photo array a second time and failed to identify Snyder, although she said his eyebrows looked familiar.

Police confiscated Snyder's shorts and he later went to the police station to have them returned. When he arrived, police detained him while they summoned the victim, who then identified Snyder as her assailant. Police grilled Snyder and later claimed he made a confession, although no record of a confession was ever produced. His nose was broken during this interrogation. He was then charged with rape, breaking and entering, and aggravated sexual battery.

At Snyder's 1986 trial, the victim again identified Snyder, saying that he smelled of "a combination of oil and a basement," this statement made after the victim had learned that Snyder lived in the basement of his parents' home and worked as a cooling and heating repairman. Defense attorneys had not been informed that the victim had failed twice to identify Snyder and were not told that she learned from police where Snyder lived and worked. The jury was informed that Snyder had the same blood type as the attacker, according the rape kit evidence. Snyder was convicted and sentenced to forty-five years in prison.

When his appeals failed, Snyder contacted the Innocence Project, which undertook his case and asked for postconviction DNA testing. It was performed by the Center for Blood Research, which reported in 1992 that Snyder was excluded as the donor of the spermatozoa examined from the swab in the rape kit. The test was done again at the request of prosecutors, with the same results. On April 23, 1993, Snyder was released after Governor L. Douglas Wilder (1990–1994) signed an executive order of clemency. Snyder's conviction record was expunged and he was given $11,200 in compensation for his wrongful conviction and six years of imprisonment.

### West Virginia

Larry David Holdren, wrongly convicted in West Virginia in 1985. *Innocence Project, New York.*

A nurse living in Kanawha County was attacked while jogging along a boulevard in Charleston, West Virginia, in December 1982, by a man running toward her and wearing a hooded jacket that hid his face. He pushed her down a hill and dragged her to a storm sewer, where she was raped orally, anally, and vaginally. Running to a nearby house, the victim was transported to a hospital, where swabs were taken for a rape kit from her face, on which the assailant had ejaculated, as well as her clothing. The victim picked Larry David Holdren's photo from a police photo array, and he was also identified by another witness who said that Holdren had been near the scene of the crime. In March 1983, Holdren was arrested, and he went to trial in 1985.

Though Holdren's attorneys requested biological evidence, the hospital where the victim had been treated reported that it no longer had any evidence to provide. Holdren denied the attack and provided an alibi, which was supported by several persons. The victim identified him in court and the jury convicted him. He was sentenced to thirty to sixty years in prison. After he lost all appeals, the Innocence Project accepted his case and convinced West Virginia officials to allow postconviction DNA testing, which was performed by Forensic Science Associates in 1997. Biological evidence was located, and the spermatozoa tests excluded Holdren from being its donor. In 1999, prosecutors agreed to release Holdren, and

charges against him were dismissed in January 2000.

Holdren, who had spent fourteen years behind bars, was awarded $1 million from Charleston Area Medical Center for destroying semen evidence in his case. He was also awarded $1.65 million from the state of Virginia for its wrongful conviction of him. Holdren's problems were not at an end, however. In April 2007, he was convicted of attacking a motorist with the claw end of a hammer in a roadway argument and sentenced by Kanawha circuit Judge Irene C. Berger to five years in prison. The fifty-one-year-old Holdren apologized to the man he attacked, Robert Harper, before going to prison. The road raged manifested by Holdren was thought to be the result of pent-up anger over his wrongful conviction.

## DNA Exonerations in the Midwest

### Illinois

On September 16, 1981, a woman was walking to her car on Rush Street in Chicago's North Side. As she opened her car door, a man suddenly pushed her into the car, beat her, and brutally raped her. He took her money and a gold chain and then forced the woman into the trunk of her car. He attempted to drive the car from the premises, but a suspicious attendant who recognized the car told the man to back up and wait behind the barrier while she summoned another employee. The man jumped from the car and fled on foot.

Hearing the victim shouting from the trunk of the car, the two attendants managed to free her. The attendants gave a description of the attacker to police, which an artist later used to sketch a composite image. A police officer a short time later thought he recognized Jerry Miller as the man in the composite sketch. The officer later stated that he had seen Miller some days before the attack looking into the window of a parked car, and on this "evidence" Miller was arrested.

Jerry Miller, wrongly convicted in Illinois in 1982. *Innocence Project, New York.*

The victim was shown a police photo array of several young black men, but she told police she had followed instructions from the assailant to keep her eyes closed during the attack, fearing that he would kill her. The two parking attendants, however, identified Miller in a police lineup before his 1982 trial. A rape kit yielded little or no biological evidence in this case, although sperm were found on the fringes of the victim's slip. Miller was convicted of rape, robbery, and kidnapping by a Cook County jury on October 1, 1982, on the eyewitness identification. He was sentenced to forty-five years in prison.

In 2005, after all appeals had failed, Miller's case was undertaken by the Innocence Project, which requested postconviction DNA testing. After the court granted this motion, the Cook County Clerk's Office located the slip bearing the sperm and sent it to Strand Analytical Laboratory for testing. The lab reported that its test excluded Miller as the donor of the spermatozoa; his conviction was vacated and all charges against him dismissed. Miller was paroled in 2006, after spending twenty-four years behind bars. He was officially exonerated on April 23, 2007, after the DNA test samples were compared to those in the FBI convicted offender database, which identified another man as the attacker.

A year after Miller went to prison, another Chicago police officer identified a man as a child rapist from a police composite sketch. This man, Ronnie Bullock, like Miller, would be wrongly convicted and sent to prison. Bullock's dilemma began in 1983, when two separate sexual attacks occurred on the South Side of Chicago only a month apart and only a block away in an alley. The first of these attacks happened on March 18, 1983,

when a nine-year-old girl was walking to school. A man who appeared to be dressed as a police officer approached the girl and she instinctively fled. After chasing her down, the man dragged her to a car and drove to a nearby alley, where he raped her. On April 18, 1983, a twelve-year-old girl was approached by a man showing a police badge. He abducted the girl in the same manner as the first attack, taking her to an alley and raping her.

Both girls gave descriptions of their attacker to a police artist, who drew a composite sketch of the same person. A police officer a short time later identified Ronnie Bullock as the man in the police sketch. Bullock was a black man who lived in the area where the attacks took place. His proximity to the crimes and his resemblance to the police composite caused his arrest. Both victims identified Bullock in a police lineup. He was brought to trial on charges of deviate sexual assault and aggravated kidnapping in the first attack in May 1984 (charges in the second attack were dropped).

Bullock was convicted and sentenced to sixty years in prison. Almost immediately after his conviction, his attorneys demanded that the evidence in the case be preserved. The court ordered that the victim's panties be stored in the freezer inside the office of the Clerk of the Circuit Court. In 1987, an appeals court upheld Bullock's conviction and, in October 1990, denied his motion for postconviction relief. In 1993, his motion to have the evidence in the case undergo DNA testing was granted. After some delays in locating the evidence, Cellmark Diagnostics completed its PCR tests in October 1994, stating that the sperm and nonsperm fraction of the victim's panties were not related to Bullock.

On October 13, 1994, Bullock was released from prison without bond but was ordered to wear an electronic monitoring device while living at his parents' Chicago residence. Prosecutors conducted their own tests and the Cook County Laboratory arrived at the same conclusion. A judge dismissed all charges against Bullock, who had spent ten years in prison. Bullock had been

Alejandro Dominguez, wrongly convicted in Illinois in 1990. *Innocence Project, New York.*

the victim of mistaken identity on the part of two victims, as well as through the police composite sketch that bore his resemblance, which provided no actual evidence that he was the perpetrator. In the case of Alejandro Dominguez, there was no similarity at all between him and the description of a rapist, but he was nevertheless sent to prison for a crime he did not commit.

Dominguez, a Mexican national living in Waukegan, Illinois, was arrested in 1990 for a 1989 rape. After the assailant invaded the victim's Waukegan residence and raped her, the woman described to police a man having "shoulder-length, black curly hair, a small mustache, and a diamond stud earring." Police ignored this description in arresting sixteen-year-old Dominguez, who had short-cropped hair and no piercings in his ears. The victim had also told police that her attacker spoke to her in English and Dominguez spoke no English at that time. The victim told police that the rapist had a tattoo. Dominguez had no tattoo.

Dominguez was tried as an adult. On the advice of his counsel, Dominguez waived the right to a jury and had a bench trial before Lake County circuit court Judge Harry D. Hartel, who, despite the woeful lack of evidence, found him guilty and sentenced him to nine years in prison. Dominguez was subject to constant beatings from other inmates and tried to protect himself from being raped in the shower room by carrying a sock containing two bars of soap to use as a weapon. Always maintaining his innocence, Dominguez worked hard to learn English and managed to get his high school diploma behind bars. With credit for time served in jail before his trial, as well as day-for-day good time served at Joliet Prison, Dominguez was released on parole in December 1994.

Dominguez married and fathered a child while working hard and maintaining a clean record (he had had no criminal record before his 1990 conviction). His life may have continued undisturbed had it not been for the intervention of the U.S. Immigration and Naturalization Service. Immigration authorities, noting his conviction, moved to have him deported for failing to register as a sex offender. This he would not do, claiming that he had been wrongfully convicted and imprisoned. Dominguez retained defense attorneys John P. Curry and Jed Stone, who appealed for DNA testing in the case.

In 2001, the motion was granted by Lake County circuit court Judge Raymond McKoski, on the stipulation that the tests would be made at Dominguez's expense. Following testing, the Serological Research Institute of Richmond, California, announced that Dominguez was excluded as the source of biological material recovered from the woman in the 1989 rape. Judge McKoski and Lake County prosecutors asked that Dominguez's conviction be set aside on April 26, 2002. Prosecutor Michael G. Mermel refused to apologize, however, telling the Chicago *Tribune*, "I won't apologize for the original conviction. At the time, the science [DNA] didn't exist, and we had a credible witness."

Governor Rod Blagojevich (2003–) officially exonerated Dominguez in 2005. He was the fifth man Blagojevich had pardoned after DNA had refuted a conviction. On October 17, 2006, a U.S. district court in Chicago awarded Dominguez $9 million in compensation for his wrongful conviction and imprisonment of more than four years. During that October 2006 trial, Dominguez charged Waukegan police lieutenant Paul Hendley with causing the rape victim to falsely identify him.

## Indiana

On February 1, 1986, a woman getting off a bus in Indianapolis was attacked by a man wearing boots that laced up the front and were splattered with paint. The assailant brandished a knife and hid his face while dragging the woman to a grassy slope near a highway overpass, where he raped her. He held a knife to her throat throughout the attack. He took all of the victim's money, $6, and then ordered her to "roll away" from him. He then fled on foot. Wayne Scruggs, a black, self-employed house painter, was arrested and imprisoned in Marion County Jail, held on a $50,000 bond he could not pay. He possessed a pair of boots that laced up the front and were, like those of the attacker, splattered with paint. The victim identified Scruggs in a police photo array of two hundred photos from a police sex crimes file, and later identified Scruggs at his 1986 trial.

Scruggs had little defense and further implicated himself when he admitted that he was familiar with the area where the attack occurred. On May 13, 1986, he was convicted of rape and robbery by a jury in Marion County superior court. He was sentenced to forty years in prison. In a 1987 appeal, defense attorneys argued that Scruggs's conviction lacked sufficient evidence and that an "evidentiary harpoon" had been committed by a police officer at his trial, who stated that the victim had viewed photos of "individuals who have all been arrested for rape or sexual assault." Though the jury was admonished to disregard the officer's statement, no mistrial was ordered. The Indiana Supreme Court nevertheless affirmed Scruggs's conviction.

On December 18, 1992, Scruggs's defense counsel again appealed, arguing that the defendant had been given a prison sentence not based on the evidence presented by the prosecution. The petition also cited that by entering evidence, which was accepted by the court, of Scruggs's previous arrest for rape (for which he was not convicted), the prosecution had denied Scruggs of due process. Attorneys requested that DNA evidence which was not available at the time of Scruggs's 1986 trial be tested. In February and April 1993, defense attorneys again requested DNA testing, asking that blood samples be drawn from their defendant for DNA tests.

The court allowed the testing, which was conducted by Cellmark Diagnostics. Cellmark tested all of the items in the rape kit from the case, later reporting that the items were amplified using PCR and typed for DQ alpha using an amplitype HLA DQ alpha forensic DNA amplication and typing kit. The results excluded Scruggs as the source of spermatozoa found on the swabs from the rape kit, as well as from blood samples taken at the crime scene.

On December 17, 1993, the superior court ordered Scruggs's conviction vacated and ordered a new trial. Prosecutors declined to retry him and dismissed all charges against him. His conviction record was expunged on May 28, 1994. Scruggs served seven years and seven months behind bars for a crime he did not commit.

### Kansas

On the night of August 25, 1985, a woman left a nightclub in Topeka, Kansas, with two female friends. They sat in two cars talking until a man appeared, entering one of the cars and ordering the woman to drive to a secluded area where he raped her. The victim was shown a police photo array and picked out a man who proved not to be the assailant. Joe C. Jones was then identified by two witnesses as the perpetrator. Jones was a regular patron of the nightclub and had been present at the club before the attack occurred. The victim later identified him when police brought Jones before her. Police then obtained a pair of jeans from Jones's residence that matched those worn by the attacker, according to the victim.

Jones claimed that he had left the nightclub and was in a store at the time of the attack. A store clerk supported his alibi, stating that Jones was wearing clothes different from those worn by the assailant. On February 13, 1986, a Shawnee County jury convicted Jones and he was sentenced to life on a charge of kidnapping, plus ten to twenty-five years on the rape charge. On February 2, 1987, the Kansas Supreme Court denied Jones's appeal, which was based on new evidence that another man had committed the crime. That man was questioned and denied committing the rape (he was later convicted of sexual assaults with the identical modus operandi). A second appeal in 1989 was also denied, after Jones's attorneys stated that their client was homosexual and was psychologically incapable of committing a rape on a female.

Jones's attorneys then appealed for postconviction DNA testing, which was granted. Forensic Science Associates (FSA) analyzed the vaginal swab taken from the rape kit in the case, and it reported on October 25, 1991, that the semen on the vaginal swab excluded Jones as the donor. FSA was asked to retype Jones's blood, and it reported on April 13, 1992, that it had replicated its findings and again announced that Jones could not have supplied the semen on the vaginal swab. The court vacated Jones's conviction on July 17, 1992, after a judge ruled that DNA was admissible. Prosecutors stated that it would not retry Jones, and he was released after spending over six years behind bars.

## Michigan

The vicious rapist who invaded a woman's home in Clinton, Michigan, on the night of April 30, 1994, carefully eliminated any clues of his attack. Wearing a nylon stocking mask tied at the top, the intruder attacked the twenty-eight-year-old married woman while she slept, tying her hands behind her back and blindfolding her with her underwear. The assailant leisurely raped the victim several times in various rooms of the house. When she complained that she could no longer feel any sensation in her hands, he removed the handcuffs and tied her hands in front of her.

The rapist then ejaculated in the victim's mouth, forcing her to swallow the semen. He then forced her to drink soda to wash down the semen and then used her panties to wipe out any remaining semen. Before leaving, the assailant wiped off the soda can and removed the phone from its hook. A short time later, the victim contacted police but could only supply a sketchy description of her attacker. She said she had only a few glimpses

of the man, a white male standing 6 feet 0 to 6 feet 2 inches and weighing between 200 and 225 pounds. She aided a police artist in putting together a composite sketch, but, after looking at it, the victim said it was only 60 percent accurate.

Police thought that the sketch resembled forty-three-year-old Kenneth Wyniemko, who, as of July 14, 1994, was being held on unrelated misdemeanor charges. He was placed in a police lineup and the rape victim identified him, although he did not quite match her original description of the attacker. Wyniemko stood 5 feet 11 inches and weighed 198 pounds at that time. Despite the attacker's attempt to destroy evidence of his assault, semen had been found in the crotch area of the victim's underwear and on bedsheets.

Wyniemko's trial began on October 31, 1994, his court-appointed attorney having little more than a weekend to prepare for trial. A serologist tested the rape kit samples and reported that the antigens were consistent with a donor of type A blood. The victim and Wyniemko had type O blood, but the victim's husband had type A. The prosecution admitted that the semen could have come from the victim's husband. In addition to the "positive" identification of Wyniemko in court by the victim, prosecutors offered a prison informant who stated that Wynniemko had confessed the crime to him. For that doubtful testimony, the informant was spared a life sentence for an unrelated conviction.

A Macomb County jury convicted Wyniemko on fifteen counts of criminal sexual conduct, armed robbery, and breaking and entering. On December 15, 1994, he was sentenced to forty to sixty years in prison, the harshest possible sentence and one delivered by a judge, who felt the defendant deserved the

Kenneth Wyniemko, wrongly convicted in Michigan in 1994. *Innocence Project, New York.*

maximum prison term because he had "shown no remorse." Wyniemko had indeed shown no regret for a crime he insisted he did not commit.

When all appeals failed, Wyniemko appealed to the Cooley Innocence Project at the Thomas M. Cooley School of Law in Lansing, Michigan. Through one of its attorneys, Gail Pamukov, who worked pro bono on the case, evidence from the case was secured for postconviction DNA testing. That evidence consisted of a cigarette butt left behind by the arrogant rapist (he had stopped to smoke a cigarette between his several rapes of the victim) and semen-stained nylons. This and other evidence was tested by the State Police Forensic Science Division. STR testing reported in June 2003 that Wyniemko was excluded as a donor of the spermatozoa. His conviction was overturned on June 17, 2003, and he was released after serving over eight years behind bars. The fifty-four-year-old Wyniemko, a resident of Rochester Hills, Michigan, was awarded $3.7 million in an out-of-court settlement with Clinton Township in 2005.

## Missouri

The wrongful conviction and imprisonment of Steven Toney could be attributed to fate as well as mistaken identity. On the night of September 30, 1982, a twenty-one-year-old woman returning to her apartment building in Richmond Heights, Missouri, in the heart of the St. Louis metro area, was met at the entrance by a black man she did not know. The man followed her into the building and, when she put her key into the lock of the door of her apartment, he threatened her with a knife and then dragged her outside to a wooded area, where he raped her and sodomized her orally before fleeing. The woman then returned to her apartment, where her fiancé was sleeping. She woke him, told him about the

Steven Toney, wrongly convicted in Missouri in 1983. *Innocence Project, New York.*

attack, and then bathed while her boyfriend called police.

Steven Toney was soon selected by the victim as her assailant. Toney had served almost three years on a conviction of forgery, kidnapping, and robbery. At the time of the rape, he was under arrest on a bad check charge. Fate had made him available to the police. His photo was shown to the victim, who identified him from a photo array of four other persons. She later identified him in a police lineup and after listening to his voice. A gas station attendant stated that he saw Toney near the crime area at the time of the rape. Toney's prior criminal record was emphasized by prosecutors, as well as his habitual drug abuse.

Toney's attorneys offered little defense, stating that their client was asleep at his grandmother's home at the time of the attack. They pointed out that he had completed high school and was a Vietnam War veteran with an honorable discharge. He was convicted of rape and sodomy and given two life sentences. New defense attorneys appealed the case, alleging that their client had been subjected to multiple constitutional violations, including a violation of due process, exclusion of exculpatory evidence, ineffective assistance of counsel, inappropriate sentencing, and inappropriate standard of evidence. The lawyers asked for postconviction DNA testing, which was done in 1996 and showed that the biological evidence from the rape kit excluded Toney as the donor of the spermatozoa.

In that year, Toney was released from prison in Moberly, Missouri, supplied with $16 and a free ride back to St. Louis. His exoneration brought him no compensation since Missouri had passed a law denying compensation to anyone exonerated before August 28, 2003. Toney went to work for a car rental agency, surviving on a meager salary. His twenty-five-hour-a-week job consisted of returning rented cars to lots, which kept him outdoors. He enjoyed the job because it prevented him from being as cooped up as he had been during the thirteen years of his wrongful imprisonment.

**John Briscoe, wrongly convicted in Missouri in 1983.** *Innocence Project, New York.*

On October 1, 1982, one day after the woman in Richmond Heights was raped, the crime for which Steven Toney was wrongly convicted, another woman in a St. Louis suburb was attacked by a black man who broke in to her apartment, threatened her with a knife, robbed her of jewelry and money, and then raped her. The assailant, following the attack, brazenly sat in a brightly lit room with the victim, and both smoked cigarettes. Before he left, the attacker told the victim that his name was John Briscoe. While police officers were present in the victim's apartment, the assailant brazenly phoned the victim several times, identifying himself with each call as John Briscoe. The calls were traced to a pay phone in the neighborhood of Briscoe's home.

The victim was transported to a hospital where biological swabs were taken for the rape kit. The victim was later shown a police photo array from which she picked Briscoe's photo and she later identified him in a police lineup. She also identified him at his 1983 trial, where he offered little in defense. A forensic expert testified that a hair found at the crime scene showed characteristics similar to Briscoe's head hair. In less than two hours, a jury convicted Briscoe of forcible rape, sodomy, burglary, robbery, stealing, and armed criminal action. He was sentenced to forty-five years in prison.

During the course of his many appeals, Briscoe petitioned the St. Louis district attorney's office to locate the biological evidence in his case so that it could undergo postconviction DNA testing. He was originally told that the evidence could not be located, and the petition was denied. Centurion Ministries, located in Princeton, New Jersey, undertook his case in 2000. In response to persistent requests for DNA evidence in the case, investigators were told in 2001 that the evidence could not

be found and was presumed destroyed. In 2004, an inventory was conducted at the St. Louis Police Laboratory and the three cigarette butts smoked on the night of the 1982 rape had been found in a freezer (the assailant has smoked one cigarette, the victim two).

The district attorney's office, however, told defense attorneys that it had not been told of the existence of the cigarette butts until July 6, 2006. DNA tests were conducted and showed that Briscoe had been excluded from smoking any of the cigarettes, but saliva found on one of the butts showed that another man, who was then serving time in a Missouri prison, had smoked the cigarette. This man, who could not be prosecuted because of the statute of limitations in the case, was known to Briscoe and it was logically concluded that he had used Briscoe's name when committing the rape. At age fifty-two and after spending twenty-three years behind bars for a crime he did not commit, Briscoe was released on July 19, 2006.

In another St. Louis rape case, which occurred on January 31, 1984, Larry Johnson was wrongly convicted of rape, sodomy, robbery, and kidnapping and sentenced to prison for life. The evidence that would eventually exonerate him was stubbornly withheld by St. Louis prosecutors until the Innocence Project filed a suit against the prosecutors, who continued the delay and obfuscation tactics that kept Johnson wrongly behind bars for years.

The victim was attacked in her car by a masked assailant wearing a sweatshirt and scarf. He threatened the victim with a knife while he drove her to an alley where he raped and sodomized her for two hours. Following the attack, the

**Larry Johnson, wrongly convicted in Missouri in 1984.** *Innocence Project, New York.*

victim drove home, called police, and was later taken to a hospital where rape kit evidence was collected. She worked with a police artist the following day to put together a composite sketch, saying that the assailant was clean-shaven. After being shown about 140 photos, the woman selected one photo showing a black man wearing a mustache. The police artist was then told to add a mustache to the composite sketch, which he did.

Larry Johnson was identified by the victim later that day in a police lineup. He had facial hair, which contradicted the victim's original description. At Johnson's 1984 trial, the victim's identification was the prosecution's chief evidence. When defense attorneys asked about the evidence collected for the rape kit, the prosecutor objected and the judge, who had traditionally opposed allowing forensic evidence into evidence, sustained the objection. Johnson was convicted and sentenced to life.

In 1986 Johnson lost an appeal based on his challenge of jury selection. He later contacted the Innocence Project, which focuses on DNA post-conviction testing, and it undertook his case. That organization, however, ran into stiff resistance from the district attorney's office. Attorney Barry Scheck, director of the New York–based Innocence Project, claimed that St. Louis prosecutors purposely withheld evidence to prevent DNA testing in six rape cases, including Johnson's. In 2000, he sued the prosecutors. Prosecutors denied obstructing justice, stating that they were complying with federal laws and that processing the evidence took considerable time. They further claimed that Scheck and the Innocence Project were inflicting undue anguish on the rape victims—a traditional argument from prosecutors reluctant to see DNA testing that might bring about vacated convictions and new trials.

Prosecutors then stated that they had planned to review more than 1,400 pre–1994 convictions to determine if DNA evidence existed, and if it did, whether or not it made any sense to order that testing. They claimed that it took about ten hours

to review each case before making a decision to order DNA testing, or 14,000 hours, or 350 weeks (at forty-hour weeks), or 6.7 years to address the cases in question, not to mention the millions of dollars in man hours such labors would consume. (In rough accounting to maintain the conservatively estimated 10,000 innocent persons behind bars—although probably four to eight times that number actually exist—it was costing a state average of $1.8 million per person per twenty years at $90,000 per year per person if the amortized yearly prison costs are to be accepted.)

The first DNA tests affirmed Fred Hamilton's rape conviction. Prosecutors crowed over this triumph, stating that the Innocence Project was wasting government time and money and was "re-victimizing the victim." The second case, however, which dealt with Larry Johnson, was a different matter. Prosecutors announced on July 26, 2002, that DNA testing had excluded Johnson from being the donor of the spermatozoa found on the rape kit and the victim's sweater and panties. Exonerated after serving eighteen years in prison, Johnson was released on July 30, 2002.

To establish Lonnie Erby's innocence, the Innocence Project had to compel the St. Louis circuit attorney to provide evidence for DNA testing. Erby had been convicted in 1986 of three sexual attacks occurring in St. Louis, Missouri, on July 26, 1985, August 22, 1985, and October 1, 1985. All of the victims were teenagers waylaid at night on lonely streets and taken to alleys or garages, where they were raped, the attacker brandishing either a knife or a gun. All of the victims later identified Erby as their assailant.

Erby's defense counsel provided witnesses who testified that Erby had been elsewhere at the time of the attacks, but he was nevertheless found guilty and

Lonnie Erby, wrongly convicted in Missouri in 1986. *Innocence Project, New York.*

sentenced to 115 years in prison on charges of kidnapping, rape, sodomy, sexual abuse, attempted robbery, and stealing. After the Innocence Project filed a civil suit against the circuit attorney's office in 2000, coupled to the fact that Missouri enacted its first postconviction DNA statute in that year, the rape kit evidence in all three cases was released. Forensic Science Associates and the St. Louis Police Laboratory both excluded Erby as the donor of the spermatozoa in all of the cases. After seventeen years in prison, Erby was released on August 25, 2003.

On April 15, 1996, a twenty-six-year-old white woman attempted to park a car in a St. Louis lot before going to work. She mistook a black man wearing a baseball cap for a parking attendant and gave him her car keys. He then attempted to attack her with a screwdriver. The woman threw her purse onto the car seat and, after struggling with her assailant, fled. She noticed that the man was bleeding at the time. The victim ran to a nearby garage and called police.

The victim described her attacker as a black man with a "David Letterman gap" between his teeth who was wearing a baseball cap. She said he stood about 5 feet 10 inches tall. Based on a composite police sketch, which the victim helped an artist create, Antonio Beaver was identified by a St. Louis police officer and was placed in a lineup with three other men, two of whom were police officers. Only Beaver and the other man wore baseball caps and only Beaver, who stood 6 feet 2 inches tall, had chipped teeth (but no "David Letterman gap").

The victim identified Beaver in the lineup and later at his trial in April 1997, where he was charged with first-degree robbery. Defense attorneys stated that the fingerprints (other than the victim's) found in the victim's stolen car, which had later been found abandoned in East St. Louis, did not match Beaver's prints. Beaver

Antonio Beaver, wrongly convicted in Missouri in 1997. *Innocence Project, New York.*

was, however, convicted and sentenced to eighteen years in prison. After all appeals failed, Beaver applied for postconviction DNA testing, which was performed in October 2006. Results from the examination of the blood left in the victim's abandoned car showed that Beaver was innocent. The forty-one-year-old Beaver was officially exonerated on March 29, 2007, after spending ten years in prison.

### Ohio

Walter D. Smith, wrongly convicted in Ohio in 1986. *Innocence Project, New York.*

In July 1985, Walter D. Smith, a black man who resided in Columbus, Ohio, was accused by three women of having raped them several years earlier. Smith, who was awaiting trial for unrelated charges, was identified by all three rape victims. He denied committing the sexual attacks but eyewitness testimony brought about his conviction in two of the three rape cases in 1986. He was sentenced to 78 to 190 years in prison.

Behind bars, Smith became a model prisoner, acquiring a business degree from Wilmington College and completing a drug rehabilitation program. He appealed his conviction several times and requested postconviction DNA testing in 1987. DNA testing was performed in 1996 and showed that Smith was innocent of the two rapes. He was paroled on December 6, 1996, after serving ten years in prison.

The same kind of mistaken identity that landed Smith in prison sent Donte Booker behind bars for a rape he did not commit. His case began on November 11, 1986, when a white woman was attacked in her car in a parking lot at her office building in Beachwood, Ohio. The assailant, a black man who had asked her where he could find a telephone, followed her to her car and, brandishing a knife, drove the car to a loading dock behind the building where he raped the woman. He ordered her from the car and she fled on foot to a nearby building where she called police.

After the victim's car had been recovered, she noticed that a toy gun had been taken from it by the attacker, along with $8. The victim helped a police artist draw a composite sketch of her attacker, but she failed to identify anyone from a police photo array shown to her. In February 1987, Donte Booker was arrested over a charge involving a toy gun. When a police officer remembered that a toy gun had been stolen from the car of the rape victim, Booker's photo was placed among a police photo array and shown to the victim. She picked Booker out of the array, identifying him as her assailant. She also identified a toy gun obtained from Booker as the toy gun stolen from her car.

At Booker's 1987 trial, prosecutors offered the eyewitness identification of the victim as their chief evidence. Prosecutors stated that the Ohio Bureau of Criminal Investigation had collected semen on the victim's slip, but there was not enough to perform ABO blood typing. Further, prosecutors said, a Negroid hair had been found that could have come from Booker. He was convicted and sentenced to ten to twenty-five years in prison.

Behind bars, Booker refused to show remorse or take part in a rape rehabilitation program, insisting that he was innocent of the crime for which he had been sent to prison. He attempted on his own in 2000 to have the Ohio Bureau of Criminal Investigation perform DNA testing on the evidence it had retained, but his request was denied. After his 2002 parole, Booker contacted W. Scott Ramsey, asking that Ramsey file a motion requesting that the evidence in his case be subjected to DNA testing. The motion was granted, and, on January 25, 2005, DNA tests were announced, stating that Booker was excluded as a contributor of the spermatozoa found in the rape kit. He was officially exonerated on February 9, 2005, when his conviction was overturned.

Where Donte Booker spent fifteen years behind bars for a crime he did not commit, Brian Piszczek served four years in prison because a victim mistakenly identified him as her sexual attacker. A woman home alone in her Brook Park, Ohio, residence heard a knock on her door early in the morning of July 29, 1990. Looking through the peephole, she saw a man who said he was with the woman's friend and that the friend was then parking her car. The woman thought she recognized the man and opened the door. The man immediately produced a knife, slashed the victim's neck, breast, and stomach, and then raped her.

Two months later, the victim picked Brian Piszczek's photo from a police photo array. The victim also identified Piszczek at his trial, where, after one hour's deliberation, a Cuyahoga County jury convicted him on June 25, 1991, of rape, felonious assault, and burglary. He was sentenced to fifteen to twenty-five years in prison. Attorneys for the Innocence Project, which had undertaken his case, filed a release of evidence motion. It was granted and DNA testing was performed by Forensic Science Associates on the swabs taken from the rape kit and from the victim's nightgown.

FSA reported on July 6, 1994, that Piszczek was excluded as the donor of the semen found in the samples. Prosecutors then asked a judge to overturn Piszczek's conviction and the judge declared Piszczek not guilty on all charges on October 6, 1994. He had served four years in prison. Piszczek was later awarded $105,000 for his wrongful conviction and imprisonment.

In the 1999 Akron, Ohio, murder-rape trial of Clarence Elkins, the testimony of a six-year-old child brought about a conviction. Again, it was a case of mistaken identity that the child realized four years later. The child (Brooke Sutton; her name was later released by the media) was sleeping on the night of June 6, 1998, at her grandmother's house in Barberton, Ohio, when an intruder broke in and attacked fifty-eight-year-old Judith Johnson, who was legally blind. He beat her with a blunt instrument, raped her, and then strangled her to death. During the attack, the woman's screams awoke the child, who ran into the kitchen to see her grandmother struggling with a man. She ran back to her bedroom and the man followed her.

The girl had no recollection of events after that, awakening the next morning to find her grandmother dead. She went to the house of a neighbor, who called police. While waiting for police to arrive, the girl told the neighbor that the assailant looked like her uncle, Clarence Elkins, or so the neighbor later said. Police investigators soon realized that the child had been hit by the attacker with a blunt instrument, presumably knocked unconscious before she was raped.

Clarence Elkins lived in Magnolia, Ohio, in Carroll County, a forty-five-minute drive from the Barberton home of Judy Johnson, his mother-in-law. While detained and interrogated by police, Elkins told them that he had been in several bars in Waynesburg, Ohio, when the murder-rape occurred, before going home; several witnesses supported his story. Barberton police found no fingerprints at the scene of the crime and no signs of forced entry.

Investigators concluded early on that Elkins, a press operator working in Malvern, Ohio, was the perpetrator in that he had access to Johnson's home and that he had reportedly been arguing with Johnson over his troubled marriage with her daughter, Melinda Elkins. Prosecutors at Elkins's trial admitted that biological evidence had been collected at the crime scene, including hairs, but that testing of the hairs excluded Elkins. Prosecutors relied chiefly on the testimony of Elkins's six-year-old niece, who testified on the stand for forty-five minutes. The girl said she only saw the attacker briefly and in poor lighting. Beverly Kaisak, a family friend, asked the girl in her room a short time after the attack if the assailant's voice was that of her uncle. The girl replied, "I think it sounded like him."

The niece told the court that the attacker had "a mean face." Becky Dougherty, assistant summit county prosecutor, then asked, "You're sure that it was Uncle Clarence?"

"Yes," the girl replied, "because of his face."

Elkins was convicted by a Summit County jury of murder, attempted murder, and rape and sentenced to life in prison. Melinda Elkins, whose mother and niece were the victims, never had any doubt that her husband was innocent. She had gone walking with him after he returned from the bars that night, she said. She and family members spent more than $100,000 in their attempt to prove him innocent. They hired a private detective, Martin Yant, who poked holes in the prosecution's circumstantial case, pointing out that prosecutors had used letters sent to a friend of Johnson's in which the victim said she was afraid of Elkins and called him derogatory names.

Yant focused on a man who was romantically involved with Johnson. He had suffered a head wound as a child and carried a sawed-off pool cue for protection, implying that this might have been used as the murder weapon. Beverly Kaisak, who lived briefly with this man, later stated that he had returned home on the night of the murder with scratches on his back, claiming that he had been "with a wild woman." The man bore a striking resemblance to Elkins.

In 2002, the niece, then ten, recanted her identification of Elkins. She remembered that the attacker had been wearing cowboy boots and Elkins owned none. The attacker, she said, had brown eyes, but Elkins's eyes were blue. Elkins requested postconviction DNA testing, but his petition was denied, the court stating that such testing would not prove Elkins innocent, a judicial position that was to prove erroneous.

Elkins continued to maintain his innocence, as did his wife, who was dedicated to seeing her husband set free. The family contacted the Ohio Innocence Project, which undertook Elkins's case in spring 2004. Twenty law students at the University of Cincinnati's College of Law, working under the direction of Louis Bilionis, dean of the college, began to investigate the case, locating the rape kit evidence and requesting DNA testing. The petition was granted and DNA testing of a swab from the rape kit, hair, and skin cells from underneath the fingernails of the deceased victim and a hair found in the child's clothes showed that Elkins was innocent. The Ohio Innocence Project made a motion for a new trial, but the petition was denied.

Little hope remained for Elkins, until his wife Melinda realized that her husband might be able to solve his own case. While he was behind bars at the Mansfield Correctional Institution, another man, the very suspect detective Yant had investigated, Earl Eugene Mann, was imprisoned at the same facility. Mann had been convicted of raping three girls in 2002 and given a seven-year sentence. Melinda Elkins had read of this conviction, knowing that Mann, a sexual predator with a long criminal history who had escaped from a halfway house only five days before her mother had been killed, lived with the next door neighbor to whom her niece had run to after recovering from her own attack.

Melinda Elkins had always wondered why the neighbor, Tonia Brasiel, Mann's common-law wife, had her blood-covered niece wait for thirty minutes on her porch before she called police. She also recalled a message that her niece had left on a neighbor's answering machine: "Somebody killed my grandma." She had not said "my uncle Clarence," but "somebody." After learning that Mann had been sent to the same prison that housed her husband (ironically sent to the same cell block where Clarence Elkins was held), Melinda Elkins contacted her attorney to discuss how to obtain a DNA sample from Mann without his knowledge. The attorney, Jana Deloach, suggested that, if Mann smoked, Clarence Elkins might obtain one of his cigarette butts and mail it home for DNA testing.

This is exactly what was done. Elkins, seeing Mann extinguish a cigarette, retrieved the butt, placed it in his Bible, and then transferred it into a small plastic bag and mailed it to an uncle two weeks later. The butt was DNA tested and showed that saliva from the butt was that of Earl Mann and that it matched the vaginal swab taken from Johnson and the niece's underwear. The results were

shown to Ohio state attorney general James Petro, who later commented, "I am always one who believes that DNA is pretty darn compelling." He launched a six-week investigation in 2005 and became convinced of Elkins's innocence. In an unprecedented move, he publicly pressured the local prosecutor to exonerate Elkins. "The whole concept of the justice system is to seek justice," Petro stated.

In December 2005, prosecutors admitted that Elkins had proven his innocence and asked the court to vacate his conviction. Elkins was officially exonerated when released on December 15, 2005, to be reunited with his wife Melinda and family members. Melinda Elkins, a heroic woman who refused to accept her husband's guilt and doggedly sought justice for him and got it after he had spent over six years behind bars for a crime he did not commit, was the subject of a motion picture. Mann, who reportedly confessed to the murder-rape of Johnson and the sexual attack on Brooke Sutton, has not been tried for these crimes at this writing.

# DNA Exonerations in the Southwest

## Oklahoma

In Oklahoma City in 1985, an attacker confronted a woman returning to her apartment complex, robbed, raped, and sodomized her. The victim could not identify any suspects, including Jeffrey Pierce, who worked with a landscaping crew about the apartment complex. Though police pointed out Pierce to the victim, she said he was not the assailant. But several months later, when police showed the victim a photograph of Pierce wearing a tan shirt, the same color shirt the victim had described the attacker as wearing, the victim identified Pierce as her assailant.

In 1986, the victim identified Pierce at his trial, and prosecutors further offered the testimony of Joyce Gilchrist, a forensic scientist at the Oklahoma City Police Laboratory. Gilchrist stated that hairs collected from the victim's residence, where

Jeffrey Pierce, wrongly convicted in Oklahoma in 1986. *Innocence Project, New York.*

the attack took place, matched Pierce's hair. A jury convicted Pierce of robbery and rape and he was sentenced to sixty-five years in prison. In 2001, the FBI Crime Laboratory ran DNA tests from samples taken from the rape kit and pronounced Pierce innocent. The bureau also refuted the claims of Joyce Gilchrist, who was accused of performing shoddy forensic analysis in the case and falsely testifying against Pierce. After serving fifteen years in prison as an innocent man, Pierce was released in May 2001.

Before his release, Pierce, a white man, befriended another inmate, a black man named Arvin Carsell McGee Jr., who had also been convicted of rape, a crime McGee insisted he did not commit. When Pierce was freed by DNA, he told McGee, "It's not over," encouraging McGee to have hope. "He gave me that faith," McGee later recalled, a faith that would eventually see DNA bring about his freedom too. McGee's case began on October 29, 1987, when Cyndi Doe, a twenty-year-old woman who worked in a Tulsa, Oklahoma, laundry, was attacked, tied up, and left in a rest room. The assailant later returned to the laundry and carried Doe over his shoulder to her car, drove her to a secluded wooded area, and raped and sodomized her. He then locked her in the trunk of his car, but she managed to escape and found the keys to her car in the ignition and the assailant gone.

Doe returned to the laundry, where police officers were investigating the report of a robbery. Doe jumped from her car, running hysterically into the laundry to shout to officers that she had been raped. Doe initially picked out another man from a police

Arvin Carsell McGee, Jr., wrongly convicted in Oklahoma in 1989. *Innocence Project, New York.*

photo array but then changed her mind four months later, when she picked out a photo of McGee. On March 7, 1988, McGee was arrested and charged with rape, kidnapping, robbery, and forcible sodomy.

The victim identified him in court, but her confusing statements led to a mistrial. A second trial ended with a hung jury. All the while, McGee's defense attorneys claimed that their client had been suffering from an injury requiring surgery that would have made it impossible for him to commit the crime.

In a third trial, however, McGee was convicted on all charges on June 22, 1989, and was sentenced to a total of 298 years in prison. After all appeals failed, the Oklahoma Indigent Defense System requested postconviction DNA testing on McGee's behalf. The results from testing by the DNA reference laboratory showed that McGee could not have been the donor of the spermatozoa collected in the rape kit. He was officially exonerated by Judge Linda G. Morrissey on February 26, 2002, and released from prison after serving over twelve years behind bars.

In September 2002, the DNA samples used to exonerate McGee were sent to the state's crime database where they were matched to Edward Alberty, who was then in an Oklahoma prison. Alberty was charged with the Doe rape, even though the statute of limitations in the case had expired in 1994 and prosecutors held little hope for a conviction. Before leaving prison, McGee said, "There are a lot of guys like me in this yard. Don't be so quick to judge."

McGee later sued the Tulsa police department for his wrongful conviction. A state's attorney at that civil trial argued that "there is no constitutional guarantee that only the guilty will be convicted." The jury disagreed and awarded the forty-four-year-old McGee $14.5 million in compensation.

### Texas

Texas, which leads the United States in meting out capital punishment, also leads the country in exonerating wrongly convicted persons. As of April 2007, twenty-nine men had been exonerated through DNA testing, thirteen from Dallas alone. Most of these cases involved rapes, where DNA testing from samples taken from rape kits proved extremely effective. Like other cases around the world, 75 percent of those wrongful convictions stemmed from mistaken eyewitness identification. Most of those mistaken identity cases involved whites identifying blacks or Latinos. More than half of wrongly convicted defendants nationwide were black. In addition to race, class also played a role in many of these cases, where defendants were poor, uneducated, unskilled, and language deficient.

In April 1981, in Dallas, Texas, a woman awoke to find an attacker on top of her in her bed. He wielded a butcher knife, slashing her hands, neck, and back while raping her. At first the victim told police she could not identify the assailant since the attack took place an hour before sunrise, and the room was dark. Officers asked her to view a police photo array. Seeing a photo of Larry Fuller, she identified him as the attacker, saying that he looked "a lot like the guy."

At his August 1981 trial, Fuller was also identified as the assailant by a forensic expert, who stated that the semen from the victim's rape kit, which had been serologically tested, included him as a nonsecretor, and that the blood type of the rape kit fluid matched the victim's blood type. Fuller was convicted of aggravated rape and sentenced to fifty years in prison. Postconviction DNA testing, however, excluded him from being the donor in the spermatozoa collected in the rape kit. His conviction was vacated on October 31, 2006, and he was released from prison after serving twenty years behind bars. On January 11, 2007, Governor Rick Perry (2000–) officially

Larry Fuller, wrongly convicted in Texas in 1981. *Innocence Project, New York.*

exonerated Fuller by granting him a full pardon.

The fate of James Waller, also of Dallas, mirrored that of Fuller. In the early morning of November 2, 1982, a man invaded a Dallas home where two white boys, seven and twelve, were sleeping. He tied up the twelve-year-old and sodomized him orally and anally, threatening to hurt him

James Waller, wrongly convicted in Texas in 1983. *Innocence Project, New York.*

if he told anyone about the assault. One night later, the boy identified Waller, a black man, after seeing him in a corner store near the apartment complex where Waller and the victim lived. The manager of the apartment complex reported to police ten weeks after the attack that she had found Waller's address book outside the victim's apartment.

Waller explained at his 1983 trial that he had left his address book behind in his apartment after his family was ordered to vacate the premises following his arrest and that the new tenants probably threw it out. He said he was sleeping with his girlfriend at the time of the attack, and the girlfriend and a cousin confirmed his alibi. Based on eyewitness identification, however, he was convicted of aggravated sexual abuse and sentenced to thirty years in prison.

After serving ten years behind bars, Waller was released on parole in 1993. He still maintained his innocence and, using his own money, secured DNA testing in 2001, which proved inconclusive. The Texas Department of Public Safety reported that, in performing its test, the sample from the rape kit was consumed. Still Waller persisted, and in 2002 had the hairs found at the crime scene DNA tested, which excluded him.

Further, with the aid of the Innocence Project, extracts from the rape kit were located and DNA tested by Orchid Cellmark, which reported in 2006 that both Waller and the victim were excluded as donors of the semen analyzed. Waller's conviction, after twenty-three years, was vacated on December 19, 2006, and Governor Rick Perry officially pardoned him on March 9, 2007. He was later awarded $250,000 compensation for his wrongful imprisonment. Governor Perry, among his many other duties, was kept busy reviewing one DNA case after another, routinely granting through his term of office official pardons to wrongly convicted Texans. These included Billy Wayne Miller, David Shawn Pope, Keith E. Turner, and Entre Nax Karage.

Miller had been convicted in 1984 of aggravated sexual assault with a deadly weapon in a Dallas rape case occurring on the night of September 26, 1983. Miller had been identified by the victim through his license plate, which was one digit different from the number the victim had provided to police. Given a life sentence, Miller appealed for DNA testing, which was done in 2006 by the Texas Department of Public Safety. The test results excluded Miller from the spermatozoa taken from the rape kit. He was released in May 2006, and Governor Perry granted him a pardon on December 20, 2006.

In July 1985, a Garland, Texas, woman was attacked and raped by a knife-wielding assailant. The victim later identified David Shawn Pope, who had been evicted from the same apartment complex where the attack occurred. He was then living in his car, which was searched. A knife was found that was similar to the butcher knife the assailant had taken from the victim's kitchen and used in the assault. Messages left on the victim's answering machine were later matched to Pope's voiceprint, which was instrumental in bringing about his conviction for aggravated sexual assault in 1986. This method is no longer used in the courts.

When all appeals failed, an anonymous tipster came to Pope's rescue, calling prosecutors in January 1999 and telling

Keith E. Turner, wrongly convicted in Texas in 1983. *Innocence Project, New York.*

them that Pope was innocent, which prompted them to employ DNA testing in his case. In 2001, DNA tests showed that Pope was excluded as the donor of the samples taken from the rape kit, which pointed to another man as the perpetrator, a convicted felon serving time in another state. Pope was released and exonerated by Governor Perry that year after spending fifteen years behind bars.

Three years before the Garland attack, a woman in Dallas, Texas, accused a coworker, Keith E. Turner, of raping her. Turner provided an alibi for the 1982 attack, but eyewitness identification, based solely on the sound of his voice, brought about his 1983 conviction on a charge of aggravated sexual assault and his twenty-year prison sentence. Released on parole in 1987 after being behind bars for four years, Turner sought vindication, which was achieved in 2005 when DNA testing showed him innocent. He was exonerated through a pardon from Governor Perry on December 22, 2005.

In 1994, the fourteen-year-old girlfriend of Entre Nax Karage was found murdered behind a store in East Dallas. Not until 1997 was a suspect arrested for the crime—Karage—whom prosecutors theorized had murdered the girl after finding her with another man. The only clue linking Karage to the crime, however, was some blood from the girl found in the car of his trunk, a car that the girl had been driving. Karage was tried before Judge Karen Greene at a bench trial and, not having a solid alibi, was

David Shawn Pope, wrongly convicted in Texas in 1986. *Innocence Project, New York.*

Entre Nax Karage, wrongly convicted in Texas in 1997. *Innocence Project, New York.*

found guilty of murder and sentenced to life in prison.

Karage requested DNA testing, which was performed in 2004, the results not only showing that Karage was innocent of the murder but that the DNA samples matched those of another person previously convicted of a similar crime. Karage was released and, on December 22, 2005, Governor Perry exonerated him with a full pardon, the same day Perry signed a pardon for Keith E. Turner. On that day, Governor Perry stated, "I believe that a full pardon for innocence must be supported by strong evidence, such as forensic DNA tests. In both of these cases [Turner and Karage], new DNA evidence proves that these men are innocent."

A. B. Butler Jr. of Tyler, Texas, received a pardon from Governor George Bush in 2000, shortly before Bush became president. In Butler's case, a twenty-five-year-old white woman in Smith County, Texas, claimed that Butler had raped her in 1983. She identified Butler, a black man, from a police photo array, at a police lineup, and in court at his 1983 trial. Convicted of aggravated kidnapping (rape was a factor in the charge in that the assailant abducted the woman from a parking lot), Butler was sentenced to ninety-nine years in prison.

Butler attempted on his own to obtain postconviction DNA testing but failed on appeals. He then secured an attorney, who in 1997 got permission for the tests, which proved inconclusive by Cellmark Diagnostics. In 1999, however, DNA samples were sent to the New York City Medical Examiner's Office, where newly developed Y chromosome DNA testing was conducted. (Y chromosome DNA testing can isolate male DNA more accurately.) The results showed that Butler was innocent of the rape. After serving over sixteen years in prison, Butler was released in January

A. B. Butler, Jr., wrongly convicted in Texas in 1983. *Innocence Project, New York.*

2000 at age forty-five, and Governor Bush officially pardoned him in May of that year.

Three years earlier, Governor Bush pardoned Kevin Byrd, wrongly convicted of a 1985 rape in Houston, Texas. The assailant in this case, who invaded the victim's home and assaulted the twenty-five-year-old pregnant white woman (while her two-year-old daughter slept

Kevin Byrd, wrongly convicted in Texas in 1985. *Innocence Project, New York.*

at her side), took twenty minutes in raping her before cutting the phone line and fleeing. The victim initially described her attacker as a white man with a strange skin tone she described as "honey brown color."

Four months later, while grocery shopping with her husband, the victim saw Kevin Byrd and told her husband that he was the man who had sexually attacked her. The following day, police arrived at Byrd's job site, L&B Realtors, where he worked as a carpenter. He was asked to go with them to headquarters and he complied, thinking officers were investigating a recent burglary at his firm. When he arrived at the police station, he was charged with rape.

Other than the victim's identification of Byrd, the case against him was thin and even the presiding judge at his 1985 Harris County trial questioned the shallow police work built for the prosecution. He was convicted and given a life sentence. DNA evidence in the form of a rape kit had been present at Byrd's trial, but DNA testing did not begin until 1989, four years after Byrd went to prison. In July 1997, however, DNA testing was conducted and results showed that Byrd was innocent. In an unusual move, the presiding judge in his case, as well as the prosecutor and the local sheriff all signed a petition sent to Governor Bush, asking that Byrd be officially pardoned.

Bush was hesitant, agreeing that he would sign the pardon only after a court hearing validated the new DNA findings. Following that hearing, Byrd's conviction was overturned and, in October 1997, Governor Bush signed the pardon. Byrd, who had spent twelve years behind bars, was later given $50,000 in compensation, but, after attorney fees and taxes, he had $8,000 to use in rebuilding his life. Kevin Byrd's freedom had actually been brought about by the whim of an anonymous Harris County employee.

It had been customary, because of an ever accumulating backlog of evidence, for Harris County to destroy all evidence in convictions that had been upheld in appeals. The evidence in Byrd's case should have been destroyed in 1994, but someone drew a line through his name, indicating that his file and the DNA evidence it held be preserved, and it was that evidence which finally brought about Byrd's release and exoneration.

In the case of Roy Criner, who had been wrongly convicted of murder and rape in 1990, Governor Bush again insisted that credible authorities support the DNA testing that exonerated Criner. He received overwhelming sanctions and signed Criner's pardon on August 14, 2000. Criner and his attorneys had struggled for a decade to obtain that official signature. Criner, a burly white logger whose language was laced with vulgarities, more than any other evidence presented in his case, brought about his own conviction through bragging statements he had made to friends. He undoubtedly regretted making those statements after the battered body of Deanna Ogg, a sixteen-year-old vagabond (some reports had her age at fourteen), was found near an old logging road near New Caney, Texas, on September 27, 1986.

Criner had boasted earlier to three friends that he had picked up a young girl and "had to get rough with her."

Roy Criner, wrongly convicted in Texas in 1990. *Innocence Project, New York.*

When one of the friends saw a newspaper story about Ogg's body being discovered, he showed it to Criner and said, "This is an awful lot of coincidences." Criner immediately responded, "I didn't rape her. I took her to her grandmother's house in New Caney." It was already known that Ogg had been expected at her grandmother's trailer home in that town but never arrived. Those statements were used to hammer Criner at his 1990 trial, prosecutors arguing that, if the girl Criner admitted picking up was not the girl who had been raped and murdered, then two girls at the same time were en route to their grandmother's home in New Caney—a coincidence too rare to be believed by a jury.

Criner was not brought to trial until four years after Ogg's murder, and, even then, he was not charged with killing her, only raping her, since his self-incriminating statements to friends only encompassed the possibility of a sexual attack. The three friends testified against Criner, but their statements were inconsistent before presiding Judge John C. Martin and a jury. Maurita Howarth, a forensic scientist, testified that tests of a clump of blond hairs clutched in the victim's hand eliminated Criner as the source, and that semen samples recovered from the victim were inconclusive. Defense attorneys showed a timeline alibi which indicated that Criner was at work some distance from the crime scene when Ogg was murdered.

A jury nevertheless convicted Criner of aggravated sexual assault and, on May 1, 1990, he was sentenced to ninety-nine years in prison. Criner applied for DNA testing, which was granted, and those tests excluded Criner from contributing the genetic material found on the victim. Though this proved innocence, Criner's hopes of release were dashed when local and state officials refused to grant him a new trial. A district judge did order that new trial, but the Texas Court of Criminal Appeals in May 1998 overturned the ruling by a 5–4 majority.

Writing for the majority, Judge Sharon Keller opined that "the DNA test is not proof that he

[Criner] is innocent. It's negative evidence, instead of positive evidence. . . It would not have made a difference in the jury's verdict. . . Nobody knows for sure. But no state ever says, 'I'm not sure. Let's just give him a new trial.' Before trial, it's up to the state to prove that he's guilty. Now, it's up to him to prove that he's innocent." Judge Keller went on to state that no DNA evidence from Criner was found because he had not ejaculated or might have been wearing a condom, albeit these scenarios had never before been presented in Criner's case. The semen that was found, Judge Keller said, could have been produced through consensual sex before the killing, another scenario also never before presented.

In this case, Criner had to try and try again. A cigarette filter was then DNA tested and the cells on the filter determined that a male and female had smoked the cigarette. The female was Ogg, but, as the test results confirmed, Criner was eliminated as a contributor on the cellular material on the filter. Further, the male contributor to the cigarette filter also proved to be the contributor of the spermatozoa found in the victim. These tests were performed by two separate labs coming to the same conclusion.

The results were shown to Judge Michael Mayes in July 2000, who concluded that Criner was innocent and signed a request for an official pardon. That request was also signed by prosecutor D. A. McDougal and Sheriff Guy Williams. Governor Bush, however, did not sign the pardon until, in August 2000, the Texas Board of Pardons voted unanimously (18–0) to set Criner free after he had served ten years in prison. On August 14, 2000, Governor Bush signed that pardon, stating he believed "that credible new evidence raises substantial doubt about the guilt of Roy Criner and that he should receive a pardon."

DNA testing also brought about the exoneration of Billy James Smith, a black man in Dallas, Texas, but his attorneys, like those representing Criner, had to struggle to bring that testing into existence. In 1986, Smith was accused by a white woman of abducting her at knifepoint from a laundry room and taking her to a remote grassy area, where he raped her. The assailant placed a hat over her face to prevent her from identifying him and told her he lived in the area before fleeing. The victim, who had been working in the laundry room of an apartment complex managed by her

**Billy James Smith, wrongly convicted in Texas in 1987.** *Innocence Project, New York.*

boyfriend, told her boyfriend that she had been raped and described a black man she had seen earlier in the complex.

The boyfriend, accompanied by the victim, went to Smith's apartment, and when he appeared on the balcony, the victim identified Smith as her assailant. The boyfriend called police and Smith was arrested and charged with aggravated sexual assault. Evidence from a rape kit was not tested, but it was entered into Smith's 1987 trial. Prosecutors argued that since the victim had not had sex with anyone in twenty-four hours prior to the attack, the semen had to belong to the perpetrator, Smith.

Smith claimed to be asleep in his own apartment at the time of the attack and this alibi was supported by his sister, who lived with him. He was nevertheless convicted of aggravated sexual assault and sentenced to life imprisonment. In 2001, Smith requested DNA testing, but this was denied, as were subsequent requests. Prosecutors argued that the victim, despite her denials that she had had sex prior to the attack, might have had sex with her boyfriend. In this instance, it appeared that the state was protecting the victim from having to admit her sexual conduct with her boyfriend, an argument that defense attorneys found ridiculous.

Defense attorneys persisted, and in 2005 the Texas Court of Criminal Appeals granted Smith the DNA testing, the results showing that Smith was excluded as being a contributor to the spermatozoa found in the victim. He was released in July 2006, after serving nineteen years behind bars. "I have lived a long, lonely, secluded life in jail," he said upon his release. "I don't have many friends and sometimes I would cry myself to sleep and ask God to take me away. The only way I was able to survive the jail time was because of my faith in God."

Of all of the men in Texas convicted of rape in the past twenty years, Anthony Robinson was the most unlikely suspect. A university graduate who had served honorably in the U.S. Army, Robinson had no criminal record. Yet he was thrown into a police hopper chiefly because he was black and available. On January 8, 1986, he was stopped by campus police at the University of Houston. Officers had set up a road block at a parking lot and rushed toward a car occupied by Robinson, who was retrieving that car for a friend. He was yanked from the car and put under arrest, charged on the spot with raping a white female student.

The victim had told police that her attacker was black, was wearing a plaid shirt and a mustache, and smelled of smoke. Robinson was clean shaven and had never smoked. Her assailant, she said, had no money and apologized to her after raping her, saying he had just been released from prison and had not had sex in a long time. Robinson was found with $169 in his pocket and had never been in prison.

At Robinson's 1987 trial, the victim identified him as she had in a police lineup earlier. She was very convincing to the jury and, in fact, prosecutors called her a "dream witness," in that she was intelligent, articulate, and attractive. Represented by a court-appointed attorney, Robinson claimed innocence and offered to provide a blood sample to be tested in order to prove that innocence. Unfortunately, DNA testing was not conducted at that time to offer him any vindication. His attorney pointed out that the fingerprints found at the crime scene did not match Robinson's, and that the victim's initial description of her assailant did not match Robinson. A jury, however, found him

guilty of sexual assault and he was sentenced to twenty-seven years in prison.

In an effort to reduce the overpopulation of Texas prisons, Robinson, a model prisoner, was selected for parole and released in November 1996. He was nevertheless still guilty under the law of a crime he continued to insist he did not commit. Working as clerk in an oilfield supply firm, he saved his money until he could afford to hire attorney Randy Schaffer, who had experience with DNA appeals.

Schaffer overcame considerable resistance from the Harris County district attorney's office but finally managed to get DNA testing approval on the victim's rape kit. The test proved him innocent, but the state insisted that the samples be tested by its own laboratory. The same results were produced and announced on September 19, 2000. The Texas Board of Pardons voted unanimously to recommend Robinson's pardon on November 7, 2000. Governor Bush signed that pardon on November 14, 2000.

Robinson, who worked hard to bring about his own exoneration, eloquently testified before the Texas Senate to convince legislators to pass a new law that would properly compensate wrongly convicted persons such as himself. Up to the time of Robinson's exoneration, the state paid a flat $25,000 in compensation to such wrongly convicted persons, along with $25,000 for medical expenses. State Senator Rodney Ellis, after reviewing Robinson's case, wanted to upgrade that compensation to an equitable status and used Robinson as his poster child.

In April 2001, the articulate Robinson pleaded with legislators to be fair to those the state had damaged through wrongful convictions and imprisonments. He was so convincing that the Compensation to Persons Wrongfully Imprisoned bill was approved a few weeks later. Under the new law, each person proved to have been wrongfully imprisoned was to receive $25,000 for each year of wrongful incarceration. Under that law, Robinson received $250,000 for his ten years behind bars.

Robinson eventually became an attorney, graduating from the Thurgood Marshall School of Law in August 2006.

Obtaining DNA testing for those claiming to have been wrongly convicted in Texas was historically an arduous and often disappointing effort. The cases of Brandon Moon and Gregory Wallis, both white, graphically display the reluctance of officials to cooperate with DNA testing. Moon was charged with the April 27, 1987, aggravated sexual assault of a woman in El Paso, Texas. An assailant wearing a stocking mask accosted the woman in the hallway of her apartment building and robbed and raped her.

The woman identified Moon from a police photo array and at a police lineup, but she told police that she really did not get a good look at the assailant because of the short period of time occurring during the attack and because the hallway was dimly lit. At Moon's December 1987 trial, the victim again identified Moon and a serologist from the Texas Department of Public Safety testified that Moon could not be excluded from the rape kit samples, although the woman's husband and son were excluded. Moon insisted that he was elsewhere at the time of the attack with his girlfriend, who supported his alibi.

Prosecutors, however, were permitted to introduce the testimony of another woman who had recently been raped in the same El Paso area and also identified Moon as her attacker. This convinced the jury to find Moon guilty. He was sentenced to seventy-five years in prison. In 1989, Moon was allowed DNA testing, but the 1990 results (RFLP DNA testing) only excluded him from one sample, semen taken from a bedspread in the victim's home, while the rape occurred in a hallway. Further, tests could not be compared with samples from the victim as these samples were not made available.

Moon then asked that more improved DNA testing be conducted and that the samples from the victim be provided. His petition was denied. In 1996, the Texas Department of Public Safety con-

ducted DNA tests in the case, but Moon was not informed of the results from this testing until 2004, and even then he learned that the results were limited since reference samples were not admitted, despite repeated requests for these samples.

The obfuscation and delay tactics by prosecutors and police in Moon's case came to an end when Texas passed its postconviction DNA testing statue in 2001. New STR-based DNA testing was conducted by a DPS lab in El Paso in 2002, and the results showed that Moon was excluded from all available samples. Even more DNA tests were performed, showing that the victim's husband and son were also excluded from the samples. Moon was released from prison in December 2004 and officially exonerated the following year. He had been behind bars for seventeen years, waiting on a DNA testing process that was hampered throughout by bureaucratic foot-dragging.

Brandon Moon, wrongly convicted in Texas in 1987. *Innocence Project, New York.*

Those same stalling techniques were used against Gregory Wallis, who was convicted in 1989 of raping a woman in Irving, Texas, on January 6, 1988. The woman gave a description of her assailant to police, but detectives developed no leads and, in desperation, distributed a flyer at the local jail. An inmate told investigators that Gregory Wallis had a tattoo similar to the one described in the flyer by the victim. On the strength of this information, Wallis was, many months later, identified by the victim from a police photo array.

A jury at Wallis's trial ignored his alibi, which was supported by his wife, and convicted him. He was sentenced to fifty years in prison. Michelle Moore of the Dallas County public defender's office, who represented Wallis, asked for postconviction DNA

Gregory Wallis, wrongly convicted in Texas in 1989. *Innocence Project, New York.*

tests, and the Southwestern Institute of Forensic Science conducted tests from samples of the rape kit in 2005. But the results showed that 1 in 452 persons had the same portion of the DNA profile that the perpetrator and Wallis shared.

This inconclusive evidence prompted prosecutors to attempt to confirm their conviction by offering Wallis a deal: he would be released from prison if he agreed to register as a sex offender for life. This Wallis adamantly refused to do, insisting that he was innocent of the crime. Moore then arranged for Orchid Cellmark to perform more sophisticated DNA testing in 2006, and its results showed that Wallis was excluded from the profile taken from the rape kit samples and from cigarette butts smoked by the assailant. Wallis, after serving seventeen years behind bars, was released from prison on March 2006 and the Texas Court of Criminal Appeals granted his writ of habeas corpus on January 10, 2007. Like so many others before him, Gregory Wallis had to fight an uphill battle before winning exoneration.

## DNA Exonerations in the Far West

### California

On September 30, 1979, someone entered the Tustin, California, apartment of Diana and Kevin Lee Green (born in 1959). Finding the pregnant Diana Green alone, he raped her and struck a severe blow to the middle of her forehead, which caused amnesia and rendered her unable to speak. The physical attack, physicians later stated, also caused the death of the fetus Diana Green was carrying.

Kevin Green, a former Marine corporal, was charged with second-degree murder, and his trial began on September 22, 1980. He claimed that he was away from the apartment when the attack took place, having gone to get a cheeseburger. When he returned, he saw a man leaving the premises in a van.

**Kevin Lee Green, wrongly convicted in California in 1980.** *Innocence Project, New York.*

Green stated that when he entered his home, he found his wife in a semiconscious state and called police. Officers responding to that call noted that the burger Green had brought from the hamburger stand was still warm and an employee at the fast food outlet testified that Green had been at the location at the time he claimed.

On October 2, 1980, an Orange County jury found Green guilty of second-degree murder (of the fetus), attempted murder (against his wife), and assault with a deadly weapon. Even though spermatozoa had been found and preserved in a rape kit from the attack, Green was not charged with sexual assault. On November 7, 1980, he was sentenced to fifteen years to life. Green's conviction had been based on his wife's testimony, even though she had trouble signing her own name at the trial.

Diana Green stated that she and her husband had quarreled on the night of the attack, after she refused to have sex with him due to her advanced pregnancy. She said that in her comatose state all she could remember was that her husband was beating her. (Kevin Green had complained about not having sex with his pregnant wife to some of his friends.) Dr. Martin Brenner, a psychiatrist, testified on behalf of the prosecution that he had examined Diana Green and that, despite her terrible injuries, she was a reliable witness. Defense attorneys, however, were denied the right to have their own medical expert testify as to the reliability of the witness's mental condition and to her reliability in testifying against her husband.

Kevin Green petitioned the California Supreme Court in 1982, but the court affirmed his conviction. In 1990, Green came before the parole board, but his wife testified against him and he was denied parole. In 1996, he requested postconviction DNA testing, which was granted. The tests from the samples of the rape kit showed that Green was innocent of being the contributor of the spermatozoa found in the victim on the night of the attack. And when the DNA profile was run through the state database, another man, Gerald Parker, was identified as the depositor of sperm in Diana Green.

Before and during the time of the DNA testing and results, detectives had been investigating the background of the forty-one-year-old Parker, who had attacked and raped several women and children in Orange County over the past two decades. The "Bedroom Basher," as he had been dubbed by the press, broke into homes, sexually attacked his victims, and then bashed them to death with blunt instruments.

Green had persistently claimed that he had not attacked his wife and that another man was responsible. The fact that Green was a former Marine and that another Marine in his old outfit, Sergeant Gerald Parker (born in 1955), had been under suspicion of having attacked Diana Green, caused investigators to rethink the case, even before Green's DNA vindication.

Investigators' suspicions congealed to the conclusion that the attack on Diana Green was made by Parker, not Kevin Green, after DNA evidence firmly linked Parker to the crime. Parker was then in prison on other charges. Officials realized that Green had been convicted solely on the testimony of his disoriented wife. He was released from prison on June 20, 1996, after serving seventeen years, receiving an apology from Judge Robert R. Fitzgerald: "You're about to wake up from a nightmare. . . I want to congratulate you on the end result, and the court, on behalf of society, apologizes to you for your incarceration. I wish you have a good and happy remainder of your life." Green openly wept.

Green immediately went to St. Louis, Missouri, where he was reunited with his second wife, Darlene Busby, whom he had married in prison on July 2, 1985, after Diana Green divorced him. Busby had remained loyal to him, believing in his innocence throughout his sixteen years of wrongful imprisonment. In October 1999, California Governor Joseph Graham "Gray" Davis Jr. (1999–2003) awarded Green $620,000 in compensation for that wrongful imprisonment.

Parker, the real perpetrator, met his judicial fate eight months before Green received financial compensation. Charged with attacking Green's wife and murdering her fetus, Parker confessed to this attack, as well as five rape-murders, admitting that he was the "Bedroom Basher." Convicted on October 20, 1998, Parker was sentenced to death on January 21, 1999, by Judge Francisco Briseno in Santa Ana, California. Judge Briseno told Parker that just one of his vicious homicides would have warranted the death penalty. He added, "That the defendant would repeat these acts six different times is beyond belief."

Many a wrongfully convicted and imprisoned person has a hard time believing in justice. Leonard McSherry, in March 1988, was charged with raping a six-year-old child in Long Beach, California. The girl was kidnapped from a park near her home, driven to a house, and raped. A rape kit was assembled after the child arrived at a hospital and she positively identified McSherry as her assailant from several police photo arrays and in a live police lineup.

The girl's four-year-old brother also identified McSherry from a police photo array and a neighbor stated that she saw McSherry in the park where the girl was abducted a short time before the kidnapping took place. The victim also identified the home of McSherry's grandparents, where she had been taken and attacked and she was able to describe interior details of that house.

McSherry was convicted of kidnapping and rape in 1989 and was sentenced to forty-eight years in prison. His defense attorneys had challenged the credibility of the witnesses, implying that police had coached the children in their identifications, as well as providing details about the home in which the girl was attacked. They further maintained that police had been predisposed to the belief that he was the attacker, keeping him under close surveillance before his arrest, even though he did not match the original descriptions given of the assailant. In 1992, his attorneys asked that biological evidence be tested, but the court denied the request on the grounds that the type of testing then available would not provide sufficient proof of innocence.

In 2001, McSherry's lawyers obtained approval for DNA testing, which excluded McSherry as the perpetrator. When the DNA results were compared with the state DNA database, the samples matched another man, who was then serving a prison sentence for kidnapping and molesting another young girl in 1997. On April 29, 2003, California Governor Gray Davis signed legislation awarding McSherry $481,000 in compensation for the thirteen years he spent behind bars. The day McSherry received the check, he was sitting in a jail cell on charges of loitering and parole violation, charges his attorneys claimed had been trumped up by police in retaliation for his prior vindication. McSherry was nevertheless convicted of those charges and sentenced to eighteen months in prison.

By the time Mark Diaz Bravo was wrongly accused of raping a woman in Los Angeles, DNA testing had been widely accepted by many states as a reliable means of identifying biological evidence. In Bravo's case, however, that early forensic science offered him no salvation. On February 20, 1990, a longtime female psychiatric patient at the Metropolitan State Hospital in Los Angeles told a guard that she had been raped that afternoon in her hospital room by an attendant. She named several persons as her attacker, but Bravo was singled out as the perpetrator and was arrested the next morning, charged with rape.

The victim later identified Bravo as her assailant and he was brought to trial in 1990, where he pleaded innocent, saying that he was not on duty at the hospital at the time of the attack and was far from the crime scene, attending meetings, an alibi

that was supported. His attorney claimed that before the trial, he asked the district attorney's office to conduct DNA testing on the evidence collected at the crime scene, but no testing was done. The prosecution later stated that no such request had been made by the defense.

The prosecution, however, did provide biological evidence in the form of blanket found at the crime scene, which contained male deposits. A forensic serologist stated that the blood type found on the blanket was found in only 3 percent of the population from which Bravo could not be excluded. Bravo was convicted and sentenced to eight years in prison. He made many appeals, all of which were denied, including a petition to the California Supreme Court seeking to admit new evidence.

In October 1993, however, the Los Angeles superior court granted Bravo's motion for postconviction DNA testing, which was performed on samples taken from the blanket used at Bravo's trial and panties worn by the victim at the time of the attack. On December 24, 1993, the results were announced, showing that Bravo and the victim were both excluded as donors to the stains found on the items tested. Exonerated through this DNA test, Bravo was released on January 6, 1994, at the order of a superior court judge.

Following his release, Bravo worked at the reception center of the California Youth Authority in Norwalk, California, a short distance from the hospital where he had wrongly accused of rape. He put himself through law school and was studying for a master's degree in nursing while living with his wife, Rosanne, a registered nurse, and his son, who was in his twenties, in Diamond Bar, California. His wife had never failed to believe that he was innocent from the moment of his arrest to the minute he was released from prison. On February 14, 2004, Valentine's Day, the forty-five-year-old Bravo had a very special valentine for his wife Rosanne: a check from the State of California in the staggering amount of $7,075,367.82. This was one of the highest paid compensations ever made to a wrongly convicted person.

Hermez Moreno, Bravo's attorney, who had fought hard through the years to bring about his client's exoneration, stated at that time that he would receive "more than 30 percent but less than 50 percent" of that payment as his contingency fee. Though no one ever doubted that Moreno had earned that hefty fee, some critical prosecutors had long been claiming that the increasing rash of exonerations in the past two decades had been brought about by clever defense attorneys who zeroed in on certain types of criminal cases (rapes or other crimes having substantial biological evidence at hand) simply to cash in on millions from compensation resulting from DNA testing.

This kind of sour grapes criticism, however, did not address the fact that all of the attorneys and the myriad law students working for the many statewide Innocence Projects labored for nonprofit organizations and, despite their hopes that DNA testing might prove their clients innocent, there was no guarantee that this would be the end result of their exhaustive work. These dedicated, principled people labored long in their pursuit of justice and whenever they triumphed through DNA, much of the compensation from subsequent awards went to pay for their heavy expenses in research and legal costs, and more went to fund investigations into new cases that held no promise of financial return.

James Ochoa, another wrongly convicted Californian, was fortunate enough to receive a prison release and exoneration after overcoming mistaken identity, unreliable and limited forensic science, and government misconduct that reached back to the bench of the presiding judge at his 2005 trial. (By the time of this writing, however, Ochoa has not received any compensation.) That jurist was superior court Judge Robert Fitzgerald, the same judge who had released another wrongly convicted Orange County resident, Kevin Green, with apologies nine years earlier in 1996.

Ochoa's woes began at 12:30 A.M., May 22, 2005, when a young Hispanic male approached two other young Hispanic men sitting in a parked

Volkswagen Jetta in Buena Park, California. Brandishing a gun, the robber demanded that the two men in the car give him their wallets, which they did, both containing about $600. The bandit then ordered the driver to give him the keys to the car and directed both men to step out of the vehicle. He then drove off in the stolen car. The victims immediately called police, telling officers that the robber had worn a black baseball cap and a flannel shirt.

James Ochoa, wrongly convicted in California in 2005. *Innocence Project, New York.*

After the victims described the bandit, the responding officer immediately identified James Ochoa as a suspect. Earlier that night the officer had questioned Ochoa and two of his friends as they sat on the front porch of Ochoa's home, a few blocks from the scene of the robbery. The officer had searched Ochoa and his friends but found none of the contraband or drugs he suspected they might have. Now he concluded that Ochoa had carjacked the Jetta, which was later found abandoned a short distance from Ochoa's Buena Park residence.

The officer showed a photo of Ochoa on his laptop computer to the two victims, who said that he "looked like" the robber. When the stolen Jetta was found a half hour later, the victims identified a gray shirt and black hat left in the car as having been worn by the attacker. As police were towing the car, a black BB gun fell from beneath the rear fender of the car and the victims identified this as the weapon the robber had wielded.

Two hours later, at 3:00 A.M., a police bloodhound was brought to the scene of the crime and given the scent of the robber wearing the black hat. The bloodhound reportedly took officers directly to Ochoa's front door. The victims were brought to Ochoa's home at 8:00 A.M. They identified Ochoa as the robber while he stood on his front lawn, without a shirt and wearing handcuffs since he was already under arrest. Two months later, the victims identified Ochoa as the perpetrator while he stood in a police lineup.

Prosecutors at Ochoa's 2005 trial had to admit that the biological evidence in the case was not sufficient to convict the defendant. The Orange County Crime Laboratory had examined the black baseball cap, gray shirt, BB gun, and steering wheel of the stolen car and reported that DNA testing excluded Ochoa as having a connection to these exhibits. Further, a latent fingerprint found on the car's gearshift knob did not match the victims or Ochoa.

In his defense, Ochoa insisted that he was at home with his family at the time the crime occurred, and five relatives supported that alibi. His attorney, Scott Borthwick, who had taken the case pro bono, could offer little help to his client when facing a judge, who seemed bent on sending his client to prison. Most damaging was the strange and unpredictable conduct of the presiding judge, Robert Fitzgerald, who had had a long history of bizarre behavior on the bench since becoming a judge in 1981.

Fitzgerald's decisions had seen many reversals, mostly due to sloppy or injudicious behavior on his behalf. Typical was a murder conviction that was thrown out by a California court of appeals after Fitzgerald had not bothered to tell a jury about the presumption of innocence, the prosecutor's burden of proof, or the meaning of reasonable doubt.

Appellate judges overturned a 2001 murder conviction in Fitzgerald's court because of Fitzgerald's rude and sarcastic remarks to defense attorneys in front of the jury. The California Supreme Court determined in 2002 that Fitzgerald's rulings had wrongly sent a man to prison for life without parole. In 2003, Fitzgerald ignored and defied a voter-approved state proposition regarding punishment for nonviolent drug abusers. In 2004, Fitzgerald substantially reduced the bail of a violent bank robber, who was released on a small bond and promptly shot a Santa Ana police officer.

The controversial antics of this jurist had, however, long been recognized, when, in 1991, he made national headlines by writing a poem for a man he was about to sentence to prison. It read: "The sentence I've chosen / To you may seem cold / You'll pay and you'll pay / All the while you'll grow old / One day you will die / A funeral a warden will hold / For you will serve your entire natural life / And not be paroled."

Fitzgerald wrote no poetry for Ochoa, but he did, according to defense attorney Borthwick "everything in his power to sabotage my client's case." Even before the trial began, Fitzgerald displayed his anger when Ochoa refused to change his plea to guilty. Ochoa demanded that all of the evidence in the case be shown to the jury and Fitzgerald responded by telling him that he promised to send Ochoa to prison for life if he was found guilty and then went on to describe the horrid living conditions in prison. He told Ochoa that faith in a jury could be misplaced and that few persons in his court were ever acquitted. Judge Fitzgerald added, "Innocent people get convicted, too."

Though Fitzgerald did not interrupt the opening statements of deputy district attorney Christian Kim, he repeatedly interrupted Borthwick's arguments, editing them and lecturing the defense attorney on petty rules, as well as criticizing him for stepping six inches beyond the podium. During the trial, Fitzgerald actually altered statements by witnesses. When one of the victims admitted to Borthwick's questioning that he was actually facing a wall with his back to the robber and did not really see his face, Judge Fitzgerald interrupted and said pointedly to the jury, "The witness could see his face."

After the first day of trial, as Ochoa sat brooding in his cell at Theo Lacy Jail, he realized that he was facing a judge who seemed dedicated to sending him to prison for life. Terrified of that prospect, Ochoa, on the following morning, December 8, 2005, told attorney Borthwick that he was going to take the plea bargain deal and plead guilty. Despite his attorney's objections, he did exactly that, delighting Fitzgerald, who told the jury that the case was over, a surprise to the jurors, most of whom believed that the prosecutor had little or no case. "That plea," said Borthwick, "was the direct result of the inexcusable bullying tactics of Judge Fitzgerald."

Ochoa was sentenced to two years in prison, serving fourteen months of his term until a man named James T. McCollum was imprisoned at the Los Angeles County Jail and held on a carjacking charge. His DNA was entered into the CODIS database, and it matched the biological evidence collected in the May 2005 Buena Park robbery and carjacking. The match was noticed by Buena Park officer Peter Montez, who immediately informed the Orange County district attorney. The district attorney's office filed a people's petition for immediate habeas corpus relief on October 18, 2006. Ironically, on the following day, October 19, 2006, Judge Robert Fitzgerald was compelled to vacate the conviction of James Ochoa, the young man Fitzgerald had so dedicatedly sent to prison.

On October 20, 2006, prison officials told Ochoa that he was being set free. He was startled, since no one had even told him about the CODIS match or that his conviction had been vacated, or that he had been exonerated and was now a free man. He was not represented by an attorney at that time. Given a new set of civilian clothes at the expense of the district attorney, Ochoa was greeted by a representative of the district attorney's office, who bought him lunch outside the prison and then drove him back to his family residence in Buena Park in Orange County.

### Idaho

On February 24, 1982, nine-year-old Daralyn Johnson was kidnapped while walking to her elementary school on a street in Nampa, Idaho, near Boise. Several days later, her body was found in a ditch along the Snake River. She had been raped before being killed. Police rounded up hundreds of suspects and eventually narrowed their investiga-

tion to Charles Irvin Fain, who lived a block from the victim's house. The only clue relating to Fain was that he had light brown hair similar to that found on the victim's body.

Fain, however, was an unlikely child molester and killer. He had served honorably in Vietnam as a member of the 101st Airborne Division, although he had difficultly adjusting after discharge, moving between Idaho and Oregon while he picked up odd jobs. He never had any difficulty with the law. After an initial interrogation, Fain was grilled a second time and asked if he would take a lie detector test. He agreed and the results showed that Fain was telling the truth when denying that he had anything to do with the murder of Daralyn Johnson. This was refuted by an FBI forensic expert, who stated that hairs from Fain examined under a microscope indicated that those hairs matched the hairs on the victim.

That testimony caused Fain to be charged and brought to trial in 1983. In addition, prosecutors provided two jailhouse informers who claimed Fain confessed while sharing a cell with them, describing in lurid detail how he raped and murdered the girl. One of the informers, Ricky Chilton, who was facing 230 years in prison on various charges, was released from prison three years after testifying. He later recanted his testimony, saying that prosecutors had pressured him into falsely testifying against Fain.

Fain said that he was at his father's home in Redmond, Oregon, at the time of the crime, but only his father corroborated his alibi. Fain's attorney tried to introduce the lie detector tests, which were performed at the request of the police. This was denied by the court, as such results have been routinely and universally excluded from trials. A jury convicted Fain of rape and murder and he was sentenced to death.

The condemned man, however, had two attorneys, Frederick Hoopes and Spencer McIntyre, working tirelessly to prevent his execution and bring about his exoneration. Through their appeals, postconviction DNA testing was allowed, and the results from mitochondrial DNA testing in early 2001 showed that the pubic hairs found in the victim's socks and underwear, which had been used to convict Fain did not belong to him. Alan Lance, the state's attorney general and a conservative Republican, had closely reviewed this case, and when the initial DNA results were shown to him, he ordered another test by a second lab in Virginia. The same results determined that Fain was innocent.

Lance had already come to believe that a great injustice had occurred in the Fain case, and that prosecutors had manipulated the poorly managed case against him. He ordered Fain's conviction dismissed and gave prosecutors sixty days to retry Fain. When they declined, the fifty-two-year-old Fain was set free on August 23, 2001, after having served more than seventeen years in prison for a crime he did not commit. Fain had become the eleventh person released from death row in the United States due to postconviction DNA testing. (Idaho is a conservative state that is home for countless retired police officers from western states, and its draconian procedures and harsh punishments reflect the severe views of such citizens.)

Officials in this case did not agree with Fain's exoneration through DNA. Prosecutor Richard Harris was still convinced of Fain's guilt, relying on the dubious testimony of his two jailhouse informers. Judge James Doolittle, who sentenced Fain to death, also resisted the irrefutable evidence that showed Fain innocent: "If I had the slightest doubt, I certainly would not have imposed the death penalty." Doolittle in his mind believed Fain guilty, but that was not proof, as pointed out by Fain's attorney, Hoopes: "We just can't kill people who we are sure are guilty."

The deadly problem here went to the rooted, unfounded beliefs of Harris and Doolittle. They resisted the truth because it proved that they had wrongly sent an innocent man to the death house (although reversals of Idaho's death sentences stand at 82 percent, highest in the nation). Out of official arrogance or scientific ignorance, they blindly and stupidly refused to accept that truth. They are not the exceptions in a judicial system gluttonous for convictions at any cost, where innocent persons are devoured along with the guilty without principled and discerning discrimination, or, seemingly, conscience.

### Montana

Like Fain's conviction in Idaho, eighteen-year-old Jimmy Ray Bromgard was wrongly convicted and sent to prison on faulty forensic evidence dealing with human hair. Bromgard was accused of invading a home in Billings, Montana, on March 20, 1987, and sexually attacking an eight-year-old girl, before stealing a purse and fleeing. Following the attack, police collected the victim's underwear and bedsheets, which contained semen stains. Several pubic hairs were found on the sheets. The victim described the attacker to a police artist, and when the composite sketch was completed a officer thought he recognized the image as that of Bromgard, who later agreed to participate in a police lineup.

The victim identified him in this lineup, which was videotaped, but she told police she was not certain. She repeated her uncertainty after viewing the videotape and again in court during Bromgard's 1987 trial. Since the semen found on the victim's underwear could not then be typed—DNA was still in its embryonic stages—prosecutors relied on evidence provided by a forensic expert, Arnold Melnikoff, who stated that the pubic hairs collected from the bedsheets matched those of Bromgard. He went on to state that there was less than a 1 in 10,000 chance that the hairs did not belong to Bromgard. The expert actually made up this statistic in that there was no standard by which to statistically match hairs through microscopic inspection.

**Jimmy Ray Bromgard, wrongly convicted in Montana in 1987.** *Innocence Project, New York.*

Prosecutors pointed out that a checkbook from the victim's stolen purse had been found only a block from Bromgard's house.

Bromgard's defense counsel did little to counter the evidence put forth. In fact, the attorney made no opening statement, did no investigation, offered no expert to challenge the forensic scientist so sure about the hairs, and filed no motion to suppress the girl's identification of his client, which she had publicly admitted was only "65 percent sure." Further, this lawyer did not prepare a closing statement, and, after Bromgard was convicted, failed to file an appeal.

The only defense mounted was Bromgard's statement that he had been at home asleep when the attack took place and that none of his fingerprints were ever found in the house the perpetrator invaded or on the checkbook found later. Though the prosecution's case was weak, the defense was even weaker. The jury convicted Bromgard on three charges of sexual intercourse without consent, and he was sentenced to forty years in prison.

In 2000, Bromgard was turned down by a parole board because he had refused to take part in a sex offender program, which demanded his admission of guilt. Still maintaining his innocence, he filed several appeals, which were denied. He finally contacted the Innocence Project, which undertook his case. Students and an attorney connected with the project worked hard to locate the evidence in Bromgard's case, and postconviction DNA testing was allowed. Samples found on the victim's underwear were tested and showed that Bromgard could not have been the donor of the spermatozoa in the samples. He was released in 2002, after spending fourteen years in prison.

Following the Bromgard exoneration, the ACLU filed a class action suit against seven Montana counties for failing to provide adequate representation for indigent defendants. Arnold Melnikoff, the forensic expert testifying against Bromgard (the onetime director for the forensic science division of the Montana Department of Justice), was by then working in Washington State. The many hundreds of cases in which he testified were reviewed by peer scientists, who reported that he had frequently concocted the "facts" used as evidence against defendants. All of his "evidence," the reviewing scientists decreed, was the product of "junk science" and not reliable in any court of law.

Melnikoff had also testified in the Montana rape case of Paul D. Kordonowy in Richland County, Montana, in 1990. His testimony regarding hair comparisons chiefly brought about a conviction and a thirty-year sentence. (Kordonowy was exonerated through DNA testing in 2003 after spending thirteen years in prison.) Melnikoff also testified in a rape case against Chester Bauer in Centerville, Montana, in 1983. Bauer was finally exonerated in 1997 through DNA testing. This kind of "junk science" has sent many other wrongly convicted persons to prison. (See Chapter XV, "Inept Defense and Government Misconduct.")

## DNA Exonerations in Canada
### Manitoba
At 8:30 P.M., on December 23, 1981, someone inside the Ideal Doughnut Shop in Winnipeg, Manitoba, wrapped twine around the neck of the only shop employee, sixteen-year-old Barbara Stoppel, and fatally choked her with it. She was found unconscious and rushed to the St. Boniface Hospital. The attractive, vivacious high school girl never regained consciousness and died without identifying her assailant, who had robbed the till before leaving.

John Doerksen witnessed the crime, or so he said. Doerksen told police that he had arrived at the shop about 8:15 P.M. and found the door locked. But he saw a tall man inside rummaging through items at the counter and finally taking money from the till. Doerksen later said he believed a robbery was in progress, but, instead of calling police, he retrieved a baseball bat and followed the man for several blocks when he left the shop. He confronted the man at the Norwood Bridge, he said, but when the tall man pulled a knife, he backed away. He returned to the shop and saw police investigating the robbery and removing the unconscious Stoppel. He went home, drank five beers, and then went to the police with his story.

The descriptions of the robber and killer Doerksen gave to police varied, so they referred him to a hypnotist at the University of Manitoba who might be able to help Doerksen clarify his description of the assailant. On January 6, 1982, he called police to say that he had seen the culprit at the Norwood Hotel, telling officers that if the man he had seen was not the killer, he was certainly his twin brother. The police detained a man named Dubé, but he proved to have an alibi. A short time later, Doerksen identified another man as the perpetrator, a newspaper reporter, also with an alibi.

On March 13, 1982, Doerksen viewed a police lineup but failed to identify anyone, including the tallest person there, Thomas Suphonow. A police sergeant, knowing that Doerksen had earlier described the man as being tall, suggested that the witness concentrate on the tallest person, Suphonow. An identification was then made and Suphonow was arrested and charged with the murder-robbery.

Doerksen's uncertainty at the lineup was shored up by police when they later took him to a cell where Suphonow was sitting and Doerksen then made a positive identification, saying that Suphonow was clean shaven when in his cell and looked like the suspect, but in the lineup looked different with a heavy beard. In a second lineup, several other witnesses supported Doerksen and identified Suphonow as the man they had seen through a window of the locked shop close to the time of the assault and robbery.

At his three trials—the first a mistrial, the second a conviction in 1983, and a third in 1985—Suphonow claimed that he was at a garage having his car repaired at the time of the robbery-murder. But police reported at the 1983 trial that they had timed the distance from the garage and shop and

testified that Suphonow would have had enough time to leave the garage and commit the crime. Further, Thomas Cheng, a jailhouse informer, stated in the first two trials (his statement was read into the record of the third trial) that Suphonow admitted to him while they were jailed together that he had robbed the doughnut shop. Cheng faced twenty-six counts of fraud, which were later dropped in exchange for his testimony.

The Manitoba court of appeals overturned Suphonow's 1983 conviction on the grounds that the trial judge had made several reversible errors. Acquitted in 1985 as a result of this ruling, he was set free after serving four years in prison but was not officially exonerated until June 8, 2000, when Winnipeg police announced that DNA proved in 2000 that he had not killed Stoppel. Suphonow was awarded $2.6 million (Canadian) in 2001 as compensation for his wrongful conviction and imprisonment. Suphonow moved with his wife to British Columbia, where he spent some of his award money on restoring an 1891 house in Westminster. "To tell you the truth," Suphonow said, "no compensation can pay for all the years."

In 1990, James Driskell, another resident of Winnipeg, was charged with the murder of his friend, Perry Harder. Investigators from the Royal Canadian Mounted Police found three hair samples in Driskell's van they said belonged to the victim. Solely on the basis of this evidence, Driskell was convicted in 1991 and sent to prison for life. His attorneys appealed and secured postconviction DNA testing, which was performed by Forensic Science Services. The results of the testing showed that the hairs did not belong to Harder, and Driskell was released in November 2003.

Driskell had spent twelve years behind bars for a crime he did not commit. The Justice Department did not fully exonerate Driskell until February 15, 2007, when officials stated that the jury at Driskell's trial had been "seriously misled" on issues involving the reliability of key witnesses and the failure of prosecutors to disclose information to Driskell's defense attorneys.

## Newfoundland

In 1995, Randy Druken was convicted of stabbing to death his twenty-six-year-old girlfriend, Brenda Young, and sent to prison for life. His conviction had been chiefly brought about by a jailhouse informer who claimed that Druken had confessed the murder to him while both shared a prison cell. That witness recanted his testimony in 1999, saying that police had pressured him into making false statements. Druken was released at that time on bail, pending a new trial.

While awaiting trial, Druken's attorneys secured postconviction DNA testing, which proved that the cigarette smoked at the crime scene and had earlier been used as evidence against Druken had not been smoked by Druken but by another person, the actual killer. Prosecutors declined to retry Druken in 2000. As early as 1998 investigators had learned that Randy's brother, Paul Druken, might have been the actual killer, based on evidence that he was with the victim shortly before her death.

Druken served his time at the Atlantic Institution, a maximum security center in Renous, New Brunswick, where dangerous convicted criminals were housed. He faced constant danger from fellow inmates who savagely punished any inmate convicted of killing children or women. Druken later recalled that "there were times that. . . I even wanted to kill myself. And, again, I had to think of reasons why not to." He sought relief by getting books from the prison library that related the horrors of the Jewish holocaust. "I had to try to find strength in other people's ordeals that they were going through when they were trying to survive." Upon his release and later exoneration, Druken did not readjust well, having become addicted to drugs while in prison, a habit he struggles with to this day.

Another Newfoundland murder—a matricide—also saw an innocent man go to prison. On January 2, 1991, Gregory Parsons found his mother dead in the bathroom of her St. John's home with numerous stab wounds in the head and torso. Par-

sons rushed outside, screaming to his wife that his mother was dead. Within twenty-four hours, Parsons was a suspect, but he was not brought to trial until 1994, after thirty witnesses were assembled to testify that Parsons's mother, Catherine Carroll, feared her son. Some claimed that the woman had often said she was afraid he would stab her to death. All of this was rumor and hearsay, but the prosecution nevertheless offered such shoddy statements as credible evidence. "What we had," said Jerome Kennedy, Parsons's defense attorney, "was a man being convicted on rumor, innuendo and gossip. It was referred to at the trial as 'hearsay from the hearse.'"

Defense attorneys were able to show a jury that the victim was a hopeless alcoholic who abused drugs and would say anything for attention. The prosecution had no physical evidence, no murder weapon, and no eyewitnesses. It did have a tape Parsons had made earlier. In 1988, as a would-be rock drummer, he had cowritten crude lyrics to a now incriminating amateur song entitled "Kill, Kill, Kill," with savage lines that ended with "Stab once. Stab twice. Kill your parents. Ha, ha, ha, ha."

This and the wash of hearsay "evidence" brought about Parsons's murder conviction. He was sentence to life in prison. His conviction was overturned in 1996, after the Newfoundland court of appeal determined that the evidence at his trial, particularly the song lyric, was highly prejudicial and should not have been admitted. The court believed Parsons had written those incriminating lyrics as an adolescent lark. Yet Parsons was not offered exoneration until February 1998, when his attorneys persuaded officials to allow postconviction DNA testing, which exonerated the twenty-six-year-old Parsons and pointed to another suspect, thirty-one-year-old Brian Doyle, who was arrested in Ontario.

Parsons was given $650,000 in compensation on "humanitarian grounds." After spending eleven years behind bars, however, Parsons took exception to the terms of the compensation: "I don't agree that it's humanitarian. I asked [former premier]

Brian Tobin for a job, and now, all of a sudden, it's a humanitarian thing." Parsons wanted honest work, not a payoff, but he was nevertheless grateful for the cash that would provide his family with "groceries."

### Northwest Territories

Like many another innocent person sent to prison, Herman Kaglik had to fight for his life behind bars while wrongly imprisoned for a rape he did not commit. Kaglik was a thirty-five-year-old plumbing and heating contractor living in Inuvik, when his thirty-seven-year-old niece accused him of raping her. Based solely on her statements in 1992, Kaglik was convicted and sentenced to four years in prison. In 1993, Kaglik was again placed on trial when his niece accused him of several more rapes and he was again convicted and given another six years.

In 1996, Kaglik's attorneys secured postconviction DNA testing, which proved in all instances that Kaglik was not the donor of the spermatozoa, and he was declared innocent. After spending fifty-two months behind bars, Kaglik remarked, "Thank God for science." In 2000, he was awarded $1.1 million in compensation for his wrongful conviction and imprisonment. That was achieved by his hard-working attorney, Hersh Wolch, who obtained a $10 million compensation for another wrongly convicted Canadian, David Milgaard, the biggest award for a wrongful conviction in Canadian history.

The fact that Kaglik refused to admit guilt while in jail brought severe punishment from guards, as well as other inmates. Said Kaglik, "It was a daily grind of fighting for your life and trying to convince people you were innocent. Every day I was in there [prison] I did that. I didn't care if I got killed."

### Ontario

On October 3, 1984, nine-year-old Christine Jessop disappeared from her home in Queensland, Ontario, Canada. On December 31, 1984, her bat-tered body was found close to her home. She had been stabbed to death. Police soon focused their suspicions on her next-door neighbor, twenty-three-year-old Guy Paul Morin. There were several other suspects in the area, one who had been found spraying out the back of his truck, another who had previously been charged with molesting a five-year-old girl, but both of these suspects had alibis that satisfied police.

During Jessop's disappearance, police interviewed neighbors including Morin, who told one constable, "I bet that little Christine is gone." The policeman interpreted that remark as an admission of guilt, especially since Morin repeated the same remark to several other persons. A police dog later sniffed and then barked at the Morin car, which was parked next to Morin's house, when the entire area was searched and this, too, police believed implicated Morin, thinking that the girl had sometime or other been in Morin's car. Morin did not join in the search for Jessop and this, too, caused police to become suspicious of Morin. (The small town police of Queensland apparently had not heard that many a guilty killer has joined in the search for his or her victim to allay suspicion from investigators. A classic example was Richard Loeb, who, with his friend Nathan Leopold Jr., had murdered Bobby Franks in Chicago in 1924 simply as an experiment to prove that they were smarter than any detective. Loeb not only gave detectives tips on how to find the missing boy but actually led search parties combing rural areas in that melancholy quest.)

An autopsy revealed that a gold chain embedded in the victim's flesh had trapped several hairs. A cigarette butt was also found near the body. On February 22, 1985, when undergoing a police interview, Morin was asked if he smoked and he said no. That interview was conducted in a police van for two and a half hours. Officers recorded only the first forty-five minutes because the tape ran out. In part of the unrecorded interview, according to police, Morin allegedly stated that Jessop was an innocent child but added, "All little girls are sweet and beautiful, but grow up to be corrupt." According to the officers, no mention was made to Morin that he was under suspicion, but he nevertheless blurted, "I am innocent."

On the strength (or total lack of it) of these alleged statements, Morin was arrested on April 22, 1985, and charged with the Jessop murder. During pretrial proceedings an FBI profiler offered a "psychological profile" of the suspect, which stated that Morin matched the profile of the killer better than four other suspects, who had been investigated and then dismissed as the likely perpetrator. Because of the widespread pretrial publicity, the venue for Morin's trial was moved to London, Ontario. His trial began on January 6, 1986. Prosecutors claimed that Morin had lured the victim into his car after she returned home from school, sexually attacked her, and then killed her and hid her body in some nearby woods.

Prosecutors' "evidence" consisted of the fact that Morin was at home at the time the girl disappeared and had the opportunity to abduct and kill her. His statements to police on February 22, 1985, were positioned as an admission of guilt. A hair embedded in the victim's neck reportedly matched Morin's hair, and three hairs found in Morin's car allegedly matched the hair of Christine Jessop. Gordon Hobbs, an undercover police officer who was in jail with Morin before his trial, testified that Morin had made stabbing motions toward his chest in demonstrating how he killed the girl.

Defense attorneys pointed out that Morin worked on the day the girl disappeared, leaving work at 3:32 P.M. and stopping at a shopping mall lottery booth, a grocery store, a gas station, and two other stores before arriving home at between 5:30 and 6:30 P.M. By that time, Jessop's parents had arrived home and discovered their daughter missing. After thirteen hours of deliberation, the jury acquitted Morin on February 7, 1986. Morin was set free after fifty weeks in custody.

Prosecutors appealed the verdict and the trial, claiming that the trial judge had made fundamental errors while instructing the jury, which prejudiced the Crown's right to a fair trial. (Specifically the judge had told the jury that if it had a reasonable doubt regarding the evidence presented by the prosecution, it should give the benefit of the doubt to the accused.) The court of appeals sanctioned a second trial, there being no double jeopardy right in Canada. Morin's attorneys challenged this motion, but the Supreme Court of Canada upheld the ruling of the Ontario court of appeal.

Morin went back to trial in 1992. The same "evidence" was submitted by the prosecution and Morin offered an alibi, stating that he was at home at the time of the kidnapping-murder of Jessop. His mother and father supported this alibi, which prosecutors depicted as a ploy by the Morin parents to allow their son to get away with murder. A jailhouse informer, Robert Dean May, told the court that Morin had confessed to the Jessop killing while they were in prison together. A jury deliberated for a week, and, on July 30, 1992, found Morin guilty of first-degree murder. He was sentenced to life in prison.

In 1995, Morin's attorneys secured permission for postconviction DNA testing, which, at the time of his conviction, was not a sophisticated forensic science in Canada. Test results disclosed that the hairs used in part to convict Morin had not come from him, that the hairs found in his car had not come from the victim, and that a cigarette butt used in evidence had not been smoked by him. On January 23, 1995, Morin's conviction was dismissed and a directed verdict of acquittal was entered.

Morin had been exonerated and an inquiry into his wrongful conviction was launched on September 3, 1996. The inquiry found that police, prosecutors, and forensic experts involved in the case had been inept at best and at worst might have fabricated or altered evidence. On January 24, 1997, the Ontario government awarded Morin and his parents $1.25 million in compensation for his wrongful conviction and imprisonment. Ontario attorney general Charles Harnick officially apologized to Morin. At that time, a whistleblower at the Ontario Center of Forensic Sciences (CSF) informed authorities that the hairs examined in the Jessop case had been contaminated and that such knowledge was common gossip at the institution. This was later obliquely admitted by Norman Erickson, retired head of CFS biology section.

### Saskatchewan

On January 31, 1969, the body of twenty-year-old Gail Miller, a nursing assistant, was found in a snow-clogged alley in Saskatoon, Saskatchewan. She was partially clad and her throat had been slashed. She had been stabbed twenty-seven times before she had been raped. Police soon picked up David Milgaard, a sixteen-year-old drifter who was passing through Saskatoon with three friends. Police quickly concluded that Milgaard had sexually attacked and murdered Miller, particularly when one of his friends, Nichol John, told police that she saw Milgaard stab Miller.

Brought to trial in 1970, Milgaard had reason for hope when John took the stand and said she could not remember the incident. Prosecutors, however, were able to introduce her original statements to police, which were admitted into evidence. Fur-

ther, some of Milgaard's other friends stated that Milgaard had talked about killing Miller after seeing a story about the murder on TV. Milgaard was convicted and sentenced to life in prison.

In 1997, Joyce Milgaard, who had remained loyal to her son, always believing him to be innocent, invested her own money and money from other relatives to have DNA testing done on the case. She also enlisted the aid of Centurion Ministries, which helped her secure permission for the testing. The test results, which examined samples of the blood on Miller's gloves and the semen on her clothes, showed that David Milgaard was not the contributor of either the blood or semen. The test results, when run through police databases, also showed that the real rapist and killer was Larry Fisher, who was then in prison serving a life term.

Milgaard, released in 1993 and his conviction dismissed, was not exonerated until Fisher was convicted of the Miller murder in 1999. Milgaard was later given $10 million in compensation for his wrongful conviction and imprisonment, which had kept him behind bars for twenty-three years. This was the largest compensation ever made to an exonerated person in Canadian history.

# X

# *False Confessions*

PEOPLE MAKE FALSE CONFESSIONS FOR VARious reasons, from the inexplicable to the prosaic. Many confess out of fear and intimidation. One of the most common motivations is created by threats. Police, when interrogating suspects, have habitually and wrongfully threatened certain execution, particularly in capital cases of murder, kidnapping, or rape. If the suspect confesses, the interrogator states, such cooperation will produce a lenient sentence that will save his or her life. When such tactics fail, police have routinely resorted to physical violence, beating the subject in places on the body where such damage will not be too evident. They employ psychological terror techniques by keeping the suspect in an isolated area, in the dark, without food or water, beyond human contact.

Such techniques work most effectively with retarded persons or those having low IQs. In such cases, the will to resist and defy such intimidation is almost nonexistent. These victims arm their interrogators with their own apprehensions and innermost fear of persecution. Interrogators play on their paranoia and schizophrenia, repeatedly predicting doom and destruction, so that naturally fearful persons are consumed by desperation and panic. Typical was Delbert Ward, a fifty-nine-year-old farmer with an IQ of 69, who, after hours and hours of interrogation by a half dozen burly offi-

cers, confessed to murdering his brother, a crime he did not commit.

Those whose lives have been dominated by authority figures are also vulnerable to such techniques. Their pliable, malleable personalities will succumb, the trained interrogator knows, to any demand, acquiesce to any proposed scenario, in a frantic move to escape the reprimand or judgment of the policeman, who replaces the stern father or draconian clergyman of yesterday. The policeman plants "the fear of God" in such persons. They are also highly susceptible to autosuggestion (or interrogative suggestibility), subliminal inference, and subtle hypnosis that implants guilt and compels a blurting admission, truthful or not. (See "The Ordeal of Beverly Anne Monroe," in Chapter III, "Suppression and Fabrication of Evidence.")

Although rare, some false confessions stem from a desire to protect friends or relatives the confessing party believes to be innocent but will likely be convicted unless he or she preempts that conviction by making a false confession. In one classic instance, a husband and wife, both innocent, were being held on serious criminal charges and the husband confessed to a crime he did not commit so that his wife could return home and take care of their children. In other instances, parents have falsely confessed to crimes in order to protect their children, while sons and daughters have done the same thing in an effort to protect their parents.

Amnesia brought on by a blow, a physical disorder, or drug or alcohol abuse has often convinced an innocent person that he or she is guilty of a crime, which a normally functioning memory would exclude. False confessions come from persons awakening from deep alcoholic states, fierce hangovers that produce not only head-splitting headaches but prison sentences. (See "The Guilty Out of the Blue," in Chapter VI, "The Real Culprit Stands Up.")

Many persons have confessed simply to get attention, dark notoriety instead of bright celebrity. Such limelight seekers perversely covet Andy Warhol's fifteen minutes of fame—or infamy as the case may be. These "habitual confessors" have little or no regard for propriety or righteous self-image, and are the slavish creatures of the media. Where the hero has an hour of bright fame, the antihero or public enemy has an hour of shocking infamy as a false confession produces an unsavory but memorable moment.

Others making a false confession are goaded by jealousy or revenge. One woman confessed to serial killings she had nothing to do with in order to keep a wayward lover in tow, even though they would be sent to separate prison cells (see this chapter, "False Confession in the 1990s"). They would nevertheless share a common destiny behind bars together, keeping their bond (to her deranged thinking) intact. Another woman confessed to a murder she did not commit in order to obscure the fact that she was having an affair when her husband was slain. "I would rather be known by the world as a murderer," she said after her prison release, "than an adulterer, a fallen woman."

Some confess to a crime simply to gain the sanctuary and security of prison, itinerant and disenfranchised persons having no purpose or independent role in life. Others confess to expiate the guilt of another offense, whether criminal or not. Still others confess to mask the guilt of an actual, more serious crime. The motivations of such persons are myriad and never beneficial to anyone, bringing injury and damage to themselves while thwarting the actual solving of a crime and the apprehension of the true perpetrator. Sometimes a false confession will take root in a minor misstatement that mushrooms to an admission of guilt, while one unthinking comment after another, like toppling dominoes, sends an otherwise innocent person to prison.

## "Guilty" Though Innocent

A classic example of being in the wrong place at the wrong time, or making the wrong statement at the wrong time, epitomized the case of Louis DeMore, who made the remarkably uncanny mistake of informing police that he fit the description of the man they were after. DeMore moved to St. Louis, Missouri, from Chicago in April 1934, the same day a man attempted to rob a streetcar.

When the attempted robbery failed, the bandit fled, only to stop running as police officer Albert R. Siko caught up with him. The robber stopped so suddenly that Siko passed him, and, as he did so, the robber grabbed the patrolman's gun and fired three bullets into Siko. The only clues at the crime scene were the bullet shells and a gray hat. Later that night at a restaurant, police officers were discussing the case. DeMore, who was leaving the restaurant, overheard the description of the bandit and exclaimed to officers that it matched him.

This astounding statement led police to arrest the out-of-towner, when they learned that he had registered at his hotel under an assumed name, presumably because he wished to start a new life after leaving his wife. DeMore was identified by the streetcar driver and apparently the dying Siko, who nodded at seeing DeMore before slipping into a coma and dying the next day. Three female streetcar passengers were unsure of the identification. The prisoner was jailed for murder, and learned erroneously from other prisoners that he would be executed if found guilty. "That's how they treat cop killers in this state," a fellow inmate said. To escape death, DeMore quickly confessed to the crime and was convicted just as quickly in 1934. Ironically, he was sentenced to death, a fate he had attempted to avoid by making his false confession.

Police arrested George Couch just ten days after arresting DeMore, and, after searching the man's apartment, found the gun that had killed Siko, the gun that DeMore said he had thrown into the river. Perplexed police asked DeMore how a gun thrown into the river could come into Couch's possession. DeMore then admitted he had confessed only to save his life, which was never in danger until he made that false confession, and had hoped the real killer would eventually be caught. Couch, who had spent ten years in prison for an Indiana armed robbery, was convicted and sent back to prison, where he was later killed by another inmate. DeMore was pardoned on October 1, 1934, by Missouri Governor Guy Brasfield Park (1933–1937).

Nine years after DeMore was pardoned, two murders occurred on two different continents in the same year, 1943, both producing false confessions that sent innocent persons to prison. For nearly forty years, Rose Ada Robinson (1903–1943) ran the John Barleycorn Tavern in Portsmouth, England. After her husband died, she kept the bar going until November 29, 1943. On that morning, a cleaning woman and a sailor found Robinson's body lying on the bedroom floor. The house had been ransacked and police determined that Robinson had been strangled to death by someone who was probably right-handed. Robinson was rumored to stash large amounts of money, and police surmised that nearly £400 had been taken in the robbery-murder.

A few weeks after what came to be known as the John Barleycorn Murder, officials arrested Harold Loughans on minor charges. While in police custody, Loughans said he killed Robinson. After being charged with murder and put on trial, Loughans retracted his confession. He said that he

had spent the night in a bomb shelter and presented witnesses to testify on his behalf that he had never been anywhere near the John Barleycorn.

Famed British pathologist Sir Bernard Spilsbury told the jury that Loughans could not have possibly committed the murder because his right arm and hand had been injured in an accident and therefore he did not have sufficient strength to strangle anyone. Loughans was acquitted of the murder. Following the trial, it was revealed that Loughans had once before pleaded guilty to a crime that he did not commit. On his deathbed in 1963, Loughans once again claimed he killed Robinson.

A month after Rose Robinson was murdered in England, a man was killed in Connecticut, and as in the Robinson case, a false confession was made which allowed police to solve the crime with alacrity. Because she did not want to have her sexual wantonness made public, Delphine Bertrand, born in Canada in 1890, confessed to a Connecticut murder she did not commit on December 24, 1943. Bertrand told police that, on the night her supposed fiancé, James Streeto, was killed, she was tied up in a bedroom. Her story, however, did not seem plausible. The marks on her wrist were not those of an alleged three-hour struggle to free herself. Further, a bullet wound was found under Streeto's left armpit, though no gunshot wound was mentioned by Bertrand. Moreover, an autopsy revealed that the victim had eaten a large meal, not a light one as Bertrand claimed.

At that point, Bertrand's story changed completely. She confessed to murdering Streeto after the two had fought over his refusal to marry her, though she still failed to mention the bullet wound. She pleaded guilty to a charge of manslaughter on April 11, 1944, and received a sentence of ten to fifteen years at the women's correctional facility in Niantic, Connecticut.

Police Captain Leo Carroll, who had supervised the investigation in the Streeto-Bertrand case, continued to have doubts about Bertrand's guilt. Two years after Bertrand went to prison, Carroll learned that three men were in the cottage on the night of the murder, two of them admitting it after their arrest and pleading guilty in July 1946. The third man had been in the bedroom with Bertrand, though not as an intruder but as a lover. When released, Bertrand said that she had made a false confession, preferring to be known as a murderer than as a loose woman. She was subsequently deported to her native Canada when news of the her false confession and release was announced. It was then learned that Bertrand was an illegal alien, prompting immigration authorities to deport her to her native Canada.

While Bertrand sought to protect her image by falsely confessing, Ralph W. Lobaugh falsely confessed to three heinous murders in Indiana and consequently was sent to death row, as officials later concluded, to either escape a wife he detested (he may have been a latent homosexual) or to enjoy the basic security and support afforded inmates in prison.

In one of the most unusual cases in American criminal history, Lobaugh voluntarily confessed to three slayings he did not commit and spent twenty-eight years in prison after the man who actually committed the crimes had been executed. On June 10, 1947, the thirty-year-old Lobaugh entered a Kokomo, Indiana, police station and confessed to three unsolved rape-murders in the Fort Wayne, Indiana, area. He told police that he had developed a guilty conscience after going to traffic court with his forty-three-year-old wife, who had been arrested for drunk driving. He said, "I have an urge to kill. Something tells me to kill somebody. I was afraid I would kill my wife."

Lobaugh claimed he killed nineteen-year-old Anna Kuzeff, whose partially clothed body was found strangled on August 6, 1944; thirty-year-old Mrs. Dorothea Howard, who was found severely beaten in an alley on March 7, 1945, and died nineteen days later; and thirty-eight-year-old Billie Haaga, who stumbled beaten and bleeding into a farm house outside Fort Wayne on February 2, 1944, and died three days later. Police tested Lobaugh's confession by having him find the murder sites. He took detectives to the sites involving two of the slayings, thus confirming his confession of the murders of Kuzeff and Howard, but could not do so in the Haaga case. Lobaugh denied any involvement in the murder of nineteen-year-old Phyllis Conine, whose death was similar to those to which Lobaugh confessed. Lobaugh was charged with the murder of Kuzeff on June 11, 1947. He pleaded guilty at his trial and was sentenced to death.

In August 1949, Franklin Click, a married man with a record of two automobile thefts, confessed to the murders of Kuzeff, Haaga, and Conine. He was arrested after a woman he raped wrote down his license plate number and called police. Click went to the woman's house posing as a potential house buyer. As she showed him around, Click looped his belt around her neck, took her to his car, drove into the country, and raped her. Driving her back home, he promised to buy her and her children Christmas presents if she did not go to the police.

During a lie detector test police asked Click a routine question about Kuzeff. Click grew violent and threatened to tear the controls off the lie detector if they asked further questions about Kuzeff. Pursuing the same line of questioning, police worked on Click round the clock until he confessed. Regardless of his confession, Click pleaded not guilty during his trial. He nonetheless was convicted by the jury after more than ten hours of deliberation, and sentenced to die in the electric chair.

The police and prosecutors were in a quandary. Two crimes to which Lobaugh had confessed were, according to the facts, committed by Click, executed on December 30, 1950. Furthermore, a third man, Robert Christen, confessed to killing Howard and was sentenced to life in prison. Governor Henry F. Schricker (1941–1945; 1949–1953) commuted Lobaugh's sentence to life in 1949, but refused to pardon him on the grounds that he was "a degenerate and a homosexual, not a fit person to be free on the streets of any city, but not guilty of killing any of these three women."

Lobaugh was eventually pardoned in 1977 by Governor Otis R. Bowen (1973–1981), who ordered an investigation into the case after he learned that two unrelated men had been separately convicted and imprisoned for the same murder (which, if nothing else, proved that the Indiana judicial system at that time did not know its left hand from its right). After thirty years of incarceration, Lobaugh, sixty, was moved to a work release center and then paroled. Two months later, however, Lobaugh chose to return to the penitentiary, saying that it was the only home he knew.

That may have explained why Sam Thompson also made a false confession to murder. Thompson not only wrongly sent himself to prison for a crime he did not commit, but made sure that his close friend Lemuel Parrot shared the same fate. (Christopher Ochoa would do the same thing in 1988, making a false confession for a murder in Austin, Texas, he did not commit, sending himself to prison, along with his best friend, Richard Danziger; see this chaapter, "False Confessions in the 1980s.")

In 1947, bakery employee Kenneth Taylor was murdered in Kinston, North Carolina. At the time, Lemuel Parrott and Sam Thompson were in Winston-Salem, more than 150 miles to the northwest. Thompson nevertheless confessed to the crime and implicated Parrott. As a result of this confession, Parrott was found guilty of first-degree murder and sentenced to death; Thompson was convicted of second-degree murder and sentenced to thirty years imprisonment.

Parrott was unsuccessful in his appeal, but he was granted a retrial after Thompson retracted his confession and admitted the two were in Winston-Salem at the time of the killing. The State Bureau of Investigation corroborated Thompson's retraction, and Parrott was retried and found not guilty. Thompson remained imprisoned, though it was obvious that he was not responsible for Taylor's death. Lenoir County, where Parrott had been

convicted and acquitted, later charged Thompson with perjury, but because he had served almost twelve years of his sentence, the charge was dropped and Thompson was paroled in 1959.

In the case of Robert Williams, his false confession, he insisted, had been made to prove the justice system fallible. He was right, but his "test" of that system cost him seventeen years of his life. Robert Williams confessed twice to murders he did not commit. In 1956, at age eighteen, Williams confessed to the murder of a Palos Verdes, California, man, believing he would never be convicted. He confessed to get the attention of a former girlfriend, who was about to marry another man.

To prove to authorities that an innocent man could be wrongly convicted, he then confessed to a second murder. He spent the next seventeen years in prison, many of them in solitary confinement. Paroled in 1975, Williams tried to clear his name. After he produced a letter that placed him in a corrections camp at the time of the first murder, a judge released him from his parole on May 31, 1978.

Louis William Bennett, unlike Williams, had no inclination to test the U.S. judicial system, particularly when he could not test his own memory. Because of an alcoholic blackout, Oklahoma resident Bennett could not be sure he had not murdered a friend. Rather than risk pleading innocent and facing the death sentence, he pleaded guilty and got life in prison. Police told Bennett, an alcoholic, that his fingerprints had been found on a doorstop, and that he was believed to be the murderer in the beating death of his friend, seventy-year-old Fred Ernest in Bartlesville, Oklahoma.

Bennett had been on a binge for several days. Unable to recall his actions, he assumed that he had committed the crime and pleaded guilty to manslaughter. Sentenced in July 1957 by Judge Jesse Worten to a thirty-five year prison term, Bennett later would remember only that he had painted a doorstop for Ernest. After Bennett had served three and a half years in jail, Leonard McClain, a Texan sentenced to life at the Huntsville

Prison for murder, admitted he had beaten Ernest to death with a hammer ten days before slaying his Dallas landlady.

FBI agents then talked with Bennett and used a lie detector to help prove his innocence. The wrongly convicted man was released in December 1960 and given an unconditional pardon by Oklahoma Governor J. Howard Edmondson (1959–1963). Bennett left jail to visit his mother for Christmas; authorities gave him a bus ticket to Lawton, Oklahoma, a new khaki suit, and a $5 bill. The reprieved man declared, "I am bitter at no one at all."

Six months after Bennett was released from prison in Oklahoma, a gruesome murder in Paris, France, produced a false confession that remains unexplained to this day. The body of seven-year-old Dominique Bessard was found lying in a pool of blood in the cellar of her home on July 7, 1961, in Paris. Her throat was slit nearly to the bone and her stomach slashed three or four times with a knife. Rather than be injected with truth serum, Jean-Marie Deveaux, a nineteen-year-old assistant of Dominique's father, confessed to the horrible crime.

Deveaux's confession came on September 1, 1961, just three days after he had feigned an attack on himself because he believed the police suspected him of the murder. His confession, however, did not quite match the conclusions of the forensic and pathology experts. Deveaux told how he had first stabbed the girl in the stomach and then cut her throat, contrary to findings that her throat must have been cut first because she had lost so little blood from her abdomen.

Deveaux, however, told police over the phone that Dominique had been murdered before it was known she had been killed. On February 7, 1962, Deveaux was found guilty of murder and sentenced to twenty years in prison by Judge Combas. Because of the efforts of his lawyer and his priest, Father Boyer, Deveaux spent only six years in prison. There he cut his wrist deep enough to

sever a tendon before his conviction was overturned on the basis of his false confession.

John Jeffers confessed to a crime he did not commit in order to get attention and make a name for himself (shades of Robert Williams, who falsely confessed to murder in California in 1956). Jeffers was a seventeen-year-old junior high school dropout. He had stolen a car and had been sent to a juvenile detention center in Indiana in 1977. He was derided as an unimportant punk by more hardened juveniles at the center, and to improve his status, he went to authorities and confessed to raping and murdering a young woman two years earlier.

That sensational case had captured headlines, which Jeffers intended to share. On March 1, 1975, Lindy G. Alton and his twenty-three-year-old girlfriend, Sherry Lee Gibson, of Knox County, Indiana, drove to a remote lover's lane outside of Vincennes, Indiana, and parked Alton's car. Another car with a man and woman inside pulled alongside of them and the man, brandishing a gun, ordered Alton to climb into the trunk of his car. Gibson's body was found a short time later near Monroe City, Indiana, in an abandoned farmhouse that had been set on fire. She had been raped and then repeatedly stabbed to death.

Jeffers went to guards at the juvenile facility where he was being held to say that he and another teenager, who was by then serving in the military in Germany, had abducted, assaulted, and murdered Gibson. Police, eager to solve this notorious and nagging crime, readily accepted Jeffers's statements, despite his claims being at odds with the actual facts of the case.

The other teenager was extradited from Germany and returned to Indiana, where he emphatically denied having anything to do with the Gibson slaying, but he remained in jail for nine months until the surviving victim, Lindy Alton, insisted that the serviceman had nothing to do with the attack, reminding officials that the assailants were a man and a woman. Then Jeffers recanted a portion of his confession, saying that the other teenager (whom he apparently hated and vengefully tried to incriminate) had nothing to do with the crime. He nevertheless continued to depict himself as the perpetrator.

Jeffers convinced interrogators of his guilt by providing more facts about the rape-murder, which he had undoubtedly gathered during interrogations and from press coverage of the case. It was enough to bring about his 1978 conviction and a thirty-four-year prison sentence. Jeffers committed suicide in 1983.

Twenty-seven years later, in fall 2001, Ella Mae Dicks, forty-seven, walked into an Atlanta, Georgia, police station to tell her brother, a detective, that she and her former husband, sixty-year-old Wayne G. Gulley, had committed the crime in Vincennes, Indiana. Dicks, of Toccoa, and Gulley, of Oakbrook Terrace, Georgia, were both taken to Knox County, Indiana, where they were indicted for the Gibson killing. Gulley was convicted and sentenced to fifty years at the Wabash Valley correctional facility. Dicks was sent to prison for fifteen years.

Two years before John Jeffers went to officials with his false confession, another seventeen-year-old, Lloyd Lindsey of Illinois, also sent himself to prison for a crime he did not commit by admitting that he and two others had murdered three little girls and their brothers—raping one of the girls—in Chicago. Lindsey and two of his friends were initially accused of this crime by a boarder in the home where the crime occurred, as well as by the surviving brother of the victims. Though the other defendants were acquitted, Lindsey, who had made a confession (most likely coerced), was convicted in 1975 and sent to prison for forty to eighty years.

In 1979, the Illinois Supreme Court ordered Lindsey's release, but not based on his false confession. The court reviewed the case and reversed Lindsey's conviction and prohibited a new trial, concluding that the two witnesses against him, the boarder and the brother, had not provided credible

evidence to bring about that conviction: "The inconsistencies of the testimony [of the prosecution witnesses] were not only contradictory but diluted the evidence to the level of palpable improbability and incredulity." The case against Peter Reilly, a teenager who confessed to murdering his mother, was also rife with incredulity. Reilly was nevertheless sent to prison, until a firestorm of protest pressured officials into looking closer at the so-called evidence that wrongfully sent Reilly to prison.

Barbara Gibbons, Peter Reilly's mother, shown in 1945; she was brutally killed on September 28, 1973, her confused and dazed son confessing to the murder. *History Inc./Jay Robert Nash Collection.*

Writer William Styron wrote in the introduction to Joan Barthel's book *A Death in Canaan* that the polygraph "is to my mind this book's chief villain, and the one from which Peter Reilly's most miserable grief subsequently flowed." The lie detector was not even admissible as evidence in a Connecticut courtroom, and yet Reilly, eighteen, was indicted for the murder of his mother, Barbara Gibbons, based on the results of a polygraph test administered when he was sleep deprived and had been told repeatedly that he had murdered his mother and simply did not remember it (shades of Beverly Anne Monroe; Chapter VI).

On the evening of September 28, 1973, Reilly returned from a church meeting and found his mother dying on the bedroom floor of their small house, five miles outside Canaan, Connecticut. Her throat had been slashed so severely that her head was almost severed from her body. Her ribs, thighs, and nose were broken. Peter called the ambulance service and friends for help.

The police came and took Peter to police headquarters, where he was searched. Police records show that no sign of blood was found on him. Police found a strange fingerprint on the open back-

The four-room cottage where Peter lived with his mother on Route 63, Falls Village, outside of Canaan, Connecticut; Barbara Gibbons was killed in the kitchen. *History Inc./Jay Robert Nash Collection.*

door of the Reilly house, a door that was always locked. The police also found a barbershop razor Peter used for crafts, and they claimed this was the murder weapon.

During the next twenty-four hours, as his friends' parents tried to locate and help him, the police kept him awake, hungry, and alone. They began questioning him the next morning at 6:00 A.M. The entire afternoon he spent attached to the polygraph device. The technician, Sergeant Tim Kelly, talked as if Peter had done the deed, and Peter gradually came to believe that he had. After twenty-five hours of questioning, Peter Reilly signed a statement that he killed his mother.

People in town set up the Peter Reilly Defense Committee to raise money for the $50,000 bond. After five months, a woman who did not even know him paid his bond, and he went to stay with a friend's family. Peter Reilly's trial began on March 1, 1974, and lasted seven weeks. His attorney, Catherine Roraback, focused his defense on how Peter had been manipulated into agreeing that he had murdered his mother. Ultimately the jury found him guilty of manslaughter in the first degree.

Before the sentencing, Joan Barthel of the defense committee wrote to a number of celebrities, trying to get them involved. Arthur Miller, Philip Roth, Martin Segal, Paul Newman, Joanne Wood-

ward, William Styron, William F. Buckley, Mike Nichols, Elizabeth Taylor, Jack Nicholson, and many others contributed and signed petitions. Regardless of their efforts, Peter was given a sentence of six to sixteen years in prison.

The defense committee hired a new attorney, T. F. Gilroy Daly, who asked for a retrial on the basis of new information. Playwright Arthur Miller brought in Dr. Milton Helpern, the former chief medical examiner of New York City, to review all the information. At the appeal hearing, Helpern testified that there was no way Peter could have committed the crime and stayed free from bloodstains. Dr. Herbert Spiegel of Columbia University, an expert on hypnosis, could find no sign that Peter had lost his memory of any of the minutes while he was in his home. He noted that Peter's self-esteem was so low that he could easily be led to "accept as a fact something he knows nothing about."

The appeal hearing started on March 25, 1976, and became a virtual trial, with new witnesses and a reevaluation of old evidence. The appearance of brothers Tim and Michael Parmalee was instrumental to the appeal. Tim, who had not been fingerprinted at the time of the trial, had since been arrested for an unrelated matter and had his prints taken. It was his print that was found on the backdoor of the house following the murder of Reilly's mother. Tim Parmalee claimed that he used that door when he visited, though others had already testified that that door was always locked. A wallet that Barbara Gibbons had bought on the day of her death had also been found sometime after the murder, and a large amount of money was missing from it.

The new evidence convinced Judge John Speziale "that an injustice has been done, and that the result of a new trial would probably be different." Peter was released, and, having graduated from high school between hearings, went into ambulance technician training while living with the family of a friend. His mother's murder remains unsolved.

Peter Reilly with friend Geoffrey Madow and his adopted "grandmother," Hannah Lavigne, receive a phone call on March 25, 1976, stating that Reilly has been granted a new trial; he was released and all charges dropped before that trial began. *History Inc./Jay Robert Nash Collection.*

## Confessions from False and Real Perpetrators

On May 26, 1978, Eric Christgen, a four-year-old boy from a prominent St. Joseph, Missouri, family, was found sodomized and choked to death in a wooded area outside of town. A police search led to twenty-four-year-old Melvin Lee Reynolds, who was rumored to have molested his three-year-old nephew. Reynolds was repeatedly questioned by police but denied any wrongdoing. After persistent interrogation, he confessed the Christgen murder in 1979. He was tried and was sentenced to life imprisonment at the Missouri state penitentiary.

Had the Christgen killing been an isolated case, Reynolds may have remained behind bars for the rest of his life. Yet that murder was eventually linked to a string of slayings committed by a psychopathic serial killer who had been sent to the same Missouri State Penitentiary twenty years earlier. For two decades, this wily murderer had

feigned insanity to escape punishment. Even after committing several killings, he was released from mental institutions and paroled from prisons.

When a stumbling bureaucracy failed to free this man, he often escaped to kill again. This killer used many aliases, including Richard Clark, Richard Lee Grady, Albert Price, Ron Springer, and Dwayne Wilfong. Under these false identities he was separately tried and convicted, without authorities realizing that the various identities represented the same man, and all of the crimes had been committed by the same person.

That person was Charles Ray Hatcher, born on July 16, 1929, in Mound City, Missouri, to an alcoholic ex-convict father and an unstable mother. Hatcher's father reportedly abused him. When Hatcher was six years old, he was present when his eight-year-old brother was accidentally electrocuted. In 1945, Hatcher moved with his family to St. Joseph, Missouri—the same town where Melvin Lee Reynolds was born nine years later and where the Christgen boy would be murdered.

Hatcher's boyhood was crippled by crime. He was often in trouble with the authorities for automobile theft, burglary, and forgery. In reform school and later in prison, Hatcher was a victim of homosexual rape. On May 18, 1959, Hatcher, then twenty-six, was released from prison. On June 26, Hatcher tried to kidnap sixteen-year-old Steven Pellham at knifepoint as he delivered newspapers. Hatcher was arrested shortly after the attempted abduction while driving a stolen car. On November 20, 1959, he was convicted of auto theft and intent to kill and was sentenced to five years in the Missouri State Penitentiary.

In the penitentiary, Hatcher became the primary suspect in the stabbing death of inmate Jerry Tharrington on July 2, 1961. Although he was never charged with that crime, prison officials kept Hatcher in solitary confinement for much of the rest of his prison term. Hatcher wrote a letter to prison officials acknowledging that he needed psychiatric help. They viewed Hatcher's request as the work of a manipulative repeat offender and denied it. Hatcher was released from prison on August 24, 1963, and, six days later, on August 30, 1963, was arrested for burglarizing a store in Maitland, Missouri. Freed on bond, Hatcher, using the name Dwayne Wilfong, was arrested for burglarizing a business in Iola, Kansas.

On March 7, 1964, Hatcher escaped from the Allen County Jail in Iola. On May 28, 1964, he was sentenced to eighteen months in the Oklahoma State Penitentiary for car theft in Oklahoma City. On September 20, 1965, he was sentenced to five years in the Missouri State penitentiary for the burglary in Maitland. On December 7, 1967, he was sentenced to the Kansas State Penitentiary for one to five years for car theft in Kansas City, Kansas. On August 21, 1969, He escaped from a prison farm.

Years later, when Hatcher finally began to confess to his many assaults and murders, he explained his motivation to authorities: "I kill on impulse. It's an uncontrollable urge that builds and builds over a period of weeks, until I have to kill. It doesn't matter if the victims are men, women, or children. Whoever is around is in trouble."

That "uncontrollable urge" struck on August 28, 1969. Hatcher abducted and murdered twelve-year-old William Freeman in Antioch, California. The following evening, as Roger Galatoire was walking his dog in a deserted area in the hills outside San Francisco, he saw a man lying on the ground not far from the path. Assuming the man was drunk, Galatoire kept walking. As he returned, he saw that the man was sitting up and had with him a small, naked boy, who jumped up as Galatoire approached. The man grabbed the boy by the neck and threw him to the ground and began beating him. Galatoire ran to the nearest house and called police. Two police officers arrived and arrested the man, who later gave his name as Albert Price. He had raped and beaten the boy.

While being held for the assault, Hatcher made a superficial suicide attempt and began to affect behavior that he repeated during all subsequent detentions. He refused to talk to police or doctors, and, when he did speak, his statements were irrational. His behavior suggested paranoid disorder. Once the authorities had correctly identified him, they gained access to Hatcher's criminal record. Even so, court-appointed psychiatrists found Hatcher insane.

On September 30, 1969, Hatcher was sent to the California State Hospital at Atascadero. After a period of treatment, Hatcher was found competent to stand trial, but psychiatrists again found him insane and returned him to the state hospital. This cycle was repeated four times before Hatcher escaped on June 2, 1972. One week later, he was arrested for car theft in Sacramento under the alias of Richard Grady. As before, Thatcher refused to speak to police and acted seriously disturbed. As Grady, he was sent to the California State Hospital, where the staff identified him as Albert Price.

Hatcher's psychotic behavior caused hospital officials to request his transfer to the state prison hospital. He was transferred in April, and in August was moved to San Quentin. Although Hatcher seemed desirous of being apprehended and punished, he also appeared to fear confinement. Two days after arriving at San Quentin, Hatcher wrote to the public defender and asked to stand trial for the assault of the boy in San Francisco.

Hatcher was tried on December 12, 1972, and, five days later, was found guilty of lewd and lascivious conduct. In January 1973, a judge again committed Hatcher to the state hospital as a mentally disturbed sex offender. Late in March 1973, Hatcher was caught trying to escape. Then hospital officials returned him to court for sentencing as untreatable and as a security and escape risk. In June 1973, Hatcher was finally placed in the maximum security prison at Folsom.

Hatcher was paroled on May 20, 1977, on the condition that he take an elaborate mix of antipsychotic drugs and abstain from alcohol, apparently a component in many of his crimes. Five days later, he violated parole. Although Hatcher committed numerous other crimes and was actually arrested at various times, authorities never caught up with him until he turned himself in to the St. Joseph State Hospital under the name of Richard Clark on July 30, 1982.

As Richard Clark, who complained of voices in his head, Hatcher had come almost directly from kidnapping, raping, and murdering eleven-year-old Michelle Steele. He was found competent to stand trial and was indicted for first-degree murder. While awaiting trial, Hatcher slipped a note to prison guards, saying that he wanted to talk to the FBI.

FBI agent Joseph Holtslag arrived to talk to Hatcher, who would communicate only in writing. Hatcher hinted that he had other murders to confess, but wanted the agent to guess the first murder he had in mind. To entice Holtslag into his bizarre game, Hatcher gave him information that led to the discovery of a body outside Davenport, Iowa. It became clear that Hatcher had killed mentally retarded James Churchill, thirty-eight, who had disappeared in June 1981. Hatcher eventually admitted killing sixteen people, and Holtslag, who had served in the St. Joseph area for sixteen years, perceived where Hatcher had been leading him.

Four years earlier, four-year-old Eric Christgen had been abducted from a play lot in a mall in downtown St. Joseph. His body was found the following day in a wooded area near the river, just a mile upstream from where Michelle Steele's body had been found. The boy had been sodomized and asphyxiated. Holtslag had participated in the FBI aspects of the Christgen investigation, and knew at that time that the man convicted of the murder, Melvin Lee Reynolds, was, despite his confession, an unlikely suspect.

It also became clear to Holtslag that Hatcher wanted to have Reynolds released from prison and to punish the St. Joseph authorities for botching the Christgen case. Finally, Holtslag came to understand that Hatcher was trying to ensure that his complete confession would guarantee him the death sentence. After mailing Holtslag a written confession to the murder of Eric Christgen, Hatcher was indicted on capital murder charges.

Missouri authorities quickly realized that the investigation into the Christgen murder had been botched. After Eric Christgen had been killed, the FBI, chiefly Holtslag, predicted another attack by October or November. When authorities finally pieced together Hatcher's complicated past—unearthing one false identity after another—they discovered how accurate the FBI's prediction had been. On September 4, 1978, Hatcher had been arrested in Omaha, Nebraska, for a sexual attack on a seventeen-year-old boy. Between the autumn of 1978 and the spring of 1982, Hatcher was arrested for molesting a teenage boy, attempting to stab a seven-year-old boy, and fighting over payment for sex with a young man, all in Omaha. He was also arrested in Lincoln, Nebraska, for molesting a man and, in Des Moines, Iowa, for attempting to stab a man.

In Bettendorf, Iowa, Hatcher was arrested for trying to abduct an eleven-year-old boy from a mall. Hatcher was not jailed for any of these arrests. His ability to feign insanity assured him a stay in the local mental hospital and a speedy release. Worse, authorities never sent Hatcher's fingerprints to the FBI, so his crimes were never linked. Hatcher was discharged from a mental health facility in Iowa on May 7, 1982. On July 27, 1982, he tried to abduct nineteen-year-old Stephanie Ritchie from the mall in St. Joseph. The next day, he tried to abduct ten-year-old Kerry Heiss from another shopping center. On July 29, 1982, he kidnapped, raped, and murdered eleven-year-old Michelle Steele.

On October 13, 1983, a judge in St. Joseph accepted Hatcher's guilty plea to the murder of Eric Christgen and sentenced Hatcher to life in prison. The next day, Melvin Reynolds walked from prison a free man, after spending four years behind bars for a wrongful conviction that his own inexplicable false confession had brought about.

In 1984, more than two years after Michelle Steele's murder, Hatcher went to trial. On September 21, 1984, he was found guilty of capital murder. Although Hatcher took the stand and asked for the death penalty, the jury decided on life imprisonment. At various times Hatcher had complained of being driven to crime by voices in his head.

Hatcher may have seen execution as a way of silencing those voices—if indeed he really heard them or was feigning insanity once more in the hope of being sent to a hospital from which he could escape. He had also expressed fear of reprisal in prison from another inmate on whom he had informed years before.

Unpredictable and erratic behavior caused Hatcher to be closely watched in prison. Nevertheless, on December 7, 1984, his body was found hanging from an overhead pipe in his cell. Electrical cord was wrapped around his neck and his hands were tied behind his back with a shoelace. Investigators theorized that Hatcher had placed the cord around his neck, tied his hands in front of his body, and then stepped through his tied hands before jumping off the toilet and strangling himself to death. Some claimed that he had been murdered in typical prison revenge for informant activities. If Hatcher actually committed suicide, it was probably because he despaired of escape, that he had exhausted all ruses and used up all identities under which might murder again.

The mystery of Hatcher's death equals that of Reynolds's confessing to a crime he did not commit. Where Reynolds and Hatcher confessed to the same crime, several disturbed family members in Georgia vied to share guilt in a double murder four years before Hatcher died in his prison cell. On January 11, 1980, in the Carnesville, Georgia, home of Walter McIntosh, sixty-nine, his niece, Judy McIntosh, twenty-eight, and Jimmy Drinkard, forty-two, were shot to death while the disabled World War II veteran sat eating in his kitchen. At first denying the crimes, McIntosh abruptly switched his testimony and confessed, pleading guilty by reason of insanity. He was sentenced to life imprisonment at Central State Hospital in Milledgeville, where he died of leukemia four months later.

Franklin County Sheriff Joe Foster said that he never believed McIntosh was guilty when, on August 17, 1984, Emma Heard, twenty-five, another of McIntosh's nieces, and Dorothy Mae Rucker, twenty-five, Heard's friend, confessed to slaying Judy McIntosh and Jimmy Drinkard. Heard had been a suspect for some time and had been indicted for the murders in September 1982. The state did not proceed with the case owing to lack of evidence. Franklin County deputies arrested Heard again on July 10, 1984, and she was held without bond until she and Rucker were tried and convicted of manslaughter and sent to prison. Foster explained that "the whole thing was over money, family money, and who was going to get it."

## Dreams and Visions Turned into False Confessions

Another type of false confession is interpreted or manufactured from the statements of persons claiming to have dreams or visions of a murder related to an actual homicide under investigation. Neighbors, friends, or even distant members of a community may dwell on a slaying to the point where their random speculations, conjecture, and theories coalesce and congeal into what appear to be facts. Rarely, however, do persons go to the police with such nagging visions, lest they be considered unbalanced, hallucinatory, or, in the worst possibility, an actual suspect. Steven Linscott of Oak Park, Illinois, however, did exactly that, naively offering detectives the mental images he conjured after a neighbor was murdered.

On October 4, 1980, Karen Ann Phillips was found dead in her Oak Park apartment, where

Steven Linscott, who allegedly "confessed" to a 1980 Illinois murder. *Center on Wrongful Convictions/Northwestern University/Jennifer Linzer.*

she had been viciously attacked and sexually molested. Linscott, a Bible student who lived near the murder scene, told friends he had had a vision or dream on the night of Phillips's murder. His friends encouraged him to go to the police, suggesting that his vision might help investigators solve the killing. Two days later, on October 6, 1980, Linscott contacted the Oak Park police and related his dream to detectives. Linscott told police about details of a similar murder, but not specifically the Phillips killing. In his description of that murder, Linscott offered a few details similar to the Phillips murder, but none of these details were exclusively known to the killer or the police.

Linscott's "dream" related that Phillips (or another person in a similar murder) had been beaten severely with a long, thin weapon and that she had died in a passive position. The weapon, in reality, was long and thin, a tire iron, which had been used to repeatedly beat the victim. Phillips had been found with her hands in a Hindu position, indicating that she had passively accepted her fate, or so the police concluded from the scene of the crime, which they quickly linked to Linscott's vision. Perhaps Linscott was psychic or even clairvoyant in receiving and retaining a telepathic image about this crime. Many others have the same "gift."

Spiritualist William Lees, who had performed séances for Queen Victoria, envisioned several Jack the Ripper murders occurring in London's East End in 1888, and was so terrified by his gory visions that he fled to the Continent. Lees returned after five of the murders and, when getting off a bus, saw a man he intuitively felt was the killer. He followed this man to a mansion and then confronted him, who turned out to be William Gull, physician to Queen Victoria. Gull, however, had suffered a stoke in 1887 that had left him partially paralyzed and there was no way this invalid could have committed the energetic acts of Jack the Ripper, as Scotland Yard concluded after hearing Lees describe his "visions."

Police in the past have consulted mediums such as Peter Hurkos (whom police unsuccessfully involved in the Boston Strangler murders) in their attempt to identify perpetrators in the course of solving crimes. Detectives with the small, unsophisticated police force in Oak Park, however, did not view Steven Linscott as a beneficial spiritualist coming to their aid in solving the Phillips murder. They conveniently viewed him as the actual killer.

Police arrested Linscott on November 25, 1980, and, based on his statements to them, charged him with the rape and murder of Phillips. Police had handwritten and tape-recorded statements Linscott had made voluntarily to them regarding his "dream," which investigators considered a confession. He was brought to trial in 1982, where those statements were put into evidence as Linscott's "confession." Forensic scientists also bore evidence against him. A state expert, Mohammad Tahir, testified that several hairs found on Phillips's body, as well as the bed and carpet in her apartment, were consistent with hair samples of Linscott, which the defendant had provided. Although this was a telling point in his 1982 trial, it was later learned and widely accepted that only a few hair samples—all that were available in the Linscott case—invariably failed to provide effective comparisons and that microscopic hair comparisons in general were of little or no value.

Prosecutors John E. Morrissey and Jay C. Magnuson stated in court that forensic scientists in the case reported that biological evidence recovered at the crime scene had to stem from an O secretor, which included Linscott and a small population group. The prosecutors, however, did not point out that biological evidence examined in the case actually showed that it originated from a nonsecretor of any blood type, which would include a considerable majority of the population.

On June 16, 1982, a Cook County jury acquitted Linscott of raping Phillips but convicted him of murdering her, and Judge Adam M. Stillo sentenced him to forty years in prison. Attorneys representing Linscott convinced the Illinois appellate court to reverse Linscott's 1982 conviction on August 7, 1985, maintaining that his original conviction was based on insufficient evidence. The Illinois Supreme Court approved Linscott's release on bond on October 31, 1985. After three years in prison, Linscott was released on November 1, 1985. The Illinois Supreme Court, on October 17, 1986, however, stated that there had been sufficient proof of guilt in Linscott's 1982 trial, but with enough reservations to remand the case back to the appellate court, which was instructed to consider the issues raised by Linscott's attorneys that had not yet been addressed.

On July 29, 1987, the appellate court reversed Linscott's 1982 conviction once again, this time citing prosecutorial misconduct, specifically that prosecutors had misled jurors in presenting hair and blood evidence. Expert Tahir again testified as to his hair analysis in the case but admitted that he could not remember the characteristics of the hairs he had tested, which were minimal samples, at best. On January 31, 1991, the Illinois Supreme Court affirmed the appellate court reversal of Linscott's original conviction, which still allowed prosecutors to retry the defendant. Cook County state's attorney Jack O'Malley had had enough. After DNA tests officially exonerated Linscott of raping the victim (although he had not been convicted of the rape of Phillips at his 1982 trial), O'Malley dropped charges against Linscott on July 16, 1992. O'Malley did not concede that Linscott was innocent, only that he had insufficient evidence to support another trial against him. Official exoneration came on December 19, 2002, from Governor George Ryan, who pardoned Linscott as an innocent person.

A year after Steven Linscott was convicted and sent to prison because he described a murder vision to police, a child in the Chicago area was attacked and murdered. This heinous crime was described in a vision by another Illinois resident, who, like Linscott, cooperated with police in detailing aspects of the murder and, like Linscott, went not only to prison but to the Illinois death row, along with a fellow defendant who was a borderline retarded man. This case involved Rolando

Cruz and Alejandro Hernandez, and it eventually saw their exoneration and the ruination of police and prosecutorial careers built on reshaping a "vision" into a confession and then supporting that false confession by manipulating evidence and committing perjury to bring about a flagrant wrongful conviction.

While she was recuperating from the flu, ten-year-old Jeanine Nicarico was abducted from her bed by someone who broke into her Naperville, Illinois, home, about thirty-five miles southwest of Chicago on February 25, 1983. Her sister returned home to find the door ripped from its hinges and Jeanine gone. Her battered body was found two days later by hikers in a DuPage County woods. The girl had been raped and then bludgeoned to death. Police determined that Nicarico had been struck several times to the head. They believed that more than one person might be involved after finding one footprint on the front door of the Nicarico home, as if the intruder had literally kicked down the door, and different footprints outside a rear window.

A year later, three Wheaton, Illinois, area men were charged with the kidnapping and murder—Rolando Cruz, Alejandro Hernandez, and Stephen Buckley (charges against Buckley were dropped within a short time). When originally interrogated about the Nicarico murder, Cruz told Lieutenant James Montesano and other Wheaton police officers about a vision he had seen, and he related facts about the case, which, the police later insisted, only the killer or killers would have known. Later, however, it was proven that what Cruz related were then publicly known facts. "I was just a smart-aleck punk then," Cruz was later

**Kidnapped from her Naperville, Illinois home on February 25, 1983, 10-year-old Jeanine Nicarico was found battered to death two days later.** *History Inc./Jay Robert Nash Collection.*

Rolando Cruz told police that he had "visions" about the murder and related what police said were facts that only the killer would know (they were facts already published in newspapers), and he was convicted of the Nicarico murder through his "confession" and was sentenced to death, only to be exonerated in 1995. *Center on Wrongful Convictions/Northwestern University/Loren Santow.*

quoted as saying, "and was showing off." Still later, he denied ever making those statements, which were not recorded by police.

Hernandez was a borderline retarded man who was prone to fantasies, as was his acquaintance, Cruz. During initial questioning the two men began to incriminate each other, trying to earn rewards—as much as $10,000—that police had offered for information leading to the arrest of the culprit or culprits. One officer claimed that Hernandez had incriminated himself during interrogation, although he did not record those incriminating statements until several years later. Other officers involved with interrogating Cruz said that they did not make notes or later claimed that the notes they did make were either destroyed or lost.

The 1985 trial for Cruz and Hernandez was rooted to the statements both men had allegedly made to officers, and Cruz's "vision" was offered as a confession, which largely contributed to convictions against both men. In addition, several witnesses testified that both men had admitted having intimate knowledge about Nicarico's murder. This testimony was suspicious to some involved in the investigation and one detective working on the case claimed that Cruz and Hernandez were innocent, reportedly resigning from the force over the matter.

Following their convictions in 1985, Cruz and Hernandez were sentenced to death. Cruz fought

hard through an appeals process that produced two more trials. Hernandez also endured three trials and was awaiting a fourth when Cruz's attorneys made a breakthrough in establishing their client's innocence. During Cruz's third trial, one of the investigators, Lieutenant James Montesano, changed his story about the vision Cruz had described that landed him on death row—if, indeed, he ever made such a statement.

Montesano's admission, more than any other factor, caused the state's case against the two men to collapse. Further, DNA tests revealed that neither Cruz nor Hernandez was the culprit and in fact pointed to a repeat sex offender and murderer, Brian Dugan, who later confessed that he alone had attacked and murdered Nicarico. This forensic evidence, though meaning much to the universal justice community, had little effect on the DuPage police and prosecutors, since they had placed little faith in DNA and all other forensic science involved in the case.

The case against Cruz and Hernandez was dismissed on November 3, 1995, and both men were later released, after spending more than a decade in prison for a crime they did not commit. Brian Dugan, although DNA evidence pinpointed him as Nacarico's killer and he admitted murdering the girl, was never charged in this killing in that he plea-bargained a deal for other crimes in exchange for that confession, which he positioned as hypothetical testimony. Cruz, Hernandez, and Buckley later filed a suit in federal court against DuPage County, which agreed to pay the three men $3.5 million.

Following the exoneration of Cruz and Hernandez, seven DuPage County officials were indicted for fabricating evidence and wrongly convicting the two

Alejandro Hernandez, who was convicted along with Rolando Cruz of the Nicarico slaying, based on what police called his "confession," but, he, too, was exonerated with Cruz in 1995. *Center on Wrongful Convictions/Northwestern University/Loren Santow.*

men. The seven included three former DuPage County assistant state's attorneys—Robert Kilander, who had become a county judge; Thomas Knight, who had gone into private law practice; and Patrick King, who had become an assistant U.S. attorney. The four officers who worked on the Cruz-Hernandez case in the DuPage County Sheriff's Department and were indicted were Montesano, Lieutenant Robert Winkler, and detectives Thomas Vosburgh and Dennis Kurzawa.

All were at trial in 1999 and, ironically, testifying against them was Rolando Cruz. King and Kilander were acquitted by the presiding judge and the other five defendants were acquitted on June 5, 1999, following a thirteen-week trial. Jurors told reporters after the trial that the greatest roadblock to convicting the prosecutors and police officers was the unreliability of Rolando Cruz's testimony—he had long been branded a liar.

Oddly, the statements of Rolando Cruz were accepted carte blanche by those same prosecutors and officers, or so they said in constructing the case against him and Hernandez. Paradoxically, Cruz was disbelieved by a jury deliberating in a case against those very prosecutors and officers. It might be concluded that those jurors accepted the rationale that Cruz's so-called vision was indeed a confession, but one that proved to be a false confession after all, helping to bring about *two* exonerations—the case against himself and Hernandez and the case against the seven men, who had sent him and Hernandez to death row.

As Cruz and Hernandez had initially cooperated with Illinois police, Robert Lee Miller Jr., a black man in Oklahoma City, Oklahoma, was also eager to cooperate with police in solving several home break-ins that had resulted in two murders in 1986–1987. Miller had a severe drug problem and often hallucinated, but he was a prime suspect after making a marathon "confession" in the form of relating his visions or dreams.

On September 2, 1986, eighty-three-year-old Anna Laura Fowler was found raped and murdered in her Military Park apartment in Oklahoma City. The assailant had broken into her home and attacked her. Four months later, on January 11, 1987, ninety-three-year-old Zelma Cutler, living in the same area, suffered the same fate. Nothing had been taken from the apartments and no murder weapon was found. Both victims had died from suffocation and police conjectured that they had died from the weight of the man attacking them. Knowing that the assailant was a black male and an A secretor, police canvassed the area, asking twenty-three black men to provide blood samples. One of these was Miller.

Miller was asked to come to a police station to see if he could help police solve the two murders. The drug-addicted Miller, flattered that he might be instrumental in aiding the police with his visions, told officers that he could "see through the killer's eyes." Employing a hidden camera unknown to Miller, police encouraged Miller to expand upon his wildest theories and describe what he saw through "the killer's eyes." For twelve hours Miller rambled on, relating some facts about both cases that were publicly known while inserting discrepancies and blatant errors. Detectives David Flowers and David Shupe guided him in his meanderings, urging him to focus on himself whenever concentrating on the killer, but Miller repeatedly stated in these instances, "It's not me."

Despite the inconsistencies uttered by Miller—at one point he stated that one of the victims was only a few years older than he was when she was eighty-three and he was twenty-eight—the videotape was offered to prosecutors as Miller's "confession." Charged with rape, burglary, and murder, Miller was tried on May 9–19, 1988. The evidence at Miller's trial consisted of three hairs the prosecution said belonged to Miller, type A blood samples that also belonged to Miller (as they did to many others), and his nearly incoherent twelve-hour taped "confession," which even the most astute jurors found difficult to follow. He was nevertheless found guilty and, on May 27, 1988, received two death sentences for the two murders and 725 years on two counts of rape and two counts of burglary.

Miller's appeals were handled by Lee Ann Peters, an energetic attorney in Oklahoma City public defender's office, who took note of the fact that a convicted rapist named Ronald Clinton Lott, who lived in the area at the time of the Military Park rape-murders, had not been blood sampled at the time Miller and two dozen other men had been examined and had their blood samples taken. Upon checking, Peters discovered that Lott's gun had been fingerprinted and those prints matched fingerprints found in the homes of the two murdered women.

Lott had confessed to two rapes at the same time Miller's case was in its pretrial status, and prosecutor Barry Albert, who was handling both the Lott and Miller cases, informed the judge in Miller's case that exculpatory evidence in Miller's case involved Lott, but the judge seemed unconcerned. Albert absented himself on the basis of conflict of interest and was replaced by district attorney Robert "Cowboy Bob" Macy, and assistant district attorney Ray Elliott, who were informed by Albert about Lott's possible involvement with the murders of Fowler and Cutler, but these prosecutors reportedly hid that evidence when prosecuting Miller.

By 1994, Peters had left the public defender's office and those replacing her told Miller that he might be able to cut a deal with prosecutors if he pleaded guilty—his two death sentences would be commuted to life imprisonment. He refused because DNA testing had excluded him from having raped either of the two murder victims. New DNA tests were made in 1996 and again showed that Miller was innocent, but this time Lott was identified as the rapist of the two murdered women. Tim Wilson, then Miller's public defender, stated that "if we had a different district attorney, I'm quite sure Robert Miller would be dismissed."

Cowboy Bob Macy bristled at Wilson's remark and replied, "It will be a cold day in hell when I let Tim Wilson decide for me what cases I will file and not file. Two judges and a jury all found

Robert Miller knew things about the murders only someone who was there would have known. It's my job to bring that case to [another] trial."

Prosecutors still refused to release Miller, saying that even though he was proven innocent of raping the two victims, he was still guilty of killing both of them—assuming Miller *and* Lott had invaded both homes together, a point never made in Miller's trial—basing their view on Miller's so-called dream confession. Prosecutor Elliott stated in 1999, "At a minimum, he [Miller] was the lookout for Ronald Lott."

Macy knew, however, that exculpatory evidence had been suppressed in Miller's original trial. He also knew that Miller's so-called confession was little more than gibberish and that whatever facts he had related in that seemingly endless "confession" were publicly known at the time Miller stated them. Macy had no way to go except to try to get Lott to implicate Miller. Lott had already plea bargained a forty-year prison sentence by confessing to raping the two women. If he implicated Miller, prosecutors said, he would not receive a death sentence in the two murder cases. Lott refused and prosecutors dropped their case against Miller, who was released on January 22, 1998, after spending nine years in prison. Lott was later tried, convicted of murdering Fowler and Cutler, and sentenced to death.

## False Confessions in the 1980s

A seventy-four-year-old woman was attacked while sleeping in her Ogden, Kansas, home in July 1981. The assailant struck the struggling woman several times about the head, causing her to bleed. He then raped her vaginally and burglarized her home before fleeing. A short time later, a traffic accident occurred near the victim's residence, involving Eddie James Lowery, a nineteen-year-old soldier stationed at Fort Riley, Kansas. Police immediately focused on Lowery as the perpetrator in the rape.

Eddie James Lowery,
convicted of a Kansas rape
in 1982 on a false
confession. *Innocence
Project, New York.*

Lowery was held all day and kept under constant interrogation. He asked for a lawyer but was told by officers that he did not need one. Interrogators throughout their grilling gave Lowery details about the crime while denying him food and sleep. Finally Lowery parroted those details back to his interrogators in a confession and was officially charged with rape, aggravated battery, and aggravated burglary.

Lowery recanted his confession at his two trials in 1981 and 1982. His defense attorney attempted to have his client's confession suppressed, but the court ruled that since the confession had been made voluntarily it would be allowed as part of the trial record. That false confession served as the main evidence used by prosecutors, although they did provide some forensic evidence to support Lowery's statements. Serologists provided evidence from the victim's clothing and bedding, as well as from the rape kit, to show that it was type A blood, the same as the victim, and that semen on the bedsheets came from a type O secretor, which was Lowery's type, as it was with most of the population. This was matched with bloodstains on Lowery's pants that resulted from the traffic accident.

Lowery's first trial resulted in a hung jury, but he was convicted when tried again in January 1982 and sentenced to eleven years in prison. He served nine and a half years of that sentence before being paroled in 1991. At that time, Lowery was ordered to register as a sex offender every year from the time of his parole, a stigma that gnawed at Lowery, who had throughout his trials and incarceration insisted that he was innocent.

With his own savings, he secured a new attorney, Barry Clark, who requested postconviction DNA testing. Lowery paid for that DNA testing,

which was conducted on swabs from the rape kit, and semen from the bedding and from the victim's nightgown. In 2002, the results of that testing showed that the semen on the bedding and nightgown was the same as the semen found in the vaginal swabs, but the contributor of that spermatozoa was not Lowery, who was thus proved innocent. Based on these results, the district court of Riley County, Kansas, vacated Lowery's conviction in April 2003.

Six months after Lowery was wrongly sent to prison, a rape-murder case in Virginia engulfed another man, who subsequently made a false confession that would send him to death row. On June 4, 1982, Rebecca Lynn Williams, the nineteen-year-old mother of three children, was sexually attacked and fatally stabbed in her apartment in Culpepper, Virginia. She lingered long enough to provide a few sketchy details about her attacker. The case remained dormant until a year later when police arrested twenty-two-year-old Earl Washington, a farmhand, in Fauquier County, charging him with burglary and malicious wounding.

Washington, who had an IQ of 69, had been arrested in 1983 for burglary and appeared to be an easy mark for police eager to solve the Williams case. Kept in custody for two days by interrogators, Washington was provided with details of the Williams case. At the end of that exhausting interrogation, he confessed to raping and murdering Williams, as well as four other serious crimes, including three additional rapes. In fact, he had committed none of these crimes. Washington was brought to trial in 1984, and four of his "confessions" were thrown out as being inconsistent with the actual facts of those four cases, and because witnesses could not identify him as participating in those crimes.

Earl Washington's
rehearsed false confessions
got him a death sentence
in 1984. *Innocence Project,
New York.*

The court, however, let his confession stand in the Williams case.

That confession contradicted the actual facts, and his defense attorney asked the court to throw it out, particularly since his client had recanted that confession. In his confession, Washington stated that he did not know the race of his victim or the address of the apartment where she had been murdered. He said that he had stabbed her two or three times, whereas Williams had been stabbed thirty-eight times. He said that his victim was short, whereas Williams was 5 feet 8. He said that no one was in the apartment other than the victim at the time of his attack, whereas two of Williams's three children were sleeping in the apartment at the time.

Washington's confession was obviously rehearsed. Before he signed it, police took him three times to Williams's address and had to coach him in picking out that address. That confession was the only evidence the prosecution used in convicting Washington. A state psychologist testified at the trial that Washington was competent when he signed the confession, but that expert did not point out that the defendant suffered from a mental disability that allowed him to be easily led. He would meekly agree with any authority figure—in this case the police interrogators—asking him leading questions. Like most persons with low IQs, he sought their approval at the expense of his own judicial fate.

Serology tests in the case were inconclusive but showed that the seminal fluid found on a blanket at the scene of the crime did not match Washington, a serious point that went unchallenged by Washington's defense attorney. Prosecutors offered a shirt belonging to the victim, which they said Washington had identified, but this shirt had been given to police six weeks after the crime by members of the victim's family.

Washington was convicted and sentenced to death after the jury recommended execution on January 20, 1984. Washington, in May 1984, pleaded guilty to the 1983 burglary charge and was sentenced to two consecutive fifteen-year sentences. He was moved to death row to await execution for the Williams murder, which was set for September 5, 1985. His direct appeal failed and his case seemed hopeless when he could not find an attorney to make further appeals. A fellow inmate, Joseph Giarratano, whose death sentence had been commuted to life imprisonment, came to his aid by contacting Marie Deans, who worked at the prison as a representative of the Virginia Coalition on Jails and Prisons (now defunct).

After scores of attorneys declined to take on Washington's case, Deans persuaded a New York legal firm to represent Washington pro bono, Eric M. Freedman becoming his attorney and securing a stay of execution for him only nine days before he was scheduled to die. Washington remained alive, his lawyers making another appeal in 1991, but a three-judge panel of the federal appeals court decided, despite the many obvious errors in Washington's signed confession, that his confession stood as reliable.

In 1993, in their final appeal, Washington's attorneys argued before the U.S. Court of Appeals for the Fourth Circuit that their client had been denied his constitutional right to effective assistance of counsel at trial since the defense had failed to introduce exculpatory biological evidence. The court, however, stubbornly clung to Washington's "confession," stating that the failure of Washington's defense attorney at his trial was harmless in light of the other evidence, the "confession."

Having exhausted all other appeals, Washington's lawyers directly requested a pardon from Virginia Governor L. Douglas Wilder (1990–1994), who said that a DNA test must be performed on the biological evidence before he ruled on the application. In October 1993, DNA testing showed that Washington was excluded from being the donor of the spermatozoa in the Williams case. Prosecutors countered this irrefutable evidence by claiming that the semen left at the scene of the crime had been deposited by a Washington accomplice, even though the recorded statements of

Williams before she died clearly said that only one assailant had been present.

Instead of granting a pardon, Governor Wilder, on January 14, 1994, commuted Washington's death sentence to life imprisonment without the possibility of parole. He remained behind bars for another six years until his attorneys convinced the new governor, James S. Gilmore III (1998–2002), to order another DNA test. Most of the biological evidence had deteriorated, but a blue blanket that had been at the scene of the crime was unearthed and this was tested for the first time in 2000. The results showed that the spermatozoa from that blanket excluded Washington, and comparisons made in the state crime database pointed to another man, a convicted rapist, as the actual culprit in the Williams case. Governor Gilmore granted Washington a full pardon on October 2, 2000, but he was not released until 2001. The Virginia Department of Corrections pointed out that Gilmore had refused to pardon Washington's lesser charges in the burglary conviction. The department determined that Washington would have been eligible for parole on January 25, 1989, for the burglary conviction, so it ordered Washington's release on February 12, 2001, granting his release from prison to parole supervision. Earl Washington spent seventeen years behind bars for a crime he did not commit.

Like Washington, Eddie Joe Lloyd, a native of Michigan, spent seventeen years behind bars. Like Washington, Lloyd was also wrongly convicted on a false confession, but the motivation for that confession, according to Lloyd, was designed to entrap the real killer, not himself. The victim in that case was sixteen-year-old Michele Jackson, a Detroit high school honor student who disappeared at a bus stop near her home on the snowy morning of January 24, 1984. Search neigh-

Eddie Joe Lloyd supposedly "confessed" while trying to help Detroit police solve a 1984 murder. *Innocence Project, New York.*

bors found her strangled body in an abandoned garage.

Some time passed before Lloyd, who was then residing in a mental institution after having a violent altercation with a clerk in a welfare office, contacted police. In a letter, he offered to help detectives solve the Jackson murder, giving details about the killing that were otherwise available in local newspaper reports. Lloyd did state one fact that had not been publicly known. When interviewed, Lloyd said he had heard in some store he had visited that a bottle had been used in the sexual attack on the girl. A green bottle had been found at the scene of the crime, which the assailant had employed for that purpose.

A detective, also according to Lloyd, after interviewing him three times at the mental hospital, asked him if he would cooperate in helping police "smoke out" the actual killer by writing a detailed confession. Lloyd agreed, dictating, with the help of the detective, a six-page confession, which he signed. The confession was also audiotaped. The confession was not used to catch anyone except Eddie Joe Lloyd. After it was published, Lloyd was arrested and charged with killing Jackson.

At his 1985 trial, Lloyd's attorney portrayed him as sane at the defendant's insistence, although the attorney wanted to plead him insane. "With a psychiatric plea," the attorney said, "we might have had a chance. If he's not goofy, there's not a dog in Texas." Prosecutors provided untested biological evidence, semen found on the victim's undergarments and on a piece of paper stuck to the green bottle. They wholly relied on Lloyd's manufactured confession, which convinced a jury in a half hour's deliberation to find him guilty.

Wayne County circuit court Judge Leonard Townsend openly complained that he could only sentence Lloyd to life imprisonment since no death penalty existed in Michigan, but that "the only justifiable sentence, I would say, would be termination by extreme constriction [hanging]." In response to his sentence, Lloyd said, "I never killed anybody in my life and I wouldn't."

After all his appeals failed, Lloyd, who had spent much time in prison studying legal and forensic matters in his case, contacted the Innocence Project in 1995. Students for the project began a search for the biological evidence and found it with the aid of the Wayne County prosecuting attorney's office. Forensic Science Associates tested the biological evidence in the case and announced that the results showed Lloyd innocent of the crime. Its tests were duplicated by the Michigan State Crime Lab, which came to the same conclusion. Lloyd's release and exoneration in 2002 proved that he had been wrongly convicted by police manipulating a mentally impaired person, but Lloyd himself thanked God for his freedom, saying that DNA was "God's signature. God's signature is never a forgery."

The year 1985, a hallmark period for wrongly convicted persons sent to prison on false confessions, also saw Kirk Bloodsworth of Maryland go to death row for a killing he did not commit. That murder occurred on July 25, 1984, when Dawn Venice Hamilton, age nine, went to play outside her cousin's apartment in Rosedale, Maryland, near the Golden Ring Mall. She was found dead—beaten with a rock, sexually assaulted, and strangled to death—in a wooded area nearby a few hours later. Two boys fishing in the area told police that they had seen the victim enter the woods with a man with curly blond hair. Their statements were echoed by neighbors, who also said they had seen a tall, slim man with curly blond hair in the area on the day of the murder.

A police artist put together a composite sketch from these descriptions, which was released to TV stations that aired the illustration and to news-

Kirk Bloodsworth, sentenced to death on a false confession. *Innocence Project, New York.*

papers that published the sketch. An anonymous caller phoned the police and said that the sketch looked like a man named "Kirk." A short time later, Kirk Bloodsworth's wife filed a missing persons report and the name "Kirk" alerted an officer working on the Hamilton case. Bloodsworth was taken in for interrogation and explained that his marriage was on the rocks and that he had gone away to stay with friends, planning to return to his home in Cambridge, Maryland. But when he did, he came to realize that the relationship would not work. He did not know why his wife filed a missing persons report, since she knew he would be out of town.

In the course of the investigation, police learned that Bloodsworth had stated that he had done something terrible on the day of the Hamilton killing that would affect his relationship with his wife and mentioned a bloody rock. This was construed as a confession that he had killed the Hamilton girl, although he later stated that his so-called confession was false in that he meant that he had forgotten to get food his wife had requested—the "terrible thing"—on the day of the murder, and that he mentioned the bloody rock during interrogations simply because police showed him a rock while questioning him.

Five witnesses also identified Bloodsworth as the man they saw go into the woods with Hamilton, although the man had been described as being 6 feet 5, very thin, and with blond curly hair. Bloodsworth stood 6 feet 0, was heavyset, and had bright red hair. FBI lab experts who had been called into the case testified that no biological evidence linked Bloodsworth to the case simply for the lack of it. Bloodsworth was convicted and sentenced to death.

In a 1986 appeal, attorneys for Bloodsworth argued that police had neglected to closely examine more likely suspects in the case, particularly one man who had helped in the search for the girl and found her underpants hanging on a tree branch, and yet another man who more closely resembled the composite police sketch of the suspect. The

Maryland appeals court agreed that Bloodsworth's first trial had been tainted and that prosecutors had withheld evidence. In July 1986, it overturned the first trial and ordered a new trial. In 1987, however, Bloodsworth was convicted at the second trial, although he was given a life sentence instead of death.

After spending more than two years on death row, Bloodsworth joined the general prison population, which was dangerous for him in that fellow convicts preyed on child molesters. He avidly read everything the could find about DNA, and learned that British police had recently solved some murders through that newly developing forensic science. He asked Robert E. Morin, his court-appointed attorney, to seek DNA testing in his case. Morin realized that the FBI had examined the scant biological evidence and had originally reported that little or nothing could be determined, but Morin believed that DNA had made great strides since that time and asked that the biological evidence be reexamined.

Morin sent the victim's shorts, which contained a semen stain about the size of a dime, along with a stick found at the scene and an autopsy slide, to Edward Blake, who operated the only private lab conducting DNA tests at the time, Forensic Science Associates (FSA) in California. Results from the PCR-based DNA testing, which took more than a year to conclude and for which Morin paid $10,000, were announced on May 17, 1993, stating that Bloodsworth could not have been the donor of the spermatozoa found in the evidence. To resolve questions about the labeling on the original samples, FSA then requested another fresh sample of blood from Bloodsworth. Again he was proven innocent, according to the June 3, 1993, announcement by FSA. The FBI crime lab then duplicated the testing and came to the same results: Kirk Bloodsworth was innocent.

Bloodsworth was released from prison on June 28, 1993, and in December 1993 was pardoned by Maryland Governor William Donald Schaefer (1987–1995), becoming the first person to be exon-

erated from death row through DNA testing. Dozens would follow in his wake. He was paid $300,000 in compensation for the ten-year period of his incarceration (time of arrest to his release) at $30,000 per year. Bloodsworth remarried and continued to live in Cambridge, working as a crab and commercial fisherman on Maryland's eastern shore.

Also in 1985, Dennis Brown, a black man, was wrongly convicted on a false confession. Where Bloodsworth's oblique comments had been reshaped into a confession, Brown confessed at the point of a knife, according to statements he later made when recanting that confession. In September 1984, a man invaded a home in Covington, Louisiana, and sexually attacked the woman who lived there. The victim later told police that her assailant was black and wore a bandana over his face below the eyes. She said that she had seen the man's face long enough to describe it to a police artist, who sketched a composite illustration of the attacker.

Dennis Brown, a seventeen-year-old black, was asked to participate in a police lineup, but he was told that he was not a suspect and that he was simply gong to be a "filler." He agreed and, to Brown's amazement, the victim picked him out of that lineup and he was charged with rape. During a prolonged interrogation, Brown later insisted, police threatened him with a knife until he made a confession.

The confession was used in court to convict him and send him to prison for life. A serologist reported that the biological evidence collected from the victim's sanitary napkin showed that the assailant had type O blood and was a secretor, stating that Brown also had type O, which was shared by 40 percent of the black population. With the

Dennis Brown made his "confession" at knifepoint in Louisiana. *Innocence Project, New York.*

assistance of the Innocence Project New Orleans, Brown obtained postconviction DNA testing on the biological evidence, which in 2003 showed him to be innocent. Brown was released from the Louisiana State Penitentiary at Angola in 2004, after spending nineteen years behind bars.

Where police in Louisiana had used physical coercion to exact a false confession from the teenage Brown, officers in Pennsylvania quickly solved a rape-murder case by pressuring a young retarded man into making a false confession. On the night of August 12, 1987, elderly Edna Laughman was viciously attacked and murdered, her body found hours later by relatives. One of those relatives was her nephew, Barry James Laughman, who had an IQ of 70. The twenty-four-year-old Laughman was a common laborer who rode his bicycle to work because he could not understand or pass his driver's examination. He was afraid of the dark and carried a flashlight whenever he ventured outside after sunset.

When Edna Laughman failed to appear at her relatives' home on the night of August 12, 1987, to have her usual dinner—she lived in a ramshackle wooden frame house in Oxford Township, with only a single lightbulb and no running water—relatives went to her home two doors away and found it locked. They had to force their way inside and there found the old woman's naked corpse, choked to death on pills that had been forced down her throat, a fact later determined by police.

At first, investigators focused on a neighbor, Royce Emerson, who had been seen at the time of the crime behind his house, which was close to the victim's home. They quickly gave up looking for that suspect when seeing Barry Laughman act nervously, which was his habitual emotional response whenever he was in the presence of authority figures. Laughman was interrogated by two officers who later claimed that he made a full confession to them, admitting that he beat his aunt, forced the pills down her throat, which caused her to choke to death, and then had sex with the corpse. His confession consisted of fifty-three questions

and answers, printed in the same handwriting by one of the officers; the officer wrote "yes" for Laughman's responses to any question that incriminated him.

An officer who examined the victim's body noticed bruise marks on her neck, which he later stated in court had come from the killer's fingers. One finger mark was missing, the officer added. The officer had concluded that that missing finger mark proved Laughman's guilt since his pinkie finger had been injured and was unworkable since childhood, a bit of self-styled Sherlockian deduction that had no basis in forensic fact. But it impressed a naive jury, as did a confession that had not been taped or otherwise corroborated by anything other than the initials of the two interrogating officers.

The biological evidence at the trial was inconclusive, so Laughman was convicted on the strength of his confession or the lack of it. In 1988, he was convicted of murder, rape, robbery, and burglary and sentenced to life in prison. In appeals, Laughman's attorneys secured postconviction DNA testing, but in 1993 Cellmark Diagnostics reported that their PCR/DQ Alpha DNA tests showed inconclusive results. Ten years later, in 2003, David J. Foster and William C. Costopoulos of the firm of Costopoulos, Foster & Fields took over Laughman's case and asked that the biological evidence again be tested under the advanced technologies of DNA. Unfortunately, the attorneys were told by officials, the biological evidence could not be found.

Pete Shellem was an investigative reporter for the Harrisburg Patriot-News who had been writing a series of articles on the Laughman case. He challenged the confession, believing it to be coerced or fabricated, and then undertook an exhausting search for the missing biological evidence. He traced the evidence to a former anthropology professor at Penn State University, who had initially analyzed eighteen swabs and six microscopic slides with fluids from Edna Laughman's body. Shellem then traced the professor to Germany, where he had taken up residence. He admitted that he had retained the biological evidence in the Laughman case. That evidence was turned over to Orchid Cellmark for Y-STR DNA testing in November 2003. The results from that testing excluded Laughman as the killer.

Laughman was released from prison but kept under supervised house arrest, since prosecutors planned to retry him. On August 26, 2004, however, Adams County District Attorney Shawn C. Wagner announced that all charges against Laughman had been dropped, officially exonerating a retarded man who had spent sixteen years behind bars. Attorney Costopoulos credited Laughman's freedom to a dogged reporter's unwillingness to give up his search for the missing biological evidence: "I believe Laughman would have served the rest of his natural life in jail for a murder he did not commit if not for Pete Shellem."

Officers in Pennsylvania coerced another man, Bruce Godschalk, into confessing to two rapes he did not commit a year before Langham was sent to prison on the basis of a false confession. This time, however, in addition to setting Godschalk free, a county and a town in Pennsylvania would pay dearly for his wrongful conviction and imprisonment—more than $2 million.

In the summer of 1986, two women in the same apartment complex in King of Prussia, a suburb of Philadelphia, were raped, and a third woman in the area reported seeing a man expose himself to her. All three women, who did not know each other, provided police with details that allowed a

Bruce Godschalk "confessed" to two rapes in a Philadelphia suburb in 1987. *Innocence Project, New York.*

police artist to make a composite sketch of the same assailant, which was broadcast on local TV and printed in newspapers. On December 30, 1986, police were contacted by a caller who said that the sketch resembled Bruce Godschalk, who worked as a landscaper in the area where the rapes occurred. (This was the same manner in which Kirk Bloodsworth had been identified.)

Godschalk was brought in for questioning, and, after prolonged interrogations, he signed a taped confession on January 13, 1987. Before his trial in May of that year, however, Godschalk recanted his confession, saying that it was false and had been made under threats from police. The confession, prosecutors stated, contained information about the two rapes that had not otherwise been made public. Defense attorneys countered by saying that police had provided that information to Godschalk in manufacturing his false confession.

In addition to the confession, one of the victims identified twenty-six-year-old Godschalk at his 1987 trial, and a jailhouse informant also testified that Godschalk had admitted to committing the crimes to him. A serologist testified that tests on the biological evidence did not exclude Godschalk. He was convicted of two counts of forcible rape and two counts of burglary and was sentenced to ten to twenty years in prison.

After all of his appeal motions, including a request for postconviction DNA testing, were denied, Godschalk, in 1995, contacted the Innocence Project, which undertook his case. (The statewide Innocence Projects only investigate cases where DNA can be employed.) Even with the aid of local counsel and the Innocence Project, Godschalk had an uphill battle. He had struggled for seven years to obtain permission for DNA testing, but Montgomery County prosecutors adamantly prohibited such DNA testing and statewide judges backed these prosecutors, even though it was Godschalk's constitutional right to have such testing.

Godschalk all along had insisted that he was innocent and had been denied parole when he refused to enter a sex offender program in prison. His only hope of salvation was DNA, but Montgomery County District Attorney Bruce L. Castor Jr. repeatedly denied him that right. The Innocence Project, however, had already obtained a copy of Godschalk's "confession," which prosecutors refused to release until 1999. It was sent to an expert, who analyzed it and then reported that Godschalk had falsely confessed. Even in the light of these results, Castor refused to release biological evidence for DNA testing.

In November 2000, the Innocence Project and Godschalk's attorneys filed a Section 1983 civil rights complaint against Montgomery County in an effort to obtain the biological evidence. Federal district Judge Charles R. Weiner ruled that Godschalk had a constitutional right to have the evidence DNA tested and ordered Castor to release it for that purpose. Castor filed a motion to dismiss, which was denied. Still Castor delayed, until consenting to release the evidence in spring 2001. Then prosecutors delayed further by setting protocol for the delivery and testing of the evidence until the Innocence Project filed a motion for summary judgment in June 2001.

More obfuscation by prosecutors surfaced when, in response to the June 2001 motion, prosecutors informed Godschalk's attorneys that they had sent the biological evidence to a laboratory and had it tested without the consent of the defense. Prosecutors reported that their lab's testing of the evidence produced no results and, in the course of its secret testing, the evidence had been consumed. Moreover, Castor had secured an affidavit from the police officer who had conducted the interrogations with Godschalk and had obtained his "confessions."

The Innocence Project accused Castor's office of false representation, saying that though prosecutors had said that all of the crime scene evidence had been sent to the lab, a carpet sample from one of the crime scenes had not been received by the lab. Castor's office responded by saying the sample had not been introduced as evidence at Godschalk's trial and was therefore irrelevant. That sample, however, had been used at Godschalk's trial to tie him to the scene of one of the two rapes for which he was convicted and imprisoned. Prosecutors then admitted that they had entrusted the delivery of the biological evidence to its lab to the very officer who had obtained Godschalk's

confession, and that this investigator also had removed the carpet sample from the crime scene.

That carpet sample was located in October 2001, and it was divided, with two separate labs—Cellmark Diagnostics in Maryland testing for the prosecution and Edward Blake's Forensic Science Associates of California testing for the defense—conducting tests of the biological evidence in January 2002. Profiles were identified in both rapes as having come from the same assailant, the results from both labs announcing that Godschalk had been excluded.

David Rudovsky, a Philadelphia attorney representing Godschalk, asked Judge S. Gerald Corso to order Godschalk's release on the grounds that DNA testing had proved "he is factually innocent." But Castor still refused to release Godschalk, claiming that the tests had been flawed. The Godschalk case, thanks to Castor's truculent behavior in defying the DNA results, which had become universally recognized as the definitive identification system, made national headlines. The *New York Times* asked Gary Harmor, a forensic serologist in San Francisco with a widespread reputation for reliability, to examine the results from both labs that had tested the biological evidence. This Harmor did, stating from his results that "both profiles match each other, and can only come from one person in the world [involved in both rapes]. And that person is not Bruce Godschalk."

Overwhelmed by conclusive evidence and having no other legal recourse, the court released Godschalk from prison on February 14, 2002. His confession, his attorneys pointed out, had been proven false after DNA had proved him innocent. This District Attorney Castor stubbornly refused to believe, saying that, confronted with the DNA evidence, "the tie goes to the defendant," as if describing a neck-and-neck race that had little or nothing to do with the conclusive evidence at hand.

Bruce L. Castor Jr. was not the only prosecutor who had to be dragged kicking and screaming into the modern reality of DNA. Castor arguably enabled defense attorneys to mount subsequent civil suits that claimed willful persecution against Godschalk in his arrest, conviction, and imprisonment—unnecessarily prolonged by Castor after DNA had cleared him—consuming more than fourteen years of Godschalk's life. Officials realized this when Montgomery County awarded Godschalk compensation of $740,000 and Upper Merion, Pennsylvania, paid him an additional $1.6 million for destroying the best years of his life.

In the case of Dennis Fritz, police relied on jailhouse informers to provide them with Fritz's "confession," one he never made about the rape and murder of twenty-one-year-old waitress Debra Sue Carter, who was raped and murdered in Ada, Oklahoma, on the night of December 7, 1982. On the night of the murder, Carter was seen arguing with Glenn Gore at the Coachlight, a popular drinking spa on the outskirts of town where she worked. She had known Gore since high school and she appeared to be afraid of him, telling a friend later that night that she did not want to stay alone in her apartment. But she did not tell her friend what or who troubled her. Several hours later, another friend found Carter in her home, her naked body lying in a pool of blood. She had been raped and killed, but not before putting up a fight, according to police investigators.

Even though Glenn Gore had been seen arguing with the victim on the night of the murder, he was never a police suspect. His fingerprints and biological samples were never taken, while he was allowed to spread rumors and gossip about two other men, which implicated them in the crime. The case went unsolved for five years, until the public pressured law enforcement to find and punish Carter's killers. Ronald Keith Williamson became the chief suspect. He had once been a town hero,

Debra Sue Carter, raped and murdered in Ada, Oklahoma, December 7, 1982. *History, Inc./Jay Robert Nash Collection.*

playing on the Asher High School baseball team that won a state championship and earning a contract with the Oakland Athletics.

All that evaporated when Williamson turned to drink. He returned home to live with his mother after a failed marriage. At twenty-eight, he led an aimless life, boozing and carousing in bars at night and causing disturbances. He

Dennis Fritz falsely confessed to murdering Debra Sue Carter and went to prison for life. *History, Inc./Jay Robert Nash Collection.*

had been charged in two rapes but was exonerated after proving that the acts were consensual. Over the years, the reported incident between Carter and Gore had changed to the point where Williamson and his good friend, Dennis Fritz, a married high school teacher, became the subject of that report and not Gore, which Gore himself encouraged. Both men, town gossips said, "made her [Carter] nervous."

Williamson was arrested and charged with first-degree murder, as was Fritz. Police first focused on Williamson, arguing that his background of rape accusations made him a likely candidate for the Carter killing. Williamson took two polygraph tests, but the results were inconclusive. He lived near the scene of the crime, however, and police felt that indicated his culpability, along with his bad reputation. Further witnesses, including Gore, testified that Williamson had been in the Coachlight on the night of the murder. A jailhouse informer testified that Williamson had said that he would harm his mother the same way he had Carter, and this was introduced in court as Williamson's "confession." Another jailhouse informant came forward to seal Fritz's fate, providing a two-hour taped testimony in which he

Ronald Keith Williamson falsely confessed to killing Debra Sue Carter and was sentenced to death. *History, Inc./Jay Robert Nash Collection.*

recited Fritz's "confession" of killing Carter to him.

At the 1988 trial, a forensic expert testified that the seventeen hairs collected at the crime scene matched those of Williamson and Fritz. A serologist stated that the semen collected from the victim suggested that the perpetrators were nonsecretors, which fit Williamson and Fritz. A jury convicted both men. Williamson was sentenced to death and Fritz to life behind bars. All appeals filed by separate attorneys for both men were denied. Fritz contacted the Innocence Project in time to learn that his codefendant had filed for postconviction DNA testing. An injunction on Fritz's behalf was made to ensure that the biological evidence would not be totally consumed on tests for Williamson alone until the cases were joined for joint DNA testing on behalf of both Williamson and Fritz.

DNA tests were performed in 1999, and the results showed that neither Williamson nor Fritz had donated the spermatozoa found in Carter's body.

Dennis Fritz today; he served eleven years in prison. *Innocence Project, New York.*

Further, those tests—run through DNA databases housing the profiles of convicted felons—showed that the actual rapist and killer was Glenn Gore. When he heard the news of the DNA test results, Gore, who was being held in a minimum security facility on a separate charge, escaped. He was recaptured and later tried and convicted of raping and murdering Carter and sentenced to death. Williamson and Fritz, exonerated after serving eleven years in prison, were released in April 1999. Williamson died in 2004.

Chicago police did not rely on jailhouse informants to manufacture a confession for Ronald Jones. They simply beat it out of him, according to Jones, after he had been arrested and charged with the rape and murder of twenty-eight-year-old Debra Smith, a mother of three whose body was found in a South Side Chicago alley on the night of March 10, 1985. She had been beaten, raped, and then stabbed repeatedly in the neck and face. Her body was naked from the waist down, except for a single sock. Investigators followed a trail of blood from her body to an abandoned motel.

No arrests in the murder were made until police picked up Ronald Jones on October 5, 1985, charging him with Smith's rape and murder. Jones had a bad record, with two felony convictions for burglary and robbery. He had been charged with raping Barbara Benson in June 1985, but charges in the case had been dropped. The proximity of that charge to the murder of Smith three months earlier convinced police that Jones, who lived nearby, was the culprit.

During his interrogation by Chicago detectives Steven Hood and John Markham, Jones made a confession. But later he insisted that Hood and Markham had beaten that confession out of him. Jones testified at his 1989 trial that Hood beat him

Dennis Fritz and Ronald Keith Williamson in court, April 15, 1999, when all charges against them were dismissed. *History, Inc./Jay Robert Nash Collection.*

Ronald Jones' "confession" was beaten out of him by Chicago police to bring about his 1989 conviction. *Center on Wrongful Convictions/Northwestern University/Loren Santow.*

about the head with an object resembling a blackjack and that Markham cautioned Hood not to "hit him like this because he will bruise." Markham then proceeded to punch Jones in the stomach, according to Jones. The confession was suspicious in that some details provided by Jones were obviously erroneous. Jones stated in his "confession" that Smith was a prostitute, but she had no record of prostitution.

In addition to the confession, prosecutors put on the stand Barbara Benson, who had earlier accused Jones of raping her, although that case had been dismissed. Prosecutors were allowed to introduce this irrelevant evidence on the grounds that it established a pattern of criminal behavior by Jones. Prosecutors were contradictory in their presentation of the biological evidence, stating that Jones had ejaculated and was the source of the semen found on the victim, but that that the quantity of semen discovered on the victim at the scene of the crime was insufficient to test or identify the culprit. Further, Jones, who was then addicted to drugs, had been seen panhandling from Smith a short time before her murder, according to another witness.

On July 17, 1989, Jones was convicted by a jury and Judge John E. Morrissey sentenced him to death. Jones's case seemed hopeless after his appeals were denied, but in 1994 Richard Cunningham, an assistant appellate public defender, requested Judge Morrissey to authorize a DNA test in the case, telling Morrissey that such technology had not been available at the time of Jones's trial. Judge Morrissey denied the request, but Cunningham reminded the judge that prosecutors at Jones's original trial had stated that the semen found at the scene of the crime belonged to Jones. "Save arguments like that for the press," Judge Morrissey replied. "They love it. I don't."

Cunningham would not give up, and, with the aid of Gary O. Pritchard, appealed to the Illinois Supreme Court, which reviewed the case and reversed Morrissey's ruling, ordering DNA testing in 1997. Forensic Science Associates conducted PCR-based DNA testing and announced results which showed that Jones was not a donor of the spermatozoa found in the victim. The court ordered a new trial, but prosecutors decided to drop charges against Jones on May 17, 1999, and he was released from prison after spending fourteen years behind bars. He had overcome his alcohol and drug addictions and had become a model prisoner who never incurred a single offense in prison.

Like others before him, Christopher Ochoa confessed to a murder he did not commit and, in the process, sent himself to prison, as well as his best friend, Richard Danziger. Ochoa's journey to prison began in the early morning hours of November 24, 1988, when someone entered a Pizza Hut in Austin, Texas, and raped and fatally shot the manager, twenty-year-old Nancy DePriest. She was found still alive, tied with her bra. She had been raped and shot in the head. She died before she could describe her assailant.

Since the place was locked at the time, police concluded that someone had entered with a master key, available to any Pizza Hut employees. Christopher Ochoa and Richard Danziger, who were roommates, worked in another Pizza Hut in the Austin area. When a Pizza Hut waitress saw them together shortly after the DePriest murder, they were eating and drinking together, and she thought they were toasting each other over the accomplishment of the crime. Police brought both men in for questioning in late November 1988.

Danziger and Ochoa were interrogated sepa-

Christopher Ochoa falsely confessed out of fear to a Texas murder in 1989. *Innocence Project, New York.*

rately and police quickly came to believe that Danziger knew more about the rape-murder than was known publicly, although, as a Pizza Hut employee, he may have gotten inside information from other employees previously interviewed by police. Ochoa was interrogated at great length and police reported that he had confessed, implicating his close friend Danziger. That confession, as Ochoa later related, took place over a two-day period, with one night when Ochoa was held in a hotel room. He was, according to his later statements, subjected to nonstop intimidation.

Officers told the twenty-two-year-old Ochoa they knew he was guilty and had the evidence to send him to death row. They told him that he would be placed in a cell where he would be nothing more than "fresh meat" to savage prisoners who preyed on young men for their sexual pleasure. He resisted giving officers what they wanted until interrogators began pounding on the table at which he sat and yelling at him constantly. One threw a chair at him that narrowly missed his head. A detective tapped his arm to show him where the needle would go when he received a lethal injection at his execution, a fate that would befall him unless he confessed. "White guys always walk," the interrogator said. "Hispanics get the needle."

Told that Danziger was in the next room and was willing to implicate him in the crime—a lie—Ochoa was exhausted after forty-eight hours of questioning and thought that his only recourse was to either keep quiet and be executed or make a false confession and get life in prison. He chose life, signing a confession officers had prepared for him, which also implicated his friend Danziger.

Ochoa's confession said that both he and Danziger had planned to rob the Pizza Hut and that he had tied up DePriest, raped her, and then fatally shot her. Danziger was made of tougher stuff, refusing to admit his guilt even though he was put through the same intimidating interrogation. He provided an alibi for the time of the murder, saying that he had been with a girlfriend. He was dumb-founded by Ochoa's confession, saying that he had no idea why his friend would implicate him.

Both men were brought to trial and were convicted on the strength of Ochoa's confession. Ochoa was convicted in 1989 of murder and aggravated sexual assault, Danziger in 1990 of aggravated sexual assault. They were given life sentences. Both would have rotted behind bars had it not been for another prisoner, Achim Josef Marino, who was already serving three life sentences. In 1999, Marino began sending letters to officials and the media in Austin, claiming to have committed the Pizza Hut rape-murder. In his missives he stated that he was puzzled by Ochoa's confession, wondering why an innocent person would confess to a crime he had not committed. Marino had a religious conversion after participating in AA meetings in prison, which compelled him to make his admissions. He said he did not know Ochoa or Danziger.

After police received more letters from Marino, they began to reinvestigate the DePriest case. They interviewed Marino, who provided information about items stolen at the time of the Pizza Hut murder and never recovered. He told them where these items could be found and they were found. Marino's confession ostensibly exonerated Ochoa and Danziger, so officers reinterviewed Ochoa in prison. But he clung to his original confession, later saying that if he had not endorsed that false confession, he would somehow be denied eventual parole. Danziger had nothing to say, since he had suffered brain damage in prison from savage beatings by other prisoners.

Ochoa had second thoughts about escaping his wrongful imprisonment and contacted the Wisconsin Innocence Project, which could bring about his exoneration through postconviction DNA testing. The Innocence Project would serve as a third party source that could prove his innocence without his repudiating his false confession and jeopardizing the possibility of a parole.

Keith Findley and John Pray, who headed the Wisconsin organization, encouraged students at the University of Wisconsin law school to conduct a thorough investigation. Subsequently they unearthed biological evidence from the DePriest case that had been tested as early as 1989 by Forensic Science Associates, with inconclusive results. At the instigation of the Wisconsin organization, the evidence was again tested by FSA, which reported that Ochoa and Danziger had been excluded as the donors of the spermatozoa found in DePriest, and confirmed that the actual donor, as he had claimed earlier, was Achim Marino.

Both Ochoa and Danziger were exonerated and released in 2001. Danziger had to be released into medical care. He was later awarded $9 million compensation for his wrongful conviction and imprisonment, as well as the irreparable physical damage done to him in jail. Ochoa received $5.3 million, went on to graduate from law school, and became the poster child for the Innocence Project. He later stated that he "wished that I had stood up to the police," and apologized for sending his friend Danziger to prison. Danziger had proved his mettle as an innocent person and had refused to lie himself and his friend into prison.

Ochoa was simply a coward who tried to save his own hide, but in so doing squandered the life of his best friend. Police instinctively knew Ochoa was a coward when they applied fear tactics in their interrogations with him. Those unethical, illegal tactics compelled that cowardice into making a false confession. In essence, Ochoa committed perjury in making his false confession, induced by police fear tactics, that sent another innocent man, Danziger, to prison and mental oblivion (at one point after his release, Ochoa reportedly offered to pay Danziger $500,000 compensation for doing this). Christopher Ochoa was not the stuff of heroes, simply another cringing, weak-willed victim of oppressive police tactics and he had plenty of company.

Where fear of execution compelled Ochoa to make a false confession, fear of being labeled a homosexual drove Rodney Woidtke to falsely confess to murdering Audrey Cardenas, a young intern reporter for the *News-Democrat* in Belleville, Illinois.

On June 26, 1988, Cardenas's body was found in a creek behind Belleville East Township High School a week after she had disappeared. A drifter named Rodney Woidtke was found wandering about the area and was arrested. He was mentally ill and was not taking his medication. Woidtke was interrogated over a period of three days and made three confessions. Only part of the third confession was taped, and it made no more sense than the first two confessions as it was laced with errors and inconsistencies about the true facts of the murder, points that were made by the conscientious chief investigator, D Wayne Heil, to those who eventually prosecuted Woidtke.

State's attorney John Baricevic charged Woidtke with the Cardenas murder and scheduled his trial. Brian Trentman, an attorney with only one year of trial experience, was appointed Woidtke's defense lawyer by the court. At the time, Trentman was representing Dale R. Anderson on unrelated minor matters. Anderson had been very active in the Cardenas murder, telling friends that he had been providing police with suggestions on how to solve the case. He kept files on the investigation and often stated that the culprits behind the Cardenas murder were his former bosses at the Illinois Department of Public Aid, where he had once been employed as a caseworker. (He had also been employed by the St. Clair County sheriff's department as a jailer.) Anderson was another police suspect in the Cardenas murder, but he was not investigated after Woidtke was charged.

Trentman waived Woidtke's right to a jury trial and pleaded his case before Judge Richard Aguirre in 1989. He did a miserable job in cross-examining chief investigator Heil, never asking Heil if he thought the evidence against Woidtke showed his client to be guilty. Heil later stated that if he had been asked that question, he would have said no. Using Woidtke's confession, Judge Aguirre took only a few minutes to find him guilty and sentenced him to forty-five years in prison.

Anderson, meanwhile, was enraged at the Woidtke conviction, not because an innocent man had been sent to prison but because his former bosses at the Illinois Department of Public Aid had not been sent to prison for the murder of Cardenas. In a mad effort to implicate those former employers, Anderson murdered a pregnant woman and her three-year-old son. Before killing the woman, he forced her to write a note that his employers at the Illinois Department of Public Aid had killed Cardenas.

Investigator Heil was so upset about the Woidtke conviction that he reportedly quit his job and went to work investigating the Cardenas murder all over again, believing that Anderson was the guilty party. He allegedly interviewed Anderson in prison and got a confession from him, presenting this to Trentman, who refused to submit it for appeal. Judge Aguirre reviewed the Woidtke case but refused to acknowledge new evidence and upheld his original decision.

In 2000, the Illinois Fifth District Court of Appeals overturned Woitke's conviction and ordered a new trial, ruling that Trentman had had a conflict of interest in representing Woidtke and Anderson at the same time and that evidence existed which pointed to Anderson as the killer of Cardenas. Further, the court questioned Woidtke's confession after noting the comments of a clinical psychologist who had testified for the prosecution and stated his belief that Woidtke, whom he depicted as a paranoid schizophrenic and homophobe, had confessed to prove to the police and the public that he was not a homosexual. The court described Judge Aguirre's conduct in the case as "unconscionable."

St. Clair state's attorney Robert Haida decided to retry Woidtke, using the same useless false confession. In 2001, when the defense made a shambles of the their client's false confession, Woidtke was acquitted and released. That retrial was condemned by the mother of the slain Cardenas, Billie Fowler, who said that Woidtke's second trial "had nothing to do with finding out the truth, finding out what happened to my daughter. [It was] all about making sure that they convinced the public that they didn't make a mistake. But, guess what? They did make a mistake—and they got caught."

## False Confessions in the 1990s

The victim of a savage rape in New York's Central Park on April 19, 1989, for which five black teenagers from Harlem were sent to prison, abandoned her anonymity in 2003 with the publication of her memoir, *I Am the Central Park Jogger: A Story of Hope and Possibility*. Trisha Meili, a twenty-eight-year-old investment banker, had been jogging in Central Park when she was viciously attacked in the north end of the park near 102nd Street. The park at that time had been invaded by scores of petty thieves, muggers, and purse snatchers. Meili was found unconscious, raped, and almost beaten to death, her skull caved in with a heavy object. She was unconscious for twelve days, and when she regained consciousness, she could recall nothing.

Dozens of youths, mostly blacks and Hispanics, had been rounded up and questioned about the case. Police suspicion focused on five blacks, ages fifteen to seventeen—Anton McCray, Kevin Richardson, Kharey Wise, Raymond Santana, and Yusuf Salaam. All were charged with the assault and gang rape of Meili. All of the boys gave rambling statements that passed for confessions, and these false confessions were chiefly used to bring about their convictions. The only other evidence offered at trial was hair from one of the defendants found on the victim. McCray, Santana, and Salaam were tried together in 1990, Salaam being the only one to take the witness stand. All three were convicted of rape and given prison sentences of five to ten years. Wise and Richardson were tried three months later, where hairs from the victim were shown to have come from Richardson. Within twelve days, he was convicted of attempted murder and rape and was sentenced as a juvenile to five to ten years. Wise was convicted of sexual abuse and assault and was sentenced as an adult to five to fifteen years in prison.

Yusuf Salaam falsely confessed to attacking the Central Park jogger in NYC. *Innocence Project, New York.*

Kharey Wise, like Salaam, falsely admitted attacking the jogger in 1989. *Innocence Project, New York.*

All was not settled in this highly publicized case, however, after the court received a vexing report from a DNA expert on July 13, 1990. The expert stated that analysis of the semen taken from the victim did not match any of the five black youths who had been sent to prison. "That means," the expert declared, "there is another rapist who is still at large." More troubling news came when, in January 2002, Matias Reyes, who was serving thirty-three years for the rape and murder of a twenty-four-year-old pregnant woman, Lourdes Gonzalez Serrano, in Manhattan, told a guard at the Clinton Correctional Facility that he wanted to talk to someone about the Central Park jogger case. Reyes told an investigator that he had undergone a religious experience that compelled him to confess to that crime (a statement made shortly after the statute of limitations had run out), and that he and he alone had attacked and raped Meili.

DNA testing showed that the semen found in Meili had come from Reyes. Further testing showed that the hairs found on Richardson had not come from the victim. Moreover, Reyes provided details of the attack and rape that only the assailant would have known and had never been related by the five convicted black teenagers. He described in detail how he attacked the woman, struck her head with a dead tree branch, and tied her with her own shirt, looping it around her neck and also gagging her with it—a technique he had employed in his other rapes, which were a matter of record—and how he had inflicted a peculiar wound on her cheek, which came from his ring, one having a cross, a wound that the victim bore to that day.

Reyes's confession was corroborated by the DNA profile that proved he was the donor of the spermatozoa in the case and the mitochondrial DNA testing that proved that hairs found on the victim came from him. The confessions of the five black youths were, in light of the positive DNA evidence, dismissed as false. On the recommendation of the Manhattan district attorney, the convictions of McCray, Wise, Santana, Salaam, and Richardson were overturned on December 19, 2002, and all five were released.

Frederic Saecker, convicted in 1989 in Wisconsin on self-incriminating statements. *Innocence Project, New York.*

Frederic Saecker of Wisconsin made several self-incriminating statements which passed for a confession that sent him to prison for fifteen years, following his conviction for sexual assault, kidnapping, and burglary in 1990. A year earlier, in June 1989, a thirty-nine-year-old woman clad only in underwear had been kidnapped from her home in Bluff Siding, Wisconsin. The assailant raped her and let her out of his car on a lonely road. She gave a sketchy description of the attacker and police seemed to have no clues in the case until they found Saecker near the victim's home wearing a bloody T-shirt.

Arrested on suspicion, Saecker was questioned at length and gave several versions of his whereabouts on the night of the kidnapping-rape. Most damaging, he made several statements that appeared to incriminate him, which police accepted—too readily, as it turned out—as a confession. Brought to trial in 1990, prosecutors had to rely on that confession because Saecker did not resemble the description the victim had given to the police. He was nevertheless convicted of burglary, kidnapping, and sexual assault, and sentenced to fifteen years in prison.

In 1993, Saecker's mother paid Genetic Designs, a private lab in North Carolina, to conduct post-conviction DNA testing. The tests showed that Saecker could not have been the donor of the spermatozoa found in the victim. A request for a new trial was denied until 1996. At that time, the case was reviewed and the district attorney realized that the confession Saecker had made was false; coupled to the DNA evidence, Saecker was factually innocent. He dismissed all charges against the defendant, who was released from prison after having serving six years behind bars.

As profiled earlier in this chapter, many false confessions are made by persons suffering from mental disabilities or retardation. Few are ever tested for their mental capability prior to interrogation. Knowing that a suspect is retarded, police take unethical advantage in manipulating such a submissive person into making a confession that is false but is used to send him to prison. Four such cases in the 1990s typify false confessions coming from retarded persons, those of Anthony Gray, Lafonso Rollins, David Allen Jones, and Douglas Warney.

Anthony Gray, a resident of Calvert County, Maryland, was arrested in 1991 for the rape and murder of thirty-eight-year-old Linda Mae Pellicano. During his police interrogation, the mentally retarded Gray was told that two other codefendants had already implicated him in the crime and that if he did not confess, he would be executed. Terrified, Gray signed a confession prepared for him and then testified against the other two men. Having little or no real facts by which to tie those men to the crime, however, his testimony failed to bring about convictions. One of those men was found innocent and the other case was dismissed. Only Gray was left to hold the bag.

Based on his confession, Gray was convicted of murder and rape and sent to prison for life in 1991. The following year, however, a conscientious prosecutor, Calvert County state's attorney Robert Riddle, reviewed Gray's case and came to believe that he had not committed the crime that sent him

to prison. Riddle urged police to reopen their investigation, which they did, but little or no new evidence was uncovered until 1997, when police arrested Anthony Fleming for breaking and entering. In an effort to plea-bargain that charge, Fleming began to feed details about the Pellicano murder to officers, who then suspected that he had been involved in that crime.

DNA testing was made on the biological evidence taken from Pellicano and results showed that the donor of the spermatozoa was Fleming, not Gray. Fleming, confronted with this evidence, confessed to the crime and was sentenced to life imprisonment. Gray, who had been exonerated in the process, was released in 1999, fifteen months after Fleming confessed, after serving seven years in prison. Prosecutor Riddle was on hand to greet Gray as he left prison, saying to gathered members of the press, "There was justice today." Gray, however, was still asking questions about his wrongful conviction: "They were trying to get me the death penalty for something I didn't do. Why should I die for something I didn't do?" No one gave him an answer. There was none.

Lafonso Rollins was a seventeen-year-old Chicago ninth grader when he was arrested in 1993 and charged with a series of robberies and rapes of four elderly women living in a South Side housing complex. After being interrogated at some length, Rollins meekly signed a confession written by police that detailed the robberies and two sexual assaults. This false confession was used at his 1994 trial to convict him and send him to prison for seventy-five years.

Rollins filed for DNA testing through his public defenders, and in 2004 he was excluded as the donor of the biological evidence taken from the victims. His exoneration showed that his signed confession had been false. He was released after serving ten years behind bars to changed circumstances: his sister had been shot and killed and his grandparents had died.

David Allen Jones, also a retarded man with an IQ of between 60 and 73, made a false confession that was created and coaxed by Los Angeles police interrogators that sent him, in 1995, to prison for life for three rape-murders he did not commit. In 1992, four women believed to be prostitutes were brutally slain near the 97th Elementary School in Los Angeles. The body of Crystal Cain was found on September 30, 1992, about a quarter mile from the school. Also in that month, the body of Tammie Christmas was discovered. On November 16, 1992, the corpse of thirty-two-year-old Debra Williams was found in a stairwell leading to the boiler room of the school, and on December 16, 1992, the body of forty-two-year-old Mary Edwards was found inside a carport next to the school. All four women had been strangled to death.

In late December 1992, David Allen Jones, who had an IQ equivalent to that of an eight-year-old and worked part-time as a custodian, was arrested on an unrelated matter. A drug abuser who lived on 101st Street, close to where the murders had occurred, Jones had a record of abusing prostitutes and became a prime suspect in the four murders. Detectives went to work on him, subjecting him to prolonged interrogations. During the three-day interrogation, Jones admitted that he had fought with all of the slain women, putting some of them into a choke hold, but he claimed he did not really hurt them. He said he fought with them when they demanded more money and drugs for their "services."

During the interrogations, detectives showed Jones photos of the crime scenes and fed him details about each murder. When he stated contradictory information about the murders, interrogators corrected him and Jones parroted those corrections into his so-called confession. The detectives continued providing Jones with leading questions and when he appeared unclear as to where the murders occurred, detectives drove him to those sites and had him pose at the locations, pointing to the area where each body had been found—all of this taped, like his interrogations, and very much staged.

Charged with the murders of Christmas, Edwards, Williams, and Cain, Jones went to trial. No biological evidence linked him to the crime and an expert who examined the hairs left on the victims stated that they had not come from Jones. Prosecutors were left with Jones's confession to bring about his conviction, which they did in 1995. Convicted of rape and murder in the Edwards case and manslaughter in the deaths of Williams and Christmas (he was acquitted of the murder of Cain because her death did not fit the "pattern of murder" in the other three cases and attributed to Jones), he was sentenced to thirty-six years to life in prison.

In prison, Jones attempted to make appeals and also wrote to the FBI, but he had to have another inmate write those letters; Jones couldn't even spell his own name correctly. He claimed that if DNA had been used in his case, he would not have been sent to prison. When civil rights attorney Constance L. Rice was asked to evaluate the widespread corruption of the LAPD in the Ramparts Division, she reviewed Jones's case and stated that his confession was absurd. "This is nothing but detectives trying to put a fabricated story in the mind of a retarded man," she said. "You could have convinced him that he was Spiderman for the afternoon."

Jeffrey C. English, a former federal prosecutor and inspector general for the Los Angeles Police Commission, agreed that detectives had put words in Jones's mouth, but pointed out that their action was an acceptable police practice. Jones, however, was not ignored thereafter. Pursuant to California's new postconviction DNA statute, he was entitled to have his case biologically reviewed. Represented by the Post Conviction Assistance Center (PCAC), Jones applied in 2002 for that postconviction DNA testing.

Two of the rape kits in three of the cases had been destroyed, but Jones's attorneys were informed that a new wrinkle had developed. The LAPD had been pursuing cold rape-murder cases involving almost a dozen prostitutes killed from 1990 to 2000, and all of these slayings, including the murders for which Jones had been convicted, had the earmarks of a serial killer who had been operating before Jones was arrested and long after he had gone to prison. In that investigation, DNA had determined that all of the murders were committed by a person with a type A blood (Jones had type O blood), and that the profile in all the cases fit another black man named Chester Dwayne Turner (born in 1966 in Warren, Arkansas), who was already in prison on a rape conviction.

In 2002, DNA tests on the two remaining cases showed that Jones was excluded as the donor of the spermatozoa, but that Turner was indeed the guilty party. Jones's convictions were dismissed and he was released on March 4, 2004, after spending nine years behind bars. The real killer, Turner, was charged with murdering ten women on April 30, 2007, and was convicted and sentenced to death on May 15, 2007. His total victims, according to police estimates, may have been as many as fifteen or twenty, including the murders for which Jones was originally charged.

Douglas Warney of Rochester, New York, like Gray, Rollins, and Jones, suffered from a mental disability that placed his IQ at 68. His mind had been further eroded through AIDS-related dementia. He, like Gray, Rollins, and Jones, willingly gave police a false confession in the murder of sixty-three-year-old civil rights activist William Beason (a.k.a. Solomon Israel), one of the organizers of the Million Man March, a confession that was rife with inconsistencies and errors but was used to send him to prison.

Douglas Warney, who falsely confessed to murdering William Beason in 1996. *Innocence Project, New York.*

Beason was slain in his Rochester, New York, home on January 3, 1996. He was found lying on his back with puncture wounds to his neck and chest. He had been stabbed nineteen times but apparently put up a struggle, as indicated by wounds on his left hand.

Found in the clothing hamper in his bathroom was a bloodstained knife, a bloodstained towel, and several blood-soaked tissues. Police had no clues until they received a phone call from Douglas Warney, who told officers that he had known the victim and maybe he could help solve the crime. He explained that he had cleaned Beason's house and shoveled the snow from his walks and driveway in the past.

Police invited Warney to visit them and then put him under interrogation. During that prolonged session, Warney provided some details of the crime, but defense attorneys later believed that these facts were fed to Warney by questioning detectives—that the victim was wearing a nightgown and had been cooking chicken and that the murderer had cut himself on a knife and wiped it on tissues deposited in the bathroom. Warney also mentioned another man who was investigated but was residing in a mental institution at the time of the killing. Warney's "confession" contained many errors, including the location of the corpse and how the clothing was disposed of by the killer after the murder.

The results from the Monroe County Public Safety Laboratory, which made serology tests of the blood from the scene of the crime, provided only sketchy information. The victim had type O blood, whereas Warney had type A. The blood on the knife was consistent with the victim's blood, a serologist testified, but both the victim and Warney were excluded from the blood on the towel and on the tissues. Blood scrapings from beneath the fingernails of the victim did not yield sufficient enough materials for testing.

Employing Warney's shaky confession, prosecutors were able to obtain a second-degree murder conviction at his 1997 trial. His past robbery conviction did not aid him during the trial; prosecutors said that he had beaten his victims, and that he had been released from prison in 1993, only three years before the Beason slaying. His mental condition was not considered at his trial, even though Warney, only a short time before Beason had been murdered, had been admitted to a psychiatric unit at Strong Memorial Hospital "after allegedly pulling fire alarms and reporting false incidents."

Warney was sentenced to twenty-five years to life, but his case was taken up by the media, many New York reporters and columnists insisting that he had been wrongly convicted on a false confession that had been engineered by interrogating detectives. Bob Herbert, a columnist for the New York *Times*, wrote that "Warney's confession appears to be the ranting of a man who has only a passing acquaintance with reality." William Easton, one of Warney's original defense attorneys, stated, "I think this case is a cautionary tale to anyone who believes that the criminal justice system operates in a fair and flawless way."

The Innocence Project undertook Warney's case, but it had tough sledding with local officials when it sought postconviction DNA testing. The district attorney's office stated to the court that "DNA results now would add nothing significant to what we already know or what the jury knew at time of trial." This position was supported by New York Supreme Court Justice Francis Affronti, who, in 2004, denied DNA testing for Warney, ruling that Warney's defense had not met the legal threshold to require testing and that claims by his attorneys that such testing could show someone else as having committed the murder were "too speculative." Someone else, however, had murdered Beason, and DNA would prove it not only to the staid Justice Affronti but to the rest of the world as well.

Warney's case was again appealed. Without notifying Warney, his attorneys, or the Innocence Project, Rochester prosecutors—in an apparent effort to cover up their own actions—ordered DNA testing on the blood splatter gathered from the case and the fingernail scrapings from the victim, the bloody towel and tissues. This was done by the Monroe County Public Safety Laboratory, which conducted STR-based DNA testing. The results showed Warney innocent, and shortly thereafter the tests were entered into the national DNA profile database, where the real culprit was identified. A DNA profile matched Eldred Johnson Jr. who was already in a New York prison, serving a life sentence for a murder he had committed in Utica, New York.

Investigators interviewed Johnson in prison and he admitted that he had murdered Beason, he did not know Douglas Warney, and he had committed the slaying alone. After serving nine years in prison, Warney had his conviction vacated. He was released from prison on May 16, 2006. Warney's defense attorney, Donald Thompson, had the last word: "We now know that Douglas Warney is actually innocent and always has been."

Where police have manipulated retarded persons into making false confessions, they have employed the same interrogation tactic with those debilitated by alcohol- or drug-related problems. Such persons suffer memory blackouts that are routinely filled in by detectives and blindly accepted by suspects. This type of "confession" sent Ronnie Mark Gariepy and Franklin Thompson to prison for crimes that had not committed.

Gariepy, of Hutchinson County, Texas, had a lifelong problem with alcohol. When he was accused by his thirteen-year-old stepdaughter of raping her in 1992, his only defense was that he could not remember the attack. Police soon discovered that there was no evidence to support the girl's claim, but knowing Gariepy's drinking problem, they assumed that he had committed the act while drunk and simply had no recall or, worse, could easily take advantage of his routine blackouts.

Gariepy was brought in for questioning and, during his prolonged interrogation, he denied sexually assaulting the girl. Detectives worked on him, finally persuading Gariepy that he might have committed the crime during a drunken blackout. After signing a confession to an act he could not remember, he pleaded guilty and was sent to prison for twelve years. Eighteen months later, however, the girl recanted her accusation, saying that anger had prompted her statements against her stepfather following a domestic argument.

Local authorities believed the girl, supporting Gariepy's postconviction innocence claim in two appeals made to the Texas court of criminal appeals, but the court denied those appeals, without judicial comment. Paroled in 1999, Gariepy, who had been a model prisoner, sought to clear his name and was supported by the Texas Board of Pardons, which urged then Texas Governor George W. Bush to grant a pardon. Bush issued that pardon on August 15, 2000, officially exonerating the forty-one-year-old Gariepy.

In the case of Franklin Thompson, drugs compelled him to sign a false confession that sent him to prison. On February 6, 1994, the body of forty-one-year-old Jacqueline Oaki was found in a school parking lot in Joliet, Illinois. She had been beaten and killed after being run over by a car. For some time, Robert Ezell was considered a suspect. A 911 phone call placed from his home had been made by a hysterical woman whose voice was identified as Oaki's. But when police arrived to check on that call, they found no one in Ezell's home except Ezell, who claimed that his young nephew had been playing with the phone.

Two years later, Officer Brian Lewis, who had found Oaki's body in the school parking lot, was promoted to the homicide investigation unit of the Joliet Police Department. In reviewing the Oaki cold case, he remembered that Franklin Thompson, a factory worker, had known Oaki. Lewis asked Thompson to visit him at the police station to discuss the case. Thompson complied. He had no serious criminal record and was a decorated Vietnam War veteran. Thompson had, however, recently lost a well-paying job that he had held for more than two decades over his use of drugs.

When he arrived at the station, however, Thompson was not asked to "discuss" the Oaki case but was put under interrogation by Lewis. During his questioning, Lewis waved a file folder in front of Thompson and said it contained conclusive evidence which would prove Thompson had murdered Oaki by purposely running over her with his car.

Thompson, confused and still suffering from the effects of drug use, told Lewis that he had been at a party with Oaki and had driven her to her parents' home, where she obtained $20 to buy crack cocaine from James Culpepper, who hosted the party. He said he drove Oaki back to the party and she bought the drugs. Lewis managed to get Thompson to sign a statement that Oaki had been run over, but Thompson stated that her death had been accidental and that he had not been responsible.

Following Thompson's signed "confession," police charged the forty-eight-year-old with the first-degree murder of Oaki on October 2, 1996. He was brought to trial in 1997, where prosecutors acknowledged that there was no physical evidence linking Thompson to the crime and that DNA had excluded him as the source of hairs recovered from the victim. Further, tire prints at the scene of the crime did not match Thompson's car, a 1991 Pontiac Sunbird. Prosecutors relied wholly on Thompson's half-baked "confession" to wring a conviction from a jury. He was sentenced to twenty-four years in prison by Will County circuit court Judge Stephen D. White.

In a 1999 appeal, the Third District Illinois Appellate Court upheld Thompson's conviction, denying relief. As a last resort, Thompson's family contacted the Center on Wrongful Convictions and its counsel, Jane E. Raley, filed a postconviction petition that was denied by Judge White. Raley filed another appeal and, at the same time, requested a full pardon from Illinois Governor George H. Ryan (1999–2003). Two days before he left office, Ryan signed pardons for scores of condemned Illinois prisoners, as well as many others who were not on death row, and that included Thompson, who was exonerated on January 11, 2003. After more than six years in prison, Thompson was a free man.

Many false confessions are motivated by real and understandable causes. Some, however, have no foundation in reality and originate in minds controlled by ambiguous but commanding emotions. Laverne Pavlinac made just such a false confession, her motivations so bizarre and strange that psychiatrists are baffled by it to this day. To understand it, the police and courts involved with her could only seek an explanation in the arcane line that describes such motivations: "The heart has its reasons of which reason does not know."

Laverne Pavlinac and John A. Sosnovske (or Sosnovski) were sent to prison for life in 1991 for a 1990 Oregon strangulation they never committed, even though, at the time of their conviction, Pavlinac insisted they did, in one of the most fantastic false confessions on record. They were released on November 27, 1995, three weeks after serial killer Keith Hunter Jesperson, the so-called Happy Face Killer, was convicted of the murder and sent to prison for life.

In 1995, Keith Hunter Jesperson, who claimed to have slain more than 160 female victims (a total of eight women murdered in five northwestern states are attributed to him and he confessed to four slayings, one each in Washington and Wyoming and two in Oregon), began to send letters to news outlets in which he took responsibility for the murder of twenty-three-year-old Taujna Bennett of Portland, Oregon. Jesperson, was a divorced thirty-five-year-old father of three in 1990, when he worked as a long-haul truck driver in the Northwest.

In January 1990, Jesperson, a resident of Selah, Washington, met Bennett, a mildly retarded woman, in a Portland bar. He later beat, raped, and strangled her to death, driving eastward with her body in his truck until he reached the Columbia River Gorge, just east of Portland. There he tossed his victim's body down a remote embankment.

Serial killer Keith Hunter Jesperson, whose murders were inexplicably claimed by Laverne Pavlinac, and whose false confession sent her and John A. Sosnovske (or Sosnovski) to prison for life in 1991. *History Inc./Jay Robert Nash Collection.*

Each of Jesperson's letters was adorned with a smiling face, earning him the sobriquet of the "Happy Face Killer." After leading investigators to the exact location where Bennett's decomposed body was earlier found with the rope around her neck that Jesperson used to strangle her, Jesperson was convicted and given a life sentence. He had also taken detectives to a blackberry thicket where he had buried his victim's purse, and contents from her purse were then found after that site was excavated. The conviction of Jesperson brought about the release of Pavlinac and Sosnovske, who had spent four years in prison for the Bennett killing.

Pavlinac, a middle-age homemaker, had gone to the police after officials found Bennett's body, confessing to the murder. She said that her live-in boyfriend, Sosnovske, had forced her to help him murder Bennett. Pavlinac recited details of the case that she, as later admitted, had read in newspaper accounts. She was nevertheless convincing after she provided police with a cutout section of denim cloth that appeared to be missing from the fly of Bennett's jeans. She also led detectives to the approximate area where the killer had dumped the corpse (this too she culled from newspaper reports).

Investigators at first discounted her admissions, but, as time went on and many police interrogations ensued with her, Pavlinac sounded more and more convincing. She was actually parroting back to these interrogators information that they provided to her, including the fact that the victim had been strangled with a rope. In a later interrogation, Pavilinac told police that she held the rope tight around Bennett's neck while Sosnovske raped her. Not checking their own statements to this strange woman, detectives then accepted Pavilinac's information about the rope as originating with *her*.

During her trial, however, Pavlinac claimed that she had made up the entire story, implicating Sosnovske so she could escape an abusive relationship with him. Another report held that she made up the murder tale in order to punish the younger Sosnovske, who was about to leave her, and had been venting the eternal wrath of a woman scorned. The jury nevertheless convicted the pair in 1991 because Pavlinac's taped "confession" was so convincing.

Both Pavlinac, sixty-two when released in 1995, and Sosnovske, then forty-two, had been sentenced to life in prison. Sosnovske had pleaded no contest in 1991. Marion County circuit court judge Paul Lipscomb, ruling from Salem, Oregon, set aside Sosnovske's conviction and sentence, stating that his civil rights had been violated because Pavlinac's lies had implicated him in the Bennett murder. Judge Lipscomb chastised Pavlinac for fabricating the accusations against her former lover, Sosnovske, and refused to set aside her conviction and sentence. He did, however, order her release. He stated that serving a prison term for a crime one did not commit amounted to cruel and unusual punishment.

Pavlinac remarked at the time of her release, "I'm kind of upset with the way my case wasn't investigated. They just took my word for it and didn't try to find out anything else." She added, "These things don't happen except in the movies." It had happened, however, in real life, to John Sosnovske.

# *Railroading and Framing*

THE RAILROADING OR FRAMING OF PERsons throughout history in the courts of the world has been, until the modern age, a matter of political, social, or religious genocide, particularly with nationalities, religious sects, and individuals who seemed to threaten the established systems and leaders of those ages. The peoples of conquered nations were typically decreed under the laws of the conquerors slaves without human rights.

Beginning with the earliest civilizations, noncitizens had little recourse in a court of law, and their privation was justified through their stateless class. Courts summarily ordered the torture, imprisonment, and execution of these hapless millions after branding them enemies of the state. Their trials, such as they were, consisted of false testimony, and in some rare instances elaborate trials, where forged documents and perjury brought about imprisonment or death by fire, rope, ax, and sword with judicial alacrity.

Countless individuals lost to history have been the victims of such injustice. One man became a classic example of governmental and judicial framing—Jesus of Nazareth, a Galilean whose great teachings and reported miracles—from walking on water to raising Lazarus from the dead—had electrified the countryside. His arrival in Jerusalem

in A.D. 33 during the Passover festival prompted great throngs to shout, "Hosanna! Blessed is he who comes in the name of the Lord!" Then Jesus entered King Herod's temple and overturned the tables of moneylenders doing business there, stating that they had turned the temple into a den of thieves.

To many leading Hebrew religious leaders, chiefly the high priest, Caiaphas, Jesus represented a serious challenge to their authority. His prosaic but meaningful teachings had persuaded thousands of Jews to accept him as the Messiah. Widespread reports of his miracles also frightened and alarmed Caiaphas and the Jewish judicial authority, the Sanhedrin. On orders of the Sanhedrin and Caiaphas, guards from Herod's temple were sent to the Garden of Gethsemane, where they arrested Jesus while he was with his disciples. The guards were led to his whereabouts by one of his followers, Judas Iscariot, who kissed Jesus as a way of identifying him (the proverbial kiss of death).

In a rigged trial presided over by Caiaphas, Jesus was asked by several priests, "Are you the Son of God?" He reportedly replied, "You say that I am." This was interpreted as blasphemy, and, under the old Hebraic laws, he was condemned to death. By executing Jesus, Caiaphas and others could rid themselves of a dangerous religious rival who, in their eyes, threatened to bring about the destruction of their orthodoxy and authority. However, that death was not so easily arranged.

Roman rule dominated Judea and Jerusalem as it did most of the known world, and Jesus was sent to the Roman governor, Pontius Pilate, for official condemnation, under the accusation of the Sanhedrin that Jesus had committed sedition by claiming to be king of the Jews—a claim he did not make. Pilate, a crafty and cautious man whose secret agents had documented the travels and reported miracles of Jesus, was disinclined to condemn this good rabbi. He talked briefly with Jesus, who gave him no cause to condemn him. Pilate was also troubled after his wife had warned him not to injure Jesus, describing a dream filled with bad omens about his case. There was a report that Pilate's wife had even attended some of Jesus' sermons and had become a secret follower.

Pilate at first refused to condemn Jesus, saying that he found no guilt in him (or that he had not committed any crimes against the Roman Empire) and sent him to King Herod, who was just as apprehensive as Pilate in condemning the rabbi. Herod sent Jesus back to the Sanhedrin, which again condemned him and returned him to Pilate. The governor stalled, apparently looking for a way he might spare Jesus and escape responsibility for his death. There existed a custom at that time, according to the Gospels, that a prisoner was released at the Passover.

Before a mob, Pilate offered to release either Jesus or a bandit and insurrectionist named Barabbas. Many of Barabbas's followers, who had assembled with the mob, shouted down those demanding that Jesus be set free. Barabbas was released and Jesus was sent to Calvary (Golgotha), an area outside the walls of Jerusalem, where he was put to death by crucifixion. Pilate repeatedly washed his hands after making the decision, as if to cleanse himself of the injustice he had meted out. That wrongful conviction and execution would eventually topple the Roman Empire and alter the course of the world for centuries to come.

## Joan of Arc and Other Martyrs of Judicial Framing

Fifteen centuries after Jesus' crucifixion, an inspired and inspiring girl in France translated his teachings into military action that would rid her country of foreign invaders. She was Joan of Arc (Jeanne d'Arc, 1412–1431). She would share the fate of her God, for where Jesus of Nazareth was wrongly framed and condemned for blasphemy, Joan would be wrongly sent to the stake for heresy, following an equally framed trial.

Compelled by the voices of St. Michael, St. Catherine, and St. Margaret, Joan, who would be called the "Maid of Orleans," had a mission to free France from the English. While Henry VI of England sat on the French throne (in 1422, the infant king, with the aid and support of France's Philip of Burgundy, was proclaimed king of France), Joan, an unschooled girl from the village of Domre-my-la-Purcel, sought out the dauphin, Charles VII (1403–1461), the rightful heir.

The perceptive peasant girl identified the dauphin in a crowded palace court, although she had never met him. (She may have been psychic, telepathic, or clairvoyant, or all in one, beyond the voices she said she heard.) She told the startled dauphin that she had a divine mission to free France of the British invaders.

After talking with Joan in private, Charles was convinced of her mission and gave her command of an army of five thousand men. On April 29, 1429, Joan invaded Orleans and on May 8, 1429, at the head of her troops, even after being wounded, she

Joan of Arc, who said she was counseled by Heavenly voices to free France, is shown in 1429, when she led a 5,000-man army that liberated the city of Orleans from English troops. *History Inc./Jay Robert Nash Collection.*

A statue of Joan of Arc in the Cathedral at Reims, France; to the French she was a gift from God, to the English a heretical witch. *History Inc./Jay Robert Nash Collection.*

miraculously recaptured the city from a powerful English army. In September 1429, she was wounded while trying to capture Paris, and in December 1429, she and her family were ennobled with the surname of du Lis. Her knighthood was short-lived, however.

On May 23, 1430, Joan was captured by Burgundians during the siege of Compiègne, some later claiming through the connivance of Charles VII, whose coronation Joan had proudly witnessed at Reims on July 17, 1429. Charles, his detractors claimed, had become fearful that the enormously popular Joan might replace him on the throne.

The Burgundians sold Joan to the English six months later, who charged her with witchcraft and heresy. Pierre Cauchon, the bishop of Beauvais and friend of the English, claimed jurisdiction for the trial. Rather than trying Joan in a civil trial for crimes of war, Cauchon wanted her tried in a church tribunal for heresy because of the voices she claimed to hear.

**Actress Ingrid Bergman playing Joan of Arc in an epic 1948 film based upon the exploits of the teenage warrior. *History Inc./Jay Robert Nash Collection.***

Joan's disgraceful and unfair trial, framed at Rouen by Cauchon and a group of ecclesiastics loyal to the English throne, revolved around her claims that she had acted on these divine voices, that she wore men's clothing, and that she refused to accept the authority of the Church. During sixteen inquisition sessions, Joan was asked questions such as, "Did the saints speak in English or

A copy of Joan of Arc's retraction of her confession, which sealed her fate and sent her to a fiery death; she had been framed with false documents and testimony by her chief judge, Cauchon. *History Inc./Jay Robert Nash Collection.*

French?" and "Does God hate the English?" On March 27, 1431, she was formally tried before thirty-seven clerical judges at Rouen Cathedral.

Before the court, Joan admitted that she had disobeyed the "voices" in trying to escape from prison and in urging the attack on Paris. The court asked if she had disobeyed revelations from God. Indeed, had she obeyed the devil? Finding that "she sets herself up as an authority, a doctor, a master," the tribunal charged her with heresy.

On April 18, 1431, the inquisitors pleaded with Joan to recant her testimony, but she refused. With her execution imminent, she made a last-minute appeal to the pope. But then she disavowed her earlier testimony with a signed confession, most probably coerced, admitting that "I have previously sinned, in falsely pretending to have had revelations from God and his angels." She was sentenced to life imprisonment.

Forced again before a tribunal, Joan retracted her confession, insisting that her revelations were divine. On May 30, 1431, she was excommunicated and ordered executed by the bailiff of Rouen. Placed high on a pyre, she was crowned with a miter that read "Relapsed heretic, apostate, idolater," and slowly burned before a crowd.

When Joan endured the flames without crying out, many in the witnessing throng shouted for her release, some saying that she had been sent by heaven. Some dissenting clerics who were present later condemned the execution as murder and denounced Cauchon and his slavish followers for framing an innocent girl. Cauchon himself was astounded at Joan's brave death. Her entire body was consumed by the flames, but, it was reported, her heart remained intact and wholly uninjured.

On June 16, 1456, Joan's conviction was annulled and she was proclaimed innocent. More than four hundred years later, "to advertise the intimate union between patriotism and the Catholic faith," interest in Joan of Arc was revived. In 1909, she was beatified by Pope Pius X (1835–1914; as pope, 1903–1914). She was canonized in 1920 as a saint by Pope Benedict XV (1854–1922; as pope, 1914–1922). Long before that time, Joan of Arc was honored as one of France's greatest heroes and is celebrated with an annual festival in France on May 30. The memory of Pierre Cauchon is celebrated by no one.

The world would see Cauchon's equals as monstrous religious magistrates who sat in judgment of countless framed victims of the Spanish Inquisition, which began less than fifty years after Joan was consumed by flames and would continue its dreadful persecution of "heretics" for the next four centuries. The Inquisition practiced horrible methods of torture to compel accused heretics into confessing or to force others into pointing out heretics, who were then burned at the stake.

When Queen Isabella of Castile (1451–1504) and King Ferdinand II of Aragon (1452–1516) married in 1469, they united Spain and, after prolonged wars, drove most of the Moors from the country. The monarchs responded to widespread hatred for Jews by ordering all Jews out of the country through the Alhambra Decree of 1492.

In the same year Queen Isabella commissioned three small ships to explore the West Indies under the command of Christopher Columbus. Many Jews, however, disinclined to leave prosperous businesses or long-established homes, converted to Catholicism. These conversions were then de-

nounced as false, made as a guise by Jews to remain in Spain where they could secretly practice their religion and continue to control the country's economy, gain important political and religious posts, and covertly chart the course of the nation, while undermining the authority of the Catholic Church.

Ferdinand II embraced this concept and, at the suggestion of his most zealous religious advisers, established the Inquisition to combat such imagined subterfuge, increase the authority of the monarchy, and weaken local political opposition. A papal inquisition had been established in Aragon in 1232 during the era of Albigensian heresy. Queen Isabella gave tacit approval, although she may have had reservations; no inquisition had existed in Castile prior to this time.

The reestablishment of the Inquisition actually began in Castile, after Isabella was convinced by a Dominican priest from Seville, Alonso de Hojeda (no relation to the explorer who accompanied Columbus on his second voyage in 1493), that Seville was overrun by converted Jews pretending to be Catholics (Conversos). This assertion was corroborated by Pedro Gonzalez de Mendoza, archbishop of Seville (1428–1495), and a fanatically zealous Dominican monk, Tomàs de Torquemada (1420–1498). Torquemada would become

Joan of Arc dying in the flames at Rouen, France, on May 30, 1431. She uttered no cries and it was later claimed that her entire body was consumed except her heart which was wholly intact; she was canonized a saint in 1920 by Pope Benedict XV. *History Inc./Jay Robert Nash Collection.*

Queen Isabella of Castille, who hesitantly approved of the establishment of the Spanish Inquisition. *History Inc./Jay Robert Nash Collection.*

Pope Sixtus IV refused to endorse the Inquisition, but gave reluctant approval after the Spanish monarchs threatened to withhold their military and financial support from the Vatican. *History Inc./Jay Robert Nash Collection.*

the chief inquisitor of this draconian institution as well as the confessor and adviser to Queen Isabella and King Ferdinand.

Torquemada imported his religious terrorism to the New World through appointees traveling with Christopher Columbus, and they inflicted horrible punishments on natives in the new lands reluctant to embrace the Spanish version of the Catholic religion. The Spanish Inquisition was never under the control of the Vatican, although Pope Sixtus IV grudgingly sanctioned its existence after Ferdinand threatened to withhold his troops in the defense of the Papal States against the Turks. The Spanish Inquisition was in the exclusive service of the Spanish monarchy until it was officially abolished on July 15, 1834.

Clerics representing the Inquisition accompanied explorer Hernán Cortés to Latin and South America, intimidating natives as well as Cortés's own men with savage punishment for any perceived offense to their religion. Protestant monarchs of Europe embraced the same terrorist tactics as they persecuted anyone practicing a faith other than their government-backed religions, giving rise to the innumerable witchcraft trials in France and England, where dozens were

burned alive at the stake. The number of persons wrongly imprisoned in Spain during the Inquisition is not known. At least 40,000 converted Jews were singled out for some sort of chastisement by the Inquisition, half the number of those who chose to migrate from the country after the fall of the Moors. But the numbers of those departing may have been as high as 800,000.

An accused heretic is being turned on the rack by torture experts of the Inquisition, which targeted Jews, Protestants and homosexuals as its victims. *History Inc./Jay Robert Nash Collection.*

In the carefully preserved records of the many tribunals under the Inquisition, at least two thousand persons were put to death after being framed as heretics; some historians put the numbers of wrongly convicted persons much higher. In Mallorca in 1691 alone, records show that thirty-six crypto-Jews were burned to death as heretics. Jews fleeing to Portugal found no relief in that country, which established its own Inquisition in 1532. While purging Jews from Spain in the fifteenth century, the Inquisition focused on persecuting and eliminating Protestants from Spain in the following century.

Victims in this period ranged from a dozen to two hundred but may have been much higher, particularly when the trials of all Muslim converts to Christianity were included in the tribunals in Granada, Aragon, Valencia, and elsewhere in southern Spain. Of the almost 50,000 trials registered with the Inquisition from 1560 to 1700, most dealt with heresy, but many other offenses—from bigamy to solicitations and superstitions—were in included. By the early sixteenth century, witchcraft became the focus of the Inquisition, a mania that had earlier spread across Europe, and one that brought about countless wrongful convictions and

A torture chamber employed by the Spanish Inquisition; those who refused to confess to heresy were often put to death and those who made confessions were spared, but their lands seized and most were banished. *History Inc./Jay Robert Nash Collection.*

An Inquisition victim convicted as a witch is shown wearing a miter labeling him a heretic. *History Inc./Jay Robert Nash Collection.*

executions. During the auto de fe (trial) at Logrono, Spain, six persons were framed as witches, convicted of witchcraft (superstition), and burned alive on November 7–8, 1610.

The Inquisition also targeted homosexuals and tried them on then universal European laws against sodomy, coupling this offense to heresy. In Zaragoza, more than one hundred men were put to death after being convicted of this crime between 1570 and 1630. Not unlike the witchhunts of the 1950s in America, anyone wishing to get rid of someone in Spain for any reason needed only to bring an accusation of heresy and attending crimes. Without substantiation, Inquisition tribunals simply framed these judicial victims to suit the protocol of the auto de fe before sending them to prison for life or to the stake. This secretly operating judicial system would be embraced by countries the world over, especially in Nazi Germany, communist Russia, and fascist Italy during the 1930s and early 1940s, where more than 20 million railroaded persons (or twice that number, according to some estimates) forfeited their lives.

These judicial systems encouraged armies of informers to come forth. The Inquisition at first offered to reconcile anyone who had fallen from grace without severe punishment within a month after the local tribunal issued an edict. When these persons came forward to absolve themselves, they were initially treated with understanding and kindness but then obligated to name all of their accomplices, whether they existed or not, under the threat of torture or even death. Informers were encouraged to point out enemies of the state under the Inquisition's promise (which was upheld) that such denunciations would remain anonymous.

Tens of thousands of informants were thus entrapped and began denouncing their neighbors and relatives to save their own lives. Those tried and convicted through such denunciations forfeited their property and assets to the Inquisition, which funded its widespread operations from looted wealth in a never-ending cycle of persecution.

## Elizabeth Barton, Thomas More, and Mary, Queen of Scots

During the height of the Inquisition in Spain, many other countries adopted its techniques, framing victims under the guise of national or religious security. England's Henry VIII (1491–1547), who had married one of Isabella's daughters, Catherine of Aragon (1485–1536), and who broke with the Vatican over his bigamous marriages, wholeheartedly embraced the techniques of the Inquisition in summarily dispatching his enemies, real or imagined. One of these persons was an annoying but spiritually enlightened young woman named Elizabeth Barton (a.k.a. Fair Maid of Kent, Holy Maid of Kent; 1506–1534).

Barton was afflicted with a nervous condition and a sporadic skin ailment, and her unpredictable ailments were interpreted in 1520 as manifestations of supernatural power. Born of peasant parents, Barton, at the age of fourteen, was sheltered by an innkeeper at Ashford, Kent, where she displayed uncontrollable seizures and said she saw visions.

Barton correctly predicted the death of one of the innkeeper's children (although the child was ill before the prediction). At nineteen, Barton slipped

England's Henry VIII, in 1511, who ordered the death of Elizabeth Barton after she denounced his oppression of the Catholic Church, and who made Thomas More his foremost minister, later arranging for More's wrongful conviction and execution. *History Inc./Jay Robert Nash Collection.*

into a trance for a week and delivered esoteric diatribes on sin, virtue, and the Ten Commandments. She was thought to be controlled by the Holy Ghost, and even Henry VIII, after hearing stories about the girl, sent his closest adviser and friend, Sir Thomas More (St. Thomas More; 1478–1535), to investigate. More visited Barton and reported later to Henry that she had no spectacular powers.

Others, however, were more apt to believe in Barton's powers. After she moved into the rectory of John Cobb at Aldington, Barton was visited by Archbishop Warham of Canterbury, who became quickly convinced that she was a holy seer. He endorsed her divine powers, saying to doubters that he would "not hide the goodness of the works of God." Miracles were attributed to the maid: women who could not suckle their infants suddenly were bursting with milk, altar candles gave birth to flames, when Barton pointed at them, and the ill and crippled were restored to health after she laid hands upon them, or so it was written, or so it was said.

Barton was sent to the convent of St. Sepulcher's at Canterbury, where she convinced the nuns of her purity and her prophetic powers and became a novitiate. On one occasion, supposedly before three thousand people, Barton, dressed in a nun's habit, lay in a trance for three hours before a statue of the Blessed Virgin. She spoke in strange voices, describing the joys of heaven and the torments of hell.

Thousands flocked to her; she became a symbol of goodness, and scores of tracts and books were written about her, referring to her as the Fair Maid

of Kent, the Holy Nun of Kent, and the Holy Maid of Kent. In the accounts of some historians, however, she became a tool in the hands of nobles opposed to Henry, particularly the marchioness of Exeter, the countess of Salisbury, the bishop of Rochester, and others.

These highborn persons subtly convinced Barton to render prophecies against Henry, criticizing his treatment of Queen Catherine of Aragon and damning him for his association with Anne Boleyn (c. 1501–1536). Elizabeth Barton then assumed a regal attitude, openly forbidding the king to divorce Catherine. She said that if Pope Clement VII (1478–1534) permitted the divorce, he would die. Clement did not sanction the marriage to Boleyn, and consequently the English Parliament, Henry's stooge organization, passing the Act of Supremacy in 1534, which created the Church of England with Henry at its head.

Insisting that Henry would die within seven months after divorcing Catherine, Barton commented that Henry "is like Saul. He will never be king in the eyes of God." When Henry drove through Canterbury, Elizabeth Barton stood in the way of his coach, warning him that he was imperiling his soul and courting the tortures of hell. Henry ignored her.

Worse for Barton, she aligned herself with Henry's political foes, especially Cardinal Thomas Wolsey (1471–1530), which incurred the enmity of Henry's chief minister, Thomas Cromwell (c. 1485–1540). He sent Thomas Cranmer (1489–1556) to interview the young woman, with Cranmer reporting that "she never had visions in all her life. All that she ever said was feigned of her own imagination, only to

Cardinal Thomas Wolsey, British prelate who fought against Henry's interference with the Catholic Church in England, and who obliquely supported Elizabeth Barton's denouncements of the king. *History Inc./Jay Robert Nash Collection.*

satisfy those, who resorted to her and to obtain worldly gain." Cranmer's evaluation of Barton, which branded her a heretic, served Henry's purposes. After he become archbishop of Canterbury in 1533, Cranmer slavishly voided Henry's marriage to Catherine and announced the validity of his marriage to Anne Boleyn.

Based on Cranmer's assertions, Barton was charged with heresy and witchcraft. Cranmer reportedly obtained a confession from her, undoubtedly coerced, in which Barton said that she was an imposter and that she had been possessed by Satan, a confession she allegedly repeated after being taken from London Tower to Tyburn, where, on April 20, 1534, she was tied to a stake. She had by then been convicted at a trial rigged by Cranmer, which framed her guilt and brought about her mandated execution.

As the faggots piled about her were torched, Barton cried out, "To say the truth, I am not so much to blame considering that it is well known to these learned men that I am a poor wench without learning." She shrieked as the flames consumed her. According to Henry's direct order, Barton's head was severed from her body and buried separately from the rest of her remains.

Barton would be followed in death the next year by one of England's greatest men, Thomas More, who had first interviewed Barton for Henry VIII and found the girl harmless. Although the intellectual and well-reasoning More found no supernatural powers present in Barton, as he reported, he shared her views about his sovereign. As a steadfast Catholic, More opposed Henry's religious transgressions against the Vatican's edicts concerning his intention to annul his marriage with Catherine of Aragon so that he could wed Anne Boleyn. More also opposed Henry's outlawing of the Catholic Church, and the establishment of the Church of England, with Henry as its supreme head.

Before that time, More had established himself as a foremost humanist scholar, lawyer, and statesman, occupying many important public offices.

From 1510 to 1518, he served as one of the two undersheriffs of London, earning a reputation as an honest and upright official. In 1517, More had become Henry's counselor and was knighted after completing a mission to Holy Roman Emperor Charles V. He became secretary and personal adviser to Henry, who befriended him and respected his intellectual capabilities. Henry used More as his liaison to Cardinal Thomas Wolsey, archbishop of York and chancellor of England. More then became England's Lord Chancellor (1529–1532).

Pope Clement VII, who refused to annul Henry's marriage to Catherine of Aragon, prompting Henry to abandon the Catholic Church and establish his own state-controlled religion in England. *History Inc./Jay Robert Nash Collection.*

Prior to that time, More authored a *History of King Richard III* (1513–1518), a critical biography that obliquely attacked tyrannical monarchs, and *Utopia* (1515), a novel depicting a tranquil island where no one owns private property and all religions are tolerated. More's brilliant but subtle writings veiled his deep-seated opposition to the rise of Protestantism, which took deep root in England, when Pope Clement VII refused to annul Henry's almost twenty-year marriage to Catherine of Aragon, who had failed to provide him with an heir, and to endorse his new marriage to Anne Boleyn, who might provide that heir.

More asked Henry to relieve him of his office as chancellor when Henry began to defy the pope and moved toward the establishment of his own church. Henry, who held More in high regard, had been offended when, in 1530, More parted with leading English aristocrats and churchmen who had signed a petition to Clement VII, requesting that he annul the marriage between Henry and Catherine. More would not affix his signature to that document. Henry nevertheless retained More as his chancellor until agreeing to More's request

Anne Boleyn, whom Henry married after Parliament annulled his marriage to Catherine of Aragon, an act that Thomas More did not endorse. *History Inc./Jay Robert Nash Collection.*

to resign. When More did not attend the coronation of Anne Boleyn in 1533, Henry became enraged and More was subsequently charged with accepting bribes. These accusations were dismissed after they were proven false.

Henry next tried having his ministers accuse More of conspiring with Elizabeth Barton, who had opposed Henry's annulment and was executed in 1534. More successfully defended himself against this charge by pointing out that he had, at Henry's request, interviewed Barton and reported back to Henry that she was a naive young woman who had no real saintly visions. Further, he provided the courts a copy of a letter he had sent to Barton, warning her not to interfere in state matters. These charges, too, were dismissed.

Henry knew that More represented serious opposition in England to his defiance of the pope and his marriage to Anne Boleyn. He took the extraordinary step of attempting to frame More on charges of treason through his lickspittle minions. On April 13, 1534, More was asked to appear before a royal commission and swear his allegiance to the Act of Succession. More accepted Parliament's right to declare Anne Boleyn the legitimate queen of England, but he refused to take the oath because the act contained a clause that gave Henry the right to deny the authority of the pope and legislate religion in England. Four days later, More was charged with treason and imprisoned in the Tower of London.

While awaiting trial, More wrote his *Dialogue of Comfort Against Tribulation.* He was deprived of his books and eventually his writing materials, as well as visits from family members. More's fate had already been decided by Henry. On July 1, 1535,

More was brought before a panel of judges, headed by the new Lord Chancellor, Sir Thomas Audley, and included members of Anne Boleyn's family. This kangaroo court attempted to trick More into denying Henry's right to head the Church of England, but More wisely chose not to answer any questions on that matter, believing that he could not be convicted if he did not utter any such denials.

Henry's henchman, Thomas Cromwell, then presented a witness, Richard Rich (c. 1496–1567), who had been knighted and made Solicitor General in 1533. Rich, who had many times in the past asked More to employ him in some official capacity but had been repeatedly refused, took vengeance by falsely testifying that More, in his presence, had denied Henry the right to be the legitimate head of the church.

This perjury was made evident by two others, Richard Southwell and a man named Palmer, who had been present at the time Rich said More made these statements, and who testified that More had made no such statements. On the strength of Rich's lies, however, More was convicted and sentenced to death. Rich would become infamous in making other perjured statements against those thought to be the enemies of Henry. He rose to the post of Chancellor of England and, ironically, brought about the ruination of Thomas Cromwell, the man who used him as a judicial tool to end More's life.

More was beheaded at the Tower of London on July 6, 1535. He was beatified by Pope Leo XIII

Thomas Cromwell, henchman to Henry VIII, who prosecuted Thomas More on trumped up charges of treason, bringing about his wrongful conviction and death sentence through the perjured testimony of Richard Rich. *History Inc./Jay Robert Nash Collection.*

Sir Thomas More, England's foremost scholar and enlightened minister, who was executed on July 6, 1535, following his wrongful conviction on false charges of treason. *History Inc./Jay Robert Nash Collection.*

(1810–1903) in 1886, and canonized by Pope Pius XII (1876–1958) in 1935. Known as the patron saint of lawyers, More is considered one of the wisest leaders of England in its time, where Henry is most remembered as a brutal tyrant.

As Henry had framed Thomas More, the king's only child and daughter, Elizabeth I (1533–1603), framed her cousin, Mary, fifty-two years after More had gone to the headsman. Mary, Queen of Scots (Mary Stuart, 1542–1587) was the only daughter of James V (1512–1542) of Scotland and Mary of Guise (1515–1560), who was descended from the royal house of France. Her father died when she was only six days old. The infant queen was sent to France when she was five and brought up in regal splendor in the court of Henry II (1519–1559) and Catherine de Medici (1519–1589). She was taught to speak French, Italian, Latin, and Spanish, so that by the time she achieved adulthood she was more a citizen of France than Scotland.

In November 1558, Elizabeth Tudor succeeded to the throne of England, meaning that Mary stood next in line by virtue of her blood ties to Henry VIII. Her position was strengthened by the Catholic population of Britain. Catholics regarded Elizabeth's claim as illegitimate because of Henry's divorce from Catherine of Aragon and subsequent marriage to Anne Boleyn. When Henry of France died in 1559, Mary was named Queen Consort of France.

Following the death of her French husband, Mary returned to Scotland in August 1561. She was greeted with scorn by Queen Elizabeth, who

publicly shunned her and denounced her claims to the throne as mere pretensions. Complicating matters was Mary's tenuous position among the Scottish nobility, which was slow to lend support to the foreign queen and too preoccupied with clannish feuding to be of much help in the early years of her reign. In July 1565, Mary was joined in marriage to Henry Stewart, the Earl of Darnley (1545–1567), and a descendant of the Tudor dynasty, an ill-fated union that Queen Elizabeth refused to sanction. (Some accounts hold that Elizabeth secretly encouraged Darnley to wed Mary in order to ultimately depose her and exile her back to France, if not have her murdered.)

For his part, Darnley displayed a growing indifference that bordered on dislike toward his wife. In March 1566, he had Mary's private secretary and trusted adviser, David Rizzio (c. 1533–1566), murdered before her very eyes. Convinced that Darnley was going to murder her too, Mary took up with James Hepburn, the Fourth Earl of Bothwell (1534–1578), with whom she began a publicized affair.

On February 9, 1567, Darnley was strangled in his private residence outside Edinburgh, allegedly by Bothwell's agents and a clique of ambitious Scottish noblemen. Bothwell then made his advances toward the queen. He reportedly abducted Mary, most likely with her approval, on April 24, 1567, and made her his bride three weeks later. Their marriage lasted only a month, until usurping Scottish nobles captured them.

On June 15, 1567, Bothwell was exiled to Norway. Mary was imprisoned on the island of Loch Levin to await her fate. Deposed in favor of her infant son, James I (James VI of Scotland;

Mary Stuart, Queen of Scots, wrongly convicted on false conspiracy evidence and executed on February 8, 1587. *History Inc./Jay Robert Nash Collection.*

1566–1625), Mary, in a last desperate grab for power, raised an army of six thousand men. However, this poorly led force was thoroughly routed at the battle of Langside by the Earl of Moray on May 13, 1568.

Mary fled to England where she naively hoped her cousin Elizabeth might give her political sanctuary. The Protestant queen was not kindly disposed toward the Scottish usurper. Mary was imprisoned for her role (unsubstantiated as it was) in the murder of Lord Darnley and remained a captive for eighteen tortuous years. Outside the stone walls of Sheffield Castle, however, the English Catholics had not forgotten her, nor had they abandoned hope that she would one day sit on the throne of England.

There were many intrigues and wild plots to assassinate Elizabeth and restore a Catholic to power. Cognizant of the dangers posed by Mary, Elizabeth's ministers advised her to eliminate her rival, but not until the Babington Plot (1586) was made known did the English queen move against her cousin. Before that time, in 1580, Mary had been removed to another prison, Chartley Hall in Staffordshire, where she was placed under strict observation by Sir Amyas Paulet, an ardent Puritan and zealous supporter of Elizabeth I.

Anthony Babington (1561–1586), the man who provided Elizabeth with the reason to eliminate Mary, was born in rural England. He and his family were secret Catholics at a time when their religion was severely persecuted by the Protestant government of Elizabeth I. When Mary fled to England for protection in 1868, Babington was only a boy, serving as a page to Mary's jailer, and he became Mary's most ardent supporter. In 1580, after convincing Queen Elizabeth

Queen Elizabeth I of England, who connived with her ministers to eliminate her cousin, Mary, Queen of Scots, and whom she feared threatened her throne. *History Inc./Jay Robert Nash Collection.*

that he was a staunch Protestant, Babington was accepted at court and remained there for two years.

Babington nevertheless schemed against Elizabeth and, in 1582, he traveled throughout Europe, organizing Catholic Englishmen of wealth and power. He planned to overthrow Elizabeth with their help and an invading Spanish army, expecting the downtrodden Catholics in England to rise up against their oppressors and replace Elizabeth with Mary. He was reportedly supported in his resolve by Catholic missionaries in London.

Mary received letters from Babington, which he had carried from the Continent, all from English noblemen who were Catholics and promised to rescue her. He also carried letters from Mary to these Catholic conspirators. All the messages were written in code, which convinced Babington that such correspondence was safe.

In 1586, Babington entered into a conspiracy with John Ballard to assassinate Elizabeth and foment a Catholic uprising. Sir Francis Walsingham (1532–1590) and Robert Cecil (1563–1612), who advised the queen on domestic and foreign policy matters, knew of the plot from the beginning. Walsingham was the queen's cunning spymaster, adept at deceit, as was the manipulative Cecil, a hunchback who was called "my elf" or "my pygmy" by Elizabeth.

Elizabeth became aware of Mary's correspondence through Walsingham. After intercepting some of Mary's correspondence with foreign Catholics, Walsingham had his most talented cryptographers decipher the letters. He not only informed Elizabeth that Mary was plotting against her, but, at Elizabeth's clever instigation, introduced messages of his own subtle design into the correspondence. The aim was to expand the Babington plot until Mary and her conspirators were completely compromised.

In a surprise move, Walsingham ordered the arrest of John Ballard, a leading conspirator. Ballard promptly confessed to the plot, providing Walsingham with all the pieces of information

Sir Francis Walsingham, Elizabeth's intelligence chief and spymaster, who caused forged documents to be created and used in convicting Mary, Queen of Scots, of conspiracy to usurp the throne of England. *History Inc./Jay Robert Nash Collection.*

Walsingham needed to prove his case against Mary, Babington, and the others. Those details of the plot not provided by Ballard were invented by Walsingham and his cohorts.

Upon Ballard's arrest, Babington went into hiding, but he and other conspirators were hunted down and imprisoned in the Tower of London. Babington lost his nerve at the end and tried to shift the blame to Ballard. The other conspirators, except Mary, also blamed each other. Babington then begged Elizabeth for mercy. She responded by sending him to the block and the executioner's ax on September 20, 1586. The same fate befell the rest, including Mary.

Mary's treason conviction was based on a single letter in which she allegedly expressed her approval of the conspirators' plan to murder Elizabeth. The damning passage, which Walsingham insisted was in Mary's own handwriting, was undoubtedly a forgery. Walsingham probably had had the incriminating words inserted into one of Mary's letters, which he knew would bring about her execution. Elizabeth relied on Walsingham in all matters of foreign policy and state and he became, next to the queen, one of the most powerful persons in England.

Walsingham had earlier established the most extensive spy network the world had ever seen, placing secret agents throughout Europe, especially in the Catholic courts of Spain, Italy, and France, to ferret out Catholic plots against Elizabeth. To that end, he sent poet Christopher Marlowe to study at a Catholic seminary in Rheims, where plots against Elizabeth were being hatched. Marlowe's reports identified those going to England to overthrow the queen.

Marlowe later became a celebrated playwright and Walsingham's homosexual lover, but he was mysteriously murdered in a tavern brawl that may have been staged to bring about his permanent disappearance. Walsingham had a penchant for using writers as spies. William Fowler, the Scots poet, worked for him at one time or another, as did Matthew Royston. Some reports have it, without any substantial evidence, that Ben Johnson was also a Walsingham agent.

Many of the so-called plots against Elizabeth were probably invented by the insidious Walsingham. He jailed many innocent persons, accusing them of committing espionage in order to enhance his image of spy catcher with his sovereign. The Babington plot, however, was very real, to his great benefit. Walsingham chartered that plot through his most astute and assiduous spy, Anthony Munday, who lived in Rome and infiltrated the English College there, exposing many Catholic plots and identifying many anti-Elizabeth spies for his spymaster. At home, Walsingham relied on John Dee and Thomas Phelippes, both scholars of ancient ciphers and codes, to decode Queen Mary's mail, which was intercepted by another Walsingham spy, Gilbert Gifford, who posed as an ardent Catholic and had gained Mary's confidence.

Through these men, Walsingham framed a detailed and seemingly well-documented case against Mary, one that eventually spelled her doom. Mary's correspondence, according to Dee and Gifford, who was also a cryptographer of sorts, contained secret treasonable statements. One letter of Mary's in particular was used by Walsingham to prove that Mary had been part of the Babington plot, and it brought about a death warrant from Elizabeth. It was likely, however, that Walsingham himself, or Dee or Gifford acting under his direction, concocted this forgery, perhaps with Elizabeth's collusion, in order to eliminate Mary.

The technique of providing forged documents would be employed by Elizabeth's minions in many similar cases to come. Roderigo Lopus, a Portuguese Jew who had become a member of the College of Physicians, was reportedly involved in an attempt to poison Elizabeth in 1593. An incriminating letter that Lopus allegedly sent to conspirators was used to convict him, and he was hanged in Tyburn on June 7, 1594.

Elizabeth was convinced that as long as Mary was alive to lend encouragement, the threat of a Catholic uprising would always be a danger. Mary was charged with conspiring to overthrow Elizabeth on forged documents provided by Walsingham. She was removed from Chartley Hall and taken to Fotheringhay Castle and tried for complicity in the Babington Plot on October 11, 1586.

In support of charges brought against her, letters to Babington were offered as evidence. Mary protested that she had never seen them before. "A packet of letters that had been kept from me almost a whole year came into my hands about that time, but by whom sent I know not," she said.

Denied legal counsel in a framed trial, Mary's conviction was a certainty. A sentence of death was supported by both houses of Parliament as well as Elizabeth I, who tacitly approved of her rival's wrongful conviction and sentence. On February 8, 1587, Mary, Queen of Scots, was beheaded at Fotheringhay Castle believing that history would vindicate her memory. When King James I came to power, ironically through the large efforts of Robert Cecil, he constructed a lasting monument to his mother.

The Babington Plot and Mary's execution fueled the fear of Catholic insurgencies and assassinations for decades to come. Catholics in England lived perilously and, often as not, became scapegoats for any number of crimes simply because of their religion. Two Catholic men, as

Sir Edmund Berry Godfrey, a powerful London magistrate, was murdered in 1678, a slaying for which three innocent persons were convicted and executed, framed by anti-Catholic agents and officials. *History Inc./Jay Robert Nash Collection.*

well as a Protestant, went to the gallows for a sensational murder they did not commit, even after their accuser repeatedly recanted his statements.

The justice of the peace for Westminster, a borough of Greater London, fifty-six-year-old Sir Edmund Berry Godfrey, left his home on October 12, 1678. His servants became worried when he did not return that night. On October 17, 1678, Godfrey's body was found lying face down in a ditch on the south side of Greenbury Hill, now Primrose Hill. He had been strangled and stabbed to death with his own sword.

Godfrey's murder caused an uproar in London as he was enormously popular and considered one of the city's most upstanding citizens. Godfrey's reputation for diligence and courage was enhanced by his refusal to join the mass exodus from London in 1665 to escape the plague. Godfrey stayed and reminded his colleagues that they too were obliged to continue their work. When a notorious felon dared officials to enter a hospital full of plague victims to arrest him, Godfrey boldly accepted the challenge and was later knighted for his courage.

A postmortem examination revealed that, following his abduction, Godfrey had not eaten for two days. Since his shoes were clean, authorities reasoned that he had been abducted and killed elsewhere. It quickly became evident that Godfrey's murder had not been motivated by robbery, as money and jewelry were found on his body. Further, it appeared that Godfrey had been murdered indoors and his body brought to the location where it was discovered. His chest bore a deep stab wound and was covered with bruises. Rope burns were found on his neck, which was broken.

White wax, similar to that used by Roman Catholic priests in their masses, was found on his clothing. Popular opinion held that Godfrey, a staunch Protestant, had been murdered by Catholics. On December 21, 1678, a Catholic silversmith, Miles Prance, was arrested for making fraudulent statements while a suspect in a religious conspiracy. After he was tortured, Prance implicated Robert Green, an employee of the queen's chapel, Henry Berry, a porter, and Lawrence Hill, a servant, as Godfrey's murderers. The three men were arrested, but Prance withdrew his accusations prior to the trial. Several days later, Prance repeated the accusations, apparently coerced by authorities into restating them.

The three defendants were convicted and condemned. Hill and Green, who were Catholic, were hanged on February 21, 1679, at Tyburn, and Berry, a Protestant, was hanged the next week. Later, Prance admitted again that his accusations were false, and may have been made under threats from anti-Catholic forces. The fact that Prance was a habitual liar was evidenced on June 15, 1686, when he pleaded guilty to a perjury charge. He was fined and directed to stand in the pillory and to be whipped during a journey from Newgate to Tyburn.

Despite the execution of three workingmen convicted of killing Godfrey, the magistrate's murder most likely began in high places in England, and was prodded through the agitation of a virulent anti-Catholic named Titus Oates (1649–1705), who allegedly pressured Prance into framing Hill, Green, and Berry. Early in 1678, Godfrey received the formal complaint of Oates, whose allegations regarding seditious activity by Catholics came to be known as the Popish Plot. Oates claimed that well-placed people in the court of Charles II planned to overthrow the government and restore Catholicism as the state religion. Oates, unaware of Charles's conversion to Catholicism, also argued that the plotters intended to murder the king.

Godfrey, believing that the plot had been invented by Lord Shaftesbury, an influential and strongly anti-Catholic member of Parliament, did nothing about Oates's statement, and refused to swear out warrants for those he named. When Godfrey's body was discovered, however, Oates used the murder to stir the public into a frenzy, claiming that Godfrey had been murdered by Catholics to prevent him acting on Oates's deposition.

Because of Godfrey's refusal to pursue Oates's charges and also because of the manner in which

Oates later exploited Godfrey's death, it was suspected that the inventors of the Popish Plot were responsible for Godfrey's murder. Another theory states that Godfrey was murdered by Philip Lord Pembroke, whom he had convicted of manslaughter for stomping to death Nathaniel Coney on February 4, 1678.

Nevertheless, three lowborn men—Robert Green, Lawrence Hill, and Henry Berry—went to their deaths as the convicted killers of Godfrey. Oates used the executions of these two Catholics to support his wild theories about the Popish Plots. A priest of the Church of England, Oates had became rabidly anti-Catholic at an early age and decided to convince the British public that the pope wanted to seize the government and make Catholicism the official religion of England.

In order to prove that there was a popish plot, according to some reports, Oates and his friends arranged to murder Godfrey and place the blame on Catholics. Oates had earlier agitated against a schoolmaster, hoping to take his place, when he was fired. He later joined the Catholic Church and studied at a Spanish seminary, apparently to learn realistic detail to add to his denunciations of the Church.

In 1678, Oates and a fanatical friend, Israel Tonge, began to spread rumors that the pope was planning to seize the government of England, kill the king, put his Catholic brother James II on the throne, and reinstate the Catholic Church as the official Church of England. While Tonge tried to convince Charles II, Oates made a deposition to the local magistrate, Godfrey, who, upon Godrey's refusal to endorse that deposition, was murdered. When the two Catholic men who worked in Godfrey's home—Green and Hill—were accused of the murder and executed, the public hailed Oates as a national hero and paid attention to his other accusations. Perhaps as many as thirty-five people were railroaded in kangaroo trials and hanged as a result of those false accusations. As a reward, Oates was given a pension.

The terror that Oates instigated began to subside in a few months, however, and people began to question the truth of his claims. In 1685, he was convicted of perjury. Condemned to stand for three days in the pillory, he almost died the first day. His complete sentence called for imprisonment, but he was to stand in the pillory for one day in each of five different locations each year for the rest of his life. He was also to be whipped regularly. When Protestants William and Mary ascended the throne in the Glorious Revolution of 1688, they released Oates.

## Framing the Innocent in Early Scotland

During the eighteenth century, two rival Scottish clans, the Stewarts and the Campbells, clashed over land. The Hanover government seized the lands of Charles Stewart of Ardsheal after he fled to France, and Colin Campbell of Glenure, the "Red Fox," was appointed to oversee and collect rents for the region. Campbell chose James Stewart (c. 1702–1752) of the Glen to help him, but in spring 1751 Stewart was ordered off the land and all the Stewart tenants were directed to vacate their homes by May 15, 1752.

On their behalf, Stewart went to Edinburgh and secured a bill of suspension on April 18, 1752, and returned home to organize a protest. Campbell also traveled to Edinburgh and influenced Lord Haining to strike down the bill Stewart had won. On May 14, 1752, Campbell was riding home with a servant, Mackenzie, a sheriff, and his nephew, Mungo Campbell, a lawyer.

During the ride, Campbell was shot dead in the Wood of Lettermore. Mungo Campbell later altered his description of the murderer to fit Allan Breck Stewart, the foster son of James Stewart, and James Stewart was incriminated as a conspirator. A short time later in the day, James Stewart remarked when he heard the news, "Well, whoever did the deed, I am the man they will hang for it."

During the proceedings, Allan Breck Stewart was in France and the trial of James Stewart was presided over by a Campbell clan leader and decided by a jury composed of eleven Campbell members. Although there was little or no evidence to prove that Stewart was guilty of murdering Campbell, Stewart was nevertheless convicted in what was essentially a kangaroo court that framed him with false evidence. Protesting his innocence, James Stewart was hanged. According to Stewart legend, the actual murderer was Donald Stewart.

Where James Stewart was framed and executed for a crime he did not commit, a young servant woman in Glasgow was framed for a murder committed by her employer. On July 4, 1862, affluent Glasgow accountant John Fleming left town for the weekend, leaving his father, James Fleming, at home with a female servant, twenty-five-year-old Jessie McPherson. After John Fleming returned on July 7, 1862, his father claimed that McPherson had disappeared.

When John Fleming unlocked the door to the servant's basement bedroom, however, he found her half-naked, bloody body lying on her bed. An inspection of the house indicated that she had been killed in the kitchen and her body dragged to the bedroom. The murder weapon, a meat chopper, was found in the kitchen. Police observed that the type of wounds indicated that the murderer had been an old man or woman, since the murder blows had been wielded by someone with limited physical strength.

The elder Fleming, about eighty, claimed he had heard screams the night his son left town and attributed them to a visitor he assumed the girl had admitted to her room. When McPherson did not appear the next morning, he fixed his own breakfast, he said, believing she would eventually return. The old man's flimsy story, coupled with bloodstains on two of his shirts, made him the prime suspect in the murder and he was detained for questioning.

On July 9, 1862, however, a local pawnbroker reported to police that a former servant of the Flemings, Jessie McLachlan (1834–1899), had pawned silver in the shop, which had been stolen from the

Fleming home the night of the murder. Further investigation showed that bloody footprints in the dead woman's bedroom and discarded bloody clothing found at the scene of the crime belonged to McLachlan. With this new evidence, James Fleming was released and McLachlan arrested and charged with the murder.

Jessie McLachlan claimed she had gone to the Fleming residence on Friday night to drink with Jessie McPherson and the old man. When the three ran out of liquor, she was sent out to buy more. On returning, she found McPherson lying on the floor moaning. McPherson, though injured, revived enough to tell McLachlan that, while she was gone, she had quarreled with Fleming about his persistent sexual advances. The old man had then followed her to her room and hit her in the head with a heavy object. Later in the evening, Fleming went crazy again and killed McPherson. He promised not to harm McLachlan if she would help him cover up the crime and gave her the silver to pawn, claiming to need money.

Despite the fact that James Fleming had a reputation as a lecher and had once been formally sanctioned by his church for "the sin of fornication" with one of his female servants, he remained free while the statements of his former servant were dismissed. Jessie McLachlan was tried for Jessie McPherson's murder in September 1862 at Glasgow. She was found guilty and sentenced to die on October 11, 1862.

On October 3, 1862, the execution was postponed due to strong popular feeling that McLachlan had not received a fair trial. On October 13, 1862, a Crown commissioner, George Young, was appointed to review the case. When the Home Secretary received the commissioner's findings on October 24, 1862, McLachlan's sentence was commuted to penal servitude. She served fifteen years of her sentence before being released. In 1887, she joined her son in Port Huron, Michigan, where she died in 1899.

James Fleming was never prosecuted in the case, although public suspicion caused his family to relocate. Many believed that James Fleming, after killing McPherson, had intimidated McLachlan into helping him cart the body to the basement room, where she bloodied her clothes and left bloody footprints, thus incriminating herself, as Fleming planned. Further, Fleming, though he was wealthy, ordered Fleming to pawn the candlesticks on the ruse that he needed money, knowing that this action would further incriminate her in the murder. He had cleverly framed the naive, frightened servant girl for a murder that he had committed.

## Framing the Leaders of Chicago's Haymarket Riot

Chicago's Haymarket Riot of 1886 marked the bloodiest battle to date between labor and management in America, but it was really a confrontation between radical elements of the emerging labor movement and the Chicago police, a force that had been labeled by labor as a tool of big business. At the center of this storm was the unions' struggle to establish an eight-hour workday. During the mid-1880s organized labor had scored great triumphs, the first of which was the organization of workers on Jay Gould's Southwestern Railroad System in 1885.

Following this achievement, the membership of the Knights of Labor skyrocketed in one year from 100,000 to 700,000 members. In 1886, labor leaders turned their attention to establishing an eight-hour workday. Since the most radical elements of the labor movement were headquartered in Chicago, it became the hub of this activity. The labor chiefs set May 1, 1886, as the date for a nationwide strike to pressure management into granting an eight-hour workday.

However, many of the most extreme radical groups were divided on what measures to take to ensure success. The anarchists, under the direction of Johann Most, advocated violence at all costs. Most insisted that the labor movement be of "a violent revolutionary character," and claimed further that "the wage struggle alone will not lead us to our goal."

Dynamiting the property of the rich was advocated by such anarchist publications as *Alarm,* published by Albert Richard Parsons. According to *Alarm,* dynamite "will be your most powerful weapon, a weapon of the weak against the strong." Such widely publicized revolutionary tactics were not lost on the authorities, particularly in Chicago, then a hotbed of anarchist activities.

The May 1, 1886, rallies across the nation saw between 200,000 and 300,000 workers gather in peaceful demonstrations and call for an eight-hour workday. The following night, anarchist George Engel, a leather-lunged rabble-rouser, addressed a large throng at the Bohemian Hall in Chicago. He urged workers to blow up all police stations, slaughter the police, and free all the prisoners so they could join union ranks to help battle the business tycoons. On May 3, 1886, violence erupted in Chicago at the McCormick Harvester Plant, where 50,000 workers had gone on strike.

Anarchist August Spies was present and led a large number of members of the Lumber-Shovers Union in a clash with scab workers. As the picketing workers battled scab employees, police charged into their midst, attacking the strikers. Officers fired point-blank into a line of strikers, killing one worker and injuring scores more. Labor leaders instantly responded by sending out thousands of flyers in English and German calling for a mass meeting at Haymarket Square the next

Chicago strikers attacking a police van outside the McCormick Harvester Plant on May 3, 1886, one day before the Haymarket Riot took place. In this earlier riot, one striker was killed and many others wounded. *History Inc./Jay Robert Nash Collection.*

night, when, the anarchists' circulars promised, labor leaders would "denounce the latest atrocious acts of the police."

About three thousand workers began to fill up Haymarket Square on the night of May 4, 1886. There was much milling about and little organization. Mayor Carter Henry Harrison Sr. (1825–1893; as mayor, 1879–1887), who owed much of his electoral support to labor, wanted to demonstrate that he was the workingman's friend.

Chicago Mayor Carter H. Harrison, Sr. met with the strikers early on the night of May 4, 1886, assuring his police that those assembled at Haymarket Square were peaceful and he went home at 7:30 P.M.; less than three hours later mayhem and murder bloodied the streets of his city. *History Inc./Jay Robert Nash Collection.*

He told Police Captain John "Clubber" Bonfield to hold his 180 policemen in reserve, saying that he did not expect trouble. But if violence erupted, he would call off the meeting. By 7:30 P.M., a few speakers addressed the crowd in docile terms, and Mayor Harrison went home, believing nothing would happen. He felt that Chicagoans had nothing to fear from the union workers since Harrison and the Chicago city council had, in April 1886, already approved a local law assuring workers of an eight-hour workday.

On Jefferson Street, August Spies climbed onto a large wagon and shouted loudly to the jostling crowd, "Please come to order. This meeting is not called to incite any riot!" When Albert Richard Parsons next shouted, "To arms! To arms!" his meaning was ambiguous; workers did not know whether Parsons wanted them to attack the authorities or merely arm themselves. Many in the crowd were already armed with pistols, knives, and clubs. One member of the crowd held a bomb that he had recently made.

May 4, 1886, 10 P.M.: Teamster Samuel Fielden, left, arm upraised, addressing a crowd of striking laborers at Haymarket Square, Chicago, at the time a bomb exploded among police ranks, killing eight officers and wounding sixty-seven others. Many more strikers were killed and wounded that night. *History Inc./Jay Robert Nash Collection.*

At this point, a lanky man with a full white beard and long white hair mounted the wagon. He was an English-born teamster, Samuel Fielden, and he screamed at the crowd, "You have nothing more to do with the law! . . . Throttle it! Kill it! Stab it! Do everything you can to wound it!" The die-hard anarchists of the labor movement in Chicago were clustered about the wagon and thus were the most responsive to Fielden.

As Fielden continued his bombastic harangue, members of the crowd began to shout back that action should be taken immediately, that certain men of authority and business should be shot or hanged. After he concluded his speech, Fielden stepped down from the wagon. At about 10:00 P.M., a police officer shouted that the meeting was closed and everybody should return home. When the workers failed to disperse, Captain Bonfield ordered his men forward.

As Bonfield and his police began to close in on the wagon, Fielden yelled to the officers, "We are peaceable!" At that moment—some later claimed the word "peaceable" was a signal—a round, cast-iron dynamite bomb was thrown over the heads of the workers from the area of the wagon, landing di-

rectly in front of the advancing police ranks. The bomb exploded with an ear-splitting roar and cut down the police like a row of corn beneath a giant scythe. The crowd and the police were stunned and amazed. This was the first time dynamite had been used as a weapon in America and shock was visible on the faces of all present.

The police were decimated. Eight officers were fatally wounded and another sixty-seven seriously injured, almost half of the police force assembled in the area that night. The police regrouped within minutes and charged the workers, pistols blazing. The workers fled in all directions, but many were cut down by the intense fire. Long after the throng fled, guns could be heard popping down the streets. Many workers were killed and dozens were wounded; the exact toll was never determined. The leading anarchists escaped, and the bomb thrower was never identified. Police quickly arrested the chief anarchist labor leaders in the next few days and charged them with murder.

At a quick trial, beginning on July 15, 1886, presided over by Judge Joseph Easton Gary, eight anarchists—Michael Schwab, Samuel Fielden, Louis Lingg, Albert Parsons, August Spies, George Engel, Adolph Fischer, and Oscar Neebe—were found guilty of inciting to riot and murder. Early in the trial, defense attorney William Foster realized that his clients would all be rail-roaded either to the gallows or to prison, as Judge Gary denied almost every motion Foster made. In his closing argument, Foster sarcastically told a jury (perhaps too prophetically for the sake of his clients): "If these men are to be tried. . . for advocating doctrines opposed to

The type of bomb used during the Haymarket Riot; no one was ever identified as being the bomb-thrower. *History Inc./Jay Robert Nash Collection.*

Chicago Police Captain Michael J. Schaack, who witnessed the bombing and who felt that dozens of strikers should have been executed for the widespread slaughter of his officers; he later wrote a 700-page book about the bombing. *History Inc./Jay Robert Nash Collection.*

our ideas of propriety, there is no use for me to argue the case. Let the sheriff go and erect a scaffold. Let him bring eight ropes with dangling nooses at the ends. Let him pass them around the necks of these eight men, and let us stop this farce now."

Prosecuting attorney Julius Grinnell, in his closing argument, placed on the jury the obligation of crushing bloody anarchy before it destroyed a law-and-order society: "You stand between the living and the dead. You stand between law and violated law. Do your duty courageously, even if the duty is an unpleasant and severe one."

The jury delivered its verdict on August 20, 1886. All but Neebe were sentenced to death. August Spies, George Engel, Adolph Fischer, and Albert Richard Parsons were sent to the scaffold in Chicago. Louis Lingg committed suicide in his cell before the mass hangings. On November 10, one day before the executions, Governor Richard J. Oglesby (1885–1889) commuted the death sentences of Samuel Fielden and Michael Schwab, who were then given life sentences. Oscar Neebe was sentenced to fifteen years in prison. All of the condemned men, except Parsons, were German-born anarchists.

Parsons, the only American-born defendant, was born in Montgomery, Alabama, on June 20, 1848. His forefathers had fought in the American Revolution, and as a teenager, he fought in the Confederate Army during the Civil War (enlisting at age fifteen), under the command of his older brother, General W. H. Parsons, a celebrated Rebel cavalry commander. After working as a reporter in Galveston and Houston—he was a correspondent for the Houston *Daily Telegraph* in 1869—Parsons had moved to Chicago in 1873, where he became deeply involved in socialist politics and formed the first printers union.

As time went on, he adopted anarchist views. According to many historians, Parsons and the others were singled out for persecution by Melville E. Stone of the Chicago *Daily News,* who, in the words of one journalist, "railroaded" these men "to the gallows. . . because they were labor agitators and outspoken enemies of the capitalist system." As far as Parsons was concerned, Stone had a personal ax to grind in that Parsons had recruited union members from Stone's printing staff.

Before the execution date, one of the condemned men, Louis Lingg, committed suicide in his jail cell by exploding a dynamite cap in his mouth. The other four men mounted the gallows inside the Chicago jail on November 11, 1887. The gallows had been built at the north end of the jail, as high as the second tier. More than 180 people, including 50 newspaper reporters, filled makeshift pews beneath these high gallows.

At 11:50 A.M., Spies, Fischer, Engel, and Parsons were paraded along the second floor tier, accompanied by a dozen heavily armed deputies. The condemned men wore white shrouds that fell to their ankles. Beneath these shrouds, their hands were manacled behind their

November 11, 1887: Four anarchist labor leaders— August Spies, Albert Richard Parsons, Adolph Fischer and George Engel—all wearing burial shrouds, were hanged in Chicago for the bombing at Haymarket Square a year-and-a-half earlier, despite widespread efforts to have their death sentences commuted. *History Inc./Jay Robert Nash Collection.*

backs. Once on the gallows, the four were placed under waiting nooses and their feet tied together.

A guard moved behind all four men, dropping the nooses around their necks and tightening them, fixing the knots under each man's left ear. Fischer, who seemed the calmest, smiled weakly when the guard affixed the rope around his neck, saying almost as if joking, "Don't draw it so tight. I can't breathe." All was in readiness. The guards left the platform and it appeared that the prisoners would not be allowed to say any last words.

Spies suddenly boomed, "You may strangle this voice but my silence will be more terrible than speech!" Shouted Engel, "Long live anarchy!" Fischer repeated the same words in German, "Hoch die Anarchie!" Parsons then said, "Shall I be allowed to speak?" He looked at the impassive crowd before him and said, "Oh, men of America . . ." Sheriff Matson, standing to the side, said something to Parsons in a low voice. Parsons replied loudly, "Let me speak, Sheriff Matson!" He then turned to the crowd again and said, "Shall the voice of the people be heard. . ."

At that moment, the executioner pulled a lever that released the platform on which all four men stood and they shot downward together, Parson cut off in midsentence. None of the nooses had been fixed correctly, and all four men slowly strangled to death. It was later claimed that this sloppiness on the hangman's part was deliberate. The authorities wished to cause the condemned men as much pain as possible, it was claimed, in retribution for the deaths of the eight police officers. Fischer, a giant of a man, struggled violently in his death throes, writhing wildly at the end of the rope. Four doctors stood next to the dangling men, checking their pulses and heartbeats. All died within eight minutes.

The remaining three anarchists languished in jail until Governor John Peter Altgeld (1847–1902), an idealistic reformer, pardoned Fielden, Schwab, and Neebe on June 26, 1893. This act caused a tornado of criticism that swept Altgeld from office in the following election. His actions had been dic-

tated through conscience after he had reexamined the case and found that Judge Gary had committed flagrant improprieties and displayed great prejudice against the anarchists during a trial that had obviously framed the defendants.

A champion of human rights, the German-born Altgeld was the first Democratic governor of Illinois (1892–1896) since the Civil War, and he aroused tremendous opposition when he pardoned three conspirators. Altgeld set a precedent when he based the pardon on his conviction that the imprisoned men were wholly innocent; he did not offer clemency based on a presumption of guilt.

Illinois Governor John Peter Altgeld determined that the trial of the original eight defendants in the Haymarket bombing had been framed by Judge Joseph Gary, and he pardoned the three surviving defendants—Samuel Fielden, Michael Schwab and Oscar Neebe—an act that destroyed his political career. *History Inc./Jay Robert Nash Collection.*

Altgeld was elected to the superior court but remained silent about the Haymarket case. Four years later, he was elected governor of Illinois and he immediately began to study the trial records, an exhaustive investigation that revealed gross prejudice and improprieties by presiding Judge Joseph Easton Gary. He resolved to set part of the matter straight by pardoning the remaining three men—Schwab, Fielden, and Neebe—who had been languishing in prison. Altgeld, writing an 18,000-word executive order entitled *Reasons for Pardoning*, set Schwab, Fielden, and Neebe free on June 26, 1893. His argument was the defendants were either innocent or guilty, and he could not free guilty men as an act of political generosity. He determined that they were innocent.

This heroic decision cost Altgeld his political career, as he knew it would. He was attacked by the press across the nation, scathing editorials condemning him as an anarchist and traitor in Detroit,

New York, Chicago, and Philadelphia. Chicago's conservative city fathers, who had held up Judge Gary as a champion of law and order and a bastion of American ideals, were incensed that Altgeld would describe them as bigots.

Some of these leaders insisted that Altgeld's only motivation for the pardon was to seek revenge on Judge Gary for an 1889 decision where Gary had reversed a judgment in the amount of $26,000, which was to be paid to Altgeld by the city of Chicago for damage to Market Street property owned by Altgeld. The real reason for Altgeld's pardoning of the three accused men, as history has proven, was his determination to uphold justice at any cost, including his own political and professional career.

Before issuing his pardon, Altgeld had remarked to the great Chicago criminal lawyer Clarence Darrow, "If I pardon the Haymarket anarchists, from that day on I will be a dead man." Following the release of Schwab, Fielden, and Neebe, Altgeld's career all but collapsed. He ran for the governorship in 1896 and was soundly defeated by Chicago's moneyed class. Labor suffered equally at the loss of Altgeld, with workers losing their eight-hour workday and the reforms Altgeld and others had worked hard to establish.

In 1899, Altgeld ran for mayor as an independent candidate. He polled only one-sixth of the vote and then retired to private law practice. He lost most of his property and had suffered heavy business reverses in 1902, when he joined the law offices of his friend, Clarence Darrow. Following a speech on March 12, 1902, at the Joliet Theater, defending the Boers in their attempt to stave off subjugation by the British in South Africa, Altgeld suffered a cerebral hemorrhage and died six hours later in a small hotel room.

Clarence Darrow was on hand at the train station to receive the body shipped from Joliet, Illinois. The body lay in state at the Chicago Public Library for two days while tens of thousands filed past the bier. Darrow gave one of the most moving speeches of his career during the funeral services. "In the days now passed, John P. Altgeld, our loving chief, in scorn and derision was called John Pardon Altgeld by those who would destroy his power. We who stand today around his bier and mourn the brave and loving friend are glad to adopt this name." (Darrow was a celebrated agnostic, which explains the posture of his following remarks.) "If, in the infinite economy of nature, there shall be another land where crooked paths shall be made straight, where heaven's justice shall review the judgments of the earth if there shall be a great, wise, humane judge, before whom the sons of men shall come, we can hope for nothing better for ourselves than to pass into the infinite presence as the comrades and friends of John Pardon Altgeld, who opened the prison doors and set the captives free."

The Haymarket Riot and Altgeld's pardoning of three labor leaders connected to it did much to set back the cause of labor. Not until decades later would millions of workers join the labor unions. Until that time, the attitude toward unionism and workers was brutally summed up by police Captain Bonfield, who thundered following the slaughter of his officers in 1886, "The trouble is that these strikers get their women and children mixed up with them, and we can't get at them. I would like to get three thousand of them in a crowd without their women and children and I will make short work of them!"

## Framing for Revenge and Bigotry

On February 22, 1900, Nash R. Broyles, the city recorder of Atlanta, Georgia, received a letter that maligned his moral character in an obscene manner. It was signed "Grant Jackson." The next day, the police picked up a black man named Grant Jackson, whom Broyles knew. Police also arrested Jackson's friend William Broughton a day later. The case against Jackson was dropped when it was discovered that he could not write.

Suspicion fell on Broughton, who had written several missives for his friend. Inducing Broughton to write a letter to his mother asking her to send him clothes in jail, the police decided his handwriting matched the letter to Broyles.

Broyles appeared as a witness at the trial and also qualified as a handwriting expert when he said that he had some previous experience judging writing samples when he served as U.S. commissioner in Atlanta. Dissimilarities were explained away by Broyles and two other so-called experts, one who claimed to be qualified for the task because he was a traveling auditor for Standard Oil and the other because of long experience in bank work.

Broughton maintained steadfastly that he had never heard of the letter until police showed it to him. He was nevertheless tried and found guilty. Broughton was sentenced to five years in prison and fined $500 plus prosecution costs.

Not long after Broughton was sent to jail, Broyles received a letter from Charley Mitchell of Birmingham, Alabama. Mitchell claimed that Broughton was a friend of his, and that another friend, Becky Lou Johnson, had actually written the obscene letter. When Mitchell wrote to Broyles again, Broyles invited him to come to Atlanta for a conference.

Mitchell, flattered, walked into Broyles's trap and soon admitted that he had penned the letter to take revenge on Jackson after they had had a dispute over a twenty-cent loan and a scarf pin. Mitchell had not known that Jackson could not write, and though he had intended to frame Jackson, he had indirectly framed Broughton. Mitchell was found guilty and sentenced to a five-year term and a fine of $100 plus prosecution costs. Broughton was pardoned on May 18, 1900. Broyles made no apology to Broughton, but he never again claimed to be a handwriting expert.

Whereas William Broughton had been framed into prison through an obscene letter, hardworking George Edalji, of Indian blood, was the recipient of obscene statements scrawled in large letters on the walls of buildings in his local village and later in a series of letters from an anonymous person. Those statements were written by local bigots who went further in oppressing a foreigner out of bigotry by framing him into prison for crimes he never committed.

George Edalji was born in 1876 to a man of Indian descent, the Reverend Shapurji Edalji, and his wife, an Englishwoman, in the small mining village of Great Wyrley, Staffordshire, England. In 1888, obscene messages and insults about the Edaljis were scrawled on the sides of village buildings. A servant girl was arrested on libel charges but released for lack of evidence. She left the village, but the messages continued. Tradesmen in the area then began receiving orders for goods ostensibly ordered by the Edaljis, but they neither ordered the goods nor had the money to pay for them.

In 1892, the chief constable for the village, G. R. Anson, found a key to the front door of the local grammar school and accused teenager George Edalji of stealing it. The sixteen-year-old boy denied it, but Anson insisted that he was guilty, despite the fact that he had found the key on the front doorstep of the Edalji home, an unlikely place to hide the key. Moreover, Anson accused George Edalji of writing obscene letters to his own parents. The racial hate campaign on the part of the letter writer continued. Then, on August 17, 1903, the village was shocked to learn that a rash of animal maimings had occurred. A pit pony had been gutted and cattle in the area had been slaughtered with a sharp instrument.

Local police immediately accused George Edalji of the heinous crimes. Police stated that Edalji's coat was examined and animal bloodstains had been found on it. His razor bore the hairs of the horse that had been slain and horsehair on Edalji's coat also matched those of the slain horse. The accused man's boots, police insisted, were caked with mud from the area where the cattle and horse had been slain and mutilated. Edalji, by then a struggling solicitor, was arrested, convicted, and sentenced to seven years at hard labor. After serving three years, Edalji was released. In 1906, in an effort to clear his name, Edalji wrote a series of articles for a small newspaper, *The Umpire*. One of its readers was Arthur Conan Doyle, creator of Sherlock Holmes.

Writer Arthur Conan Doyle, creator of the immortal Sherlock Holmes, championed many wrongfully convicted persons; in 1906 he took up the cause of George Edalji, an Indian in England, who had been sent to prison for animal maiming and obscene writings, proving the man's innocence. *History Inc./Jay Robert Nash Collection.*

Doyle read Edalji's articles and sent for him. Upon meeting Edalji, Doyle observed that he was myopic and wore thick glasses. Doyle took the young man to an eye specialist, who told the famous author that, in his opinion, Edalji was nearly blind. Doyle concluded that Edalji could not have traversed the bushy terrain of Great Wyrley on the night of the animal maiming and killings and that the frail youth certainly could not have wielded a razor in the dark. Armed with a letter from Scotland Yard giving him authority to investigate the case, Doyle visited the constabulary at Great Wyrley where, to the consternation of the local police, he examined the so-called evidence that had convicted Edalji.

The razor supposedly used to kill and maim the animals was examined by an expert, who claimed that the hairs on it came from the elder Edalji. The hairs on George's coat were, indeed, horsehair, but Doyle learned from tight-lipped officers that this coat had been mixed with blankets used by the slain horse *before* it was introduced as evidence. The horsehair came from the blanket, not the slain horse. Moreover, the blood on the coat was from uncooked meat Edalji had been carrying about on the night of the animal slayings. Doyle inspected the area where the maiming took place, taking samples of the loam and having another expert compare it with that on Edalji's old boots, which were still held in evidence. The mud on the boots was completely dissimilar to that of the area where the animals had been maimed.

Then Doyle obtained several of the obscene letters written about and to the Edaljis. He had a top handwriting expert compare them to Edalji's writing. The expert stated that George Edalji had not written the obscene letters. Doyle then examined the background of some of Edalji's classmates and discovered one unbalanced youth who had had the habit of slashing pillows and writing obscenities on walls. The youth later became a sailor.

The anonymous letter writer of years earlier had talked about going to sea. Doyle came to believe that this youth, Royden Sharp, who had been a classmate of Edalji's, developed a deep-seated hatred for foreigners, especially Persians, and that it had been Sharp who conducted the smear campaign. He may also have been the slayer of the animals, but Doyle learned that another youth, Harry Green, had confessed to the animal slayings and maiming, but the police had suppressed his confession and arranged to have him move to South Africa. Certain members of the local constabulary obviously framed evidence against Edalji out of racial prejudice and hatred.

Doyle assembled his evidence and presented it to the Gladstone Commission of the Home Office, which studied his findings and then cleared Edalji of the animal maiming, but commission members insisted that Edalji had written several anonymous obscene letters to his own parents, despite the findings of the handwriting experts. Enraged, Doyle wrote a series of thundering articles for the London *Daily Telegraph*, which convinced the public that George Edalji was not only innocent but had been wrongly convicted on framed evidence.

The solicitor was never fully cleared, but the intense controversy surrounding his case led to the establishment of the Court of Criminal Appeal. Doyle emerged from this investigative interlude with the image of an author who possessed many of the skills demonstrated by his immortal Sherlock Holmes, especially his deductive reasoning and keen sense of observation. Like Holmes, Doyle was a champion of the underdog and this was never more in evidence than in the Oscar Slater case of 1908, a murder mystery that immersed Doyle in a prolonged campaign to vindicate a wrongly convicted man. (See Chapter I, "Fighting for Justice.")

## The Framing of Jack Johnson

John Arthur "Jack" Johnson, born in Galveston, Texas, on March 31, 1878, became heavyweight boxing champion of the world on December 26, 1908, by knocking out Canadian world champion Tommy Burns in Sydney, Australia. He proved to be a colorful, brawling, and raucous champion, whose arrogance and defiant attitude earned him the enmity of most whites. He was hated—mostly because he was black—as much as he was loved. Johnson, a cautious counterpuncher who always began his fights slowly and then increased aggressive pressure in later rounds, was a man who admittedly liked to punish his opponents, black or white. He was undoubtedly one of the great prizefighters in the history of the ring.

Many of Johnson's fights were brawling affairs that he won against clubbing fighters like Victor McLaglen in 1909. (McLaglen went on to become a great film actor, winning an Academy Award for his role in John Ford's 1935 classic movie, *The Informer*.) He beat Frank Moran, Tony Ross, Al Kaufman, and the great middleweight champion

Middleweight champion Stanley Ketchel, known as "The Michigan Assassin," left, and heavyweight champion Jack Johnson, just before their classic ring battle in 1909; Ketchell knocked down Jackson, but Jackson came back to knock out Ketchel. *History Inc./Jay Robert Nash Collection.*

The first great black heavyweight champion, John Arthur "Jack" Johnson, who won the title in 1908 when he knocked out Tommy Burns in Sydney, Australia. *History Inc./Jay Robert Nash Collection.*

Stanley Ketchel, who fought Johnson as a heavyweight, in one of the wildest matches ever fought. In 1910, he met retired American world champion James J. Jeffries, who had been urged to come out of retirement to defeat Johnson and regain the crown as a white prizefighter. Jeffries, who had retired with his title intact, had been urged to fight Johnson by many

dignitaries, including writer Jack London who wrote to Jeffries and encouraged him to "wipe that smile off his [Johnson's] face."

Jeffries made no bones about his motivation in meeting Johnson: "I am going into this fight for the sole purpose of proving that a white man is better than a Negro." Racial superiority and race hatred permeated the match, which took place on July 4, 1910, in Reno, Nevada, where an arena had been specially built for the occasion. More than 22,000 people packed the arena, almost all of them white and chanting, at the urging of the fight promoters, "Kill the nigger! Kill the nigger!" A band at ringside played over and over a racist song entitled "All Coons Look Alike to Me."

The fact that Jack Johnson had the courage to enter the ring surrounded by thousands of racists thirsting for his blood (and despite many warnings

Promoted as the "Fight of the Century," former heavyweight champion James J. Jeffries battled heavyweight champion Johnson in Reno, Nevada, July 4, 1910, a boxing match rife with racism and where Johnson's life was threatened; Johnson won the fight, prompting bigots in Chicago to frame Johnson on a morals conviction in 1913, causing him to flee the county. *History Inc./Jay Robert Nash Collection.*

to him that, if he appeared to be winning over Jeffries, he would probably be shot to death by white spectators) is a tribute to his indomitable fortitude. The battle was fairly even, despite the fact that Jeffries had not been in a ring for six years and had lost more than one hundred pounds in an effort to get into fighting weight. In the later rounds, Johnson's powerful blows began to tell on Jeffries, who was knocked down twice. After fifteen rounds, his managers refused to let him come out of his corner (or Jeffries himself refused). Johnson left Reno, without incident, with $225,000 in winnings, as well as the grudging respect of most white boxing enthusiasts, who accepted him as a true champion.

Johnson lost his crown on April 5, 1915, in Havana, Cuba, to the towering white champion, Jess Willard. Johnson fought Willard in Havana because he was a wanted fugitive in the United States. In 1912, Johnson fell in love with a white woman, Lucille Cameron. He persuaded her to become his mistress and later married her. (Johnson had married another white woman, Etta Duryea, in late 1910 or early 1911; she committed suicide in September 1911.) He took Cameron across a state line and thus violated the Mann Act, which was enacted into law by the U.S. Congress on June 25, 1910, to combat the white slavery operators who were importing thousands of girls from different states and Europe to stock their whorehouses.

The Mann Act specifically indicted anyone transporting a woman across a state line for "im-

moral purposes," which were interpreted to mean that such women would be compelled into acts of prostitution. However, the woman Johnson took with him was his lover and would later become his wife. Cameron's mother disapproved of her daughter's relationship with Johnson and contacted the Department of Justice, claiming that Johnson had abducted her daughter.

U.S. marshals arrested Johnson in Chicago on October 18, 1912, charging him with transporting Lucille Cameron across state lines for "an immoral purpose" in violation of the Mann Act. Cameron, however, refused to cooperate with officials and the charges were dropped. Cameron then married Johnson, but the prizefighter was not beyond the abiding wrath of those who hated him and wanted him publicly disgraced with a conviction and prison sentence.

Officials next produced a white woman, Belle Schreiber, who said that Johnson had provided a ticket for her so that she could take a train from Pittsburgh to Chicago, later testifying in court that Johnson had bought her that ticket for the explicit purposes of "prostitution and debauchery." Schreiber was an admitted prostitute who had made a deal with Chicago officials—her bordello operations would not be molested as long as she provided evidence that would send Jack Johnson to prison.

Johnson was brought to trial in 1913 and convicted of white slavery by an all-white jury, based solely on Schreiber's testimony. The presiding judge prevented his attorneys from challenging Schreiber's false statements. There was no evidence to prove that Johnson had ever known this woman and there was no mistaking the fact that officials and many leading businessmen working with white boxing promoters in Chicago hated Johnson simply because he was black. These influential persons not only brought about Johnson's indictment "to teach that grinning nigger a lesson," but reportedly railroaded his conviction by providing false witnesses and manipulated evidence against him.

Johnson was released on bond while his lawyers filed appeals. Then, disguising himself as a baseball player for a minor league black team, he fled Chicago for Canada and remained a fugitive for seven years. Johnson roamed the world, defending his title in other lands. After he was defeated, he went on fighting for small prize money. Finally, weary of running and hiding, Johnson returned to the United States from Mexico on July 20, 1920, and surrendered to federal marshals. He served a ten-month sentence at the U.S. penitentiary at Leavenworth, Kansas, where he organized and supervised an athletic program and devised inventions that he later patented. When he stepped out from prison on July 9, 1921, he was greeted by a host of friends and a brass band playing his favorite tunes.

Though Johnson continued fighting, his ring career was in decline. He had only two fights in 1928, losing both of them, and then boxed in exhibition matches thereafter. Johnson invested his money in some small businesses, eventually opening a nightclub in Harlem, which reportedly later became the celebrated Cotton Club (taken over in the early 1930s by white gangsters Owney Madden and Big Frenchy DeMange).

A lover of fast cars, Johnson was often stopped by police for speeding. On one such occasion, he was stopped for driving at 91 miles per hour and was told that he would have to pay a $50 fine. Johnson handed the cop a $100 bill, telling him to keep the balance since he would be driving just as fast when he returned the same way a short time later. Johnson's wild driving caused five car crashes. He died at age sixty-eight in his sixth car crash (slamming his Lincoln Zephyr into a telephone pole) in Raleigh, North Carolina, on June 10, 1946. He was buried in Chicago's Graceland Cemetery next to the remains of his first wife, Etta Duryea. Johnson was inducted into the Boxing Hall of Fame in 1954.

The flamboyant Johnson is shown in 1921, shortly after he was released from Leavenworth after serving ten months on a 1913 conviction of violating the Mann Act, a conviction that was framed by racist officials who resented a black man reigning as heavyweight champion of the world. *History Inc./Jay Robert Nash Collection.*

## The Framing of Leo Max Frank

The Leo Frank case was one of the most sensational miscarriages of justice in the history of American jurisprudence. Leo Max Frank (1884–1915) was railroaded for a murder he did not commit. He was convicted because he was a Jew. He was lynched because he was a Jew. Though evidence clearly showed his innocence then and later, this murdered man was not exonerated for decades because he was a Jew.

Born in Cuero, Texas, on April 17, 1884, Frank was an infant when his family moved to Brooklyn, New York. He was a quiet, studious youth who wore thick glasses. Frank attended Cornell University in 1906 and graduated with a degree in mechanical engineering. He found work as a draftsman with the B. F. Sturtevant Co. of Hyde Park, Massachusetts, and six months later, he returned to Brooklyn to work as a testing engineer for the National Meter Co.

Frank's uncle, Moses Frank, was the majority stockholder in the National Pencil Company, organized by New York and Atlanta businessmen for several hundred thousand dollars in 1907 (now Scripto). It was housed in a rundown four-story brick building located on Forsyth Street in Atlanta.

Moses Frank offered the job of superintendent of this new factory to his nephew, Leo, who accepted. Leo Frank spent eight months in Germany learning about pencil-making equipment, which he would have to test and retest while supervising the Atlanta company's operations. By late 1907, Frank had moved to Atlanta and had taken charge.

Lucile Selig, who married Leo Frank in 1909; she was composed throughout the trial, as was her husband, never believing he would be convicted. *History Inc./Jay Robert Nash Collection.*

In 1909, Frank met Lucile Selig, the daughter of a wealthy manufacturer of detergents and disinfectants. The couple married in 1910. Both the Frank and Selig families were distinguished, cultured members of Atlanta's Jewish community. The intellectual Frank, though nervous and shy in public, was an articulate and often eloquent writer. He was also a workaholic, slaving over company paperwork in the evenings at home and on weekends. He worked long office hours during the week and was constantly trying to improve the quality of lead in the pencils his firm sold. At twenty-nine, he was considered one of the most promising businessmen in Atlanta. To honor this brilliant young businessman, the Jewish community elected Frank president of the B'nai B'rith Association. There was never a suggestion of impropriety in anything Leo Frank did.

In spring 1913, the firm, because it had run out of brass to bind the pencils, had temporarily laid off nine teenage girls who worked on the assembly line, including thirteen-year-old Mary Phagan, who lived fourteen miles from Atlanta in Marietta. She was a week from turning fourteen. She arrived at the pencil factory a little after noon on Saturday, April 26, 1913, to collect her back pay.

Entering Frank's office, Mary asked for her pay and Frank handed her an envelope containing $1.20, one day's pay. She asked if the new shipment of brass had arrived and Frank told her that it had not. The girl left his office and Frank settled down to more paperwork at his desk. He later said that, a few minutes later, he heard a thumping sound, but he attributed this to workmen who were replacing rotten planking on the fourth floor of the building. As he worked on a financial report, Mary Phagan was being sexually attacked and strangled to death in another part of the factory.

At 1:00 P.M., Frank went to the fourth floor and found the two workmen, Harry Denham and J. Arthur White. White's wife was also present, having brought her husband his lunch. Frank said he was going home for lunch and told the workmen he would return at 3:00 P.M. He left the building, accompanied by Mrs. White. Before she stepped out of the front door, Mrs. White saw a large black man sitting on a box beneath the stairway near the front door. He was twenty-nine-year-old Jim Conley, the building janitor. Mrs. White stepped outside with Frank, and Frank locked the front door. He then went home, arriving at 1:20 P.M., according to the family maid, who served him a light lunch. He took a catnap and then went to watch a parade on Peachtree Street that was celebrating Confederate Memorial Day. At 3:00 P.M., Frank returned to the factory, went to his office, and worked until 6:00 P.M.

As Frank was leaving the factory, his night watchman, Newt Lee, was about to lock the front door after him, when John M. Gantt approached the superintendent. Frank leaped backward, expecting trouble. He had fired Gantt a week earlier because his payroll was a dollar short. Gantt explained that he only wanted to retrieve two pairs of shoes he had left in his locker. Frank permitted him to go inside the building, accompanied by watchman Lee, and get the shoes. Both men reappeared within minutes, Gantt holding his shoes. Lee locked the factory door from the inside and Gantt sauntered off, while Frank went to Jacob's Pharmacy, where he bought his wife a box of candy. He

Mary Phagan, thirteen, who was brutally assaulted and murdered in 1913, at an Atlanta, Georgia, pencil factory where she worked. *History Inc./Jay Robert Nash Collection.*

then went to the home of his in-laws, the Seligs, where he was to meet his wife and have dinner.

Frank's encounter with the heavy-drinking Gantt had unnerved him. He called the factory three times that night, until he finally got watchman Lee on the phone at 7:00 P.M. He asked Lee, "Is everything all right?" Lee assured him that there was no trouble at the factory. Undoubtedly Frank thought that Gantt might return and cause problems, which is why he called, but that call was later used against him in his murder trial. The prosecution claimed Frank called to see if the body of his victim had been discovered. (This was one of the many paradoxical positions taken by investigators, who accused Frank of bringing attention to himself in making those calls, while, according to the contention of the police, he had murdered Mary Phagan and took few pains to hide the body in a building for which he was the superintendent, a mindless murder plan that only a moron would have enacted and, as police knew, Frank was no moron.)

At 3:30 A.M., Lee, who had traversed the entire building fifteen times during his watch, went to the basement to go to the "colored toilet," a washroom reserved for black employees. (In this predominately racist era in the South, almost every business and factory had four separate washrooms for males and females, two for white employees, two for blacks.) Lee flashed his lantern to a corner, where it appeared someone had piled some rags. When he approached the pile, he froze. There was the body of Mary Phagan, her long blond hair matted with blood. A cord used to tie pencils into bundles was tied around her neck so tightly that it had penetrated the flesh. Her tongue protruded black from her mouth and her staring blue eyes had dust on them. Her clothes were torn, indicating that she had been sexually molested.

Terrified, Lee tried to reach Frank at home, but there was no answer. Then he called police, sobbing out his report. He knew that he would be the first to be suspected of violating and murdering this innocent white girl. After getting Lee's report

at Atlanta police headquarters, Sergeant L. S. Dobbs dispatched Detectives W. W. Rogers, John Black, and J. S. Starnes to the pencil factory to investigate. The three detectives went to the police car in front of the station to find newspaperman Britt Craig of the Atlanta *Constitution* sleeping off a drunk in the back seat. They took him along on the call and thus provided Craig with the most sensational story of his career.

The detectives arrived at the factory within fifteen minutes, and a quaking Newt Lee guided the officers to the basement, shining his lantern on the remains of Mary Phagan. "Great Jesus in the morning!" gasped Starnes. "It's a white woman!" Part of the head and face had been covered by a makeshift bandage torn from Mary Phagan's petticoat, as if the killer had clumsily tried to conceal the method of his murder. One of the victim's eyes had been blackened as if she had been hit during a struggle. A small gold bracelet on her left wrist had cut into her as if a powerful grasp had forced it inward on the flesh.

Newspaperman Craig knelt next to the body to retrieve two scraps of paper with notes scribbled on them. The first read, "He said he wood love me and land down play like night witch did it but that long tall black negro did buy his self." The second note read, "Mam, that negro hire doun here did this i went to make water and he push me doun that hole a long tall negro black that hoo it was long sleam tall negro i wright while play with me."

Craig looked up at Newt Lee, a tall, slim black man, who was so nervous that he almost collapsed and had to be supported by one of the detectives. "Symbolic retribution," Craig said. "Girl murdered in pencil factory identifies her killer."

The detectives directed the beams of their flashlights onto the quivering face of Newt Lee, who screamed, "It looks like he's trying to put it off on me!" Handcuffs were produced, and Newt Lee was arrested on "suspicion." He was taken to jail and locked in a cell.

At 7:00 A.M., these same detectives arrived at Frank's home to ask him if he knew a Mary Phagan.

He could not remember her name. Starnes told him that she had gone to his office to collect her pay the previous day. Frank, half-dressed, said he only knew the girls through their payroll numbers. "I would have to check."

"We'll give you a chance to check," Starnes told him. "That little girl was murdered in your factory yesterday."

Mrs. Frank asked her husband what the police wanted, calling to him as he stood with the detectives at the front door of his house. Replied Frank, "A little girl is dead." He was asked to identify the girl and Frank asked if he could finish dressing and have his breakfast.

Starnes shouted at him, "We have a damn murder on our hands and you want breakfast! We're going now! Come on!"

Frank accompanied the officers. He was easily bullied, being a nervous man who avoided confrontation. The detectives had no right, of course, to order him about. They had no warrant for his arrest. This was simply a ploy. They had already identified the body of Mary Phagan hours earlier, when one of the girls who worked with her identified the body. Moreover, they knew that Mary had gone to collect her pay from Frank, and they knew what time she had entered the factory. Yet Frank went to the Bloomfield Mortuary and told detectives, "That's the girl I paid off yesterday." He was then taken to the factory and shown the place in the basement where the girl had been found.

"Do you have any idea who did it?" Frank asked the detectives.

"We've arrested Newt Lee," he was told by Newport Lanford, chief of detectives.

"I'm going to have to tell the owners about this," Frank said, and asked if he could go. Lanford told him he could leave, but that they would talk to Frank that afternoon. Later that day, Lanford grilled Frank about his movements on Saturday, the day of the murder, asking him to repeat over and over again exactly where he was in the factory when Mary Phagan arrived, and when he left the building. On Monday, detectives brought Frank to

headquarters for more questioning, telling him, "Newt Lee has been saying things." Newt Lee had said nothing. He had repeatedly and without changing his story told how he found the body. He never implicated his employer, Frank.

Chief Lanford, who obviously disliked Frank, kept the young man waiting outside his office and then suddenly threw open his office door and stuck out his hand, flicking it contemptuously at Frank, almost shouting, "Come here!" Frank meekly obeyed and Lanford began to grill him about timecards at his factory. Just then, a voice boomed outside Lanford's office, that of attorney Luther Z. Rosser, one of the best criminal lawyers in Atlanta: "That man is my client and I am going into that room! Keep me out and I will get a writ of habeas corpus!"

Lanford threw open the door and said, "I didn't know this man had a lawyer. What's he need a lawyer for?"

Rosser ignored the bullying Lanford and turned to Frank: "You make no statement unless I am present." Police Chief John Beavers then appeared in Lanford's office and Rosser told both Beavers and Lanford that the police were acting in a ridiculous fashion, that the Phagan girl obviously fought with her attacker and that, if Frank was the killer, he would be marked with scratches and bruises. Frank then, at his attorney's request, took off his coat, tie, shirt, and undershirt. "Not a mark on him," Rosser said.

Frank volunteered, "This is the suit I wore Saturday. If I had killed her, my clothes would be covered with blood."

Lanford said that Frank could have changed his shirt and underwear and Frank said all his clothes were at home and he invited the police to inspect them. The police were fishing, of course, not sure who murdered Mary Phagan. They did go to Frank's home and inspected Frank's clothing. Other detectives smeared what appeared to be blood on one of Newt Lee's shirts found in his shack and confronted the terrified watchman with it. He sobbed that he had not worn the shirt in a year. A city chemist examined the shirt, reporting that the stain on Lee's old shirt was not blood at all, and had been applied by hand. Meanwhile, detectives sorted through all of Frank's clothes, clean and dirty, taking inventory. They found nothing stained.

Frank was by then composed and ready to go back to work. "I've got to get to the factory," he told his wife after the detectives left his house. "This whole episode has really broken down our production schedules." When Frank arrived at the factory, he discovered that all the women had been sent home. They had become hysterical when one of the factory machinists, R. P. Barrett, a self-styled detective, insisted that he had found on his lathe five tiny bloodspots and strands of blond hair. This "discovery" indicated that Mary Phagan had been murdered on the second floor, the same floor where Frank's office was located.

Then police brought Frank in for more questioning and he was asked if he wanted to talk to Newt Lee. He agreed and was brought before Lee, who was handcuffed to a chair. "Newt, you'd better tell them everything you know," Frank said to his watchman.

Lee's face was coated with tears. He sobbed, "Look at me, Mr. Frank. Handcuffed, handcuffed all the time."

Replied Frank, "Well, they've got me, too."

"Before God, I don't know anything," Lee cried.

"If you do," warned Frank, "you'd better tell them or we will both go to hell."

Meanwhile, more than 20,000 people attended the funeral of Mary Phagan. The Atlanta press had seen to that. The *Constitution,* the *Journal,* and the *Georgian* vied with each other daily in printing anything sensational about the case. They retold the story of Mary's tragic murder every day in spectacular fashion and gruesome detail. The *Georgian,* a Hearst paper, whipped its readers into a vengeance-seeking frenzy with such headlines as "Body Dragged by Cord After Terrific Fight," and "Grandfather Vows Vengeance." Its narrative passages offered horror-filled descriptions: "In the room where Mary Phagan was attacked and paid out her young life to the brutality of her assailant, across the floor where her limp form was dragged, down the stairs and down through the trap door into the dirty basement where her body was found."

Other suspects were arrested. John M. Gantt was placed in a cell until his alibis were checked and he was, in the eyes of the police, proven innocent. Gordon Bailey, the black elevator operator in the pencil factory, was also arrested and then released, terrified because of the stigma placed on him. Frank was arrested on April 29, 1913, the very day Mary Phagan was buried in Marietta. A short time later, Frank was charged with murder and scheduled for trial. Newt Lee was kept in a cell, awaiting a separate trial, one that never arrived. He would be freed the day Leo Frank was convicted.

The prosecution was headed by Hugh Mason Dorsey, an underhanded, politically ambitious solicitor general for Fulton County. He hired Pinkerton detective Harry Scott, whom Frank had previously hired to find out the facts in the case. Scott visited Frank in his jail cell and cleverly pretended that he was still working for him. He told Frank that he had to be absolutely sure that he was in his second-floor offices until 1:00 P.M. The prosecution had the statements from physicians examining the body of Mary Phagan, which fixed the time of death *before* 1:00 P.M. Frank confirmed to Scott that he did not leave the factory until 1:00 P.M. Next, the police took statements from all the factory workers, which caused janitor Jim Conley, a black, to come under police scrutiny.

On May 1, 1913, a factory employee reported Conley washing a stain off his shirt in the factory. Police arrested him minutes later, claiming that he was washing Mary Phagan's blood off his shirt. Conley denied it, saying that he was preparing to appear before police to make a statement and that he did not "want to go around all those white people in a dirty shirt." He was asked to write down a few lines on a piece of paper so police could compare his handwriting with the two notes left at the murder site. Conley laughed and told detectives, "Boss, I can't write." He added that he could not read either. Conley could not have written the notes, or at least that is what he wanted the police to believe.

Conley was nevertheless locked up until police could check his claim about being drunk in a saloon on the day of the murder. Mary Pirk, a factory employee, had already accused Conley of murdering Mary Phagan, when Pirk appeared before a grand jury on April 28, 1913. Her claim was supported by another factory worker, Mrs. E. M. Carson, who informed the grand jury that she had told Conley before his arrest that he was lucky he was not in jail; she also told him that he knew Leo Frank was innocent. Mrs. Carson stated that Conley admitted to her that Frank had nothing to do with the crime.

When Frank heard about Conley's claim that he could not write, he told police, "But I know he can write. I have received notes from him asking me to lend him money. In the drawer in my safe, you will find the card of a jeweler from whom Conley bought a watch on the installment plan and you will find Conley's signed receipt. He can write." Meanwhile, Frank occupied Cell 2 in the Atlanta jail tower. He had a bunk that hung suspended from the wall by chains, a bare table and chair, and a slop bucket. He wore the business suit he had on when arrested, but his wife made sure that he had changes of shirts and underwear. She also made sure that Frank received home-cooked meals each day. He ate in silence and refused to make any statements to Dorsey, who persisted in trying to hammer a confession from him.

Frank never spoke to his guards and only briefly to his own defense attorneys. On a rare occasion, he said to one of his attorneys, Leonard Haas, "Do you really think they can pin this crime on an innocent man?" Most of Frank's concerns seemed to be centered on the pencil factory and whether the publicity about the Phagan murder had hurt business. He avidly read the daily newspaper accounts regarding his case.

Atlanta police by then were pressured every day by the newspapers to solve the city's "crime of the century." Lanford and Beavers, with the help of the conniving Dorsey, then fabricated a ridiculous story, compelling a local whorehouse madam, Nina Formby (or Faby or Fomby, she gave many aliases), to sign a statement that Frank had been one of her most regular customers, that he craved sex insatiably, and that on the day of the murder he desperately tried to get Mrs. Formby to give him a room at her place so he could bring Mary Phagan to the house, where she could be revived. When incredulous newsmen asked Lanford why Frank would want to carry a dead girl through the streets of Atlanta in broad daylight with parades going on and the streets busy with people, Lanford lamely replied, "He didn't know the girl was dead then."

The police, particularly the detectives investigating the Phagan case, pressured and threatened many persons to testify against Frank. One of these was Minola McKnight, the black cook who worked for the Franks. She was threatened by police into making statements that impugned Frank's honesty and portrayed him as an adulterer. McKnight's husband was being kept in jail on trumped-up charges, literally as a hostage to her testimony. Yet Mrs. McKnight eventually took the stand to defend Frank, repudiating a damaging affidavit forced from her earlier by the police, knowing full well what was in store for her because she had decided to tell the truth, despite the consequences.

Behind Dorsey's actions and those of the police was Georgia's powerhouse political leader, Tom Watson (1856–1922), an old-time populist whose hatred for Jews exceeded even his intense hatred for blacks and Catholics. Watson was the "gray eminence" in this tragedy, a southern Cardinal Richelieu, pulling the legal strings from which Frank helplessly dangled. His racist newspaper, the *Jeffersonian,* constantly hammered away at Frank, libeling him regularly as a "lascivious sodomite," a pervert, and a child killer throughout his long trial.

Watson was well aware that many people had pinpointed Conley as the real killer and that Conley had told his own defense lawyer that he had attacked and killed the Phagan girl. Watson, however, was after bigger game. His attitude, and that of his many followers, was best summed up in a comment attributed to Watson: "Hell, boys, we can lynch a nigger any time in Georgia, but when do we get the chance to hang a Yankee Jew?" More than any other, this vicious anti-Semite was responsible for the legal railroading and subsequent lynching of Leo Max Frank.

Though Watson planned and schemed to crucify Frank, one person stood in the way—Jim Conley. It was obvious to Watson's police cronies that Jim Conley was becoming an embarrassment to them. They found the notes he had written to Frank in the safe at the pencil factory. Detectives went to Conley's cell and he admitted that he had lied and that he could write. "White folks," the big black man smirked, "I'm a liar." He said he had lied because he knew they would say he had written the notes. He went on to say that he had been nowhere near the factory on the day of the murder.

Detectives ordered Conley to duplicate the wording on the notes found at Mary Phagan's side. He did so and even the untrained detectives admitted that Conley's handwriting and that on the notes were almost identical. Conley knew that, too. He cleverly concluded that he would admit writing the notes but not being their author. On May 24, 1913, Conley called a detective to his cell and said, "I did write those notes. This is the truth. I wrote those notes because Mr. Frank asked me to."

Beavers and Lanford seized on this absurd story to establish evidence against Frank. They had their orders from both Dorsey and the political bigwigs representing Tom Watson. They coaxed Conley into signing a confession, careful to point out to Conley the exact time Frank reportedly ordered Conley to write the notes, at about ten minutes before 1:00 P.M. on the day of the murder, knowing that Frank had witnesses who would testify that he had left the factory by that time. Conley said that Frank ordered him to write the notes and also to carry Mary Phagan's body from the second floor to the basement, that Frank intended to pin the killing on Newt Lee, the "tall lean black man."

A portion of the affidavit of the prosecutor's chief witness, James Conley, which was the first affidavit by a black man in the South that brought a white man to trial on a capital charge; Conley was the actual killer of Mary Phagan and the prosecution knew it. *History Inc./Jay Robert Nash Collection.*

(This had been Conley's intent all along, hoping that Lee would be blamed for the rape and murder. But when that crude plan became obvious to police and himself, Conley adopted the plan of blaming Frank, by saying that Frank had ordered him to write those notes, still blaming Lee.)

Conley said that Frank had threatened to pin the murder on him if he did not do as he was told. Of course, Conley, the real killer, had written the notes, not at Frank's command, but for the exact reason he claimed Frank had told him to the write the notes: Conley murdered the girl and then wrote the notes to pin the crime on Newt Lee, never believing for a minute, at that time, that he could get away with blaming a white man for his crime. To Watson, Dorsey, and most of the police in Atlanta involved in the case, however, Frank was not a white man—he was a detested Jew. This the shifty, calculating Conley also came to understand when listening to his interrogators. Their rabid racism was much more intensely directed at "that moneyed Jew" than any black man.

In jail, Conley saw a turnkey and a detective working on the Frank case talking together. He called them to his cell. A black woman scrubbing the floor nearby heard the following conversation among the three:

"What's a kike, mister?" Conley asked the detective.

"A kike? That's the worst kind of human being— a Jew," replied the detective.

Leo Max Frank, the reticent and mild-mannered manager of the pencil factory, who was charged with the Phagan murder because he was Jewish. *History Inc./Jay Robert Nash Collection.*

"Worse even than a bad black man?" Conley said.

"Worse than anybody and worse than anything," added the jailer.

Even before confirming in his mind that it was Frank that officials had set out to railroad, Conley suspected that he *could* blame a white man for his crime and get away with it in Georgia, as long as the white man was a Jew. Before taking the stand to testify against his employer, Conley, through remarks made to him by prosecutors and law enforcement officers, knew that they knew he had killed Mary Phagan. He also knew that the most powerful men in Atlanta had no intention of convicting him for that crime. They were going to convict Leo Frank. They were going to execute him. The cunning Conley also realized that they could get away with it too, while appearing to be racially tolerant in not conveniently and traditionally pinpointing a black man, Conley, as the actual killer.

Conley's confidence and self-assurance grew when he realized that officials did not want him, even though they knew he was guilty. They wanted the Jew. Everything had been thrown into that dirty basement with Mary Phagan's body, all ethics and scruples and any sense of justice in Georgia. Knowing all this, that the state was conspiring with him to protect his guilt and convict an innocent man, Jim Conley grew stronger at each hearing, appearing smug and arrogant. He might spend some time behind bars, but he would live. Leo Max Frank would die for Conley's heinous crime.

Dorsey would use Conley as the state's leading witness against Frank. The solicitor general seized on Conley's claim, without exposing his knowl-

A proclamation of the Leo Frank Protest League, an organization that realized Frank was being railroaded for murder he had not committed. *History Inc./Jay Robert Nash Collection.*

edge that Conley had committed the crime, which Dorsey learned from witnesses and from Conley's own lawyer. He relentlessly built a fake case against Frank, suborning witnesses and fabricating evidence with the collusion of the police.

Behind Dorsey and the police was the despicable and powerful Tom Watson, directing events from his mansion at Hickory Hill, sending out hundreds of rural anti-Semites who marched around the Atlanta courthouse during Frank's trial, and, on occasion, into the courthouse, shouting racial slurs and obscenities, demanding during the trial that Frank be hanged and that legal proceedings against "this damned pervert" were just a waste of time and money. They terrorized the jurors with signals such as running their fingers across their throats as if they were razors, indicating that they would kill any juror who did not vote guilty.

The nation's press covered the entire farce, and for the most part, condemned the state's tactics. Tens of thousands rallied to Frank's support. A large defense fund was gathered from Jews and non-Jews alike, and the B'nai B'rith came into its own, chiefly with the help of donors to Frank's defense fund, people who were shocked at the medieval treatment Frank was receiving. In Georgia, however, the racists and bigots, at Watson's direction, had taken control. During Frank's long trial, Dorsey and his assistants ignored proper procedures, brushed aside established facts and the trial record itself. It ter-

Leo Frank at his 1913 murder trial. His wife Lucile sits behind him. *History Inc./Jay Robert Nash Collection.*

rorized witnesses by creating a nightmare image of Frank as a murderous sex fiend.

Frank's attorneys were hampered and hamstrung at every turn. The trial judge, Leonard Strickland Roan, agreed with the high-handed Dorsey on every point of law. Roan tolerated outrageous behavior by Dorsey. Frank sat passively and did not react to Dorsey's prejudicial accusations. He refused to be provoked and was dubbed by the press "The Silent Man of the Tower."

Frank told his wife and a few friends that he would measure his statements, lest he bring down the wrath of the anti-Semites on his fellow Jews in Atlanta. In so doing, he limited, even injured, his own defense. He was a man who believed that he was living in a civilized society, where justice would triumph. He clung to this idea and was eventually murdered for it.

Throughout the trial, Rosser and Haas attempted to conduct their own investigation of the murder, hiring the foremost detective in America, William J. Burns, head of the Burns Detective Agency. Despite his considerable efforts, Burns met with little success. He and his assistants were denied information. The police prevented them from interviewing key witnesses and charged them with criminal activities. Burns, while checking some court records, was almost lynched by a group of Tom Watson's rabid supporters. One of these Watson advocates was an Atlanta hardware salesman, William J. Simmons, who sat through Frank's trial hooting for conviction.

Simmons later went to see W. D. Griffith's *The Birth of a Nation,* gripping the armrests of his seat in excitement as he witnessed scenes depicting the long dormant Ku Klux Klan in heroic action. The film, coupled with Simmons's obsessive hate for Frank, caused him to lead what he called the Knights of Mary Phagan up Stone Mountain one night in 1915 and torch a huge cross that had been erected there, reestablishing the dreaded Ku Klux Klan.

Frank's most damaging enemy was the killer himself, Conley, who appeared as a witness against Frank and testified in court that Frank had molested and killed the Phagan girl. With some clever acting that convinced many in the court that he was nothing more than an uneducated black man, Conley appeared nervous and claimed that he carried the girl's body to the basement and wrote the notes under Frank's orders, saying that he had acted out of fear that Frank, a white man, would arrange to have him charged with the murder, unless he did as he was told.

Despite a spirited defense, Frank's lawyers were unable to shake Conley from this position, which was, of course, a lie Conley used as a shield against admitting his own guilt in the case. Further, Conley brazenly told unsupported lies about Frank bringing whores to his office to have sex, and that he, Conley, had seen Frank having sex with women in his office and other areas of the factory, and that Frank had tried to seduce many of the factory girls in his employ. These tales were undoubtedly carried to Conley by detectives who had earlier attempted to blacken Frank's reputation through the paid statements of the bordello madam, Nina Formby.

Private detective William J. Burns, later head of the Bureau of Investigation, who attempted to find evidence that would vindicate Frank, but who was rebuffed and threatened by officials in Atlanta, Georgia. *History Inc./Jay Robert Nash Collection.*

Frank's mother, Mrs. Rudolph Rhea Frank, who was apprehensive during her son's murder trial, knowing well the deep-seated anti-Semitism in Atlanta. *History Inc./Jay Robert Nash Collection.*

Frank's defense counsel was later attacked for mishandling his case. Reuben Arnold, who headed the defense, along with Rosser and Haas, was joined by four more attorneys hired by the Franks and Seligs. They and the defendant were all well dressed, and the Frank and Selig family members sitting nearby wore fashionable, expensive attire. The witnesses against Frank were dressed in simple clothes. Conley, who was the star witness against Frank, wore clothes that were almost rags, attire dictated by the shrewd Dorsey. Before the trial, Conley was provided with a fine suit to wear in court, but this was taken away from him and a shabby suit with frayed lapels and cuffs replaced it. "I'm gonna look bad in court," Conley said, when donning the old suit. "No," one of the prosecutors told him. "You'll look like the poor, simple Negro you are. It's all those rich Yids wearing New York suits, who will look bad."

Conley's manufactured down-home image was contradicted by the image of Leo Frank. His natural reticence was interpreted as a sign of guilt, although he took the stand in his own defense, offering a brilliant statement in the fourth week of his trial. Frank told the jury, in part, "I know nothing about the death of little Mary Phagan. I had no part in causing her death nor do I know how she came to her death after she took her money and left my office. I never even saw Conley in the factory or anywhere else on April 26, 1913. . . . The statement of Conley is a tissue of lies from first to last. . . . Conley's statement as to his coming up and helping me to dispose of the body, or that I had anything to do with her or with him that day,

is a monstrous lie. The story as to women coming into the factory with me for immoral purposes is a base lie and the few occasions that he [Conley] claims to have seen me in indecent positions with women is a lie so vile that I have no language with which to fitly denounce it. . . .

"Gentlemen, some newspaper men have called me 'The Silent Man in the Tower,' and I have kept my silence and my counsel advisedly, until the proper time and place. The time is now; the place is here, and I have told you the truth, the whole truth." With that, Frank left the witness stand. He had impressed the court and moved the jury with his sincere, direct statements, but he was battling for a life, his own, which had already been claimed by Tom Watson and his racist fanatics. He was found guilty and sentenced to death.

Before Judge Roan sentenced Frank, he was visited by William Smith, the court-appointed lawyer for Jim Conley. Smith told Judge Roan that his client had admitted to him not once but many times that he had raped and murdered Mary Phagan. Roan as much as told Smith that such statements were "inadmissible" in the Frank case since they violated client-attorney confidences. He went on to sentence Frank to death. Frank's lawyers filed an appeal with the U.S. Supreme Court, which denied the appeal, with Justices Charles Evans Hughes and Oliver Wendell Holmes writing strong dissenting opinions. Stated Holmes in part, "Mob law does not become due process of law by securing the assent of a terrorized jury. We are not speaking of mere disorder, or mere irregularities in procedure, but of a case, where the processes of justice are actually subverted." Judge Roan had considerable reservations about his own actions. Before his death a short time later, he wrote a letter to Georgia Governor John M. Slaton (1911–1912; 1913–1915), an honest and courageous man. Judge Roan expressed his reservations about Frank's guilt to Governor Slaton.

The governor had by then come to his own conclusion that Frank was innocent, and that he had been railroaded by Dorsey, the police, and Tom

Watson. Reporters, too, had gone to Slaton with their doubts about Frank's guilt, one of these being a young newspaperman working for the Atlanta *Journal,* Harold Ross, later founder of the *New Yorker.* Ross provided the governor his research on the case, stating, "Conley's own lawyer told me that his client admitted killing that girl. What are you going to do about it?"

John Slaton would do more than any other governor had ever done on behalf of a wrongly convicted person. He conducted his own investigation through trusted state police investigators, and he learned that Frank was innocent and Jim Conley was the real murderer. Only twenty days before he was to leave office in 1915, Slaton commuted Frank's death sentence to life imprisonment, believing that the true facts of the case would later emerge in a calmer atmosphere, and Frank would be exonerated and freed, and that the true culprit, Conley, would be properly punished. The commutation was a heroic move on Slaton's part, as he well knew the political repercussions and that his decision would end his career in Georgia. He also knew that Tom Watson and his brutish hordes would react violently.

On the day of the commutation, Atlanta police feared violence and urged all Jews in the city to close their shops and stay indoors, or even leave Atlanta. Thousands of Jews left Atlanta by car and train. Hundreds of Jewish children were boarded on trains by their parents, while scores of Watson's sneering supporters shouted threats at little boys and girls. Police stood by and did nothing. A drunken Watson brute wielding a club and leading others staggered in the direction of a group of Jewish children about to board the train.

A towering policeman suddenly barred his way, bringing his nightstick down on the thug's head and knocking him unconscious to the pavement. Only two other officers, out of a contingent of thirty white officers (there were no serving black police officers in the city) at the station that day, joined this officer, who shouted to the crowd, "Anyone who attempts to harm these children will get what this

man got!" He pointed his club at the unconscious thug. The crowd of toughs retreated. The three officers kept watch until the train pulled out of the station. The next day, all three were suspended.

The reaction to Slaton's commutation of Frank was like a time bomb exploding. Thousands of Watson's followers and the even more rabid members of Simmons's Knights of Mary Phagan (later changed to the Knights of the Ku Klux Klan), heavily armed, stormed onto the grounds of the governor's mansion, some of them barging into the mansion and screaming, "Where is that Jew-loving son of a bitch?" Slaton had fled the mansion with his family and gone into hiding.

A regiment of horse-mounted national guardsmen wielding swords went into action, and for two days

Georgia Governor John M. Slaton, who conducted his own investigation into the Phagan killing and learned that James Conley, not Frank, was the guilty party; he bravely commuted Frank's death sentence to life imprisonment, an act that wrecked his political career. *History Inc./Jay Robert Nash Collection.*

the troops battled bloodthirsty mobs bent on killing Governor Slaton or any Jew they could find on the streets of Atlanta. There were even cries for the life of Slaton's wife, "a notorious liberal." Slaton escaped the state with his family and remained in exile for years. He had been warned by Watson and his minions, as well as several state officials, not to return to Georgia where he "would be killed." John Slaton foresaw his fate when he commuted Frank's death sentence, but this brave man accepted the consequences rather than "let an innocent man be murdered."

Tom Watson then began to lobby for mob action and the lynching of Leo Frank, who had been confined in Milledgeville Prison Farm following

Populist leader Tom Watson, the most powerful politician in Georgia, a virulent anti-Semite, who decreed Frank's wrongful conviction and urged his murder by a lynch mob. *History Inc./Jay Robert Nash Collection.*

Slaton's last-minute reprieve. There, a berserk inmate, William Green, crept up on Frank's bunk in an open prison barracks and slit his throat as he slept. Frank survived, thanks to the quick action of another prisoner, a doctor, who was able to close the wound and stop the bleeding. Twenty-five stitches were used to close up the ugly wound.

Frank's survival incensed Tom Watson. "He's going to slip away," he told friends. Watson thought Frank might prove his innocence while he lived, so he urged his readers to take the law into their own hands. Green was one of them. When Green failed, Watson called on the Knights of Mary Phagan, led by the racist Simmons, to avenge the death of the murdered girl. It was also Watson who stated in his newspaper that he saw "the invisible power" of these "knights" bringing justice in the Frank case, thus providing Simmons with another title, which Simmons quickly reshaped into "The Invisible Empire of the Ku Klux Klan."

Watson then published an article that, in any other state, would have caused his arrest for inciting to riot and murder. In this article, Watson declared, "The next Jew who does what Frank did is going to get exactly what we give to Negro rapists." He had pronounced Leo Frank's death sentence. Simmons and his Knights of Mary Phagan responded quickly to this order, spreading their "invisible power" over Georgia on the night of August 16, 1915. They cut the telephone wires to the Milledgeville Prison Farm and then packed eight cars full of "knights" and drove to the institution from Marietta.

The first to see the headlights of the cars approaching the prison was trustee J. W. Turner. He rushed up to a guard on duty and shouted, "They are coming for Frank! Get him out the back way!" The guard said nothing, turning away. Turner and another trustee. Bruce, then went to the warden's office, but guards there ignored their warning about invaders coming for Frank and ordered them to return to their barracks. The lynch mob, about twenty-five men, broke through the front gates of the prison farm without opposition from guards. Only three of them wore masks. They split into four parties, as if practicing a drill they had earlier rehearsed, and began their systematic search for Frank.

One group stormed into the home of Warden Smith and snapped handcuffs on him. A man poked a rifle into Smith's face and shouted, "We have come for Leo Frank. You will find him tomorrow on Mary Phagan's grave. You can come with us, if you want."

"Damned if I go any place with you," Smith shouted back.

Smith was held prisoner as the rest of the prison guards were rounded up and handcuffed. None resisted the invaders. Another group ran to a barracks and raced to the second floor. They searched the bunks of sleeping men and found Frank, a large bandage still covering the vicious knife wound to his neck. The invaders had been informed of this bandage and used it to identify the man they were seeking. Frank was grabbed by his hair, arms, and legs and yanked from his bed. As he moaned in pain, the invaders handcuffed him and then hauled him out of the barracks to a waiting car.

After the invaders departed with Frank, Warden Smith broke free. He had difficulty contacting police in Augusta, since the phone wires had been cut. It took him a half hour to convince state officials and police that Frank had not been rescued by a group of his Jewish friends but dragged from the prison by a lynch mob headed for Marietta. By the time state police began to pursue the mob, the abductors had an hour's head start. Sheriffs from several towns in a fifty-mile radius put together car posses, the first time autos were used for such purpose in Georgia, and the lawmen began a desperate search for Frank and his kidnappers. William Frey, an ex-sheriff, was driving down Roswell Road near Marietta at about 7:00 A.M. when the caravan of "knights" passed him. He later stated that he thought he saw Frank sitting between two men in the backseat of one of the cars. Frey kept driving in the opposite direction.

A short time later, the caravan came to a stop on Roswell Road next to a giant oak tree outside of Marietta. About thirty men jumped out of the cars, some wearing masks, but most not. Surveyors working along a nearby railroad track that dawn began to walk toward the group, but men in the lynch mob waved them off with pistols. A farmer named Chandler was driving a team of horses in a nearby field and witnessed Frank being pulled from one of the cars. He left his team and, while hiding behind thick bushes, witnessed the mob lynching of Leo Frank.

Frank was placed beneath the oak tree and a heavy rope was put about his neck. He wore only a nightshirt. His hands were handcuffed and someone knelt to place handcuffs about his feet. Chandler, standing close behind some bushes in terror, heard the following conversation: "Mr. Frank, we are going to do what the law said to do—hang you by the neck until you are dead. Do you want to say anything before you die?" (This was said by the ringleader, who was identified as a former Marietta police officer.)

Frank stood coolly staring back at his self-appointed executioners. He said nothing for some moments and then he replied, "No."

Then the ringleader asked a question that belied the stated purpose of the lynch mob: "We want to know if you are guilty or innocent of the murder of Mary Phagan."

Frank refused to dignify the question of a lynch mob leader. Instead, he calmly held up his handcuffed hands, elevating a finger bearing his wedding ring. He said in a firm voice, "I think more of my wife and my mother than I do of my own life. Would you return my wedding ring?"

A member of the lynch mob slipped the ring from Frank's finger. The ring was later returned to Mrs. Frank through a reporter, who said he was handed the ring by a man on an Atlanta street before running off. Members of the lynch mob then placed Frank on a small, battered table, tied the end of the rope to a branch of the oak tree, and kicked the table out from beneath him. Frank jerked downward, his body convulsing as he strangled to death. The mob stood silent, watching him die. When his body was at last lifeless, swaying gently from the rope, the murderers walked casually back to their cars and drove away.

Chandler ran into Marietta, where a ceremony honoring the slain Mary Phagan was beginning in the town square. "They got him! They got him!" Chandler shouted to the crowd. First hundreds, then thousands, followed Chandler pell-mell on foot, in carriages, in cars, to the site of the lynching. There the throngs stood to view Frank's swaying body. An amateur photographer took photos showing scores of gaping men, women, and children standing beneath the hanging corpse. These photos were displayed for fifteen years

Lynch-mob members and spectators proudly pose with the swinging corpse of Leo Max Frank, who was dragged from a prison farm and summarily hanged near Marietta on the night of August 16–17, 1915, an event that gave rebirth to the dormant Ku Klux Klan in Georgia. Copies of this grisly photo sold for decades on postcards in Georgia candy shops and drugstores. *History Inc./Jay Robert Nash Collection.*

in the windows of small Georgia shops and on post-cards sold for a nickel in rural drugstores.

The rage felt by citizens across the land over the lynching was universally expressed by the press, even in Georgia, but it solved nothing. The members of the lynch mob were never arrested, although most of them were well-known. On hearing the news, former governor Slaton wept openly. Thomas E. Watson, who had released the forces of malice, ignorance, and prejudice, gave a gloating interview to the press on the front porch of his mansion at Hickory Hill, in which he commended Frank's killers for meting out "Georgia justice."

Then Watson stepped inside his mansion to meet with Hugh Dorsey, telling his obedient prosecutor, "Hugh, my boy, for what you did for the great state of Georgia, I'm going to send you to the United States Congress. 'Congressman Dorsey'—how do you like the sound of that?" Dorsey loved the sound of it. He served two terms as a member of Congress from Georgia. Then he returned to Boss Watson and told him he wanted to be a U.S. senator. Watson turned him down, saying that he, Tom Watson, intended to run for that office. He did, beating Dorsey badly and winning the post. Dorsey, meanwhile, was elected governor of the state (1917–1921).

Watson became a U.S. senator from Georgia in 1920. When he died of bronchial asthma on September 26, 1922, none of his fellow senators sent condolences. His written legacy was published in 1915, a rabid anti-Semitic diatribe against Frank and Jews in general. Thomas E. Watson was the epitome of southern white racism, a fanatical bigot to the core and a hideous embarrassment to the human race.

Many years later, troubled with an uneasy conscience, Hugh Dorsey insisted from his deathbed, "Frank was guilty! Guilty! I have the files to prove it!" No such files existed. William Simmons, who had worked so well for Dorsey and Watson, went on to establish his "Invisible Empire" of the Ku Klux Klan, bringing hundreds of thousands to its hooded ranks, a secretive organization of hate and prejudice that would dominate southern politics for the next five decades. Following World War I, John Slaton returned to Georgia, where he devoted his life to his private law practice. He died in 1955. Two years later, the Georgia legislature honored this heroic man by establishing the John Marshall Slaton Memorial, referring to him as "the incomparable Georgian." Green, the man who had slit Frank's throat, was pardoned ten years later by Governor Eugene Talmadge (1933–1937; 1941–1943) and died a few years later, a sick old man.

The real murderer of Mary Phagan, Jim Conley, was convicted of being an accessory after the fact to the killing and was sent to a chain gang to serve a year and day. In 1919, Conley was convicted of instigating a riot that caused the death of one man and he was sent to prison for fourteen years. After his release, Conley continued to live in Atlanta, where he died in 1962, at age seventy-six. He had confessed to killing Mary Phagan to his lawyer, William Smith, to his common-law wife at the time of the murder, Annie Maude Carter, and later to a fellow convict. Those confessions were pointed out to authorities in Georgia at the time of Frank's trial, but no one acted on them.

The site of Frank's lynching became a KKK shrine. Each year on the anniversary of Frank's lynching, members of the hooded empire met at night with blazing crosses to celebrate their grotesque triumph. The old oak tree was finally cut down and the site now lies buried beneath four lanes of Interstate Highway 75. Frank himself summed up the incredible miscarriage of justice involving a man who came to be identified as America's Alfred Dreyfus. Before being sentenced to death, Leo Frank stood before Judge Roan and said in a calm voice, "The issues at the bar were lost. The poison of unspeakable things took their place."

In the spring of 1982, Alonzo Mann, who had been a fourteen–year-old black office boy working in the pencil factory, made a statement in which he insisted that, on the day of Mary Phagan's murder, he saw Jim Conley carrying the unconscious body of Mary Phagan from the second floor to the basement of the factory. Frank did not accompany Conley and was not even in the building. Conley told him at the time, "If you ever mention this, I'll kill you!" Mann returned home and told his mother, who cautioned him not to say anything about Conley. Mann, at age eighty-five, came forward, saying that he had tried to tell his story many times and as early as 1953, when Conley was still alive, but southern newsmen dismissed his story.

Mann persisted, taking a lie detector test, which he passed, and signed detailed affidavits. "I know deep down in my heart what I saw," said Mann in 1983, "and that Frank did not do this." Because of Mann's statements, the Georgia pardon board weighed the new evidence and considered giving Frank a posthumous pardon. "I pray to God that they will give Leo M. Frank a pardon," Mann said at the time. "It would be the Christian thing to do. He did not commit that crime." On December 22, 1983, the Georgia's board of pardons denied the posthumous pardon.

Board chairman Mobley Howell stated, "After an exhaustive review and many hours of deliberation, it is impossible to decide conclusively the guilt or innocence of Leo M. Frank. There are too many inconsistencies in the accounts of what happened." Jewish organizations, however, continued to petition the board, which in 1986 reversed itself and granted Frank an equivocating pardon, based on the state's "failure to protect the person of Leo Frank and thereby preserve his opportunity for continued legal appeal on his conviction, and in recognition of the state's failure to bring his killer to justice, and as an effort to heal old wounds." Seventy-three years after his legal persecution and lynching, Leo Max Frank had received grudging justice in Georgia.

## Framing the Innocent in the 1920s

Just as the KKK lynch mob murdered Leo Max Frank in Georgia in 1915, members of the Ku Klux Klan framed and lynched hundreds of victims in the 1920s throughout the American South and Southwest for crimes they did not commit. Unable to lynch its prey in the northern state of Illinois in 1923, the local KKK (there were more than 50,000 dues-paying KKK members in Chicago alone at that time) simply framed the victim into a prison sentence.

Jim Montgomery, born in 1893, was convicted on rape charges in Waukegan, Illinois, in 1923 after local members of the Ku Klux Klan framed him for the crime. In response to Montgomery's attempt to organize black protests against segregation and degradation in the suburban Chicago community, the KKK bribed sixty-two-year-old Mamie Snow into charging that Montgomery had raped her. In a trial that lasted twelve minutes, Montgomery, a black man, was found guilty by an all-white jury and sentenced to life imprisonment.

It was not until 1944, after Montgomery had served twenty-one years in jail, that attorney Louis Kutner listened to Montgomery's pleas to investigate his case. Kutner discovered that no medical evidence confirming rape had been introduced into the trial, and, after searching through hospital records, he found that a physician had determined that Snow was a virgin. Finally, Kutner and his associates broke into the KKK offices in Waukegan and uncovered evidence of the plot to frame Montgomery.

On June 27, 1947, a writ of habeas corpus was heard at which the doctor who had examined Snow admitted that the KKK had forced him not to testify, and that the prosecutor had been involved in the cover-up. On August 10, 1947, after twenty-four years of incarceration, Montgomery was released. He was handed the usual $10 granted to ex-convicts upon release. Though the law allowed Montgomery to sue for compensation, his case for unjust incarceration was never heard.

Where the KKK framed Jim Montgomery in Illinois in 1923, a French police inspector in the same year framed an innocent man into prison to advance

Guillaume Seznec, the owner of a sawmill in Morlaix, France, was framed for a 1923 murder by an ambitious police inspector, Pierre Bony; Seznec was released in 1947, but not exonerated until 1954, before being shot as a Nazi collaborator, admitted he had manufactured false evidence against him. *History Inc./Jay Robert Nash Collection.*

his corrupt career, which culminated before a firing squad after he had been convicted of being a war criminal and Nazi collaborator. This case began with Guillaume Seznec (c. 1875–1954), who owned a sawmill in Morlaix, France. Seznec had agreed to aid his friend, Pierre Quemeneur, in selling Cadillacs to the Soviet Union. Quemeneur needed money and Seznec had considerable cash. The two decided that Seznec would provide Quemeneur with $4,000 in gold for his home near Brest. On May 23, 1923, the sale was made with a waiter at a Brest hotel observing the transaction.

The next day, both men left in a Cadillac for Paris. Along the way, the car continually broke down. According to Seznec, Quemeneur took the train to Paris, while he returned to his sawmill in the rundown car. Quemeneur still had not returned home by June 4, 1923, and on June 12, 1923, his sister reported him as missing to the police. The next day, she received a telegram, apparently signed by Quemeneur, in which he stated he would soon be home. He never returned, nor was his body ever found, but young Sûreté inspector Pierre Bony was sure that Quemeneur's companion had killed the missing man.

Achille Vidal was in charge of the investigation, but it was Bony who charged Seznec with the murder after all three had journeyed to Houdan, where Quemeneur was last reported seen, and it was Bony who vowed to prove Seznec was the murderer. Immediately after arriving in Le Havre, Bony discovered Quemeneur's luggage, which contained the missing man's contract for the sale of his home.

The inspector claimed that the contract had been typed after Quemeneur had been killed, and that it, like the telegram, had been forged by Seznec. He asserted that he would find the typewriter and prove his theory. By then, Seznec's property had been searched three times without yielding a shred of evidence to incriminate him. Shortly after Bony arrived at the sawmill, he emerged carrying the typewriter, posing for the press to photograph him holding the typewriter on July 6, 1923. Many wondered why the machine, allegedly purchased on June 12, 1923, could look new and not be covered with dust after sitting in a sawmill for more than two weeks.

Not unexpectedly, the size of the typewriter matched the size of a box taken into the sawmill by a police officer before Bony arrived. The officer left the building without the box. The only evidence against Seznec was that provided by Bony (or suppressed by him). Seznec's lawyer, Maitre Bienvenue, had remembered that his earlier statement concerning the whereabouts of his client the day he allegedly sent the telegram to Quemeneur's sister was incorrect.

Bienvenue had spent the day with Seznec and would provide the accused with an alibi. Bony would not let the truth stand in the way of his career, and Bienvenue was not heard from until well after the trial. As for the one man who clearly identified Quemeneur two days after he was murdered, Bony denounced him in court as unreliable. Le Her, a tram conductor, had spoken with Quemeneur on May 26, 1923, but his testimony, along with only three others, counted for little against more than one hundred witnesses for the prosecution, all provided by Bony.

The trial, which was held in the Palais de Justice at Quimper, opened on October 24, 1924, at the Finistre Assizes. Defending Seznec was Maitre Moro-Giafferi, who had earlier defended the notorious serial killer, Henri Desire Landru, known as the "French Bluebeard." Before this prestigious advocate could give his closing speech, he left the court to fill his appointment as a minister in the new government in Paris. Junior counsel Marcel

Kahn closed the case for the defense, but Bony's "evidence" overwhelmed the arguments of the younger attorney and Seznec was found guilty.

Seznec was sentenced to penal servitude for life and sent to French Guiana. After his trial, further evidence that Bony had suppressed was made known. A magistrate at Plouviers, M. Herve, had received a signed statement from five sailors that, on the night of May 27, 1923, a man had been shot on the Brest estate owned by Quemeneur. This information was purposely misplaced by Bony, and following a new trial for Seznec, police harassment caused Herve to lose the case. So exhausted and harassed was the attorney that Herve entered a psychiatric facility for treatment.

In July 1947, Seznec was released from prison after the penal colony at French Guiana was closed. He lived with his daughter, Jeanne Seznec, who had since married Le Her, the man who testified about having met Quemeneur. Le Her often beat his wife, and one day Jeanne shot him. She was found not guilty of manslaughter, the very verdict she had fought so hard to obtain for her father without success. The truth was not made known until Bony died.

Bony, it was shown, had collaborated with the Nazis during World War II. For that he was convicted and condemned. Only seconds before his execution, he informed a priest that he had framed Seznec. He was shot to death at the Mont Valrian fortress. A former colleague of Bony's, Leon Sacre, then corroborated the dying words of the corrupt inspector. As for the typewriter, Bony had purchased that himself, and even typed the forged contract in the shop where he bought it. Jeanne Seznec, who had always declared her father's innocence, announced to the world that Le Her was the true killer of Quemeneur.

Jim Montgomery had been framed for racial hatred in Illinois, and Guillaume Seznec had been framed in France to advance the career of an ambitious French police officer. In the case of Floyd Flood, a policeman in St. Louis, Missouri, framed him simply because Flood's girlfriend had refused to date the officer. Arrested in St. Louis without a charge against him, Floyd Flood soon found himself on trial for a bank robbery in Freeburg, Illinois, on August 23, 1924.

Flood, however, had not visited Illinois in more than a year. The First National Bank in Freeburg was held up by six men; two remained in the getaway car, while four entered the bank with revolvers and forced bank president Russell E. Hamill to retrieve money from the vault while cashier Susie Wolf and bookkeepers Minnie Holst and Emma Wolf looked on. More than $10,000 was stolen, but some of the money was new and easily traceable.

Police arrested James Breene and Ralph Southard in Jonesboro, Arkansas, and Flood was taken into custody in St. Louis. Flood's arresting officer stated the man was picked up for being a "bad egg," though Flood had no criminal history. Flood countered that he was arrested because his girlfriend had refused to date the arresting officer, and the girlfriend supported that claim. The police dressed Flood up like one of the bank robbers and, while the Wolfs were watching, ordered him to say "stick 'em up." After that, he was taken to Illinois to stand trial.

At St. Clair County circuit court before Judge George A. Crow, Breene, Southard, and Flood were tried on December 2–5, 1924. Prosecutor Hilmar C. Lindauer had no problem convicting Breene and Southard, but the bank president and several witnesses, who had identified the first two defendants, could not positively identify Flood. In his defense, attorney Joseph B. McGlynn clearly proved that Flood had indeed been in St. Louis at the time of the robbery, with testimony from several witnesses to support that contention. The jury, however, ignored the evidence supporting Flood and found him guilty along with Breene and Southard. All three were sentenced to ten years to life in prison on December 18, 1924.

A glimmer of hope came for Flood when Breene and Southard confessed to the crime and stated that they had never met Flood before their trial. With the arrest in Ohio of two more bank robbers who named the real members of the gang, McGlynn felt his chances for freeing Flood were much better. Along with Breene and Southard, the bandits were Benjamin Ingram, John Lyons, Brice McConnell, and Arthur Richardson.

Flood, however, remained in prison for more than a year because the Bankers Association opposed his pardon while members of the gang were at large. The last two robbers were finally caught and convicted, and Flood was pardoned and released on January 21, 1926. Flood considered suing the St. Louis police officer who had framed him, but attorney McGlynn advised against it: "Be thankful you're out of prison. Going after that crooked cop would be like chasing the devil. You'll only wind up in hell."

## The Scottsboro Boys and Other Victims of the 1930s

The Scottsboro case (1931–1937) was a classic civil rights battle that exposed southern prejudice in grim definition, involving the alleged rape of two white women, Ruby Bates and Victoria Price, by nine black youths who were framed and sent to prison for crimes they did not commit. On the night of March 25, 1931, the nine, who ranged in age from thirteen to twenty-one, boarded a freight train bound from Tennessee to Huntsville, Alabama, to look for work.

Price and Bates were also on the train illegally with seven male companions, all white. According to Price, the nine blacks picked a fight with the white men as the train rumbled through Jackson County, Alabama. The blacks threw the white youths off the train and then gang-raped Bates and Price. One of the men who was thrown from the railroad car reported the incident to the sheriff, who promptly organized a posse that intercepted the train at the next stop, Paint Rock, Alabama.

The nine blacks—Roy Wright, thirteen; his brother Andy, seventeen; Clarence Norris, nineteen; Olin Montgomery, seventeen; Ozzie Powell, sixteen; Haywood Patterson, seventeen; Charles Weems, twenty-one; Willie Robertson, seventeen; and Eugene Williams, thirteen—were taken off the train and jailed in Scottsboro, where they were charged with rape.

A local physician stated that neither of the two women showed any signs of rape, nor did they seem greatly upset. These facts mattered little to the hot-headed residents who organized a lynch party after news of the arrests leaked out. The deputy sheriffs moved the prisoners to separate jails, where they were kept in solitary confinement while awaiting trial. They were returned under heavy guard to Scottsboro a week later.

The case captured the attention of the national media when deliberations began shortly afterward. A total of 102 national guardsmen were positioned outside the courtroom to prevent the thousands of southerners from ransacking the building and lynching the prisoners. Judge A. J. Hawkins had difficulty finding a lawyer willing to handle the emotionally charged case. Eight of the nine were found guilty, solely on the testimony of Bates and Price, which was questionable, and sentenced to die. Only because of Roy Wright's young age was the jury inclined to show mercy in his case.

News of the verdict sparked waves of protest in the more liberal-minded North. A May Day parade in Harlem attracted 300,000 blacks and

The nine black youths in custody by National Guardsmen at Scottsboro, Alabama, March 1931, all charged with raping two white women. *History Inc./Jay Robert Nash Collection.*

The Scottsboro boys under heavy guard are led into court. *History Inc./Jay Robert Nash Collection.*

whites. The NAACP and various left-wing groups like the International Labor Defense League (ILD) rallied to the cause, popularizing the slogan "The Scottsboro Boys Shall Not Die." The Alabama Supreme Court eventually overturned the conviction of Eugene Williams because he was under the legal age but upheld the convictions of the seven others.

On November 7, 1932, by a 7–2 margin, the U.S. Supreme Court struck down the ruling of the Alabama Supreme Court on the grounds that the selection of defense lawyers had been insufficient. A new trial was ordered and a change of venue granted, not to Birmingham as the defense had hoped but to Decatur in rural Morgan County. Deliberations began on March 27, 1933. This time the defendants were represented by famed Manhattan criminal attorney Samuel S. Leibowitz, whose fees were being paid by the ILD.

Famed criminal lawyer Samuel Leibowitz is shown with the Scottsboro nine; he took over the defense of the Scottsboro Boys at a new trial in 1933, after the Alabama Supreme Court reversed the original convictions on the grounds that the defendants had not been properly represented by legal counsel. *History Inc./Jay Robert Nash Collection.*

This struck a note of discord among members of the National Association for the Advancement of Colored People (NAACP), who charged that the group was using the case to promote domestic communism. The NAACP withdrew its support. Meanwhile, Leibowitz promised the black community in Harlem that he would "march those Scottsboro boys up Lenox Avenue!"

Price appeared on the witness stand and repeated essentially the same story she had told earlier. However, Ruby Bates shocked and outraged the white community by recanting her earlier testimony. She said the story had been concocted to avoid possible arrest for vagrancy. Members of the Ku Klux Klan, who had been present through much of the proceedings, talked of lynching the defendants and their attorney.

The sentiment was echoed in more subtle terms by state's attorney general Thomas E. Knight Jr., who demanded a guilty verdict. He believed, as did many others, that Bates had been bought off by northern interests. "Show them," he said, "that Alabama justice cannot be bought and sold with Jew money from New York." Judge James E. Horton, a veteran of the bench for nearly twenty-five years, was unconvinced. Two months after the trial began, Judge Horton ruled that the available evidence did not support a guilty verdict because Price's testimony was not only "uncorroborated, but it also bears. . . indications of improbability and is contradicted by other evidence."

However, the affair was far from over. In December 1932, Haywood Patterson was tried for a third time in the courtroom of Judge William Washington Callahan, who promised to "debunk" the Scottsboro case. (Horton had been

Victoria Price, testifying against the Scottsboro Boys in court, 1931. *History Inc./Jay Robert Nash Collection.*

Judge James Edward Horton leans over the bench to hear a physician state at the 1933 trial of the Scottsboro Boys that there was no physical evidence to prove that the two young women had been raped; further, Ruby Bates recanted her accusations and Judge Horton threw out the case. The youths were then tried separately, four released in 1937 and four sent to prison. *History Inc./Jay Robert Nash Collection.*

pressured into withdrawing from the case.) Ruby Bates was not present for the hearing. She was in a New York hospital at the time, but one of the white men who had ridden on the train that night, Orville Gilley, corroborated Price's story.

Patterson was easily convicted. The appeals process reached the U.S. Supreme Court a second time. While reviewing the case of Clarence Norris, the justices on the high court concurred that the convictions should be overturned on the grounds that blacks had been "systematically excluded" from jury duty in the Deep South. An angry Governor Bibb Graves (1927–1931; 1935–1939) expressed his displeasure. "This decision means that we must put the names of Negroes in jury boxes in every county!"

Year five of the Scottsboro affair began on January 20, 1936, when Patterson went to trial a fourth time. After a three-day trial, he was found guilty and sentenced to

Ruby Bates, who, like Price, identified all of the nine black youths as her attackers at the 1931 trial in Scottsboro, Alabama; all were convicted and eight of the nine were sentenced to death. *History Inc./Jay Robert Nash Collection.*

seventy-five years in prison. "I'd rather die!" Patterson said. In July of that year Thomas Edmund Knight Jr., who now served as lieutenant governor of Alabama, met with Leibowitz at his offices in Manhattan. They proposed a tradeoff.

In return for the freedom of four of the defendants, the defense had to agree to plead guilty to four of the other cases, with Ozzie Powell to be tried separately. In 1937, Clarence Norris was again convicted and sentenced to die. Andy Wright and Charles Weems were likewise found guilty, and the men received prison terms of ninety-nine and seventy-five years. Powell entered a guilty plea on a stabbing charge and was sentenced to twenty-years. The state in turn dropped the rape charges against Roy Wright, Williams, Powell, Robertson, and Olin Montgomery.

World War II temporarily diverted attention from the Scottsboro case. On January 8, 1944, Wright and Clarence Norris were released on probation. Weems was later freed, and Powell's release followed in 1946. Haywood Patterson escaped from prison on July 17, 1948. He settled in the North but wound up in jail on a murder charge. He died in prison in 1952.

The last surviving member of the Scottsboro defendants, Clarence "Willie" Norris, sixty-four, was pardoned by Alabama governor George C. Wallace (1963–1967; 1971–1979; 1983–1987) on October 25, 1976, after spending the previous six years trying to clear his name. Two days after Norris received his pardon, Ruby L. Bates Schut died of natural causes in Yakima, Washington. At the time of her death, she was involved in litigation with the National Broadcasting Corporation, charging NBC with libel, slander, and breach of promise for

Clarence Norris leaves Kilby Prison in Montgomery, Alabama, in 1946. *History Inc./Jay Robert Nash Collection.*

Andrew Wright, last of the
Scottsboro Boys to go free, 1950.
History Inc./Jay Robert Nash
Collection.

their telecast of a docudrama titled *Judge Horton and the Scottsboro Boys.* She was sixty-three. Throughout the ordeal, there was strong evidence of double-dealing and fraud in the prosecution's case. In 1950, Haywood Patterson wrote his memoir, *Scottsboro Boy.* Leibowitz went on to become a respected judge, standing firmly on the side of law and order.

Where the Scottsboro boys were railroaded because of their race, a New Jersey resident was framed because of his out-of-state status. When gas station attendant Lonnie Russell was gunned down in Asheville, North Carolina, by bandits on September 27, 1932, Gus Langley was nearly four hundred miles away. The fact that Langley was a native of New Jersey and was driving an automobile bearing license plates from his home state proved to be the only shred of evidence linking him with the murder of Russell. Langley and his partner, Wilcey Johnson, were taken from Wilmington to Asheville and indicted for murder.

Charges against Johnson were eventually dismissed, but Langley went to trial on December 20, 1932. An insurance agent present at the gas station the day before the murder testified to having observed a car with a New Jersey license plate in the vicinity and had talked to its driver. A cell mate of Langley's stated that he had heard him say that he killed Russell but had enough witnesses in Wilmington to testify to the fact that he had not been in Asheville on September 27, 1932.

There were no witnesses, however, to say where Langley had been on September 26, the day he drove back to Wilmington. The perjured testimony of the cell mate who was released from custody after appearing on the witness stand, coupled with the lack of an alibi for September 26, resulted in Langley's framed conviction of first-degree murder. He was sentenced to die in the electric chair.

Twenty-five minutes before Langley was to be strapped into the chair, his defense lawyer secured a temporary stay of execution, after it was discovered that the presiding judge in the trial had failed to mention the critical words "first-degree" murder when he pronounced sentence. Langley's plight stimulated an outpouring of letters from Wilmington residents, who claimed he was being railroaded by North Carolina and its court officers, who were prejudiced against northerners.

There were six more stays of execution and a decision by the governor to commute his sentence to life imprisonment before he was conditionally released to New Jersey authorities. On August 5, 1936, law enforcement authorities from Asheville finally admitted that Langley was innocent. Langley received a formal pardon from Governor John C. B. Ehringhaus (1933–1937).

Politics instead of facts brought about the framed conviction of the governor of North Dakota, who had been elected as a Republican against the great Democratic tide that took Franklin Delano Roosevelt into the White House in 1932. William Langer (1886–1959) earned a reputation as an independent-minded politician for his vigorous prosecution of the North Dakota railroads that failed to pay rent on leased sites in 1914. These actions earned Langer plaudits from the state's Nonpartisan League, which was gaining control of the Republican Party in the state.

With the help of the largely agrarian Nonpartisan League, Langer became the only Republican ever to win the governor's chair in 1932, the same year Franklin Roosevelt was swept into office as president on a Democratic landslide. Langer ran into trouble when the state learned that the new governor was soliciting cash contributions from state employees in the form of a 5 percent levy on wages. He argued that such actions were necessary to sustain the Republican Party in the state.

In his dual capacity as governor and state relief administrator, Langer, it was claimed by his political opponents, had forced CWA employees to subscribe to the weekly *Leader,* a political organ published by his staff. In June 1934, the U.S. charged Langer with "conspiracy to obstruct the orderly operation of an Act of Congress." The trial was held in Bismarck, and Langer and four political associates were found guilty. Langer was sentenced to eighteen months in prison and assessed a $10,000 fine.

After being forcibly removed from office at the order of the North Dakota Supreme Court on July 17, 1934, Langer filed an appeal claiming that the judge in the case was prejudicial and had railroaded his wrongful conviction. In a stunning reversal, the U.S. court of appeals handed down a ruling in May 1935 that the state had failed to prove "overt acts" of political corruption against the governor. Armed with what he considered to be a mandate, Langer ran for governor and won a second term of office in 1937. Three years later, he was elected to the U.S. Senate.

## Framing by the Long Arm of Law Enforcement

Earl Patrick Charles, born in 1953, was framed for two murders he did not commit in Georgia. Without a shred of evidence against him and possessing a rock-solid alibi, Charles was nevertheless found guilty of murdering two men he had never seen. On October 3, 1974, the seventy-six-year-old owner of the Savannah Furniture Company, Max Rosenstein, and his forty-two-year-old son, Fred Rosenstein, were shot in the head and killed with bullets from a .22-caliber pistol.

The two assailants also struck seventy-year-old Myra Rosenstein, Max's wife, in the head with a tape dispenser before making off with $1,007 in cash. While this crime was taking place, Charles and his friend, Michael Williams, were working at a Kwik Pep Service Station in Tampa, Florida,

about three hundred miles from Savannah, Charles's hometown and site of the killings.

Fingerprints at the crime scene did not match those on file for Charles, who had been jailed as a youth for burglary and shoplifting. Nor did either of the eyewitnesses, Myra Rosenstein and Bessie Corcelius, identify Charles as the killer. However, a detective, F. W. Wade, eager to be credited for a "collar" (arrest), managed to have Charles arrested in Florida. After a police lineup that was reportedly rigged, Charles was extradited to Georgia and tried on two counts of murder, armed robbery, and aggravated assault.

On May 15, 1975, a jury found Charles guilty of all charges except aggravated assault, despite testimony by Charles's employer, Robert Zachary, that Charles was working during the shooting. For some reason, the jury chose to believe Wade's claim that Zachary had earlier said that the defendant was not working. The jury sentenced Charles to death by electrocution, to which Judge George Oliver agreed, despite misgivings.

The persistence of Flossie Mae Charles, Charles's mother, helped free her son. At her urging, Lemon Harvey, a Tampa police officer who monitored Zachary's employees at the employer's request, recalled that Zachary's statement was true, since Charles had not yet been fired by the service station manager. Charles's lawyer, John Sullivan, managed to obtain a new trial, but the retrial never took place. On July 5, 1978, district attorney Andrew Ryan decided not to prosecute the case again, and Charles was freed.

The wrong done to Charles resulted in a lawsuit against Wade for violating the defendant's rights. An April 1980 trial found the detective innocent of the charges, but a federal judge reversed this decision in 1983 and awarded the wrongly convicted man $417,000. Charles dropped the suit when it became clear that Wade could not pay the damages, and the city of Savannah agreed to pay him $75,000 for the thirty-seven months he had wrongly spent on death row.

Where a Georgia police officer had framed Charles, more than one officer in Philadelphia rigged the evidence that brought about the wrongful conviction and imprisonment of Neil Ferber for a gangland slaying he did not commit. Philadelphia police had long been known to employ heavy-handed tactics in coercing suspects, particularly under the reign of "Supercop" Frank Rizzo (Chapter V, "Conviction by Coercion"), and Ferber's case was no exception. Officers added a new wrinkle to their underhanded techniques—railroading.

Two witnesses, a husband and wife, said they saw Ferber shoot to death Chelsais "Steve" Bouras and his dinner companion, Jeanette Curro, while they were eating in the Meletis Restaurant in South Philadelphia on the evening of May 27, 1981. Bouras was an underworld figure and police immediately believed that the slayings were gangland related.

Two killers had entered the restaurant wearing ski masks, which one took off after fleeing the restaurant. That person was identified by the couple as Ferber. The woman identified Ferber from a police photo array, but when she saw him later in a police lineup, she said she could not make a positive identification. Her husband nevertheless did make a positive identification, telling police the he was sure that Ferber was one of the two gunmen.

Ferber was brought to trial with no evidence other than the initial identification and the added testimony of a jailhouse informer, Gerald Jordan, who claimed that Ferber had confessed the murders to him while they were held together at the Philadelphia detention center. Prosecutors offered no other evidence to bring about Ferber's conviction and his death sentence in 1982.

After two years, while Ferber waited for execution on death row, some upstanding members of the Philadelphia district attorney's office and some homicide detectives of the Philadelphia police department expressed doubt about Ferber's conviction. The court was informed that Jordan had failed a lie detector test before making his testimony, a fact not disclosed to Ferber's defense attorneys. Then Jordan recanted his testimony.

On his last day in office, January 3, 1986, district attorney Edward G. Rendell went to common pleas Judge Robert A. Latrone, requesting that he grant Ferber a new trial based on Jordan's recantation. Latrone vacated Ferber's conviction and granted him a new trial. The new district attorney, Ronald D. Castille, refused to retry Ferber and he was released. Ferber almost immediately filed a wrongful conviction and imprisonment suit against the city of Philadelphia, telling the court that he had experienced a nervous breakdown and developed bleeding ulcers because of that wrongful conviction, demanding $4.5 million in damages, which a jury awarded him in 1993.

That award was undoubtedly influenced by a series of articles published in the Philadelphia *Inquirer*, which claimed that Ferber had been railroaded into prison on framed evidence supplied by Daniel Rosenstein, a detective with the Philadelphia police Homicide Division, and police artist Dominic Frontino, who had drawn a sketch of Ferber. Judge John Herron in the Court of Common Pleas overturned the award but stated his belief that Ferber had indeed been framed by corrupt officers.

Judge Herron depicted Ferber's wrongful conviction as a "Kafkaesque nightmare of the sort, which we normally characterize as being representative of the so-called justice system of a totalitarian state." Further, he stated that Philadelphia police officers had "withheld important information, tampered with identification evidence, and misled judicial officers." The city of Philadelphia did not wait for Ferber to file a federal suit, granting him $1.9 million in compensation for his wrongful conviction. Former district attorney Rendell described that award as "fair and appropriate and a fraction of what a jury would have awarded."

The Ferber case added one more stain to the Philadelphia police department, which, like all other metropolitan police departments in the

United States, had its share of corrupt officers willing to frame suspects. In the railroading case of Steven Manning, however, the framers were not local police officers but, according to the Chicago *Tribune*, members of the vaunted Federal Bureau of Investigation.

On June 3, 1990, James Pellegrino, who operated a trucking business in the Chicago area, was found dead, his body floating in the Des Plaines River. His head was wrapped in a plastic bag and a towel, and his hands and ankles were bound by duct tape. He had been killed by a single bullet fired into the back of his head.

When informed of her husband's death, Joyce Pellegrino told police that her husband had left their home on May 14, 1990, telling her that Steven Manning, a former Chicago police officer and a partner in Pellegrino's business, had "ripped him off for a lot of money," and that he intended to get it back. He also told her, Mrs. Pellegrino insisted to police, that if he turned up dead, she should contact the FBI and tell agents that Manning had killed him.

The Federal Bureau of Investigation already knew about Steven Manning, since he had long been working with those Chicago agents as an undercover operative and secret informer. Manning, however, had disliked the job and told agents that he would no longer work for the bureau.

Manning later filed a civil harassment suit against the FBI and claimed that when he tried to quit his role as an undercover informant, agents attempted to compel him to continue. The FBI took vengeance on Steven Manning for that lawsuit, a vendetta so severe that he would be framed for kidnapping and murder and sent to prison and the death house.

Following the discovery of Pellegrino's body, Manning was arrested and charged with the murder, and locked up in the Cook County Jail to await his trial. His cell mate at that time was a notorious felon named Thomas Dye who had ten prior convictions and a recent burglary conviction that brought him a fourteen-year sentence. It is uncertain whether or not Dye directly contacted prosecutors or was contacted by FBI agents first—both stories are on record—in offering to provide evidence that would convict Manning.

The state's attorney's office knew Dye was an infamous liar and jailhouse snitch, but assistant state's attorneys William G. Gamboney and Patrick J. Quinn offered Dye a chance to reduce his burglary sentence by getting that evidence. He was wired by Illinois officers or by FBI agents, the latter being the most reliable version of events, according to Chicago *Tribune* reports. Dye was instructed to engage Manning in conversations and get his confession on tape.

The conversations Dye secretly recorded with Manning involve several criminal activities, but much of this involved Manning's experience with criminals as a police officer. Later, however, Manning's comments were twisted to mean that he himself had conducted those activities. Nowhere in those conversations with Dye, however, did Manning ever incriminate himself in Pellegrino's murder.

When Dye turned over the tapes to officials, he claimed that he had obtained Manning's confession. But when officials listened to the tapes, they heard nothing audible from Manning that provided such a confession. Dye then explained that Manning had made the confession during a two-second inaudible portion of one of the tapes. He said that Manning had grabbed him by the arm, bending him backward and putting a finger to his head as if it was a gun, saying, "This is how I killed Pellegrino."

In Manning's 1993 trial, Dye testified against him and the tapes he had secretly recorded were entered into evidence with the approval of circuit court Judge Edward M. Fiala Jr., a decision that proved to be a serious judicial error in that there was no mention of Pellegrino on the tapes and the conversation between Dye and Manning made no reference to the case then being tried. The tapes indicated at worst that Manning had a sordid past involving criminals, which could be said of many police officers dealing day to day with such male-factors, but the tapes did not necessarily define Manning as a criminal.

Joyce Pellegrino also testified at the trial, repeating comments she said her husband had made to her. The jury convicted Manning on this next-to-nothing evidence, and after he waived his right to a jury sentencing, the judge sentenced him to death. Following that sentencing, Dye's fourteen-year-sentence was reduced to six years. A short time later, he was paroled, never serving most of those six years, and was placed in the federal witness protection program, a long-established FBI sanction.

Manning's attorneys appealed, and the Illinois Supreme Court ruled on April 16, 1998, that Judge Fiala's admission of the Dye tapes constituted a judicial error since the tapes made no mention of the crime for which Manning was being tried and for which he was convicted, while otherwise offering prejudicial references to other crimes the jury might construe to be associated with Manning. The court also ruled that the statements made by Joyce Pellegrino regarding her husband's comments to her, which were allowed at Manning's trial, should have been excluded as hearsay.

Manning remained on death row for another twenty-one months until prosecutors dismissed the murder charges against him in 2000, following investigative reports on the Pellegrino case by the Chicago *Tribune*. In November 1999, reporters related that Manning's 1993 conviction had been deeply flawed by the prosecutor's use of unreliable and untrustworthy jailhouse snitches such as Dye. Though momentarily set free, Manning was nevertheless rearrested and sent to Missouri to begin serving a hundred-year sentence for a previous kidnapping conviction.

Steven Manning, however, fought the kidnapping conviction in Missouri through appeals and on January 24, 2005, won a stunning victory in a federal court in Chicago—a jury exonerated him of both the Pellegrino murder and the Missouri kidnapping. Manning, the jury stated, had been framed for both of these crimes by two FBI agents, apparently bringing about malicious prosecutions and convictions against Manning for his refusal to continue to work with the bureau as an informer and for filing a harassment suit against the FBI after agents had attempted to compel him to continue in that role.

A six-week trial presided over by U.S. district Judge Matthew Kennelly ended after jurors deliberated for six and a half days, finding FBI special agents Robert Buchan and Gary Miller liable for Manning's wrongful 1993 conviction of murdering James Pellegrino. Buchan was also found liable for framing Manning on the Missouri kidnapping case. The jury found that both FBI agents had maliciously and intentionally inflicted emotional distress on Manning. Both the Illinois and Missouri convictions were overturned and prosecutors dropped all charges in both cases.

Manning was awarded $6.6 million in damages and was finally free after serving fourteen years in prison for two crimes he did not commit. On hearing the verdict, Steven Manning said, "It's a long, long way from death row to complete vindication." His attorney, Jon Loevy, had more to say: "It's a very unusual thing that the jury would find FBI agents framed somebody not just once but twice for capital crimes."

Spokesmen for the FBI responded to this decision by stating that they "respect the jury system, the work of this jury and its verdict." They then stated that they were still confident that "the agents who were sued did not engage in any misconduct in this matter." How the FBI could reconcile a jury verdict it "respected" and one that found its own agents guilty of misconduct with its own statements that those agents were innocent of such misconduct is beyond reasonable speculation, resting with the uneasy (if not frightening) conclusion that the FBI, in this instance, had reasons of which reason does not know.

Beyond its terse response to this devastating verdict, which indicted the ethics and conduct of the Federal Bureau of Investigation, U.S. attorney

Patrick J. Fitzgerald and Richard K. Ruminski, acting special agent in charge of the bureau's Chicago office, stated that they would have no further comment. FBI spokeswoman Cynthia Yates stated that both Buchan and Miller remained with the bureau.

## Railroading Through Racial Prejudice

In Groveland, Florida, in 1949, four young black men were arrested for raping a seventeen-year-old white divorcée. Their framed convictions of three of these young men sent them to prison and they would not be cleared until 1971, more than twenty years later. Once the rape was reported, Lake County officials and Groveland volunteers organized a posse to track down Charles Greenlee, Walter Lee Irvin, Samuel Shepherd, and Ernest Thomas. Greenlee, Irwin, and Shepherd were taken into custody while the search continued for Thomas. Once they cornered Thomas, an angry mob shot him to death. The other three prisoners were arraigned and charged with rape.

Tensions in Groveland flared as the trial date neared. Mobs of angry whites rioted. They firebombed black homes and beat black residents. The National Guard eventually restored order to the community, where tensions continued to run high against the defendants. Defense attorneys felt that selecting an impartial jury would be difficult, and they requested a change of venue. The request was denied and the three defendants were tried in Lake County, amid rampant prejudice.

Greenlee, Irvin, and Shepherd were found guilty by the all-white jury on circumstantial evidence. The prosecution's entire case was based on the fact that investigators had found a tire print at the scene of the crime that police said matched those made by Irvin's car. It was believed, but never substantiated, that once Irvin and the others were arrested, Lake County Sheriff Willis McCall ordered a deputy to drive Irvin's automobile to the scene so that those "planted" tire tracks could then

be used as evidence. Charles Greenlee, sixteen, was sentenced to life in prison, while Irvin and Shepherd were to be executed. Defense attorneys appealed the death sentences to the state supreme court, which reaffirmed the decisions.

Refusing to give up, the defense appealed to the U.S. Supreme Court, which ordered a new trial in April 1951. Irvin and Shepherd were taken from prison for questioning. While transporting the two convicted men back to Lake County, Sheriff McCall shot Shepherd dead and critically wounded Irvin, maintaining that the men had attempted to escape and he used his weapon in self-defense. Irvin survived and told a coroner's jury that McCall was unprovoked and had intended to kill both men to stop them from testifying. The all-white coroner's jury sided with the sheriff and ruled that Shepherd's death was "justifiable." A grand jury investigation, however, brought about another trial for Irvin.

A change of venue was approved for the second trial and the proceedings were held in nearby Ocala, Florida. With a team of defense lawyers that included Thurgood Marshall, Irvin refused a plea bargain for a life sentence and was again convicted and sentenced to death. He was returned to Raiford State Penitentiary, and the St. Petersburg *Times* began its investigation of his case.

In 1953, following the election of LeRoy Collins as Florida's governor, the *Times* revealed its findings and reported that "great doubt" existed in regard to whether Irvin and the others were actually guilty. Sparked by the newspaper reports, letters and petitions representing thousands of citizens demanding that Governor T. LeRoy Collins (1955–1961) pardon Irvin began arriving in Tallahassee.

In 1955, Collins commuted Irvin's death sentence to life in prison, and Lake County circuit court Judge Truman G. Futch organized a grand jury to investigate Collins's activities. After the grand jury ruled Collins was within his legal rights to commute the sentence, Futch said the governor had shown himself "an innocent victim of the

Communists by helping to save a Negro in the Groveland rape case from the electric chair."

In 1961, after serving eleven years of his life sentence, Charles Greenlee, then twenty-seven, was paroled. Walter Lee Irvin's freedom finally came when he was paroled in 1969. Irvin died of a heart attack the following year when he returned to Groveland for the first time since his sentence to attend the funeral of a friend. In 1971, all four men were finally cleared of any wrongdoing in the Groveland incident.

Race prejudice in Groveland, Florida, had brought about the wrongful convictions of three black youths, but racism that translated into false convictions was not confined to the American South, where blacks over the decades were routinely railroaded into prisons and chain gangs. It was evidenced in Nova Scotia, Canada, when a Mi'kmaq Indian, Donald Marshall Jr., was framed for a murder he did not commit. Marshall was sent to prison for life and remained behind bars for eleven years, until the truth of his railroading was exposed.

Marshall, a seventeen-year-old Indian, lived on the Membertou Reserve outside of Sydney, Nova Scotia. His father, Donald Marshall Sr., was the grand chief of the Mi'kmaq Nation. On the night of May 28, 1971, Marshall met a casual acquaintance, Sandford "Sandy" Seale, a seventeen-year-old black youth who was returning home, and they walked through Wentworth Park. Before midnight, they encountered Roy Ebsary and Jimmy MacNeil, two other youths known to both of them. Marshall and Seale asked the older Ebsary and MacNeil for change to take the bus home and Seale, believing that Ebsary had money, urged him to dig into his pocket and provide some change. (It was later claimed that Seale had demanded the money in a threatening manner.)

Ebsary reacted by producing a knife and plunging it into Seale's abdomen and then turned on Marshall, slashing him on the arm. Marshall fled while Seale sank to the ground, fatally wounded. Marshall ran into another acquaintance, fourteen-year-old Maynard Chant, telling him about the stabbing. Both boys returned to the park to see if they could assist Seale and found him alone on the ground clutching his abdomen. Chant tried to cover Seale's wound while Marshall ran to a nearby house, where he asked the residents to call the police.

Police arrived and ordered an ambulance to take Seale to the City Hospital, where he died forty hours later. Marshall was also taken to the hospital that night in a patrol car. En route to the hospital and after he arrived he told how Ebsary had stabbed Seale. He accurately described Ebsary and MacNeil, but the interviewing Sydney police officers did not take a formal statement; in fact, they did not take a formal statement until after Seale died.

The Sydney police did nothing to apprehend Ebsary and did not return to the scene of the crime in Wentworth Park. Nor did they order the crime scene sealed off to preserve evidence that might be found there. They did not interview any suspects, did not search the area, and did not question any witnesses. They did nothing at all.

The case was taken over the next day, May 29, 1971, by Sergeant John Macintyre of the Sydney police department. Ignoring the fact that Marshall had caused the police to be summoned to the scene of the crime and gave a detailed account of how Seale had been attacked (the victim died before identifying his assailant on the night of May 29, 1971), Macintyre, without a shred of evidence, decided that morning that the culprits were Seale and Marshall, not Ebsary, and that Seale and Marshall, a black and an Indian, had tried to rob two white youths, Ebsary and MacNeil, and that Marshall had fatally stabbed Seale, coming to this utterly baffling conclusion through no knowledge of motivation on Marshall's part. Macintyre completely disregarded the fact that it was Marshall who tried to save Seale's life.

Macintyre made no effort to contact Ebsary or MacNeil, but he did interview the terrified fourteen-year-old Chant, who was on probation and was apprehensive of going to jail. He also interviewed sixteen-year-old John Pratico, who was under psychiatric care and said he had seen Marshall and Seale running through Wentworth Park on the night when Seale was stabbed. Both Chant and Pratico underwent prolonged interrogations by Macintyre and other Sydney police officers and both falsely stated that they had seen Marshall fatally stab Seale.

On June 4, 1971, Macintyre charged Donald Marshall Jr. with the murder of Seale. Marshall's trial was a farce. Prosecutors took the false statements of Chant and Pratico at face value, while Marshall's defense attorney allowed that testimony to go unchallenged; the trial judge admitted it into evidence, also without questions. Marshall was convicted and sentenced to life in prison. Ten days after that conviction, Jimmy MacNeil, who had been with Ebsary and had not been interviewed by Macintyre or any other Sydney police officer, came forward, telling police that he was present with Ebsary when Seale was stabbed and that it was Ebsary who had committed the stabbing, not Marshall.

The Royal Canadian Mounted Police (RCMP) was asked to investigate MacNeil's claim. The RCMP investigation amounted to little more than filing a report which dismissed MacNeil's statements out of hand and supported Sergeant Macintyre's investigation and Marshall's conviction. This report was never given to Marshall's defense attorney or to the new attorney handling Marshall's appeal, which was denied.

Donald Marshall Jr. was lost to memory as he languished behind the prison walls of Dorchester Penitentiary. In 1981, however, two RCMP officers, after hearing from relatives of Ebsary that the wrong man had been imprisoned for the slaying of Seale, interviewed Marshall. He gave Ebsary's version of the event, saying that he and Seale were pressuring Ebsary for money, which the officers translated as an attempted robbery. They then interviewed Chant, the key witness against Marshall, and were startled when Chant

recanted his testimony, saying that he had been intimidated by local police into giving false testimony against Marshall. It became apparent that Marshall had been framed for a crime he had not committed based on race hatred for Indians.

On the phone with one of the officers, Ebsary then admitted stabbing Seale. Marshall was allowed bail on July 29, 1982, while his attorneys prepared for a new trial. That trial never took place. The court of appeal overturned his conviction on May 19, 1983, and, after prosecutors declined to retry Marshall, he was officially exonerated. Ebsary was charged with second-degree murder two days after Marshall's acquittal. He was convicted in 1985 and received a three-year sentence, but the court of appeal reduced it to one year, believing that Ebsary had acted in self-defense.

On September 26, 1984, Marshall was awarded $270,000 in compensation for his wrongful conviction and imprisonment. His attorneys had sued provincial officials and police for $14 million. Marshall was arrested on a new charge of attempted murder on January 2, 2006, allegedly trying to run over a man with his motorcycle. A judge ordered him to undergo psychiatric treatment. This charge too, Marshall and others claimed, was based on race hatred.

The bigotry that had imprisoned three blacks in the notorious Groveland, Florida, conviction and had ensnared Donald Marshall Jr. in a wrongful murder conviction was repeated in San Francisco, where bias against Asians produced the same results, framing and imprisoning a Korean for a murder he did not commit. Chol Soo Lee, born in 1952, arrived in the United States from Seoul, South Korea, in 1964. He was a troubled adolescent and fought his way through junior high school, where he was taunted and persecuted as a foreigner. He served thirteen months in a California Youth Authority institution, which was only a prelude to more serious crimes for which he would be convicted.

In 1973, Chol Soo Lee allegedly shot and killed a rival gang leader named Yip Yee Tak on a crowded San Francisco street in broad daylight. A series of Chinatown murders plagued the Bay Area at that time, and caused Mayor Joseph Alioto (1968–1976) many sleepless nights. There was considerable pressure on the police to come up with a suspect, any suspect. Homicide investigator Frank Falzon arrested Lee after recovering a bullet lodged in the ceiling of his apartment.

Ballistics tests tended to show that it was the same type of bullet used to kill Yip Yee Tak. Eyewitnesses were located by the prosecution, and their testimony helped convict Lee in 1973. The Korean immigrant received a life sentence in San Quentin for the murder of Yip Yee Tak. The plight of Chol Soo Lee drew the attention of many prisoner activist groups and the leaders of the San Francisco Asian community. There were calls for a new trial on the grounds that the defendant had been railroaded by shaky, unreliable testimony, and the skimpy facts in this case supported that claim. The Chol Soo Lee Defense Committee was organized, and in 1982 a second trial was ordered.

On September 3, 1982, a San Francisco jury found him not guilty of murdering the Chinatown gang figure. However, Lee was still in a bind. He sat on San Quentin's death row for the 1977 murder of Morrison Needham, a member of the white racist Aryan Brotherhood and a fellow prison inmate. Lee had killed Needham in a prison knife fight, which he claimed to be a matter of self-defense. The jury disagreed, and he was sentenced to death.

This second murder conviction was overturned in 1983, when a Sacramento appeals court ordered a new trial on the grounds that the presiding judge had failed to inform jurors that Lee could have been found guilty on a lesser charge of second-degree murder if they believed he acted in self-defense. In a plea bargaining arrangement, Chol Soo Lee agreed to plead guilty to one count of second-degree murder in return for a sentence of time served. The case concluded on August 25, 1983. Lee was granted a final release from custody, and he returned to the Korean neighborhood of San Francisco and went to work in a community center.

Racism in Chicago has often bubbled to the surface to produce riots and counterriots. A major influx of black workers into northern industrial cities prior to World War I contributed to a racially tense atmosphere as blacks and whites vied for scarce jobs in the industrial sector. World War I then produced a labor shortage; blacks and whites migrated to the city, and ghetto neighborhoods expanded. The integration of previously insulated ethnic communities often led to bloody racial confrontations. These problems resulted in a full-blown race riot in Chicago that left twenty-three blacks and fifteen whites dead.

On July 27, 1919, several black youths swimming off the segregated 29th Street beach in Lake Michigan were pelted by rocks. One of the boys, fourteen-year-old Eugene Williams, was struck on the head by a rock, lost consciousness, and drowned before his friends could rescue him. When a white police officer, Dan Callahan, refused to arrest the white man who had thrown the rock, angry blacks began to riot. Mayor William Hale Thompson (1915–1923; 1927–1931), at first reticent to call the National Guard because of a feud with Governor Frank Lowden (1917–1921), was forced to put partisan political issues aside and seek help.

Organized gangs of white youths from the South Side attacked public places such as trolley cars, buildings, and hotels. The gangs, which included the Ragen Colts, the Aylward Club, the Dirty Dozen, Lorraine's, and Our Flag, were composed of Irish and Germans who believed they had a duty to protect the neighborhoods. An area hospital was soon filled to capacity with the injured. The region of the South Side from 31st to 35th Streets was virtually destroyed by arsonists and looters. The National Guard finally quelled the fighting in Chicago, but the unrest soon spread to other American cities, including Washington, D.C.; Charleston, South Carolina; Knoxville, Tennessee; Longview, Texas; and Omaha, Nebraska.

Racial hatred had long infected the predominately white Chicago police department since those 1919 race riots, as well as the mostly white court system. Until recent years, innocent blacks, especially those without money, were routinely railroaded to prison along with the guilty simply because they were easy prey, allowing the police to take credit for solving crimes expeditiously and to add convictions to ambitious prosecutors. (By 1995, black officers made up 25 percent of the Chicago police force, with 9 percent being Hispanic.)

Racial hatred against blacks was still running high in Chicago during the 1970s, when police were confronted by the violent actions of the terrorist gang known as the Black Panther Party. Any black arrested during that time was looked on by white police officers as a potential terrorist, intent on mayhem and murder. Several white officers involved in solving a 1977 murder on Chicago's North Side held that same attitude, when two blacks were arrested and put on trial for that crime.

On November 13, 1977, two armed blacks entered Mel's Red Hots, a hot dog stand at 3927 North Broadway, to rob it and shot and killed an employee, Charles Cuccion, and the owner, Melvin Kanter. The killers fled, leaving no clues behind, but two weeks later Phyllis Santini, who had made money in the past by providing testimony for prosecutors (she was known as a "professional witness") contacted police to tell officers that she had heard Perry Cobb and Darby Tillis, two young black men, talking about the robbery as if they had committed the crime.

On December 5, 1977, a number of Chicago police officers, guns drawn and pointing, burst through the door of a room occupied by Cobb at the Wilmot Hotel on Chicago's North Side, finding Cobb naked and dripping from a shower. He was arrested and charged with the murders at Mel's Red Hots. A short time later, Tillis, whom Cobb knew only in passing, was also arrested and both were held for trial. In addition to Santini's testimony, police offered a watch they had found in

Cobb's room which had been taken from Cuccion during the robbery. Cobb insisted that he had purchased the watch from Johnny Brown for $10. Brown was Santini's boyfriend.

Santini would later state that she had actually driven the getaway car for Cobb and Tillis on the night of the robbery-murder, but years later she admitted lying about that. She had really spent the night with her boyfriend, Johnny Brown, telling officials that she would do anything to protect Brown. Another witness was rounded up by the police, Arthur Shields, a bartender who worked at Terminal Liquors, across the street from the hot dog stand.

In the first two attempts to try Cobb and Tillis (both resulting in hung juries), Shields stated that he had seen two black men standing inside the door of the hotdog stand at the time of the robbery-murders, but he could not identify either one. On the night of the crime he had told two police officers that Tillis regularly patronized his bar and was definitely not one of the two men he had seen. At the third trial in 1979, however, Shields said that Cobb and Tillis were the two men he had seen. In cross-examination, he admitted that he had earlier said that neither Cobb and Tillis was on the scene, but said that at that time he was responding to mug shots of both defendants and had told police that all blacks looked alike in photographs.

An all-white jury convicted Cobb and Tillis and both men were sentenced to death. Judge Thomas Maloney's actions during the three trials all but railroaded Cobb and Tillis into prison. He had not allowed defense attorneys to have two witnesses take the stand—Patricia Usmani, who would have testified that Santini had admitted to her that she and Brown had committed the crime, and Carol Griffin, who would have testified that Santini had told her that she expected to receive a substantial payment for testifying against Cobb and Tillis (she did, $1,200).

In 1983, the Illinois Supreme Court reversed the 1979 conviction based on Maloney's many judicial errors. Prosecutors, however, tried Cobb and Tillis a fourth time, and were surprised to see one of their own number come to the aid of the defendants. He was Michael Falconer, who had recently graduated from the DePaul University College of Law and had become an assistant state's attorney when the fourth trial for Cobb and Tillis began. Falconer, who had read about the case, had intimate information to relate about Santini, testifying that he had spent one summer working in a factory where Santini also worked. Santini had told him that she and her boyfriend, Johnny Brown, had committed the robbery-murders.

This testimony, however, did not wholly convince the jury, which was hung. A fifth and unprecedented trial for Cobb and Tillis was ordered—making theirs the longest court case in U.S. history up that time. In 1987, at a bench trial, circuit court Judge Thomas A. Hett found both men not guilty and ordered their release on January 20, 1987. Santini and Brown were never charged with the robbery-murders and the conviction of Cobb and Tillis had all the earmarks of racist railroading. Judge Maloney was later convicted and sent to prison for taking bribes from underworld figures in exchange for their acquittals. Cobb and Tillis were each given approximately $140,000 in compensation for their wrongful convictions and the nine years they spent behind bars for a crime they did not commit.

Police officers and the presiding judge in the Cobb-Tillis case had undoubtedly framed the defendants because of racial prejudice, but their bias was bland compared to the flagrantly racist railroading of a Texas defendant. Clarence Lee Brandley was twenty-nine years old when he was convicted in 1981 of the August 23, 1980, rape and strangling murder of sixteen-year-old Cheryl Dee Fergeson. The girl was the manager of a visiting Bellevue High volleyball team at Conroe High School in Conroe, Texas, where Brandley worked as a janitor. Fergeson disappeared when she went in search of a restroom. Her body was found two hours later, following the game, concealed in a storage area in a loft of the school auditorium.

Brandley, the only black janitor working at the school when Fergeson was murdered, was fingerprinted and provided hair samples, as was the case with another janitor, Henry Peace. Both took polygraph tests and reportedly passed. Peace later stated that the officer conducting the interrogations of both men told them, "One of you two is going to hang for this." Also according to Peace, the officer turned to Brandley and said, "Since you're the nigger, you're elected." Brandley was arrested by Texas Ranger Wesley Styles several days later when Brandley was unable to prove his whereabouts at the time of the crime. All of the other janitors—Peace, Sam Martinez, John Sessum, and Gary Acreman—provided alibis for one another.

During the investigation and at Brandley's trial, the other three white janitors gave the same story, so closely related in detail that some believed they had been coached by police. They all said they had seen Fergeson go to the girls rest room and then saw Brandley approaching with some toilet paper. They said they warned Brandley that the girl was occupying the restroom, but Brandley said he was going to supply the boy's restroom. They all said that Brandley was missing for about forty minutes, the time that elapsed before a search was conducted for the missing Fergeson.

Peace stated he told Brandley at the time that he had searched the loft above the auditorium and found nothing, but that Brandley led him back to the loft to conduct a more thorough search and then found the girl's body, taking her pulse and, when finding none, notified authorities. It was determined that only Brandley had keys to the auditorium. Brandley said he had disappeared for thirty minutes, not forty-five, so that he could listen to a radio and smoke a cigarette.

The all-white jury in Brandley's first trial in 1980 learned little from the prosecution. A blood spot was found on the victim's blouse that belonged to neither Fergeson nor Brandley, and the crucial sperm recovered from the victim's body had vanished or had been destroyed without being tested.

The jury was unable to come to a unanimous verdict, so a mistrial was declared. The sole dissenting juror, William Srack, later reported that he received thousands of threatening phone calls, many of them racial in nature. During his holdout debates with other jurors in the jury room, fellow jurors called him a "nigger lover."

The jury in Brandley's second trial in February 1981 also consisted of white members only. The prosecution in this second trial offered a new witness, a junior student at the school, Danny Taylor, who worked with the custodians. He testified that once he was standing with Brandley and some female students passed by. Brandley then said, "If I got one of them alone, ain't no telling what I might do." The Harris County medical examiner testified that the belt worn by Brandley was consistent with the weapon used by the killer to strangle Fergeson to death.

Further, the prosecutor told the jury that Brandley might be a necrophiliac in that he had a second job at a funeral home and then suggested that he could have raped the girl after she was dead. Though the defense objected to this inflammatory remark, the presiding judge overruled the objection. The jury found Brandley guilty and recommended the death penalty. The judge promptly agreed.

Brandley's attorneys started the appeals process on his behalf immediately, spurred on by what they considered incontrovertible evidence that their client had been framed. Physical evidence in the case—including body and pubic hair found on the victim's body that could not have been Brandley's—was "accidentally" discarded, according to police. In fact, of the 309 exhibits at Brandley's trial, 166 were missing. Also missing was a photo showing Brandley wearing a belt on the day of the killing, which was unlike the belt the medical examiner had described as the likely murder weapon. Police also, according to defense lawyers, had ignored information from Brenda Medina, who told them that the man she lived with, James Dexter Robinson, a former janitor at the high school, had confessed the murder to her in 1980.

Brandley was granted two stays of execution in January and March 1985 due to the incompetent handling of the investigation. He was nevertheless scheduled for execution on January 17, 1986, but Brandley's lawyers got another stay of six months on the argument that the "lost" evidence had deprived Brandley of a fair trial. Medina's statements were initially dismissed by prosecutors, who termed the woman "unreliable." Brandley's execution was again set, this time for March 26, 1987.

By this time, Brandley had become a national figure and civil rights activists raised $80,000 for his defense fund. A thousand people marched in Conroe in support of the condemned man. He was then championed by James McCloskey, a former seminary student and celebrated attorney for Centurion Ministries in Princeton, New Jersey, who had a long and dedicated career in bringing about exonerations of wrongly convicted persons. With an investigator, McCloskey persuaded one of the janitors, Acreman, to provide new statements, which were videotaped. Acreman supported Medina's earlier statements in saying that Robinson alone had abducted and murdered Fergeson. Though he later recanted his videotaped comments, Acreman was quoted by new witnesses as saying that Brandley did not kill the girl and he knew the identity of the real murderer.

Only six days before Brandley's scheduled execution on March 26, 1987, a judge granted another stay. In September 1987, special state district Judge Perry Pickett, seventy-one, a jurist known for his fair decisions, held an evidentiary hearing in the case, listening to the testimony of Robinson, Acreman, and Texas Ranger Styles. Both Robinson and Acreman appeared to compromise each other, while Styles was shown as a racist. Judge Pickett condemned the police and prosecution in the case, stating, "The conclusion is inescapable that the investigation was conducted not to solve the crime but to convict Brandley." He went on to say that the testimony he had heard "unequivocally establishes that Gary Acreman and James Dexter Robinson are prime suspects and probably were responsible for the death of Cheryl Dee Ferge-son." He recommended that the Texas court of criminal appeals grant Brandley a new trial.

After fourteen months of heated debate, the court ordered a new trial on December 13, 1989. On January 23, 1990, Brandley was released from prison on bond. The prosecution would not give up on its next-to-nothing case against Brandley and appealed to the U.S. Supreme Court. On October 1, 1990, the high court upheld the state court's order for a new trial, and the prosecution quit the case, exonerating Brandley.

In another crime in Texas, another black man was railroaded into prison, and he too became a national cause célèbre. On August 23, 1982, a Kentucky Fried Chicken restaurant was robbed in Balch Springs, Texas, a Dallas suburb. Within days, twenty-four-year-old Lenell Geter, a black man born in 1957, was arrested and charged with the robbery because an elderly white woman became suspicious when she noticed that Geter often went to a park after work, a park close to the scene of the crime. During his trial, five eyewitnesses identified him, although seven coworkers testified that Geter had been at work fifty miles away in Greenville, Texas, at the time of the robbery.

On the basis of the eyewitness identification, Geter was convicted and sentenced to life. Afterward, two more fellow workers gave depositions stating that Geter was at his desk during the robbery. Geter's story gained national attention after the television program *60 Minutes* covered the story, and his friends, family, and the NAACP fought his case. His lawyers claimed that the conviction stemmed from racism and that he had been framed. After serving sixteen months in prison, Geter was granted a new trial and was freed on December 14, 1983.

On March 21, 1984, prosecutors announced that they were dropping charges against Geter. Subsequently Geter established the Geter Justice for All Foundation, an organization that distributes the names of civil rights agencies and lawyers to defendants. Geter's case also became the basis for a television movie, *Guilty of Innocence: The Lennell Geter Story* (see Filmography).

## Framing Victims Around the World

Racial hatred had nothing to do with the framed and railroaded execution of a former prime minister of Pakistan. Politics and power had everything to do with it. Zulfikar Ali Bhutto (1928–1979), the prime minister of Pakistan, was framed for an assassination he did not commit and was hanged. Following the overthrow of the Pakistani government, amid political strife caused by accusations of corruption in the government and a lopsided victory during elections on March 7, 1977, the ousted prime minister was tried, convicted, and sentenced to die by firing squad for allegedly ordering the assassination of a political foe.

Bhutto, who came to power in 1971 after the end of the war with India, had been prime minister of Pakistan since 1974, when he ended martial law. With opposition to his rule growing, a military coup led by General Mohammed Zia ul-Haq took place on July 5, 1977. Zia Ul-Haq had Bhutto imprisoned in September and tried for the murder of Nawab Mohammad Ahmed Khan, who was machine-gunned to death on November 11, 1974, during an attempt on the life of his son, Ahmad Raza Kasuri, who opposed Bhutto.

The former prime minister was found guilty of murder. Charges of political corruption and electoral fraud were subsequently set aside on March 18, 1978, mainly on the testimony of Bhutto's director of security, Masood Mahmud, who was held captive for two months before confessing with a promise of immunity. According to Bhutto, Mahmud's confession and testimony was "dishonest and utterly unreliable." Also considered by many to be dishonest were the entire proceedings, because Zia ul-Haq apparently influenced the decision of the jury in a blatantly framed trial. An appeal of the conviction was turned down on

February 6, 1979, by the Pakistan Supreme Court, which upheld the lower court's decision.

Death by hanging was substituted for a firing squad and Bhutto, along with the men he allegedly ordered to commit the crime—Mian Mohammed Appas, Arrad Iqbal, Rana Isti Khar, and Guylam Mustafa—were executed on April 4, 1979. Tara Masih, at the time Pakistan's first and only hangman since Pakistan had become a nation, said of Bhutto, "He was the only man I hanged, who I was convinced was an innocent man."

Bhutto's judicial plight in Pakistan was repeated in Iran, where civil rights and basic freedoms are routinely ignored and suppressed, when the liberal-minded mayor of Tehran was railroaded into prison by right-wing clerics who thought he posed a threat to their tyrannical, oppressive regime. Arrested on April 4, 1998, on charges of misappropriating public funds, Gholamhossein Karbaschi, born in 1954, the reform mayor of Tehran, Iran, went into custody amid a storm of violent protest. A moderate who had done much to institute reforms, Karbaschi had been singled out by conservatives, particularly Chief Judge Mohammad Yazdi, for a show trial.

A crowd of more than four thousand persons, mostly students, protested in Tehran on April 14, 1998, after it was announced that Karbaschi would be placed on trial. More than three hundred police officers of Tehran's riot police waded into the crowd at Tehran University, swinging clubs in an attempt to disperse the throng. Students fought back and more than thirty were arrested. Karbaschi's supporters claimed that he was being persecuted for having cleaned up Tehran, a city of 8 million, and established parks and meeting areas with funds received from heavy taxation levied against powerful merchants, who make up the financial base of the conservative clergy.

The following day, April 15, 1998, Karbaschi was released from jail, thought to be a sign that conservatives wanted to ease national tension. Karbaschi was nevertheless brought to trial in June 1998. He called the court action a sham built on false confessions and torture. He told the court, "You set up a group of seventy men, most of whom have little more than a high school education, and put them in charge of this investigation. They take each person into a basement and emerge with a confession. What is the meaning of this?"

On July 23, 1998, Karbaschi was found guilty and sentenced to five years in prison, three years for embezzling public funds and two years for misappropriation of government money. He was also banned from holding office for twenty years and given the additional sentence of sixty lashes, but the flogging was suspended because of Karbaschi's prestigious standing. Karbaschi denied taking any public funds and his attorney vowed that he would be set free, cleared of all charges. This did not happen, but an appeals court did reduce Karbaschi's sentence from five years to two years on December 24, 1998.

Obviously Kabaschi had been jailed because he had begun to pry open that closed society. He began by establishing parks where open discussions and debates could ensue and forums could gather—one of the most dangerous threats to the right-wing government of Iran, the freedom of speech.

In the same year Karbaschi was railroaded in Iran, a Catholic priest was railroaded in Guatemala by a right-wing military junta for the murder of his bishop, a slaying that the militarists themselves had orchestrated after that courageous prelate had condemned them for the murder of dissidents. Bishop Juan Jose Gerardi, a senior Roman Catholic prelate in Guatemala, was killed on April 26, 1998. He was found in the garage of his residence at the San Sebastian Church in Guatemala City, Guatemala. His head had been crushed by a concrete block.

Only two days earlier, Bishop Gerardi had released a human rights report on the country's thirty-six-year civil war, which ended in 1996. The report detailed countless atrocities and mass murders, which Gerardi attributed to right-wing death squads or military units, blaming these government units for more than 80 percent of the 150,000 deaths and 50,000 disappearances during the war.

On July 23, 1998, Reverend Mario Orantes Najera, who worked with Bishop Gerardi, assigned to the San Sebastian diocese, was arrested and charged with killing Gerardi. Police stated that the priest had murdered his bishop by having his German shepherd, Baloo, maul and bite the prelate before he, Orantes, dropped a concrete block on Gerardi's head, killing him. Prosecutors insisted that the murdered clergyman's body bore many dog bites.

Many in Guatemala believed that the charges against Orantes were false, based on fabricated evidence. Many more were convinced that the priest had been charged and jailed as a smokescreen behind which the real killers could hide, the actual murderers being members of the very death squads Bishop Gerardi had identified. Orantes called the charges "absurd," but he was nevertheless held without bond and jailed. Also arrested with the priest was a church cook, Margarita Lopez, and twenty-four-year-old Carlos Enrique Vielman. Held in prison until February 1999, Orantes was released pending trial. He immediately fled to the United States, where he sought refuge, as well as medical help for an ailment.

Extradited back to Guatemala in 2000, Orantes was tried and convicted, sentenced to twenty years in prison. In June 2001, three others charged with Gerardi's murder, retired Colonel Byron Disrael Lima Estrada and his son, army captain Byron Miguel Lima Oliva, and former presidential bodyguard, Jose Obdulio Villaneuva, were convicted. The three men were sentenced to thirty years in prison. This was the first time important military figures had been convicted of human rights violations, in addition to murder. There was talk of indicting even members of the military high command in the Gerardi murder, but that came to nothing. In October 2002, a Guatemalan court of appeals reversed the verdicts, annulled the sentences, and freed all four prisoners, including Father Mario Orantes Najera.

The body of Bishop Gerardi was exhumed and examined in order to confirm the police and military claims that the victim had been repeatedly bitten by Orantes Najera's dog. Seven experts reported that the body bore no such bite marks. The dog, Baloo, was so infirm at the time of the attack, it was reported, that the animal could barely use its hind legs and most of its teeth were missing. Five members of Guatemala's military high command were suspected of being the actual killers of Bishop Gerardi, but none were ever charged or brought to trial.

Being an important person in Pakistan, Iran, or Guatemala did not protect those persons from being framed for crimes they did not commit. In Mexico, one of the most corrupt countries in the world for the past century, being an American citizen presents an open invitation to any venal and corrupt Mexican official—and these have always been in preponderance—to railroad such persons into prison in order to flagrantly seize assets, cash, or subsequent payoffs for crimes created out of thin air.

No other country in the Western Hemisphere, except for Colombia, is as plagued with widespread political and police corruption, with billion-dollar drug cartels, and decades-long crime waves of mass murders, kidnappings, and extortion that approaches national anarchy. Mexican officials on all levels seemingly are powerless to curb the crime or actually collude with a criminal element that appears to control the country.

Overpopulated and underdeveloped, Mexico is a mock democracy, corrupt to its social marrow and controlled by about four hundred elite families that have held power for generations, surviving the reform revolutions of Benito Juarez, Francisco Madero, Emiliano Zapata, and Pancho Villa. These families of landed gentry, going back to the time of the Spanish conquerors, control all branches of the government, maintain a small middle class, and economically deprive the millions of impoverished Mexican citizens of a decent wage. In the latter respect, it is the true source of illegal mass immigration from Mexico, where millions of desperate Mexicans illegally enter the United States in search of work, in search of a wage, in search of basic survival for themselves and their starving families.

These landed families who control vast estates, as they have over the centuries, also support the powerful drug cartels, participating in their billion-dollar spoils, while they insidiously orchestrate an illegal alien problem that has reached epidemic proportions over the past two decades, with an estimated 7 million to 15 million Mexicans being smuggled into the United States each year to escape the death-dealing poverty of their miserable country. (There may be as many as 20 million illegal Mexican aliens in the United States as of this 2007 writing.)

Mexico's cities, particularly border towns like Tijuana, Matamoras, and Juarez, have for several decades been among the most dangerous places for any foreign tourist to visit. Thousands of human rights violations have been recorded as tourists, chiefly U.S. citizens, have been arrested on trumped-up charges, tortured into making false confessions, and imprisoned through railroaded convictions so that crooked police, judges, and lawyers can extort thousands from their family members and friends before releasing these innocent persons.

Typical of such blatant offenses was the case of Mario Amado. In June 1991, Amado, a twenty-nine-year-old fence installer from Los Angeles, California, and a U.S. citizen, visited Tijuana, where he was arrested for being drunk and disorderly. Only a few hours later, Amado was reportedly found dead by his own hand in his cell, according to his Mexican jailers. They stated that Amado had committed suicide by hanging himself with his own sweater, which was tied to the bars of his cell at one end and around his neck at the other.

A subsequent investigation into Amado's supposed suicide revealed that, according to a Los Angeles coroner, the victim had been severely beaten before death and suffered massive injuries, and that the welt on his neck had been caused by a thin cord, not his sweater. The conclusion was that Mario Amado had simply been murdered by his Mexican guards, savagely beaten and then garroted to death. The motivation for such a murder can only be speculated, but it is known that any defiance shown to Mexican police or warders is immediately met with violent retaliation and those woeful victims too impoverished to provide extortion payments are summarily lost in Mexico's utterly corrupt penal system or, worse, disappear forever, presumably under ground.

Also in 1991, Jennifer Whitt, a twenty-four-year-old student from Texas, was arrested while she was visiting Reynosa, Mexico. She was charged with having more than the legal limit of Valium, even though she had no more than the legal amount prescribed by a Mexican physician who was treating her bursitis. Whitt languished inside a filthy Mexican prison for ten months while her parents paid more than $30,000 in "legal fees" to bail her out. She was finally released on September 29, 1992, only to die that very night of a bronchial attack. Only a few days earlier, a Mexican judge newly assigned to the Whitt case ruled that the young woman had broken no law.

On August 14, 1992, William Yost, a young Peace Corps volunteer, was detained in a Mexico City jail after being brought from Oaxaca, where he had been detained and had paid a fine of $1,400 for "failure to register his vehicle," according to Mexican authorities. The next day, Yost was found dead in his cell. Mexican jail officials said he was either given a gun or obtained the weapon himself, and committed suicide by shooting himself in the mouth. Yost, facing minimal charges, had no reason to take his own life and it was logically concluded that Yost had simply been murdered by his Mexican guards.

Mexico City, a metropolis teeming with more than 25 million persons (the most populous city in the world), who mostly live at the poverty level, can be as dangerous for tourists as any Mexican border town. The poverty here is so intense that tens of thousands live in cardboard shacks, their children running naked through garbage-strewn areas covering miles, all drinking from water carrying raw sewage and with no toilet facilities available. Police routinely target tourists as extortion victims, selecting those who appear to have money but few political connections. Randy Lee Rogers, a Florida welder on vacation in Mexico City in 1993, was just such a victim, according to one report, spending fifteen hellish months in a Mexico City jail on drug charges.

Arrested by the Mexican federal police, Rogers later claimed that he was tortured for twelve days before he signed a forced confession. "I saw them treat Mexicans like dogs and they treated me the same," said Rogers. He related that they beat him in the chest and testicles, gave him electric shocks in the abdomen, and repeatedly applied a torture called *tehuacanazo*—blasting a combination of seltzer water and chili powder into his nostrils. Another popular torture in Mexico, according to Amnesty International, which has documented thousands of such cases, is to jam a suspect's head into a plastic bag filled with ammonia fumes. Amnesty International issued a report on Mexican police abuse in 1992 entitled "Torture with Impunity."

Where U.S. citizens are open prey to Mexican officials, Mexicans are simply victims expendable in any numbers, particularly those who bring criticism and disapproval of those officials and their blatantly corrupt policies. Teodoro Cabrera García and Rodolfo Montiel Flores were typical. Environmental activists from Pizotla, Guerrero, both men worked with the Organization of Peasant Environmentalists of the Mountains of Petatlán and Coyuca de Catalán. Soldiers arrested Cabrera García and Flores in May 1999, killing another man, Salomé Sánchez Ortiz, at the time. Soldiers held the two men illegally for two days and tortured them before turning them over to prosecutors.

On August 28, 1999, a district judge sentenced Cabrera García to ten years in prison and Flores to

seven years, for drug peddling and possession of weapons. Defense attorneys for both men claimed that the military planted the weapons and drugs that formed the basis of the charges against the two, an accusation confirmed in a July 2000 report issued by the government National Human Rights Commission. Soldiers forced the activists to sign incriminating confessions, which were then used against them in court.

Journalists attempting to expose the widespread police and judicial corruption in Mexico have been routinely harassed into silence, wrongly imprisoned, or, if their crusades went unchecked, simply murdered. Two reporters were killed in 2000. José Ramírez Puente, a radio journalist, was stabbed to death in April in Ciudad Juárez, Chihuahua. Pablo Pineda, of the Matamoros daily *La opinión,* was killed in the same month. As usual, officials issued ambiguous reports on these murders, where motives of the perpetrators were not specified and identities of the killers went undisclosed. On June 22, 2000, gunmen fired on *TV Azteca* news anchor Lilly Tellez as she traveled by car in Mexico City.

Tellez escaped unharmed, but the driver and bodyguards accompanying her were wounded. Threats had been repeatedly made against Tellez in retaliation for her reporting on drug trafficking. Legal harassment is routinely practiced against any journalist criticizing governmental operations. Melitón García of the Monterrey daily *El Norte* published a report in May 2000 that described how easy it was for him to obtain a false voter credential. Prosecutors charged him with falsifying documents.

Mexico's judicial system has long been utterly corrupt, with only a few valiant jurists willing to defy the venal judiciary system. Such corruption was widespread in urban as well as rural areas. The respected Human Rights Commission of Mexico City, an agency of the city government, reported that the main suspect in the high-profile murder case of television personality Francisco "Paco" Stanley, gunned down in 1999, had been framed by prosecutors.

Prosecutors refused to accept the commission's recommendation that charges be dismissed against the suspect. Instead, prosecutors began a campaign of intimidation against the commission. This, in turn, led the commission in May 2000 to issue a stinging report accusing the office of the attorney general of Mexico City of playing politics with judicial investigations. The office had opened four "notoriously unfounded" investigations against a judge, who had ruled against the attorney general in Mexico City.

Mexico, to appease international criticism and reportedly attempt to institute reforms, established its National Human Rights Commission in 1992, but widespread violations continued. On January 14, 1999, Human Rights Watch, a New York–based watchdog group, released a two-year study of Mexico's human rights violations, reporting that up to that time, "[Mexican] authorities are more likely to close ranks and deny that even well-documented abuses ever took place than they are to insist that those responsible be brought to justice."

The report studied the Mexican provinces of Baja California and Tamaulipas, which border the United States, Jalisco and Morelos in central Mexico, and Oaxaca in the south, the latter province being the location of the leftist Popular Revolutionary Army, which had staged attacks against government troops and installations. In retaliation, state and federal police arbitrarily detained suspected guerrilla sympathizers, torturing many persons into signing blank papers that were later filled out by police to implicate others.

Typical of these forced and forged confessions was a 1996 police document involving three Oaxaca men who had accused another person of rebel activity. The document was written and signed by the three Oaxaca men in Spanish, who could neither write nor read the language, knowing only their Indian tongue. A Mexican judge threw the document out as a blatant forgery.

This action was an exception, according to Human Rights Watch, since most Mexican judges rarely discount questionable confessions, even after defendants retract them, and these judges paradoxically consider any evidence legal, including evidence obtained through illegal means. Judges and prosecutors routinely do nothing about complaints of human rights violations. Little had changed at this 2007 writing, with Mexico still considered to be an uncivilized country by human rights organizations, one where anyone in authority can flaunt the law and inflict savage and sadistic punishment on any naive or gullible person, foreign or domestic, while considering these victims their rightful prey.

# XII

# *Perjured Testimony*

T HOSE OFFERING PERJURED TESTIMONY have lied countless defendants into prison and, in some cases, to execution. Some perjurers are motivated by a desire to exercise power over the destiny of others. These fabricators exercise a subtle sadism for which they take no legal responsibility; the pain and suffering they inflict on their victims is seemingly administered impartially by the state. These liars appease their "conscience" by endorsing the state's conviction.

Others perjure themselves to take revenge on a rejected lover, a former business partner, or a person of higher social or economic standing. Still other perjurers are motivated by monetary rewards, cash payments from prosecutors, or, if the witness is a convicted felon, a reduced prison sentence. Some perjurers are desperate to shield their own guilt for crimes they themselves have committed, conveniently framing another for those crimes.

Perjurers throughout history have lied about their neighbors, denouncing them so that, as part of their reward for identifying a dangerous enemy of the state, they receive the forfeited or seized property or lands of those they have wrongly accused. Others will lie in court to cancel a debt or to eliminate a relative in line for an inheritance. Perjury has been committed to destroy political opponents or crusading reformers threatening the gluttonous economies of inequitable corpora-

tions, including the underworld, or challenging unjust laws, oppressive working conditions, or social evils.

The justice systems in all countries and in all ages, so eager to justify their existence (particularly today when such judicial systems support billion-dollar industries employing police, attorneys, judges, and court employees) have too readily embraced the doubtful testimony of perjurers and knowingly accepted perjured testimony to support such systems. Further, when such perjury is planted in a closed case, police and prosecutors are often reluctant to recognize it at the risk of ruining the credit for a conviction. Such inaction is comparable to that of physician refusing to cut out a cancerous tumor because the patient my die, when the patient is already dying of the disease.

To be sure, there are honest police and officers of the court dedicated to meting out justice, but their good and mostly unrecognized work is overshadowed by widespread corruption in their midst. Investigations revealed that in the Los Angeles Police Department, for example, thousands of innocent persons were imprisoned on the false testimony of arresting officers seeking bribes and payoffs, or simply to increase their number of "collars."

In modern times, the perjurer has a greater chance of being exposed through the investigation and cross-examination of defense attorneys, when the lawyers have the money to conduct such investigations, supported by reliable forensic experts. In the past few decades, the media has become more alert to perjury, and DNA testing has brought about an impressive number of acquittals. Its impartial scientific process, if properly conducted, can ensnare a lying witness. Investigative reporters for newspapers and periodicals (a dying breed in comparison to the mindless bloggers comprising that modern Tower of Babble, the Internet, who routinely disseminate slander and libel, unchecked by law) have, through their time-honored and credible work, exposed perjurers and brought about many exonerations.

Historically, though, the victim has been subject to the nonexistent mercy of the perjurer. No greater example exists of perjurers who lied simply to exercise power over the fate of others than those youthful fabricators of long-ago Salem, Massachusetts. Superstition and fear enabled these cunning liars to destroy their neighbors. This was an age when people actually believed that witches flew on broomsticks, wizards wafted above villages and towns in bilious clouds of smoke, and the devil stalked the land in a tangible and misshapen form to randomly claim human souls.

## The Witchcraft Perjury Victims of Salem

In 1692, the elders of Salem, Massachusetts, were overwhelmed by a witchcraft craze that swept their little community into the horrors of heresy and wholesale executions. Thirty innocent persons were wrongfully convicted on the most flagrantly perjured testimony in American history. Twenty of these victims paid with their lives after a group of hysterical girls accused them of consorting with the devil.

Salem would be forever linked with supernatural evil and the brutal customs of the Inquisition used to exterminate sinister spirits in its midst. It was a time of mass hysteria and ignorant fears that

The peaceful town of Salem, Massachusetts in 1692, disrupted with fear and apprehension when a witchcraft craze seized the minds of its 1,700 residents. *History Inc./Jay Robert Nash Collection.*

crushed common sense and drove reason from the human mind. It was an age that embraced nightmare apprehensions to establish baseless facts. It was an era when witches, warlocks, wizards, and their animal familiars sprang to reality from bedeviled imaginations. The true motivation for creating this unbelievable hoodoo environment, however, had nothing to do with purging ancient evil from the human soul.

The accusers, a cabal of lonely girls who would have otherwise died in obscurity, gained spectacular attention and the actual power to decide who lived and who died. This terrible recognition was their goal, a lethal vanity they lived to regret. More sinister were those who coached and subtly directed the girls, relatives for the most part, bent on acquiring their neighbor's possessions, which would be forfeited to the accuser through perjured testimony and wrongful conviction. Others gave perjured testimony in support of the accusers and against the defendants to rid themselves of unwanted wives, settle old business scores, or simply destroy someone they did not like. Many others perjured themselves to save their own lives. A pointing finger could spell doom in this fear-crazed period, a mania that would not see its like again in America until the coming of Senator Joseph McCarthy in the communist witch-hunts of the 1950s.

Salem and the surrounding communities operated on theocratic principles, governed after 1690

The slave Tituba, right, telling witch and Devil tales to several impressionable girls living in superstitious Salem, Massachusetts, which prompted the witchcraft mania of 1692. *History Inc./Jay Robert Nash Collection.*

Pastor Samuel Parris prays while his 9-year-old daughter Elizabeth collapses from a recurrent seizure caused, the girl and her friends claimed, by Salem citizens controlled by the Devil and turned into witches, warlocks and wizards. *History Inc./Jay Robert Nash Collection.*

by Mosaic laws applied to the temporal and the spiritual alike. Inhabitants lived by a rigid code of laws that not only regulated their every move but governed their very thoughts. Though the pursuit of witches in Europe was all but nonexistent by the time of the New England mania, the Puritans were suddenly awash with witches and witch-hunts that would see the imprisonment of close to two hundred suspected witches and the execution of nineteen alleged witches and one lone wizard before the madness waned.

The witch-hunts began in Salem in February 1692 in the home of the Reverend Samuel Parris, who, since 1689, was the pastor of the First Church at Salem. Parris had been a merchant in the West Indies (some later rumored that he had trafficked in slaves along the Spanish Main), and financial reverses brought him to the ministry. Coming from Boston to Salem, which then boasted a population of 1,700, Parris brought along two slaves he had acquired in the West Indies, a man called John Indian and his wife, Tituba.

When not scrubbing floors, washing, slaughtering farm animals, or emptying slops, Tituba whiled away the hours by telling ghost stories to Parris's nine-year-old daughter, Elizabeth, and her cousin, eleven-year-old Abigail Williams.

So provocative were Tituba's tales that the girls invited their friends to gather each evening at the parsonage to hear the slave's twaddle. These included Ann Putnam, twelve, Mercy Lewis, seventeen, Mary Walcott, seventeen, Elizabeth Hubbard, seventeen, Elizabeth Booth, eighteen, Susan Sheldon, eighteen, Mary Warren, twenty, and Sarah Churchill, twenty. The group, later known as the Circle Girls, was entranced and terrified by Tituba's voodoo blathering.

The slave told their fortunes in ominous tones, working her voice into strange pitches. She seemed to induce tables to tip crazily and bring about strange knockings and other noises the girls unhesitatingly ascribed to spirits and the devil. Some of the younger girls reportedly fell into hypnotic trances, or claimed to do so, as they competed to shine at adolescent ceremonies. As the meetings went on, the girls' conduct became unpredictable and wild. Most of these girls were lonely sorts, unattended by young men, embittered by their lot in life. They were unschooled and only two of them could write their name. Ann Putnam, who would wreak the most havoc, was epileptic. Three of the girls were domestic workers who willingly testified against their employers, bringing about their gruesome deaths.

Pastor Parris, who was later described as a man "narrow and bigoted," became alarmed at his daughter's odd behavior. Elizabeth Parris and Abigail Williams appeared to throw fits at all hours of the day—especially when called on to perform their routine chores. They became hysterical and pulled at their hair. They went into uncontrollable convulsions. The Reverend called in a friend, Pastor Deodat Lawson, who sat in the Parris home one night and watched horrified as Abigail Williams became nearly insane. In his account of the Salem witch trials, *A Brief and True Narrative*, Lawson recalled how he watched the Williams child "run to the fire, and begin to throw fire

An elderly woman accused of being a witch is seized by Salem officials in early 1692; dozens of such innocent persons were jailed, and twenty of them convicted of witchcraft were executed. *History Inc./Jay Robert Nash Collection.*

brands about the house and run against the back as if she would run up the chimney."

Lawson was also present when Abigail Williams went berserk during a prayer meeting at the parsonage. She interrupted the meeting many times by shrieking and stomping the floor. In tandem, little Elizabeth Parris shouted incoherent phrases interpreted as obscenities. Elizabeth hurled a Bible across the room, striking her strict and startled father.

Much disturbed, Lawson later wrote that "after psalm was sung, Abigail Williams said to me, 'Now stand up and name your text.' And, after it was read, she said, 'It is a long text.'" In the afternoon, Lawson remembered that Abigail, "upon my referring to my doctrines, said to me, 'I know of no doctrine you had. If you did name one, I have forgot it.'"

This was heresy, and the baffled adults perceived the certain workings of the devil. A local doctor named Gregg was summoned, and he observed the girls go through their tantrums. "I know of nothing else to say save to declare them both bewitched," pronounced the good doctor.

"Who bewitched you?" demanded Parris of his daughter and niece. They stood mute before him with staring eyes and tightly closed lips. The slave Tituba stepped forward, the sinister catalyst of the horrors to come, and offered a remedy: "Take four ounces of rye meal, mix it with children's water [urine], roll it in a biscuit, bake it in ashes, and feed it to the dog. If the dog gets sick, the girls will tell who bewitched them."

Any reasonable adult would have dismissed Tituba's prescription as gibberish, but Parris was not a reasonable adult. He ordered the repugnant concoction fed to the family dog, and the animal not unexpectedly vomited. Then, with Tituba coaching the two girls, a plethora of names spilled forth from their mouths. The first person named as a witch was, quite naturally, Tituba, who made no denial and added that Satan compelled her to sign her name in his book and vow to work mischief upon all children.

The demented slave was put in jail, where she remained throughout the witchcraft trials. (How Tituba, who could not write, managed to sign her name in the devil's book was never revealed; the fact that she enjoyed her stay in jail with no labors to perform was well recorded.)

A cane-wielding demagogue, Sir William Phips, the first governor appointed to rule the newly reorganized Massachusetts Colony, toured the jails in Boston, Ipswich, Cambridge, Andover, and Salem and found them brimming with accused witches and other slavish followers of Satan. He wasted no time in establishing a witchcraft court, appointing four Boston and two Salem men to preside over this court as judges.

The court only existed to rid the colony of witches. The fact that the governor had no power to create courts and that this court was illegal was ignored. Deputy Governor William Stoughton was appointed chief justice. The other judges were John Hathorne, Jonathan Corwin, Major Bartholomew Gedney, Wait Winthrop, Pe-

Witches Hill in Salem, where those convicted of witchcraft were hanged; the entire community was required to watch the executions. *History Inc./Jay Robert Nash Collection.*

ter Sargent, Major John Richards, and Captain Samuel Sewall.

The trials ensued in late February 1692, and those brought before the judges stood accused by girls whose parents and relatives had old scores to settle. Most of those tried and convicted of witchcraft were avowed enemies of Ann Putnam, mother of her twelve-year-old namesake, Ann Putnam, who testified in all but one of the cases that resulted in the death penalty. The mother coaxed and counseled her daughter in every instance.

The first "witch" tried in Salem (those accused in Boston and other communities were sent to Salem to stand trial) was a sixty-year-old woman, three times married, Bridget Bishop. As the keeper of a rowdy inn between Salem and Beverly, Bishop had a rather soiled reputation. Twelve years earlier she had been tried as a witch but freed for lack of evidence, a fact known to the accusing girls.

Bishop was brought into court on June 2, 1692, following an examination in which nine Puritan women stripped her in her jail cell in a fruitless search for "witch marks" (marks on the flesh such as birthmarks, moles, and scars that could be interpreted as brandings by the devil).

The moment this hapless woman appeared, those who accused her of being a witch—Ann Putnam, Abigail Williams, Mercy Lewis, Elizabeth Hubbard, and Mary Walcott—fell from their benches and rolled in paroxysms of pain, screaming and ranting that Bridget Bishop was pinching

them and thrusting long needles into their flesh. Such a hysterical display greatly moved the Puritan throng and visibly upset the dour-faced judges.

Judge Hathorne began the inquisition: "Bridget Bishop, what do you say? You here stand charged with sundry acts of witchcraft made upon the bodies of Mercy Lewis and Ann Putnam and others."

"I am innocent," Bishop replied. "I know nothing of it. I have done no witchcraft."

Hathorne addressed the girls as some were still in spasms, rolling their eyes and wincing in what appeared to be intense pain. "Look upon this woman and see if this be the woman that you have seen hurting you." The judge turned to Bishop: "What do you say now that you see they charge you? Do you confess?"

"I never hurt them in my life. I never saw these persons before. I am innocent as the child unborn."

"What contract have you made with the Devil?"

"I have made no contract with the Devil. I never saw him in my life."

One of the bewitched accusers, Mercy Lewis, jumped to her feet and shouted, "Oh Goody Bishop [most women in this formal era were referred to as goodwife, "goody" for short, and men "good man" or "good men"], did not you come to my house the last night and did you not tell me that you would torment me?"

Hathorne let the exclamation stand without rebuke, an interruptive technique used by the girls that was consistently tolerated during all the trials. The judge then turned back to the accused: "Tell the truth in this matter. How come this person to be tormented and to charge you with doing it?"

"I am not come here to say I am a witch and to take away my life." Bishop knew full well that an conviction for witchcraft could result in condemnation and execution.

As the mania spread throughout the courtroom, spectators succumbed to the swelling fever. Marshall Herrick claimed that Bridget Bishop had once entered his bed chamber as a ghost and added, "She is by some of the afflicted persons charged with murder."

To this hearsay, Hathorne persisted, "What do you say to these murders you are charged with?"

"I am innocent," cried the exasperated woman. "I know nothing of it."

Witnesses full of suspicion and fear, and overcome by their own nightmares, came forward to testify against Bridget Bishop. William Stacey claimed that "about fourteen years gone I had the small pox and Bridget Bishop did visit me and profess a great love for me in my affliction. After I got well, Bridget Bishop got me to do some work for her for which she gave me three pence which seemed to me as if it had been good money, but I had not gone over three or four rods before I looked into my pocket where I put the money but could not find it.

"Sometime afterwards I met the said Bishop in the street going to the mill. She asked me whether my father would grind her grist. I asked her why she asked me that and she answered: 'Because folks count me a witch.' Then I told her I knew my father would grind it. But being gone about six rods from the said Bishop suddenly my off wheel here sunk down into a hole upon plain ground and I was forced to get one to help me get out. Afterwards I went back to look for the hole where the wheel sunk in but could not find any hole.

"After that, in the winter, about midnight, I felt something between my lips pressing hard against my teeth and it was very cold, insomuch that it did wake me, and I got up and set upon my bed and at the same time I did see the said Bridget Bishop at the foot of the bed and it was as light as if it had been day. It was either the said Bishop or her shape she having then a black cat and a black hat and a red coat. And the said Bishop or her shape clapped her coat close to the legs and hopped upon the bed and about the room and then went out.

"Sometimes afterwards I met the said Bishop by Isaac Stone's hill and, after I had passed by her, my horse stood still with a small load going up the hill, and the cart fell down. Then I went to lift a bag of grain of about two bushels, but could not budge it with all my might.

"I fully believe that the said Bishop was instrumental in the death of my daughter, Pricilla, about two years ago. The child was a likely, thriving child and suddenly screeched out and so continued in this unusual manner for about a fortnight and so died in a lamentable manner."

A Salem man, Samuel Gray, then testified that Bridget Bishop had entered his bedroom as a specter in 1678. The ghostly apparition, Gray stated, stood between his bed and the cradle of his child. He called out to her, "In the name of God what do you come for?" The phantom departed, he said, and, thinking it all a dream, Gray went back to sleep. "Then I felt something come to my lips cold and thereupon I started and looked up and again I did see the same woman with something between her hands holding it before my mouth and the child in the cradle gave a great screech as if it were greatly hurt and she disappeared, and when I took the child I could not quiet it in some hours." Gray added, almost in tears, that his once healthy child "pined away and was never well, although it lived some months in a sad condition and so died." Gray raised an arm and pointed a finger. He identified that murderous ghost of fourteen years earlier as one and the same, Bridget Bishop.

John Hale testified that Bishop kept her inn open at all hours of the night to those "who were drunk and played at shovel board." When a neighbor, John Trask, at the request of his wife, entered the inn to complain of the noise, he was insulted. After Trask threw the game pieces into the fire, his wife Christiane became bewitched, a spell that was broken only after many months of intense prayer and church communion.

Trask's wife then suddenly died. Of this Hale stated, "As to the wounds which Christiane Trask died of I observed three deadly ones. A piece of her windpipe was cut out and other one about through the windpipe and gulle to the veins they call jugular so that I then judged and still do be-

The hanging of Bridget Bishop, June 10, 1692; she was the first innocent person to die during the witchcraft mania in Salem, Massachusetts. *History Inc./Jay Robert Nash Collection.*

lieve it impossible for her to do so without some extraordinary work of the Devil or witchcraft."

Sam Shaltoch insisted that his fitful, sick child had been made ill by Bridget Bishop, who had cast a spell over him. An argument with the accused, stated John Lauder, caused Bishop to enter his bedroom late at night in 1684 and sit on his stomach. "She presently laid hold of my throat and almost choked me and I had no strength or power in my hands to rise or help myself and in this condition she held me." One of the innkeeper's employees, John Blye, testified that Bishop kept "poppets [puppets] made up of rags and hoggs brussels with headless pins in them" in holes in the basement walls of the inn's cellar. A half dozen more, including Bishop's husband, Edward, condemned her as a witch.

Susan Sheldon was one of the "witch bitches," as the original accusing coterie of girls was labeled by old George Jacobs, whom they accused of being a witch. Susan Sheldon claimed that "on the second day of June 1692, I saw the apparition of Bridget Bishop and immediately appeared two little children and said they were twins and told Bridget Bishop to her face that she had murdered them by setting them into fits whereupon they died."

A solemn jury found Bridget Bishop guilty. Chief Justice Stoughton did not pause in signing her death warrant, which read: "Whereupon Bridget Bishop, alias Oliver, at a special court held at Salem the second day of this month of June before William Stoughton, Esquire and his Associate Justices of the said court, was indicted for practicing and exercising on the nineteenth day of April last past and diverse other days and times certain acts

of witchcraft in and upon the bodies of Abigail Williams, Ann Putnam, Mercy Lewis, Mary Walcott, and Elizabeth Hubbard of Salem, whereby their bodies were greatly afflicted, pined, consumed, wasted, and tormented. To which indictment Bridget Bishop pleaded not guilty and put herself upon God.

"Whereupon she was found guilty of the offense and witchcrafts and sentenced to death. Therefore, in the name of their majesties William and Mary, now king and queen of England, we command you Sheriff George Corwin that, on Friday next, being the tenth day of June, to conduct the said Bridget Bishop from their majesties' jail in Salem to the place of execution and there cause her to be hanged until she be dead."

Corwin carried out the order on June 10, 1692, and, confirming the convicted witch as being dead, cut down her body and buried her next to the scaffold. On hand for the execution was witch-hunter Cotton Mather (1663–1728), who would go on to become a chronicler of witchcraft in Puritan America. Although he initially endorsed the witchcraft trials in Salem, he later diplomatically joined the popular view that they had been unfair.

In the beginning, however, he, like most others, saw a witch at the top of every tree or a wizard lurking behind every building.

Mather claimed that a moment before Bridget Bishop was hanged, she looked toward the church and her withering, evil glance caused a giant timber to be torn loose from the building and slam

The trial of Rebecca Nurse, who was convicted of witchcraft on the perjured testimony of the girls claiming to have been bewitched and tortured by her and many others serving the evil pursuits of the Devil. *History Inc./Jay Robert Nash Collection.*

The official examination of Rebecca Nurse before her trial; she was condemned and hanged on July 19, 1692. *History Inc./Jay Robert Nash Collection.*

through a distant wall. Mather left it to another to record how the pathetic woman turned into a raving lunatic on the gallows, ferociously fighting with executioners for the last seconds of her life.

Soon after the first Salem witch was executed, her husband, Edward, who "gladly followed her to the gallows" to witness her "just execution," took his third wife. The trials ground on all summer. On July 19, 1692, five more women were convicted as witches—Sarah Good, Elizabeth Howe, Susanna Martin, Rebecca Nurse, and Sarah Wilds—and were taken to the Salem scaffold and hanged on July 19, 1692. Sarah Good was a seventy-year-old beggar woman no one liked. When she was refused alms, she would curse the niggardly passerby. She was the first person arrested for witchcraft in Salem.

Sarah's husband, John Good, a known drunk, testified that "my wife often appears to be possessed of the Devil." Elizabeth How of Topsfield, also seventy, escaped from the Salem jail and was later found walking in a daze through the forests around Boston. Susanna Martin came from Amesbury and was seventy-two. Rebecca Nurse, seventy-one, had been involved in many lawsuits with the Putnam family. All of these people were accused of "tormenting" the "witch bitches" and were hanged for it.

Seventy-five-year-old George Jacobs was the first male witch to be convicted. Jacobs had to struggle against senility while combating the dozens of "bewitched" girls and men accusing him. In Jacobs's preliminary hearing, the judge pointed to several of the Circle Girls and stated, "Here are them that accuse you of witchcraft."

"Well," Jacobs replied quietly, "let us hear who they are and what they are."

"Abigail Williams," announced the judge.

Jacobs looked at the wide-eyed eleven-year-old and laughed.

"Why do you laugh?" the judge asked.

"Because I am falsely accused. Do you think this is true?"

"What do you think?" the judge queried.

"I never did it."

"Who did it?"

"Don't ask me."

The judge pointed to one witness. "Sarah Churchill accuses you. There she is."

"I am as innocent as a child born tonight. I have lived in Salem thirty-three years. If you can prove I am guilty, I will lie under it."

Sarah Churchill then spoke in a monotone as if in a trance: "Last night I was afflicted at Deacon Ingersoll's and Mary Walcott said it was a man with two staves, it was my master." (Jacobs walked on two canes and he was Sarah Churchill's employer.)

Jacobs would not look at the lonely girl, who worked for him on his ten-acre farm, but turned to the judge, pleading, "Pray do not accuse me, your worship. You must judge rightly."

He was ignored as the judge concentrated on the witness. "What book did he bring to you, Sarah?"

"The same the other women brought."

"The Devil can go in any shape," the judge prompted.

"He appeared to me on the other side of the river and hurt me."

"Look here," the judge pointed out, "she accuses you to your face. It is not true?"

"I never wronged no man in word or deed," said Jacobs.

"Here are three evidences."

Jacobs grew disgusted with the farce. "You tax me for a wizard, you may as well tax me for a buzzard!"

"Is it no harm to afflict these?"

"I never did it."

"But how comes it to be in your appearance?"

"The Devil can take any likeness."

"Not without their consent."

"Please, your worship. I am silly about these things as the child born last night."

"You argue you have lived so long, but Cain might have lived long before he killed Abel and you might have lived long before the Devil got you."

"Christ hath suffered three times for me."

"What three times?"

"He suffered the cross and the gale."

Sarah Churchill, in keeping with the brazen conduct of all the allegedly bewitched girls, stepped closer to the accused and shouted, "You might as well confess if you are guilty."

"Have you heard that I have any witchcraft?"

"I know that you live a wicked life," Sarah offered.

"Let her make it out."

"Does he ever pray in his family?" the judge asked Sarah Churchill.

"Not unless by himself."

"Why do you not pray in your family?" the judge admonished Jacobs.

"I cannot read."

"Well," harrumphed the judge, "but you may pray for all that. Can you say the Lord's Prayer? Let us hear you!"

Old George Jacobs glared at the judge, and, following more allegations by Sarah Churchill that he compelled her to write her name in the Devil's book, Jacobs turned angrily toward the judge and said, "Well, burn me or hang me, I will stand in the truth of Christ."

When Jacobs was examined in court for a second time, Ann Putnam, Abigail Williams, and Mercy Lewis, who were all to testify that he was a witch, fell on the floor when he appeared, going into frothy fits.

The judge wasted no time in asking the girls, "Is this the man who hurts you?"

"This is the man!" Abigail Williams screeched and sank back into her fit.

Ann Putnam shouted, "This is the man that hurts her and brings her the book, and she should be as well as his granddaughter!" (One of Ann's rel-

The trial of George Jacobs, kneeling and pleading for his life, lower right; he was found guilty of witchcraft and hanged on August 19, 1692. *History Inc./Jay Robert Nash Collection.*

atives was involved in a suit with Jacobs some time before, and it was her father, Thomas Putnam, who accused Jacobs of bewitching his daughter.)

The judge pointed his finger at the accused. "Mercy Lewis! Is this the man?"

Mercy Lewis could barely manage to interrupt her fit to bubble, "This is the man. . . He almost kills me." She then resumed rolling her eyes and twisting her body on the floor.

Mary Walcott had to struggle against the fit she claimed Jacobs was then imposing on her to burst forth, "This is the man! He used to come with two staves and beat me with one of them!"

The judge spun around to Jacobs. "What do you say? Are you not a witch?"

"No," the old man mumbled, tired, "if I were to die presently." Asked by the court if Mercy Lewis's statement was correct, Jacobs responded, "Why, it is false."

Vicious little Ann Putnam shouted, "Yes, you told me you had been so [a witch] for forty years." Then she and Abigail Williams held out their hands, palms up. There were pins sticking in their palms, and they cried out that Jacobs had caused this to happen during the testimony.

The judge took the pins as conclusive evidence. "Are you not the man that made a disturbance at a lecture in Salem?" he asked Jacobs.

"No great disturbance. Do you think I use witchcraft?"

"Yes, indeed," the judge snapped.

"No, I use none of it!"

The remainder of the testimony in the trial of George Jacobs no longer exists. It is known that his granddaughter Margaret was badgered into confessing that she was bewitched by her grandfather. A day before Jacobs was executed, the child became violently insane. Only hours after Jacobs and four other convicted witches were hanged, the ten-acre Jacobs farm was seized by Sheriff Corwin. Sarah Jacobs, George's ailing wife, had her wedding ring torn from her finger. She too was convicted of being a witch, but her execution was delayed and the witchcraft delusion subsided. When released, Sarah Jacobs married John Wilds, whose wife had been hanged.

It soon became apparent that the authorities were more lenient with those who confessed to being a witch than those who denied it. In fact, the twenty victims of the Salem madness were executed because they refused to admit they were witches. Dozens of persons, and then hundreds from the area around Boston, were rounded up and imprisoned on suspicion of practicing witchcraft, which was also treason against the theocratic government. Cotton Mather defined witchcraft and treason as one and the same offense, writing that such acts mean "a renouncing of God and advancing a filthy Devil into the throne of the Most High; 'tis the most nefandous high treason against the majesty on high."

Rather than suffer execution, most Puritans who stood accused confessed to anything demanded of them. Their admissions were, they knew, along with the judges and juries who heard them, quite ridiculous, but such confessions functioned to cleanse the spirit and thereby exonerate the living flesh. To confess was to live. Deliverance Hobbs and her daughter, Abigail, were both accused, and they both readily confessed and were spared the hangman's rope.

To save her life, Deliverance Hobbs taxed her imagination to the utmost: "I was at a meeting of witches yesterday morning and there were present Proctor and his wife, Goody Nurse, Giles Corey and his wife, Goody Bishop, and Burroughs, the preacher. He [Burroughs, who was hanged later as a conjurer, a wizard] told us to bewitch all the village, but to do it gradually, assuring us we would prevail. He administered the sacraments with red bread, and red wine like blood. I saw Osborne [Sarah Osborne, a convicted witch, who died in jail], Sarah Good, Goody Wilds, and Goody Nurse distribute the bread and wine, and a man in a long crowned hat [the devil] sat next to the minister [Burroughs], and they sat at a table and filled out the wine in tankards.

"I did not eat or drink, but all the rest did, therefore they threatened to torment me. The meeting was in the pasture by Mr. Parris' house. I saw Abigail Williams run out to speak to the others, then I was struck blind and could see no more. Goody Wilds told me if I would sign the book, she would give me some clothes and would not afflict me any more. I saw Goodman Corey and a woman from Boston trying to break my daughter's neck."

The case against the Reverend George Burroughs, who graduated from Harvard in the class of 1670 and became pastor of the First Church in Salem in 1680, was trumped up by the scheming Putnam family. He was branded the chief wizard in the witch trials, the man who conducted black witch masses and administered the witch's sacrament in the dark of night in Reverend Parris's pasture. When Burroughs's first wife died in 1681, he ordered rum from John Putnam to be used at her funeral. Burroughs never paid for the rum and then moved to Maine some years later. Thomas Putnam, John's brother, was the constable who traveled to Maine and arrested Burroughs for witchcraft and brought him back to Salem to stand trial.

The onetime Salem minister had been married three times, and his first two wives had died mysteriously. The Circle Girls believed, or so they told the court, that the Reverend Burroughs had murdered them and organized the great witch coven of Massachusetts. It was to the sinister pasture meeting that Burroughs summoned Ann Foster and a host of others. Foster was a widow from Andover and a confessed witch.

To save herself from the gallows, Foster created the broomstick legend. Her testimony and that of many others, all intimidated, some tortured by being tied hand and foot and hung upside down until blood ran from their noses, sealed the fate of George Burroughs, wizard.

Ranted Foster, "The Devil appeared to me several times in the shape of a bird as I never saw the like before, and I have had the gift of striking the afflicted down with my eye ever since. I know the bird was the Devil, because he came white and vanished away black. The Devil told me I should have this gift if I would believe him, and he told me I should have prosperity.

"He came to me three times, always as a bird, and the last time was about a half a year since and sat upon a table. He had two legs and great eyes, and Carrier's wife [Martha Carrier, another accused witch] came to me about three weeks ago and persuaded me to hurt these people. One time I bewitched a hog of John Lovejoys to death, and I hurt some persons in Salem. Goody Carrier wanted me to bewitch two children of Andrew Allins, and she had two poppets made and stuck pins in them to bewitch the said children by which one of them died and the other was very sick.

"Carrier came to me and wanted me to go to the meeting of witches. So we got upon sticks and went said journey [flying in the air on broomsticks]; and I saw Burroughs, the minister, there, and he spake to all of us. There was about twenty-five persons there met together and I tied a knot in a rag and threw it into the fire to hurt Timothy Swan, and I hurt the rest by squeezing poppets and almost choked them.

"When we rode on a stick to the meeting the stick broke as we were carried in the air above the tops of the trees and we fell, and I hung fast about the neck of Goody Carrier and we were presently in the village and my leg was much hurt. I heard some of the witches say there was 305 in the whole country, and that they would ruin this village.

"There was present at the meeting two men besides Burroughs. One of them had gray hair and used to attend public meetings [Jacobs] to worship God. About three or four years ago, Martha Carrier told me she would bewitch James Hobbs' child to death, and the child died in twenty-four hours."

For telling these absurd tales, couched against Burroughs and Martha Carrier, who were both hanged and for whom the Salem witch-hunters harbored special animosities (those who confessed were well aware of such animosities and thoroughly briefed by the accusers as to events, people, and places), Foster was reprieved from the gallows only to die in jail.

The confession of the hysterical Abigail Hobbs, daughter of Deliverance, was also used against Burroughs to convict him. A judge leaned over the frightened girl and asked her, "Did Burroughs bring you any of the poppets of his wives to stick pins into?"

"I don't remember."

It was then established that Burroughs provided poppets of his wives for Abigail Hobbs to stick pins into. When the judge inquired, "Did you know of any poppets pricked to kill her [one of Burroughs's deceased wives]?" the girl provided the rationale for all of those who stood accused and saved their lives through lies.

"No, John Proctor told me better to afflict than be afflicted, and then I should not be hanged. He brought me a poppet and a thorn to afflict Ann Putnam last Friday." This pathetic girl later committed suicide.

In jail the heavyset Burroughs was thoroughly examined for witch marks, but none were found. When entering the court, he became so angry that he jumped backward and knocked down many who were prepared to bear witness against him. The testimony of twelve-year-old Ann Putnam damned him completely.

"On April 20, 1692, at evening I saw the apparition of a minister at which I was grievously affrighted and cried out, 'O, dreadful, dreadful, here is a minister come! What are ministers converts to? Whence come you and what is your name for I will complain of you, though you be a minister, if you be a wizard?' Immediately I was tortured by him, being racked and almost choked by him and he tempted me to write in his book, which I refused with many outcries. And I told him I would not write in his book though he tear me all to pieces, but told him that it was a dreadful thing for him which was a minister that should teach little children to fear God should come persuading poor creatures to give their souls to the Devil.

"'Tell me your name that I may know who you are?' Then he told me his name was George Burroughs, and that he had three wives and that he had bewitched the first two of them to death, and that he killed Mrs. Lawson, and also killed Mr. Lawson's children, because he went to the Eastward with Sir Edmon and preached to the soldiers and that he had bewitched a great many soldiers to death at the Eastward, and that he had made Abigail Hobbs a witch and several more, and he also told me that he was above a witch; that he was a conjurer."

Five more terrible examples of devastating witchcraft—Martha Carrier, George Jacobs, John Proctor, John Willard, and the "wizard" George Burroughs—were solemnly escorted to the gallows on August 19, 1692, and hanged until dead. Burroughs made a moving speech on behalf of his innocence. He denounced the witch-hunting in such a convincing manner that many in the crowd had second thoughts. According to one story, his avowed foe, Cotton Mather, saw a threat to his master scheme of purging the land of evil, and, riding wildly through the dense gathering on horseback, he shouted down the minister and ordered the hangman to perform his duty, which he did.

Families and relatives of those condemned were compelled to pay the hangman's fee, as well as fees for maintaining the accused in jail. Discharges and reprieves also incurred fees, meaning that many of the less notorious who were suspected of witchcraft could buy their way to freedom from the money-loving Puritans.

Following the execution of George Burroughs, the witch trials became more bizarre. Giles and Martha Corey were accused of being witches so that the Putnams and others could seize their sizable property, or so it was later reported. The general rule of thumb in Massachusetts seemed to be that the death penalty was not invoked for those who admitted being witches, but their possessions were seized and invariably reverted to the accusers as payment for cleansing the community of devil-worshiping witches. Corey owned a considerable tract of land and was one of the richest men in the community. When he was tried for witchcraft, rather than admit or deny anything, he stood mute.

Corey, an enfeebled eighty-one-year-old, angered the court by protesting Judge Hathorne's treatment of his wife Martha. In jail, he was tortured until he agreed to testify against her. She was sentenced to death. At his own trial, Corey shrewdly refused to utter a word. He repeatedly resisted either admitting or denying he was a witch. He intended to preserve his land for his sons and daughters.

Before his trial began, the old man bravely stood up to Judge Hathorne and stated: "I will not plead. If I deny, I am condemned already in courts, where ghosts appear as witnesses and swear men's lives away. If I confess, then I confess to a lie, to buy a life, which is not life, but only death in life. I will not bear false witness against any, not even against myself, whom I count least."

Corey was promptly convicted of witchcraft and treason. As if to emphasize the exaggerated sequence of nightmare events in Salem, a death penalty from the Dark Ages was resurrected—*peine forte et dure*. This was the only execution of that medieval custom ever carried out in America. Giles Corey was pressed to death.

Although no complete description of Corey's execution has survived, this traditional torture death is thus described in John Swain's *History of*

The slow Medieval execution of pressing to death was revived in Salem and applied to elderly Giles Corey, who had refused to admit practicing witchcraft, and was executed by rocks and heavy stones piled upon his chest on September 19, 1692, the only such recorded execution in the Western World. *History Inc./Jay Robert Nash Collection.*

*Torture:* "The victim was stripped and tied to the ground with his arms and legs extended; a square board was then placed on his chest, upon which weights were laid until he pleaded or life became extinct. The torture occasionally lasted three days. A triangular board was sometimes placed under the victim's back, which had the effect of breaking his spine, thus bringing the torture to a more rapid termination."

In Corey's case, the board was not used. Rocks were piled directly on top of his chest, his hands and feet stretched and staked down. He died in great pain. According to later apocryphal reports, every now and then through the long hours of his dying, Corey cried out in irony, "More weight!"

The hatred and vengeance in Cotton Mather waned considerably when he viewed the old man's body, which had been placed in Potters Field in Salem, a huge boulder still atop his crushed chest. He realized for once the inhumanity of the trials and executions and was quoted as saying over Corey's body, "O sight most horrible! In a land like this spangled with churches Evangelical inwrapped in our salvations, must we seek in moldering statute books of English court some old forgotten law, to do such deed? . . . This poor man, whom we have made a victim hereafter will be counted as a martyr!"

The last insane acts of the Puritans in their spectacular witchcraft trials were grotesque and unconscionable. Robert Calef, in *More Wonders of the Invisible World Discovered,* states that two dogs were tried at Salem for witchcraft, one being the familiar of John Bradstreet, who rode on the dog's back as would a witch on a broomstick. The dog was convicted for "afflicting them and they all would fall into fits at the dog looking upon them. Whereupon the said dog was tried and hung for a witch."

No records of these dog trials now exist (the Puritans no doubt found them then as inhuman as we do today); the ledgers of record were destroyed. It is known that the animals were held in halters by bailiffs before the judge and made to answer charges by barking, which was produced by goads and prongs rammed by the bailiff up the animal's anus. Dogs were hanged head downward.

The last executions occurred on September 22, 1692, when Martha Corey, Mary Esty, Alice Parker, Mary Parker, Ann Pudeator, Wilmot Reed, Margaret Scott, and Samuel Wardwell were hanged as witches. Almost two hundred people were still held in various jails, many of whom, like the Coreys, had been constantly moved from Andover to Boston to Salem in an "around the horn" technique later popular with certain police departments to prevent relatives and friends from contacting the accused, another Puritan first.

Before most of the accused were permanently freed in early 1693, several notable prisoners escaped, including John Alden of Boston, whose father would be immortalized by Henry Wadsworth Longfellow. The Circle Girls were brought to Alden's Boston trial and committed all sorts of slanders against this esteemed hero of the Indian wars. One of his accusers screamed in court, "There stands Alden! A bold fellow with his hat on before the judges. He sells powder and shot to the Indians and French, and lies with Indian squaws and has Indian papooses!"

The hanging of Samuel Wardwell in Salem, Massachusetts, September 22, 1692. *History Inc./Jay Robert Nash Collection.*

Alden was forced to stand on a chair and face the girls; the accusers went into their tired act, falling into faints. As Alden's hand was placed on each apparently unconscious girl, she revived immediately. Revolted by such shamming, the logical Alden turned to the judge and said, "What's the reason *you* don't fall when I look at *you*? Can you give me one?" The judge grew red-faced and nonplussed. Alden was sent to Boston prison, where he remained for fifteen weeks, until he escaped. He was later recaptured in New York but released.

Though many sued the government for private lands and possessions seized during the hysteria, petitioners had to wait until 1711 before damages were awarded. The state of Massachusetts, however, has never reversed the witchcraft convictions.

The relatives of Giles and Martha Corey were eventually given £79 for their property loss. The Burroughs family received £50. These payments were forthcoming almost twenty years after the trials had become an ugly, unwanted memory. Abigail Faulkner and Elizabeth Proctor, who were both sentenced to death and reprieved because of pregnancy, were released to find that they had been legally declared dead and therefore cut off from their property and inheritances.

The Salem jury repented its convictions in 1696, four years after it found thirty persons guilty of witchcraft. In a petition signed by all twelve members, the jury stated that they "were not capable to understand, nor able to withstand [thus stating that the Devil brought about the trials], the mysterious delusions of the Powers of Darkness and Prince of the Air, but were, for want of knowledge in ourselves and better information from others, prevailed with to take up such evidence against the accused, as on further consideration and better information we justly fear was insufficient. . . We fear we have been instrumental with others, though ignorantly and unwittingly, to bring upon ourselves and this people of the Lord the guilt of innocent blood. . .

"We do therefore hereby signify to all in general, and to the surviving sufferers in especial, our deep sense of, and sorrow for our errors, in acting on such evidence to the condemnation of any person. And we do hereby declare that we justly fear that we were sadly deluded and mistaken, for which we are much disquieted and distressed in our minds. . .

"We do heartily ask forgiveness of you all whom we have justly offended, and do declare according to our present minds we would none of us do such things again on such grounds for the whole world. . . "

Only one of the judges, Samuel Sewell, who later helped disperse damage funds to the families of the trial victims, admitted his error. He confessed the total guilt of the court and took "the blame and shame of it, asking pardon of all men" in 1702. The despicable Judge Hathorne went to his grave believing in the witchcraft convictions and executions, as did Stoughton and others. Hathorne's great-great grandson, author Nathaniel Hawthorne (who added a *w* to his name to avoid the stigma of his murderous ancestor), branded his Puritan forefathers for the superstitious bigots they were in *The Scarlet Letter*.

The Reverend Samuel Parris, in whose home the great religious pogrom began, was eventually driven from the town's precincts by enraged citizens. The ten girls who first pointed their fingers at the old, the feeble-minded, and those whom their parents and adult counselors wanted to get rid of were kept away from each other in late 1692 and with the separations came silence. Most of these girls married and settled into obscure lives. Ann Putnam was reinstated by her church in 1697.

In 1706, Putnam confessed to committing fraud and perjury during the witch trials. This confession was read in the First Church of Salem by the new pastor, Joseph Green: "I desire to be humbled before God for that sad and humbling providence that befell my father's family in the year about 1692; that I, then being in my childhood, should by such a providence of God be made an instrument for the accusing of several persons of a grievous crime, whereby their lives were taken

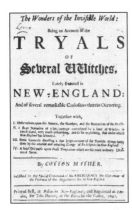

Cover of the book written by witch-hunter Cotton Mather, which detailed the trials of those convicted of witchcraft in Salem, Massachusetts, in the dark year of 1692. *History Inc./Jay Robert Nash Collection.*

away from them, whom now I have just ground and good reason to believe they were innocent persons. And that it was a great delusion of Satan that deceived me in that sad time, whereby I justly fear I have been instrumental, with others, though ignorantly and unwittingly, to bring upon myself and this land the guilt of innocent blood. . . I desire to lie in the dust, and to be humbled for it, in that I was a cause, with others, of so sad a calamity to them and their families, for which cause I desire to lie in the dust and earnestly beg forgiveness of God, and from all those unto whom I have given just cause of sorrow and offense whose relations were taken away or accused." In the end, however, Putnam did not blame herself. In her mind, the one who orchestrated and administered the trials, who had brought about the wrongful conviction and execution of thirty innocent persons, was the devil himself.

The following wrongly convicted persons were tried and condemned at the Salem witch trials in 1692 (twenty were executed): Bridget Bishop, hanged, June 10, 1692; Mary Bradbury, convicted, September 6, 1692, escaped; Reverend George Burroughs, hanged, August 19, 1692; Martha Carrier, hanged, August 19, 1692; Sarah Cloyce, convicted, September 6, 1692, reprieved; Giles Corey, pressed to death, September 19, 1692; Martha Corey, hanged, September 22, 1692; Rebecca Eames, convicted, September 17, 1692, reprieved; Mary Esty, hanged, September 22, 1692; Abigail Faulkner, convicted, pleaded pregnancy; Ann Foster, died in jail; Sarah Good, hanged, July 19, 1692; Dorcas Hoar, convicted, September 6, 1692, reprieved; Abigail Hobbs, convicted, September 6, 1692, reprieved, later committed suicide; Elizabeth Howe, hanged, July 19, 1692; George Jacobs, hanged, August 19, 1692; Mary Lacy, convicted, September 6, 1692, reprieved; Susanna Martin, hanged, July 19, 1692; Rebecca Nurse, hanged, July 19, 1692; Sarah Osborne, died in jail; Alice Parker, hanged, September 22, 1692; Mary Parker, hanged, September 22, 1692; Elizabeth Proctor, convicted, pleaded pregnancy; John Proctor, hanged, August 19, 1692; Ann Pudeator, hanged, September 22, 1692; Wilmot Reed, hanged, September 22, 1692; Margaret Scott, hanged, September 22, 1692; Tituba, held in jail; Samuel Wardwell, hanged, September 22, 1692; Sarah Wilds, hanged, July 19, 1692; John Willard, hanged, August 19, 1692.

## Professional Perjurers and Perjury from Actual Culprits

Throughout the ages, "professional" witnesses, seeking profit and position, routinely perjured themselves in testifying against others. Typical was John Waller (a.k.a. John Trevor), who was convicted for committing highway robbery against John Edglin. Waller's testimony, later found to be false, was what caused his death. During Waller's trial, it emerged that Waller, using the name John Trevor, attended hearings and trials as often as many judges and attorneys, testifying falsely against the accused to obtain the reward money.

Convicted of perjury, Waller was sentenced to two years in prison and required to pay a fine. He also had to undergo the indignity of the pillory. On June 13, 1732, Waller, locked in the pillory bareheaded with his crime advertised in large letters, was pelted to death by an angry crowd. The next day the coroner's statement read, "Willful murder by persons unknown."

Waller made a handsome living through perjury until his lies caught up with him. Two decades after his ironic death in a pillory, a gang of British thieves not only earned their money through perjury, but actually arranged for crimes to occur so that these liars could then testify against innocent persons and receive rewards for bringing the "culprit" to justice.

In 1756, an innocent man was condemned as a thief and sentenced to die. His accusers, it turned out later, were a gang of liars, who committed crimes that they could blame on others and perjure in court against those victims as a means of obtaining reward money. On a December day in London, Joshua Kidden met a man in a pub and agreed to accompany him to Tottenham to remove property from a house before it could be seized for failure to pay rent. Once in Tottenham, however, Kidden was told that the goods could not be removed that day and he received eighteen pence for his time. The two men set off again on the road to London.

Mary Jones, who later said she had been to Edmonton to see a man who owed her £19, was traveling that same day, accompanied by a Marshalsea police officer, Stephen Macdaniel, and a friend, John Berry. During the journey, she explained, her horse fell and she had to walk the animal until it calmed down. As she returned to the chaise, two men accosted her, one pinning her arms and the other threatening to murder her with a large knife. They grabbed her purse and ran.

Berry whipped the horse and overtook the robbers. One escaped but Macdaniel captured the second man, who was positively identified by both Jones and Berry as Joshua Kidden. Kidden objected, explaining that the man he had accompanied to Tottenham had lagged behind him on the road, robbed Jones, attempted to thrust money into his hand, and then took off to relieve himself in a ditch. Kidden was then arrested by the officer. His story was discounted and he was convicted and hanged.

The £40 reward money was divided between Jones, Macdaniel, Berry, and a constable. Several months after Kidden's execution, the efforts of Blackheath high constable Joseph Cox exposed Jones's story as a fraud concocted to get the reward money. Berry, Macdaniel, and Jones were charged with the willful murder of Kidden.

Found guilty and sentenced to death, they were all immediately reprieved because of doubts that the unsupported allegations against them legally amounted to murder. The case was dismissed when the attorney general declined to argue the question, fearing that it might negatively affect the incentive system of rewards, if it were felt that a witness, by giving evidence, might be endangering his life. The gang moved to another area and went on framing people and then giving perjured testimony against them to collect reward money.

Many criminals throughout history, to offset suspicion against themselves, have falsely testified against innocent persons, avoiding convictions that were wrongly applied to others. Thomas Harris, who was hanged for a murder he did not commit, was posthumously cleared when it was discovered that the chief witness for the prosecution had committed the crime. Landlord of the Rising Sun Inn on the York-Newcastle Road, Harris was convicted and executed for murder in 1819. It was later learned that the killer was a bartender at the inn who hated his employer and framed him for the crime through perjured testimony.

When thieves stole a herd of horses and then blamed another, a seething rage was born inside the wrongly convicted man, who was retarded. That rage would explode years later in a mass murder. Born in Auburn, New York, William Freeman (1824–1847), a black with Indian and French blood, belonged to a family that exhibited a deep strain of insanity. His brother and sister were certified insane and Freeman's father died of brain disease.

Freeman grew up without schooling, living a carefree life in Auburn's small black community. Although neighbors thought him to be "addle-brained," Freeman was nevertheless a happy-go-lucky youth who never got into trouble. In 1840, however, he was falsely accused of stealing horses.

The perjured testimony that brought about his conviction was provided by the horse thieves themselves, who rightly believed that the weak-minded Freeman was incapable of defending himself. Freeman was given a five-year term in Auburn Penitentiary.

Embittered over his wrongful conviction, Freeman became sullen and disobedient. Guards responded to Freeman's refractory behavior by brutalizing him. He was repeatedly flogged, and a guard struck Freeman on the head so hard with a board that his skull was permanently damaged and he was deafened in one ear.

Before he was released in September 1845, prison officials realized that Freeman was demented, accelerated by their savage treatment of him. When he was finally set free, he wandered about Auburn babbling to himself about "getting my pay." He came to believe that wealthy, popular John G. Van Nest, who owned a farm three miles south of Auburn, had something to do with his imprisonment. On March 12, 1846, Freeman appeared at the Van Nest home, demanding his "pay."

Van Nest ordered him from the premises, but Freeman produced two knives and stabbed Van Nest to death, then killed his wife and two small children. He was caught the following day and jailed, charged with mass murder. The prisoner, considered "a fiend" and "a monster," caused great excitement in the community. The pastor of the church Van Nest attended mounted the pulpit and demanded Freeman's life. Only a strong guard around the city jail prevented a mob from dragging the prisoner outside and lynching him.

Freeman's fate was predetermined in the minds of everyone except William Henry Seward, former governor of New York and later Abraham Lincoln's secretary of state. He undertook Freeman's defense, entering a plea of insanity for him on July 21–23, 1846. The court determined the prisoner could tell right from wrong, and the obviously biased Judge Bowen Whiting ruled that Freeman was sane. Freeman was put on the witness stand by Seward and he made a poor showing. He sounded confused and at times acted like an imbecile.

In his summation Seward expressed shock that the state would try "a maniac as a malefactor." He made an impassioned speech that ended with an exhortation to jury members to judge his client as they would a white man, saying "he is still your brother, and mine. Hold him to be a man." He went on to quote the words of another black man, John Dupuy: "They have made William Freeman what he is, a brute beast. They don't make anything else of any of our people but brute beasts. But when we violate their laws, they want to punish us as if we were men." (Fifty years later, these words from this famous case, avidly read and researched by British author H. G. Wells, undoubtedly inspired Wells to write his chilling 1896 novel, *The Island of Dr. Moreau*, which saw three film versions, 1933, as *The Island of Lost Souls*, 1977, and 1996, all of which portray a mad doctor on a remote island transforming wild beasts into men and then savagely punishing them for human offenses they do not understand.)

Seward's eloquent effort to save his client was useless, since Judge Whiting, in his highly prejudicial instructions to the jury, pressured it into a verdict of guilty. On July 24, 1846, Judge Whiting sentenced Freeman to death, but Seward appealed the verdict and sentence. The U.S. Supreme Court ruled that Judge Whiting had made serious errors in his court conduct and dismissed the verdict, ordering a new trial.

Seward visited his client in jail to find him critically ill with tuberculosis. Freeman died in his Auburn jail cell on August 21, 1847. An autopsy

William Henry Seward, who later became Lincoln's Secretary of State, defended William Freeman on mass murder charges in 1846, in one of the first insanity pleas, winning a second trial for his client, who died behind bars before that trial began. *History Inc./Jay Robert Nash Collection.*

was performed by Dr. Amariah Bingham, who examined Freeman's brain, concluding that it "presented the appearance of a chronic disease," which posthumously supported Seward's courtroom claims of Freeman's insanity.

For Seward, the defense of Freeman and of Henry Wyatt, another black charged with murder, proved to be a feather in his cap politically. Wyatt had also become a victim of the existing brutality in prisons. After endless beatings and forced starvation, his mind snapped and he killed a fellow inmate, James Gordon.

Again Seward attempted to save his client on grounds of insanity, but he lost this case too, and Wyatt was executed by hanging at Auburn Penitentiary on August 17, 1846. Seward's law business nevertheless boomed and he became celebrated nationwide as a champion of the oppressed. He was also vilified by racists and threatened with violence. Seward's defense of Freeman was a legal landmark for the insane charged with serious crimes, who, up to that time, had received little or no consideration in U.S. courts.

A not dissimilar case involved a leading Kentuckian who was assassinated during a political vendetta. Two of his political opponents were convicted and imprisoned for the crime, the chief witness against these men being the man who most probably committed the murder. William Goebel of Covington, Kentucky, had been a state senator since 1886. His personal life became inextricably involved with his political life. He killed a man because of politics before he was himself assassinated for the same reason.

Regarded as a reformer, Goebel fought against extending the powers of big business when they harmed citizens. John L. Sanford, the chief executive officer of the Farmers and Drovers National Bank of Covington, was an important influence in Kenton County, which was plagued by bitter political fighting for many years. The fight between Sanford and Goebel became personal when Goebel opposed some banking regulations that Sanford favored.

Sanford then worked successfully to oppose Goebel's election to appellate judge, a position Goebel coveted. In April 1895, Goebel bought the local newspaper, the *Ledger,* but the change in ownership was not made public. Almost immediately, an article appeared claiming that Sanford's support of Joe Blackburn in the upcoming U.S. Senate election was based on Blackburn's brother, the governor of the state, pardoning a Sanford relative for forgery and embezzlement before he was even tried.

On April 11, 1895, Sanford spotted Goebel walking with W. J. Hendricks, the attorney general of Kentucky, after a meeting at the courthouse. Keeping his right hand in his pocket, Sanford shook hands with Hendricks and then said to Goebel, "I understand that you assume the authorship of that article." When Goebel replied, "I do," the two men simultaneously pulled pistols from their pockets and fired. Goebel's bullet hit Sanford in the forehead, killing him. Sanford's bullet ended up between Goebel's body and clothing but did no damage.

A hearing was held five days later at which a number a witnesses said they thought Sanford fired first. Another politician also testified that he had earlier heard Sanford threaten to kill Goebel. The grand jury refused to indict Goebel for murder. In the election of November 1899, Goebel was, by the first count, defeated for the governorship of Kentucky by William S. Taylor by 2,383 votes. On January 2, 1900, Goebel and supporters challenged the results on eight different counts, all of which implied that the Republicans had stolen the election by rigging the votes.

Caleb Powers, the newly elected Republican secretary of state, rounded up hundreds of angry mountain people and had them march on Frankfort in protest. Rumors flew that they were there to shoot someone. Everyone who had a gun started carrying it. On January 30, 1900, as Goebel was walking toward the state house, he was fatally shot through the chest, apparently from the direction of the window in Caleb Powers's office. Taylor called out the militia, which was waiting close by, to break up the angry crowds. Within hours, the Democrat-controlled state election board declared that Goebel had won the election after all. The Republicans tried to take the matter to the U.S. Supreme Court, but it refused to act.

The dying William Goebel was sworn in as governor of Kentucky on February 3, 1900, just hours before he died. J. C. W. Beckham, who had been elected lieutenant governor, immediately became governor. One of his first acts was to establish an investigative board to find out who shot Goebel. Over the coming months, twenty men were arrested, though only five were ultimately tried: Caleb Powers, Berry and James Howard, Garnett Ripley, and Henry Youtsey. Ripley went to trial first and was acquitted, as was Berry Howard. Youtsey was found guilty and sentenced to prison for life, although he spent much of the next seven years appearing as a witness at other men's trials.

Powers's trial began on July 9, 1900, before a "special" jury of twelve Democrats who had voted for Goebel. One witness quoted Powers as saying, "If we can't get [Goebel] killed, I will kill him myself if necessary." Henry Youtsey had been seen aiming a rifle and trying out its angle of view from Powers's window. Judge Cantrill left the jury little doubt that he was out to get Powers, who was found guilty and sentenced to life in prison. James Howard was also found guilty and also sent to prison for life. Powers and Howard appealed the decisions, and an equally Democrat-laden jury was chosen for the October 1901 retrial. Many prosecution witnesses were less positive than they had been before. Two of them frankly admitted that the prosecutor had paid them for their testimony. Powers was again found guilty and the verdict was again appealed.

A third trial began on April 7, 1903, with James Howard as the defendant. This time, the prosecution had new witnesses, including Youtsey, who turned state's evidence and claimed he had let Howard into Powers's office and heard the shot seconds later. Howard was again found guilty.

Powers's third trial the following August took place before a new judge, also a Goebel Democrat. Youtsey was encouraged to testify that he turned state's evidence because he had been tortured in prison and forced to change his testimony. The Democratic jury again found the man guilty, this time changing the penalty to death. The appeals court quashed this verdict too, and a fourth trial was demanded.

In December 1907, the Republicans controlled the state, and a different atmosphere prevailed at trial. This time, Youtsey was identified as the actual killer. The jury was unable to reach a verdict and a fifth trial was scheduled. Powers and Howard, however, had had enough. They asked through their attorneys that Republican Governor Augustus E. Willson (1907–1911) grant them pardons, which he did. Willson blamed Youtsey for the conspiracy, since he had consistently provided perjured testimony that kept Powers and Howard behind bars illegally for eight years.

In the case of a wrongly convicted Florida railroad worker, the actual killer paid two informants to commit perjury in order to escape a murder conviction. On October 17, 1901, a railroad worker found the body of an engineer, Harry E. Wesson, in the Florida Southern railway yard. Wesson had been shot once in the head by a .38-caliber pistol, which lay a few feet from his body; his pockets were turned inside out, but $130 in a roll of bills was hidden in his overalls.

Citizens of Palatka, Florida, were enraged at the cruel murder, and Sheriff R. C. Howell brought a number of suspects into the Putnam County Jail for questioning. The jailer, Hagan, overheard J. B. Brown, a former brakeman on one of the trains, talking to a prisoner, Lucius Crawford: "Keep your mouth shut and say nothing." Within an hour, Brown was arrested.

Investigation revealed that Brown had held a grudge against Wesson since he was fired following a dispute with a conductor. Edward Ponder, a porter, said Brown had told him in September that he was going to get his pistol and kill Wesson.

Brown claimed he played cards until about 11:30 P.M. the night of the murder, and found out about the killing the next morning at another card game. According to some of the other players, Brown had seemed excited at the game and had money; he also whispered on the side with Jim Johnson, another player.

On this evidence, Brown was held as the main suspect, while the others were released. Brown's cellmate, Alonzo Mitchell, then told the sheriff that Brown had just confessed to him that he and Jim Johnson had plotted together to murder Wesson for his money. When Henry Davis, another prisoner, corroborated that he also had heard Brown confess, the case was brought to trial.

Brown was prosecuted by state's attorney Syd L. Carter on a charge of first-degree murder before Judge W. S. Bullock on November 19, 1901. Defense attorneys were A. M. Allred and John E. Marshall. The accused man testified on his own behalf, consistently maintaining his innocence and denying that he had made a confession at the coroner's inquest. He said he did not own a pistol and had never made a threat against Wesson's life. When Bullock refused to admit Brown's alleged confession because Brown had refused to sign it, saying it was incorrect, a court reporter testified from his records about Brown's statements at the inquest.

The two-day trial ended on November 20, 1901, with Brown convicted. Bullock sentenced Brown to be hanged. An appeal to the Florida Supreme Court affirmed the conviction and sentence. As Brown was led to the gallows and a rope adjusted around his neck, the death warrant was read, which had the name of one of the jurors instead of Brown's as the convicted man. The hanging was canceled over the error in announcing the wrong name for the condemned man. A plea was made to the governor of Florida, and the sentence was commuted to life imprisonment.

In 1902, the case against Jim Johnson, who had been jointly indicted with Brown, was dropped. In 1913, as Johnson was dying, he confessed that he had shot Wesson and that Brown had had nothing to do with it. It was also learned that both Mitchell and Davis had committed perjury in falsely testifying against Brown, and that Johnson, who had been imprisoned with both Mitchell and Davis, had paid both of the prison informers to commit perjury.

On October 1, 1913, Governor Park Trammell (1913–1917) granted Brown a full pardon. After serving twelve years in prison, Brown was released physically disabled. Sixteen years later, in 1929, the State of Florida granted the infirm and destitute Brown a relief fund of $2,492, to be paid in monthly installments of $25, for his "faithful service. . . during the period of this wrongful imprisonment." It is not known how much longer Brown lived to collect these miserable stipends.

A black laborer in Alabama shared the same fate as Brown and was tried and convicted six times for the same murder and lived with six separate death sentences. He too had been framed by the perjured testimony of the real killer, but he did not wait for an exoneration he believed would never come. Instead, he broke out of prison and escaped into oblivion.

On an evening in April 1909, James McClurkin rode after a thief who had stolen some seed from his Alabama barn. The next morning, a member of his household discovered McClurkin's body near the home of a black man named John Body. The victim's head was severely beaten. The authorities proceeded against another black man, Ervin Pope, though the evidence police gathered to convict him was circumstantial. Body put the murder on Pope, telling police on the night of the murder that he heard a man say, "Ervin, Ervin, I ain't going to do nothing."

The police discovered that Pope visited the McClurkin mill the day of the murder and allegedly encouraged the hired mill hand to sleep in a place other than the barn that evening. They also discovered some seed in Pope's lumber yard and dug up a pair of shoes bearing what appeared to be particles of human skin and blood stains.

Several problems existed with the prosecution's case. First, the incriminating shoes were two sizes too big for Pope and had been worn by a person whose left foot had a large bunion. Pope's left foot had no such bunion. Second, there was nothing suspicious in Pope's presence at McClurkin's mill; it was the best mill in the county and Pope frequented it on a regular basis. Third, a chemical analysis could not determine that the stains on the shoes were human blood.

Further, Body's testimony was highly questionable and suspicious when police arrested him for McClurkin's murder but released him following Pope's first trial. After his release, Body fled the county. Nevertheless, the jury convicted Pope of murder on Body's statements and sentenced him to be hanged. The U.S. Supreme Court heard the case and ordered a new trial; Pope was again convicted and sentenced to death. This happened three more times until the Supreme Court refused a sixth trial, condemning Pope to his execution. Alabama Governor Emmet O'Neal (1911–1915) commuted his sentence in 1914, but Pope escaped prison and was never recaptured. It was reasonably surmised that Body was the real culprit in the McClurkin murder and that the head injuries the victim had sustained shortly after that slaying had been a result from Body's struggle with McClurkin. To evade conviction, Body blamed Pope in his perjured testimony, before fleeing.

## The Perjured Case of Tom Mooney and Warren Billings

For twenty-two years, Thomas Jeremiah Mooney (1882–1942) chose prison over freedom. His choice was based on moral principles. To accept anything less than an outright pardon from the governor of California was, in his view, an admission that he was responsible for bombing the San Francisco Preparedness Day Parade on July 22, 1916, a terrorist act that left ten persons dead and forty seriously injured. Mooney and his young protégé,

Warren Knox Billings (1893–1972), were arrested, charged, and convicted of murder, based on the perjured evidence of two unreliable witnesses. Even the presiding judge in the case, Frank Griffin, expressed his doubts. He called the Mooney conviction "one of the dirtiest jobs ever put over." The clamor for the release of Mooney and Billings would echo through the state

The Preparedness Parade in San Francisco, July 22, 1916, a patriotic event that urged America to prepare to go to war in Europe and one marred by a terrific explosion that killed ten persons and wounded forty more. *History Inc./Jay Robert Nash Collection.*

house of California for the next two decades before justice would finally be served.

Tom Mooney was the son of an Irish immigrant who arrived in the United States from County Mayo. His father, Bernard Mooney, was active in the Knights of Labor, whose involvement in the fledgling labor movement left an indelible impression on his son. Following Bernard Mooney's passing in 1892, Mary Mooney moved with her children to Holyoke, Massachusetts.

Mooney's baptism into left-wing causes began at an early age. Reprimanded by a Catholic priest for habitual truancy and for sneaking off to a Protestant church to sample free candy, Mooney quit the parochial school to enroll himself in the public school. The experience made him a "rebel," according to his later admission. In 1907, Mooney formally entered labor union politics by running as a nominee for delegate to the International Molders Union convention in Philadelphia, but lost by seven votes.

Later that year, Mooney took his life savings and sailed to Europe, where he hoped to fulfill his aspirations to become a great artist. While strolling through an art museum in Rotterdam, Mooney was approached by Nicholas Klein, an American delegate to the International Socialist Convention.

Klein noticed the membership pin of the Molders Union that Mooney wore proudly on his lapel.

For the next two days, Klein and Mooney discussed the objectives of the labor movement and the class struggles between workers and management. Mooney spent the remainder of his stay in Europe observing laborers and the socioeconomic problems they confronted. When he returned to the United States, he found the country in a panic. From that time, he dedicated himself to the socialist cause. He joined the party and began subscribing to *Appeal to Reason,* the socialist news organ. In 1908, Mooney traveled with Eugene Victor Debs on the "Red Special" as the unsuccessful socialist candidate for president barnstormed the country.

Mooney joined the International Workers of the World (IWW, or Wobblies) in March 1910. He went to San Francisco later that year to run as the socialist candidate for judge of the superior court; he lost. In May 1911, Mooney founded *Revolt: The Voice of the Militant Worker,* along with Austin Lewis and Cloudsley Johns. Over the next few years, Mooney immersed himself in radical causes on the West Coast, including the struggle to free James and John McNamara, who were accused of bombing the *Los Angeles Times* Building on October 1, 1910. Mooney and his compatriots in the IWW charged publisher Harrison Gray Otis with a frame-up, but the McNamaras pleaded guilty and received long prison terms. The case galvanized the labor movement and set the stage for the violent management-labor clashes that were yet to come.

In May 1913, Mooney, his wife Rena, and Warren Billings were caught up in one of San Francisco's bitterest strikes. Outside linemen who belonged to the Electrical Worker's Union walked off the job in a dispute over wages with the Pacific Gas and Electric Company of California. The use of explosives by labor agitators during this strike presaged the kind of class warfare predicted by left-wing leaders such as Klein, Emma Goldman, Joe Hill, Alexander Berkman, and others.

Warren Billings, who had come from New York to join forces with Mooney, was promptly arrested and charged with possession of dynamite. He was sentenced in November 1913 to two years in Folsom Prison. A month later, Mooney was arrested on a charge of plotting to blow up the PG&E Towers that spanned the Carquinez Straits. Since no dynamite was actually found, the jury acquitted Mooney and a codefendant. Attorney John J. Barrett, who represented Pacific Gas, remarked bitterly to defense lawyer Maxwell McNutt that a day of reckoning was coming: "Well, Mac, you got Mooney out of this, but we put a red shirt on him and we will get something on him someday."

They only had to wait three years. In July 1916, the Mooneys were in San Francisco attempting to organize the streetcar motormen. The abortive attempt to get them to walk off the job to protest working conditions ended ignominiously with the arrest and imprisonment of Rena Mooney. The motormen, it seemed, were not interested in incurring the wrath of their employer. Billings, who had been released from prison earlier following a wrongful conviction, joined Mooney in this labor fight. Both were exhausted by the events in San Francisco and were making plans to vacation near the picturesque Russian River, when a momentous event occurred that changed their lives forever.

For days, the local businesses advertised the Preparedness Day Parade scheduled for July 22, 1916. America would soon enter the European War, and the parade was to be a show of patriotic support for the Allied cause, which the United States had firmly endorsed. The IWW, the radical trade unionists, and Thomas J. Mooney, among others, opposed America's entry into the Great War (World War I) on moral principles. They had made their feelings known in the radical press and consequently emerged as likely suspects when a power-

Damage and dead at Market and Steuart Streets in San Francisco, after a bomb exploded at 2:06 P.M., July 22, 1916, an explosion almost immediately attributed to anarchists or left-wing labor leaders. *History Inc./Jay Robert Nash Collection.*

IWW labor leader Tom Mooney, who was wrongly convicted of planting the lethal bomb at San Francisco's Preparedness Parade on July 22, 1916; his trial was rife with perjured testimony offered by biased prosecutors. He was sentenced to death, but reprieved and released and exonerated twenty-one years later. *History Inc./Jay Robert Nash Collection.*

ful dynamite bomb exploded near the intersection of Market and Steuart Streets, killing ten people. The frightful blast could be heard blocks away.

When the bomb went off, Mooney was on the roof of the office building where he rented space, more than a mile from the devastation. "Mrs. Mooney and I were in her studio on the fifth floor of the Eilers Building," Mooney later explained. "A large flag covered the window. We could not see the parade so we went up on the roof. On the roof was Wade Hamilton, an Eilers employee with a small camera making pictures. In the sweep of his camera, he caught us as well as the parade. A clock down on the street also was in the picture. In three of his pictures, the clock showed the time to be 1:58 P.M., 2:01 P.M., and 2:04 P.M. The time of the explosion was 2:06 P.M."

The prosecution claimed that Mooney had the pictures retouched. It was the district attorney, Charles Fickert, however, who actually tried to have the hands on the clock altered by photo developers. Fickert was the political tool of the United Railroads, with which Mooney had frequently bumped heads in his efforts to gain recognition for the union. Hours after the explosion, Fickert and Martin Swanson, a burly private detective employed by the railroads, moved in and quietly took control of the police investigation from Chief David Augustus White, who had no shortage of suspects and leads involving the bombing.

It was conceivable that secret agents from the kaiser's government had planted the bomb. Resentful Mexicans opposed to General John Pershing's recent military incursion into their country were another possibility. Neither could the members of the Black Hand be discounted. Fickert, however, had settled on Mooney and Billings as the perpetrators, and worked hard to manufacture the proof, since so little evidence was found by police at the bomb site.

The San Francisco *Chronicle* posted a reward of $14,100 for the capture of the "bomb fiends." The chamber of commerce supplemented this amount by putting up an additional $5,000. On July 26, 1916, Warren Billings was taken into custody by San Francisco police officers. The SFPD had promised the jittery public that those responsible would be behind bars within forty-eight hours. This was followed by the arrest of Edward D. Nolan, Israel Weinberg, and Belle Lavin, who were only nominally connected to the radicals.

Lavin's only "crime" was that she kept a rooming house that was frequented by members of the labor movement. All had been seized by police without the benefit of warrants. Unaware that they were wanted by the police, the Mooneys blissfully went on a picnic to Montesano. When they saw the headlines in the newspaper that told of Billings's arrest, Mooney wired Chief White to advise him that he was returning to San Francisco on the twenty-seventh to tell his side of the story.

On August 1, 1916, district attorney Fickert presented his case to the San Francisco grand jury. A prostitute and accused murderer named Estelle Smith and an unemployed waiter named John McDonald supplied damaging testimony

Labor leader Warren Billings, who was wrongly convicted along with Mooney, was released eight months after Mooney in 1939, returning to his old homestead to sit in its ruins. *History Inc./Jay Robert Nash Collection.*

against Billings and Mooney to open the hearing. McDonald testified that he had observed Tom Mooney standing at the corner of Market and Steuart, carrying the suitcase that police believed contained the bomb.

The shaky testimony led to an eight-count murder indictment against Mooney, Billings, Nolan, and Weinberg. Fickert's evidence against Nolan consisted solely of his past friendship with Mooney and some explosives allegedly found in his basement. None of the eyewitnesses could place him at the scene of the blast. The district attorney also supplied the motive, stating that the defendants had gathered at Market Street to bomb company officials from United Railroads. During the trial, Fickert amended this story to say that the real target was Preparedness headquarters, located across the street.

The celebrated trial of Tom Mooney began on January 3, 1917, before Judge Griffin. After hearing McDonald's testimony, the prosecution called a surprise witness: Frank C. Oxman, a traveling businessman from Durkee, Oregon, who said he had arrived in San Francisco on July 22, 1916, and watched the parade. Oxman told the court that he saw the whole thing unfold, from the time that Weinberg, Mooney, and Billings first appeared on the street to the moment they planted the bomb (contained in a black satchel) next to the wall of the saloon, where it went off.

It was subsequently shown that Oxman was induced to commit perjury. At the time of the explosion, he was nowhere near San Francisco but was transacting business in Woodland, California. He was tried for attempted subornation of perjury in September 1917 but was predictably acquitted. In 1921, McDonald signed an affidavit admitting that his testimony was false and that he had identified Mooney and Billings after being ordered to do so by police. In both instances, the sizable reward was an important factor in the decision by Smith, McDonald, and Oxman to perjure themselves.

That perjured testimony, however, greatly impressed the jurors, who retired on February 9, 1917, to consider their verdict against Mooney. After ten ballots, they voted to convict, based solely on the unreliable testimony of McDonald and Oxman. Judge Griffin sentenced Mooney to hang, but, before that sentence could be carried out, President Woodrow Wilson (1856–1924; terms: 1912–1916; 1916–1920) intervened with California Governor William Dennison Stephens (1917–1923). Mooney's sentence was commuted to life imprisonment at San Quentin, commencing a twenty-one-year fight for exoneration. Billings, also convicted, was sentenced to spend the duration of his life incarcerated at Folsom Prison.

Years passed. In 1930 and again in 1935, the governor of California refused Mooney's petition for an official pardon. Owing to the fact that Billings was a two-time convicted felon, his case could only be reviewed by the California Supreme Court. Mooney, on the other hand, was permitted to appeal his case directly to the governor. The two men parted ways when Billings made it known that he would accept a parole. Mooney maintained that accepting parole was tantamount to an admission of guilt.

Eight years after the National Commission on Law Observance and Enforcement expressed doubt over the outcome of Mooney's 1917 trial, a Gallup poll conducted in January 1938 revealed that most Americans believed the two men were the victims of a serious miscarriage of justice, convicted on the basis of their political beliefs and not for the crime they had been charged with.

The fall elections of 1938 brought a Democrat to the California state house for the first time in forty-four years. The new governor, sixty-two-year-old Culbert Levy Olson (1939–1943), reopened the Mooney case and determined that the Preparedness Day bombing was not the work of Tom Mooney. The prisoner was transported from San Quentin to the state capitol in Sacramento in January 1939. Before a large gathering of the press, Governor Olson announced that he was granting Tom Mooney an unconditional pardon. Accompanied by labor organizer Harry Renton

Bridges of the A. F. of L, Mooney greeted a throng of well-wishers, a free man for the first time in two decades. "Governor Olson, I shall dedicate the rest of my life to work for the common good. . . Dark and sinister forces of fascist reactionism are threatening the world," he exclaimed.

Later that year, the case of Warren Billings was referred to the California Supreme Court. Only three of the original judges who had turned down his 1930 application remained. Acting under the recommendation of Governor Olson, Billings was ordered released on October 15, 1939. When asked what he wanted most now that he was a free man, Billings replied, "A ripe persimmon. Boy, do I want a ripe persimmon!"

## Perjury That Sent Robert Elliott Burns to a Chain Gang

Robert Elliott Burns (1890–1955) was America's Jean Valjean, a quiet, intelligent man who was convicted by two robbers providing false testimony for a crime they alone had committed and for which Burns was sent to the living hell of a Georgia chain gang. A successful accountant in New York, Burns enlisted the day after World War I was declared in 1917. He served with distinction in the medical detachment of the 14th Railway Engineers, seeing action in Flanders, Chateau Thierry, Argonne, and St. Mihiel. Upon his return, he found it difficult to obtain a job. He drifted about the country looking for work and, while on the bum and starving in Georgia, got involved in the robbery of an Atlanta grocery store.

Burns had arrived in that city a few days before, penniless, barefoot, and starving after riding the rails from New York. He went to a Salvation Army shelter where he met two men who told him they could get him a job. He followed them to the store where one of them pulled a gun and held up the proprietor. When Burns told the others he wanted no part of the robbery and began to walk away, one of them pointed the revolver at him and told

him that he was part of the robbery and would be shot unless he left with the other two thieves.

The robbers took all of $5.80. Burns was caught and tried with the two robbers, who insisted that he had participated in the robbery, even though one later recanted his perjured statements. Burns was sentenced in March 1922 to six to ten years. He was sent to the chain gang in Georgia, where he experienced unbearable living conditions, beatings, and torture. Burns resolved to escape at any price, and three months later, in June 1922, he made his escape while working on railroad repairs outside the camp compound.

Robert Elliott Burns, a former accountant, as a prisoner on a Georgia chain gang in 1922; he was convicted on perjured testimony, but he made a spectacular escape. *History Inc./Jay Robert Nash Collection.*

Burns had persuaded a huge black prisoner to bring a sledgehammer down on his leg irons and break them. He then dove into a nearby swamp and got to a road where he crawled beneath a truck and rode to the state line. Burns made his way to Chicago and got himself one job after another, working as an accountant for a lumber company and then as a real estate agent. He was able to save a considerable amount of money and, in 1924, founded the *Greater Chicago Magazine,* largely devoted to real estate in Chicago.

By 1930, the fugitive occupied a suite of offices in a modern skyscraper, made

Burns is shown in Chicago in 1929, where he relocated after his 1922 escape from a chain gang, becoming a successful editor; he was identified to officials by a scorned wife and voluntarily returned to Georgia where the State reneged on its promise to shorten his prison term. *History Inc./Jay Robert Nash Collection.*

$20,000 a year as a publisher, and was a leader in the business community. Burns's personal life, however, was miserable. When he had arrived in Chicago in 1922, he rented a room from a Mexican divorcée, Emilia del Phino Pacheo, who later went through Burns's belongings and found a letter which described life as a fugitive from the chain gang. The woman, madly in love with Burns, threatened to turn him in unless he married her. He did.

The marriage was unhappy, and in 1929 Burns fell in love with young Lillian Salo. Together they went to Emilia and begged her for a divorce. She agreed, provided that she was given substantial alimony; the papers were drawn up and signed. A short time later, Georgia officials appeared in Chicago and insisted that Burns be extradited to Georgia. They had reportedly been contacted by Emilia, who sought revenge.

The case was publicized in national newspapers and editorials throughout the country encouraged Georgia to give Burns a full pardon, stating that he had proven himself to be a hardworking, substantial citizen for seven years. Vivien Stanley, a member of the Georgia Prison Commission, arrived in Chicago and told Burns and his lawyers that, if he waived extradition and voluntarily returned to Georgia, a full pardon would be forthcoming. The governor of Illinois appeared to be leaning against extradition after receiving scores of letters from such distinguished citizens as Jane Addams and Carl Sandburg, who opposed it. Sandburg went even further, saying that the state of Georgia could not be trusted, a grimly prophetic comment. Burns, however, on the advice of his lawyers, returned there with Stanley.

Burns, who again escaped from a chain gang in Georgia in 1930, is shown looking at his book, published in 1931, a bestseller that exposed the flagrant prison abuses in Georgia, but he remained a hunted man. *History Inc./Jay Robert Nash Collection.*

In August 1929, in a small room in Atlanta, the police commission gave Burns's lawyers a few minutes to explain the circumstances but cut off arguments after a minute or so. The commission was made up of tight-lipped, uncompromising judges named Rainey, Johns, and Stanley. They said nothing but seemed impatient at the impassioned pleadings by Burns's attorneys and then motioned to a man named Stephens, who was assistant solicitor in Fulton County, Georgia.

Stephens, a short man with thick glasses and a permanent scowl, stood up and snorted derisively at Burns, "This man is a convict. He belongs in a chain gang. He is a habitual criminal. He has violated the laws of Georgia and owes Georgia a debt. We intend to collect that debt and we expect to keep this thief in the chain gang until it is collected!" Further, Stephens held up a letter he had received from Phino Pacheo vilifying the hapless Burns, proving that the old line was true about hell having no greater fury than a woman scorned.

Burns was summarily returned to chain gang hell. The state of Georgia had reneged on its promise of a pardon. In fact, state officials were incensed at the newspapers and civic leaders of *other* states telling them what they should do with their convicted felons. Burns, Georgia authorities vowed, would serve every day of his sentence with more years added because of his 1922 escape. While his case was appealed and more reasonable persons in Georgia reconsidered his case, Burns was subjected to whippings and torture. The same guards he eluded seven years earlier savagely took their revenge, beating Burns unconscious day after brutal day.

Burns decided he had to escape, and in 1930, a year after he had voluntarily returned to Georgia, he became the only man ever to escape a chain gang twice. He somehow worked his way out of his shackles on a road repair job and dashed into deep woods and kept running, outdistancing bloodhounds and searchers, eventually making his way to New Jersey where he lived under an assumed name and operated an antique shop.

After writing a series of articles about the horrors of the chain gang for New York magazines,

Actor Paul Muni, left, playing Burns in the film based on his book, *I am a Fugitive from a Chain Gang*, is about to make another escape, waiting for a fellow prisoner to break his shackles with a sledgehammer. *History Inc./Jay Robert Nash Collection.*

Burns put together his now classic book *I Am a Fugitive from a Georgia Chain Gang.* The book became a bestseller and was purchased by Warner Brothers Studios. The great actor Paul Muni starred in the film in 1932. During production, Burns secretly traveled to Hollywood and acted as an adviser to director Mervyn LeRoy, while elaborate precautions were taken to keep his identity a secret. Burns lived in constant fear that he would be recognized and taken back to Georgia.

Burns was moved from one hotel room to another during his stay in Hollywood, and even lived on the studio back lot for a time, using an alias and assuming various roles, such as that of a stagehand or a technician. Finally, his nerves shattered, Burns returned to New Jersey. The film was an enormous success when released, but *I Am a Fugitive from a Chain Gang* (the name of Georgia was removed from the title) was banned in Georgia. Although the film made Burns a national cause célèbre, the state of Georgia, or its most hardheaded officials, resolved to recapture Burns at any cost. Georgia authorities felt that the film had injured the state's image and reputation and that Burns was the cause of an undeserved stigma.

On learning that Burns was residing in New Jersey, outraged Georgia officials demanded his extradition back to Georgia. Hearings were held in the Trenton state house before New Jersey Governor A. Harry Moore (1938–1941), and these proved to be the most dramatic in Burns's sensational case. Clarence Darrow defended Burns at these hearings and presented petitions containing hundreds of thousands of names asking that Burns not be turned over to Georgia, a state that had already broken its sovereign word.

The horrors of the Georgia penal system were exposed at these hearings and, for the first time, the nation learned of the sweat box, a standup structure in which the convict had to remain upright with little fresh air, while the heat of the day turned the inside of the box into an unbearable oven. Several prisoners, it was claimed, had died in the box. Also introduced was the barrel punishment, a small barrel with iron staves over which prisoners were tied and left to roast in the sun after being whipped.

All kinds of torture weapons were displayed. The Georgia penal system was shown to be a bestial, Dark Ages organization designed to sadistically brutalize its prisoners with no thought of reform or rehabilitation. Will P. Cox, a member of the Society of Penal Information, exhibited photos of cages containing dozens of miserable convicts. Governor Moore denied Georgia's writ and defiantly refused to turn over Burns.

Georgia was dogged and continued its efforts to regain the fugitive. The police chief in the town where Burns lived received many telegrams, all worded the same: "Arrest escaped prisoner Robert Burns and return him to Georgia." The chief tore up the telegrams week after week. Georgia lawmen actually tried to kidnap Burns, but he managed to elude them. In 1941, Georgia's Eugene Talmadge (1941–1943), who had recently been elected governor on a campaign that included the return of Burns, again tried to have the fugitive brought back to the chain gang.

Again, New Jersey refused to turn Burns over, Governor Charles Edison (1941–1944) giving Tal-

Burns (sitting), who had become a tax appraiser in the early 1940s, is questioned by an official in New Jersey, where he took up residence; the State refused to turn him over to Georgia officials, which doggedly attempted to recapture him. *History Inc./Jay Robert Nash Collection.*

Georgia Governor Ellis Arnall, left, who abolished the chain gang system (calling it an "abomination"), is shown shaking hands with Burns, right, in 1945, when he commuted Burns' sentence, officially setting him free. *History Inc./Jay Robert Nash Collection.*

Robert Elliott Burns, left (with writer John T. Shuttleworth, who aided him in his fight for freedom), is shown on the steps of Georgia's State Capitol, November 2, 1945, reading his commutation signed by Governor Arnall. *History Inc./Jay Robert Nash Collection.*

madge a firm no. Burns, by then remarried and the father of two children, holding a good job as a tax appraiser, seemed to weary of the hunt. "My God," he exclaimed to newsmen. "How long will they keep this up? Am I never to have any peace?"

In 1945, Georgia Governor Ellis Arnall (1943–1947), a reformer, wiped out the horrid chain gang system in his state, calling it "an abomination." He also wanted to clear the record with Robert Elliott Burns. He "invited" Burns to return to Georgia, promising that if he did so, he would commute the fugitive's sentence. Burns, with no little apprehension, went to Georgia, and this time the state kept its word. Governor Arnall commuted Burns's sentence to time served and he was a free man.

Burns was escorted to a Pullman car and rode back to New Jersey in the luxury of his own stateroom. He noted that the last time he left Georgia, he was riding in the back of a dump truck. The great manhunt was over, and Burns would no longer have to leap from his bed at the slightest sound in the middle of the night. He lived for an-

other ten years, dying in a New Jersey veteran's hospital on June 5, 1955.

## From Perjury to Prison and the Death House

Guards at the Raiford State Penitentiary in Florida were making bets on whether or not Joseph Green Brown (a.k.a. Shabaka WaQlimi) would receive a stay of execution. Brown could hear them as he was moved to a death watch cell thirty feet from the electric chair. He was scheduled to die on October 17, 1983, following a conviction of raping and murdering Earlene Treva Barksdale, the owner of a clothing store and the wife of a prominent attorney in Tampa, Florida, which had occurred on July 7, 1973. His death warrant had been signed by Florida Governor D. Robert Graham (1979–1987) only a few weeks earlier.

Technicians constantly tested the electric chair while Brown awaited death. The electric chair was called "Old Sparky" because of malfunctions (see

Jesse Tafero, this chapter) that had agonizingly prolonged the deaths of several condemned inmates. These tests sounded like lightning bolts crackling through Brown's ears twice a day.

In the decade that Brown had been at the prison, sixteen other inmates had been executed and he was about to become number seventeen. After an execution, the stench of burning flesh permeated the cellblock and Brown thought he could detect that terrible smell again—his own. A tailor appeared and had Brown step from his cell before measuring him. When asked what the tailor was doing, he was told, "I'm making your burial suit." Brown exploded and had to be dragged back to his cell kicking and screaming.

On October 16, 1983, one day before he was scheduled to die, Brown was asked what he wanted for his last meal. He refused to order that traditional last meal. Brown had always maintained his innocence, but now that all of his appeals had failed, he glumly awaited death. Only fifteen hours before he was to be taken into the death room and strapped into the electric chair, he received a stay of execution and was returned to the cellblock housing other death row prisoners.

Brown knew his death was only postponed. His attorneys, however, continued to appeal his case. Arrested on July 8, 1973, one day after the crime, the twenty-four-year-old Brown had no criminal record. He had been identified as Barksdale's killer by Ronald Floyd, a man who hated Brown because Brown had turned him in for a robbery that Floyd then claimed had been committed by himself *and* Brown.

At Brown's 1974 trial in Hillsborough County, a jury was shown a .38-caliber handgun by prosecutor Robert Bonanno, claiming that Brown had used this weapon to rob, rape, and murder Barksdale. FBI ballistics tests had eliminated that possibility, but those tests were not revealed to the jury. The only substantial evidence against Brown was Floyd's testimony. Floyd had cut a deal with prosecutors eight months before testifying against Brown, court officials promising him leniency in his ongoing robbery case in exchange for that testimony.

While on the stand, Floyd was asked by Brown's defense attorney, a thirty-year-old court-appointed lawyer whom the state had paid only $2,800 for trying the case, if the prosecution had promised him anything for his testimony. Floyd stated that he had not received any promises. Those were perjured statements, along with everything else he said about Joseph Green "Shabaka" Brown.

Floyd's testimony nevertheless convinced a jury to return a conviction and death sentence. After failing in all of his appeals and narrowly missing execution in 1983, Brown turned to Centurion Ministries, which undertook his seemingly hopeless case. This organization, which had rescued a condemned person by proving innocence, reinvestigated Brown's case and learned that the star witness against him, Floyd, had recanted his testimony some months after Brown's conviction. It also learned that he had made a deal with prosecutors on a robbery charge in exchange for his testimony, which he had denied on the witness stand.

After attorneys from Centurion Ministries argued Brown's case, the U.S. Court of Appeals for the Eleventh Circuit reversed Brown's conviction on the grounds that the prosecution had knowingly allowed and exploited Floyd's perjured statements. On March 5, 1987, prosecutors dropped all charges against Brown and he was released from prison.

Following his release, Brown, who later went into social work in Washington, D.C., told members of the press that he was angry and bitter, complaining that the state of Florida had given him nothing at

Joseph Green "Shabaka" Brown was sentenced to death for a 1973 Florida murder, a conviction that Centurion Ministries proved had been based upon perjured testimony, and which caused Brown's exoneration and release in 1987. *Center on Wrongful Convictions/Northwestern University/Loren Santow.*

the time of his release. "They didn't give me an apology. When they released me, they didn't even give me bus fare home." Still later, Brown, then able to appreciate his freedom, said, "I'm alive. That's good enough for me."

The man who prosecuted Brown, Robert Bonanno, had become a Hillsborough County circuit judge by the time of Brown's release. Even though the appellate court had severely rebuked his conduct in the case, Bonanno remained adamantly convinced that Brown was guilty: "He's very fortunate. He should have been executed."

Where Brown had been sent to prison on perjured testimony from a man who hated him, Jesse Tafero and Sonia Jacobs were sent to prison for murdering two cops—one to the death house, the other to life behind bars—on the basis of perjured testimony by the man who was responsible for those murders.

Seeing a green Camaro parked at a rest stop on Interstate 95 in Broward County early on the morning of February 20, 1976, two suspicious officers decided to investigate. Philip Black, a Florida highway patrol officer, and Donald Irwin, a visiting Canadian constable, approached the car cautiously. Asleep in it car were Walter Rhodes, an ex-convict, Jesse Tafero, and Sonia "Sunny" Jacobs. The two officers peering through the closed windows of the car thought they saw a gun on the floor.

They tapped on the windows and asked Rhodes and Tafero to get out of the car and they did, one of them firing away at the officers, killing both of them. The three occupants then ran to the police car and drove off with it, later abandoning it after stealing another car.

Police established roadblocks, and the trio was stopped and captured at one of them. All were tested for gunpowder burns and the results indicated that Rhodes had recently fired a gun. Tafero, the tests showed, had either handled or fired a gun too. Tafero told police that Rhodes had shot the two officers and then handed him the gun so that he could drive the getaway car, a statement sup-

ported by the fact that Rhodes was driving the stolen car when stopped by police.

Rhodes insisted that Tafero had killed the two officers and offered to take a polygraph test, which he reportedly passed. But results from that test were never shown to prosecutors. Prosecutors then cut a deal with Rhodes, allowing him to plead to second-degree murder and receive a life sentence in return for his testimony against Tafero and Jacobs. Rhodes became the star witness in the 1976 trials against Tafero and Jacobs, who were tried separately but with the same evidence used in both cases.

Jailhouse informants also testified for the prosecution that Tafero and Jacobs had confessed to shooting the two officers. Two eyewitnesses also testified, one saying that he saw a man in brown (the attire worn by Tafero) spread-eagled on the hood of the police car shortly before the shooting and another said that a man in blue (the attire worn by Rhodes) ran from one side of the car to another shortly before the shooting.

It was Rhodes's testimony, however, that convinced the jury to convict Tafero and Jacobs, who were both sentenced to death. Jacobs, a twenty-eight-year-old self-proclaimed hippie, was the common-law wife of Tafero, the relationship having produced two small children. Both claimed to be innocent in the shooting. They had just accepted a ride from Rhodes, a hardened criminal who had committed perjury in sending them to death row. This Rhodes himself admitted in 1982, one year after Jacobs's death sentence was commuted to life imprisonment. He recanted that recantation and then seesawed for years between admitting the truth and maintaining the lie, viciously taunting and torturing Jacobs and Tafero and exulting in his control over their judicial destinies.

That torture came to an end for Jesse Tafero on May 4, 1990, when he was put to death in Florida's electric chair. The execution, one of the most atrocious and barbarous on record, was completely botched. After the first jolt of electricity was sent into Tafero, smoke and flames spurted from his head for a distance of a foot or more. The flames and smoke emanated from the area around a metallic skull cap, inside of which was a saline-soaked synthetic sponge meant to increase the flow of electricity to the head. The cap is the source of the electricity administered to condemned prisoners by the electric chair.

Officials stopped the execution and then ordered another jolt to be administered, which produced the same smoke and flames spurting from Tafero's head. A third jolt was then applied and physicians pronounced Tafero dead. But he had endured six or seven minutes of excruciating pain while surviving the first two jolts. His head was mutilated by the flames that had gouged out the top and sides of his skull. This brutal execution caused Florida to cease using the electric chair. But after another condemned man received a lethal injection that took thirty-four minutes to end his life, the state restored Old Sparky and all of its potential horrors.

New evidence in Jacobs's case later surfaced, including the fact that defense attorneys had never been informed that Rhodes had failed his lie detector test. After a federal appeals court determined that only Rhodes could have fired the fatal shots that killed the two officers, Jacobs was granted a new trial. Instead of retrying her, prosecutors offered her a deal. If she entered a plea in which she promised not to file a civil suit while still maintaining her innocence, she would be released. Jacobs, then forty-five and eager to see her children, agreed and was released on October 9, 1992. She moved to Los Angeles, where she taught yoga, and then moved to North Carolina to join her children and grandchildren.

Perjury in Florida involving two murders had sent an innocent man to the electric chair and his wife to life in prison. Perjury in Illinois also involved two murders, but it sent four persons to prison after a brutal robbery and two murders occurred on May 12, 1978, in Homewood, Illinois. That crime involved four black defendants, two of whom were sentenced to death and two sent to

prison for life. This case, dubbed the "Ford Heights 4," was permeated with perjured testimony, junk science, and widespread misconduct by police and prosecutors.

On that spring night, Lawrence Lionberg and Carol Schmal, both white and recently engaged, were abducted from a gas station in a predominately white suburb and driven to almost all-black East Chicago Heights (later known as Ford Heights). Abductors dragged the couple into an abandoned townhouse, raped Schmal, and then shot each victim in the back of the head.

Three witnesses the came forward to describe how four black men—Verneal Jimerson, Willie Rainge, Kenneth Adams, and Dennis Williams—had entered the townhouse with the victims, raped Schmal seven times, and then killed the victims execution style. The first of these witnesses was Charles McCraney, who lived close to the murder scene and saw six to eight blacks going in and out of the abandoned townhouse, including Kenneth Adams and Willie Rainge. Following the arrest of Rainge and Adams, a jailhouse snitch, David Jackson, who had been incarcerated with Rainge and Adams after they were jailed, later testified that he heard them discussing the crime, talking about killing a man and "taking" sex from a female victim.

The third witness was the strangest of all. Seventeen-year-old Paula Gray, an uneducated black teenager, like McCraney, lived near the crime scene. While being interviewed by police, she told officers that Rainge, Adams, Williams, and Jimerson had all been inside the townhouse and had kept a disposable cigarette lighter burning to provide the light by which all four of the blacks raped the white woman. Gray repeated this story before a grand jury but later refused to testify in court against the four men, recanting her earlier statements. For her refusal, she was charged as an accomplice and was convicted in 1978 of murder, rape, and perjury, and sent to prison for fifty years.

Gray's trial and that of the four men was awash with racial prejudice as evidenced in the

Verneal Jimerson, who was one of the Ford Heights 4, convicted of two murders in 1978, in Illinois, was exonerated and released in 1996. *Center on Wrongful Convictions/Northwestern University/Loren Santow.*

Dennis Williams, who, along with three others, was wrongly convicted of a double murder in 1978 in Illinois and who was proven innocent and released in 1996. *Center on Wrongful Convictions/Northwestern University/Loren Santow.*

Kenneth Adams, wrongly convicted and sentenced to death with Dennis Williams of a double murder in 1978, was shown to be innocent and released in 1996. *Center on Wrongful Convictions/Northwestern University/Jennifer Linzer.*

Willie Rainge, wrongly convicted with Adams and Williams for a 1978 double murder in Chicago. *Innocence Project, New York.*

jury selection. Leroy Posey was the seventeenth potential juror called for voir dire. Posey, a black pump operator from Chicago's South Side, had noticed that prosecutors had routinely stricken other potential black jurors with peremptory challenges. After answering several questions, Posey asked permission to speak, which was granted. He said, "It's obvious that the state's attorneys want an all-white jury. They don't want me here." Posey had thus set the stage for later accusations that the "Ford Heights 4" trial was based on racial bias.

While prosecutors obliquely used Paula Gray's prior perjured statements without her presence in court, there was little evidence against the defendants in addition to McCraney's and Jackson's thin testimony. Serology evidence showed nothing except that the victims and the defendants were type O blood, the most common in the population. Three hairs reportedly were found in Williams's car that matched one of the victims, but these hairs could not be uniquely identified, as was then claimed, and only through DNA could such hairs provide definitive identification. But that forensic science was not then employed and would be years in development. Microscopic examinations

of at least *two* hairs might offer *probable* identification, but not a *positive* one. The forensic expert testifying as to the reliability of the three hairs found stated that two of the hairs were similar to that of Schmal and one hair similar to that of Lionberg. Prosecutors, however, substituted the word *similar* with *matched* when referring to the hair evidence.

In 1979, three of the defendants were convicted of abduction, murder, and rape, Rainge receiving a life sentence and Adams seventy-five years; Williams was sentenced to death. Jimerson was convicted in 1985 and was also sentenced to death. Adams lost his appeals, but Williams and Rainge were granted new trials and were again convicted based on the eyewitness testimony and the perjured testimony of Paula Gray that had brought about Jimerson's conviction.

Williams had won a new trial in 1983, but prosecutors, to make sure that his death sentence from his first trial was upheld, went to the imprisoned Pauls Gray and offered her a deal. If she reverted to her original testimony that implicated Williams and Jimerson, her fifty-year sentence of perjury would be drastically reduced. Gray eagerly took this offer and testified in court against Williams in

Paula Gray, whose perjury sent Williams, Adams and two others to prison and received a prison sentence for refusing to again testify against the defendants. *Center on Wrongful Convictions/Northwestern University/Jennifer Linzer.*

his 1983 retrial, her statements sealing Williams's death sentence and convicting Jimerson and sending him to Illinois's death row. About two years after offering her perjured testimony, Gray was released from prison.

A team of journalism students from Northwestern University, led by Professor David Protess, began to investigate the case. With the help of attorney Mark Ter Molen of the Chicago firm of Mayer, Brown & Platt working pro bono, they unearthed a police file that related how another witness had come forward at the time of the crime to identify four black men at the scene of the crime and none of these persons were Jimerson, Williams, Adams, or Rainge. One of the actual killers, Arthur "Red" Robinson, had been named by the witness, whose statements had been obviously suppressed by police and prosecutors.

Based on this new evidence, Jimerson appealed in 1995, which caused the Illinois Supreme Court to unanimously reverse his conviction, ruling that prosecutors had used known perjured testimony from Gray after cutting a deal with her to provide that perjured testimony (albeit prosecutors never admitted to doing so) in convicting Jimerson. He was released on bond and awaited a new trial. In the meantime, postconviction DNA tests in 1996 showed that none of the "Ford Heights 4" had been responsible for the rape and murders.

Those tests were run through the state's crime database and found a match, identifying Robinson as one of the rapists and killers. Robinson confessed to raping Schmal and murdering her and Lionberg, naming three accomplices, one who had

died from a drug overdose, another who was already in prison serving time for a murder, and a fourth accomplice, who was convicted along with Robinson for the Lionberg-Schmal murders and sentenced to life.

All four innocent men were released and exonerated in 1996, when Illinois Governor Jim Edgar (1991–1999) granted pardons to them all. Jimerson had spent eleven years on death row, and the other three had been behind bars for eighteen years each. The four men settled claims against the Chicago police department for an aggregate $36 million, a staggering penalty for using perjury and framing to bring about their wrongful convictions and imprisonment. Employing honesty and ethics at the time the crime occurred, not to mention to extensive court costs involved in prosecuting four innocent men, would have saved the city of Chicago that money and protected the lives of those men.

A lot less money was spent on convicting two prisoners of a murder committed behind bars. Convictions for murders in prison are mostly brought about through the testimony of fellow convicts. Little or no other evidence is usually found to challenge the statements of those hardened criminals, despite the fact that such testimony is always questionable and often perjured. One such case involved Willie Brown and Larry Troy, who were then serving time in the Union correctional institution in Raiford, Florida, when they were accused of murdering fellow inmate Earl Owens, stabbing him to death in his cell.

Both were convicted in 1981 on the dubious testimony of three other convicts, two with known mental problems. The third was reportedly sane, but he was almost as dangerous to the prosecution as he was to the defense attorneys representing Brown and Troy. The third witness was Frank Wise, who was serving time for killing a cousin of Troy, and he had stated to prosecutors that he hated Brown and Troy so intensely that he wanted both of them executed, whether or not they were guilty of killing Owens. Wise told a court that he saw Brown and Troy leaving Owens's cell shortly before his body was found. This testimony sent Brown and Troy to death row.

While filing unsuccessful appeals and awaiting execution, Brown was interviewed by an anti–death penalty activist, Esther Lichtenfels, who fell in love with him and, over the next several years, spent her life savings, an estimated $70,000, to have his case investigated. Her cause was aided in 1987, when the Florida Supreme Court reversed Brown's and Troy's murder convictions, based on its discovery that prosecutors had not shared with the defense the highly prejudicial statements made to them by Wise prior to the convictions.

Lichtenfels then took it upon herself to get enough evidence to prevent Brown (and subsequently Troy) from having to face a second trial in the Owens killing. Wearing a wire, she got permission to interview Wise in prison. Wise told her that he had committed perjury in the Owens case and that he would recant that perjured testimony if Lichtenfels gave him $2,000. All of his conversation was recorded and played to prosecutors, who then dropped all charges against Brown and Troy in the Owens murder.

Brown, who served out his time for a prior robbery conviction, was released in 1988 and married Lichtenfels. Brown, however, took to drugs and later robbed two banks and was sent back to prison. Troy was released in 1990, after serving time for another murder. He was later arrested for peddling cocaine and sent back to prison. Both Brown and Troy were career criminals who had been legitimately imprisoned for crimes they committed, but, in the instance of the Owens murder, they were innocently convicted on perjured testimony.

In one of the most blatant perjured murder cases in Missouri history, Ellen Reasonover was sent to prison for life for a robbery and murder that took place on January 2, 1983, at a gas station in Dellwood, Missouri. Late that night, the white gas station attendant, nineteen-year-old James A. Buckley, had been robbed and killed, shot seven times. When she heard of the crime, twenty-four-

year-old Ellen Reasonover told her mother that she had stopped at that very service station to get change from Buckley for a laundromat. Her mother urged her to contact the police and tell them what she knew in order to help solve the crime.

Reasonover called the next day, identifying herself as Sheila Hill (she was afraid of involving herself with the crime as several family members had criminal records), and told police Captain Dan Chapman that she had seen two black men lurking about the station when she went to get change. She agreed to meet Chapman and revealed her true identity. She was asked to view mug shots and selected two photos of convicted black men as possibly being involved in the service station robbery-murder. She then agreed to take a stress test, a modified form of a lie detector test, which she passed.

Police became suspicious of Reasonover after learning that the two men identified by her had been in prison at the time of the Buckley slaying. Officers wrongly concluded that she had made these identifications in order to deflect possible suspicion from herself. Though she had no criminal record, police soon learned that a half brother had killed his girlfriend and her sister and another half brother had robbed a supermarket. Further, in 1978 Reasonover herself had been accused but not charged with the robbery of a service station where she worked.

On January 7, 1983, police gave Reasonover another stress test, which she failed. She was not represented by an attorney when she was placed under arrest and charged with robbing another service station. While in jail, was placed in several cells with other inmates, two of whom—Rose Jolliff and Mary Ellen Lyner—would later testify against her. At the same time, Marsha Vogt, a police officer posing as a jail inmate and wearing a hidden microphone, was placed in Reasonover's cell. Nothing incriminating was taped.

Prosecutor Steven H. Goldman brought Reasonover to trial for the robbery of the other service station on July 12, 1983, hoping that a conviction would establish a criminal history for Reasonover that would more easily allow him to then try her for the robbery and murder of Buckley. Without anything other than innuendo, Goldman achieved his ends, obtaining a robbery conviction, which brought Reasonover a seven-year prison sentence. Four months later, Goldman tried Reasonover for the January 2, 1983, robbery and murder of Buckley.

Goldman's two star witnesses were jailhouse snitches Jolliff and Lyner, who both testified that Reasonover had admitted killing Buckley. She was convicted and sentenced to life imprisonment, without the possibility of parole for fifty years. Reasonover remained behind bars for the next sixteen years, filing one appeal after another, until, in 1999, a federal judge reviewed her case and overturned her convictions, stating that she had been essentially railroaded by prosecutors using perjured testimony to obtain those convictions. Five years later, Reasonover was awarded $7.5 million in compensation.

Perjured testimony by David Falcon, who had the ambition to become a confidential informant for Florida law enforcement, sent an innocent man to death row for a murder he did not commit. Falcon's perjury was compounded by the perjured statements of a second man, John Berrien. The murder occurred on September 13, 1983, when Delbert Baker was shot three times, his throat cut, and his expensive gold jewelry was taken from his beauty school in Auburndale, Florida. The following year, Falcon contacted police to tell them that Baker's killer was Juan Roberto Melendez, who had been born in Brooklyn, New York, in 1951 and had been raised in Puerto Rico, before moving to Lakeland, Florida.

Falcon said that Melendez had confessed the Baker killing to him, but that he did not know all the details of the murder. He said, however, that another man he identified, John Berrien, also of Lakeland, could provide the details that would bring about Melendez's conviction. Berrien was picked up and interrogated at length. After being threatened with the death penalty, he implicated Melendez, but the information he gave was loaded with inconsistencies and errors. Berrien said that his cousin, George Berrien, had accompanied Melendez to Baker's school on the day of the murder and that he knew that Melendez was armed with a .38-caliber handgun and that, after the robbery-murder, he described the jewelry he had taken from Baker.

Police, however, in following the "leads" of Falcon and John Berrien, could find no evidence that implicated either Melendez or George Berrien, other than the claims of Falcon and John Berrien. In searching George Berrien's car—the alleged getaway car—they found no blood or any other forensic evidence that might normally be present after the blood-soaked crime had been committed. They never found a weapon or recovered the jewelry. George Berrien emphatically denied any participation in the crime and stated that Melendez had nothing to do with it, restating those views for defense attorneys at Melendez's September 1984 trial. George Berrien, ostensibly Melendez's coconspirator, was never charged. John Berrien, following Melendez's trial, would be sentenced to two years house arrest as an accessory to first-degree murder.

Melendez at his trial maintained his innocence, offering an alibi—he had been with a girlfriend on the night of the murder. Prosecutors offered no evidence other than the statements of Falcon and John Berrien. Melendez was found guilty of first-degree murder and, on September 21, 1984, was sentenced to death. Had Melendez's attorney, Roger Alcott, been able to enter into evidence the tape-recorded statements he had secured from another person, Vernon James, Melendez would probably have been released. James stated to Alcott that he had been involved in the Baker slaying, along with two others, and that Melendez had nothing to do with the robbery-murder.

Alcott, however, was prevented from entering this evidence, which was never shown to the judge or jury in the case, and was blocked by prosecutors, who termed it hearsay. When Alcott called James to the witness stand, he took the Fifth Amendment and refused to give testimony. Melendez went to death row, filing one appeal after another, all failing. In 2000, however, Melendez's case was taken over by Rosa Greenbaum, who worked for Capital Collateral Representative (CCR), a public defender organization that represents defendants whose sentences and convictions have been affirmed on direct appeal.

Greenbaum learned of the James tape and, with the help of Alcott and defense investigator Cody Smith (who had been with Alcott when the James tape was recorded), discovered that prosecutor Hardy Pickard had possession of that tape since Melendez's 1984 conviction. The tape was secured from Pickard and entered into evidence in a new appeal. Greenbaum also offered a dozen witnesses, who testified in two new hearings that they had heard from Vernon James how he and two others had been responsible for the Baker robbery-murder and that the wrong man, Melendez, had been sent to death row for that crime.

The defense, through attorney Martin McClain, also showed that Falcon, who had launched the perjured case against Melendez, had a grudge against the defendant and that he had made his perjured statements in exchange for a deal with prosecutors. Falcon had been charged with breaking into a residence, which was dropped after he testified against Melendez. He lied when he told the court that he had received no consideration for his testimony.

After reviewing this new evidence and testimony, circuit court Judge Barbara Fleischer overturned Melendez's conviction on December 5, 2001. Judge Fleischer also ruled that the sworn statements made by John Berrien to prosecutor Pickard before Melendez's trial contradicted his testimony in court and that Pickard had misled the jury about Falcon's reason for testifying against Melendez. The new evidence, she said, had "seriously damaged" the state's case.

Pickard declined to retry the fifty-year-old Melendez, who was released on January 3, 2002, becoming the ninety-ninth person freed from death row in America since the resumption of capital punishment in 1976. He had spent seventeen years on Florida's death row. Vernon James was never tried for the Baker slaying, as he had been murdered in 1986, his killer serving five years in prison on a manslaughter conviction. Said attorney McClain of Melendez's wrongful conviction and wrongful seventeen-year imprisonment, "The system is not premised on the notion that the prosecutor wants to win, but that he wants justice to be done. The way this [Melendez case] was done is not consistent with that notion."

Where Florida police encouraged Falcon to falsely testify against Melendez by offering him a deal for his perjured statements, police in Alabama actually helped a perjurer concoct his false statements in sending an innocent man to death row. Walter "Johnny D" McMillian, a black man, was convicted and sentenced to death in 1988 for the November 1, 1986, murder of Ronda Morrison, an attractive eighteen-year-old white clerk and junior college student. The girl's body was found in the backroom of a drycleaners in Monroeville, Alabama, following a robbery. She had been shot three times. McMillian had been arrested and charged with the murder on the statements of a career criminal, Ralph Bernard Myers, who was also a suspect in the case.

Myers, who was white, initially told police he had given McMillian a ride to the drycleaners, placing him at the crime scene. Both Myers and McMillian were charged with the robbery-murder and tried in separate cases. Judge Robert E. Lee Key Jr., who presided at McMillian's trial (which lasted only a day and a half), wholly relied on Myers's statements—expanded when Myers testified in court that he saw McMillian kill the clerk—to send McMillian to Holman State Prison to await execution.

The jury at McMillian's trial ignored the testimony of six witnesses, all black, who insisted that McMillian was at home at a fish fry when the robbery-murder occurred. Myers, meanwhile, was permitted to plead to the reduced charge of third-degree robbery. The case was rife with race prejudice from the start. Local white residents resented the fact that McMillian had a white girlfriend and that his son had married a white woman. At the time of his arrest, the Monroe County sheriff said to McMillian, "I ought to take you off and hang you like we done that nigger in Mobile, but we can't."

McMillian's fate had been decided long before he went to trial. Two weeks after his arrest, McMillian was placed on death row and there awaited his trial. So prejudiced were local residents that McMillian's attorneys managed to change the venue to Baldwin County, a locale known worldwide as the home of famed novelist Harper Lee, author of *To Kill a Mockingbird*. The change of venue had no effect on McMillian's fate, sealed by a jury that convicted him but nevertheless voted 7–5 against the death penalty. Judge Lee, however, thought that too lenient and sentenced McMillian to death.

McMillian lost a direct appeal, but attorney Bryan Stevenson of the Equal Justice Initiative of Alabama came to his rescue, working pro bono to acquire documents proving that in his initial police interrogation, Myers stated that McMillian had nothing to do with the crime. Stevenson also obtained statements from four doctors who saw Myers following his arrest, and all four stated that Myers had complained to them that police had coerced him into falsely implicating McMillian. A tape was later found which indicated that police had forced Myers to help them frame McMillian through Myers's perjured statements.

Even though the trial court barred postconviction relief based on this new evidence, the Alabama Court of Criminal Appeals ordered a new trial for McMillian, stating that prosecutors had suppressed exculpatory and impeachment evidence (in the latter case of Myers's perjured testimony), denying access to this evidence by McMillian's defense attorneys. In 1998, prosecu-

tors dropped all charges against McMillian, who had been exonerated and set free in 1993.

At the time of his release, McMillian described his six-year nightmare behind bars in written testimony at a subcommittee hearing on July 23, 1993: "I was wrenched from my family, from my children, from my grandchildren, from my friends, from my work that I loved, and was placed in an isolation cell, the size of a shoe box, with no sunlight, no companionship, and no work for nearly six years. Every minute of every day, I knew I was innocent."

Prosecutors lamely admitted that the case against McMillian had been "bungled" but made no mention of police coercion and framing or of a deal prosecutors may have made with Myers for his perjured testimony. Two other witnesses who had also testified against McMillian later admitted that they, like Myers, had lied. McMillian received an undisclosed settlement for his wrongful conviction, and his case undoubtedly influenced Alabama to pass a 2001 statute that authorized compensation for exonerated prisoners.

Since 1975, Alabama has executed thirty-four convicted murderers, but the state acquitted in subsequent reviews and retrials seven men who had been sent to death row—McMillian, Charles Bufford, Gary Drinkard (see Chronology, 1993), Louis Griffin, Larry Randal Padgett, James "Bo" Cochran, and Wesley Quick—one innocent person on death row for every five executions, a frightening rate of error. (See Chapter IX, "The Near Miracle of DNA.")

Quick, for instance, was tried three times for the 1995 murders of two teenagers in Birmingham, Alabama. His first trial was ruled a mistrial because of jury misconduct, but he was convicted in a second trial in 1997 and sentenced to death. The second trial was overturned in 2001, when an appeals court determined that the judge in the second trial refused to allow defense attorneys to use their notes in challenging witnesses who may have committed perjury, and denied those attorneys access to the trial transcript of the first trial.

In the third trial, Quick, a white man, was acquitted after a jury believed him when he stated that the prosecution's star witness, Jason Beninati, had actually killed the two victims. Beninati, who was a jailhouse snitch, claimed that he had come upon the crime scene just after the two teenagers were murdered, and saw Quick at that time. Beninati was never charged with the murders.

Cochran, a black man, was convicted in 1976 of murdering Stephen Ganey, the assistant manager of a grocery store in Birmingham, Alabama, and was sentenced to death. Four trials occurred, the first a mistrial, followed by two trials at which he was convicted (both overturned) and a fourth trial at which he was found innocent in 1997, after spending twenty years on death row. In the two trials where Cochran was convicted, the two separate juries were each made up of eleven white jurors and one black juror. In his 1997 trial, the jury was made up of seven black jurors and five whites.

Cochran's two convictions involved questionable testimony thought to be perjured. At his third trial, his more experienced attorneys successfully argued that it would have been impossible for their client to move the body of Stephen Ganey under the trailer of a mobile home park, as prosecutors contended, while being chased by police officers.

A year after Walter McMillian went to Alabama's death row for a murder he did not commit, an Illinois man was sentenced to death for a murder committed by someone else. On August 1, 1989, a jury found Joseph Burrows, born in 1946, guilty of murdering an eighty-eight-year-old farmer, William Dulin, in his Iroquois County home southeast of Kankakee, Illinois, on November 8, 1988. Burrows was condemned to death and sent to death row, where he continued to claim innocence, insisting that he had never been in Iroquois County. Four witnesses at his trial for the murder of Dulin testified that he was sixty miles from Iroquois County at the time of the killing.

Working against Burrows in that trial, however, was the fact that he had earlier been convicted of burglary and other crimes, and his criminal record weighed heavily in favor of a conviction. Burrows began counting the days until his execution. Then, in July 1994, Gayle Potter, the woman who had first implicated Burrows in the Dulin murder, admitted killing Dulin herself.

A drug addict and dope dealer, Potter stated that she had gone to see Dulin, a retired mechanic, to ask for money so that she could buy drugs. He refused, she recalled for police: "He pushed me out the door. . . and I reached into my purse and pulled out my gun." This startling revelation soon unraveled the case against Burrows. Potter's gun had been originally found at the scene of the crime, as well as her blood, coming from a head gash during her struggle with Dulin. She had been arrested six hours after Dulin's murder while attempting to cash a check in the amount of $4,050 in Dulin's name.

Potter nevertheless testified that Burrows was the actual killer, while Ralph Frye, a man with an IQ of 76 and a friend of Burrows, admitted being at the scene and supported Potter's version of the events. In exchanged for their perjured testimony, Potter was sent to prison for thirty years and Frye received a twenty-seven-year sentence, while Burrows was condemned to death.

The case began when an uncle of Burrows, a man who had taught his nephew the tricks of burglary, broke into Potter's home. She later suspected the uncle and confronted him. He told her that Burrows had been the burglar, believing that his nephew "was in the clear," since he was never in Iroquois County. He further believed that Potter

Joseph Burrows was sentenced to death for the 1988 murder of a farmer in Iroquois County, Illinois, his conviction based upon the perjured testimony of two alleged eyewitnesses; his conviction was reversed and he was released in 1994. *Center on Wrongful Convictions/Northwestern University/Loren Santow.*

would say nothing to the police about Burrows, since she was a cocaine addict and a drug dealer.

Potter, however, did more than that. Just as the uncle had blamed Burrows for the break-in, Potter blamed Burrows for her killing of Dulin, both as an act of revenge for the break-in and as a way to escape punishment for a murder she had committed. She knew that she was identifying a man with a long criminal record, a convicted felon the police would readily accept as Dulin's killer.

After Potter confessed and Frye recanted his testimony—he said that police had coerced him to name Burrows as Dulin's murderer—Judge John Michaela overturned Burrows's murder conviction on September 2, 1994. After spending five years and ten months on death row, Burrows was released, returning to live with his wife and children in Homer, Illinois. "I never have been able to understand how that jury found me guilty," he said following his release. "I never claimed to be a saint. . . but I'm no murderer." On Burrows's left arm is a tattoo he acquired while on death row: "Die Free." Ralph Frye's murder conviction was vacated. He was convicted of perjury and sentenced to ten years in prison.

In the many cases already depicted, perjurers were responsible for sending one or more innocent persons to prison for one-case crimes. In Canada, however, a perjurer sent many innocent men behind bars involving many different cases for no reward other than the perverse satisfaction it gave her. Many habitual liars whose fabrications are accepted as truth over a period of time come to realize that their lies can be an effective tool for revenge. Their lies escalate to perjury when they figure in legal cases, ostensibly stemming from upstanding citizens.

In Ottawa, Canada, perjured statements by thirty-year-old Cathy Fordham sent an innocent man to prison, as well as many before and after him. Fordham was the close friend of Christine Thompson, the common-law wife of Jamie Nelson, a chef. When the couple separated, a bitter custody battle over their child ensued.

Throughout the custody battle, Fordham stood side by side with Christine Thompson and toe to toe against Nelson, assuming the role of Thompson's surrogate avenger. In 1992, Fordham accused Nelson of sexually assaulting his own son and then changed her mind. In 1994, she accused Nelson of physically attacking her, and this charge she stood by, filing a formal complaint. Nelson insisted that all he did was hold the woman's wrists after she flailed at him with her fists. Nelson was nevertheless convicted and jailed for sixty days. In 1996, Fordham again accused Nelson of physically attacking her, and he was again convicted and sent to jail for 120 days.

Shortly after serving that time, Nelson was again accused by Fordham, but this time of a brutal rape. Nelson had little or no defense and was denied bail, based on the details provided by Fordham, which described him as a brutal rapist, and, most importantly, Nelson's criminal record, which Fordham herself had created through her charges against him. While in custody, Nelson came to believe that the woman had systematically brought about his destruction and that there was little hope for him.

Nelson, in utter despair, attempted to kill himself in his jail cell. He made a noose out of a bedsheet, and after lights out and his cell mate fell asleep, he jumped from a sink. His kicking awoke the cell mate and he was taken down. "I had just served 120 days for nothing," Nelson said. "I was picturing the worst and I thought my solution [suicide] would be easier."

In a seven-day bench trial before Ontario court justice Hugh Fraser, Nelson was defended by attorney Ken Hall. He was prosecuted by assistant Crown attorney Mark Moors, who had no evidence against Nelson except the testimony of Cathy Fordham. It was simply her word against Nelson's, and the judge believed Fordham, who said that Nelson had taken revenge on her for his being jailed earlier by invading her apartment in Vanier, Ontario, where he viciously beat and raped her. She said that she had not reported the sexual attack to police until April 29, 1996, because she lived in fear of reprisals. Nelson was arrested the next day by police with drawn guns when he pulled into the driveway of his home with his son in tow.

Fordham took the stand and cried as she described the sordid details of the attack to Justice Fraser. Nelson took the stand to deny Fordham's allegations and supplied witnesses who testified that he had been elsewhere when the attack had taken place. Justice Fraser found Nelson guilty of rape and assault, and, on November 14, 1996, sentenced him to three and a half years in Millhaven Federal Penitentiary. Nelson refused to participate in a sexual offender program, insisting that he was innocent. Consequently he was placed in solitary confinement for fifteen months.

Meanwhile, Fordham, who apparently believed that she had the power to imprison anyone she chose to accuse, established herself as an authority on men caught up in Canada's court system. She continued to create entrapments after she became the leader of a group home for such men called the Vanier Community Support Center. A police investigation into her activities later revealed that the home was a snake pit of drugs, alcohol, and sex. While supervising this home, Fordham used the courts as a weapon for meting out her own brand of justice. She reported breaches of court orders that never occurred but nevertheless sent innocent men behind bars.

In January 1998, Fordham accused twenty-six-year-old Andre Emile Masson of raping her, an accusation that brought about his arrest in Vanier. In August 1998, she accused Allan Kamen of raping her while she was praying at a grotto in Vanier, while another man, Phillippe Francois, stood by and watched. Ottawa police sergeant Paul Turner thoroughly investigated the charge and discovered that Kamen and Francois had solid alibis and were nowhere near Fordham at the time she said she had been sexually assaulted by Kamen.

Looking deeper into Fordham's background, Turner discovered that she had filed fifty-five com-

plaints against men, including Nelson, and he came to believe that she was a serial liar and a perjurer and had caused great public mischief; he arrested her under that charge. A short time later, she was charged with making false police complaints and threatening to kill a former boyfriend.

Nelson, meanwhile, served every day of his sentence, 1,047 days, before his parole and release in 1999. In 2000, as the details of Fordham's insidious and evil career unfolded, prosecutors came to realize that Nelson, like so many other men, had been victimized by Fordham's perjury (she was never charged with that offense), and that Justice Fraser, who had noted at Nelson's 1996 trial that Fordham's testimony was not "perfect," had greatly misjudged Fordham's credibility and had been misled by her adroit lies. This was all illustrated by Todd Ducharme, Nelson's attorney, who filed an appeal in 2000 asking that Nelson be exonerated.

Crown attorney Scott Hutchinson was convinced that Nelson had been wrongly convicted on the perjury of Fordham and asked the court to acquit Nelson, which it did. Following the acquittal, Hutchinson shook Nelson's hand and said, "The right thing happened today."

Said Ducharme, "It's a cautionary tale—people make false accusations, and they make false accusations about serious crimes like sexual assault. I hope it [his client's wrongful conviction] makes people remember why people accused of crimes are presumed innocent."

When Fordham was informed of Nelson's acquittal and exoneration, she appeared startled, saying, "I had no idea this was going on. If I had known something about this I would have done something to try and fight it. I would never accuse anybody of anything they didn't do."

Cathy Fordham had filed fifty-five complaints against men, seven of which involved serious sexual assault charges. She had successfully brought about their conviction and imprisonment through a bureaucratic judicial system that took her lying word as truthful evidence. Fordham was convicted of public mischief in 2000 and was sentenced to six months in prison. Most of the men she victimized, including Nelson, believed that the sentence was paltry and that Fordham should have been sent to prison for many years.

Fordham's conviction was brought about in part by Nelson's testimony. Following her conviction, the thirty-four-year-old Nelson walked from the courtroom where he had been convicted four years earlier. He sat down on the courthouse steps and said, "Now we get to the accountability of this story. . . I finally feel that I am a free man. . . Of course, it crossed my mind that all she [Fordham] had to do was see me and make a call to police and I'd land in jail again, charged with something I didn't do. . . I do know that if I hold out and wait for her to apologize, I'll be a very old and very gray man."

Four innocent men wrongly convicted and sent to prison in Illinois did not have to wait until they were old men to see freedom and exoneration, but they did wait for years before they were released. Their troubles began on July 18, 1997, when the badly burned body of fifty-six-year-old Sindulfo Miranda was found in his Mercedes-Benz, which had been set on fire. The victim was a furniture dealer living in the Logan Square neighborhood of Chicago.

Miranda had been kidnapped and tortured (his hands and feet had been jabbed with scissors and he was sodomized with a broomstick) before being murdered, according to police, who had little to go on during this initial investigation. It was believed that the kidnappers intended to hold the wealthy Miranda for ransom, but when that came to nothing, they angrily murdered him. Four months later, Miguel LaSalle contacted police and gave them the names of five men he said committed the crime: Robert Gayol, Omar Aguirre, Luis Ortiz, Edar Duarte Santos, and Ronald Gamboa.

LaSalle told detectives that he was in Ronnie's Bar (owned by Gamboa), when he overheard the five men planning to kill Miranda. Later he saw the five men with Miranda and, while the kidnapping, torture, and murder of Miranda was occur-

ring, he actually was talking to one of the kidnappers, Santos, on his cell phone. Reacting to these statements, Chicago police arrested all five men on November 7, 1997, charging them with Miranda's murder. Gamboa was acquitted and released, but the other four men, though claiming innocence, later began turning on one another to save themselves.

Following his arrest, Aguirre, after lengthy interrogations, made a false confession that implicated Santos. Aguirre was convicted by a Cook County circuit court jury in 1999 and was sentenced to fifty-five years in prison. Santos, with Aguirre's testimony stacked against him, held out in the Cook County Jail until 2002, when he too confessed in exchange for a twelve-year sentence. With good behavior time and the time he had already spent in Cook County jail, he could look forward to release in 2003.

Ortiz had already been convicted of murder and sentenced to life imprisonment, but he too cut a deal with prosecutors. In exchange for his testimony against Gayol, he was offered a reduction of his life sentence to twenty-five years. He accepted and testified against Gayol, who was convicted in 2001 and sentenced to life in prison.

The irony of this selling out and plea bargaining was that all four convicted men were innocent. Following an FBI investigation into Chicago gang operations, the Bureau reported that, among many murders committed, the Miranda slaying had been performed by members of the Latin Kings street gang and specifically pointed out that the five men who had been identified by LaSalle had nothing to do with the murder of Miranda. After reviewing the FBI report, Chicago prosecutors appeared before a Cook County judge on December 18, 2002, to announce that Gayol, Ortiz, Aguirre, and Santos, as well as the suspected Gamboa, were all innocent of the Miranda murder. The four men were immediately released from prison and their convictions overturned.

In an apparent effort to deflect future wrongful suits by the five men, Cook County state's attorney Richard Devine stated that the four convicted men had actually sent themselves to prison by making false confessions and that police officers and prosecutors should be commended for "doing the right thing" in acknowledging the innocence of the four convicted men and announcing their exoneration. Police and prosecutors, however, had to bear the brunt of the responsibility for blindly accepting LaSalle's statements and pressuring the defendants into making false confessions and guilty pleas, as well as perjured statements from themselves in an effort to escape an unjust network that conspired to wrongfully imprison them. LaSalle, the man who had wrongly fingered the five men, was charged with making false statements and was tried in September 2003 but was acquitted, his attorneys successfully arguing that though he had made some "errors" those "errors were honest ones."

# XIII

# *Crimes That Never Happened*

Throughout recorded history inno-cent persons have been sent to prison or even executed for crimes that never happened. This bizarre scenario occurs more fre-quently than anyone might imagine. Missing per-sons are presumed kidnapped or murdered, and, on wholly circumstantial evidence, wrongly ac-cused suspects are imprisoned or even executed on the false presumption that they have abducted or murdered the missing person.

In many disappearance cases, the missing per-son either returns home or is found in a different location, and the wrongly imprisoned suspect is released. In some cases, however, the wrongly convicted person has been executed. Most of these cases belong to deep history when commu-nication and identification systems were poor or nonexistent, and law enforcement and the judici-ary made decisions on hazardous speculation.

Other cases that sent innocent persons to prison have been based on crimes that did not occur but were the work of fabricators who wanted to pun-ish or take revenge on enemies or deflect criminal investigations away from themselves. (See also Chapter XI, "Railroading and Framing.") Still other cases have been profiled as capital crimes when they actually resulted from accidents or sui-cides, invariably misdiagnosed by medical examin-ers or pathologists.

The true victims in such cases—wrongly con-victed persons—have little recourse when officials have accepted the alleged crimes as real and actual. Thorough investigation into the accusers often ex-poses the nonexistent crimes and the accusers' mo-tivations, but such probing is expensive and usually exceeds the financial resources of the accused. As often as not, defense attorneys, prosecutors, and police, as well as investigative journalists, launch their own postconviction investigations into the supposed crimes, as well as the accusers' back-ground, frequently bringing about exonerations.

Often an officer of the court or a journalist prompts an investigation, but some accusers, hec-tored by a troubled conscience, confess the fabri-cation of a crime for which an innocent person has been sent to prison. Career criminals have little or no conscience, as in the case of bootlegger Roger Touhy, sent to prison for a kidnapping that was fabricated by the colossal swindler, "Jake the Bar-ber" Factor (see this chapter).

Others fake their own murder in order to take posthumous revenge on relatives and friends by implicating them with manufactured or false evi-dence before they commit suicide. Still others have died through an accident, later wrongly inter-preted as a murder that is then pinned on some-one. It has even happened that persons have falsely admitted to crimes that never happened to bring punishment on themselves and others. The confessing party believed that evidence against him or her was overwhelming and that a confession would draw a lighter punishment. This has seldom been the case.

To be wrongly convicted for an actual crime is justice at its worst. To be wrongly convicted of a crime that never happened absurdly compounds the dilemma of such innocent persons, who not only must prove their innocence but must also prove that the crime for which they were convicted had no basis in fact.

## Early Murder Cases Without Bodies or Evidence

The mother of the Perry family, Joan, and her two grown sons, John and Richard, were servants on the estate of Viscountess Camden in Chipping, England, employed directly under the aristocratic lady's steward, seventy-year-old William Harrison. In 1659, an intruder broke into Lady Camden's house and stole about £140. The thief was never found. On August 16, 1660, the seventy-year-old Harrison disappeared during a trip to collect rents.

Mrs. Harrison sent her servant John Perry to find him. When Perry did not return, young Edward Harrison went after him and found Perry, who claimed that the elder Harrison had disappeared. Shortly before Edward Harrison and John Perry returned, a poor woman had found a hat, comb, and collar. The items, belonging to the elder Harrison, proved to be bloody; the woman led them to where she had found them, but there was no sign of a body. After John Perry returned, the justice of the peace ordered Perry to be kept in custody while a further search was made.

John Perry, when taken before the magistrate, explained his own disappearance by claiming he had been lost. However, before he had been detained and while he was in custody, Perry began telling a variety of contradictory stories to explain why he had not returned to Gloucestershire. On

August 24, 1660, the judge again questioned John Perry, asking him why he had confessed to several different people, saying that Harrison had been murdered by a tinker to one, by a neighbor to another, and telling a third that the corpse had been hidden in a bean silo. Perry then confessed, saying that Harrison had been killed by Perry's own mother and brother, claiming that they had long been nagging him to let them know when Harrison was going to collect rents, so they could rob and kill him.

According to Perry, Joan and Richard robbed Harrison before Richard Perry strangled the man while Joan Perry stood by. The three relatives had planned to take the body to a cesspool in the garden, but when John went to make sure there were no passersby, the body was spirited away by an unknown party. Perry said he had taken the hat, collar, and comb of his master and thrown them into the highway where they were later found.

Joan and Richard Perry bitterly denied John's accusations, but he refused to change his story, further implicating his sibling by identifying as the murder weapon a piece of knotted, looped rope that fell from Richard's pocket. Joan Perry and her son Richard were also arrested and jailed.

The three were indicted for robbery and murder. The Perrys were tried in September 1660 at the Gloucester Assizes, charged with robbery and murder. Pleading guilty to robbery when the judge refused to try a murder case for lack of a body, they remained in jail for some time. The Perrys believed that, without the existence of Harrison's body, they had no defense. They also believed that Charles III would pardon them and they would benefit from the Indemnity and Oblivion act, which provided exoneration for those accused of crimes that could not be proven.

John Perry eventually changed his story again, saying he had confessed previously in a fit of madness. Although Harrison's body was never found, Joan, John, and Richard Perry were all found guilty and hanged in spring 1661 on Broadway Hill. John Perry was left dangling in chains as additional punishment for fabricating an alibi—falsely recanting his confession.

Two years later, William Harrison returned very much alive to Chipping Camden with a complicated and ludicrous tale of having been kidnapped, taken to the coast of Kent, carried away to Turkey, and thrown into jail, then rescued by a Turk, who wanted an Englishman with "some skill in physick" as a slave.

After nearly two years as a slave, Harrison explained, he was released when his master died, and managed to slowly work his way back to England via Portugal. The probability that Harrison had wanted to disappear, perhaps because he had embezzled funds or knew too much about some business deal, so depressed his elderly wife, who had been in a deep state of melancholy since his disappearance, that she hanged herself not long after his return. Harrison was never charged with any wrongdoing, but authorities had clearly convicted and executed three innocent persons.

Like the Perrys, William Shaw, a tradesman in Scotland, went to the gallows for a murder that never happened. Shaw, a well-to-do upholsterer in Edinburgh, Scotland, did not approve of the man his daughter, Catherine Shaw, had chosen to marry. In fact, he despised John Lawson, calling the man a profligate and ordering his daughter never to see him again. Catherine nevertheless continued her liaison with Lawson, and, when Shaw discovered her defiant behavior, he confined her to her room.

Shaw informed her that a man of his choosing, Alexander Robertson, would be her husband. Catherine defied her father's authority, declaring in several confrontations that she would sooner die than marry Robertson. One such argument in October 1721 ended with loud screams and protestations heard by another tenant, James Morrison. Shaw locked his daughter in her room and stormed from the building.

Not long after his departure, Morrison heard groans coming from the Shaw apartment and even heard Catherine cry out, "Cruel father, thou art the cause of my death." Morrison summoned a constable and they entered Catherine's room, finding the woman with her throat slit and a knife lying beside her. Before she died, witnesses claimed she acknowledged with the nod of her head that her father had stabbed her.

Shaw returned with bloodstains on his shirt and was confronted with the sight of his daughter. Although he claimed that the stains appeared after he removed bandages from an earlier bloodletting when his daughter had tried to cut herself, the jury quickly found Shaw guilty. He was sentenced to death and hanged. Prior to his execution, his last words were, "I am innocent of my daughter's murder." His body was gibbeted at Leith Walk in November 1721 to the delight of a large and uproarious crowd.

In August 1722, the room in which Catherine Shaw died was rented by a new tenant, who came across a letter written by Catherine. The letter was a suicide note blaming Shaw for her unhappy imprisonment. It was proven to be in her handwriting, and an Edinburgh magistrate ordered Shaw's body removed from its chains. Shaw, who had once been a soldier, was posthumously exonerated for his daughter's death and given a proper burial, complete with military colors flown over his grave.

Shaw went to his death blamed for a murder that was actually a suicide. Forty years later in France, another father was horribly executed for the murder of his child, which was also proven, too late, to be a suicide. The Calas family of Toulouse, France, was part of the Protestant minority. The father, Jean Calas (1699–1761), clung to his faith with the hope that his children would do the same. It came as a terrible shock to him when his twenty-eight-year-old son Marc Antoine announced his intention to convert to Catholicism.

When Marc Antoine Calas was found dead in his home in 1761, authorities assumed his father had murdered him. The evidence, however, showed that young Calas had hanged himself. When relatives found the body, they attempted to disguise the rope burns by affixing a tie to his neck. They were afraid of the inevitable scandal, some later claimed. The police concluded that the father had merely attempted to hide his crime, and that he murdered his son out of rage after he had embraced a religious faith that his father passionately opposed.

Jean Calas was tried for murder and condemned to death on the wheel, an agonizing execution. Following his death, the family property was confiscated, and his daughters were placed in a convent. In 1761, the philosopher Francois Marie Arouet Voltaire (1694–1778) became interested in the case. Voltaire launched a one-man campaign to clear the Calas family name and to restore the property of the bereaved mother and daughters.

Voltaire demonstrated to the courts that Marc Antoine had committed suicide as a result of a large gambling debt he had incurred. He had killed himself fearing the scandal that debt might incur. In March 1764, the royal councilors, meeting at the palace of Versailles, opened an official inquiry. In March 1765, the parliament of Toulouse decided that Calas had been wrongfully executed. Jean Calais was absolved posthumously of all guilt, and the family estate was returned to its rightful owners. Voltaire called his success at vindicating the Calas name "the finest fifth act the theatre can give us."

Three decades later in England, a runaway girl brought about her father's execution for murder. John Graham beat his daughter Susan mercilessly, as evident from the wails that came from behind their farmhouse walls and from the deep brown scars that marked her young body. Neighbors in the town of Cobham dreaded the day when Graham would kill the innocent child. Driven by their dread, it was they, not he, who committed murder.

Until the death of his wife Mary in 1803, Graham had been a good father and husband. After he lost his wife, he became vicious, seeming to resent his daughter's existence. In early 1804, police were sent to the troubled Graham home more than once to confront him for abusing his child, so when several days passed and no one had seen Susan, neighbors assumed the worst, that Graham had finally murdered her.

Once arrested, a pale and frightened John Graham gave a different explanation, saying his daughter had run away the day before. With Graham in prison awaiting trial for murder, searchers turned his home inside out looking for a body or other evidence of foul play. They found nothing and Graham again claimed his innocence. A merciful judge granted him three months of freedom to find his daughter and prove his innocence.

Graham set off but could not find Susan and spent some of his borrowed time tracking down a look-alike. In three months, he returned with the girl, confident of acquittal. One observant woman sitting under the witness box noticed that this "Susan Graham" lacked the scars of abuse the original had carried. She arose and declared, "She's no more Susan Graham than I am." The terrified girl then admitted being an impostor, and Graham, still saying he was not guilty of murder, admitted he had bribed the girl into testifying in desperation of preserving his life.

The judge and jury, convinced that the bribe meant "guilty," convicted Graham of murdering his missing daughter and sentenced him to death. Graham was hanged and buried in a grave in the prison precincts. Then the real Susan Graham showed up. A Mrs. Carter saw her first when the girl strolled into Cobham. Taking her by the wrist, the woman brought the girl to the town inn, presented her to the shocked customers, and said, "They hanged an innocent man when they executed her father—and all of you did it!"

## More Mythical Murders

Jesse and Stephen Boorn were simple farmers from Manchester, Vermont. Their sister Sally married Russell Colvin, considered by the townsfolk to be an eccentric personality, if not feebleminded. It came as no surprise in Manchester when Colvin suddenly disappeared in May 1812. He had the wanderlust in him and had run off before, sometimes staying away for weeks on end. This time, though, Colvin stayed away for seven years.

In the spring of 1819, seven years after Colvin vanished, Uncle Amos Boorn had a vivid dream in which he spoke with the ghost of Colvin. The ghost led him to the precise spot where he was buried. Three times Amos claimed to have received a nocturnal visit from the ghost, and, on each occasion, the burial spot was always the same, a burned-out silo on the Boorn property.

A few days later, a boy and his dog dug up some old bones found near the family home. Recalling that Stephen and Jesse had quarreled with Colvin shortly before he vanished, residents of the town demanded an investigation. The proof of guilt seemed incontrovertible. Jesse was brought to the justice of the peace on April 27, 1819, and examined for four days. He accused his brother Stephen of murdering Colvin and named several likely burial spots where the remains might be found.

Stephen faced a grand jury, which returned an indictment for murder, though the bones near the stump were later determined to be those of an animal. The most damaging testimony came from a convicted forger named Silas Merrill, who had shared a jail cell with Jesse Boorn and testified that Jesse had told him about the quarrel. According to Merrill, Stephen had struck the fatal blow and Colvin's body had been buried under the same cellar old Amos had dreamed about.

The case was riddled with hearsay and rumor. The most puzzling aspect was the absence of a body. Despite all this, Jesse and Stephen were convicted of murder on January 28, 1820, and sentenced to death. Jesse's sentence was later commuted to life imprisonment.

As the days passed and his scheduled execution loomed, Stephen Boorn's hopes began to fade. At the last possible moment, Colvin was located in New York City (another report said New Jersey). He knew nothing about the plight of his brothers-in-law until a Manchester man named James

Whelpley noticed an article in the New York *Evening Post* that questioned the whereabouts of Colvin, if in fact he was still alive. The story had been placed by friends of the Boorns, who were anxious to stave off a hanging.

Colvin returned to his hometown, where he refused to reconcile his differences with Sally but willingly appeared before the magistrate to help clear Jesse and Stephen Boorn. The state's attorney entered a motion of nolle prosequi, so that the case would proceed no further. The Boorn case was the first wrongful murder conviction recorded in U.S. jurisprudence.

Sixty years after the Boorns were vindicated with the arrival of a living "corpse," a clergyman in Denmark went to his death for killing a man who was indeed alive. The pastor of the church at Veilby, Denmark, began having uncontrollable fits of violent temper, which he regarded as periods of fighting the devil. When Soren Qvist felt one of these fits coming on, he would try to isolate himself in his house. This was not always possible. When a domineering and crooked farmer, Morten Bruns, tried to court Qvist's daughter, the pastor threatened him and told him to stay away. Qvist tried to compensate when he gave a job to Bruns's brother, Neils Bruns. However, Qvist fired the brother when he did not do his work.

Morten Bruns was enraged when his brother was fired and saw an opportunity for revenge against Qvist. That night, he dug a body from the cemetery, took it to the pastor's home, dressed it in one of Qvist's gowns, and buried it in the parsonage garden. Bruns's loud complaints and

The "murder" of Russell Colvin in 1819 in Manchester, Vermont, a slaying for which two brothers were convicted and sentenced to death, but were released after Colvin reappeared very much alive. *History Inc./Jay Robert Nash Collection.*

neighbors' sighting of someone digging in the garden caused authorities to disinter the body. It was identified as Neils Bruns.

The pastor, convinced he had killed Bruns in an unremembered fit of rage, willingly stood trial in 1880. He was found guilty of murder and sentenced to be executed. He refused all help in getting the sentence commuted and was hanged. Twenty years later, after Morten Bruns died, a man appeared at the parsonage looking for him. It was Neils, his brother. Morten had paid him to leave town and never come back. He did not return until Morten died and the payments stopped coming.

A desire for revenge, which had created a nonexistent murder in Denmark, also prodded an unfaithful wife to bring about the execution of her lover in Arkansas for a murder that existed only in her imagination and subsequently in the minds of officials. George and Rebecca Watkins moved to Marion County, Arkansas, from Kansas in 1886. Soon Rebecca Watkins took an interest in Charles Hudspeth, and a year later, George Watkins vanished. Officials could find no trace of him and began to believe the rumors that he had been killed and his body hidden by Rebecca and Hudspeth. Both were arrested, and Rebecca Watkins then told police that Hudspeth had murdered her husband so that they could wed.

Hudspeth, on Rebecca's statements, was convicted and sentenced to death in 1887, but was reprieved when the Arkansas Supreme Court overturned the conviction, ruling that Judge R. H. Powell had wrongly barred testimony that depicted Rebecca's character as amoral and untrustworthy. Tried again, Hudspeth was again convicted and again sentenced to death. On December 30, 1892, he was executed by hanging in Harrison, Arkansas.

The following year, W. F. Pace, Hudspeth's attorney, reportedly located the missing George Watkins, who had been living in Kansas. George Watkins had abandoned his wife, he said, after she proved to be unfaithful. Further, Rebecca Watkins,

it was then concluded, had lied about Hudspeth murdering her husband, knowing that accusation to be false, in order to punish Hudspeth for threatening to leave her, as had her husband.

Vengeful neighbors in Nebraska brought about the hanging of an innocent man in 1887, the same year Hudspeth was wrongly convicted of murdering a man who was still alive. William Jackson Marion went to the hangman in Gage County, Nebraska, on March 25, 1887, proclaiming his innocence to the very end. He had been convicted of murdering a business partner, John Cameron, eleven years earlier.

Marion and Cameron became friends when they boarded together in Clay County, Kansas. In May 1872, they traveled to Gage County, Nebraska, to visit Marion's in-laws, John and Rachel Warren. Before they left or en route to the Warren home, Marion and Cameron signed an agreement that Marion would buy a team of horses from Cameron for $315, giving Cameron $30 as a down payment, with the understanding that Cameron would keep the horses until the balance was paid off.

After a short visit with the Warrens, Marion and Cameron departed, saying they were going to work on the western railroads. Marion returned to Gage County a few days later without Cameron and offered no explanation as to his whereabouts. Marion continued to live in the area, but his tough-minded business practices incurred the anger of several neighbors.

These neighbors harbored deep resentment of Marion and, for years, spread the false rumor that he had killed Cameron to acquire the horses without paying for them. When a badly decomposed body was found in 1883 on a former Indian reservation, neighbors insisted, based on the clothes, that the corpse belonged to the missing Cameron.

On this shabby evidence, Marion was arrested and eventually tried for murdering Cameron, convicted and sentenced to death. However, his conviction was overturned by the Supreme Court of Nebraska on a technicality—a judge had sentenced Marion to death when this was thought to be the exclusive prerogative of a jury. It was later determined that the law, by the time of Marion's original trial, had been changed to allow judges to mete out such justice. Marion was nevertheless re-tried and again convicted and executed in 1887.

In 1891, John Cameron reappeared in Gage County, Nebraska. He was shocked to learn that his friend Marion had been wrongly convicted and executed for a murder he did not commit. Cameron explained that he had set out with Marion to work on the railroads and then decided to go to Mexico in order to escape the family members of a girl he had wooed in Kansas, believing that they would compel him to wed the girl. Marion received posthumous exoneration through a special proclamation issued by Nebraska Governor Kay A. Orr (1987–1991) on March 27, 1987, the 100th anniversary of his wrongful hanging.

Where angry neighbors vengefully took the life of the innocent William Marion, a disgruntled Alabama farmworker concocted a murder theory that was also based on skeletal remains and resulted in a trial almost identical to the Nebraska case. That theory, despite its repudiation by knowledgeable scientists, sent an innocent man to prison for life.

In the spring of 1912, two fishermen found some skeletal remains along the bank of the Warrior River in Blount County, Alabama. The bones were thought to be those of an adult female and a child. When learning of this, James House, a farmworker, began talking to local police. He believed that the remains were probably those of Jenny Wade Wilson and her nineteen-month-old child, who had disappeared in 1908 after Jenny divorced William Wilson. House had no love for Wilson, having occasionally worked for him as a tenant farmer and often arguing with him about wages.

House theorized that Wilson had murdered his former wife and child after Jenny visited the Wilson farm seeking financial support. House said that, after the rancorous divorce, he had seen Jenny go to the Wilson house carrying a basket, presumably holding her child. He said he followed footprints from the house that had been left the following day and led to the Warrior River, where he found a "child's cloth" and blood on a rock. When asked why he had not made such disclosures in 1908, at the time Jenny and he child disappeared, House gave vague answers.

James Embry, Blount County solicitor, came to believe House's unfounded accusations as fact and persuaded a grand jury to indict Wilson for the murder of his former wife and child. Wilson was brought to trial in 1915, where Embry offered to a jury the testimony of a jailhouse informer, Mack Holcomb, who had shared a cell with Wilson while Wilson awaited trial. Holcomb stated that he had overheard Wilson tell a relative visiting him in jail, "If you tell anything, I will tend to you when I get out." More witnesses stated in court that Wilson had threatened to kill Jenny if she ever contacted him again following their bitter divorce.

Wilson, who said that he was innocent, offered many witnesses who testified that Jenny had never visited the Wilson home after she divorced and left the county with her child. Defense attorneys also provided a medical expert, Dr. J. E. Hancock, who stated that he had carefully examined the skeletal remains, particularly the teeth, this being one of the first murder cases in Alabama where odontology surfaced in detailed testimony. Hancock said that the teeth in the skull of the adult belonged to an elderly person and that the teeth in the skull of the child were second teeth usually found in a child of four or older, not a nineteen-month-old child. Wilson was nevertheless found guilty by a jury and was sentenced to life imprisonment by Judge J. E. Blackwood on December 18, 1915.

Judge Blackwood had misgivings about the case from the beginning and privately told officials that he had doubted some of the prosecution witnesses, especially House, who harbored deep animosity toward Wilson, and the jailhouse informer Holcomb, whose own sentence was cut short after he testified. Through third parties, Blackwood contacted Dr. Alex Hrdlicka, curator of physical anthropology at the renowned Smithsonian Institution in Washington, D.C., who closely examined the skeletal remains found on the bank of the Warrior River. Dr. Hrdlicka reported that the remains were actually those of four very old persons, probably the bones of long-dead Indians who once dwelled in the area and where it was commonplace for tribal burial squads to inter the remains of their members along the banks of the river.

Upon receiving this report, Judge Blackwood, who no longer had jurisdiction of the Wilson case, asked Alabama Governor Charles Henderson (1915–1919) to grant clemency and issue a pardon that would bring about Wilson's release. Before Governor Henderson could act, however, Wilson's attorney located Jenny Wade Wilson and her eleven-year-old child alive and well in Vincennes, Indiana. The lawyer accompanied her and her child back to Blount County, Alabama, where both appeared in the flesh before astonished officials and residents on July 8, 1918. On that very day, Governor Henderson granted a full pardon to William Wilson, who was immediately released from prison.

Ten years later in Alabama, revenge was at the root of a murder conviction involving the disappearance of a fourteen-year-old girl. On the southern bank of the sluggish Alabama River in Lowndes County, Alabama, there lived a young black woman named Louise Butler, who became fond of George Yelder, a fifty-five-year-old neighbor. Louise was a jealous, possessive woman who resented the attention Yelder showed to Topsy Warren, her fourteen-year-old niece.

One day in 1928, after returning from a visit to Montgomery, Louise found Topsy chatting with Yelder, who had just given her a shiny new half-dollar. Louise marched Topsy out to the woodpile and administered a severe beating. Then the girl disappeared from the county, and rumors began to circulate that she had been murdered.

Sent to investigate, Deputy Sheriff "Buck" Meadows listened to a wild story told by Louise's twelve-year-old daughter Julia, who claimed to have witnessed her mother chop up Topsy with an ax and discard the body parts in a burlap sack. When nine-year-old niece Anne-Mary corroborated the story, separate murder indictments were returned against Butler and Yelder for the death of Topsy Warren on April 17, 1928.

The trial was held in the courtroom of Judge A. E. Gamble. Both parties maintained their innocence, but were convicted and sentenced to life imprisonment on April 26, 1928. A week after they had been imprisoned at the Alabama State Penitentiary, word reached county authorities that Topsy Warren was alive and living with relatives in Dallas County.

Topsy was located and brought back to Hayneville for identification before Judge Gamble and solicitor Calvin Poole. An official pardon was granted in June 1928, and the pair was officially released. Sheriff Meadows later theorized that the two juvenile "eyewitnesses" had been coached into giving false testimony by a man who bore a personal grudge against George Yelder.

## The "Kidnapping" of Jake the Barber

Roger "The Terrible" Touhy (1898–1959) was a prominent bootlegger who operated with a small gang in the northern suburbs of Chicago during the 1920s. Born in Chicago, the son of a policeman, Touhy moved with his large family (two sisters and five brothers) from Chicago to the suburb of Downer's Grove, Illinois, in 1908, after a kitchen stove blew up in their Chicago home and killed his mother.

Touhy's childhood was normal. He attended St. Joseph's Grade School in Downer's Grove and graduated in 1911. He was an altar boy in the local Catholic church and went to work as a Western Union messenger in his early teens. He later became a telegraph operator and manager of a small Western Union office, a job he kept until 1915, when he was fired for union activities.

Moving to Colorado, Touhy continued to be a telegraph operator, working for the Denver & Rio Grande Railroad. During World War I, Touhy enlisted in the U.S. Navy and taught Morse code to naval officers at Harvard University in 1918. When mustered out of the service, Touhy sought adventure by traveling to the boom towns of Oklahoma, where he worked as an oil rigger and engineer. He bought and sold oil leases and built up a nest egg of $25,000 before returning to Chicago in 1922.

Following his marriage, Touhy purchased several trucks and founded a trucking firm with his brother Tommy. By 1926, Touhy, Tommy, and their brother Eddie began distributing illegal beer and liquor, controlling most of Chicago's northwestern suburbs. Touhy hired a top chemist to establish a brewery.

With his partner, Matt Kolb, Touhy produced what was considered to be the best Prohibition beer in the Midwest at a cost of $4.50 a barrel, which they sold for $55 a barrel. Touhy paid off police in Des Plaines and other suburbs with barrels of beer or cases of bottled beer (he had his own bottling plant at the time) so that his lucrative bootlegging could continue unmolested.

In late 1926, Touhy and Kolb began installing slot machines in suburban saloons until hundreds of these one-armed bandits were raking in thousands of dollars each week. So famous was Touhy's beer that Al Capone began ordering hundreds of barrels from him. One order brought a payment of $30,000.

At the time, Touhy's headquarters were located at The Arch, a roadhouse in Schiller Park, Illinois. Capone, coveting the northern territories controlled by Touhy, sent two representatives, Frank Rio and Willie Heeney, to negotiate a Capone takeover of this area.

Touhy had no real gang at the time. He was a middle-class brewer with a long list of saloon clients. He met with Heeney and Rio while a parade of farmers and off-duty policemen, all friends of Touhy's and numbering in the dozens, marched through Touhy's offices, brandishing submachine guns and shotguns, playacting as gangsters. These otherwise peaceful, law-abiding citizens snarled out lines like, "Hey, boss, you want we should take out that mob in Skokie?" Or, "We took care of those nine punks from Detroit, who tried to horn in on your business, boss—they're all floating face down in the Fox River," Or, "You got trouble with that guy Capone, boss?—just give us the word and we'll send about four companies of the National Guard to the South Side of Chicago with some armored cars, the ones with the heavy machine guns."

The show of force unnerved Capone's men, Rio reporting back to Scarface Capone that the "Touhy mob is tough and big. He must have a hundred guys up there, all killers. Touhy hardly talked to us. He spent most of the time on the phone giving orders to have guys bumped off. He's got every local cop for fifty miles and the National Guard behind him."

The phone conversations were also part of Touhy's playacting. Aside from a few truck drivers, Touhy had no gang. Yet Capone believed he was up against a powerful organization and continued to play a cat-and-mouse game with Touhy, repeatedly sending emissaries to see Touhy but getting no results.

Touhy rebuffed all of Capone's attempts to install whorehouses and gambling dens in the northern suburbs. At one point, Touhy told Capone gunmen that he had "two hundred guys out here from every penitentiary in the United States and from Canada." He then invited the gunmen to attend a party the following Saturday night, asking that they bring Capone along. "Most of my guys will be here," Touhy said.

On Saturday night, Touhy closed The Arch down. Several squads of county police arrived to raid the place only to find it locked up. As he suspected, Capone had contacted his stooge, Cook County Sheriff Peter Hoffman, ordering him to raid the Touhy headquarters and arrest Touhy's entire gang, thus putting his competitor out of business.

However, there was no one to arrest. Capone meanwhile continued to send representatives to Touhy, including Murray "The Camel" Humphreys and James "Red" Fawcett. When Humphreys got tough with Touhy, the bootlegger went to a wall rack containing several submachine guns and began fingering one of them. Humphreys panicked, thinking he was about to be killed. He offered Touhy his new $16,000 roadster: "If you drive me back inside the Chicago city limits, I'll give you the car. I want to get home alive."

"Go on back to Chicago, both of you," Touhy told them. "You won't get hurt."

Both men left hurriedly. A few minutes later, Fawcett returned and told Touhy that the cowardly Humphreys disgusted him. "Listen, Touhy," Fawcett said. "For five grand I'll kill that s.o.b. Humphreys on the way back to the city, and for another five thousand I'll go to Cicero and knock off Frank Nitti [Capone's top enforcer]. What do you say?"

Touhy declined the offer: "I've got my own boys for little jobs like that."

The frustrated Capone, angered at having to pay Touhy $37.50 a barrel for beer, had Touhy's partner, Matt Kolb, kidnapped and ransomed for

Roger "The Terrible" Touhy, a peaceful bootlegger who dominated Chicago's northwest suburbs in the late 1920s and whose successful territory was coveted by Chicago crime czar Al Capone. *History Inc./Jay Robert Nash Collection.*

$50,000. Capone called Touhy to tell him that he had learned of Kolb's kidnapping and offered to act as a go-between to bring about Kolb's release.

Touhy personally delivered the $50,000 to Capone, boldly marching through an army of bodyguards stationed in Capone's Chicago headquarters in the Metropole Hotel. He threw the money onto Capone's desk and demanded to know where Kolb was. Capone nervously counted the money and replied, "Now, Rog. I want you to know that I had nothing to do with this. I like Matt. I'm trying to help him."

"Sure you are, Al," Touhy said sarcastically.

"I'll get this dough into the right hands and we'll get Matt out of this mess right away," Capone promised.

Within the hour, Kolb was released from a Capone hideout a few blocks away. Capone went on buying beer from Touhy but resented paying a premium price. In 1931, his gangsters once more kidnapped Matt Kolb but demanded no ransom. They merely shot him to death and dumped his body in a ditch.

In 1933, Touhy, whom the press had dubbed "The Terrible," stemming from the horror stories told about him by Capone men, was arrested by Melvin Purvis of the FBI and wrongly charged with kidnapping millionaire St. Paul brewer William A. Hamm, a crime that actually was committed by the Barker Brothers. Touhy and three others were found not guilty. Touhy's arrest and acquittal were widely publicized and noted by swindler John "Jake the Barber" Factor (1894–1984), who hatched a plot to frame Touhy for a crime that never happened. Factor, who had used many aliases in his million-dollar scams, was about to be deported to his native England to face charges of fraud, which were certain to put him behind bars for decades. He would use Touhy, the docile bootlegger, to permanently evade deportation and conviction.

John Factor was born in poverty in London. At an early age, he moved to the United States with his family, settling in Chicago. In an immigrant ghetto on the West Side, he learned the art of sneak thievery and petty racketeering. By the time he was in his teens, Factor was inventing schemes to swindle others. To keep himself in walkabout money, Factor became a barber, first in a West Side shop and later graduating to a posh salon at the Morrison Hotel in downtown Chicago. Here Factor met high-rolling confidence men, and he soon joined forces with several swindlers specializing in postal con games. He was indicted for mail fraud in 1925 but escaped a prison sentence.

Through his contacts, Factor met Al Capone, crime boss of Chicago during the 1920s, and through Capone, many other racketeers, including Jack "Legs" Diamond of New York. In 1930, Factor convinced Diamond, then cash heavy from bootlegging and other rackets, to invest in a wild scheme whereby Factor would swindle hundreds of thousands of British investors. Reportedly armed with $500,000 of Diamond's money, Factor and several confederates left for London. He established himself in a luxury suite in Grosvenor Square, using various aliases, such as Harry Wise and J. Gest. With him was his right-hand man, Arthur Jack Klein.

Factor then pumped a fortune into establishing the Broad Street Press, which published a number of financial publications, including *City News, Stock Exchange Observer, Financial Observer,* and *Finance.* These publications were written and edited by Factor's shrewd stock-swindling henchmen for the sole purpose of promoting useless stock. Factor had undoubtedly studied the career of British swindler Horatio William Bottomley, who had successfully bilked enormous sums from British investors in the previous two decades, promoting useless stock through his financial publications.

After buying millions of ten-shilling shares in Vulcan Copper Mines and Rhodesia Border Mines at bargain basement prices, Factor peddled these worthless stock certificates through two dozen specially trained salesmen, with Klein overseeing their door-to-door pitches. Factor ingratiated himself with the Prince of Wales and other British dignitaries, while his photo appeared in newspapers with leading social figures. He was accepted as a brilliant financier who was bringing financial prosperity to the small British investor through his development of companies reported to be laden with priceless copper and diamonds. The reports, of course, came from Factor's own financial newspapers, which were given away free to millions of readers and urged readers to buy the worthless Vulcan and Rhodesia stocks.

Factor and his minions gleaned more than an estimated $5 million from gullible British investors before fleeing England a few steps ahead of Scotland Yard. Yet Klein and several other so-called directors of the Broad Street Press and the empty copper and diamond companies were arrested and tried in 1931. These included Herbert John Spellen, Frederick Newbery, and the firm's solicitor, Barnett Leon Elman. All of them, including Klein, received long prison terms. Factor, however, had slipped through the Scotland Yard net and had returned to the United States.

Jack "Legs" Diamond, who expected to receive several million dollars in return for his investment in the Factor scheme, suddenly learned that Factor

British swindler John "Jake the Barber" Factor, who bilked millions out of British investors and fled to Chicago and the protection of crime boss Al Capone. *History Inc./Jay Robert Nash Collection.*

intended to renege on his bargain. Diamond threatened to have Factor killed, but Diamond himself was murdered. His death has been attributed at one time or another to many of his underworld rivals, from Dutch Schultz to Charles "Lucky" Luciano. Some reports have it that Factor arranged for Diamond's murder.

The British government pressed U.S. authorities to extradite Factor to England to stand trial for his swindles, but authorities in Chicago, where Factor had heavily bribed officials and also used his influence with Al Capone, informed the British that Factor had "committed no crimes in Illinois" that would affect British laws. The British continued to press extradition demands through U.S. officials, battling through the U.S. court system against Factor's highly paid attorneys.

Chicago, with a huge Irish immigrant population, was decidedly anti-British, which was dramatically and ridiculously demonstrated by one of the city's most autocratic mayors, William Hale "Big Bill" Thompson (1869–1944). After hearing that King George of England might visit the United States, Thompson publicly stated, in an attempt to curry

Al Capone, Chicago crime boss who gleaned $50 million each year from his rackets, but whose greed demanded that he take over Touhy's bootleg area either by force or cunning. *History Inc./Jay Robert Nash Collection.*

favor with Irish voters, "If King George comes to Chicago, I will punch him in the nose!" Thompson was also on Capone's payroll, as were most of the city's alderman and high-ranking police officers, as well as top state officials. Illinois Governor Lennington "Len" Small (1921–1929), who pardoned hundreds of Capone's most vicious gangsters during the 1920s, was later indicted for money laundering and bribes but escaped conviction.

In 1933, just when it appeared that Factor was about to lose his battle with immigration officials, he was reportedly kidnapped by the bootlegging gang headed by Roger "The Terrible" Touhy and held for a large ransom. It was later paid, and Factor was released. "I was treated like a dog," Factor claimed, and he was held as a witness against the Touhy gang. His son, Jerome Factor, was also kidnapped a short time later, reportedly by the same gang, and Factor claimed that he paid $50,000 for his son's safe return. The car in which Jerome Factor had been kidnapped was later identified as belonging to Al Capone, Factor's close friend.

The kidnappings were hoaxes, cleverly devised to prevent Factor from being extradited to England to stand trial and face certain conviction for his gigantic swindle there. Since he had to testify against Touhy and his men, Factor was held in jail as a material witness and put in a cell to "protect him from gangland reprisals." This was also nonsense, since Touhy's so-called gang was nothing more than a small group of entrepreneurial bootleggers. Lending credence to Factor's claim of being kidnapped was the earlier charge against Touhy for kidnapping Hamm, the brewery magnate.

Touhy did, however, control a lucrative territory coveted by Al Capone and his chief henchman, Murray "The Camel" Humphreys. By framing Touhy for the faked Factor kidnapping, which Capone arranged with Humphreys's connivance, Factor could use Touhy as an excuse to fend off his extradition, and Capone and Humphreys could take over Touhy's Far North Side bootlegging operations.

Capone lieutenant and killer, Murray "The Camel" Humphreys, who failed to make a deal with Touhy on his boss's behalf and then conceived of framing him for a crime that never happened. *History Inc./Jay Robert Nash Collection.*

Factor and his attorneys were familiar with a federal law stating that if a person held to be extradited is not removed within sixty days of his arrest, he can be released under a writ of habeas corpus and thereby permanently evade extradition. That was exactly what happened. Factor stayed in jail, ostensibly in "protective custody" so that he could testify against the Touhy gang, and this period of time exceeded the sixty days.

Factor identified Touhy and others as his kidnappers, and these men, convicted on Factor's lies, were sent to prison for life. Factor's lawyers then appeared and informed authorities that their client had been held in jail over the sixty-day limit and was therefore, according to the U.S. Statute of Limitations, ineligible for extradition. He was released and left Chicago for Los Angeles, where he began investing his stolen millions in real estate.

In 1943, Factor was back in the news when he and ten others were convicted in a mail fraud that manipulated liquor warehouse receipts. Factor was sentenced to six years in the federal prison at Sandstone, Minnesota. He entered Sandstone in August 1943 and was released in February 1948. Factor returned to Los Angeles and continued his

Police officers manhandling Roger Touhy after arresting him for allegedly kidnapping "Jake the Barber" Factor in 1933, an abduction that never occurred. *History Inc./Jay Robert Nash Collection.*

mysterious real estate investments. Moreover, he began to pump considerable sums into newly built Las Vegas casinos, including 65 percent interest in the Stardust Hotel and Casino. Factor continued to give heavy donations to politicians at the local, state, and federal level. He contributed $20,000 to the campaign of John Kennedy and $5,000 to that of Richard Nixon in 1959.

In that same year, 1959, Roger Touhy, who had been sent to prison for life for kidnapping Factor in 1933, was released from prison in Illinois. The judge who released him announced that the Factor kidnapping had been a hoax. Touhy had written a best-selling book, *The Stolen Years,* in which he pilloried Factor and Murray "The Camel" Humphreys for framing him and his men. Only twenty-three days after his parole, Touhy was killed on the porch of his sister's home in Chicago by shotgun blasts, a killing undoubtedly urged by Factor and most certainly carried out by Humphreys's gunmen.

So controversial was this slaying that federal authorities moved to have Factor deported to his native England, using as their case

Factor testifying against Touhy in 1933, claiming that he had been forced to pay the bootlegger $50,000 to release him and that his son was also kidnapped by Touhy. *History Inc./Jay Robert Nash Collection.*

Factor's 1943 conviction and other shady practices, along with the Touhy killing, including parole violations. Formal deportation proceedings against Factor began in December 1962, but President Kennedy (who had received a $20,000 donation from Factor in his presidential campaign), on Christmas Eve of that year, granted Factor a full pardon. Three years later, in 1965, the federal government charged Murray "The Camel" Humphreys with stock manipulation in regard to an overnight stock transaction arranged by Factor, which netted Humphreys $42,000.

Factor admitted helping Humphreys make this money on an inside deal, saying that he was merely returning a favor, since Humphreys had arranged to have his son returned to him after the 1933 kidnapping. In truth, according to reliable sources, Factor was repaying Humphreys for killing Roger Touhy, who had exposed his faked 1933 kidnapping. Humphreys could certainly have helped in getting Jerome Factor released in 1933, since it was Humphreys who arranged the faked kidnapping.

In 1933, the year Jerome Factor was released after allegedly being kidnapped, Touhy and three others were convicted with testimony that was later determined to be perjured. False evidence reportedly proving that Touhy and others were

Factor is surrounded by gun-toting guards, protecting him against another so-called Touhy kidnapping, the guards being Capone enforcers. *History Inc./Jay Robert Nash Collection.*

"Jake the Barber" with Chicago Police Captain John Stege; his complaint against Touhy was supported by another police officer, Detective Daniel A. "Tubbo" Gilbert, who provided manufactured evidence at Touhy's 1933 trial. *History Inc./Jay Robert Nash Collection.*

Roger Touhy at his 1933 trial for kidnapping Factor; he was convicted and sent to prison to serve 199 years. *History Inc./Jay Robert Nash Collection.*

guilty of kidnapping Factor was provided to the court by a Chicago police captain who had been on Capone's payroll for years, Daniel A. "Tubbo" Gilbert.

Gilbert personally supervised the manufacture of false evidence against Touhy, including forged documents and false witnesses who eagerly gave perjured testimony against Touhy at Gilbert's behest and under his threat of retaliation, should that false testimony be ineffective. (William Drury, a former Chicago police officer, threatened to expose Gilbert's longstanding ties with the Chicago outfit. He was murdered in Chicago on September 26, 1950, while backing his car into his garage. His two shotgun-wielding assassins were never apprehended, the same kind of gangland slaying that took Touhy's life nine years later.)

Touhy was sent to Joliet Prison to serve 199 years. For almost a decade, Touhy tried to prove his innocence in the Factor kidnapping, spending his bootleg fortune on expensive lawyers. He was a model prisoner but came to believe he would never be released. A short time later, he agreed to join a prison break that included six other veteran convicts: Basil "The Owl" Banghart, Eugene O'Connor, Edward Darlak, Martlick Nelson, Edward Stewart, and St. Clair McInerney.

On October 9, 1942, Touhy and the other six men escaped Joliet. Using a makeshift rope ladder, the seven men scaled a wall to a guard tower and then slipped over it to freedom. Touhy and the others became public enemies on the FBI's most wanted list. Bureau agents cornered the escaped convicts in a Chicago boardinghouse in December 1942. McInerney and O'Connor chose to shoot it out with agents and were killed in a wild battle. Touhy and the others were returned to Joliet.

Touhy persisted in attempting to prove his innocence in the Factor kidnapping, and his lawyers successfully argued his case before federal Judge John P. Barnes, who declared the Factor kidnapping "a hoax." The wrongly convicted Touhy was released from prison on November 25, 1959. By then he was broke and ailing. He returned to Chicago to live with a sister. As he was entering his sister's home on the night of December 17, 1959, Touhy was met with several shotgun blasts, which almost tore his body in half.

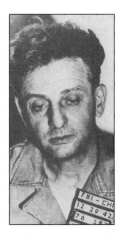

Touhy in 1942, returned to prison after a daring escape, with more years added to his sentence. *History Inc./Jay Robert Nash Collection.*

While being rushed to a hospital, Touhy told newsmen riding in the ambulance, "I've been expecting it. The bastards never forget!" According to best reports, Touhy's execution had been ordered by "Jake the Barber" Factor and carried out by his old enemy, Murray "The Camel" Humphreys, who had never forgiven Touhy for frightening him half to death in 1931, and for the demeaning remarks Touhy had made about him in his book, *The Stolen Years*, published shortly before Roger "The Terrible" Touhy was released from prison.

With Touhy dead, Factor continued to pile up his millions in California through real estate investments,

Roger Touhy, after learning that his kidnapping had been labeled a hoax by federal Judge John P. Barnes; the former bootlegger was released on November 25, 1959. *History Inc./Jay Robert Nash Collection.*

aided mightily by local politicians and other influential residents. He kept his ties to the presidency, or attempted to do so. In 1968, Factor paid more than $350,000 in contributions and loans to Hubert H. Humphrey in his unsuccessful bid for the presidency. He went on making charitable contributions almost to the day of his death on January 22, 1984.

December 17, 1959: The end of Roger Touhy, who lays dying on the porch of his sister's Chicago home, fatally shot by gunmen most probably sent by his old nemesis, Murray "The Camel" Humphreys. *History Inc./Jay Robert Nash Collection.*

Factor once handed out $20 bills to more than a thousand blacks in Fayette, Mississippi, calling a press conference and announcing to newsmen, "I know what it is to be poor and hungry and to be discriminated against." He later contributed $1 million to establish a youth center in Watts, a depressed black area of Los Angeles. At the same time, Factor contributed $6,000 to the election campaign coffers of Los Angeles district attorney Joseph A. Busch. This inventive swindler, once described by the *Los Angeles Times* as a "prominent Democratic philanthropist," died peacefully in bed and was buried in the Hollywood Cemetery alongside stellar actors and actresses he had wined and dined in life.

## Crimes of the Imagination

In June 1951, North Carolina farmer Mack Ingram, born in 1907, needed to borrow a wagon to harvest his hay crop. The forty-four-year-old black man walked to the house of a white neighbor, Aubrey Boswell, and mistakenly followed one of the Boswell children across a field before realizing it was not the father. In the afternoon, Ingram was arrested and charged with assault with intent to rape.

Willa Jean Boswell told authorities that Ingram had chased her for an extended time and kept watching her. The seventeen-year-old girl told police that the closest Ingram came to her was twenty-five feet, but he would not stop looking at her. Ingram, the father of nine children, said he mistook the girl for her father because she was wearing dungarees and a hat.

Prosecutor W. Banks Horton wanted Ingram to stand trial. Recorder Ralph Vernon, having duties comparable to a justice of the peace, deemed Ingram guilty of "assault on a female" and sentenced him to two years of hard labor. A North Carolina law stated that an assault could occur without physical contact.

The National Association for the Advancement of Colored People (NAACP) took up the issue, helping Ingram appeal his case. In November 1951, a mistrial was ordered when a mixed jury could not reach a verdict.

One year later, an all-white jury in Yanceyville upheld the assault ruling despite agreeing that the farmer never came within fifty feet of the girl. In March 1953, the North Carolina Supreme Court reversed the lower court decision. After serving two years behind bars for a crime that never happened, Ingram was released.

In 1965, another crime that never happened began when an impoverished California couple claimed they abandoned their seriously ill three-year-old daughter in the restroom of a San Francisco gas station, believing it was the only way to get her the medical attention she desperately needed.

Eight years later, in 1973, the bones of a girl were found in a shallow grave near where the couple, Antonio Rivera and Merla Walpole, had lived at the time they abandoned their daughter, Judy. In March 1975, the couple, now divorced, were tried and convicted of murder. Prior to sentencing, the convictions were reversed on a technicality, and in November, charges against them were dismissed when ten-year-old Judy was found living in San Francisco with her adoptive parents.

In the instance of James Dixon, a Chicago police officer obtained a wrongful conviction for a crime that never happened. The twenty-four-year-old Chicagoan was jailed for 362 days for allegedly shooting Sergeant Richard Scanlon in August 1975 after Scanlon intervened in a fight between Dixon and his grandfather. Charged with attempted murder, Dixon spent nearly one year in jail after pleading guilty to the lesser charge of aggravated battery.

In August 1976, state's attorney investigators were tipped by a phone caller that Scanlon had shot himself with an illegal pen gun. Soon Dixon's plea was withdrawn and all charges stricken. Scanlon was charged with official misconduct and obstruction of justice and suspended from the police force.

Dixon was awarded a $50,000 settlement for his wrongful arrest and imprisonment, which was approved by U.S. district court Judge Julius J. Hoffman, resulting from an out-of-court decision made by attorneys for Dixon and the city corporation counsel's office. Dixon had sued several police officers for $1 million. A similar incident occurred with Dixon earlier when he was held three years for murder. The Illinois appellate court overturned that conviction, saying police improperly withheld knowledge of a critical defense witness from Dixon's lawyers.

Where Dixon was falsely imprisoned for an attack on a Chicago police officer that never occurred, Gary Dotson, also a native of Chicago, was accused of savagely raping sixteen-year-old Cathleen Crowell, a rape that never happened. On the night of July 9, 1977, a police officer in a patrol car found Crowell standing beside a road in Homewood, Illinois, not far from a mall where she worked as a fry cook and cashier in a Long John Silver's seafood restaurant. The officer noticed that the girl's clothes were in disarray and heavily stained with dirt.

Crowell tearfully explained that a car followed her when she walked from the mall. It stopped to let out two of three young male occupants, who grabbed her and threw her into the backseat. The car sped off while one of the young men, she said, tore away her clothes, raped her, and then scratched letters on her stomach with the shard of a broken beer bottle. She stated, "I tried to fight him off, but I couldn't."

Gary Dotson was convicted in 1979 for a 1977 Homewood, Illinois, rape that never occurred and went to prison for fifty years; he was one of the first persons to be exonerated through DNA testing, released from prison in 1989. *Center on Wrongful Convictions/Northwestern University/Loren Santow.*

Crowell was taken to South Suburban Hospital where an apparent semen stain was found in her panties during the rape kit examination. Several pubic hairs were also obtained. The superficial scratches on her abdomen, according to an examining physician, did not provide legible letters, which officers later interpreted to mean "love" and "hate." Crowell's background was checked and she proved to be a good student at Homewood-Flossmoor High School, where she studied Russian and was a member of the junior varsity swimming team.

Three days after the attack, Crowell worked with a police artist to create a composite sketch of her assailant, one she described as a white man with stringy hair. Two days later, she viewed a photo array of suspects and selected one of Gary Dotson, a high school dropout from a working-class family. Crowell later claimed that police had pressured her into identifying Dotson, saying that he matched the composite sketch she had helped create, but police would consistently deny any intimidation of the witness.

Dotson was arrested in his Country Club Hills home a short time later and charged with rape. The fact that he was then wearing a full mustache that he could not have grown within five days was dismissed by police and prosecutors. He went to trial in May 1979 in Markham, Illinois, where Crowell testified against him in open court, identifying him as her attacker: "There's no mistaking that face." Further damning Dotson was the testimony of a forensic expert, who was no forensic expert at all. He was Timothy Dixon, a state police forensic scientist who claimed that he had done his graduate work at the University of California–Berkeley. In fact, he had attended a two-day extension course at that institution.

Dixon claimed his examination from the rape kit revealed that a type B blood secretor had contributed to the semen stain found, and it matched Dotson, who was a type B blood secretor. Dixon stated that only 10 percent of the white male population has such blood types, and this testimony thus strongly supported Crowell's claims. Dixon did not tell the court that Crowell was also a type B blood secretor and the stain could have emanated from her. Further, Dixon did not tell the court that type O blood might have been involved and that would have included two-thirds of the population. Dixon also falsely stated that the pubic hairs recovered were "microscopically similar" to Dotson's.

These empty claims were supported and exaggerated by prosecutor Raymond Garza, who stated that the hairs "matched" Dotson's, a common misrepresentation in many wrongful conviction cases. Garza further discounted the four witnesses testifying for Dotson, who said that he had been with them when they were drinking beer and going to parties on the night of the attack. Garza called the witnesses "liars," saying that since none of their statements had any inconsistencies they were not reliable.

Public defender Paul T. Foxgrover challenged Garza's statements as prejudicial, but Judge Richard L. Samuels overruled defense objections in all instances. Dotson was convicted of aggravated kidnapping and rape, and sentenced to twenty-five to fifty years in prison. In 1985, Crowell recanted her charge against Dotson, saying that she had fabricated the entire attack. She had married a Homewood classmate, David Webb, and moved to New Hampshire, where she told her Baptist minister, Carl Nannini, that she had pangs of guilt for fabricating a story that had sent an innocent man to prison. She had invented that tale, she said, because she feared that she had become pregnant after having sex with another classmate, David Bierne, and, to create a cover story in the event that the pregnancy was real, she tore her clothes and inflicted the superficial wounds on her stomach and then accused Dotson.

Illinois Governor James R. Thompson (1977–1991) disbelieved Crowell-Webb and refused to grant Dotson a pardon. Thompson was most likely responding to an article in the *Chicago Tribune* that had reported Crowell-Webb's recantation with disdain, describing the woman as "unstable." Thompson did commute Dotson's sentence to the six years he had already served, granting him a parole on May 12, 1985, but he was charged with violating that parole after his wife charged him with an attack and after he had been in a barroom fight. His parole was revoked in December 1987.

A new attorney representing Dotson challenged the forensic evidence presented against Dotson in his 1979 trial. In 1985, following Crowell-Webb's recantation, and in one of the early American cases where DNA was used in an attempt to exonerate a convict, Dotson's attorney arranged to send the rape kit evidence to Dr. Alec Jeffreys in England for RFLP analysis, Jeffreys having been a pioneer in developing DNA. Because the sample was badly degraded, results were inconclusive.

Samples were then sent to American DNA pioneer Edward T. Blake, a forensic serologist who had received his Ph.D. at the University of California–Berkeley and had established Forensic Science Associates (FSA) in Richmond, California. The tests conducted by Blake and his colleagues showed that the spermatozoa found on Crowell's panties did not come from Dotson but could have been contributed by her boyfriend. The FSA tests were confirmed by Henry C. Lee, a scientist working with the Connecticut state police.

Blake had great success in helping establish DNA as the world's most reliable identification system. By 2003, he had become one of the world's most sought-after DNA experts, responsible for more than forty postconviction DNA exonerations in the United States and Canada, working closely with Barry Scheck and Peter Neufeld of the nonprofit Innocence Project at the Benjamin Cardozo School of Law in New York City, which had been involved in bringing about half of the DNA exonerations in the United States. Blake was also responsible for aiding prosecutors and police in identifying more than one hundred actual perpetrators of capital crimes.

FSA findings in the Dotson case were corroborated by the crime lab of the Connecticut state police because Blake refused to follow DNA criteria set down by the FBI and established under federal law, and therefore his testing was unacceptable to the Bureau and many state law enforcement agencies. Blake, who refused to submit his firm's credentials to the FBI, stated, "Just because a lab has credentials [it] doesn't mean it produces accurate work. What the FBI and crime lab managers are trying to do is say that the only thing that we will trust are those people we tell you we should trust." In twelve cases where FSA brought about exonerations, the tests in those cases were not accepted by the Bureau or run through the FBI's DNA database, thus losing an opportunity to identify an actual culprit who might have been located through such identification and apprehended.

Dotson's lawyer aggressively attacked the original prosecution case, pointing out that Crowell had recanted and that her statements at the time of Dotson's trial were unsupported. She claimed that she fought with her attacker, making scratches on his chest, but Dotson bore no such scratches when examined five days later when arrested. Crowell had also described in detail the car used to kidnap her, but Dotson and his friends owned no such car. Further, assistant Cook County state's attorney Garza had claimed in court that Crowell was a virgin, when this was not the case.

On August 14, 1989, Judge Thomas R. Fitzgerald ruled that evidence in the Dotson case was not substantial enough to support a conviction and he overturned the 1979 conviction, with approval from prosecutors, who declined to proceed with a new trial. Dotson was released, one of the first Americans to be exonerated by DNA.

Claims of rapes that never occurred have sent many innocent men to prison (Chapter XII, "Perjured Testimony") and have cast doubt on the statements of actual rape victims. In one of the most outlandish false rape claims, a black New York teenager turned the state's police and judicial system upside down, before it was proven that she had concocted a fantastic story of being raped when no such crime had ever taken place.

On November 28, 1987, fifteen-year-old Tawana Brawley, born in 1972, was found in the courtyard of the Pavillion apartment complex in Wappingers Falls, New York, inside a plastic garbage bag, dog excrement smeared on her body, her hair crudely chopped, burn marks on her legs, and the words "KKK" and "Nigger" scrawled in charcoal on her chest. Brawley had been missing for four days. Through family members, Brawley said she had been abducted, raped, and sodomized by six white men, who then put her in a bag and left her in the road. At the hospital, a black policeman asked Brawley who had assaulted her. She reached toward his badge and then scrawled "white cop" on a piece of paper.

The case immediately created turmoil. Actor Bill Cosby and *Essence* magazine offered a $25,000 reward for information. Heavyweight boxing champion Mike Tyson donated a $100,000 scholarship for Brawley. Three black activists took charge of the case, lawyers Alton H. Maddox Jr. and C. Vernon Mason, and religious leader Reverend Al Sharpton. Sharpton accused New York Governor Mario Cuomo of racism and compared state attorney general Robert Abrams to Adolf Hitler. Following her advisers' instructions, Brawley refused to give any further details.

The case became more confused by charges of an unjust legal system. Brawley's story was inconsistent. She initially claimed to have been beaten and raped; later she said there was no rape, but other kinds of sexual abuse had occurred. Forensic tests revealed no evidence of sexual assault or a beating. Three months after the incident, Brawley's family added a charge of theft, saying $600 worth of gold jewelry had been stolen. Her family also claimed Brawley had been left outdoors, but tests showed no signs of exposure, and several people had seen her at the Pavillion complex during the time when she said she had been left outside.

Other witnesses at the Pavillion described seeing Brawley alone on foot the morning after she was supposedly abducted. Brawley's mother, Glenda, said she and her sister had tried to report Tawana's disappearance several times, but that police did not respond until Saturday at 2:02 P.M., seventeen minutes after the girl was found. Charges of cover-up and conspiracy were made, and there were demonstrations. Sharpton, Mason, and nine others, including folk singer Pete Seeger, were arrested at a Tawana rally in Brooklyn on April 4, 1988. Sharpton served a fifteen-day jail sentence for his part in the rally.

Brawley was advised not to testify until a new special prosecutor was named. When Governor Cuomo refused to replace Abrams, Brawley remained unavailable as a witness in her own case. By May 1988 acting police chief of Wappingers Falls, William McCord, said, "A lot of local people feel it's just a story. . . . All these people investigating, and they keep coming up with nothing to go on. It's hard to believe six people would be involved in a crime and no one knows anything about it." By September 27, 1988, a grand jury had completed a 170-page investigation of Brawley's story, finding no evidence of kidnapping, rape, or any other crime. Attorney General Abrams said, "We have the facts. We have solved the case. The allegations she [Brawley] had made are false."

Abrams attributed the controversy that surrounded the trial to the "hucksterism and opportunism" of her advisers. On April 2, 1989, Samuel M. McClease, who said he had proof that would

discredit Brawley's advisers claiming he had been hired by Sharpton to bug Mason and Maddox, was brought to trial on perjury charges. The ten tapes he gave federal prosecutors turned out to be blank. McClease said someone had substituted the blanks for the ones he said would have proved his charges.

Long before the Brawley trial took place, Sharpton, Maddox, and Mason launched an all-out racial attack on white politicians. One of the men named later by Brawley and her advisers as part of the rape gang was New York prosecutor Steven Pagones. But when Brawley appeared before a grand jury, her story fell apart. The jury concluded that she had concocted the disgusting tale and smeared her own body with dung and racial epithets to avoid punishment from her stepfather for staying out late. The jury completely exonerated Pagones.

The New York prosecutor immediately filed a multimillion-dollar defamation suit against Brawley, Sharpton, Maddox, and Mason. Brawley went into hiding, refusing to answer the defamation charges or the many subpoenas ordering her to appear in court. In 1991, a default judgment against her was registered in Pagones's favor. It was not until October 9, 1998, that damages of $198,000 were awarded to Pagones. In ordering Tawana Brawley to pay that amount to Pagones, state Supreme Court Justice S. Barrett Hickman stated, "It is probable that in the history of this state, never has a teenager turned the prosecutorial and judicial systems literally upside down with such false claims."

Three months earlier, Sharpton, Maddox, and Mason, Brawley's so-called advisers, had been ordered to pay Pagones $345,000 for defaming him. Maddox had insisted through the years that Pagones was "involved in the abuse" of Tawana Brawley. Mason told "everyone within the sound of my voice" that Pagones "raped, kidnapped, and sodomized Tawana Brawley." Sharpton, the most vocal and demonstrative of the three black advisers, stated, "I am again repeating Steven Pagones was involved . . . and if I'm lying, sue us."

In the face of the verdict, Sharpton refused to apologize to Pagones for ruining his life. In fact, he seemed to glory in the conviction, which he considered racist, stating that it would elevate him among his followers—many of New York's 130,000 poverty-level blacks. Sharpton likened himself to the martyred Martin Luther King Jr., a posture that resulted in widespread criticism.

Two years after Tawana Brawley falsely claimed that she had been attacked by a group of savage white men, a woman died in Shelburne, Nova Scotia, through a freak accident. On February 20, 1989, Janice Johnson fell down the basement steps of her home and was found later by a neighbor gasping for breath. Her death was initially ruled an accident by a coroner's jury.

At the time of her mishap, her husband, Clayton Johnson, was on his way to his job as a high school teacher. He appeared to be a loving and reliable spouse, until it was rumored that he had taken out and collected on a $125,000 life insurance policy for his wife. Moreover, shortly after Janice Johnson's death, he married an attractive twenty-two-year-old woman who had been his mistress.

Police and prosecutors were gripped by rumors and gossip promoting the story that Janice Johnson had not died accidentally but had been murdered by her husband so that he could marry his mistress and collect insurance money in the bargain. In 1993, the court ordered the body of Janice's body exhumed, and several pathologists examined the injuries she had sustained. Two of them concluded that she had been beaten to death, her head hammered by either a baseball bat or a two-by-four. This was the evidence used at Clayton Johnson's trial, where, on May 4, 1993, he was convicted of first-degree murder by a jury in Halifax and sentenced to life imprisonment.

On March 8, 1994, the Nova Scotia Court of Appeal dismissed Johnson's appeal, and the Supreme Court of Canada dismissed Johnson's appeal on February 2, 1995. Meanwhile, Johnson's attorneys, along with the Association of the Defense of the Wrongly Convicted, persuaded the court in 1998 to reexamine Janice Johnson's body, which was again exhumed and reviewed by a host of Canadian and U.S. pathologists, including some from Northern Ireland, who concluded that Mrs. Johnson had died accidentally.

One of the pathologists re-created the accident to show that she had fallen backward down the stairs to the basement in a freak fall that produced repeated blows to the back of her head, not dissimilar to that of her being struck repeatedly by a heavy instrument. A court vacated Johnson's conviction, and when prosecutors declined to retry him, he was released in 1998.

# XIV

# *Language Barriers and Prejudicial Publicity*

POOR COMMUNICATION HAS SENT MANY wrongly convicted persons to prison, particularly immigrants. Inept translators fail to accurately render defendants' statements or alter their comments to the point where they implicate themselves or make no sense when they attempt to establish their innocence. This was epitomized in the classic Old Shakespeare case in New York, where Ameer Ben Ali was wrongly convicted of murder in 1891. (See Chapter V, "Conviction by Coercion.")

In Pennsylvania, a company boss was slain in a labor dispute, and three immigrants who could communicate only in their native Hungarian went to death row simply because they could not make a jury understand them. The murder on New Year's Day 1890 of Michael Quinn, a furnace boss at the Edgar Thompson Steel Works in Braddock, Pennsylvania, provided some insight into the lives of immigrants who worked in the steel mills and how their native languages isolated them from the English language that ruled the law of the land.

Quinn, along with four hundred men, had decided to work on New Year's Day. A group of immigrant Hungarian workers, angry over low wages, poor working conditions, and seven-day workweeks, fueled by the alcohol consumed in celebrating the new year, became indignant with workers who had willingly sacrificed their holiday.

More than two hundred Hungarians, armed with clubs, ax handles, and shovels, assaulted the men at work. Many were badly beaten before the workers drove the Hungarians back. Quinn was among the badly injured and died five days after the attack. Fifty-four men were arrested within several days of the attack. Although it was unclear who had killed Quinn, police charged three of the Hungarians, Andrew Toth, Michael Sabol, and George Rusnok, with the crime on February 4, 1891.

The trial for these three defendants provided no language experts to cope with their native Hungarian tongue. None could intelligently speak or write in English, and they could hardly communicate with their attorneys, let alone testify on their own behalf. A jury nevertheless returned a verdict of first-degree murder against all three defendants and sentenced them to death by hanging. The Pennsylvania Supreme Court reviewed the case and affirmed the judgment of the trial court on June 5, 1891.

In contrast to pretrial public sentiment, which ran strongly against the Hungarians, a movement with influential advocates such as Andrew Carnegie and Charles M. Schwab began to form. Arguing that the Hungarians, with their slight knowledge of English, had not received as impartial a trial as three Americans fluent in English would have received, these industrial tycoons requested that the governor commute the three men's sentences to life imprisonment. The pleading pointed out that the three defendants could barely speak English, could not write a word of it, and did not understand their pleadings, defense, or even the remarks made by their attorneys on their behalf.

The request was granted on February 25, 1892. By September 1897, Sabol and Rusnok had been pardoned. Because there had been direct testimony against Toth, Governor Daniel Hartman Hastings (1895–1899) refused to grant him any further clemency. A second application for a pardon, filed in 1902 by Toth's son, was refused. In 1911, a rumored deathbed confession to the murder by a man named Steve Toth rekindled the fight to gain freedom for Andrew Toth.

A review of the evidence, which included a Hungarian translator who was able to understand Toth's arguments and alibis, revealed that it was highly unlikely that Andrew Toth had attacked Michael Quinn. Toth received a full pardon on March 17, 1911, from Governor John Kinley Tener (1911–1915) and was released from prison after serving nearly twenty years. When a petition to the state requesting financial compensation for Toth was turned down, Andrew Carnegie, Toth's former employer in the steel mills, arranged for Toth to receive $40 a month for the rest of his life.

## A Failure to Communicate

Convinced that Henry Lambert was innocent of murdering J. Wesley Allen, his wife, and fifteen-year-old daughter on May 12, 1901, Maine Governor Percival P. Baxter (1921–1925) freed him after he had spent nearly twenty years in prison. A French Canadian who spoke little English, Lambert was convicted on circumstantial evidence and sentenced to life in prison even though the trial judge believed he was innocent. Throughout his trial, Lambert communicated poorly with his attorneys and could not be understood on the witness stand when no interpreter was available, all of

which contributed to his conviction. He was released from the state prison in Thomaston on July 24, 1923, and given a new suit and $50.

Where Lambert was unable to make himself understood in court in his native French, Rafaello E. Morello, who spoke only Italian, sent himself to prison with words from his own mouth that were misinterpreted by a so-called language expert. To the Essex County, New Jersey, courts, it seemed like a clear-cut case of murder. Police had found a gun in the hands of Rafaello Morello, who lay wounded in his bedroom. His wife lay next to him, dead of a bullet wound. Morello, a native Italian who had recently emigrated to America, explained through an interpreter at his trial that he was "responsible" for his wife's death. In 1918, Morello was found guilty of murder and sentenced to life imprisonment.

During the trial, however, the word "responsible" was either misused by the interpreter or misconstrued by the courts. The truth was that, when the U.S. draft board had ordered Morello to report for duty in the armed services, his wife of only a few months had killed herself. Upon finding her body, Morello took the gun and attempted to follow his wife to the grave. He had not meant that he had *killed* his wife; the fact that he was going to join the U.S. forces in World War I was what had driven his wife to commit suicide, and for which he felt *indirectly responsible*. While in prison, Morello mastered English well enough to finally explain his plight to welfare workers. They worked to get his name cleared, and, after serving eight years for his wife's suicide, he was finally freed in 1926.

Morello's native Italian had been wrongly interpreted in court, but, with another Italian immigrant, Tony Marino, his language was reshaped intentionally to make it appear that he had confessed to a crime he did not commit. In 1923, sixteen-year-old Tony Marino left Italy for the United States to improve his life. Marino's vision of America was dreamy and his knowledge of the language nonexistent. This proved to be a dangerous combination when, in 1925, the young immigrant was falsely charged with murder and processed through the Illinois judicial system. His hopes for a free life in the land of milk and honey turned into twenty-two years of despair and confinement behind bars.

Marino maintained his innocence, but his cries went unheeded by the judge-appointed interpreters assigned to his case. One interpreter was the very police officer who had arrested Marino. He and another interpreter lied to Marino, which caused him to sign a waiver of a trial by jury stating that he pleaded guilty. In reality, Marino had no idea what he was signing. At his trial he was found guilty of killing a man and sent to prison for life.

Marino did not give up. He used the time to learn English and study judicial procedure. Twenty-two years later, when he was finally granted a new trial in the circuit court of Winnebago County, Illinois, he spoke for himself and explained the injustice perpetrated in his case. The state's attorney agreed that Marino had suffered a miscarriage of justice and that his constitutional rights had been limited, but he also said that, under Illinois law, it was too late to remedy the situation. Marino had one final hope, the U.S. Supreme Court.

Marino wrote to the court himself, and the justices responded in kind. They examined the evidence and on December 22, 1947, unanimously voted to free him. "This case presents a flagrant example of deprivation of due process," Justices William O. Douglas and Frank Murphy jointly stated.

Marino's fate was shared by a young Puerto Rican man in Massachusetts who went to prison because he did not understand the police document he signed—a confession to a murder he did not commit. Twenty-one-year-old Santos Rodriguez emigrated from Puerto Rico to Springfield, Massachusetts, where he worked as a busboy in a restaurant.

Rodriguez had learned only enough English to do his job when he was arrested in 1954 for the murder of Mildred G. Hosmer in Springfield. He was convicted of second-degree murder on the basis of a signed confession that he later said had been forced from him by police. Officers had interrogated him in a language he did not understand, he said, and he signed a document he could not read, which was that confession. He was sentenced to life in prison.

When Rodriguez was an inmate at Norfolk Prison Colony in January 1957, Lucien Peets, being held on another charge, confessed to the accidental killing of Hosmer and was indicted for manslaughter. Peets was sentenced to eighteen to twenty years in prison. Rodriguez was granted a full pardon by Governor Foster Furcolo (1957–1961) and released after thirty-nine months in prison. The state of Massachusetts granted him $12,500 in compensation.

Ahmed Kassim also signed a confession he did not understand. In his case it had been written by the very man who brought about his wrongful conviction for murder. In 1958, Kassim, born in 1928 and then living in Buffalo, New York, was convicted of first-degree manslaughter in the knifing death of a Lackawanna resident. Though he was unable to speak fluent English, Kassim's "confession" was admitted in court. His words were actually those of an ambitious district attorney.

Kassim was sentenced to five to ten years in prison for the murder. In 1965, the conviction was vacated on the grounds that the confession was involuntary, and that the defendant could not understand the language in which it was written. A year later, the indictment was dismissed and Kassim was released.

On December 26, 1984, the State of New York passed a bill enabling Kassim and a second man, William Fisher, who had been wrongly convicted in a similar case years earlier, to sue the state for damages. Under the new law, Kassim collected $501,653 for denial of his civil rights, mental anguish, and loss of income.

The wrongful conviction of a man known as "Dummy" had nothing to do with misinterpreted foreign languages. The man was unable to hear or speak. They called Donald Lang "Dummy" because he could only articulate three words: "home," "water," and "finished," having lost his hearing during infancy when a crib collapsed around him. The injuries Lang sustained doomed him to a life of menial jobs, second-rate treatment, and whatever charity he could receive from the courts and the Illinois Department of Mental Health.

The twenty-year-old Lang was unloading trucks near the South Side Chicago housing project where he lived when police arrested him on November 12, 1965, for the murder of a prostitute whose body was found outside a tavern the previous night. Witnesses told police that Lang had been in the company of the woman, and the presence of blood on his clothing tended to corroborate the belief that he had committed the murder. Illinois law mandated that a prisoner who could not communicate with his lawyer could not be judged fit to stand trial. It was ruled that Lang should be institutionalized until he learned and understood sign language. His IQ fell into the 90–100 range, according to clinical tests.

Attorney Lowell Myers, the only practicing lawyer in Illinois who could understand sign language, agreed to represent Lang for the small fee of $250. For the next five years, he dedicated himself to the seemingly impossible task of securing a trial for his client. Meanwhile, he succeeded in moving Lang from the Illinois Security Hospital at Chester, where he had been raped and assaulted, to the more sedate environment at the Dixon State School, where, it was hoped, he would learn rudimentary communication skills.

Myers dug deep into legal precedents. He unearthed a little-known statute from English law that asserted the right of a deaf mute to stand trial to prove his innocence. In September 1970, the Illinois Supreme Court voted to grant Lang a trial. By this time, though, the circumstantial evidence submitted by the state years earlier had evaporated. Lang was freed on February 2, 1971, and his life story was told by Ernest Tidyman in his book *Dummy*, later made into a movie.

Five months after Lang was released a second prostitute was found murdered in a grimy transient hotel on Chicago's West Side. In July 1971, Lang was seen checking into a by-the-hour motel with thirty-nine-year-old Earline Brown, a known prostitute. A short time later, Lang emerged without the woman. A couple renting the same room hours later found Brown in a closet, badly beaten and strangled to death.

Lang was positively identified as having taken Brown to the room. Overwhelming evidence proved him guilty—there was blood from the victim on his sock, which he had attempted to hide by rolling the sock down when arrested. His face was scratched and his right hand injured, wounds apparently suffered in a fight with his victim. Further, Lang drew a picture of his victim for an arresting detective, one that fairly portrayed Brown in an Afro hairstyle, a sketch that Lang then crossed out, as if to tell the officer that he had killed her, or so the officer interpreted.

This time the state went to trial better prepared. The evidence in the Brown slaying was convincing, and a guilty verdict was returned. Judge Earl Strayhorn sentenced Lang to fourteen to twenty-five years in prison. Four years later, the conviction was overturned on the same grounds that the court had denied Lang a trial the first time around. The court's rationale was that a defendant must be able to communicate with his attorney and participate in his own defense.

Lang was remanded to the Department of Mental Health and Developmental Disabilities (DMH), where, for the first time, he began to learn sign language. Then inexplicably the training sessions were cut off. The DMH argued that Lang was neither retarded nor mentally ill, and was therefore ineligible to remain in custody. The state returned him to a cell in the county jail.

In December 1987, after seventeen years of shuttling back and forth between state agencies and the county jail, Lang was recommitted to the DMH for another six months, ostensibly exonerated. Judge Marjan Staniec recommended that the agency intensify its efforts on training Lang to communicate. "It is shocking to the conscience that after seventeen years of commitment and training very little indeed has been done to understand him, his motivations, and perhaps his sense of despair and frustration and to communicate with him in any depth," Staniec added. Many believe, however, that Lang was a clever serial killer who may have slain several other women and knew how to use his disability in mounting his "silent" defense, one who had hoodwinked his attorney, Lowell Myers, as well as the Illinois court system.

## Prejudicial Publicity Leading to Wrongful Convictions

The press has long functioned as a vigilant sentinel in making the crooked straight and righting many wrongs, but its two-edged sword can also cut away support for innocent persons when media moguls dictate the outcome of trials before they begin. On some occasions the press has irresponsibly provided avid readers with unsupported scandal about the accused, creating a universal atmosphere of guilt and prejudicing the views of juries that send innocent persons to prison. This was the case of William Allison MacFarland.

When MacFarland returned home to Newark, New Jersey, from New York City on October 17, 1911, where he had stayed overnight with his six-year-old son, he found his wife, Ruth MacFarland, dead. A doctor suggested an autopsy to which MacFarland objected on the grounds that he and his children might be subjected to the bad publicity and insinuation of a postmortem examination.

The autopsy, however, was ordered and revealed that the deceased was the victim of cyanide potassium poisoning. MacFarland, originally from Maine, had lived in Newark just a few months. He explained that he brought some potassium home from the factory where he worked, making a jewelry cleaning solution of it for his wife. He said he put it in an old bromide bottle and carefully labeled it and, explaining to his wife what he had done, showed her two similar bottles. Mrs. MacFarland frequently used bromide for her headaches. After his arrest, McFarland was released but kept under surveillance.

MacFarland did not destroy a number of letters written to him by Florence Bromley, a young woman with whom he had been intimate for two years. The county prosecutor, a man named Mott, learned from the widower that the bottle had been changed in a way that his wife could easily have picked up the wrong one, and that the poison label had been changed between the time when Mott first saw it and when the authorities seized it as evidence. MacFarland was charged with murder.

The press covered the love affair and the wife's death for weeks, including excerpts from the love letters. MacFarland was tried before Chief Judge Gummere in Newark beginning on January 28, 1912. The trial lasted just three days. His liaison with Bromley was portrayed by the prosecution as an affair in which the younger woman threatened public exposure and suicide if MacFarland did not marry her. MacFarland, who did not take the stand, was found guilty of first-degree murder and sentenced to death. His execution was automatically stayed when a demand for a new trial was made.

MacFarland testified at the second trial, which began on October 14, 1912. He admitted to being unfaithful and said he had tried for years to force his wife to divorce him, had feared retribution from the dissatisfied Bromley, but had not tried to kill his wife or force her to commit suicide. His attorneys argued that their client had been wrongly convicted through prejudicial publicity, the press assuming the role of jury and judge. He was found not guilty. After the verdict, MacFarland rushed off to the marriage clerk to get a license to marry Bromley, but technical difficulties forced the couple to wait another year. They were finally married on October 1, 1913, at Niagara Falls.

420 I AM INNOCENT!

A year after MacFarland finally found bliss at Niagara Falls, a British subject who worked for the German embassy in London was wrongly sentenced to death after being indicted by a hostile press following the outbreak of World War I. Nicholas Emil Herman Adolph Ahlers worked for the German consul-general in London, holding the position of German consul in Sunderland. When war broke out, he was arrested and charged with "High Treason with the Statute of King Edward III (1351) in that he adhered to the King's enemies in his realm giving to them aid and comfort in his realm."

Ahlers was so charged because he had become a naturalized British subject in 1905 and consequently had committed treason. He was therefore betraying his country, England, which had just gone to war with Germany.

In his defense, Ahlers contended that he merely followed instructions from the German consul in London by sending the following message to Germans then residing in England, in anticipation of war being declared: "All able-bodied men from the age of seventeen to forty-five must try to find their way to Germany." This message was sent to German reservists in England.

Hostilities were officially declared by England at 11:00 P.M. on August 4, 1914, and Ahlers's messages were sent out as late as August 5. Ahlers insisted that he did not learn about the British declaration of war until August 6, 1914, and when he did, he immediately ceased sending the messages. He added that only eight German reservists received the message as well as money to return to Germany.

Public feeling at the time of Ahlers's arrest was so intense that the court chose to split hairs and place Ahlers on trial in December 1914. Justice Shearman thought very little of the prosecution's case and instructed the jury that, in his opinion, Ahlers was not guilty. The jury, however, filled with patriotic zeal and responding

to the widespread negative publicity generated by the case, convicted the accused. Under the existing and ancient laws of treason, Shearman had no choice but to sentence Ahlers to death.

In appeal, however, Lord Reading, presiding as Lord Chief Justice, studied the summation by Justice Shearman in the original trial and the judge's favorable remarks toward the accused. These remarks played a large part in saving Ahlers from the gallows in that they caused the higher court to quash the conviction. Ahlers was released.

## Prejudicial Press, a Biased Court, and Sacco and Vanzetti

The Sacco-Vanzetti case rivaled the sensational French cause célèbre, Alfred Dreyfus. The case became a state of mind and an intellectual point of view that captivated the United States for decades, following a trial blatantly biased by the local and national press and conviction of two illiterate Italian immigrants, Nicola Sacco (1891–1927) and Bartolomeo Vanzetti (1888–1927). Widespread and unceasing prejudicial publicity, more than any other factor, brought about the convictions and death sentences of these two men.

Nicola Sacco, an assembly-line shoemaker, who was convicted and sentenced to death for robbery and murder in 1921. *History Inc./Jay Robert Nash Collection.*

Bartolomeo Vanzetti, who, along with Nicola Sacco, was convicted and sentenced to death for robbery and murder in 1921. *History Inc./Jay Robert Nash Collection.*

Sacco worked in a factory making shoes, and Vanzetti was a self-employed fishmonger. Both men were ardent radicals and devout anarchists, who went armed on the streets and gave rabble-rousing speeches in which they urged the violent overthrow of the U.S. government. To the police in Massachusetts, along with leading members of the judiciary, these men were dangerous, capable of any crime. When the pair stood accused of a brutal robbery involving the murder of two men, establishment forces in the state had no qualms in judging Sacco and Vanzetti out of hand.

At the time, the nation was undergoing emotional trauma created by radicals who had tried to blow up dozens of political leaders in 1919. In response to these anarchist attacks, U.S. attorney A. Mitchell Palmer had ordered federal agents to arrest every radical in the country. The agents ran amuck, illegally breaking into homes and offices, beating up suspects, and arresting thousands of persons, many of whom were innocent.

These wholesale arrests were known as the Red Raids, and the publicity attending them frightened Americans who read the newspapers of the day. They saw all radicals as dark-complexioned immigrants bent on mass destruction and death, the very image of Sacco and Vanzetti as portrayed endlessly in the nation's press.

Two crimes, each occurring four months apart, presaged the fate of Sacco and Vanzetti. The first happened on the morning of December 24, 1919, in Bridgewater, Massachusetts, a manufacturing center about thirty miles south of Boston. On that day, a party of men, all "foreign-looking" according to witnesses testifying later, stopped a truck carrying the payroll of the White Shoe Company.

Two men got out of a car and fired at the truck, one blasting it with a shotgun, when the driver refused to turn over the payroll. The driver, however, was armed and fired back. With that, the two men leaped back into the car with the other robbers and the auto sped off. An Overland car, which was thought to be the auto in which the robbers escaped, was later found in a Bridgewater garage.

The location of the April 15, 1920, robbery in South Braintree, Massachusetts, where gunmen shot and killed two guards carrying a company payroll; the bandits made off with more than $16,000, a crime later attributed to Sacco and Vanzetti. *History Inc./Jay Robert Nash Collection.*

Attendants stated that it was owned by a man named Boda. Police ordered the garage owner to contact them when Boda came to pick up his car.

On April 15, 1920, Frederick A. Parmenter, cashier for the Slater and Morrill Shoe Company, and a guard, Alexander Berardelli, were transferring almost $16,000 in cash from one company building to another along the main street of South Braintree, Massachusetts. It was 3:00 P.M. on a sunny afternoon and few people were about. Some workers moved along the street conducting business, and two men idled next to a fence separating the two shoe company buildings.

The two men stood in the path of Parmenter and Berardelli, and, as the cashier and guard came abreast of them carrying the payroll, the two men blocked the sidewalk. Berardelli, carrying a bag with payroll money inside, stepped into the gutter to avoid them, but one of the men suddenly jammed a gun into his ribs and fired several times, killing him. The gunman picked up the money bag.

Parmenter, who had been walking behind the guard by some ten feet, saw the cold-blooded murder and dropped his money bag. He immediately ran across the street, the other gunman running after him, firing two bullets that struck the cashier in the back and killed him on the spot. The second murder was probably committed to prevent Parmenter from later identifying the robbers. The killers then picked up the second bag of money, and both men ran to the street.

At that moment a car, later identified as a Buick, roared around a corner, raced up to the two waiting men, and stopped for a few seconds as the robbers tossed the money bags inside and dove into the backseat. The Buick raced down the street and out of sight. The robbery and murders took place in less than four minutes, one of the most shocking crimes in Massachusetts history to that date. Like the abortive Bridgewater robbery months earlier, the robbers and thieves were described as a group of "foreign-looking" men.

The Buick used in the South Braintree robbery had been stolen and was found two days later in a rural area. Tracks from another car led away from the area where the Buick was found, and detectives concluded that the tire tracks belonged to the Overland parked in the Bridgewater garage. On May 5, 1921, Boda and three other men later identified as Sacco and Vanzetti and a man named Orciani appeared at the garage, asking for the Overland. The owner, Johnson, told the men that his wife had to perform an errand before he could release the car to them.

Mrs. Johnson ran next door to a neighbor's house to call police, as detectives had earlier instructed the owner to do when Boda called for his car (this had been done on previous occasions since the Bridgewater raid without police response). Meanwhile, Johnson chatted with the Italians, who seemed to grow increasingly nervous. The garage owner pointed out to Boda that the Overland had improper plates. The men began to talk quietly in Italian and then abruptly left the garage, Boda and Orciani riding away on a motorcycle, the other two men, reportedly Sacco and Vanzetti, on foot.

Several carloads of armed police officers arrived a few minutes later. Learning that the suspects had left, the police fanned out in all directions, searching for them. More police were called into the dragnet, and that evening an officer got aboard a streetcar and noticed two swarthy-looking men sitting together. He took no chances, drawing his gun and ordering the two men off the streetcar.

Both men had guns, and these weapons were pocketed by the arresting officer. They gave no resistance and identified themselves as Nicola Sacco and Bartolomeo Vanzetti.

Inside one of Sacco's pockets, police found some radical literature, including a leaflet written by Sacco that was later used against him at his trial. The compromising document read, "Fellow workers, you have fought all the wars. You have worked for all the capitalists. You have wandered over the countries. Have you harvested the fruits of your labors, the price of your victories? Does the present smile on you? Does the future promise you anything? Have you found a piece of land where you can live like a human being? On these questions, on this argument, and on this theme the struggle for existence Bartolomeo Vanzetti will speak. Admission free. Freedom of discussion to all. Take the ladies with you."

Charged with carrying concealed weapons, both men pleaded guilty. They were then asked what they were doing in Bridgewater, and they said they were going to see a friend. They were held on suspicion of committing the Bridgewater and South Braintree robberies. Sacco was able to prove that on the day of the Bridgewater robbery, he was at work, but unfortunately had no alibi for April 15, 1920, the day of the South Braintree robbery, which was his day off. Sacco was charged with the South Braintree robbery. Vanzetti could provide no alibi for the dates of either robbery, and he was charged with both crimes.

Vanzetti was tried first for the Bridgewater robbery, appearing before Judge Webster Thayer at Plymouth, Massachusetts, on June 22, 1920. He was convicted on questionable evidence, and Judge Thayer, an avowed foe of radicals with a thick streak of prejudice toward foreigners, gave Vanzetti the maximum sentence of between ten and fifteen years in prison. Then both Sacco and Vanzetti were tried together in Dedham, Massachusetts, in June 1921. Their conviction was almost a certainty from the outset. The judge who presided over Vanzetti's trial in Plymouth and sen-

Judge Webster Thayer, who presided over the Sacco and Vanzetti trial and showed a decided bias toward both defendants, calling them "anarchist bastards." *History Inc./Jay Robert Nash Collection.*

tenced him to prison was the presiding judge in the Dedham trial.

Judge Thayer was one of the most conservative jurists on the Massachusetts bench, an outspoken foe of liberals, and he saw the radical movement as a dangerous threat to democracy. He was openly prejudiced in the case but refused to remove himself from the bench. It was later stated that, either during or following the Dedham trial, Judge Thayer boasted, "Did you see what I did with those anarchist bastards?"

The prosecutor, Frederick Katzmann, hated anarchists as much as the Back Bay Webster Thayer. Said Katzmann, "I will crucify those damned God-hating radicals!" Twelve archconservative jurors helped Katzmann drive the nails into the creaking boards of the Sacco and Vanzetti case. Worse, the nation's press had convicted Sacco and Vanzetti out of hand, linking their anarchist politics to every recent terrorist act.

The defendants were portrayed as inhuman beasts preying upon innocent Americans. Such prejudicial publicity was fueled by terrorist acts like the one on September 16, 1920, when a terrific explosion from a horse-drawn cart filled with explosives and shrapnel-like metal stalled at Broad and Wall Streets in Manhattan, killing thirty-eight people and wounding hundreds more during the lunchtime rush hour. It was concluded that the driver of the cart, who was reportedly killed, had been an anarchist, willing to sacrifice his life (not unlike the myriad Muslim suicide bombers in the 1990s and 2000s) in the fanatical service of his cause.

The fact that Sacco and Vanzetti were self-proclaimed anarchists put them in league with the Wall Street bombing. This event and many others, including the highly publicized federal seizure of more than 10,000 suspected anarchists and 446 deportations of their leaders in 1920–1921, including Emma Goldman and Alexander Berkman, caused the public to focus on Sacco and Vanzetti, who became the icons of anarchist terrorism. Although the two immigrants had many literary champions—columnists and authors—the press in America at that time was decidedly conservative and could be correctly positioned in today's perspective as right-wing.

The publishers of most of the newspapers and periodicals editorialized and campaigned against Sacco and Vanzetti, urging their conviction, if not execution, for the bloody Braintree robbery. The two defendants were mercilessly profiled as murderous zealots day after endless day in the press, prejudicial publicity that created a mania bordering on the kind of mass paranoia that would grip the nation eighty years later, following the September 11, 2001, attacks by al-Qaeda. To the press, Sacco and Vanzetti were ruthless terrorists guilty of endorsing and advancing the politics of assassination, and they were easily perceived as being guilty of the crime for which they stood accused.

In addition to an adversarial press, the defendants faced a hostile judge and jury, who had been deeply influenced by that press. Adding to this almost insurmountable problem, Sacco and Vanzetti made a crucial error in the selection of their defense attorney. On poor advice from friends, the two anarchists chose Fred Moore to defend them. Moore was a wild California bohemian who supported leftist causes.

Moore had long hair and rumpled clothes, and he arrogantly flaunted his radical views in front of Thayer and the jury, agitating them with every word he uttered. Jury members later stated that they found the defense attorney "repulsive." Moore challenged the court at every opportunity and used Sacco and Vanzetti for his own political cause and ends. He wore garish ties and outlandish clothes that seemed rented from a costume shop.

On more than one occasion, Moore relaxed outside the courtroom in his dirty bare feet.

The defense attorney set a pattern of open confrontation with the court that immediately put his clients in jeopardy. He fought every minor rule and regulation, and his remarks to the bench were provocative and insulting, arousing Judge Thayer's considerable ire. Before the trial commenced, Moore retained additional counsel in the form of John and Thomas McAnarney, but even these respectable and able lawyers could do little to help Sacco and Vanzetti, since Moore continued to be the lawyer of record and controlled the defense.

Every move Moore made was political, and he disregarded the advice of his fellow attorneys. Moore exhausted the jury system in Dedham for weeks as he dismissed more than seven hundred prospective jurors, such selections then being limitless. If a prospective juror wore a conservative suit, he was dismissed. Anyone who worked in a bank or a brokerage house was dismissed. Said a disgusted Thomas McAnarney after the trial, "Every time I wanted a man on the jury whom I felt to be honest, he [Moore] would make an exception to it. Whenever he was addressing the court, it was quite similar to waving a red flag in the face of a bull!"

John McAnarney realized after the first disastrous day that Moore's unpredictable and flamboyant actions would certainly send his clients to the death chamber. McAnarney went to noted trial lawyer William G. Thompson and pleaded with him to take over the defense. "I told him that the lives of two innocent men were at stake," McAnarney later said. Thompson agreed to take on the case. When Thompson appeared the next morning, Moore adamantly refused to withdraw from the case and screamed hysterically, "You will not deny me my shining hour!"

Moore stayed on, taking a week to impanel the jury. The trial finally opened with Katzmann relating in detail the robbery and murders that occurred in South Braintree. Meanwhile, the defendants fidgeted and whispered to each other, glancing furtively at the judge and jury. They spoke broken English and communicated poorly with their attorneys. Sacco, the shoemaker, was thought to be the more suspicious of the pair. Even the fact that he made shoes and that both the South Braintree and Bridgewater robberies were of shoe firm payrolls seemed to implicate him.

Sacco shown with his son and wife, Rosina, a photo taken some years before he was tried and convicted of robbery and murder. *History Inc./Jay Robert Nash Collection.*

Born on April 22, 1891, Sacco was married and had one child. Vanzetti, a fishmonger, was a confirmed bachelor, born on June 11, 1888. They were lifelong friends who emigrated from Italy to the United States in 1908, and were bonded by their common zeal for anarchy. The prosecution pointed out that in 1917 and 1918 both men shirked their duty by evading the draft in World War I, fleeing to Mexico and remaining there until the war was over. Even their own defense attorneys admitted that their clients acted suspiciously, but this was no doubt due to their precarious political posture. The attitude of the accused was later described in the press as "the consciousness of guilt." In other words, the defendants looked and acted guilty. Therefore, the illogical conclusion was that they *were* guilty.

The prosecution brought forth a small army of witnesses who positively identified both Sacco and Vanzetti as being members of the South Braintree robbery gang. Immediately after the robbery, these same witnesses could not give a clear description of the killers. However, after careful coaching and prodding on the part of Katzmann and his aides, these witnesses suddenly recalled, thirteen months after the crime, the exact identities of Sacco and Vanzetti.

Michael Levangie, a gatekeeper at a South Braintree railroad crossing, was typical of those

Vanzetti and Sacco are shown during their 1921 trial where the evidence was flimsy and the press had convicted the pair long before the jury's verdict was announced. *History Inc./Jay Robert Nash Collection.*

who bore witness against the defendants. Following the robbery, he stated, "I saw nobody. I was too damned scared to see anyone. All I saw was the muzzle of that damned gun and I turned and ran for the shanty and they put a bullet through the shanty." In court, however, it was a different matter. Levangie described one of the killers in precise detail, saying that the driver of the getaway car was "dark complexioned, with cheekbones sticking out, black hair, heavy brown mustache, slouch hat, and an army coat."

Assistant prosecuting attorney Harold P. Williams asked Levangie if he had seen that man since, and the witness, without hesitation, pointed at the defense table and replied, "Yes, sir. Right there!" Levangie's testimony was attacked vigorously by the defense, who pointed out that other witnesses had described the driver as blond and sallow-complexioned. This meant very little to a judge and jury, who had already come to a decision.

Dozens of witnesses were company employees who swore that Sacco and Vanzetti were the culprits. Lewis L. Wade was the exception. He testified for the prosecution, but when he was asked to identify Sacco as one of the bandits, Wade said, "Well, I ain't so sure now. I have a little doubt." Two weeks later, after having worked for Slater and Morrill for sixteen years, Wade was fired.

Fifty-nine witnesses testified for the prosecution. Many of these were so-called ballistic experts. One firearms expert positively identified the bullets that killed Parmenter and Berardelli as having come from the gun Sacco had when he was arrested in Bridgewater. Another ballistics expert testified that the bullets were "consistent," therefore having been fired by the same weapon.

The defense called ninety-nine witnesses to the stand, many stating that they had seen Sacco and Vanzetti on the day of the murder at locations far distant from the scene of the crime. A clerk in the Italian consulate in Boston swore in a deposition that Sacco had been there on the day of the robbery, filling out a form to obtain a passport for a return trip to Italy. Others came forth to say that, at the time of the robbery, they were buying fish from Vanzetti in Boston.

After thirty-seven grueling days, the trial came to an end. Judge Thayer, for all of his seething bias, summed up the trial fairly and impartially for the jury. The jury, not surprisingly, returned a verdict of guilty on July 14, 1921, convicting both men of first-degree murder. When hearing the verdict, Sacco leapt to his feet shouting, "*Siamo innocenti!* They kill an innocent man! They kill two innocent men!" On November 1, 1921, Judge Thayer sentenced both men to death.

Thus began a seven-year ordeal for the condemned men as their attorneys, friends, and relatives, as well as the legions of supporters they had collected, fought battle after battle to save their lives through appeals. Many appeals were filed, and stays of executions were granted. Thousands picketed the Massachusetts statehouse and government buildings, demanding a pardon for Sacco and Vanzetti. On the literary front, the fires blazed for the pair. Heywood Broun, the giant columnist for the New York *World,* wrote so many columns defending the pair that his boss, Herbert Bayard Swope, fired him for a brief period.

Joining the cause were such distinguished literary lights as poet Edna St. Vincent Millay

Vanzetti and Sacco are shown leaving court, en route to prison to await execution. *History Inc./Jay Robert Nash Collection.*

Heywood Broun, influential columnist for the New York *World*, who stumped for the commutation of Sacco and Vanzetti, writing so many "free Sacco and Vanzetti" columns that he was fired (but re-hired) by *World* publisher Herbert Bayard Swope. *History Inc./Jay Robert Nash Collection.*

Celebrated poet Edna St. Vincent Millay, who relentlessly campaigned for the commutation and release of Sacco and Vanzetti. *History Inc./Jay Robert Nash Collection.*

Writer and wit Dorothy Parker lobbied with her fellow scribes for years to obtain a commutation and release for Sacco and Vanzetti, but to no avail. *History Inc./Jay Robert Nash Collection.*

and writer Dorothy Parker. Robert Benchley, the humorist, also mounted podiums in defense of the convicted anarchists. Many, like Katherine Ann Porter, were arrested and jailed for their picketing and protests. Porter later described the way many of the political groups supporting Sacco and Vanzetti used the pair for their own ends, calling to mind leftist Rosa Baron. Porter had stated to Baron in Boston, before joining a picket line, that she hoped they could save the lives of the shoemaker and the fishmonger. Snapped Baron, "Alive—what for? They are no earthly good to us alive!"

Year after year, petitions and letters from famous persons around the world flooded the offices of Massachusetts Governor Alvan T. Fuller (1925–1929), asking for a new trial, for clemency, for parole, or for pardon. The letter writers included George Bernard Shaw, John Galsworthy, John Dos Passos, H. G. Wells, President Thomas Garrigue Masaryk of Czechoslovakia, Captain Alfred Dreyfus of France, and even Italian dictator Benito Mussolini.

Governor Fuller, in turn, appointed a special independent committee to reinvestigate the case, a committee headed by President Lowell of Harvard University and Judge Robert Grant. The Lowell Committee's task was to review the entire case and report to Fuller, to help guide him in his decision regarding clemency. The Lowell Committee found that, in addition to the enormous prejudicial publicity at the time of the trial, there was substantial bias on the part of Judge Thayer, but that the jury's verdict could not be challenged, and that the condemned men were guilty "beyond all reasonable doubt."

As the Lowell Committee was sifting through already yellowing archives and affidavits, Celestino Madeiros, a youthful Portuguese gunman, confessed to taking part in the South Braintree robbery and told police that Sacco and Vanzetti had nothing to do with it. Examining this confession was Judge Thayer. He concluded that Madeiros's confession had not established a "reasonable doubt" as to the guilt of either Sacco or Vanzetti.

Pro–Sacco and Vanzetti demonstrators in Boston are shown being placed under arrest. Thousands took to the streets in many major American and European cities protesting their convictions and death sentences. *History Inc./Jay Robert Nash Collection.*

Rosina Sacco and her two children, her son weeping, leave the Charlestown Prison only a few hours before the execution of her husband was scheduled on August 22, 1927. *History Inc./Jay Robert Nash Collection.*

The Massachusetts Supreme Court upheld Thayer's decision. Judge Thayer brought Sacco and Vanzetti before his bench on April 5, 1927, and confirmed the death sentence.

"You know I am innocent!" Sacco shouted. "That is the same words I pronounced seven years ago. You condemn two innocent men!"

Said Vanzetti, "Never in our full life could we hope to do such work for tolerance, for justice, for man's understanding of man as we do now by accident. Our words, our lives, our pains . . . nothing! The taking of our lives, lives of a good shoemaker and a poor fish-peddler, all! That last moment belongs to us, that agony is our triumph!"

The two men returned to Charlestown Prison to await the end in the same death house cells they had occupied for seven years. At midnight on August 23, 1927, Madeiros, who had been condemned for another murder, then Sacco, then Vanzetti were electrocuted. After being strapped into the electric chair, Nicola Sacco cried out in Italian, "Long live anarchy!" He added in English, "Farewell my wife and child and all my friends. Farewell, Mother." Vanzetti claimed innocence to the last: "I have never committed a crime, but sometimes sin. I am innocent of all crime, not only of this, but all."

The deaths of these two men resulted in nationwide mourning among the liberal-left camp because it had lost a great cause. The public in general was sickened by the executions because the condemned men had been put through an agonizing and interminable process before meeting a fate that had been judicially decreed years earlier. Waiting for death was, indeed, cruel and unusual punishment, let alone the execution itself. The funeral procession in Boston for the pair was attended by tens of thousands.

The Sacco and Vanzetti case remains almost as hotly debated today as it was in that long-ago era. Were the two men guilty? This author believes that at least one of the robberies was committed by the Joseph Morelli gang. Bartolomeo Vanzetti, according to all of the extensive evidence, was most certainly innocent, but Nicola Sacco may

Luigia Vanzetti, Bartolomeo's sister, pleads with officials on a last-minute radio broadcast to spare the lives of Sacco and Vanzetti, a plea ignored; both men went to their deaths in the electric chair a few hours later. *History Inc./Jay Robert Nash Collection.*

A rally in support of Sacco and Vanzetti in New York City, shortly before their scheduled execution on August 22–23, 1927. *History Inc./Jay Robert Nash Collection.*

Tens of thousands assemble in Boston on the start of the massive funeral procession for Sacco and Vanzetti, August 24, 1927; most authorities believe that Sacco was most probably guilty of the crime for which he was executed but that Vanzetti was actually innocent, although both men received a posthumous pardon decades later. *History Inc./Jay Robert Nash Collection.*

have been guilty—he was in South Braintree on the day of the robbery and murders and belonged to the gang that slew the cashier and guard.

The testimony of ballistics experts appeared to be the strongest evidence to support this conclusion, along with Sacco's own peculiar statements, crying out to the court when first convicted, "They kill an innocent man," then amending that blurted thought with "they kill *two* innocent men." No one could read Sacco's mind at the time, of course, but one inference that can be drawn was that his first statement was a plea for his dear friend Vanzetti, knowing that he, Sacco, was guilty, and then, to maintain their umbilical defense, he added himself, a telling slip of the tongue.

Conversely, it could be argued that Sacco's initial statement of proclaiming his own innocence was merely selfish on his part, and he realized it immediately and then amended his statement to include his friend Vanzetti. The entire case, which was chiefly brought about by widespread prejudicial publicity, and, to no lesser degree, by police coercion of witnesses and Judge Thayer's personal bias, was a miserable shambles, leaving another ugly stain of wrongful conviction on U.S. jurisprudence.

## Dr. Sam Sheppard and Others Prosecuted by Prejudicial Publicity

Beyond the Sacco and Vanzetti case, no other murder trial generated so much prejudicial publicity in

twentieth century America as did that of Dr. Samuel Sheppard (1924–1970). Sheppard and his wife, Marilyn, had been high school sweethearts who exchanged passionate love letters when Sam left his eastern Ohio hometown to study osteopathic medicine in Indiana and Southern California. Marilyn wrote that life without Sam was impossible and he wrote

Dr. Sam Sheppard and wife Marilyn on their wedding day, 1945. *History Inc./Jay Robert Nash Collection.*

back that he could not wait to see her again. Upon his return in 1945, the couple married and bought a large two-story house on the shores of Lake Erie in the Cleveland suburb of Bay Village.

Sheppard began practicing medicine at a private hospital that he owned with his father and two brothers. The couple's son, Sam Jr., or Chip, was born in 1947. Dr. Sheppard devoted himself to his thriving practice, while Marilyn was involved in school and church activities in the community. After five years of marriage, however, they began to grow apart. By 1954, Sheppard's involvement with other women was rumored, including an affair with a laboratory technician at his hospital. No discord, however, was evident on July 3, 1954, when the Sheppards threw an Independence Day party. The memories of the guests leaving that night retained an image of the Sheppard couple as one of mutual affection. Marilyn Sheppard was brutally murdered four hours later.

Shortly before 6:00 A.M. on July 4, 1954, Mayor J. Spencer Houk, a friend of the Sheppards, received a frantic phone call from Sheppard, imploring assistance, because he thought Marilyn had been murdered. Houk arrived within seven minutes. He found Marilyn Sheppard in a blood-

Housewife Marilyn Sheppard, a photo taken shortly before her murder on the night of July 3–4, 1954. *History Inc./Jay Robert Nash Collection.*

soaked bedroom, her nightgown shredded and her skull crushed with the force of twenty-seven blows from a heavy instrument.

Sheppard told investigators that he had fallen asleep on a downstairs sofa and been awakened by his wife's screams. Marilyn was four months pregnant and had recently suffered convulsions. Racing up the stairs and entering their bedroom, Sheppard said he saw a shadowy figure standing over his wife's bed. As he advanced, he was knocked down from a blow to the back of the neck. Recovering from the blow, he chased someone he described as a bushy haired figure downstairs, out the door, and along a path adjacent to the lake, where the assailant struck him again, and he lost consciousness on the sandy shore. Awakening two hours later, Sheppard limped back to his house and called his friend.

Sheppard's brother Steve, who was also a physician, diagnosed him with a broken vertebra and admitted him to the family's hospital. But he merely had lacerations, a black eye, and a chipped tooth. (A possible spinal injury caused him to wear a leather collar in public.) Investigators were skeptical of Sheppard's account of the fateful night. They determined that it should have taken him less than ten seconds to respond to his wife's screams, whereas an assailant would have needed a full minute to administer twenty-seven lethal blows. Conse-

The Sheppard home in Bay Village, an upscale suburb of Cleveland, Ohio, photographed a day after Marilyn's murder. *History Inc./Jay Robert Nash Collection.*

quently he would have had enough time to prevent his wife from being murdered.

Fingerprints had been carefully eliminated from the murder scene, including those normally found in an active household. Police concluded that the intruder or Sheppard himself had wiped the area clean of prints. The violence did not wake the six-year-old child, Chip, or stir the family's dog. The blood-stained shirt Sheppard was wearing during his pursuit of the attacker had mysteriously disappeared.

Sheppard was vehement about his innocence, even offering $10,000 for information regarding the crime. His friend Mayor Houk refused to order his arrest, but Louis B. Seltzer, the publisher of the Cleveland *Press,* launched a crusade, and police arrested Sheppard on July 30, 1954, on suspicion of murdering his wife.

Sheppard was interrogated by a team of twelve detectives but refused to break, finding strength in the Bible, he claimed. Five days later, he was released on a $50,000 bond. But on August 6, 1954, after his involvement with laboratory technician Susan Hayes became known, he was indicted for murder by a grand jury. Twenty-one-year-old Hayes was out of state at that time, but was flown to Cleveland by officials. Local newspapers trumpeted her long-running affair with Sheppard and quoted her statements that

The other woman—21-year-old Susan Hayes, identified by the *Press* as Dr. Sheppard's mistress, was brought from out of state to appear against Sheppard, claiming he planned to divorce his wife and marry her. *History Inc./Jay Robert Nash Collection.*

October 18, 1954: Dr. Sam Sheppard, right, handcuffed to an officer, is escorted to court to stand trial for murdering his wife, a trial that became the longest in U.S. history to that time. *History Inc./Jay Robert Nash Collection.*

Sheppard had lied, that their relationship was not merely platonic but they had a sexual liaison and Sheppard had talked of marrying her.

The longest-running murder trial in U.S. history to that date commenced in Cleveland, Ohio, on October 18, 1954, at the Cuyahoga County criminal courtroom of Judge Edward Blythin. The trial transcript accumulated to more than six thousand pages, added to the four hundred pages from the coroner's inquest. More than one hundred exhibits were placed in evidence. (In Sheppard's second trial, more than twenty-one hundred pages would make up a second transcript, and the police records in the Bay Village police department on this case exceeded twenty-one hundred pages.)

Sheppard was defended by William Corrigan, an Irish-born criminal lawyer, while the prosecution was presented by John J. Mahon and assisted by Saul S. Danaceau and Thomas Parrino. Thirty-one witnesses appeared before the jury, including Susan Hayes, who detailed her fifteen-month clandestine affair with Sheppard. Mahon's team sought to prove guilt by the time lapsed between the actual crime and the call to Mayor Houk, the missing shirt, and a trail of blood from the murder scene.

Corrigan countered that losing a garment was an everyday occurrence, and that the bloodstains were inconclusively matched to Sheppard. As no weapon had been found, there was no forensic evidence to connect Sheppard to the crime, Corrigan pointed out. After hearing nine weeks of testimony, the jury of five women and seven men retired on December 17, 1954. They deliberated for

more than one hundred hours, discussing 2 million words of testimony and more than two hundred exhibits from the Sheppard household. Finally, on December 21, 1954, they announced their verdict that Sheppard was guilty of second-degree murder, for which Blythin sentenced him to life imprisonment at the Ohio Penitentiary.

The jury at Sheppard's 1954 trial; it deliberated for more than 100 hours in an impossible attempt to review 2 million words of testimony and 200 exhibits, finally reaching a verdict, finding Dr. Sam Sheppard guilty of second-degree murder; he was sent to prison for life. *History Inc./Jay Robert Nash Collection.*

Corrigan immediately filed for an appeal. The weight of the trial was devastating to the Sheppard family. Two weeks after the conviction, on January 7, 1955, Sheppard's mother put a gun to her head and committed suicide. Ten days later, the elder Dr. Sheppard succumbed to illness and grief. Sam Sheppard twice stood the public humiliation of attending graveside ceremonies handcuffed to a sheriff.

The defense offered new evidence indicating that the murderer was a left-handed person with the strength of a woman, which is why he or she had to administer twenty-seven blows to bring Marilyn Sheppard's life to an end, and which would have exonerated the hefty, right-handed Sheppard, but the appeal was rejected three times during the following year. Years passed as Corrigan doggedly pursued the appellate process to higher courts.

Corrigan died in 1961, and Sheppard's hopes began to wane. In 1963, he started corresponding with a wealthy German divorcée, Ariane Tebbenjo-hanns, and a romance blossomed. His appeal was taken up by F. Lee Bailey, then just six years out of law school. Bailey brought the process to the highest stage, when the final appeal reached the U.S. Supreme Court in the spring of 1966.

J. Spencer Houk, the mayor of Bay Village, is shown with his wife, waiting to testify at Sheppard's trial; both were close friends of the Sheppards. *History Inc./Jay Robert Nash Collection.*

Dr. Sam Sheppard sits next to his defense attorney, William J. Corrigan, who argued enthusiastically on behalf of his client. *History Inc./Jay Robert Nash Collection.*

Dr. Sam Sheppard, right, is shown with wealthy German divorcée Ariane Tebbenjohanns (whom he married in 1966) and with new attorney F. Lee Bailey, who won for his client a second trial from the U.S. Supreme Court on the grounds that the original conviction had been tainted by prejudicial publicity, the first such opinion in U.S. legal history. Bailey was then successful in winning an acquittal for Sheppard at the second trial in 1966.

After almost twelve years in prison, Sheppard won a new trial on June 6, 1966, on the grounds that the original conviction had been tainted by prejudicial publicity, the first such opinion in U.S. legal history. Following that hearing, a federal judge stated that Sheppard's original trial had been tainted by "massive, pervasive, and prejudicial publicity." The U.S. Supreme Court reaffirmed this decision in an 8–1 vote, stating that inflammatory media coverage and the failure of Judge Blythin to sequester the jury in Sheppard's 1954 trial had denied Sheppard a fair trial.

Ohio, however, would not give up easily. The case was again remanded to the Cuyahoga criminal court in Cleveland. While he was out on appeal, Sheppard married Ariane. On October 24, 1966, accompanied by F. Lee Bailey, he reentered the courtroom in Cleveland, now presided over by Judge Francis Talty.

Bailey aggressively attacked the slipshod police work at the murder scene that possibly ruined fingerprint evidence. Bailey forced coroner Dr. Samuel Gerber to admit that, while he had testified that the murder was committed with a surgical instrument, he could not identify its type. Prosecutor John T. Corrigan (no relation to William Corrigan) countered with testimony from Gerber's assistant, who said she had discovered Sheppard's pocket watch covered with flecks of blood.

The absence of blood on Sheppard was always a major issue in this case. Marilyn Sheppard was coated with blood about the head, having received at least twenty vicious blows from a blunt instrument. When investigators had arrived at the original crime scene, they could find no blood on Sheppard. It was suspected then, but not fully detailed until more than four decades later, that Sheppard had staged the murder. He had, in his first interrogations and initial trial stated that he had taken his wife's pulse before he was knocked unconscious the first time. Had he done that, Marilyn's blood, one expert insisted, would have remained on his fingers, but no blood was found on his hands when detectives first saw him.

The theory that he had staged the murder also claimed that he had pulled his wife's pajamas down to her feet and opened the top to bare her body to make it appear that the invader's motivation was to rape the victim, yet forensic evidence (stated by the defense to be faulty at that time) indicated no sexual molestation of the victim. Further, the bedroom had apparently been ransacked by the invader, with drawers removed from dresser bureaus. But according to hindsight evaluation, they had been carefully dumped onto the floor as if to to create the appearance of a burglary. Yet only a few items of little value had been taken. Marilyn's watch and Sheppard's watch were missing but found on the premises later. This led an expert to later claim that Sheppard, in staging the murder, had no intention of ridding himself of anything in the house that had real value.

Bailey persevered in the second trial. He questioned every document. He reexamined every

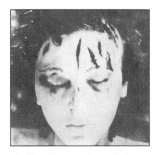

Marilyn Sheppard in death; her skull bore many cuts and blows, and this, along with other evidence, indicated that she had resisted a sexual attack and that her killer had retaliated with brutal savagery. *History Inc./Jay Robert Nash Collection.*

The living room of the Sheppard house, with rummaged drawers and items in disarray indicating that the motive for the killing was robbery. Detractors of Dr. Sheppard later claimed he staged the scene for that purpose. *History Inc./Jay Robert Nash Collection.*

Police found Dr. Sheppard's medical bag overturned in the hallway of his home and initially believed that the killer was searching for drugs. *History Inc./Jay Robert Nash Collection.*

Evidence suppressed by Cleveland police at Sheppard's 1954 trial—a tooth fragment found beneath Marilyn Sheppard's bed. *History Inc./Jay Robert Nash Collection.*

Evidence suppressed by Cleveland police at Sheppard's 1954 trial—an unidentified piece of red leather found beneath Marilyn Sheppard's bed. *History Inc./Jay Robert Nash Collection.*

piece of evidence, challenging the credibility of the prosecution's case and planting considerable doubt in the minds of the jurors. On November 16, 1966, more than twelve years after the crime was committed, Sheppard was acquitted of his wife's murder.

One of the salient factors and weapons employed by Bailey in his defense was that Sheppard had been the victim of prejudicial publicity generated by the Cleveland *Press* and other newspapers that assumed the role of the prosecution in the case and brought about the original conviction through their jaded coverage of the story, which, in turn, planted bias in the minds of the jurors in the first trial. That jury was not sequestered, and its members were free to come and go during that trial and read whatever reports were available.

Bailey illustrated for the jury how Dr. Sam Sheppard had been the victim of newspapers seeking circulation, not justice. Working closely with the press at that time, and before Sheppard was officially charged with murdering his wife, was Samuel Gerber, the coroner who had nominally been in charge of the investigation at the onset, or at least he appeared to be in charge in that he gave out all of the official statements at that time to reporters recognizing him as their immediate contact and official source of information. Gerber, prior to any police investigation into Sheppard, concluded that Sheppard was guilty and stated his belief to Louis Seltzer, editor of the Cleveland *Press*, then Cleveland's leading newspaper.

When police did not act, Seltzer unleashed a savage monthlong campaign through his newspaper, demanding that Sheppard be arrested and charged with his wife's slaying. Almost every available *Press* reporter was assigned to this task, providing each day countless reams of editorial indictment against Sheppard. Public animosity toward Sheppard had been whipped to a frenzy by Seltzer and his minions, who did not stop there. After Sheppard was brought to trial, the *Press* published the name of each juror sitting in judgment of Sheppard, reportedly so these jurors could be personally lobbied before hearing any evidence.

Sheppard's attorneys begged for a change of venue, stating, and rightly so, that the trial should be moved from the Cleveland area, where almost universal prejudice was held against their client. That request was denied, and, in Bailey's perspective (one of the chief issues in his arguments in the 1966 trial), this prejudicial atmosphere created by the *Press* had brought about his client's original wrongful conviction.

Louis B. Seltzer, editor of the Cleveland *Press*, who decided early on that Sheppard was guilty of murdering his wife and launched a pretrial crusade to convict him in the pages of his newspaper. *History Inc./Jay Robert Nash Collection.*

Seltzer ran an editorializing image in the Cleveland *Press* that accused police and officials of shielding Sheppard. *History Inc./Jay Robert Nash Collection.*

Another edition of the *Press*, appearing only three weeks after Marilyn Sheppard's murder, all but accused Dr. Sheppard of killing his wife. *History Inc./Jay Robert Nash Collection.*

Life outside of prison, however, brought no relief to Sheppard. He returned to medical practice in Youngstown, Ohio, but was served with two wrongful death suits. After five years of marriage, the relationship faltered, and Ariane filed for divorce, claiming that Sheppard had physically threatened her. Moving to Columbus, Ohio, Sheppard fought drug addiction and the loss of professional trust. He became a professional wrestler (blatantly capitalizing on his tainted reputation by billing himself "Killer Sheppard") and married the nineteen-year-old daughter of a fellow grappler. His third marriage was over in six months, his bride beseeching him to attend to his faltering health. He had by then become an alcoholic. He deteriorated rapidly, and, on April 6, 1970, Dr. Sam Sheppard died of a liver disease at the age of forty-six.

The case did not die with Sheppard's demise. His son, Samuel Reese "Chip" Sheppard, who was seven at the time of the murder and had been taken from the Sheppard house on the night his mother was found slain, later sought to vindicate his father's name, bringing a civil suit against the

state of Ohio in 1998 and asking that his father be pronounced innocent. The 1966 trial had acquitted Dr. Sam Sheppard, but the verdict did not officially pronounce his innocence or extend a full pardon.

In the course of this civil trial, many forensic experts came forward to argue the case once more. Dr. Cyril Wecht, in a hindsight evaluation of Gerber, the chief official lobbying for Sheppard's 1954 conviction, stated, "I don't know who created the term 'Napoleon Complex,' but it was made for Gerber. He was about five foot two and he loved to tell people what to do, even though he was not a criminalist and he never spent one day in a pathology residency. He ran the Sheppard crime scene and he screwed up royally." Wecht and many others came to believe that the real killer of Marilyn Sheppard was the family handyman and window washer, Richard Eberling. He had worked for some time for the Sheppard family, and his complimentary remarks to Marilyn were thought at the time to be good-natured and well-intentioned.

When Eberling later became a suspect, those remarks were interpreted to mean that he lusted after her. It was believed that, with Sam Sheppard sleeping off a heavy night of drinking on the downstairs couch, Eberling entered Marilyn's bedroom and attempted to seduce her by pulling down her pajamas while she slept. When she awoke and fought off his

Coroner Samuel Gerber, who became a self-appointed public arbiter on the Sheppard case, testified for the prosecution at Dr. Sheppard's trial in 1954; although he was considered an expert in pathology, much of his testimony was misleading and confusing. *History Inc./Jay Robert Nash Collection.*

advances—easily interpreted by a blue collar mentality as a rejection of his class and station in life—Eberling went berserk and savagely and repeatedly struck her with a blunt instrument, killing her.

In her fight with Eberling, a struggle not well recorded by Geber's 1954 investigation, theorists stated that Eberling was cut up and bloodied and that the trail of blood leading from the bedroom was his. DNA testing in the 1990s, prompted by the civil trial, proved that that trail of blood belonged to neither Marilyn nor Sam Sheppard but came from a third party. Further DNA tests used Eberling's blood and bodily fluids, but these findings proved inconclusive. Eberling, who had been imprisoned for the rape-murder of a ninety-year-old widow, died behind bars in 1998, without making any admissions. At the time of his death, Eberling was bald. At the time he worked for the Sheppard family, however, he had a thick, bushy head of hair.

The civil trial launched by Sam Sheppard's son did not result in vindication. In 2000, a jury voted 8–0 not to declare Dr. Samuel Sheppard innocent. The media, however, or its most influential elements—television and the motion picture industry, had long ago declared in dramatic presentations that Sheppard was a classic victim of wrongful conviction and imprisonment. The long-running TV series *The Fugitive*, as well as the feature movie by the same name, was based on the Sam Sheppard case.

Where Sam Sheppard had been pilloried by the Cleveland *Press* into a wrongful conviction, David

Dowaliby of Midlothian, Illinois, was wrongfully convicted on shabby evidence and chiefly because the trial judge allowed the jury to view gory crime photos that prejudiced jurors' views in their decision to bring about that conviction. This case began when seven-year-old Jaclyn Dowaliby vanished from her Midlothian home on the night of September 9, 1988. The girl's body was found four days later in a rural area outside Blue Island, Illinois. She was wrapped in a blanket that had been taken from her bed. Her badly decomposed body showed a rope tied tightly about her neck and by which her assailant had strangled her to death.

Dowaliby and his wife Cynthia told police that when they had gone to sleep on the night of September 9, 1988, Jaclyn was in her bed, and police concluded that an intruder had broken the glass of a basement window to get inside the home, where the girl was abducted. The Dowalibys cooperated with officers, each volunteering to take lie detector and drug tests, which they passed. Police knew that the girl's biological father might be a suspect since he had a criminal record, but, upon checking, they discovered that the man was in prison at the time of the murder. An uncle, Rob Kenny, was also suspected, but he provided an alibi, although that alibi was later disputed by witnesses.

Although there was little or no evidence, police, having been pressured by widespread publicity that was decidedly prejudicial to the parents, arrested both David and Cynthia Dowaliby, charging them with the crime. They had, by that time, determined that the glass in the window through which the intruder reportedly entered the home had been broken from the inside, not the outside.

Beyond that, prosecutors at the Dowalibys' 1990 trial had four witnesses who

David Dowaliby, wrongly convicted in Illinois in 1990 for killing his daughter; prejudicial publicity was widespread in the case. *Center on Wrongful Convictions/ Northwestern University/Jennifer Linzer.*

implicated the Dowalibys, including a star witness named Everett Mann, who testified that he saw a man with a "nose structure" similar to that of David Dowaliby near the area where Jaclyn's body was found. Mann, however, had a history of mental illness, and the man he claimed to have seen had been viewed by Mann from a distance of seventy-five yards on a dark, moonless night.

Before the case went to jury deliberation, Cook County circuit court Judge Richard A. Neville delivered a directed verdict of not guilty to Cynthia Dowaliby. David Dowaliby was another matter. The jury had been persuaded to convict him based on two sets of photos, both prejudicial and one erroneous.

Jurors viewed police photos that showed marks on the doorframe leading to Jaclyn's bedroom which prosecutors interpreted as fist marks, in the belief that David Dowaliby, a man portrayed often in uncontrollable rage, had made by slamming his fists into the wood. The other set of photos detailed the gruesome body of the child in death.

Dowaliby was convicted and sentenced to forty-five years in prison. His appeal was denied by Judge Neville and there seemed little hope for him, until two men began writing an article about the case, Rob Warden, an award-winning investigative Chicago journalist and director of the Center on Wrongful Convictions at Northwestern University Law School, and David Protess, a professor at that law school. Warden, who had been instrumental in providing evidence that had brought about other exonerations of wrongly convicted persons, as had Protess, with the aid of his investigative students, unearthed new evidence on the Dowaliby case when writing that article.

They determined that the glass broken in the basement window used by the intruder had not been broken from the inside, as originally concluded by police, which cast suspicion on the Dowalibys, but from the outside, indicating that an intruder had actually been present on the night of the abduction. Further, the marks on the door leading to the victim's bedroom had been made

long before the Dowalibys had occupied the home, proving that David Dowaliby had not made these marks with his fists in any kind of emotional outburst, which had also been wrongly surmised by police and the jury. It was also learned that three of the prosecution witnesses in the case later admitted that they had lied and that Mann had recanted his testimony.

With this new evidence in hand, Warden and Protess convinced Chicago attorney Robert L. Byman of the law firm of Jenner & Block to file motions for acquittal. In 1991, the appellate court reviewed the new findings and found that Mann's testimony had been "preposterous" and that Judge Neville had seriously erred in allowing the prejudicial crime scene photos to be shown to the jury.

The court ruled that there was no evidence supporting David Dowaliby's conviction, and it ordered his conviction overturned without ordering a new trial. Prosecutors appealed to the Illinois Supreme Court, which refused to review the case in 1992, bringing about the exoneration and release of David Dowaliby.

Prejudicial pretrial publicity and the prejudicial photos showing the body of his dead daughter had sent David Dowaliby to prison. In the instance of a flagrant abuse of publicity in Canada, a radio reporter in Quebec was sent to prison after the station he once worked for launched a crusade to bring about his wrongful conviction. On the night of October 25, 1982, France Alain, a nineteen-year-old engineering student at Laval University in Quebec, was shot in the right hip by an assailant who was not apprehended. Alain was rushed to a hospital where she died minutes later. She was the former girlfriend of radio reporter Benoit Proulx.

Police routinely interviewed Proulx, along with others, and then determined that no perpetrator could be identified and left the case open without making any charges. In 1990, station CHRC, through station reporter Andre Arthur and John Tardif, a retired Quebec police detective who had worked on the case in 1982, expressed the opinion on air that Proulx had murdered

Alain out of jealousy and revenge after the victim had reportedly dumped him in favor of another man.

Proulx promptly filed a defamation suit against the station and specifically against Tardif and Arthur, having had previous confrontations with the latter—Proulx had picketed the station after leaving its employ in a labor squabble. The repeated stories told about Proulx in airings by station CHRC, as well as the widely publicized defamation suit brought by Proulx, caught the attention of Paul-Henri Paquet, a Quebec resident who contacted the radio station, saying that he had briefly seen Alain's attacker five minutes after the shooting. (Paquet never explained why he had not gone to the police with this evidence eight years earlier when the crime had occurred.)

A Crown attorney had also listened to the CHRC broadcasts and hired Tardif to launch a new investigation focusing on Proulx. Part of that investigation involved the statements of witness Paquet, who was put in contact with Tardif by someone at CHRC after he had contacted the station—Proulx later claiming that his enemy Arthur had done this. Paquet told Tardif that he could identify the assailant through "his eyes," so Tardif showed him photos of Proulx, covering Proulx's face except for his eyes, and Paquet then identified him as Alain's killer. Later he claimed that Proulx's entire face was not that of the attacker.

Based upon this flimsy or almost nonexistent evidence, Crown attorneys charged Proulx with the killing in 1991. On November 10, 1991, prosecutors obtained a conviction of first-degree murder from a jury in a Quebec. Proulx was sentenced to life imprisonment. After reviewing the case and determining that Proulx had been wrongfully convicted through malicious prosecution, where no evidence to bring about that conviction existed, the Quebec court of appeals, on August 20, 1992, set aside Proulx's guilty verdict and entered a verdict of acquittal. The court made no specific mention of the prejudicial publicity generated by station CHRC, which had launched the arrest and trial against Proulx.

After serving two years in prison, Proulx was released. A Quebec court awarded him compensation in the amount of $1.6 million in 1997, but this ruling was overturned on appeal. In 2001, Proulx was awarded $2.2 million in compensation by the Supreme Court of Canada, which ordered the city of Quebec to pay that amount without challenge. It was a high price to pay for listening to useless radio chatter.

# XV
# *Inept Defense and Government Misconduct*

THE CONVICTION OF INNOCENT PERSONS has been brought about in simple and complicated ways—mistaken identity, coercion, perjury, false confessions, fabricated crimes, suppression of evidence, insufficient evidence, language barriers, prejudicial publicity, and railroading and framing. Other than mistaken identity, the most common cause of wrongful conviction is inept representation by the defense or misconduct by police or prosecutors.

In an always burgeoning judicial system attempting to catch up with overpopulation and its commensurate increase of serious crime, innocent persons are lost in that vast and grinding system or discarded by poorly paid, understaffed, and overworked defense attorneys. Conversely, police and prosecutors, to expedite their toppling caseloads, routinely shuttle their cases to quick convictions by violating codes of ethics and abandoning normal police and court procedures.

Largely contributing to the breakdown of the judicial system is an uncontrolled population explosion. In the United States alone, the population has more than doubled within eight decades, from 132 million persons in 1940 to more than 300 million in 2007 (including as many as 25 million illegal immigrants, mostly from Mexico and the Far East). There are not enough police or court officers to cope with the increased crime generated by

that ever-expanding population, and every effort to increase the number of such professionals, inherently demanding increased budgets and finances to meet that increase, is met by legislators with political indifference at best, or unthinking stern resistance at worst.

In most state cases, the defense attorney appointed as a public defender for the indigent poor defendant is addressing dozens of other cases and has little or no time to prepare a solid defense. Many states do not provide sufficient funds for defense attorneys to hire expert witnesses, let alone conduct their own investigations, where larger budgets to address these necessary expenses for police and prosecutors are well in place.

Many defense attorneys are woefully inexperienced, being recent law school graduates or being ill versed in criminal law; their legal specialty may be corporate contracts or copyright violations. Still other defense attorneys, through exhaustion, conflict of interest, or willful neglect, suppress conscience and professional principles in providing a pedestrian and halfhearted defense that all but guarantees the client's conviction. Such cases do not trickle through the courtrooms of America, but are part of a continuing flood that carries the innocent to prison or even death row.

## Ineffective and Inadequate Counsel

As many cases that are vacated and not retried suggest, the person released from prison might not be "actually innocent." Such a label was attached to Troy Lee Jones, a native of Fresno, California, who was convicted of murdering his girlfriend, Carolyn Grayson, in 1981, in Bakersfield, California, by shooting her to death with six bullets. Jones's conviction was overturned because he had one of the most inept defense attorneys in recent decades, whose shabby conduct all but assured Jones's conviction in 1982. Jones had a stormy relationship with Grayson, who at one point threatened to testify against him in a burglary-murder case, in which an elderly woman, Janet Benner, had been strangled to death.

Grayson had told Jones's brother, Marlow, that she had seen Jones choke the old woman to death. Marlow Jones, who had no love for his brother, later told police and prosecutors that his brother had told him that he planned to kill Grayson to keep her quiet about the Benner slaying. A few weeks before Grayson's bullet-riddled body was found, Jones was seen threatening Grayson with a tire iron. All of this was later presented at his 1982 trial.

Jones was found guilty, based on circumstantial evidence and hearsay statements, which included a description by a witness who said Grayson had told her daughter that she was going to Oakland, California, with Jones, only one day before her body was found in a field. Jones was sentenced to death, remaining for fourteen years on San Quentin's death row. His case was nevertheless reviewed in 1996 by the California Supreme Court, which found that his defense attorney had been ineffective when representing his client.

That attorney, the high court determined, had failed to conduct an adequate pretrial investigation, obtain an important and relevant police report, speak with potential witnesses, or seek pretrial investigative funds that were available and might have enabled him to properly challenge the prosecution's case. During the cross-examination of one witness at Jones's 1982 trial, the attorney elicited damaging testimony against his own client, the court pointed out. The court vacated Jones's conviction and ordered a new trial, additionally pointing out that the evidence suggested Jones was guilty but did not prove his guilt beyond a reasonable doubt. Prosecutors, with witnesses either dead or not available (one was in prison serving time for a murder), dropped all charges against Jones in November 1996, and he was released from San Quentin. Jones was never officially exonerated, officials pointing out that his release did not indicate "actual innocence."

In the case of a Cuban refugee who was wrongly convicted through inadequate defense counsel, his actual innocence would be pronounced by the state that would compensate him for that wrongful conviction with millions of dollars. Seeking freedom and a better life, Robert Miranda fled Cuba in 1980 during the Mariel boatlift and subsequently moved to Las Vegas, Nevada, where he got a job in a car wash and spent most of his time detailing cars. The following year, in August 1981, Miranda was arrested and charged with the murder of Manuel Rodriguez Torres, a thirty-year-old Mexican who worked at the Stardust Hotel. Rodriquez Torres was found stabbed to death in the kitchen of his Las Vegas apartment, which police determined had been burglarized.

Miranda was identified to police as the culprit by a fellow Cuban émigré with whom he had been quarreling. He was assigned at his 1982 trial a public defender, Thomas W. Rigsby, who had graduated from law school about a year earlier and had little or no experience in capital cases. (The assignment reportedly was made by Clark County public defender Morgan Harris.) A complaint filed years later alleged that the Las Vegas public defender's office maintained a policy in 1981 dictating that it would apply only minimal investigation and defense for minorities that did not belong to the Mormon Church.

According to later complaints, Rigsby failed to call several witnesses Miranda suggested would provide an alibi, including a key eyewitness. Years later these witnesses were located and testified on Miranda's behalf. The attorney also, according to Miranda, urged his client to plead guilty, which Miranda refused to do, maintaining his innocence throughout. Miranda's fifteen-day trial ended with a conviction and death sentence. He would remain on death row for fourteen years while filing appeals and staving off execution.

The credibility of Miranda's innocence claim was supported by the fact that before his trial, the state offered him a plea bargain deal. If he confessed to murdering Rodriguez Torres, he would be guaranteed a prison sentence of no more than ten years and would not face the death penalty. Miranda refused, telling prosecutors that he was innocent, a position he maintained while suffering year after year on death row.

Miranda did not really understand the death sentence he received. In his native Cuba, where communist dictator Fidel Castro sent people to death with a nod of his autocratic head, receiving a death penalty meant that you would almost immediately be executed. For this reason, Miranda tried to kill himself three times in prison. His trial attorney had never explained to him that in the United States, a defendant who receives a death sentence has the right to file many appeals to stay that execution or even win a new trial or exoneration.

Miranda's suffering came to an end in 1996, when new attorneys representing Miranda uncovered new evidence and filed an appeal, which had been brought about in part by the public defender's office. Clark County senior district Judge Norman Robison reviewed the case and ruled that Miranda's original defense attorney, Rigsby, had bungled the case and that Miranda had been a victim of inadequate defense, along with mitigating misconduct by two homicide detectives in Las Vegas regarding witnesses in the case. Judge Robison overturned Miranda's conviction, stating, "The lack of pretrial preparation by trial counsel . . . can-

not be justified." Miranda was released a short time later.

Miranda continued to suffer for many years, unable to find steady work. His attorneys, however, filed a suit against Clark County, and, in 2004, the county paid Miranda $5 million in compensation after reaching a settlement with his attorneys. While fighting for that compensation, Miranda, two years earlier, expressed no bitterness toward his adopted country. "I can't blame America," he said. "America didn't do this to me. A judge and a lousy lawyer did. The judge is dead now, and I am alive. There is a God."

The same year Miranda was wrongly convicted in Nevada, four Mexican defendants met the same fate in Chicago, sent to prison for life following a mass murder that had stunned the city. In what was later called the Milwaukee Avenue Massacre, four members of the Sanchez family were shot to death in Chicago in 1982 by feuding members of the Varela family. Police followed leads from witnesses, quickly arresting and charging Rogelio Arroyo, Isauro Sanchez, Joaquin Varela, and Ignacio Varela with mass murder. Their trial that year was a disaster of perjured eyewitness testimony, two simultaneous trials—one a bench trial for three of the defendants, a jury trial for the fourth—and marked by woefully inadequate legal counsel all around.

Interpreters also botched most of the statements made by the defendants, particularly those of sixteen-year-old Joaquin Varela, who made an ambiguous statement about witnesses testifying against him, which was wrongly construed to be a confession. Only one eyewitness put all four defendants at the scene of the crime, Leoncio Quezada, who, later reports disclosed, was probably drunk at the time of the murders, he being a survivor of the attack. Defense attorneys failed to effectively challenge Quezada's statements and those by others testifying for the prosecution, as well as challenge the judge's decision to include Joaquin Varela's supposedly self-incriminating statement. All four were convicted and sent to prison for life.

In 1990, Gilberto Varela made a collect call from Mexico to Margo DeLay, an immigration researcher at the University of Chicago. Varela confessed to her on the phone that he and three others, who had all fled to Mexico, had killed the four Sanchez family members and that the four imprisoned men had been wrongly convicted of the crime. This new evidence, along with other new revelations, brought about a successful appeal for Arroyo and the other three men. In 1991, all four men were released on orders of Illinois Governor James R. Thompson (1977–1991).

Where language problems and judicial errors compounded the deficiencies of the defense attorneys in the Arroyo case, the murder case of a Washington State defendant occurring two years later was lost before it began by a defense attorney almost indifferent to his client's plight and lethal fate. In the case of Benjamin Harris, of Spokane, Washington, his defense attorney, Murray Anderson (died in 1994), treated Harris's case as if it were an annoying chore, or, in the evaluation of the trial judge, as if he were defending a "shoplifting charge," when his client was being prosecuted for murder with the real possibility of being sentenced to death.

Harris was a local character who was chummy with police and prosecutors, thinking of himself as a "consultant" to detectives by giving them his theories on one case or another. He frequented a local coffee shop patronized by detectives, prosecutors, and legislators, going from table to table, shaking the hands of men who thought him an amusing or eccentric person who spiced their morning coffee with feeble jokes and outlandish crime theories.

Harris deluded himself into believing he was part of the political in crowd, a notion that eventually landed him behind bars. Bank robber Willie "The Actor" Sutton cautioned any suspect against becoming too friendly with police, stating at one time to this author, "Sit down with cops and you get up with handcuffs." Harris, however, was not a suspect until he made himself one in the shooting death of Jamie Lee Turner, who was killed in the summer of 1984.

Turner's body was found near the garage of his home in the Hilltop area of Tacoma. He had been shot in the head and neck. Rumor had it that Turner had been involved in crimal activities and some of his shady associates wanted him dead. Following the murder, Harris went to detectives he knew to state that he was not involved in the crime but might be able to help investigators solve it. The information Harris volunteered led police to arrest Gregory "Gay Gay" Bonds, who was charged with Turner's murder in July 1984.

Bonds admitted to the killing but told police it was a murder-for-hire job and Harris had hired him. On August 10, 1984, Harris was charged with paying Bonds to kill Turner. Within ten weeks, he was convicted and sentenced to death. He was represented by experienced defense attorney Murray Anderson, who treated his client as if he had committed a minor infraction instead of a capital offense that could end in his execution. Anderson made hardly any preparation for the case, which was to be tried in Pierce County superior court.

The attorney spent less than two hours in conference with Harris before the trial and did twelve hours of additional work. He talked with only three of thirty-two persons who might have been called to testify on behalf of Harris, and he did not contact a single person Harris listed who would vouch for him and his whereabouts at the time of the Turner killing.

Most of the key elements of the defense case were handled by Anderson's assistant, Thomas Haist, who had graduated from law school only six months earlier. Early in the case, Anderson failed to challenge the prosecutor's decision to seek the death penalty, a routine motion that probably would have been successful, according to many sources.

To escape a murder-for-hire conviction that would have brought the death sentence, Anderson decided to have his client plead guilty to actually killing Turner. If he personally committed the murder, he could not be convicted of hiring someone else to do it. He would thus be found guilty of simple murder, which was not punishable by death, or at least that was Anderson's muddled theory.

Anderson actually put his client on the stand to make this admission. Said Harris later, "Murray forced me to make a confession." That confession entailed Bonds and Harris waiting in ambush for Turner and both of them shooting the victim, one firing a bullet into the head, the other sending a bullet into Turner's neck. Allen Ressler, the Seattle attorney who later took over Harris's appeals, said of Anderson's defense theory, "It was about as stupid as it can get."

The story Harris told only convinced a jury that he was responsible for the murder, and they convicted him on October 31, 1984. He was sentenced to death. Bonds was tried in a separate trial, represented by a competent attorney, and was acquitted. For ten years, Harris awaited execution on death row at Washington State Penitentiary near Walla Walla, while one appeal after another was denied. Twice he came within weeks of execution but received stays that reprieved him from those death warrants.

In 1994, U.S. district court Judge Robert Bryan reviewed the Harris case and overturned the 1984 conviction, ruling that Harris's case was so flawed as to raise serious doubt regarding his guilt, blaming defense attorney Anderson for a wrongful conviction. Judge Bryan exemplified Anderson as "the one person in the courtroom, who is professionally obligated to display a sense of loyalty and advocacy [and] has described Harris in such a way that left him with little or no credibility, no humanity and no means to be identified as a peer of the jury." Harris was officially released in 1997 but kept in a psychiatric facility on a court order, after prosecutors agreed with his appeal attorneys that he might have become unbalanced during his imprisonment.

Where Harris's attorney had put together an incompetent defense plan that all but assured his client's conviction, an impoverished defense budget and a misunderstanding of the law on the part of another defense attorney helped send a man to death row in Texas. In 1983, Federico Martinez Macias was accused of hacking to death an El Paso, Texas, couple who had once hired him as a gardener. His accuser was Pedro Levanos, a landscape worker who said he had first met Martinez Macias when he asked him to cash a check for him at an El Paso currency exchange.

Levanos had been arrested by police after eyewitnesses had identified him at the crime scene. He at first denied being one of the two men who had invaded the home of the elderly couple intent on burglarizing the residence. When he was confronted with property found in his own home that had been taken from the crime scene, Levanos cut a plea bargain deal, saying that he would name the killer in exchange for a reduced sentence.

Levanos then told police that he drove Martinez Macias to the crime scene where Martinez Macias entered the home and killed the couple while Lavenos remained in a car nearby. He later admitted that he had entered the home too and helped Martinez Macias tie up one of the victims, Robert Haney, but he insisted that he had not murdered anyone. Levanos testified against Martinez Macias at his 1984 trial, as did a jailhouse informant who claimed that Martinez Macias had admitted to him that he had committed the burglary-murders. A nine-year-old friend of Martinez Macias's daughter stated that she had seen the defendant return home on the day of the crime with blood on his shirt and hands.

The defense counsel for Martinez Macias was a former prosecutor who had been appointed by the court, reportedly a good trial lawyer. He approached the trial as would a prosecutor, relying only on police reports and documents. He conducted no investigation himself, since his defense budget was $500. The attorney spent one hour preparing for trial and forty-five minutes for sentencing after his client was convicted.

During the trial, he failed to call two alibi witnesses who would have placed Martinez Macias at another location at the time of the crime. He did not cross-examine a witness who said that he had been at the scene of that crime when he was not and did not cross-examine the nine-year-old girl whose testimony was later revealed to be false. The conviction of his client was all but assured through his inefficient defense, although he later attributed his failure to a misunderstanding of Texas law in the case.

Martinez Macias was convicted and sentenced to death. He waited on death row for nine years, once coming only hours away from execution before receiving a stay. Martinez Macias's fortunes improved when one of the largest and wealthiest law firms in the United States, Skadden, Arps, Slate, Meagher & Flom, was assigned his case during postconviction. A partner in that firm, Douglas Robinson, based in Washington, D.C., had volunteered with the American Bar Association to take on a capital case involving an indigent person. Robinson and his firm spent a good deal of money pro bono to discover that Martinez Macias had been victimized by his own defense counsel.

The firm spent more than $1 million in rooting out discrepancies in the case, providing new witnesses who would testify on their client's behalf, and showing that Martinez Macias could not have been present at the time of the burglary-murders. Further, the firm, through its own investigators, proved that Levanos had completely fabricated his story about their client and was, in fact, the actual burglar and murderer. Robinson presented a 173-page petition to two federal courts, one of which brought about the reversal of Martinez Macias's conviction in 1992 and resulted in a new trial.

A federal judge ruled in the appeal, "The errors that occurred in this case are inherent in a system that paid attorneys such a meager amount." The judge added, "We are left with the firm conviction that Martinez-Macias was denied his constitutional right to adequate counsel in a capital case in which actual innocence was a close question. The State paid defense counsel $11.84 per hour. Unfortunately, the justice system got only what it paid for." At that time, Texas maintained no statewide

system to represent indigent defendants and had no meaningful criteria for the appointment of trial counsel. Prosecutors declined to retry Martinez Macias, and he was released from prison.

Federico Martinez Macias left Texas with his wife and resettled in Mississippi as a landscape gardener. In reflecting on his wrongful conviction, he stated, "I've had some of the worst representation and some of the best. Money makes a big difference." His grim but accurate portrayal of how the American judicial system treats impoverished defendants was echoed by U.S. Supreme Court Justice Ruth Bader Ginsberg, who once remarked, "I have yet to see a death penalty case among the dozens coming to the Supreme Court on eve-of-execution stay applications in which the defendant was well-represented. . . . People who are well-represented at trial do not get the death penalty."

Three years after Martinez Macias was wrongly convicted in Texas, another murder defendant in the neighboring state of Oklahoma was sent to death row through the inefficient behavior of a defense attorney who came to court with a damaged brain. In 1985, Kathryn Wilhoit was found dead on her bed in her Osage County, Oklahoma, home. Neighbors had responded to the cries of her two infant daughters. Her estranged husband, Gregory Wilhoit, an ironworker, was immediately suspected of murdering the woman, who had also been raped by her assailant. More than twenty bite marks were found on her body.

During the 1987 trial, two dentists who claimed to be experts in forensic odontology testified that the bite marks perfectly matched the teeth of the defendant and that the bacteria left behind by the attacker were rare and matched Wilhoit's. The defense made little or no effort to save its client from death row.

Gregory Wilhoit was sentenced to death due to a faltering defense attorney. *History Inc./Jay Robert Nash Collection.*

Wilhoit's attorney, who had suffered brain damage following a recent accident (for which he reportedly had become addicted to drugs and alcohol), did not examine the dentists' reports, which were available to him before trial. He did not call any odontologists to challenge the testimony of the two dentists testifying for the prosecution. Within two weeks, Wilhoit was convicted and sentenced to death.

While awaiting execution on Oklahoma's death row, Wilhoit befriended another condemned inmate, Ronald Keith Williamson, who had been sentenced to death for a sensational murder in Ada, Oklahoma. They became convinced of each other's innocence and helped each other file appeals that would eventually bring about their exoneration. (See Ronald Keith Williamson, in Chapter X, "False Confessions.")

When public defender Mark Barrett was assigned to Wilhoit's case, the future began to brighten for him. Barrett was convinced that Wilhoit had been wrongly convicted through inadequate counsel and worked hard to save his client's life. He located and got statements from eleven dentists who were forensic odontology experts, refuting the testimony of the two dentists who testified against Wilhoit at his 1987 trial. They said that the bite marks had not come from Wilhoit and that the bacteria left behind by the assailant was not rare, as the two dentists had claimed.

The Oklahoma Court of Criminal Appeals agreed with Barrett's arguments and evidence and vacated Wilhoit's conviction, ordering a new trial, which took place in 1993. When prosecutors attempted to use the same evidence against Wilhoit they had employed in the original trial, the trial judge stopped proceedings, saying that the prosecution had no case. He acquitted Wilhoit, who was then released from custody.

In the case of a California defendant charged with two rapes, a defense attorney was so sloppy in his routine legal chores that he hardly presented any defense at all and compounded his inefficiency by forgetting to file a motion to preserve important

evidence that might later exonerate his client. Albert Johnson was convicted in 1992 of two rapes, both occurring within a short period of time in Contra Costa County, California. He was sentenced to an aggregate total of thirty-nine years behind bars for both sexual attacks. At his trial, his defense attorney failed to challenge eyewitnesses and did not, on direct appeal, request that the rape kit in one case be preserved for possible DNA testing in the future. That rape kit was destroyed.

In the second rape, however, where police misconduct was clearly demonstrated by Johnson's appeal lawyers—he had been identified as the culprit by a victim who had been manipulated by a detective who knew Johnson since childhood—the rape kit was preserved. In October 2002, DNA tests were conducted on the rape kit from the second attack and results showed that Johnson was innocent of that crime. Over the protests of prosecutors who admitted Johnson's innocence in the second rape but insisted he was guilty of the first rape, Johnson was exonerated and released in March 2003. The court ruled that he had been wrongly convicted chiefly on inadequate counsel and police misconduct in the second rape case.

In another case where a defendant was charged with murder, a defense attorney thought it wise to keep his client from testifying on his own behalf, a poor tactic that backfired when the jury presumably interpreted that refusal as an admission of guilt. In Philadelphia on December 22, 1992, Eric McAiley, a small-time drug dealer, was shot to death in what was thought to be a dispute with a drug supplier who felt he had been shortchanged by McAiley.

A short time later, thirty-four-year-old William Nieves, who was also a penny-ante drug dealer, was interrogated but released when witnesses could not identify him as the man who had stepped from a Cadillac to shoot McAiley to death. Nine months later, a previously uncertain witness told police that Nieves was the killer.

Nieves hired attorney Thomas Ciccone Jr., who had represented him in minor charges a decade earlier but had not handled a capital case. Ciccone asked for a $10,000 retainer but then agreed to take a $2,500 down payment to defend Nieves. The prosecution's star eyewitness was a thirty-four-year-old prostitute who gave conflicting reports when testifying against Nieves at his two-day trial in July 1994. She had told police months earlier that two heavyset black men shot McAiley to death, but nine months later, she said that a burly Hispanic man committed the murder.

Nieves was Hispanic but had a slight build. This discrepancy was ignored by the court. Most damaging, however, was the conduct of Ciccone, who provided little or no defense, calling no witnesses and advising his client not to take the witness stand. Ciccone reasoned that keeping his client from the witness stand would prevent prosecutors from questioning Nieves about his prior criminal record.

Found guilty of first-degree murder, Nieves was sentenced to death. On appeal, John McMahon Jr., a former prosecutor, represented Nieves, arguing that his client had been inadequately represented by Ciccone, who had denied Nieves the right to testify for himself. In 1997, the trial judge ordered a new trial for Nieves, but prosecutors appealed the ruling, which prolonged a decision for three years.

The Pennsylvania Supreme Court agreed with the defense and supported the 1997 ruling on February 17, 2000, vacating Nieves's conviction and ordering a new trial, ruling that Nieves had been represented by ineffective assistance of counsel. At his new trial, Nieves's attorneys were able to show from police documents that an FBI informant could have testified that other persons had committed the McAiley murder. Nieves was acquitted on October 20, 2000, and released three days later.

## Prosecution Misconduct

At approximately 6:30 P.M. on the evening of January 14, 1976, nine-year-old Lisa Cabassa accompanied her eleven-year-old brother Ricky as they walked to a friend's house. The girl complained of a headache and said she was returning home, only a few blocks away on Chicago's South Side. When Ricky Cabassa returned home about two hours later, his family discovered that Lisa was missing. After searching the neighborhood, they called police at 9:00 P.M. A desperate search was made, but the girl was not found until the following day, January 15, 1976, two miles away in an alley. She had been sexually molested and strangled.

Vaunted Cook County medical examiner Robert Stein believed that the girl had fought for her life and that one man held her down while another raped her; then the men exchanged roles, finally murdering Lisa Cabassa. The fact that Stein emphatically stated that *two* men were involved caused police to look for multiple suspects and may have influenced the identification of two men who were wrongly sent to prison for hundreds of years.

A few days after the heinous crime was publicized, a neighborhood businessman, Frank Martin, posted a reward of $5,000 for information that would identify the abductors and killers of little Lisa. Responding to that reward was thirty-two-year-old Judith Januszewski, who worked as a secretary in a real estate office in the neighborhood where the girl had been abducted. After talking with the woman on January 19, 1976, four days after the girl's body had been found, Martin alerted police, saying that Januszewski had important information on the case.

Detectives reportedly talked with her on the phone, and she said that she had seen two young black youths struggling with a young white girl on the evening of January 14 at the corner of Saginaw and 86th Street, a short distance from her office. The detective wrote down that Januszewski had seen this happen at "6:37 P.M.," a precise time Januszewski would later disavow. She did not specifically identify Lisa Cabassa as the girl even though she had known Lisa for more than a year. A short time later, Januszewski helped a police artist create composite sketches of the two men she had seen with the girl.

In routine police interviews over the ensuing months, police interrogated sixteen-year-old Keith Jones. He had come to the attention of detectives when Januszewski notified officers that Jones had been calling her with what sounded like threats about her earlier statements to police. Jones was grilled, and he implicated Michael Evans and James Davis. Jones also said that Paul Terry looked like one of the police sketches drawn from the descriptions of Januszewski. Jones would later deny identifying the three youths.

Evans, Davis, and Terry were brought in for questioning. Januszewski identified all three men in police lineups, even though she had originally said only two youths had been struggling with the girl. Evans was indicted for kidnapping, rape, and murder. Waiving a jury trial, he was tried before Cook County circuit court Judge Earl E. Strayhorn. Januszewski testified against Evans, but her credibility was challenged after prosecutors admitted that she had worked at her office on the night of the kidnapping-murder until 8:00 P.M., whereas the parents of the victim had stated that Lisa Cabassa had left her home about 6:30 P.M. on the night of her murder. (This discrepancy was detailed in an in-depth account of the case written in 2003 by Chicago *Tribune* reporters Maurice Possley and Steve Mills, who stated that the time difference "was changed to fit Januszewski's account.")

Convicted before Judge Strayhorn, Evans's conviction was later vacated by the same judge after he discovered that Januszewski had received payment from prosecutors for her testimony. Evans was then retried with Terry and Davis, who had also been charged with the

Michael Evans, wrongly convicted through prosecution misconduct in a 1976 Chicago murder.
*Center on Wrongful Convictions/Northwestern University/Jennifer Linzer.*

crime. Based on Jones's recantation, the charges against Davis were dropped, and in April 1977, Evans and Terry were tried by a Cook County court jury with Judge Frank W. Barbaro presiding.

Defense attorneys immediately challenged Januszewski's testimony, based on the time discrepancy that had risen in Evans's first trial. The prosecution's star witness brushed off that discrepancy, saying that she had never told anyone, including the police, that she saw the victim with the two black youths at "6:37 P.M.," and that the detective to whom she had been talking at that time "made that up out of his own head."

Paul Terry, who was wrongly convicted with Michael Evans for a 1976 Chicago murder. *Innocence Project, New York.*

The jury had doubts, and after some deliberation sent Judge Barbaro a note stating, "We are deadlocked unalterably. What shall we do?" Barbaro replied, "It is your duty to continue to deliberate." The judge later received another note from the jury, stating, "In almost four additional hours of deliberation, we cannot reach a unanimous decision."

At this point, defense attorneys moved for a mistrial. Judge Barbaro would have none of it, again instructing the jury to "continue to deliberate." An hour later, the jury returned a guilty verdict against Evans and Terry on all charges. They were sentenced to more than four hundred years each for kidnapping, rape, and murder. They would likely have been sentenced to death, but their convictions took place eighteen months before Illinois reinstated the death penalty.

The First District Illinois Appellate Court upheld the convictions and sentences in December 1979, where defense attorneys had challenged Januszewski's credibility. The court, however, ruled that her "testimony, if believed, was not so improbable, doubtful, or vague as to raise a reasonable doubt as to the defendant's guilt."

Lead prosecutor Thomas M. Breen had some lingering doubts. Breen left the state's attorney's office to become a defense lawyer and was instrumental in bringing about the exoneration of Gary Dotson in 1989 through DNA testing, the first person in the United States to be so vindicated. He also worked to exonerate Rolando Cruz in 1995. (For Dotson, see Chapter XIII, "Crimes That Never Happened"; for Cruz, see Chapter X, "False Confessions.")

When working on the Cruz case with Lawrence C. Marshall, a professor of law at Northwestern University (who later became legal director for the Center on Wrongful Convictions, established in 1999), Breen expressed suspicions that Evans and Terry might have been innocent. Marshall probed the case with the assistance of Karen Daniel, a legal member of the staff of the Center on Wrongful Convictions, aiming at postconviction DNA testing for both Evans and Terry.

Daniel, along with attorney Jeffrey Urdangen and two Northwestern University law students, Anne Hunter and Ann Jerris, presented a motion before the circuit court to have DNA testing done on behalf of Evans and Terry, as well as James Davis, who had originally been implicated in the murder. Tests made in September 2002 excluded all three men as donors of the spermatozoa found in the victim. Prosecutors insisted on additional testing, implying that the two convicted men were still guilty but that an unidentified accomplice may have been the ejaculator.

Even after additional tests proved the defendants innocent, prosecutors stalled until May 23, 2003, when they agreed that Evans and Terry deserved a new trial. The men remained in prison for another three months before truculent prosecutors dropped all charges against them on August 22, 2003. Both Evans and Terry were set free, after serving twenty-seven years behind bars for a gruesome crime they did not commit.

Where Evans and Terry were convicted through the misconduct of prosecutors who improperly argued their case, two men in San Fran-

cisco were convicted of murder and sent to prison by prosecutors who were later shown to have suppressed evidence in that sensational case. In 1989, San Francisco was undergoing a savage war between rival drug gangs attempting to control the Sunnydale and Hunter Point neighborhoods, which were crammed with low-rent housing projects populated mostly by blacks and other minorities.

More than forty persons had been killed in this ongoing drug war. One of those deaths involved eighteen-year-old Roderick "Cooley" Shannon. On the night of August 19, 1989, Shannon was chased by a group of men through San Francisco's streets. After Shannon became trapped in a convenience store parking lot in Visitacion Valley, he was beaten and shot to death.

Police were under tremendous pressure to curb the violent drug war, and several San Francisco officers bent the law in bringing about two wrongful convictions in the Shannon slaying in order to appease the public outcry. Two young girls, Pauline Maluina and Masina Fauolo, claimed to have witnessed Shannon's murder, one of them being a friend of his. Both identified Antoine "Soda Pop" Goff and John J. Tennison as the slayers. The testimony of these two girls, despite a total lack of physical evidence, brought about the 1990 convictions of Goff and Tennison.

Goff and Tennison were each sentenced to twenty-seven years to life in prison. Both were sent to maximum security prisons, Goff to Solano Prison near the Oregon border, where inmates were routinely savaged by guards. An inmate had once been thrown into a tub full of scalding hot water, and Goff once witnessed a tower guard shoot an inmate in the head to quell a prison yard melee. Tennison was sent to Mule Creek State Prison, where the same brutal conditions existed. Jeff Adachi, who had been Tennison's court-appointed public defender, consistently believed that his client was innocent.

While Tennison and Goff filed one appeal after another, attorneys Ethan Balogh and Elliot Peters undertook their case pro bono. During a prolonged investigation urged by the indefatigable Adachi, defense investigators began to turn up widespread misconduct on the part of the prosecution and police in the case. They learned that prosecutors and police had bullied one of the girls (Maluina) testifying against Tennison and Goff into changing her statements after she recanted her identification of the two men. At the time of the trial, the prosecution had failed to turn over to defense attorneys information on a secret payment fund for witnesses and a polygraph test conducted on one of the girls after she recanted. One of the girls had reportedly been paid $2,500 for her testimony.

Further, the prosecution had failed to provide the defense with the statements of two eyewitnesses who had contradicted the testimony of the two girls, and, most importantly, a taped confession from a man who admitted to murdering Shannon but was told by police to remain silent after they advised him of his Miranda rights. The man who confessed was Lovinsky (or LaVinsta or Lavinster) Ricard Jr., who had been picked up on a drug charge in November 1990 and had been identified by Chante Smith.

Ricard's statements were cited in a later appeal, but the court dismissed Ricard's "confession" as untrustworthy. In 1992, Smith backed away from her 1990 statements about Ricard, saying that she had not really been an eyewitness to the Shannon murder, but had heard the details from someone else and refused to support her earlier statements about Ricard, saying that she did not want to appear in court.

The defense attorneys specifically pointed out in their appeal that assistant district attorney George Butterworth had purposely withheld all of this evidence from Tennison's lawyers at the time of the trial and placed additional responsibility for police misconduct on retired Police Chief Prentice Earl Sanders and Inspector Napoleon Hendrix for subverting or hiding evidence. Sanders later denied tampering with witnesses. He had retired on a police chief's annual pension of $188,718.00.

On August 26, 2003, U.S. district Judge Claudia Wilken vacated Tennison's conviction and ordered a new trial in her 103-page ruling that Tennison's constitutional right to a fair trial had been violated after prosecution and police withheld evidence that might have proven him innocent. San Francisco district attorney Terence Halliman later said he would not retry Tennison, stating that the case against him had been "improper, and it resulted in the reversal of this conviction and, worse, the conviction of an innocent person. He's been locked up for thirteen years for a crime he did not commit." Tennison was released from prison on August 29, 2003.

Goff's exoneration followed shortly. Lovinsky Ricard Jr., who by then had moved to another state, was interviewed by police in September 2003, saying that he had confessed to police in San Francisco on February 9, 1990, under pressure, but that he later recanted that confession and asserted he had nothing to do with the murder of Shannon. His confession had already been dismissed as unreliable in an appeal filed by the defendants many years earlier, so police had little to use against him. He was never charged with the murder.

Withholding exculpatory evidence by prosecutors in the case of Goff and Tennison paled in comparison to the conduct of prosecutors in the 1996 murder conviction of a sixteen-year-old boy in New Orleans. Their conduct outlandishly flaunted the rules of court procedures and behavior. Prosecutors in this case not only manipulated evidence but prevented defense witnesses from appearing in court.

At 10:26 P.M., on the night of May 2, 1995, Michael Gerardi and his date, Connie Baben, emerged from a New Orleans restaurant and were confronted by three armed men, one of whom shot Gerardi in the face and killed him. The killer then rummaged through the victim's pockets as Baben fled screaming down the street.

Baben called police and initially told them that, in all the confusion, she doubted that she could recognize the killer. She did say that the murderer was shorter than Gerardi. In a police interview some days later, Baben again told detectives that she was unclear as to the killer's identity: "I don't know. It was dark, and I didn't have my contacts or my glasses, so I'm coming at this with a disadvantage."

Having no clues or evidence, detectives began canvassing jailhouse snitches, turning up one who was willing to finger an innocent sixteen-year-old boy for a killing he did not commit. The snitch was James Rowell, who had been jailed on nine counts of armed robbery. His attorney asked him if he had information that might reduce his impending sentence, and Rowell said he could solve the Gerardi killing. He named a casual acquaintance, Shareef Cousin, as Gerardi's killer.

Cousin, who was black, was arrested and charged with first-degree murder, but he had a solid alibi that vexed prosecutors. At the moment Gerardi had been killed, Cousin was riding in a car with several other basketball teammates and their coach, Eric White, who was driving them home after a game. White testified that he dropped Cousin at his home at 10:45 P.M., almost twenty minutes after Gerardi had been killed on the other side of town. Further, the game had begun at 9:30 P.M.

Prosecutors nevertheless brought Cousin to trial in 1996 with no evidence other than the perjured statements of James Rowell and the revised statements of Connie Baben, who testified that she was "100 percent" certain that Cousin was Gerardi's killer. Cousin's "iron-clad" alibi was shattered when the prosecution showed a tape of the basketball game, which indicated that that game had not begun at 9:30 P.M. but ended at that time, and that Cousin had enough to time to murder Gerardi. White, who had been a witness for Cousin, charged prosecutors with altering that tape, but he was ignored, and Cousin, who was tried as an adult, was convicted and sentenced to Louisiana's death row.

The public outcry against this wrongful conviction and imprisonment was so widespread that *Time* magazine and other publications took up

Cousin's cause, charging prosecutorial misconduct. There was more than ample misconduct to show to the Supreme Court of Louisiana when defense attorney Clive Stafford-Smith filed his appeal in 1998.

Stafford-Smith was able to show that Rowell had recanted his perjured statements about Cousin and that prosecutors had illegally altered the tape of the basketball game to the wrong timetable. Further, Stafford-Smith showed that three of Cousin's teammates had arrived in court to testify on behalf of Cousin, but defense attorneys could not find them. They had been diverted to the district attorney's office in another building and thus did not testify for Cousin.

The high court reversed Cousin's conviction on April 14, 1998, citing the prosecution's improper use of hearsay (Rowell), but it did not depict or comment on the prosecution's withholding of exculpatory evidence. A new trial was set for January 11, 1999. Before that time, prosecutors attempted to persuade Cousin to sign a confession that he had murdered Gerardi, promising reduced prison time, but he refused. On January 8, 1999, prosecutors dropped the murder charge against Cousin, but he remained in prison on four counts of robbery that had earlier been coerced from him in a plea-bargained arrangement.

Where the prosecutors in the Cousin case blatantly performed misconduct that brought about an exoneration, prosecutors in Lawrence County, Pennsylvania, undid their murder conviction by improperly barring a defense attorney from questioning a witness in a 1998 trial. That case involved forty-year-old Thomas H. Kimbell Jr., who was described by prosecutors as a onetime crack addict with a violent temper. Witnesses claimed that Kimbell was lurking about a trailer located outside New Castle, Pennsylvania, and occupied by Bonnie Dryfuse, her two daughters, Jacqueline, age seven, Heather, age four, and her niece, Stephanie Herko, age five. All were murdered on June 15, 1994, repeatedly stabbed to death and their throats slit.

Although there was no physical evidence that linked Kimbell to the crime, three jailhouse snitches testified that Kimbell, while awaiting trial, had told them that he had killed four people, which helped to bring about Kimbell's conviction of four charges of first-degree murder on May 8, 1998. He was sentenced to death. On appeal in 2000, however, the Pennsylvania Supreme Court vacated the original conviction and ordered a new trial, based on the prosecutor's motion to exclude testimony that most probably would have brought about Kimbell's acquittal.

That testimony had been given by defense witness Marilyn Herko, the mother of one of the murder victims and the sister of Tom Dryfuse. Herko said that she was talking to her sister-in-law, Bonnie Dryfuse, a little after 2:00 P.M. on the afternoon of the killings. Bonnie Dryfuse, shortly before she was murdered, abruptly ended that phone conversation with Herko, according to Herko's statements at the 1998 trial, by saying, "I got to go. Somebody just pulled up in the driveway."

Thomas W. Leslie, Kimbell's defense attorney, then attempted to have Herko repeat earlier statements she made to police about that phone call, in which she said that Dryfuse had said that her husband, Tom Dryfuse, was then driving his car into the driveway of the mobile home. Dryfuse had testified that he had not arrived at home until after 3:00 P.M. to find the bodies. Had Herko's original statement been admitted in court, that testimony would have placed Dryfuse at the scene of the crime an hour before he claimed he was at the mobile home and would have implicated him in the murders.

Leslie, however, was prevented by the prosecutor from further questioning Herko on her statements. The prosecutor had wrongly stated in his motion that Leslie was barred from asking such questions on the basis that he could not impeach his own witness, a motion that was sustained by Judge Glenn McCracken Jr. The high court stated that Leslie had been deprived of the opportunity of revealing that Tom Dryfuse "was at the scene of the murders during the time he claimed to be elsewhere. . . . This obviously worked to the benefit of the prosecution." At a new trial, both of Herko's statements were exposed to a jury, which found Kimbell innocent. He was released from prison on May 3, 2002.

## Police Misconduct

Local or state police had nothing to do with the widespread misconduct of law enforcement in the wrongful conviction of Peter J. Limone and three other men. That sullied case was properly placed at the door of the Federal Bureau of Investigation, and even within the office of its director, J. Edgar Hoover. Limone and three other men had been selected by a high-ranking Mafia figure as "fall guys" in the syndicate murder of hoodlum Edward "Teddy" Deegan, who had been shot to death (with six bullets) on March 12, 1965, in an alley in Chelsea, Massachusetts, a suburb of Boston.

For two years, police searched for the killer or killers but developed no clues or leads. Then Joseph "The Animal" Barboza, a high-placed Mafia hit man who was also one of the FBI's most protected informants in its Boston office, agreed to cooperate with local prosecutors in bringing about the convictions of four men he said were responsible for murdering Deegan. In 1968, Boston prosecutors brought to trial Peter J. Limone, Louis Greco, Henry Tameleo, and Joseph Salvati, with Barboza as the key prosecution witness.

Barboza, who had been granted immunity in exchange for his testimony, stated that Limone and the other three men had murdered Deegan, providing details of the shooting.

FBI Director J. Edgar Hoover, who had been informed by his own agents that a Boston murder for which Peter J. Limone and three others had been wrongly convicted and sent to prison in 1968, had been committed by Mafia/syndicate killers, but he did nothing about it. *History Inc./Jay Robert Nash Collection.*

Barboza, who had long been an informant for the FBI, had already admitted to Bureau agents that he had participated in the Deegan murder, along with Mafia killer Vincent "Jimmy the Bear" Flemmi. That information, however, was not revealed until many years later.

Almost solely on Barboza's perjured testimony, Limone, Greco, Tameleo, and Salvati were convicted and sentenced to death. All four innocent men escaped execution in 1974, when Massachusetts abolished capital punishment. Their sentences were commuted to life. Greco and Tameleo died in prison, but Limone and Salvati continued to languish behind bars decade after miserable decade. Both would probably have died in prison, but for the decision of the U.S. Department of Justice to thoroughly investigate the Boston FBI office, which for years had been rumored to be working hand in glove with the New England Mafia under the direction of crime boss Raymond L. S. Patriarca.

In the early 1960s, when President John F. Kennedy entered the White House, the new U.S. attorney general, Robert Kennedy, began pressuring FBI chief J. Edgar Hoover to attack and demolish the national crime syndicate, which was then largely controlled by the old American Mafia bosses. For decades, since his appointment as chief of the Bureau in 1924, Hoover had steadfastly maintained that no such national crime syndicate existed and that it was a myth created by flamboyant and irresponsible journalists.

Hoover had taken this position, ridiculous as it was, in order to avoid committing most of his FBI forces against a widespread organization he believed was too powerful to be destroyed. Had he accepted the syndicate's existence and launched an all-out attack against it, he believed he would be proven to be ineffective and that the Bureau and its annual budgets would suffer drastically. Rather than combat the syndicate, Hoover ignored it, until the media and national politicians proved its existence and prodded him to take action against it.

Hoover halfheartedly began a campaign against the syndicate in the mid-1960s. However, he

launched an attack against his Boston office with the syndicate's approval. A 2000 investigation of that office by the U.S. Department of Justice showed willing collusion between the syndicate and the Bureau, as clearly evidenced in the wrongful conviction of Peter J. Limone. (The framing of Limone and others was not dissimilar to the railroading of Roger Touhy in Chicago in 1933 by Al Capone and his ally, Jake Factor; see Chapter XIII).

Internal memos generated by the Boston FBI office revealed that Barboza, Flemmi, Stephen Flemmi (Vincent's brother), and James Bulger had long wanted to kill Deegan, who had been causing trouble—invading rackets controlled by the New England syndicate (Mafia). A memo written by FBI agents H. Paul Rico and Dennis Condon stated their informants' intent two days before Deegan was slain. It said that before the murder was committed, the overall don (boss) of the New England syndicate, Raymond L. S. Patriarca, had to approve of it, which, the agents went on to say, he did.

Hoover received a memorandum from his Boston office a week after Deegan was killed: "Informants report that . . . Vincent James Flemmi and Joseph Barboza, prominent local hoodlums, were responsible for the killing." Hoover's office responded on June 4, 1965, demanding to know the progress of the Boston office in developing Vincent Flemmi as an informant. It made no mention of the fact that Flemmi had been identified as Deegan's killer. On June 9, 1965, the Boston office replied to Hoover that Flemmi was in a hospital recovering from gunshot wounds received during his services with Patriarca, but "potentially could be an excellent informant."

Barboza was held in the same high esteem by the Boston FBI agents. Following his testimony against Limone and the three others, he was placed in the federal witness protection program, the first person to enter that program. At that point, later Department of Justice investigations revealed, Hoover and the FBI accepted without protest the fact that Limone had been framed for the Deegan killing by the Bureau's own syndicate informants, and knew that the informants had actually performed the murder.

Evidence of this railroading was supported in December 2000 by an affidavit submitted to Middlesex superior court Judge Margaret Hinkle, who had lifted attorney-client privilege so that Joseph J. Balliro Sr., lawyer for Vincent Flemmi, could divulge information about his client. Balliro's statement detailed how Flemmi had told Balliro that Limone and the three other men were innocent of murdering Deegan. Flemmi by that time was dead.

Judge Hinkle vacated Limone's conviction and ordered his release from prison in January 2001. Two weeks later, Judge Hinkle vacated the conviction of Salvati, who had been paroled in 1997. Judge Hinkle could do nothing for Greco and Tameleo since they had died in prison. Hinkle at that time stated, "The conduct of certain agents of the Bureau stains the legacy of the FBI." It was further shown that Boston FBI agents had even coached Barboza in his testimony against Limone and others and had organized and orchestrated the prosecution's case. (Two Chicago FBI agents were later shown to have done the same thing in railroading one of their own informants, Steven Manning; see Chapter XI.)

F. Lee Bailey, who had briefly represented Barboza in the 1970s, stated in one of the committee hearings on corruption in the FBI Boston office that he was convinced the Bureau had coached Barboza. Said Bailey, "He told me he had quite a bit of help. I believe the testimony was furnished." Another witness at those hearings was Jeremiah T. O'Sullivan, who headed the New England organized crime strike force and later became a U.S. attorney in Boston. O'Sullivan testified that he knew at the time that Bureau informants had committed murder and were nevertheless being protected by the FBI. He cited his fear of reprisals from the Bureau as his reason for not taking action, adding, "With the FBI, if you go against them, they will try to get you."

The corruption ran into the marrow of the Boston office. One of its special agents, John J. Connolly, who recruited James "Whitey" Bulger as an informant, worked hand in glove with Bulger in many rackets, gleaning a kickback from the illegal profits those million-dollar rackets produced. James J. "Whitey" Bulger, born on September 3, 1929, was a longtime criminal who had done time in many prisons, including Alcatraz, and headed Boston's Winter Hill Gang with coboss Stephen Flemmi.

Bulger had controlled almost all of the rackets in Boston for decades, including the lucrative drug trade. Finally in the mid-1990s, police and federal agencies began to close in on him. Flemmi would later be convicted of money laundering and extortion and sent to prison for ten years while still facing murder charges in Oklahoma and Florida.

Connolly, his paid informant at the FBI, informed Bulger that he was going to be arrested in 1994, and Bulger went on the run, moving about the United States for the next five years with his mistress, Catherine Greig. They reportedly left the country in 1995 or later. On August 19, 1999, Bulger was named as one of the FBI's most wanted fugitives (becoming the 458th such fugitive so named by the Bureau), with a $1 million price tag on his head. Bulger's brother, William Michael Bulger, had at one time been the president of the Massachusetts state senate and later became the president of the University of Massachusetts.

In his memoir William Bulger described his older brother as "mischievous." It was claimed at one time, without supporting evidence, that William Bulger had brought about his sibling's early prison release and had given him considerable political protection. William Bulger, after admitting that he had talked to his brother on a pay phone while he was on the run, was fired in 2003 from his position as president of the University of Massachusetts by Massachusetts Governor Mitt Romney (2003–2007).

Whitey Bulger's odyssey around the world was described by former protégé Kevin Weeks, who took control of the Winter Hill Gang after Whitey's flight and remained boss until he was arrested and turned informant. Bulger is considered the Bureau's most wanted man only after Osama bin Laden. Reportedly possessing millions from his rackets, Bulger was seen in London in 2002, in Uruguay in 2005, in Ireland in 2006, and walking about the streets of Rome, Italy, in 2007, still accompanied by Greig. His freedom was not shared by the FBI agent who worked so closely with him and reportedly helped Barboza frame Limone and the three other men. John J. Connolly was convicted of racketeering in 2002 and sent to prison for ten years.

Connolly received a much shorter prison term than the wrongly convicted Peter J. Limone, who spent more than three decades behind bars for a murder he did not commit. He was convicted through the collusion of syndicate killers and their Boston protectors, the FBI. The sixty-seven-year-old Limone returned to his wife of forty-five years. Olympia Limone had remained faithful to him, believing in his innocence. They settled in Medford, Massachusetts, where they have four children and eight grandchildren.

On July 26, 2007, U.S. district Judge Nancy Gertner awarded Peter Limone, seventy-three, and Joseph Salvati, seventy-five, $101.7 million in compensation for their wrongful conviction and imprisonment. The award capped a prolonged civil suit against the FBI, which was argued by attorneys for Limone and Salvati. They had not asked for a specific amount but pointed out to the court that other wrongfully convicted persons had been awarded $1 million for each year behind bars.

Judge Gertner had nothing but scathing remarks for the Bureau's behavior in this case: "The FBI's misconduct was clearly the sole cause of this conviction. The government's position is, in a word, absurd. No lost liberty is dispensable. We have fought wars over this principle. We are still fighting these wars." Said Salvati, who had been in prison for more than twenty-nine years, "Nothing can compensate for what they've [the FBI] done." Limone, who had been in prison for thirty-three years, stated that Judge Gertner's decision had been "a long time coming. . . . What I've been through—I hope it never happens to anyone else."

The egregious behavior of the Boston FBI office that wrongfully sent Limone and three others to prison in 1968 was repeated by Baltimore police six years later. Police officers knowingly supported the lies of a drug peddler and suppressed exculpatory testimony from an eyewitness in bringing about the wrongful conviction of an innocent man in 1974.

On April 29, 1974, an armed robber entered a Crown Food Market in Baltimore, Maryland, shooting and killing security guard Ray Kellam during the robbery. Shop assistant Jackie Robinson was interviewed by police and, as an eyewitness to the crime, originally described the assailant as a light-skinned black man standing 5 feet 8 inches tall, weighing about 140 pounds.

Police nevertheless arrested Michael Austin, a dark-skinned black man who stood 6 feet 5 and weighed more than 200 pounds, and charged him with the robbery-murder. Found in Austin's wallet was a card with another man's name on it, who police thought to be an accomplice. The man was interrogated and then released and never charged, but the card was nevertheless used as evidence against Austin.

Robinson, whom prosecutors portrayed as a civic-minded college student, became the chief witness against Austin. He had changed his description of the assailant by that time so that it fit the description of the towering Austin, who was convicted and sentenced to life in prison. After all appeals failed, Austin contacted Centurion Ministries, a nonprofit organization that seeks to exonerate persons it believes have been wrongly convicted. The organization hired Baltimore attorney Larry A. Nathans to represent Austin on appeal.

Nathans and a private investigator unearthed new evidence showing that Robinson, the prosecution's star witness against Austin, was actually a drug-peddling high school dropout with a serious heroin addiction; he died from a heroin overdose in 1997. Robinson's family told an investigator that Robinson was unreliable and had been involved in drug peddling. Robinson's brother, John Robinson, stated that Jackie Robinson had confessed to him before his 1997 death that he had testified against a man who was wrongfully sent to prison.

Moreover, the investigation revealed that Robinson changed his mind about his original physical description of the killer after police pressured him into identifying Austin from a police photo array that contained only six photos. At the time, police had threatened Robinson with drug charges unless he identified Austin, which he did. Following his cooperation, he was not charged on drug violations.

Police misconduct in this case turned out to be more widespread than suspected when it was revealed that another eyewitness, Eric Komitsky, the store's assistant manager, had gone to police immediately after the crime and told them that the killer was not taller than himself and that he was absolutely sure because he had faced the killer eyeball to eyeball. Komitsky stood 5 feet 9 inches tall. Komitsky's report was not provided to either prosecutors or defense attorneys at the time of Austin's trial.

Joseph Wase, the prosecutor who tried Austin, when later reviewing the new evidence, stated that the new revelations convinced him that he should not have tried the case. Former Baltimore mayor Kurt Schmoke, a onetime state and federal prosecutor, also reviewed the new evidence and then asked the city's top prosecutors help free Austin. The case was vacated, and Austin was released from prison on December 28, 2003, after prosecutors dropped all charges.

In January 2004, Maryland Governor Robert L. Ehrlich (2003–2007) exonerated Austin by granting him a full pardon. In the same year Austin was given $1.5 million in compensation. Austin was proven innocent of a crime for which he had spent twenty-seven years behind bars. Said Governor Ehrlich, who personally greeted and shook hands with Austin after granting him the pardon, "I apologized to him, although words are very difficult to come by." When asked about the compensation for Austin, Ehrlich replied, "What's a year worth? What's a month worth? What's twenty-seven years worth?"

The state of Wisconsin enacted a law that entitles any wrongfully convicted person to $2,500 for each year of wrongful imprisonment, or a total of $25,000. But that law, like other state laws with caps for financial compensation, is presently being challenged.

Police in Dallas, Texas, have been accused on more than one occasion of gross misconduct in sending innocent persons to prison. In the rape case of a black construction worker, those accusations bore fruit. An eighteen-year-old woman living in North Dallas, Texas, was gang-raped in her residence on August 1, 1982, by three young black men. Six months later, the victim identified a black man, James Curtis Giles, a married construction worker living in Duncanville, Texas, twenty-five miles distant from the scene of the crime, as one of her three attackers. The victim had doubts about him in court since the assailant was shorter and younger than the defendant, who had gold teeth, which the victim had not initially described to police. Giles was, however, chiefly convicted on the victim's testimony in 1983 and sentenced to thirty years in prison.

Released on parole in 1993, Giles, who had insisted all along that he was innocent of the crime, was compelled to list himself as a sex offender and report regularly according to his parole regulations. These conditions nagged and haunted him to the point where he contacted the Innocence Project in New York, asking for help in clearing his name. After repeated pleas from Giles, the Innocence Project decided to investigate his case. Its investigative and legal efforts (the organization has brought about dozens of exonerations where DNA can been applied to such cases) revealed that misconduct by Dallas police had contributed largely to Giles's conviction.

In May 1983, several weeks before James Curtis Giles was tried, the police learned from detectives in Indianapolis, Indiana, that a suspect being held there on a murder charge, a black man named Stanley Gay Bryant, had information on the Dallas rape. In an attempt to plea-bargain that murder charge, Bryant told Indianapolis detectives that he was present when two black teenagers raped a woman in Dallas (he blamed the other two, saying that he was not a participant when he was). Bryant identified the two young blacks as James Earl Giles, known as "Quack," and Michael Anthony Brown.

James Earl Giles, who was no relation to James Curtis Giles, had a record as a violent teenager and lived across the street from the Dallas rape victim. He was nevertheless not charged with that rape, nor was Brown or Bryant, who had offered to testify against James Earl Giles and Brown in that rape case but was never called. The police had already arrested James Curtis Giles for the crime and had gotten an identification of him from the victim, and they settled for that.

Dallas police never gave the defense attorneys for James Curtis Giles the exculpatory information they received from Bryant and that information was not disclosed to the Innocence Project by prosecutors until August 2003. DNA was subsequently tested in the case, which showed that James Curtis Giles was not the donor of the spermatozoa found in the rape kit, but confirmed that Bryant and Brown were two of the perpetrators. Brown had died in 1985 in jail while serving time for another gang rape.

DNA testing for James Earl "Quack" Giles was not done since Dallas police had destroyed the evidence in the rape case in 2003, the year in which Dallas prosecutors admitted to the Innocence Project that the exculpatory evidence from Bryant had been withheld by police. Dallas prosecutors did not admit the police had destroyed that evidence until December 2006.

When Dallas police realized that the disclosure of the Bryant statements would impugn their case, detectives (with the possible collusion of prosecutors) destroyed biological evidence. If Quack Giles had been identified through DNA, it would endorse their suppression of evidence in the Bryant statements and add railroading and framing to the conviction of James Curtis Giles.

Quack Giles died of cancer in 2000 while serving a prison sentence for assault and robbery.

James Curtis Giles was cleared by state district Judge Robert Francis in February 2007, with the endorsement of Dallas prosecutors. On June 21, 2007, the Texas Supreme Court granted his writ of habeas corpus, which officially exonerated him. There was nothing magnanimous related to these court actions, which had been wrenched from a judiciary system seemingly bent on sending innocent persons to prison. The Innocence Project had diligently and expertly extracted one poisonous fang after another that had been sunk into the flesh of James Curtis Giles's human history.

In one of the most startling and shocking cases involving police misconduct, Pennsylvania police sent an innocent man to death row for a murder committed by a clever killer who initially duped police into believing they had the right suspect. Somewhere in the investigation of that case, officers realized their mistake but nevertheless supported the statements of the real killer and even provided false evidence to prosecutors, while one of the investigators stowed away exculpatory evidence in the attic of his home.

Jay C. Smith, the eccentric principal of Upper Merion High School in Montgomery County, Pennsylvania, was an ideal fall guy in a murder planned by a teacher at that school, William S. Bradfield Jr. Smith was a married womanizer who collected pornography that accented bestiality. His wife divorced him but returned to live with him when she contracted cancer. She died while living with him. His older daughter was a heroin addict, as was her husband, and his younger daughter was emotionally troubled.

Smith, who kept guns in his home and his car, was convicted of impersonating a Brink's messenger, illegally collecting more than $34,000 in cash from a Sears store on August 27, 1977. When he attempted to repeat the crime at another Sears store, a manager recognized his impersonation. The day before Smith was to be sentenced for this crime in Harrisburg, Pennsylvania, one of his teachers at Upper Merion High School, Susan Reinert, left her Ardmore, Pennsylvania, home with her two children, ages ten and eleven, at 9:20 P.M., on Friday, June 22, 1979.

Reinert, who was married, was not discovered until the following Monday, June 25, 1979. Her battered, naked body was found stuffed into the trunk of her car, which was located at a parking lot of a Harrisburg motel. Her two children were never found and were presumed murdered. Investigators learned sometime later that Reinert was having an affair with another Upper Merion teacher, William Bradfield, who was also having an affair with another teacher at the school, Sue Myers. Bradfield at first denied any sexual relationship with the married Reinert, saying that she was too "mousy" and unattractive to interest him, but that she had avidly and annoyingly pursued him despite his attempts to avoid her unwanted attentions.

Bradfield's attitude toward Reinert changed when it was learned that he was the beneficiary of a $750,000 life insurance policy on Reinert. Under pressure from police, Bradfield finally admitted being involved in Reinert's death. He had organized the killing, he said, but he had not actually killed the woman. That gruesome chore, he said, had been performed by Jay C. Smith. Bradfield, of course, knew that Smith was to be sentenced in Harrisburg on the same day that the body of Reinert was found in the Harrisburg motel.

Smith was arrested and charged with the actual murder of Reinert, although he emphatically claimed innocence. Bradfield, in exchange for his stated conspiracy theory, received three life sentences. He did not testify against Smith at his 1985 trial, but statements Bradfield had made to others were used at that trial, which outlined and supported the concepts of Bradfield's murder-for-hire claim. Smith, however, received three death sentences, one for Reinert's death and two more for her missing children. During the trial, Smith's attorneys attempted to put the full responsibility on Bradfield, but Bradfield had a solid alibi: he

spent the weekend Reinert disappeared with three reputable high school teachers in Cape May, New Jersey.

An autopsy of Reinert seemed to confirm the time period specified by Bradfield, a pathologist stating that the victim had been severely beaten twenty-four to thirty-six hours before her death, which had occurred early Sunday morning, June 24, 1979, when she was injected with a fatal dose of morphine. Police by that time knew otherwise, but suppressed evidence that would have shown Bradfield could have murdered Reinert and that Smith had nothing to do with this crime.

Following his conviction, Smith continued to file appeals but seemed unlikely to avoid the death penalty. Said Smith, "From the moment you are in that cell, when they tell you you're going to be electrocuted, you contemplate it all the time. It never leaves your mind, and they never let it leave your mind." His fate was also on the mind of two dogged investigative reporters, Pete Shellem and Laird Leask of the Harrisburg *Patriot-News*, who felt from the beginning that the state's case against Smith was questionable. (In 2003, Shellem brought about the exoneration of another wrongfully convicted person, Barry Laughman, by tracking down missing biological evidence that proved Laughman innocent of a murder through DNA testing; see Chapter X.)

The reporters wrote consistently over the years that police had suppressed evidence in the case, and this was endorsed in March 1992, when a box of evidence was removed from the attic in the home of Jack Holtz, a Pennsylvania state trooper who had led the investigation against Smith. In that box was a comb marked with the name of Smith's army reserve unit (he had been a colonel). At Smith's trial, prosecutors had produced an identical comb linking it to Smith that was alleged to have been found beneath Reinert's body in the trunk of the car. The comb found in the box was never entered as evidence in court, but the one that was used as an exhibit allegedly had Smith's hairs in its teeth, according to FBI hair analyst

Michael P. Malone, who testified for the prosecution and whose testimony chiefly contributed to Smith's death penalty.

Years later Malone was discredited. He had made so many errors in capital cases that he may have contributed to dozens of wrongful convictions, if, indeed, he had not made outright fabrications of evidence in his assertions and testimony, which was alleged by others, including another FBI forensic expert. Smith called Malone "Agent Death," in claiming that he had fabricated reports about hair analysis and that he could find hair under a microscope where none ever existed in routinely sending innocent persons to death row. The comb was part of the fabricated evidence presented against Smith at his 1985 trial.

Also found in Holtz's magic box of evidence was a letter addressed to Holtz written by crime author Joseph Wambaugh, stating that he had offered $50,000 to Holtz's deceased partner, Sergeant Joseph Van Nott, for police information before Bradley and Smith were arrested. This was in clear violation of police procedures, which prohibited investigators from receiving outside money for police work without the approval of the commissioner. At the time, Wambaugh was planning to write a book on the sensational murder case, which he did. It became a best-seller under the title *Echoes in the Darkness*.

In a postscript to his letter to Holtz, Wambaugh stated, "Since I would start the legwork [on the book] immediately, we should be very careful about being seen together for the sake of your job. As far as witnesses would know, I received all my information from news stories and anonymous tips." Reporters Shellem and Leask later reported that Holtz, a twenty-three-year veteran of the Pennsylvania state police, had received $45,000 from Wambaugh in the same year Smith was convicted and sentenced to death. Holtz earned a salary of $35,000 a year, yet, after Smith was sent to prison, according to Shellem and Leask, he bought a Porsche 944 and purchased a resort home in North Carolina.

In addition, twenty-three notebooks on the case were found in Holtz's box; only notebook number thirteen was missing. That missing notebook, according to Smith's attorney, William C. Costopoulos, covered a period when Holtz was dealing with jailhouse snitch Raymond Martray, who later testified against Smith in court, saying that Smith, while awaiting trial in jail with him, admitted to murdering Reinert. Costopoulos also claimed that Bradfield had told Holtz that he alone had killed Reinert and that Smith had had nothing to do with the murder. In 1992, the attorney asked Judge Robert L. Walker to put all the evidence found in Holtz's box in the care of a court-appointed custodian. At the same time, Costopoulos asked Judge Walker to ask prosecutors why the evidence held in Holtz's residence was not made available to Smith's defense.

Costopoulos had long suspected that his client was framed by Bradfield and with the collusion of police. In 1991, he was given rubber evidence lifters containing sand that had been taken from the bare feet of Reinert, that evidence found in a police locker at the end of the trial but never given to the defense until six years after Smith was convicted and sent to death row. That evidence supported the defense claim that Reinert had not gone to Harrisburg but to the Jersey shore to meet Bradfield, who was at that location according to his own alibi. He killed her there and then drove her body to Harrisburg, leaving it in the car at the motel parking lot. From the sand taken from Reinert, it was logical to conclude that she had been murdered on a beach where Bradfield was staying, while Smith was nowhere near that location.

Smith had already won an appeal granting him a new trial, based on the fact that his original conviction had been brought about by inadmissible hearsay evidence. Costopoulos then inventively argued that his client should be set free without a second trial, based on a double jeopardy clause in the state constitution. In almost all instances, double jeopardy applied to those initially acquitted of a crime, where Smith had been convicted.

Costopoulos, however, argued that Smith's civil rights would be violated by a second trial where the state employed the same charge since the state itself, through its own police misconduct, had caused the original trial to be reversed.

The Pennsylvania Supreme Court surprisingly agreed, stating that the prosecution's case against Smith had been so egregiously manufactured through police misconduct that compelling the defendant to face the same charges amounted to double jeopardy. The court, basing its decision on the sand evidence and the secret deal Holtz had made with jailhouse snitch Martray, barred a retrial, and Smith was released from prison on September 18, 1992. The prosecution protested, rightly stating that Smith had won his freedom through legal technicalities but was not "actually innocent."

Bradfield, meanwhile, died at Graterford State Prison in 1998. He had cleverly framed Smith for a murder he personally committed, but he had not been clever enough. He had set up Smith for months before killing Reinert, telling coworkers and friends that Smith was evil and was planning to kill Reinert, even though Smith had no motive to do so, other than a minor run-in with Reinert at school when she brought her children unannounced into his office.

After Reinert left his office, his secretary said that Reinert's children were "good kids," and Smith reportedly replied, "I hate all kids," a remark Bradfield later heard and constantly repeated in order to implant the later conclusion that Smith had somehow decided to murder Reinert. Murdering Reinert simply because her children annoyed him, to the minds of workers at Upper Merion High School, was not that far-fetched for him as a well-known eccentric.

Those persons, other than the insightful and crusading newsmen Shellem and Leask, as well as the alert Costopoulos, failed to ask themselves why Smith would murder Reinert and her children, and then drive the body to Harrisburg. They also failed to ask themselves why he would then somehow return home and then drive back to Harrisburg to face sentencing on the Brink's theft, somewhere along the way disposing of Reinert's two children, if he had not done so earlier. None of it made any more sense than the case presented against Smith in the first place.

A year after Smith was convicted in Pennsylvania, Arthur Mumphrey was convicted and sent to prison for raping a thirteen-year-old girl in Conroe, Texas, a crime he did not commit, while local police, before that wrongful conviction, had the real rapist in custody. On February 28, 1986, a thirteen-year-old girl was walking along the railroad tracks outside of Conroe, followed closely by two black men, who suddenly grabbed her and carried her to a wooded area where both men repeatedly raped her while drinking wine. She finally fled and police later picked up Steve Thomas, who said that he would provide information on the case if he could get a plea bargain deal.

Police offered him a deal and Thomas then admitted he had been involved with the crime. But he claimed that the chief offender was a man named Arthur Mumphrey, who had raped the girl. In exchange for a fifteen-year prison sentence, he agreed to testify against Mumprhey, who was convicted on Thomas's testimony in 1986 and sent to prison for thirty-five years.

Before the conviction, Charles Mumphrey, Arthur's fifteen-year-old brother, told police that he committed the crime, but officers told him that he was lying. He admitted that he had fabricated the story, also admitting that he knew nothing about the details of the sexual attack. His aim was to take the blame for his older brother in order to be tried as a juvenile and receive a light sentence.

Released on parole in 2000, Mumphrey was sent back to prison two years later for parole violations.

Arthur Mumphrey, wrongly convicted on perjured testimony used by Texas police. *Innocence Project, New York.*

During that time, he hired Eric Davis, an experienced defense attorney, who filed a motion for postconviction DNA testing. But Davis was told by the Texas Department of Public Safety (DPS) that it had no such biological evidence. After three searches, all urged by Davis, the evidence of the rape kit in the case was found in a refrigerator at the DPS storage facility.

DNA tests conducted in 2005 proved that Steve Thomas and another unknown man had been the donors of the spermatozoa in the 1986 rape, but that Mumphrey was innocent. Exonerated, Arthur Mumphrey was released from prison on January 27, 2006. He had remained behind bars for almost eighteen years because of the perjured statements of the real culprit and the willingness of police to accept his lying testimony.

In the same year Texas police wrongly sent Mumphrey to prison, detectives in Riverside County, California, fabricated evidence that would send another man to prison for a rape he did not commit. The crime occurred sometime between 11:30 and 12:00 P.M., April 8, 1986, when a black man entered a shoe store in Lake Elsinore, California, to sexually attack the lone female employee. She was robbed at gunpoint and raped, the assailant wiping the semen from his genitals onto her sweater. Immediately after the attacker fled, the woman called police and was taken to a hospital where a rape kit was assembled and the sweater kept as evidence.

The victim was later taken to a police station and shown Lake Elsinore High School yearbooks but failed to identify her assailant. She was next taken to a briefing room at the station where she was shown a wanted poster for Herman Atkins, a black man wanted on an unrelated charge. She was then shown a police photo array from which she picked Atkins's photo, identifying him as her assailant.

Another witness, a waitress working at a restaurant that was next door to the shoe shop, told detectives that she had seen Atkins in the restaurant earlier on the day of the rape, but only after she too was shown the wanted poster for Atkins. Detective Danny Miller, who supervised this case, also secured a signed statement from a man named Eric Ingram, stating that Ingram identified Atkins as a known gang member and that he had seen him in the Lake Elsinore area in early April 1986, only days before the crime occurred.

Herman Atkins, wrongly convicted after California police rigged his identification. *Innocence Project, New York.*

These statements were presented by the prosecution in Atkins's 1988 trial, along with a forensic expert who claimed that blood tests from the case showed that the perpetrator was blood type A and PGM 2+1+, a blood type consistent with the victim and Atkins. The expert also stated that Atkins was within a population of 4.4 percent of the population (both Caucasian and Negroid) that could have committed the rape. In summation, the prosecution stated that the forensic evidence "corroborated" the claim that Atkins was the perpetrator.

Atkins provided an alibi for the time of the crime and testified on his own behalf. His defense attorney argued that he was a victim of mistaken identity. The jury did not believe this and convicted Atkins of two counts of forcible rape, two counts of forcible oral copulation, and robbery. He was sentenced to more than forty-five years in prison.

After all appeals failed, the Innocence Project undertook his case in 1993, seeking postconviction DNA testing, which prosecutors resisted, saying the biological evidence could not be found. Two years later, the sweater with the semen stains and the swabs from the rape kit had been located, but prosecutors refused to turn this over for testing.

In 1999, the Innocence Project filed a motion to compel the prosecution to release the evidence for

DNA testing, which was granted. The evidence was sent to Forensic Science Associates in Richmond, California, which announced that Atkins had been excluded from the spermatozoa evidence found in all the samples. He was released from prison in February 2000 and filed a suit against Riverside County.

During that period, a private investigator tracked down one of the witnesses, Eric Ingram, whose signed statement against Atkins had been submitted as evidence by Detective Danny Miller. Ingram signed a sworn statement that he had never told Miller anything about Atkins and that he had never seen Atkins. This and other evidence that irrefutably proved police misconduct in the Atkins case were shown to a jury in a civil federal trial, which decided in Atkins's favor, awarding him $2 million in compensation in April 2007. He had been represented at that trial by the same attorneys heading the Innocence Project that had brought about his exoneration through DNA testing seven years earlier.

Police in the case of a high school student in Peekskill, New York, were so focused on him that they all but ignored any other suspect in the brutal rape-murder of a fifteen-year-old girl on November 15, 1989. Her murderer remained in the area and lived under the nose of the police, until he murdered another female in Peekskill four years later. This killer allowed an innocent youth to go to prison for his crime and remain behind bars for another thirteen years, while the unconscionable killer kept silence in another cell.

Angela Correa had left her home on Main Street that day to take pictures for her photography class. Her killer was smoking crack near Griffin's Pond when he spotted the girl and dragged her into some woods. He beat her and raped her, and then strangled the girl with his hands, hiding her body in a depression in a wooded area behind Hillcrest Elementary School and covering her naked body with leaves. He then went home to his wife and son. He was twenty-nine-year-old Steven Cunningham.

The child's body was discovered on November 17, 1989. Her clothes and cassette player were found nearby. News of this murder swept through the town, sending the victim's relatives, friends, and classmates into mourning. One bereaved classmate, sixteen-year-old Jeff Deskovic, became a suspect early on, after police noted that he had been late for class on the morning following Correa's disappearance. He also appeared to detectives to be overly disturbed by his classmate's death, visiting her wake three times. (It is not known if Peekskill police were aware of the fact that many killers attend their victims' funerals, but it might be concluded that was the case since they made a point of remembering those multiple visits by Deskovic.)

Police concentrated on Deskovic, although he had no criminal record and appeared to be an upstanding and sincere youth. He was interviewed eight times by detectives, four times in December 1989 and four times the following month. Deskovic was eager to solve the murder of his classmate, telling police that he was trying to gather facts about the case in his own "investigation." He desperately wanted the killer found. As far as the police were concerned, they had the killer—Jeff Deskovic. In some rare murder cases, the killer actively participates in the investigation of his own crime, providing leads and clues to detectives in an effort to deflect attention away from himself. Some of these arrogant killers are motivated by brimming pride and conceit.

This was the case with Richard Loeb, who, with Nathan Leopold Jr., randomly selected Bobby Franks, the child of a Chicago millionaire, to kidnap and murder in 1924, to see if they could get away with "the perfect crime." Both Loeb and Leopold

Jeff Deskovic, wrongly convicted after New York police inveigled him into a confession. *Innocence Project, New York.*

were the pampered sons of millionaires and Loeb thought himself superior to any living creature. Loeb provided detectives with his theories about the Franks murder and even went along with detectives while they searched remote Chicago areas before the child's body was found. That crime, Loeb learned, was not perfect—none ever is—and he and Leopold went to prison.

The profile of the killer provided to Peekskill detectives by the New York Police Department seemed to support their suspicions that Deskovic was too eager to work with police to solve his classmate's murder. In 1982, another youth, Steven Linscott, went to police in Oak Park, Illinois, in an effort to help them solve a brutal murder. His volunteered information and "visions" about the case made him the chief suspect, and he was later wrongly convicted of that murder and sent to prison (Chapter X). Like Linscott, the equally naive Deskovic, during his prolonged interrogations with police, also provided a "confession."

In late January 1990, police asked Deskovic to take a polygraph test, but they did not tell him he was a suspect. The sixteen-year-old boy believed that if he took the test and passed, he would be encouraged to work with police to solve the crime. In an eight-hour session, the exhausted Deskovic was grilled without being given any food but was offered coffee. Three lie detector tests were administered that day, interrupted by intense interrogations by detectives. At the end of six hours, Deskovic reportedly "confessed" to the killing, but his statements alternated from the first to third person and back, as if he were trying to tell police what was in the mind of the actual killer.

Deskovic told detectives that he lost his temper and hit the girl over the head with a plastic bottle and held his hand over her mouth "too long." He began to weep, the session ending when the boy was under the table in the interrogation room, curled up in a fetal position. He was charged with the murder and brought to trial where Legal Aid Society attorneys put up a feeble defense. DNA tests on the evidence found at the crime scene showed that Deskovic was not the donor of the spermatozoa found on the victim and her clothes.

However, prosecutors did not wait for those results and presented the case to a jury, which convicted Deskovic of first-degree rape and second-degree murder in January 1991. The jury ignored the DNA results, which were by then at hand. Prosecutors pointed out that more DNA testing could not be performed since the victim's clothes had been "lost."

To explain the original DNA results, which cleared Deskovic, prosecutors said that Deskovic had murdered the victim out of jealousy since he learned that she had consensual sex with an unknown male, who had deposited the semen. In so doing, prosecutors cruelly and ruthlessly defamed the dead girl, as well as offering an absurd theory with no evidentiary support in their desperate effort to gain a conviction.

Prosecutors to this day, while stubbornly considering a retrial, rely on the "consensual partner" argument in an effort to continue to inculpate a defendant exonerated by DNA. In so doing, these prosecutors literally make themselves and their communities liable to defamation suits, even from rape victims whose identities have been shielded by the press since those identities can be accessed through police and other records and pose a threat of being made public by others with the possible intent of extortion or blackmail.

Prosecutors in the Deskovic case got their conviction through an argument that, in the opinion of this author, libeled a dead girl. Before sentencing, Deskovic pleaded with Judge Nicholas Colabella that he was innocent and had not killed his friend Angela Correa. Judge Colabella sentenced him to prison for fifteen years to life. When all appeals failed, the Innocence Project agreed to represent Deskovic and moved to have new DNA testing, which was entered into the New York State DNA database.

In September 2006, results from that DNA test showed a match with a convicted felon serving a twenty-year prison sentence for murder—Steven

Cunningham. He had been convicted of strangling to death with his hands—the same method he had used to murder Angela Correa—Patricia Morrison, the mother of three, in her Peekskill apartment in 1993, after she refused to give him money to buy crack cocaine or let him sell her videocassette recorder for that purpose.

Detectives then interviewed Cunningham in prison, showing him a picture of Angela Correa. He bristled at the sight of her image, blurting, "I never saw that woman in my life." Detectives told him he was lying—they already had the DNA evidence to prove him guilty of killing the girl. One of the detectives, Arthur Mohammed, asked Cunningham how he wanted to be remembered by his mother and son. He then urged him to confess to "free Angela's soul and end her family's suffering." Cunningham then confessed to having killed the girl. He was convicted of second-degree murder in that case and, on May 3, 2007, was sentenced to twenty years, those years added to his sentence for the Morrison murder, making the forty-seven-year-old Cunningham eligible for parole in 2033.

By that time, Deskovic was free. He had been released on September 20, 2006, after spending fifteen years in prison. He was officially exonerated on November 2, 2006, when the court dismissed Deskovic's indictment on the ground of actual innocence. He was present in the courtroom to see Cunningham sentenced for the murder of his classmate, as was the victim's mother, Angela Vasquez.

In court, Cunningham refused to look at Deskovic or Vasquez while the mother's written statement was read to him: "Because of his own inadequacy and failure at life, a man who amounts to nothing, took the life of a daughter, who means everything to me." She had written that she did not want Cunningham's apology "for his senseless act, because sorry means nothing. . . . We do not know what kind of human he is. Not only did he take these lives [Morrison and Correa], but he allowed another child [Deskovic] to be blamed and sacrificed like a lamb."

Another lamb sent wrongfully to prison was Peter Rose, convicted of raping a thirteen-year-old girl in Lodi, California. While walking to a school bus stop on November 29, 1994, the girl was grabbed from behind and dragged into alley, where a man sexually assaulted her. She told police immediately after the rape that she did not recognize her assailant. Officers Ernie Nies and Matt Foster mercilessly grilled the girl, who

Peter Rose, wrongly convicted after California police pressured a witness to identify him as a rapist in 1994. *Innocence Project, New York.*

continued to tell them she could not identify her attacker. The officers denigrated her, calling her a liar and telling her to remove a necklace with a cross on it that hung about her neck, saying that she did not deserve to wear it.

Again and again, using every kind of pressure and method of coercion, the officers pounded away at the girl. At one point, she shouted, "I'm telling you I don't know who it was!" The girl's aunt, who had problems with Peter Rose in the past, suggested to the girl and to police that Rose was the attacker, although she had no evidence to support this suggestion. Rose had no history of violent crime or sexual assault, and was the hardworking father of three children.

The girl finally relented to police pressure and named Rose as her attacker. To support the girl's statements, prosecutors offered serology evidence that said Rose could not be excluded as the donor of the sperm found on the victim. He was convicted of kidnapping, forced oral copulation, and rape in 1996 and sentenced to twenty-seven years in prison. At sentencing, Rose wept while telling the judge he was innocent.

Following years of unsuccessful appeals, Rose's case was undertaken by the Northern California Innocence Project (NCIP) at Golden Gate University School of Law in San Francisco in December 2002. Under the direction and supervision of NCIP director Susan Rutberg and attorney Janice

Brickley, students began to locate and assemble evidence on Rose's behalf. They determined that semen samples still existed in the case, and they filed a motion for postconviction DNA testing.

DNA tests showed that Rose, as well as the girl's boyfriend, were excluded as donors of the spermatozoa found on the victim's clothing. The court vacated Rose's conviction and ordered his release from Mule Creek state prison. On October 29, 2004, the thirty-six-year-old Rose was set free. A few days later, the victim, then twenty-three, contacted reporter Jeff Barker at the Stockton *Record*, recanting her 1994 statements about Rose, telling Barker, "I am not sure. I wasn't sure [at the time of the crime]."

The victim went on to say that police pressure had caused her to make her wrongful accusations about Rose. She stated that she had told police at the time that she had never seen the face of her attacker. Wrote Barker, "[She] went along with the police because they seemed to have evidence lined up against Rose." They had no evidence other than the statements they had coerced from the victim.

Officers Nies and Foster had reportedly badgered the girl when interrogating her, suggesting that she might not have been raped after all and that she was making it all up, one saying, "It wasn't forced, was it?" Another said, "Who did you really get in a fight with and why did you end up behind that house?" The girl, after many hours of this kind of pressure, finally stated, "My aunt talked to his girlfriend and his girlfriend said he wasn't home. Maybe it could be Pete [Peter Rose]."

This tentative comment was converted into a declarative statement by the officers, becoming a positive identification, when, at best, it was nothing more than a desperately groping supposition on the part of a harassed teenager. The police, according to her story, had portrayed her as being a promiscuous person if indeed she had not been raped. To vindicate herself, the victim was compelled to identify a real person as the perpetrator to make that rape a reality in the eyes of the police. The girl thus was victimized *twice*, once by her attacker and again by the police during their relentless interrogations.

In reviewing the exoneration of Rose, NCIP director Susan Rutberg said, "Something is terribly wrong with this picture. A vulnerable crime victim is browbeaten into identifying an innocent man, and then years later, the real rapist is still out there." Rose filed a civil suit seeking damages. The city of Lodi and other authorities settled with his attorneys in January 2007, compensating him in the amount of $1 million for sending him behind bars for eight years for a crime he did not commit.

A year after Rose was wrongfully convicted, an innocent teenager in Kentucky was accused of an arson-murder, and, like Jeff Deskovic eight years earlier, he became the chief suspect after he tried to help police in that case. On the night of December 14, 1997, eighty-two-year-old Sam Davenport and his seventy-six-year-old wife Lillian were murdered by an intruder who entered their home in Whitley County, Kentucky. He struck both victims on the head before setting their home on fire.

Both victims, who had lived at the residence for forty-six years, died about 12:30 A.M. of smoke inhalation. A short time earlier, two youths, seventeen-year-old Larry Osborne and fifteen-year-old Joe Reid, were riding past the Davenport home on a motorbike. They heard the sound of breaking glass, and Osborne stopped a few minutes later at a pay phone to report what they had heard to his mother, Pat Osborne. She then called police, who saw that the Davenport home was in flames when they arrived.

Police had been vexed by a number of recent murders in the area and, without any foundation, suddenly concluded that Pat Osborne was behind it all, that she was a criminal mastermind who had directed a number of capital crimes. In fact, Osborne had an IQ of 54 and experienced difficulty in performing simple chores. They settled on her seventeen-year-old son, Larry, even though it was Larry Osborne who had alerted his mother and, through her, the police, to the crime.

To get to Osborne, police picked up gullible teenager Joe Reid on December 15, the day following the murders, and grilled him for several hours. Reid told police that he and Osborne had nothing to do with the deaths of the Davenports or the arson firing of their home. He repeated the same story in a second interrogation on December 16, 1997. In a third, four-hour-long interrogation, detectives supplied all known details of the crime and even showed Reid a map of the Davenport home.

Reid took a lie detector test at that time, which police said he failed. All of this was taped, except for a forty-minute period. After that lull, Reid was again taped, saying that Osborne had committed the crime while he stood outside the Davenport home. Police told him that they would inform prosecutors that he had been cooperative. "Is that going to get me out of all of this stuff?" the naive fifteen-year-old boy asked.

Osborne was arrested on December 31, 1997, and charged with arson and the murders of the Davenports. Police had actually constructed the crime for the witness Reid to parrot back to them in a rigged confession. Moreover, they did not inform Reid that he had the right to an attorney—he was never cross-examined on his testimony nor was he ever represented by counsel. Police misconduct was compounded by the prosecution in Osborne's 1999 trial by introducing Reid's testimony in court.

Reid, however, could not be cross-examined by Osborne's defense attorney, since he was dead, having drowned in an accident in Jellico, Tennessee. The defense argued that Reid's testimony was not admissible in that he was deceased and therefore not available for cross-examination. The motion was overruled by the presiding judge, and Osborne was quickly convicted on that inadmissible testimony and sentenced to death.

On appeal, the Kentucky Supreme Court reversed Osborne's conviction, saying that prosecutors had introduced hearsay evidence to bring about that conviction—the testimony of the dead Joe Reid. It ordered a new trial, where Reid's statements were not admitted. Twenty-two-year-old Osborne was acquitted on July 31, 2002, and, after spending three years on Kentucky's death row, he was released, becoming the first death row inmate in Kentucky to be exonerated since capital punishment was reinstituted in 1976.

## Forensic Science Misconduct

Forensic science (Chapter VIII) is not infallible in determining all of the evidence needed to bring about convictions, and that includes DNA. Many a DNA expert and even entire crime laboratories have been shown incompetent or capable of making intentional errors in manipulating test results to bring about wrongful convictions. In regard to crime labs, the chief cause for concern is sloppy categorization and classification by forensic science experts. This affects most police crime labs.

In October 2004, the *Washington Post* reported that the police crime lab in Houston, Texas, was disorganized and ineffective. An internal investigation discovered 280 abandoned and mislabeled boxes of evidence in murder cases from 1979 to 1991, boxes that contained a human fetus, body parts, guns, and other weapons, all unearthed and unaddressed in a police property room. The boxes contained evidence involving more than 8,000 open and closed capital cases and had been placed in the property room predating DNA testing, which began in Houston in 1992. Those boxes contained evidence that brought about many convictions, but their contents had reportedly become so degraded that DNA testing might prove ineffective.

Typical of the disorganization of the Houston lab was the case of Josiah Sutton, who was convicted of the 1998 rape of a Houston woman that involved two attackers who abducted her and raped her in the backseat of a car. The victim identified Sutton and a friend who was later released. Sutton was convicted the following year and sentenced to twenty-five years in prison, based partly on the victim's identification. She had originally described the chief assailant as 5 feet 7 inches tall and weighing 135 pounds, where Sutton was 6 feet tall and weighed 200 pounds.

Forensic experts from the Houston Police Department Crime Laboratory had testified at Sutton's trial that DNA testing of the semen found in the backseat of the car matched that of Sutton and another unknown black male. This was the key testimony that had sent Sutton to prison. When the operations of the Houston Police Crime Laboratory were later exposed as shoddy and ineffective, the DNA report it had issued on Sutton was obtained by reporters who sent it to other forensic experts for review and evaluation. William Thompson, a renowned criminology professor at the University of California–Irvine, was one of the experts who responded with a scathing report on the Houston lab findings, saying that its DNA tests on the Sutton case were unsound and had been the work of amateurs.

Thompson's report led to new DNA testing that exonerated Sutton, showing that only one male had deposited the spermatozoa in the victim, and that Sutton was excluded as the donor. Sutton was released from prison in 2004, after serving four years. Sutton was later officially pardoned and given $118,000 in compensation for his wrongful conviction. The real culprit, Donnie Lamon Young, a convicted felon, was identified in 2006 as the rapist in the police DNA database.

A year after Sutton was released, the state of Texas was compelled through DNA testing to release another wrongly convicted man, George Rodriguez, who had been convicted in 1987 of a Houston rape and sent to prison for fifty years. He had been sent to prison largely on the testimony of Jim Bolding, who headed the Houston Police Department Crime Laboratory. Bolding stated that the lab's serology testing proved that Rodriguez was the culprit, and a hair definitely linked him to the victim.

After all appeals failed, the Innocence Project undertook Rodriguez's case in 2002. It learned

that the biological evidence in the case had been destroyed in 1995, but the single hair that had largely contributed to his conviction was still available for testing. Unlike the earlier microscopic testing conducted on that hair by the Houston police lab, that hair was subjected to more reliable DNA testing that excluded Rodriguez, who

George Rodriguez, wrongly convicted in Texas on misleading serology reports. *Innocence Project, New York.*

was exonerated in September 2005 after prosecutors dismissed all charges against him.

Shoddy forensic science figured largely in one of Canada's most controversial cases. Fourteen-year-old Steven Truscott was convicted in 1959 of murdering a classmate and became the nation's youngest person ever to be convicted and sentenced to death. In his case—woefully cluttered with contradictory forensic science evidence—pathology took a leading role in an attempt to fix the time of the victim's death, crucial to that questionable conviction.

On June 9, 1959, Truscott went on a short bicycle ride with twelve-year-old Lynne Harper near an air force base outside of Clinton, Ontario. Truscott later said that he left the girl somewhere on a bridge and then went home. When Harper did not return home, a search for her ensued, ending on June 11, 1959, when her body was found in some woods. She had been raped and strangled to death. Based on eyewitnesses who saw the children together, Truscott was charged with the murder and was convicted and sentenced to death on December 8, 1959, after a fifteen-day trial.

Truscott was held on Canada's death row for six terrifying weeks before his sentence was commuted to life imprisonment on January 22, 1960. The youth continued to file appeals, but all failed. In 1966, a book entitled *The Trial of Steven Truscott* by Isabel Le Bourdais seriously questioned the speedy police investigation in the case, as well as the conduct of prosecutors in the trial procedures. The book became a best-seller in Canada and provoked a firestorm of protest that advocated Truscott's innocence. In response, the Supreme Court of Canada reviewed Truscott's case but found no irregularities in the case and ruled 8–1 against granting a new trial.

A good prisoner with an unblemished record, Truscott was paroled in 1969. He moved to Guelph, Ontario, where he lived under an assumed name. He married and had three children. Truscott sought exoneration, and in 1997, his case was undertaken by celebrated defense attorney James Lockyer, who had brought about the exoneration of another wrongly convicted Canadian, Guy Paul Morin. (See Chapter IX, "The Near Miracle of DNA.") Three years later, Truscott proclaimed his innocence on a CBC television program entitled *The Fifth Estate*, in which his case was profiled as a wrongful conviction and new evidence was revealed suggesting that police had rushed to judgment in performing an overly hasty investigation.

Federal officials began reviewing the case in 2001 after Truscott and attorneys from the Association in Defense of the Wrongly Convicted made an appeal to the federal justice minister, who appointed former Quebec Judge Fred Kaufman to assess the case. After a lengthy investigation Kaufman's report was released on November 29, 2005. The report stated that there was probably a miscarriage of justice in Truscott's case.

This assertion was endorsed earlier on October 28, 2004, when federal minister of justice Irwin Kotler referred the case to the Ontario Court of Appeal, telling the court that there was a reasonable basis to conclude that a miscarriage of justice had occurred in Truscott's case. Kotler had by then reviewed Kaufman's report.

Debate centered on the original pathology report made by coroner John Penistan, who fixed the time of death on the evening when the victim was with Truscott. But other pathologists, reviewing the case decades later, took issue with that conclusion. With the consent of her family, the girl's remains were exhumed on April 6, 2006. Medical examiners reported that they found no DNA evidence in the body that might have exonerated Truscott.

Several witnesses by then, all of them children at the time of the crime, altered or recanted their original statements to police, so that this testimony became useless in determining Truscott's guilt. Most importantly, more than one adult witness had seen a strange man parked in a yellow car close to where the girl's body was later found. One of those witnesses, Bob Lawson, a farmer who owned the property where the body was discovered, said he initially reported seeing this man to guards at the Royal Canadian Air Force Base near Clinton, but they dismissed his report.

Everything then focused on the actual time of death. On June 29, 2006, forensic entomologist Sherah Van Laerhoven told a court of appeal that in her examination of the case, flesh flies had not begun laying eggs or larvae on Harper's body until about 11:00 A.M., June 10, 1959, making it too late for Truscott to have been her killer. This challenged the original time of death fixed by John Penistan, which allowed Truscott to have killed the girl before returning home that night.

On July 7, 2006, renowned pathologist Bernard Knight testified that, after reviewing all available evidence, he had concluded that Penistan's pathology case against Truscott was without merit. Knight, who had written one of the standard works on pathology and was considered to be one of the world's foremost authorities on the subject, threw out Penistan's use of stomach content to pinpoint Harper's time of death: "It's so inaccurate, it's hardly worth doing. There are so many errors in it that it's impossible to give an accurate time of death."

All of the evidence pointed to Truscott's actual innocence, but he had not received official exoneration from Canadian officials at the time of this writing. Officials and forensic experts debated his case in a seemingly endless reluctance to make closure, with an apprehensive view to the staggering

**Bernard Webster, wrongly convicted in Maryland on faulty evidence from a forensic expert.** *Innocence Project, New York.*

compensation that might result. Most believe Truscott to be innocent, including this author, but the judicial system of Canada had the last word and it remained silent.

Although DNA could not be applied to vindicate Truscott, it has exonerated dozens of others around the world. As DNA testing was developed into a reliable forensic science, many an innocent person went to prison after juries relied on other forensic experts whose findings amounted to little more than guesswork. In the 1983 trial of Bernard Webster, who was charged with break-in and rape in Towson, Maryland, the previous year, a forensic serologist claimed to have matched Webster's semen to the crime, but that testimony proved to be misleading and served only to support the prosecutor's case.

Webster was sent to prison for thirty years, but in October 2002 DNA testing proved that he was not a donor of the biological evidence found in the case. Consequently he was released after spending twenty years behind bars for a crime he did not commit. A serologist providing faulty forensic science evidence also largely brought about the conviction of Anthony Michael Green in 1988 for a rape that occurred in that same year in Cleveland, Ohio. That "expert" testified that a washcloth containing sperm from the rapist was definitely linked to Green, who was sentenced to between twenty to fifty years in prison.

In 2001, Forensic Science Associates, at the request of the Innocence Project, conducted DNA testing on the washcloth and reported that Green was excluded as the donor of the spermatozoa found on it. Green, thirty-five, who had been imprisoned for thirteen years, was released on October 9, 2001, and officially exonerated on October 18, 2001. Green, by 2004, had received settlements of more than $2.6 million in compensation for his wrongful conviction and imprisonment.

Two years after Green's Ohio conviction, a serologist in Massachusetts testified in the case against Marvin Mitchell, a black man accused of abducting an eleven-year-old girl from a bus and raping her in Dorchester, Massachusetts, on September 22, 1988. Mitchell was picked up the next day as the victim was driven about her neighborhood in a police car and randomly selected him as her assailant, although she had originally described the attacker as clean shaven and Mitchell wore a mustache and goatee.

At Mitchell's 1990 trial, David Brody of the Boston police crime laboratory admitted that serology tests excluded Mitchell from being the donor of the sperm in the rape kit, but then went on to say that he could not be excluded as a possible suspect. Due to this extraordinary and contradictory testimony, Mitchell was convicted of forcible sexual intercourse and forcible unnatural sexual intercourse on January 23, 1990. He received a sentence of nine to twenty-five years in prison.

After all appeals failed, David Kelston and attorney Noah Rosmann took Mitchell's case and had postconviction DNA testing performed by Cellmark Diagnostics in 1997, which excluded him as being a donor to the rape kit, officially refuting the statements of David Brody. Mitchell's conviction was vacated by the Suffolk superior court on April 23, 1997, and prosecutors dropped all charges against him the following month. He was free after serving more than seven years in prison.

In the past two decades many forensic experts, or those who claimed to be experts, were proven to be incompetents or frauds whose courtroom testimony sent innocent persons to prison. Pamela Fish was one such "expert." In 1988, Fish testified in the case against Donald Reynolds and Billy Wardell, both black, who had been accused of robbing and raping a University of Chicago student and attempting to rape another student in 1986, both victims being white. Both men had been identified by one of the victims, although it was Fish's testimony that would send both men to prison.

Fish, who worked as a serologist for the Chicago police crime lab, stated that the semen recovered from one of the victims could only have come from 38 percent of the male population, and that included Reynolds. The truth was that more than 80 percent of black males could have been the source. Fish suppressed evidence produced at the Chicago police crime lab by forensic expert Maria Pulling showing that hair samples taken from the victim did not match either Reynolds or Wardell. Fish's "positive" testimony clinched the conviction for prosecutors.

Both defendants had requested DNA testing in the case, but the motion was denied by Cook County circuit court Judge Arthur J. Ciseslik. When sentencing Reynolds and Wardell, Ciseslik gratuitously stated, "You weren't satisfied with [robbing] the victims. You were going to have some fun with some white girls." He sentenced them each to sixty-nine years in prison.

On appeal, the higher court ruled that Ciseslik was within his rights to deny the DNA testing, but his remark about "white girls" was racist and might have influenced the severity of the sentence. The sentences for both defendants were reduced to fifty-five years each. They remained behind bars for nine years until postconviction DNA testing was granted, the 1997 results showing that both Reynolds and Wardell were innocent.

Prosecutors protested the reversal on the grounds that eyewitness testimony in the case was more meritorious than the scientific evidence. This was a startling and illogical statement since it is widely known that eyewitness identification, more than any other source, has brought about the greatest number of wrongful convictions throughout history. It was not known if prosecutors, in taking that weak stance, were actually minimizing Fish's original testimony, which DNA utterly disproved. Prosecutors finally conceded that Reynolds and Wardell were innocent on November 16, 1997, when Judge Daniel J. Kelley vacated their convictions and ordered their release from prison.

Pamela Fish was also instrumental in bringing about the wrongful convictions of three other Illinois men, all black and all innocent—John Willis, Marion Pendleton, and Dana Holland. Willis had been accused of committing a number of robberies and rapes in Chicago in 1989 and 1990 and was convicted of two of the rapes in 1992 and 1993, based on shaky eyewitness reports. Fish testified in one rape case against Willis that tests on the biological evidence recovered from the victim were inconclusive, a falsehood in that serology tests at the Chicago police crime lab had already excluded Willis from being the perpetrator.

Willis's appeals were denied, even after he informed the court that he had learned the identify of the real culprit, Dennis McGruder. In 1999, however, DNA testing in both rape cases showed that Willis was not the donor of the spermatozoa. He was released after serving seven years in prison. McGruder was identified as the real perpetrator of both of crimes after the DNA tests were run through the DNA database. He pleaded guilty and was sentenced to prison.

Dana Holland was accused of committing two crimes in February 1993 in Chicago. The first offense occurred when two black men attempted to rob and rape thirty-eight-year-old Ella Wembley on February 8, 1993. She appeared with blood running from knife wounds in her neck and face when she flagged down a police car at Ashland Avenue and 79th Street. She was taken to Holy Cross Hospital and told officers en route that two men had attempted to abduct and rape her, but she fought them off and fled after one of the men slashed her with a box cutter.

The second offense occurred on February 22, 1993, when officers entered an alley off 77th and Paulina streets, where they found a woman being raped in the backseat of

**Dana Holland, wrongly convicted on the shabby evidence of serologist Pamela Fish.** *Center on Wrongful Convictions/ Northwestern University/ Jennifer Linzer.*

a car. The woman, who was pregnant, broke loose and fled to the arms of police, while her black assailant jumped out of the car and fled in the opposite direction.

An officer followed the tracks left by the attacker in the snow to an apartment building on Paulina Street. There the officer saw Dana Holland dumping garbage into a can. Holland was taken into custody while his apartment building was searched. An officer found a pair of wet gym shoes he said belonged to Holland and seemed to fit the tracks in the snow trailing from the scene of the crime. Holland was brought before the rape victim, twenty-two-year-old Dionne Stanley, who initially said Holland was not the assailant. A few minutes later, she changed her mind and accused him of the attack. He was charged with aggravated criminal assault.

Police investigating the February 9, 1993, attack found a wallet left by Wembley in the backseat of the car where she had been briefly held before escaping. The car was traced to its owner, Gordon Bolden, who was Holland's uncle, but had been registered under the name of Jerald Bolden, who was also a nephew of Gordon Bolden. Jerald and Gordon Bolden, along with Holland, all lived at the same address on Paulina Street. On March 6, 1993, Wembley identified thirty-one-year-old Gordon Bolden and Holland as the two men who had attacked her, and both were charged with armed robbery and attempted murder.

Bolden and Holland waived a jury trial and went before Cook County circuit court Judge David A. Erickson for the Wembley attack in February 1995. Wembley identified the two men as her attackers, explaining that they had forced her into the front seat of a car while she was waiting at a bus stop. Inside the car, she resisted and Holland slashed her repeatedly with the box cutter. Despite her bleeding injuries, she escaped the car and ran three blocks to find a police car.

Bolden refused to take the witness stand, but Holland was eager to establish his innocence, testifying that he had nothing to do with the Wembley attack. He had been arrested for that offense only because he had been charged in the Stanley rape two weeks later and that Bolden had committed the Wembley assault with another man. Holland also stated that, in the Stanley rape, it was Bolden alone who had assaulted the woman and left his sperm at the scene of the crime.

Prosecutors wrongfully mixed the Wembley and Stanley cases, when, in summation, they stated that the evidence in the Stanley case corroborated Wembley's identification of Holland, but there was no corroborative evidence to convict Bolden. Judge Erickson found Bolden not guilty and Holland guilty. Judge Erickson accepted the prosecution's argument that evidence in the separate Stanley case (the wet gym shoes), for which Holland had not yet been convicted, was enough corroboration to convict Holland in the Wembley attack. Before being led back to jail, Holland pleaded with his uncle, Bolden, to "clear me out of this . . . it's my life!" Bolden remained silent.

On March 24, 1995, Holland was sentenced to twenty-eight years in prison for the Wembley attack, and he served more than two years before being tried for the second offense, the Stanley rape. He opted for a bench trial in April 1997 before Cook County circuit court Judge Themis N. Karnezis. At that trial, prosecutors did not depend on the wet gym shoes to convict Holland but relied on a report by Pamela Fish, a serological analyst who worked for the Chicago police department crime lab. In her report, filed seven months after Holland had been sentenced in the Wembley case, Fish stated that the amount of semen recovered in the Stanley case was insufficient for DNA testing.

In making this false statement, Fish undoubtedly knew that the evidence in the Stanley case was sufficient for PCR (polymerase chain reaction) DNA testing, the very type of DNA testing that had brought about the exoneration of fifteen wrongly convicted persons, including two in Illinois, Steven Linscott (Chapter X) and Gary Dotson (Chapter XIII). Based on Fish's report, Judge Karnezis denied a defense motion to have the biological evidence DNA tested. The prosecution therefore relied on the testimony of Stanley to bring about Holland's second conviction, which, unorthodox as it was, had predicated his first conviction without the second conviction being on record.

Stanley, however, proved to be a truculent witness. She had given birth to a child and moved to Milwaukee, Wisconsin, refusing to testify in Holland's 1997 trial. She was arrested under orders from prosecutors and brought to the Cook County jail, where she was held as a material witness. Stanley remained in that jail for thirty days before going to court to testify against Holland. She admitted to defense attorneys that she had initially said Holland was not her attacker, but then went on to identify him as that assailant, a man who had raped her three times.

Gordon Bolden then appeared for Holland. He testified that he had sex with Stanley but had not raped her, that the sex was consensual. He knew, of course, that he could not be prosecuted under the law, which at that time restricted prosecution to three years from the time of the crime under the then present statute of limitations. (That law was later eliminated in regard to DNA cases.) Bolden also stated that the wet gym shoes found by police were his. Holland then took the stand to say that he had been awakened at 6:00 A.M. on February 22, 1993, when his uncle, Bolden, entered the apartment building where he lived and he gathered up some garbage to dump it outside, which is where and when police arrested him for the Stanley rape.

Lauren Freeman, assistant state's attorney, told the court that the testimony from Bolden and Holland was "absolutely preposterous" and that both men had "made a mockery of the court" in providing such statements. Judge Karnezis found Holland guilty and sentenced him to ninety years in prison, thirty years for each charge against him, which Holland would begin serving after completing his twenty-eight year sentence for the Wembley attack, a total of 118 years in prison.

After all appeals failed, Holland wrote to the Center on Wrongful Convictions at Northwestern

University, which undertook his case. A team of law students went to work on the case—Ann Jerris, Anne Hunter, John Capone, Steve Heiser, Ashley Brandt, Brian Dunn, Greg Swygert, Jacquie Johnson, and Erin Smith. They located the evidence in the Stanley case, which was the linchpin to Holland's conviction in the Wembley case, and the center's staff attorney, Karen Daniel, filed a motion for postconviction DNA testing. Judge William S. Wood accepted the motion and on July 30, 2002, ordered Orchid Cellmark of Princeton, New Jersey, to conduct DNA testing.

On September 23, 2002, Kristin D. Koch, an analyst for Orchid Cellmark, announced that the results from the DNA testing of the biological evidence in the Stanley case excluded Holland as being the donor of the spermatozoa. The report refuted the 1995 statements of Pamela Fish, who had insisted that there was insufficient evidence available for such testing. Further DNA testing was done on the same evidence, and the same results were announced.

Gordon Bolden further provided a signed statement to the law students that he was the driver of the car when another unnamed person attacked Wembley and that Holland had had nothing to do with that crime either. Exonerated of the Stanley rape, Holland was nevertheless retried on the Wembley case in June 2003. Wembley again testified, but she gave uncertain statements that were shown as such in cross-examination by defense attorneys Karen Daniel and Thomas Geraghty, director of the Bluhm Legal Clinic at the Northwestern law school, who represented Holland.

Wembley had stated that Bolden was the driver, and the second man who slashed her was lighter-skinned and lighter in weight than Bolden. Holland was darker toned and heavier than Bolden at the time of the crime, factors emphasized by the defense. Cook County circuit court Judge James B. Linn, although he made no mention of Fish's false statements about the biological evidence in the case, determined at this bench trial that Stanley's statements could not be corroborated and that though he believed her description of the attack against her,

Marion Pendleton, wrongly convicted on misrepresentations by serologist Pamela Fish. *Innocence Project, New York.*

he had a reasonable doubt about Holland being her attacker. He acquitted Holland, who was released on June 6, 2003, after spending ten years in prison.

Pamela Fish was involved in several other cases where her testimony, or the lack of it, helped send innocent persons to prison. By the time her egregious testimony was revealed in the Holland case, Fish had already been shown to be grossly incompetent, at least, in the convictions of four Chicago youths—Marcellius Bradford, Calvin Ollins, Larry Ollins, and Omar Saunders—who were wrongfully sent to prison for the rape and murder of Lori Roscetti, a Chicago medical student. (See Chapter V, "Conviction by Coercion.") Marion Pendleton was another victim of Fish's statements. He had been accused of abducting a nurse from a bus stop on Chicago's South Side on October 3, 1992, and dragging the woman into an abandoned building where he robbed and raped her at gunpoint.

Although the victim identified Pendleton, a black man, as her assailant, there were many discrepancies in her description of the attacker. She initially said that the rapist weighed 170 pounds, where Pendleton weighed 135 pounds. DNA testing was not done in the case because Chicago police crime lab analyst Pamela Fish said there was not enough evidence in the rape kit taken from the victim to provide reliable testing. Pendleton was convicted in 1996 and sent to prison for twenty years.

Like Holland before him, Pendleton was championed by the Center on Wrongful Convictions at the Northwestern University law school, which filed a motion for postconviction DNA testing. The biological evidence that Fish had said in 1996 was insufficient for DNA testing was indeed sufficient. DNA tests showed that Pendleton was innocent of raping the nurse in 1992, and, on the announced results of that testing, was released from prison on November 30, 2006. On December

8, 2006, his conviction was vacated, and prosecutors announced his exoneration by stating that they had dropped all charges against him.

An unrelated but just as muddled case involving gross forensic misconduct occurred in West Virginia. A nurse was attacked in Rand, West Virginia, on December 16, 1984, as she was walking home from work. The victim identified William O'Dell Harris in a police lineup and later at his 1987 trial. She originally told police that she was acquainted with Harris, who lived in her neighborhood. Harris was arrested and charged with first-degree sexual assault on July 25, 1985. He was a juvenile at the time, but the state's motion to transfer the case to adult status was granted on May 16, 1986. He did not go to trial for almost three years after the offense.

At his trial, Harris insisted that he was innocent, but he was identified in court by the victim, and Frederick Salem Zain, chief serologist for the West Virginia state police, emphatically testified that the genetic markers in the semen left by the attacker matched those of Harris and only 5.9 percent of the population. Harris was convicted of second-degree sexual assault by a jury after a four-hour deliberation. On October 18, 1987, he was sentenced to ten to twenty years in prison.

After losing all appeals, Harris's prospects suddenly brightened on November 10, 1993, when the West Virginia Supreme Court of Appeals authorized special habeas corpus proceedings on any case involving Fred Zain, who would later be discredited as a forensic authority for falsifying and fabricating evidence in more than 130 cases (some later stated as many as 4,500 cases) from 1979 to 1989, including many murder and rape cases.

In 1989, Zain left West Virginia and moved to Texas, where he became San Antonio's chief

William O'Dell Harris, wrongly convicted on testimony of failed serologist Fred Zain. *Innocence Project, New York.*

serologist, reportedly falsely testifying in many cases that also resulted in wrongful convictions. After three years in that office, he was fired and retired to Florida. He was later indicted on perjury charges but was never convicted of his extensive corruptive forensic practices. In many instances, Zain never performed tests and simply made up his testimony in capital cases out of whole cloth. Where the conscientious Virginia serologist Mary Ann Burton posthumously brought about the exoneration of many wrongly convicted persons, the conscienceless serologist Zain sent many more innocent persons to prison.

On May 1, 1995, Dr. David Bing of the Center for Blood Research Laboratories reported that DNA testing excluded William O'Dell Harris as the donor of the spermatozoa found on the victim. On October 10, 1995, his conviction was vacated. He had served seven years in prison and one year in home confinement while forensic testing was being performed. His exoneration would be followed by the release of several more persons who had been victimized by Fred Zain's false testimony, including Gerald Wayne Davis and his father, Dewey Davis.

A Kanawha County woman who knew the Davis family claimed that when she went to their home to do some laundry on February 18, 1986, Gerald Davis took her to his bedroom and raped her on his waterbed. Chiefly based on her positive identification and the forensic testimony of Fred Zain, who said that spermatozoa found on the victim was linked to Davis, Gerald Davis was convicted and sentenced to prison for fourteen to thirty-five years. His father, Dewey Davis, who allegedly stood by and did nothing while his son attacked the woman, was also convicted and given a ten- to twenty-year sentence.

Gerald Wayne Davis, wrongly convicted on testimony from failed expert Fred Zain. *Innocence Project, New York.*

Since Fred Zain had been involved in the case,

DNA testing was conducted, which stated that Davis was not linked to the rape. Prosecutors refused to accept this exoneration and retried Davis in 1995, stating that he had not ejaculated during the rape and therefore the DNA results did not apply. A jury refuted that claim and acquitted Davis on December 4, 1995. All charges against his father, Dewey Davis, were dropped. Both men spent eight years behind bars.

Dewey Davis, father of Gerald Davis, also wrongly convicted on Zain's faulty testimony. *Innocence Project, New York.*

Zain had also testified in the case of Glen Woodall, who was convicted of sexually attacking two women in Huntington, West Virginia, in 1987. Both victims identified Woodall, a gravedigger, from his "cemetery" smell, they said. He was found guilty by a jury on July 8, 1987, of sexual assault, kidnapping, and aggravated robbery and was given two life sentences. But when Zain's credibility was challenged, Woodall's attorneys sought postconviction DNA testing, which proved that Woodall was not linked to the two attacks. He was released on May 4, 1992, the first person exonerated of a conviction largely brought about by the false statements of Fred Zain. Woodall was later given $1 million in compensation.

Yet another Zain victim was James Richardson, convicted in 1989 of murder and rape. Zain positively stated that Richardson was directly linked to the murder and rape, while reporting that his "findings" excluded three other suspects. DNA testing in 1996 completely disproved Zain and exonerated Richardson, who received $2 million in compensation for having spent nine years of a life sentence behind bars. In its special report on Fred Zain, the West Virginia

Glen Woodall, wrongly convicted on the false statements of serologist Fred Zain. *Innocence Project, New York.*

Supreme Court of Appeals stated that Zain's misconduct, in more than 130 cases, involved "overstating the strength of results . . . reporting inconclusive results as conclusive," and "repeatedly altering laboratory records" that were "the result of systematic practice rather than an occasional inadvertent error." Further, the court stated that Zain's "supervisors may have ignored or concealed complaints of his misconduct."

Zain was also instrumental in wrongfully sending Gilbert Alejandro to prison for twelve years, following a 1990 conviction for aggravated sexual assault in Uvalde County, Texas, in that same year. The victim in that case was attacked in her apartment while the assailant held a pillow to her face. The victim identified Alejandro from a police composite sketch and later in a police lineup. Her testimony was in question, but Fred Zain testified in open court that he had positively matched Alejandro's biological profile in his DNA testing. It was later determined that Zain had not even completed his examination of the rape kit evidence when he gave that testimony.

A subsequent and reliable DNA test was made, and it showed that Alejandro was not the donor of the spermatozoa found in the crime. His conviction was vacated, and he was exonerated and released in 1994, after having served three years in prison, a sentence mostly based on the misstatements of Fred Zain. Though DNA has become the greatest scientific tool in reliably identifying the right person from the wrong person in any criminal case where such science can be brought to bear, its validity and credibility lie within the hands of the DNA experts supervising and analyzing the results of its tests. In the many criminal cases reviewed by such people as Pamela Fish and Fred Zain, DNA was, unfortunately, held by the wrong hands.

# Chronology

Note: More than 560 additional wrongful conviction cases not covered in the main text of this work appear in this Chronology. Entries are shown by year of conviction. Some of the entries in this Chronology, as is the case for a few illustrative main text entries, profile those who were not released from prison, including some who were executed, but who were believed innocent of the crimes for which they were convicted. Others, as is also the case with some main text entries, were released after having been wrongly convicted, but those convictions were overturned on technical legalities that do not necessarily signify "actual innocence." The names of all wrongly convicted persons appear in boldface in all entries for this Chronology.

**590 BC:** Subject of an apocryphal book, **Susanna** (or Susannah) was falsely charged with adultery by Jewish elders. Convicted, she was ostracized and subjected to the death penalty by stoning. The wife of Joachim, she was later exonerated by Daniel during the Hebrews' captivity in Babylonia. Her false accusers, who had lusted after her, were put to death.

**AD 385: Priscillian** (or Priscillia) was a religious reformer who established the Priscillianist religious sect. He was an ordained priest and consecrated bishop of Avila, Spain, but the synod of Saragossa excommunicated him for heresy in 380. He was wrongly convicted and sentenced to death for sorcery, and he and other leaders of the sect were executed in 385.

**524:** Philosopher **Anicius Manlius Severinus Boethius** (c.480–524) was accused of plotting against Theodoric the Great, king of the Ostrogoths. He was wrongly convicted of treason and imprisoned at Pavia in 524. While awaiting his execution, he wrote the seminal work of his career, *The Consolation of Philosophy*.

**1315:** Personal favorite of Philip the Fair of France, **Enguerrand de Marigny** (1260–1315) quickly fell out of favor when Philip died in 1314. He was seized by feudal lords and, after a wrongful conviction, led to the gallows for practicing witchcraft and sorcery on April 30, 1315.

**1324:** By 1324, **Alice Kyteler** was a four-time bride and a three-time widow. All three of her husbands had died of a mysterious disease with strikingly similar symptoms: before they died, the nails fell off their fingers and toes, and they went prematurely bald. The deaths began in 1302, when Alice's first husband, William Outlawe, died suddenly, followed by Adam le Blund in 1311, and Richard de Valle shortly after. All three men were wealthy and left their money to Kyteler. In 1324, Kyteler was living in the village of Kilkenny, Ireland, when her latest husband, Sir John le Poer, became ill and his hair began falling out. Relatives of her dead husbands became suspicious and told Sir John that Kyteler was slowly killing him. On their request, he forced his way into her bedroom and reportedly found an array of poisons and items for satanic worship and witchcraft. Sir John immediately summoned authorities from the Catholic Diocese to investigate. Kyteler and several others, including a son from her first marriage, William Outlawe, and her servant, **Petronilla de Meath**, were charged with practicing witchcraft. Kyteler refused to appear before the bishop for formal proceedings. A group of her supporters held the bishop at bay inside his home at Kilkenny Castle. For eighteen days, they protested his actions, charging him with defamation of character. Kyteler fled to England. At her trial, Kyteler was found guilty in absentia. Her son begged for reconciliation with the Church and was released. Petronilla de Meath, however, confessed under torture, claiming that Kyteler had taught her about satanic worship. Meath was condemned for witchcraft and executed. The Kyteler case marked the first time charges of witchcraft were brought in Ireland, and Petronilla de Meath was the first woman burned at the stake in Ireland for allegedly practicing witchcraft.

**1391:** The first secular trial in Europe for witchcraft took place in Paris at the Grand Chatelet Criminal Court beginning on October 29, 1390. The proceedings were public, almost two dozen lawyers and judges were consulted in an extensive appeals process, and the degree of guilt of the defendants was debated and carefully delineated, with specific acts charged as witchcraft. The trial ended with two convicted witches being burned alive on August 19, 1391. The deposition of Jehan de Ruilly, which charged that **Jehenne de Brigue,** also known as La Cordire, had used sorcery to heal him and was a witch, started the trial. When diagnosed with a week to live, Ruilly had been told by Jehenne that he was under a spell cast by Gilette, with whom he had two children. Helping him make a wax doll of Gilette, Jehenne denied any knowledge of witchcraft when Ruilly recovered and said he had been "unhexed" by Jehenne.

Sentenced to die by burning, de Brigue was given a postponement based on the judgment that she was pregnant. When this proved untrue, she appealed her case to the Parlement of Paris, and the trial was reopened on August 2, 1391. When the court decided that Jehenne was holding back, she was tortured into a confession. Ruilly's wife, Macette de Ruilly, was implicated in the accused woman's statements. Arrested, Macette initially denied everything but confessed after being tortured on the rack. Her case was joined with that of de Brigue. Both reiterated their confessions, most probably after having been tortured again. Their trial was reviewed by the Parlement of Paris and passed under the scrutiny of several judges and lawyers before the defendants were sentenced and burned together on August 19, 1391.

**1419: Joan of Navarre** (Joanna, 1370–1437) married John V, the Duke of Brittany, in 1386, with whom she had eight children. After her husband's death in 1399, she married England's Henry IV and maintained a friendship with her stepson after he succeeded his father. During a period of anti-French sentiment in Britain, she was wrongly imprisoned for witchcraft, 1419–1422.

**1435: Agnes Bernauer** (c.1410–1435) was falsely arrested and wrongly convicted of witchcraft and exe-

cuted on October 12, 1435, by being drowned in the Danube at Straubing, Bavaria, under orders from Ernest, Duke of Bavaria–Munich after it was revealed that she married his son, Albert. She was later honored by her husband with a marbled grave, and a festival in her honor occurs every four years.

**1441:** British court astronomer **Roger Bolingbroke** was accused of sorcery and attempting to conjure up spirits of the deceased in July 1441. Though he renounced his faith in the black arts in the presence of the Archbishop of Canterbury, Bolingbroke was found guilty by the King's Counsel and wrongfully hanged and quartered at Tyburn in 1441. Bolingbroke claimed that his actions were guided by **Margerie Jourdemayne,** who was known as "The Witch of Rye" since 1430, when she had been imprisoned at Windsor Castle for sorcery. Released in 1432, Jourdemayne disappeared for eight years, resurfacing in time to be ensnared in Bolingbroke's tales. Bolingbroke also implicated **Eleanor** (or Elianor) **Cobham,** daughter of Reginald Cobham, Lord of Stirborough. Because of Bolingbroke's statements, the young woman was wrongfully convicted of witchcraft, heresy, and treason and was made to offer public penance in the streets of London before beginning a life prison sentence in Chester Castle, Kenilworth (some accounts state that she was sent to the Isle of Man Prison). Cobham was the Duchess of Gloucester. She and her husband, Humphrey, Duke of Gloucester, had many enemies, some of whom disapproved of Eleanor's actions. Others were simply conspiring against the duke, who had angered the bishops when he accused Cardinal Beaufort, Bishop of Winchester, and the Archbishop of York of malfeasance, when Henry VI was a minor. Bolingbroke committed perjury in making his remarks about Eleanor at the instigation of political enemies, as well as to save himself from execution, an effort that failed to save his life. Eleanor stood trial for allegedly directing two others to make a wax statue in the image of Henry and to put it over a slow-burning fire on July 23, 1441, when she, Jourdemayne, and Thomas Southwell reportedly gathered in a churchyard at Paul's Cross, with effigies of demons and of the king. The slowly melting wax images were supposed to cause Henry's similar slow death. If Henry had died, her husband, as the closest heir, would have ascended to the throne. Found guilty, Eleanor was sentenced on November 9, 1441, to do public penance three times in London, in which she was to bring offerings to the alters of three churches, before going behind bars for life. Jourdemayne was found guilty as a traitor and a relapsed heretic and was burned at the stake.

**1453: Jacques Coeur** (c.1395–1456), a merchant who built a fortune through commercial trading and manufacturing, became counselor to France's Charles VII and administered the royal finances. Among his many creditors were members of the aristocracy and the royal family. In 1451, nobles schemed to seize his estates, and he was falsely accused of treason. He was wrongly convicted at Poitiers, France, on June 5, 1453, and condemned, but reprieved and sent almost penniless in exile to Rome.

**1485:** Imprisoned in the Tower of London by Henry VII in 1485, **Edward, Earl of Warwick** (1475–1499), who was thought by some historians to be simpleminded, was falsely accused of conspiracy for which he was wrongly convicted and subsequently executed along with Perkin Warbeck, who had attempted to escape his tower imprisonment. During his imprisonment, rumors were rampant that Edward had escaped, and that he had been crowned in Ireland; to dispel these rumors, Edward was exhibited for one day in 1487 at the Tower of London, officials announcing that Lambert Simnel had impersonated Edward to illegally acquire the Irish crown. Edward was kept thereafter incognito in the Tower of London for eleven years until he was beheaded on November 28, 1499.

**1529:** In 1529, twenty-seven-year-old **Desle la Mansenée** (c.1502–1529) was tortured for witchcraft. When she could stand no more, the young French woman told the authorities what they wanted to hear. "Confessing" to such actions befitting a witch, Mansenée said she had denied her Catholic faith, brought on hailstorms, flown through the air on an anointed stick, danced at the sabbat, and used black powder to poison cattle. With that, the youthful wife and mother was convicted of homicide, renouncing the Catholic religion, and committing heresy. Witchcraft was not even mentioned in her verdict or sentence. The inquisitor-general of Besancon exacted several accusations from the citizens of Anjeux. Many accusations came willingly from those interrogated. Others, like the one that came from Mansenée's son, in which he said his mother went backwards on a twisted willow stick to the sabbat, were undoubtedly forced. Promising anonymity, the inquisitor-general collected the necessary gossip and hearsay, arrested the woman, and tortured her. Hoping to end her suffering, condemned Mansenée confessed to being a witch and even provided the names of accomplices. On December 18,

1529, Mansenée was hanged and her body burned on wrongful convictions of homicide and heresy.

**1581: James Douglas** (1525–1581), a powerful Scottish clan leader, who was the Fourth Earl of Morton and regent of Scotland during the minority of King James VI of Scotland, also King James I of England (1566–1625), had brought about the abdication of Mary, Queen of Scots (1542–1587), the mother of James VI-I (his father being Mary's second husband, Lord Darnley). Douglas was falsely accused and wrongfully convicted of murdering Lord Darnley (Henry Stuart, Duke of Albany, 1545–1567), second husband of Mary, Queen of Scots, through the collusive efforts of the ambitious Esmé Stuart (First Duke of Lennox, First Earl of Lennox, 1542–1583) and king James VI, resulting in Douglas's execution by decapitation on June 2, 1581, at Edinburgh, Scotland. Douglas had admitted that Lord Bothwell (James Hepburn, Duke of Orkney, Fourth Earl of Bothwell, 1534–1578), third husband of Mary, Queen of Scots, had told him the "design" of Darnley's assassination, but Douglas emphatically denied that he had taken part in that murder in Edinburgh on February 9, 1567 (the bodies of Darnley and one of his servants were found the following day). Douglas's head was placed on display for eighteen months before being reunited with its body.

**1587: William Davison** (c.1541–1608) was employed by Queen Elizabeth I as Scottish secretary, 1586–1587, and whom she falsely accused and imprisoned, 1587–1589, for obtaining her signature with unnecessary haste on the death warrant of Mary, Queen of Scots. Elizabeth made this charge so as to make it appear that she had been unreasonably pressured into having Mary beheaded, when, in truth, Elizabeth had conspired with Robert Cecil and Francis Walsingham to wrongly condemn Mary and bring about her death in order to remove a threat to her throne.

**1589:** The hysterical testimony of three children doomed to death on the gallows in April 1593 an old woman, her husband, and her daughter. The unfounded charges of witchcraft were brought against seventy-six-year-old **Alice Samuel** of Warboys, in Huntingdon, by the three precocious daughters of Robert Throckmorton. On November 10, 1589, ten-year-old Jane Throckmorton developed the symptoms of what appeared to be influenza. Mrs. Samuel stopped by to pay her respects, and it was not long afterward that the other girls became similarly afflicted. Jane's accusations of witchcraft were given credence by Dr. Philip Barrow of Cambridge University, who examined the children. In September 1590, the wife of Sir Henry Cromwell, grandfather of the Protector (Oliver), encountered Alice Samuel. She died ten months later after describing "bad dreams" and physical suffering she had endured. These afflictions were blamed on Samuel, who was indicted for witchcraft along with her husband and daughter. The three were tried at Huntingdon and found guilty after five hours' deliberation. They were hanged forthwith.

**1590**: **Rebecca Lemp**, the mother of six young children and the wife of accountant Peter Lemp, was one of thirty-two prominent women burned for witchcraft at Nordlingen, Swabia, in 1590. Unlike alleged witches from other districts whom the clergy attacked, Mrs. Lemp was persecuted by lawyers, Conrad Graf and Sebastien Roettinger, who were led by Burgomaster George Pheringer. They had Mrs. Lemp jailed for witchcraft, but, in writing to her husband, she decried her innocence, stating that she would not suffer torture or death for a crime she did not commit. Mrs. Lemp's jailors tortured her on five different occasions, ultimately forcing her to confess. A second note to Lemp from his wife recanted her confession. She also wrote of needing some relief, in the form of poison, from the pain she endured. The letter was found, and the court dictated a confession letter for Mrs. Lemp. Lemp did not believe the letter, however, and petitioned the court to show mercy and release his wife. In response, Rebecca Lemp was tortured and sentenced to death. She was burned alive on September 9, 1590.

**1590**: After being tortured by her employer, a servant girl in North Berwick, Scotland, accused several people, including teacher Dr. **John Fian** (a.k.a.: John Cunningham), of an intricate witchcraft conspiracy to kill James VI. Seventy people were incriminated during the famous trials of the North Berwick Witches in 1590. Fian, singled out as the leader, was charged with witchcraft and high treason on December 26, 1590. He was accused of conspiring with the devil to wreck a ship on which the king had voyaged, of worshiping the devil, bearing the devil's mark, robbing graves, and experiencing "ecstasies and trances." When Fian refused to confess to any of the charges, he was subjected to thrawing, a procedure in which his head was bound with rope and the rope pulled in different directions. Then he was put in the "boots," a vise used to crush the legs. After being tortured with pins, Fian confessed to all of the charges, but he later retracted the confession. He then suffered more torture, including another session with the vise, but he maintained his innocence.

The king's council, as well as James VI, personally condemned Fian to death. Fian was strangled and burned in the Castle Hill of Edinburgh in late January 1591.

**1596**: Thomas Darling, fourteen, of Burton, England, claimed to have witnessed "visions of hell" after being separated from his uncle in a forest near his home. The next day, he complained of illness, and of strange green cats and angels that tormented him. A physician stated that the boy did not suffer from any physical malady, but may have suffered from a "spell." Young Thomas lent credence to the suspicions by telling of a "little old woman . . . with three warts on her face" who had bewitched him after he tipped over her egg basket. An elderly woman named **Alice Gooderidge** was seized and accused of being a witch. She was forced to implicate her husband and her mother, Elizabeth Wright, after the inquisitor nearly burned her feet off in front of an open fire. The case reached a swift conclusion when the exorcist, John Darrell, arrived in the village on May 27, 1596, to rid the boy of his "demons." Darrell was in fact a trained ventriloquist, who staged a "conversation" with a devil so that Tom Darling might be cured. Though he had admitted to staging the entire affair, Darling was physically coerced into admitting that he had been possessed and then cured by the exorcist. Gooderidge, who had been sentenced to twelve months in prison, died in her cell.

**1598**: Four members of a French family, a brother, two sisters, and a son, were condemned as werewolves and charged with practicing witchcraft in 1598, in Naizan, France. A wolf attacked the sister of a teenager, Benoit Bidel, and, as Bidel struggled with the wolf, he later said, he saw that the front paws were human hands. Because Perrenette Gandillon was in the area of the attack, she was murdered by furious peasants. Another sibling, **Pierre Gandillon**, was charged with witchcraft, lycanthropy, murder, cannibalization of men and animals, and making hail. Pierre Gandillon confessed after being tortured. His son, **Georges Gandillon**, admitted under torture to becoming a werewolf and slaughtering two goats. A sister, **Antoinette Gandillon**, was charged with becoming a werewolf, attending the sabbat, and creating hail. Pierre, Georges, and Antoinette were wrongfully convicted of the charges and burned to death.

**1601**: Accused of witchcraft by Rupprecht Silberrad, a member of a witch-hunting faction in the town council of Offenburg, Germany, **Else Gwinner** was brutally tortured on five occasions over a period of two months before she was wrongfully convicted of witchcraft and executed by being burned to death on December 21, 1601. Silberrad claimed Gwinner had used witchcraft to cause the death of Silberrad's son. The accusation was motivated by Silberrad's wish to destroy George Laubbach, Gwinner's father and Silberrad's adversary on the town council. To obtain a confession, weights were attached to Gwinner's body, thumbscrews were applied, and she was hanged by her wrists. Gwinner never confessed, not even when the judges flogged her daughter, forcing her to lie about her mother. While the thumbscrews drew an admission of copulating with a devil, she later retracted the confession. At one point, the pain of the torture became so excruciating that cold water was thrown in her face to revive her. Less than two months after Gwinner's execution, the other town councilors arrested Silberrad. This late attempt at justice proved to be in vain, for Silberrad regained his position through the intervention of the Catholic Church and continued his witch-hunts.

**1603–1630:** The Bishop of Eichstatt, Germany, Johann Christoph, led a witch-hunt in which 113 women and nine men were burned and more than 150 others were convicted of witchcraft in Germany from 1603–1630. By 1627, Christoph came under pressure from the townspeople for confiscating the property of convicted witches. In an effort to prove that his crusade was strictly religious and not personal, the bishop, after twenty-four years, stopped seizing estates. The trials often consisted of victims being arrested on the basis of circumstantial or insubstantial evidence, and then being tortured into admitting they were witches. The defendants were not allowed any legal representation, there was no testimony from witnesses, and the victims were allowed to see a priest only after being sentenced. One such defendant was **Anna Kaser**, who was charged with attending a sabbat, a meeting of witches, in 1629. The charges came out of forced confessions of previous trial victims. After hours of brutal torture, Kaser confessed to being a witch. She was beheaded and burned at Neuberg.

**1618: Margaret Barclay** lived with her husband Archibald Dean in the town of Irvine, County of Ayrshire, England, in 1618. She did not get along with her in-laws so she went before the church court seeking arbitration in a domestic quarrel. Church officials advised her to forget about the matter and try to reconcile the differences in an amicable way. Margaret was not satisfied with this advice and continued to speak out against her in-laws. When the brother-in-law left for France in the company of the town provost Andrew Tran, Mar-

garet said she hoped the ship would sink to the bottom of the sea and that crabs would eat the passengers up. These comments were said in anger, but there was little reason to believe that Margaret Barclay had engaged in any deliberate sabotage. When a passing tramp named John Stewart reported that a vessel had sunk near Padstow, England, Barclay was accused of witchcraft. Stewart was taken to prison where he confessed under torture that Barclay had sought his aid against "such persons as had done her wrong." According to Stewart, she had fashioned a waxen model of the ship her brother-in-law sailed on and an image of Provost Tran. The demonic ceremony was witnessed by a local townswoman named Isobel Insh and her young daughter, who told of a dog emitting a strong light from its mouth, which permitted Barclay to go about her work. Stewart, Insh, and Barclay were subjected to unspeakable tortures. John Stewart committed suicide in his jail cell shortly before the trial began. Isobel Insh escaped to the church belfry, but fell off the roof and died. The accused witch Barclay was placed in a stock, and heavy iron bars were placed across her legs until she pleaded for mercy. "All I have confessed was in agony of torture, and before God, all I have spoken is false and untrue," she said. A court of elders convicted her of witchcraft. She was strangled and burned at the stake.

**1618:** Sisters **Margaret Flower** and **Philippa Flower** confessed under torture to destroying by witchcraft the eldest son of their former employer, Francis, the Earl of Rutland, who had fired the two from his employ. In her confession, Philippa told how she had stolen the right-hand glove of Lord Henry Rosse and given it to her mother, alleged witch Joan Flower. Joan Flower reportedly stroked an evil cat named Rutterkin with the glove, placed the glove in boiling water, pricked it several times, buried the glove, and spoke an oath against Rosse. The girls were tried before judges Sir Edward Bromley and Sir Henry Hobart in Lincoln and wrongfully convicted. They were executed in March 1618.

**1628:** In Germany, on June 28, 1628, **Johannes Junius** (c.1573–1628), the burgomeister of Bamberg, was examined, without torture, on the charge of witchcraft. He claimed to be wholly innocent, to have never renounced God and knew nothing of witchcraft. On June 30, 1628, thumbscrews were applied, but he still did not confess, or cry out in pain. Then came leg vices, but still no confession or pain. He was stripped and found to have a bluish mark on his right side, that, when pricked, did not draw blood. Yet, when confronted without torture on July 5, 1628, he confessed.

Junius was accused of participating in a witch gathering and was reportedly heard to have said, "I renounce God in Heaven and his host, and will henceforth recognize the Devil as my God." It was alleged that his paramour had taken him to sabbats (Black masses where the devil was worshipped), and that, when he wished to be transported, a black dog would appear at his side. He would mount it, and the dog would raise itself in the devil's name and fly off. He confessed on July 7, 1628, that two months earlier, on a day following an execution, he was at a witch dance at the Black Cross when Beelzebub had come to ridicule and taunt them. Junius was ordered to kill his son and two daughters. A week before his arrest, he had been met by the devil in the form of a goat, he said, and told that he would soon be imprisoned. On August 6, 1628, he ratified his confession, stating that he would stake his life on it. He was found guilty and burned at the stake. Before dying, Junius wrote a memorable letter to his daughter Veronica, smuggled from his prison cell by a friendly guard, which began: "Many hundred thousand good nights," and went on to apologize for making his false confessions, but emphasized that he had been horribly tortured into making his admissions.

**1631**: **Dominic Gordel** was charged in 1631 with engaging in sorcery, attending satanic gatherings, and committing acts of deviltry. Those testifying against him included four children and persons already convicted as witches. Authorities of his French village asked him if the accusations were valid, a fatal question with no way out. Gorbel answered no. His subsequent torture ran from painful thumbscrews on his hands to excruciating vise grips and to be stretched on the rack, to the eventual, intolerable, fatal burning. His defense ranged from, "Jesus, Maria. I do not even know what a sabbat is," to "I am dying! I am broken! Father everlasting, help me! I deliver myself into the hands of the good angels." Gordel's cries went unheeded as torture and interrogation intensified. The priest, who first begged to be believed, later begged to die: "I cannot take any more!" he cried. All the while, he maintained his innocence and for it eventually gained his final desire of death. In the end, the man was taken to the Tower of La Joliette near a fire with a guard, where he was burned to death.

**1645**: **Joan Williford**, **Joan Cariden**, and **Jane Holt**, known as the "Faversham Witches," were wrongly convicted and executed for witchcraft in Faversham, Kent, England, on September 29, 1645. Their deaths were mandated by the local inquisitors after Williford

was forced to "confess" to having entered into a covenant with the devil twenty years earlier. Holt, Elizabeth Harris, and Joan Argoll were named as three other witches in a case typical of the witchcraft persecutions of seventeenth-century England. Although accurate court records do not exist from that time, popularly published chapbooks detailing the Faversham witch confessions served to fan the witchcraft hysteria that spilled over into the early years of the eighteenth century.

**1647**: **Achsah Young** (or Alse Young), a resident of Windsor, Connecticut., was tried and wrongly condemned as a witch, and appears to be the first person on record in New England to be so charged. Young was hanged at Windsor on May 26, 1647. Existing records give no other details of this precedent-setting case.

**1650**: **Ann Green**, an unmarried maid working in the home of Sir Thomas Read in Duns Tew, Oxfordshire, England, miscarried in her fourth month of pregnancy as the result of the strenuous housework she was performing. Under torture, she confessed to causing the fetus's death and was convicted of murder. She was hanged at Oxford Castle on December 14, 1650. Green's body hung from the gallows and was beaten by castle guards for more than half an hour before it was cut down and the soldiers realized that she was still breathing. In an attempt to carry out the death sentence, soldiers stood on her chest and again beat her with their weapons. Afterwards, her body was taken to a physician for an autopsy (doctors could only then perform such "experimental" practices with the bodies of convicted felons), but the medical examiner determined that she was still alive. Under the doctor's care, Green recovered. Many believed her triumph over death proved her innocence, an intervention from God that provided a divine acquittal. Prosecutors attempted to retry Green, but several high-ranking officials defeated their plans, announcing that her miraculous survival proved that she had been wrongly convicted. Green was then officially acquitted of the murder of her child. Fully recovered, Ann Green was released. She later married and bore three children before her death in 1659, nine years after her failed execution.

**1652**: **Joan Peterson**, who was called "The Witch of Wapping," stood trial for witchcraft in London in 1652. Witnesses were bribed to speak against her. She was accused of making threats, and her servant testified that one night she had talked at great length with a squirrel. Others testified on her behalf, saying she could cure headaches and "unwitch" cows. Sir John Danvers, one of the judges at the trial, influenced the other justices to convict Peterson. She was found guilty, sentenced to death, and hanged at Tyburn on April 12, 1652.

**1653: Anne Bodenham** (1573–1653) was servant and mistress to Dr. Lamb, the personal physician to the Duke of Buckingham, and lived with him at his manor. Lamb practiced alchemy and magic on the side, which compelled a superstitious mob to stone him to death in the streets of London in 1640. Following the death of her benefactor, Bodenham began to capitalize on his name and reputation. She took up residence in Wiltshire, where the townspeople of Fisherton Anger looked upon her as a sorceress. Neighbors would frequently ask her to prepare special potions, deliver incantations, and foretell future events. One of her regular clients was the wife of Richard Goddard, a paranoid woman, who believed that her two daughters were trying to poison her. Goddard's wife asked Bodenham to prepare a special poison made of dried vervain and dill, which she used unsuccessfully against her daughters. In 1653, the year of her death, Bodenham began dispensing legal advice to the son-in-law of Richard Goddard. She allegedly called on demonic forces to help her in this endeavor. (The ceremony was described in Nathaniel Crouch's *Kingdom of Darkness,* published thirty-five years later in 1688.) Not long after this, Anne Bodenham's alleged sorcery came to light, when Mrs. Goddard's daughters complained that their mother had consulted a witch, who prepared a deadly potion to kill them. Ann Styles, a servant girl who acted as the go-between for Bodenham and her customers, verified their claim in order to save herself from the scaffold. She described how her employer changed herself into a black cat and wrote in the book the names of all who had sold their souls to the devil. To give credence to these accusations, Styles went into fits during Bodenham's witchcraft trial. Two witch symbols were reportedly found on Bodenham's body, the final determinant of her guilt. Anne Bodenham was hanged at Salisbury, Wiltshire.

**1661: Florence Newton,** called the "Witch of Youghal," was charged with two counts of witchcraft on March 24, 1661, in Youghal, Ireland. The first charge involved bewitching Mary Longdon, a servant girl, and the second was causing the death of David Jones. The Irish courts treated witch trials like regular criminal trials, and so the defendant was not tortured. The evidence presented in her case was certainly unreasonable by today's standards. Longdon testified that the witch (Newton), angered by some slight, had knocked her

down and kissed her. Thereafter, she had experienced visions and such symptoms as vomiting needles and being pestered by continuous showers of stones on her head. As soon as the witch of Youghal was arrested, Longdon's symptoms stopped. Newton was found guilty and probably executed, though the records are not complete.

**1662:** People living in Scotland in 1662 believed in witches. They found witches everywhere. Their preachers were witches; butchers who charged too much for meat were witches. If one's neighbor was too noisy, that neighbor was a witch. But **Isobel Gowdier** carried her belief to an extreme when she declared on April 13, 1662: "I am a witch!" Much of what people knew of witches they learned from Gowdie. She said she first became a witch in 1647 when she met the devil in an Auldearne church. Here she made a pact, denying Christian baptism and receiving the new name of Janet and the devil's mark on her shoulder. She accepted rebaptism in the blood the devil sucked from her and swore allegiance by placing one hand on her head and the other on the sole of her foot. The ceremony concluded with the devil, like a minister, reading from the pulpit. Acting in her new capacity Gowdie said she would ride on straw, crying, "Horse and hattock, in the devil's name." From that vantage point, she could shoot down any Christian who saw her and did not bless himself. Occasionally, she would turn herself into an animal by repeating a certain charm, or she might shoot elf arrows to injure or kill people. Today, psychiatrists would readily deduce that Gowdie was certifiably insane. In 1662, however, people knew her only as Witch Gowdie, who was tried and wrongly convicted for witchcraft. Court records fail to detail her ultimate fate, but she was most likely executed, the usual fate of those convicted of witchcraft in her superstitious era.

**1662:** Two elderly English women were wrongly indicted in England on charges of witchcraft. They represented just two of hundreds who were falsely accused and convicted of witchcraft. The people of Lowestoft, England, attributed great powers to the frail and aging **Rose Cullender**. The woman supposedly worked in association with another so-called witch, **Amy Duny,** in casting spells on neighborhood children. Both were later labeled the "Bury St. Edmunds Witches." A court trial before Sir Matthew Hale, who later became chief justice of England, concluded that Cullender knowingly and maliciously caused the children of Edmund Durent and Diana Bocking to vomit pins and nails. Witness Susan Chandler described how and where she found the "Devil's mark" on Cullender's body. Chandler also swore that her daughter had been bewitched, vomited pins, and screamed the name of Rose Cullender. Additional testimony indicated that Cullender threatened John Soam after his harvest cart brushed her window. Strangely, the cart overturned two or three times that same day and would no longer pass through a gate it had gone through hundreds of times before. Evidence mounted against witch Cullender, when Robert Sherringham swore that she set lice in his clothes after he accidentally damaged her house with an axle-tree. The jury was instructed by Justice Hale to decide two key points: one, were the children (who could not attend the trial because it sent them into spellbound fits) truly bewitched and, two, was it Cullender and Duny who had bewitched them? Convinced by the "evidence," the jury returned after thirty minutes with a verdict of guilty. The children immediately recovered, and the women were executed.

**1668–1669**: In July 1668, Gertrude Svensen, eighteen, accused fifteen-year-old Eric Ericson of abducting and bewitching several children from the village of Elfdale in Dalecarlia, Sweden. Her accusation sparked a series of trials and executions that displayed just how thoroughly the fear of witchcraft had penetrated seventeenth-century Europe. By May 1669, the number of accused witches had increased so rapidly that Sweden's Charles XI, in an attempt to save many people from death, asked that the accused be redeemed through the prayers of his kingdom. His plea, however, only served to heighten the witch hysteria. On August 14, 1669, a Royal Commission at Mora, Sweden, had "discovered" seventy witches, and on August 25, 1669, these wrongly convicted persons, almost all women, were burned to death en masse. Of the several "afflicted" children, fifteen were also burned, thirty-six were ordered to run the gauntlet and to receive public whippings once a week for a year, and still twenty others received lighter sentences of lashings. As word of the **Mora Witch Trials** spread, the fear of Satan was hardly quelled. Prisons throughout Sweden and Finland were filled with accused witches, until, finally, Urban Hjarne, a doctor, proved at Stockholm in 1675 that the witchcraft mania was not based on fact, but on anxious accusations. The purge ceased, though some continued to insist on sightings of and dealings with Satan.

**1670**: **Thomas Weir** had served as a major in command of troops protecting Edinburgh and also had participated in evangelical Protestant prayer meetings until 1670, when the seventy-year-old man suddenly denounced himself for crimes of witchcraft, incest, adultery, and bestiality. He also incriminated his sixty-year-old sister, **Jane Weir**. Thomas Weir's trial began on April 9, 1670, charged with adultery, bestiality, incest with his sister, Jane, and his stepdaughter, as well as the attempted rape of his sister when she was age ten. Jane Weir was also tried on charges of sorcery, incest, and consulting with devils, witches, and necromancers. Both Weirs were convicted and sentenced to be strangled and burned to death. Weir was executed on April 11, 1670, between Leith and Edinburgh, and his sister was executed the next day at the Grass Market in Edinburgh. Weir and his sister were both undoubtedly deranged and had made their confessions through intimidation and their own delusions.

**1711**: **Magee Island Witch Trial** took place on March 31, 1711, at Carrickfergus, Ireland. Like many such trials, the "evidence" was based on the convulsions or fits, which apparently attacked a teenager. Mary Dunbar, eighteen, perpetrated these fits, but the idea of witchcraft was begun before Dunbar's arrival. There was rumored to be a poltergeist in the home of James Haltridge, who lived with his wife, widowed mother, and young servant. A child also was known to have entered this house, possibly with another mischievous child. Strange noises and events, such as sheets and covers left in disarray, were said to have occurred in the bedroom, but never with someone inside the room. Haltridge is said to have frightened away the poltergeist, but it reportedly returned in February 1711. His mother, the recipient of most of the attacks, died soon after feeling a sharp pain in her back. Dunbar arrived to take care of the young Mrs. Haltridge and, after learning of the poltergeist, decided to envision her own demons and feign sickness. The girl accomplished her convulsions and vomiting with such dexterity that seven women she accused were tried for witchcraft, and an eighth narrowly escaped being tried. The evidence, other than Dunbar's testimony, consisted of articles the girl vomited in the presence of others, including pins, buttons, feathers, yarn, and other small objects. Judge Anthony Upton did not feel the women, who were all upstanding churchgoers, were guilty, but Judge James MacCartney thought differently, as did the jury, which found all guilty. The women were sentenced to one year in prison and made to appear in the pillory four times.

**1712**: The residents of Walkerne, England, were afraid of **Jane Wenham**, who was thought to be a "wise woman." Once, in 1712, the elderly woman reportedly asked Matthew Gilson, a farmhand, for some straw. When he refused to sell her any, she allegedly cast a spell on him, which caused him to fill his shirt with manure and to request straw from everyone he met. Gilson told the story to his employer, who denounced Wenham as a witch. Offended, Wenham filed a warrant for defamation of character, but the judge urged her to settle the disagreement out of court before Pastor Gardiner, the local clergyman. Gardiner, who believed in witches, told Wenham to live with her neighbors without arguments, and Gilson's employer paid a one-shilling fine for the insult. Not long afterward, the minister's servant, Anne Thorne, claimed that Wenham had caused her to suffer from a "running spell." Thorne, who had a dislocated knee, said she had been able to run until she met Wenham, and that she told Wenham she was going to Cromer to collect sticks for a fire. Thorne explained that Wenham told her to get sticks from a nearby oak tree, take off her dress and apron in order to carry the sticks, and then the woman pinned the material together to secure the load. Thorne then rushed home to the minister, screaming: "I am ruined and undone!" On Thorne's unsupported accusations, Wenham was arrested, placed in jail for several days, and searched for marks of the devil. In 1712, she stood trial, accused of "conversing familiarly with the devil in the form of a cat," and, reportedly, some "magic salve" and "magic cakes" were found in her home. After sixteen people testified against her, Wenham was convicted and she received the death penalty. Judge Powell, however, was able to secure a reprieve and a pardon for Wenham. She died in 1730.

**1716**: In early eighteenth-century England, people often practiced fraudulent "magic" to manipulate their gullible neighbors into giving them donations and gifts in order to protect themselves from harm. **Mary Hicks**, one of these primitive "sorceresses," told authorities that she and her eleven-year-old daughter, **Elizabeth Hicks**, had made a pact with the devil. Hicks was questioned after her neighbors reportedly began to vomit pins. The two illiterate females admitted under torture to devil-worship and were convicted of witchcraft. Hicks and her child were hanged at Huntington on July 28, 1716.

**1748**: Bertrand Francois Mahé La Bourdonnais (1699–1753), an honored French naval officer, whose successes included capturing Madras from Britain in 1746, was wrongly convicted of conspiracy, after a long dispute with Joseph Dupleix, French governor-general of all possessions in India. He was sentenced to the Bastille in 1748. He was vindicated, however, after two years of incarceration and released in 1750.

**1749**: Sister **Maria Renata** had devoted fifty years to the Premonstratensian convent, near Wurzburg, Germany. In 1745, one young nun, Cecilia Pistorini, was troubled by cramps, contortions, foaming at the mouth, and hallucinations, thought to be signs of demonic possession. Another older nun accused Renata of bewitching the younger sister. Renata was brought to trial before the abbot of a neighboring monastery, Father Oswald Loschert. Her rooms were searched and alleged witch salves, noxious herbs, and a sabbat-going dress were found. She was then interrogated for several months and finally whipped with a consecrated rawhide. During the ordeal, Renata confessed that, as an eight-year-old, she had given herself to Satan, at eleven had been seduced, and then learned the craft of Satanism as a teenager. She had entered the convent to effect its destruction. While there, she had bewitched several people, caused six nuns to become possessed, and desecrated the host. She was condemned on thirteen counts of sorcery, heresy, and apostasy, and defrocked on May 28, 1749. A secular court sentenced her to burn at the stake on June 21, 1749.

**1752**: Captain **Peter De la Fontaine**, a French officer, was tried in Paris in 1750 for running off with a rich man's daughter, but acquitted after the girl testified that it was her own idea. His mortal wounding of a fellow officer in a duel forced him to flee the continent. After stops in a Turkish jail and the port of Amsterdam, and a five-year sojourn in Surinam, he arrived in London. There De la Fontaine, who had acquired a sizeable fortune, met a swindler named Zannier, who claimed he was under a criminal charge and needed bond money. Convinced that Zannier owned an estate in Ireland, De la Fontaine put up the £300 bond. He never saw the money again. To add to his trouble, he married two women at the same time and was eventually arrested for bigamy. While De la Fontaine awaited trial at Newgate Prison, Zannier visited him, once again claiming friendship. The captain was so enraged that he beat the swindler with a broomstick until he was subdued by warders. Zannier, in vengeance, charged De la Fontaine with forgery. The swindler supplied false evidence to convict the Frenchman. Even though one witness testified that the forged signature appeared to be that of Zannier, De la Fontaine was wrongly convicted and sentenced to death. He was spared, but exiled to the colony of Virginia. In 1752, De la Fontaine boarded a ship full of other convicts and later went on to establish one of the first families of Virginia.

**1786**: Fourteen-year-old **Robert Cox** was dragged screaming to the gallows in Holborn, England, on December 18, 1786, for a crime he probably never committed. Cox was one of three men arrested for the murder of Duncan Robinson, who was accosted by pickpockets in Holborn on November 16, 1786, as he walked down the street with Michael Hunt. The assailants were identified as Michael Walker and Richard Payne. Hunt believed Cox was the boy he saw as the two older men attempted to make their escape. The fact that the boy was associating with a gang of robbers was enough to convict him of murder in the stabbing death of Robinson. At his trial, the judge conceded as much by stating that "though he had not struck a blow, yet it was a maxim in law that persons connected for a felonious purpose, if any evil consequences ensued, were all equally answerable for the guilt."

**1798**: While working at the Bell Inn, a roadside tavern outside of London, **John Jennings** was accused of the armed robbery of a traveler. The victim's marked coins were found in Jennings's possession, leading to his speedy trial and execution in 1798. A year later, however, it was discovered that the real robber was a man named Brunnell, the owner of the Bell Inn. Apparently, Brunnell had planted the marked coins on the sleeping Jennings, when he learned from the victim that the coins he had stolen had been marked. Only when Brunnell was sentenced to death for another crime did he confess that he had framed Jennings to protect himself.

**1803**: **Joseph Samuels** was transported to New South Wales in 1803 for the murder of a police constable. He steadfastly maintained his innocence, right up to the moment he faced the hangman on the gallows in Sydney, Australia. The assembled crowd took pity on Samuels, who said the actual murderer, a man named Simmonds, stood among them. The noisy mob demanded that Samuels be set free. The provost marshal however, ordered the "drop." The rope broke, however, and Samuels fell to the ground unconscious. After two more execution attempts failed, the marshal petitioned the governor for a reprieve. Simmonds was arrested and was later convicted of murdering the constable, and hanged. Samuels had by then been set free and, ironically, stood in the crowd, where Simmonds had earlier stood, to see the real culprit executed.

**1805**: Two Irish immigrants, thirty-four-year-old **Dominic Daley** and twenty-seven-year-old **James Halligan**, were arrested on November 12, 1805, and charged with murdering farmer Marcus Lyon, near Wilbraham, Massachusetts. Both were tried at Northampton, where a thirteen-year-old boy, Laertes Fuller, testified in court that he had seen both men with the victim's horse. The horse had been seen aimlessly wandering about three days before Lyon's body was discovered. Under the law, no one under the age of fourteen could give legal testimony, but the trial judge illegally admitted Fuller's statements. No other evidence was presented, and both men were convicted and sentenced to death. They were hanged on June 5, 1806, at Northampton, before a crowd of more than 15,000 spectators. At the time and thereafter, it was widely held that Daley and Halligan had been the victims of anti-Irish sentiment, then rampant in the United States; this bias, coupled to the suspicious behavior of the man who captured them and received a $500 reward in the process, caused widespread belief that the two men were innocent. That they had been wrongly convicted under the law through inadmissible testimony was a fact not lost on Massachusetts Governor Michael Dukakis (1983–1991), who posthumously pardoned Daley and Halligan in a special 1984 proclamation.

**1809**: Born of Yorkshire, England, parents, **Mary Bateman** (a.k.a.: The Yorkshire Witch; 1768–1809) began thieving at the age of five, stealing her father's clothing and hiding these to exchange for other items with neighbor children. In 1778, she moved to Leeds, where she became a seamstress, but she spent most of her time telling simple-minded customers that she was a seeress and possessed powers that would bring them good fortune. She told fortunes and was well paid for it. She later married a hardworking laborer, John Bateman, who was devoted to his wife, but was repeatedly milked of his money by her. For many years, Mary operated occult swindles under the guise of having magical powers, until she was charged with theft, murder, and witchcraft. Of the latter charge, she was innocent and wrongly convicted. Bateman was executed on March 20, 1809. Before she was hanged, Bateman proclaimed her innocence.

**1831**: Two white missionaries to the Cherokee Nation, **Elihu Butler** and **Samuel Austin Worcester**, were arrested and charged with illegally living with the Cherokees in New Echota, Georgia, without having a state license. Both men were convicted and sentenced to hard labor for four years, serving on a chain gang. The two missionaries had protested the state's seizure of Cherokee lands in 1829, after gold had been discovered in Dahlonega, Gordon County, Georgia, and after the State required all whites living in the Cherokee lands to obtain a license, which the missionaries refused to do. To suppress their protests of the illegal seizure of the Cherokee lands, state officials muzzled them by wrongly convicting and imprisoning them. In an 1832 appeal to the U.S. Supreme Court, Chief Justice John Marshall ruled that Georgia had no constitutional right to extend any state laws over the Cherokees, including the illegal seizure of their lands, and ordered the missionaries released. State officials ignored the ruling and kept the missionaries on the chain gang for sixteen months, before releasing them in time to join the mass migration of more than 17,000 Cherokees (the Trail of Tears) from northwest Georgia to Oklahoma. The State of Georgia did not repeal its Cherokee laws until 1979, at which time it issued posthumous pardons to Butler and Worcester.

**1835:** In March 1835, two men were wrongly convicted of murder in England. Both were hanged. **Edward Poole Chalker**, a farm laborer, had been convicted in March 1835 of murdering a gamekeeper. Adamantly claiming his innocence, he was nevertheless hanged within forty-eight hours. According to a 1752 act "for better preventing the horrid crime of murder," convicted killers were normally executed within two days. Seven years later, another man admitted committing the crime for which Chalker had paid with his life.

**1835:** At Waterford Assizes that same month an Irish peddler known as Daniel Savage was sentenced to die for killing his wife ten years earlier. He was positively identified by only one witness. When shaved to make the hangman's job easier, his sister visited him and, perplexed, explained: "He's not my brother . . . doesn't look anything like him." Soon after Savage's death, it was discovered that the man hanged was a mentally retarded person, **Edmund Pine**, and not Daniel Savage (who was never found). Partly in response to the deaths of Chalker and Pine, the 1752 law was eventually changed.

**1881: Johann Gawenda**, after being beaten by a police officer, confessed to murdering sixteen-year-old Katarina Sroka, who had been missing from her village in Germany. Gawenda said that a man named Gallus had helped him in the crime by providing a hoe with which he beat the girl to death. Gawenda was sentenced to death, but his sentence was later commuted to twenty years in prison, while **Gallus**, convicted as an accessory to the murder, was sent to prison for ten years. A year after both men went to prison, Sroka was found living in another village. She said she had run away from home without notice to get a job as a domestic servant. Both Gawenda and Gallus were then released from prison.

**1884: Mary Lefley** lived with her husband in Lincolnshire, England. Her husband farmed and also made deliveries. One day in May 1884, her husband was out making deliveries, and she put a bowl of rice pudding in the oven for him before she left the house to go to the market. When Lefley returned, he ate the pudding and lay down to rest. He woke up in extreme pain and went to a neighbor's house. A doctor was summoned, but he could do little for the ailing Lefley, who stated that his wife's pudding had not "tasted right," before dying a short time later. The pudding was examined, and, after arsenic was found in the dish, Mary Lefley was arrested and tried. Mary Lefley argued that she was innocent, but she was found guilty and condemned to death. Still expecting a reprieve, Lefley screamed "Murder!" as hangman James Berry took her to the scaffold. The hangman later stated that he had learned that a farmer confessed to the crime in 1893 on his deathbed. The farmer reportedly bore a grudge against Lefley because Lefley bested him in a bargain. Years later, he went to the Lefley home, saw the unattended food, and placed the arsenic in the pudding.

**1886: James Lee** was convicted of murdering police inspector Simmons outside Romford, Essex, although there was some uncertainty about his guilt. He was executed at Chelmsford by hangman James Berry, who served as public executioner between 1884 and 1892. In 1886, before Berry executed a man named Martin, a convicted murderer, Martin confessed to Lee's crime.

**1886: Willie Sell** was convicted of murdering his parents, brother, and sister on March 8, 1886, in Neosho County, Kansas. He was sentenced to life imprisonment, but he was exonerated when he received in 1907 a full pardon from Kansas Governor Edward W. Hoch (1905–1909).

**1892:** Delteena Davis, a young woman from East Cambridge, Massachusetts, had been missing for several days, when her body was found floating in the Mystic River. The girl's mother accused Delteena's suitor, **James Albert Trefethen**, and his cousin, William H. Smith, of throwing her off the Wellington Bridge and into the icy waters on December 23, 1891. Trefethen disavowed any responsibility, claiming that she had committed suicide. Trefethen had been courting Davis for years. In July 1891, the young woman announced that she was pregnant with his child. Trefethen by then had lost interest and sought to end the relationship. He began ignoring Davis and treating her coldly. On the night of her disappearance, the jilted young woman was to confront him in town to discuss the matter. Whether or not that meeting occurred was later much in debate. Trefethen and his cousin were placed on trial in February 1892 at the courthouse in East Cambridge for the murder of Davis. Smith was acquitted, but Trefethen was found guilty and sent to prison. He appealed, and witnesses came forward to testify that they had been with him at an inn at the time of Davis's death. There was also evidence that Davis had been seeing another man, who may have impregnated her and killed her. In September 1893, Trefethen was granted a retrial and was acquitted on all murder charges.

**1894**: James and **Patrick Groake**, were tried for manslaughter, allegedly having kicked their mother to death in their rural home outside of London. James Groake was acquitted, but Patrick, his older brother, was found guilty and sentenced to twenty years in prison. Seven years later, James, on his deathbed, confessed that he had actually committed the murder. Patrick Groake was released and lived another thirty years, dying in 1930.

**1895**: On February 19, 1895, James Mahoney was arrested by police in Boston, Massachusetts, and charged with picking the pocket of May Ivers. She had $3 and small change at the time. A second man involved in the crime had escaped. Mahoney was released on bail, and the police resumed their search for the accomplice. Through the description provided by two female store detectives and a witness to the theft, an ex-convict named **Joseph Ward** was arrested. Ward, who often used the alias "Winston," was found guilty of robbing the $3 plus change from Ivers and was sentenced to five years in the state prison. During the trial, he refused to testify on his own behalf because he feared that his past criminal record would influence the jury to return an even harsher sentence. Later, Mahoney, who had also been sent to prison on the same charge, told police that his partner had not been Ward, but a New Yorker named Dooley. The resemblance between the innocent man and Dooley was a strong one, which had resulted in Ward's wrongful conviction. On January 30, 1896, Massachusetts Governor Frederic T. Greenhalge (1894–1896) granted Ward a formal pardon in what had been a case of mistaken identity.

**1895**: A decapitated human body, with portions of the chest removed, was found near the village of Stary Multan in Russia's Vyatka province in 1895. A group of Votyak villagers were tried for practicing human sacrifice, with the district police officer getting peasants to confess by forcing them to take an oath in front of a stuffed bear, an animal spiritually venerated by the tribe. Two of the villagers were convicted in the local court, but the sentences were suspended by a Senate Appeals Division on the grounds that there had been violation of due process during the **Votyak Trials**. A retrial ended in acquittal.

**1896**: In the late summer of 1896, a well-dressed crook named Tyler passed counterfeit money in Evansville, Vincennes, and Terre Haute, Indiana. About the same time, **Percy B. Sullivan**, an insurance agent from a prominent Bowling Green, Kentucky, family made calls in those towns. Police tracked Sullivan, and he was arrested in St. Louis by a U.S. Marshal and sent back to Indianapolis. After several Evansville residents were shown Sullivan's photograph, he was identified as the man passing the counterfeit money and a grand jury indicted him on November 12, 1896. He was tried and convicted on December 8, 1896, received a four-year sentence, and was fined $100. He began serving his term at the South Prison at Jeffersonville, but then was transferred to the Michigan City Prison. Later the real criminal, Tyler, was arrested and confessed to passing counterfeit notes in the three Indiana towns. Authorities showed Tyler's and Sullivan's pictures, which were not labeled, to victims, who identified Tyler as the counterfeiter. Tyler's was then tried, convicted, and sentenced. On May 12, 1898, President William McKinley (1843–1901; term of office, 1897–1901) granted a full pardon to Sullivan and he was freed.

**1898**: Convicted of murdering Hattie McCloud at Buckland, Massachusetts, near Shelburne Falls, **Jack O'Neil** claimed he was innocent and the victim of anti-Irish prejudice. At his execution, on January 7, 1898, he said: "I shall meet death like a man, and I hope those who see me hanged will live to see the day when it is proved I am innocent, and it will be, some time." Months later, a soldier from Shelburne Falls fighting in Cuba confessed to the murder. A reporter who interviewed the killer obtained a deathbed confession from him, which he sent back to *Boston Post* newsman Dan W. Gallagher.

**1900**: **Michael J. Synon** was convicted of murdering his wife in Illinois and sent to prison for life. On appeal, in 1902, defense attorneys proved to an appeals court that their client could not have committed the murder in that he was miles away from the scene of the crime.

Synon's conviction was vacated, charges were dropped against him, and he was released from prison.

**1900:** After his twelve-year-old daughter disappeared from a small German village, **Franz Bratuscha** and his wife admitted that Bratuscha had murdered the girl, and his wife had cut up the corpse and both had eaten her body, but inspectors found no traces of their admitted cannibalism. Bratuscha was sentenced to death, his sentence later commuted to life in prison, while his wife was sent to prison for three years as an accessory to the killing. Both were released in 1903, when the daughter was found living in a nearby town. Bratuscha and his wife were uneducated peasants, prone to superstition and hallucinations, as was the case with another German case in 1881 (see **Johann Gawenda**, Chronology, 1881).

**1901:** After John Edwards, a white man, was killed in Stroudsburg, Pennsylvania, the victim's wife, Kate Edwards, admitted the crime, but said that her black lover, **Samuel Greason**, had helped her murder her husband. Both were convicted and sentenced to death. While awaiting execution, Kate Edwards gave birth to a child of mixed race, a daughter, whom Edwards admitted had been sired by Greason. At that time, Edwards said that she alone had killed her husband. Greason was exonerated and released in 1906.

**1905:** On September 7, 1905, **Jasper Jennings** and his sister Dora Jennings, of Portland, Oregon, were accused of killing their father, Newton M. Jennings. In January 1906, Jasper was tried separately, convicted of first-degree murder and sentenced to be hanged. In November of that year, the Oregon Supreme Court reversed the conviction due to false testimony by a prosecution witness. At a new trial, the charges against Jasper Jennings were dismissed after Dora Jennings had told others that she committed the crime. Dora Jennings was later convicted and imprisoned.

**1905:** Following the armed robbery and murder of Hans Peterson, a storekeeper operating a shop on Chicago's West Lake Street, **Joseph Briggs** was arrested and charged with the killing. Briggs, a railroad worker, had been located in a tavern close to the scene of the crime and had been arrested shortly after the robbery. Briggs insisted at his trial that he was innocent of the robbery-murder. There was no physical evidence linking Briggs to the crime—the police never recovered either the murder weapon or the cash taken—but three witnesses testifying against Briggs brought about his conviction. He was sentenced to death, his execution by hanging scheduled for June 16, 1905. On an appeal,

it was revealed that the first witness against Briggs, William Portee, a shop employee wounded during the attack, had failed to identify Briggs when he was brought to his hospital bedside while he was recuperating. Portee stated at a subsequent coroner's inquest that he could not identify Briggs, yet, five months later at Brigg's trial, he identified him as the robber. The second witness, Albert Piemental, a boy in his early teens, also failed to identify Briggs in a police lineup, but later identified him in court. The third witness, Matilda Peterson (no relation to the dead shopkeeper), stated in court that she had seen Briggs in the store a day before the robbery, when he asked for change from a $10 bill. Police theorized that Briggs had been "casing" the store by seeking change at that time. When reviewing Briggs's appeal, the Illinois Supreme Court reversed the conviction in a unanimous decision on December 20, 1905. The court held that the trial judge erred in preventing the defense from challenging the inconsistent statements of Portee and allowing the prosecution to put leading questions to the teenager, Piemental, as well as prohibiting the defense to impeach Matilde Peterson's statements. A second trial was ordered, at which time Briggs was acquitted and set free.

**1906:** **Moses Walker**, a poor black farmer from Lauderdale County, Mississippi, was arrested and charged with attempted murder in the fall of 1906. He was accused of firing bullets into the home of a white farmer named Harrington. A load of metal slugs had been found embedded in the wall of Harrington's house. Police took Harrington at his word, and Walker was taken into custody and charged with felonious assault with intention to kill. Walker's trial began in the Circuit Court on January 18, 1907. He was found guilty on the sole testimony of Harrington and ordered to serve ten years at hard labor in the state penitentiary. An appeal to the Mississippi Supreme Court was denied. Five years later, after Harrington had died, his widow explained that the shooting had been a "frame-up" against the black man, whom her husband deeply resented. Walker was granted a pardon from Mississippi Governor Earl L. Brewer (1912–1916). The state awarded him $500 as compensation.

**1907:** On November 26, 1907, Bob Henderson, Beulah McGhee, and **David Sherman** were to be hanged for the murder of a man named Hix in McMinnville County, Tennessee. A stay of execution was granted, however, by Governor Malcolm Rice Patterson (1907–1911). The hangings were rescheduled for January 27, 1908. The sentences of Henderson and Sherman were commuted to life imprisonment on January 23, 1908. Prior to execution, McGhee confessed that Sherman had had nothing to do with the murder of Hix, saying that Sherman just happened to be asleep in the same house as the victim. McGhee repeated his confession to the sheriff while on the scaffold. Based on McGhee's statement and a petition by Attorney General Fletcher, who felt that Sherman was completely innocent of the crime and did not even know a murder had been committed until the next day, Sherman was granted a full pardon by Governor Patterson on January 13, 1911. The board of pardons pointed out to the governor that Sherman's conviction turned out to be "quite a remarkable case of a miscarriage of justice."

**1907: Robert Mead Shumway** was convicted and sentenced to death for the murder of his employer's wife in Gage County, Nebraska. Only circumstantial evidence was offered at his trial, and one juror held out for acquittal until being pressured by others into voting guilty (the juror was so distraught at having sent an innocent man to death that he later committed suicide). On March 5, 1909, Shumway was executed by hanging. The following year, Shumway's employer confessed on his deathbed that he had murdered his wife.

**1907: John Vickers** and **Hampton Kendall** were convicted of a murder in North Carolina, but both were pardoned by North Carolina Governor Locke Craig (1913–1917) in 1916, after another man confessed to the crime.

**1908**: Six of Mary Kelliher's close relatives died mysteriously in Boston, Massachusetts, during a three-year period. A July 1908 postmortem on her daughter revealed the presence of arsenic. Examination of other bodies—including Kelliher's husband, sister, sister-in-law, and two other children—revealed arsenic. No evidence could be found to connect **Mary Kelliher** with the crimes until the district attorney ordered the furniture in her home examined. The mattress, on which all six of the victims died, revealed large quantities of arsenic, suggesting that it had been impregnated with the poison. The people sleeping on the bed had evidently absorbed it through their skin. Kelliher was convicted and sent to prison. In appeal, however, her attorneys argued that the prosecution's theory had been faulty in that the mattress could have easily been soaked with arsenic by accident or through other means and by persons other than Kelliher. She was exonerated and released, after having spent fifteen months in prison.

**1910**: When one of the most prominent politicians in Omaha, Nebraska, phoned police to report a suspicious-looking suitcase on his porch, authorities discovered a crudely constructed bomb inside the bag. Only hours later, **Frank Erdman** was arrested and charged with attempted murder on May 22, 1910. Erdman, a small-time hoodlum, had recently argued with the politician, who was connected to gambling operations in Omaha. John O. Yeiser, a lawyer, was doubtful whether someone who really wanted to a kill another man would do such a sloppy job. Reports said the suitcase contained a visible white string that stretched to a porch railing. Yeiser visited Erdman in jail and offered to defend him free of charge. The prisoner said it was no use. Even though he did not plant the bomb, Erdman said, he did not have an alibi and admitted to hating the politician. On trial, the prosecution had nine witnesses testify that Erdman was in the vicinity of the politician's house on the day of the murder. Two young girls testified they saw the suspect at around 2:15 P.M. The reason they were so sure of the time was that it followed their religious confirmation, of which they happened to have a picture. To counter the evidence, Yeiser secured an astronomer from Creighton University, who testified that by the angle of the sun's shadow, the photo was taken at 3:20 P.M. Erdman, however, was convicted and sent to prison. Ultimately, the Nebraska Supreme Court released Erdman, based on additional evidence that supported Yeiser's argument about the exonerating photograph. For several years after the incident, investigators took photos at the church on May 22 at 3:20 P.M. and found that the sun's shadow matched the original picture, thus proving Yeiser's argument that the girls had been mistaken as to the time of their confirmations.

**1910: Oscar Krueger** was arrested in 1910 on charges of mailing a "lewd, lascivious, obscene letter" to an unmarried New York woman, who had answered a want ad in the classified section of the *New York Journal*. Krueger was convicted with only circumstantial evidence, and the testimony of several handwriting analysts, who found his writing similar to that in the letter. Convicted on February 2, 1911, Krueger was sentenced to serve eighteen months in the federal penitentiary in Atlanta, Georgia. After many appeals, Krueger was granted a retrial, where it was shown that the handwriting analyses in his first trial were inconclusive and that he had been convicted on insufficient evidence. On January 18, 1912, Krueger received a full pardon from President William Howard Taft (1857–1930; term of office, 1909–1913) after serving almost one year for a crime he did not commit.

1911: **Will Evans** was convicted of raping a woman in Pulaski County, Illinois, and sentenced to ninety-nine years in prison. A few days after his sentencing, Evans's attorney provided the trial judge with a concrete alibi in the case in the form of a sworn statement from the Chief of Police in Cairo, Illinois, who said that he had personally arrested Evans for burglarizing a train car at the time the rape in Pulaski County occurred. The judge ignored the alibi, stating that Evans was "probably in prison rightfully, but upon the wrong charge." This slipshod and illegal decision permitted the State to keep Evans in prison until 1932, when Illinois Governor Louis L. Emmerson (1929–1933) granted him a pardon, based on the fact that he had been the victim of mistaken identity.

1913: **Francisco Garcia** was convicted and sentenced to prison for manslaughter in New Mexico. An appeals court overturned his conviction in 1916, ruling that it was "physically impossible for him to be guilty."

1914: In a case of mistaken identity, **Herbert Andrews**, a cashier from a large Boston department store, was tried and convicted on seventeen counts of passing bad checks. A Suffolk County jury accepted the sworn testimony of seventeen witnesses, who positively identified Andrews as the man who had written the checks. Based on their testimony the cashier was found guilty on February 26, 1914, and sentenced in May to fourteen months in prison on Deer Island. The bad checks kept reappearing, however, even with Andrews behind bars. Suspicion swung to Earle Barnes, a Denver man posing as a visiting socialite. He lived extravagantly, writing checks that came back with the terse explanation "no account." Barnes was arrested on June 12, 1914. Given the overwhelming evidence of guilt and the pile of bad checks bearing his handwriting, Barnes confessed to Captain Armstrong of the Boston Police Department. He was arraigned two days later and pleaded guilty to the same judge who had sentenced Andrews. Barnes's plea was admitted, and he received a sentence of eighteen months at Deer Island. One mystery remained unsolved: Why seventeen witnesses had been so quick to identify Herbert Andrews, who did not resemble Earle Barnes in any way. Andrews was released following Barnes's conviction.

1916: **Ernest Wallace** was convicted of the June 16, 1916, murder of Jacob Levine, a Chicago saloonkeeper. An eyewitness to the shooting identified Wallace as the gunman, but three other persons present at the time said that the robbers all wore masks. Wallace was sentenced to die on the gallows, but through the efforts of Attorney O. J. Wray and five concerned Chicagoans the condemned man was granted a second trial by the Illinois State Supreme Court on June 21, 1917. Wray had worked tirelessly to exonerate his client without receiving a salary. Wallace's conviction was later overturned because of insufficient evidence (the testimony of the lone eyewitness was successfully challenged), and he was released.

1916: The case of **Ernest Haines**, a teenager of subnormal intellect, became a rallying cry among the foes of capital punishment in the state of Pennsylvania. If World War I had not intervened, the death penalty might have been abolished as a result of Haines's wrongful conviction. Haines, along with his friend Henry Ward Mottern, sixteen, was convicted of the August 2, 1916, murder of his father and sentenced to death. There was no hard evidence linking Haines with his father's death, only the testimony of Mottern, who did not suffer the same defects of mind. Mottern's statements were later deemed reversible error by the state supreme court because he discussed a burglary allegedly planned months earlier. Haines was granted a new trial that resulted in his acquittal. Mottern, who had pleaded guilty before, could not be granted a second trial under Pennsylvania law. Instead, the Board of Pardons commuted his sentence to life imprisonment on January 1, 1918, after several earlier unsuccessful attempts. The publicity of this trial led to new demands to end capital punishment, but the issue soon died when war was declared.

1916: On October 7, 1916, **Thomas Bambrick** was executed in the electric chair at Sing Sing Prison in Ossining, New York, but prison warden Thomas Mott Osborne was convinced that he died an innocent man. Bambrick was convicted in 1915 of the murder of New York City police officer George Dapping in September 1915. Evidence was uncovered after his conviction that convinced the warden that Bambrick was innocent, and that Bambrick knew the actual murderer, but had refused to reveal his identity and preferred to go to his death rather than risk being known as a "squealer."

1917: In May 1917 Mrs. Julia May Hess, a visitor to the city of Mobile, Alabama, was robbed and murdered by strangulation and/or drowning. The cause of death was never completely determined, and there is still doubt about who committed the crime. Two men died for it, but only one claimed he killed her. Fisher Brooks and **Albert Sanders**, two black men, matched a description of the cab drivers who picked up Mrs. Hess and were indicted for murder. Both men were sentenced to death, despite Sanders's protestations that he was innocent. Brooks confessed and told the court that his friend had nothing to do with the crime. Fisher Brooks was hanged on August 3, 1917. Sanders followed nearly a year later on July 19, 1918. Up to the last minute, Sanders maintained his innocence, giving an hour by hour description of his movements the night of the murder. The court did not budge. Commenting on the affair, the *Mobile Register* said that the city "is to be praised and congratulated that it passed through the long and trying ordeal with self-control, satisfied that the law would serve and that the guilty would be punished."

**1917: Luigi Lanzillo**, twenty, was convicted of murdering Morris Goldstein in New Haven, Connecticut, in 1917. A gun found near the scene of the murder was traced to Lanzillo, who declared that his brother, Carmello, had taken it without his permission. Carmello Lanzillo and two accomplices were hanged for the murder in 1918. Luigi, who had nothing to do with the crime, was jailed for ten years, despite a signed confession from the three condemned prisoners that he was innocent of the murder for which he was charged. On May 7, 1928, the State Board of Pardons granted Lanzillo his release after Mrs. Sylvester Z. Poli, the wife of a millionaire theater mogul in New Haven, came forward to make an impassioned plea on his behalf.

**1918:** Whether **George Harold Lamble** (a.k.a.: George Brandon) actually killed Edith Janney and her fiancé, Edward Kupfer, on the night of August 22, 1918, remains a matter of serious speculation. The plight of Lamble led to new calls for the abolition of the death penalty in New Jersey and public censure of New Jersey Governor Edward I. Edwards (1920–1923). Kupfer and his girlfriend were on their way back to Perth Amboy, New Jersey, from Highland Park, when they picked up two hitchhikers. The men were later identified as George Lamble and Charles Perchand, Perchand acting as a chauffeur. During the drive into Rahway one of the two men shot the young couple and dropped their bodies on the side of the road. Apprehended some months later, the men accused each other of the crime, Lamble maintaining that he was never in the car and Perchand that he was only driving the car when the shots rang out. The prosecutor believed Perchand. Edward Schwartz of the Newark Police Department reportedly matched fingerprints taken on the side of the automobile against those of Lamble's and Perchand's, which were on file. Based on this evidence, a conviction was secured against Lamble, who was executed in the electric chair at Trenton, on August 23, 1921, amid loud protests from the Executive Committee of the Citizen's Union of New Jersey that the governor had repeatedly ignored requests for a stay of execution. Up to an hour before Lamble's death, Edwards was "out of the office" and could not be reached. The handling of the case by defense attorneys was also attacked. One lawyer was later disbarred for refusing to continue his work when funding ran out. Sheriff David Knott of New Jersey led the fight to abolish the death penalty in the wake of the Lamble execution, saying, "He even wrote a letter in his last hour of life insisting that he did not commit the crime for which his life was taken. The point is that his vehement protest of innocence has created a doubt." The evidence that sent Lamble to the electric chair, the fingerprint matching by Edward Schwartz, was also in question, particularly in a time when such identification was, in the United States, still in embryonic stages, and errors in making fingerprint identification at that time were commonplace.

**1918: Robert Loomis** was convicted of murdering Bertha Myers during a burglary in Easton, Pennsylvania. Myers apparently interrupted a burglar who had entered her home and was killed when she discovered the intruder. Two fingerprint experts testified at Loomis's trial that a latent fingerprint found on a jewelry box inside the victim's home was matched to Loomis, who was sent to prison for life. On appeal, Loomis was granted a new trial, when an appellate court determined that the trial judge had prejudiced the jury against the defendant. That trial ended with a second conviction, but Loomis was granted a third trial on the same grounds, one in which he was acquitted in 1921, after his attorneys were able to compel prosecutors into admitting that Loomis was not the source of the latent fingerprint.

**1918: Frank Ewing**, a black man, was convicted of raping a white woman in Davidson County, Tennessee, the attack occurring on June 24, 1918. Ewing provided an alibi at the time of his trial through his white employer, who, unfortunately, remembered the wrong time Ewing was working for him, a period that did not support his alibi. Ewing was sentenced to death, but before the scheduled execution, the employer went to officials to show them his work record book, which clearly demonstrated that Ewing was at work fifteen miles from the scene of the crime when it occurred. Officials ignored this exculpatory evidence, and Ewing was executed by hanging on May 21, 1919.

**1919**: **Alf Banks** and **Edward Hicks** were two of fifty-one blacks convicted of murder after a 1919 racial uprising near Elaine, Arkansas, ended in the death of five whites and 200 blacks. Banks, Hicks, and ten other rioters were originally charged with first-degree murder and sentenced to death. Following the trial, the decision was reversed because of a technicality, and Banks and five of his codefendants were retried and once again found guilty and sentenced to death. The Arkansas Supreme Court once again reversed the decisions of the lower courts, and, in 1923, all of the men who had stood trial for murder were freed.

**1919: Louis Benevente** was convicted and sent to prison for robbing a baking company in New Jersey of $192. His conviction had been brought about by a company employee, John Dougherty. Benevente was paroled in 1924 and, in 1931, Dougherty confessed that he had falsely accused Benevente of the robbery to cover up the fact that he had lost the company money himself while playing dice. In 1939, the New Jersey legislature awarded Benevente $5,000 in compensation for the five years he had spent behind bars.

**1920**: In December 1920, in North Carolina, **Cecil Hefner** was found guilty of second-degree murder in the death of Glenn Lippard and was sentenced to fifteen years in prison. On April 4, 1921, Hefner was pardoned by North Carolina Governor Cameron Morrison (1921–1925) after the prosecutor, Solicitor Huffman, with the concurrence of Judge Thomas J. Shaw, proved in a post-trial investigation that Hefner was not present when Lippard was murdered.

**1920:** In 1920, in Virginia, **Joseph S. Williams** was convicted of voluntary manslaughter for the death of his wife and was sentenced to five years in prison. She had died of a brain hemorrhage, and Williams was suspected of striking her. Following an appeal, a new forensic investigation disclosed that there had been no outward sign of physical violence to the woman's head. When the Virginia Supreme Court ordered a retrial, the state, realizing that it had insufficient evidence, chose not to prosecute and Williams was released.

**1920:** Four black men in rural Alabama, **Willie Crutcher**, **John Murchison**, **Jim Hudson** and **Cleo Staten**, were wrongly convicted and sent to prison for life on perjured testimony of murdering a white man, John McClendon, who disappeared on August 6, 1920, and whose body was later found atop Brindlee Mountain. All four were sent to prison for life, three dying behind bars before Otis McClendon, the nephew of the murder victim, admitted in 1926 to the murder, saying

that he had slain his uncle in a murder-for-hire scheme with John McClendon's wife, Myrtle, in exchange for forty acres of farmland and two mules. Murchison was released from prison at that time and given $750 compensation. Otis McClendon was murdered a short time later, reportedly by Cleve King, Myrtle's new husband. Neither Cleve King or Myrtle McClendon King were charged in John McClendon's murder or that of his nephew.

**1922: Maurice F. Mays**, a black man, was accused of murdering Mrs. Bertie Linsey, a white woman, shooting her to death while she lay in bed early in the morning of August 30, 1919, in Knoxville, Tennessee. Mays was convicted on the eyewitness testimony of Ora Smyth, the only witness to the crime. Before Mays was executed, a mob of more than 1,000 whites attempted to storm the Knox County Jail in an effort to lynch Mays, but they were prevented from reaching him by state troops. Widespread rioting then ensued in Knoxville, where seven persons were killed, one white man and six blacks. Following Mays's hanging, Sadie Brown Mendil, a white woman living in Virginia, confessed to having murdered Linsey, saying that she had dressed as a black man (darkening her skin with charcoal) and had shot Linsey because Linsey was having an affair with her husband. Virginia authorities found Mendil's confession credible and notified Tennessee officials, who dismissed the exculpatory evidence out of hand.

**1922: Cooper Johnson** and **Bennie Young** were convicted of murder after making false confessions and sent to a Texas prison for life. Both men were released in 1934, following the identification of real perpetrator.

**1925**: On March 23, 1925, Mr. and Mrs. Edward Palombizio were found shot to death in their Chicago home. **Ralph Reno**, a godfather to the couple's daughter, was suspected and surrendered to the police. He was a suspect because of the testimony of an eyewitness, who named Reno as the killer, but gave a physical description of a man bearing little resemblance to Reno. On the basis of this illogical statement, Reno was convicted of the murders and sentenced to death. In 1926, Reno was granted a stay of execution pending appeal a mere seven hours before he was to have been executed. A new trial was ordered, the original eyewitness changed her testimony, and Reno was acquitted. He was finally released in 1928, but claimed to have suffered a nervous breakdown due to the ordeal. "Everything that I had built up in my first thirty-six years was gone—money, job, home, wife and baby, and my good health," he said.

**1925: Anastacio Vargas** of Austin, Texas, was convicted of murder in 1925, and was sentenced to life in prison. The conviction was reversed on appeal, and Vargas was tried again, but he received another conviction and a sentence of death. In the final stages of preparation for execution, his head had been shaved and he had been served his last meal. With four hours left to live, a look-alike killer confessed to the crime. A judge investigated the case and commuted Vargas's sentence to life imprisonment. In 1929, the wrongly convicted man was granted a full pardon and released after four years in the Bexan County Jail. He sued the state for damages and was given an award of $20,000 in 1965. Although the state appealed, the award was affirmed.

**1925: Junius Wilson** was convicted of rape in North Carolina, but when he was declared insane, he was sent to a state mental hospital for blacks. Charges against him were dropped sometime in 1970, but he remained a prisoner in a mental facility until the early 1990s.

**1926**: On August 23, 1925, fourteen-year-old Mary Vickery disappeared from her home in Coxton, Kentucky. In September 1925, the badly decomposed body of a female was found in a nearby mine shaft. A short time later, Marie Jackson, a friend of the missing Vickery, went to officials with a terrifying tale. She said that she and Vickery, on the day of Vickery's disappearance, hired a cab driven by **Condy Dabney**, a miner turned taxi driver, who was the married father of two children. The three had lunch together, Jackson said, and then drove to a secluded area, where Dabney made sexual advances to Vickery. When she protested, he struck her over the head with a large stick and Vickery fell to the ground, Jackson said. Dabney then forced Jackson to take the body to the mine shaft and warned her that she would be killed by him or his friends if she ever told authorities about the murder. Based on Jackson's statements, Dabney was charged with Vickery's murder in March 1926 and brought to trial a short time later. Prosecutors, other than Jackson's testimony, had little evidence. The corpse found the previous year was so badly decomposed that it could not be positively identified as that of Vickery. Several witnesses contradicted Jackson's statements as to the time when the crime occurred, and others claimed that a cab driver named William Middleton had given her and Vickery a ride, but he did not accompany them after letting them out of his taxi. A jailhouse informant, who was a friend of Jackson's, testified that Dabney had offered him $15 if

he falsely stated that Jackson was lying. Dabney took the stand to say that he was innocent and that he had never had Vickery in his cab, but had driven Jackson several times. A jury convicted Dabney on March 31, 1926, and he was sentenced to life at hard labor. About a year later, a police officer in Williamsburg, Kentucky, eighty some miles distant from Coxton, noticed the name "Vickery" on a hotel register. The name sounded familiar and he interviewed the young girl, discovering that she was the very person for whom Dabney had been convicted of murdering. Vickery explained that she had run away from home without leaving any notice after quarreling with her stepmother. When Vickery's existence was announced, Dabney's conviction was vacated, and he was released from prison in March 1927. Jackson was convicted of perjury on March 27, 1927, and sent to prison. She had concocted the story about Dabney to get the $500 reward money Vickery's father had posted for information regarding his missing daughter.

**1927**: On April 12, 1927, before Judge J. F. Pullen of the Superior Court of Sacramento County, **James Willis** was sentenced to San Quentin for five years to life for first-degree robbery. Willis, twenty-seven, the son of a prominent California physician, was a drug addict, had a prior police record, and had been convicted twice in Washington State. Willis had been convicted of three separate robbery incidents in Sacramento on March 19, 1927, and was identified by all of the victims. However, at about the same time, Vincent Bohac, twenty-three, confessed to Detroit police that he had committed the Sacramento crimes. In turn, Bohac was identified by all three victims and sentenced in May 1927. Because of Willis's past record, however, he was not pardoned until August 18, 1927.

**1927**: A night guard for Midland Steel Products Co., in Ohio, Jasper Russell, was murdered on March 13, 1927, by Alex Maynor. After Maynor was arrested, he implicated **Joseph Weaver**, and the two were put on trial in 1927. Maynor was convicted of manslaughter and received a life sentence. Weaver was convicted of murder and sentenced to die. For two years, Weaver's lawyers fought to keep him from going to the electric chair. After his conviction was upheld by an appeals court, authorities planned to execute Weaver in 1929. Days before the execution, Maynor came forward, withdrawing his accusation against Weaver. Three days later, the Ohio Supreme Court ordered a retrial, stating that inadmissible hearsay evidence had been presented at the first trial. During the retrial, on April 5, 1929,

Judge W. R. White directed the jury to acquit Weaver on the grounds that the government had not proven Weaver's guilt at the first trial. Set free, Weaver left the Cuyahoga County Jail, declining to shake Maynor's hand, saying: "Why should I shake his hand? He's luckier than I am . . . I should have been free these last two years. He lied me into prison and saved his own life in the bargain."

**1927: Gangi Cero** was convicted of first-degree murder in a Boston slaying and was sentenced to death. Only four hours before he was to be executed, a stay was granted after defense attorneys had located an eyewitness, who identified another man as the killer. Cero's conviction was vacated, and he was retried and acquitted. He was released from prison in 1929.

**1928**: In August 1928, someone stole four cabs within five days and robbed each of their drivers in Los Angeles. Police arrested **Elmer P. Jacobs** for stealing a car and included him in a lineup of suspects in the cab thefts. All four taxi drivers identified Jacobs as their assailant. Even though he had pleaded guilty to grand larceny and been sentenced to prison, Jacobs was forced to appear before Judge Emmett H. Wilson on October 30, 1928. The drivers appeared in court and positively identified Jacobs as the robber. Jacobs tried to establish alibis, but he was found guilty on four counts of robbery. One month later, he was sentenced to fifteen years to life in prison. During the same week, police arrested four men who confessed to robbing the taxi drivers and stealing their cabs. After police verified their stories, Jacobs was freed and all charges against him were dropped in December 1928.

**1928**: In the same month Jacobs was acquitted, thirty-year-old **Mary Berner** was arrested in Chicago and sent to prison for forgery. She had quit her job at an insurance company about the same time that a number of the company's checks disappeared. Fortunately, Emma Lutz later confessed to the crimes for which Mary Berner had been wrongly convicted. A year and a half prior to Berner's arrest in December 1928, a woman fitting Berner's description cashed fraudulent checks, always for amounts less than $50, at approximately sixty banks in the Chicago area. Since Berner had left her job at the same time as some checks were found missing and because she had been positively identified by witnesses, a grand jury found her guilty. She refused to plead, but the judge entered the guilty plea for her and sentenced her to a year's probation. Berner never finished her sentence, for, in April 1929, Lutz confessed to the charges against Berner and was

then tried, convicted, and sentenced to one year in prison.

**1928:** In October 1925, two men, Henry Sweet and Carmen Wagner, were murdered near Eureka, California. Two Native Americans with mixed blood, **Jack Ryan** and Walter David (described by the local press at the time as "half-breeds"), were charged with the slayings. David was released for lack of evidence, and Ryan was acquitted in a jury trial on charges of killing Wagner. Stephen Metzler was then elected the new district attorney on the promise he would solve the Sweet-Wagner murders or resign. David was reportedly abducted by thugs working for Metzler and was killed when he refused to admit the two murders or implicate his friend Ryan. Metzler then charged Ryan with the murder of Sweet. Ryan was beaten in a nightlong ordeal of third-degree interrogations and finally admitted murdering Sweet. He was sentenced to life imprisonment and was released on parole in 1953 from San Quentin after having spent twenty-five years behind bars. He had maintained his innocence throughout and up until his death in 1978. A later investigation revealed that Ryan's confession had been coerced and that Metzler had paid a woman to testify against Ryan at his 1928 trial. In 1996, California Governor Pete Wilson (1991–1999) posthumously issued a full pardon to Ryan.

**1929**: Mistaken testimony by a dying man caused two twenty-year-olds to be wrongly convicted of murder. Virgil Romine was shot in the abdomen at about 1:30 A.M. on January 7, 1929, in Herculaneum, Missouri. Before being taken to the hospital where he died, Romine told Deputy Sheriff J. W. Dugan that his attackers had caused trouble at the Artesian Park Filling Station the previous month and had returned to an adjacent restaurant, where Romine was shot. **Alvin Craig** and **Walter Hess**, who had stolen money from a slot machine at the filling station, were arrested and charged with Romaine's murder. Their trial began on April 18, 1929, with defense attorney Albert S. Ennis arguing that bloody clothes, including a shirt with a bullet hole found by a crew from the State Highway Department, proved that the uninjured defendants were innocent. The jury felt otherwise, however, and Craig and Hess were convicted and sentenced to ten years. While the pair awaited appeal, Mamie "Babe" Woolem told police that she, Louis Taylor, Joe Muehlman, and Radford Browning were at the filling station on the night of the murder, and that Taylor had shot Romine. The other three also confessed and pleaded guilty in court in May 1930. Browning and

Muehlman were sentenced to ten years in prison, while Taylor, who had a chest injury matching the bullet hole in the shirt found after the crime, received a life sentence. Woolem, who helped Taylor take care of his injury, was also found guilty and sentenced to life on Taylor's testimony that his former girlfriend had planned the robbery of the filling station and had given Taylor the gun. Hess and Craig were pardoned by Missouri Governor Henry S. Caulfield (1929–1933) within a year after their sentencing.

**1929:** On March 14, 1929, **Robert Coleman**, twenty-two, of Clayton County, Georgia, came home to find his eighteen-year-old wife murdered. He called the police, who found the murder weapons, a block of wood, a poker, and a flat iron, inside the house. They also found Coleman's overalls, recently washed, with stains that appeared to have been from human blood. Coleman suspected a man named Starks. However, Starks was never questioned. Instead, Coleman was arrested, tried, found guilty, and sentenced to life in prison. In 1932, an inmate named Davis in the Georgia prison told officials that another convict named Starks had admitted killing a Clayton County woman in 1929. Following an inquiry, Davis's statements were corroborated, and Coleman was granted an unconditional pardon by Georgia Governor Eugene Talmadge (1933–1937; 1941–1943) on April 14, 1933. The Georgia legislature awarded him $25,000 in restitution on March 27, 1941.

**1929: Joseph Barbato**, thirty-seven, was convicted of murdering Mrs. Julia Musso Quintieri in her Bronx, New York, rooming house on September 15, 1929, after she reportedly rejected his sexual advances. In December 1929, a jury convicted Barbato of first-degree murder. Judge James M. Barrett of the Bronx County Court sentenced him to death, and he was sent to Sing Sing to await execution in the electric chair. In July 1930, the Court of Appeals ruled that Barbato's conviction was invalid because the police coerced a four-word confession from him. A doctor, who had earlier examined the defendant, concluded that he had been beaten by police while in custody. Assistant District Attorney Solomon Boneparth put forward a motion requesting Barbato's release, which was accepted and acted upon by Judge Barrett, who officially released Barbato on November 26, 1930. Judge Barrett told the freed man: "Tomorrow is Thanksgiving Day and you ought to pray to God. You have much to be thankful for."

**1929:** Convicted of the murder of James B. Smith, a New York tobacco and candy salesman, in 1929, twenty-year-old **Gerald Growden** was freed after serving eight months of his sentence. His innocence was established after Lawrence Hein and Harry Lancaster confessed to the murder and provided enough details to make it clear that Growden was not with them at the time of the murder. Growden had originally been convicted on eyewitness testimony and on the testimony of inmates who knew him when he was in prison before his trial and said he had bragged about the murder. He was freed on June 18, 1932, after having been convicted and sentenced the previous October.

**1929:** In fall 1928, a German college student named **Philipp Halsmann** went on a mountain climbing expedition to the Zillertaler Alps in Austria with his father. Near the Olperer Massif, the father sustained a fatal fall. Investigators believed, however, that the death of the senior Halsmann involved murder. A bloodstained stone was found near the scene where the elder Halsmann had died, and it was thought to have been the murder weapon, but there was no hard evidence of the boy's guilt. Philipp Halsmann was nevertheless found guilty and sentenced to life in prison in early 1929. Serologists, however, began a new investigation, and these forensic scientists proved that the blood on the rock was not that of the senior Halsmann, The son was retried in spring 1929 and acquitted. The sensational nature of the trials resulted in the creation of a special laboratory for blood analysis at the Institute of Forensic Medicine at the University of Innsbruck.

**1929: H. A. Clements** was convicted and sent to prison for a Texas robbery after he had been identified by an eyewitness. The identification was discredited in 1929, and Clements was released from prison.

**1930:** Three robberies on the night of December 7, 1930, in Syracuse, New York, brought two men to the attention of the police: Vincent Starowitz, twenty-four, just released from prison, and twenty-year-old **Joseph Nedza**, on probation for the same burglary that sent Starowitz to prison. Samuel Meyers, a hotel proprietor shot during one of the robberies, identified the two from photographs. After arresting Nedza and Starowitz, police dressed them as the robbers had been dressed and invited two gas station attendants to identify the men, which they did. Faced with the positive identification, Starowitz confessed and, in the process, referred to his partner as "Jimmie." The men were quickly indicted for first-degree robbery. Albert Sherwood, arrested in Utica, was also brought to Syracuse, but, when several witnesses failed to identify him, he was returned to Utica to face other charges. In February 1931, Nedza and Starowitz were tried before Judge

William L. Barnum in Onondaga County Court. Evidence was admitted that showed the criminal records of both men, specifying that they had been convicted of burglary in the past. Nedza testified that he was at his hotel on the night in question, and he had a number of witnesses to support the claim. The jury nevertheless found both men guilty, and they were each sentenced to thirty-five years in Auburn Penitentiary. Nedza's attorney, Irving Devorsetz, was certain that his client was innocent. He continued to see Starowitz, who soon confessed that his partner in the crimes had been Albert Sherwood, not Joseph Nedza. Meyers, the hotel proprietor, then identified Sherwood in a lineup of twenty convicts, and a motion was made for a new trial for Nedza. Judge Barnum then dismissed all charges against Nedza, who was freed after serving three months.

**1931:** Anthony Huegler and his wife Emma owned a small delicatessen-grocery on Reid Avenue in Brooklyn, New York. They were hardworking people who kept only small amounts of cash in their drawer. A sinister-looking young man with a cap pulled down over his face entered their store on February 5, 1931, and held up the couple at gunpoint. He left the store with $70 taken out of the till. The police combed the neighborhood for a suspect matching the description provided by the Hueglers. Based on the sketchy information provided, **Anthony J. Barbera** was arrested on suspicion because he had been observed in the neighborhood for several days, and a gun found in his car provided the police with enough circumstantial evidence needed to sustain an arrest. Barbera protested that he had nothing to do with the holdup. He said that he had taken his fiancée to a movie theater on Myrtle Avenue that night, twelve miles from the Brooklyn delicatessen. A Kings County Grand Jury returned a first-degree robbery indictment against Barbera. The case was heard by Judge A. I. Nova on March 24–25, 1931. Despite compelling evidence from defense witnesses, who corroborated the young man's alibi, the jury believed the Hueglers, who admitted that the robber had a cap pulled low over his face, but they were still able to identify the perpetrator. Barbera was found guilty. While awaiting sentencing, the police arrested a second man, Harold Sorenson, who had a long record of delicatessen robberies. District Attorney William F. X. Geoghan was satisfied that Sorenson, not Barbera, committed the robbery after Sorenson related the exact words spoken by Mrs. Huegler in the store. On March 30, 1931,

Sorenson's confession was read to Judge Nova. Barbera was freed minutes before his scheduled sentencing.

**1931:** The key witness in a March 18, 1931, Minneapolis, Minnesota, robbery made a wrong identification, which led to the conviction of **George B. Slyter**. The actual robbers committed an identical crime the night before Slyter was to be sentenced. The record was quickly corrected, and the real thieves were arrested and sentenced. Two gunmen held up Aaron Oxendale, who was working at a Minneapolis garage, and Oxendale later gave police a description of the men. A few days later, Oxendale thought he saw one of the men who had robbed him and called the police. They arrested Slyter. He was convicted, although he denied knowledge of the crime and said he had been at a St. Patrick's Day party the night of the robbery. Though his mother and sister were able to verify this alibi, they gave different versions of the affair. In addition, Slyter had a prior criminal record, which could have doubled the sentence, turning a five to forty-year term into a ten to eighty-year term. The same garage, however, was robbed again on April 24, 1931. Oxendale recognized the bandits as the same ones who had robbed him earlier. He immediately confessed his error to the court. The following morning, after everyone had gathered for the sentencing, Slyter was set free.

**1931:** In April 1931, during the robbery of a New York City speakeasy, Peter Sardini killed a bystander. He and **Pietro Matera** were tried, convicted of murder, and sentenced to death. Just before the scheduled executions, Sardini said Matera was not his accomplice in the robbery. Because of the uncertainty about Matera's guilt, New York Governor Franklin D. Roosevelt (1929–1932) commuted Matera's sentence to life in prison in 1932. Matera was exonerated in 1960, after the wife of Sardini's real accomplice admitted on her deathbed that she had wrongly identified Matera to protect her husband. After almost thirty years behind bars for a crime he did not commit, Matera was set free.

**1931: Henry Cashin** was convicted of a New York murder and was sentenced to death on the testimony of a lone witness, a woman with questionable character. The woman recanted her statements in 1933, and Cashin's conviction was vacated and he was released from prison.

**1931: Julius Krause** was sent to prison for life after confessing to a robbery-murder in Ohio. Police had pressured him into falsely confessing after telling him that he would never be acquitted and would most probably go to the electric chair unless he confessed. One of the actual robbers made a deathbed statement in 1935, naming his real-life partner in the robbery-murder, a man who was not Krause. After officials refused to act on this information, Krause escaped from prison in 1940, and tracked down the perpetrator, extracting a confession from him, which he also made to authorities. Though Krause had brought about his own exoneration in the 1931 robbery-murder, he voluntarily returned to prison to serve out eleven more years behind bars for the prison escape, He was released in 1951.

**1932:** **Theodore Jordan** was convicted of the murder of F. T. Swift in Klamath Falls, Oregon, and sentenced to hang. There was evidence that Jordan's confession had been coerced during a beating following his arrest. Following a public outcry, his sentence was commuted to life imprisonment. He served twenty-two years and was paroled in 1954. In 1964, Jordan was arrested for shoplifting in Portland. He left the state in violation of his parole and was sentenced to three years to be served concurrently with the original life sentence, which was again in effect. He appealed the original murder sentence, and it was reversed in 1964. However, he remained guilty of shoplifting.

**1933:** When former boxer Mickey Erno and his friend Socks Brewer sold a diamond ring, they split the profits. **William Dulin** and Fred Hayes had also been in on the deal. After Dulin and Hayes discovered the deception, they were understandably upset. When Mickey Erno's body was found under a bridge in Long Beach, California, on January 17, 1933, with a bullet in the head, Dulin and Hayes were indicted for his murder. Mayme Proctor, a close friend of Hayes, testified at their trial in April 1933 that Hayes had told her in detail how the crime had been committed. He had said that nobody could "double-cross him and get away with it," she told the court. Proctor's testimony seemed quite damaging, until the defense proved that she had been threatened by police with a jail term if she did not testify. Despite the disclosure of police coercion, the case against Hayes was still strong, but evidence of Dulin's involvement was sketchy at best. Near the end of the trial, Hayes accepted full responsibility for the murder. However, both Hayes and Dulin were found guilty and sentenced to life imprisonment. Dulin's conviction was appealed, but not overturned. Finally, in 1936, at the request of a number of officials, including Dulin's trial judge, who believed Dulin to be innocent, California Governor Frank Merriam (1934–1939) pardoned Dulin.

**1933:** In 1913, John Holmberg, Frank Adams, and Marie Schmidt were seen for the last time near Fairbanks, Alaska. The following year, the bones of Holmberg were found on a sandbar in the lower Kuyouyok River. Natives found the body of Schmidt further down the river, but it was swept away by high tide before they could retrieve it. Adam's body was never found. Police sought Thomas Johnson, known as "Blueberry Tom," for the murders, but could not find him. Twenty years later, in Brooklyn, New York, a Danish seaman, **Thomas Peter Jensen**, was arrested for the murders. In the courtroom of Magistrate Malbin, Jensen was identified as "Blueberry Tom" by Frank Ely Allen, and he was convicted and sent to prison for murdering Holmberg, Adams, and Schmidt. However, Ely's identification of Jensen proved to be a case of mistaken identity, and the wrongly convicted Jensen was released on July 10, 1934, by Martin C. Epstein, the U.S. commissioner in Brooklyn.

**1933:** When the Bank of the United States collapsed in 1930, losing $443 million of investors' money, the bank's president, Bernard K. Marcus, and vice-president, Saul Singer, and Singer's son, Herbert, a law clerk, went down with it, all convicted of embezzling $8 million. The two executives and the clerk were found guilty of misappropriation of funds from several large loans, which led to the bank's collapse. Marcus and the elder Singer were sentenced to three to six years in Sing Sing. Herbert Singer was sentenced to three months to three years in the state penitentiary. Judge George L. Donnellan said their worst offense was moral, not legal, and it was based upon greed. Prosecutors also tried **Isidor Jacob Kresel**, the counsel for the bank, who advised bank officials on a complicated scheme in which bank funds were transferred to different accounts and "paper companies" to help certain affiliates pay off outstanding loans. Many of Kresel's counterparts at other institutions were aware of this banking practice and frequently used it; the difference, they admitted, was that Kresel was caught. Kresel's defense attorney argued that no one involved had profited or lost anything on the financial maneuvers; thus, no crime had been committed. Nonetheless, in November 1933, a jury found Kresel guilty. He was barred from practicing law, and was sentenced to an eighteen-month prison term. This decision also was overturned in January 1935, when an appeals court found a lack of evidence necessary for conviction and further found that the jury had been instructed incorrectly as to what constituted criminal conduct. Kresel was released after officials admitted that he had committed no crime.

**1933: Herschel McCarn**, **William Hathaway**, and **Glenn Davis** were convicted and sent to prison for an Alabama bank robbery, but were pardoned in 1940 after appeal attorneys proved that the trio had been the victims of mistaken identity.

**1933: David Lamson** (1903–1975) advertising manager of Stanford University Press, was convicted and sentenced to death for murdering his wife, Allene Lamson, in their Palo Alto, California, home on Memorial Day 1933. The woman's injuries were in question in that she may have accidentally struck her head when falling, but prosecutors convinced a jury that Lamson had struck the fatal blow. Prosecutors also advanced an unfounded theory that a "love triangle" had motivated Lamson's murder, but the defendant's counsel failed to rebut that unsubstantiated argument. This argument stemmed from two love poems written by an old friend of Lamson's, Sara Kelley, but the poems had actually been submitted for publication to the *Stanford Illustrated Review*. The defense relied upon the "accidental death" theory, but did not explore the possibility that Allene Lamson might have been killed by a third party, ignoring a report from a Stanford student, John Venderlip, who had informed campus police that he had seen a suspicious stranger near the Lamson residence on the night of Mrs. Lamson's death and early in the morning following that death. On September 16, 1933, defense attorney Edwin Rea was almost nonchalant after the jury, deliberating for eight hours, returned a guilty verdict of first-degree murder, which mean death. "Take it on the chin, kid," Rea whispered to his client. On appeal, Lamson saw three more trials, two resulting in hung juries and one aborted due to jury list irregularities. Before a fifth trial was ordered, prosecutors, realizing that they had little evidence to begin with, dropped all charges against Lamson, and he was released from prison on April 3, 1936. He moved to Los Angeles, where he remarried (to screen magazine writer Ruth Smith Rankin) and raised his daughter, Allene Genevieve Lamson. Abandoning the advertising profession, Lamson wrote screenplays and published eighty-nine short stories, many of which were published in the *Saturday Evening Post*. He later moved to Los Altos, California, where he became a maintenance manager for United Airlines, dying there in 1975 at age seventy-two.

**1934**: During the strain of the Great Depression, **Louis J. Weitzman** loaned $108,000 to Eli Daiches, the owner of the Thomas M. Bowers Agency, a Chicago advertising firm. As collateral, Weitzman, a relative of Daiches' wife, received stock in the company, and he became the chairman of the board of directors and the actual owner of the firm. Daiches transferred life insurance policies worth $317,000 at the same time, designating his company as the beneficiary. On March 3, 1934, as Daiches was driven from his apartment in a limousine, another car pulled up, and a young man, armed with a double-barreled sawed-off shotgun, got out of his car. He walked leisurely toward the limousine and fatally shot Daiches in the chest and head. Then the killer returned to his car and drove slowly away in the morning rush hour. A local reporter, Harry Read, discovered the connection between the loan and the insurance policy, and he also learned that Weitzman had two cousins with police records, and two brothers, Irving and Leon, who operated a bakery in Chicago. Irving Weitzman was implicated in the murder plot along with Jerry Pilot and a man named Toner. Pilot was suspected of being the killer and Toner as Pilot's assistant. In early April 1934, Pilot was murdered and Toner was killed as he went home from Pilot's funeral, both shot to death with the same gun responsible in the Daiches murder. Irving Weitzman was tried for the Daiches murder, and on February 23, 1935, he was found guilty and sentenced to a life term; however, after an appeal and a retrial, he was acquitted, his wrongful conviction based upon insufficient evidence.

**1934: Nancy Louise Botts** was convicted of forgery in Kokomo (Howard County), Indiana, and sentenced to two to four years in prison after seven merchants insisted that she was the culprit. Botts, who claimed that she had never in her life been in Kokomo, was exonerated in 1936, when Indiana Governor Paul V. McNutt (1933–1937) pardoned her, following the confession of a woman named Dorsett, who had been passing the bad checks. Botts was awarded $4,000 in compensation by the state legislature for her wrongful conviction and imprisonment.

**1934: Ovid Matthis** and **I. L. Southerland** were convicted and sent to prison for a Texas bank robbery through erroneous identification, but they were later released when another man confessed to the crime. Texas Governor W. Lee "Pappy" O'Daniel (1939–1941) pardoned both men.

**1935**: During President Franklin D. Roosevelt's New Deal administration in the 1930s, the main solution to the U.S. Depression crisis in agriculture was to cut down production by supplementing government subsidies to cooperating farmers. Though the tactic successfully raised agricultural prices, it devastated tenant farmers, laborers, and sharecroppers in the South. Landlords grabbed acreage reduction benefits intended for the tenant farmers and even dispossessed sharecroppers and tenants, who then became disenfranchised laborers and went on relief. Blacks and whites together reacted by organizing tenants' unions, not for the first time. An earlier Alabama Sharecroppers Union in the Depression years was violently broken up by the authorities. The most effective new organization was formed in Arkansas. Socialists H. L. Mitchell and Clay East, advised and backed by Norman Thomas and the Socialist Party, formed the **Southern Tenant Farmers' Union**. Earlier efforts in Arkansas had been quickly repelled by violence, and, in 1919, a Phillips County union of blacks was massacred. By 1935, the new interracial movement included Socialists and ministers, with 10,000 members in eighty local branches. The group focused on peaceful action, but was met with massive mob violence, with local whites and absentee corporations trying to break the union through harassment, threats, beatings, and murder. Despite all this, the union endured, struggling unsuccessfully against great odds to change the economic structure of the area. A reign of violence in March 1935 continued for about two and a half months as terrorist tactics against the union prevailed in northeastern Arkansas, with meetings broken up and members falsely accused, jailed, and wrongly convicted on fraudulent charges. Relief was cut off, and members were evicted by the hundreds as vigilante bands patrolled the highways. Organizers were beaten, mobbed, tortured, and slain. On Norman Thomas's return to New York, he began a nationwide radio broadcast with a denunciation of what he had seen: His broadcasts brought national attention to the mob violence, terrorism, and massive wrongful convictions. Public pressure eventually forced these activities to diminish and finally stop.

**1935: Harry Pyle** was convicted in Kansas on murder and robbery charges and sentenced to a life term in 1935. A district court upheld the conviction, and later the Kansas Supreme Court refused to reverse it on appeal. On November 20, 1941, Pyle wrote a petition himself for a writ of habeas corpus, charging that the prosecution used perjured testimony and had suppressed evidence in convicting him. He submitted the document to the Kansas Supreme Court, along with a letter from witness Truman Reynolds, who said police had employed coercion in Pyle's case, threatening to send him to prison for burglary if he did not testify

against Pyle. Pyle also sent a letter from a prosecuting attorney in the case, which said: "The evidence at the trial of Murl Hudson certainly shattered the conclusions drawn from the evidence produced at your trial." The court still denied the appeal. About six months later, Murl Hudson was tried for involvement in the same robbery and murder for which Pyle had been convicted. Evidence presented at Hudson's trial proved that Pyle was not guilty. Pyle then wrote to the U.S. Supreme Court, which held that the new proof "clearly exonerates petitioner," and he was finally released. According to the old proverb, this was truly a case of God helping someone who helped himself.

**1935:** In May 1935, **Arthur O'Connell**, twenty-six, was convicted and sent to prison for eight to twelve years for sexually attacking a thirteen-year-old girl in Boston, Massachusetts. The victim and her thirteen-year-old girlfriend identified O'Connell and testified against him in court. A month later, the companion told police that the crime had never happened and that the girls had accused O'Connell "just for fun" after he stopped on the street to briefly talk to them. O'Connell was released from prison in June 1935 (this kind of wrongful identification would be repeated in England in 1976, when some girls wrongly identified **Stefan Ivan Kiszko** for a crime he did not commit as "a joke"; see Chronology, 1976).

**1935: Geither Horn** confessed to a murder after police took him to an open grave in Franklin County, Washington, and threatened to bury him alive with the victim if he did not sign a confession. He signed the confession and spent twenty-four years in prison, released in 1959 after officials realized that he had been coerced by local police. Horn, after his 1959 prison release, was awarded $6,000 for his wrongful conviction and imprisonment.

**1936:** Frequently arrested, put in prison, and sent into exile during the czarist regime, **Aleksei Ivanovich Rykov** (1881–1938) supported Lenin and the communist revolution in Russia in 1917. After Lenin's death in 1924, he became the president of the Soviet of People's Commissars, serving from 1924–1930. However, he was dismissed from his position because of his opposition to Joseph Stalin. He publicly retracted his disagreements with dictator Stalin and was reinstalled as commissar for posts and telegraph from 1931–1936. In 1936, he was falsely accused and convicted of involvement in a conspiracy to assassinate Stalin and was executed for treason in 1938. Rykov was only one of thousands of such wrongly convicted persons who suffered imprisonment or execution during Stalin's massive political purges in the mid-1930s.

**1936:** On December 18, 1936, in Manhattan, New York, **George Chew Wing** (1904–1937) was convicted of the November 29, 1935, Chinatown murder of Yip Chow. Wing had been identified as one of the four masked men who took part in the first Chinese homicide in more than twenty years. He was executed on February 8, 1937, but later it was discovered that he had been falsely identified and that perjured testimony had been used against him. An alleged coconspirator had named Wing in exchange for a plea-bargained lesser sentence.

**1936: John Brite** and his brother, **Coke Brite**, who owned property at Horse Creek, California, in Siskiyou County, had had a dispute with Charles Baker and Fred Seaborn, who convinced local deputy sheriffs Martin Lange and Joseph Clarke to arrest the Brites in order to use the Brite property for some business enterprises. On August 30, 1936, the deputies crept up on the Brites at their camp. Thinking they were being attacked by a gang of thieves, the brothers reportedly opened fire, killing Seaborn, Lange, and Clarke. Baker fled the scene and reported to officials that the Brites had committed the triple slaying. They were brought to trial, convicted of the murders on Baker's testimony and the testimony of a ballistics expert, who said that the bullets taken from the three slain men had come from guns owned by the Brites. The brothers were sentenced to death. Their sentences were later commuted to life imprisonment, and they continued to file appeals without success. Mystery writer Erle Stanley Gardner later undertook their case and hired an investigator named McClure, who showed that Baker had lied in his statements about the Brites and that the ballistics evidence had been bogus. He proved that the Brites had not killed anyone in the firefight and that Baker may have been the perpetrator. The Brite brothers were released from prison in September 1951.

**1937:** Shortly before midnight on October 6, 1937, Albert Dillulio was fatally shot in the doorway of a barbershop on Forty-eighth Street in Manhattan, New York. **Thomas Kapatos**, twenty-two, was eventually arrested and charged with killing Dillulio. He was tried for second-degree murder at the General Session Court of Manhattan in 1938. Two guns that were identified as the murder weapons were found in his possession. He was convicted and sentenced to twenty years to life in prison, despite the fact that key witnesses were not allowed to testify. Michael Danise, one of those wit-

nesses, was present at the time of the shooting and had witnessed two others fleeing the area. However, neither of these men was suspected. Kapatos was granted a parole in 1960. A year later, however, he was back in prison, convicted of receiving stolen goods. He served another year's sentence, which resulted in revocation of his parole hearing on the murder charge. Then on July 9, 1962, federal Judge Edmund Palmieri ordered the prisoner released after attorney Joseph Aronstein filed for a writ of habeas corpus. The state prosecutor in the original trial had prejudiced the jury, according to Judge Palmieri. The available evidence would not have been enough to convict Kapatos at the time.

**1937: Charles Lee Clark**, thirty-nine, was accused of shooting to death the owner of a Michigan store during a holdup by three men in 1937. Despite sworn affidavits from Clark's landlady claiming that Clark was home during the killing, he was convicted and sentenced to life imprisonment; Michigan had earlier done away with capital punishment. For the next three decades, Clark turned down offers of a commuted sentence or parole, arguing: "If I accepted a parole, it meant I would still have that mark on my record." His determination was rewarded when it was finally proven that the one eyewitness to the murder, the store owner's daughter, had been coaxed by police to identify Clark as the killer. Clark was released in 1968 after a new trial overturned the conviction. In December 1971, the State of Michigan agreed to pay Clark $10,000, awarded on January 28, 1972, in compensation for having spent thirty years behind bars for a crime he did not commit.

**1937: Anthony Piano** was convicted of a robbery in Pennsylvania, but was released from prison seven months later and exonerated after the real perpetrator had been identified. Piano had been identified by an eyewitness who later admitted to mistaken identity error.

**1938:** The wife of Texan W. S. Cochran was allegedly raped by a black man, **Bob White**, who was tried, convicted of rape, and sentenced to death in 1938. After an appeal, the Texas Court of Criminal Appeals overturned the conviction. White was tried and convicted again, although he claimed police beat him to make him confess. The U.S. Supreme Court struck down the decision and ordered a new trial. During jury selection for the third trial in June 1941, Cochran walked into the courtroom and fatally shot White in the head. Cochran gave his gun to the prosecutor, turned himself over to authorities, and a week later, after deliberating ten minutes, an all-white jury acquitted him of murdering White.

**1939**: **Samuel Curbow** and **J. C. Strickland** were convicted of a Texas robbery in January 1939, following their identification by several eyewitnesses. Both were indigent and without funds and were not appointed any legal representation at their trial. In 1940, the actual perpetrators confessed to the robbery, and both men were released from prison. Curbow and Strickland were given official pardons by Texas Governor W. Lee "Pappy" O'Daniel (1939–1941), who was characterized by actor Charles Durning in the 2000 film, *O, Brother Where Art Thou*.

**1943**: **William Marvin Lindley** was convicted and sentenced to death for murder in Los Angeles, California. Prosecutors at his 1943 trial used the dying statements of the victim to bring about that conviction, saying that she had identified her assailant as Lindley. Mystery writer Erle Stanley Gardner championed his case and, after conducting his own investigation, showed that the police had manufactured evidence against Lindley and that Lindley had been at another and distant location at the time of the murder and could not therefore have been at the scene of the crime. Lindley received a stay of execution and was released from prison in 1963.

**1945**: On October 22, 1945, Sophie Wright, a seventy-year-old widow, was attacked by two men in her New York City apartment. **Thomas Oliver**, eighteen, of Brooklyn and Eddie Lee Wilbur, a neighbor of the victim, were arrested the next day. Mrs. Wright identified both men at their trial, which resulted in a conviction. They were sentenced to from ten to twenty years in Sing Sing. In December 1946, District Attorney Frank Hogan received a letter from Oliver proclaiming his innocence, claiming that he had been wrongly convicted. Hogan ordered a new investigation in which Wilbur admitted that Oliver had no part in the attack, and that he implicated Oliver in fear of his real partner. Oliver, however, had been convicted on testimony by the victim. Mrs. Wright was finally convinced that Wilbur's partner was another man. Meanwhile, with Wilbur's assistance, the police arrested James W. Campbell. Campbell was quickly convicted and sent to prison for attacking Wright, and Oliver was freed. New York Governor Thomas E. Dewey (1943–1954) allowed Oliver to sue the state for false imprisonment. Before the suit was filed, however, Oliver was found guilty of another felony. He received a suspended sentence because of time wrongly served, but was forced to drop his lawsuit.

**1946**: **Edward Hodsdon** was convicted and sentenced to fifteen years in prison for assaulting a woman with intent to rape in Presque Isle, Maine. He was identified by the victim, whose testimony brought about his conviction. In 1952, Edward Kennison, arrested on an unrelated charge, confessed that he, not Hodsdon, had committed the assault. Hodsdon's conviction was vacated, and he was released from prison.

**1947**: **William S. Green** was convicted of a Pennsylvania murder, but was released and exonerated in 1957, following the recantation of the chief witness for the prosecution, who admitted that he had lied when he said he saw Green at the scene of the murder. The witness said that he had been paid $100 to provide false testimony against Green by a homosexual, who had been beaten by Green after Green had refused his solicitations.

**1948**: On January 27, 1948, a group of young black men entered the North Broad Street junk shop of seventy-three-year-old William Horner in Trenton, New Jersey, saying that they wanted to buy a mattress and a stove, but the group suddenly demanded the owner's receipts, $50, while he was in the back room. One of the robbers threw or wielded a soda pop bottle that crushed Horner's head, killing him, while another clubbed his common law wife, Elizabeth, into unconsciousness. When she was revived by police, she said she could not give specific descriptions of the robbers, only that she had seen at least three black men in the store. A witness said he had seen two light-skinned blacks walk from the store at the time of the robbery. Another witness claimed that he had seen black "teenagers" flee the store, running to a car driven by another black youth. The murder created widespread pressure on the police to produce the culprits, which was typified on January 29, 1948, by a *Trenton Evening Times* editorial crying out for vengeful blood, entitled "The Idle Death Chair," and saying that the state's official instrument of death was not being employed enough to thwart the murders of people like Horner. Police patrol cars swarmed into black neighborhoods, pulling young black males in for questioning. On February 6, 1948, police detained twenty-three-year-old Collis English, who had been stopped for driving his father's car without permission. He was put through extensive interrogations and soon he signed a confession, implicating five other blacks, all six men later being dubbed the "Trenton Six." English, a Navy veteran with a rheumatic heart condition, had a low mental aptitude, as police knew, and was easily coerced into his confession, as he later claimed when recanting his statements. On February 11, 1948, English was arraigned on a charge of murdering Horner. Charged with English was his thirty-five-year-old brother-in-law, **McKinley Forrest**, who had gone to police headquarters a few days earlier to inquire why his relative was being held and was then himself seized as a suspect in the Horner case. The other four included twenty-three-year-old Ralph Cooper, twenty-four-year-old **John McKenzie**, twenty-four-year-old **James Thorpe**, and forty-year-old **Horace Wilson**. All but Wilson signed confessions, and all who signed those confessions later recanted them, saying that they had been coerced. Forrest had signed a confession that admitted that he had swung the bottle that killed Horner, and police produced a receipt he allegedly signed with his own name that proved he had been in Horner's store a week before the killing. Both the confession and the receipt were suspicious from the start in that Forrest was illiterate and could only sign his name with an "X." Thorpe had only one arm, one being amputated following an accident only eight days before the Horner slaying, and none of the witnesses ever testified that they saw a one-armed man fleeing the place. Witnesses also stated that the getaway car was a green Plymouth, while police insisted that the robbery car was a black Ford, the one in which they had found English. Prosecutor Mario Volpe nevertheless publicly stated that the case against the six men was "overwhelming." When asked about the recanted confessions, Volpe said that the recantations were part of a group conspiracy wherein the defendants "agreed and planned to act crazy in order to produce or provide an avenue of escape." An all-white jury agreed with Volpe, when, on August 6, 1948, after deliberating for seven and a half hours, it found all six men guilty. All six were immediately sentenced to death and sent to the New Jersey State Prison's Death Row. The conviction caused international response, which widely claimed that the Trenton Six had been legally lynched on the flimsiest of evidence and they were likened to the pilloried Scottsboro Boys of the 1930s (see Chapter XI: "Railroading and Framing"). There appeared no hope for the condemned men until Bessie Mitchell, English's sister, a New York seamstress, viewed the conviction as a travesty of justice. She petitioned the Trenton NAACP to raise money for an appeal, and, when that organization was disinclined to support an unpopular and apparently losing case, she turned to the Communist Party, which championed the Trenton Six through its legal arm, the Civil Rights Congress, which, in a 1949 appeal, con-

vinced the New Jersey Supreme Court to reverse the convictions and order a new trial. By then the Communist Party backed away from the case, as it was drawing too much attention from powerful anti-Communist forces led by Wisconsin Senator Joseph McCarthy. Funds from the NAACP supported the retrial of the defendants, who were then represented by George Pellettieri and Ruth Rabstein (who fell in love during the case and later married), along with many other attorneys from New York and Philadelphia. The second trial began in March 1951 and resulted in the acquittals of Forrest, McKenzie, Thorpe, and Wilson on June 14, 1951. English and Cooper were found guilty on circumstantial evidence. English died in prison a year later when his rheumatic heart gave out, and Cooper, whose plight seemed hopeless, cut a deal with prosecutors wherein he admitted the murder in exchange for time served and a parole in 1954.

**1948:** On March 2, 1948, in New York City, **Samuel Tito Williams** was convicted of the 1947 murder of a fifteen-year-old Brooklyn girl and sentenced to death. On November 16, 1949, the day before Williams was to die in the electric chair, New York Governor Thomas E. Dewey (1943–1954) commuted his sentence to life imprisonment. In 1963, after sixteen years in prison, Williams's conviction was overturned because his confession had been coerced. He was released and later received compensatory damages from the state for "malicious prosecution."

**1949**: In December 1949, longshoreman **Jean Dehays** was tried in Nantes, France, with Rene Floriot defending him against charges of robbery and assault. Dehays had confessed to his crime, but it was speculated that police had beaten the confession from him. At his trial, Dehays appeared on crutches with one leg in a cast. When asked why the defendant was in this condition, officers explained that he had fallen down the stairs at the police station. Dehays was sentenced to ten years of hard labor. Four years later, Rene Dutoy and Raymond Pruvot confessed to the crime for which Dehays had been convicted, absolving him of the robbery. At the hearing to obtain rehabilitation at the ensuing trial, Floriot told the court, "You will never stop the police from beating up suspects." Dehays was then officially released without compensation.

**1949: John Stoppelli** was convicted of drug trafficking in Oakland, California, following his 1948 arrest, along with four other men. He had been convicted in a federal court after one of his fingerprints was identified on a package of heroin. The four men told police that

Stoppelli was not a member of their drug gang, and Stoppelli provided an alibi—that he had been registering with his probation officer in New York City, three thousand miles away, at the time of the crime. These seemingly stolid defense arguments met with no success, but famed San Francisco criminal attorney Jake Ehrlich did not give up on his client. He contacted a fingerprint expert at the FBI's crime lab and had him examine the fingerprint that had sent Stoppelli to prison. The report the expert returned stated that the print did not match that of Stoppelli. The court, however, refused to accept this as new evidence, saying that the FBI report was nothing more than a reexamination of old evidence. In 1951, President Harry Truman (1884–1972; term of office, 1945–1953) commuted Stoppelli's conviction to time served, and he was released from prison.

**1950**: **Leonard Kirkes**, wrongly convicted of second-degree murder in late 1950, spent more than two years behind bars for a crime he did not commit. Kirkes, a former California highway patrolman, was convicted of the August 1942 murder of twenty-year-old Margaret Senteney and was sentenced to life imprisonment at San Quentin. The victim's body had been found in the foothills above the town of Carpinteria, and, for eight years, the case remained unsolved. Local Sheriff John Ross gleaned every bit of evidence he could in the case, all of which amounted to little more than snippets of gossip and rumor. Ross had actually found the body of Senteney, bruised and garroted, along with Kirkes. Although Ross told Kirkes to be careful in inspecting the crime scene, Kirkes reportedly trampled footprints and tire tracks nearby. Kirkes, a graduate of Vanderbilt University, church member, and the married father of a young boy, went off to serve in the Aleutians during World War II, returning to his job as a state motorcycle cop after the war. Ross continued to work with him, but suspected him all along as the killer, and, when a woman in Carpenteria filed a complaint that Kirkes had molested her ten-year-old son, Ross jailed the cop, hoping that a witness would then come forward with more evidence in the Senteney case. A friend of the slain woman did just that in September 1950, saying that she had seen the victim get into Kirkes's 1939 coupe Ford the night before Senteney's death. This witness, more than any other evidence, brought about Kirkes's conviction. In 1953, granted a retrial, he won acquittal when the higher court ruled there had been misconduct by one of the prosecutors and an error made by the judge while instructing the jurors. Further, Kirkes's attorneys were

able to provide information about the star prosecution witness, who was then residing in a mental institution. Psychiatrists stated that the woman had had mental problems dealing with reality long before she testified against Kirkes. In May 1953, a California Supreme Court jury spent fourteen minutes in deliberation to clear Kirkes. Walking out of court a free man, Kirkes said: "I would have appealed this case for the rest of my life."

**1950: Timothy Evans**, a dull-witted man who may have been retarded, falsely confessed to murdering his infant daughter, Geraldine, in London, England. Evans later recanted his confession, saying that "the other man" had committed the crime. After Evans was executed by hanging, the "other man" and true murderer, John Reginald Halliday Chistie, a subtle serial killer, was found to have not only killed the child but Evans's wife and many other victims. Evans and his family had lived in the same building with Christie, 10 Rillington Place, which became a horror house in London when one rotting body after another was discovered behind the walls, under the floors and buried in the small backyard garden. The British government granted Evans a posthumous pardon in 1966 in its belated recognition of his innocence.

**1950: Joseph Smith** was convicted of a May 1950 armed robbery in Pennsylvania. He was released from prison in July 1963, after the real perpetrator confessed that Smith had been framed for the crime.

**1951: Emma Jo Johnson** was convicted of murder in Nevada, but was released from prison in 1954 after a court determined that no crime had been committed.

**1951: George White** was convicted of a November 1951 robbery in Texas. Without funds to hire legal counsel, the court failed to appoint an attorney to represent him. The real robber confessed to the crime in 1959, and White was released from prison, receiving a full pardon from Texas Governor Price Daniel (1957–1963).

**1952**: Following a 1952 conviction for felony murder, to which **Joseph Antoniewicz**, **William A. Hallowell**, and **Edward H. Parks** had all pleaded guilty, the three youths—all under eighteen years old at the time of their arrest—spent sixteen years of life sentences in prison before the decision was overturned. Judge Edmund B. Spaeth Jr. ordered the release of Antoniewicz, Hallowell, and Parks on February 13, 1968, after evaluating the testimony from a Philadelphia medical examiner, who said the man killed had died of coronary heart disease and not from an attack by the youths during a robbery nine days earlier.

**1953:** A woman sentenced to life for killing her husband with an ax was freed by a judge, who rejected a controversial agreement between Britain and the United States empowering the latter to prosecute crimes committed by civilians accompanying the U.S. Air Force. On March 10, 1953, Master Sergeant Edward Covert was slain by his wife as he slept in their home in Heyfort, England. The country had no jurisdiction to prosecute the wife due to a section of the 1950 Uniform Code of Military Justice, and she was sent back to the United States, where she received life imprisonment by a court-martial of the U.S. Air Force. Mrs. **Clarice Covert** was freed in late fall of 1955 by Federal District Judge Edward A. Tamm, who ruled that the section of the military code by which she was sent home was unconstitutional.

**1953:** A California man who studied Buddhism in his youth and lived in a Japanese monastery, **John David Provoo,** later enlisted in the U.S. Army and rose to the rank of sergeant. When he was captured on Corregidor in 1942, at the age of twenty-five, Provoo became, according to his fellow prisoners, an informer for the Japanese and was connected with the execution of a U.S. officer. No charges were brought against him after the war, and he re-enlisted. In 1949, however, he was indicted for treason and was sentenced to life imprisonment in 1953. A year later, the U.S. Court of Appeals for New York reversed the conviction on technical grounds. The court ruled that the ex-sergeant should have been tried in Maryland, where he was first arrested, and that he should not have been cross-examined on the issue of homosexuality, as it was irrelevant and "prejudicial." Provoo was again indicted, this time in Baltimore, Maryland, but, in March 1955, his case was thrown out when U.S. District Court Judge Roszel C. Thomsen ruled that he had been "denied the right of speedy trial within the meaning of the Sixth Amendment." The dismissal of Provoo's case was upheld by the U.S. Supreme Court in October 1955.

**1953: Darrell Parker** was convicted of murdering his wife in Nebraska after confessing to the killing. His conviction was vacated, and he was released in 1969 after defense attorneys proved that the confession had been coerced. In 1988, attorneys representing another man, who had just died, released a signed confession from their client that he had been Mrs. Parker's murderer.

**1953: Kenneth Massey** was convicted of a January 1953 armed robbery in Texas. He was released from

prison in November 1954, after the actual perpetrator admitted the robbery. Texas Governor Allan Shivers (1949–1957) granted Massey a full pardon.

**1953:** On the testimony of an eyewitness, **Arthur Emery** was convicted of robbing a bus driver in Washington State. He was released after the witness recanted the identification and released in January 1954, seven months after being incarcerated. Emery was pardoned by Washington Governor Arthur B. Langlie (1941–1945; 1949–1957) and was awarded $13,000 in compensation by the state legislature.

**1956: Edward A. McMullen** was charged with a murder committed during a robbery. McMullen, however, did not fire the murder weapon. Nevertheless, he was found guilty and sentenced to life in an Ohio prison in 1956. McMullen's attorney learned of his client's innocence in 1963, when it was revealed that police had suppressed ballistic evidence of the gun in question. The evidence proved that the murder weapon had been used during a previous burglary committed by three other men. This information had been known to the prosecution, but not to McMullen's defense attorneys. The conviction was overturned in 1965 by the Ohio Supreme Court's ruling in *McMullen v. Maxwell*. McMullen was acquitted at a retrial.

**1960: Robert Lee Kidd** was convicted and sentenced to death for the December 13, 1954, murder of seventy-one-year-old Alfred Clarke during the robbery of Clarke's antique shop in San Francisco, California. On appeal, Kidd's attorneys were able to convince the court that Clarke was alive several hours after their client reportedly murdered him. Kidd was released from prison in 1962, after having spent two years behind bars.

**1960: Clyde Kennard,** a young black man, was convicted of burglarizing $25 worth of chicken feed in Forrest County, Mississippi. He was sentenced to seven years of hard labor. Because of failing health, Kennard was given clemency and released from prison in 1963, dying six months later. In-depth studies on this case performed by high school students in Lincolnshire, Illinois, determined that Kennard had been framed and sent to prison in order to prevent him from becoming the first black student to attend Mississippi Southern College (later renamed the University of Southern Mississippi). Years after that conviction, his accuser signed an affidavit exonerating him. Mississippi Governor Haley Barbour (2004– ), after receiving a request from the students, refused to issue a posthumous pardon for Kennard, but one of his spokespersons stated on May 4,

2006, that Barbour recognized that Kennard was innocent. Judge Bob Helfrich of the Forrest County Circuit Court, where Kennard had been convicted forty-six years earlier, vacated Kennard's conviction and exonerated him, saying on May 17, 2006: "I am compelled to do the right thing, and that is to declare Mr. Kennard innocent, and to declare that the conviction of Mr. Kennard is hereby null and void."

**1961: Clarence Earl Gideon** (1910–1972) was convicted of breaking and entering with intent to commit larceny after a pool hall/beer joint, owned by Ira Strickland Jr., in Bay Harbor (Bay County), Florida, at the outskirts of Panama City, had been burglarized on June 3, 1961. Impoverished, Gideon was compelled to defend himself and, with no legal knowledge, was easily convicted. On August 27, 1961, he was given the maximum sentence by Judge McCrary of five years in prison. While behind bars, Gideon, who had no formal education, researched and taught himself the law, and filed many appeals on his own behalf. All failed, until he wrote a five-page letter to the U.S. Supreme Court, which agreed to hear his case and assigned the brilliant attorney Abe Fortas to represent him. Fortas argued before the court that "you cannot have a fair trial without counsel." In little more than three hours after closing arguments from Fortas and Bruce Jacob, representing the State of Florida, the court unanimously (9–0) ruled in Gideon's favor, saying that he had been wrongly convicted because he had been denied the right of counsel. On August 5, 1963, Gideon was retried, with W. Fred Turner as his defense counsel. Turner proved that the lone witness against Gideon, Henry Cook, had most likely been a lookout for a group of youths who had routinely burglarized taverns. Gideon was acquitted. On November 11, 1963, U.S. Attorney General Robert F. Kennedy commented on this precedent-setting case, saying: "If an obscure Florida convict named Clarence Earl Gideon had not sat down in prison with a pencil and paper to write a letter to the Supreme Court; and if the Supreme Court had not taken the trouble to look at the merits in that one crude petition among all the bundles of mail it must receive everyday, the vast machinery of American law would have gone on functioning undisturbed. But Gideon did write that letter, the court did look into his case; and he was retried with the help of competent defense counsel, found not guilty and released from prison after two years of punishment for a crime he did not commit. And the whole course of legal history has been changed." Gideon's dramatic struggle to gain freedom was profiled in the 1980 made-

for-TV film *Gideon's Trumpet*, starring Henry Fonda as Gideon.

**1961: Darryl Beamish,** a deaf mute, was convicted and sentenced to death for the 1959 axe murder of twenty-two-year-old socialite and chocolate heiress Jillian Brewer in Perth, Australia. He received several stays from the gallows until his sentence was commuted to life imprisonment. He was released in 1977, after serving fifteen years, but was not exonerated until 2005, when, during his fifth appeal, his attorney, Tom Percy was able to convince the appeals court that he his client had not understood anything that happened at the police station where he was interrogated for the killing or at his subsequent trial. Moreover, Percy provided evidence that serial killer Eric Edgar Cooke, who had terrorized Perth for fifteen years with a half dozen brutal murders, confessed to the Brewer killing. Beamish's conviction was overturned in April 2005, and he was finally cleared. Percy was also instrumental in bringing about the exoneration of another wrongly convicted Australian, John Button (see Chronology, 1963).

**1961: Willie Comer** was convicted and imprisoned as being one of the men who robbed a café in Pennsylvania. Four months after entering prison, Comer was released and all charges against him were dismissed after a codefendant confessed that Comer had not been part of the robbery, the real perpetrator naming his actual accomplices.

**1962: Vinzenz Kuehn** had a record of sexually molested little girls, but it is believed the fifty-two-year-old Kuehn was wrongly convicted of the violent rape and murder of thirteen-year-old Petra Giese on April 23, 1962. Giese's strangled, raped, and partially dissected body was found in a wooded area near Bruckhausen, Germany. It was believed that her killer had removed and eaten the fleshy parts of her body, which were never found. Police suspected Kuehn after a nearby resident reported seeing a rare Goggomobile Isar, a combination motorcycle and automobile, in the area on the day of the girl's murder. Only 522 of these vehicles existed and Kuehn, who owned one, was soon traced. When it was learned that he had a sexual proclivity for young girls, he was quickly arrested. Without a concrete alibi on the day in question, Kuehn was found guilty, but the judge sentenced him to only twelve years in prison and ordered him to undergo psychiatric treatment. Two months after Giese's death, another body was found north of Bruckhausen. A second police department handled the homicide and had they been aware of the particulars in the Giese case, Kuehn might not have been convicted. Kuehn was released after serving six years. The murder of Petra Griese, it was later confirmed, had been committed by rapist-murderer and cannibal Joachim Kroll (born in 1933; a.k.a.: The Ruhr Hunter),

**1963: George Whitmore Jr.,** a dim-witted youth, was manipulated into confessing to the murder of Janice Wylie, a celebrated Manhattan slaying, for which he was convicted and imprisoned. Whitmore was later released when pharmacist Richard Robles admitted killing Janice, the niece of writer Philip Wylie, and her roommate Emily Hoffert.

**1963:** On the night of February 9, 1963, seventeen-year-old Rosemary Anderson was run down and fatally crushed by a car driven by her killer in Perth, Australia. The girl died in a hospital the next day without regaining consciousness. Her boyfriend, nineteen-year-old **John Button,** was convicted of manslaughter, despite his claims of innocence. He was released on parole in 1969, but continued his fight for exoneration. In 1992, writer Estelle Blackburn took up his cause, and, following her research, stated that the real perpetrator had been serial killer Eric Edgar Cooke. Journalist Bret Christian conceived and arranged for car-crash evidence to be presented by Rusty Haight, a car-crash expert, who examined Button's Simca car, stating that no hair, skin, skin smears, or clothing imprints had been found on the car. His statements were supported by the owner of a car Cooke had stolen and crashed on the night of Anderson's fatal attack. Cooke himself, who was hanged for the murder of John Sturkey, had confessed several times to killing Anderson to his widow, Sally Cooke. (In all, six murders had been attributed to Cooke.) In 2002, the West Australian Court of Criminal Appeals overturned Button's conviction and exonerated him the following year, awarding the fifty-nine-year-old Button $460,000 in compensation (largest paid in Australia) for the five and a half years he had spent in prison. West Australia Attorney General Jim McGinty admitted that the compensation was almost three times more than the previous record payout of $160,000, but added that "the toll on him [Button] continues to be huge and affected all aspects of his life, including his work capacity."

**1964:** On September 27, 1964, twelve-year-old Edith Connor was raped and murdered in Philadelphia. **Lou Mickens-Thomas** was convicted and sentenced to life in prison for this crime, chiefly on the testimony of Agnes Mallatratt, a so-called forensic expert working at the Philadelphia crime lab. The girl's body had been found in an alley three doors away from Mickens-Thomas's shoe repair shop, the proximity of the corpse leading police to arrest the defendant without any other cause. Mallatratt testified that she had found microscopic wax and bristle particles on the body that were similar to particles found in the defendant's home. The particles could have been present within an area of a half block of the scene where the body was found, but this area was not examined by Mallatratt, who stated in court that her credentials included her being a graduate of Temple University, that she had done postgraduate work in zoology, botany, and biology, and that she was a hematologist. Years later, she was exposed as a fraud, that she had not even graduated high school, and that all of her forensic work was questionable. In 1995, Lou Mickens-Thomas was released from prison on the executive order of Governor Robert Patrick Casey (1987–1995).

**1965:** A Bronx, New York, man, **Arthur Barber**, born in 1941, was arrested, tried, and convicted for the murder of Elijah Williams, which occurred on December 19, 1965. Williams was a bookie and numbers runner with whom Barber had quarreled. A jury convicted Barber of first-degree murder despite evidence that the police had conducted their interrogation in a brutal, shocking manner, questioning him for an extended period of time without arraignment, denying him permission to call an attorney, and neglecting to advise him of his right to remain silent lest he incriminate himself. His conviction was upheld in the appeals courts, and Barber began serving his life sentence. He clung to the faint hope that the federal courts might free him, but, as the years passed, the chances grew remote. A defense attorney then filed an appeal a decade later, one that produced surprising results. On September 10, 1975, Federal Judge Constance Baker Motley ruled that the actions of the police at the time constituted a "pattern of lawlessness, which shocks the conscience." In a twenty-page opinion, Motley cited evidence that Barber had been arrested without probable cause and beaten by police. She ordered his immediate release.

**1967:** On May 11, 1967, fifty-five-year-old Joseph Gagnepain, toll keeper of the Mississippi River booth at Chester, Illinois, was murdered, the perpetrator taking $11 in bills and approximately $40 in change from the booth. Two days later, police found a revolver and some change in a box in a car owned by **Jerome Miller**, who had been working in St. Louis, Missouri. Miller was arrested, and at his trial, his defense attorney, Robert H. Rice, who had been practicing criminal law for sixteen years, advised Miller to plead guilty in that he had no real defense and by making that plea he could possibly avoid the death penalty. Rice made this statement in open court on September 5, 1967. Miller pleaded guilty and was sentenced to 199 years in prison. On May 26, 1970, the Fifth District Illinois Appellate Court found that Miller did not fully comprehend the consequences of his guilty plea. The court vacated his conviction and ordered a new trial. On November 16. 1970, Miller was acquitted at a jury trial in Washington County (to where the venue had been relocated). Miller sued the State for wrongful conviction and imprisonment, but he was denied compensation by the Illinois Court of Claims on September 7, 1978.

**1968: William De Palma,** thirty, of Whittier, California, was arrested and convicted of armed robbery based on forged fingerprint evidence. For the sixteen months following his sentencing, De Palma remained in McNeal Island Prison in Washington State. When the fingerprints that had brought about the conviction were exposed as forgeries, De Palma was freed. On August 12, 1975, he was awarded a $750,000 settlement for the time he spent in prison. It was the highest compensation ever given to an individual for a wrongful conviction to that time.

**1968:** On December 2, 1967, fifty-six-year-old Robert Brewer was shot and killed by a black man robbing the Giles Food Market, a convenience store in South Baltimore, Maryland. A short time later, **Walter Lomax** went to a police station because he heard that there was a warrant for him. He was told that the warrant was for his brother, Michael, for nonpayment of child support. For reasons never explained to him, Lomax was then put into a lineup and was identified as the man who had robbed the Giles Food Market and killed Brewer. That identification was the lone evidence that convicted Lomax and sent him to prison for life. When all appeals failed, Lomax turned to Centurion Ministries, which undertook his case. That dedicated and diligent organization unearthed exculpatory evidence that later convinced a judge to vacate Lomax's conviction on December 13, 2006. Lomax was released from prison after having served thirty-nine years behind bars. Part of the exculpatory evidence unearthed by Centurion Ministries included a doctor's report that stated that Lomax had been wearing a plaster cast on his right arm from the hand to elbow up to the day of the crime, a cast resulting from injuries he received when slashed by several gang members who attempted to molest his sister at a dance. Witnesses at the time of the crime did not report any problems with the assailant's right arm.

**1969:** On June 14, 1969, Police Officer Aaron "Sonny" Liberty was shot and killed in Woodville, Mississippi, while attempting with other officers to arrest a suspect at a crowded pool hall, where more than fifty persons attempted to prevent that arrest. Liberty was mortally wounded in the fray, shot four times in the back with .22-caliber bullets. Before dying, Liberty fired off both barrels of his riot gun into an alley down which he believed his assailant was fleeing. He wounded **Leon Chambers,** who was arrested and charged with Liberty's murder. Before Chambers went to trial, Gable McDonald several times confessed to having killed Liberty, but as quickly recanted his confessions. He was called as a witness at Chambers's trial by both the prosecution and defense, but defense was not permitted to challenge some of McDonald's statements, the court ruling that it could not impeach its own witness. Chambers was convicted and sentenced to death. On appeal, Chambers's attorneys argued that the court had denied their client due process because the presiding judge had barred most of the evidence showing that McDonald had shot Liberty and not their client. The appeal court upheld the argument, stating that McDonald was an adverse witness because his exculpatory recantation was inculpatory of Chambers and that Chambers's right to confront and cross-examine an adversary did not depend on which side, defense or prosecution, happened to first call him as a witness. The court overturned Chambers's conviction, and he was released in 1973.

**1970: Edmond D. Jackson,** twenty-six, was convicted in 1970 of murdering bartender Harold Dixon in a Queens, New York, holdup and sentenced to two concurrent terms of twenty years to life in prison. Attorney Helen Bodian doggedly fought to have Jackson's conviction overturned, and, in 1978, federal District Court Judge Vincent L. Broderick dismissed the former mechanic's murder conviction. The judge ruled that the defendant had been convicted solely on the testimony of four people who could not possibly have seen the gunman for more than a few seconds. The U.S. Circuit Court of Appeals upheld the ruling and criticized officials in Queens. The court stated that the evidence against Jackson was circumstantial at best, and that police had ignored another suspect. Jackson was released and spent Christmas with his family for the first time since he was imprisoned eight years earlier for a crime he did not commit.

**1971:** Convicted in 1971 of the sexual assault and murder of a California widow, Agnes Lehmann, near the Grant Park band shell in Chicago, Illinois, **Wilbur McDonald** insisted that he was innocent, but was sentenced to a prison term of 100 to 150 years. On August 14, 1973, Lester Harrison, forty-nine, confessed to murdering Lehmann and three other women in Grant Park, providing details about the murder weapon and position of the bodies that had not been made public and that only the killer could have known. After a twenty-minute private hearing in the chambers of Criminal Court Judge Frank J. Wilson with McDonald and his attorney, Frederick A. Cohn, who had long worked on McDonald's appeal, the wrongly convicted man was released from the Pontiac State Penitentiary, where he had served twenty-two months. In 1974, McDonald was granted a full pardon.

**1971: Lawyer Johnson** was convicted and sentenced to death in Massachusetts for the first-degree shooting murder of thirty-year-old James Christian on December 17, 1971, in Boston's Roxbury neighborhood. The prosecution's chief witness against Johnson, Kenneth Myers, who was also a suspect in the case, testified that he witnessed Johnson's shooting of Christian. Before Myers identified Johnson, he identified the killer as someone else, picking that person out of some police photos, but he changed his mind after officers told him that the man in the photo was in prison, and Myers then named Johnson. Myers's prints were on the weapon used to kill Christian, but he explained that, after he witnessed the shooting, along with his girlfriend, he picked up the gun and, frightened, hid it. He later took police to the spot where the gun was hidden and refused to identify the girlfriend. In 1982, all charges against Johnson were dropped and he was released after an eyewitness, who had not testified at Johnson's original trial, came forward to identify Myers, the state's chief witness as the real murderer.

**1971: Arthur Allan Thomas** was convicted and sent to prison for life for murdering Harvey and Jeanette Crewe in 1970 in their farmhouse at Pukekawa, New Zealand. Crusading newspaperman Pat Booth of the Auckland *Star* led a campaign to exonerate Thomas, one in which police were shown to have planted evidence in the case. (A cartridge case had been planted at the scene of the crime, reportedly by Dr. Jim Sprott, who provided forensic evidence in the case.) Thomas's

conviction was overturned and he was released from prison with a full pardon in 1979.

**1971:** On June 28, 1971, Charles Erdman, a customer inside of a 7-Eleven store on Crain Highway near Aquahart Road in Glen Burnie (Anne Arundel County), Maryland, tried to stop a robbery and was shot to death by the robber. Linda Packech later told police that she had seen the assailant's face when he briefly lifted his mask, and she identified **Guy Gordon Marsh** as the perpetrator. On her testimony, Marsh was convicted and sent to prison for life. In 1987, Packech admitted that she had lied and had given perjured testimony in Marsh's case. Defense attorneys proved that she was a heroin addict and had been in jail at the time the crime was committed so that she could have identified no one at the time of Erdman's murder. Packech told a prosecutor and a reporter that she had been pressured into identifying Marsh by a county police detective, who was convinced of Marsh's guilt. Marsh's conviction was vacated, and he was released from prison after having been behind bars for fourteen years.

**1972: Gene Howard Williams,** twenty-five, was convicted of rape and served more than a year in an Oklahoma prison, including eight-and-a-half months of solitary confinement, because of a clerical error. The actual culprit was thirty-six-year-old Harold Gene Williams, but because both men were known as "Gene," their prison files became mixed up. Although the wrongly accused was released, he was diagnosed as a paranoid schizophrenic (a condition that may have developed during his wrongful imprisonment). On October 29, 1976, as recompense for his "lost year," Gene Howard Williams was awarded $125,000 in damages by a federal court jury.

**1972: Elmer "Geronimo" Pratt,** a leading member of the Los Angeles Black Panther Party, had been targeted by the FBI and local police officers. He was arrested on December 4, 1970, and charged with the murder of Caroline Olsen, a white schoolteacher, who had been killed on a Santa Monica, California, tennis court on December 18, 1968. He was tried in spring 1972 at a Los Angles Superior Court, where LAPD evidence and the testimony of Julius Carl "Julio" Butler, a prominent member and leader of a local black church, brought about his conviction. He was sentenced to life imprisonment, but Centurion Ministries took over his case and conducted a four-year investigation that eventually showed that Butler was an FBI and LAPD informant, as well as an informant for the Los Angeles District Attorney's Office (which Butler always denied), and that covert FBI tapes of Black Panther operations at the time of Olsen's murder showed that Pratt was at a Black Panther meeting in Oakland, California—400 miles north of the crime scene—at the time the victim was slain, evidence that was confirmed by FBI agent Wesley Swearingen, who stated: "My supervisor and several agents on the racial squad knew that Pratt was innocent because the FBI had wiretap logs proving that Pratt was in the San Francisco area several hours before the shooting of Caroline Olsen and that he was there the day after the murder." In overturning Pratt's conviction, Orange County Superior Court Judge Everett Dickey ruled that Butler had lied about Pratt at his trial. Pratt was exonerated of the Olsen murder and released in 1997.

**1973**: **Aaron Owens**, twenty-eight, was convicted in 1973 for the May 13, 1972, murders of an Oakland, California, couple and sentenced to life at San Quentin. Owens steadfastly insisted that he was innocent, and during a parole hearing in November 1980, he was granted a new trial. He had been convicted because an eyewitness had identified his distinctive mutton-chop sideburns. However, he was able to help the prosecutor identify someone whom he believed to be the real killer, a man who, indeed, bore a startling resemblance to him. On March 4, 1981, it was determined that Owens had been the victim of mistaken identity, and he was granted his release after nine years in prison.

**1973: Terry Lee Wanzer** was convicted of aggravated rape and sodomy in Clayton County, Georgia. Paroled in 1981 after eight years behind bars, he was officially pardoned in 1991 and, in 1996, was awarded $100,000 by the State of Georgia for his wrongful conviction and imprisonment.

**1973:** On July 12, 1973, twenty-four-year-old **Allan E. Thrower** of Cleveland, Ohio, was convicted of first-degree murder in the August 1972 ambush death of Columbus, Ohio, police officer Joseph Edwards. Thrower was convicted in spite of his claims of innocence, a lack of motive, and the testimony of three alibi witnesses, who swore that Thrower was in Detroit on the night of the murder. The only evidence against Thrower was the testimony of Edwards's partner, Charles W. McFadden. Throwers's conviction was affirmed on appeal, and, after serving five years of his sentence, an internal police investigation revealed that McFadden had perjured himself when testifying against Thrower. When McFadden's perjury and that of a police detective, who had falsely testified at the trial that he heard two of the alibi witnesses plotting to perjure

themselves, were discovered, a new trial was ordered and Thrower was released. In 1979, all charges against Thrower were dropped.

**1973:** In September 1973, **Christopher Spicer** was convicted of the murder of Donnie P. Christian in North Carolina. The North Carolina Supreme Court overturned that conviction the following year, stating that the trial judge had made several reversible errors, particularly when Spicer's defense attorneys were prohibited from cross-examining a jail informant, Charles Pennington, whose testimony—he said in court that Spicer, his cellmate, had confessed to killing Christian—largely convicted Spicer. Pennington's bond had been reduced from $5,000 to $400, and he was released from jail after he offered his testimony. Defense witnesses stated that Pennington never shared a cell with Spicer, and it was pointed out that the trial judge had wrongly pressured defense attorneys into withdrawing a request for an inappropriate instruction to the jury by the judge. At Spicer's retrial in February 1975, a jury deliberated only fifteen minutes before acquitting him.

**1973: Samuel A. Poole** of North Carolina was convicted in 1973 of first-degree burglary and attempted rape, and received a mandatory death sentence. The chief evidence presented by the prosecution consisted of a button believed to have come from a shirt owned by Poole, a gun he owned, which seemed to match the description of the gun seen by the victim, and the fact that Poole was in the vicinity of the crime when it occurred. The North Carolina Supreme Court, however, determined that there was a lack of substantial evidence to prove that Poole was the actual home-breaker, and his case was overturned and he was released in 1974.

**1973: Stephen Downing**, seventeen, was convicted and sent to prison for life for the murder of Wendy Sewell in Bakewell, Derbyshire, England. Downing, who had no reading skills and was considered mentally retarded with the mental capacity of an eleven-year-old, simply signed a confession prepared by police and one that he did not understand. The Court of Appeal reviewed the case in 2001 and overturned Downing's conviction, releasing him from prison after he had served twenty-seven years behind bars. The court ruled that Downing's conviction was "unsafe," meaning that insufficient evidence had wrongly brought about that conviction, added to a false confession. Downing's exoneration had been brought about chiefly through the efforts of crusading newspaper editor Don Hale, of the

*Matlock Mercury*, who, for his considerable efforts in this case, was made an Officer of the British Empire.

**1973:** On March 9, 1973, someone broke into the home of **Johann Ernst Sigfried "Ziggy" Pohl** in Queanbeyan, New South Wales, Australia. The intruder murdered Pohl's wife, Kum Yee Pohl, stole items, and then fled. Pohl was almost immediately accused by local police of murdering his wife and, in November 1973, he was convicted on circumstantial evidence of murder and sentenced to life in prison. After serving ten years in prison, Pohl was released on parole. In 1990, the true killer, Roger Bawden contacted officials and confessed to murdering Mrs. Pohl. The court later overturned Pohl's conviction, and, after he was granted an unconditional pardon, Pohl was awarded $200,000 in compensation.

**1973:** On the night of May 22, 1973, two gas station attendants, twenty-year-old Ronald Rider and sixty-eight-year-old Harvey Hodges, were murdered during the course of two separate robberies in Mobile and Baldwin counties in Alabama. Police interrogated seventeen-year-old **Michael Pardue** for extensive periods without informing him of his rights until thirty hours into the first interrogation. He was threatened with the death penalty if he did not confess, although Pardue did not know that Alabama at that time had no death penalty. Pardue confessed to the Rider and Hodges robbery-murders, as well as to killing an unknown man whose skeleton had been located while he was under interrogation, the remains later identified as that of forty-three-year-old Theodore White. In a trial lasting less than two hours, Pardue was convicted and given three life sentences. Prosecutors in his case, including Baldwin County District Attorney Jimmy Hendrix, were later sent to prison for drug smuggling, jury tampering, and extortion, but none of this then determined the fate of Pardue, who escaped from prison three times, in 1977, 1978, and 1987. In each instance, he was recaptured within a few days. He was given two additional life sentences for these escapes and was labeled a habitual offender. On appeals, Pardue's convictions were vacated twice in 1994 by the Alabama Supreme Court, based on police misconduct. He was tried again in 1995 in Mobile County and convicted by a jury that listened to twenty-two-year-old audiotapes of his confession in the Hodges slaying that had been taken at the Saraland Police Station. Pardue was sentenced to 100 years in prison, but an appeals court overturned this conviction on the grounds that his confession had been coerced and that he had been denied access to legal counsel. Prosecutors in Baldwin and Mobile counties dropped all charges against Pardue in all of the murder cases in 1997, but he remained in prison on the convictions for his prison escapes. Those convictions were vacated by the Alabama Supreme Court in 2000. Prosecutors, however, refused to drop charges on those convictions until Pardue pleaded guilty to those escapes in exchange for a parole. He was then released after serving twenty-eight years in prison. (The man who had gathered the evidence that sent Hendrix and a sheriff's top investigator, Bobbie Stewart, to federal prison, Patrick Swiney, had been a former police officer on several Alabama forces and had turned in his badge at the Gulf Shores Police Department in Baldwin County in protest of widespread police corruption. He was later convicted of murdering his wife and her former husband and sent to prison for life in what many persons believe to be a framed case and in retaliation for his whistle-blowing.)

**1974:** **John Henry Knapp** was convicted and sentenced to death in Arizona in 1974 for the arson-deaths of his two children in his Phoenix home in 1973. Arson detectives at his several trials claimed that there was evidence of "flammable liquid fire" at the scene—a gas can with unidentifiable fingerprints on it—but it was later discovered that these arson "experts" had no fire training or education and relied chiefly on burn pattern myths. Knapp was released in 1987, after evidence indicated that the fire had been accidental, most probably caused when his young daughters were playing with matches. Eleven days after the fire, Knapp reportedly confessed to burning his daughters alive while he stood outside his home sipping coffee, but he recanted that confession, saying that it had been produced by a terrible migraine headache and because he was trying to protect his wife, whom, he believed, would commit suicide if she were charged with the crime. (She fled the state after the fire, was later granted immunity, but did not testify at Knapp's trials.) He was nevertheless tried twice again, his third trial in 1991 resulting in a hung jury. Knapp, in and out of prison from 1987 to 1992, made an agreement with the prosecution wherein he pleaded no contest and was finally released in 1992, still maintaining his innocence. Though released, some officials believed that either Knapp or his wife were the culprits and that the daughters did not accidentally set fire to the Knapp residence, as was the general belief following Knapp's prison release.

**1974:** Four men, members of a California motorcycle gang—**Richard Greer, Clarence Smith, Thomas**

Gladish and **Ronald Keine**—were convicted and sentenced to death for the kidnapping, rape and murder of a college student, William Velton, a homosexual, in Albuquerque, New Mexico, in 1974. The only evidence against the four men was the testimony of a part-time motel maid, Judith Weyer, who said she had witnessed the crime, and two other witnesses, who said they had seen the bikers in Albuquerque at the time of the crime. The bikers, who had been arrested in Oklahoma City on robbery charges, tried to prove that they were not in Albuquerque at the time of the Velton murder-rape by showing receipts for gas and other items they had purchased, unfortunately with stolen credit cards. The *Detroit News* launched an investigation into this case (three of the defendants were from Detroit), and its reporters learned that Weyer had been pressured by police and prosecutors into fabricating her story and providing perjured testimony against the four men. In 1976, Kerry Rodney Lee, a homeless drug addict who occasionally worked as an informant for the Drug Enforcement Administration, entered a South Carolina police station, where he confessed to the kidnapping-murder, identifying the murder weapon, which he said he had stolen from the father of a one time girlfriend. When contacted in Detroit, Weyer admitted that she had fabricated her testimony against the motorcycle members under police pressure. Greer, Smith, Gladish, and Keine were released in 1976.

**1974:** Four persons—**Gerard Conlon**, **Paul Hill**, **Patrick Armstrong**, and **Carole Richardson**—who were known as the "Guilford Four," were wrongly convicted of an IRA bombing in London. After serving fourteen years in prison, all four were released on October 19, 1989.

**1974:** Following a 1972 double shooting in Birmingham, Alabama, **Freddie Lee Gaines** was charged with killing Johnny Lee Swanson and Mary Ann Wright, and was convicted of murdering Swanson in 1974 and sentenced to thirty years in prison, released in 1985. A man in Florida confessed to the shootings in 1990, which brought about Gaines's exoneration. He was given $1 million compensation in 1996, the second person in Alabama to receive such compensation for a wrongful conviction (the first being one of the Scottsboro Boys convicted in 1931).

**1974:** Convicted and sentenced to die for the 1972 beating death of transit worker James Corry in Boston, Massachusetts, **Laurence Adams** escaped death when the U.S. Supreme Court abolished capital punishment. His sentence was commuted to life. It was later discov-

ered that the police had withheld evidence in Adams's case, where witnesses had identified another perpetrator. After a trial witness recanted her testimony, Adams's conviction was vacated, and all charges against him were dropped. He was released in 2004.

**1974:** Another Boston resident, **Ella Mae Ellison**, was convicted of the first-degree murder of Boston police detective John Schroeder, who had been slain during a 1973 robbery. Apprehended within twenty-four hours, three black men—Anthony Irving, Nathaniel Williams, and Terrell Walker—claimed that a woman had been behind the crime, two of the defendants, Williams and Irving, agreeing in a plea-bargain arrangement to testify against Ella Mae Ellison, whom they called "Sue," and who, they said, had shot and killed Schroeder. The two defendants pleaded guilty to second-degree murder, while their testimony convicted twenty-seven-year-old Ellison of first-degree murder and sent her to prison for life. Prior to this conviction, Ellison had no criminal record, although she admitted that she had on occasion, given rides in her car to Williams and Irving. In 1976, Williams and Irving recanted their statements, saying that there had been no fourth person in the robbery-murder and that they had invented "Sue" in order to get a lighter sentence through their plea-bargained and false testimony. Ellison's conviction was vacated, all charges against her were dropped, and she was released from prison in 1978, after having served five years behind bars.

**1974:** **Betty Tyson** and **John Duval**, two prostitutes in Rochester, New York, were convicted and sentenced to twenty-five years to life for the May 24, 1973, murder of fifty-two-year-old Timothy Haworth, an Eastman Kodak consultant from Philadelphia. Both had been arrested after two teenagers named them as Haworth's killers. The teenagers, Jon Jackson and Wayne Wright, were both held in jail as material witness and both later stated that detectives threatened to charge them with Haworth's murder if they did not testify against Tyson and Duval. One of those witnesses later stated that a detective put a gun to his head and said he would kill him if he did not give perjured testimony in court against Tyson and Duval. There was no physical or forensic evidence linking either suspect to the murder. The tire tracks of Tyson's car were different from that of the killer's. Tyson, however, confessed after being handcuffed to a chair for twelve hours and being kicked by interrogators. (The detective who supervised the case was convicted in 1980 for faking evidence in an unrelated case.) In 1997, Wayne Wright recanted his perjured testimony, and a police report showed in the same year that Jackson had denied ever seeing Tyson or Duval with the victim. Tyson's conviction was vacated in 1998, and she was later awarded $1.25 million in compensation. Duval was released in 1999, at age forty-seven, but received no compensation because he had lied twice to the parole board in prison, in 1995 and 1997, admitting his guilt, when he knew he was innocent. His attorney, Gilda Sherrod-Ali, stated that her client "believed that was the only way he could get out."

**1974:** On September 12, 1970, John Eddie Mitchell, a newspaper boy for the Harrisburg *Patriot-News*, was stabbed and then bludgeoned to death, his body found beneath a car in a garage. The $32 he had collected that day from his paper route was missing. A sledgehammer coated with blood and hair was found, and this, along with the garage in which the victim had been found, belonged to the father of Mitchell's best friend, fourteen-year-old **Steven Crawford**. He, as well as several other neighborhood boys, routinely questioned and fingerprinted, but the case remained dormant until two state police officers, who had held onto some bloody fingerprints from the car where the boy's body had been hidden (he was either stuffed beneath the car or crawled there to escape his assailant), turned over the prints to Harrisburg Detective Walter D. Simpson, who identified three partial palm prints as Crawford's. This identification was confirmed by police official John C. Balshy. The prints were then given to the Bureau of Alcohol, Tobacco and Firearms in Washington, D.C., but that agency reported that there was no way to date the prints. The dilemma faced by police was whether or not Crawford had made the prints on the car—he was often in and out of that garage, as were many other boys—before Mitchell was murdered or had left the prints at the time the boy was killed. The problem was solved in November 1972, when the prints were turned over to State Police chemist Janice Roadcap. She performed a test on November 29, 1972, for blood on a section of the print, witnessed by Simpson and Balshy. All later reported that they observed a chemical reaction producing a positive indication for blood *only* on the ridges of the print. This became the chief theory of the prosecution's case, that since the blood only appeared on the ridges, it was on Crawford's hand after he had killed Mitchell, and that the blood was not therefore splashed onto one of Crawford's prints that had existed on the car prior to the murder. In Crawford's 1974 trial, Roadcap testified that Mitchell's blood was on Craw-

ford's hands when he left his prints, proving that he was the killer. Crawford was convicted and sentence to life in prison. After all appeals failed, fate intervened. On October 2001, two boys rummaging through a dump found an old briefcase that had once been owned by Simpson, who had died in 1994. The briefcase contained Roadcap's original notes from her testing of the blood splashes and Crawford's prints. It clearly showed that she and the two officers had altered the results of that report, deleting information on the test she had conducted by eliminating a reference that the chemical reaction had shown positive indication for blood on the ridges *and the valleys* of the print, which indicated that Mitchell's blood had been splashed onto Crawford's print while it already existed on the car before the killing and did not therefore confirm that he had murdered Mitchell, as Roadcap had falsely testified. Armed with this new evidence, which was detailed in many published articles by crusading reporter Pete Shellem of the *Harrisburg Patriot-News*, a new appeal was made on Crawford's behalf by his attorney Joshua D. Lock. Crawford had been tried three times, his case sent back twice because of trial errors. Before the third trial in 1978, where he was again convicted on the Roadcap evidence, Crawford refused a plea-bargain deal, which would have seen his release at that time for time served. He had all along maintained his innocence. He was released from prison in 2002 on orders of Judge Joseph H. Kleinfelter. Prosecutors later refused to retry him for a fourth time. Roadcap had worked on innumerable cases in eleven counties as a state police crime lab "expert" from 1967 to 1991, when she retired. She contributed evidence in the wrongful conviction of Barry James Laughman (see Chapter X: "False Confessions").

**1974: Edward Baker** was one of several men convicted for the brutal robbery and murder of an eighty-five-year-old retired man in Philadelphia in 1973. The victim had been murdered with an ice pick. Sent to prison for life, Baker had been identified as the chief assailant by Donahue Wise, who confessed to the killing and who also identified sixteen-year-old Clifford Walker as an accomplice. In exchange for this identification, Wise was allowed to plead to second-degree murder, facing no more than a three- to twelve-year sentence. Centurion Ministries undertook Baker's case, and, through its prodding, Wise confessed in 1996 that he alone had committed the murder and that he had falsely accused Baker in order to avoid the life sentence that was given to Baker. Upon hearing this confession from Wise, a court vacated Baker's conviction. Prosecutors threatened to retry him, until Centurion provided information that would support a concrete alibi for Baker—the organization's excellent research could prove that Baker, on the night of the killing, had traveled to the north side of Philadelphia (the murder occurred in South Philadelphia) to attend the funeral of a friend's aunt and that he had stayed overnight at the home of the friend's sister—and that it was prepared to provide eleven witnesses who would support that alibi. The prosecution, on February 11, 2002, dismissed all charges against Baker, who had been released from prison in 1999. The dropping of the charges exonerated him.

**1974: Edward Ryder** was convicted of a prison murder, but was granted executive clemency and ordered released in 1993 by Pennsylvania Governor Robert Patrick Casey (1987–1995). Centurion Ministries conducted an investigation in this case and unearthed an eyewitness, who identified the real perpetrators. Ryder's conviction was vacated in 1996.

**1975: Jerry Banks**, who was rabbit hunting in November 1974, south of Atlanta, discovered the bodies of thirty-eight-year-old Marvin W. King, a high school band instructor, and one of his former students, Melanie Ann Hartsfeld, both white and both killed by shotgun blasts. Banks, a black, stopped a motorist and asked him to call the police while he stayed at the crime scene. The police charged him with the murder, saying he had used his own shotgun to murder the two victims. Banks claimed that he had not used his weapon that day and asked police why he would call them if he had murdered two people he did not know, a question officers never answered. Banks was convicted and sentenced to death on two counts of murder. The motorist, Andrew Eberhardt, then came forward to tell authorities that he had identified himself to the police and had been questioned by officers after summoning them at Banks's request. His testimony had been withheld from Banks's defense attorneys. Further, it was proved that shotgun shells found near the crime scene and chiefly used to convict Banks had been placed there after Banks's arrest. The lead investigator of the case, Philip S. Howard, Banks's defense attorneys pointed out, had a terrible record as a police officer who falsified evidence. He had been fired from one police force, resigned from another, and had been convicted of forgery, chiefly that he had "tampered with and manipulated evidence involving [shotgun] shells." Banks's conviction was overturned and he was released in 1980, when the appeals court determined that prosecutors

knowingly withheld exculpatory evidence in his case. Banks later committed suicide after his wife divorced him. His estate was awarded a settlement that benefited Banks's children.

**1975: Jonathan Treadway** (or Treadaway), twenty-one, was convicted and sentenced to death for sodomizing and suffocating six-year-old Brett Jordan in the Jordan home in Phoenix, Arizona, in 1974. Two county medical examiners, who performed an autopsy on the Jordan boy, determined the cause of death as suffocation and found evidence of sodomy. The prosecution used a partial palm print found on the windowsill of the Jordan home and hair samples found on the boy's body as evidence that Treadway was the killer. The defendant admitted that he had been window-peeping at the Jordan home, but that he had never touched the child. Treadway, who was convicted and sentenced to death, spent three years on Death Row before his conviction was reversed because evidence of a prior criminal act by Treadway had been improperly introduced in the original trial. The Arizona Supreme Court ordered a new trial based upon incompetent defense. Treadway was retried in 1978 and released following the testimony of five pathologists from five other states, who stated that, on the basis of their examination of tissue slides and photographs of the Jordan boy's body, there had been no sodomy and the boy had died of either pneumonia or bronchitis. The county medical examiners, who had performed the Jordan autopsy in 1975, admitted that they had not conducted microscopic examinations of body tissues before reaching their conclusions. Jurors meeting with attorneys after Treadway's 1978 retrial said they had voted to free Treadway because the prosecutors had failed to provide sufficient evidence that Treadway was even in the Jordan home. Treadway was freed immediately after the acquittal.

**1975: Johnny Ross**, a sixteen-year-old black, was convicted and sentenced to death for the rape of a white woman in New Orleans, Louisiana, in 1975. Ross had confessed only after he was severely beaten. His trial lasted but a few hours. His case was taken up by investigators working for the Southern Poverty Law Center. Based on the new evidence unearthed by these investigators, Ross was released in 1981, after serology tests proved that his blood type was inconsistent with that of the rapist.

**1975: Clarence Chance** and **Benny Powell** were convicted of robbing a Los Angeles gas station and killing an off-duty deputy sheriff in the process. Both men were sentenced to life without the possibility of parole. After many appeals, an investigation into police conduct in the case revealed that officers had coerced confessions from Chance and Powell. The Los Angeles County Superior Court overturning their conviction in 1992, ruling that, in addition to mistaken eyewitness testimony, police in the case had encouraged perjured eyewitness testimony, suppressed exculpatory evidence, and may have intentionally framed the defendants. In releasing Chance and Powell, Los Angeles County Superior Court Judge Florence-Marie Cooper formally apologized to the defendants for the "gross injustice" of the seventeen years they had spent in prison. "Nothing can be done to return to you the years irretrievably lost," she added. Both men each later received $3.5 million in compensation for their wrongful convictions and imprisonments.

**1975: Gregory Bright** and **Earl Truvia** were convicted of second-degree murder and sentenced to life without parole for the killing of Elliott Porter in New Orleans. Their conviction had been brought about by an eyewitness who claimed that she saw the pair dragging the victim in a building of a housing project where they all lived. The coroner's report on the case was at odds with the statements of this witness in that its recorded time of death of the victim did not coincide with the timeline presented by the witness. That report was not given to the jury. The jury did not know at the time that the witness suffered from visual hallucinations and was judged a paranoid schizophrenic, who was also a prostitute using many aliases and used an alias at the time of the trial of Bright and Truvia. In February 2002, Bright and Truvia were granted an evidentiary hearing that had been brought about by the Innocence Project New Orleans (IPNO) and one where the unreliability of the prosecution's star witness was exposed, as well as the fact that this woman was addicted to heroin and that police supplied her with cash for her drug habit in exchange for her testimony. Moreover, IPNO and its pro bono attorneys showed that prosecutors had withheld from defense attorneys police reports describing other suspects in the case. The convictions of both men were vacated and a new trial was ordered, this ruling upheld by the Supreme Court of Louisiana. On June 24, 2003, the New Orleans District Attorney's Office dropped all charges against Bright and Truvia, and both men were released from prison after having served more than twenty-seven years behind bars.

**1976**: Thirty-year-old **Larry Thomas Smith** was convicted of killing drug dealer Brady Greenlease in 1976. With a criminal record that included passing bad checks and attempted breaking and entering, and testimony by the victim's girlfriend, the only eyewitness, who stated that she saw Smith commit the murder, Smith was sent to prison for life. Five years later, the eyewitness admitted that she had been high on angel dust when the murder was committed and confessed that she did not know what had happened. Other witnesses suddenly were pointing a finger at another suspect, who, at the time, was in West Virginia awaiting extradition to Ohio. After he spent five years behind bars, the state of Ohio set Smith free with $230 and an apology.

**1976: Jorge de Los Santos** was wrongly convicted of murdering an apartment building superintendent in Newark, New Jersey, spending more than ten years in prison before it was revealed that the star witness against him had made a secret deal with prosecutors, who dropped charges against this witness in exchange for false testimony; de Los Santos was freed in 1986, after the witness had a change of heart, visiting him in prison and apologizing for falsely testifying against him.

**1976: Bernard Vindiola** was wrongfully convicted of fatally shooting T. J. McCoy shortly after midnight on July 22, 1976. McCoy, a security guard at the Peek-A-Boo Bar in Fowler, California, had been shot to death, while trying to break up a bar brawl. Two brothers, Bernard and Eddie Vindiola, were reportedly involved, along with their sisters and several friends. Four witnesses in the dimly lit bar said they thought Bernard Vindiola had killed McCoy, but their statements were hazy and inconclusive. Christina Vindiola told officers that night that Eddie had shot McCoy, but later said she implicated Eddie only because she was angry with him. Bernard Vindiola alone was convicted of second-degree murder and was sentenced to five years to life. The conviction was reversed on appeal, based on the grounds that only hearsay evidence identified Bernard, rather than Eddie, as the murderer, and because the judge excluded evidence of Eddie's prior felony convictions, which might have impeached his self-serving testimony. Eddie Vindiola had been arrested for a parole violation on the day of the murder and was known to be carrying a gun. His girlfriend had been involved in the brawl that McCoy was trying to break up when he was shot. The higher court also questioned the reliability of the eyewitness account. After a prosecution witness admitted that she had earlier told police that Bernard had not committed the crime, a statement not admitted in Vindiola's trial, the prosecution dropped the charges, and Bernard Vindiola was released.

**1976: Ernest "Shujaa" Graham**, who had been sent to a California state prison in 1973 following a conviction for a $35 robbery, was convicted in 1976, along with codefendant **Eugene Allen**, of killing a state correctional officer and sentenced to death following a second trial in that year. Graham, who was a leader of the outlawed Black Panther Party behind bars, was retried, and, in his fourth trial in 1981, he and Allen were acquitted of murdering the prison guard, the Supreme Court of California reversing the original 1976 conviction based on the fact that prosecutors improperly used their preemptive challenges to exclude black jurors (Graham and Allen were black) from the 1976 trial.

**1976:** In 1976, twenty-three-year-old **Stefan Ivan Kiszko** was convicted and sent to prison for life for murdering eleven-year-old Lesley Molseed on October 5, 1975, in Rochdale, Lancashire, England. Three teenage girls had stated that Kiszko had flashed his body to them shortly before Molseed was murdered, and police had focused upon the reclusive young man, whose only social contact with the world was his mother and aunt, from the time the girls had pointed him out. His case was reviewed in 1989, and his conviction was overturned and he was set free in 1992, when it was learned that he could not produce sperm. The murderer of Molseed had ejaculated onto her clothing after killing her. The three teenage girls who had identified Kiszko later recanted their statements, saying that they had made their remarks in 1976 as "a joke." (this same kind of wrongful identification also victimized **Arthur O'-Connell** in 1935, when some girls purposely and wrongfully accused him of a crime he had not committed "for fun"; see Chronology, 1935).

**1976: Michael Damien**, **Joseph Eastridge**, and **Nick Sousa**, all members of the Pagan motorcycle gang, were convicted of the November 1974 stabbing death of John Battle in Washington, D.C. Battle had been one of three black men who had shot at Pagan members after they left a birthday party. The gang members chased Battle down a street and stabbed him to death. The defendants were picked up by police in their car after they had been circling the crime scene, unfamiliar as they were with the area. All three men were convicted on the testimony of Dorothy Willetts, Sousa's girlfriend, who gave police conflicting statements after the killing and said that her boyfriend Sousa and Eastridge had confessed to the Battle slaying. All three men were sen-

tenced to life in prison. After all appeals failed, Centurion Ministries undertook their case. Meanwhile, Sousa and Damien were paroled in 1995, and Eastridge was paroled in 2005. In that year, after Kate Germond of Centurion Ministries tracked down witnesses who refuted Willetts's statements, U.S. District Court Judge Rosemary Collyer exonerated all three men, saying that "the court finds that this is the rare case in which petitioners can prove their actual innocence of the crime charge as well as violations of their constitutional rights at trial. The petition is supported by evidence unearthed by Centurion Ministries, a non-profit prison advocacy center, during an eight-year investigation of the case." Damien and Sousa had served twenty years behind bars, and Eastridge had been in prison for thirty years.

**1976: J. L. Ivey Jr**. was convicted and sent to prison for murder and robbery in Erie County, New York. His conviction was vacated in 1981 by an appeals court, after the court ruled that the prosecutor in the case, Albert Ranni, had committed many errors that were improper and prejudicial. After being retried and acquitted, Ivey was released from prison in 1982. Three years later, he won a judgment against the state for his wrongful conviction and imprisonment.

**1977:** Sentenced to death for the robbery-murder of a seventy-four-year-old barber named Eberhart in Madison County, Georgia, **Henry Arthur Drake** has been wrongfully convicted upon the testimony of William Campbell, who actually committed the robbery-murder, and who plea-bargained his own conviction for that testimony. In 1981, Campbell recanted his testimony, signing an affidavit that stated Drake had had nothing to do with the crime and that he had been convicted on perjured testimony. Wrote Campbell: "My name is William Campbell and I was a witness in the trial of Henry Arthur Drake for armed robbery and murder. I lied at his trial. I said Henry was the one who killed the barber, Mr. Eberhart, and that I tried to stop Henry from killing him. But what I said were lies. I was the one who killed Mr. Eberhart. Henry wasn't even there. He didn't have anything to do with it. . . . I lied about Henry because I thought Henry had done me dirty. I thought Henry had turned me in." Drake and Campbell had been tried separately as codefendants in the robbery-murder, with Campbell falsely testifying at Drake's trial that he was sitting in the barber's chair getting a haircut when Drake robbed and murdered Eberhart. Campbell had earlier been convicted and sentenced to death, believing that his conviction had been brought about by Drake who had secretly cooperated with officials, which he had not. At Drake's first trial (he was tried three times and convicted twice), a medical examiner stated that the bloodstains found at the scene of the crime indicated that there had been two assailants, but those stains were never matched to Drake and no physical evidence linked him to the crime. Following Campbell's 1981 confession, the Georgia Circuit Court of Appeals vacated Drake's death sentence in 1984 and ordered a second trial, where the jury was hung, ten jurors voting for acquittal. Drake was convicted in a third trial in 1987. Six months later, however, the medical examiner in the original case stated that the bloodstains at the scene of the crime did not necessarily support the claim that two attackers had been involved. This testimony, more than anything else, caused the Georgia Board of Pardons and Paroles to exonerate Drake and release him in 1987.

**1976: Vernon McManus**, The football coach at Lamar University in Beaumont, Texas, was convicted and sentenced to death for the July 24, 1976, murders of his estranged wife's parents, Paul Harvey Cantrell and Mary Bright Cantrell, in their Baytown, Texas, home. The chief witness against him at his 1977 trial was his hostile wife, Paula, who admitted that she had had problems with her parents, saying that McManus recommended using hired killers to get rid of the Cantrell couple, and, after she agreed, he told her he had paid $20,000 to hired killers to do the job. Paula McManus testified that her husband called her on the night of the murder to tell her that the killers were near the vicinity of the Cantrell house and for her to leave, which she said she did, returning the next day to find her parents dead. McManus, his wife also stated, had told her that the killers had forced him to go with them to the murder scene, and he was present when the Cantrells were murdered. Paula McManus was sent to prison for life, and her husband waited on Death Row for ten years until he was released in 1988. From the time of his trial, McManus insisted that he was innocent and that his wife alone had arranged for the murders. He pointed out that his defense attorney at his trial was romantically involved with his wife, which explained his less than enthusiastic defense of his case. In 1988, the 1977 murder trial was reversed after McManus was granted a writ of habeas corpus, the court stating that the McManus trial involved improprieties relative to jury selection, and a new trial was ordered. Prosecutors, however, had no longer at hand the thin evidence origi-

nally used against McManus, and all charges against him were dropped.

**1976:** Charged with molesting his girlfriend's thirteen-year-old son in Dalton (Whitfield County), Georgia, twenty-two-year-old **Wayne Cservak** was convicted and sentenced to ten years in prison. One of the jurors at Cservak's trial, Jim Thomas, a chemist with a small company, felt that Cservak had been wrongly convicted (he had held out in exhaustive arguments against eleven other jurors until agreeing to convict). Using his children's inheritance money, Thomas hired an experienced trial lawyer in Dalton, Robert Adams, to represent Cservak in his appeals. Said Adams later: "It's unheard of—not only in Georgia legal history, but in the entire American legal history as far as I can tell." In an appeal, the accusing boy told prosecutors in a Conasauga Judicial Court that he had lied and had fabricated his story that Cservak had repeatedly molested him over a two-week period. He said that he had overheard his mother and Cservak talking about plans to be married, a marriage the boy did not want to happen. Cservak's conviction was vacated in 1998 and prosecutors dropped all charges against him, releasing him from prison.

**1976: James Landano** was convicted of killing a police officer during an armed robbery in Kearny, New Jersey. Sent to prison for life, he wrote to the Centurion Ministries, which later uncovered a suppressed police memo that stated that the only eyewitness to the killing had identified a person other than Landano. His conviction was vacated in July 1989 based on the disclosure of that police memo, but Landano was not retried until nine years later. On July 27, 1998, after deliberating for less than one hour, a jury acquitted Landano, fully exonerating him of a crime he had not committed and for which he had served thirteen years in prison.

**1976:** On December 21, 1976, the Ohio National Bank in Columbus, Ohio, was robbed of $1,207 by two black men. In the course of the robbery, Berne Davis, a seventy-four-year-old security guard, was shot to death "execution style," according to police. The bank's security camera did not record the event in that it had no film. Robert Simpson became a key witness in the case, identifying **Timothy Howard** and **Gary Lamar James** as the bank robbers. Both men were convicted and sentenced to death, but their sentences were commuted to life terms after Ohio declared capital punishment unconstitutional in 1978. After all appeals failed, Howard and James contacted Centurion Ministries, which undertook their case, and through the efforts of its attorneys and investigator, Martin Yant, were able to locate an FBI report that showed how corrupt Columbus police detectives had manipulated perjured testimony against both men. Further, three fingerprints had been found at the scene of the crime that did not belong to either Howard or James, and this evidence had not been disclosed to the defense. Another suppressed police report showed that bank employee Michacla M. Hollenbach had said she could identify the robbers, but did not identify James in a police photo array shown to her. The FBI agent who had been involved in the case, was instrumental in exposing the misconduct of the Columbus police and subsequently, in appeal, helped to bring about the freedom of Howard and James, who were set free in 2003. In 2006, Howard was awarded $2.6 million in compensation, and, in 2007, James received $1.5 million. James had received less than Howard in that his legal fees were less and his lost wages were deemed to be less. Both men had been behind bars for twenty-seven years. During that time, Howard's father died, his mother contracted colon cancer, his son, Timothy Howard Jr., was paralyzed in a drive-by shooting, and two of his grandsons had been born. Howard did not live long to enjoy the award money. He died from a heart attack in 2007.

**1978: Harllel Jones**, thirty, of Cleveland, Ohio, was convicted of second-degree murder for the August 7, 1970, shooting death of John H. Smith, and was sentenced to life in prison. A member of a black nationalist organization, Afro Set, he was accused of ordering the random shooting in retaliation for the death of a fellow member. His lawyers appealed when they found that the prosecution had withheld evidence. Jones was implicated by a codefendant and admitted triggerman who turned FBI informant to avoid first-degree murder charges. In 1977, after Jones had spent five years in prison, Victor Harvey and two other witnesses testified that Jones did not pull the trigger. Jones was released by U.S. District Court Judge Frank J. Battisti pending a new trial. The original prosecutor, John T. Corrigan, vowed to retry the case, but his efforts failed when key witnesses could not be located. Corrigan was forced to recommend dismissal of the case on October 18, 1978, and Jones remained free.

**1978:** Sixteen-year-old **Larry Hicks**, who had no criminal record and had been a good student, and who was trying to earn his high school degree by working at part-time jobs, was convicted and sentenced to death in 1978 on two counts of murder. Hicks, a black teenager, had been accused of stabbing to death two persons in

Gary, Indiana, and the only evidence against him had been the statements of two women who claimed that they had seen Hicks waving a knife while arguing with the victims, who died of stab wounds. When only two weeks from execution, the warden of the prison where Hicks was imprisoned asked two attorneys, Niles Stanton and Kevin McShane, to review the case. The lawyers obtained a stay of execution and hired an investigator (paid for by the Playboy Foundation) who conducted extensive interviews with the two witnesses who had testified against Hicks. Both women recanted their testimony. Hicks was retried and acquitted in 1980, after it was proven that the eyewitnesses against him at his original trial had committed perjury, while other witnesses supported his alibi. At the retrial, Stanton convincingly showed how Hicks's original attorney had failed to investigate his client's alibi, thoroughly interview witnesses against him, examine the red stains on his jeans (which police stated was blood when they proved to come from rust), and failed to examine the knife police said had been used in the murders. Stanton further showed that the knife on exhibit could not have made the death wounds on the victims, and only a different kind of knife, one with a longer, narrower blade, could have made those wounds.

**1978: Anthony Ray Peek**, a black drifter from New York staying in a halfway House in Winter Haven, Florida, was convicted and sentenced to death in 1978 for murdering Erma Carlson, a sixty-five-year-old nurse, in her Winter Haven, Florida, home in 1977. Peek's fingerprints were found in the victim's car, as well as a "Negroid" hair, according to an analyst at Peek's trial. Peek offered witnesses who swore that he was present at the halfway house on the night of the murder, and the defendant claimed that he had left the prints in the victim's car when he found it empty the day after the murder, but had never entered Carlson's home. Polk Circuit Curt Judge John Dewell overturned Peek's conviction in 1983, stating that the state's hair analyst had wrongly identified the hair found in the victim's car to be Peek's. At Peek's second trial in 1984, he was again found guilty and sentenced to death, the trial judge making the racial slur that the defendant's family members were "niggers." The second trial was overturned because the trial judge had wrongly allowed a prior conviction of rape against Peeks to be introduced into his second murder trial. A third trial in 1987 brought about Peek's acquittal in the Carlson murder after expert testimony in his first trial was proven to be false. Peek's rape conviction stood, and he remains at this writing at the Everglades Correctional Institution, eligible for parole in 2010.

**1978: Charles Ray Giddens** received a death sentence in 1978 for killing a clerk in Oklahoma. His conviction had been brought about by the testimony of Johnnie Gray, who had also been arrested as a suspect in the same crime, but who was not charged. Giddens was freed in 1981 after the Oklahoma Court of Criminal Appeals reversed his conviction, stating that Gray's uncorroborated testimony came from a person who had much to gain in blaming Giddens for a crime he might have himself committed, and, as such, his testimony did not support a conviction.

**1978: David A. Gray** was convicted of raping a fifty-eight-year-old woman in Madison County, Illinois, and sent to prison for sixty years (the woman died while he was in prison from thirty-three stab wounds). Gray had been tried twice, the first trial ending in a hung jury. He was convicted in a second trial on the testimony of a jailhouse snitch who claimed that Gray had admitted raping the woman. In 1998, DNA testing on a quilt containing biological evidence in the case excluded Gray or the victim's husband as the perpetrator. Gray's conviction was overturned in 1999 and he was released.

**1978:** On May 29, 1978, **Fritz Yngvar Moen** (1941–2005) was convicted of the April 11, 1978, rape and strangulation murder of Sigrid Heggheim in Trondheim, Norway, and sentenced to twenty years in prison. He had confessed to the murder, but later recanted the confession, saying that police coerced his admission. He was, on December 18, 1981, convicted of a second rape and murder strangulation, that of Torunn Finstad, whose body was found in Trondheim on October 4, 1977. Five more years were added to Moen's sentence. On appeal, the conviction of the Heggheim murder was vacated after it was learned that Moen, who was deaf and partly paralyzed could not have pursued the victim across a field, knocked her down, and then used his own clothes to strangle her. Moen, who died on March 28, 2005, was also posthumously exonerated of the Finstad murder, having been cleared in both cases through DNA and after another man made a deathbed confession in December 2005 that he had raped and killed the two women.

**1978:** On December 18, 1978, in Manchester, England, fifteen-year-old **Paul Blackburn** was convicted of the attempted rape and murder of a nine-year-old boy, which had occurred on June 25, 1978. Blackburn had been interrogated several times by police and after a four-hour grilling confessed to the crime. He later re-

canted his confession, but it stood to bring about his conviction and sentence to prison for life. On appeal in March 2003, the court learned that police pressured the boy into falsely confessing, as an expert then testified, and also learned that Blackburn's older brother, Fred, had also confessed to the crime and recanted, as well as two other teenagers interrogated by police. The court overturned Blackburn's conviction on May 24, 2005, and he was released from prison after serving twenty-seven years behind bars.

**1978: Edward Charles Splatt** was convicted of murder in South Australia and sent to prison for life. He was released six years later after a Royal Commission determined that he was innocent. He received a full pardon and was later awarded $270,000 in compensation.

**1978: Terry Harrington** was convicted of the first-degree murder of a victim in Pottawattamie County, Iowa. The Iowa Supreme Court overturned Harrington's conviction, ruling that several police reports indicated that another person was a likely suspect in the case and that these reports had been withheld from defense counsel. The court also noted that a witness who testified against Harrington at his trial admitted in a post-conviction hearing that he had lied because police and prosecutors had pressured him. Harrington was released from prison in 2003.

**1978:** Following the brutal rape and ice pick murder of an eleven-year-old girl at a housing project in Philadelphia, Pennsylvania, **Matthew Connor** was convicted of this crime and sent to prison for life. In 1989, Centurion Ministries, which had undertaken his case, persuaded the district attorney's office to reexamine Connor's case. It discovered police misconduct involving hidden reports proving that the original trial testimony against Connor was false. Connor was released from prison in March 1990.

**1979: Brett Allen Bachelor**, twenty-one, was sentenced in 1979 to serve fifteen years for the brutal strangulation murder of a seventy-five-year-old apartment manager in Hyde Park, Florida. During his trial, Bachelor pleaded with the court, saying: "Please, I'm innocent. You should believe me. I'm innocent!" In July 1980, Circuit Court Judge Arden Mays Merckle ordered Bachelor released from prison, where he had served eight months of a fifteen-year sentence. Bachelor was released when, during a second trial of codefendant **Kenneth Mullins**, also indicted in the 1978 murder, evidence showed that a key witness had mistakenly identified Bachelor as the killer. Bachelor was freed on his own recognizance, and both he and Mullins were acquitted of all charges.

**1979: Cornell Avery Estes,** sixteen, was convicted of murdering Donna M. Turner and sentenced to twenty years in prison. Less than one year later, Estes was freed when another man confessed to murdering Turner. In March 1984, the Maryland Board of Public Works awarded Estes $16,500 in damages to compensate him for the time he had been wrongly confined. The announcement of Estes's cash award was tempered by the fact he was serving a three-year prison term for breaking and entering. .

**1979:** Following a 1979 South Carolina murder conviction, where **Michael Linder** was sentenced to death for killing a highway patrol officer, defense attorneys brought about Linder's acquittal two years later. Prosecutors had originally stated that Linder had murdered the officer without provocation, but Linder had all along insisted that he had shot in self-defense after the officer fired six shots at him. At Linder's retrial, evidence from the ballistics division of the state's crime lab supported the defendant's claim of self-defense, and Linder was released in 1981. He was subsequently convicted of kidnapping and assault and sent to prison for life.

**1979:** Three men—**Ross Dunn**, **Timothy Anderson** and **Paul Alister**, known as the Ananda Marga Trio— were convicted of conspiracy to commit murder by planting a bomb in Sydney, Australia, and each spent seven years behind bars until a judicial inquiry into their questionable convictions was conducted by Justice Wood in 1985, who determined that the three men were innocent, which brought about their prison release in 1986 when they were granted unconditional pardons. Each received $100,000 in compensation.

**1979:** Working as a logger in Yreka, California, in 1978, **Patrick "Hootie" Croy** attended a party that was made up of his fellow Native Americans. In a confrontation with police following a reported robbery, Croy shot and killed a police officer. He was convicted of felony murder in that he intentionally committed a robbery that resulted in the officer's death. On appeal in 1985, the California Supreme Court vacated Croy's conviction and death sentence on the grounds that the judge at his 1979 trial had read the wrong instructions to the jury, allowing the jury to convict Croy of robbery even when he had no intent to steal. Retried in 1990, defense attorneys showed that Croy had acted in self-defense, believing that the officer was trying to kill him, pointing out the tension that then existed between

combative Native Americans and police. The jury agreed and acquitted Croy, and he was released from prison after serving ten years behind bars.

**1979: Eric Jackson** (a.k.a.: Eric Knight), was convicted and sentenced to twenty-five years in prison for the arson fire that consumed Walbaum's Supermarket in Sheepshead Bay, New York, where six firefighters died while battling the blaze. Jackson had been identified by a police informant, and police later claimed that he had confessed to setting the fire. Granted a new trial on appeal in 1994, Jackson's defense attorneys successfully argued that their client's confession had been coerced. A police arson investigator stated that the fire could have been caused by faulty electrical wiring. Jackson was acquitted.

**1980:** After he was arrested on suspicion of raping a pregnant woman in Miami, Florida, **Jerry Frank Townsend**, a mentally retarded man with an IQ of an eight-year-old child, who worked as a carnival roustabout in Hallandale, Florida, confessed to that crime as well as six murders in the area, dating back to 1973. Townsend, during prolonged police interrogations, confessed to all of the crimes after detectives took him to the crime scenes and gave him details on each of the murders and the rape. He was convicted of the first-degree murders of Naomi Gamble, Barbara Brown, and Terry Cummings in Broward County in 1973. He also confessed to the 1979 murder of thirteen-year-old Sonia Marion. In 1982, Townsend confessed to two more murders in the Miami area, that of Ernestine German and Thelma Bell. He was given seven life sentences, one each for the six murders and one for the rape, serving those sentences in the Polk County Correctional Facility. In 1998, the mother of Sonia Marion asked a Fort Lauderdale police detective to review the murder of her daughter, believing that another person might have killed her child. The detective's investigation turned up several discrepancies in the Townsend case, which led to DNA testing on the girl's shorts in 2000 (she had been raped before being murdered). DNA testing exonerated Townsend of two of the six murders, that of Cummings and Gamble, where biological evidence was extant. The DNA results were tested against other Florida felons in the DNA database in 2001, which showed that the murder-rapes of Cummings and Gamble had been committed by fifty-three-year-old serial rapist-killer Eddie Lee Mosely, who had been institutionalized in a state mental hospital and had been declared incompetent of standing trial in dozens of rapes and murders attributed to him. It was then determined that Townsend had falsely confessed to all of the crimes for which he had been convicted. Such false confessions are routine when coming from mentally retarded persons, who desire to satisfy any challenging authority figures, which, in his case, were the detectives, who obviously and easily manipulated his confessions. Townsend's convictions were vacated, and he was exonerated and released on June 15, 2001, after having spent 21.5 years in prison. Townsend's exoneration also brought about the posthumous exoneration of wrongly convicted **Frank Lee Smith** (see Chapter IX: "The Near Miracle of DNA," under DNA Exonerations in the South, Florida), who had been sent to prison in 1989 for some of Mosely's myriad crimes.

**1980:** On February 4, 1980, a man pulled a shotgun from beneath his coat and shot twenty-eight-year-old George Sneed while he waited on the porch of a friend's Boston apartment building. The man convicted of the crime was twenty-one-year-old **Christian Amado**, identified by a witness from a photograph as resembling the man he had seen murder Sneed. The witness testified on the stand, however, that Christian Amado was positively not the murderer, although Amado and the man in the photograph were one and the same. Amado was nevertheless convicted of first-degree murder on October 29, 1980, in Suffolk County Superior Court and sent to prison for life. Two years later, his defense attorney, appealing the 1980 decision before the Massachusetts Supreme Court, won an acquittal for his client, who, justices ruled, had been convicted on insufficient evidence. Christian Amado was released in 1982.

**1980:** In 1979, twenty-four-year-old **James Newsome**, a black man, was stopped outside of Wrigley Field in Chicago by two police officers who trained guns on him, believing that he had recently committed an armed robbery. He was released after the officers heard his alibi, but one of the officers thought Newsome resembled a police sketch of a suspect in an armed robbery, where grocery store owner Edward Cohen had been killed. Two eyewitnesses to that robbery-murder had already picked out another suspect in that case from a police photo array, and Newsome bore little resemblance to the police composite sketch, being taller and many years younger than the suspect, and having a mole not shown in the sketch. He was nevertheless placed in a police lineup where he was told that he had been identified as Cohen's killer (it was later determined that police had prompted witnesses to identify Newsome). In 1980, Newsome was

convicted of the robbery-murder and sentenced to life, but, in 1989, with the help of Norval Morris, a law professor at the University of Chicago, Newsome was able to obtain a court order demanding that Chicago police submit the unidentified fingerprints from the crime scene where Cohen had been murdered to the Automated Fingerprint Identification System. The fingerprints were processed, and a Chicago police officer reported falsely that the database search yielded no prints matching anyone filed in that database. Five years later, in 1994, Chicago police officials admitted that there had been a match of those prints, those of Dennis Emerson, who was on Illinois' Death Row, convicted of another murder. Newsome was released on December 6, 1994, but was electronically monitored at his home until January 5, 1995. His conviction was overturned and he filed a civil suit, which resulted in the City of Chicago awarding him $15 million in damages, $1 million for each year he had spent behind bars on November 21, 1997. Philip Beck, the attorney representing Newsome in that suit, had a life-sized replica of Newsome's prison cell made and displayed in court, and, while the jury stared at this grim exhibit, Beck and his client unraveled one prison horror story after another. Following this litany, Beck reminded the jury that as bad as prison can be, "it is a hundred times worse when you know you are innocent."

**1980:** Eighteen-year-old **David Wayne Robertson** was convicted in 1980 on two counts of first-degree murder in the shooting deaths of a Baltimore woman and her grandmother. The murder-for-hire took the lives of twenty-three-year-old Mary Thompson and eighty-three-year-old Maria Zisser, and put Robertson in prison for life. In 1983, Robertson's conviction was overturned by the Maryland Court of Appeals on the grounds the judge had given improper instructions to the jury at his trial. The court also ruled that a codefendant in the trial had perjured himself by implicating Robertson in the murder. At a 1984 retrial, a jury acquitted Robertson of all charges, and he was released after serving nearly four years in Patuxent Institution in Jessup. Michael J. Schindler and Tony E. Thompson are currently serving life sentences in prison for the murder of Thompson and Zisser.

**1980:** Lawyers for **Robert Wallace**, who was convicted and sentenced to death for murdering a Georgia police officer in 1980, filed an appeal with the U.S. Court of Appeals for the 11th Circuit, which determined that Wallace had not been competent to stand trial. In his retrial, Wallace was acquitted when disclosures showed that the shooting of the police officer had been accidental. Wallace was released in 1987.

**1980:** Half brothers twenty-three-year-old **Earnest Lee Miller** and twenty-eight-year-old **William Riley Jent** were convicted of the first-degree murder of a twenty-year-old woman known only as Tammy in July 1979 on the Lacoochee River, Pasco County, Florida. Both men were tried in separate trials presided over by the same judge in 1980. Both were found guilty, chiefly on the testimony of three eyewitnesses, who had been part of a drug and alcohol party. Though defense attorneys pointed out that the witnesses were drunk at the time of the brutal murder, the defendants were found guilty and both were sentenced to death. In 1981, The Florida Supreme Court upheld the convictions and sentences and both men came close to execution in 1983, but they received a stay from a federal judge, who stated that exculpatory information had been withheld from the trials of Miller and Jent. The actual identity of the murder victim was established in 1986. She was Linda Gale Bradshaw, and it was also disclosed that her time of death occurred when Miller and Jent were elsewhere, according to their unshakable alibis. Strong suspicion was then shifted to a former boyfriend of Bradshaw's, who had been convicted of a similar crime in Georgia. A federal district court ordered a retrial in 1987, stating that exculpatory evidence had been suppressed in the 1980 trial. Both were tried again in 1988 and released, after they agreed to plea to second-degree murder. Miller and Jent loudly repudiated their pleas when leaving the courtroom. Two of the three witnesses who had testified in the 1980 trial recanted their testimony, saying that they had been coerced by police into making their statements against Miller and Jent. Because of the error-ridden 1980 trial the Pasco County Sheriff's Department awarded Miller and Jent $65,000 compensation in 1991 in settling a wrongful arrest suit, clearly showing the innocence of both defendants.

**1980: Gary Nelson** was convicted and sentenced to death for the 1978 rape and murder of a six-year-old girl in Chatham County, Georgia. He was represented at his trial in 1980 by a single lawyer who had never tried a capital case, and who was being paid an hourly rate of between $15 and $20 to defend his client while struggling with financial problems and an expensive divorce. The attorney was denied his request for a cocounsel and funds for an investigator, and, after such court refusals, did not seek any expert witnesses, believing that funds for those witnesses would also be denied. This attorney's closing argument consisted of no more than 225 words. (He was later disbarred for unrelated matters.) Nelson, however, was proven innocent when it was revealed that prosecutors had suppressed evidence supporting Nelson's claim of innocence and information that implicated another man. No fingerprints or eyewitnesses linked Nelson to the crime, and it was shown that prosecutors had manufactured false scientific evidence in the form of a hair found on the victim's body, alleging that it had come from Nelson, which was supported by the director of the Savannah Crime Lab, but this was later refuted by FBI lab experts. The Savannah Lab, it was later determined, had never examined the hair. Police, it was learned, had also suppressed information from an alibi witness who could have cleared Nelson. The defendant lost two appeals wherein prosecution and police misconduct were termed "harmless error," until the Georgia Supreme Court finally granted Nelson a new trial, where, in 1991, in addition to all of the previously stated misconduct of police and prosecutors in this case, it was revealed that a police detective had lied about the alleged murder weapon in the case. Nelson was acquitted and released after having spent eleven years on Georgia's Death Row, watching during that terrible ordeal fifteen others go to the electric chair.

**1980: Joyce Ann Brown** was convicted of robbing a Dallas, Texas, fur company with another black female, a robbery in which one of the proprietors was killed. One of the women, the actual shooter, was later captured and confessed to the crime, saying that Brown had nothing to do with the robbery-murder, and, in fact, she did not know or ever meet Brown. Given a life sentence, Brown was released nine years after her conviction proving that she was working on the other side of the city when the crime occurred.

**1980: Douglas Harry Rendell** was convicted of murder and sent to prison for life in New South Wales, Australia, but, upon appeal in 1989, the court determined that the evidence presented in his case, which had been provided by the same expert who had testified in the 1982 wrongful convictions of Alice and Michael Chamberlain (see Chapter IV, "Insufficient Evidence"), had also presented unreliable evidence in the Rendell case. Rendell's conviction was overturned and he was given a pardon. He was later awarded $100,000 in compensation for the nine years he had spent behind bars.

**1980:** On November 3, 1979, jogger John McGinest was killed by a shotgun blast in an alley in Long Beach, California. Police investigating the case early on focused upon thirty-year-old **Thomas Lee Goldstein**, an ex-Marine and heavy drinker who lived in the alley in an unheated $85-a-month garage. Goldstein, who was at the time an engineering student at Long Beach City College, had been arrested for public drunkenness and disturbing the peace, but had no record of violent crime. Police, two weeks after the murder, interviewed Goldstein and searched his premises, finding no forensic or physical evidence that linked him to the killing. He was nevertheless arrested and given a lie detector test, that polygraph examination proving to be inconclusive. (Goldstein asked for a second polygraph test, which was denied.) Two witnesses testified against Goldstein at his 1980 trial, the first being a jailhouse snitch aptly named Edward Fink, who said that Goldstein had confessed to murdering McGinest while they shared a cell at the Long Beach jail. The second person was Loran Campbell, who claimed to be an eyewitness and who insisted Goldstein was the perpetrator. He was found guilty and sentenced to twenty-five years to life in prison, plus two years for using a gun in a felony. Goldstein served twenty-five years of that sentence in some of California's toughest prisons—San Quentin, Folsom, and the maximum security prison at Tehachapi (where most incorrigible female convicts were also held). He spent all of his spare hours in the prison libraries studying law and was awarded a paralegal certificate, filing one habeas corpus petition on his own behalf after another. Goldstein was able to provide in one appeal evidence that proved that Edward Fink's testimony was bolstered through lies in that Fink had said he had received no leniency for his own crime when, in fact, he did, in exchange for his testimony against Goldstein. The second witness, Campbell, recanted his original statements, saying that he had been overeager to aid police and that investigators had pressured him to identify Goldstein. In 2002, Magistrate Robert N. Block delivered an extensive opinion that stated that Goldstein had been wrongly convicted. He vacated Goldstein's conviction and ordered him released. Judge Dickran Tevrizian of the Federal District Court of Los Angeles agreed, as did a three-judge panel of the U.S. Court of Appeals for the Ninth Circuit. Goldstein was released from prison on April 2, 2004, after prosecutors declined to retry him. He went to work as a paralegal for the firm that had handled his recent defense, Hadsell & Stormer, in Pasadena, California, working with his counsel, Ronald O. Kaye, in preparing a damage claim against the officials who had wrongly sent him to prison.

**1980: Luis Carlos Arango** called police to his Dade County, Florida, home to report a robbery and the murder of his roommate, Jario Posada. Three armed men had invaded their apartment, Arango told police, taking their money and shooting Posada to death. Two of the bandits fled through the kitchen door, he said, while a third man, who had done the shooting, jumped off a bedroom balcony. Police searched the area, but did not thoroughly search the area beneath the balcony since it was getting dark. They shortly concluded that Arango had killed his roommate and charged him with the murder. He was convicted with circumstantial evidence in 1980 and sentenced to death. On appeal in 1986, the Florida Supreme Court vacated Arango's conviction, deciding that he had not gotten a fair trial in that prosecutors had withheld exculpatory evidence from the defense. Police had subsequently found a handgun and some of its bullet casings beneath the balcony where Arango said the assailant had fled. The gun had been purchased two days before the robbery-murder by Antonio Garcia at the Tamiami Gun Shop, and police lab analyses of the casings showed that it had been used to kill Posada. None of this had been shown to Arango's defense attorneys. The court vacated Arango's conviction and ordered him released from prison.

**1980: George Parker** was convicted of manslaughter for a killing committed in Howell Township, New Jersey, and sentenced to twenty years in prison. He had made a false confession, which he later recanted at his second trial in 1985, when he was acquitted, following the conviction of Patricia Pope who was the actual killer and who was convicted and sent to prison. Parker said that he had falsely confessed because he loved Pope's two children and believed Pope was pregnant with his child at the time of the killing.

**1980: Andrew Lee Mitchell** was convicted and sentenced to death for the December 26, 1979, murder of Keith Wills, a clerk who worked at a fireworks stand outside of Troup, Texas. Mitchell spent thirteen years on Texas's Death Row before he was released from prison and exonerated in 1993, when exculpatory evidence was presented that proved that Wills was alive several hours after Mitchell had reportedly killed him. This evidence had been withheld from Mitchell's defense, suppressed by the local sheriff's department.

**1980: Terry Pinfold** and **Harry MacKenney** were charged with murdering a convicted felon, Terrence Eve, who disappeared from Dagenham, Essex, England, in November 1974. Pinfold was convicted of

Eve's murder and MacKenny was acquitted of murdering Eve, but convicted of murdering four other persons, and both were sent to prison for life, these convictions brought about by the sole testimony of another felon, John Bruce Childs. In 1986, Childs recanted his testimony, saying that he had been coerced into making false statements against Pinfold and MacKenney by police and prosecutors, and that Eve was reportedly alive and living in London under an assumed name. A court of appeals vacated the convictions of Pinfold and MacKenney in 2003.

**1981:** On February 21, 1981, an intruder broke through a window in the Jonesboro, Louisiana, residence of a twenty-two-year-old math tutor, beating the woman with a heavy wooden stick and repeatedly raping her. The victim later identified sixteen-year-old **Michael Anthony Williams**, a sophomore at Jonesboro High School, as her assailant. The victim had been tutoring Williams in math a year before the attack, and said that the boy had become infatuated with her, visiting her at her father's store, where, on one occasion, he refused to leave and was jailed for breaking a glass and striking the woman, as well as threatening to take her into some woods and beat her. Williams was released on February 5. 1981, sixteen days before the rape occurred. Other than the victim's identification, there was no physical evidence linking Williams to the crime. At his May 1981 trial, Williams was again identified as the attacker by the victim, who said that she had known him since he had been a little child. A jury convicted him of aggravated rape within one hour, and he was sentenced to life imprisonment without parole at the Angola State Penitentiary. All appeals failed, and Williams remained behind bars without his father (who died while he was in prison; his mother had died when he was a child) or his four brothers and two sisters contacting him after 1990. In 2003, his case was undertaken by the Innocence Project New Orleans. That organization sought post-conviction DNA testing in his case, which was granted by Assistant District Attorney Douglas Stokes, who had been Williams's defense attorney at his 1981 trial. In fall 2004, Forensic Science Associates performed DNA testing and reported that evidence from the victim's clothing (the rape kit was no longer available) excluded him from being the donor of the spermatozoa. In December 2004 and January 2005, the North Delta Crime Laboratory retested the same evidence and came to the same conclusion. DNA tests were made from the same evidence in February 2005 by Orchid Cellmark, with the same conclusion.

Williams's conviction was vacated and prosecutors refused to retry the case, exonerating him on March 11, 2005. He was then released from Angola State Penitentiary, given $10, but no bus ticket. Williams moved into a one-bedroom apartment in downtown Baton Rouge, Louisiana. When entering the apartment for the first time, he noticed blue paint peeling from the trim, but he was nevertheless delighted, saying: "It needs a little cleaning, but it's definitely better than a prison cell." The forty-year-old Williams, who had earned his high school degree while behind bars, had been imprisoned for 23.5 years.

**1981:** After his arrest at Miami International Airport in 1981 for grand theft, **Anibal Jaramillo-Restrepo**, a twenty-seven-year-old illegal Colombian immigrant, was linked to the December 1980 slayings of two Colombian men. Jaramillo-Restrepo's fingerprints were found on several items at the Miami townhouse where Gilberto Caicedo and Candelario Castellanos were bound and gagged, then machine-gunned to death. During his trial in April 1981, Jaramillo-Restrepo said he had been at the house the night before the murders helping Caicedo's nephew clean out the garage, but that he had nothing to do with the killings. Although authorities could not determine when Jaramillo-Restrepo left the prints, a jury found him guilty on two counts of first-degree murder. The one man who might have cleared him, Edison Caicedo, disappeared before the trial. The jury recommended life imprisonment, but Dade County circuit Judge Ellen Morphonios-Gable sentenced Jaramillo-Restrepo to death. In July 1982, the Florida Supreme Court overturned the death sentence, arguing that the suspect's fingerprints at the scene were insufficient to convict him. The ruling marked the first time a man had been removed from Death Row since the reinstitution of the death penalty in 1972. Jaramillo-Restrepo literally "jumped for joy" when released from Death Row, according to his attorney, Louis Casuso, but, on the day he left Death Row, he was arrested by agents of the Bureau of Alcohol, Tobacco and Firearms for lying on a form when he purchased a .45-caliber pistol from a gun shop in 1980. A federal judged sentenced him to four years in prison for this offense in 1983, but he was eventually deported to his native Colombia, where he was reportedly murdered in Medellin.

**1981: Van Bering Robinson**, twenty-two, was found guilty of killing an Albuquerque police officer and robbing a shoe store, and sentenced to life imprisonment in 1981. Phil Chacon had been shot and killed while pursuing a robbery suspect on his motorcycle. Two years later, a jury in a second trial reversed the guilty verdict and acquitted Robinson of both charges. In March 1983, the New Mexico Supreme Court had overturned the lower court ruling in Robinson's first trial, stating that the prosecutors had prejudiced the testimony of an eyewitness, who testified that Robinson was innocent, in an effort to impeach him. Robinson's lawyer, James Toulouse, called the police investigation "inadequate" and "undirected." Although Robinson was exonerated in Chacon's death, he still faced an eight-and-a-half-year prison sentence for crimes he had allegedly committed that were unrelated to the murder.

**1981: James Emmons Kimball** was inebriated and under the influence of tranquilizers when, in 1981, he drove with a female friend to a liquor store in Lansing, Michigan, where he approached a clerk and demanded money. As the clerk started to hand over the cash, Kimball said he had only been kidding and would not take funds from someone who was so good-looking. Protesting that he had abandoned the crime, Kimball was nonetheless convicted and sentenced to a three-to-five-year prison term for robbery. In a retrial in a Leelanau County Circuit Court, the Michigan Court of Appeals reversed the conviction, ruling that a mid-crime change of heart is a legitimate defense. Setting legal precedent, the court noted that the "traditional view" is that an attempted crime has been committed after a person makes an intentional, overt act, but ruled that a person who voluntarily abandons a crime before it is completed has negated the danger and so removes the cause for prosecution.

**1981: Clifford Henry Bowen**, convicted and receiving three death sentences in Oklahoma in 1981, was released in 1986, and all charges were dropped against him the following year after the U.S. Court of Appeals for the Tenth Circuit overturned his 1981 conviction. The court pointed out that prosecutors offered no physical evidence that linked Bowen to the crime, where three men were slain execution style while they sat at a poolside table at an Oklahoma City motel at 2 A.M. on July 6, 1980. Prosecutors at Bowen's trial had failed to disclose information about another police suspect in the case, Lee Crowe, a South Carolina police lieutenant, and, had Bowen's defense attorneys known of this suspect, Bowen would have most probably been acquitted. Crowe had a strong resemblance to Bowen, and, where Bowen provided twelve witnesses who stated that he was 300 miles away from the scene of the crime, Crowe had no alibi. Further, it was proven that Crowe carried

the same kind of gun and unusual ammunition that had been used in the slayings. Three witnesses at the motel slayings had identified Bowen as the killer who walked up to the three victims, shooting them at point-blank range, but their statements were later discredited when Bowen was released in 1986. He died ten years later in 1996.

**1981:** On October 12, 1980, a seventeen-year-old girl was raped by a man driving a blue car. The rapist attacked the victim on a secluded road south of Sea-Tac Airport in Seattle, Washington. **Steve Gary Titus**, the married thirty-one-year-old manager of a seafood restaurant, who drove a blue car, was arrested and charged with the rape after the victim picked out his photo from a police photo array. While in court testifying against him, the victim became hysterical, which all the more readily convinced a jury that she was telling the truth. Titus was convicted on March 4, 1981, but before sentencing, investigative reporter Paul Henderson of the Seattle *Times*, who had earlier begun probing the case, unearthed one discrepancy after another, chiefly those created by Police Officer Ronald Parker. Henderson not only exposed Parker's altering of evidence, but pointed to the existence of the real perpetrator, serial rapist McDonald "Mac" Smith. (Henderson would be awarded the Pulitzer Prize for this investigation into the Titus case.) With this evidence in hand, a judge vacated Titus's conviction, and Seattle prosecutors dropped all charges against Titus, who was then released from jail. He had by then lost his wife and job, but he filed for damages, only to drop dead of a heart attack at age thirty-five a few weeks before that civil trial began. His son was later awarded $2.6 million in compensation for his father's wrongful conviction. Ironically, the corrupt police officer, Parker (who never apologized to Titus for the wrong he did to him), who died in 1987, and Titus were buried in the same cemetery, resting for eternity only fifty feet distant from each other. On Titus's gravestone read the words: "He fought for his day in court/He was used, deceived, betrayed and denied justice even in death." No editorial comment appeared on Parker's stone.

**1981: Clarence Womack** was convicted and sentenced to death for killing Arthur Bullock during the robbery of a market in Montgomery, Alabama, but his conviction was vacated and he was released from prison in 1988. An appeals court ruled that Womack's conviction had been brought about through perjured testimony, ineffective assistance of counsel, and official misconduct when exculpatory evidence had been withheld.

**1981: Robert Charles Cruz** was convicted and sentenced to death for hiring three men to murder the owner of a business he wanted to acquire in Phoenix, Arizona. The 1981 conviction was vacated on appeal by the Arizona Supreme Court, which determined that prejudice had been demonstrated in court against the defendant. A new trial was ordered, and two more trials ended in hung juries. Cruz was convicted in a fourth trial, which was also overturned by the Arizona Supreme Court, ruling that the prosecution had made serious errors. A fifth trial revealed that prosecutors had pressured witnesses and had made egregious deals to bring about Cruz's conviction. He was acquitted of all charges in a jury trial and released from prison in 1995.

**1981: Nathaniel Carter** was convicted and sentenced to twenty-five years to life for stabbing to death sixty-year-old Clarice Herndon in Queens, New York. The victim was Carter's ex-wife's foster mother. His ex-wife, Delissa Carter, testified against him at his trial, bringing about his conviction. Two years later, Delissa Carter went to authorities to say that she had lied, and that she had killed Herndon. Judge John J. Leahy, of the State Supreme Court in Queens, vacated Carter's conviction and ordered the thirty-three-year-old Carter released from the Correctional Facility at Fishkill, New York.

**1981: Felix Rodriguez** and **Russell Weinberger** were convicted for the beating and strangling murder of optometrist Charles Langley. The body of the sixty-three-year-old Langley had been found in his Kensington Avenue office on January 15, 1981, in Philadelphia, Pennsylvania. His pockets had been turned inside out, and his wallet was missing. Detective Frank Suminski was assigned to investigate the case. When he learned that a man named "Russell" had gone to the Episcopal Hospital on the day of the murder, he tracked down twenty-three-year-old Russell Weinberger, a furniture mover with a third-grade reading ability and an IQ of 60 to 65. When first questioned, Weinberger said he knew nothing about the Langley robbery-murder, but he said that Felix Rodriguez, a man he knew in the neighborhood, "liked to beat up old men." The twenty-two-year-old Rodriguez was then brought in for questioning. A Puerto Rican immigrant, Rodriguez spoke only Spanish and he later said that, during his interrogation, a translator told him that if he signed a piece of paper, he could go home. He signed a confession of murder. Weinberger also confessed, but the police

records of his confession and that of Rodriguez could not be supported since only Suminski worked on the case (he died in 2000). Weinberger pleaded guilty to third-degree murder and was sentenced to fifteen to thirty years in prison. Rodriguez was convicted by a jury and was given a life sentence. Both men would have been forgotten had it not been for a conversation in November 2001 when a woman asked Philadelphia Police Captain Alan Kurtz to solve the 1980 murder of her grandmother, Anne Ruane. Captain Kurtz learned that a fingerprint had been lifted from the case, but, in that day, no computers existed by which to compare the print with other crimes. Kurtz had the print run through the Automated Fingerprint Identification System, and it matched that of forty-six-year-old Anthony Sylvanus, who was in prison serving a term for robbery since 1981. Kurtz asked Sylvanus about Ruane's murder, and he confessed to killing her. Syvanus then confessed to several other "cold" cases—the slaying of eighty-eight-year-old Grace Woolsey in Mount Airy, Pennsylvania, in July 1980, the beating and stabbing death of fifty-five-year-old Anna Knuttel in her Philadelphia store on November 11, 1980, the murder of eighty-seven-year-old Vincente Morelli in January 1981, and the killing of Langley a short time later. He said that in two of the murders, including Langley, he had been assisted by Ramon Ortiz. Kurtz located Ortiz in jail, where he was serving time for theft. He admitted to being an accomplice of Sylvanus in the two murders. In October 2002, Rodriguez, Weinberger, as well as Sylvanus and Ortiz stood before Common Pleas Judge Benjamin Lerner who, after reviewing Sylvanus's and Ortiz's confessions, stated that "there's no doubt about the two new guys' involvement. None whatsoever." Prosecutors, however, stubbornly clung to the convictions of Rodriguez and Weinberger, pointing out to the court that Sylvanus and Ortiz had failed lie detector tests (polygraph tests were not admissible at trials, but were mentioned at this evidentiary hearing). Still, Sylvanus and Ortiz insisted that they had murdered Langley, where Rodriguez and Weinberger had insisted all along that their confessions, which had convicted them, were false and that they had recanted those confessions shortly after their convictions and maintained their innocence for twenty-one years behind bars. Weinberger had been denied a parole in 1997, after telling a parole board that he was innocent and for which the parole board charged him with "denial of crime [and] failure to take responsibility." The state now had two separate sets of killers for the same crime. To solve its dilemma and save its face, the prosecution told Rodriguez and Weinberger that they would authorize their prison release if they would plead guilty to reduced charges and for the time already served. Judge Lerner had no comment on this arrangement, even though he had "no doubt" that Sylvanus and Ortiz were guilty of murdering Langley. Believing there was no other way to freedom, Rodriguez and Weinberg took the prosecution's deal. Weinberger was the only one released. Rodriguez remained behind bars to serve as much as an additional twenty years on a parole violation for a previous and unrelated burglary conviction.

**1982**: In October 1980, a white woman working as an attendant in a gas station in Hammond, Indiana, was abducted from the station by two black men. They beat her and then both raped her before dropping her off at a remote area. The victim was first taken to a police station and then to a hospital where a rape kit was assembled. The victim identified **Larry Mayes** as one of her assailants from a police photo array, although she had failed to identify him in two police lineups. The only significant physical description given of one of the attackers was that he had a gold tooth and Mayes had a gold tooth. Fingerprints found at the scene of the crime did not match Mayes's fingerprints, and the biological evidence examined through serology tests did not provide conclusive results. On July 8, 1982, Mayes was convicted of rape, robbery, and unlawful devious conduct on the testimony of the lone eyewitness, and sentenced to eighty years in prison. After all appeals failed, the Innocence Project at the University of Indiana in Indianapolis undertook his case in 1996. Fran Hardy, a criminal law professor, supervised four law school students in their search of the biological evidence, which prosecutors said had been lost. The students searched for a number of years for that evidence until one law student, Resa Overhoudt, was able to convince a conscientious court clerk to conduct a thorough search of the evidence room of the Hammond Courthouse. The evidence was located. The Innocence Project in Indianapolis was joined by the New York Innocence Project in filing a motion to have the biological evidence DNA tested. New prosecutors in the case, alerted to the defense's request for that DNA testing, once again interviewed the victim, who told them that Hammond police had hypnotized her before she made the final identification of Mayes from the photo lineup. The DNA testing was performed in 2001, and the results showed that Mayes was excluded as the donor of the spermatozoa in the case. His conviction was vacated

and prosecutors dropped all charges against him. The fifty-two-year-old Mayes was released from prison on December 21, 2001, after having served 18.5 years behind bars for a crime he had not committed. He became the 100th person exonerated by DNA in the United States During the time he spent behind bars, Mayes's father, son, and daughter had died. He went to live with his mother, working at a job referred to him by a sympathetic prison guard. Represented by John Stainthrop of the People's Law Office of Chicago, Illinois, and Barry Scheck and Nick Brustin of the New York law firm of Cochran, Neufeld & Scheck, Mayes won a $9 million award from a jury in a civil suit against the City of Hammond and Police Chief Captain Michael Solan in U.S. District Court for the Northern District of Indiana, on August 23, 2006.

**1982:** Following the rape of a female student at Dickinson College in Carlisle, Pennsylvania, in May 1982, **Willie Nesmith** was identified by two witnesses who said he was near the scene of the crime. He was tried twice, the first trial ending in a hung jury. He was convicted in a second trial and sentenced to nine to twenty-five years in prison. After serving nine years, Nesmith sought exoneration following his parole, which was achieved in 2000, after DNA testing showed him innocent.

**1982:** On March 31, 1981, a man inquiring about the sale of a waterbed in Jacksonville, North Carolina, sexually attacked the woman selling the bed in her home, raping her vaginally at gunpoint and then stealing some jewelry before fleeing. The victim later identified **Leo Waters** as her assailant. Serology reports at his 1982 trial showed that the victim and Waters were both type O blood, which had been found in the rape kit, and prosecutors stated that Waters could not be excluded from a white population of 35.5 percent. This evidence brought about Waters's conviction of rape, sexual offense, and robbery with a dangerous weapon. He was sentenced to life in prison. Attorney Mark Raynor, who took over Waters's case in February 2002, helped him secure post-conviction STR DNA testing by Laboratory Corporation of America, performed in January 2003, and which showed Waters innocent of the crime. Prosecutors had the same tests replicated by the North Carolina State Bureau of Investigation Laboratory, which announced the same results. All charges against Waters were dismissed on November 20, 2003, and Waters was released. He was officially exonerated in August 2005, when Governor Michael Easley (2001– ) granted Waters a full pardon.

**1982:** An intruder wearing a ski mask robbed and raped a woman in her Long Island, New York, home in 1978. Since the woman could not identify the assailant, she reported only the burglary to police. In 1981, the woman returned home to presumably find the same man waiting for her. He robbed and raped her again. The victim identified **Kerry Kotler** as her assailant after selecting his photo from a police photo array, again at a police lineup, and again through voice identification. He was convicted of rape, burglary, and robbery for both the 1978 and 1981 crimes and was sentenced to twenty-five to fifty years in prison. In 1989, the Innocence Project in New York undertook his case, securing post-conviction DNA testing the following year by Forensic Science Associates, which conducted PCR DNA testing, and announcing that Kotler was excluded as the donor of the biological evidence in the case. Further DNA tests were conducted after prosecutors argued that the spermatozoa could have been a mixture of the offender and a consensual partner. The Center for Blood Research, however, excluded both Kotler and the woman's husband. Kotler's convictions were vacated, and he was released from prison in 1992, after having served 10.5 years in prison. He was later awarded $1.5 million in compensation by the State of New York. Three years later, however, in 1995, Kotler was again arrested and charged with waylaying a woman on a New York roadway while pretending to be a police officer and then raping the victim. Following the rape, the assailant produced a water bottle and rinsed off the victim. When the woman asked why he was doing that, "he told me that he just wanted to get rid of any evidence." Kotler was identified as the attacker and, in 1997, was convicted on the very evidence that had earlier released him from prison—DNA. He was sentenced to seven to twenty-one years in prison.

**1982:** In September 1982, **Bruce Nelson** was convicted of rape and murder in Allegheny County, Pennsylvania, based upon the testimony of Terrence Moore, who confessed to taking part in the crime, but claimed that Nelson had choked the victim to death after both had sexually assaulted the woman. Nelson was sentenced to three life terms plus thirty-four years. His attorneys appealed for post-conviction DNA analysis in 1990, and tests were performed the following year, resulting in Nelson's exoneration on August 28, 1991.

**1982:** Following the July 1982 shooting death of a Houston, Texas, police officer, nineteen-year-old **Ricardo Adalpe Guerra** was charged with the murder even though the killer, who was riding with him in his car when he had been stopped by the police officer for a routine traffic violation, had also been killed in the shootout along with a passerby, and the gun used to murder the officer was found in the hand of the other dead man. The chief witness against Guerra was the ten-year-old son of the murdered bystander, who identified Guerra at his October 1982 trial. Though the defense pointed out that the gun used by the killer was in the hand of that dead killer, prosecutors maintained that Guerra was the actual shooter and that he had placed the gun in the dead man's hand. Guerra was found guilty and sentenced to death, spending nearly fourteen yeas on Death Row and coming within only three hours of execution in 1992. On appeal in 1994, a judge vacated the conviction, stating that prosecutorial and police misconduct had been widespread in the case in that prosecutors had intimidated witnesses into testifying against Guerra and that police had manipulated evidence to help bring about that conviction. The judge's ruling was upheld by the U.S. Fifth Circuit Court of Appeals, which caused Guerra to be removed from Death Row in Huntsville, Texas, to the Harris County Jail to await a new trial. The Harris County district attorney's office dropped the case because, it admitted, six key prosecution witnesses were unable to testify since their testimony had been influenced by police and that there was "overwhelming evidence" that Guerra was innocent. Guerra, who had been an illegal Mexican in the United States when arrested—a factor emphasized by prosecutors at his trial and one in which they wrongfully suggested that he deserved the death penalty for that illegal status—was deported back to his native land, Monterrey, Mexico—the Mexican Government had intervened directly on his behalf—where he was killed in a car accident in August 1997.

**1982:** On December 5, 1981, Bobbie Russell, mother of two, was raped and murdered in her Birmingham Terrace apartment in Toledo, Ohio. Police found her strangled to death with a cord from lights of a Christmas tree she had only days earlier decorated. Her six-year-old son and two-year-old daughter were inside the apartment when the crime occurred. The boy, Jeffrey, repeatedly stated to police that "Danny killed my Momma. . . Danny killed my Momma. . . Danny killed my Momma." **Danny Brown** had been dating Russell for several months up to the time of her murder and was almost immediately charged with the murder. Jeffrey Russell also told police that he saw Brown and another man enter his apartment through a window and saw Brown arguing with his mother before running to his bedroom and hiding under the bed. He later discovered his mother dead and ran to neighbors for help. Jeffrey identified Brown in a police lineup and later at Brown's 1982 trial. Though Brown had alibi witnesses, and his defense attorney, Jon Richardson, pointed out that there was no physical evidence linking him to the crime, the jury chose to accept the boy's statements, which had emanated from a traumatized incident. Brown was convicted of aggravated murder and aggravated burglary and was sentenced to prison for life. When all appeals failed, defense attorney Jeffrey Gamso contacted Centurion Ministries in New Jersey, asking their help. This organization, headed by founder James McCloskey, undertook Brown's case and secured postconviction DNA testing on the case, which excluded Brown as the donor in the rape (he was not convicted of rape) and indicated the actual perpetrator was Sherman Preston, who had been sent to prison for life following his conviction of murdering Denise Howell, of Toledo, in 1983, a rape-murder case that bore striking similarities to the Russell rape-murder. In 2000, Preston was found guilty of murdering Russell and given another life sentence. Following the announcement of the DNA testing, Brown took and passed a polygraph test. He was released in April 2001, after having spent 18.5 years in some of Ohio's toughest prisons—Mansfield Correctional Facility, Richland Correctional Facility, and the infamous Lucas Correctional Facility in southern Ohio, where, in 1993, rioting took the lives of one prison guard and nine convicts. Upon his release, Brown stated that he was not bitter about his wrongful imprisonment, but he wanted to see improvements in a judicial system that wrongfully sent persons to prison. He said that his favorite book, which he read often in prison, was Victor Hugo's *Les Miserables*, the story of Jean Valjean, who endured one prison horror after another in nineteenth-century France.

**1982: Lesly Jean**, a marine stationed at Camp Lejuene, North Carolina, was convicted of raping a Jacksonville, North Carolina, woman and was sentenced to life in prison. His conviction was brought about through his identification by the victim. His attorney, Mike Glazier, showed in appeal that prosecutors had withheld exculpatory evidence in his case, and his conviction was vacated in 1991, when he was released after prosecutors declined to retry him. In 2001, DNA testing showed that Jean was excluded as the donor of the spermatozoa from the biological evidence in the rape kit. On February 9, 2001, North Carolina Governor Mike Easley (2001– ) officially pardoned Jean, mak-

ing him eligible for $150,000 in compensation for the nine years he spent in prison. Said Jean: "You know that old saying, 'When someone knocks you down, you need to get back up'? Well, sometimes it's not that simple to get back up." Glazier, who fought doggedly for nine years to establish Jean's innocence, did help him get back up and went on to aid other wrongfully convicted persons. He became a state representative (Dem.) for Cumberland County, sponsoring a bill that would assure defendants proper police treatment, wherein all police lineup identification procedures would be videotaped to prevent police officers from inadvertently or purposely steering witnesses to suspects and urged the establishment of the first state Innocence Commission to review all possible wrongful convictions.

**1982:** On the night of December 11, 1980, a gunman entered a Burger King in Orange, California, leaping over a counter and forcing three employees at gunpoint to a walk-in cooler. The gunmen then went to the back office, where he found Walter Horace Bell Jr., the nineteen-year-old night manager, counting out the evening's receipts. The gunman forced him to open the safe and then shot Bell in the back of the head, killing him. Six days later, police arrested **DeWayne McKinney** for the crime. McKinney had been a street gang member and had a police record. He was identified by one of the Burger King employees as the gunman, even though he was much shorter than the man originally described by the witness. Three more witnesses identified McKinney as the perpetrator of the robbery-murder. Deputy District Attorney Tony Rackauckas asked for the death penalty, telling the jury that his witnesses had proved McKinney's guilt, saying: "About the only way to bring in better evidence is if we had a movie of it." The jury decided that McKinney was guilty, but should be sent to prison for life without parole. While filing appeals that proved unsuccessful, McKinney survived two knife attacks, a bout with tuberculosis, and a failed suicide attempt when housed in California's most dreaded prisons, including San Quentin and Folsom. He studied hard and earned his high school equivalency degree. In 1999, McKinney's fortunes improved when two prison inmates confessed to having been involved in the Burger King robbery-murder, and they named the killer. In 2000, a judge of the Orange County Superior Court, at the suggestion of Rackauckas, vacated McKinney's conviction based upon eyewitness error and police misconduct (police officers had lied to witnesses, saying that McKinney had been found with the proceeds from the robbery of the Burger King). Upon his release from prison, McKinney met with Raukauckas and, in a photo op arranged by an enterprising reporter of the *Los Angeles Times* who got the exclusive, shook the hand of the man who had sent him to prison eighteen years earlier (and had even sought his execution), saying that he would not only endorse Raukauckas's election to the post of Orange County District Attorney, but that he would campaign door-to-door for him. That endorsement sealed Raukauckas's election. McKinney was later awarded $1.7 million in compensation for his wrongful conviction. He had by then married and moved to Hawaii with his share of the settlement, about $1 million, after paying off contingency amounts to attorneys and covering court costs. In Hawaii, McKinney invested wisely in real estate and bought a franchise for ATM machines all over the main island of Oahu, becoming within a few years a multimillionaire, certainly a real-life tale that matched the fabulous and fictional story of Edmond Dantès, the wrongly convicted protagonist of the novel *The Count of Monte Cristo* by Alexandre Dumas, père.

**1982: Raymond Girdler** was convicted of setting fire to his home in Yavapai County, Arizona, in which his wife and child died. A prosecution expert testified that flammable liquid had been found in Girdler's residence. On appeal, however, other experts proved that the fire was started from natural origins. After serving eight years in prison, Girdler's conviction was vacated, and he was released from prison in 1991.

**1982: Lee Perry Farmer** and Charles Huffman went to an apartment in Riverside, California, in June 1981 to collect a drug debt. One of the visitors shot and killed eighteen-year-old Erich Allyn Schmidt-Till, the roommate of the person they intended to see, and then fled. Both men were tried in 1982, but Huffman was acquitted, while Farmer was sentenced to death. Farmer always maintained that he was innocent of the shooting, but he nevertheless spent eight years on San Quentin's Death Row, until, in 1989, the California Supreme Court ordered a new trial. A jury in 1991 found him guilty again, but recommended life, which removed Farmer from Death Row. Meanwhile, his attorneys continued to file appeals, claiming that Huffman had been the killer of Erich Allyn Schmidt-Till. Huffman had confessed to his attorney that he had entered the apartment and shot the victim, and he made that confession to several other persons. In 1997, the Ninth Circuit Court of Appeals vacated Farmer's murder conviction, ruling that Farmer had incompetent coun-

sel at his first trial in ignoring Huffman's confession at his 1991 trial. On January 15, 1999, a Riverside County Superior Court jury acquitted him of the Schmidt-Till murder, believing that Huffman had been the real and only perpetrator. Farmer was released from prison after serving eighteen years behind bars. Another conviction for burglary in the same event had been satisfied with time served. Farmer, while at San Quentin, had become deeply religious and served as an inspiration to many fellow convicts, preventing the suicides of two of those inmates. Upon his release, Farmer went to his mother's home in Colton, California and, when entering, his mother's dog, believing him to be an intruder, promptly bit him. He laughed off the experience and then went with his family to a Burger King, where he bit into a Whopper, a meal he had dreamed about for more than two decades.

**1982: Damaso Vega** was convicted of murdering the sixteen-year-old daughter of his best friend in Long Branch (Monmouth County), New Jersey. He was set free in 1989 after a Superior Court judge ruled that the three chief witnesses against him had committed perjury at his trial. Centurion Ministries, which had undertaken Vega's case, had shown at an evidentiary hearing earlier the recantations from all three witnesses. The judge at that time apologized to Vega for his wrongful imprisonment and complimented Centurion Ministries for its in-depth and meticulous investigation into this case.

**1982: Colin Warner** was convicted of second-degree murder in Kings County, New York. His codefendant later confessed that he had acted alone and that Warner had nothing to do with the slaying. Warner's conviction was vacated, and he was released from prison in 2001.

**1982:** On October 27, 1981, Ulra Elma Thompson, seventy-six, was found raped and suffocated in her apartment in Oklahoma City, Oklahoma. No fingerprints were found at the scene of the crime, but, after items from the victim's apartment along with the key to that apartment were found in the home of **Malcolm Rent Johnson**, who had been detained for an unrelated parole violation, police charged Johnson with the Thompson rape and murder. Johnson said that he had gotten the items from Thompson's apartment, along with the key (which was reportedly found on Johnson's bed stand), from a third party. Johnson was convicted on this evidence and, to a greater degree in the rape charge, on the evidence of a so-called forensic expert, Joyce Gilchrist, who worked for the Oklahoma City Police Department. Gilchrist testified that six biological samples taken from the murder victim's bedroom matched Johnson's blood type. She also testified that hair fragments found at the murder scene matched Johnson, and fibers also found at the crime scene matched a blue cotton shirt Johnson owned. This was the first time Gilchrist testified as a fiber expert. Johnson was convicted and sentenced to death, executed on January 6, 2000. In the following year, Gilchrist was suspended with pay after the FBI reported that, after reviewing eight cases in which she had testified, Gilchrist had misidentified evidence or made other serious mistakes in six of those cases. The evidence that Gilchrist reportedly examined in the Johnson case, chiefly the spermatozoa taken at the crime scene, was refuted by another crime lab expert, Laura Schile, who signed a July 30, 2001, memo stating that "spermatozoa is not present." After stating that the evidence reportedly analyzed by Gilchrist did not exist, Schile resigned from the Oklahoma Police Department crime lab, citing a hostile work environment as her reason. Gilchrist was fired in September 2001. Earlier, two appellate courts ruled that Gilchrist gave false testimony about semen evidence in the 1992 rape and murder trial of **Alfred Brian Mitchell,** whose death sentence was overturned in August 2001. One of the court rulings called her testimony "untrue." Johnson was by no means exonerated through the misconduct of Gilchrist. He had been convicted of two rapes in Chicago and was thought to be a danger to the community, and all state officials felt that his execution was warranted on evidence other than that falsely presented by Gilchrist. Defense attorneys felt that without that false evidence being presented against their client, there was a chance that the jury might not have convicted Johnson and he would not have been executed. DNA testing did not exist at the time of Johnson's trial, but it did later exist and come to the rescue of another Gilchrist victim, **Jeffrey Pierce** (see Chapter IX: "The Near Miracle of DNA"; also see **Curtis McCarty,** Chronology, 1986).

**1983**: In October, Marine Corps corporal **Lindsey Scott,** twenty-five, was convicted of the rape and attempted murder of the wife of a fellow Marine at the Quantico, Virginia, Marine Base, where he was stationed. Scott maintained his innocence throughout the trial, saying that he had been shopping and dining when the crime was committed on April 20, 1983. Scott was sentenced to thirty years in the military prison at Fort Leavenworth, Kansas. In July 1987, the U.S. Court of Military Appeals reversed the conviction on the basis that Scott's civilian attorney had fallen "far short of rea-

sonable competence" in not investigating the defendant's alibi. Although Scott had provided his attorney, Ervan E. Kuhnke, with the details of his whereabouts on the evening of April 20, 1983, Kuhnke failed to introduce any mention of those details in Scott's defense, saying that he had never expected the case to come to trial. Scott's family and supporters had charged that Scott was convicted in the first trial because he was black and the victim was white. The thirty-year sentence and an $18,000 pay forfeiture imposed on Scott were set aside at the time of the reversal, and Scott was released from prison. On February 19, 1988, a jury at Scott's second trial acquitted him of the charges.

**1983: John C. Skelton** was convicted and sentenced to death for the 1982 murder of Joe Lee Neal, a former Skelton employee, who was blown up in Odessa, Texas, after someone planted dynamite beneath his pickup truck. In 1989, the Texas Court of Appeals, in a 2–1 split decision, acquitted Skelton, who claimed (with witnesses) that he had been 800 miles away from the crime scene at the time of Neal's bombing death. (Skelton's presence was not necessary to have brought about Neal's death.) The court specified that Skelton had been convicted on weak circumstantial evidence, and that there was a "strong suspicion or probability that appellant committed the capital offense" in the evidence prosecutors provided, but that no moral certainty existed to justify Skelton's conviction. He was acquitted and released in 1990. On August 15, 2006, the seventy-seven-year-old Skelton, a native of Knoxville, Arkansas, was convicted of threatening to kill Terry Lee Jacobs, of Midland, Texas, over a $300,000 debt, reportedly telling Jacobs that he would be shot in the head unless the debt to his business associates was paid. Nancy Neal, daughter of the slain Joe Lee Neal, sat throughout the Skelton-Jacobs trial, and, when learning that Skelton was facing twenty years in prison on the Jacobs conviction, stated: "It doesn't bring back my father, but at least John Skelton will go to prison—he'll die in prison." Skelton reportedly stated that "I will kill any liar that says I threatened to kill anyone".

**1983:** A thirty-seven-year-old Mexican citizen, **Pedro Torres,** was arrested for drinking beer in the parking lot of a Dallas, Texas, convenience store. When police ran his name through their computer, they discovered that Torres was wanted for the murder of eighteen-year-old Manuel Ortega on April 17, 1983. Torres, who was in the United States illegally, was arrested, tried, and convicted despite his claim that he was 250 miles from the crime when the murder was committed. Torres was sentenced to seventy-five years in prison. Three months later, the trial judge received information that Torres's alibi might be sound. He had Torres's original attorney, Carlos Garcia, file a motion for a new trial. When Torres's work records, which for some reason Garcia had neglected to introduce as evidence in the first trial, were examined, it became clear that the wrong Pedro Torres had been arrested and sent to jail. In April 1985, the conviction was reversed and Torres was released.

**1983: Anthony Silah Brown** was convicted of the first-degree murder of a deliveryman and sentenced to death in Florida in 1983. He was retried in 1986 and won an acquittal after the prosecution's chief witness confessed to having committed perjury in the first trial.

**1983:** On December 10, 1982, twenty-year-old Carmen Zink, of Woodward, Indiana, was killed after she struggled with a purse-snatcher in Fort Wayne, Indiana. A man claiming to be the getaway driver in the robbery told police that Zink's killer was **Charles "Charlie Red" Smith**, a black male and resident of Fort Wayne (born on October 10, 1953), and, in exchange for his testimony, all charges were dropped against this accomplice. Smith was brought to trial in 1983, where he provided a solid alibi, but the alibi was prohibited from being entered into evidence at the trial because Smith's inept attorney had failed to file a pretrial alibi notice, according to the presiding judge. Smith was convicted on September 21, 1983, that conviction chiefly based upon the testimony of the accomplice, who had plea-bargained for his statements in court. On October 18, 1983, Smith was sentenced to death by Allen County Superior Court Judge Alfred W. Moellering. The Indiana Supreme Court stayed Smith's execution and granted a second trial in 1987, based on the fact that Smith had not received adequate representation. Smith's alibi was admitted into evidence at that Allen County retrial, where the accomplice recanted his testimony, and where Smith, on May 9, 1991, was acquitted of Zink's murder and released.

**1983: Juan Ramos** was convicted and sentenced for raping and murdering Mary Sue Cobb in Cocoa, Florida, on April 23, 1983. A bloodhound was used to smell Ramos's scent and then taken to a room where five knives and five blouses were on display, the dog reportedly stopping at the knife and blouse taken from the scene of the crime. It was later learned that only one set of the knives and blouses had blood on them, and that the hound had simply detected the blood, not the specific crime scene evidence. A jailhouse snitch testified against Ramos, but his statements were discred-

ited later when it was learned that, in exchange for his testimony, prosecutors reduced his prison sentence to two years from the seventy years he faced in a conviction. The Florida Supreme Court reviewed his case and ordered a new trial, stating that the prosecution in Ramos's first trial improperly used evidence brought against him (use of the bloodhound, which the court determined was unreliable). He was acquitted in his second trial and released in 1987.

**1983: Richard Neal Jones** was convicted and sentenced to death in Oklahoma in 1983, along with three codefendants, all charged with the murder of Charles Keene of Grady County, Oklahoma. Jones steadfastly maintained that he had passed out when three others committed the murder and that he had had nothing to do with the crime. The Court of Criminal Appeals of Oklahoma reviewed his case and remanded it for retrial, stating the original trial was tainted by the admission of prejudicial hearsay and inflammatory photos. The court also endorsed Jones's assertion that the prosecution at that trial was guilty of misconduct and that there had not been "overwhelming" evidence in the case to convict him. Jones was supported by a new witness, who stated that Jones had, indeed, passed out, before and during the crime. The statements of this new witness were then supported after one of the codefendants confessed to his own role in the murder. Jones was released in 1987 and acquitted the following year.

**1983: Vincent Jenkins** (later changed his name to **Habib Warhir Abdal**), a black man, was convicted and sentenced to twenty years to life for raping a white woman in a Buffalo, New York, nature preserve in May 1982, when she had been separated from her husband. The woman later told police that the rapist wore a hood and had blindfolded her. The victim failed to identify Jenkins in a lineup four months later, but did identify him in a subsequent police lineup. DNA tests later confirmed that there were two contributors of spermatozoa, neither of which belonged to Jenkins, who was released in September 1999 after having spent seventeen years in prison.

**1983:** The 1983 conviction and 1984 death sentence given to **Jesse Keith Brown** (who represented himself at his 1983 trial) for the murder of John Horace McMillen during a home invasion in Spartanburg, South Carolina, was chiefly brought about by Brown's half brother, who was the actual killer, and whom prosecutors allowed to plead to a lesser charge in exchange for his false testimony. A new trial for Brown was ordered by the South Carolina Supreme Court in 1986, and, in 1988, Brown was again convicted and sentenced to death. Because of improper jury instructions during the second trial, the Supreme Court ordered a third trial, which occurred in 1989 and at which Brown was acquitted after new evidence showed that his half-brother was the killer. Brown was convicted in a third trial on charges of robbery related to the McMillen murder, indicating that his actual innocence in the murder was in question.

**1983:** Convicted in 1983 of raping a white woman in Ada, Oklahoma, in August 1982, **Calvin Lee Scott**, a black man, was sent to prison chiefly on hair samples, which a state serologist said linked him to the crime (hair samples being the most tenuous of identification systems, particularly when limited amounts are examined microscopically). Scott, who originally had been brought to the attention of police through an anonymous tipster (the victim was able to identify her assailant only as a black man standing between five-foot-eight-inches to five-foot-eleven-inches tall) was sentenced to twenty-five years in prison, but, in 2003, post-conviction DNA testing showed him to be innocent, and that another person, already in prison for an unrelated crime, was the perpetrator and for which no prosecution was made due to the statute of limitations in the case. Scott was not released because he was still serving time for an assault, which occurred while he was in prison.

**1983:** Convicted of rape in Oklahoma and sent to prison for sixty-plus years, **Thomas Webb** was exonerated in 1996, after defense attorneys successfully argued in appeal that police misconduct in his case was evident through the manipulation of the victim's identification in police photo arrays and lineups and DNA tests proved his innocence.

**1983: Calvin Johnson** was convicted of rape, aggravated sodomy, and burglary in 1983 for assaulting two women in College Park, Georgia, on March 7, 1983, and March 9, 1983. In both instances, the attacker assaulted the victims from behind, using a belt to choke them and lead them around their apartments in locating items and cash, which he stole before sexually assaulting the victims. The victims could describe the assailant as a black man, but detectives believed that the modus operandi of the attacker matched the same procedures described in an earlier robbery-rape for which Johnson was convicted (he pleaded guilty only to the robbery), and he was thus charged with the two March 1983 rapes and robbery. Both victims identified Johnson as the perpetrator, and serology reports stated that in

both crimes the assailant had been an ABO type O blood secretor, which matched Johnson and about 40% of the American black population. Johnson was sentenced to life in prison. His conviction was confirmed in 1989, but he filed through the Innocence Project for a new trial on April 26, 1994, requesting post-conviction DNA testing. LabCorp examined the nonsperm samples in the cases and reported on November 11, 1997, that results were inconclusive. Forensic Science Associates then conducted PCR-based DNA testing and announced that Johnson was not the donor of the spermatozoa in both cases. On June 15, 1999, a judge ordered a new trial for Johnson, who was released that year after prosecutors declined to retry his case. He had served 15.5 years behind bars.

**1983: Joseph Beringer** and **Kenneth Beringer** were convicted of the 1981 murder-for-hire slaying of Joanne Barkaukas in Cook County, Illinois, chiefly on the testimony of James Galason, an eighteen-year-old mental patient, who had conspired with the woman's husband, Edward Barkauskas, to kill the victim in order to share money from her life insurance policy. In order to receive a lenient sentence, Galason said that his roommates, brothers Joseph Beringer and Kenneth Beringer, had actually committed the crime, Joseph being the person who shot Mrs. Barkaukas while she was waiting at a bus stop, and Kenneth being at the wheel of a getaway car. An eyewitness, Harvey Webb, however, testified that he saw Galason alone shoot and kill Joanne Barkaukas and that the Beringers were not present at the scene of the crime. Edward Barkaukas testified that he had never met the Beringers and had met only with Galason. Barkaukas, Galason, and the Beringer brothers were convicted and sent to prison for life, but, in 1987, an appellate court overturned the cases against the Beringers, branding the prosecutor with "brazen misconduct." The court stated that State's Attorney Kenneth Wadas had wrongly accused Galason of forming a conspiracy with defense counsel at the trial to exonerate the Beringers, and that Wadas, in his closing arguments had wrongly disparaged the integrity of the defense counsel. The court decided that there was no factual evidence in the cases of the Beringers and vacated their convictions. Both men were released from prison after prosecutors dropped all charges against them.

**1983: Oscar Lee Morris** was convicted and sentenced to death in Long Beach, California, for killing a gay man in a bathhouse in 1978. That conviction was brought about by the testimony of Joe West, who was then imprisoned for another offense. West stated that Morris said to him that he "wanted to kill someone" and specified the victim. In 1988, appeal attorneys exhibited the misconduct of the prosecutor during Morris's trial, upon which the California Supreme Court acted, ordering an evidentiary hearing into the case. The court vacated Morris's death sentence, but it did not overturn his conviction. Morris was removed from Death Row after having spent six years awaiting execution, but he was retained in prison on a life sentence without parole while an ongoing investigation ensued. The hearing uncovered misconduct by the prosecuting attorney in the case, Arthur Jean Jr., who later became a Los Angeles County Superior Court judge. Jean had misrepresented the motives of his star witness, West, by saying that "[there] is no evidence, not a shred, and you would have it if it existed, if Mr. West got any benefit from this, that is, in the handling of his criminal case." Records, however, clearly showed that West had received, in exchange for his testimony against Morris, a reduced sentence on a felony auto theft charge, as well as termination of his prison sentence for a parole violation. Morris nevertheless remained in prison for another eleven years. His accuser, West, recanted his statements about Morris in a sworn statement a few weeks before his death in 1997, saying that he had fabricated the entire case against Morris. In 2000, a Los Angeles Superior Court overturned Morris's 1983 conviction, and, after prosecutors declined to retry him, he was released. In a later deposition, Jean stated: "I wish I wasn't on record having participated in giving him [Morris] something less than a perfect trial, but I am. It's an embarrassing situation that I didn't do well at the trial, and I didn't handle things well. And misjudgments occurred, and I made them. And it's tough to look people in the eye and 'fess up with them sometimes.'"

**1983:** Brothers **Raymond Mickelberg**, **Peter Mickelberg**, and Brian Mickelberg were all convicted of stealing gold bars from the mint at Perth, Australia, in 1982, the bars estimated to be worth $650,000. The conviction against Brian Mickelberg was dropped, but Raymond and Peter Mickelberg were each sentenced in 1983 to twenty years in prison, Raymond serving eight years and Peter serving six years behind bars, until they were paroled. The brothers consistently claimed innocence and filed many appeals to have themselves exonerated. On their eighth appeal in 2004, defense attorneys were able to show widespread misconduct by detectives involved in the case, proving that detectives

Tony Lewandowski and Don Hancock had mercilessly beat Peter Mickelberg in a prosecutor's office and later fabricated evidence that brought about their convictions. Lewandowski committed suicide in May 2004, after the court ruled that the Mickelbergs had been wrongly convicted because of police misconduct. The Mickelberg convictions were overturned after the court determined that the brothers had been framed.

**1983: Angel "Sammy" Toro** was convicted and sentenced to life in prison for the 1981 killing of Kathleen Downey, the desk clerk at a Howard Johnson Inn in Dorchester, Massachusetts, during the course of a robbery. His conviction was vacated and charges were dropped in 2004, after witnesses recanted their statements, saying that police had pressured them into making false testimony against Toro while new evidence implicated another person in the crime. Toro was released from prison.

**1983: Alvin McCuan**, **Debbie McCuan**, **Scott Kniffen**, and **Brenda Kniffen** were all convicted of abusing their children in Bakersfield (Kern County), California, based upon the testimony of their own children. They were given sentences that amounted to life terms and were not released for fourteen years, until Kern County Superior Court Judge Jon Steubbe vacated their convictions and ordered the wrongly convicted couples released from prison on August 12, 1996. The children by then had recanted their testimony, all saying that they had been pressured and threatened (some were no more than six years old at the time) by prosecutors and social welfare workers into repeating the accusations that the prosecutors created. None of the abuse was supported by any forensic or physical evidence, and, in fact, the crimes never happened. While serving time in prison, the married couples had been separated from each other. The McCuans and Kniffens were only a few of the dozens of persons wrongly accused (with many convicted and sentenced to prison) in the witch hunt Bakersfield trials, where no child abuse existed except those planted in the minds of more than sixty impressionable children by prosecutors, a mania at that time that equaled the Salem Witchcraft Trials. (See Chapter XII: "Perjured Testimony;" **John Stoll**, Chronology, 1984; **Jeffrey Eugene Modahl**, Chronology, 1986.).

**1983:** A black man invaded an apartment shared by three young white women in Brighton, Massachusetts, on December 8, 1980. He robbed and raped all three women. Two of the victims later identified **Charles Rodriquez**, an immigrant from Trinidad, saying that he spoke with a distinct accent. One of the victims said she thought the assailant had been circumcised, where Rodriguez had not. Based on the identifications, and with no physical or forensic evidence to tie him to the crime, Rodriguez was convicted and was given four consecutive eighteen to twenty-year sentences. Post-conviction DNA testing in 1999 excluded Rodriguez from being the donor of the spermatozoa in the biological evidence. On May 11, 2001, a judge vacated Rodriguez's conviction and ordered a new trial. When prosecutors refused to retry him, he was released from prison.

**1983: Richard McKinley**, of Homestead, Florida, was convicted of sexually molesting an eleven-year-old girl, after prosecutors told a jury that his blood type was matched to semen taken from the biological evidence in the rape case. A police officer also testified that he caught McKinley with "his pants down." He was sentence to life in prison, but, on November 15, 2003, post-conviction DNA testing excluded him as the donor of the spermatozoa found in the rape kit. McKinley was released from prison after accepting a plea bargain deal with prosecutors, wherein he admitted to committing a lesser offense. The court ruled that the twenty years he had thus served behind bars satisfied a sentence for that offense.

**1983: Peter Vaughn** was convicted and sent to prison for the armed robbery of a Star Market in Suffolk County, Massachusetts, on January 6, 1983. Two months later, while Vaughn was in custody, a security camera tape showed that the same culprit robbed the same market. In pointing out this irrefutable evidence at Vaughn's trial, defense attorneys moved for a directed verdict of acquittal, which was denied by the presiding judge. An appeals court vacated Vaughn's conviction and entered a verdict of acquittal, stating that the "only rational explanation" for the evidence was that "the same person was involved in both robberies," and therefore Vaughn did not commit either robbery.

**1984**: On January 8, 1983, a seventeen-year-old girl was abducted outside of her boyfriend's home in Newburgh, New York, her gun-wielding attacker taking her to a nearby woods and raping her orally, vaginally, and anally. The victim later identified **Victor Ortiz** as her assailant. He was convicted of rape and sodomy by a jury on January 17, 1984, and sentenced to twenty-five years in prison on February 15, 1984. After all appeals failed, Ortiz contacted the Innocence Project in 1994, which undertook his case after a student working for that organization found that the biological evidence in the case still existed (the Innocence Project, unlike Cen-

turion Ministries and other like organizations, confines itself to capital cases where DNA testing can be performed). After the Orange County District Attorney's Office granted permission for post-conviction DNA testing, Forensic Science Associates made tests on the rape kit evidence, along with samples of Ortiz's blood. It later announced that Ortiz was excluded as the donor of the spermatozoa, and his case was vacated and charges dropped. He was released in October 1996, after having served 11.5 years in prison.

**1984: Ulysses Rodriguez Charles** was convicted of a 1980 Massachusetts rape, but he was exonerated in 2001 and his conviction was vacated in 2003. Charles was released after seventeen years of wrongful imprisonment, claiming that he had been personally targeted by a police officer who withheld evidence in a vendetta to wrongfully convict him. His conviction for aggravated rape, robbery, unlawful confinement, and entering armed with intent to commit a felony was overturned when DNA evidence showed that the semen found on the victim's bed sheets did not match his own.

**1984: Frederick Daye** was sent to prison for life following his San Diego, California, conviction on rape, kidnapping, and vehicle theft. The rape victim identified him from a photo lineup before identifying him again in a live lineup. A conventional serology test reportedly matched Daye's blood type and semen stain found on the victim's pants. A second defendant in this case, tried separately, stated in 1990 that Daye had no part in the crime. Daye served ten years behind bars until his release in 1994, after DNA testing by Cellmark Diagnostics in 1994 confirmed that Daye's semen did not match those found on the victim's pants. Daye, considered a victim of mistaken identity, was awarded $389,000 in compensation.

**1984**: Convicted and sentenced to death in 1984 for murdering Dolores Dye during a car theft in the parking lot of a store in Gretna, Louisiana, **Curtis Kyles** was the victim of a frame-up, tried and convicted five times, and coming close to execution, until a habeas corpus petition to the U.S. Supreme Court in 1995 saved his life. Kyles was tried in November 1984, a trial that ended in a hung jury. He was tried a month later and convicted. An informant testifying against him, it was later revealed, was the actual killer, who had planted evidence in Kyles's apartment, which included a spent cartridge from the murder weapon and the victim's purse, that was later used against Kyles in court. An eyewitness positively identified Kyles as the assailant and so testified at his trial. Less than thirty hours before Kyles's scheduled execution, the U.S. Supreme Court ordered a new trial, stating that the prosecution had failed to disclose exculpatory evidence to Kyles's defense attorneys before the trial. A third trial ended in a deadlock, a fourth trial ended as a mistrial, and after a fifth trial, prosecutors dropped all charges against Kyles. New evidence had implicated the informant as the actual killer, and the eyewitness later signed an affidavit that police had urged her to make a false identification of Kyles. Exonerated, Kyles was released in 1998.

**1984:** After a rape victim was sexually assaulted in her Dallas, Texas, home on the night of February 18, 1984, **Eugene Ivory Henton** was convicted of sexual assault and sentenced to four years in prison. He was paroled, but sought post-conviction DNA tests, which were arranged by Michelle Moore of the Dallas County Public Defender's Office. That DNA testing showed that Henton was not the donor of the spermatozoa collected in the rape kit of the case. His conviction was overturned on September 1, 2005, and, through his attorney, Robert Udashen, he was granted habeas corpus by the Texas Court of Criminal Appeals on February 15, 2006, which essentially exonerated him for a crime he did not commit.

**1984: Donald Wayne Good** was convicted of breaking into a Dallas, Texas, home on June 9, 1983, tying up a mother and daughter and raping the mother. He was arrested when a police officer thought he resembled a police composite sketch, which had been created from the description of the victim. Good was tried three times, the first ending in a hung jury. He was tried again in 1984 and convicted of rape, sexual abuse, and burglary and given a life sentence. Good was given a third trial in 1987 and was again convicted and received the same sentence, both convictions based upon eyewitness identification. Paroled in 1993, Good registered as a sex offender and, in 2002, pleaded guilty to a property crime and was given a five-year sentence. Because that crime violated his parole his life sentence was reinstated. The Dallas Public Defender's Office then requested and got post-conviction DNA testing for the rape conviction, the April 2004 test showing that Good was not the donor of the spermatozoa found in the rape kit. On November 17, 2004, the Texas Court of Criminal Appeals vacated the rape conviction, and the district attorney's office dropped all charges against him for that conviction. He nevertheless remained in prison to serve out his sentence for the property crime.

**1984: Steven Shores** was convicted and sent to prison for 35 years for the 1982 slaying of off-duty security guard Garrison Hester in Chicago, Illinois. His conviction was brought about through the questionable testimony of two El Rukn Gang members who had also been suspects in the murder. Shores appealed his conviction many times without success, until Shores's attorneys were able to provide new exculpatory evidence in a third habeas corpus petition to convince U.S. District Court Judge Paul Plunkett (who had earlier denied a second appeal) that Shores deserved another hearing, which was granted, also convincing the Cook County State's Attorney's Office that Shores was not guilty and causing prosecutors to drop all charges on the condition that Shores make an Alford plea on a related charge. This he did and was released in 1996.

**1984:** On October 10, 1983, a fifteen-year-old girl was attacked by a knife-wielding assailant when she entered the backyard of a friend's home in St. Louis, Missouri. After a rape kit was assembled at a hospital, the victim was shown a police photo array of suspects, but failed to identify anyone, including **Anthony D. Woods**, whose photo was present. The next day, the victim was sitting on her porch and saw Woods walk by her home and said he had been her assailant. Friends and neighbors captured Woods and held him for police. The victim later positively identified him while he was in jail awaiting trial, which took place in 1984. Prosecutors explained at the trial that the victim had failed to identify Woods in the police photo array because the photo showed Woods in an earlier photo displaying a lighter skin tone (he was black) and a hairstyle different from the one he was wearing when arrested. He was convicted and sent to prison for twenty-five years. Woods served eighteen years of his sentence before he was paroled in May 2002. He was nevertheless compelled to list himself as a sex offender, to which he objected, having all along maintained his innocence. In November 2002, Woods contacted his trial attorney, Christelle Adelman-Adler, asking for her continued assistance. She secured post-conviction DNA testing in the case, which was performed by Paternity Testing Company (PTC), which, because the original samples had been degraded, employed Y-STR DNA testing and captured a partial profile that excluded Woods as the donor of the spermatozoa. His conviction was vacated on April 21, 2005, and all charges were dropped against him. Following his exoneration in 2005, Woods was given $328,500 in compensation for his wrongful conviction and imprisonment.

**1984:** On November 16, 1983, a twenty-eight-year-old woman, while walking to her home in Lowell, Massachusetts, was accosted by a man who dragged her to a nearby yard and sexually assaulted her. The next night, another victim was attacked by a knife-wielding assailant only one hundred yards from the site of the previous crime. She nevertheless struggled with her attacker and managed to escape. The second victim told police that the attacker had been wearing a hooded red sweatshirt and a khaki military-style jacket. On the night of the second attack, police stopped and questioned **Dennis Maher**, a sergeant in the U.S. Army. Searching Maher's car, they found a hooded red sweatshirt and an army field jacket, as well as an army-issue knife. He was arrested and charged with the two attacks in Lowell, as well as an earlier rape occurring in Ayer, Massachusetts, which is where Maher was stationed at Fort Devens. All three victims gave different descriptions of their assailant, but nevertheless identified Maher in police photo arrays. At his 1984 trial, Maher was charged with both Lowell attacks as well as the attack in Ayer. Biological evidence was available but never tested. He was convicted on the identifications of the victims and sentenced to life imprisonment. After all appeals failed, Maher wrote to the Innocence Project in New York in 1993. That organization repeatedly tried to locate the biological evidence in the case, but was told by prosecutors that it could not be located. The case was then taken over by the New England Innocence Project, and Aliza B. Kaplan and law student Karin Burns diligently began a search for that evidence. Their search culminated in 2001, when Whitney J. Brown, first assistant clerk at Middlesex Superior Court, told them that the evidence was stored in the vault of the courthouse. Boston criminal defense attorney J. W. Carney, Jr., who had originally prosecuted Maher, helped the New England Innocence Project secure post-conviction DNA testing on all of the cases. The results from Forensic Science Associates showed in March 2003 that Maher was excluded from being the donor of the spermatozoa. On April 3, 2003, Middlesex County Superior Court Judge Charles M. Grabau, after reviewing the DNA testing and with the consent of Middlesex County District Attorney's Office, vacated Maher's conviction, and ordered a new trial. Prosecutors then dropped all charges against him, and he was released from custody after having served nineteen years behind bars. Maher told the victims, who had mistakenly identified him: "What happened to you really happened. I hold no grudge against you. I hope that you got your

lives back together." Neither did he blame Carney, who prosecuted him and apologized to him for the system that wrongfully sent him behind bars. There was nevertheless a void in Maher's life that he could never fill and for which he said: "I lost nineteen years. I should be retired from the military, getting a pension and starting a second career. I should be married with children. You can't make up for that." He did blame his defense attorney for bungling his case (the attorney was later disbarred for malpractice and was dead by the time Maher was released). Maher went to work as a night shift mechanic for a trash company, and he did meet someone, Melissa Valcourt, who married him in 2005, a union that produced two children, Joshua Elijah and Aliza Karin Lucy, the second child named after the attorney and law student who had worked so hard to set him free. Maher, who relocated to Tewksbury, Massachusetts, had helped pass a 2004 Massachusetts bill to compensate wrongfully convicted persons. He received $550,000 in compensation, although he had filed a suit seeking $1.5 million.

**1984:** On September 24, 1984, **John Stoll** went to trial on charges of widespread child abuse in Bakersfield, California, which resulted in his conviction and sentence to what amounted to a life term, until, on appeal, it was learned that four child witnesses against him had fabricated their accusations. His conviction was vacated and he was released in 2004. Stoll was only one of many victims in widespread child abuse cases involving dozens of adults and children in Bakersfield, where, as recantations from the children and other evidence later showed, prosecutors had manipulated and created the charges out of whole cloth. (See **Alvin McCuan**, Chronology, 1983).

**1984: Robert Brown** and **Elton Houston** were arrested and charged with a gang-related murder in Chicago, which had been committed by three men in a Buick Riviera. Brown was convicted at a bench trial where a witness identified him as one of the men riding in the Buick. He was sentenced to thirty-five years in prison. Houston was tried separately, that trial ending in a hung jury. At a second trial, where two eyewitnesses testified that Houston had also been in the Buick, Houston was also convicted and sentenced to thirty-five years in prison. The three real perpetrators of the crime were identified by a member of the El Rukn street gang, who was then cooperating with a federal probe on the gang's activities in 1985. Two of the men identified by the gang member confessed to the killing in 1989, and the convictions of Brown and Houston were vacated and both men were released. Cook County, Illinois, awarded both men $1.1 million in compensation in 1993 for their wrongful imprisonments.

**1984: Larry Fisher** was convicted of the 1983 rape and murder of an eighteen-year-old high school student in Meridian, Mississippi. Pretrial media coverage of the case was extensive since a series of similar crimes had occurred in the same area. Fisher's attorneys asked for a change of venue, which was denied. He was convicted and sentenced to death in 1984. The Supreme Court of Mississippi reversed Fisher's conviction and sentence, ruling that the widespread media coverage had created prejudicial publicity and a change of venue was required. Fisher was tried again in 1985 and was acquitted of all charges in that case, but he remained in prison because of an unrelated rape conviction.

**1984:** On October 14, 1983, Olga Delgado was raped in her room at the Bronx Park Motel by a black man, whom she later identified as twenty-eight-year-old **Marion Coakley**. She identified him in a police photo array and then persuaded two more witnesses to also identify Coakley. At his 1984 trial, Coakley insisted that he had been at a Bible class at the time of the crime, and eight witnesses testified in support of that alibi. He also insisted that he be given a lie detector test, and he passed that polygraph test. He was nevertheless convicted by a jury and sentenced to between five and fifteen years in prison. Defense attorneys then had serological tests made of the rape kit evidence, which showed that Coakley had not been the donor of the spermatozoa. Further, doubts about the motives of Delgado's accusations against Coakley were made when it was disclosed that she had filed a $10 million suit against the motel where the crime allegedly occurred and that the crime might have been fabricated by her in order to receive such a settlement in a civil suit. An appeals court vacated Coakley's conviction in 1987, and, after the district attorney dropped all charges against him, he was released from prison.

**1984: Alberto Ramos**, twenty-two, was convicted in 1984 and sentenced in 1985 to prison for twenty-five years for child abuse, but he was exonerated in 1992 after it was shown that police had tortured him into making a false confession and that prosecutors had withheld exculpatory evidence from his trial lawyers. In 2003, Ramos was awarded $5 million in compensation. While in prison, he had been sodomized, beaten, and several times attempted suicide. Ramos was one of five wrongly convicted persons, who were known as the Bronx Five, in child abuse cases that had no foundation in reality.

**1984: Sylvester Smith** was convicted of raping two small girls in Brunswick County, North Carolina, and was given two life sentences. One of the girls was the daughter of Smith's girlfriend, and Smith was the father of the girlfriend's young son. In 2004, the two girls, by then in their mid-twenties, came forward to say that their grandmother had pressured them into falsely saying that Smith had sexually molested them when their nine-year-old cousin had repeatedly raped them, that cousin then twenty-nine and serving a life term in prison for murder. The grandmother wanted to protect the nine-year-old boy, but all she did was nurture a future killer. Smith was acquitted at his second trial, and all charges against him were dismissed. Though exonerated, North Carolina Governor Mike Easley (2001– ) refused to give Smith a pardon, that refusal most likely based upon the fact that Easley had been the prosecutor in Smith's case (along with Wanda Bryant, who later became a state appeals court judge), and that, according to his critics, Easley could not bring himself to admit that he had sent an innocent man to prison for ten years.

**1985: Scott Fappiano**, after a jury could not reach a verdict in 1984, was convicted the following year of rape, sodomy, burglary, and sexual abuse committed on December 1, 1983, in Brooklyn, New York. At that time, an intruder ordered his victim to tie up her husband, a NYPD officer, with wire cord and then repeatedly raped the woman, forcing her to commit oral sex. The victim subsequently described her assailant to police as a white Italian male and picked Fappiano out of a police photo array and, thereafter, in a police lineup, but her husband failed to identify him as the attacker. Following his conviction, Fappiano was sentenced to between twenty to fifty years in prison. During his incarceration and through his appeals, extensive DNA testing ensued, conducted by LifeCodes, Cellmark, and New York's Office of the Chief Medical Examiner (OCME). The OCME determined in 2006 that DNA results excluded Fappiano and the victim's husband from the male portion of the extracts taken from sweatpants worn by the victim shortly after the attack. Fappiano's 1984 conviction was overturned on October 6, 2006, and, after twenty-one years in prison, he was released. The perpetrator was not found.

**1985: David Brian Sutherlin**, a black man, was convicted in June 1985 of raping a woman in St. Paul, Minnesota, but, in 2001, the Ramsey County Attorney's

Office ordered a systematic review of pre-1995 convictions to determine if DNA testing would have altered the outcome of those cases. In Sutherlin's case, where he was chiefly convicted on the tentative identification of the victim, serology testing proved inconclusive. DNA testings in 2001, however, excluded Sutherlin as being the donor of the spermatozoa in the case, and, when compared to others filed in the State DNA database, another man was identified as the perpetrator of the St. Paul rape, although the perpetrator was then imprisoned for unrelated convictions and could not be tried for the rape because of an existing statute of limitations law. Sutherlin, though exonerated of the rape charge, remained imprisoned, based upon two murder convictions in July 1985.

**1985: Carlos Lavernia**, a Cuban immigrant, was arrested in August 1984, and was convicted the following year of the aggravated rape of a woman jogger running through the Barton Creek Greenbelt in Austin, Texas, on June 2, 1983. Based on the victim's description, a police artist assembled a composite image of the assailant, and Lavernia was later put into a police lineup, where the victim identified him, saying at the time that Lavernia was the only one in the lineup who "anywhere near resembles" the police sketch of the attacker. Convicted, he was sentenced to ninety-nine years. Lavernia served fifteen years behind bars before DNA testing in 2000 proved him innocent of the crime and brought about his release. Lavernia had throughout maintained his innocence, correctly claiming that he was a victim of mistaken identity.

**1985:** Charlene and **George W. White** were both shot when a masked gunman invaded their home in Enterprise, Alabama, on February 27, 1985. Mrs. White died, but her husband survived, White being charged with Charlene's murder sixteen months later. He was convicted and sent to prison for life, but that conviction was overturned in 1989 on the grounds of insufficient evidence. All charges against White were dismissed in 1992, and he was released from prison.

**1985: Steven Avery** was convicted of raping a woman in Manitowoc County, Wisconsin, chiefly on the victim's eyewitness testimony and despite the fact that Avery provided sixteen witnesses that put him elsewhere at the time of the crime. He was released from prison in 2003 after DNA evidence proved that he was not the donor of the spermatozoa found in the rape kit of the case. In April 2007, however, Avery was convicted of shooting and killing photographer Teresa Halbach near his family's auto salvage lot in rural Man-

itowoc County, on October 31, 2005. Avery became the first exonerated person to be later convicted of murder.

**1985: Larry Youngblood** was convicted of kidnapping, child molestation, and sexual assault after a ten-year-old boy was abducted from a carnival in Pima County, Arizona, in October 1983. Based chiefly on the victim's identification (who at one time told police that his attacker had a disfigured eye), Youngblood was convicted and sentenced to ten and a half years in prison. When appealing his conviction, Youngblood's attorneys maintained that the biological evidence in the case had been improperly stored, which had caused it to become degraded (none of it was used at Youngblood's trial), and that his due process rights had been violated through the destruction of this potentially exculpatory evidence. His conviction was set aside and he was released from prison in 1988, but the Supreme Court reversed the Arizona Court of Appeals ruling, reinstating his conviction. While filing more appeals, Youngblood remained free, but was sent back to prison in 1993, when the Arizona Supreme Court reinstated his conviction. He was released on parole in 1998, but was sent back to prison the following year after failing to register his address as a sex offender. His attorneys asked police to test the degraded evidence in the case, and this they did, employing new, sophisticated DNA technology. The results showed that he was excluded from the evidence, and he was released from prison in August 2000, the same year in which prosecutors dropped all charges against him. The DNA profile in the case was submitted to the national convicted offender database in early 2001, where Walter Cruise was identified as the assailant in the 1983 attack. Cruise, who was blind in one eye (as the victim had originally stated), was at that time serving out a sentence in Texas for an unrelated offense. Cruise was convicted of the Arizona sexual attack in August 2002, and sentenced to twenty-four years in prison.

**1985:** On November 8, 1983, the bodies of Susan Hamwi and her infant child, Shane Hamwi, were found dead in her Fort Lauderdale, Florida, home. Susan had been stabbed and strangled to death with a phone cord and her child had died from neglect. She had not had any contact with anyone after a friend called her on November 1, 1983. Susan had had bitter ongoing divorce proceedings with her brutal husband, Paul Hamwi, who had beaten her many times in the past. Hamwi, however, was not the focus of police investigators in the case, who apparently decided early on, without supportive evidence, that **John Gordon Purvis** (born in

1942), the town "weirdo," had been responsible for the murder. Fort Lauderdale police detectives Rich Martin and Rick Rice concentrated on Purvis, who was brought in for questioning where, according to Purvis's mother, who was standing nearby, the detectives shouted and intimidated Purvis in a prolonged interrogation. Despite the fact that the detectives knew they had no forensic evidence linking Purvis to the crime, they recalled Purvis for another interrogation, making sure that his mother was not present. Purvis had led a reclusive and sheltered life and was easily frightened; he was later diagnosed as suffering from acute schizophrenia. He spent most of his time in the company of his mother or his protective stepbrother, Mike Bartlett. While Purvis was alone in the interrogation room, Martin and Rice went at him with an intense grilling, pressuring him into making a confession. He later recanted that confession, which was judged at his April 1985 trial to be inadmissible, but a jury nevertheless found him guilty and he was sentenced to life imprisonment. While all of his appeals failed, an alert and conscientious detective in Aspen, Colorado, while investigating the beating of a woman by Robert Wayne Beckett Jr., learned something about the Hamwi case. The woman told detective Gary White that Beckett had told her that his father, Robert Wayne Beckett Sr., had murdered a woman in Florida. White knew of the Hamwi case and called Fort Lauderdale detectives Martin and Rice, but they seemed disinterested in developing any new leads in the case and did not follow up on the Beckett statement. This information actually surfaced in May 1985, only one month after Purvis went to prison and while his direct appeal was pending and State Attorney Michael Satz was aware of this exculpatory evidence. Satz and his investigator, Barbara Barton, conducted some additional investigation, which was halted when Fort Lauderdale prosecutor Robert Carney ordered Barton to close her investigation. None of the exculpatory evidence was disclosed at that time to Purvis, his attorney or his guardian. Purvis continued to languish in prison. That changed when two bright detectives, Bob Williams and Tim Bronson, were newly assigned to the homicide division of the Fort Lauderdale police department. They learned, while reviewing old cases, about the remark made by Beckett and pursued that lead until Robert Wayne Beckett, Sr. admitted killing Susan Hamwi, along with Paul Serio, and that both killers had been given $14,000 by Paul Hamwi to murder his wife. With this evidence in hand, Purvis's conviction was vacated, all charges against him

dropped, and he was released from prison on January 15, 1993. Beckett Sr., Serio, and Paul Hamwi were all convicted of the murder and given life sentences.

**1985:** On October 28, 1983, social worker Colleen Maxwell, was robbed at gunpoint by three black men while she was escorting a resident of a group home for mentally handicapped adults to a transit station in Dorchester, Massachusetts. The resident, thirty-nine-year-old Charles Bartick, was struck on the head by one of the assailants before the robbers fled. Maxwell ran to her car and attempted to block the car that the robbers were driving and was then fatally shot by one of the perpetrators. Seven minutes later, **Louis Santos**, a black man, was arrested about a mile from the scene of the crime. Bartick was taken to an interrogation room at a police station where he identified Santos as the killer of Maxwell. Based on this identification, Santos was convicted and sentenced to life behind bars. In 1988, the U.S. Supreme Court vacated his conviction after ruling that the trial judge had wrongfully admitted into evidence Bartick's identification of Santos at the police station, where Santos was the only black man not in a police uniform. Santos was acquitted by a jury at his second trial on March 16, 1990, and released.

**1985: Melvin Mikes** was convicted of the 1980 robbery-murder of the owner of a fix-it shop in Long Beach, California. He was sentenced to twenty-five years to life. The Ninth Circuit Court vacated the conviction in 1991, based upon insufficient evidence (Mikes's defense attorney failed to provide an available alibi witness at his trial, which constituted ineffective assistance of counsel). The Los Angeles County District Attorney's Office appealed the vacated conviction to the U.S. Supreme Court, which, in 1992, refused to hear the case, and Mikes was then released.

**1985: Russell Burton** was convicted of raping three teenage girls in Harris County, Georgia, and sentenced to life in prison. On appeal, it was shown that the prosecution had no evidence of the sexual attacks, two of the girls claiming that they bathed after the attack and the third, after being examined following the so-called attack, showed no new sexual activity, the latter police report withheld from defense attorneys at Burton's trial. It was also shown that Burton had had eight warts removed (burned off) from his genitals only a few days before the so-called attack, which, according to a physician, made it "impossible" for him to have sex. Further, witnesses reported that he was with them watching television on the night of the so-called attack before he went to pick up his wife from her night job. A federal district court vacated Burton's conviction, which was upheld by the Eleventh Circuit Court of Appeals in January 2002. Burton was released from prison in May 2002.

**1985:** Hotel executive Ray Liuzza, thirty-four, was shot and killed on a New Orleans Street on December 6, 1984. "Why did he have to shoot me?" the dying Liuzza asked police when they arrived at the scene. His attacker, whom he did not identify, had fired five bullets into Liuzza, three in the back. The killer had taken a gold ring from his finger. Kevin Freeman and **John Thompson** were originally charged with the murder and robbery. Freeman, in exchange for his testimony against Thompson, cut a deal wherein he received a five-year sentence as an accessory after the fact. Before Thompson was tried on the Liuzza murder, however, three people saw Thompson's picture in a newspaper and identified him as the perpetrator of an attempted carjacking. He was convicted of that crime before being tried for Liuzza's murder, for which he was also convicted, based on Freeman's testimony. That testimony had been bolstered by Thompson's attempted carjacking conviction. In the Liuzza case, Thompson was sentenced to death. He languished at Angola on Death Row, staving off execution until 1999, when intentionally hidden blood evidence surfaced in the attempted carjacking robbery. It showed that the blood type of the perpetrator was not the same as Thompson. The conviction in the attempted carjacking robbery was vacated, which led to the overturning of the Liuzza murder. Thompson, who had been taken off Death Row, was retried in 2003. Freeman was not available to prosecutors as a witness since he had been killed in 1995 by a security guard while reportedly attempting to break into some parked cars. A new witness, Sheri Hartman Kelly, however, was available. She had witnessed the Liuzza shooting from her apartment balcony and had clearly seen the killer, but had fled New Orleans out of fear. She had been found in Tennessee in 2000 by the investigating team working fourteen years on Thompson's behalf (including New Orleans defense attorney Robert Glass and Philadelphia lawyers Michael Banks and J. Gordon Cooney). Kelly told the court that Thompson had not been Liuzza's killer, who had short-cropped hair and a muscular build. Thompson at that time was slender and had a tall Afro hairdo. Thompson took the stand to insist upon his innocence, and his attorneys exposed the behind-the-scenes deal between prosecutors and Freeman at Thompson's original trial. A jury, after deliberating less than an hour, ac-

quitted the forty-year-old Thompson, who was released on May 9, 2003. He had been behind bars for eighteen years for crimes he had not committed.

**1985:** During a home invasion in Randallstown, Maryland, on October 20, 1984, Charles "Squeaky" Jordan and his eighteen-year-old stepdaughter, Lisa Brown, were killed by an armed robber. Linda Jordan, Brown's mother, who was wounded in the head during the attack but survived, later identified the assailant as **Christopher Conover**. Her statements were supported by an FBI forensic expert, who testified at Conover's 1985 trial that two hairs he microscopically examined that had been found at the crime scene matched that of Conover. Sent to prison for life, Conover's appeals failed. In the mid-1990s, he contacted the Innocence Project in New York, which agreed to undertake his case in 1998. That organization brought about post-conviction DNA testing in the case. The tests showed in 2003 that Conover was excluded as being the donor of the hairs. Conover's murder conviction was overturned, but prosecutors threatened to retry Conover on the robbery. Conover then took an Alford Plea—one that did not admit guilt but did concede that the prosecution might have enough evidence to bring about a conviction—and the forty-eight-year-old Conover was released from prison, after having served eighteen years behind bars.

**1985: Angelo Martinez** was convicted and sentenced to life in prison for the April 10, 1985, murder of seventy-year-old Rudolph Marasco in Queens, New York. Martinez's conviction was vacated and all charges against him dropped when the actual killer was identified. He was exonerated and released from prison in 2002.

**1985: Derrick Jamison** was convicted of murdering a bartender in Cincinnati, Ohio, and sentenced to life in prison. He had been convicted largely on the testimony of eyewitness Charles Howell, a codefendant, who received a lesser sentence in exchange for his testimony against Jamison. On appeal in 2002, Jamison's conviction was vacated and a new trial ordered after it was disclosed that the prosecution suppressed evidence that would have challenged Howell's statements, as well as police information that showed the discrepancies of Jamison's physical characteristics and those of the perpetrators as described by other eyewitnesses. Howell at this time stated that he could recall nothing about the murder, and all charges were then dropped against Jamison and he was released from prison.

**1985: Susan Cummings** was convicted of murder, but was released from prison after two informants recanted their identifications of her. Washington State Governor Gary Locke (1997–2005) issued Cummings a pardon in 2004.

**1986**: **Timothy Hennis**, a U.S. Army staff sergeant stationed at Fort Bragg, North Carolina, was convicted of raping and murdering Kathryn Eastburn in her Fayetteville, North Carolina, home on May 7, 1985, as well as raping and stabbing her two young children (ages five and two) to death. Police, after the bodies were found (a 22-month-old child remained unharmed in a crib), focused upon Hennis as the primary suspect after they learned that he had bought a dog from Mrs. Eastburn a week earlier. (Mrs. Eastburn's husband was an Air Force captain who was serving overseas.) Hennis was sentenced to die in the state's gas chamber. Prosecutors in this case offered two witnesses who identified Hennis with the murder, one stating that Hennis was in the driveway of the Eastburn home at the time of the killings, the other, a bank employee, saying that Hennis appeared to be the man using Eastburn's stolen ATM card at a cash station shortly after the murders. In 1988, the North Carolina Supreme Court granted Hennis a new trial based on the prosecution's inflammatory use of a slide show during Hennis's trial in which prosecutors showed gruesome photos of the murder victims to the jury just above a photo of Hennis, this prejudicial technique allowed by the trial judge. The court also stated that the two witnesses in Hennis's trial gave testimony that was, on the part of the one identifying Hennis near the Eastburn home, "tenuous," and that of the bank employee to be "extremely tentative." At Hennis's second trial in 1989, his defense attorney, Gerald Beaver, provided a new witness, who was a neighbor of the Eastburns, and who bore a resemblance to Hennis, stating that he often walked near the victims' home and wore clothing that earlier witnesses said had been worn by Hennis. The first witness, who had placed Hennis near the crime scene, stated that police had pressured him into making the identification, and the second witness, the bank employee, was discredited when Beaver was able to show through bank records that the misuse of Eastburn's ATM card had occurred before that bank employee arrived at work. It was shown that blood, semen, and hair samples from the case did not match Hennis and that the two eyewitnesses testifying against him at his first trial had several times contradicted themselves. Memory expert Elizabeth Loftus, formerly of the University of Washington, testified about the fal-

libility of eyewitness recollections, her statements challenging the testimony of one of the eyewitnesses, who claimed to have seen someone dressed in military clothes at the time of the murders. Hennis was acquitted and released from prison after having spent two years on Death Row.

**1986**: A twenty-two-year-old woman working at a dry cleaning shop in Indianapolis, Indiana, identified fifteen-year-old **Harold Buntin** as the person who raped and robbed her in 1984, although she had previously identified another man to the police. Buntin was not tried until April 1986, but, fearful that he would be wrongly convicted, fled the state. He was convicted in absentia and sentenced to fifty years in prison. In 1994, Buntin was located in Florida and returned to Indiana, where he began serving his fifty-year sentence. After all appeals failed, his mother and two sisters raised $4,000 to have two post-conviction DNA tests made on the biological evidence from the case, and both tests showed that Buntin was not the donor of the spermatozoa found in the rape kit. In April 2005, a judge vacated his conviction and exonerated Buntin, ordering his prison release after prosecutors dropped all charges against him. That release did not occur for two years because a court clerk misfiled the judge's order, and Buntin remained behind bars even after state officials had pronounced him innocent. In a badgering trail of family complaints against bailiffs and court officials, the order was finally located in storage, and Buntin was released on April 20, 2007. "I feel like somebody has to answer for that," Buntin said at the time he left prison. "I never should have been in jail—and I spent two more years there after they knew I was innocent."

**1986: Bruce Dallas Goodman**, a welder, was convicted of murdering his girlfriend, twenty-one-year-old Sherry Ann Fales Williams, of Salt Lake City, Utah, in November 1984. He appealed to the Rocky Mountain Innocence Center (RMIC), an organization that secured DNA testing in his case, which proved him innocent of the crime and caused his release in 2004, after serving almost nineteen years in prison. The RMIC had succeeded in getting post-conviction DNA testing in four cases, with Goodman as the only person seeing exoneration up to January 2006, the limited effectiveness of this organization attributed to its woeful understaffing and limited finances. Goodman, who was not eligible for compensation, and who found little work, was the first person in Utah to successfully employ a state law that allowed inmates to petition for DNA testing of old evidence. (Two other Utah men were earlier exonerated through DNA testing when the State's own expert was persuaded by friends of the convicted men, without an official petition to the State, to retest DNA samples in their case—see **Jed Gressman** and **Troy Hancock**, Chronology, 1993.)

**1986:** Following the 1985 death of two-year-old Charles Gregory in Chicago, **LaVale Burt**, nineteen, was accused of shooting the boy to death by the child's mother. Burt was convicted of murder, but, while awaiting sentencing, the victim's grandmother went to officials to state that she had found a .22-caliber pistol in the possession of her daughter, which she believed had caused the boy's death. When the daughter, the mother of the dead child, admitted that the boy had been killed accidentally, Burt was exonerated and released.

**1986: Wiley Fountain** was convicted of raping and robbing a woman who was abducted from a bus stop in Dallas, Texas, on the night of January 15, 1986, by a knife-wielding assailant. He had been arrested only one block away from the scene of the crime on the same night of the attack, matching, according to police, the description given by the victim. At the time of Wiley's 1986 trial, Southwestern Institute of Forensic Sciences analyzed the biological evidence from the rape kit, but its test were inconclusive. On March 26, 2002, the Dallas County District Court granted post-conviction DNA testing, which had been requested by Michelle Moore of the Dallas County Public Defender's Office. The Texas Department of Public Safety Laboratory in Garland, Texas, reported that its results showed that the male profile from the vaginal swab from the rape kit did not match that of Fountain or the victim's husband. Fountain had been released from prison in 2001 on parole but returned to prison for parole violation when he could not find a job or pay fees as a registered sex offender. Due to the new DNA findings, he was released from prison on September 27, 2002, and Governor Rick Perry (2000– ) exonerated Fountain by granting a full pardon to him based on innocence on March 18, 2003. Of the 112 DNA tests for separate cases conducted by the Texas Department of Public Safety since 1999 through January 2007, twenty-six were for Dallas County. In that period, post-conviction DNA tests were increased to show that DNA tests, including those conducted by private labs, accounted for thirty-two Dallas County cases, twelve resulting in exonerations, nine affirming convictions, and six pending at the time of this writing.

**1986: Victor Larue Thomas** was convicted of robbing, kidnapping, and raping a store clerk in Texas in 1986 and sentenced to life in prison based solely on eyewitness testimony. He requested post-conviction DNA testing, which was performed in 2002, the results showing that he was innocent of the crime. Thomas was released from prison after having served fifteen years behind bars.

**1986:** Shortly after 2 P.M., on November 12, 1984, eleven-year-old Margaret "Peggy Sue" Altes was kidnapped from a park on the south side of Indianapolis, Indiana. Five days later, hunters found her body in a field in Hancock County. She had been raped and stabbed to death. The last person to see the girl alive was her mother who, along with other relatives, had long suspected **Jerry Watkins**, the girl's brother-in-law, of having earlier molested the girl, along with other female relatives. Watkins provided an alibi at his 1986 trial, proving that he was at work until 3:30 P.M. on the day of the crime and thereafter with his wife running errands until attending a revival meeting that night and later learning of the girl's disappearance. Prosecutors offered a serology report on the case showing that semen taken from the victim was found to have a B indicator, suggesting a B or AB donor. Watkins had type O blood, but a lab technician testified that the B indicator could have been contaminated and suggested that Watkins could still be the donor. Dennis Ackeret, a jailhouse snitch, testified in court that Watkins had confessed to raping and murdering the girl while the two were together in a holding cell. Watkins was convicted and sentenced to sixty years in prison. In his several appeals, Watkins's attorneys provided five witnesses who signed affidavits that Ackeret had admitted to them that he had lied about Watkins's so-called confession. Moreover, DQ Alpha DNA testing was conducted, which indicated that Watkins could not have been the sole donor of the spermatozoa found on the victim, if he was a donor at all. The judge at that appeal ruled that this DNA evidence was nothing more than an extension of the serology evidence provided at Watkins's original trial, and his appeal was denied. In 2000, more sophisticated STR DNA testing was conducted on the biological evidence, and it positively excluded Watkins from the crime. The State of Indiana replicated the testing and came to the same results. Watkins's conviction was vacated, and he was released from prison in July 2000, after spending 13.5 years behind bars. He was later compensated by Indianapolis and Hancock County in a payment of $475,000. The DNA profile was then submitted to the Indiana State Police database, which identified Joseph Mark McCormick as the donor of the spermatozoa. He was arrested in August 2001 and charged with the Altes rape-murder. McCormick, in a plea-bargain deal, admitted to helping several other men abduct the girl and to sexually molesting her, but denied killing her. He was given a twenty-year prison sentence, but released within three years. McCormick's statements to police led to the arrest of Kenneth Munson, Hugh Munson, and William L. Beever, who were all charged with the Altes kidnapping, rape, and murder. Charges were later dropped against Beever and Hugh Munson. Police were unable to provide enough evidence to convict Kenneth Munson of the murder, but accepted his admission that he was guilty of battery in the case, and he received a six-year sentence. The actual killer of Margaret "Peggy Sue" Altes was never identified. On August 2006, Indianapolis police offered a reward for information leading to the arrest of Joseph Mark McCormick, who vanished after failing a drug test as part of his probation.

**1986:** On December 5, 1984, the naked body of sixteen-year-old Theresa Fusco was found in a wooded area of Lynbrook, New York. She had been missing for about a month, last seen on November 10, 1984, at the Hot Skates Roller Rink, where she worked. Six months earlier, on June 12, 1984, another girl, fifteen-year-old Kelly Morrissey, had disappeared from the same area. Another girl, nineteen-year-old Jacqueline Martarella, disappeared in Oceanside, New York, in March 1985 (her body was found on April 22, 1985, near a golf course at Lawrence, New York, four miles from the scene where Fusco had disappeared). The Morrissey and Martarella cases were never solved, but, in the Fusco case, police believed they had identified the men who had raped and murdered the girl. In March, police began questioning a number of persons reportedly involved with the missing girls, including **John Restivo**, who, along with a brother, owned a small moving business. Restivo, during interrogation, mentioned two other men, **Dennis Haltstead** and a sometimes employee, **John Kogut**. In late March 1985, Kogut was brought to police headquarters for interrogation. He was a twenty-one-year-old high school dropout and an unemployed landscaper. He was given a polygraph test and then given two more lie detector tests. After studying these tests, police concluded that Kogut had been lying about his involvement in the Fusco murder. Kogut was again put under intense interrogation, one that lasted for eighteen hours in which detectives shouted at him and told him that he had failed three polygraph tests, saying to him over and over again that

he, Restivo, and Halstead had abducted Fusco, raped her repeatedly and then murdered her. Detectives fed Kogut many of the details of the Fusco killing and then wrote out for Kogut several versions of a "confession." At the end of the exhausting interrogation, Kogut signed the sixth version of that "confession," one in which he said that he, Restivo, and Halstead were driving about in Restivo's van on November 10, 1984, when they spotted Fusco and invited her to get inside the van, which, according to the confession, she did voluntarily. When she shouted that she wanted to get out of the van, the men held her down, stripped her and she was raped by Halstead and Restivo. The men then drove to a cemetery, where the victim was taken out of the van. Either Halstead or Resitivo, Kogut's confession said, handed him a rope and said: "Do what you got to do." He then used the rope to strangle Fusco to death, he said. The men then rolled the body in a blanket and dumped it at another location, according to the confession. Based on this confession, Kogut, Restivo and Halstead were all charged with the rape and murder of Fusco. Police searched Restivo's van and a forensic science expert later testified at their separate trials (Kogut was tried in 1986, Restivo and Halstead in 1987) said that two hairs found in the van had been microscopically examined and that they matched that of Fusco. Prior to Kogut's trial, Robert Fletcher, a teenage friend of Kogut, reportedly told authorities that Kogut had been mixed up with a Satanic cult and was deeply enmeshed in pornography. Fletcher allegedly committed suicide later in Rosedale, Queens, New York. Satanic cult signs were found near the scene where Martarella's raped and strangled corpse had been discovered. The girl had reportedly kept a diary and had allegedly written one entry where she recorded a date with Kogut, who had, at one time or another, according to some friends, had burned the sign of an inverted cross on his arm. On May 9, 1985, officials said that they believed at least twelve members of a Satanic cult had been abducting, raping and murdering virgins as "sacrifices," in and about Long Island, New York, and these victims included Morrissey, Martarella and Fusco. They believed that even though Kogut was in custody at the time of the Martarella murder, Halstead and Resitivo, then still at large, had murdered Martarella as a "sacrifice" that would deflect suspicion by officials against their associate Kogut. This wild theory aside, Kogut was convicted in May 1986 of the Fusco murder and sentenced to thirty-one years in prison. Halstead and Restivo were convicted in November 1988 and each sentenced to thirty-three years in prison. After all appeals failed, Centurion Ministries undertook all three cases, and the Innocence Project began researching the Restivo case three years later. Post-conviction DNA testing was conducted repeatedly, and each time results showed that all three men in the Fusco case had been excluded, pointing to another unknown male as the donor of the spermatozoa found in the biological evidence. The hair evidence that had earlier brought about the three convictions was discredited by experts. All three convictions were vacated in 2003, and the three men were released from prison. Kogut was retried, but acquitted in 2005. By then all charges against Halstead and Restivo had been dropped. Kogut moved to New Jersey where, in early 2006, he was charged with burglary.

**1986: Gloria Killian**, a law student, was convicted of the 1981 murder of coin collector Edward Davies, seventy-one, who was found shot to death in his kitchen in Rosemont, California, near Sacramento. Killian's name was mentioned by an associate of Gary Masse who was initially arrested and charged with the murder, and she was arrested in December 1981, but all charges against her were dropped in May 1982. After Masse was convicted and while he awaited sentencing, he reportedly plea-bargained a deal with prosecutors by naming Killian as the mastermind of the attempted robbery and killing. Based on next to nothing evidence, Killian was convicted in 1986 and sentenced to prison for thirty-two years to life. Masse received a twenty-five-year-sentence instead of the expected life sentence. While in prison, Killian was in charge of the prison law library and aided several inmates in filing successful appeals. She was interviewed in 1992 in prison by Joyce Rider, a wealthy woman interested in justice, and who was the mother of astronaut Sally Rider. Convinced of Killian's innocence, Rider hired William Genego, an attorney specializing in post-conviction cases, to investigate Killian's case. (Rider would spend more than $100,000 in an effort to see Killian exonerated.) Genego was able to find court documents that showed prosecutors had cut some sort of deal with Masse in order to bring about Killian's conviction, and, in March 2002, a federal judge ruled that her case had been rife with perjury, prosecutorial misconduct, and ineffective assistance by trial counsel. He vacated her conviction, and Killian was released from prison after serving more than eighteen years behind bars. She later founded the Action Committee for Women in Prison.

**1986: Jeffrey Eugene Modahl** was convicted on ten charges of child molestation in Bakersfield, California, based on accusations from several children. He was sentenced to forty-eight years in prison until his conviction was overturned by Superior Court Judge John I. Kelly, who found that prosecutors had pressured and threatened the children into falsely accusing Modahl, who was released from prison in May 1999, after spending fifteen years behind bars. Modahl was only one of many wrongly convicted persons ensnared in the Bakersfield witch-hunts of the mid-1980s. (See: **Alvin McCuen**, Chronology, 1983; **John Stoll**, Chronology, 1984.)

**1986:** On December 17, 1986, **Rudolph Holton** was sentenced to death for the June 23, 1986, strangulation murder of Katrina Graddy. The victim had been found in a burning house in Hillsborough County, Florida, which had been set afire after her death. She had also been raped, the neck of a glass bottle inserted in her anus. Graddy, ten days earlier, had reported to police that she had been raped by a person known only as "Pine." Holton, a drug addict with a long criminal record for car theft and burglary dating back to 1979, was identified by a truck driver, Carl Schenck, as having been near the crime scene as did several other witnesses. Holton claimed that he had been in the abandoned house before the murder to secretly take drugs. At Holton's 1986 trial, an FBI crime lab technician claimed that three hairs found in the victim's mouth could possibly belong to Holton (both the victim and Holton were black). Based on the questionable hair evidence and witness recantations, Holton's attorneys convinced a Circuit Court judge to overturn Holton's conviction on November 2, 2001, affirmed by the Florida Supreme Court on December 18, 2002, which ordered a new trial. Prosecutors dropped all charges against him on January 24, 2003, and Holton was released from prison after having served sixteen years behind bars. Holton did not fare well after release. In early 2003, he was arrested and charged with aggravated assault for threatening his nephew with a machete. He was arrested on December 11, 2003, and charged with aggravated battery after punching his wife and then beating her with a golf club. He was convicted of this crime on June 21, 2004, and sentenced to two years in prison. Holton was released on August 29, 2005.

**1986: Joe C. Jones** was convicted and sent to prison for life for the August 24, 1985, kidnapping and rape of a woman in Topeka, Kansas. The attack occurred after three women left a Topeka nightclub and sat talking in their parked cars. A man ordered one woman out of one of the cars and got into the car with the victim, ordering her to drive off. After asking the woman for her name and address (she gave a fake name and address), the man raped the woman. The victim picked out a different man as her attacker after viewing a police photo array, but later identified Jones when he was brought face to face with her. Police searching Jones's house found a pair of jeans that looked similar to those the victim said the attacker had been wearing. At Jones's trial, however, a market employee said that Jones was in his store at the time of the attack and that he had been wearing clothing different from that described by the victim. Jones was a member of the nightclub attended that night by the victim and had been at that location before the attack occurred. An appeal in 1987 was filed on Jones's behalf in which his attorneys claimed that another man, who had been convicted of two similar sexual assaults, could have been the perpetrator. The motion for a new trial was denied. Attorneys in a second appeal argued that Jones was a homosexual, who would not have been psychologically suited to committing the rape. The appeal was denied on March 3, 1989. In 1991, defense attorneys requested post-conviction DNA testing. This was initially done by Cellmark Diagnostics, but that lab was unable to produce any results from the rape kit evidence. It suggested that further DNA testing be conducted by Forensic Science Associates (FSA), which, on October 25, 1991, announced that its tests excluded Jones from being the donor of the spermatozoa in the biological evidence. FSA was then asked to retype Jones's blood type in another DNA test, which, on April 13, 1992, showed that Jones could not have contributed the semen found on the vaginal swab. On July 17, 1992, a judge vacated Jones's conviction and ordered a new trial. Prosecutors dropped all charges against him, and he was released from prison. Jones had spent 6.5 years behind bars for a crime he had not committed.

**1986:** On January 14, 1986, a twenty-six-year-old woman sleeping in her apartment in Somers Point, New Jersey, was sexually attacked by an intruder who raped her orally, anally, and vaginally. She originally told police that she believed the assailant was a black man, but was uncertain since there had been so little light in the bedroom where she was attacked. Sixteen days later, she underwent hypnosis and provided certain facts as to the assailant, this time sure that he had been a black man. She worked with a police artist to create a composite sketch of the attacker and, three weeks later, picked out a photo of **Clarence McKinley Moore** from a police photo array, identifying him as her assailant. Police had

targeted Moore as a serial rapist, believing that he had committed as many as five rapes in Cape May and Atlantic counties. Moore lived in a neighboring county and owned a successful masonry firm. He owned his own home as well as an apartment building and was happily married with three children. At his trial, Steven Rosenfeld, the prosecutor, made several racial remarks about Moore, saying that because his wife was white Moore had a predilection for white women, remarks that an appeals court later labeled "outrageous." On the testimony of the victim, Moore was convicted and sentenced to life in prison. After all appeals failed, he contacted Centurion Ministries in 1995 (founded by James McCloskey in 1983 and named after the centurion present at the crucifixion of Jesus Christ, who stated, according to the Gospel of Luke: "Surely, this one was innocent."). Kate Germond, McCloskey's close associate, studied the case and believed Moore innocent. Centurion hired attorney Paul Casteleiro to make appeals for Moore, which brought about a ruling from an Atlantic County Court that the hypnosis-inspired testimony of the victim in Moore's case was inadmissible. This was backed up by an appeals court and Moore's conviction was vacated, and he was released from prison in 2001. He had lost his business, his home, and his family while spending fifteen years behind bars for a crime he had not committed. Moore was the seventh person freed from a life term by Centurion Ministries.

**1986:** Rev. **Nathaniel O'Grady** was convicted and sent to prison for child abuse while operating a day-care center in the Bronx, New York, although there was no foundation in fact for the conviction, as was shown when his conviction was vacated and he was released in 1996. One of the children testifying against O'Grady at his 1986 trial was so confused (and apparently poorly coached) that he identified the judge as his abuser. O'-Grady was one of the Bronx Five who had been wrongly convicted of child abuse, based on the false and coached accusations of several children. The other four included **Alberto Ramos** (see Chronology, 1984), and three others also tried, convicted, and sent to prison—twenty-one-year-old **Albert Algerin**, twenty-seven-year-old **Franklin Beauchamp**, and twenty-nine-year-old **Jesus Torres**—who all worked at the day-care center—in 1986, and whose convictions were also later vacated.

**1986:** **Francis Featherstone**, reportedly a high-ranking member of the Westies, an organized crime group operating on the West Side of Manhattan, was convicted and sent to prison for the murder of forty-one-year-old construction worker Michael Holly in Manhattan, New York. His conviction was vacated, and he was released six months later after prosecutors came to believe that another person had committed the crime.

**1986:** On June 7, 1983, Raymond John Oliver, a clerk in a 7-Eleven outlet in Springfield (Lane County), Oregon, was killed in the course of a robbery. **Christopher Boots** and **Eric Proctor** were charged with the murder, but charges were later dropped. When both filed a wrongful imprisonment suit, police took revenge by recharging them with the same offense and reportedly providing false evidence in the process. Both were convicted and sentenced to prison for life. Post-conviction DNA testing showed that both were innocent, and they were released from prison in 1994. In 1998, Boots and Proctor each received $1 million compensation for their wrongful imprisonment.

**1986: Curtis McCarty** was convicted and sentenced to death for the 1982 stabbing and strangulation murder of teenager Pamela Kaye Willis in Oklahoma City, Oklahoma. The primary evidence against McCarty at his 1986 trial was provided by forensic crime lab expert Joyce Gilchrist (see Jeffrey Pierce, Chapter IX: "The Near Miracle of DNA"), whose testimony and research were wholly discredited. The Oklahoma Court of Criminal Appeals overturned McCarty's 1986 conviction, based upon the misconduct of District Attorney Robert H. Macy, and because Gilchrist had omitted important information from her forensic reports. Macy was the district attorney for Oklahoma County for twenty-one years, sending seventy-three persons to Death Row—more than any other prosecutor in the United States—twenty of whom were executed. Macy had said publicly that executing an innocent person was a sacrifice worth making in order to keep capital punishment in the United States McCarthy was tried a second time in 1989 and was again convicted and sentenced to death. The conviction was upheld on appeal, but McCarty's death sentence was reversed. In 1996, a new penalty phase trial was conducted and McCarty's death sentence was reinstated. In May 2001, DNA testing, which had been arranged by the Innocence Project, showed that McCarty was excluded from the biological evidence in the rape-murder of Willis, and all charges against him were dismissed on May 11, 2007, by Oklahoma District Court Judge Twyla Mason Gray, stating that his convictions had been tainted by Gilchrist's false evidence. Gilchrist was the leading forensic "expert" in twenty-three cases ending in death sentences, eleven persons involved in those convictions and sentences having been executed. Gilchrist, who worked on more than 1,100 criminal cases, proved to be a disaster for forensic science, casting unsupported, but long-lasting doubt about the work of otherwise credible and reliable forensic experts.

**1986:** After a farmworker died in a strawberry field in Clackamas County, Oregon, eighteen-year-old **Santiago Ventura Morales** was charged with the murder. An immigrant from Mexico, Ventura Morales spoke neither Spanish nor English, but Mixtec, an indigenous language, which greatly hampered his defense. The interpreter at his trial attempted to tell the judge that he could not communicate with Ventura Morales, but the judge refused to believe that a Mexican defendant could not speak Spanish. Convicted and sentenced to life in prison, Ventura Morales appealed through his attorney Paul De Muniz, who also provided information that another man was the actual killer. Ventura Morales was released in 1991 and all charges against him were dropped. He received a scholarship from the University of Portland and graduated with a degree in social work, later working in the Oregon Law Center as a community outreach worker. His attorney, De Muniz, became a justice of the Oregon Supreme Court.

**1986: Ernest Ray Willis** was convicted of murdering Gail Joe Allison and Elizabeth Grace Belue in Iraan (Pecos County), Texas, after the victims died in a fire that was labeled arson, and was sentenced to life imprisonment. An appeals court later determined that the prosecution had wrongly administered medically inappropriate anti-psychotic drugs without Willis's consent, drugs that made him appear indifferent to the charges in court, a demeanor (created by the prosecution through the drugs) for which the prosecution vilified the defendant, calling him "cold-hearted" and being a "Satanic demon." The court further ruled that prosecutors had suppressed exculpatory evidence and that Willis had received ineffective legal representation. A new arson specialist re-examining the fire stated that no "accelerant" had been used to start the fire, as originally contended in Willis's trial, but that the fire had started accidentally through "flashover burning." The district attorney dropped all charges against Willis in 2004, and he was released from prison, later receiving $430,000 in compensation for his wrongful conviction and imprisonment.

**1986: Richard McArthur** was convicted of murder in Alberta, Canada, but, in 1999, the Alberta Court of Appeals acquitted him.

**1987**: On the night of March 1, 1986, Juanita White returned from work to her home in Waco, Texas. Her body was found the next day. She had been beaten and raped. According to the coroner, White had either died of injuries from a blunt instrument or had been smothered or strangled to death. Police arrested and charged **Calvin Washington** with the crime. Prosecutors at Washington's 1987 trial said that the defendant was in the possession of the victim's car the day following the murder and that he had sold items burglarized from the victim's home on the night of the crime. Jailhouse snitches testified for the prosecution, stating that Washington had admitted the burglary to them in prison and they also said that Washington bragged that he had bitten the victim several times while raping her to leave his "trace marks." Washington was convicted and sent to prison for life. After all appeals failed, Washington's attorneys secured post-conviction DNA testing on the case. The results showed that the blood on one of Washington's shirts, which had been used in evidence by the prosecution, did not come from White and that the biological evidence in the rape kit showed that Washington was not the donor of the spermatozoa, but, in fact, the contributor had been Bernard Carrol. Although Carrol had been a suspect in the White case, he was never prosecuted. Carrol admitted to a friend that he had raped an elderly woman who had been one of White's neighbors. Three years later, Carrol committed suicide. Washington, in 2001, was released from prison after serving thirteen years behind bars. There was a grimly ironic twist to the Washington case in that the victim, Juanita White, was the mother of David Wayne Spence who, along with two others, had committed the Lake Waco murders, the brutal stabbing killings of three teenagers on July 13, 1982, and for which Spence wrongfully blamed convenience store owner **Muneer Mohammed Deeb** as masterminding and for which Deeb was wrongly convicted and sent to prison. (See Deeb, Chapter IV: "Insufficient Evidence," Reams of Unreliable Evidence.) Spence, who was executed in 1997, claimed innocence up to the last moment of his life, and some later thought that Waco resident Terry Lee Harper, who allegedly had bragged of committing the Lake Waco murders may have been one of Spence's accomplices. When police went to Harper's home in 1994 to arrest him for the murder of an elderly man, he, like Bernard Carrol, committed suicide, blowing off his head with a shotgun.

**1987: Gordon "Randy" Steidl** was convicted of murdering newlyweds Karen and Dyke Rhoads in their Paris, Illinois, home, stabbing them more than fifty times, their bodies later found on July 6, 1986, after their home had been set on fire. Testifying against Steidl were Deborah Reinbolt and Darrell Harrington, known alcoholics, Reinbolt claiming that she had provided the knife used in the murder case and had even held Karen Rhoades down while either Steidl or his co-defendant, Herbert Whitlock, murdered the twenty-six-year-old woman. Harrington claimed that he had been asleep in Steidl's car and was afterward shown the murder weapon by Steidl. In separate trials, Steidl was sentenced to death in 1987 and Whitlock to life imprisonment. Both witnesses later recanted their statements, and Steidl won an appeal where the court determined that he had been defended by inadequate counsel. He was not retried and the fifty-two-year-old Steidl was released on May 28, 2004, but Whitlock remained in prison.

**1987: Jimmy Lee Mathers**, Ted Washington, and Fred Robinson were convicted of the June 8, 1987, home invasion and murder of Sterleen Hill in Yuma, Arizona. The Arizona Supreme Court set Mathers free in 1990, after reviewing the case and finding that there was "a complete absence of probative facts" in the case prosecutors had presented at his trial. The court further stated that the evidence offered at the trial had "nothing to do with Mathers." The court set aside Mathers's conviction and death sentence and officially acquitted him.

**1987: Edward Green** was convicted through mistaken identity of two rapes occurring in Washington, D.C., on July 3 and August 5, 1987, but in February 1990, Cellmark Diagnostics tested DNA samples from the rape kits in his cases and reported that he could not have been the donor of the semen samples. Green was later released following a short prison sentence on unrelated drug charges.

**1987:** Following the burglary of his apartment in Virginia Beach, Virginia, where the fiancée of **Craig Bell** was murdered on the night of October 4, 1986, Bell, a twenty-five-year-old U.S. Navy officer, was charged with the killing. Bell told police that he was sleeping in a bedroom and that his fiancée was watching television when he heard a disturbance and found the woman dying from stab wounds. Calling police, Bell told officers that someone had entered the apartment through a window (a screen had been removed and a window broken). Fingerprints, human hairs, and clothing that did not belong to Bell were found, but police ignored this evidence after neighbors told them that Bell and his fiancée had been quarreling shortly before the killing. Prosecutors at Bell's trial ignored the statements of neighbors who said that they had heard glass breaking and had seen a man climb through the window of Bell's residence. They focused on blood samples, saying that the perpetrator had left type O blood samples at the scene of the crime and that Bell had type O blood (as did 36 percent of the population). Prosecutors then offered a motive, which was unsubstantiated, claiming that Bell had murdered his fiancée because he was bisexual. The jury accepted this wild-eyed murder motive and convicted Bell on August 7, 1987. He was sentenced to twenty years in prison. Two and a half months later, while Bell awaited his transfer to a prison in the Virginia Beach Jail, police arrested Jesse Calvin Smith, who they found peeping into windows late at night at the very same apartment complex where Bell's fiancée had been slain. A detective, recalling the recent Bell case, confronted Smith, who quickly admitted that he had entered the Bell residence through the window, removed his clothes, and, panicked when the woman awoke, stabbing her and then fleeing through the same window. Bell, with Smith's confession in hand by police, was released from jail. Smith was later convicted and sent to prison for life.

**1987: Eric Clemmons**, while serving a fifty-year term for the murder of a gang member in St. Louis, Missouri, was tried and convicted in 1987 of the stabbing murder of a fellow inmate, Henry Johnson, in the yard of the Jefferson City Prison. Bloodstains from Johnson were found on his shirt and cap, and prison captain A. M. Gross stated in court that Clemmons, after being arrested for the killing quoted Clemmons as saying, "I guess they got me." In filing his own appeals, and later through the representation of attorney Cheryl Pilate, Clemmons was able to show that Fred Bagby was Johnson's real killer, even though Bagby had himself been stabbed to death three months after Johnson's murder. He was able to show that Gross's statements about him had not been challenged at his trial and then provided a memo from Gross to another prison official that stated that Gross had been informed immediately after the Johnson killing that Bagby had been the murderer. In 1997, the state reversed Clemmons's conviction in the Johnson killing, ordering a new trial, where an expert testified that the bloodstains Clemmons had on his shirt and cap were the result of the fatally wounded Johnson running into him after having been stabbed by Bagby in the prison yard. Clemmons was acquitted.

**1987:** Private pilot **James Jordan Denby**, forty-seven. was forced by Nicaraguan Sandinista gunfire to land his Cessna–172 single-engine plane on December 6, 1987, on a beach about 150 miles southeast of Managua. Denby, a native of Carlinville, Illinois, who owned a ranch in Costa Rica, was forced down and captured when his plane flew over Nicaraguan territory. Denby was charged with transporting guns to the right-wing Contra rebels, who opposed the leftist ruling Sandinistas. The first U.S. citizen charged with such a crime, Eugene Hasenfus, parachuted from his cargo plane laden with arms that Sandinistas shot down. He was sentenced to thirty years, but served only one month before his release. Denby, however, was freed on January 30, 1988, after spending seven weeks in custody, claiming innocence. He was absolved of any wrongdoing by a judge in Nicaragua on February 8, 1988.

**1987: Mark Webb** was convicted of the February 1985 rape of a woman in Tarrant County, Texas. The victim identified him, and serology tests did not exclude him as being the perpetrator. Webb was sentenced to thirty years in prison. Paroled in 1997, he was returned to prison for parole violation. DNA testing was conducted on his case, which showed that Webb was innocent of the 1985 crime, and he was released from prison in 2001.

**1987:** On the night of February 1, 1986, police in Savannah, Georgia, entered the home of **Samuel Scott**, arresting him and **Douglas Echols** on charges of raping a young woman earlier that evening. The victim had accompanied police to Scott's home, saying that Echols was one of three men who abducted her that night when she left a nightclub and put her into a car and then took her to Scott's home, where she was raped, later escaping when the abductors fell to arguing. The victim later positively identified Scott from a police photo array as the man who raped her, while, she said, Echols held her down. Both Scott and Echols at their 1987 trial said they were victims of mistaken identity and they provided witnesses, who said they were with Scott and Echols at a restaurant at the time of the crime. Rape kit evidence at the trial proved to be inconclusive, but both men were convicted, Scott sent to prison for life and Echols to five years in prison. Echols was paroled in 1992, but Scott, who remained in prison, saw all appeals fail. He contacted the Innocence Project, which arranged for post-conviction DNA testing. Those tests showed in July 2001 that Scott was excluded as the donor of the spermatozoa retrieved from the rape kit, and after all possible consensual sex partners were also eliminated, Scott, who had been released on parole in September 2001, was exonerated. All charges against Scott and Echols were dismissed on October 7, 2002.

**1987: Albert Ronnie Burrell** and **Michael Ray Graham Jr.** were convicted and sentenced to death in 1987 for the murder and robbery of a retired construction worker and his wife, William and Callie Frost, in Union Parish, Louisiana, on August 31, 1986. Burrell was arrested after his former wife, Janet Burrell, contacted the local sheriff, Larry Averitt. She told officers that, on the night of the murders, she had seen her former husband with a wallet, containing $2,700, that belonged to the construction worker and that he was holding a rifle used in the killings. Graham, a friend of Burrell, was also arrested at this time. Graham was placed in a cell shared by Olan Wayne Brantley, a jailhouse informant, who quickly told officers that Graham had confessed to the murders. Brantley was then placed into a cell housing Burrell, who was considered to be a mildly retarded schizophrenic, and Brantley shortly thereafter told officers that Burrell, too, had confessed to the murders. Burrell's former wife then attempted to recant her statements about Burrell, telling officials that she had made false statements about her former husband to improve her position in a child custody dispute, but she was threatened with loss of custody if she publicly recanted her statements. Assistant District Attorney Dan Grady, to whom this case had been assigned, objected to seeking an indictment, but, according to an affidavit Grady submitted thirteen years later, District Attorney Tommy J. Adkins ordered him to present the Burrell-Graham case to a grand jury so that Union Parish Sheriff Averitt would not be embarrassed at falsely arresting Burrell and Graham. Burrell and Graham were tried separately, but both resulted in convictions and death sentences. For thirteen years, Burrell and Graham made every available appeal, and, at one point, Burrell was only seventeen days away from execution at Angola, the Louisiana State Penitentiary, when his former wife publicly recanted her statements about him. It was then learned that Brantley, who had testified against both Burrell and Graham, had been granted leniency in a pending case against him in exchange for his testimony. This deal was not disclosed prior to the trial and defense attorneys also learned that Brantley had provided to prosecutors three other jailhouse confessions in other criminal cases. When all of this was disclosed to the Louisiana Attorney General's Office, a new trial for Burrell was ordered in March 2000 by Judge Cynthia Woodward. Prosecutors, rather than see all of their dirty laundry washed in a new trial, dismissed all charges against Burrell and Graham on December 27, 2000, based on "a total lack of credible evidence.".

**1987:** On July 28, 1987, **Timothy Atkins** was convicted of one count of murder and two counts of robbery in the slaying of Vincente Gonzalez on New Year's Day, 1985, in Venice, California. Two black men had stopped Gonzalez's car on a street and shot him after taking a necklace from his wife. Atkins, who had been arrested and charged with the crime three years before his conviction, had seen his trial delayed because of an accident he incurred while in jail awaiting that trial. Denise Powell, a local resident, had told neighbors that she knew who the perpetrator was, and when police interviewed her she said that a number robberies and shootings had been committed by a man named "Atkins." She later identified Timothy Atkins as the man who killed Gonzalez. He was sentenced to life imprisonment, but, after all appeals failed, the Innocence Project at San Diego's California Western School of Law (established in 1999 by Justin Brooks) undertook his case in 2002. Several law students researched his case, attempting to locate Powell, who had disappeared. Wendy Koen, one of those students located Powell after she had been arrested in 2006 on drug charges and, in an interview, got Powell to recant her identification of Atkins (Powell had earlier told Atkins's sister, Sheila, that she had lied to police at the time and, in fact, never knew who killed Gonzalez). This written recantation, along with other evidence, was submitted to Los Angeles Superior Court Judge Michael Tynan, who had presided over Atkins's trial twenty-three years earlier. On February 9, 2007, Judge Tynan vacated Atkins's conviction, releasing the thirty-nine-year-old man from prison. He was officially exonerated after prosecutors refused to retry him.

**1987: David Munchinski** was convicted and sentenced to life in prison for the 1977 murders of James Peter Alford and Raymond Gierke at Bear Rocks, Pennsylvania. The victims were known drug dealers, and the star witness against Munchinski was labeled a liar by the defense. Based on this and the fact that prosecutors had hidden exculpatory evidence from the defense, Munchinski's conviction was vacated, and he was released from prison in 2004.

**1987: Raymond Carter** was convicted of the September 18, 1986, murder of Robert "Puppet" Harris, in Philadelphia, Pennsylvania. His conviction was brought about through the corrupt practices of police detective Thomas Ryan, who, it was later learned, had paid a witness $500 to testify against Carter, a woman that Ryan was then dating. In January 1997, Common Pleas Judge Joseph I. Papalini, when learning of Ryan's misconduct, vacated Carter's conviction, stating that if the information about Ryan's relationship with the witness had been disclosed at Carter's 1987 trial, Carter would probably not have been found guilty. Prosecutors declined to retry Carter. The fifty-year-old Carter was then released from the Pennsylvania State Prison at Dallas. Officer Ryan later pleaded guilty to a federal corruption charge and was sent to prison for ten months, where the man he had victimized, Raymond Carter, had spent ten years behind bars for a crime he had not committed.

**1987: Susan Mowbray** was convicted and sentenced to life in prison for the murder of her husband, William Mowbray, in Cameron County, Texas. Mowbray insisted all along that she was innocent. On appeal in 1996, the court ruled that prosecutors had concealed a blood splatter report during her original trial that indicated her husband had committed suicide. The court vacated Mowbray's original conviction and ordered a new trial, which occurred in 1998, when the exculpatory forensic evidence was finally shown and where Dr. Herbert MacDonnell testified that William Mowbray most likely took his own life. Susan Mowbray was acquitted and released from prison.

**1987: Teng Xingshan** was beaten by police until he confessed to murdering his wife, who had been missing in China. Condemned to death, Xingshan was executed by gunshot. His wife, however, was identified as being alive in June 2005.

**1988: Robert Craig Cox** was investigated in the December 30, 1978, beating death of nineteen-year-old Sharon Zellers, a clerk at Disney World in Orlando, Florida. Cox, who had been staying with his family at the same motel where the victim was killed, required surgical treatment the day after the murder for an injury to his tongue (he claimed that he had bitten his tongue during a bar fight). Cox's blood type O was the same as the victim's and it was believed that a boot print at the crime scene might have come from one worn by Cox, but when the boot print did not match that of Cox, and the blood evidence proved insufficient, and that there was no evidence establishing the fact that Cox and Zellers ever met, Cox was not charged with Zeller's murder and was no longer considered a suspect. In 1986, Cox was convicted of a California kidnapping, a crime

that seemed to Florida officials to have the earmarks of the Zellers killing. Cox was extradited to Florida, where he was tried, convicted, and sentenced to death in 1988 for the Zellers murder, but the evidence in that trial proved to be no more substantial than what had been discovered in the police investigation of 1978. On appeal, the Florida Supreme Court determined that Cox had been convicted only on "a suspicion" of guilt. The court vacated his conviction and ordered him released in 1989, after he had spent one year on Florida's Death Row. Cox was returned to California to serve out his sentence for the kidnapping conviction. When Cox was released in California, he returned to his native Springfield, Missouri, where police believed that he had something to do with the disappearances of his mother and two teenage girls. He was not charged with those disappearances, nor was he arrested in Plano, Texas, where he was suspected of a kidnapping. In 1995, however, Cox, a former army ranger, was convicted of an armed robbery in Decatur, Texas, and was sentenced to life in prison, being eligible for parole in 2025.

**1988: Byron Halsey** was convicted in 1988 for the November 1985 rape-murders of his girlfriend's children, eight-year-old Tyrone Urquhart and his seven-year-old sister Tina, in Plainfield, New Jersey. The girl had been beaten and then strangled to death, the boy had been killed by a savage beast who had hammered nails into his skull. Halsey's conviction had been brought about by his own confession, made after a grueling thirty-hour interrogation where he went without sleep. Although he recanted this confession, Halsey's blood type was matched to that of the perpetrator, and, in five hours of deliberation, the jury found him guilty. He was sentenced to death. Halsey came close to death several times, but received stays while filing appeals that were unsuccessful. He then contacted the Innocence Project in New York, which was able to secure post-conviction DNA testing, which showed in 2007 that he was not the donor of the spermatozoa in the biological evidence from the two victims, and, in fact, the DNA tests showed, after being run through the New Jersey DNA crime database, that the perpetrator had been forty-nine-year-old Clifton Hall, who lived next door to Halsey and his girlfriend at the time of the attacks, and who had testified against Halsey at his 1988 trial. Hall's DNA was on file after he was convicted and sent to prison for three savage sexual attacks in 1993. On May 15, 2007, Superior Court Judge Stuart Peim vacated Halsey's conviction, and Halsey was released on a bail of $55,000, which had been raised by church groups in Plainfield. On July 9, 2007, prosecutors dropped all charges against Halsey, who, exonerated, had spent twenty-two years in prison for a crime he had not committed.

**1988: Miguel Castillo** was convicted of murdering Rene Chinea, a fifty-year-old Cuban refugee, whose body was found in Castillo's apartment in Chicago on May 18, 1988. He was sentenced to life imprisonment, but, in 2001, the medical evidence in the case was re-examined, and it was determined that Chinea had died no later than May 9, 1988, while Castillo had been in jail on an unrelated charge at that time and had not been released until May 11, 1988, which made it impossible for him to have committed the murder. Following his release from prison, the City of Chicago awarded Castillo $1.2 million in compensation for his wrongful conviction and imprisonment.

**1988:** On the night of September 27, 1987, Jose Antonio Rivera was chased through Kelly Park in the Bronx by a group of teenagers with whom he had been feuding. Apprehended by the group, Rivera was killed after he was stabbed and bludgeoned to death by a baseball bat and heavy sticks. Rivera's girlfriend identified **Jose Morales** and **Ruben Montalvo** as the killers, and her sole testimony brought about their convictions on second-degree murder and fifteen-year prison sentences. The real culprit was Jesus Fornes, who confessed the killing to a priest and told the defense attorney about his own guilt, but later remained silent on the advice of his own attorney. Fornes died in 1997, and both the priest and Fornes's attorney came forward to officials with the confession, since Fornes's death relieved them of any responsibility to keep his statements confidential. Based on this new evidence, Judge Denny Chin of the U.S. District Court in Manhattan vacated the convictions of Morales and Montalvo and ordered their released from prison on July 24, 2001.

**1988:** On March 14, 1987, cab driver Jean Ulysses was found dying in his taxi on a Brooklyn, New York, street. A fatal bullet had entered his right cheek. Nicky Roper, a police informant, told police to contact Carolyn Van Buren. Detectives were then told by Van Buren that she had seen **Anthony Faison**, who lived in the area, shoot Ulysses in the course of a robbery while his good friend, **Charles Shepard** stood lookout. Faison and Shepard were arrested and charged with the murder. Although no physical or forensic evidence linked either man to the crime, Van Buren's testimony sealed their fate. She admitted that she was a drug addict and had drunk ten beers on the night she witnessed the shoot-

ing, but the jury nevertheless believed her story. Faison and Shepard were found guilty of second-degree murder on May 31, 1988. Both were sentenced to life imprisonment. On a direct appeal, New York State Supreme Court Justice Robert Kreindler denied a motion for Faison to be released to marry his pregnant girlfriend, saying: "In the eyes of the law he is legally dead." Faison refused to accept that fate, and, from the moment of his incarceration, he began writing letters each and every day to anyone and everyone who might be able to help him and Shepard. In all, he wrote 62,000 letters to politicians, attorneys, state and local officials, private detectives, and simply any citizen of the Republic he thought might champion his case. (Prison inmates called him "The Writer.") In January 1999, one person positively responded, Michael S. Race, a private detective in Long Island, New York, who had been a homicide detective for twenty-three years. He had received a letter from Faison in which the imprisoned man expressed his fear that Van Buren, whom he had heard had AIDS, might die before she recanted her statements and forever keep him and Shepard in their prison cells. Race tracked down Van Buren and wrote back to Faison, saying: "She admits that the whole story is a lie!" Van Buren told Race that Roper had cooked up the story about Faison and Shepard so that they could split a $1,000 police reward. Race then tracked down Roper, who admitted that he had arranged the fake story Van Buren gave so that he could get even with Faison, a construction worker, who had, at one time, refused to recommend Roper for a job with his firm. Van Buren's statements to Race contradicted the actual murder of Ulysses. She had said in her original deposition (not challenged at that time by either police, prosecutors, or defense) that Faison had shot the cab driver through the window of the driver's side of the car, but, as Race established from police reports, the window of the cab had been closed and unbroken when police found the victim dying and that the only way the victim could have been shot was by someone sitting in the back eat of the taxi. Race then contacted attorney Ron Kuby, providing the attorney with eleven fingerprints taken from the interior of the cab, none of which matched either Faison or Shepard. The prints did match, however, a man named Arlet Cheston. Armed with the fingerprint evidence and the signed statements of Van Buren and Roper, Kuby filed a new appeals motion. Judge Kreindler, who had thirteen years earlier permanently closed the book on Faison and Shepard, reviewed the new evidence assembled by the meticulous Race and submitted in an appeal by Kuby, and vacated the Faison and Shepard convictions, ordering their release on May 14, 2001. Both men had been behind bars for more than thirteen years. In 2003, each was awarded $1,650,000 for their wrongful imprisonment.

**1988: Alfredo Domenech** and **Ivan Seranno** were convicted and sentenced to life in prison for the May 29, 1987, murder of Juan "Junior" Martinez on a Philadelphia street. There was no physical or forensic evidence linking either man to the killing, which occurred during a drug deal gone wrong. A lone witness, Rene Thompson, a known prostitute, testified that she had seen the face of the killer, who shot Martinez from the driver's side of a car, identifying Domenech as the killer. The car sped off after Martinez was fatally shot and fell to the pavement. A few minutes after the police arrived, Thompson, standing with officers, saw a car pass by and identified it as the one with the killer. Police stopped the car and immediately arrested Domenech and Seranno, who were in the car. In a 2002 appeal, a new witness, identified only as John Doe in the court records, stated that he had seen Martinez shot and that Domenech and Seranno were not present at the shooting. Witness Thompson by then was dead. Attorney Jerome M. Brown, who represented both defendants for years and had provided exculpatory evidence in the appeal, had long ago argued that the identification of his clients by Thompson was ridiculous in that they had driven by the crime scene twice when looking for girls. "It makes no sense," Brown stated, "because who comes back to the scene of a murder five minutes after it occurs?" Edward McCann, chief of the homicide of the District Attorney's Office, along with Assistant Attorney Ann Ponterio, concurred after talking with the new eyewitness, whom they found credible and that his testimony would absolve Domenech and Seranno of the crime. At their urging, Common Pleas Court Judge D. Webster Keogh vacated the convictions and, after all charges were dropped, ordered the release of forty-two-year-old Domenech and thirty-six-year-old Seranno from prison. They had been behind bars for eighteen years.

**1989: Warren Douglas Manning** was convicted and sentenced to death for the 1988 murder of a South Carolina state trooper. At Manning's trial, prosecutors claimed that Manning, who had been stopped for driving with a suspended license, suddenly grabbed the officer's gun, pistol-whipped him with it, and then shot the trooper to death before fleeing. Defense attorneys insisted that Manning had fled the scene when the

trooper stopped another car, and it was the occupant of that second car who had shot the officer. Further, defense attorneys offered witnesses who said they saw Manning minutes after he fled and that there were no bloodstains on him, which, the defense said, would have been present if he had committed the murder. Manning's conviction was overturned in 1991, and he was tried again in 1993, which resulted in a mistrial. Manning was tried a third time in 1995, and he was again convicted and sentenced to death. On December 29, 1997, the South Carolina Supreme Court overturned the 1995 conviction, the court saying that the trial court had abused its discretion by granting the state's motion to change venue for the selection of the jury. A fourth trial in 1997 resulted in a mistrial, but dogged prosecutors would not give up and brought Manning to trail again for a fifth time in 1999. This time, he was represented by a death penalty attorney, David Bruck, who proved that the state's case was entirely circumstantial. Bruck stated in his argument to the jury: "If there wasn't any case against Warren Manning, then we wouldn't be here. But, the law requires that the state prove him guilty beyond a reasonable doubt. Without that, the law says you cannot find him guilty." After three hours of deliberation, Manning was acquitted, but this did not indicate that he was "actually innocent."

**1989:** Activists **Moses Chikane**, forty-one, **Patrick Lekota**, forty-one, **Geinumuzi Malindi**, **Pope Molefe**, thirty-seven, and the Reverend **Tom Manthata**, forty-nine, were released on December 15, 1989, from prison after their convictions for treason and terrorism were overturned by the Appeals Court in Bloemfontein, South Africa.

**1989: Melvin Todd Beamon** was convicted of a murder in Montgomery, Alabama, following his confession, which Beamon later claimed had been beaten out of him by police in a grueling, nonstop seventeen-hour interrogation. His conviction was vacated after an eyewitness came forward to exonerate him.

**1989: Terry L. Nelson** was convicted and sentenced to forty years in prison for murdering drug dealer Marvin Butler outside a nightclub in Centreville, Illinois. Nelson's conviction had been achieved through the testimony of three jailhouse snitches who claimed that Nelson had confessed to the murder to them while in jail and awaiting trial. On appeal, Nelson's attorneys argued that the statements of one of the witnesses had been inconsistent and that another had recanted his statements. The Fifth District Illinois Appellate Court ordered a new trial, but when the St. Clair County State's Attorney's Office dropped all charges against Nelson, he was released in 1998. Two other men were later convicted and sent to prison for Butler's slaying.

**1989:** At about 3 A.M., on August 17, 1988, twenty-two-year-old Noreen Malloy, the night manager of a McDonald's fast-food outlet in Duquesne, Pennsylvania, was finishing her shift. As she was walking to her car, she was stopped by a man wearing a nylon mask, a hat, and a woman's trench coat. He demanded her money, but Malloy fled toward her car in a parking lot, the man in pursuit. He caught up with her, pistol-whipped her, and then shot her in the back, killing her. He then fled across the parking lot, discarding his hat, nylon mask, and the trench coat, disappearing into some nearby woods of Kennywood Park. Another McDonald's employee, Jerome Wilson, witnessed the attack and shooting, and later told police that the assailant had been **Drew Whitley**, whom he said he had identified by his voice and shape of his head and the way he walked, although Wilson admitted that he had not clearly seen the attacker's face. Wilson lived in the same building as Whitley. His testimony was used in Whitley's 1989 trial, where a prison informer, Gary Starr, also testified against Whitley, saying that Whitley had confessed to the murder of Malloy while both were at the State Correctional Institution in Pittsburgh, Pennsylvania. Starr was a twice-convicted murderer on Death Row whose sentence was reduced to life in exchange for testifying against Whitley. A technician from the Allegheny County Crime Laboratory testified that the hairs found in the nylon mask were similar to Whitley's hairs, but admitted that he could not state so conclusively. The technician also stated that the saliva found in the nylon mask did not match that of Whitley. The prosecutor in his closing arguments wrongly stated that the hairs the technician described as "similar" had been "matched" to Whitley. Whitley was convicted of second-degree murder and sentenced to life imprisonment. In 1995, Cellmark Laboratories conducted post-conviction DNA testing on some of the rooted hairs found in the nylon mask, but the testing proved inconclusive and that the hairs had been consumed in the testing. The thirty-nine hairs without roots that had also been found in the mask were not thereafter available, explained prosecutors, since they had been lost in a flood of the Allegheny County Police Evidence Room. In 2001, Whitley's case was undertaken by the Innocence Institute of Point Park University, its director being Bill Moushey, a staff member of the *Pittsburgh*

*Post-Gazette*. Students from the university worked under the direction of Moushey in learning investigative reporting, and many worked to uncover more evidence in the Whitley case. In 2005, Whitley's attorney, Scott Coffey, was told that the thirty-nine rootless hairs found in the nylon mask had been found—this discovery reportedly brought about by the students. Mitotyping Technologies performed DNA testing, on these hairs and reported on February 28, 2006, that Whitley had been excluded from the hairs. Prosecutors then sent five hairs found in the discarded hat to their own lab for testing and the same results were announced—Whitley was innocent. On April 25, 2006, Allegheny County Common Pleas Judge Anthony Mariani vacated Whitley's conviction and ordered a new trial. District Attorney Stephen A. Zappala Jr. dropped all charges against Whitley on May 1, 2006, when he was released from the State Correctional Institution at Greensburg, Pennsylvania. When released, Whitley said to reporters what he had said to them throughout his 16.5 years of wrongful imprisonment: "I am an innocent man."

**1989: Shawn Drumgold** was convicted of first-degree murder in the shooting death of twelve-year-old Tiffany Moore. The *Boston Globe* conducted a deep investigation into this case, which raised serious questions about the validity of Drumgold's conviction. Moore had been fatally shot while sitting on the front stoop of her Boston home on the night of August 19, 1988, while a drive-by shooting occurred. After several prosecution witnesses admitted that their testimony had been coerced by police, prosecutors moved to have Drumgold's conviction vacated. He was released in 2003.

**1989:** Two eyewitnesses brought about the conviction and life sentence of **Algie Crivens** for the 1989 murder of Cornelius Lyons in a Chicago parking lot. A direct appeal to the state court failed, but another appeal to a federal court convinced a judge to vacate Crivens's conviction and order a new trial. It had been shown that a witness had heard a fellow inmate confess to the Lyons murder, identifying him as Marcus Williams, but he had not been allowed to testify at Crivens's trial. Another witness then came forward to state that he had seen Williams shoot and kill Lyons. At his second trial, Crivens was acquitted after winning a directed verdict of not guilty. Illinois Governor George H. Ryan (1999–2003) then officially pardoned Crivens.

**1989:** In October 1989, seventeen-year-old **Herman May** was convicted of raping and sodomizing a female student at the University of Kentucky in Frankfort on

May 22, 1988. The victim, who had gone to California on vacation one month after the attack, identified May from a police photo array brought to her by a Frankfort detective who had flown to California with the photos. A forensic expert at May's trial said that the hairs retrieved from the victim were "as good of a match as I have ever had." (Microscopic examination of hair in criminal cases has since come under more severe scrutiny as to its reliability.) May was sentenced to two concurrent twenty-year prison terms. After all appeals failed, May contacted the Kentucky Innocence Project at the Salmon P. Chase College of Law, where a team of KIP members, including Marguerite Thomas, Gordon Rahn, Diana Queen, and, especially, Chase College law students Beth Albright and Debbie Davis, and University of Kentucky law student Chris Turner, undertook his case. They learned that the victim had originally described her attacker to police as a thin man in his twenties with long, stringy, greasy dark brown hair. May had been seventeen at the time and had bright red hair. They learned that May had always maintained his innocence and had refused to accept counseling for sex offenders, which had caused him to be denied parole, signifying that May had opted to remain in prison rather than admit to having committed a crime he had not done. The law students diligently tracked down the biological evidence in the case, which, at first, seemed to have been lost, once in a courthouse that had burned down and then in another building to which it had been transferred before the fire, but which was later flooded. The students nevertheless located the intact evidence, which was submitted to post-conviction DNA testing. The rape kit evidence was also submitted to Y-chromosome testing. In both instances, May was excluded as the donor of the spermatozoa. May's conviction was vacated, and he was released from prison on September 18, 2002.

**1989: Clarence Braunskill** was convicted and sent to prison for selling cocaine, his Suffolk County, New York, conviction based upon a tape recording of a seller's voice and the testimony of an undercover detective. His brother, Leonard Braunskill, spent years tracking down the real drug seller, who confessed, which brought about Braunskill's release from prison in 1997. In 2001, Braunksill was awarded $1 million in compensation for his wrongful conviction and imprisonment.

**1989: Robert "Bob" Kelly** and **Dawn Wilson** of the Little Rascals Day Care Center in Edenton, North Carolina, were convicted of Satanic child abuse in a mania that gripped the town for several years and involved ninety children accusing twenty adults of ritual sexual child abuse, including the mayor and the sheriff with 429 separate offenses. Kelly and Wilson were given life sentences of the seven adults eventually charged. Three adults were released after charges were dropped, and two were allowed to plead to no contest. Kelly and Wilson were set free in 1997 after their error-ridden convictions were vacated, and they were acquitted and all charges dropped against them two years later. None of the charges, it was later painfully discovered, had any basis in fact, and the children had been coached into making false accusations.

**1989: Harold Wilson** was convicted of murdering three persons in Philadelphia and received three death sentences. On appeal, Wilson's original conviction was vacated based upon the racial practice of District Attorney Jack Mahon, who attempted to eliminate blacks from jury selection and exclude any "smart people who will analyze the hell out of your case. . . . They take those words 'reasonable doubt' and they actually try to think about them." (Here was a man wholly subscribing to the words of H. L. Mencken, who once wrote that "nobody ever went broke underestimating the intelligence of the American public.") Wilson's second trial in 2003 ended with a mistrial. At his third trial in 2005, DNA evidence had been admitted, showing that he had been excluded from the murders. On November 15, 2005, a jury agreed with that testing and acquitted Wilson on all charges.

**1989: Jack Davis** was convicted and sent to prison for life for sexually assaulting, mutilating, and murdering Kathie Balonis in Bexar County, Texas. His conviction was brought about by forensic "expert" Fred Zain, who testified that the blood found under the victim's body came from Davis. Zain changed his testimony in 1992 at an evidentiary hearing, stating that the blood came from Balonis. Davis's conviction was vacated in 1992, and he was released from prison. He was later awarded $600,000 in compensation for his wrongful conviction and imprisonment. Zain had testified in innumerable criminal cases that had brought about convictions and imprisonments that were later proven to tainted with his false testimony (see Chapter XV: "Inept Defense and Government Misconduct").

**1990**: Connie Nardi, a thirty-one-year-old mother and divorcée, left a bar in Mantua, Ohio, on the night of August 14, 1988, accompanied by twenty-one-year-old Troy Busta, both driving off on a motorcycle. Nardi's half-naked body was found floating in a pond in Geauga County by a fisherman the next day. The woman had been strangled to death. Busta was arrested and interrogated several times, finally naming **Randy Resh** and **Robert Gondor**, both twenty-four-year-old laborers, as the actual killers. Busta, when one of his defense attorneys reportedly asked him earlier if he would go along with "setting up" other suspects, allegedly replied that he would "do anything to get myself out of this. I ain't sitting in no [electric] chair for somebody else." In a plea-bargain agreement with prosecutors, Busta, who claimed that he was present when Nardi was murdered, but was not her actual killer, pleaded guilty in his 1989 murder trial, receiving fifteen years to life. He testified the following year in the 1990 trial of Resh and Gondor, describing in detail how the two men had murdered Nardi, but with inconsistent statements. Resh and Gondor knew Busta and saw him leave the bar with Nardi and then return sometime later, but they, too, left the bar to go to another pub and a pizza parlor before returning to the bar, where they again met up with Busta. Their absence from the original bar was used by prosecutors to claim that they had left the bar, driven to meet Busta and Nardi, and murdered the woman before returning to that bar. There was no evidence linking both men to the crime, but they were nevertheless convicted on the questionable statements of Busta and sent to prison for life. On December 26, 2006, following ten years of post-conviction appeals, the Ohio Supreme Court vacated the 1990 convictions of Resh and Gondor, based on insufficient evidence and the unreliable credibility of Busta's testimony. Resh was retried in April 2007, where he was acquitted, and prosecutors dropped the case against Gondor. Both men, after sixteen years in prison, had been released on bond in January 2007, following the high court's December decision.

**1990: Carl Lawson** was convicted and sentenced to death for the July 27, 1989, murder of eight-year-old Terrence Jones in East St. Louis, Illinois. Lawson had recently broken up with the boy's mother, Pamela Burts, but had continued to live in her home. He said at his 1990 trial that he had not been at the residence at the time the boy was killed, although a Pro Wing sneaker he wore fit one of the bloody footprints found at the crime scene. Seven other bloody footprints not identified as belonging to Lawson, however, were also found at the murder scene. Fingerprints found on a beer bottle and a matchbook were also used in evidence against Lawson. He was represented at his trial by William Brandon who, incredibly, had been appointed as his public defender even though Brandon had previously

been an assistant state's attorney who had actually been part of the prosecution's team at Lawson's arraignment. Brandon did not have the footprints and fingerprints tested since he lacked funds to hire such experts, and, when he requested funds for that purpose, trial Judge Michael O'Malley denied him such funds. With little defense, Lawson was convicted by a St. Clair County jury and sentenced to death. The Illinois Supreme Court reversed the conviction, stating that Brandon's role as Lawson's attorney constituted a "conflict of interest," in that he had earlier been part of the prosecuting team dedicated to imprisoning Lawson. Tried again, a hung jury could not determine his guilt and, in a third trial, Lawson was acquitted. In that third trial, it was learned that the blood at the crime scene was wet when a number of people entered the Burts residence before the police arrived, and the footprints that originally convicted Lawson could have been made by anyone at that time. Another suspect in the case, who had never been investigated, died by the time that Lawson was set free on December 12, 1996. Lawson was officially exonerated by Illinois Governor George Ryan (1999–2003) on August 1, 2002.

**1990: Christina Hill**, a seventeen-year-old girl from Roxbury, Massachusetts, was convicted at a bench trial of poisoning to death Henry Gallop, that conviction brought about in part by Boston *Herald* reporter Michelle Caruso, who reportedly pressured another girl to falsely testify against the defendant. Hill had been given an undetermined sentence and was incarcerated at the Department of Youth Services. Roxbury District Court Judge Gordon A. Martin found Hill guilty of second-degree murder. Under the state's dual trial system, Hill's attorneys requested a jury trial. On January 28, 1991, a jury acquitted Hill and she was set free. In testifying at that trial, reporter Caruso took the Fifth Amendment to avoid incriminating herself.

**1990: Harold Coleman Hall** was convicted and sentenced to life imprisonment for the 1985 murders of Nola Duncan and her brother David Rainey in Los Angeles. Following seventeen hours of interrogation, Hall had confessed to the killings, but on the witness stand gave an impassioned plea to the jury, recanting his confession and insisting that he was innocent. His conduct on the witness stand convinced the jury not to seek the death penalty. Hall was convicted in April 1990, and sentenced to life imprisonment without parole. Hall worked in the prison law library, filing his own petitions. In 1994, an appellate court overturned his conviction of Rainey's murder for lack of evidence, and, in

2003, his conviction for the murder of Duncan was vacated and a new trial ordered, based upon new evidence that showed police and prosecutors had offered the court a questionable confession and unreliable statements from a jailhouse informant. Further, it was determined that the informant had admitted to fabricating information in his testimony. Hall had claimed that his confession had been coerced by the same Los Angeles police officer who was later found wrongfully accessing data from a police database when spying on Hollywood celebrities in conjunction with private detective Anthony Pellicano, who had been imprisoned for that offense. The officer later retired with a full pension. Hall was released from prison in 2004 by Los Angeles County Superior Court Judge William Pounders, who stated that there was no physical or forensic evidence connecting Hall to the crime, and after the Los Angeles District Attorney agreed to dismiss all charges against him, based on the passage of time and the unavailability of potential witnesses.

**1990: Jesus Avila** was convicted of attempted murder, resulting from a shooting at a wedding party in Los Angeles. His conviction was vacated in July 2002, and he was released, after Avila's brother admitted to the shooting.

**1990:** Gang member Deron Jones was shot and wounded by two men on August 18, 1989, in the Mission Hill Housing Project in Boston, Massachusetts. Police Officer Terrence O'Neil, who pursued the gunmen, said that **Christopher Harding**, an alcoholic who lived in the area, had been one of the gunmen and had also shot at him. On the testimony of O'Neil, Harding was convicted of two counts of assault with intent to murder on May 25, 1990, and was sentenced to between ten to twelve years in prison. His conviction had been brought about by the testimony of gang members and Officer O'Neil. Released on parole in October 1996, Harding filed for a new trial in 1997, after several gang members said he had had nothing to do with the Jones shooting. On December 22, 1997, Superior Court Judge Volterra granted Harding's motion for a new trial, and at a subsequent hearing, the testimony of gang members, as well as the testimony of another police officer, showed Officer O'Neil had falsely testified and had misrepresented ballistics evidence. Prosecutors announced in January 1998 that they would not retry Harding, who was, in January 2000, awarded $480,000 for his wrongful conviction. Officer O'Neil was fired by the Boston Police Department the following month "for lying under oath and other breaches of department rules in the [Harding] case." Harding had spent seven years behind bars.

**1990: Jeffrey Blake** was convicted of the June 18, 1990, murders of Everton Denny and Kenneth Felix in New York City, his conviction brought about by the testimony of a lone eyewitness. Blake's conviction was overturned and he was set free in 1998, after prosecutors admitted that the testimony from their star witness had been false.

**1990: Harold Hill, Dan Young Jr.**, and Peter Williams were arrested and charged with the 1990 murder of thirty-nine-year-old Kathy Morgan, whose body was found by firefighters answering a fire alarm. Hill, sixteen at the time, had been arrested on unrelated charges when he was interrogated by Chicago police detectives John Halloran and Kenneth Boudreau. He confessed to sexually attacking and murdering Morgan, along with Young and Williams. He later recanted his confession, saying that he had been beaten by the detectives, Young was then interrogated, and he, too, confessed, even though he had an IQ of 56, which qualified him as being mentally retarded. Williams was the last to be interrogated, and he also confessed to the crime, but later recanted that confession, as had Young, saying that he had been handcuffed to a radiator in the interrogation room and, because he had not been allowed to go to a rest room, urinated on himself. The confessions were suspect from the beginning since Young and Hill had implicated Williams, and Williams himself had confessed to a crime that he could not have committed as it was proven that he was in jail at the time of the crime and charges against him in the Morgan slaying were dropped before Young and Hill were brought to trial. The victim had been sexually attacked, and a forensic expert testified that bite marks on her body had been matched to the teeth of both of the defendants. Hill and Young were convicted and sentenced to life imprisonment. On appeal, when post-conviction DNA testing was permitted, both Hill and Young were excluded from being the donors of the biological evidence in the rape kit. The bite mark evidence was also discredited at that time. The convictions of Hill and Young were vacated, and all charges dropped against them in 2005 when they were released from prison.

**1990:** On March 26, 1988, thirty-seven-year-old Danny Josephs was shot to death in Brownsville, a section of Brooklyn, New York. **Lamont Branch** was convicted and sent to prison for life for this murder, but he was set free in 2002, after his brother, Lorenzo Branch, confessed to the killing.

**1990:** On February 21, 1989, the body of Lonnie Malone was found in a culvert near Bug Hollow Road in Sumner County, Tennessee. A coroner soon reported that the victim had died of several stab wounds, and, without any linking evidence, Sumner County Sheriff officials immediately focused upon **Ronnie Marshall** and **Robert Spurlock** as the suspects. Both men were convicted and sentenced to life imprisonment. The convictions of both men were vacated after the real killer confessed to murdering Malone.

**1990: Dennis Counterman** was convicted and sentenced to death for the arson murder of his three children on July 25, 1988, in Allentown, Pennsylvania. Following the fire, his wife, who was heavily sedated, gave contradictory statements to detectives (she was on a breathing tube in the hospital when detectives interviewed her), mostly through nods of her head that were later construed as an accusation that her husband had set the fire. Janet Counterman, who was mentally retarded, also said that her husband was sleeping when the fire began, and that she woke him and he tried to put out the fire until overcome with smoke inhalation. Neighbors later testified that they saw Counterman outside in the backyard screaming for help while the house was afire. Counterman was sent to a prison that was only two blocks away from where his house burned down and there awaited an execution that never came. On appeal, his conviction was vacated in 2001, after it was learned that exculpatory evidence had been withheld from his defense—chiefly the known history of his six-year-old son Christopher, who had started many fires in the home. Prosecutors threatened a new trial, and Counterman agreed to an Alford Plea, which admitted no guilt and was satisfied by time served. He was released from prison in October 2006.

**1990: Troy Hopkins** was convicted of murdering thirty-seven-year-old Curtis Kearney in Richmond, Virginia. Following his trial, several witnesses came forward to say that Hopkins was innocent, and, in 1992, another man admitted to committing the murder. After his conviction was vacated on appeal, a higher court reinstated the conviction. Hopkins was paroled in 2001, but he was exonerated in 2005 when Virginia Governor Mark Warner (2002–2006) issued him a full pardon.

**1991: Clarence Richard Dexter**, born in 1941, was found guilty of murdering his wife, Carole, in Missouri in 1990, following a marriage of twenty-two years. He was sentenced to death, but it was later learned that his trial attorney had been ill and was under investigation for tax fraud, problems that caused that lawyer to give little attention to Dexter's case, where he failed to challenge evidence given by a serologist. The Dexter home, the defendant insisted, had been invaded in a botched robbery by an unknown assailant who killed his wife. In 1997, the Missouri court of appeals overturned Dexter's conviction, stating that prosecutors were guilty of misconduct. An in-depth reexamination of blood evidence, which had chiefly convicted Dexter, determined that the serologist testifying against Dexter had made several errors and that expert admitted that he had overstated his case. A retrial was ordered, but prosecutors declined to proceed and charges against Dexter were dismissed. He was released in 1999, dying on April 10, 2005, in Butler, Missouri. Part of his small estate included a quilt Dexter had made while living on Missouri's Death Row. The quilt contained portraits he had made of eight other inmates he had known and who had been put to death while he awaited his own execution.

**1991:** Prosecutors charged **Andrew Golden**, a high school teacher, with the 1989 drowning murder of his wife, Ardelle, in Winter Haven, Florida. The woman's body was found floating in a lake close to a boat dock located near the Golden home, a partially submerged Pontiac, which Andrew Golden had recently rented, also nearby. Police stated that Golden had killed his wife to collect $350,000 in life insurance policies he had taken out on his wife's life so that he could pay of more than $200,000 in personal debt. Officers theorized that Golden had thrown his wife into the lake and then sent the car in after her to make it appear that she had accidentally driven the auto into the lake and had drowned by mishap. The medical examiner, however, reported no signs of foul play and had ruled Ardelle Golden's death an accident. Although prosecutors in Golden's 1991 trial offered no real evidence that Golden murdered his wife—there was no confession, no physical evidence, and no eyewitness testimony—he was convicted and sentenced to death. In 1993, the Florida Supreme Court stated, in a unanimous decision, that the state had convicted Golden with insufficient evidence, saying that it had "failed to show beyond a reasonable doubt that Mrs. Golden's death resulted from the criminal agency of another person rather than from an accident." The court vacated Golden's conviction and ordered his release, which occurred on January 6, 1994. Two years later, however, Golden was charged with molesting two young girls, ages eight and nine. He pleaded guilty to engaging in indecent behavior with a child and was sentenced to fifteen years in prison. John Gioffreddi, Golden's attorney, attributed his client's transformation into a pedophile as the result of his wrongful murder conviction and the two years he spent on Death Row awaiting execution.

**1991:** On November 15, 1990, a woman living in Madison, Wisconsin, allowed a black man into her apartment after he told her that he was her upstairs neighbor and needed to use her phone for an emergency. Once inside the apartment, the man took the woman's money and tied a scarf around her head before sexually assaulting her. The victim provided a description that was used to create a composite police sketch, which was widely distributed. A few days later, **Anthony Hicks** was stopped for a routine traffic violation. A witness thought that Hicks resembled the person in the sketch, and he was arrested and charged with rape and robbery. Hairs left at the crime scene were identified as having come from Hicks, but a serologist testified that tests on the limited spermatozoa left at the scene of the crime proved inconclusive. Hicks was convicted and sent to prison for twenty years. After all appeals, a new defense attorney secured post-conviction DNA testing, which showed, after one of the root hairs from the crime scene was examined, that Hicks was excluded. He was released in 1997 after serving five years in prison. On October 13, 2000, a jury in Madison, Wisconsin, awarded Hicks $2.6 million compensation, a judgment made against his defense attorney Willie Nunnery. The attorney, according to the judgment, had failed to seek DNA testing at Hicks's trial or use a witness, who would have provided an alibi for Hicks. An appeals court reversed this decision in 2002, stating that it was not enough that prosecutors had declined to retry Hicks for his exoneration to be established, proof of innocence which the court said he had not established in his civil case against Nunnery (this in light of DNA testing that exonerated Hicks).

**1991:** An almost identical case to Hicks's dilemma began on December 23, 1990, when a twenty-two-year-old woman in Irvington, New Jersey, was abducted from a dark street by a black man wielding a .38-caliber handgun, dragging the woman into an alley and then through several backyards, before stealing $60 from her and then vaginally and orally raping her. The assailant warned the victim to remain at the scene of the crime for ten minutes before fleeing. The woman went to a nearby house and police were called. A rape kit was shortly assembled at the hospital where she was treated that night. The victim later identified **John Dixon** from a police photo array. She viewed another police photo array on January 4, 1991, again identifying Dixon, who was arrested on January 18, 1991, and charged with kidnapping, sexual assault, robbery, and unlawful possession of a weapon. (In 2001, New Jersey abandoned the use of police photo arrays after determining that it was an unreliable identification system.) Public defender Regina Marrow was assigned to Dixon's case, but, according to Dixon's later claims, did little with it. Dixon had immediately requested DNA testing be made in his case, but nothing was done in that regard. The defendant stood only five-feet eight inches tall and weighed 150 pounds, where the attacker described by the victim was six-feet tall and weighed 200 pounds. Little was done with this discrepancy. On advice from his attorney and out of fear that he would get a more severe sentence if he were convicted on a not guilty plea, Dixon, in July 1991, pleaded guilty to first-degree kidnapping, first-degree robbery, and two counts of first-degree aggravated sexual assault, and unlawful possession of a weapon in the third degree. Dixon, prior to this time, had written two letters to Judge Leonard Ronco, who presided in his case, stating that he was innocent and pleading that DNA testing be conducted. Following his guilty plea, Dixon appeared before Judge Ronco for sentencing on November 12, 1991. Judge Ronco at that time asked the prosecutor: "It's not relevant to this case, is it, DNA?" The prosecutor replied: "I doubt it." Defense attorney Marrow stated: "It may be relevant only to the extent that the State never moved to have Mr. Dixon examined." She also cited the existence of the rape kit and that her client had repeatedly asserted that DNA would prove him innocent. Judge Ronco denied the motion to grant DNA testing and sentenced Dixon to forty-five years in prison. After all appeals failed, including another request for DNA testing in 1996, Dixon contacted the Innocence Project, and a student located the biological evidence, which, in September 2000, the Essex County prosecutor's office agreed to have DNA tested and, in fact, paid for that testing. Deputy Chief Assistant Prosecutor Robert Laurino felt that the evidence against Dixon had been thin and that the defendant's consistent requests for DNA testing had created doubts about his guilt. DNA testing showed that Dixon had been excluded as the contributor of the spermatozoa in the rape kit. His case was vacated on November 29, 2001, by Essex County Judge Harold Fullilove. When prosecutors declined to retry him, Dixon was released from prison after having been behind bars for ten years.

**1991: Adam Riojas Jr.**, of Oceanside, California, was convicted in 1991 of killing Jose Rodarte in Los Angeles, chiefly on eyewitness identification. Though he insisted that he was innocent, that he was at home at the time of the murders, and that he had offered an alibi witness, he was sentenced to fifteen years to life in prison. In 2001, Adam Riojas Sr., who bore a strong resemblance to his son, admitted to several persons shortly before his death that year that he, not his son, had murdered Rodarte. This confession was submitted to the California Parole Board in 2004 by attorneys representing the California Innocence Project, which had undertaken Riojas's case. The lawyers showed the board a statement from a deputy district attorney, whose remarks were on record, that he was "seriously concerned that the inmate may have been wrongfully convicted." The board unanimously voted to grant Riojas a parole, which Governor Arnold Schwarzenegger (2003– ) did not oppose. Riojas was released on April 26, 2004, although his parole release did not indicate "actual innocence" or exoneration.

**1991: Thomas Merrill** was convicted and sentenced to life without parole for the 1989 robbery and double murder at a coin shop in Orange County, California. On appeal, his conviction was overturned in 1995, and he was acquitted at a jury trial and released, based upon prosecutorial misconduct (prosecutors had failed to inform defense counsel of exculpatory witness evidence) as well as police errors and/or misconduct.

**1992**: Convicted of the 1990 murder of Leonard Jamison in Chicago, Illinois, **Melvin Bentley** was sentenced to life imprisonment. According to two eyewitnesses, Leroy Stephenson and Daniel Washington, Jamison was shot to death when Bentley and Jamison exchanged gunfire in the parking lot of a tavern across from the Ford Heights Police Station, an area police had identified as a heroin and crack cocaine marketplace. Stephenson was a cousin of the murdered victim, and Washington was only fifteen at the time he said he saw the shooting. The testimony of the two witnesses secured the prosecution's conviction of Bentley, but both recanted their initial reports. The Cook County Public Defender's Office later obtained sworn statements from Stephenson and Washington in which both witnesses said that the lead investigator in the case, who at the time of the recantations had been convicted of bribery and sent to a federal prison, had coerced them into falsely witnessing against Bentley. Washington had earlier told this investigator and other policemen that the man he saw shoot Jamison had been

himself wounded in the hand during the exchange of gunfire. Bentley bore no such wound. Gary Hadden, however, who had been another suspect in the Jamison case, had been shot in the hand, but he was not investigated by police. (Hadden was convicted in an unrelated murder case and sent to prison for ninety years.) Prosecutors, as well as police, were aware of Washington's statements before Bentley's trial, according to Bentley's lawyers, but suppressed those statements during Bentley's 1992 trial. In 2000, Bentley was offered a prison release by the Cook County State's Attorney's Office on the proviso that he make no attempt to obtain a new trial. Bentley had consistently claimed innocence in the Jamison killing. He realized that, if he insisted on a new trial, he would have to remain in prison and that might take years. He accepted the release, given with the tacit admission by Cook County authorities that they had convicted an innocent person.

**1992:** On September 20, 1990, a graduate student at the University of Chicago was raped and robbed. The victim later told police her assailant was a black man, and she identified **Richard Johnson** from a Chicago police photo array. When police failed to find Johnson, he was profiled on *America's Most Wanted* TV show, which led to his arrest in Florida. Arrested for the 1990 rape and robbery on August 8, 1991, Johnson was again identified by the victim in a Chicago police lineup. Before Johnson went to trial in 1992, biological evidence in the rape kit showed the presence of H antigens, indicating that they came from a person who was a secretor. Serology testing showed that examinations of blood and saliva from both the victim and Johnson and determined that neither the victim or Johnson was a secretor so that Johnson could not have been the contributor to the spermatozoa recovered from the victim or her clothing. Though this evidence was available to Johnson's defense counsel, the attorney did not make any use of it. Further, DNA testing was then available, and the attorney did not request that it be compared to the biological evidence from the victim, Johnson nor the victim's husband. Johnson was convicted of rape and robbery and sentenced to thirty-six years in prison. Johnson sent a letter to the Public Defender of Cook County in February 1993. He complained that he had had inept or deficient legal representation, pointing out the fact that his lawyer had not availed himself of all the evidence in the case that, in Johnson's view, would have exonerated him, especially DNA testing. That testing was granted, and DNA testing showed him innocent of the crime. His conviction was vacated on March

8, 1996, and he was released from prison after having been behind bars for four years.

**1992:** On June 1, 1991, a woman in Austin, Texas, who was three months pregnant was raped by an intruder who had broken through a latched screen door of her home. The victim later told police that she was able to clearly see the attacker's face in a well-lighted living room, where he assaulted her. She identified **Ben Salazar** from a police photo array, also saying that Salazar bore the same tattoo worn by the assailant. He also smoked the same cigarettes as had the attacker. Salazar was arrested in October 1991, and charged with aggravated rape. His wife provided an alibi, but the victim's identification, as well as a serology report on the rape kit that said Salazar could not be excluded and that the blood samples came from only 1 percent of the Hispanic population, brought about his conviction on aggravated sexual assault. He was sentenced to thirty years in prison. Salazar's attorneys, David Shulman and Karyl Krug, secured in December 1994 a court order to preserve the rape kit evidence, but the Department of Public Safety reported that it was then unable to locate the evidence. In October 1996, the rape kit evidence was located in a freezer. The court granted DNA testing of the evidence in February 1997, which was conducted by GeneScreen, a private laboratory in Dallas, Texas. This lab performed PCR-based DQ Alpha and polymarker testing on the evidence and announced that Salazar was excluded as the donor of the spermatozoa in the biological evidence. In October 1997, the Department of Public Safety also tested the evidence and came to the same results. Salazar was released on bond on October 27, 1997, while a third DNA test using Salazar's blood was conducted (to prevent any claims of evidence tampering while the evidence was "lost"), and the same results were announced. On October 30, 1997, Salazar's conviction was overturned. Governor George W. Bush (1995–2000), following the recommendation of the Texas Board of Pardons and Paroles, granted Salazar a full pardon on November 20, 1997. He had been imprisoned for five years.

**1992:** A woman waiting for a bus in Dorchester, Massachusetts, on the night of March 19, 1991, was kidnapped at knifepoint by an assailant, who raped her and then, before fleeing, told her to go to a Boston skating rink the next night and bring $100. The following night, Boston police arrested **Anthony Powell** at the skating rink and charged him with rape and kidnapping. The victim identified him as her assailant, and he was convicted in 1992 and sentenced to twelve to twenty years

in prison, despite his consistent claims that he was innocent. After all appeals failed, the Committee for Public Counsel Services appointed attorney Julie Boyden to Powell's case. She was able to secure post-conviction DNA testing of the samples in the rape kit. Testing showed that Powell was excluded from being the donor of spermatozoa in the rape kit evidence. On March 8, 2004, Superior Court Judge Robert Mulligan, who had presided over Powell's 1992 trial, vacated the original conviction and ordered a new trial. Prosecutors did not retry Powell, who was released from prison after having served twelve years behind bars.

**1992: Quedellis Ricardo "Rick" Walker**, a black man, was convicted of murdering his ex-girlfriend, Lisa Hopewell, in her Cupertino, California, home on January 10, 1991. The thirty-four-year-old Hopewell, a Princeton graduate with a serious drug addiction, had been found bound with duct tape and stabbed to death in her condominium off Stevens Creek Boulevard. Walker, who had been arrested for stealing Hopewell's car after an argument a year earlier, was named as her killer by Rahsson Bowers, who had been arrested for the crime. Bowers stated that he and Walker, an auto mechanic in East Palo Alto, had invaded Hopewell's condominium, but it was Walker who had killed the woman. Walker's fingerprints were found on the duct tape and his alibi—he claimed that, at the time of the Hopewell murder, he had been at a motel smoking crack cocaine with another woman—fell apart when that woman denied having been with him. His defense attorney failed to summon witnesses who might have supported his alibi, and, on Bowers's testimony, Walker was convicted in April 1992, and sentenced to twenty-five years to life. After all appeals failed, he was fortunate enough to find an attorney, Alison Tucher, a onetime San Francisco prosecutor turned defense attorney, who was the daughter of a friend of Walker's mother. She worked for years to find evidence that would exonerate her client, finally locating five witnesses who stated that Walker was not at the scene of the crime and that he had been framed by Bowers, the actual killer, who was shielding an unknown accomplice. Tucher also discovered that Bowers had cut a deal with prosecutors to receive a lighter sentence by agreeing to testify against Walker. After losing one appeal in 1999, Walker's next appeal through Tucher was successful, when, on June 9, 2003, Santa Clara County Superior Court Judge Kevin Murphy ordered Walker's release from prison. After disclosures of police and prosecutorial misconduct in the case, Bowers's perjured testimony, and defense attorney and trial errors, Walker's conviction was vacated and he was not retried by prosecutors. He received $421,000 in compensation for the thirteen years he had been behind bars.

**1992: Anthony E. Bragdon** was convicted of assault with intent to rape. He was released on parole in 2002 after serving ten years in prison. In March 2003, his conviction was vacated, and he was exonerated after it was learned that the forensic evidence that had brought about his conviction, provided by FBI forensic expert Michael Malone, had been fabricated. Malone had testified that carpet fibers found on the victim's clothing were traceable to Bragdon's home.

**1992:** After Felix Ayala was shot to death on a Bronx, New York, street in 1990, a woman identified twenty-year-old **Milton Lantigua** as the killer. She said she had seen the shooting from her bedroom window, and police, shortly after the shooting, drove her about the neighborhood in a patrol car. She then spotted Lantigua and made the identification. Lantigua's first 1990 trial resulted in a hung jury. Prosecutors then offered him, before the second trial, a deal where, if he pleaded guilty to a weapons violation, his sentence would be limited to time served. Lantigua, who had insisted all along that he was innocent, refused. He was retried in 1992 and found guilty of second-degree murder. He was sentenced to twenty years to life in prison. On appeal in 1996, a court learned that the woman identifying Lantigua for the Ayala murder had recanted her testimony before his 1992 trial, but that that recantation had been withheld from the defense by prosecution. Moreover, she again denied seeing anyone kill Ayala since she was with a man in her bedroom at the time of the killing. The court vacated Lantigua's conviction and ordered his prison release after prosecutors declined to retry him. The State of New York awarded Lantigua $300,000 compensation in 2004, and the City of New York awarded him $1 million compensation the following year.

**1992:** On August 20, 1992, a man groped Lissette Saillant on a street corner in East Elmhurst, Queens, New York, which resulted in a struggle with her date, Wilfredo Cesacro, who was shot dead by the assailant. Saillant later identified **Lazzaro Burt** as the killer. Burt was convicted and sent to prison for life. After his appeals failed, attorneys for a Wall Street firm represented Burt pro bono in 2001 and paid for a private detective, Michael Race, to probe the case. Race located Saillant, who admitted that police had pressured her into identifying Burt. At the same time, the Queens District Attorney's Office began an investigation into the Burt case after an arrested drug dealer said that another man, Jarrett Smith, who was a Burt look-alike, had killed Cesacro. Another witness identified Smith as the killer, and he was convicted and sent to prison for life for the Cesacro murder. Burt was exonerated and released from prison on September 26, 2002, after spending ten years behind bars. His attorney, Ron Kuby, filed a $30 million lawsuit against officials and the state, which was widely publicized. In 2003, twenty-eight-year-old Ronald Laws accused Burt of trying to kill him, shooting him in the leg while the two were in a car together. Laws had waited a month to report the incident, and on his testimony Burt was again put behind bars, waiting in jail for ten months for a trial. Burt was acquitted at that trial, his defense attorneys saying that Laws was a "low-level street hustler and a con man," who was trying to get some sort of payment from Burt from the expected compensation for his first wrongful imprisonment. His attorney believed that Laws could have shot himself in the leg to make the scam work. Said lawyer Kuby: "I think the Queens District Attorney's Office should declare a moratorium on future Lazzaro Burt prosecutions."

**1992: Nathaniel Lewis** and **Jimmy Williams** were convicted and sent to prison for raping a woman in Akron, Ohio. The victim recanted her identification of both of these men in 2002, and they were released from prison after their convictions were vacated and all charges dropped against them. Williams was awarded $750,000 in compensation by the State of Ohio in 2003. Lewis received $662,000 in compensation in 2005.

**1993:** On May 30–31, 1991, an eleven-year-old girl, who was home alone in her residence in Tulsa, Oklahoma, was assaulted and raped at the pool at her residence by a stranger the girl later described as having red hair and a pock-marked face. Tulsa resident **Timothy Durham**, twenty-nine, fit the victim's description, and he was arrested and later identified by the girl as her assailant. Further, hair and DNA tests pointed to Durham as the culprit. Durham was convicted in 1993 of first-degree rape, forcible sodomy, and attempted robbery. He was sentenced to 3,120 years in prison, where he was constantly abused by fellow inmates, who had labeled him a pedophile. Durham, at his trial, had a solid alibi—he and his father had driven on the day of the attack to Dallas, Texas, for skeet-shooting—but this alibi and the eleven witnesses supporting Durham's alibi were ignored. The Innocence Project launched an investigation in 1996 that proved that the forensic science case presented against Durham in court was the product of "junk science," and that it was "riddled with quality control problems" so severe they converted "solid science into junk." Dr. Edward Blake of Forensic Science Associates retested the semen sample used in the original case against Durham and unequivocally excluded Durham as the source of the semen left at the scene of the crime. After three and a half years of wrongful imprisonment, Durham was released in 1997.

**1993:** On August 18, 1993, Dalton Pace, a dealer in junk autos, was robbed and murdered in Decatur, Alabama. Chiefly because of the statements of two family members, a thirty-seven-year-old carpenter, **Gary Drinkard**, was convicted of the crime and sentenced to death. When Drinkard became a suspect in the case, police interviewed his adopted daughter, Kelly Drinkard Harvell, who, at first, said that her father was at home when Pace was killed, but later said that Drinkard was not at home at the time of robbery-murder. Another family member, Beverly Segars, Harvell's half sister, agreed to wear a police wire to entrap Drinkard, but the tape resulting from her talk with Drinkard produced only garbled responses. Segars nevertheless on the witness stand stated that Drinkard had told her that he had difficulty in handling Pace during the robbery when not realizing how big the victim had been. Segars's common law husband, Rex Segars, also stated that Drinkard had told him that he had stolen $2,200 from Pace. In his own defense, Drinkard stated that he was at home on the night of the murder, suffering from an injury to his back. His two attorneys, both having little criminal trial practice, failed to call two physicians to testify that Drinkard's back injury would have prevented him from attacking Pace, a much larger man. They also failed to call a family acquaintance who visited the Drinkard home on the night of the murder and saw that Drinkard was in so much back pain that he could hardly move about. In 2000, the Alabama Supreme Court overturned Drinkard's conviction and ordered a new trial. Attorneys and investigators from the Southern Center for Human Rights then discovered that Harvell may have changed her testimony under police pressure, when it was learned that she had been charged earlier by the managers of a Panama City, Florida, motel of stealing money from them. Harvell then admitted that charges against her in Florida were pending for grand theft and possession of a controlled substance. Robert Lambert, Beverly Segar's son, then stated that his mother's word could not be counted on, and that he would not believe her statements even un-

der oath. Two new witnesses, Thomas Carter and Willodene Brock, then stated that they were both at the Drinkard home on the night of the murder and insisted that Drinkard was present and did not leave his home until 10 P.M., the Pace murder having occurred two hours earlier. Drinkard was then released after having spent seven years in prison, five of which were on Death Row.

**1993:** On Labor Day 1991, **Jed Gressman** and **Troy Hancock** met a hitchhiking woman while driving on the shore of Yuba Reservoir State Park in Utah. The woman was later assaulted and raped and she, at first, accused another man of the crime, then changed her identification to Gressman and Hancock, along with providing different details of the sexual assault. Gressman and Hancock were nevertheless convicted in 1993 and sent to prison. Friends and relatives, however, paid to have their case researched, providing supportive information that they were innocent and persuading the state's own DNA expert to retest the available forensic science evidence in the case. The expert, using advanced processing not available at the time of the conviction of Gressman and Hancock, reported that the two men could not have committed the crime. They were both released in 1996, three and a half years after going behind bars, when Juab County Attorney David Leavitt dropped the case, abandoning a second trial. Said Leavitt at that time: "It made more of an impression on me than any other case of my career." Gressman stated: "I knew that someday the truth would come out. I knew that if I became bitter, it would hurt me." Gressman's refusal, however, to admit any guilt while in prison brought about additional punishment. He refused to attend sex-offender classes, and at a parole board hearing, he later recalled, "they told me unless I took those classes, they would never let me out." When he adamantly refused, seven more years were added to his sentence. His release and that of Hancock came about through DNA testing a short time later.

**1993:** In two separate attacks occurring one month apart in 1992 at the same apartment complex in Louisville, Kentucky, one seventy-year-old woman was raped and the same assailant attempted to rape a second woman. Both women identified **William Gregory**, a black man, who lived in their same apartment complex. In addition to the identification, prosecutors offered forensic evidence in the form of Negroid hairs found in a cap left by the assailant and which, prosecutors said, belonged to Gregory. He was convicted of rape, burglary, and attempted rape and sentenced to seventy years in prison. After all appeals failed, Gregory contacted the Innocence Project that brought about post-conviction DNA testing. In 2000, DNA test results showed that Gregory was excluded as the donor of the spermatozoa in the rape kit. Released from prison on July 5, 2000, the forty-five-year-old Gregory became the first person to be exonerated through mitochondrial DNA testing alone and the first person in Kentucky to be exonerated by DNA testing. He was later awarded $3.9 million in compensation for the seven years he had spent behind bars.

**1993:** On September 18, 1992, sixteen-year-old Kendrick Thomas, along with three other youths, was walking on South Paulina Street in Chicago when they encountered thirty other black youths who began chasing them for several blocks, shooting at them. Thomas was struck in the head by a bullet and died. The three surviving youths, led by Dedrick Warmack, reviewed Chicago police photo arrays and lineups and identified twenty-four-year-old **Xavier Catron** as the person who had shot Thomas. Based on this identification, Catron was convicted in 1993 of murder and sentenced to thirty-five years in prison. Years later, Rick Strasser, a journalist at WGN-TV, who had been reviewing the case, received a letter from Catron, one in which Catron insisted that he was innocent and that he had been wrongly convicted. Strasser interviewed the victim's father, Anthony Thomas, who told Strasser that he believed that Catron had not killed his son. In October 1996, Thomas wrote to Cook County Judge James Schreier to state that "I feel that Xavier was not involved." Strasser then interviewed the three witnesses, and all recanted their statements in written affidavits, which were submitted to Judge Schreier, along with a petition from Catron. Warmack again recanted his testimony in court, and, on January 31, 2000, Judge Schreier vacated Catron's conviction. Prosecutors dismissed all charges against him, and he was released from prison. The three witnesses all said they had been either pressured or coerced into making their statements by police. Chicago Police Detective John Holloran, who had appeared in an earlier hearing, denied that charge, telling the court that the three youths had volunteered their identifications of Catron without any coaxing from officers.

**1993: Andrew Adams** was convicted and sentenced to life imprisonment for the March 19, 1990, murder of retired teacher Jack Royal in Newcastle on Tyne, England. His appeal was reviewed when his attorneys argued that the jury had been biased in its verdict, several members of that jury having made disparaging remarks about the defendant during his trial. The court found that Adams's defense counsel had failed to present exculpatory evidence at the trial, which might have proven the client innocent. Adams's conviction was overturned on January 12, 2007, and he was released from prison.

**1993: Timothy Brown**, who was mentally retarded, was arrested in 1991 and charged with the November 13, 1990, murder of Patrick Behan, a deputy sheriff of Broward County, Florida. His trial did not take place until two years later, when he was convicted and sentenced to prison without parole. That conviction was secured through a garbled confession Brown made to two detectives, James Carr and Eli T. Graham. After all of his appeals failed, Brown's prospects brightened when the *Miami Herald* began publishing a series of investigative articles probing the flimsy case in 2001. At that time, Gwenda Johnson informed officials that her estranged husband, Andrew Hughray Johnson, a former sheriff's employee, had admitted to murdering Behan. Two undercover agents posing as drug dealers interviewed him, taping a boastful admission of that murder in which Johnson provided details of the 1990 slaying. Johnson and his wife later recanted their statements as simply "brag," and, in 2002, Broward County Sheriff Ken Jenne concluded that he did not have enough evidence to arrest Johnson for the Behan murder. Meanwhile, the *Herald* unearthed police misconduct in the case, describing how police secured Brown's confession, which was improperly conducted from the beginning when interrogators failed to make Brown understand his rights under the Miranda rule. Based on this evidence, U.S. District Judge Donald Graham vacated Brown's conviction in March 2003, and Brown was released from prison on May 14, 2003, much to the credit of the *Miami Herald* and his two devoted federal public defenders, Timothy Day and Brenda Byrn. (Brown was released on a minimal $5,000 bond, which he and his impoverished family could not pay, but Roschell J. Franklin, of Franklin Bail Bonds, personally made the payment.) Detectives Carr and Graham had by then retired from the Broward County Sheriff's Department, Carr reportedly stating that he had been forced into retirement because of his handling of the Timothy Brown case.

**1993: Weldon Wayne Carr** was convicted and sentenced to life in prison for the April 7, 1993, arson-murder of his wife in Sandy Springs, Georgia. On appeal, the Georgia Supreme Court vacated Carr's conviction, ordering a new trial after ruling that Carr had been convicted on insufficient evidence. The Georgia Supreme Court ordered all charges against Carr dropped in June 2004 since prosecutors had not brought Carr to a new trial, after prosecutors admitted that they could not find an arson expert to support their theory of the crime, if, indeed, there had been a crime and not simply an accidental fire that took the life of Mrs. Carr.

**1993: Henry Myron "Hank" Roberts**, sixty-three, was convicted of murdering his nephew in Baltimore, Maryland, despite the fact that he was seriously wounded during the killing and claimed that another man he could not identify had committed the crime. Police produced the murder weapon, a gun registered to Roberts, which detectives said he had thrown into a run, where it was washed downstream. Roberts denied this claim, saying that the run never had more than six inches of water in it. He said that his gun had been missing for some time. Roberts was sentenced to fifty years in prison. In April 2002, twenty-nine-year-old Robert Tomczewski, who had a long record of criminal violence, pleaded guilty to the nephew's murder, saying that he had used Roberts's gun, which he had stolen a year earlier from Roberts, to shoot the nephew and Roberts. Tomczewski was sentenced to ten years in prison. Meanwhile, prosecutors reported that they had attempted to locate Roberts in prison, but could not find him so that he could be officially exonerated and released from prison. He was already under ground, having died of a heart attack on December 22, 1996, just outside of his prison cell, which is as far as he got to the freedom he deserved for having been wrongly convicted and imprisoned for more than three years.

**1993: Patrick Hurley** was convicted of a sexual assault in Grant County, Washington, but was released from prison in 1996, after the victim recanted her testimony against him, saying that she had fabricated the entire story. Hurley's public defender, Tom Earl, had offered little help to him at his trial. Earl was disbarred for life in May 2004 after it was shown that he had been charging defendants for his services when the state had provided such expenses to him as a public defender.

**1994: Gary Gauger** was convicted and sentenced to death by Judge Henry L. Cowlin on January 11, 1994, for the April 8, 1993, murders of his mother and father, Ruth and Morris Gauger, at a farm in McHenry County, Illinois, which was close to the Wisconsin border. This conviction, as it was later learned, was brought about by a false confession made by Gauger that was coerced by the police during their interroga-

tions of him, and the testimony of a jailhouse informant, Raymond Wagner, who shared a cell with Gauger in the McHenry County Jail while Gauger awaited trial. Wagner, who had twice been convicted of felonies, claimed that Gauger had confessed to the murders. Forensic experts also testified in this case, but their statements had to be argued by the prosecution as supporting its case and did not necessarily incriminate Gauger. On March 8, 1996, the Illinois Appellate Court unanimously reversed Gauger's conviction, stating that Judge Cowlin should have granted a motion to suppress Gauger's confession because the police interrogations had been unconstitutional. The court also stated that the police arrest of Gauger without probable cause prohibited Gauger's courtroom statements, which should not have been admitted. The court remanded the case, further stating that Judge Cowlin was in error in allowing Gauger's coerced statements to be read into the trial transcript. Police, when initially interrogating Gauger, told him that he had failed a lie detector test and that his clothes soaked with his parents blood had been found, both statements being untrue. In a hypothetical discussion with police, Gauger said that if he had performed such a heinous deed, he must have experienced a blackout at the time since he had no recollection of murdering his elderly parents, who were both in their seventies. His statements were quickly construed to be a confession, although they were nothing of the kind. Gauger was set free. In June 1997, federal investigators probing a conspiracy involving a Wisconsin motorcycle gang called the Outlaws acquired evidence that proved that members of this gang had killed Gauger's parents. They unearthed a tape on which gang member Randall E. Miller stated that he had killed the Gauger couple, but had left no evidence to link him to the crime. Miller and another gang member, James Schneider, were indicted on thirty-four counts of conspiracy, including the Gauger murders. Schneider confessed to the murders in 1998, and Miller was convicted of those murders in 2000. Gauger went on to establish a small but successful business, later becoming an outspoken opponent of the death penalty, and at one point stating: "Until this happened [his parents' murders and his own wrongful imprisonment and death sentence], I really believed in the criminal justice system.".

**1994:** On August 28, 1992, a black man forced his way into the apartment of a white female student at Rutgers University in New Brunswick, New Jersey, stating the need for money to get back to New York City. After taking her money and credit cards, the man raped the victim. After the assailant fled, the victim called police and described the attacker and his clothes. She was taken to a hospital where a rape kit was assembled. Police later showed her a photo array of suspects, which included **McKinley Cromedy**, but she failed to make any identification. Eight months later, the victim saw Cromedy on the street and called police, identifying Cromedy as her assailant. He was charged with aggravated sexual assault, robbery, burglary, and terrorist threats. Although saliva and blood samples were taken from Cromedy, no forensic evidence was introduced at his trial in 1994. Hair samples found at the scene of the crime did not match Cromedy nor did the fingerprints also found at the scene of the crime. Cromedy's defense attorney did not seek DNA testing, believing that the case was so overwhelming against Cromedy that the risk of such tests was too high. Cromedy was convicted on the victim's testimony in August 1994, and sentenced to sixty years in prison. Cromedy was granted a new trial on appeal and was again convicted. DNA was not requested by defense attorneys at that second trial. Post-conviction DNA testing was requested later, and this was performed on the rape kit by the New Jersey State Police Crime Laboratory on December 8, 1999, excluding Cromedy as the donor of the spermatozoa. Prosecutors declined to retry him, and he was released from prison on December 14, 1999, after serving 4.5 years behind bars.

**1995: Kulaveeringsam Karthiresu**, a Tamil refugee arriving in Canada in 1991, was convicted of the May 2, 1993, shooting death of Sivapiragasam Namasivayam outside a house in Scarborough, Ontario, Canada, and was sent to prison for life. In 2000, an appeal court quashed the conviction and ordered a new trial, based upon insufficient evidence provided by the prosecutor in the 1995 trial. Prosecutor Phil Kotanen, who had very little evidence other than innuendo to begin with, decided to drop all charges rather than proceed with a second trial. Karthiresu, at age thirty-seven, and after having spent six and a half years behind bars for a murder he had not committed, was released by Toronto Superior Court Justice David Watt, who stated: "You were wrongly convicted. I cannot return to you the time you spent in custody. What I can do is apologize to you on behalf of the administration of justice. You, sir, are free to go." Karthiresu had all along maintained his innocence and had testified at his trial that another man had committed the murder. Upon his release, Karthiresu stated: "It was hell. I didn't do this crime. I'm going home now. I'm a free man." He had nothing but bitter thoughts about his captors in prison, adding: "They laughed at me when I told them I was innocent and they kept me in maximum security because of that."

**1995: Jonathan Jones**, thirty-six, was found guilty of murdering Harry and Megan Tooze, whose bodies were found on July 26, 1993, at their farm in South Wales, England. Jones had, at the time, been living with Cheryl Tooze, the daughter of the victims, in nearby Orpington, Kent, England. The only evidence linking Jones to the double murder—the victims had been killed with shotgun blasts—was a thumbprint on a piece of china in the Tooze home, albeit as the common-law husband of the victims' daughter, Jones had reason to often visit the Tooze home. Sentenced to life in prison, Jones appealed, his attorneys claiming that prosecutors had misrepresented his alibi, and, when it was proven that Jones had been talking with two workmen in Orpington at the time of the slaying, his conviction was overturned on April 25, 1996, and Jones was released from prison.

**1995:** Based on the allegations of thirteen-year-old Donna Perez, the foster daughter of police detective Robert Perez, forty-three persons in Wenatchee, Washington, were accused of widespread child molestation and incest, all forty-three adults arrested and charged with 29,726 offenses of child sex abuse involving sixty children. Many of the accused were convicted and sent to prison, including Pastor **Robert Roberson** and his wife **Connie Roberson**, who ran a food bank in Wenatchee and the local Pentecostal Church. All were later exonerated (the Robersons received a $3 million settlement) when it was learned that the children had been coached and manipulated into making their accusations and that there had been no foundation for the accusations that had launched this massive latter-day witch-hunt.

**1995: Lee Long** was arrested in 1994 and held as a suspect in a rape in Queens, New York. The investigating officer at that time called Long's girlfriend, who confirmed to the detective that Long had been with her at her apartment at the time the crime occurred. Long was released, but he was again arrested for the same crime in 1995, and was convicted of rape, sexual abuse, and robbery. Sentenced to eight to twenty-four years in prison, Long's case was reviewed by a lawyer from the Queens Legal Aid. After talking with Long in prison, he believed him to be innocent, and the lawyer tracked down the detective who had first investigated the rape case in 1994, but whose report had not been used in

Long's 1995 trial. The detective confirmed Long's alibi, and in June 2000, his conviction was vacated and he was released from prison.

**1995: Alan Gell** was convicted of murdering Allen Ray Jenkins, a fifty-six-year-old retired truck driver. His body was found in his Aulander, North Carolina, home on April 14, 1995. He had been shot twice with a shotgun. Two teenagers, Crystal Morris and Shanna Hall (the latter was Gell's former girlfriend), testified that they had seen Gell kill Jenkins during a robbery. No physical or forensic evidence linked Gell to the crime. The shotgun was found by police after Morris and Hall told them where it was hidden. Morris and Hall plea-bargained ten-year prison sentences by pleading guilty to second-degree murder in exchange for their testimony against Gell, who was sentenced to death. On appeal, the court learned that prosecutors had withheld an audiotape where one of the witnesses admitted that she had "made up the story," and the statements of seventeen persons who testified that the victim was alive on the day Gell reportedly killed him. Gell was retried in February 2004, and, after the jury deliberated less than three hours, was acquitted.

**1995:** On March 11, 1994, sixty-seven-year-old M. Geneva Long was raped, stomped to death, and placed on a bed before being set on fire in a rooming house in Harrisburg, Pennsylvania. Andrew Dillon, later proven to be a serial killer, who confessed to raping and stomping to death four elderly women, and who occupied a room next door to the victim, was questioned by police. He was released after a convicted child molester, in an effort to get his sentence reduced, fingered James A. Carson as Long's killer. Carson, after a ten-hour interrogation by police, who had Carson's terminally ill mother call him at that time and beg him to confess, finally broke down and gave detectives what they wanted. He said that he and **David Gladden**, a mentally retarded man who had been released from prison only four hours before Long had been killed after serving a term on a burglary charge, had killed Long. Based on Carson's testimony, Gladden was convicted and sent to prison for life, but an appeals court overturned his conviction in February 2007, releasing him from prison, after it was determined that he had not received adequate counsel—his trial attorney had insisted that Carson was the killer and did not attempt to implicate Dillon, the most probable killer, after being told by police that the district attorney had eliminated Dillon as a suspect, a murder to which Dillon later pleaded guilty.

**1995: Ross Sorrels**, who had been the former director of a group of troubled teenagers, America for Youth Foundation, was convicted of raping a five-year-old girl in Clark County, Washington. He was exonerated after post-conviction DNA testing cleared him, and, in 2002, after the actual rapist was convicted of raping the girl as well as her two sisters while living with the mother of the three girls. Sorrels was released from prison in 2003.

**1995: Michael Piaskowski** was convicted, along with five other men, of the 1992 beating murder of Tom Monfils in Green Bay, Wisconsin. All six men worked as mill workers as did Monfils, who was found with a forty-pound weight tied around his neck. A federal judge vacated Piaskowski's conviction, a ruling upheld by the Seventh Circuit Court of Appeals on July 10, 2001, which stated: "The record is devoid of any direct evidence that Piaskowski participated in the beating of Monfils, and available circumstantial evidence at most casts suspicion on him. This is a far cry from guilt beyond a reasonable doubt." Piaskowski was then released from prison.

**1996**: In November 1995, Lemuel Cruz was outside the crowded Sunset Park social club, Con Sabor Latino, a nightclub in Brooklyn, New York. The area was packed with Latin Kings gang members, and when he accidentally bumped into one of them without apologizing, more than twenty-five gang members began shouting "kill the black guy!" and "Latin Kings! Latin Kings!" Cruz, who was Hispanic but had dark skin, was knocked to the ground, and scores of gang members, like savage beasts, began beating and kicking and stabbing him. In the melee, several were slashed and cut. When the fight ended, Cruz lay dead, his throat slit. **Hector Gonzalez**, who was not a member of the Kings, moved from one stricken person to another in an effort to help them. He tore his shirt into strips and used this as bandages in attempt to stop the bleeding of several victims. As he knelt next to these victims, his pants became speckled with their blood. Based upon the statements of a lone eyewitness, Gonzalez, the Good Samaritan, was arrested on December 2, 1995, and charged with murdering Cruz. In addition to the eyewitness, prosecutors at Gonzalez's 1996 trial offered a serology report that maintained that the murder victim's blood was found on the defendant's clothes, but the blood type identified was shared by more than 50 percent of New York's population. On this shabby evidence, Gonzalez was convicted of murder and sentenced to fifteen years to life in prison. Three members of the Latin Kings were also convicted and sent to prison for the murder. Some years later, FBI agents began to probe into the criminal activities of the Latin Kings and, in the process, reviewed the Cruz murder, interviewing several persons who said that Gonzalez was nowhere near the victim when he was attacked and, in fact, was standing ten to fifteen feet away, which corroborated Gonzalez's own statements to Brooklyn police. Bureau officials then ordered post-conviction DNA to be conducted on Gonzalez's bloodstained pants, which had been preserved as evidence. The test showed that the blood on Gonzalez's pants had come from two of the victims he had tried to help and none had come from Cruz. His attorney, Glen Garber, a protégé of Barry Scheck, cofounder of the Innocence Project in New York, contacted Scheck, who, along with Garber, contacted an assistant district attorney involved in the original prosecution of Gonzalez. Scheck and Garber told the prosecutor that they were prepared to file a motion for Gonzalez's prison release unless the prosecutor agreed to order Gonzalez's release. The prosecutor clung to some kind of conviction, however, saying that he would agree if Gonzalez pled guilty to the lesser charge of participating in a riot. Scheck and Garber refused. They then contacted the district attorney, who, in the face of DNA evidence, agreed to have his office make a motion in court to have Gonzalez's conviction vacated. On April 24, 2002, two detectives escorted Gonzalez from the Eastern Correctional Facility in Napanoch, a maximum-security prison, to the New York courtroom of Judge Alan Marrus, who had presided in Gonzalez's trial six years earlier. Judge Marrus vacated Gonzalez's conviction with the agreement of prosecutors that they were dropping all charges against him. "Mr. Gonzalez," Judge Marrus said, "you are a free man." He turned to embrace his mother, Gladys Gonzalez, who had always claimed that her son was innocent. "I am the happiest mother in the world," she said. The twenty-five-year-old Gonzalez stated: "I feel great. I feel better than great!" Barry Scheck told members of the press that day: "In this case, a sole eyewitness and [blood] evidence with little probative value sent an innocent man to prison."

**1996: Kum Yet Cheung** was convicted of the 1995 attempted murder of two men outside a Denny's Restaurant in Emeryville, California, and was sentenced to twenty-nine years in prison. That conviction was overturned, and Cheung was tried again in 1999 and was again convicted. The First District Court of Appeal reviewed both convictions and vacated the sec-

ond conviction, based upon the evidence that an eyewitness had erred, that defense counsel had failed to properly translate another man's taped confession from Cantonese and to have it admitted into evidence, that exculpatory medical records had been withheld from the defense, and that the prosecutor had allowed a witness to lie on the stand. The court agreed that Cheung's lack of understanding of the English language hampered his case from his arrest through his two convictions. He was released in 2002 after having spent seven years behind bars.

**1996:** On August 11, 1995, a motorcyclist drove past a driveway where three young men were standing in Boston's Dorchester neighborhood, firing at them. Tennyson Drakes, eighteen, was killed, and two others were wounded. The man on the motorcycle then turned around and rode slowly past the victims, firing at them while they writhed on the ground. Several witnesses later identified **Marlon Passley** as the killer, four of them identifying him from police photo arrays and later in court. Passley was convicted in 1996 and sentenced to life imprisonment without parole. After new evidence was unearthed in the case, the District Attorney asked the court to vacate Passley's conviction in 2000. Passley had already been released the previous year.

**1996:** Another Boston resident, sixteen-year-old **Donnell Johnson**, was convicted of another drive-by killing, the shooting death of nine-year-old Jermaine Goffigan, who was counting his candy after trick or treating on Halloween night 1994, and was fatally struck by a bullet while sitting in front of his grandmother's home in Boston, Massachusetts. The shooting was the result of gangland violence, which had been plaguing the Academy Homes housing development. In two trials, one before a judge in March 1996, a second before a jury in November 1996, Johnson was convicted. He was sentenced to eighteen to twenty years in prison. An unrelated drug investigation led to the surfacing of new evidence in Johnson's case, where police misconduct in withholding evidence was revealed. When eyewitnesses recanted their testimony, Johnson's conviction was vacated. He was released from prison in 1999 and was fully exonerated, with Suffolk County District Attorney Ralph C. Martin II and Boston Police Commissioner Paul Evans personally apologizing to Johnson for his wrongful conviction.

**1996:** A rape victim in San Diego identified eighteen-year-old **Kevin Baruxes** as her assailant, providing police with a detailed description of Baruxes, including tattoos and the specific clothing he wore during the attack. Baruxes, at his 1996 trial, provided an alibi, and his defense attorneys pointed out that no physical evidence linked their client to the crime. He was nevertheless convicted and sentenced to fifteen years to life, given an aggravated sentence after the victim said that Baruxes had made racial remarks to her during the attack, which constituted the offense as a hate crime. (Baruxes was white.) Sometime later, the former fiancé of the victim sent an email to the San Diego District Attorney's Office, stating that he believed that the victim had been wrongfully sent an innocent man to prison. Witnesses then testified that the victim was a habitual liar (she had also accused Baruxes's brother of sexually attacking her). The victim subsequently recanted her testimony against Baruxes, whose conviction was vacated and all charges against him were dropped. The twenty-six-year-old Baruxes was released from prison in 2003 on orders from the San Diego Superior Court. Baruxes, who had spent more than seven years behind bars, was awarded $265,000 for his wrongful conviction and imprisonment. It is not clear if any rape ever occurred in this case.

**1996: Jose Salazar** was convicted of the shaking death of infant Adriana Krygoski while babysitting the girl in her Los Angeles home. He was sentenced to fifteen years to life, but, in 1999, prosecutor Dinko Bozanich publicly stated that the testimony of Deputy Coroner James Ribe was false in that case and many others, that Ribe had wrongly made innocent deaths appear to be the result of violence or sexual abuse. The Krygoski child had suffered several falls before she had been put into the care of Salazar. The conviction was vacated in August 2003, and Salazar was released from prison.

**1996:** On January 29, 1995, a jubilant Murray Barnes left Creola's Bar at 2904 Laussat Street in New Orleans, after collecting $1,000 in the bar's Super Bowl pool. He was robbed at gunpoint and killed. Freddie Thompson, an alcoholic barfly with a criminal record, told police that the perpetrator was **Daniel L. Bright III**. Bright was arrested and tried for the robbery-murder in 1996, with Thompson testifying against him. Other than that testimony there was no physical or forensic evidence that linked Bright to the crime. He was nevertheless convicted of first-degree murder and sentenced to death. The Supreme Court of Louisiana found that the evidence in that case was insufficient to bring about a conviction of first-degree murder and robbery and ruled that Bright's conviction be adjusted to second-de-

gree murder. On May 25, 2004, the court vacated Bright's conviction and ordered a new trial, based on its findings that prosecutors had withheld from the defense the fact that its star witness, Thompson, was drunk on the night of the crime and that he was a convicted felon who had recently been charged with a parole violation. Prosecutors dismissed all charges against Bright, and he was released from prison after having served eight years behind bars.

**1996: Rodney Addison** was convicted of the shooting murder of Lewis Jackson in Baltimore, Maryland, and sent to prison for life. His conviction was overturned on appeal in 2005, when defense attorneys showed that exculpatory evidence had been withheld from the defense at his trial, that evidence including the statements from three witnesses who refuted the testimony of the prosecution's sole witness. Addison's conviction was vacated, and he was released from prison after prosecutors dropped all charges against him.

**1996:** On July 21, 1994, four men described later as being Latinos snatched three cases containing black pearls valued at $1.5 million from jewelry vendors in Queens, New York. The vendors were returning to their hotel in Elmhurst from a gem show in Manhattan when the attackers grabbed the cases. In their escape, the robbers tried to carjack an off-duty police officer, who drew his gun. One of the attackers grabbed the barrel and the officer fired, wounding the robber before the robber knocked him unconscious. Ironically, at the same time, **Napoleon Cardenas** was showing a .380-caliber semiautomatic pistol to two friends in his girlfriend's apartment and the gun accidentally went off, wounding him in the hand. Cardenas went to St. John's Queens Hospital for treatment. The off-duty police officer and one of the vendors who had been injured by the robbers were being treated for their injuries in the same room where doctors were inspecting Cardenas's gunshot wound. When the officer asked how he had gotten the wound, Cardenas gave vague answers, and he was thought to be a suspect in the robbery. He was placed in a police lineup, but none of the venders identified him. With a recent conviction for credit card fraud, Cardenas was awaiting sentencing and then fled to the Dominican Republic. His brother, **Carlos Cardenas**, was later interrogated by police, who believed that he, along with his brother, Napoleon Cardenas, had been part of the jewelry robbery. On the strength of the gunshot wound received by his brother, Carlos Cardenas was tried and convicted of robbery in May 1996 and sentenced to eight to twenty-five years in prison. A year later, Napoleon Cardenas returned to the United States, served his four-month jail term for credit card fraud and was then convicted and sent to prison for the 1994 gem robbery. In 2005, Napoleon Cardenas had surgery performed on his injured hand, and the bullet fragments were later used by attorneys from the Queens Legal Aid to file a motion. The fragments proved that they were aluminum and not from the copper casings used by police and therefore Cardenas could not have been shot in the hand by the off-duty police officer as had been contended at his trial. He and his brother passed lie detector tests and were both released from prison in 2007.

**1996: Beth LaBatte** was convicted and sentenced to life in prison for the 1991 murders of two sisters, Ceil Cardigan, eighty-five, and Ann Cardigan, ninety, in Kewaunee County, Wisconsin. Her case was undertaken by the Innocence Project at the University of Wisconsin's Law School, which secured post-conviction DNA testing. That testing showed that blood on items connected to the murder did not belong to LaBatte. The thirty-nine-year-old LaBatte was released from prison in 2006, after prosecutors dismissed all charges against her.

**1997**: The conviction and death sentence in the case of **Alfred Rivera** in 1997 had been brought about by three jailhouse informants. In exchange for leniency on unrelated charges, these informants testified that they saw Rivera enter an apartment in Forsyth County, North Carolina, and that they subsequently heard gunshots that took the lives of two persons. (Both Rivera and the victims were black.) Rivera's defense counsel insisted at his trial that the three informants had conspired with the actual killer to tell their stories in order to frame his client. The trial judge, however, barred the testimony of a witness who claimed to have had knowledge of that conspiracy. That ruling was judged by the North Carolina Supreme Court to be in error, and it ordered a retrial. In 1999, Rivera went back to trial, where his attorneys were able to provide the witness that corroborated the conspiracy to frame Rivera. Other defense witnesses then testified that Rivera was elsewhere at the time of the crime. He was acquitted and released after having spent thirty-two months behind bars.

**1997: Jeremy Sheets**, a white supremacist, was tried, convicted, and sentenced to death for the September 23, 1992, rape and murder of a seventeen-year-old black girl, Kenyatta Bush. An honor student, Bush's throat had been slashed and her body dumped in some woods outside of Omaha, Nebraska. In 1996, police arrested Adam Barnett on a charge of possession of illegal weapons. During his interrogation, Barnett admitted in a taped confession that he and fellow white supremacist Jeremy Sheets had raped and killed Bush in a racist retaliation against black men who dated white women. In exchange for this plea-bargained confession, Barnett was not charged with first-degree murder in the Bush case and the weapons charge was dropped. He asked and got a promise from officials that his safety in prison would be maintained, believing that black inmates might kill him. While he was behind bars, threats from black prisoners were made, and Barnett, believing that he could be killed at any time, hanged himself in his prison cell, his death reported as a suicide (if, indeed, that was the case). Sheets was then brought to trial, convicted of first-degree murder and sentenced to death on the taped confession of Barnett, who could not corroborate those statements since he was dead. The Nebraska Supreme Court overturned Sheets's conviction in September 2000, stating that Barnett's tape recording, which had convicted Sheets, was "unreliable" and "highly suspect," and was inadmissible in that Sheets's attorneys were not able to cross-examine the witness, who was dead by the time of Sheets's trial. In 2001, prosecutors appealed for a new trial before the U.S. Supreme Court, which refused to hear that appeal and Sheets was released. Though it was proven that he had been wrongly convicted, the decision did not inherently signify that Sheets was innocent. Investigators learned before his trial that he had shaved his head in the fashion of the skinheads, a white supremacist group, was obsessed with Nazi drawings, and had, at one point, threatened a black neighbor.

**1997**: Convicted and sentenced to death, **Joaquin Martinez**, a Spanish national, had been found guilty of the 1995 murders of Douglas Lawson and his girlfriend, Sherrie McCoy-Ward, in their home at Clair Mel, Florida, which was east of Tampa. Lawson had been shot several times and McCoy-Ward stabbed more than twenty times as she tried to flee the house. Police and prosecutors had little to link Martinez to the crime, other than the fact that Martinez had once worked at a warehouse with Lawson. Sloane Martinez, however, who was the defendant's estranged wife, told police that she suspected her husband of murdering the couple, and she agreed to wear a wire to record a conversation she had with Martinez, which was later aired in court. The tape was barely audible, however, and contained no direct statements from Martinez about the murders, but prosecutors contended that "several re-marks . . . could be interpreted as incriminating." Fur-ther, Martinez's girlfriend testified that he had left their home on the night of the murder and returned with a swollen lip and scuffed knuckles, as if he had been in a fight. During the trial, a police detective volunteered the opinion that Martinez was guilty, an assertion that was repeated by the prosecution in closing arguments. Because of this improper statement, the Florida Supreme Court, in 2000, overturned the 1997 convic-tion, ordering a new trial. In Martinez's second trial, prosecutors did not seek the death penalty, and most of its case had evaporated. Sloane Martinez and the defen-dant's girlfriend changed their stories, mostly recanting earlier statements, and Circuit Court Judge J. Rogers Padget then refused to admit the tape originally aired in the first trial because it was inaudible. Moreover, the jury learned for the first time that the victim's father, who had been the evidence manager for the Hillsbor-ough County Sheriff's Office, had prepared the tran-script of the inaudible tape and had offered a $10,000 reward for the apprehension and conviction of his son's killer. In less than two hours, a jury acquitted Martinez, and the news of his release was broadcast internation-ally since this case had drawn the attention of many no-table worldwide figures. Pope John Paul II had earlier made an appeal that Martinez's life be spared, and that plea had been echoed by King Juan Carlos of Spain. When hearing that Martinez had been set free, Spain's prime minister, Jose Maria Aznar, stated: "I am happy that this Spaniard was declared not guilty. I have always been against the death penalty and I always will be."

**1997:** Arrested for the May 20, 1995, rape and bur-glary in Lake Charles, Louisiana, **Allen Coco** was iden-tified by the victim on June 20, 1995, after reviewing two sets of police photo arrays. The victim told police that, following the rape and burglary, she had gotten hold of the knife the assailant had been wielding and used it to stab the attacker in the buttocks, which caused him to jump out a window in his flight. Coco, arrested shortly after the identification, bore no stab wound in the buttocks. He did bear many tattoos that had not been mentioned by the victim. During Coco's 1997 trial, a serologist testified that the blood left be-hind by the assailant, which came from the wound in-flicted by the victim, matched that of Coco, a type of blood present in only 5.8 percent of black Americans. This evidence and the identification of the victim brought about his conviction of aggravated rape and aggravated burglary in a bench trial on November 7,

1997. He was sentenced to life. The Innocence Project New Orleans undertook Coco's case in 2003, securing post-conviction DNA testing in 2005. In March 2006, ReliaGene conducted the tests and announced results that proved that Coco was neither the donor of the blood left at the scene of the crime nor of the sperma-tozoa found in the rape kit evidence. The state per-formed its own tests and came to the same conclusion. A judge vacated Coco's conviction in July 2006 and or-dered a new trial, which, after further state DNA tests that confirmed Coco's innocence, prosecutors declined to make. Coco was released and exonerated after hav-ing served a total of 11.5 years behind bars, nine of which were served in his actual sentence.

**1997: Jose D. Vasquez** was convicted of murdering fifteen-year-old Corey LeSure in 1994, in Aurora, Illi-nois, that conviction chiefly achieved by prosecutors us-ing a jailhouse snitch, Larry Wilkinson, who claimed to be an eyewitness to the murder. Vasquez was sent to prison for fifty years, until the Illinois Appellate Court learned that Wilkinson's testimony was rife with incon-sistencies and lies. Before identifying Vasquez, Wilkin-son had identified another person. Vasquez's attorneys showed the court that the detective supervising the case, Marshall Gauer, who was called "The Sheik," had lied when saying that he had only talked to Wilkinson two or three times, when records showed that Wilkin-son, while in an Iowa prison, had placed 384 collect calls to Gauer when arranging for his testimony against Vasquez, testimony reportedly prepared and coached by Gauer. The court ordered Vasquez's conviction va-cated, but Kane County prosecutors told Vasquez that they would drop all charges against him only if he pleaded guilty to a lesser charge. Believing he would re-main indefinitely behind bars while awaiting appeals from prosecutors, Vasquez accepted the deal and he was released in 2000.

**1997:** The United Kingdom established its Criminal Cases Review Commission in 1997, which, until July 2006, had reviewed more than 8,500 cases. The Com-mission sent about 4 percent of appeals back to court for new trials, and about two-thirds of those cases, more than 220, resulted in overturned or vacated con-victions.

**1997: Ronald Reno** was charged in 1996 and con-victed in 1997 of the felony possession of a handgun in Fresno, California, after police found a handgun in his truck. Reno, who had already received three prior felony convictions, was a four-time loser with this con-viction and was sentenced to twenty-five years to life, although he claimed that someone else had left the gun in his truck. His attorney had unwisely urged him to cut a plea-bargain deal with prosecutors, saying that to do otherwise would mean a stiffer prison sentence, but the sentence he received could not have been stiffer. In 2001, while working in the admissions office of the prison, Reno saw a list of new admissions that included the man who had left the gun in his truck, Preston Marsh. He talked with Marsh, who, at some risk to himself, agreed to admit that the weapon had been his and not Reno's. After this confession, Reno was released from prison in 2002, after agreeing with prosecutors that he would accept a larceny charge for time served, but without a three-strikes sentence.

**1997: Mark Reid** was convicted of the November 1996 kidnapping and rape of a white woman in Hartford, Connecticut. The victim initially told police that the assailant was a light-skinned black man, with freckles about the eyes, about five feet seven inches tall, who grabbed her at night when she was walking home from a bar, dragging her to a park, choking her, and threatening to kill her unless she stopped struggling. He held a sharp instrument to her side she thought might be a knife. When she stopped struggling, the assailant forced her to perform oral sex and put on a condom before raping her vaginally. While still emotionally upset, the victim identified Reid from a photo array of eight photos, although Reid bore no freckles and stood six feet tall. In addition to the victim's testimony in court, prosecutors also relied on hair evidence. A forensic expert stated that the Negroid hairs retrieved from the victim were similar to that of Reid, although he admitted that he could not prove that they were identical. Reid was found guilty of first-degree sexual assault and first-degree kidnapping and was sentenced to twelve years in prison. Post-conviction DNA testing was performed on the biological evidence in the case in 2003, and it showed that Reid was not the donor of the spermatozoa. It also showed that the hairs examined and used as evidence at his trial were those coming from a Caucasian. Reid was released from prison after having spent 5.5 years behind bars.

**1997: Dwight Labran**, a twenty-four-year-old black man with no prior convictions, was convicted of first-degree murder in New Orleans. Prosecutors had only one witness against Labran, the owner of the car in which the body was found, who named Labran as the killer. Labran provided an alibi, witnesses saying that he was having dinner with family members at the time of the crime. The jury, however, chose to believe the witness and convicted Labran, who was sentenced to life in prison without parole. (Several members of the jury argued for the death penalty.) When all appeals failed, Labran turned to the newly created Innocence Project New Orleans (IPNO), which undertook his case, several law students, including Candace O'Brien, searching through records and compiling evidence on his behalf. IPNO learned that the witness testifying against Labran had, at the time of the killing, outstanding warrants against him for firearms and drug violations and that that witness provided a false name to police and prosecutors and thus avoided becoming a suspect in the killing as well as evading arrests in the pending warrants. All of this information was known to prosecutors, which was withheld from Laban's defense attorneys. After IPNO provided an appeals court a ninety-page document that detailed this information, the court vacated Labran's conviction in 2001, ruling that he had been convicted on perjured testimony. After the district attorney dropped all charges, Labran was released from prison after having served four years behind bars. He was the first person to be exonerated through the considerable and noble efforts of the IPNO.

**1997:** On June 16, 1994, an intruder invaded the home of Carl White Jr. in Jackson, Mississippi, shooting him in the leg while robbing the home and threatening White's wife, Gloria, and his daughter, Jamilla, at gunpoint. White later died of his wound. This robbery had been repeated four other times in the Jackson area, where other victims had been shot in the leg. **Cedric Willis** was identified in the White robbery and murder by Gloria and Jamilla White. Although Willis was not identified in three of the other robberies, he was identified as the robber in the fourth robbery. He was convicted in 1997 and sentenced to life in prison. After DNA testing cleared him, Willis was granted a new trial in 2005. The presiding judge refused to admit the testimony of the Whites, and, on a joint motion by the defense and prosecution, the judge dismissed all charges against Willis, who was set free.

**1997:** Leonard and Lena Walters were shot dead on February 23, 1997, in Lake of the Ozarks, Missouri, after Leonard Walters was showing a car he wanted to sell. Jessica Cox told police that **Danny Wolfe** had killed Leonard Walters in the backseat of the car while she was at the wheel in a demonstration drive. She testified at his trial that, after Wolfe shot Leonard Walters, he went into the Walters home and shot and killed Lena Walters. A forensic expert testified at Wolfe's 1997 trial that hairs found on the victim in the backseat of the car came from Wolfe. He was convicted and sentenced to death. In 2003, the Missouri Supreme Court vacated Wolfe's conviction on the grounds that he had received inadequate counsel at his trial, specifically that his defense attorney had not challenged the forensic evidence, which was later tested and proven to have come from Cox, who the defense all along had insisted was framing Wolfe. The results of the new hair testing undermined the reliability of Cox's statements.

**1997: Diomedes Polonia** was convicted of attempted murder and sent to prison for the shooting of Thomas Hosford in the Bronx, New York. Horsford identified Diomedes Polonia as "Freddy" Polonia (Pedro "Freddy" Polonia, who was the actual culprit and the brother of Diomedes), and he was thus convicted. Before fleeing to Puerto Rico, Pedro Polonia signed a confession that he had shot Hosford, but he later remained silent when located in Massachusetts. Diomedes Polonia's conviction was vacated, and he was released from prison in January 2003, when the identification error was shown to an appeals court.

**1997: Johnnie Beck** fired two bullets from a rifle into nineteen-year-old Jeffrey Watts, in a Burger King parking lot in Whiteville, North Carolina, on November 24, 1995. Watts, a relative of state senator R. C. Soles, was killed, and the eighteen-year-old Beck was charged with first-degree murder, although he maintained all along that he had shot in self-defense after Watts had stabbed his twin brother, Ronald Beck, several times in the chest and then sliced off Johnnie Beck's finger when he came to his sibling's rescue. Beck's 1997 trial was tainted by jury tampering and other prosecutorial errors. He was nevertheless convicted of second-degree murder and sentenced to ten years in prison. The conviction was later vacated, and Beck was set free in June 2006.

**1997:** In December 1994, Joy Jones Goebel was murdered in Richmond County, North Carolina, and Johnnie Ray Knight soon confessed to the murder, leading officers to her body, which was hidden in a wooded area. Two months later, Knight said that the real killer was his uncle, **Jerry Lee Hamilton** (who had been convicted in the 1970s for second-degree murder). Knight said that he and Hamilton had both raped the victim before Hamilton killed her. Hamilton was brought to trial, and convicted and sentenced to death on the testimony of his nephew, Knight. On appeal, it was shown to Richmond County Judge Michael Beale that Knight had lied at Hamilton's trial when he said he had re-

ceived no deals from officials for his testimony against Hamilton. A letter hidden by the prosecution later surfaced, one written by Knight to the Sheriff's Department before Hamilton's trial and in which Knight asked officers to visit him in prison, stating: "Come talk to me and maybe we can work out a deal." By that time, postconviction DNA testing had shown that only Knight was the donor of the spermatozoa found in the rape kit done on the victim and that Hamilton had been excluded. Judge Beale vacated Hamilton's conviction in 2003.

**1997:** On September 21, 1996, fifteen-year-old Johnny Escalante was fatally shot in the back while sitting in the passenger seat of a truck driven by his older brother, Gabriel, after leaving a party outside of Pritchett, Texas. Without any evidence to link him to the crime, **Jason Barber**, whose family owned the property where the party was held, was convicted in June 1997 of the killing and sentenced to thirty-five years in prison. In summer 2000, Barber's attorney, Melvyn Brouder, of Dallas, received a tip and instructions where to find the murder weapon, which had never been located. A .357-caliber Magnum, which had been used to kill Escalante, was located under a barn in Upshur County, which led to the arrest of another man, William Shane Wood. Barber was then released from prison.

**1997: David Wayne Kunze** was convicted of the December 16, 1994, bludgeoning murder of the fiancé of his ex-wife in Vancouver (Clark County), Washington. The victim's son described the attacker as a man between the ages of twenty-five to thirty and with dark hair, where Kunze was in his mid-forties with reddish blonde hair. Kunze was convicted in July 1997 solely on a reported earprint left on a door of the victim's house. At his trial, a so-called earprint expert from the Netherlands, Cor Van der Lugt, stated that he was "one hundred percent confident" that the print matched Kunze. The Dutch expert explained in detail how the print matched, but his explanation was so filled with hyperbole that the jury did not understand any of it and simply accepted his statements carte blanch. Kunze was sentenced to life, but, in his 1999 appeal, a court reviewing the earprint evidence ruled that there was no such reliable evidence on record, that no peer-reviewed studies existed to support the Dutch expert, and that the FBI reported that it does not use such evidence. The court vacated Kunze's original conviction, ordering a new trial. He was released on $500,000 bail in August 2000. His second trial ended in a mistrial, but he was released from prison when prosecutors announced that they would not retry him, dropping all charges against Kunze.

**1998**: **Gilbert Amezquita** was convicted and sent to prison for brutally beating a woman in Houston, Texas. The victim's family owned the plumbing firm where Amezquita worked. In November 2006, however, the Texas Court of Criminal Appeals stated its belief that the real culprit was Gilbert Guerrero and ordered Houston prosecutors to either retry Amezquito or set him free. Prosecutors announced in February 2007 that they would not retry Amezquito, and he was released. In May 2007, the Texas Board of Pardons and Paroles recommended that Amezquito be granted a pardon on actual innocence.

**1998:** Following the abandonment of white apartheid in South Africa and the takeover of political power and the government by the black majority under Nelson Mandela, outbreaks of racial violence increased. In the area around Benoni, South Africa, a number of white farmers had been murdered, reportedly by blacks who had formerly worked for these landowners. Racial tension was running high in April 1998, when white farmers banded together to form armed groups that patrolled their lands at night against intruders. One of these farmers, forty-two-year-old **Nicholas Steyn**, saw several blacks crossing his property on April 11, 1998. He stepped from his home, according to one account, and fired a shot that killed a six-month-old black girl being carried on the back of her cousin, who was wounded. Steyn was jailed, refusing bail, saying that he feared for his life if he were released. Initially charged with murder and attempted murder, Steyn was convicted on lesser charges. On March 4, 1998, Steyn was convicted of culpable homicide and assault and imprisoned. Steyn insisted that he had fired only as a warning and did not aim at the children. When the case was reopened, based upon Steyn's claims, a forensic expert testified that the fatal bullet had ricocheted off a telephone pole, proving that Steyn had fired a warning shot and had not intended to kill anyone. Steyn was given a suspended sentence and released on March 24, 1998, which nevertheless caused widespread rioting among blacks.

**1998:** On April 7, 1997, a masked gunman entered the grocery story owned by Tommy Vanhoose in Bridge City, Louisiana, a short distance from New Orleans. The gunman demanded all of Vanhoose's money, and, when he refused to turn over the cash, the gunman shot and killed Vanhoose and fled the store, discarding the ski mask, gloves, and shirt, and firing more shots at nearby witnesses as he ran to a waiting car, diving through the open window of the passenger seat. The car then sped off at high speed, driven by an accomplice. A few hours later, police found **Ryan Matthews** and **Travis Hayes**, both seventeen, in a car that fit the description of the car used by the killer of Vonhoose. Both youths were arrested and charged with the crime. Both had low IQs, Matthews at 71, which classified him as borderline mentally retarded. The badly frightened Hayes was immediately subjected to a prolonged interrogation, at first telling officers that he and Matthews had had nothing to do with the attempted robbery and murder. After six hours of grilling, Hayes confessed to the crime, admitting that he was the driver of the getaway car and that Matthews had gone into the store where he heard gunshots and then Matthews ran out to the car and got inside and he drove off. (Matthews never confessed to the crime.) Witnesses at the scene of the crime testified that Matthews had fired shots at them while making his escape and one witness had retrieved the ski mask and turned this over to police. One witness, a woman, viewed a police photo array later and tentatively identified Matthews, but was more certain that he was the killer when testifying later in court. Another witness, who was driving a car he used in an attempt to block the getaway car, said he saw the gunman's face in his rearview mirror. He and others in his car later identified Matthews at a police lineup a few hours after the killing. Both boys were tried separately, Hayes in 1998 and Matthews the following year. In both trials, defense attorneys offered forensic evidence that excluded both Hayes and Matthews as having worn the ski mask, glove or shirt abandoned by the perpetrator. Further, a defense witness, who had examined the car in which Hayes and Matthews had been found, said that it could not have been the getaway car in that the window of the passenger seat was inoperable and had been for some time before the crime had been committed, showing how the window could not be opened or rolled down. Prosecutors offered several eyewitnesses who positively identified Matthews at the scene of the crime, even though they had originally described the perpetrator as no taller than five-foot eight-inches tall, when Matthews stood six-foot tall. Hayes was convicted and sentenced to life in prison. In Matthews's 1999 trial, which took place over three days, the defense and prosecution offered the same evidence, but the trial judge was later accused of pressuring a jury into a hasty verdict. On the second day of that trial, the State presented its evidence until 10 P.M. that night. The defense then made a motion to rest, but Judge Henry Sullivan denied the request and ordered the defense to make its closing argument, which it did. The defense then moved to rest once more, but Judge Sullivan denied this motion and ordered the jury to deliberate. At 4:20 A.M. the following morning, the jury sent Judge Sullivan a note stating that it was unable to reach a verdict. Judge Sullivan ordered the jury to continue deliberating and forty minutes later, at 5 A.M., May 6, 1999, the jury returned a verdict of guilty. Two days later, Judge Sullivan sentenced Matthews to death, telling him not to feel sorry for himself because he was responsible for his own problems. Matthews's defense attorneys, William Sothern and Clive Stafford-Smith of the Louisiana Crisis Assistance Center, however, did not give up on their client and doggedly pursued post-conviction DNA testing. That testing on the ski mask discarded by the killer excluded Matthews as the perpetrator and pointed to another man as the real culprit, Rondell Love, who was serving a twenty-year term on a manslaughter conviction. Love had been found guilty of murdering Chandra Conley, who was found with her throat slashed in 1997, a short time after Vanhoose had been killed. He had reportedly bragged to fellow prisoners that he had committed the Vanhoose murder, and after defense attorneys heard of this, they had the DNA evidence involving Matthews run through the state DNA crime database, where biological evidence linked Love to the Vanhoose slaying. In April 2004, Judge Sullivan, who had sentenced Matthews to death, ordered him released from prison on a $100,000 bond, confining him to house arrest at his mother's residence until a hearing could be held. His conviction was vacated on August 9, 2004, and a new trial was ordered. Prosecutors insisted on more DNA tests, and these were made (five DNA tests in all), which came to the same results—that Matthews was innocent. Prosecutors dropped all charges against him on January 19, 2007. Hayes remained in prison until, in December 2006, he, too, was released from prison. Hayes was also exonerated in 2007.

**1998:** In mid-December, 1998, **Wang Youcai**, thirty-two, and **Qin Yongmin**, forty-four, two of China's leading dissidents, were charged with endangering state security. Both Wang and Qin had attempted to set up the China Democracy Party, an opposition party to the communist dictatorship that had ruled China since the late 1940s after the fall of Chiang Kai-shek's regime. Wang, the actual founder of the new party, had been a

student at Beijing University in 1989, and had taken part in the pro-democracy demonstrations in Tiananmen Square, which had been ruthlessly suppressed by the communists. For his role in that political uprising, Wang had served a year in prison, 1991–1992. In 1998, Wang was charged with "colluding with foreigners" in attempting to set up the opposition party, illegally sending e-mail to "foreigners," and using a computer, which had been purchased with "foreign money." His ally, Qin, was not even given a copy of the indictment against him before he and Wang were brought to a closed trial, where the press was barred and no news of the ongoing events was reported. Both men were wrongfully convicted and given prison terms.

**1998: Richard Alexander** was convicted of two rapes occurring two years earlier in South Bend, Indiana, through the identifications of two victims. Sentenced to seventy years in prison, he was exonerated in one case through post-conviction DNA testing, and, because the second offense was almost identical in modus operandi to the first, prosecutors agreed to vacating his second conviction. He was released from prison on December 12, 2001, after having served more then five years behind bars.

**1998:** In November 1998, twenty-three-year-old **Donna Anthony**, of Somerset, England, was convicted of murdering her two babies by smothering them to death to gain the sympathy of her husband. She was largely convicted and sentenced to life imprisonment on the testimony of Sir Roy Meadow, a pediatrician and academic professor, who claimed that the odds of cot death (SIDS), which had been claimed by the defense, was one in seventy-three million when, in fact, the odds were one in 200. (Meadow's testimony in many other cases—see **Sally Clark**, Chronology, 1999—was later discredited as false.) Anthony's conviction was overturned on appeal, and she was released in January 2003. Meadow had written a 1977 academic paper entitled "Munschausen Syndrome by Proxy," claiming that certain parents fabricate their child's illness, advancing the credo that "one sudden infant death is a tragedy, two is suspicious and three is murder, until proved otherwise." In many of the cases for which he testified against defendants, it appears that Meadow did not do any family heritage research to determine, as was often the case, that sudden infant deaths had occurred multiple times in the family history of such antecedents.

**1998:** Charged with two 1998 armed robberies in Irvine, California, sixteen-year-old **Arthur Carmona**, the nephew of a police officer, was tried as an adult and convicted and sentenced to twelve years in prison. The case drew widespread attention in Orange County after it was disclosed that police and prosecutorial misconduct had been rampant in bringing about Carmona's conviction. Irvine Mayor Larry Agran and film actor Esai Morales actively pursued a new investigation, which showed that no eyewitnesses had identified Carmona in a police lineup until police compelled him to wear the hat that the gunman had worn. Further, police had repeatedly lied to Carmona in saying that they had the evidence that would prove that he had committed the robberies. Police, it was determined, had coerced witnesses, wrongly categorized evidence, and skewed the identification process. Prosecutors had compounded that misconduct by further coercing witnesses. In 2000, the Orange County Superior Court vacated Carmona's conviction, stipulating that all charges be dropped against him. He was not released, however, until he signed a stipulation that he would not sue the Irvine Police Department or the Orange County District Attorney's Office, an agreement that later prevented Carmona's attorneys from winning compensation from the county government that had wrongfully kept him behind bars for two years.

**1998:** On August 25, 1997, several men entered the Quality Finance offices in eastern Johnston County, North Carolina, and, during a holdup, shot Alice Wise in the chest and face (she later lost an eye). Three of the men were later apprehended, and two of them cut a plea-bargain deal wherein they named **Terence Garner** as the man who shot Wise. Garner was tried and convicted on their testimony, as well as the eyewitness testimony of Wise and her employer, and sentenced to thirty-five years in prison. One of the real robbers told police that the man shooting Wise was named "Terrance." A short time after Garner's conviction, Terrance Deloach, a cousin of one of the accomplices, confessed to the robbery and admitted shooting Wise. He later recanted that confession. Garner's attorney, Mark Montgomery of Durham, North Carolina, worked for four years to bring about his client's acquittal and, on appeal, showed that Deloach had confessed to committing the crime for which Garner had been convicted. (At the time, Deloach was serving time in a New York prison after being convicted of an armed mugging, but sheriff's detectives from Wayne County tracked him down and obtained his signed confession.) Another codefendant at Garner's original trial, Kendrick Henderson, maintained from the start that

Garner was innocent. Based on this evidence and the fact that Garner had recently passed a polygraph test, a judge vacated Garner's 1998 conviction in February 2002, with the consent of Johnston County District Attorney Tom Lock, who had originally prosecuted Garner. Lock dropped all charges against Garner in June 2002, and he was released from prison after serving four years for a crime he had not committed.

**1998: Steve E. Snipes** was convicted of the armed robbery of a convenience store in Goldsboro, North Carolina, based upon the sound of his voice, which store employees said he had tried to disguise. No other evidence linked him to the crime. While Snipes served out his prison sentence in seventeen different prisons, another man, Terrance Wyatt, bragged about committing the robbery. When this and other exculpatory evidence was presented to Superior Court Judge Tom Lock (a former prosecutor), he ordered Snipes's prison release in 2003 and vacated his conviction. Paul Green, Snipes's attorney, had petitioned North Carolina Governor Mike Easley (2001– ) to grant Snipes a pardon, but that petition remained in the governor's hands for almost three years (from April 2004), until Easley signed that pardon in January 2007, officially exonerating Snipes. Wyatt was later indicted for the robbery, but not brought to trial.

**1998: Wesley Ronald Turley** confessed to a sexual assault in Dallas, Texas, after he pleaded guilty in what he thought would be a ten-year sentence of community supervision. He said on appeal that he had made that plea because he had run out of money to pay a lawyer in a second trial, where he faced a long prison term. Turley was later imprisoned for violating the terms of the community supervision, but, in 2002, his accuser recanted her testimony, saying that she had fabricated the sexual attack because she did not like Turley and his relationship with her mother. Turley was then exonerated.

**1999: Mendell** and **Victoria Banks**, a black couple living in Choctaw County, Alabama, both confessed to killing their infant child and were convicted of manslaughter and sent to prison, but both, who were mentally retarded, had made false confessions and were later exonerated when it was learned that Victoria Banks had a tubal ligation intact since 1995 at the time the newborn child was reportedly killed and therefore making it impossible for pregnancy to occur. The child's body had never been found before, during or after the trial of the Banks's and it was concluded that the child never existed and the crime never happened. Banks and his wife were released in 2003.

**1999:** Rafael Perez, a Los Angeles police officer belonging to the elitist unit called Community Resources Against Street Hoodlums (CRASH), went public in detailing the massive corruption of fellow officers in this unit, which had brought about almost one hundred false arrests and wrongful convictions. Perez confessed to authorities that he and others physically abused and terrorized innumerable Los Angeles citizens, stole weapons and drug money, and even participated in drug trafficking. They also, he said, planted drugs and weapons on innocent persons to gain wrongful convictions. Police investigators corroborated Perez's allegations, and ninety-nine writs of habeas corpus were granted. Huge settlements were awarded to the wrongly convicted persons, **Javier Ovando** receiving $15 million in November 2000 from the City of Los Angeles, and $11 million in a bulk settlement was made to twenty-nine others. Another LAPD victim was **Charles Harris**, who was convicted and sent to prison in 1998 for possessing and selling cocaine, but it was later learned that the drugs had been planted on him by police officers in their widespread victimization of blacks and Latinos in Los Angeles. Harris's conviction was vacated, and he was released from prison in 2000. By 2001, 142 civil cases in this enormous police scandal had been filed, two being dismissed and forty-two settled. The City Attorney's Office estimated that $125 million would most probably be paid out in settlements while investigators reviewed more than 8,000 cases and defense attorneys reviewed an additional 15,000 cases, all now questionable through the worst police scandal in Los Angeles history.

**1999: Armand Villasana** was convicted of the 1998 kidnapping and raping of a white woman in Springfield (Greene County), Missouri. Following the attack, the victim was shown a police photo array of six photos, showing five white men and one Hispanic suspect, Villasana, whom the victim identified as her assailant. Villasana's defense counsel was never shown the bench notes from the state crime laboratory, which would have aided the defendant's case. The notes were later obtained by Villasana's second attorney, Shawn Askinosie, those notes showing that biological evidence was available. Villasana had been convicted on the victim's testimony, but never sentenced, although he remained in prison for seven months until Askinosie moved to have

the biological evidence tested. STR-based DNA testing exonerated Villasana, causing his prison release in 2000.

**1999:** Forty-six persons, about one-third of the black population, were arrested in a July 1999 drug sting in Tulia, Texas, and most were convicted on false confessions (believing that they would receive lesser punishments; others who did not confess did, indeed, receive more severe prison terms) based on the unsupported statements of undercover police officer and informant Tom Coleman, who as a "gypsy" police agent worked in that capacity for small police departments having little funds for undercover work. Almost all of the defendants were later exonerated, and a collective $6 million settlement was made.

**1999: Robert Justin Kaupp** was convicted and sent to prison for life for stabbing to death fourteen-year-old Destiny Thetford, his half-sister's friend, in Harris County, Texas. On appeal, his conviction was overturned, and Kaupp was exonerated in a U.S. Supreme Court decision of May 5, 2003, in which the court determined that Kaupp's confession had been coerced by police, who ignored a more likely suspect at hand.

**1999:** British lawyer **Sally Clark** (1964–2007) was convicted of murdering her two infant sons in 1996 and 1998 in Wilmslow, Cheshire, England, when she and witnesses claimed that the boys had died from cot death (called Sudden Infant Death Syndrome/SIDS in the United States). She was sent to prison for life, but on appeal it was proven that prosecutors had withheld important information from the defense and that the testimony of certain forensic experts had been falsely positioned. One such expert testifying at her original trial was pediatrician and professor Sir Roy Meadow, who said that the chance of two children from a well-to-do family, as was the case with Clark (whose husband was also an attorney), suffering cot death was one in seventy-three million when in reality, the ratio was one to 200. The conviction was upheld in October 2000, but, in January 2003, during a second appeal where prosecutorial evidence was proven to be false, Clark's conviction was overturned and she was released from prison. Her three years behind bars, however, destroyed her will to live and she became an alcoholic, dying from that disease on March 15, 2007.

**1999:** Three children were shot, one fatally, after three men invaded a home in Sacramento, California, while in search of marijuana on October 6, 1998. A police informant identified **David Quindt** as a man who had been seeking guns shortly before the shooting, and one of the wounded children, with some coaching from family members, later identified him as the gunman. Qunidt said he had been seeking weapons to defend himself from a murder threat. He was convicted and sentenced to life without parole. A codefendant, **Anthony Salcedo,** was also charged, but was not convicted when his trial ended with a mistrial. The Sacramento District Attorney's Office then received a tip that Quindt was innocent and that three other men had committed the home invasion and shooting. In 2000, Quindt was released from prison after having served fourteen months in prison, after the Sacramento Superior Court vacated Quindt's conviction and all charges were later dropped against him and Salcedo. The true perpetrators were charged, and all three were convicted and sent to prison. Quindt, who bore a remarkable resemblance to that of the actual killer, received $17,200 in compensation for his wrongful conviction and imprisonment.

**1999: Robert Farnsworth Jr.** was convicted of robbing $2,289.20 from a Wendy's Restaurant in Jackson, Michigan on March 11, 1999, after confessing to police in a prolonged interrogation. Farnsworth was a manager of the restaurant, who claimed he had deposited two bags of receipts on that day at the night depository of the restaurant's bank. When only one bag was reported by the bank as received, Farnsworth was fired and subsequently arrested by police. He was convicted in July 1999 on his confession, which he had recanted, saying that police had coerced him into making a false admission. A bank employee testified that it was "absolutely impossible" for a deposit placed in the night depository to be lost. In February 2000, the owner of a car wash dropped a deposit bag in the same bank depository and it too, was reported missing. The owner had the bank inspect the depository, and his bag of receipts was found in the bank container along with the missing Wendy's bag of receipts, as well as another bag of receipts from a third company that had yet to be reported missing. On May 8, 2000, a judge ordered Farnsworth's conviction vacated and officially released him from custody, as well as ordering all police records involving Farnsworth destroyed.

**1999:** On January 9, 1999, thirty-three-year-old **Pamela Sue Reser**, of McMinnville, Oregon, was arrested and charged with raping her four small children. No physical or forensic evidence was offered during her five-day trial in 1999. The children testified that they had been forced to have sex with their mother and her boyfriend, and other men (no one other than Reser was

brought to trial). Reser was convicted of seventeen counts of first-degree rape, eight counts of sodomy, and four counts of first-degree sexual abuse. She was sentenced to 116 years in prison. "Eventually, my children will talk about this and the truth will come out," Reser told her attorney after being sentenced. She believed all along that the children's foster mother had caused the children to make the false accusations. In May 2002, Oregon state police officers, while working on another case, learned that Reser's four children had recanted their accusations. The officers interviewed all four children, who said they had fabricated their stories against their mother (although they did not give the source or motivation for those false accusations). One of the children took a polygraph test, which supported the recantations. Based on this new evidence, Yamhill County Circuit Court Judge John Hitchcock vacated Reser's conviction and ordered a new trial on May 31, 2002. The prosecutor then dismissed all charges against her and she was released from prison. While admitting that he had no case against Reser after her children made the recantations, he stated: "It was one of the stronger cases I prosecuted." One can only imagine the fate of those prosecuted with lesser evidence by this prosecutor.

**2000**: A rape victim was attacked on the night of February 23, 1999, in Dallas, Texas. The victim was abducted when a Caucasian male jumped into her van while she was waiting for a stoplight to change. Brandishing a gun, he ordered the victim to drive to a deserted industrial area, where he vaginally assaulted her and then forced her to perform oral sex. He then ordered the victim to drive to another area, where the attacker got out and fled on foot. Following the victim's description of the assailant to police, made at a hospital (the victim drove herself to the hospital) a short time after the attack when rape kit evidence was collected, a Dallas police officer, four hours later, saw **Andrew Gossett** going through items stored in a parked pickup truck. When later hearing of the description from the rape victim, the officer thought Gossett fit the assailant's profile, and he arrested Gossett the next day. The victim identified Gossett from a photo array and later in court. Despite the fact that advanced DNA testing was then available, no tests in the case were conducted. Gossett was convicted of aggravated sexual assault on February 10, 2000, and sentenced to fifty years in prison. In December 2006, post-conviction DNA testing was performed on the biological evidence from the rape kit in the case, and its results showed that

Gossett was not the donor of the specimens tested. On January 2, 2007, Gossett was released from prison and, a few months later, exonerated by the Texas Court of Criminal Appeals, which granted Gossett his application for habeas corpus.

**2000:** Late at night on February 26, 2000, the body of thirty-eight-year-old Kathleen Thompson was found on a street in Eau Claire, Wisconsin. The woman had been strangled to death. Thompson was last seen at 3 A.M. after walking out of the Eau Claire police station, where her husband had been jailed following a violent argument. Since the husband was behind bars at the time of his wife's murder, he was never a suspect in the case. Eau Clair Police Chief Jerry Matysik immediately focused upon **Evan Zimmerman**, a former Augusta, Wisconsin, police officer, who had been romantically linked to Thompson in the past. Zimmerman was picked up and interrogated for some time, giving inconsistent answers as to his whereabouts on the night of the murder. Zimmerman had reportedly been drinking for some time before and during the crime, and his statements were made in "an alcoholic haze." Zimmerman was convicted in 2000 and sentenced to prison for life. When all appeals failed, Zimmerman turned to defense attorney Keith Belzer, of La Crosse, Wisconsin, and Keith Findley and John Pray, cofounders (in 1998) of the Wisconsin Innocence Project at the University of Wisconsin in Madison. More than a dozen law students working under the direction of Findley and Pray unearthed considerable evidence that proved that Zimmerman's conviction had been achieved through little or no substantial evidence. Zimmerman's own statements to police, they learned, had never been documented, either written down or taped, and that his statements were inconsistent with the facts in the case. In 2003, the District Court of Appeals concurred with defense, vacating Zimmerman's original conviction and ordering a new trial, ruling that Zimmerman had not gotten a fair trial in 2000. Because of pretrial prejudicial publicity in Eau Claire, the new trial was moved 200 hundred miles away in Juneau, Wisconsin, where, on April 29, 2005, while in mid-trial, Eau Claire County District Attorney Rich White asked Eau Claire County Circuit Court Judge Benjamin Proctor to throw out the case, stating that he lacked the evidence to show "beyond a reasonable doubt" that Zimmerman had murdered Thompson. The overjoyed fifty-eight-year-old Zimmerman leaped to his feet and embraced attorney Belzer and Innocence Project founder Findley. The exonerated Zimmerman later emerged from court hold-

ing up a T-shirt that read: "Freed by the Wisconsin Innocence Project." That organization had brought about several exonerations of wrongly convicted persons in recent years.

**2000: Cees Borsboom** was convicted of the June 2000 murder of a ten-year-old girl in Schiedam, Netherlands, and sent to prison for life. DNA tests showed him innocent and that another man, Wik Haalmeijer, had committed the killing, and who later confessed to murdering the girl. Borsboom was exonerated and released from prison in December 2004. Borsboom's wrongful conviction was attributed to errors made by prosecutors and police, who ignored exculpatory information before and during Borsboom's trial.

**2000:** Trucking contractor **Rick Tabish** and topless dancer **Sandy Murphy** were convicted of robbery, burglary, larceny and murder on May 19, 2000, after a jury found them guilty of killing multimillionaire casino owner Ted Binion in Las Vegas, Nevada, on September 17, 1998, by forcing him to swallow a mixture of black tar heroin and Xanax, a sedative used for the withdrawal of heroin addiction. Prosecutors had stated that the pair had murdered Binion in order to seize his $50 million estate. Tabish had been building a vault in the desert where Binion reportedly planted $8 million in silver. He was arrested while clearing out the vault following Binion's death, but claimed that he was doing this on the instructions of the gambling tycoon. Murphy, who stood to inherit $1.5 million of Binion's estate, was sentenced to twenty-two years in prison. Tabish was given a twenty-five-year prison sentence. Evidence at the pair's trial had been mostly gathered by private detective Tom Dillard, who had been hired by the Binion family, and it was he who had persuaded police to officially charge the pair with murder. On appeal, defense attorneys showed that Binion had been a longtime heroin addict and had become deeply depressed in March 1998, after the Nevada Casino Gaming Control Board permanently barred him from ever entering his family's casino, its decision based upon his drug abuse habit and his relationships with known crime syndicate/Mafia figures. The defense proved to the court that, on the day of his death, Binion received a month's supply of prescribed Xanax and later that day bought twelve balloons of black tar heroin from a Las Vegas drug dealer. It became obvious to the court that Binion was responsible for his own overdose death and, in 2003, the court vacated the convictions of Tabish and Murphy and ordered a new trial. Both were retried in 2004 and acquitted.

**2000: Christopher DiStefano** was convicted of the April 1996 murder of his high school girlfriend, Christine Burgerhoff, in Lackawanna County, Pennsylvania, following an eleven-hour interrogation that ended in his confession written by detectives and signed by him. The interrogation, which was not taped, was filled with direct and indirect threats, altered by offers of leniency. He was convicted of third-degree murder in February 2000, and sentenced to fifteen to forty years in prison. The Pennsylvania Superior Court vacated that conviction in 2001, ruling that DiStefano's confession had been coerced, and ordered a new trial. Without the confession, however, prosecutors had no case. They nevertheless convinced DiStefano to plead no contest to misdemeanor involuntary manslaughter, and he was released.

**2001: Antonino "Nino" Lyons** was convicted of drug trafficking, carjacking, and distributing counterfeit clothing in a federal case in Cocoa, Florida, where Lyons owned a chain of clothing stores. Federal prosecutors offered the testimony of twenty-six convicted felons against Lyons at his 2001 trial, these prison informants stating that Lyons had sold them more than $6 million in cocaine. No other evidence—drugs, testimony from nonfelons, wiretaps, tape recordings—supported the questionable statements of these witnesses. On appeal, Lyons's attorneys provided to the court many letters from federal prisoners who stated that they had refused to provide perjured statements against Lyons to federal prosecutors in exchange for reductions of their sentences. His attorneys also provided the appeals court with exculpatory documents that were belatedly given to the defense. Those documents, the court determined, proved that there was no reliable evidence against him. In 2004, a federal judge vacated Lyons's conviction, dismissed all charges against him, and ordered his release from prison.

**2002: Angela Canning** was convicted and sentenced to life in prison in London, England, for murdering her three children, in 1989, 1991, and 1999, although her defense counsel argued that the deaths had been caused by Sudden Infant Death Syndrome (SIDS), or, as it is called in England, cot death. Much of the forensic evidence or testimony that brought about her conviction had been provided by Professor Sir Roy Meadow, whose statements were later discredited (he had testified in numerous cases, presenting statistics that had no support in reality that sent several women to prison). The Court of Appeals overturned Canning's conviction in 2003 and set her free.

**2002:** In March 2002, **Julie Rea Kirkpatrick** was convicted on circumstantial evidence of stabbing to death her ten-year-old son, Joel Kirkpatrick, as he slept in his bedroom in Lawrenceville, Illinois, on October 13, 1997. Kirkpatrick, who was sentenced to sixty-five years in prison, told police that a masked intruder had invaded her home, murdered her son, and attacked her, hitting her and stabbing her in the arm before he fled by smashing through two glass doors. Her chief accuser was her ex-husband, Len Kirkpatrick, who had recently become a deputy sheriff and had reportedly vowed to "destroy" his wife, who had been in a bitter custody suit over the custody of their son. After her case was featured on the TV show *20/20,* serial killer Tommy Lynn Sells confessed to the murder. In 2004, Kirkpatrick's conviction was vacated on the grounds that the prosecutor had no legal authority to try her. In 2006, she was acquitted in a second trial.

**2002: Dominque Brim**, fifteen, was convicted of retail fraud and felony assault after leaving a Sears store on April 15, 2002, in Lincoln Park, Michigan, taking more than $1,300 in unpaid merchandise and biting a security guard when he attempted to stop her. After being arrested, the suspect was taken to a police station where she gave her name as Dominque Brim, along with her address and stated that she was fifteen years old. Two weeks later, Brim was charged, although she claimed that she had not been at the Sears store on April 15. After Sears employees identified Brim as the culprit, a judge convicted Brim. Sears officials later checked their security video cameras and realized that the person involved in the April 15 incident was not Brim. That person was later identified as twenty-five-year-old Chalaunda Latham, who was a friend of Brim's sister and used Brim's identity when stopped by the Sears security guard. Before Brim was sentenced, a judge vacated her conviction and exonerated her. Latham was not charged since Sears employees had already wrongly identified Brim as the culprit.

**2002:** Texas Governor Rick Perry (2000– ) exonerated **Thomas Wayne Williams** by issuing him a full pardon after he had been wrongly convicted and sentenced to life imprisonment on drug charges that were later proven to be fabricated by a ring of corrupt Dallas, Texas, police officers who were shaking down persons for payoffs.

**2002:** On March 6, 2000, a car crash in Seattle, Washington, killed David Taylor and critically injured **Michael Lee Sipin**, who was later convicted of vehicular homicide—his blood alcohol level at the time was

11—although he maintained he had been the passenger, not the driver. Sipin's conviction was vacated in 2005, when an appeals court ruled that the prosecution had used a computer program named PC-Crash to simulate the March 6 crash, while an expert of that program did not provide to the jury at Sipin's trial an accounting for multiple impacts in the crash and the changing dimensions and angles inside the vehicle. Further exonerating Sipin were eyewitnesses, who testified that he was not the driver of the car and that Taylor had been behind the wheel. Sipin's trial was the first such case where such crash software was presented in Washington.

**2003**: After a fire broke out in the Cass County (Missouri) Medical Center on January 24, 2001, twenty-year-old **Jennifer Hall**, a respiratory therapist, was charged with committing arson, which caused more than $23,000 in damage. She was convicted and sent to prison, remaining at the women's maximum security facility at Vandalia from July 25, 2003, to July 23, 2004, until a judge vacated her conviction. A second defense attorney hired an expert to examine the evidence of the fire and discovered a copper head at the end of a wire that had caused a short and had created the fire. Prosecutors nevertheless retried Hall in 2005, but a jury, when reviewing the new evidence, acquitted her.

**2003:** In November 2001, Susan Christie disappeared from her apartment in Perth, Australia. Her estranged husband, **Rory Kirk Christie**, was charged with her murder, although the woman's body was never found. Christie, in his defense, claimed that after their marriage broke up, his wife had become an alcoholic, that "she stumbled down that path and subsequently she'd gone missing. They charged me with her disappearance." A very small quantity of blood was found in the missing woman's home, and a drop of blood from a nosebleed was found on one of Christie's ties, and this became the only evidence that brought about Christie's conviction and life sentence in 2003. An expert on blood-splattering, however, later showed in an appeal that the evidence used at Christie's trial was insufficient for a conviction. Christie's conviction was overturned, and he was set free, going to live in Manitoba, Canada, where he was rejoined with his young son, who had been living there with his grandparents after his mother's disappearance. His attorneys had worked at no cost, and the defense reportedly cost $1 million to bring about Christie's exoneration.

**2003: Christopher Bennett** was charged with vehicular homicide after the van in which he was riding crashed in May 2001 on a street in Paris Township (Stark County), Ohio. Killed in the crash was Ronald Young, forty-two. Neither Bennett nor Young had been wearing seat belts. Bennett had fled the crash, fearing that he would be wrongly accused of the accident, and remained at large for two years. He entered a guilty plea on the poor advice of his attorney, who told him that he would get a lesser sentence in light of the fact that the prosecution had an eyewitness who would put him behind the wheel and that state crash expert Toby Wagner (a state trooper) would testify that he was the driver. (Wagner's testimony was later refuted by crash reconstruction expert Ricky Stansifer.) In February 2003, Bennett was found guilty and sentenced to prison for nine years. After several months in prison, his amnesia, which he had suffered from the crash, wore off, and he vividly recalled the crash, claiming that he had not been the driver, but that Young had been behind the wheel. This was later supported by a witness, and his defense attorneys, along with the Ohio Innocence Project, provided a car crash expert who showed that Young's injuries were those consistent with hitting an airbag and the van had only an airbag for the driver, while Bennett's injuries had been received by striking the windshield while sitting on the passenger side of the van. Bennett's conviction was vacated by the Fifth District Court of Appeals in 2006.

**2003:** In February 1999, **John Robert Ballard**, a white man, reported to police in Golden Gate, Florida, that five persons in a car had driven past his neighbor's apartment and fired shots into a bedroom window. The occupants of that residence were nineteen-year-old Jennifer Jones and twenty-two-year-old William Patin. Based on Ballard's descriptions, one person in the car, a known drug gang member, was charged with the shooting. Ballard attended a going-away party at the Jones-Patin apartment on March 6, 1999. The couple had announced that they were relocating to Texas. (Police later surmised that their decision to move had been based upon the month earlier drive-by shooting, which officers believed was caused by a drug dispute with Jones who was a known dealer of marijuana and who kept large sums of cash in her bedroom, where she sold the drug, and competing drug distributors.) Two days later, friends and relatives found Jones and Patin bludgeoned to death in their apartment. The coroner found that, through his examination of the blood splatter, the couple had been killed while standing upright and had violently defended themselves from several persons who had administered the death blows with either bats, pipes, or other objects. Ballard, who had a string of burglary convictions from 1986, became the chief suspect in the case because he lived across the street from the slain couple, was often in their home socializing, and reportedly had left his fingerprints in the home and one of his hairs was reportedly found clutched in the dead hand of Jennifer Jones. In May 2001, he was charged with first-degree robbery (of an estimated $1,000, an amount seen by a friend in Jones's possession at the farewell party) and first-degree murder of both Jones and Patin. The hair evidence figured largely against Ballard, although an expert forensic witness stated that since Ballard was a regular visitor to the Jones-Patin apartment, the hair from his arm could have been easily transferred from a carpet or upholstery to Jones's hand. Five other hairs were found in Jones's hand that did not belong to Ballard. The Ballard fingerprints found in the apartment were not on the bodies, but on furniture. After the prosecution rested its case, Ballard's attorneys asked for a judgment of acquittal, based on the argument that the prosecution had not proven its case beyond a reasonable doubt and that the fingerprint and hair evidence had been left by their client at the murder scene before the killings occurred. Circuit Court Judge Lauren Miller denied the motion. After the jury convicted Ballard of robbery and murder, Judge Miller, on May 23, 2003, sentenced him to fifteen years in prison for the robbery and to death for the two murders (the jury had voted 9–3 for the death penalty). The convictions and sentences were appealed, and the Florida Supreme Court agreed with defense attorneys that Ballard had been convicted on circumstantial evidence that was insufficient and left reasonable doubt. On February 23, 2006, the court overturned the convictions of robbery and murder, vacated those convictions, and ordered a judgment of an acquittal. The thirty-seven-year-old Ballard was then released from the Union Correctional Institution at Raiford, Florida.

**2003: Angel M. DeAngelo** was convicted and sentenced to life in prison in April 2003 for murdering Brooklyn gang member Thomas Palazzotto. His conviction was overturned in 2004 after federal Judge John Gleason learned that witnesses testifying against DeAngelo had provided perjured testimony and that one of them, a gang leader, might have been the actual killer. In ordering DeAngelo's release, Judge Gleason stopped short of stating that federal prosecutors had prior knowledge of the perjury. DeAngelo was a working man, who had never belonged to any gang.

**2003: Malik Taj Mohammad** was arrested and charged with the murder of Malkani Bibi over a property dispute in Pakistan. Relatives of the slain Bibi told court officials that they had buried the victim, who had been kidnapped and killed by Mohammad. He was convicted on this testimony and sent to prison for life. Bibi, however, was found very much alive in 2006, living in the eastern Pakistan city of Gujarat, where she had been imprisoned in 2004 for theft. The Supreme Court of Pakistan, after seeing Bibi alive, vacated Mohammad's conviction and ordered his release in 2006, ordering a lower court to conduct an investigation to determine how a man could be convicted and imprisoned for a crime that never happened. It was not determined just whose body Bibi's relatives had buried when making their false accusations, but Mohammad's defense attorneys accused the accusers of a conspiracy in their effort to acquire the property, which had been originally in dispute.

**2004**: Based on the statements of one woman and the alleged statements of several child victims, eighteen persons were tried in Pas-de-Calais, France, charged with being members of a secret pedophile network that preyed upon children. Of the eighteen persons, one committed suicide while in prison awaiting trial, four admitted the crimes, and thirteen others denied any responsibility, these thirteen later being exonerated as having been wrongly convicted through the inept court procedures of the presiding magistrate, Fabrice Burgaud. The massive wrongful convictions had been termed the **Outreau Affair.**

**2004: Reshenda Strickland** was convicted of shoplifting in Clark County, Washington, based on the testimony of two eyewitnesses. While Strickland served out a jail sentence, a surveillance tape of the store revealed that Strickland's sister, who had originally claimed to have been in Atlanta at the time of her sister's arrest, was the real thief. Reshenda Strickland was released with apologies after she had spent three months in jail.

**2005: Corey Eason** of McLean County, Illinois, was convicted in March 2005 of three counts of failing to notify the police of his change of address after having been posted on the Illinois sex offender registry on the Internet since 2002. Eason, while awaiting sentence, contacted officials to state that he had never been convicted of any sex-related crime, and, in fact, his name had been posted after he had been released from prison in 2002, following a drug-related conviction (dealing in cocaine). The Illinois State Police investigated Eason's claims and determined that he was correct. His name had been wrongly added to the sex offender list on the

Internet, but prosecutor Mark Messman could not explain the error, other than stating that "it's a system [the online Internet sex offender registry] run by people and mistakes can happen." Eason's three convictions were vacated, and all charges against him were dropped on October 25, 2005. (This was a classic example of the unreliability of information on the Internet, even when coming from police officials, and where libel is routine and rampant.)

**2005: Lisa Hansen**, twenty-five, was convicted of stealing her company receipts, although she claimed that she had made the deposit in a bank depository in Grand Rapids, Michigan, on September 3, 2005. She was fined $400 and sentenced to perform forty hours of community service after her attorney urged her to plead guilty to avoid a more severe sentence. Prior to her conviction, she had failed a lie detector test. A security official for the bank testified at her trial that none of the many security cameras at the bank had recorded Hansen's presence on the night she claimed to have made the deposit. On August 9, 2006, a bank employee found the deposit bag from Hansen's firm lodged in the bank depository. A judge vacated Hansen's conviction, and she was officially exonerated. She said that the operator of the polygraph had unnerved her by accusing her of lying and pressuring her into making mistakes. The security official at the bank had no explanation of why his bank's security cameras had not recorded Hansen's visit to make the deposit. A similar wrongful conviction involved another misplaced bank deposit in Jackson, Michigan. (See **Robert Farnsworth Jr.**, Chronology, 1999.).

**2005:** New York Stock Exchange trader **David Finnerty** was convicted in a federal case of cheating customers by employing interpositioning of buy and sell orders (where, instead of matching those orders, a trader can repeatedly trade for his company's proprietary account, gleaning a slight difference in pricing). A federal judge in 2007 vacated Finnerty's conviction and entered a judgment of acquittal after the judge ruled that federal prosecutors failed to prove that interpositioning was fraudulent or was a deceptive practice.

**2006**: On February 27, 2006, a white man robbed a bar in West Palm Beach, Florida. The bartender was forced at gunpoint to turn over the receipts from the cash register before the robber fled. Some residents told police that **Cody Davis** had been bragging that he had committed several robberies in the area. Davis was arrested and charged with the robbery of the Foster's Too bar. Two witnesses identified him from a police photo array, but one witness said that the robber had a tattoo on his hand (Davis had no such tattoo). A ski mask has been found outside the bar, but witnesses never said that the robber had used a ski mask. It was nevertheless being tested during Davis's trial, information on that ongoing test never made known to Davis's defense counsel Sim Gershon. Davis was found guilty by a jury on October 16, 2006, and sentenced to three years in prison. Four months after Davis went to prison, DNA testing on the ski mask was completed by the Palm Beach County Sheriff's Office Crime Laboratory. The results showed another man's profile, matching Jeremy Prichard, who was then behind bars awaiting trial on unrelated charges. Prichard bore a distinctive tattoo. Confronted with the DNA evidence, Prichard confessed to the Foster's Too bar robbery, along with three other similar robberies. The District Attorney's Office immediately ordered Davis's release from prison, and he was set free on March 9, 2007.

# Filmography

**Note:** The following films appear under the A to Z names of real persons who have been wrongly convicted (or wrongly accused or imprisoned) throughout history and appear in the text of this work. Some film entries offer fictionalized characters known to be based on these actual persons. There are countless exclusively fictional examples of falsely accused persons appearing in films, *Ben Hur*, *To Kill a Mockingbird*, *Dark Passage*, *The Count of Monte Cristo*, *The Children's Hour*, *The Hunchback of Notre Dame*, and *My Cousin Vinny*, to name a few. This filmography addresses the best-known actual persons appearing in this work and does not claim to be all-inclusive. Where several films on the same subject were produced, the author selected the production most significantly representing that case while including as addenda in such entries other films on the subject. Each entry offers the film title, year of U.S. release, running time (at time of original release), country where the film was produced, producer and/or distributor, color or black-and-white, director, writer(s), leading players, and a brief synopsis.

## Emmanuel "Manny" Balestrero
### (Chapter VII)
*The Wrong Man*; 1956; 105 min.; U.S.; Warner Bros.; b/w; directed by Alfred Hitchcock; writers: Angus MacPhail, Maxwell Anderson (based on a story by Anderson); leading players: Henry Fonda (as Balestrero), Vera Miles, Anthony Quayle, Harold J. Stone.

The true story of a bass player at New York's Stork Club who is mistakenly identified as a robber. Fonda gives a captivating performance as Balestrero in this frightening and claustrophobic tale. He seemed to specialize in film roles portraying victimized characters (*The Oxbow Incident*, *Twelve Angry Men*, John Ford's *The Fugitive* and *The Grapes of Wrath*, Preston Sturges's *The Lady Eve* and *Gideon's Trumpet*). Master filmmaker Hitchcock specialized in making films about such fictional victims of circumstance, more than half of his career films dedicated to the subject, including *The Lodger*, *The 39 Steps*, *Young and Innocent*, *Rebecca*, *Suspicion*, *Saboteur*, *Spellbound*, *Dial M for Murder*, *North by Northwest*, and *To Catch a Thief*. I knew Hitchcock well, and when I asked about his penchant for such films, he told me that his success was based on "showing the character victimized not only once, but over and over, until everyone in that theater is rooting for him or her, and that is one of mankind's greatest passions—saving the other person from an awful fate that could engulf anyone and everyone in that theater."

## Robert Elliott Burns
### (Chapter XII)
*I Am a Fugitive from a Chain Gang*; 1932; 93 min.; U.S.; The Vitaphone Corporation/Warner Bros.; b/w; directed by Mervyn LeRoy; writers: Howard J. Green (based on the book, *I Am a Fugitive from a Georgia Chain Gang* by Robert Elliott Burns); leading players: Paul Muni, Glenda Farrell, Helen Vinson, Noel Francis, Preston Foster, Allen Jenkins, Berton Churchill, Edward Ellis, David Landau, Hale Hamilton, Sally Blane, Louise Carter.

One of the most terrifying social docudramas ever produced, this film depicts the tragic life of Robert Elliott Burns, who was wrongly convicted and sentenced to a Georgia chain gang (the state is not specified in the film, but it was nevertheless banned in Georgia), with an utterly captivating performance by the great actor Paul Muni, essaying the role of Burns (called James Allen in the film). Following his escape, Muni makes a new life, marrying Farrell to silence her after she discovers he is a fugitive, and rising to business and social prominence, only to be betrayed by Farrell when he falls in love with Vinson (the act of a woman scorned). He returns to serve out a short term as promised by the state where he had been imprisoned. But the state reneges on its promise and, once Muni is back on the chain gang, tells him he will serve out a lengthy term for his escape on top of his original sentence. He again escapes, as did the real Burns, meeting briefly with Vinson at the end of the film, where he hears a noise and retreats into darkness. "How do you live?" Vinson calls after him. "I steal!" comes back the reply from a faceless man without a future in a darkening fadeout. Director LeRoy holds nothing back in this stark and realistic production, showing the brutal use of sweat boxes, savage whippings, and other sadistic tortures inflicted on chain gang inmates, a film that horrified and enraged the American public and eventually brought about sweeping prison reforms in the South. Burns was also profiled in the 1987 made-for-TV film, *The Man Who Broke 1,000 Chains*, directed by Daniel Mann and starring Val Kilmer as Burns.

### Rubin "Hurricane" Carter
#### (Chapter V)

*The Hurricane*; 1999; 145 min.; U.S.; Azoff Entertainment–Beacon Communications/Universal Pictures; color; directed by Norman Jewison; writers: Armyan Bernstein, Dan Gordon (based on Rubin Carter's book, *The Sixteenth Round*, and the book, *Lazarus and the Hurricane* by Sam Chaiton and Terry Swinton); leading players: Denzel Washington (as Rubin Carter), Vicellous Reon Shannon, Deborah Kara Unger, Liev Schreiber, John Hannah.

This film features a powerful performance from Washington as middleweight boxer Rubin "Hurricane" Carter, who was wrongly convicted of a triple murder and sentenced to three life terms. It also shows how a youthful black American boy and his Canadian mentor, after reading Carter's book, work for his exoneration against a decidedly racist establishment which doggedly preserves that travesty of justice.

### Alice Lynne "Lindy" Chamberlain
#### (Chapter IV)

*A Cry in the Dark* (a.k.a. *Evil Angels*); 1988; 120 min.; Aus.; Warner Bros.; color; directed by Fred Schepisi; writers: Robert Casewell (based on the book by John Bryson); leading players: Meryl Streep, Sam Neill,

Dale Rees, David Hoflin, Jason Reason, Lauren Shepherd, Bethany Ann Prickett, Alison O'Connell, Aliza Dason.

Streep is riveting as Lindy Chamberlain, the wrongly convicted mother who claimed that a dingo killed her missing daughter in the Australian outback. The circumstantial evidence against her is shown to be flimsy, but prejudicial publicity and baseless suspicion bring about her imprisonment. She was later exonerated.

### David Dowaliby
#### (Chapter XIV)

*Gone in the Night*; 1996; 190 min.; U.S.; CBS Television; color; directed by Bill L. Norton; writers: David Protess and Rob Warden (based on their book by the same title); leading players: Shannon Doherty, Kevin Dillon, James Anthony, Edward Asner, Jeanne Averill, Michael Brandon, Kevin Brief, Billy Burke, Devon Arielle Cahill, Timothy Carhart.

Dillon dynamically portrays Dowaliby, an Illinois father who was wrongly convicted of murdering a child in a sensational kidnapping-murder case, where prejudicial publicity was a decisive factor in bringing about that wrongful conviction. The film diligently shows how research and exhaustive investigation finally brought about Dowaliby's release from prison and his exoneration.

### Alfred Dreyfus
#### (Chapter I)

*The Life of Emile Zola*; 1937; 116 min.; U.S.; Warner Bros.; b/w; directed by William Dieterle; writers: Norman Reilly Raine, Heinz Herald, Geza Herczeg (based on the Matthew Josephson book, *Zola and His Time*); leading players: Paul Muni (as Zola, Academy Award), Joseph Schildkraut (as Dreyfus), Gale Sondergaard, Donald Crisp, Henry O'Neill (as Colonel Picquart).

A masterful film showing the framing and wrongful conviction of French army officer Dreyfus, the cover-up of his imprisonment on Devil's Island, and how writer Zola led the crusade to bring about his exoneration. Many other English-speaking and foreign films were made on the subject, most notably *The Dreyfus Case*, a 1930 German production with Fritz Kortner playing Dreyfus; *Dreyfus*, a 1931 British film with Cedric Hardwicke essaying Dreyfus; the 1958 British film *I Accuse!* with Jose Ferrer as Dreyfus; and the superb 1991 made-for-TV film, *Prisoner of Honor*, with Kenneth Colley as Dreyfus and Richard Dreyfuss as Colonel Picquart.

## Leo Max Frank
### (Chapter XI)

*They Won't Forget*; 1937; 95 min.; U.S.; First National/Warner Bros.; b/w; directed by Mervyn LeRoy; writers: Robert Rossen, Aben Kandel (based on the Ward Greene novel, *Death in the Deep South*); leading players: Claude Rains, Gloria Dickson, Edward Norris, Otto Kruger, Allyn Joslyn, Lana Turner, Linda Perry, Elisha Cook Jr., Cy Kendall, Elisabeth Risdon.

Norris, a northern-born teacher at a southern business school, is wrongly convicted of murdering one of his young students, Turner, by a ruthless prosecutor, Rains. He is later lynched by a mob. This stark, relentless film is wholly based on the 1913 railroading of Leo Max Frank in Atlanta, although Frank's Jewish heritage is not highlighted in the Norris profile. Turner, as the murder victim, appears only briefly at the beginning of the film, walking down a street in a tight sweater as her debut, one that secured for her a position as a contract player at MGM, where she later became a reigning star. The most terrifying aspect of this conscientious production is Rains's mesmerizing performance as a prosecutor who will stop at nothing—including the framing of an innocent man—to achieve his political ambitions. After he learns that Norris has been lynched, he turns to a reporter (Joslyn), who has created public prejudice against Norris in his mob-mongering articles, and Joslyn says, "I wonder if he did it." The Frank case was also profiled in exacting and horrifying detail in one of the best docudramas ever produced, *The Murder of Mary Phagan*, a 1988 made-for-TV film, starring Jack Lemmon as Georgia Governor John Slaton, who proved that Frank was innocent following his conviction and commuted his death sentence to life imprisonment but could not prevent Frank's lynching. Slaton's political career was destroyed by anti-Semitic politicians Tom Watson (Robert Prosky) and Hugh Dorsey (Richard Jordan), who railroaded Frank while knowing all along that a conniving black janitor, Jim Conley (chillingly portrayed by Charles S. Dutton), had raped and murdered the girl.

## Lennell Geter
### (Chapter XI)

*Guilty of Innocence: The Lennell Geter Story*; 1987; 100 min.; U.S.; Embassy Communications; color; directed by Richard T. Heffron; writer: Harold Gast; leading players: Dorian Harewood, Dabney Coleman, Hoyt Axton, Dennis Lipscomb, Debbi Morgan, Marshall Colt, Gary Grubbs, Victor Love, Paul Winfield, Alan Ackles, Dan Ammerman.

This made-for-TV film accurately profiles the false arrest and wrongful conviction of Geter (portrayed by Harewood) for a robbery he did not commit.

## Clarence Earl Gideon
### (Chronology, 1961)

*Gideon's Trumpet*; 1980; 104 min.; U.S.; Hallmark Hall of Fame Productions/CBS Television; color; directed by Robert E. Collins; writers: David W. Rintels (based on the book by Anthony Lewis); leading players: Henry Fonda, Jose Ferrer, John Houseman, Fay Wray, Sam Jaffe, Dean Jagger, Nicholas Pryor, William Prince, Lane Smith, Richard McKenzie, Dolph Sweet, Ford Rainey, David Sheiner, J. Patrick McNamara.

Excellent made-for-TV production where Fonda shines as Gideon, an uneducated ex-convict sent to prison for a crime he did not commit because he had no legal counsel at trial. The film depicts how he educates himself in prison and writes a compelling letter to the U.S. Supreme Court, which brings about judicial reform, making it mandatory that all defendants receive legal counsel.

## Timothy Hennis
### (Chronology, 1986)

*Innocent Victims*; 1996; 133 min.; U.S.; American Broadcasting System; color; directed by Gilbert Cates; writers: Scott Whisnant, Guy Waldron (based on Whisnant's book); leading players: Rick Schroeder, John Corbett, Tom Irwin, Howard Hesseerman, Rue McClanahan, John P. Connolly, Liza Snyder, Don McManus, Leon Russom, Rondi Reed.

Corbett effectively plays the role of U.S. army sergeant Timothy Hennis, who was convicted of murdering a woman and her two children in North Carolina, a heinous crime he did not commit. His attorney, portrayed by Tom Irwin, proves that his client has been the victim of mistaken identity when bringing about his exoneration.

## Inquisition
### (Chapter XI)

*Captain from Castile*; 1948; 130 min.; U.S.; Twentieth Century Fox; color; directed by Henry King; writers: Lamar Trotti (based on the novel by Samuel Shellabarger); leading players: Tyrone Power, Jean Peters, Cesar Romero, Lee J. Cobb, John Sutton, Thomas Gomez, Alan Mowbray, Antonio Moreno, Barbara Lawrence, George Zucco, Roy Roberts, Marc Lawrence, Jay Silverheels.

The always commanding Power appears in this swashbuckling epic as a young Spanish nobleman forced to flee Spain after ostensibly dispatching Sutton, a member of the dreaded Inquisition, who has caused Power's teenage sister to be murdered through torture when claiming she was a heretic. Accompanied by friend Cobb and adoring servant girl Peters, Power joins the exploratory command of Hernán Cortés (Romero at his grinning best) and sees many adventures in the New World, where Cortés decides to conquer all of Latin America. Sutton, however, has survived and arrives in the New World to threaten Power but is killed. This sweeping historical epic, superbly directed by King, wonderfully enacted by a great cast, and with one of the most stirring film scores ever offered (*Conquest* by Alfred Newman), is the stuff of great adventure. But the story is pervaded by the underlying threat of the dreaded Inquisition, where Sutton, in his best role, becomes the epitome of evil itself. As the Inquisition accompanied Cortés to the New World, it sailed earlier with Columbus, shown in many films about that great explorer, including the 1949 U.S. film, *Christopher Columbus*, with Frederic March in the leading role, and the 1985 U.S. made-for-TV production, *Christopher Columbus*. In 1992, insidious representatives of the Inquisition were profiled in two films—*1492: Conquest of Paradise*, and *Christopher Columbus: The Discovery* (in which the great Orson Welles plays the leading inquisitor, Torquemada). The Inquisition rears its grotesque head in many other films, including all of the versions of the *Pit and the Pendulum*, the most notable of these being the 1962 U.S. version with Vincent Price. Mel Brooks intended to ridicule the Inquisition in a segment of his 1981 U.S. film spoof *History of the World, Part I*, but audiences found no humor in torture and agonizing death. The 1984 Spanish film, *Akelarre*, profiles the Inquisition's trials at Logrono of the accused witches of Zugarramurdi in Navarre. In the 2006 U.S. film, *The Fountain*, the Inquisition is shown to be active in a plot to assassinate Queen Isabella of Spain.

### Harold Israel
### (Chapter VIII)

*Boomerang*, 1947; 88 min.; U.S.; Twentieth Century Fox; b/w; directed by Elia Kazan (won Academy Award for Best Director); writer: Richard Murphy (based on an article by Fulton Oursler); leading players: Dana Andrews, Jane Wyatt, Lee J. Cobb, Arthur Kennedy, Sam Levine, Taylor Holmes, Robert Keith, Ed Begley, Karl Malden, Barry Kelley, Cara Williams.

A finely crafted docudrama that profiles the shooting of a priest in a small Connecticut town and shows how a drifter (Kennedy) is arrested and falsely accused of the crime, then grilled by police without sleep until he signs a confession. The prosecutor, Andrews, has doubts about the man's guilt and, at the risk of his political career, conducts his own investigation, challenging and dismissing the many eyewitness accounts that prove to be mistaken, as well as showing in court, at hazard to his life, how Kennedy's gun could not have been used to kill the priest. Based on the Harold Israel case and the actual prosecutor in that case, Homer Cummings (who later became the U.S. attorney general), this is a masterpiece of taut film noir by stellar director Kazan.

### Joan of Arc
### (Chapter XI)

*Joan of Arc*; 1948; 145 min.; U.S.; RKO Radio Pictures; color; directed by Victor Fleming; writer: Maxwell Anderson (based on his play); leading players: Ingrid Bergman, Jose Ferrer, Francis L. Sullivan, Ward Bond, Shepperd Strudwick, J. Carrol Naish, Gene Lockhart, John Emery, Leif Erickson, Cecil Kellaway, Selene Royale, Robert Barrat, Jimmy Lydon, Rand Brooks, Roman Bohnen, Irene Rich, Nestor Paiva, Richard Derr, Ray Teal, George Coulouris, David Bond, George Zucco, Richard Ney.

An epic production in which Bergman, one of the world's greatest actresses, magnificently portrays the inspired Joan. Ferrer is the cautious dauphin, later Charles VII of France, Bond the loyal La Hire, and the bloated Sullivan convincingly portrays the conniving and underhanded Pierre Cauchon, who entraps Joan into confessing, an admission that she later retracts and for which she is burned to death at the stake. Bergman's death scene is as moving as the death scene of Maria Falconetti in the 1928 silent French classic on the same subject, *The Passion of Joan of Arc*, directed by the legendary Carl Theodor Dryer, although Dryer shot most of this film in close-ups, where Falconetti's every wince and blink is captured, taxing the tolerance of the viewer. Cecil B. DeMille offered a credible 1917 silent production, *Joan the Woman*, with Geraldine Farrar as the Maid. A 1929 silent French production, *Saint Joan—The Maid*, offers Simone Genevois in the lead role, and Angela Salloker essays Joan in the 1935 German production, *Das Mädchen Johanna*. Michele Morgan played Joan in the 1953 episodic French film, *Destinees*, and eccentric director Otto Preminger offered a petulant Joan in his 1957 British production, *Saint Joan*, with Jean Seberg in the lead role. Hedy Lamarr is Joan in brief scenes from the 1957 U.S. production of *The Story of Mankind*, and Florence Carrez plays the indomitable girl warrior in the 1962 French production, *The Trial of Joan of Arc*. Alida Valli, another great actress, appears briefly and movingly as Joan in *The Miracle of the Bells*, 1948, a film written by Ben Hecht. The most recent production dealing with the Maid was helmed by director Luc Besson in the 1999 French production, *The Messenger: The Story of Joan of Arc*, which has Mila Jovovich appearing as a temperamental teenage Joan.

### John Arthur "Jack" Johnson
#### (Chapter XI)

*The Great White Hope*, 1970, 103 min.: U.S.; Twentieth Century Fox; color; directed by Martin Ritt; writer: Howard Sackler (based on his play); James Earl Jones, Jane Alexander, Lou Gilbert, Joel Fluellen, Chester Morris, Robert Webber, Marlene Warfield, R. G. Armstrong, Hal Holbrook, Beah Richards, Moses Gunn, George Ebeling, Larry Pennell.

Jones is riveting as the black heavyweight fighter who struggles to overcome racial prejudice, maintain a relationship with a white female companion (Alexander), win the championship and lose it, before going to prison for a crime he did not commit. Although this is a fictionalized version of Jack Johnson's flamboyant career and lifestyle (he is called Jack Jefferson in the film and play), it faithfully follows real-life events and personalities, a disturbing but enlightening production that established Jones as a first-line actor. Johnson appears as himself in several silent films, *As the World Rolls On*, 1921, *The Black Thunderbolt*, 1922, *For His Mother's Sake*, 1922, and in many of his filmed fights, including the classic bouts with Jim Jeffries in 1910 and with the giant Jess Willard, to whom he lost his crown in 1916. A straightforward documentary about him, *Unforgivable Blackness: The Rise and Fall of Jack Johnson*, was produced in 2004, with film clips of Johnson.

### Donald Lang
#### (Chapter XIV)

*Dummy*; 1979; 96 min.; U.S.; The Konigsberg Company/Warner Bros. Television; color; directed by Frank Perry; writer: Ernest Tidyman (based on his book); leading players: Paul Sorvino, LeVar Burton, Brian Dennehy, Rose Gregorio, Gregg Henry.

An impacting made-for-TV production that shows how Sorvino, playing deaf attorney Lowell Myers (who died of a brain aneurysm on November 7, 2006, at age 76) defends the deaf and dumb Lang (skillfully essayed by Burton) in a sensational Chicago murder case.

### Joseph Majczek and Theodore Marcinkiewicz
#### (Chapter I)

*Call Northside 777*; 1948; 111 min.; U.S.; Twentieth Century Fox; b/w; directed by Henry Hathaway; writers: Leonard Hoffman (based on newspaper articles by James P. McGuire of the Chicago *Sun*); leading players: James Stewart, Richard Conte, Lee J. Cobb, Helen Walker, Betty Garde, Kasia Orzazewski, Joanne De Bergh, Howard Smith, Moroni Olsen, J. M. Kerrigan, John McIntire, Paul Harvey, George Tyne, Michael Chapin, E. G. Marshall, Richard Rober, Henry Kulky.

Filmed on location in Chicago, where the crime occurred, this fascinating docudrama has Stewart in the role of a skeptical newspaperman who writes a human interest story about a scrub woman who placed an ad in his paper, asking anyone with information that might exonerate her imprisoned son to call her and receive a $5,000 reward, money she saved over a decade by washing floors. Encouraged by his editor, Cobb, to seek more information, Stewart begins an exhaustive and harrowing investigation that reveals official corruption and negligence that sent Conte (who is playing a role model of Joseph Majczek) and Tyne (essaying a role model of Theodore Marcinkiewicz) to prison for a robbery-murder in the early 1930s. The techniques of the investigative reporter are shown in detail as Stewart overcomes one obstacle after another, but cannot budge an eyewitness (Garde, in a small but jarring role), who has falsely testified against the two imprisoned men for unstated motives. Stewart painfully unearths other evidence, however, and finally brings about exoneration and freedom for the wrongly convicted men. This excellent production, with its literate script, crisp direction, and stellar cast, stands as a hallmark film dealing with the wrongly convicted and offers one of Stewart's finest performances.

### Donald Marshall, Jr.
#### (Chapter XI)

*Justice Denied*; 1989; 98 min.; Can., National Film Board of Canada; color; directed by Paul Cowan; writer: Cowan; leading players: Troy Adams, J. Winston

Carroll, Nicola Lipman, Daniel MacIvor, Peter Mac-Neill, Billy Mersasty, Vincent Murray.

This incisive film tells the shocking story of how Marshall, a Canadian Indian, was singled out as a killer, when all evidence showed that someone else committed the crime, a case where prejudice apparently tainted the police investigation and corrupted the methods and modus operandi of prosecutors. Marshall spent eleven years behind bars for a crime he did not commit.

## Mary, Queen of Scots
### (Chapter XI)

*Mary of Scotland*; 1936; 123 min.; U.S.; RKO Radio Pictures; b/w; directed by John Ford; leading players: Katherine Hepburn, Fredric March, Florence Eldridge, Douglas Walton, John Carradine, Robert Barrat, Gavin Muir, Ian Keith, Moroni Olsen, Ralph Forbes, Alan Mowbray, Frieda Inescort, Donald Crisp, David Torrence, Molly Lamont.

Hepburn presents a stirring performance of the willful Mary, and March is a dynamic Earl of Bothwell in this historical epic faultlessly directed by Ford. Hepburn as Mary is shown arriving in Scotland to take her uneasy crown with the sanction of bickering clan leaders, who later murder her closest aide, Rizzio (Carradine), and plot against her through her indecisive husband, Darnley (Walton), who is also murdered until Bothwell comes to her momentary rescue. With Bothwell absent and clan leaders seeking to usurp her, Mary flees to England, where her cousin, Elizabeth I (Eldridge, who, incidentally was March's wife) imprisons her and later allows a kangaroo court and false evidence to wrongly convict her and send her to the executioner's block. Of the many films made about Mary, Ford's version is the most comprehensive and certainly the most moving, although it cuts some corners on facts. In the silent era, Mary was played by Mary Fuller in a 1913 U.S. production entitled *Mary Stuart*. She was profiled by Fay Compton in the 1923 British production, *Loves of Mary, Queen of Scots*, and Maisie Fisher played Mary in another British film in that same year, entitled *The Virgin Queen*. A year after the Ford film was released, Jacqueline Delubac played Mary in a French production, *The Pearls of the Crown*, and, in a 1940 German film, *Heart of a Queen*, Zarah Leander plays Mary. In 1962, an Italian production, *Seven Seas to Calais*, saw Esmeralda Ruspoli in the role of Mary, and Vanessa Redgrave essays the part in *Mary, Queen of Scots* in a 1971 British film.

## David Milgaard
### (Chapter IX)

*Milgaard*; 1999; 85 min.; Can.; Bar Harbour Films–Barna-Alper Productions–Marble Island Pictures/Alliance Atlantis Communications; color; directed by Stephen Williams; writers: Alan Di Fiore, Keith Ross Leckie; leading players: Ian Tracey, Gabrielle Rose, Tom Melissis, Garwin Sanford, Hrothgar Mathews, Robyn Driscoll, Jaimz Woolvett.

Tracey effectively plays David Milgaard, who was wrongly convicted of a terrible Canadian rape-murder, and how his attorneys crusaded for years to bring about his prison release and exoneration. The Milgaard case was one of the worst travesties in Canadian justice, as this film so well depicts.

## Thomas More
### (Chapter XI)

*A Man for All Seasons*, 1966; 120 min.; U.K.; Columbia Pictures Corporation; color; directed by Fred Zinnemann; writer: Robert Bolt (based on his play); leading players: Paul Scofield, Wendy Hiller, Leo McKern, Robert Shaw, Orson Welles, Susannah York, Nigel Davenport, John Hurt, Corin Readgrave, Colin Blakely, Cyril Luckham, Jack Gwillim, Vanessa Redgrave.

Superb biopic depicting the brilliant Thomas More (Scofield), onetime chancellor of England and close friend of King Henry VIII (Shaw), who is wrongly tried, convicted, and condemned for sedition when refusing to acknowledge the king's Act of Succession (which condoned his divorce from Catherine of Aragon and his bigamous marriage to Anne Boleyn). Scofield is masterful as the persecuted More, winning an Oscar for Best Actor, and McKern is perfectly insidious as the scheming prosecutor, Thomas Cromwell. The literate and inspiring script, which holds fast to the known facts, is superbly managed by pantheon director Zinnemann. More was also ably and accurately portrayed in two British films, essayed by William Squire in *Anne of the Thousand Days*, 1970, and enacted by Michael Goodliffe in *Henry VIII and His Six Wives*, 1972.

## Peter Reilly
### (Chapter X)

*A Death in Canaan*; 1978; 125 min.; U.S.; CBS Television; color; directed by Tony Richardson; writers: Joan Barthel, Spencer Eastman (based on Barthel's book): leading players: Stefanie Powers, Paul Clemens, Tom Atkins, Jacqueline Brooks, Brian Dennehy, Conchata Ferrell, Charles Haid, Floyd Levine, Kenneth McMillan.

This is an engrossing tale of a confused and exhausted teenage boy who confessed to murdering his mother, a crime he did not commit. Clemens gives a telling performance as the dazed and dumbfounded Peter Reilly, and Powers is outstanding as the female author, Barthel, who crusaded for his exoneration.

### Nicola Sacco and Bartolomeo Vanzetti
#### (Chapter XIV)

*Winterset*; 1936; 77 min.; U.S.; RKO Radio Pictures; b/w; directed by Alfred Santell; writers: Maxwell Anderson, Anthony Veiller (based on Anderson's play); Burgess Meredith, Margo, Eduardo Ciannelli, Maurice Moscovitch, Paul Guilfoyle, Edward Ellis, Stanley Ridges, Mischa Auer, John Carradine.

Based on the Sacco-Vanzetti case, where both men were executed for a 1921 robbery-murder in Massachusetts, Anderson focuses his play on the son of one of the immigrants (Vanzetti, believing most probably that he was innocent, but not including Sacco, who was most probably guilty) in the celebrated case. Meredith, in one of his best performances, plays the son of Bartolomeo Romagna (Carradine), who, after his father's execution, strives to find the truth by confronting an Italian gangster (Ciannelli), who was really responsible for the crime. Anderson undoubtedly believed that the Morello gang had committed the robbery-murder for which Vanzetti, who was most probably innocent according to the evidence in the case, was put to death. The subject was also profiled in a 1971 Italian film, *Sacco and Vanzetti*.

### Salem Witchcraft Trials
#### (Chapter XII)

*The Crucible*; 1996; 124 min.; U.S.; Twentieth Century Fox; color; director by Nicholas Hytner; writer: Arthur Miller (based upon his play); leading players: Daniel Day-Lewis, Winona Ryder, Paul Scofield, Joan Allen, Bruce Davison, Rob Campbell, Jeffrey Jones, Peter Vaughan, Karron Graves, Charlayne Woodward, Frances Conroy, Elizabeth Lawrence.

Superb filming of Miller's memorable play about the witchcraft mania that seized the small town of Salem, Massachusetts, where Puritan superstition and ignorance brought about the wrongful convictions and executions of more than twenty persons. Day-Lewis as John Proctor, victimized by one of the scheming witch girls, Ryder, gives a stunning performance as one of the tormented accused. The subject was also profiled in the 1921 silent film, *Witchcraft Through the Ages*, and, most notably, in *Maid of Salem*, 1937, directed by Frank Lloyd and starring Claudette Colbert and Fred MacMurray as young lovers caught up in the witch-hunts. A French film in 1957, *Les Sorcieres de Salem*, deals with the same subject, as does the 2002 made-for-TV production, *Salem Witch Trials*, directed by Joseph Sargent.

### Samuel Sheppard
#### (Chapter XIV)

*The Fugitive*; 1993; 130 min.; U.S.; Warner Bros.; color; directed by Andrew Davis; writers: Jeb Stuart, David Twohy, Roy Huggins; leading players: Harrison Ford, Tommy Lee Jones, Sela Ward, Julianne Moore, Joe Pantoliano, Andreas Katsulas, Jeroen Krabbe.

A far-fetched but exciting Chicago chase film, where a physician (Ford) is wrongly convicted of murdering his wife and sets out to track down the real killer, a one-armed man. This production is based on the sensational Cleveland murder of Dr. Sam Sheppard's wife and for which Sheppard was wrongly convicted. This fictional version of Sheppard's story originally began as a popular and long-running TV series entitled *The Fugitive* (1963–1967), starring David Janssen, which also produced as a TV series under the same title (2000–2001). A small-budget film, *The Lawyer*, 1970, directed by Sidney J. Furie and starring Barry Newman as a wealthy attorney wrongly accused of murdering his wife, is also based on the Sheppard case. A 1975 made-for-TV film, *Guilty or Innocent: The Sam Sheppard Case*, starring George Peppard as Sheppard and Walter McGinn as his legendary lawyer, F. Lee Bailey, left viewers wondering about Sheppard's innocence. None of these productions should be confused with John Ford's 1947 classic film, *The Fugitive*, starring Henry Fonda as a Catholic priest persecuted in a Latin American country (Mexico, during the time of Alvaro Obregon's persecution of the Catholic Church in the mid-1920s).

### Jay C. Smith
#### (Chapter XV)

*Echoes of Darkness*; 1987; 250 min.; U.S.; New World Television; color; directed by Glenn Jordan; writer: Joseph Wambaugh (based on his book); leading players: Peter Coyote, Stockard Channing, Robert Loggia, Peter Boyle, Cindy Pickett, Gary Cole.

A made-for-TV miniseries that cleverly shows how the insidious William Bradfield Jr. (Coyote) framed Jay C. Smith (Loggia) for the vicious murder of Susan Reinert (Channing) and her two children (bodies never found).

## Arthur Allan Thomas
### (Chronology, 1971)

*Beyond Reasonable Doubt*; 1980; 129 min.; New Zealand; Endeavor Productions; color; directed by John Laing; writer: David Yallop; leading players: David Hemmings, John Hargreaves, Tony Barry, Martyn Sanderson, Grant Tilly, Diana Rowan, Ian Watkin.

In this well-made docudrama, Hargreaves gives a moving performance as Thomas, the simple farmer who trusted a police inspector (Hemmings), only to be wrongly convicted of murdering a farm couple outside a small New Zealand town.

# Glossary

**Note:** This glossary, containing more than 1,000 acronyms and 2,400 terms, applies to wrongly convicted persons and shows derivative source use by occupation genres (law enforcement, legal, medical, prison, sociological, underworld, etc.). Dates of first use of terms were found through my exclusive research in trial transcripts, published laws, police and legal records and documents, and the general literature of books, periodicals, and newspapers. I did not consult Internet sources for this glossary or the bibliography (below), as they are considered by all serious scholars to be generally unreliable as to identifiable sources of recognized authority and are based on the manipulative and malleable electronic status of facile corruptibility inherent in all free Internet information bases. These online information databases paradoxically disclaim the validity of their content and thereby admit to their uselessness as genuine reference databases. Terms chiefly apply to the United States and, to a lesser degree, the United Kingdom and other countries. Historical terms, though now obsolete, are included, as they apply to many of the deep historical cases profiled in this work. Although this glossary is not definitive, I believe it to be the most comprehensive offered to date for any such work.

## Acronyms

**AAAC**  American Association for the Advancement of Criminology.

**AAC**  1. American Academy of Criminalistics. 2. American Association of Criminology.

**AACFO**  American Association of Correctional Facility Officers.

**AACP**  American Association of Correctional Psychologists.

**AAFS**  American Academy of Forensic Sciences.

**AAIAN**  Association for the Advancement of Instruction about Alcohol and Narcotics.

**AALE**  Associate of Arts and Law Enforcement.

**AALL**  American Association of Law Libraries.

**A&R**  Assault and robbery.

**AAP**  Afro-American police.

**AAPL**  1. Afro-American Patrolmen's League. 2. All-American Policemen's League.

**AAPLE**  American Academy for Professional Law Enforcement.

**AAPP**  American Association of Police Polygraphists.

**AARC**  Association for the Advancement of Released Convicts.

**AASI**  American Association for Scientific Interrogation.

**AASP**  American Association for Social Psychiatry.

**AAWA**  American Automatic Weapons Association.

**AAWS**  American Association of Wardens and Superintendents.

**ABA**  American Bar Association.

**ABAJ**  *American Bar Association Journal.*

**ABC**  Aberrant behavior center.

**ABF**  American Bar Foundation.

**ABH**  Actual bodily harm.

**ABLE**  1. Action for Better Law Enforcement. 2. Advocates for Better Law Enforcement. 3. Advocates for Border Law Enforcement.

**AC**  After conviction.

**ACA**  1. American Correctional Association. 2. Anti-Corruption Agency. 3. Association of Correctional Administrators.

**ACAN**  Action Committee Against Narcotics.

**ACAP**  American Council on Alcohol Problems.

**ACC**  Assistant chief constable.

**ACCA**  American Correctional Chaplains Association.

**ACD**   Adjourn in contemplation of dismissal.

**ACEP**   American College of Emergency Physicians.

**ACF**   Anti-Crime Foundation.

**ACFSA**   American Correctional Food Service Association.

**ACGLA**   Alcoholism Council of Greater Los Angeles.

**ACI**   Adult correctional institution.

**ACIR**   Advisory Commission on Intergovernmental Relations.

**ACJ**   1. Advisory Council of Judges. 2. Arlington County Jail. 3. Associate in Criminal Justice.

**ACJA**   American Criminal Justice Association.

**ACJC**   Assembly Criminal Justice Committee.

**ACJHSIS**   Arkansas Criminal Justice/Highway Safety Information System.

**ACJS**   American Criminal Justice Society.

**ACLR**   *American Criminal Law Review.*

**ACLU**   American Civil Liberties Union.

**ACOP**   Association of Chief Officers of Police.

**ACP**   1. Academy for Contemporary (Criminal) Problems. 2. Association of Correctional Psychologists. 3. Automatic Colt pistol.

**ACR**   *American Criminal Review.*

**ACTL**   American College of Trial Lawyers.

**ACTO**   Advisory Council on the Treatment of Offenders.

**ACU**   1. Abused child unit. 2. Anticrime unit.

**ADA**   Assistant district attorney.

**ADAPCP**   Alcohol and Drug Abuse Prevention and Control Program.

**ADCO**   Alcohol and Drug Control Office (or Officer).

**ADD-CAN**   Addicts-Canada.

**ADIT**   Alien documentation, identification, and telecommunications.

**ADL**   Anti-Defamation League.

**ADPRIN**   Automatic data-processing intelligence network.

**ADT**   American District Telegraph Security Systems.

**ADW**   Assault with a deadly weapon.

**AELE**   Americans for Effective Law Enforcement.

**A-ES**   Arson-explosion squad.

**AFI**   Association of Federal Investigators.

**AF of P**   American Federation of Police.

**AFP**   1. Air Force Police. 2. American Federation of Police.

**AG**   Attorney general.

**AHS**   American Home Security.

**AIB**   Assassination Information Bureau.

**AID**   Accident Investigation Division.

**AIDA**   Automatic intruder-detector alarm.

**AIDP**   Association Internationale de Droit Penal. *French:* International Association of Penal Law.

**AIDRB**   Army Investigational Drug Review Board.

**AIDS**   Automated Identification Division System.

**AISA**   Association Internationale pour la Securite Aerienne. *French:* International Air Security Association.

**AJ**   1. Americans for Justice. 2. Associate Judge.

**AJI**   American Justice Institute.

**AJIS**   Automated Jail Information System.

**AJJUST**   Automated Juvenile Justice System Technique.

**AJS**   1. *American Journal of Sociology.* 2. American Judicature Society.

**ALAL**   Association of Legal Aid Lawyers.

**ALECS**   1. American Law Enforcement Communications System. 2. Automated Law Enforcement Communications System.

**ALERT II**   Automatic law enforcement response time.

**ALI**   American Law Institute.

**ALJ**   Administrative law judge.

**ALR**   American Law Reports.

**AMA**   American Medical Association.

**Am J Corr**   *American Journal of Correction.*

**Am L**   *American Lawyer.*

**Am Soc Soc**   American Sociological Society.

**AO**   Arresting officer.

**AOB**   Alcohol on breath.

**AP**   All-purpose.

**APA**   1. Administrative Procedure Act. 2. Adult Parole Authority. 3. American Polygraph Association. 4. American Protective Association. 5. American Psychiatric Association. 6. Association for the Prevention of Addiction. 7. Association of Paroling Authorities.

**APAP**   American People for American Prisoners.

**APB**   All-points bulletin.

**APFF**   American Police and Fire Foundation.

**APL**   American Protective League.

**AP-LS**   American Psychology-Law Society.

**APPA**   American Penal Press Association.

**AR**   Arraignment.

**ARC**   1. Addicts rehabilitation center. 2. Alcoholic rehabilitation center.

**ARCI**   Addiction Research Center Inventory.

**ARD**   Accelerated rehabilitative disposition.

**ARI**   Alcoholic Rehabilitation, Inc.

**ARJIS**   Automated Regional Justice Information System.

**ARSU**   Alcohol rehabilitation services unit.

**ARTC** 1. Addiction Research and Treatment Center. 2. Addiction Research and Treatment Corp.

**AS** Auto squad.

**ASAC** Assistant special agent in charge.

**ASAPs** Alcohol safety action projects.

**ASC** American Society of Criminology.

**ASCA** Association of State Correctional Administrators.

**ASCLD** American Society of Crime Laboratory Directors.

**ASIL** American Society of International Law.

**ASIS** American Society for Industrial Security.

**ASL** Anti-Saloon League.

**ASMH** Association for Social and Moral Hygiene.

**ASP** 1. Arizona State Prison. 2. Association of Seattle Prostitutes.

**ASPCA** American Society for the Prevention of Cruelty to Animals.

**ASPCC** American Society for the Prevention of Cruelty to Children.

**ASSPHR** Anti-Slavery Society for the Protection of Human Rights.

**ASU** Administrative systems unit.

**ATC** Alcohol treatment center.

**ATF** U.S. Bureau of Alcohol, Tobacco, and Firearms.

**ATLA** American Trial Lawyers Association.

**ATLAJ** *American Trial Lawyers Association Journal.*

**ATPE** Association of Teachers in Penal Establishments.

**ATU** Antiterrorist unit.

**AUSA** Assistant United States attorney.

**AUTOSTATIS** Automatic Statewide Theft Inquiry System.

**AVA** Automatic voice alarm.

**AW** Assistant warden.

**AWAIC** Abused Women's Aid in Crisis.

**AWARE** Addiction Workers Alerted to Rehabilitation and Education.

**AWOL** Absent without leave.

**BAC** Blood alcohol content.

**BAFS** British Academy of Forensic Sciences.

**B&E** Breaking and entering.

**BARC** Bay Area Research Collective.

**BATF** Bureau of Alcohol, Tobacco, and Firearms. See also **ATF**.

**BCC** Board of Crime Control.

**BCII** Bureau of Criminal Identification.

**BCS** 1. Bachelor of criminal science. 2. Bureau of Criminal Statistics.

**BCTF** Border Crime Task Force.

**BDAC** Bureau of Drug Abuse Control.

**BDC** Bomb data center.

**BEAT** Breaking, entering, and auto theft.

**BET** Biker Enforcement Team.

**BF** *Bonum factum. Latin:* a good act or decree; approved.

**BFP** Bona fide purchaser.

**BHD** Bronx House of Detention.

**BIA** Bureau of Indian Affairs.

**BID** Brought in dead.

**Bid** Bureau of Identification.

**Bklyn HTF** Brooklyn Homicide Task Force.

**BLD** Burglary Larceny Division.

**BMP** Bureau of Municipal Police.

**BNDD** Bureau of Narcotics and Dangerous Drugs.

**BOCCI** Bureau of Organized Crime and Criminal Intelligence.

**B of I** Bureau of Investigation.

**B of P** Bureau of Prisons.

**B of R** Bureau of Rehabilitation.

**BOP** Breach of peace.

**BOSS** Counterintelligence branch of New York Police Department, established in 1960s.

**BP** Board of parole.

**BPT** Board of prison terms.

**Bronx HTF** Bronx Homicide Task Force.

**Brooklyn HTF** Brooklyn Homicide Task Force.

**BSP** 1. Border Security Police. 2. Bureau de Securite Publique. *French:* Bureau of Public Security.

**BSSR** Bureau of Social Science Research.

**BVR** Bureau of Vocational Rehabilitation.

**BWC** Battered Women's Coalition.

**CA** Court of Appeal.

**CABLE** Computer-Assisted Bay Area Law Enforcement.

**CACB** Council Against Cigarette Bootlegging.

**CACJ** California Attorneys for Criminal Justice.

**CADC** District of Columbia Circuit Court.

**CAMRC** Child abuse and maltreatment reporting center.

**Can Pen Ser** Canadian Penitentiary Service.

**CANY** Correctional Association of New York.

**CAPE** 1. California Association of Polygraph Examiners. 2. Classification and Placement Examination.

**CARES** Computer-Assisted Regional Evaluation System.

**CAU** Child abuse unit.

**CAV** *Curia advisari vult. Latin:* the court will be advised, will consider, or deliberate.

**CBCII**   California Bureau of Criminal Identification and Investigation.

**CBI**   Central Bureau of Investigation.

**CBNE**   California Bureau of Narcotics Enforcement.

**CC**   1. *Cepe corpus. Latin:* I have taken his body, that is, arrested the defendant. 2. Chief Commissioner. 3. Chief Constable. 4. Circuit Court (also, City, or County Court). 5. Civil Code. 6. Criminal Cases (also, Crown, Civil, or Chancery Cases). 7. Councils of America.

**CCA**   1. California Correctional Association. 2. Circuit Court of Appeals. See also **USCCA**.

**CCB**   Criminal Courts Building.

**CC; BB**   *Cepe corpus. Latin:* I have taken his body; bail bond entered (defendant arrested and released on bail).

**CCC**   1. Central community center. 2. Central criminal court. 3. Crime and Correction Commission. 4. Crime and Correction Committee. 5. Customs Cooperation Council.

**CCCJ**   California Council on Criminal Justice.

**CCCP**   Citizens Crime Commission of Philadelphia.

**CCD**   Criminal Conspiracy Division.

**CCD&C**   Commission on Crime, Delinquency, and Corrections.

**CCH**   Computerized Criminal Histories.

**CCIB**   Computerized Central Information Bank.

**CCI**   Connecticut Correctional Institution.

**CCINC**   Cabinet Committee for International Narcotic Control.

**CCJ**   1. Center for Correctional Justice. 2. Center for Criminal Justice. 3. Circuit court judge. 4. Cook County Jail. 5. County court judge.

**CCOA**   1. California Correctional Officers Association. 2. County Court Officers Association.

**CCPA**   Court of Customs and Patent Appeals.

**CCPC**   Community crime prevention center.

**CCPOST**   California Commission on Peace Officer Standards and Training.

**CCR**   Commission on Civil Rights.

**CCRB**   Civilian Complaint Review Board.

**CCrP**   Code of Criminal Procedure.

**CCTF**   California Correctional Training Facility.

**CCU**   Correctional custody unit.

**CCW**   Citizens Crime Watch.

**CD**   Chief of Detectives.

**CDC**   Criminal diagnostics and counseling.

**CDJ**   1. California Department of Justice. 2. Canadian Department of Justice.

**CDRI**   Central Drug Research Institute.

**CDU**   Civil disobedience unit.

**CEA**   1. Captain's Endowment Association. 2. Correctional Educational Association.

**CEC**   Correctional Economics Center.

**CFLETC**   Consolidated Federal Law Enforcement Training Center.

**CFR**   Code of Federal Regulations.

**CG**   Coast Guard.

**CGIC**   Comisaria General de Investigacion Criminal. *Spanish:* Comissariat General of Criminal Investigation.

**CHAOS**   CIA domestic security files and operations in U.S.

**CHC**   Chicago House of Correction.

**CHEC**   Citizens Helping Eliminate Crime.

**CHINS**   Child in need of supervision.

**CHIPS**   California Highway Patrol officers.

**CHP**   California Highway Patrol.

**CHPA**   California Highway Patrol Academy.

**CIB**   1. Criminal Identification Bureau. 2. Criminal Intelligence Bureau. 3. Criminal Investigation Bureau.

**CICC**   Criminal Injuries Compensation Commission.

**CID**   1. Criminal Investigation Department. 2. Criminal Investigation Division.

**CIEC**   Centre International d'Etudes Criminologiques. *French:* International Center of Criminological Studies.

**CII**   Criminal Identification and Investigation.

**CIU**   Criminal intelligence unit.

**CIW**   California Institution for Women.

**CJ**   1. Chief Judge. 2. Chief Justice. 3. Circuit Judge. 4. Civil Jail. 5. *Corpus juris. Latin:* body of law. 6. Court of Judiciary.

**CJIS**   Criminal Justice Information System.

**CKCJP**   Center for Knowledge in Criminal Justice Planning.

**CL**   Civil law.

**CLASP**   Citizens Local Alliance for a Safer Philadelphia.

**CLEAN**   Commonwealth Law Enforcement Assistance Network.

**CLEAR**   County Law Enforcement Applied Regionally.

**CLEMARS**   California Law-Enforcement Mutual-Aid Radio System.

**CLES**   Customs Law-Enforcement Service.

**CLETS**   California Law Enforcement Telecommunications System.

**CM**   Court-martial.

**CNAEA** California Narcotic Addict Evaluation Authority.

**CND** Commission of Narcotic Drugs.

**CNIN** California Narcotic Information Network.

**CNOA** California Narcotics Officers Association.

**CNPB** Canadian National Parole Board.

**CO** 1. Chief of Operations. 2. Commanding Officer. 3. Correctional Officer.

**COA** Correctional Officers Association.

**CONNECT** Connecticut On-Line Enforcement Communication and Teleprocessing.

**COP** 1. Chief of Police. 2. Coalition on Police.

**CP** Common Pleas.

**CPA** Connecticut Prison Association.

**CPCS** Criminal possession of a controlled substance.

**CPD** 1. Chicago Police Department. 2. County probation department.

**CPF** Commonwealth Police Force.

**CPIC** Canadian Police Information Centre.

**CPOA** California Peace Officers Association.

**CPPCA** California Probation, Parole, and Correctional Association.

**CPS** Canadian Penitentiary Service.

**CPSP** Criminal possession of stolen property.

**CPU** Crime prevention unit.

**CPW** Criminal possession of a weapon.

**CRC** California rehabilitation center.

**CRMT** Community resources management team.

**CRNPTG** Commission on the Review of the National Policy Toward Gambling.

**CRO** Criminal record office.

**CRP** Crime Restitution Program.

**CRU** Crime reduction unit.

**CSA** Controlled Substances Act.

**CSCCL** Center for Studies in Criminology and Criminal Law.

**CSCD** Center for Studies of Crime and Delinquency.

**CSCJ** Center for Studies in Criminal Justice.

**CSD** 1. Correctional Services Department. 2. Corrective Services Department.

**CSF** Correctional Service Federation.

**CSM** Correctional Service of Minnesota.

**CSNDA** Center for the Studies of Narcotic and Drug Abuse.

**CSNMDU** Center for the Study of Non-Medical Drug Use.

**CSO** 1. Cargo Security Office. 2. Cargo security officer. 3. Community service officer.

**CSP** Connecticut State Police.

**CSSU** Crime scene search unit.

**CSTI** California Specialized Training Institute.

**CUE** Concentrated Urban Enforcement.

**CURB** Campaign on the Use and Restriction of Barbiturates.

**CURE** Care, Understanding, Research.

**CUSIP** Committee on Uniform Identification Procedures.

**CVCB** Crime Victims Compensation Board.

**CVLAI** Crime Victims Legal Advocacy Institute.

**CWAC** City-wide anticrime unit.

**CWLR** *California Western Law Review.*

**CWWC** Concerned Women in the War on Crime.

**CYC** Colorado Youth Center at Denver.

**DA** District Attorney.

**DALE** Drug Abuse Law Enforcement.

**DARE** 1. Drug Abuse Research and Education. 2. Drug Assistance, Rehabilitation, and Education.

**DAS** Departamento Administrativo de Seguridad. *Spanish:* Security Administration Department.

**DAWN** Drug Abuse Warning Network.

**DB** 1. Detective bureau. 2. Disciplinary barracks.

**DBHNT** Detective Bureau Hostage Negotiating Team.

**DC** 1. Defense Counsel. 2. Detective Constable. 3. District Court. 4. District of Columbia Jail.

**DCBJ** *District of Columbia Bar Journal.*

**DCC** Detective Chief Constable.

**DCCJ** Delaware Council on Crime.

**DCJ** 1. Department of Criminal Justice. 2. District Court Judge.

**DCS** Department of Correctional Services.

**DCWDC** District of Columbia Women's Detention Center.

**DD** 1. Detective District. 2. Detective Division.

**DDA** 1. U.S. Dangerous Drug Act. 2. Director of Administration at the CIA.

**DD&J** Deacons for Defense and Justice.

**DDHA** Detective Division Homicide Assault Squad.

**DEA** 1. Detectives Endowment Association. 2. Drug Enforcement Administration.

**DEAN** Deputy Educators Against Narcotics.

**DEFY** Drug Education for You.

**DFAR** Daily Field Activity Report.

**DFI** Division of Fire Investigation.

**DHC** Detroit House of Correction.

**DHQ** Divisional Headquarters.

**DI** 1. Deputy Inspector. 2. Detective Inspector.

**DIU** Diversion investigation unit.

**DJ** 1. Department of Justice investigator. 2. Don Jail.

**DJCP** Division of Justice and Crime Prevention.

**DLPS** Department of Law and Public Safety.

**DMV** Department of Motor Vehicles.

**DND** Division for Narcotic Drugs.

**DOCS** Department of Correctional Services.

**DOD** 1. Date of death. 2. Department of Defense.

**D of C** Department of Corrections.

**D of I** Division of Investigation(s).

**D of L** Department of Law.

**DOR** Discharged on own recognizance.

**DP** Displaced person.

**DPC** Deputy Police Commissioner.

**DPI** Disorderly persons investigation.

**DPS** Department of Public Safety.

**DPs** Detention pens.

**DPSCS** Department of Public Safety and Correctional Services.

**DSA** 1. Department of substance abuse. 2. Deputy Sheriff's Association.

**DSB** Drug Supervisory Body.

**DSCDP** Delaware State Central Data Processing.

**DW** Deputy Warden.

**DWI** Driving while intoxicated.

**DYA** Department of Youth Authority.

**DYS** 1. Department of Youth Services. 2. Division of Youth Services.

**E by I** Execution by injection.

**ECAB** Early Case Assessment Bureau.

**ECCP** European Commission on Crime Problems.

**ECEO** Economic Crime Enforcement Office.

**ECS** Episcopal Community Services.

**ECST** European Convention on the Suppression of Terrorism.

**ECU** Economic crime unit.

**ED** Enforcement Division.

**EDP Crimes** Electronic Data Processing Crimes.

**EFEC** Efforts from Ex-Convicts.

**EOD** Explosive Ordinance Device.

**EPD** Excellent Police Duty.

**ERC** Elmira Reception Center.

**ESD** Emergency Service Division.

**ESP** Eastern State Penitentiary.

**ESU** Emergency service unit.

**ETDS** Electronic Theft Detection System.

**EXCEL** Ex-Offender Coordinated Employment Lifeline.

**EXIT** Ex-Offenders in Transit.

**FA** Found abandoned.

**FAAPS** Fine Art, Antique, and Philatelic Squad.

**FAAR** Feminist Alliance Against Rape.

**FACFI** Federal Advisory Committee on False Identification.

**FBI** U.S. Federal Bureau of Investigation, responsible for the investigation of federal crimes and counterintelligence, the latter authority, under its charter, including all of the Western Hemisphere, established in 1924.

**FBN** U.S. Federal Bureau of Narcotics.

**FBP** U.S. Federal Bureau of Prisons.

**FCI** Federal Correctional Institution.

**FCIP** Federal Crime Insurance Program.

**FCJ** Foreign criminal jurisdiction.

**FCPA** Foreign Corrupt Practices Act.

**FD** Fire department.

**FDA** 1. Federal Drug Administration. 2. Food and Drug Administration.

**FDEA** Federal Drug Enforcement Administration.

**FDH** Federal Detention Headquarters.

**FDLE** Florida Department of Law Enforcement.

**FICA** Federal Insurance Contributions Act.

**FJ** First Judge.

**FLETC** Federal Law Enforcement Training Center.

**FMC** Federal Maritime Commission.

**FMCS** Federal Mediation and Conciliation Service.

**FOIA** Freedom of Information Act.

**FOP** Fraternal Order of Police.

**FPC** 1. Federal Power Commission. 2. Federal Prison Camp.

**FPI** Federal Prison Industries.

**FPOA** Federal Probation Officers Association.

**FPR** Federal Procurement Regulations.

**FR** Federal Reformatory.

**FRCP** Federal Rules of Civil Procedure.

**FRD** Federal Rules Decisions.

**FRW** Federal Reformatory for Women.

**FS** Forensic Science.

**FYC** Federal Youth Center.

**GBH** Grievous bodily harm.

**GBI** Georgia Bureau of Investigation.

**GCP** Glasgow (Scotland) City Police.

**GD** Gaol Delivery.

**GL** Grand larceny.

**GNTP** Georgia Narcotics Treatment Program.

**GTC** General trial and conference part of Supreme Court.

**GTF** Gang Task Force.

**HARM** Humans Against Rape and Molestation.

**HBD** Has been drinking.

**HC** Habitual criminal.

**HCCJ** Harvard Center for Criminal Justice.

**HCN**   House Committee on Narcotics.

**HIU**   Hypnosis investigation unit.

**HLPR**   Howard League for Penal Reform.

**HMC**   Heroin-morphine-cocaine.

**HOFSL**   Home Office Forensic Science Laboratory.

**HP**   Highway Patrol.

**HQ**   Headquarters.

**IA**   Internal Affairs.

**IAAI**   International Association of Arson Investigators.

**IABTI**   International Association of Bomb Technicians and Investigators.

**IACP**   International Association of Chiefs of Police.

**IAD**   Internal Affairs Division.

**IAF**   International Association of Firefighters.

**IAFD**   Intentionally-administered fatal dose.

**IAHS**   International Association for Hospital Security.

**IAPA**   1. Inter-American Police Academy. 2. International Association of Police Artists.

**IAPL**   International Association of Penal Law.

**IAPP**   International Association of Police Professors.

**IAWP**   International Association of Women Police.

**IB**   Intelligence branch.

**IBI**   Illinois Bureau of Investigation.

**IBPI**   International Bureau for Protection and Investigation.

**IBPO**   International Brotherhood of Police Officers.

**ICA**   Institute of Criminal Anthropology.

**ICAP**   Integrated Criminal Apprehension Program.

**ICCC**   International Center for Comparative Criminology.

**ICCD**   Information Center on Crime and Delinquency.

**ICCS**   International Center for Criminological Studies.

**ICM**   Institute for Court Management.

**ICND**   International Commission on Narcotic Drugs.

**ICPA**   1. International Commission for the Prevention of Alcoholism. 2. International Conference of Police Associations.

**ICPC**   International Criminal Police Commission (Interpol).

**ICPI**   Insurance Crime Prevention Institute.

**ICPO**   International Criminal Police Organization (Interpol).

**IDAA**   International Doctors in Alcoholics Anonymous.

**IDEA**   International Drug Enforcement Association.

**IDLE**   Idaho Department of Law Enforcement.

**IFA**   International Footprints Association.

**IFK**   1. Institut for Kriminologi. 2. Institut fur Kriminologie. *Norwegian, German:* Institute for Criminology.

**IFNE**   International Federation for Narcotic Education.

**IFSPO**   International Federation of Senior Police Officers.

**IHHA**   International Halfway House Association.

**II**   Illegal immigrant.

**IFSSE**   International Fire, Security, and Safety Exhibition.

**IJA**   *International Journal of the Addictions.*

**IJCP**   *International Journal of Criminology and Penology.*

**IJOA**   International Juvenile Officers Association.

**IJR**   Institute for Juvenile Research.

**IKPK**   International Kriminal-Polizei-Kommission. *German:* International Police Commission.

**ILSR**   Institute for Law and Social Research.

**IMM**   Impairing the morals of a minor.

**INCB**   International Narcotics Control Board.

**INEOA**   International Narcotic Enforcement Officers Association.

**INSLAW**   Institute for Law and Social Research.

**INTERPOL**   International Criminal Police Commission. See **ICPC**; **ICPO**.

**IOCI**   Interstate Organized Crime Index.

**IPA**   1. International Police Academy. 2. International Police Archives. 3. International Police Association. 4. International Psychoanalytical Association.

**IPAA**   International Prisoners Aid Association.

**IPM**   Institute of Police Management.

**IPPF**   International Penal and Penitentiary Foundation.

**IRC**   1. Institute for Reduction of Crime. 2. Internal Revenue Code.

**IRGDLP**   International Research Group on Drug Legislation and Programs.

**IRS**   Internal Revenue Service.

**IS**   Identification Section.

**ISC**   1. Institute for the Study of Conflict. 2. International Society of Criminology.

**ISD**   International Security Division.

**ISDD**   Institute for the Study of Drug Dependence.

**ISI**   Institute for Scientific Information.

**ISIT**   Institute for Studies in International Terrorism.

**ISO**   Industrial Security Organization.

**ISOO**   Information Security Oversight Office.

**ISP**   1. Idaho State Penitentiary. 2. Indiana State Police. 3. Industrial Security Program. 4. Institute of Social Psychiatry.

**ISSC** 1. Institute for the Study of Social Conflict. 2. International Social Science Council.

**IST** In-Service Training.

**ISTD** Institute for the Study and Treatment of Delinquency.

**ISTOM** Interstate transportation of obscene matters.

**ISV** Institute for the Study of Violence.

**ITAR** Interstate (and foreign) travel in aid of racketeering enterprises.

**ITB** International Theft Bureau.

**ITOM** Interstate transportation of obscene matter.

**ITRC** International Terrorist Research Center.

**ITSA** Interstate transportation of stolen aircraft.

**ITSMV** Interstate transportation of stolen motor vehicles.

**ITSP** Interstate transportation of stolen property.

**IUPA** International Union of Police Associations.

**JA** Judge Advocate.

**JADPU** Joint automatic data processing unit.

**JAG** Judge advocate general.

**JATLA** *Journal of the American Trial Lawyers Association.*

**JCD** 1. *Juris Canonicis* Doctor. *Latin:* Doctor of Canon Law. 2. *Juris Civilis* Doctor. *Latin:* Doctor of Civil Law.

**JCP** Justice of the Common Pleas.

**JD** 1. *Juris* Doctor. *Latin:* Doctor of Jurisprudence. 2. *Jurum* Doctor. *Latin:* Doctor of Laws. 3. Juvenile delinquent.

**JDC** Juvenile Detention Center.

**JDI** Juvenile Delinquency Index.

**JIFE** Junta Internacional de Fiscalizacion de Estupefacientes. *Spanish:* International Council for the Investigation of Narcotics.

**JINS** Juvenile in Need of Supervision.

**JIS** Jail Inspection Service.

**JJ** 1. Judges or Justices. 2. Junior Judge.

**JJC** Juvenile Justice Center.

**JJCCJ** John Jay College of Criminal Justice.

**JJSC** Juvenile Justice Standards Committee.

**JKB** Justice of the King's Bench.

**JLS** Jail Library Service.

**JND** Juvenile Narcotics Division.

**JNOV** Judgment notwithstanding the verdict.

**JOE** Juvenile Opportunities Extension.

**JP** 1. Justice of the Peace. 2. *Justice of the Peace.*

**JPS** Juvenile Probation Services.

**JQB** Justice of the Queen's Bench.

**JSD** Doctor of Science of Law.

**JUB** Justice of the Upper Bench.

**JURIS** 1. Justice Retrieval and Inquiry System. 2. Juvenile Referral Information System.

**JUZD** *Juris Utriusque* Doctor. *Latin:* Doctor of Civil and Canon Law.

**K&R** Kidnapping and ransom.

**KB** King's Bench.

**KC** King's Counsel.

**KCJ** King County Jail.

**KMCI** Kettle Moraine Correctional Institution.

**KPM** King's Police Medal.

**KRIM** Danish association for penal reform.

**KROM** Norwegian association for penal reform.

**KRUM** Swedish association for penal reform.

**LA** Legal Adjuster.

**LACJ** Los Angeles County Jail.

**L&O** *Law and Order.*

**LAPD** Los Angeles Police Department.

**LAS** Legal Aid Society.

**LAW** Legal Aid Warranty.

**LC** 1. Leading Cases. 2. Lord Chancellor. 3. Lower Canada.

**LCLJ** Lower Canada *Law Journal.*

**LDF** Legal Defense Fund of the National Association for the Advancement of Colored People.

**LEAA** 1. Law Enforcement Assistance Act. 2. Law Enforcement Assistance Administration.

**LEADS** Law Enforcement Agencies Data System.

**LECLU** Law Enforcement Civil Liberties Union.

**LEEGS** Law Enforcement Explorer Girls.

**LEEP** Law Enforcement education program.

**LEG** Law enforcement group.

**LEIU** Law enforcement intelligence unit.

**LEOPARD** Law Enforcement Operations and Activities to Reduce Drugs.

**LEPA** Law enforcement planning agency.

**LERC** Law enforcement research center.

**LETAC** Law enforcement training advisory council.

**LETS** Law Enforcement Teletypewriter Service.

**LISC** London Institute for the Study of Conflict.

**LITE** Legal Information Through Electronics.

**LJ** 1. Law Judge. 2. Law Journal.

**LL** Law Latin.

**LLB** *Legum baccalaureate. Latin:* bachelor of laws.

**LLD** *Legum* doctorate. *Latin:* doctor of laws.

**LLM** *Legum* magister. *Latin:* master of laws.

**LO** Law officer.

**LOA** The Law and Order Association.

**LPCM** London Police Court Mission.

**LR** Law Reports.

**LSAT** Law School Admission Test.

**MADD** Mothers Against Drunk Drivers.

**MALDEF** Mexican-American Legal Defense and Education Fund.

**MAST** 1. Metropolitan Arson Strike Team. 2. Michigan Alcoholism Screening Test.

**MCA** 1. Massachusetts Correctional Association. 2. Medical Correctional Association. 3. Minnesota Corrections Authority.

**MCC** Metropolitan Correctional Center.

**MCCW** Miami Citizens Crime Watch.

**MCDC** Montgomery County Detention Center.

**MCI** Massachusetts Correctional Institution.

**MCJCC** Mayor's Criminal Justice Coordinating Council.

**MCO** Michigan Corrections Organization.

**MD** Middle District.

**MDC** Minnesota Department of Corrections.

**ME** Medical Examiner.

**MHP** Missouri Highway Patrol.

**MHTF** Manhattan Homicide Task Force.

**MINS** Minor in need of supervision.

**MIRACODE** Name of Berkeley, Calif.'s computerized criminal bank.

**MP** Military Police.

**MPC** Model Penal Code.

**MPD** Metropolitan Police Department.

**MPP** Mothers in Prison Projects.

**MPU** Missing persons unit.

**MR** Michigan Reformatory.

**MRC** Minnesota Restitution Center.

**MTU** Michigan training unit.

**MULES** Missouri Uniform Law Enforcement System.

**MVL** Motor vehicle law.

**NACA** 1. National Association for Court Administration. 2. National Association of County Administrators.

**NACCC** National Association of Citizens Crime Commissions.

**NACDL** National Association of Criminal Defense Lawyers.

**NACHEPO** National Advisory Commission on Higher Education for Police Officers.

**NACJP** National Association of Criminal Justice Planners.

**NACRO** National Association for the Care and Resettlement of Offenders.

**NADA** National Association of Drug Addiction.

**NADDIS** Narcotics and Dangerous Drugs Information System.

**NADPAS** National Association of Discharged Prisoners' Aid Societies.

**NAFI** National Association of Fire Investigators.

**NAFS** National Association for Forensic Sciences.

**NAJ** National Association for Justice.

**NAJC** National Assessment of Juvenile Correction.

**NAME** National Association of Medical Examiners.

**NAPAN** National Association for the Prevention of Addiction to Narcotics.

**NAPCRO** National Association of Police Community Relations Officers.

**NAPD** National Academy of Police Driving.

**NAPLP** National Association of Para-Legal Personnel.

**NAPO** National Association of Probation Officers.

**NAPV** National Association of Prison Visitors.

**NARA** Narcotic Addict Rehabilitation Act.

**NARCO** United Nations Narcotics Commission.

**NASAR** National Association of Search and Rescue.

**NATB** National Automobile Theft Bureau.

**NATSJA** National Association of Training Schools and Juvenile Agencies.

**NAVCJ** National Association of Volunteers in Criminal Justice.

**NBDC** National Bomb Data Center.

**NBFAA** National Burglar and Fire Alarm Association.

**NBPA** National Black Police Association.

**NBPC** National Border Patrol Council.

**NCA** Narcotics Control Act.

**NCAI** National Clearinghouse for Alcohol Information.

**NCB** 1. National Central Bureau. 2. Narcotic-centered behavior.

**NCCAN** National Center on Child Abuse and Neglect.

**NCCCD** National Center for Computer Crime Data.

**NCCD** National Council on Crime and Delinquency.

**NCCH** National Council to Control Handguns.

**NCCJ** National Coalition for Children's Justice.

**NCCJPA** National Clearinghouse for Criminal Justice Planning and Architecture.

**NCCL** National Council for Civil Liberties.

**NCCPL** National Community Crime Prevention League.

**NCCPV** National Commission on the Causes and Prevention of Violence.

**NCCVD** National Council for Combating Venereal Diseases.

**NCDA** 1. National Center for Drug Analysis. 2. National Council on Drug Abuse.

**NCDC** 1. National Center for Disease Control. 2. National Communicable Disease Center.

**NCIC** National Crime Information Center.

**NCICCCH** National Crime Information Center Computerized Crime History Program.

**NCJISS** National Criminal Justice Information and Statistics Service.

**NCJRS** National Criminal Justice Reference Service.

**NCLRev** *North Carolina Law Review.*

**NCOC** National Conference on Organized Crime.

**NCP** National Crime Panel.

**NCPA** National Crime Prevention Association.

**NCPI** National Crime Prevention Institute.

**NCPPL** National Committee on Prisons and Prison Labor.

**NCPSR** National Crime Panel Survey Reports.

**NCPV** National Commission on the Prevention of Violence.

**NCRA** National Correctional Recreation Association.

**NCS** National Crime Surveys.

**NCSC** National Center for State Courts.

**NCSCJPA** National Conference of State Criminal Justice Planning Administrators.

**NCSRC** National Centre for Social Research and Criminology.

**NCTR** National Center for Toxicological Research.

**ND** 1. Narcotics Division. 2. Northern District.

**NDAA** National District Attorneys Association.

**NDAAF** National District Attorneys Association Foundation.

**NDD** Narcotic-detection dog.

**NDI** *National Death Index.*

**NDLRev** *North Dakota Law Review.*

**NDP** National Detective Police.

**NDPs** Narcotic Detention Pens.

**NDSB** Narcotic Drugs Supervisory Body.

**NEOCIS** New England Organized Crime Intelligence System.

**NFA** No fixed abode.

**NFCF** National Fraudulent Check File.

**NFPA** National Fire Protection Association.

**NFPCA** National Fire Prevention and Control Administration.

**NHBJ** *New Hampshire Bar Journal.*

**NHSB** National Highway Safety Bureau.

**NHTSA** National Highway Transportation Safety Administration.

**NIAAA** National Institute on Alcohol Abuse and Alcoholism.

**NIC** National Institute of Corrections.

**NICD** National Institute on Crime and Delinquency.

**NIDA** National Institute on Drug Abuse.

**NIJ** National Institute of Justice.

**NIJJDP** National Institute of Juvenile Justice and Delinquency Prevention.

**NIK** Narcotic identification kit.

**NILECJ** National Institute of Law Enforcement and Criminal Justice.

**NIN** 1. Narcotics Intelligence Network. 2. National Information Network.

**NJA** National Jail Association.

**NJCCC** New Jersey Casino Control Commission.

**NJDA** National Juvenile Detention Association.

**NJLC** National Juvenile Law Center.

**NJMA** National Jail Managers Association.

**NJMP** New Jersey Marine Police.

**NJRW** New Jersey Reformatory for Women.

**NJSP** New Jersey State Police.

**NLADA** National Legal Aid and Defender Association.

**NLETS** National Law Enforcement Telecommunications System.

**NLJ** *National Law Journal.*

**NOBLE** National Organization of Black Law Enforcement Executives.

**NOCC** New Orleans Crime Commission.

**NOISE** National Organization to Insure Support Enforcement.

**NOPA** National Organization of Police Associations.

**NOV** *Non obstante veredicto. Latin:* judgment notwithstanding the verdict.

**NP** 1. Naval Prison. 2. New police.

**NPA** National Police Agency.

**NPB** National Parole Board.

**NPCC** Nebraska Penal and Correctional Complex.

**NPFFA** National Police and Fire Fighters Association.

**NPOAA** National Police Officers Association of America.

**NPP** National Prison Project.

**NPPAJ** *National Probation and Parole Association Journal.*

**NPRA** National Prisoners Reform Association.

**NPROA** National Police Reserve Officers Association.

**NPS** Narcotics Preventative Service.

**NPSB** *National Prisoner Statistics Bulletin.*

**NRCPC** National Rural Crime Prevention Center.

**NRO** Narcotic Rehabilitation Officer.

**NRS** National Runaway Switchboard.

**NRTI** National Rehabilitation Training Institute.

**NSA** National Sheriff's Association (U.S.).

**NSDF**   National Sex and Drug Forum.

**NSF**   Not sufficient funds.

**NSP**   Nebraska State Patrol.

**NSPCA**   National Society for the Prevention of Cruelty to Animals.

**NSPCC**   National Society for the Prevention of Cruelty to Children.

**NSU**   Neighborhood stabilization units.

**NSWP**   New South Wales Police.

**NSY**   New Scotland Yard.

**NTA**   Narcotics Treatment Administration.

**NTF**   Narcotics Task Force.

**NTFP**   National Task Force on Prostitution.

**NTIS**   National Technical Information Service.

**NTSB**   National Traffic Safety Board.

**NVC**   National Violence Commission.

**NWLRev**   *Northwestern University Law Review.*

**NYCCCC**   New York City's Citizens Crime Commission.

**NYCCIW**   New York City Correctional Institution for Women.

**NYCDC**   New York City Department of Corrections.

**NYCPD**   New York City Police Department.

**NYCPM**   New York City Police Museum.

**NYHD**   New York House of Detention.

**NYPD**   New York City Police Department.

**NYRM**   New York Reformatory for Men.

**NYRW**   New York Reformatory for Women.

**NYSCC**   New York State Crime Commission.

**NYSDCS**   New York State Department of Correctional Services.

**NYSIIS**   New York State Identification and Intelligence System.

**NYSNACC**   New York State Narcotic Addiction Control Commission.

**NYSNC**   New York State Narcotics Commission.

**NYSP**   New York State Police.

**NYULQRev**   *New York University Law Quarterly Review.*

**NYULRev**   *New York University Law Review.*

**NZPP**   National Zoological Park Police.

**NZPS**   New Zealand Police Service.

**OADAP**   Office of Alcoholism and Drug Abuse Prevention.

**OAR**   Offender Aid and Restoration.

**OBSP**   *Old Bailey Sessions Papers.*

**OBTS**   Offender-Based Transaction Statistics.

**OCC**   1. Oklahoma Crime Commission. 2. Organized Crime Control.

**OCCB**   Organized Crime Control Bureau.

**OCCC**   Organized Crime Control Commission.

**OCF**   Ossining Correctional Facility (New York's Sing Sing Prison).

**OCIB**   Organized Crime Intelligence Bureau.

**OCID**   Organized Crime Intelligence Division.

**OCJA**   Office of Criminal Justice Statistics.

**OCP**   Office of Consumer Protection.

**OCR**   Organized Crime and Racketeering Section.

**OCRSF**   Organized Crime and Racketeering Strike Force.

**OCS**   Organe de Controle des Stupefiants. *French:* Narcotic Drug Control Supervision.

**OD**   Overdose.

**ODALE**   Office of Drug Abuse Law Enforcement.

**ODAP**   Office of Drug Abuse Policy.

**ODOTS**   One-Day One-Trial System.

**ODS**   Office of Defender Services.

**OIPC**   Organization Internationale de Police Criminelle. *French:* International Criminal Police Organization. See also **INTERPOL**.

**OIT**   Officer in Training.

**OJARS**   Office of Justice Assistance, Research, and Statistics.

**OJDYD**   Office of Juvenile Delinquency and Youth Development.

**OJJ**   Office of Juvenile Justice.

**OJJDP**   Office of Juvenile Justice and Delinquency Prevention.

**OLEP**   Office of Law Enforcement and Planning.

**ONNI**   Office of National Narcotics Intelligence.

**OPP**   Ontario Provincial Police.

**OR**   (Release On) Own Recognizance. See also **ROR**.

**ORACLE**   Optimum Record Automation for Courts and Law Enforcement.

**ORW**   Ohio Reformatory for Women.

**OSHA**   Occupational Safety and Health Administration.

**PA**   1. Parents Anonymous. 2. Police academy.

**PAA**   Prisoners Aid Association.

**PAAM**   Prisoners Aid Association of Maryland.

**P-A-L**   Prisoner-at-large.

**P&C**   Pickpocket and Confidence Squad.

**PATH**   1. Pathologist. 2. Pathology.

**PATRIC**   Pattern Recognition and Information Correlation.

**PAU**   Police airborne unit.

**PB**   1. Patrol boat. 2. Police boat.

**PBA**   Patrolmen's Benevolent Association.

**PC**   1. Penal Code. 2. Pleas of the Crown. 3. Police Chief. 4. *Police Chief.* 5. Police Commissioner. 6. Police Constable. 7. Professional Corporation.

**PCC** 1. Pennsylvania Crime Commission. 2. Poison Control Center.

**PCCNY** Penal Code of the City of New York.

**PCI** Potential criminal informant.

**PCL** Police Crime Laboratory.

**PCO** Police Commissioner's Office.

**PCOB** Permanent Central Opium Board.

**PCOP** President's Commission on Obscenity and Pornography.

**PCR** Police-community relations.

**PCRO** Police-community relations officer.

**PCU** Protective custody unit.

**PD** Police department.

**PDID** Public Disorder Intelligence Division.

**PDP** Petty delinquency detention.

**PDR** *Physicians' Desk Reference.*

**PDSOC** Police Department Superior Officers' Council.

**PDTS** Police Detective Training School.

**PEA** Policewomen's Endowment Association.

**PEP** 1. Parent Effectiveness Program. 2. Preventive Enforcement Patrol.

**PFA** Policia Federal Argentina. *Spanish:* Argentine Federal Police.

**PFF** Police Field Force.

**PFF Inc.** Police-FBI Fencing Incognito.

**PFI** Police Foundation Institute.

**PFJM** Policia Federal Judicial Mexicana. *Spanish:* Mexican Federal Judicial Police.

**PHV** *Pro hac vice. Latin:* for this particular occasion.

**PI** Private investigator.

**PICA** Police Insignia Collector's Association.

**PID** Police Intelligence Detail.

**PILCOP** Public Interest Law Center of Philadelphia.

**PIN** Police Information Network.

**PINS** Person in need of supervision.

**PIU** 1. Precinct investigators unit. 2. Public inspection unit.

**PJ** 1. Police Judiciare. *French:* crime investigators. 2. Police justice. 3. Presiding judge. 4. Probate judge.

**PK** Principal keeper.

**PL** Public law.

**PLJ** *Pittsburgh Legal Journal.*

**PM** 1. *Police Magazine.* 2. Police Magistrate. 3. Policia Metropolitana. *Spanish:* Metropolitan Police. 4. Postmortem. *Latin:* after death.

**PMAD** Public Morals Administrative Division.

**PNC** Police National Computer.

**PNCC** President's National Crime Commission.

**PO** 1. Police officer 2. Probation office.

**POA** 1. Police Officers Association. 2. Prison Officers Association.

**POAG** Peace Officers Association of Georgia.

**POC** Prison Officer's Club.

**POF** Police officer, female.

**POM** Police officer, male.

**POP** Property Offenders Program.

**PORA** Peace Officers Research Association.

**PORAC** Peace Officers Research Association of California.

**PP&C** Pickpocket and Confidence Squad.

**PPI** Pre-pleading investigation.

**PPL** Police Protective League.

**PPS** Pennsylvania Prison Society.

**PQ** Punishment quarters.

**PROMIS** Prosecution Management Information System.

**PROOF** Parole Resource Office and Orientation Facility.

**PROP** Preservation of the Rights of Prisoners.

**PRS** 1. Property Recovery Squad. 2. Protective Research Section of the United States Secret Service.

**PSAMPP** Philadelphia Society for Alleviating the Miseries of Public Prisons.

**PS&SC** Public Service and Safety Commission.

**PSAODAP** Presidential Special Action Office for Drug Abuse Prevention.

**PSIs** Personnel Security Investigations.

**PSTD** Prison Service Training Depot.

**PSU** Public security unit.

**PTA** Prevention of Terrorism Act.

**PTI** Protect the Innocent.

**PTJ** (Cuerpo) Tecnico de Policia Judicial. *Spanish:* Technical Corps of the Judicial Police.

**PTU** Psychiatric treatment unit.

**PU** Prisoners Union.

**PV** Parole violator.

**PVA** Prison Visitor's Association.

**PVR** Police Volunteer Reserve.

**QB** Queen's Bench.

**QC** Queen's Counsel.

**QCPSA** Quaker Center for Prisoner Support Activities.

**QCSR** Quaker Committee on Social Rehabilitation.

**QD** 1. Questioned document. 2. Quick detachable.

**QJSA** *Quarterly Journal of Studies in Alcohol.*

**QPA** Queensland Police Academy.

**QPM** Queen's Police Medal.

**QPP** Quebec Provincial Police.

**RAP** Release Aid Program.

**RAPP** Radical Alternatives to Prison Plan.
**RARE** Rehabilitation of Addicts by Relatives and Employers.
**RCC** Rape Crisis Center.
**RCCP** Royal Commission on Criminal Procedure.
**RCMP** Royal Canadian Mounted Police.
**REACH** Rape Emergency Aid and Counseling for Her.
**RHKP** Royal Hong Kong Police.
**RHL** Rape Help Line.
**RIC** Royal Irish Constabulary.
**RJIS** Regional Justice Information System.
**RLDPAS** Royal London Discharged Prisoners' Aid Society.
**RLPAS** Royal London Prisoners' Aid Society.
**RMP** Radio motor patrol.
**RMPA** Royal Medico-Psychological Association.
**RNWMP** Royal Northwest Mounted Police.
**ROARE** Reeducation of Attitudes and Repressed Emotions.
**ROR** Release on Own Recognizance.
**RS** Revised Statutes.
**RSPCA** Royal Society for the Prevention of Cruelty to Animals.
**RSPCC** Royal Society for the Prevention of Cruelty to Children.
**RUC** Royal Ulster Constabulary.
**RVPA** Rape Victims Privacy Act.
**SA** 1. Special Agent. 2. State Attorney.
**SAA** Singapore Aftercare Association.
**SAC** Special Agent in Charge.
**SACRO** Scottish Association for the Care and Resettlement of Offenders.
**SADD** Students Against Driving Drunk.
**SAIC** Special agent in charge.
**SAODAP** Special Action Office for Drug Abuse Prevention.
**SARC** Sexual Assault Referral Centre.
**SCL** South Carolina law.
**SCLED** South Carolina Law Enforcement Division.
**SCLR** *South Carolina Law Review.*
**SCPAs** State criminal-justice planning agencies.
**SDCINTF** San Diego County Integrated Narcotic Task Force.
**SDCJ** San Diego County Jail.
**SDLRev** *South Dakota Law Review.*
**SDPD** San Diego Police Department.
**SDPOA** San Diego Police Officers Association.
**SEARCH** System for Electronic Analysis and Retrieval of Criminal Histories.

**SFCJ** San Francisco County Jail.
**SFLR** *San Francisco Law Review.*
**SFPD** San Francisco Police Department.
**SFSAFBI** Society of Former Special Agents of the FBI.
**SH** Station house.
**SIC** Societe Internationale de Criminologie. *French:* International Society of Criminology.
**SIU** Special investigating unit.
**SO** Sheriff's office (U.S.).
**SOA** Superior Officers Association.
**SOC** Save Our Children.
**SOCO** Scenes of crime officer.
**SP** 1. Security police. 2. Shore patrol. 3. Shore police. 4. State police. 5. Suspicious person.
**SPC** 1. Service Processing Centers. 2. Society for the Prevention of Crime. 3. Suicide Prevention Center. 4. Suicide Prevention Clinic.
**SPCA** Society for the Prevention of Cruelty to Animals.
**SPCC** Society for the Prevention of Cruelty to Children.
**SPCW** Society for the Prevention of Cruelty to Women.
**SPF** Stolen property file.
**SPI** 1. Society of Professional Investigators. 2. Southern Police Institute.
**SPIN** Southern California Police Information Network.
**SPRINT** Special Police Radio Inquiry Network.
**SPRS** State Police Radio System.
**SPSC** Scottish Prison Service College.
**SQP** San Quentin Prison.
**SRW** State Reformatory for Women.
**SS** 1. Suspension of sentence. 2. Sworn statement.
**SSA** Society for the Study of Addiction.
**SSV** Society for the Suppression of Vice.
**STAR** 1. Special Tactics Against Robberies. 2. Special Tactics and Response.
**START** Special Treatment and Rehabilitation Training.
**STJ** Special Trial Judge.
**STRESS** Stop the Robberies, Enjoy Safe Streets.
**SWAT** Special Weapons and Tactics.
**SWLJ** *Southwestern Law Journal.*
**SWLRev** *Southwestern Law Review.*
**TADARF** Toronto Alcoholism and Drug Addiction Research Foundation.
**TASC** Treatment Alternatives to Street Crime.

**TC**  1. Traffic Commissioner or Consultant. 2. Trial Counsel.

**TCJC**  Texas Criminal Justice Council.

**TDC**  Texas Department of Corrections.

**TDS**  Tennessee Department of Safety.

**TECS**  Treasury Enforcement Communications System.

**TFA**  Task Force on Alcoholism.

**TFIS**  Theft from an interstate shipment.

**TIP**  Terrorist Information Project.

**TLA**  Trial Lawyers' Association.

**TO**  1. Traffic officer. 2. Training officer. 3. Transportation officer.

**TOPCOPS**  The Ottawa Police Computerized On-Line Processing System.

**TOSCA**  Toxic Substances Control Act.

**TPBA**  Transit Patrolmen's Benevolent Association.

**TPF**  Tactical Patrol Force.

**TRACIS**  Traffic Records and Criminal Justice Information System.

**TRO**  Temporary restraining order.

**TROA**  The Retired Officers Association.

**TRY**  Teens for Retarded Youth.

**TWOC**  Taking without owner's consent.

**UBP**  Unit beat policing.

**UCC**  Uniform Commercial Code.

**UCCC**  Uniform Consumer Credit Code.

**UCMJ**  Uniform Code of Military Justice.

**UCR**  Uniform crime report.

**UCRs**  *Uniform Crime Reports.*

**UF**  Uniformed Force.

**UFAC**  Unlawful flight to avoid confinement.

**UFAP**  Unlawful flight to avoid prosecution.

**UFIRS**  Uniform Fire-Incident Reporting System.

**UISP**  Union Internationale des Syndicats de Police. *French:* International Union of Police Trade Unions.

**UJD**  *Utriusque Juris* Doctor. *Latin:* Doctor of both Canon and Civil Law.

**UNARCO**  United Nations Narcotics Commission.

**UNCCP**  United Nations Commission on Crime Prevention.

**UNCIWC**  United Nations Commission for the Investigation of War Crimes.

**UNFDAC**  United Nations Fund for Drug Abuse Control.

**UNWCC**  United Nations War Crimes Commission.

**UOC**  Uniform Offense Classification.

**UPU**  United Prisoners Union.

**URESA**  Uniform Reciprocal Enforcement of Support Act.

**USA**  United States attorney.

**USACIC**  United States Army Criminal Investigation Command.

**USBC**  United States Bureau of Customs.

**USBP**  1. United States Board of Parole. 2. United States Border Patrol. 3. United States Bureau of Prisons.

**USC**  1. United States Code. 2. United States Customs.

**USCA**  1. United States Code Annotated. 2. United States Courts of Appeals.

**USCCA**  United States Circuit Court of Appeals. See also **CA, CCA.**

**USCG**  United States Coast Guard.

**USCP**  United States Capitol Police.

**USCS**  1. United States Code Service. 2. United States Customs Service.

**USDB**  United States Disciplinary Barracks.

**USDC**  United States District Court.

**USDEA**  United States Drug Enforcement Administration.

**USDOJ**  United States Department of Justice.

**USEP**  United States Escapee Program.

**USI**  Unlawful sexual intercourse.

**USLJ**  *United States Law Journal.*

**USLW**  *United States Law Week.*

**USMS**  United States Marshals Service.

**USNCC**  United States Naval Correction Center.

**USNDRC**  United States Navy Drug Rehabilitation Center.

**USNIAAA**  United States National Institute on Alcohol Abuse and Alcoholism.

**USNIS**  United States Naval Investigative Service.

**USP**  United States Penitentiary.

**USPB**  United States Parole Board.

**USPC**  United States Parole Commission.

**USPCA**  United States Police Canine Association.

**USPHS**  United States Public Health Service.

**USPIS**  United States Postal Inspection Service.

**USPP**  United States Probation and Parole.

**USSC**  United States Supreme Court.

**USSIC**  United States Sex Information Council.

**USSS**  United States Secret Service.

**UXB**  Unexploded bomb.

**VAP**  Victim's Advocate Program.

**VCB**  Victim Compensation Board.

**VCIC**  Vermont Crime Information System.

**VIJ**  Vera Institute of Justice.

**VIN**  Vehicle identification number.

**VIP**  Volunteers in Probation.

**VPCP**  Volunteer Probation Counseling Program.

**VR**   Voluntary return.

**VTL**   Vehicle and Traffic Law.

**VU**   Vice Unit.

**VU-PD**   Vice unit–Police department.

**VVCP**   Victims of Violent Crimes Program.

**VWP**   Victim / Witness Project.

**WAD**   World Association of Detectives.

**WAR**   Women Against Rape.

**WAVAW**   Women Against Violence Against Women.

**WBSI**   Western Behavioral Sciences Institute.

**WCA**   1. Washingtonian Center for Addiction. 2. Women's Correctional Association.

**WCAC**   Women's Crusade Against Crime.

**WCS**   Wisconsin Correctional Service.

**WCSC**   World Correctional Service Center.

**WDC**   Women's Detention Center.

**WFO**   Washington Field Office.

**WHD**   Women's House of Detention.

**WHODAP**   White House Office of Drug Abuse Prevention.

**WIC**   Welfare and Institution Code.

**WPA**   Women's Prison Association.

**WPA&H**   Women's Prison Association and Home.

**WPP**   Witness Protection Program.

**WVSP**   West Virginia State Police.

**Y and CA**   Youth and Correctional Agency.

**YACA**   Youth and Correctional Agency.

**YAD**   Youth Aid Division.

**YCA**   Youth Correction Act.

**YCC**   Youth Correctional Center.

**YCI**   Youth Correctional Institution.

**YGC**   Youth Guidance Center.

**YO**   Youthful offender.

**YSB**   Youth Service Bureau.

**YSC**   Youth Studies Center.

**YSD**   Youth Services Division.

**YTS**   Youth Training School.

## Terms

**Abandonment**   1. The willful, intentional relinquishing of one's property or claim to it, without naming a new owner. 2. The giving up of an intention to commit a crime. The general view is that it may not be used as a defense in court as long as there is a clear and unequivocal intent upon the part of the accused to carry out the crime at one time. To merely walk away before the crime is committed does not necessarily make one innocent of the attempt. 3. Leaving behind one's matrimonial, parental, or custodial responsibilities, usually considered a felonious act. *Legal use.* Cf. **desertion; discharge; release; statute of limitations; waiver.**

**Abduction**   1. The forced removal or carrying away of a person. *General use.* 2. The unlawful removal of a wife, child, or ward by any means. 3. The unlawful removal of a woman for purposes of prostitution, slavery, or rape, usually constituting a felony. *Legal use.* Cf. **kidnapping**.

**Abductor**   A person who forcibly removes or carries a person away against that person's will. *Legal use.*

**Abet**   To aid in or encourage the commission of a crime. *Legal use.* Cf. **accomplice; aid and abet.**

**Abiding conviction**   A clear conviction of guilt arrived at by a careful examination of evidence. This is a term frequently used by judges during their instructions to the jury. *Legal use.*

**Abjuration**   A renunciation, made under oath, of one's rights, privileges, or position. *Legal use.*

**Abjure**   To forswear one's rights, privileges, or position under oath. *Legal use.*

**Abortive trial**   A trial stopped before the verdict is reached. *Legal use.*

**Abscond**   1. To avoid prosecution by running away and hiding. 2. To leave the area of one's parole without permission. *Legal use.*

**Absolve**   To free from guilt or responsibility. *Legal use.*

**Abuse**   *n.* An overindulgence in or improper use or treatment of drugs, alcohol, sex, or other pleasures. *v.* To mistreat a person, especially by a verbal or physical attack. *General use.* Cf. **carnal abuse; child abuse.**

**Accessory**   One who helps or provides assistance to a criminal for the commission of a crime, but is not the chief actor in the offense. *Legal use.* Cf. **accomplice; parties to crime; principal.**

**Accessory after the fact**   One who knowingly aids a felon to evade justice. Cf. **obstructing justice.** *Legal use.*

**Accessory before the fact**   One who encourages another to commit a crime or gives aid to do so, but is not present at the actual commission of the crime. *Legal use.*

**Accessory during the fact**   One who stands by during the commission of a crime without interfering or giving help, when such an act is within his power to prevent the crime. *Legal use.*

**Accidental killing**   A death that results from an act performed lawfully, where no harm was thought to be possible. *Legal use.*

**Acco collar**   An arrest made solely to fulfill an officer's quota. *Police use.*

**Accommodation arrest**   A prearranged arrest performed by corrupt police officers to hoodwink the general public. *Police and underworld use.*

**Accommodator**   One who bribes witnesses and prosecutors into bringing about a desired verdict, especially a former police officer. *Obsolete 1940 underworld use.*

**Accomplice**   One who willingly and knowingly takes part with another in the commission of a crime. *Legal use.* Cf. **abet**; **accessory**; **aid and abet**; **parties to crime**.

**Accomplice liability**   Being held criminally responsible for one's participation before, during, or after the commission of a crime. *Legal use.*

**Accomplice witness**   One who participates in the commission of a crime in one way or another, regardless of whether or not he was at the scene of the crime. *Legal use.*

**Accusation**   A formal allegation against someone stating that he is responsible for the crime in question. *Legal use.* Cf. **indictment**; **information**; **malicious accusation**.

**Accusatorial system**   A legal system based on the belief that truth and justice can best be determined by a contest where both sides on an issue present their case; the adversary system. *Legal use.*

**Accusatory body**   A group assembled to determine whether a person should be charged with a crime (e.g., a grand jury). *Legal use.*

**Accusatory instrument**   The document by which a charge is brought against someone. *Legal use.*

**Accusatory part**   The part of an indictment that states the charge. *Legal use.*

**Accusatory pleading**   A document (e.g., an indictment) in which a person is charged with the crime for which he will be tried. *Legal use.*

**Accusatory stage**   The period of a criminal investigation following the arrest of a suspect and during which time a confession or incriminating statement is sought. *Legal use.*

**Accusatory state**   The point in an investigation when the suspect has been determined. *Legal use.*

**Accuse**   To formally charge someone with having committed an offense for which he will be brought before a court. *Legal use.*

**Accused**   The defendant in a criminal court proceeding. *Legal use.*

**Accuser**   One who accuses another of a crime. *Legal use.*

**Acquit**   To certify that the accused is innocent of the charges brought against him.

**Acquittal**   Certification that the defendant is free to go as a result of a verdict of not guilty, dismissal of the case by the court, or a failure to follow proper legal procedures. *Legal use.* Cf. *autrefois* **acquit**; **jeopardy**; **nolle prosequi**; **verdict**.

**Acquitted**   To be freed from the charges brought against one. *Legal use.*

**Act**   *n.* 1. External expression of one's will. A crime requires a criminal act, either carried out or failed at. 2. A law established by the legislature. *Legal use.* 3. Pretending to be loyal, insane, sick, etc. *v.* 1. To feign one's actions. *Underworld use.* Cf. **official act**; **overt act**; **statute**.

**Actual compulsion**   Forcing another to execute an act. *Legal use.*

**Actual violence**   Physical force used on another. *Legal use.*

**Actus non facit reum, nisi mens sit rea**   For there to be a crime, the intent, as well as the act, must be criminal in nature. *Legal use.*

**Actus reus**   1. A wrongful act, which, in combination with criminal intent, constitutes a crime. 2. Behavior necessary in the commission of a crime. *Legal use.*

**Addict**   1. One who has an uncontrollable desire to use narcotic drugs. *General use.* 2. A user of opiates. *Drug addict use.* Cf. **narcotic drugs**.

**Addiction**   The state that a frequent drug or alcohol abuser experiences, involving an overpowering need for more and more of the substance of choice. *General use.*

**Adequate cause**   The grounds on which one would expect sufficient emotion produced in an average person to prevent that person from making a sensible decision. *Legal use.*

**Adequate provocation**   A cause sufficient to exclude premeditation and arouse a reasonable person to the point where his reason is obscured or his will dominated by a stronger and usually uncontrollable passion. *Legal use.*

**Adjudicate**   To judge. *Legal use.*

**Adjudicatory hearing**   The process by which the court determines whether a juvenile has been delinquent. *Legal use.* Cf. **juvenile courts; petition.**

**Admissible**   That which is fitting and proper for consideration in court. *Legal use.*

**Admission**   An acknowledgment that a certain fact is true. *Legal use.* Cf. **incriminating admission.**

**Admitting to bail**   Releasing a defendant when he posts bail. *Legal use.*

**Advocate**   A lawyer. *General use.*

**A felony**   The felony classification under New York's state penal law that carries the most severe punishment, fifteen or twenty-five years to life. This felony classification includes such crimes as murder and kidnapping. Felonies B through E cover lesser crimes and have less severe punishments. *Legal use.*

**Affective insanity**   All forms of insanity that deal with the feelings or emotions and affect one's ethical and social relations. *Medical use.*

**Affidavit**   A written statement made voluntarily and verified under oath before an authorized person. *Legal use.*

**Affidavit men**   Individuals who would swear to anything in court in return for money. They wore straw in their shoes to point themselves out to prospective customers. *Obsolete underworld use.*

**Affirmative defense**   A defense that, assuming the complaint is true, is an answer to it. The defendant has the burden of proof regarding affirmative defenses, which include insanity and automatism. *Legal use.* Cf. **alibi; coercion; duress; intoxication; self-defense.**

**Affray**   A public showing of violence by at least two people that leads to a disturbance of others in the area. *Legal use.*

**Aforethought**   Premeditation. *Legal use.* Cf. **malice aforethought.**

**Aggravated assault**   The attempt to cause or the causing of serious injury intentionally, knowingly, or recklessly with indifference to the value of human life, or causing injury with a deadly weapon. Jurisdictions punish this type of assault more severely than simple assault. *Legal and law enforcement use.*

**Aggravated battery**   An illegal application of force to another, distinguished by serious consequences or circumstances such as the presence of a deadly weapon. *Legal use.*

**Aid and abet**   To help or facilitate the commission of a crime. *Legal use.* Cf. **accessory; accomplice.**

**Airtight**   Planned to perfection, usually regarding an alibi or criminal operation. *Underworld use.*

**a.k.a.**   Alias; also known as. *General use.*

**Alford plea**   A plea in criminal court in which the defendant does not admit the act and asserts his or her innocence, but admits that sufficient evidence exists for the prosecution to convince a judge or jury to find the defendant guilty. The court, upon receiving the Alford plea, can find the defendant guilty and impose a sentence, as if the defendant had otherwise been convicted. Certain state courts, however, accept the Alford plea as an admission of sufficient facts and continue the case, which may result in conviction or acquittal. The Alford plea is a form of a guilty plea. Even though the defendant may be dismissed in a case, the same plea may be used against the defendant in future trials and can be considered a "strike" should a three strikes law apply. The nolo contendere ("no contest") plea differs from the Alford plea in that there is no admission of guilt. The Alford plea stems from the 1970 case of *North Carolina v. Alford*, argued in the U.S. Supreme Court (400 US 25).

**Alias**   A name different from one's legal name; an assumed name. *Legal use.*

**Alibi**   Evidence that a defendant was elsewhere at the time of a crime. *Legal use.*

**Alienist**   A specialist in mental diseases who gives evidence as to a defendant's mental state when the crime took place. *Legal and medical use.*

**Allegation**   1. A charge made without proof. *General use.* 2. A statement that a party in a legal proceedings will attempt to prove. *Legal use.*

**Allege**   To assert without proof or prior to proving; to make a charge or an allegation. *Legal use.*

**Alleged offender**   One who has been charged with committing a crime but has not been convicted. *Legal use.*

**Allograph**   A signature made by one person for another, usually for purposes of forgery. *General use.*

**Amentia**   An inborn lack of intelligence, reason, or mental capacity. *Legal and medical use.*

**Amicus curiae**   1. One who is asked to clarify difficult technical matters related to a trial or provide the court with expertise on a certain subject. 2. Latin for a friend of the court. 3. One who has no right to appear in court but is allowed to give evidence in order to protect his own interests. *Legal use.*

**Amnesia**   The loss or impairment of memory due to an organic traumatic experience. In a criminal proceeding, amnesia is not reason enough for one not to stand trial. *Medical and legal use.*

**Amnesty**   An act by a government abolishing and forgetting the offense of all or certain persons guilty of a crime, usually political in nature. *Legal use*. Cf. **pardon; parole.**

**Anchor**   *n.* 1. Reprieve of an execution order. *Prison use, 1929.* 2. A juror who is bribed. *Underworld use, 1936. v.* To reprieve an execution order. *Prison use.*

*Animus furandi*   Latin term meaning intent to steal. *Legal use.*

**Anticipatory offense**   A criminal act that has an additional crime as its goal (e.g., an attempt to kill someone). *Legal use.*

**Antisocial personality**   A social disorder of character marked by immoral behavior. *Sociological use.*

**Aphasia**   A disease affecting the brain which results in the loss of hearing, sight, speech, or motion or any combination of these senses. *Medical use.*

**Appeal**   A request for a completed trial case to be moved to a higher court for review. *Legal use*. Cf. **court of appeals.**

**Appearance**   Presenting and submitting oneself to the court's authority. *Legal use*. Cf. **initial appearance; nonappearance.**

**Apprehend**   To capture a suspected criminal. *Police use.*

**Apprehend the perpetrator**   To capture a suspected criminal. *Police use.*

**Apprehension**   The taking of a suspect into legal custody. *Law enforcement use.*

**Approver**   One accomplice who accuses his accomplices of the same crime and testifies at the court's discretion against his companions in hopes of reducing his own punishment. Years ago, if one failed to convince the jury of his confederates' guilt, he was hanged; a.k.a. **prover**. *Legal use.*

**Armed robbery**   Aggravated larceny committed on a person or while the victim is present, in which force or the threat of force with a deadly weapon is made. *Law enforcement and legal use*. Cf. **robbery.**

**Arraign**   To bring the accused to court to read him his rights, list the charges against him, and hear his plea. *Legal use.*

**Arraignment**   The hearing at which charges are read, the defendant is informed of rights, a plea is entered, and, if necessary, a lawyer is appointed. *Legal use*. Cf. **information.**

**Arrest**   To take a suspect into custody by authority of law in order to charge him with a criminal offense or undertake juvenile proceedings. Authority to arrest is granted by an arrest warrant, an officer's belief that commission of a felony has been perpetrated by the suspect, or for any crime committed before the officer's eyes. Private citizens may also make an arrest under certain circumstances. *General use*. Cf. **citizen's arrest; false arrest; warrant.**

**Arrestable offense**   A crime that has a sentence prescribed by law and must be handed down. *U.K. legal use.*

**Arrest of judgment**   Deferment of judgment in a court case after the verdict because of errors discovered in the record. *Legal use.*

**Arrest record**   A police department file kept to record information about the offender and offense, as well as all prior offenses, which is valuable to the judge for sentencing purposes, although often such records are prohibited at trials in that they constitute bias and prejudice. *Legal use.*

**Arrest warrant**   A written order issued by a court that authorizes arrest of the named person. *Law enforcement and police use*. Cf. **warrant.**

**Arson**   The unlawful and malicious destruction of property, especially buildings, by fire or explosion. The felony is generally categorized by degree: first degree being the burning of a residence, usually at night; second degree being the burning of any building near residential property, usually at night; third degree being the burning of any property with intent to recover insurance; and fourth degree being an attempt to burn property. *General use.*

**Arsonist**   One who commits arson. *General use.*

**Assail**   To violently attack a person. *General use.*

**Assailant**   One who attacks another. *Law enforcement and legal use.*

**Assassination**   The murder of someone, usually a person of high status, who has provided no provocation or cause of resentment to the murderer; usually the killer is hired by another party or the act is committed for political, social, or personal reasons. *General use.*

**Assault**   An unlawful attempt or threat to inflict bodily injury, which results in the victim reasonably fearing such an injury. Unlike battery, there is no physical contact. *Legal and law enforcement use.*

**Assault, aggravated.**   See **aggravated assault**.

**Assault, simple**   An attempt to injure another without aggravating circumstances (e.g., use of a deadly weapon). *Legal use.*

**Assault and battery**   Any illegal physical contact of another person. *Legal and law enforcement use*. Cf. **battery.**

**Assize**   A court session whereby judges of the Queen's Bench Division travel from one circuit town to another to hear cases brought before them. There are seven circuits in England and Wales. *U.K. legal use.*

**Attack**   To take offensive action against another in an attempt to cause harm. *General use.*

**Attainder**   The cessation of civil rights and forfeiture of estate connected with a death sentence; no longer permissible in the United States. *Obsolete legal use.* Cf. **bill of attainder**.

**Attempt**   An overt act that would have resulted in commission of the crime if not for interruption. *Legal use.*

**Attendant circumstances**   The facts surrounding an event or commission of a crime. *Legal use.*

**Attest**   To make a statement under oath; to bear witness to. *Legal use.*

**Attitude**   A sudden burst of rage. *Drug addict use.*

**Attitude arrest**   An arrest made because a police officer does not like someone's behavior. *Police use.*

**Attorney**   A person schooled in the law, admitted to practice in a jurisdiction, and authorized to advise, act on behalf of, and represent people in legal proceedings. *General use.*

**Attorney-client privilege**   The doctrine that allows communications between attorney and client to remain confidential. *Legal use.*

**Authority**   The power or right to enforce the law; jurisdiction. *Legal use.*

**Auto-da-fé**   Burning at the stake; since the fifth century.

**Automatism**   A semiconscious or unconscious state of mind that would result in involuntary actions. As a defense, one ordinarily cannot be held responsible for something he was not aware he was doing due to being in a state of automatism. *Medical and legal use.*

**Autopsy**   The examination and dissection of a corpse to determine the cause of death, required by law if the death was unnatural or violent, or if the deceased was not under a doctor's care. *Legal and medical use.*

**Auto theft**   1. Stealing a motor vehicle with the intention of permanently depriving the owner of it, distinguishable from merely using the vehicle without permission. *General use.* Cf. **joyride; motor vehicle theft**. 2. The police department division that handles any robbery involving an auto. *Police use.*

*Autrefois* **acquit**; *autrefois* **convict**   Pleas used by defendants to assert that no one is to be tried twice for the same offense if a final verdict, guilty or not guilty, was reached at the first trial. *Legal use.*

**Backing a warrant**   The endorsement of a warrant by the receiving jurisdiction. *Legal use.*

**Backlog**   The cases pending on a court's calendar. *Legal use.*

**Back time**   The unserved time that a parole violator must make up if returned to prison. *Prison use.*

**Bad rap**   1. A long prison sentence. *Prison use.* 2. A false accusation. *Underworld use.*

**Bail**   Money or other security presented to the court to allow the release from custody of a person charged with a crime while guaranteeing his appearance in court at all subsequent proceedings. If he fails to appear, the security is then forfeited. *General use.*

**Bailable action**   One where a defendant may be released from custody only upon a posted bond. *Legal use.*

**Bailable offense**   An offense for which a prisoner may be eligible for bail. *Legal use.*

**Bail bond**   An agreement between a defendant and a court or between one or more sureties designated by the defendant and a court, which grants the defendant liberty while awaiting trial and guarantees his presence in court for that trial. If the defendant jumps bail and fails to appear for trial, the surety forfeits to the state the specified amount of the bond. *Legal use.* Cf. **personal recognizance**.

**Bail bondsman**   A person who provides bail for the release of a defendant and guarantees the presence of the defendant in court. If the defendant jumps bail and does not appear, the bondsman loses the money deposited with the court. *General use.*

**Bailiff**   The officer of a court who keeps order, holds prisoners, and controls decorum. The area of his jurisdiction is the bailiwick. *Legal use.*

**Bailiwick**   A bailiff's jurisdiction.

**Ballistics**   The scientific study of projectiles in flight; in criminal law, the study of firearms. *Legal and police use.*

**Ballistics test**   A test that determines the weapon used to fire a bullet. *Legal use.*

**Bang to rights**   To be caught in a criminal act or to catch someone in the act. *Police and underworld use, 1932.* Cf. **dead bang**.

**Bargain**   A reduction in a prison sentence, usually for a negotiated guilty plea. *Law enforcement and underworld use, 1934.*

**Bark**   To inform to the police. *Obsolete 1930 underworld use.* Cf. **sing; squeak; squeal**.

**Barratry; barretry**  The practice of frequently bringing groundless legal proceedings, a misdemeanor in many jurisdictions.

**Barrister**  In English law one who argues cases before a judge. A solicitor prepares cases for trial, but the barrister tries the case. *U.K. legal use.*

**Bastinado**  A whipping or thrashing administered with a stick, especially to the soles of the feet, and used in ancient times to exact false confessions. *General use, sixteenth century.*

**Bat, go to the**  To commit perjury. *Underworld use, 1924.*

**Bat carrier**  A police informant. *Underworld use, 1925.*

**Battered child**  A child who has been injured from abuse or neglect, or one who is born dependent on a habit-forming narcotic substance. *Legal use.*

**Battered wife syndrome**  A behavior pattern in which a man physically and psychologically abuses his wife, persuades her to forgive him, seeks her love, and then repeats the cycle again and again until the wife, who hopes the marriage can be saved, becomes helpless. Relevant in connection with homicide by a battered wife and imminence-of-attack requirement of self-defense. *Legal use, twentieth century.* Cf. **self-defense**.

**Battery**  The unlawful application of force to another's person. Three legal conditions must be present: defendant's conduct, the requisite mental state, and harmful or offensive contact with the victim. A threat of harm may constitute "assault," and subsequent application of such force is battery. *Legal use.* Cf. **assault and battery**.

**Baumes Law**  New York's four-time loser law, which requires life imprisonment for anyone convicted of a fourth felony. In some jurisdictions three-time loser laws exist. *Legal use.*

**Beat the box**  To dupe a lie detector. *Underworld use, twentieth century.*

**Beat the chair**  To avoid electrocution, either by commutation of sentence or being declared innocent or insane, or by jailbreak or suicide. *Prison use, twentieth century.*

**Beef**  *n.* 1. A complaint to the police or by the police. *Underworld and police use, 1912.* 2. Information given to the police or testimony against accomplices. *Prison use. v.* To lodge a formal report or complaint about a convict's behavior. *Prison use.*

**Beefer**  An informant. *Underworld use, 1889.*

**Behavioral control unit**  A prison solitary confinement cellblock; a.k.a. **hole**. *Prison use.*

**Beheading**  A once popular form of capital punishment, especially in France, where the guillotine was invented for this purpose. In Germany, the ax was employed. *General use. v.* To remove someone's head by sword, guillotine, or ax, employed since the fifth century primarily in Germany and France for convicted felons of capital crimes; a sentence that is now abolished. *General use.*

**Belch**  *n.* A police informant. *Underworld use, 1920. v.* To inform to the police or to turn state's evidence. *Underworld use, 1898.*

**Belcher**  A police informant. *Underworld use, 1904.*

**Bench**  The judge's seat in court or a panel of judges or the judiciary at large. *Legal use.*

**Bench parole**  On probation. *Legal use.*

**Bench trial**  A trial without a jury; the judge makes the decision of guilty or not guilty. *Legal use.*

**Bench warrant**  A document ordering the arrest or apprehension of a person to compel his presence before a court, usually issued after someone has failed to appear in court, escaped custody, or violated terms of probation or parole. *Legal use.*

**Benefit of counsel**  The right granted by the Sixth Amendment guaranteeing a person charged with a crime the right to legal counsel. *U.S. legal use.*

**Bertillonage; Bertilonage**  An identification system created in the 1890s by French criminologist Alphonse Bertillon (1853–1914), in which the criminal or victim is identified by measurements of certain unchanging parts of a person's skeleton, or by any abnormalities noted in an individual. This system of identification, on which the generally discarded science of phrenology is based, was the precursor of fingerprinting; a.k.a. **bertillon system**. *Law enforcement use.*

**Bertillon system.**  See **bertillonage**.

**Bestiality**  Sexual contact between humans and animals. *Legal use.* Cf. **crime against nature**.

**Beyond a reasonable doubt.**  See **reasonable doubt**.

**Bifurcated trial**  A trial in which certain issues are decided separately (e.g., guilt and sanity, guilt and punishment). *Legal use.*

**Bigamous**  Pertaining to bigamy. *Legal use.*

**Bigamy**  The act of entering into a second marriage while a previous marriage is still valid, a criminal offense in most jurisdictions and legal grounds for annulment of the latest marriage. *Legal use.*

**Big lie**  A distortion of the truth so gross, shouted so loudly, and disseminated so widely that it is believed by many, who assume that no one would tell such an outright lie unless it were in fact true; used successfully for a time by Adolf Hitler prior to and during Germany's Third Reich (1923–1945) and by U.S. Senator Joseph McCarthy during the communist scare of the 1950s. *General use.*

**Bill of attainder** Legislation that punishes persons without a trial; forbidden by the U.S. Constitution; a.k.a. **bill of pains and penalties**. *Legal use.* Cf. **attainder**.

**Bill of indictment** A formal document accusing a person of a crime that is presented to a grand jury, which then hears the evidence. If the jurors decide there are sufficient grounds for an indictment, they return a true bill. *Legal use.* Cf. **indictment**; **presentment**.

**Billy** A policeman's baton or nightstick. *General use, 1850.*

**Billy club** A police officer's nightstick; a bludgeon. *General use.*

**Bird-lime** *n.* Time, usually the length of a prison sentence. *Underworld use, 1857. v.* To wrongly convict someone. *Australian underworld use, 1945.*

**Birdseed** 1. Money paid or anything of value given in return for information. 2. A bribe used to obtain information. *Underworld use.*

**Black cap** A square silk cap worn by an English High Court judge on Lord Mayor's Day, carried to the opening of Parliament and other formal occasions, and until the 1950s laid across his wig as he pronounced the sentence of death. *U.K. legal use.*

**Blackmail** A demand for money or other considerations under threat; extortion, shakedown, coercion, soliciting a bribe, payoff, tribute, hush money. *General use.* Cf. **coercion**; **extort**; **hush money**; **payoff**; **shakedown**.

**Blank warrant** A blanket search warrant that gives the executing officer the authority to seize anything he desires or authorizes the search of broad or multiple areas; usually this type of warrant is ruled defective and insufficient if challenged in court. *Legal use.*

**Bleat** To inform to the police. *Obsolete 1890 underworld use.* Cf. **squeak**; **squeal**.

**Blob** To inform on an accomplice; to inform the police. *Underworld use, 1925.*

**Blood identification** The serological study of blood groups, types, and grades in forensic identification of criminals who have been stained by the blood of their victims or have left stains of their own blood at the scene of a crime. *General use.* Cf. **DNA**.

**Blower** A police informer. *Underworld use.*

**Blow off** 1. To inform to the police. *Underworld use, 1925.* 2. The proof of guilt. *Police use.* 3. To steal. *Underworld use, 1936.*

**Blue room** 1. A police interrogation room, the place where the third degree is administered. *Underworld use.* 2. A solitary confinement cell in a prison, especially one where physical punishment is administered; a.k.a. **the hole**. *Prison use.*

**Board of pardons** A government board that investigates and makes recommendations for pardons and executive clemency; a.k.a. **board of parole**. *Legal use.*

**Board of parole.** See **board of pardons**.

**Bogey**; **bogy**; **bogie** 1. A police informant. *Underworld use, 1924.* 2. A police officer, especially a detective. *Underworld use, 1914.*

**Bond, appearance** One that guarantees the appearance of a defendant in court on a criminal charge; if he fails to appear, the bond is forfeited. *Legal use.*

**Bondsman** One who puts up the bail for someone charged with a crime, usually for a fee; a surety. *General use.* Cf. **bail bondsman**.

**Book** *n.* Imprisonment, especially a life sentence. *U.S. prison use, 1920.* Cf. **do the book**. *v.* 1. To sentence, especially to the maximum penalty prescribed by law. *Underworld use, 1829.* 2. To arrest and charge with specific offenses. *Police and underworld use, 1839.* Cf. **throw the book at**.

**Border warrant** A legal process that allows immigration officers to conduct preliminary questioning and searches without a warrant, usually used for the search and arrest of illegal immigrants. *U.S. legal use.*

**Bound** 1. To be placed under a legal obligation. *Legal use.* 2. To arrest someone. *Underworld use.*

**Boxed** A criminal suspect being examined by a polygraph (lie detector).

**Brady material** Any information held by the prosecution that tends to exonerate the defendant; from the 1963 case *Brady v. Maryland,* in which the U.S. Supreme Court ruled that any such information must be turned over to the defense. *U.S. legal use.*

**Brainwashing** 1. A process by which an individual is indoctrinated to a belief not his own; a coercive form of persuasion. *General use.* 2. Psychological techniques employed by police or political psychologists in a military organization in altering the thought processes of persons from whom information or services are sought. The term suggests a "scrubbing of the mind," in which all ideas deemed "dirty" by the brainwasher are given up (secrets) and "clean" ideas substituted. Brainwashing is achieved through logical arguments or incessant arguments, the latter being the Chinese method. A prisoner is kept isolated in a small cell and is addressed ceaselessly by interrogators, who point out the virtues of Marxism and the evils of democracies, denying, if necessary, basic comforts of food, sleep, and warmth to inmates until their will to resist is demolished and they embrace communism wholeheartedly as their only salvation, physically and spiritually. Constant indoctrination follows to maintain the "brainwashed" state of mind. This technique was depicted in several films dealing with the Korean War, including *Prisoner of War*, 1954; *The Rack*, 1956; and, to a devastating and impossible degree, *The Manchurian Candidate*, 1962. *Police and Intelligence use.*

**Brassey; brassy**   A police informant, from the brass buttons on police uniforms. *Underworld use, 1924.*

**Breach**   The violation of a law or obligation. *Legal use.*

**Break a case**   1. To discover the solution to a mysterious crime. *Law enforcement use.* 2. To determine, by a preliminary discussion of judges on a panel, the level of agreement or disagreement before formal opinions are written. *Legal use.*

**Breaking at the wheel**   Capital punishment in which the prisoner was strapped backward to a wheel and whirled incessantly until death ensued, or strapped to a wheel and beaten periodically and then left to die. Often used to induce false confessions. Used from the first to nineteenth centuries, mostly in Spain (Inquisition), the Middle East, ancient Greece, and Rome. *General use.*

**Bribe**   1. Money or merchandise offered, promised, given, or accepted with intent to influence action, opinion, or decisions of a public official or law officer; the giver and the taker of the bribe both commit a criminal act. *Legal use.* 2. Any gift intended to influence the taker. *General use. v.* To give or offer money or merchandise in order to influence the discharge of a legal or public duty. Prosecutors have illegally offered bribes in the form of lenient sentences to prison informants in exchange for perjured testimony. *Legal use.* Cf. **graft**; **kickback**; **solicitation of bribe.**

**Bridgeman**   The officer of a criminal court who stands between the judge and the parties to a case.

He calls the calendar and processes the paperwork. *Legal use.*

**Bucket of suds**   Information meant to deceive; lies. *U.S. underworld use, 1932.*

**Buff**   1. To commit perjury. 2. To inform to the police. *Obsolete 1910 underworld use.*

**Bull ring**   A place where the "third degree" was administered by the police. *Underworld use, 1880.*

**Bullet**   The projectile fired from a gun.

**Bullet entrance wound**   The damage done by a bullet on the way into and out of a body. The entry wound is usually a neat, round hole. The exit wound is usually much larger and not necessarily neat, especially if the bullet is a large caliber or a dumdum; a.k.a. **bullet exit wound.** *Police, legal, and medical use.*

**Bullet exit wound.**   See **bullet entrance wound.**

**Bum beef**   A groundless charge or false accusation; a.k.a. **bum finger.** *U.S. underworld use, 1928.*

**Bum rap**   A false accusation or charge. *Underworld use, 1927.*

**Bum steer**   False information or bad advice. *Underworld use, 1924.*

**Burden of proof**   The standard of persuasion that the prosecution must meet. In U.S. criminal law the accused need not prove himself innocent; he is presumed innocent until proven guilty beyond a reasonable doubt. *U.S. legal use.*

**Bureau**   1. The Federal Bureau of Investigation. *General use, twentieth century.* 2. FBI headquarters in Washington, D.C. *FBI use.*

**Bureau supervisor**   An FBI agent who coordinates the work done on a case in a certain region or between two or more field offices. *FBI use.*

**Burn up**   1. To die in the electric chair. *Prison use, 1920s.* 2. To frame an accomplice or defraud a partner. *Underworld use, 1931.*

**Burned at the stake**   Capital punishment for witchcraft, murder, robbery, and other major crimes, from ancient times to the eighteenth century in most Western countries. *General use.*

**Bust**   *n.* A police raid or arrest. *Underworld and police use, 1938. v.* 1. To inform on an accomplice. Cf. **spill one's guts.** 2. To arrest or raid. *Underworld and police use, 1938.*

**Busting**   Informing on an accomplice. *Underworld use, 1859.*

**Button**   1. A police informant. *U.S. underworld use, 1925.* 2. A policeman, from the buttons on his uniform. *Underworld use, 1918.* 3. An underworld soldier. *Mafia-syndicate use, 1940s.*

**Buzz-man**; **buzman** A police informant. *U.S. underworld use, 1920.*

**Bystander**, **innocent** A person who is in the wrong place at the wrong time; one who is innocently passing by as a crime takes place and somehow becomes involved (e.g., is hit by a stray bullet or taken hostage by criminals as they attempt to flee the police). *General use.*

**Buff** 1. To commit perjury. 2. To inform to the police. *Obsolete 1910 underworld use.*

**Buffer** A perjurer. *Underworld use, 1797.*

**Cabbage hat** A police informant. *U.S. underworld use, 1910.* Cf. **rat**.

**Cackle** To inform the police. *Obsolete 1891 underworld use.*

**Cacodaemonomania** A feeling or belief of being possessed by the devil or similar spirit and having no control over one's actions, usually seen in cases of hebephrenic schizophrenia. *Medical use.*

**Cage** *n.* 1. A jail. *Underworld and prison use, 1636.* 2. The Bellevue Hospital prison ward in New York. *Obsolete U.S. underworld use, 1891. v.* To place one in prison. *Underworld use, 1949.*

**Calaboose** 1. A prison or jail. 2. A prison cell for punishment. *U.S. underworld and prison use, 1792.*

**Calling on a prisoner** Asking the defendant why judgment should not be passed after he has been found guilty. *Legal use.*

**Camera eye** 1. A witness or detective with a good memory for faces and facts. *Police and underworld use.* 2. A police informant. *U.S. underworld use, 1920s.*

**Can** *n.* A jail or lockup. *Underworld use, 1927. v.* To place someone in prison. *Prison use, twentieth century.*

**Canary** *n.* 1. A prisoner; a.k.a. **canary bird**. *Prison use, 1725.* 2. A police informant. *Underworld use, 1930. v.* To inform on others in the hope of saving oneself. *U.S. underworld use, 1933.*

**Capacity defense** A defense that attempts to negate the accusation by showing the defendant lacked the ability to be accountable for his actions (e.g., anyone under age seven is found to lack criminal capacity). *Legal use.* Cf. **competency to stand trial**; **defense**; **insanity**; **intoxication**.

**Capias** A writ from a judge ordering police to place the defendant in custody. *Legal use.*

**Capias ad respondendum** A writ that calls for the arrest of one who has been indicted for a misdemeanor. *Legal use.*

**Capital offense** Any crime that is punishable by death; a.k.a. **capital case**; **capital crime**. *General use.*

**Capital punishment** The death penalty for capital crimes (e.g., murder); originally referred to the loss of one's head. *General use.*

**Caption** The taking element of the crime of larceny. *Legal use.*

**Captive** A prisoner, usually someone being detained or restrained by another (e.g., a wanted person or a prisoner of war). *General use.*

**Capture** To take captive (e.g., to capture a suspect or a criminal). *General use.*

**Captured conversation** Tape-recorded conversation. *Law enforcement and underworld use.*

**Career criminal** One who lives off crime. *General use.*

**Carnal abuse** 1. Defiling a female's genitals by those of a male's without penetration occurring. 2. An injury to female sexual organs in an attempt at carnal knowledge. 3. Carnal knowledge with a female under the age of consent. *Legal use.*

**Carnal knowledge** Sexual intercourse, even if only the slightest penetration by the penis is made. *Legal use.*

**Carnal knowledge of a minor** Unlawful sexual relations with a child under the age of consent. *Legal use.*

**Carnally knew** A technical term that some authorities consider unnecessary in a rape indictment. *Legal use.*

**Case** *n.* 1. Observing a prospective house to steal from, a bank to be robbed, or any other location where such crimes as murder, burglary, and rape are contemplated. *Underworld use, 1928.* 2. A judicial matter or proceeding that contests a legal question. *Legal use.* 3. A crime that requires police investigation. *Police use. v.* 1. To place a prisoner in a barren cell and feed him only bread and water. *Prison use, 1909.* 2. To carefully watch a building or potential victim with the intention of robbery. *Underworld use, 1914.* 3. To imprison someone. *U.S. underworld use, 1925.*

**Case law** The jurisprudence concerning a particular matter that has accumulated from previous court decisions similar in nature. *Legal use.*

**Case the joint** 1. To look over a place prior to robbing it. *Underworld use.* 2. To survey a place before entering in order to arrest the occupants. *Law enforcement use.*

**Catatonic** Characterized by the immobility and lack of reactions typical of catatonia schizophrenia; may be caused by mental illness or a drug reaction. *General use.*

**Catatonic death reaction** Characterized by rigid muscles, robot-like movement, and mutism, it is a stuporous condition that schizophrenics may exhibit after an emotional shock. *Medical use.*

**Catching** 1. The review of criminal complaints given by the victim to the first police officers on the scene. 2. Take on a case or assignment. *NYPD use.*

**Cattle prod** An instrument that gives electric shocks used for riot control, but sometimes illegally used in coercing suspects into confessions. *Police use.*

**Cave in** To admit one's guilt in a crime. *U.S. underworld use, 1872.*

**Cell** *n.* A unit or room of a prison where inmates are confined. *General use.* *v.* To live in a cell with another prisoner. *Obsolete U.S. prison use, 1903.*

**Central** The dispatcher who handles all emergency police calls. *Police use.*

**Central booking** The holding area for prisoners awaiting court arraignment. *NYPD use.*

**Chair** 1. The chair used for electrocution. 2. A death sentence by electrocution. *Prison use.*

**Challenge** The objection made by either the prosecution or the defense to keep a prospective juror from serving. *Legal use.*

**Challenge, peremptory** The right of the prosecution or defense to have a prospective juror removed or excused without having to give any reason for so doing. The number of peremptory challenges permissible is generally determined by court rule or statute. *Legal use.*

**Challenge of juror for cause** The right of the prosecution or defense to ask for the removal of a prospective juror for a particular reason (e.g., prejudice or bias). For removal of the juror in this case, the presiding judge must agree with the opposing attorney. *Legal use.*

**Chamber** The gas chamber used for executions. *Prison use.*

**Chamber music** An off-the-record meeting between attorneys and a judge in his chambers, where a guilty plea to a lesser charge is arranged in order to save time and money. *Underworld use.*

**Chamber of horrors** The room at police headquarters where illegal interrogations and trials take place. *NYPD use.*

**Chambers** A judge's private office. *Legal use.*

**Change of venue** Removal of a trial to another location so that a fair and unbiased jury may be selected; this is usually necessary in highly publicized cases. *Legal use.*

**Chaplaincy services** A service now provided by most U.S. prisons allowing for a full or part-time chaplain or volunteer to visit inmates and offer religious counseling and / or services. *Prison use.*

**Character evidence** Testimony or material revealing a person's reputation in the community; is sometimes admissible as evidence. *Legal use.*

**Character witness** A witness who testifies concerning another's reputation for honesty, veracity, and moral standing in the community. Usually the witness testifies for the defendant in a criminal trial, especially at the sentencing hearing. *Legal use.*

**Charge** A formal accusation that someone committed a crime (e.g., a grand jury's indictment, a criminal complaint, or a filing by a prosecuting attorney). *Legal use.*

**Chargeable** Any action that may be charged as a criminal offense. *Police use.*

**Charge of the court** Instructions the judge gives to the jury prior to its deliberations. *Legal use.*

**Charge room** A police station room where those arrested are searched and charged with a crime. *U.K. police use.*

**Charge sheet** A police record that lists persons accused of crimes, the nature of the offense, and the person making the accusation. *Legal and law enforcement use.*

**Charge to the jury.** See **charge of the court**.

**Charging document** The formal written statement that accuses a person of an offense. *Legal use.*

**Cheat** 1. To commit a fraud by trickery or deception. 2. To swindle. *General use.*

**Checkered past** Used to describe someone who has been involved in crooked or shady dealings. *General use.*

**Checkers** Police informants. *U.S. underworld use, 1925.*

**Check fraud** Writing checks with the knowledge that the bank will not honor them because the account is closed or overdrawn. *General use.*

**Cheese eater** A police or prison guard informant, cheater, or double-crosser. *U.S. underworld and prison use, 1930.* Cf. **rat**.

**Child abuse** Any cruelty committed against a child that affects the child mentally, morally, or physically. *Legal use.* Cf. **abuse**.

**Child molester** One who seeks sexual gratification from very young children. *General use.*

**Child neglect**   An intentional neglect in providing education, clothing, food, shelter, supervision, or care for a child. *Legal use.*

**Child porn.**   See **child pornography**.

**Child pornography**   Material that features children performing or involved in acts of sex. The U.S. Supreme Court has determined that child pornography is not to be protected by the First Amendment in *New York v. Ferber. General use.*

**Child snatching**   The abduction of a child by a parent or grandparent of the child who does not have legal custody of that child; a.k.a. **parental kidnapping**. *Law enforcement use.*

**Chill the beef**   To use threats or force to scare witnesses into withholding testimony or evidence; a.k.a. **chill the rap**. *U.S. underworld use.*

**Chirp**   To give information to the police. *Underworld use, 1839.*

**Chirp, turn**   Give information to the police in order to avoid prison. *U.K. underworld use, 1846.*

**Circuit court**   A court that sits in more than one place within a jurisdiction or between jurisdictions. *Legal use.*

**Circuit judge**   A judge who presides over a circuit court. *Legal use.* Cf. **court of appeals, U.S.**

**Circuit court of appeals**   The appellate court in each circuit of the United States, made up of three judges and having review power over district court decisions, in most cases, in their circuit. *Legal use.*

**Circumstantial evidence**   Indirect evidence by which principal facts may be inferred. This evidence does not result from actual observation or knowledge of the facts in question, but from other facts that can lead to deductions that indirectly prove the facts being sought. *Legal use.*

**Circus, give someone the**   To beat information out of someone. *U.S. underworld use, 1930.*

**Citation**   An order written by a law enforcement officer that requests a suspect to appear in court at a specified time and place to answer the accusation against him. *Legal and law enforcement use.*

**Citizen's arrest**   An arrest made by a private citizen, allowable in some circumstances for felonies and misdemeanors involving a breach of the peace. *Legal use.*

**Civil death**   The forfeiture of certain civil privileges and rights that accompanies a sentence to a lengthy prison term. *Legal use.*

**Civil disobedience**   Refusing to obey a law that is viewed as oppressive or immoral, in the hopes of

bringing about the law's repeal. Martin Luther King Jr. and Mahatma Gandhi practiced this type of protest. *Legal use.*

**Civil rights**   Certain rights and privileges guaranteed to all citizens by the country's constitution (e.g., freedom of speech and press granted by the First Amendment). *Legal use.*

**Civil rights of criminals**   Limitations that are placed on the civil rights of a convicted offender (e.g., loss of the right to vote). *Legal use.*

**Clam up**   To remain silent, especially when questioned by law enforcement officials. *Underworld use, 1900.*

**Classification**   The process by which a prisoner is assigned to an institution and rehabilitation program suited to his needs. It also is the cumulative file of all records concerning a prisoner from the time of sentencing to the time of release. *Law enforcement use.*

**Classification center**   A holding facility where prisoners are kept while officials decide where they should be incarcerated. *Law enforcement use.*

**Classification committee**   A group of corrections officials who meet periodically to discuss and determine treatment, housing, programming, and other matters concerning prisoners. *Prison use.*

**Classification of crime**   Crimes are often classified or grouped in statutes according to their seriousness (e.g., felonies in one class and misdemeanors in another, with different punishments for each class). Crimes are also sometimes classified by degree (e.g., first- and second-degree murder). In the United States, many police departments follow the FBI crime classifications, while others have established their own classifications. *Legal use.*

**Clean up the calendar**   A bargain with the police where one pleads guilty to a number of criminal charges, even those one did not commit, in return for a promise of a lighter sentence. This is often done with police informants exchanging false testimony against others for lenient sentences in cold case crimes. Thus the police can say they have solved more unsolved cases than they actually have, while bringing about what may be a new but wrongful conviction. *U.S. underworld use.*

**Clear**   To be free from blame or accusation. *General use.*

**Clear a case**   To remove a criminal case from further investigation either by arresting and charging a suspect or by determining that the crime was committed by a person now dead. *Police use.*

**Clearance rate**  The percentage of crimes cleared by a police department or a specific division of a police department. *Police use.* Cf. **clear a case.**

**Clear and present danger doctrine**  Constitutional law standard that allows speech to be curtailed or punished where it creates a clear and present danger of causing evils that the government has a right to prevent (e.g., falsely shouting fire in a crowded theater). *Legal use.*

**Clemency**  A kindness; refers to an act by which a state governor or a U.S. president grants a pardon (which can imply or declare an exoneration) or commutes a death sentence to life imprisonment (which does not necessarily indicate an exoneration, and is usually exercised when there is doubt about the prisoner's guilt and with the possibility of evidence being discovered in the future that may bring about that exoneration). *Legal use.* Cf. **amnesty; pardon.**

**Client**  One who engages the services of a lawyer. *Legal use.*

**Close custody**  Intense surveillance of prisoners likely to attempt escape. *Prison use.*

**Club guy**  A police officer fond of brutality. *U.S. underworld use, twentieth century.*

**Cobra-venom reaction**  A means of diagnosing insanity from hemolysis; the blood's red corpuscles are broken up when venom from a cobra or other snakes is injected. *Medical use.*

**Cocked hat**  A police informant. *U.S. underworld use, 1910.* Cf. **cabbage hat; rat.**

**Coconspirator**  A member of an illegal confederacy. *Underworld use.* Cf. **conspiracy.**

**Coconspirator's rule**  The actions and statements of all conspirators are admissible in court against each of them. *Legal use.* Cf. **Wharton Rule.**

**Code of criminal procedure**  Federal or state laws that deal with trial procedure of criminal cases and the enforcement of the penal code. *Legal use.*

**Code of Military Justice**  Laws governing all U.S. military branches. It also provides for automatic appellate review by the court of military review for certain court-martial cases. A court of military appeals consisting of three civilian judges that automatically reviews certain cases (e.g., if a charge calls for the death penalty or is against a general or flag officer). *Legal use.*

**Code 1**  A command to acknowledge or respond. *LAPD use.*

**Code 7**  A call for time out to eat. *Police use.*

**Code 3**  An emergency call instructing one to proceed at once using lights and siren. *Police use.*

**Code 2**  An urgent call instructing one to proceed at once without siren, lights being optional; proceed with traffic. *Police use.*

**Coerce**  To force or compel someone to comply. *Legal use.*

**Coercion**  Compelling someone by blackmail, threats, or force to commit an act against his will. Like duress, it can sometimes be used as a defense for the commission of a crime. *Legal use.* Cf. **duress.**

**Cold blood, in**  Used to describe an action preformed with exceptional cruelty and without mercy, especially premeditated murder. *General use.*

**Cold water ordeal**  An ancient trial method by which a common person was found guilty or innocent by casting him into a river with a rope tied about his or her torso. If the person sank to the bottom before being brought up, he was deemed not guilty, but if he or she floated, the defendant was deemed guilty for the water had rejected him or her. This "test" was applied to suspected witches in the Middle Ages and even later, an early third degree in which the defendant had no chance of survival. Someone who sank, drowned to death; someone who floated was proven to be a witch and was executed. *Obsolete legal use.*

**Collar**  *n.* 1. An apprehension, usually caught in the act. *U.S. police and underworld use, 1890.* 2. An arresting police officer. *U.S. police and underworld use, 1895.* 3. Report of violating a prison rule. *U.S. prison use. v.* 1. To grab or steal. *Underworld use, 1728.* 2. To make an arrest; usually refers to catching the criminals in the act. *Underworld and police use, 1853.* 3. To report a fellow prisoner for violating a prison rule. *U.S. prison use.*

**Collar, get the**  To be apprehended; a.k.a. **collar felt, get one's** *Police and underworld use, twentieth century.*

**Collar, give the**  To place in custody. *Law enforcement use, 1872.*

**Collar, good**  An arrest for a serious crime. *NYPD use.*

**Collusion**  A conspiracy between two or more persons to defraud another or gain an objective by unlawful or lawful means for an unlawful objective. *Legal use.* Cf. **connivance; connive.**

**Collusive**  Relating to an agreement made between at least two people that is meant to defraud another or gain an objective by unlawful or lawful means for an unlawful objective. *Legal use.*

**Come it**   To be a police informant. *Underworld use, 1812.*

**Commission**   In criminal law, the performance of a criminal act. *Legal use.*

**Commit**   1. To give information to the police. *Obsolete 1910 U.S. underworld use.* 2. To execute a criminal act. *General use.* 3. To send a person to prison or to a mental institution. *General use.*

**Commitment**   A court order that calls for someone to be placed in a mental health institution or prison. *Legal use.* Cf. **mittimus**.

**Common law**   The body of law formed from custom and prior court decisions. *Legal use.* Cf. **statute**.

**Common law contempt**   Proceedings for contempt of court that are criminal in nature. *Legal use.*

**Common law crimes**   Offenses that are tried and judged based on past courtroom decisions, as distinguished from statutory crimes. *Legal use.*

**Community facility**   A nonconfinement facility from which inmates are allowed to leave unaccompanied to look for or hold a job, get an education, or receive treatment in a program. *Prison use.* Cf. **halfway house**.

**Community treatment centers**   A facility that provides inmates with a transitional phase from the controlled atmosphere of prison life to the freedom outside. Earlier termed halfway houses, these facilities help inmates make a smooth adjustment back into society. *Prison use.*

**Commutation**   A prison sentence reduction by an act of a government official. Unlike a pardon, it does not relieve one of the legal consequences of a crime. *Legal use.* Cf. **pardon**; **parole**; **probation**.

**Comparison microscope**   An optical instrument that can view two objects simultaneously for easy comparison; it is used in ballistics to determine if two bullets were fired from the same gun. *Forensic use.* See **ballistics**.

**Comparison of handwriting**   A method of examining two writing samples to determine whether or not they were written by the same person; used during a trial to determine the authenticity of a document in question. *Handwriting analysis and legal use.*

**Competency**   1. The ability or lack of ability one has to testify before a court. Cf. **credibility**. 2. The legal admissibility of a document to be used in court. *Legal use.*

**Competency to stand trial**   A person must have the mental capacity or ability to understand the charges against him, understand the nature of the court proceedings, and consult with an attorney. *Legal use.* Cf. **insanity**.

**Competent**   Legally capable or qualified to give testimony. *Legal use.* Cf. **competent witness**.

**Competent witness**   One whom the court finds legally capable or qualified to testify in a matter. *Legal use.* Cf. **credible witness**.

**Complainant**   One who makes a formal complaint or accusation of a crime; a plaintiff. *Legal use.*

**Complaint**   A formal written accusation of wrongdoing made by a private citizen or public official and filed in a court, which specifies the offenses and names of the accused. *Legal use.*

**Complaint denied**   A prosecutor's decision not to seek an indictment or file a complaint or information against the alleged criminal for an alleged crime. *Legal use.*

**Complaint granted**   A prosecutor's decision to seek an indictment or file a complaint or information against the alleged criminal for an alleged crime. *Legal use.*

**Complaint requested**   A law enforcement office's request that a complaint or information be filed or an indictment sought by the prosecutor against an alleged criminal for an alleged crime. *Legal use.*

**Complicity**   The involvement or participation in a crime committed by another; being an accomplice. Cf. **conspiracy**.

**Compounding crime**   The offense of declining to prosecute a criminal who has committed a felony against oneself in return for a bribe or other consideration; a.k.a. **compounding a felony**. *Legal use.*

**Compulsion**   1. Being compelled or inducing another to commit a crime by use of threat or force. Generally for this to be used as a defense, the compulsion must be present and imminent, causing a well-founded fear of serious bodily injury or death if the threat is ignored. *Legal use.* Cf. **coercion**; **duress**. 2. An uncontrollable and sudden desire to act. *General use.*

**Con**   *n.* 1. A prisoner. *General use, 1893.* 2. A prior conviction. *Prison use, 1925. v.* To lie with believability. *Con artist use, 1903.*

**Conclusive evidence**   Evidence that is undeniable because of rules of law that do not allow its contradiction, or because its strength overwhelms proof to the contrary. *Legal use.* Cf. **presumption**; **proof**.

**Concurrent jurisdiction**   Jurisdiction exercised by different courts in the same territory, at the same time, and over the same subject matter. In the United States, there can be federal and state prosecution for criminal conduct; for example, an offender can be tried at the state and federal levels for robbing a federal bank. *Legal use.* Cf. **double jeopardy**.

**Concurrent sentence**   A sentence to be served in conjunction with another or others, all running at the same time; a.k.a. **sentence, concurrent**. *Legal use.*

**Condemn**   To pronounce a person guilty of a crime. *Legal use.*

**Conditional assault**   An intimidating remark or gesture that threatens one with violence if one does not comply with the request of the assailant. *Legal use.*

**Conditional release**   1. Release from prison prior to completion of a sentence; parole. 2. Release prior to one's trial on certain conditions; out on bail. *Legal use.*

**Condonation**   Forgiveness for a wrong granted by a victim. *Legal use.*

**Conduct**   One's actions or lack of action and state of mind at the time of a crime. *Legal use.*

**Coney Island**   An interrogation room. *U.S. underworld use, 1934.*

**Confess**   To acknowledge the truth of a criminal charge or accusation. *General use.*

**Confession**   A statement made voluntarily by a person acknowledging guilt to the commission of a crime and the details and facts pertaining to that crime. *Legal use.*

**Confidence game**   Obtaining money or property from another by gaining and then taking advantage of a victim's confidence through fraud, trickery, or swindling operations. *Legal use.*

**Confinee**   Inmate. *Prison use.*

**Confinement**   Imprisonment. *General use.* Cf. **solitary confinement**.

**Confinement facility**   An institution where prisoners serve out their sentence. *Law enforcement and prison use.*

**Confiscation**   When the government seizes property from a criminal without providing compensation. *Legal use.*

**Confrontation**   Having a witness and the accused face each other so that the witness can make an identification or the accused can make any objections he has to the witness. The Sixth Amendment to the U.S. Constitution requires that an accused be confronted with the witnesses against him. The right to cross-examine a witness is inherent in the right to confrontation. *Legal use.*

**Con game**   1. A crime where valuables are obtained from a victim after his confidence has been secured; a.k.a. **con job**. *General use, 1907.*

**Congeable**   Permissible or legal. *Obsolete legal use.*

**Congenital insanity**   Idiocy, a condition existing from birth. *Medical use.*

**Conjugal visit**   An agreement that allows a prisoner to have sexual relations with his spouse. *Prison use.*

**Conjuror**   A jurist, especially in criminal proceedings. *Obsolete 1900 U.K. underworld use.*

**Connivance**   Secret or indirect consent to another's commission of a criminal act. *Legal use.* Cf. **collusion.**

**Connive**   1. To conspire, consent to, or take part in an unlawful act secretly. *Legal use.* 2. To conspire or scheme with guards to break prison rules. *U.S. prison use, 1922.*

**Conniver**   One who defrauds someone by acting secretly. *Underworld use, 1930s.*

**Consecutive sentence**   A prison sentence to be served immediately after the first sentence has been served. *Legal use.*

**Consent search**   A lawful search of property or a person with the voluntary expressed consent of the person being searched or in control of the premises; such consent validates a warrantless search if freely given. *Legal and law enforcement use.*

**Conspiracy**   A confederacy formed between two or more individuals for the commission of a crime or an act, which may not be unlawful in itself but becomes unlawful when done by the joint efforts of the conspirators, or when unlawful means are used to commit a lawful act. *Legal use.*

**Conspirator**   A person taking part in a conspiracy. *Legal use.* Cf. **accomplice**.

**Conspire**   To engage in a conspiracy. *Legal use.*

**Constable**   1. A municipal officer whose duties are like a sheriff's, a title that has generally replaced constable in the United States. 2. An officer of the peace in the United Kingdom who is generally unarmed. 3. A police officer, especially one below the rank of sergeant.

**Constabulary** A police force organized in a military fashion but separate from the military. *General use.*

**Constitution of the United States** The formal document that provides the foundation for the U.S. legal and governmental systems and the rights, privileges, and freedoms of U.S. citizens. *Legal use.*

**Constitutional** Of or pertaining to a constitution or in agreement with one. *Legal use.*

**Constitutional freedoms** The basic freedoms outlined by the U.S. Constitution, specifically the Bill of Rights or the first ten amendments. *Legal use.*

**Constitutional protections** Basic protections of individuals guaranteed by the U.S. Constitution (e.g., freedom of speech, due process, and equal protection of the law). *Legal use.*

**Constitutional right** A right or privilege that is protected by and afforded to all citizens by the U.S. Constitution. *Legal use.*

**Constructive fraud** Conduct that is not actually fraudulent but is declared by law to be fraudulent because it has the consequences of actual fraud. *Legal use.*

**Constructive intent** A state that exists when one does not have an actual intent to cause a certain result but should have reasonably foreseen that one's actions would cause the result. *Legal use.*

**Constructive malice** Malice that the law infers from the evil act itself. *Legal use.*

**Constructive possession** Exists if one has the power and intent to control property. *Legal use.*

**Consul** Chief magistrates of the Roman or French republics. *Obsolete general use.*

**Contact** An ally helpful at preventing arrest or easing the toils of crime. *General use, 1931.*

**Contempt** A deliberate disregard, obstruction, or disobedience of public authority. *Legal use.* Cf. **common law contempt.**

**Contempt of court** An intentional act that is intended to obstruct, disobey, hinder, or embarrass a court in its administration of justice, or lessen its authority or dignity. May be direct, which occurs in or near the court's presence, or indirect, which does not occur in or near the court's presence. *Legal use.*

**Contempt proceeding** The trial or hearing conducted to determine whether one has been in contempt of court. *Legal use.*

**Continuance** The postponement or delay of a hearing or legal proceeding. *Legal use.*

**Continuing offense** A crime that is perpetrated over a period of time (e.g., a conspiracy). *Legal use.*

**Contraband** Any property that is unlawful to possess, produce, transport, export, or import. *Legal use.*

**Contract** 1. A murder assignment done for money or favors. *Mafia-syndicate use.* 2. A monetary inducement for a public official's help. *U.S. underworld use, 1958.*

**Contrary to evidence** Against the evidence or the weight of the evidence. *Legal use.*

**Contrary to law** 1. Illegal. 2. A jury's verdict that contradicts the law the judge gave the jury during instructions. *Legal use.*

**Contravention** 1. An act that breaks a restraint ordered by a court, deed, or contract. *Scottish legal use.* 2. An action violating the law, a contract, or a treaty. *French legal use.*

**Contributing to the delinquency of a minor** A charge brought against an adult who engages in conduct tending to make a child delinquent (e.g., providing a child with alcohol). *Legal use.*

**Contrive** To scheme or plot. *General use.*

**Controlled substance** A narcotic drug that has laws imposed on its distribution, classification, sale, and use, and is to be dispensed only by a doctor's prescription, with all other use considered illegal. These drugs are categorized by the degree of dependency: the higher the class, the greater the dependency. Class I consists of experimental drugs (e.g., marijuana); Class II consists of amphetamines, cocaine, methadone, and secobarbital; and Classes III, IV, and V consist of combinations of narcotics (e.g., codeine). *Law enforcement use.*

**Control unit** A solitary confinement cell. *Prison use.*

**Contumacy** Intentionally failing or refusing to make a required appearance in court or disobeying a court order. *Legal use.*

**Contumax** One who refuses to stand trial for the charges against him; an outlaw. *Legal use.*

**Convict** *n.* A prisoner found guilty of a crime and serving a sentence for its commission. Cf. *autrefois* **convict; malefactor.** *v.* To find one guilty of the charges brought against him. *Law enforcement, legal and prison use.*

**Conviction** A finding of guilty at the conclusion of a trial, either as the result of a jury's or judge's decision or a guilty plea. *General use.*

**Convictional criminal** One whose political, social, religious, or ethical beliefs drive him to commit crime. *Legal use.*

**Cook** 1. To murder. *Australian prison use, 1856.* 2. To be electrocuted. *U.S. underworld use, 1936.* 3. To give one an intense interrogation, especially involving the third degree. *Obsolete U.S. underworld use.*

**Cook up**   To invent an alibi. *U.S. underworld use, 1939.*

**Cool blood**   In homicidal law, pertains to one in complete control of his emotions, lacking violent passion. *Legal use.* Cf. **premeditation**.

**Cooler**   1. A jail or police station, especially a rural jail. *Underworld use, 1884.* 2. A cell for solitary confinement. *Prison use.*

**Cooped up**   In jail. *Prison use, 1887.*

**Cop**   *n.* 1. A police officer; in the nineteenth century U.K. officers wore copper stars on their uniforms. *General use, 1859.* 2. An arrest by the police. *U.K. underworld use, 1891. v.* 1. To apprehend. *Underworld use, 1827.* 2. To pilfer. *Underworld use, 1879.*

**Copper**   *n.* 1. A police officer, especially one who is tough on crime. *General use, 1840.* 2. An inmate, especially one who informs on others. *Prison use, 1885.* 3. A police informant. *Underworld use, 1891. v.* 1. To be apprehended. *Obsolete 1930 underworld use.* 2. To discover. *Underworld use, twentieth century.* 3. To become a police informant. *Underworld use, 1897.*

*Coram nobis*   Literally, in our court. A writ allowing a court to enter a correction in a judgment it already gave. *Legal use.*

**Coroner**   A public official who investigates unnatural deaths. *Legal use.* Cf. **medical examiner**.

**Coroner's inquest**   An examination of the causes and circumstances surrounding an unnatural or suspicious death, conducted by a coroner with the aid of a jury. *Legal use.*

**Corporal imbecility**   The physical inability to have sexual intercourse; impotence that need not be congenital or permanent. *Medical use.*

**Corporal punishment**   Punishment that is physical rather than pecuniary. *Legal use.*

**Corporate crime**   Crime for which a corporation is responsible because of the activities of its officers or employees. *Legal use.*

**Corpse**   The body of a dead human being. *General use.*

*Corpus delicti*   Literally, the body of the crime. The place or thing on which a crime has been committed (e.g., a murdered man's corpse or a deliberately burned-down house). Not only does *corpus delicti* refer to the material substance of a crime, but more importantly, the substantial fact that a crime has occurred. For example, a corpse is not enough to charge one with murder; there must be evidence of foul play resulting in death as well. *Legal use.*

**Correctional agency**   The department at all levels of government that handles all aspects of confinement and treatment of convicted lawbreakers and those awaiting trial. *Government use.*

**Correctional custody facility**   A prison. *Prison use.*

**Correctional custody unit**   A ship's prison. *U.S. military use.*

**Correctional day program**   A program offering education or treatment for nonresidential criminals, who are required by law to attend. *Prison use.*

**Correctional facility**   A building or an area where prisoners are confined; a prison or camp. *General use.*

**Correctional institution**   A place that deals with or houses convicted criminals for an extended period; prisons, jails, or reformatories. *Prison use.*

**Correctional officer**   A prison guard. *Prison use.*

**Correctional restitution**   A stipulation that, upon release, a prisoner is to make restitution to his victims in the form of labor, in an effort to make the offender responsible to society. Georgia, Iowa, and Minnesota have such programs. *U.S. prison use.*

**Correctional system**   The network of government agencies that are involved with correctional institutions and issues. *Government use.*

**Correctional training school**   A reformatory. *Prison use.*

**Corrections**   All government agencies or departments that are concerned with the confinement, supervision, or treatment of offenders. *Government use.*

**Corrections caseload**   The total number of prisoners assigned to a correctional agency or officer during a certain period of time. *Prison use.*

**Corrigible**   Capable of being corrected or changed, especially in reference to a criminal who is capable of being reformed. *General use.*

**Corroborate**   To support or confirm known facts or previous testimony with additional or confirming facts or evidence. *Legal use.*

**Corroborating evidence**   Evidence that supports or confirms evidence already given. *Legal use.*

**Corroborating witness**   One whose testimony supports statements made by either the victim or the accused. *Legal use.*

**Corrupt**   *v.* To act dishonestly, immorally. *adj.* Morally depraved or degenerate. *General use.*

**Corruption**   An act committed by one in an official or fiduciary capacity, who unlawfully uses his position to obtain a benefit for himself or another, contrary to his official duties and responsibilities. *Legal use.* Cf. **bribe**; **extortion**.

**Corrupt motive doctrine**   The doctrine that requires there to be knowledge of a wrongdoing for certain crimes. For example, for the commission of bribery, the acceptance of gifts or payment by public officials is required. *Legal use.*

**Cough**   1. To break down under an interrogation. *U.S. underworld use, 1901.* 2. To hand over money. *U.S. underworld use, 1906.*

**Counsel**   *n.* A lawyer or attorney. *General use. v.* To give legal advice. *Legal use.*

**Counseling and release**   A decision in juvenile court that the juvenile is to be counseled and released into an adult's custody rather than face further court proceedings. *Legal use.*

**Count**   1. A distinct offense or charge listed in an indictment, complaint, or information accusing one of the crime. *Law enforcement and legal use.* Cf. **indictment**. 2. The official counting of prisoners to make certain that none have escaped, usually conducted four times a day in large prisons, but possibly as frequently as every hour in smaller facilities. *Prison use.*

**Counterfeit**   To fabricate an imitation without authority, intending to pass it for fraudulent gain by claiming that it is the original (e.g., money, documents, or postage stamps). *Legal use.* Cf. **falsify**; **forgery**.

**Counterfeiter**   One who produces fraudulent currency, documents, or valuables. *General use.*

**Court**   1. The part of the judicial branch of government that oversees the administration of justice. Some states have both civil and criminal courts, but in most states the trial court is one of general jurisdiction: it can hear either civil or criminal cases. Cf. **criminal court**; **police court**. 2. A justice of the peace. 3. The building where legal proceedings take place. *General use.*

**Courthouse**   A building that houses one or more courts of law. *General use.*

**Court in chambers**   The part of a legal proceeding which takes place in the judge's private chamber without the presence of a jury. *Legal use.*

**Courtline**   A prison disciplinary committee that meets to determine punishments for those who break prison rules. *Prison use.*

**Court-martial**   A military court held for trying and punishing crimes committed by military personnel. *Legal use.*

**Court of appeals**   A court where review of a trial proceeding is sought by one of the parties in the case, usually an intermediary appellate court. But in some states it can be the highest court. The court consists of seven judges who have been appointed by the governor. *Legal use.*

**Court of general sessions**   A court that handles criminal cases in only some jurisdictions. *Legal use.*

**Court of last resort**   A jurisdiction's highest court of appeals. *Legal use.*

**Court of law**   A court that decides cases based on written or common law. *Legal use.*

**Court of Military Appeals**   The final court of appeals for U.S. military proceedings consisting of three civilian judges appointed by the President. *Legal use.*

**Court of record**   The court where proceedings of a particular case are written down for posterity and the public record. *Legal use.*

**Court of St. James**   The British court named for St. James Palace, at one time the seat of the court. *Obsolete U.K. general use.*

**Court order**   An order issued by a court requiring someone to do or not do a specific act. *Legal use.*

**Court reporter**   One who transcribes verbatim all that is said in a court. *Legal use.*

**Courtroom**   The room in which a court of law is held. *General use.*

**Courts of appeals, U.S.**   The intermediary appellate courts are divided into twelve circuits that have jurisdiction over most cases brought before U.S. district courts. The court's decision at this level is final, except where review is sought before the U.S. Supreme Court. Congress created this branch in 1891, and it was known as the U.S. Circuit Courts of Appeals until 1948. *Legal use.*

**Coventry Act**   The law which provided for the punishment of assaults committed with intent to disable or disfigure; named for Sir John Coventry, who was assaulted in this manner in 1671. *U.K. legal use.*

**Cover up**   Hide or destroy the evidence of a crime or provide an alibi. *General use, 1949.*

**Crab**   *n.* 1. A police informant. *Australian underworld use, twentieth century. v.* 1. To hinder or endanger another's scheme. 2. To botch or ruin one's own scheme. *U.S. underworld use.*

**Crack**   To supply the police with information. *Underworld use, 1850.*

**Creative punishment**   Punishment or sentence that is tailored to the specific crime as well as to the needs of the defendant and society; a.k.a. **creative sentence**. *Legal use.*

**Creative sentence.**   See **creative punishment**.

**Credibility**   Believability, as in how much someone's testimony should be believed. *General use.* Cf. **competency**.

**Credible**   Believable. *General use.*

**Credible person.**   See **credible witness**.

**Credible witness**   One who is to be believed in legal proceedings because of his reputation, position, intelligence or standing, knowledge of the circumstances, and lack of bias; a.k.a. **credible person**; **credibility**. *Legal use.* Cf. **competency**; **competent witness**.

**Cretinism**   An imperfect or arrested mental development with physical degeneracy, lack of physical development, or deformity. *Medical use.*

**Crime**   A wrong that the government has found to be harmful to the public and therefore may be prosecuted and is punishable in a criminal proceeding. *General and legal use.* Cf. **capital offense**; **classification of crime**; **crime, infamous**; **crime, organized**; **crime of passion**; **major crime**; **political crime**; **sex crimes**; **victimless crime**.

**Crime, continuous**   A successive series of acts that last after the crime is complete (e.g., carrying a concealed weapon). *Legal use.*

**Crime, infamous**   A crime bringing infamy to the person committing it. At common law, those who committed certain infamous or heinous crimes were deemed upon conviction to be incompetent to testify as a witness. The rationale was that such a person was too depraved to be worthy of credit. *Legal use.*

**Crime, organized**   A type of crime that is a product of groups and organizations rather than individuals. *General use.*

**Crime, quasi**   1. An offense in the nature of a crime but not classified as such. 2. A wrong committed against the public for which restitution should be made, either in the form of a forfeiture or penalty. *Legal use.*

**Crime against humanity**   Offenses of such an appalling and serious nature that they are answerable only to humanity and not a jurisdiction or person. Development of this concept occurred during the Nazi war crimes trials in 1945. *Legal use.*

**Crime against nature**   Any sexual conduct that is viewed as unnatural, including oral and anal sex. *Legal use.* Cf. **bestiality**; **sodomy**.

**Crime against property**   A crime with property, rather than a person, as its object (e.g., theft). *Legal use.*

**Crime against the law of nations**   Crimes universally understood among nations to be punishable, e.g., murder or rape. *Legal use.*

**Crime against the other**   A principle that provides that neither the wife nor husband will be made to testify against the other unless the crime was committed against the other. *Legal use.*

**Crime Control Act**   A federal law enacted in an attempt to control crime; short for Omnibus Crime Control and Safe Streets Act of 1968. *Legal use.*

**Crime-drug syndrome**   The illegal sale of drugs. *Law enforcement use.*

**Crime family**   A division of the *Cosa Nostra*/Mafia that operates in a certain area and whose members are bound together by loyalty to their boss or by blood relations. *Mafia-syndicate use.*

**Crime in the suites**   White-collar crime in offices. *Law enforcement use.*

**Crime lab**   An area where the examination of clues and evidence from the scene of a crime takes place. *Police use.*

**Crimeless**   An absence of crime or at least no detection of crime. *Law enforcement use.*

**Crimen**   Crime. *Legal use.*

**Crime of commission**   An offense that violates a specific law (e.g., murder). *Legal use.*

**Crime of omission**   An offense whose essence is the lack of action when there is an obligation to act. *Legal use.*

**Crime of passion**   1. A murder committed in the heat of the moment rather than premeditated. 2. A murder committed by one who finds that his lover or spouse is not faithful. *Legal use.*

**Crime of violence**   A category that includes, for example, murder, rape, voluntary manslaughter, mayhem, kidnapping, robbery, extortion when combined with threats of violence, assault with a dangerous weapon, or arson. *Legal use.*

**Crime partner**   One's accomplice in crime. *California prison use.*

**Crime prevention**   The reduction of the commissions of crime, which is the main activity and responsibility of law enforcement agencies. *Law enforcement use.*

**Crime rate**   The ratio of crimes reported to a specific number of residents. *General use.*

**Crime report** A complete report on a crime, including witness or victim accounts or the method of operation. *LAPD use.*

**Crime repression** The task of law enforcement agencies to reduce the opportunities for crime to be committed. *Law enforcement use.*

**Crime school** A juvenile reformatory. *U.S. prison use.*

**Crimes, common law** Criminal acts punishable by the force of common law, as opposed to those laws created by statute. *Legal use.*

**Crimes *mala in se*** Crimes that are immoral or wrong in themselves (e.g., murder, rape, arson, theft, or breach of the peace). *Legal use.*

**Crimes *mala prohibita*** Crimes prohibited by statutes because they infringe on the rights of others, not because they are necessarily evil by nature. *Legal use.*

**Criminal** *n.* One who has committed a crime. *adj.* Pertaining or connected to criminal laws, penal administration, or that which involves the element of crime. *General use.*

**Criminal, situational** One who knowingly commits a crime, well aware of that his actions are illegal, and then rationalizes his behavior as being right because of pressing circumstances. *Sociological use.*

**Criminal act** The commission of crime. *Legal use.*

**Criminal action** 1. A proceeding where the accused is brought to trial, found guilty or not guilty, and sentenced. 2. An action initiated to punish a violation of a criminal law. *Legal use.*

**Criminal anthropology** Lombrosian criminology (after Cesare Lombroso, 1835–1909), which argues that there are distinguishable types of criminals based on physical characteristics, which is also the basis of phrenology. *Legal use.*

**Criminal Appeals Act** A federal law which enables the United States to appeal certain judgments to an appellate court. *Legal use.*

**Criminal assault.** See **assault.**

**Criminal associate** One who voluntarily takes part in illegal activities with someone involved in organized crime. *Law enforcement use.*

**Criminal attempt.** See **attempt.**

**Criminal behavior** Actions that result in a harm done to society, which are punishable by law. *Legal use.*

**Criminal biopsychology** The study of psychosomatic personalities of criminals. *Scientific use.*

**Criminal capacity** Prerequisites for committing a crime, (e.g., whether the action was voluntary or due to a state of mind or age). *Legal use.* Cf. **capacity defense; insanity.**

**Criminal charge.** See **charge.**

**Criminal codes.** See **criminal statutes.**

**Criminal conspiracy.** See **conspiracy.**

**Criminal contempt.** See **contempt.**

**Criminal conversation** Having sexual relations with someone other than one's spouse, or having sexual relations with someone else's wife or husband. This is a tort based on adultery, though some states prohibit actions for it. *Legal use.*

**Criminal conversion money** The damages a convicted adulterer must pay to the injured spouse. *Obsolete U.K. general use, 1770.*

**Criminal court.** See **court.**

**Criminal.** See **professional criminal; sex criminal.**

**Criminaldom** The underworld. *General use.*

**Criminal etiology** The area of criminology that studies the biological, physical, psychological, and social makeup of an offender to show his behavior as criminal. *Law enforcement and legal use.*

**Criminal Evidence Act, 1898** The statute that, for the first time, allowed the accused the option to give evidence on his own behalf. It has been viewed as good and bad; on the one hand it allows the defendant to relate his side of the story or give evidence that would not otherwise be produced, but on the other hand, if the defendant chooses not to give testimony, the jury may view this as suspect, since he obviously does not wish to face cross-examination. *U.K. legal use.*

**Criminal fence** A place where stolen merchandise is exchanged for money or other valuables. *Police use.*

**Criminal forfeiture.** See **confiscation; forfeiture; seizure.**

**Criminal fraud.** See **fraud.**

**Criminal gross negligence.** See **negligence, criminal.**

**Criminal history information** The information kept on file of one's arrests, convictions and correctional and release records. *Law enforcement use.*

**Criminal homicide.** See **homicide.**

**Criminal informant** One who secretly provides information on criminal activities to law enforcement officials. *Law enforcement use.*

**Criminal insanity.** See **insanity.**

**Criminal intent** One's state of mind in planning and carrying out a criminal act. Many crimes require general or specific intent for the act to be criminal. *Legal use.* Cf. **mens rea; specific intent.**

**Criminalism** Behavior or conduct that is criminal. *Sociological use.*

**Criminalist**   One who is adept at criminal law or criminology. *Legal use.*

**Criminalistic**   Having a criminal nature. *General use.*

**Criminalistics**   The scientific investigation of crime. *Law enforcement use.*

**Criminalization**   The government's determination that an offense is criminal and punishable by law. *Legal use.*

**Criminalize**   To become criminal or make illegal. *General use.*

**Criminal jurisdiction**   The power of a court to hear and decide criminal cases. *Legal use.*

**Criminal justice system**   The organization of courts which deal with criminal law and enforcement. *Legal use.*

**Criminal law**   The body of law that declares what actions are criminal and prescribes punishment for them, its goal being to prevent harm to society. *Legal use.* Cf. **penal code**; **penal laws**.

**Criminal lawyer**   An attorney who specializes in and practices criminal law. *General use.*

**Criminal liability**   One's responsibility for criminal behavior. *Legal use.*

**Criminal offense**   A particular crime falling under criminal law. *Law enforcement and legal use.*

**Criminal procedure**   The steps by which a criminal case proceeds, from investigation to the end of the case; the administration of justice. *Law enforcement and legal use.* Cf. **code of criminal procedure**.

**Criminal proceeding**   Steps taken either to prevent crime or to determine and punish the guilty party for a crime already committed. *Legal use.*

**Criminal process**   A means by which a person is compelled to answer for a crime or misdemeanor, e.g., an arrest warrant. *Legal use.* Cf. **indictment**; **information**; **warrant**.

**Criminal prosecution**   A proceeding on the public's behalf in a proper court that would convict and punish the accused. *Legal use.*

**Criminal psychology**   An application of psychological techniques to studying criminals, criminal behavior, and the treatment and problems of crime; a.k.a. **forensic psychology**. *Law enforcement and forensic use.*

**Criminal registration**   Statutes in some areas that require convicted felons to register with the police so their whereabouts are known at all times. *Law enforcement and legal use.*

**Criminal sanctions**   Punishments (e.g., fines, sentences, and probation). *Legal use.*

**Criminal sociology**   A science studying societal factors affecting and developing criminal behavior. *Scientific use.*

**Criminal sociopath**   Someone who does not comprehend the difference between right and wrong. *Sociological use.*

**Criminal statutes**   Laws enacted by legislative bodies that define, categorize, and set punishments for specific crimes. *Legal use.*

**Criminal typologies**   Groupings that criminals can be classified into (e.g., professional criminal, occasional criminal, habitual criminal, convictional criminal, and abnormal criminal). *Sociological use.*

**Criminate**   To charge a person with a crime or incriminate someone. *Legal use.*

**Crimination**   The process of incriminating another; an accusation. *Legal use.*

**Criminative**   Pertaining to an accusation. *Legal use.*

**Criminator**   A person who makes accusations or incriminates. *Legal use.*

**Criminatory**   Pertaining to an accusation. *Legal use.*

**Criminogenesis**   The source of crime. *Law enforcement and scientific use.*

**Criminogenic**   That which produces crime, for example, abusing drugs and alcohol, living in slums or poverty, holding overly materialistic views, etc. *Sociological use.*

**Criminologist**   One who studies crime and criminals. *General use.*

**Criminology**   A science that examines crime, its causes, detection, punishment, and prevention. *General use.*

**Criminotechnology**   Using electronic and photographic equipment and techniques to gather evidence and track down criminals; criminological technology. *Law enforcement use.*

**Cringle**   *n.* A police informant. *v.* To give information to the police. *U.S. underworld use, 1925.*

**Crisis center**   A haven for runaway teenagers or people who leave home in emergency circumstances (e.g., a woman beaten by her husband). *General use.*

**Criterion**   The standard by which to base a judgment or decision. *Handwriting analysis use.*

**Cross-examination**   Examining a witness who was put forward by the opposition in a trial for the purpose of testing the truth of his testimony, developing it further, or for other reasons. The examination is generally limited to questioning matters covered by the direct examination. *Legal use.*

**Crown cases**  Criminal prosecutions on behalf of the Crown or public in English law. *U.K. legal use.*

**Crown cases reserved**  Questions of law that come up at criminal trial sessions and are decided later by criminal courts of appeals. *U.K. legal use.*

**Crown law**  English criminal law. *U.K. legal use.*

**Crown office**  The department that prosecutes criminal law in England. *U.K. legal and law enforcement use.*

**Crown paper**  A list of criminal cases awaiting hearing or sentencing. *U.K. legal use.*

**Crown side**  The jurisdiction of all criminal cases that come under the Crown in England. *U.K. legal use.*

**Crown solicitor**  The prosecutor for the Crown in England. The director of public prosecutions or other authority now handles public prosecuting duties. *U.K. legal use.*

**Crucifixion**  An extremely painful form of punishment in which the criminal's hands and feet are bound or nailed to a cross until he dies. *General use.*

**Crucify**  To put someone to death by binding or nailing his feet and hands to a cross, as in the case of the wrongly convicted Jesus Christ. *General use.*

**Cruel and unusual punishment**  Punishment beyond human decency (e.g., quartering, crucifixion, burning at the stake, the rack, thumbscrew, or other forms of torture disproportionate to the offense). The Eighth Amendment to the U.S. Constitution forbids infliction of cruel and unusual punishment. *Legal use.* Cf. **corporal punishment**.

**Cruelty to children**  Infliction of physical or mental suffering on a child. *Legal use.* Cf. **child abuse**.

**Crump**  One who aids lawyers in finding false witnesses. *Obsolete U.K. underworld use.*

**Culpable homicide**  Manslaughter in Scotland. *Scottish legal use.*

**Culprit**  One who has been accused, indicted, or convicted of a criminal offense. *General use.*

**Cumulative punishment**  Additional punishment given to a habitual criminal, who has been convicted more than once for the same offense. *Legal use.*

**Cumulative sentence**  A sentence of successive terms for separate crimes, which add up and accumulate; a.k.a. **sentence, cumulative**.

**Custodial arrest**  Placing a suspect in custody and informing him of his rights. *Law enforcement use.*

**Custodial interrogation**  Questioning of a suspect in custody by law enforcement officials. *Legal and law enforcement use.* Cf. **taken into custody**.

**Custody**  The actual confinement or detention of a person charged with a crime. *General use.* Cf. **close custody; maximum custody; medium custody; minimum custody; protective custody**.

**DA.**  District attorney, the prosecutor for a judicial district. *Legal use.*

**Dactylography**  The science of fingerprint identification. *Legal use.*

**Damages**  A loss in value or injury to a person, his property, or rights through a wrongful or unlawful act. *Legal use.*

**Dance hall**  The cell or hallway leading to the gallows or other execution chamber, or the chamber itself. *Prison use.*

**Dangerous criminal**  One who has been convicted of a crime of violence or one who has escaped or attempted to escape from custody by the use of force. *Legal use.*

**Dangerous instrumentality**  Anything that is inherently dangerous either by itself, such as explosives, or through careless use, such as an automobile. *Legal use.*

**Dangerous weapon**  An instrument capable of causing death or great bodily harm. *Legal use.* Cf. **aggravated assault; dangerous instrumentality; deadly weapon**.

**Date**  The date on which a convict's sentence ends or the date of his parole. *California prison use.*

**Day in court**  Usually refers to the right of a person to appear in a court of law to defend himself against charges or the right to be heard in a case where one is the complainant. *Legal use.*

**Dead bang**  1. To be caught in the act; a.k.a. **dead bang rap, dead bang to rights**. *Underworld and police use.* 2. An injection of overdiluted or bogus heroin. *Drug addict use, 1970s.*

**Dead banger, fall**  An arrest made in the act of criminal activity or with abundant evidence of guilt. *Underworld and police use.*

**Dead bang rap.**  See **dead bang**.

**Dead bang to rights.**  See **dead bang**.

**Deadly force**  Force, reasonable or unreasonable, intended or likely to cause great bodily harm or death. *Legal use.*

**Deadly weapon**  Any weapon, device, instrument, material, or substance, animate or inanimate, which, by its use or design, is capable of causing great bodily harm or death. *Legal use.* Cf. **dangerous weapon; malicious assault with a deadly weapon**.

**Deadly weapon per se**   A weapon that, through its intended use, would ordinarily result in death or great bodily harm. *Legal use.*

**Dead man**   A convict on death row. *Prison use.*

**Dead on arrival (DOA)**   A term used to describe a person who dies before reaching the hospital. *Legal use.*

**Dead ringer**   Someone who bears a striking resemblance to another, particularly those innocently but mistakenly identified as someone committing a criminal act; a.k.a. **dead spit**. *General use.*

**Dead to rights**   1. Caught in the act. 2. When the preponderance of the evidence points to guilt. *Law enforcement use.*

**Deal**   A beating or interrogation. *Underworld use.*

**Death**   Permanent cessation of all vital signs and functions; the end of life. *Legal use.* Cf. **presumption of death**.

**Death, violent**   A death caused or accelerated by another person. *Legal use.*

**Deathbed**   Something accomplished in the last hours of one's life, as in a confession. *General use.*

**Death blow**   A murderous or destructive stroke or event. *General use.*

**Death certificate**   A doctor's certificate attesting to the cause of death of a patient under his care. If a person is not under a doctor's care at the time of death or if the death is sudden, results from an accident or homicide, or occurs under suspicious circumstances, the local coroner or medical examiner determines the cause of death and issues the certificate. *Legal use.*

**Death House**   A title given a prosecutor with a long record of convictions resulting in death sentences. The attorney's surname follows the title. *General use.*

**Death mask**   A cast made of a dead person's face. *General use.*

**Death penalty**   The sentence by which life is ended as punishment for a crime or crimes; a.k.a. **death sentence**. *Legal use.*

**Death row**   Prison cells reserved for convicts awaiting execution. *General use.*

**Death warrant**   An official order to execute a death penalty. *Legal use.*

**Death watch**   The guard detail that watches over a condemned prisoner, usually in the days before an execution, to prevent escape or suicide attempt. *Prison use.*

**Deceit**   A reckless or intentional misrepresentation or deception. *Legal use.* Cf. **fraud**; **misrepresentation**.

**Deception, scientific detection of**   The field of science that attempts to determine when a lie is being told, usually through lie detector machines or tests. *Scientific use.*

**Decision**   The judgment or decree of a court. *Legal use.*

**Declaration**   A statement, usually not under oath. *Legal use.*

**Decomposed writing**   A handwriting style where down strokes and upstrokes are not connected and sometimes not even completed. *Handwriting analysis use.*

**Decomposition**   The rotting or decaying of once living matter. *General use.*

**Decoy**   A person, usually a police officer, who impersonates a civilian in the hope of attracting a criminal act. For example, a policewoman dresses as a prostitute in order to arrest men who solicit her for sex. *Legal use.*

**Decriminalization**   An official act that changes an action or omission from criminal to noncriminal. *Legal use.*

**Decriminalize**   To eliminate or decrease the criminal classification of a crime or strictness of the present law, for example, to decriminalize marijuana possession. *General use.*

**Deduce**   To trace the path of a criminal or draw conclusions from evidence gathered. *General use.*

**Deduction**   A logical method of inference where conclusions follow from premises assumed to be true. *General use.*

**Defeasance**   1. An instrument that overrides the power of another instrument or document. 2. An instrument that accompanies a judgment declaring an act void when performed. *Legal use.*

**Defect**   The absence of some legal essential, a deficiency or imperfection. *Legal use.*

**Defective delinquent**   A person who is both socially delinquent and mentally defective; criminally insane. *Legal use.*

**Defend**   1. To appear as the attorney for the accused. 2. To appear in opposition to the plaintiff in a court proceeding. *General use.*

**Defendant**   A person charged with a crime; one defending his actions or denying his guilt. *Legal use.*

**Defense**   Evidence offered by one charged with a crime to defeat or excuse the charge. *Legal use.*

**Defense attorney**  The legal representative of a defendant; a.k.a. **defense counsel**. *Legal use*. Cf. **public defender**.

**Defense of insanity**  A criminal defense asserting that the defendant lacked the required mental capacity to be held criminally responsible for his actions. *Legal use*. Cf. **insanity.**

**Deferred sentence**  A sentence that will not be carried out if the defendant fulfills certain requirements. For example, if a defendant stays out of trouble while under court supervision, he will avoid prison. *Legal use*.

**Defraud**  1. To recklessly or intentionally misrepresent the facts. 2. To cheat or trick by deceit. 3. To deprive one of property, right, or interest by the practice of fraud. *Legal use*. Cf. **collusion**; **deceit**; **fraud**; **misrepresentation**.

**Degree**  1. A classification or grade of a crime or criminal charge. *Legal use*.

**Degrees of crime**  The division of a criminal act into several levels of guilt depending on the circumstances of the act, and the division of crimes in general. For example, there are felonies and misdemeanors, and a murder may be either first or second degree. *Legal use*. Cf. **crime**.

**Deinstitutionalization**  A national trend started in Massachusetts in the early 1970s in which correctional systems use residential treatment programs along with probation and parole as alternatives to traditional incarceration. *Prison use*.

**Deliberate**  To consider, weigh, or ponder; for example, to consider a criminal act and its consequences before the commission of the act. *Legal use*.

**Deliberately**  Committed in cold blood, intentionally, purposely, and with premeditation. *Legal use*.

**Deliberation**  The process or act of deliberating, for example, a jury trying to reach a verdict. *Legal use*.

**Delict**  A wrongful act, either civil or criminal, for which legal action can be taken. *Legal use*.

**Delusion**  A belief in the existence of facts that are clearly impossible which cannot be dispelled by reasoning. *Legal use*.

**Dementia**  Deterioration of the mind, usually resulting in insanity. *General use*.

**Dementia** *praecox*  Schizophrenia, usually paranoid. *Obsolete medical use*.

**Demonstrative evidence**  Evidence that speaks for itself (e.g., a knife or gun used in a crime). *Legal use*.

**Denial**  A written or verbal rejection of the charges made; a defense. *Legal use*.

**Denounce**  To condemn a person or a thing; to accuse a person of a criminal act. *Legal use*.

**De novo**  To try anew; start from the beginning; a second time. *Legal use*.

**Deny**  To give a negative answer or reply. To claim that a statement or charge is false. *Legal use*.

**Dependency**  A state in which a person relies on something or someone. *Legal use*.

**Dependent**  To take support or direction from another. *General use*.

**Deponent**  A witness; one who testifies under oath. *Legal use*.

**Deport**  To transport someone out of the country by legal means. *General use*.

**Deportation**  The banishment, removal, or expulsion of an alien from one country to another. *Legal use*.

**Deposition**  Testimony that is given under oath but outside the courtroom and transcribed so that it may be used later at the trial proceeding. *Legal use*.

**Depraved heart murder**  The death of another person caused by extremely negligent conduct that was not intended to kill or do serious injury but that a reasonable man would realize held a very high and unjustifiable degree of risk of death or serious injury to another person or persons. There is a dispute over whether the person himself must be aware of the risk in order to be guilty of murder. Generally a person who drives an automobile at reckless speeds through streets crowded with pedestrians may be charged with murder if he strikes and kills a pedestrian, but some courts have considered a driver's conduct in then stopping to give aid or taking the injured to a hospital as inherent proof that he did not have the necessary depravity of heart to be so charged; a.k.a. **depraved mind**. *Legal use*.

**Deputize**  To designate one as a deputy. *General use*.

**Deputy**  One who is in charge when his superior is absent (e.g., a deputy sheriff). *General use*.

**Deputy sheriff**  A law enforcement officer employed by the sheriff. *General use*.

**Derangement**  All forms of mental illness except that of the natural born idiot. *Legal use*.

**Dereliction of duty**  Delinquency or neglect of one's office. *General use*.

**Derivative evidence**  Usually used to describe evidence obtained as the result of an illegal search. *Legal use*.

**Desertion**  The abandonment of one's family or station without just cause or authorization. Criminal desertion is the abandonment or willful failure to provide for a spouse who is in bad health or other needy circumstances. *Legal and military use.* Cf. **mutiny**.

**Detail** A police assignment to a special duty. *NYPD use.*

**Detain** To hold, stop, delay, arrest. *Legal use.* Cf. **detention**.

**Detainee** One who is held in confinement. *General use.*

**Detainers** A warrant filed against a person already in custody to ensure that he will be available to the jurisdiction that placed the warrant when his present term ends. *Legal use.*

**Detection** The discovery of a crime, or anything hidden, through an investigation or by accident. *Legal use.*

**Detective** An investigator, either privately employed or a member of a law enforcement agency, who detects crime and criminals and gathers information. *Legal use.*

**Detention** The act of withholding, either intentionally or accidentally, a person or a thing. *Legal use.* Cf. **confinement**; **detain**; **pretrial detention**; **preventive detention**.

**Detention center** A jail that houses prisoners waiting for trial. *Legal use.*

**Detention facility** A detention center, work camp, or honor farm. *Legal use.*

**Detention hearing** A hearing used to determine whether a defendant should be released on bond or detained in custody. *Legal use.*

**Detention in a reformatory** The detainment of a juvenile, either as punishment or as a measure of prevention, in an institution designed for juveniles. *Legal use.*

**Deter** To hinder or prevent another from acting. *General use.*

**Determent** Someone or something that stands in the way of another. *General use.*

**Determinate sentence** A fixed term of confinement, set either by statute or by the sentencing court, as opposed to an indeterminate sentence, the length of which is usually determined by the behavior of the prisoner. *Legal use.*

**Deterrence** The prevention of crimes or their repetition. *Legal use.*

**Detoxification** Medically supervised withdrawal from drug or alcohol addiction. *Medical use.*

**Devil on the neck** A torture device made of several irons that are fastened to the arms and legs and then wrenched together to break the back, used in the early nineteenth century and before to induce false confessions. *Underworld use.*

**Diagnosis center** The correctional facility or unit that determines where a prisoner will be assigned. *Prison use.* Cf. **classification center**.

**Differential association theory** A sociological theory, first published by Edwin H. Southerland in *Principles of Criminology* in 1939, which holds that crime is a condition learned through interaction with others. *Sociological use.*

**Diminished capacity** The inability to achieve the state of mind required for the commission of a crime. This concept also allows a court to regard an impaired mental state, which does not qualify as insanity, such as retardation or extremely low intelligence, as mitigating circumstances in the punishment or in the degree of a criminal offense; a.k.a. **diminished responsibility**. *Legal use.*

**Direct cause** That which sets in motion a chain of events leading to a given result. *Legal use.* Cf. **proximate cause.**

**Direct contempt** An act of contempt committed in the presence of the court. *Legal use.* Cf. **contempt.**

**Directed verdict** An acquittal by a judge in a criminal case without the case going to the jury, when it is ruled that the prosecution's case does not meet the burden of proof required by law. This usually takes place after the prosecution has rested its case and before the defense case has begun. *U.S. legal use.* Cf. **verdict**.

**Direct evidence** 1. Information given by a witness with direct knowledge to the facts of a case, such as an eyewitness. 2. Evidence which, if true, conclusively establishes a fact. *Legal use.*

**Direct examination** The first questioning of a witness by the side that called him to testify. *Legal use.*

**Directive** An order or ruling issued by a court or public official. *Legal use.*

**Disability** The lack of legal qualification or capacity. *Legal use.*

**Discharge** To release from confinement. *Legal use.*

**Discount justice** Plea bargaining, the practice of allowing defendants to plead guilty to a lesser charge (e.g., manslaughter instead of murder) to save the court the time and cost of a trial. *Legal use.*

**Discrimination**    The denying of privileges or rights because of race, age, religion, gender, or national origin. *General use.*

**Disfranchise**    To deprive a citizen of rights and privileges (e.g., the right to vote). *Legal use.*

**Disinter**    To remove from the grave, to exhume. *Legal use.*

**Dismemberment**    The removal of a person's limbs. *Legal use.*

**Dismissal**    The dropping of charges by a judicial officer without determining the guilt or innocence of the accused. *Legal use.*

**Disparity of sentences**    As a result of the substantial discretion granted sentencing judges and the Western philosophy that all offenders should be treated individually, punishment often varies greatly for similar or identical crimes. The unfairness of this system has been one of the major complaints of prisoners who have participated in prison riots. Some criminologists believe that the inequities inherent in such a system are used by many inmates as a justification for becoming career criminals. *Legal use.* Cf. **justice model of corrections**.

**Disposition**    The judicial decision which ends a trial with an acquittal, dismissal, or a verdict of guilty. *Legal use.*

**Disqualification**    Deprived of a legal right or function; without legal power. *Legal use.*

**Dissent**    A contrary opinion (e.g., a judge) who disagrees with the majority opinion. *Legal use.*

**Dissociation**    Solitary confinement. *Prison use.*

**Dissuade**    1. To advise and convince a person not to commit an act. 2. To discourage and deter a witness from giving evidence against an indicted person. *Legal use.*

**District attorney**    The prosecuting officer who represents the government in a judicial district. *Legal use.* Cf. **United States attorney**.

**District court**    A federal trial court for a specific territory of the United States or, in some states, state courts for a certain area of a given state. *Legal use.*

**District court judge**    A judge of a U.S. or state district court. *Legal use.*

**Diversion**    The suspension or termination of a formal judicial proceeding and the referral of the defendant to a treatment program. *Legal use.*

**Diversity**    A plea by a prisoner facing execution alleging that he is not the same person as the one thus sentenced. A jury is then impaneled to determine the identity of the prisoner. *Legal use.*

**DNA (deoxyribonucleic acid)**    A criminal identification method, which, in the late 1980s, became the revolutionary new "fingerprinting," one of the most reliable (if properly processed and analyzed) identification methods in criminal investigation, dependent on the basic genetic material found in all human cells. With the exception of identical twins, DNA makeup is different in every person. Genetic testing of this sort analyzes hair roots, blood, semen, and other bodily fluids for DNA. As many convictions as DNA has brought about, a great number of convicted prisoners have also been set free after DNA proved their innocence. Many police departments have sought to take DNA fingerprints of all those booked for serious crimes, but individuals and groups have fought against this procedure. By the end of 1998, only Louisiana compelled all those under arrest to provide test samples for DNA. Many states (not New York) allow DNA testing of prison inmates. According to the *National Institute of Justice Journal*, DNA samples are taken from every suspect in Britain, and British officials have solved seventeen major cases by employing DNA data since 1995. DNA, however, appears to be a fallible identification system. In summer 2004, two black men with criminal records were reported to have identical DNA patterns, which prevented authorities from charging either with a crime.

**DOA**    Dead on arrival. *General use.*

**Docket**    The record of proceedings in a court. *Legal use.*

**Documentary evidence**    Data furnished in writing or inscription, or documents of any kind. *Legal use.*

**Do the book**    To serve a life prison term; a.k.a. **do the rosary**. *Prison use.*

**Do time**    To serve a prison term. *Prison and underworld use.*

**Do tough time**    To serve a prison sentence under especially harsh conditions. *Prison use, 1860.*

**Doublage**    The law by which a French prison inmate, after finishing his prison sentence, must reside in a penal colony for the same length of time as his prison sentence, in effect doubling the sentence. *French legal use.*

**Double-cross**    To cheat, trick, or inform on a partner. *General use.*

**Double jeopardy**    Trying a defendant twice for the same crime, a practice prohibited by the U.S. Constitution. Once a decision of not guilty has been reached the disposition is final; a.k.a. **former jeopardy.** *Legal use.* Cf. **jeopardy**.

**Double-life**   Two life prison terms that run consecutively, usually imposed to guarantee there will be no parole. *Prison use.*

**Draconian code; Draconian law**   Early Greek laws known for their severe penalties. *Legal use.*

**Drag**   *n.* False arrest. *Underworld use, 1931. v.* To arrest, usually without justification. *Underworld use, 1910.*

**Dragnet; drag-net**   A police roundup of suspects. *U.S. police use, 1933.*

**Drawing and quartering**   A form of execution, existing in England from the thirteenth century, where the condemned person is hanged and cut down half alive, the entrails and sometimes the heart then cut out and drawn forth, the head chopped off, and the body severed into quarters. The head and quarters were later put on public display to thwart other would-be wrongdoers. This capital punishment was first applied to William Marise, a pirate and the son of a British nobleman, in 1241. During the reign of George III (1760–1820), Sir Samuel Romilly (1757–1818) spoke out against this punishment, labeling it barbaric and incurring the wrath of authorities, who accused Romilly of attempting to "tear down the pillars of society." The last recorded application of this punishment was in 1820, when the Cato Street conspirators were hanged and then beheaded. *General use.*

**Drop the chuck**   1. To frame a person for a crime he did not commit. 2. To testify against or inform on a colleague. *U.S. underworld use, 1934.*

**Drug abuse**   Chronic or periodic intoxication by consumption of drugs, often compulsively. *General use.*

**Drug addict**   A person who is dependent on drugs. *General use.*

**Drug addiction**   To be dependent on drugs. *General use.*

**Drug dependence**   A state caused by the repeated use of a drug in which an abuser must continue to take the drugs or go through withdrawal symptoms. *Legal use.*

**Drying room**   A police interrogation room. *U.S. underworld use, 1936.*

**Due process clause**   Two clauses of the U.S. Constitution which guarantee a person fair governmental procedures and protect against unfair governmental interference with, or the seizure of,

property. There are similar clauses in most state constitutions. *U.S. legal use.*

**Due process of law**   The regular course of the law, in which one is served with notice of any proceedings, has the opportunity to be heard and his rights protected in court, and has all the benefits of law and fundamental fairness. *Legal use.* Cf. **procedural due process; substantive due process; Warren court**.

**Due process rights**   All rights protected under due process standards. *U.S. legal use.*

**Duly**   Properly, suitably, according to all legal requirements. *Legal use.*

**Dump**   1. To throw away or abandon, especially evidence of a crime. *U.S. underworld use, 1925.* 2. To kill. *U.S. underworld use, 1936.* 3. To be given the third degree. *Prison use, 1934.* 4. To inform on, cheat, or leave your accomplices without warning or a way to escape (e.g., drive off in the getaway car). *Underworld use.* Cf. **spill**.

**Duress**   Illegal imprisonment or coercion in an attempt to force one to act contrary to his own free will. *Legal use.* Cf. **coercion.**

**Duress of imprisonment**   Wrongful imprisonment or illegal restraint of a person in order to coerce him to do some act. *Legal use.*

**Dust off**   A beating or interrogation, especially the third degree. *Police and underworld use.*

**Duty to act**   When criminal liability is based on a failure to act, there must be more than a moral duty to act. There must be a legal duty to act. Common law requires parents to aid their small children in peril, husbands their wives, ship captains their crew, and masters their servants. Therefore, parents could be charged with homicide for failing to properly attend a sick child who dies. Likewise a driver involved in an automobile accident is generally required by statute to stop and offer aid to those who may have been injured. But a passerby who merely witnesses the same accident has no such obligation. *Legal use.*

**Dying declaration**   An exception to the hearsay rule, this is an out-of-court statement made by a person who realizes he is on the brink of death, concerning how he received the mortal injuries and who caused them. If the victim then dies, the statement, properly taken, may be admitted into evidence at a trial for homicide. *Legal use.*

**Dying deposition**   A statement made to a magistrate under oath by a person who is on the brink of death.

The accused must be given the opportunity to attend and to cross-examine the witness; if he refuses to attend or cannot be found, the sworn statement of the dying person is taken nonetheless and put in writing and may be entered as evidence at a trial. *U.K. legal use.*

**Earwitness**   One who overhears a conversation or event. *Legal use.* Cf. **eyewitness**.

**Eavesdropping, electronic**   Monitoring private conversations with the aid of electronic devices (e.g., hidden microphones and tape recorders). *General use.*

**Eccentricity**   Peculiarities of mind and disposition that markedly distinguish an individual from normal, ordinary, or average people but do not amount to insanity or mental unsoundness. *Legal use.*

**Edict**   An official public pronouncement that has the same force as a law. *General use.*

**Efficient intervening cause**   A force of a new and independent nature that could not have been foreseen or anticipated, which either breaks the connection between a wrong and an injury or so interrupts the chain of events that it becomes the proximate cause of the injury. *Legal use.*

**Eighteen b lawyer**; **18b lawyer**   A private lawyer appointed under Article 35, s18(b) of New York State law to represent a defendant who cannot afford a lawyer. *Legal use.*

*Ejusdem generis*   A Latin phrase meaning "of the same kind, class, or nature," and a statutory interpretation which holds that when a statute lists some specific items with a catchall phrase following (e.g., "or other"), that phrase may be interpreted to mean restricted to others of the same general class. *Legal use.*

**Electric cattle prod**   An instrument sometimes used in the control of angry mobs or riots, and is sometimes illegally used to force confessions from suspects in third-degree interrogations. *General use.*

**Electric chair**   1. The chair in which a felon is legally electrocuted. 2. The death penalty by electrocution. *General use.*

**Electronic stimulation of the brain**   A treatment method for dealing with prisoners accustomed to fits of violence. *Prison use.*

**Electronic surveillance**   The use of electronic listening and recording devices in eavesdropping. *General use.*

**Elements of crime**   The parts of a crime that must be proved to support a conviction. *Legal use.*

**Eleventh hour**   The last possible moment, for example, the governor granting a reprieve to a condemned prisoner just before his scheduled execution. *General use.*

**Embezzlement**   A form of larceny in which someone fraudulently appropriates money or property entrusted to him by another, to his own use or benefit. *Legal use.*

**Embracer**   A person who attempts to illegally influence a verdict by tampering with a juror. *Legal use.*

**Embracery**   The crime of influencing a jury toward a particular side using corrupt means or bribery; a.k.a. **tampering with a jury**. *Legal use.*

**Emergency service unit**   A unit of law enforcement that handles shootouts, terrorism, and other acts of violence. *Police use.*

**Emotional insanity**   A mental abnormality in which ordinary reasoning ability is impaired, usually caused by excessive emotional responses to a situation or spontaneous violent excitement; a temporary passion causing complete derangement or an impulse the mind cannot resist. *Legal use.*

**Enclosure**   A fingerprint identification term describing a ridge line separation that later connects to form an enclosure. *Police use.*

**Enforce**   1. To effectively carry out or execute (e.g., enforce laws or carry out a judgment). *General use.* 2. To obtain something by force. *Obsolete general use.*

**Entrapment**   1. The act, by officers or agents of a government, of inducing a person to commit an offense not previously contemplated by that person, with the intent of prosecuting him. *Legal use.* 2. The enticement of a prostitute by an undercover police officer into soliciting the officer for sex. *Police use.*

**Epilepsy**   A neurological disorder characterized by periodic attacks of a short duration, partial or complete loss of consciousness, and sometimes convulsions or other psychomotor disorders. It is classified into three forms: (1) grand mal or major, (2) petit mal or minor, (3) psychomotor equivalent or psychic. *Medical use.*

**Equal protection clause**   A provision of the U.S. Constitution which prohibits any state from denying equal protection of the law to any person within its jurisdiction. *U.S. legal use.*

**Equal protection of the law**   A U.S. constitutional guarantee that all persons or classes of persons must be given the same legal protection as all other persons or classes in like circumstances. *U.S. legal use.*

**Escape**   To illegally remove one from custody. This crime may be committed by the prisoner himself or his legal custodian. Technically a prisoner can escape legal custody while still inside prison walls; a.k.a. **escape from custody**. *Legal use.*

**Escapee**   A person who has fled confinement (e.g., an escaped convict). *General use.*

**Escape warrant**   A warrant for the recapture of an escaped prisoner. *U.K. legal use.*

**Euthanasia**   A homicide intended to put a sick person out of misery; a mercy killing. *Legal use.*

**Evade**   To elude capture or detection by ingenuity. *General use.*

**Evenhanded justice**   A system of justice based on punishing a convicted criminal according to the crime committed and not on other factors such as race, religion, or social standing. *General use.*

**Evidence**   1. Testimony of witnesses, concrete objects, exhibits, documents, records, or other data pertaining to the issue at trial. 2. The proof on which a judgment is based. *Legal use.* Cf. **presumption; proof; testimony.**

**Evidence, circumstantial**   Testimony not based on actual knowledge or observation of the facts in question, or by any indirect evidence from which reasonable deduction may be drawn to prove the claimed hypothesis. *Legal use.*

**Evidence, hearsay**   Evidence not derived from the personal knowledge of a witness, but rather from what he has heard others say. In some jurisdictions, testimony to any out-of-court statement, even the witness's own, is considered hearsay. This evidence is generally inadmissible, although there are several exceptions (e.g., dying declarations). *Legal use.*

**Evidence, inculpatory**   Incriminating evidence which tends to establish a person's involvement in a crime. *Legal use.*

**Evidence, medical**   Evidence provided to the court by a licensed medical doctor. The evidence given can be either in the form of a document, if the physician is unable to attend the proceeding, or as testimony during the trial. This expert witness can testify to matters of fact as well as opinion concerning the case. *Legal use.*

**Evidence, rules of**   The rules of law governing the admissibility of evidence and determining what weight, if any, should be given to specific testimony, documents, or objects. *Legal use.*

**Evidentiary facts**   Facts needed to determine the ultimate facts. *Legal use.*

**Examination**   An inspection, interrogation, search, or investigation. *Legal use.* Cf. **preliminary hearing; redirect examination.**

**Examining trial**   A hearing to determine if there is probable cause for a person to be bound over to a grand jury. *Legal use.* Cf. **pretrial hearing**.

**Exception**   A formal objection during a trial to a ruling or order of a court in response to a request or an objection. *Legal use.*

**Excessive bail**   A higher bail than would be reasonably needed to prevent evasion of the law by concealment or flight, or one that is too high for the criminal charge involved or the special circumstances of the case; prohibited by the Eighth Amendment to the U.S. Constitution. *Legal use.*

**Excessive force**   Unnecessary or unjustified force due to circumstances, for example, the use of deadly force for the protection of property only. *Legal use.*

**Excessive punishment**   A sentence or fine too severe for the act committed or for the criminal record of the defendant. A sentence excessive in length may be cruel and unusual punishment, which is prohibited by the Eighth Amendment to the U.S. Constitution. *Legal use.* Cf. **corporal punishment; punishment**.

**Exclusionary rule**   This rule states that evidence obtained in violation of the U.S. Constitution is to be excluded from trial. Because of many law enforcement complaints, there are now exceptions to this rule. *U.S. legal use.*

**Exclusive jurisdiction**   The exclusive power held by a court or tribunal over all other courts or tribunals. *Legal use.*

**Ex-con**   Ex-convict. *General use, 1931.* Cf. **con.**

**Exculpate**   To clear one from blame or guilt. *General use.*

**Exculpatory statement**   A statement that can excuse, justify, or clear a defendant of fault or guilt. *Legal use.*

**Excusable assault**   An assault committed without unlawful intent, by accident or ill fortune, while using ordinary care in doing any lawful act by lawful means. *Legal use.* Cf. **assault; self-defense**.

**Excusable homicide**   The killing of a human by a person acting within the law, usually in self-defense or by accident or misadventure. The name of the act itself implies some fault, omission, or error, though one considered so trivial that the killer is excused from felony prosecution. *Legal use.* Cf. **homicide**.

**Ex delicto**   A tort or wrong; an action that grows out of a crime or a fault. *Legal use.*

**Execute** 1. To carry out an act or course of conduct to its conclusion. 2. To carry out a death sentence. *General use.*

**Execution by injection** A legal form of execution whereby the condemned person is injected with poison or air, which is far less costly than other forms of execution (e.g., electrocution). *General use.*

**Executive pardon** Power granted to a chief executive, usually the president or a governor, to nullify a judicial judgment, usually by pardoning or commuting a sentence (e.g., reducing a death sentence to life imprisonment); a.k.a. **executive clemency.** *Legal use.* Cf. **pardon.**

**Exhibit** An item of physical evidence offered to the court for inspection. *Legal use.*

**Exhumation** The removal of a body from its place of burial. This usually requires a court order and is generally only done when there is suspicion of foul play. *Legal use.*

**Exigent circumstance** A condition that arises suddenly, which allows police to make a search without a warrant because any delay might be dangerous to individuals or lead to destruction of evidence. *Legal use.*

**Ex-offender** A former offender no longer beholden to any criminal justice department. *Law enforcement use.*

**Exoneration** The removal of legal charges or suspicion against a person, which proclaims that person's innocence. *Legal use.*

**Ex parte** On only one side, referring to a legal proceeding where an issue or judgment is considered for the benefit of only one side or party. *Legal use.*

**Expert opinion evidence** Testimony given in a specific field by a person considered an authority; a.k.a. **expert testimony.** *Legal use.*

**Expert witness** One who is recognized as an authority. *Legal use.*

**Exploit** To take advantage of a person or situation unfairly or unjustly for one's own benefit. *General use.*

**Ex post facto law** A law enacted retroactively, making an act that has already taken place a crime. Prosecution in such instances is prohibited by the Fifth Amendment of the U.S. Constitution. *Legal use.*

**Express malice** For purposes of first-degree murder this includes malice, or the intention to kill or cause great bodily harm, resulting from an intent forethought. *Legal use.* Cf. **malice.**

**Expunge** To erase, purge, or seal a criminal record. *General use.*

**Expungement of record** To destroy, or seal from public view, the record of a conviction or an arrest. *Legal use.*

**Extenuating circumstances** Facts or circumstances that tend to lessen the degree of guilt. *Legal use.*

**Extort** To coerce or compel, to gain by illegal methods. *Legal use.*

**Extortion** Obtaining property from another by threatened or actual force, violence, or fear, or under cover of official right. *Legal use.*

**Extract a confession** To obtain a confession after a great deal of effort from one who is unwilling to confess. *General use.*

**Extradition** The surrender of an individual by a state or nation to another for trial or punishment pursuant to demand, for an offense committed within the territorial jurisdiction of the other state or nation. *Legal use.* Cf. **fugitive**.

**Extrajudicial confession** A confession made outside any court, judicial examination, or investigation. *Legal use.*

**Extraneous evidence** Information that is not furnished by the document in question, usually a will or contract, but comes from some outside source. *Legal use.*

**Extreme penalty** Death sentence. *General use.*

**Eyeball** An eyewitness identification, usually in a courtroom, lineup, or two-way mirror, which gives the victim or eyewitness a chance to see the suspect. *Law enforcement use.*

**Eyewitness** A person who saw the act in question. *Legal use.*

**Eyewitness identification** An identification, usually of another person by a person who witnessed a criminal act. Cf. **lineup**. *Legal use.*

**Fabricate** To invent, concoct, contrive, forge, feign, falsify, counterfeit, or make up. *General use.*

**Fabricated evidence** Evidence that was not produced as a consequence of an event or a crime, but was manufactured or distorted after the fact with the intent to hamper or divert an investigation, to block the determination of guilt, or to frame an innocent person in a wrongful conviction. *Legal use.*

**Fabricated fact** A fact which exists in statement only without a truthful basis or to which a false appearance has intentionally been given. *Legal use.* Cf. **deceit**; **fraud**.

**Fabrication** A lie or distortion. *Legal use.*

**Fact** That which is determined to be the truth; an actual occurrence, circumstance, action, event, or thing, proven by the evidence. Questions of fact are determined by the jury, questions of law by the judge. *Legal use.*

**Fact finder**    A person who attempts to determine the actual events of the case in question, especially an examiner impartial to the case, appointed by authorities to look into the facts of the matter. *General use.*

**Fair and impartial jury**    A trial jury in which each juror is fair and impartial, and has no preconceived opinion concerning the guilt or innocence of the defendant. *Legal use.*

**Fair and impartial trial**    A trial in which the defendant's full legal rights are respected and protected. This includes the right to counsel and the time needed to prepare and present a defense in a calm atmosphere where witnesses can testify and attorneys can argue without fear or intimidation; a trial where the judgment is based on the evidence presented; a.k.a. **fair hearing**; **fair trial**. *Legal use.*

**Fall**    *n.* An arrest, usually one followed by a conviction and a prison term. *v.* To be arrested or sentenced to prison. *Underworld use, 1879.* Cf. **go down**.

**Fall guy**    The accomplice who is arrested and convicted either through the regular course of justice or because he has been set up, with or without his knowledge, to take the "fall," or an innocent man who has been set up or inadvertently takes blame for a crime. *Underworld use, 1911.*

**False**    Not true. *Legal use.*

**False alarm**    1. An alarm sent when there is no reason for one, for example, a fire alarm when there is no fire. *General use.* 2. A person who is insincere or disloyal or one who passes bad information. *Underworld use, twentieth century.*

**False arrest**    One that is made without the proper legal authority and includes the unlawful restraint of liberty. *Legal use.*

**False claim**    A statement or claim not based on fact. *Legal use.*

**False confession**    An untrue confession to a crime not committed by the confessing person.

**False fact**    Simulated or fabricated evidence. *Legal use.* Cf. **perjury**.

**False imprisonment**    To confine without legal authority. Cf. **imprisonment**. *Legal use.*

**False instrument**    Any instrument representing itself as genuine but is, in fact, fabricated. *Legal use.* Cf. **counterfeit**; **false making**; **forgery**.

**False making**    An intentional duplication without alteration, such as the forgery of documents or currency. *Legal use.* Cf. **counterfeit**; **false instrument**; **forgery**.

**False token**    An untruthful document, or sign of some fact, used for fraudulent purposes. *Legal use.* Cf. **counterfeit**.

**False swearing**    Making intentional misrepresentations under oath; perjury. *Legal use.*

**Falsehood**    A willful misrepresentation or deception. *Legal use.* Cf. **perjury**.

**Falsify**    To forge, counterfeit, alter an appearance, tamper with a document, make false statements, or misrepresent. Cf. **counterfeit**; **false**; **forgery**. *Legal use.*

**Federal court**    A court, especially in the United States, established by the federal government and having jurisdiction over matters outside a state's jurisdiction (e.g., U.S. Supreme Court, U.S. court of appeals, and U.S. district courts). *General use.*

**Federal jurisdiction**    The areas of power of the federal courts. *Legal use.*

**Federal offense**    Any act prohibited by U.S. law; a.k.a. **federal crime**. *General use.*

**Fed rap**    A term in a federal institution, or a charge under a federal statute. *U.S. underworld use, 1934.*

**Feel out**    To elicit information subtly. *U.S. underworld use, 1904.*

**Feign**    To make a false pretense or appearance, or assert a falsehood as true (e.g., pretending one is ill). *General use.*

**Feigned accomplice**    A pretender who consorts with others in the planning of a criminal act in order to gain evidence, discover plans, or thwart the commission of their intended crime. *Legal use.*

**Felon**    Someone who has committed a felony. *Legal and police use.*

**Felonious**    Done with the intention to commit a felony. *Legal use.*

**Felonious assault**    An assault great enough to be charged as a felony, usually committed with a weapon; an aggravated assault as distinct from a simple assault, which is a misdemeanor. *Legal use.*

**Felonious entry**    A burglary. *Legal use.*

**Felonious homicide**    The killing of a human being without excuse or justification. *Legal use.* Cf. **heat of passion**; **homicide**; **manslaughter**; **murder**; **willful murder**.

**Felonious intent**    A conscious decision to commit a felony, an act of will. *Legal use.*

**Felonious taking**  Removing with intent to steal. *Legal use.*

**Felony**  A criminal act of graver consequence than those identified as misdemeanors, usually punishable by more than one year of imprisonment or by execution. *Legal use.* Cf. **compounding crime**; **felonious assault**; **felonious homicide**; **misdemeanor**.

**Felony murder**  A common law doctrine classifying any unintentional death which occurs during the commission of a felony as murder. Today the requirements for felony murder vary greatly by jurisdiction; a.k.a. **felony murder doctrine**; **felony murder rule**. *Legal use.*

**Fiction of law**  An assumption that what is possible is true, even if it is false. *Legal use.*

**Fictitious**  Relating to a false or assumed name. *General use.*

**Field of fire**  An area that can be adequately covered by a weapon or a group of weapons. The area differs in size depending on the range of the particular weapons. *Law enforcement use.*

**File charges**  To bring criminal charges against a person. *Legal use.*

**Final judgment**  A judicial decision that disposes of all issues. *Legal use.*

**Final plea**  The last plea entered by or for a defendant to a criminal charge. *Legal use.*

**Final sentence**  The outcome of a trial; the sentence which puts a legal dispute to rest. *Legal use.*

**Fingerprint**  Identifying marks in the epidermal surface of the fingertip that can be traced scientifically to an individual; a.k.a. **friction ridge impressions**. *Police use.*

**Fink**  *n.* A police informant. *Underworld use, 1929. v.* To inform to the police. *Underworld use, 1925.*

**Firearms acts**  Criminal statutes covering the illegal possession, sale, and use of firearms and ammunition. *Legal use.*

**First-class misdemeanant**  A person imprisoned after being convicted of a misdemeanor. *U.K. legal use.*

**First-degree murder**  Modern criminal statutes generally define murder as "first degree" or "second degree." First-degree murder typically includes those committed after premeditation; felony murders are also commonly included in this classification; a.k.a. **murder one**. *Legal use.*

**First offender**  A person without a prior criminal conviction record, often treated leniently by the sentencing judge; a.k.a. **first-time loser**. *Legal use.*

**First, second, and third degree**  Arrest, detention, and interrogation. *Police use.*

**First-time loser.**  See **first offender**.

**Fix**  *n.* 1. An act of bribery used to negotiate a deal with legal authorities. 2. One who negotiates for illegal immunity; a fixer. *Underworld use, 1920. v.* 1. To gain immunity from arrest, prosecution, or conviction through the use of bribery. *Underworld use, 1872.* 2. To place under arrest. *Police use, 1781.*

**Fixed sentence**  A prescribed and definite prison term, rather than one with maximum and minimal limits, which may be altered on the basis of good behavior. *Law enforcement use.*

**Fixed surveillance**  A stakeout located in a fixed area, as opposed to one that is mobile. *Law enforcement use.*

**Fixer**  1. One who arranges immunity through the use of bribery or otherwise facilitates criminal activities. *U.S. underworld use, 1900.* 2. One who plants or fabricates evidence, usually for the prosecution. *Obsolete 1930 law enforcement use.*

**Fix is in**  The bribe has been paid and the protection or immunity is guaranteed. *Underworld use.*

**Fix on, put the**  To arrange immunity from arrest or prosecution. *U.S. underworld use, 1929.*

**Fix the fuzz with some soft**  To bribe the police. *Underworld use.*

**Flight from justice**  The evasion of the law by one who has been accused of a crime. *Legal use.*

**Footprint**  An impression left by one's foot. *General use.*

**Force**  *n.* Restraint or violence employed against or upon another person. *v.* To compel another, often by threat or commission of violence, to submit to or perform an act against his will, especially rape. *General use.*

**Force, reasonable.**  See **reasonable force**.

**Forcible entry**  Entering or taking possession of space or land against the will of those with the legal right of possession. *Legal use.*

**Forcible rape**  The unlawful act of forcing a person to participate in or submit to sexual intercourse. *Legal use.* Cf. **rape**.

**Forensic anthropology**  The scientific study of the history of a human body, particularly bones, in determining the cause and time of death.

**Forensic ballistics**  The scientific study of projectiles in flight and the study of firearms. *Legal use.*

**Forensic chemistry.**  See **forensic medicine**.

**Forensic medicine**  The use of chemicals or medicine to deduce cause or time of death or for other legal purposes; a.k.a. **forensic chemistry**. *Legal use*. Cf. **autopsy**.

**Forensic odontology** The scientific use of teeth and/or dental records to identify physical remains or the source of bite wounds, or to obtain criminal evidence. *Legal use*.

**Forensic pathology** The scientific study of the human body in a detailed autopsy to determine the cause, time, and method of a homicide or other related crimes.

**Forensic psychology.** See **criminal psychology**.

**Forensic serology** The scientific study of blood types, bloodstains at the scene of a crime, and all other aspects of human blood involved in a crime.

**Forensics** The art or study of argumentation and formal debate used in courts of law and debate. *Legal use*.

**Forfeit** *n*. Something taken from someone for a crime or an offense. *v*. To have some property or right confiscated for a crime or offense. *General use*.

**Forfeiture** Losing the right to something because of error, default, or as a penalty for certain crimes. *Legal use*.

**Forge** To create a fraudulent copy of something with the intent of substituting the copy for the original for fraudulent or deceitful purposes. *Legal use*. Cf. **counterfeit**.

**Forger** A counterfeiter or one who alters or fabricates documents or signatures. *Legal use*.

**Forgery** 1. The intentional duplication or replication of something; the creation of a new work represented as the work of another. 2. Something that has been forged. *Legal use*.

**Foul play** A devious, unfair, or criminal act. *General use*.

**Fourth degree** Withdrawal sickness from drugs. The term is taken from police use. During interrogation of a suspect, police may use third-degree methods, those of a severe and sometimes violent nature. In dealing with a drug addict the police will sometimes hold the offender long enough for withdrawal sickness to set in, at which time he is likely to talk, hence the fourth degree. *Drug addict use, 1950s*.

**Four-time loser** A criminal with four felony convictions; in some states this makes life imprisonment the mandatory sentence; other states require only three convictins. *Law enforcement use*.

**Frame** *n*. Evidence that has been manufactured or distorted to make an innocent man appear guilty. *U.S. underworld use, 1914*. *v*. To arrange evidence so that an innocent man appears guilty. *U.S. underworld use, 1898*.

**Frame, in the** Wanted by police; refers to either an innocent man framed for a crime or a person whose picture appears framed on a wanted poster. *Underworld use, 1920s*.

**Frame-up** 1. To set up an innocent person to appear guilty and take the blame. *Underworld use, 1900*. 2. The planning of a crime, including surveillance of the site, run-throughs, and contingency plans. *U.S. underworld use, 1929*.

**Fraud** Any deceitful action in which a person distorts, withholds, misrepresents, or fabricates information in order to injure another person or deprive him of a property or right. *Legal use*. Cf. **forgery**.

**Fraudulent** Designed to carry out a fraud; based on fraud, tainted, characterized by fraud. *Legal use*.

**Freedom of the press** A right granted by the First Amendment to the U.S. Constitution, which guarantees a publication's right to report the news without prior restraint or censorship. *Legal use*. Cf. **gag law**; **liberty**; **prior restraint**.

**Freedom of religion** The U.S. Constitution protection from state-enforced religion; guaranteed freedom to hold religious beliefs without restraint or prohibition by the state. Like secular actions, the practices and actions of religion are subject to regulation for the common safety and necessity. *U.S. legal use*.

**Freedom of speech** The freedom to state one's views without fear of censorship or persecution; a right inherent to most world democracies. In the United States, the First Amendment to the Constitution guarantees freedom of speech. *U.S. legal and government use*. Cf. **liberty**.

**Fresh pursuit** The right of the police to cross jurisdictional borders in the fresh, continuous, and uninterrupted pursuit of a felon. *Legal use*. Cf. **hot pursuit**.

**Friend of the court** A person or organization not connected with a court case, but who petitions the court to be heard concerning the case due to a strong interest in the subject matter; from the Latin term *amicus curiae*. *Legal use*.

**Frisk** *n*. A pat-down search for weapons or contraband on one's person, occasionally a dwelling, usually conducted by the police. *Underworld and police use, 1789*. Cf. **stop and frisk**. *v*. To search a person, pocket, or purse, or any hiding place. *Police and underworld use, 1724*.

**Fruit of the poisonous tree**   Evidence obtained from an illegal search or interrogation, or directly derived from an illegal search or interrogation. Such evidence is generally ruled inadmissable if challenged. There are now some exceptions where certain types of illegally obtained evidence are allowed into evidence. *Legal use.* Cf. **illegally obtained evidence; poisonous tree doctrine**.

**Fugitive**   One who flees prosecution, arrest, or imprisonment. *Law enforcement use.* Cf. **extradition; fugitive from justice; fugitive warrant**.

**Fugitive Eyewitness Act**   A federal law making it a felony for a material witness in a felony case to flee in order to avoid testifying. *Legal use.*

**Fugitive Felon Act**   A U.S. federal statute which prohibits moving from state to state to avoid prosecution, imprisonment, or giving testimony. *Legal use.* Cf. **extradition**.

**Fugitive from justice**   One who commits a crime and flees from his usual residence or the jurisdiction of the court where the crime was committed, then conceals himself. *Underworld use.* Cf. **extradition**.

**Fugitive's goods**   A term used under old English law in which possessions of a fugitive could be appropriated by the British court if the fugitive fled because of the felony for which he was sought. *Legal use.*

**Fugitive warrant**   A warrant issued for the arrest of a fugitive. *Legal use.*

**Full faith and credit**   A right, guaranteed by the U.S. Constitution, ensuring that any judgments decreed by the state meet standards and are legal in the convicted individual's legal state of residence. *Legal use.*

**Furlough**   A temporary leave granted to a prison inmate. *Prison use.*

**Fuzz**   1. Any law enforcement officer or agency, or prison warden or guard. *General use, 1929.* 2. The third degree or any police interrogation. *Underworld use, 1933.*

**Gaff, stand the**   To be given punishment or the third degree. *Underworld use, 1904.*

**Gag law**   1. A court order issued in a heavily publicized trial that prohibits lawyers and witnesses from discussing the case with reporters. This measure ensures that the defendant receives a fair trial. 2. A court order prohibiting journalists from reporting certain proceedings or parts of the trial proceedings. 3. Constitutional permission given by a court for authorities to bind and gag an uncontrollable defendant at a trial so the proceedings can continue without interruption; a.k.a. **gag order**. *Legal use.*

**Gallows**   A framework of metal or wood equipped with a noose for hanging criminals. *General use.*

**Garrotte**   *n.* A device with a metal collar that continually tightens and is used to strangle prisoners; originated in Spain. *Underworld use. v.* 1. To strangle a victim by using pressure on the neck. *Legal use.* 2. To strangle and steal.

**Gassing**   A gas chamber execution. *Prison use.*

**Gault, application of**   A landmark U.S. Supreme Court ruling that governs proceedings for juvenile defendants; guarantees the right to consult a lawyer and to be notified prior to arraignment. The defendant also has the right not to implicate himself in the crime and to have witnesses present to corroborate his testimony. *Legal use.*

**Gavel**   A mallet used by a judge to bring silence to a court proceeding or to announce a recess or end of a trial. *General use.*

**General sessions.**   See **Court of General Sessions**.

**General statutes**   Laws that have been passed by the legislature. *Legal use.* Cf. **common law; statute**.

**General verdict**   A decision by the jury of either guilty or not guilty. *Legal use.* Cf. **verdict**.

**Get a valentine**   To be given a shorter sentence than expected, or to receive any favorable finding or decision. *Prison use.*

**Getaway**   *n.* An escape, especially from a crime scene. *Underworld use, 1893. v.* To flee from the place of a crime or to escape from the police or prison; a.k.a. **make a getaway**. *Underworld use, 1907.*

**Get hit with**   To receive a prison sentence or to have time added onto a sentence by the parole board. *Prison use.*

**Get hit with the book**   1. To receive a life sentence, a maximum sentence available by law, or to be required by the parole board to serve an entire sentence; a.k.a. **get the book**. *Prison use.*

**Get it in the neck**   To suffer punishment or distress. *Underworld use, 1901.*

**Get locked up**   1. To deliberately break a rule. 2. To ask to be placed in protective custody because one has informed, or because one has lost money to other prisoners while gambling and cannot pay the debt; a.k.a. **get a banner; get a shingle; get sloughed up**. *Prison use.*

**Get off**   1. To flee. *Underworld use, 1781.* 2. To be acquitted. *Underworld use, 1900s.* 3. To experience pleasure from drug use. *Drug addict use, 1960.*

**Get the goods on**   To present conclusive evidence or proof of wrongdoing. *Police and underworld use.*

**Get the works**   1. To be convicted and sentenced to prison. *Underworld use, twentieth century.* 2. To die. *Underworld use, 1927.* 3. To be given the death sentence. *Underworld use.*

**Ghosting**   Being quietly taken during the night from one jail or prison to another to prevent prisoner unrest or rioting or to hinder questioning from those outside about suspected riots, beatings, or third degree interrogations. *Prison use.*

**Ghost story**   An alibi. *Underworld use, 1899.*

**Gibbet**   A gallows: a framework with an upright pole that has one arm extending, which is used to execute prisoners by hanging. *General use.*

**Give a deal to**   To provide information while being subjected to interrogation or the third degree. *Underworld use.*

**Give a fill**   To deliberately supply false information. *Obsolete 1930 U.K. underworld use.*

**Give a pass**   1. To be reprimanded but not punished for breaking a rule. *Prison use.* 2. To refrain from prosecuting someone for a crime because he has agreed to give information to the police about other criminals and to testify against them. *Prison use.*

**Give the works**   1. To tell the entire story. *Underworld use, 1927.* 2. To murder. *Underworld use, 1929.* 3. To grill or interrogate. *Underworld use.* 4. To beat. *Underworld use, 1935.* 5. To use coercion; a.k.a. **give the business**. *Gambling use.*

**G man**   1. A government law enforcement agent, especially one working for the FBI or the Secret Service. *Underworld use, 1922.* 2. An inmate who secretly informs on other prisoners; a police informer. *Underworld use.*

**Go**   *n.* 1. Stolen items. *Obsolete 1880 U.K. underworld use.* 2. A burglary. *Underworld use, nineteenth century.* 3. A portion of drugs. *Drug addict use, twentieth century.* *v.* 1. To break out of prison. *Prison use, twentieth century.* 2. To die. 3. To be coerced, swindled, or tricked. 4. To give in to temptation. 5. A deal. *Underworld use.*

**Goat**   1. A scapegoat—a person blamed for another's crime. *Underworld use, 1886.*

**Go belly up**   To help police officials uncover criminal activities and arrest criminals. *Underworld use.*

**Go down**   1. To be convicted and sentenced to jail. *Underworld use, 1906.* 2. To steal. *Underworld use, nineteenth century.* 3. To be arrested. *Underworld use.* 4. To have parole denied. *Prison use.* Cf. **fall**.

**Go for a date**   To go to court so an execution date can be set for a prisoner sentenced to death. *Prison use.*

**Go home**   To be released from prison. *Prison use.*

**Goldfish**   1. A length of rubber hose used to beat suspects during questioning. *Police use, 1930.* 2. A prisoner in the lineup. *Police use, 1933.*

**Good behavior**   1. Lawful actions or behavior. *Legal use.* 2. The actions of a defendant, who does not break the laws regarding his original offense and who behaves lawfully. *Legal use.* 3. A reward in some prisons for inmates. For each day of "good behavior," one day is deducted from the time an inmate spends in prison; a.k.a. **goodtime allowance**. *Prison and legal use.*

**Good citizen**   One who makes an extra effort to see that a criminal is arrested, tried, and sent to prison, even though the criminal didn't steal from or harm that person. Originally the term was used by prosecuting attorneys when speaking to juries and then it was used by lawyers for the underworld. *Underworld use, 1924.*

**Good faith**   Honest intention to not deceive or defraud. *Legal use.*

**Goodtime allowance**   Prisoner incentive system advocated in 1776 by reformer Jeremy Bentham; prison time is deducted from the time that a convict spends in prison as a reward for good behavior, but the actual sentence is not reduced; a.k.a. **good time**. *Prison and legal use, 1776.*

**Go over**   To be imprisoned. *Underworld use, 1872.*

**Go over the jumps**   To be arrested or sent to prison. *General use, 1927.*

**Go to bat**   To appear in court for a trial. *Prison use.*

**Goulash**   Misleading or false information. *Underworld use, 1925.*

**Go up**   To be sent to a prison. *Underworld use, 1872.*

**Graduated release**   A program in which a prisoner, who will soon be released, is placed in less regimented confinement to help reorient him to life and responsibilities that he will confront once he is back in the community. Examples of graduated release programs are work release, school release, halfway houses, and prerelease programs that cover topics such as job hunting and how to budget. *Prison and police use.*

**Graft**   *n.* 1. Dishonest way of making a living. *Underworld use, 1886.* 2. Desired cells or favors granted by prison officials or guards. *Prison use, 1893.* 3. Part of the proceeds of a crime, usually accepted as a bribe. *Underworld use, 1901.* 4. Profit gained from dishonest business practices or fraud, or a portion of those monies that is given to corrupt officials, often politicians. *Legal use.* 5. Money or goods that will be easy to steal. *Underworld use, 1924. v.* 1. To assist a robber or pickpocket. *Underworld use, 1859.* 2. To operate in secret. *Obsolete 1920 underworld use.* 3. To use one's public office for personal gain, for example, a police officer who accepts a bribe to look away from wrongdoing or present false evidence that will either exonerate a guilty person or convict an innocent person. *General use.* Cf. **bribe**; **grift**.

**Grand embezzlement**   A felony embezzlement that exceeds the amount set by law for petit embezzlement; one that is a misdemeanor. *Legal use.*

**Grand false pretenses**   A felony charging the defendant with misrepresentation, fraud, or intent to deceive; a larger fraud than petit false pretenses. *Legal use.*

**Grand jury**   A group of citizens selected and sworn in to hear evidence and determine whether it contains enough information to indict a suspect. If the evidence against a person is not sufficient, the jury returns a "no bill." *Legal use.*

**Grand jury hearing**   A hearing usually closed to the public; a jury is selected to hear evidence of criminal actions and to decide if enough evidence exists to charge the accused and bring him to trial. *Legal use.*

**Grand larceny.**   See **larceny, grand**.

**Grand theft.**   See **larceny, grand**.

**Grant of immunity.**   See **immunity from prosecution**.

**Graphologist**   An expert in handwriting analysis. *Police use.*

**Graphology**   The science of analyzing handwriting, used to authenticate handwriting and to analyze character and personality. *Police use.*

**Grease**   *n.* 1. Money. *Obsolete 1910 underworld use.* 2. Protection money. *Underworld use, 1930.* 3. Money paid to get someone into trouble, or "on the grease." *Underworld use, 1930.* 4. A bribe. *Underworld use. v.* 1. To bribe. *Underworld use, 1900.* 2. To pay protection money. *Prison use.*

**Griddle, to be put on the**   To be grilled or interrogated by police. *Prison use.*

**Grid search**   A method used to search crime scenes, by dividing the area up into sections. *Legal and police use.*

**Grift**   *n.* 1. One who makes his living as a criminal, especially from petty crimes. *Obsolete underworld use.* 2. Money made dishonestly, usually from swindling.

*Underworld use.* 3. A theft. *Underworld use.* 4. Any confidence game. *Underworld use. v.* To steal for a living, to make a living as a professional criminal. *Underworld use, 1926.* Cf. **graft**.

**Grill**   To interrogate or question persistently. *Underworld and police use.* Cf. **griddle, to be put on the**; **third degree**.

**Gross negligence.**   See **negligence, gross**.

**Group therapy**   Psychotherapeutic treatment by one or more trained professionals who treat a group of patients simultaneously, using the group setting for peer feedback and social pressure to bring about change in individuals. *Sociological use.*

**Guided group interaction**   A treatment program for juvenile offenders in a group therapy setting. The object of the program is to change the offender's criminal self-image and actions to more conventional values and behavior. *Sociological use.*

**Guillotine**   A device with a blade that falls between two poles to behead people; invented by Dr. Antoine Louis (1723–1792) during the French Revolution and named for Dr. Joseph Ignace Guillotin (1738–1814), who favored the use of this machine as a form of public execution. A harpsichord maker named Tobias Schmidt (or Smith) used Louis's blueprints to build the guillotine. *General use.*

**Guilt**   The condition of having violated the law. *Legal use.*

**Guilt inducement schemes**   A scheme taking advantage of the victim's insecurity or physical inadequacy. *Underworld use.*

**Guilty**   1. The word a defendant uses for his plea when he admits that he committed the crime with which he is charged. *Legal use.* 2. A term which conveys a jury's verdict that the defendant committed the crime as charged. *Legal use.* 3. Having been found to have committed a crime or violation of the law. *Legal use.* Cf. **guilty but mentally ill**; **guilty plea**; **guilty verdict**; **plea of guilty**; **plea of not guilty**.

**Guilty but mentally ill**   A verdict available in some trials involving an insanity defense; a verdict meaning that psychiatrists will examine the prisoner before he goes to prison, and if he needs treatment, he will be sent to a mental health institution. *Legal use.*

**Guilty plea**   An official statement of guilt that the defendant makes in court, but only after he has been advised of his rights. Cf. **plea**. *Legal use.*

**Guilty verdict**   Official decision of a jury, which has found the defendant guilty. *Legal use.*

**Gun records**   A division in a government agency, that contains files with the serial numbers and makes of all registered weapons and information relating to permits to carry a concealed weapon. *LAPD use.*

**Habeas corpus**   Shortened form of *habeas corpus ad subjiciendum,* the model writ of habeas corpus from English common law; a.k.a. **writ of habeas corpus**. *Legal use.*

**Habeas corpus acts**   The various acts involving habeas corpus ad subjiciendum. The original act was an English statute. Similar laws have been enacted throughout the United States and are considered the primary constitutional guarantee of personal freedom. *Legal use.*

**Habeas corpus ad deliberandum et recipiendum**   A court order that authorizes removing a person from custody in one jurisdiction for prosecution in another. *Legal use.*

**Habeas corpus ad prosequendum**   A court order that takes effect when it is necessary to remove a prisoner from one area to be prosecuted in the jurisdiction where his alleged offense occurred. *Legal use.*

**Habeas corpus ad satisfaciendum**   In England, a court order desired by a plaintiff to bring a convicted prisoner to a superior court where an order of execution may be obtained. *Legal use.*

**Habeas corpus ad subjiciendum**   1. Literally, "you have the body." A court order most often used to determine if a person is being unlawfully detained or imprisoned. Habeas corpus is not used to test a prisoner's guilt or innocence. *Legal use.* 2. In Great Britain, an order issued by the Queen's Bench Division of the High Court to a person or institution holding someone in custody, demanding the presentation of the prisoner and reason for his detention. *U.K. legal use.*

**Habeas corpus ad testificandum**   Literally, "you have the body" to testify. A court order used to bring a prisoner to court to testify. *Legal use.*

**Habemus optimum testem, confitentem reum**   Literally, "we have the best witness," used to describe a person who confesses to committing a crime as charged. *Legal use.*

**Habitual criminal**   A repeat offender, who is subject to more severe penalties in most states than a first-time offender; a.k.a. **four-time loser, habitual offender**. *Legal use.* 2. A person with a long criminal record who is under frequent police surveillance and is arrested on suspicion. *Legal use.*

**Habitual drunkenness**   A condition in which a drinker readily and frequently gets intoxicated, usually indicative of alcoholism. *Legal use.* Cf. **intoxication**.

**Halfway house**   1. An alternative place of confinement for adults and juveniles who, the court feels, do not belong in prison. *General use.* 2. A housing facility for newly released or nearly released prisoners seeking reorientation to community life or for those who require counseling, usually for substance abuse. The first halfway houses were founded in nineteenth-century Europe. *General use.* Cf. **community facility**.

**Halifax Law**   The unauthorized trial and execution of a person, especially by a lynch mob or vigilantes. It is named for the Halifax parish in England, where unauthorized justice was rendered against suspected thieves. *Legal use.* Cf. **lynch mob**.

**Hall**   A hall of justice. *General use.*

**Handwriting**   *n.* 1. The individual style of handwriting that is characteristic of a person and which can be used to identify him. 2. The branch of a police department that ranks and compares handwriting samples. *Police use.*

**Handwriting, comparison of.**   See **comparison of handwriting**.

**Handwriting analysis**   The study or observation of a person's handwriting for identification purposes; each person's handwriting is as unique as a fingerprint. *General use.*

**Hang a rap on**   To charge someone with a crime or frame him for a crime he did not commit. *Underworld and police use, 1920s.* Cf. **rap.**

**Hanging DA**   A prosecutor who has obtained many convictions, especially in murder crimes subject to the death penalty. *Underworld use.*

**Hanging judge**   A judge known for giving strict sentences. *Underworld use.*

**Harassment**   1. Repeatedly annoying another or causing distress through verbal abuse (e.g., continual obscene phone calls or gestures). *Legal use.* 2. Provoking someone to violent or disorderly conduct by insults, taunts, or challenges (e.g., police harassment). *General use.*

**Harboring a fugitive**   Providing shelter or refuge to someone who rightfully should be placed in the hands of the law. *General use.*

**Harvest**   To bring in a suspect for arrest or interrogation. *Police use, 1910.*

**Hearing**   A court proceeding that is less formal than a trial. Arguments, witnesses, and evidence are presented to a judge or administrative body. *Legal use.* 2. An initial court proceeding in criminal law presenting the accused party and witnesses for the defense, usually to a grand jury. *Legal use.* Cf. **adjudicatory hearing**; **pretrial hearing**; **revocation hearing**; **sanity hearing**; **transfer hearing**.

**Hearsay**   Testimony not based on the personal knowledge of the witness, but on information obtained from others. The hearsay statement may be oral, written, or even nonverbal conduct, and typically does not describe what the witness knows personally. Hearsay is generally inadmissible, but there are many exceptions (e.g., an official police report, or the testimony of coconspirators after a conspiracy is established). *Legal use.*

**Heat**   The emotional pressure on a wanted man of knowing that a police investigation of his crime is under way. *Underworld use, 1928.* 2. A revolver. *Underworld use, 1929.* 3. An exchange of gunfire. *Underworld use, 1920s.* 4. A police officer, usually one searching for a wanted man. *Underworld use, 1930.* 5. Intense pressure from police resulting from media campaigns or public outrage. *Underworld use, twentieth century.*

**Heat of passion**   A violent, intense rage brought on by anger or fear, causing a person to lose full control over his actions so that he loses some responsibility for his actions. The heat of passion can reduce a homicide to voluntary manslaughter if reasonable provocation, immediacy, and lack of premeditation are established. *Legal use.* Cf. **homicide**; **hotblood**; **passion**.

**Heinous**   Abominable (e.g., a brutal murder). *General use.*

**Heist**; **hist**; **hyst**   A robbery, usually with a gun.

**Heresy**   An opinion, theory, doctrine, or belief judged to be contrary to what is generally accepted as the truth, especially concerning religious matters. *General use.*

**Heretic**   A person who disagrees or dissents from generally accepted dogma or beliefs, especially those held by the church. *General use.*

**High court**   A country's supreme court or highest court of appeal. *Legal use.*

**High crimes and misdemeanors**   Criminal actions that could lead to impeachment by the United States House of Representatives. *U.S. legal use.* Cf. **impeachment**.

**High degree of negligence**   Unlawful recklessness or negligence. State laws contain varying requirements for criminal liability, especially regarding the defendant's degree of knowledge of the risk. *Legal use.* Cf. **negligence**.

**Higher law**   A precept of moral or divine law, which is considered to be above the laws of a given constitution or legislature. *General use.*

**High-pressure**   *adj.* Demanding, requiring talented thieves. *Underworld use, 1925.* *v.* 1. To coerce someone into making an agreement. *Underworld use, 1922.* 2. To use a good deal of pressure in selling or influencing another. *Con artist use.*

**High-profile crime**   An unlawful act committed in the company of many witnesses in broad daylight. *Underworld and police use.* Cf. **low-profile crime**.

**Highway patrol**   A branch of state police departments authorized to enforce motor vehicle laws. Some states authorize general law enforcement powers to the highway patrol. *General use, twentieth century.*

**Hit**   *n.* 1. An arrest. *Underworld use.* 2. A rejection by parole officers. *Prison use.* 3. An assassination or murder. *Underworld and Mafia-syndicate use.* 4. An assignment to murder someone. *Mafia-syndicate use.* *v.* 1. To slay someone. *Underworld use.* 2. To be sentenced. *Underworld use, 1893.* 3. To be arrested. *Underworld use.*

**Hit-and-run**   1. A car accident followed by the flight of the negligent driver. 2. The negligent driver in a hit-and-run accident. *General use.*

**Hit-and-run felony**   Division of the Los Angeles Police Department that investigates automobile hit-and-run reports. *LAPD use.*

**Hitch**   A prison sentence. *Prison use, twentieth century.*

**Hit man**   A murderer for hire. *Underworld use.*

**Hit murder**   A killing by a hired assassin. *Underworld and police use.*

**Hit the bricks**   To escape, be acquitted, paroled, or released from prison. *Prison use.*

**Hold**   1. Jail cells where prisoners awaiting release stay. *Prison use, 1920s.* 2. A request from one jurisdiction to another that a prisoner be held until the requesting jurisdiction can take the prisoner into its custody. *Legal use.*

**Hole**   1. A prison cell or section used for solitary confinement. *Prison use, twentieth century.* 2. A punishment cell. *Prison use, 1929.* 3. A hiding spot for a criminal. *Underworld use, 1931.*

**Home free**  Having escaped arrest or fine; being acquitted; case settled; or charges dropped. *Underworld use.*

**Hoax**  *n.* A falsehood intended to trick or deceive. *v.* To fool someone into believing a falsehood to be true. *General use.*

**Hold the bag**  1. To be tricked. *Underworld use, twentieth century.* 2. To be deserted and left with all of the responsibility; to take the blame; a.k.a. **hold the sack**. 3. Of an innocent, stung by circumstantial evidence. 4. Of a gang member, tricked into taking responsibility for a crime when the rest of the gang confesses; they leave him holding the bag. *Underworld use.*

**Hold out**  1. To keep more than one's fair share of the loot. *Underworld use, twentieth century.* 2. To withhold information; keep a secret. *Prison use.* 3. To hide rations or luxuries (e.g., tobacco) from others. *Prison use.*

**Holdup; hold up**  *n.* 1. A thief who steals by gunpoint, usually from travelers. *Obsolete 1930 underworld use.* 2. A robbery at gunpoint. *Underworld use.* *v.* 1. To use violence or a threat of violence to steal or commit another crime. *Underworld use, 1887.* 2. To take someone into custody. *Obsolete 1930 U.K. underworld use.*

**Holdup man**  A man who alone, or with a gang, employs violence to rob others. *Underworld use, 1895.*

**Homicidal**  Relating to homicide; prone to homicide. *General use.*

**Homicide**  The killing of one human being by another. Homicide is not always a crime, for example, in the case of capital punishment. Murder, manslaughter, and negligent homicide are unlawful homicide. There are no degrees of murder in common law, but statutes often categorize murder as "first" or "second" degree. *Legal use.* Cf. **heat of passion**; **imminent danger**; **manslaughter**; **murder**.

**Homicide**  Any police department branch investigating all sudden and violent deaths or any attempted murder. *Police use.*

**Homicide, culpable**  The criminal killing of another with varying degrees of guilt. *Legal use.*

**Homicide, excusable**  The slaying of another human being through an accident or self-defense. *Legal use.*

**Homicide, felonious**  Homicide that is a felony, either murder or manslaughter. *Legal use.*

**Homicide, justifiable**  The intentional killing of another but without evil intent, for example, in the case of capital punishment or a killing to prevent a felony. *Legal use.*

**Homicide, negligent**  The criminal killing of another through negligence. *Legal use.*

**Homicide, reckless**  In some states, the criminal killing of another person through willfully careless behavior. *Legal use.*

**Homicide, vehicular**  The unlawful killing of another through the reckless operation of a motor vehicle, usually a car, truck, or motorboat. *Legal use.*

**Homicide by misadventure**  The accidental killing of another person while engaged in a lawful activity. *Legal use.*

**Homicide by necessity**  The legal killing of another that is required by law (e.g., capital punishment). *Legal use.*

**Homicide hours**  Midnight to 2:00 A.M.; the time of day when the most murders are committed, according to statistics of the New York City Police Department. *U.S. police use.*

**Homicide *per infortunium***  The accidental killing of another; a type of excusable homicide. *Legal use.*

**Homicide *se defendendo***  The killing of a person in self-defense during a sudden attack, in which the killer had no other reasonable option; a type of excusable homicide. *Legal use.*

**Homicide stab wounds**  The fatal and superficial wounds found on a corpse. Wounds found on the arms and hands usually suggest that the victim tried to fight back. *Forensic use.*

**Honor system**  A system of trust that allows members (e.g., prisoners) to abide by regulations without surveillance or supervision. *General use.*

**Hoosegow; hoosgow; hoosegaw**  1. A small prison or jail, possibly derived from the Spanish *juzgado*, meaning court of justice. *Underworld use, 1911.* 2. A police station. *Underworld use.* 3. The punishment cells in a prison. *Prison use.*

**Hosing**  1. A beating with a length of rubber hose; police administering third-degree punishment. *Underworld use, 1934.* Cf. **jacking**. 2. Any severe and unjust punishment or procedure. 3. The betrayal of a confidence; the act of cheating others. *Underworld use.*

**Hostile witness**  A witness who may be cross-examined by the party who called him to the stand because of his combative testimony and behavior. *Legal use.*

**Hot blood**  The mental state of a person so thoroughly enraged or aroused that his actions are uncontrollable. In criminal law, the mental state of the accused at the time the crime was committed can reduce his crime from homicide to manslaughter. *Legal use.* Cf. **heat of passion**; **mental state**.

**Hot chair**   The electric chair. *Underworld use, 1927.*

**Hot money**   Money that can be identified and linked with a crime. *Underworld use.*

**Hot pursuit**   Acts or actions taken by police while apprehending a suspect immediately after or during the commission of a crime. A situation in which police may search a captured suspect without using a warrant, an exception to the warrant requirements for a search and seizure. *Legal use.* Cf. **fresh pursuit**.

**Hot seat**   The electric chair. *Underworld use, 1928, and police and media use, 1930s.*

**Hot water ordeal**   A test under old English law. A judge would order the accused to immerse his arms up to the elbows in boiling water. After prayers and invocations, the arms were brought out and the accused party's guilt or innocence was decided by the way his arms looked—if blistered or swollen, guilty, which was mostly the case. *Obsolete U.K. legal use.*

**Housebreaker**   A criminal who unlawfully enters a residence to rob or assault people inside. *General use.*

**Housebreaking**   In criminal law, forcible entry into a residence with the intention of committing a felony inside. Under some statutes, a forcible exit after committing or considering a felony is also considered a housebreaking. A housebreaking that occurs at night is equated with burglary under some statutes. *Legal use.*

**House of correction**   A place where criminals who have committed minor offenses and are considered capable of rehabilitation are retained. *General use.*

**Hue and cry**   1. A boisterous outcry made when pursuing a criminal suspect or in calling for his arrest. 2. The chase given to a suspect or a written order calling for the arrest of the suspect. *General use.*

**Hummer**   1. Arrest of the wrong person. 2. Incorrect information, usually given on purpose. *Underworld use.*

**Hung jury**   A jury that is unable to reach a verdict after a long period of deliberations; usually resulting in a mistrial. *Underworld use, 1929.*

**Huntley hearing**   In a New York criminal case, an independent proceeding to establish the admissibility of statements made by the defendant outside of court. Derived from *People v. Huntley. U.S. legal use, 1965.*

**Hurdles**   Interrogation by police. *Underworld use, 1937.*

**Hush money**   A bribe given to a witness, policeman, or other to prevent him from testifying against or charging suspects, or to falsely testify against an innocent person framed for a crime committed by others. *Underworld use.*

**Hypnosis**   A sleepy mental state induced by a hypnotist, usually to discover answers to significant questions (e.g., what was seen during a criminal event). Some persons have been wrongly convicted on the testimony of hypnotized witnesses. *Medical and legal use.*

**Hypnotism**   The process of introducing a mental state that sometimes causes a person to remember traumatic events. The patient is subject to the inducer but will not perform actions he would not consider in a fully conscious state. *Medical and legal use.*

**Hypothetical question**   A question, usually asked of an expert witness in court, calling for an opinion based on the assumption that the facts given in the question are true. Often the answers to such questions determine the fate of a defendant, even though such expressed opinions may have no basis in fact. *Legal use.*

**Hysteria**   A type of psychoneurosis displayed by a loss of motor or sensory functions, hallucinations, or forgetfulness. Also demonstrated by an excessive emotional response or action. *Medical use.*

**Identification**   The act of identifying another person or object or having oneself identified. *General use.*

**Identification record**   The complete criminal history of an individual, usually filed under an IR number, a shortening of "identification record number"; a.k.a. **IR number**. *Police use.*

**Idiopathic insanity**   Insanity that results from a disease of the brain itself. *Legal use.*

**Ignoramus jury**   The grand jury; this was the word the jurors would write after they voted not to indict a suspect, from the Latin *We take no notice. General use.*

**Illegal**   Not authorized by the law or against the law. *General use.*

**Illegal arrest**   An arrest made without sufficient evidence that a crime has been committed or one made without the necessary warrant. *Legal use.*

**Illegal entry**   To enter a country at a wrong time or place, or to evade immigration or enter by way of fraud. *Legal use.*

**Illegal gun**   Any type of gun outlawed by statute (e.g., a sawed-off shotgun). *Legal use.*

**Illegally obtained evidence**   Evidence secured in violation of the U.S. Constitution's Fourth Amendment, which guarantees freedom from unreasonable search and seizure. The exclusionary rule, with some recent exceptions, generally excludes such evidence from admission at trial. *Legal use.* Cf. **fruit of the poisonous tree**.

**Illegal per se**   Illegal in and of itself, not because of some outside circumstance. *Legal use.*

**Ill treatment**   Cruel or improper treatment of another. *General use.*

**Illusion**   A mistaken, distorted, or perverted image or impression caused by the imagination of the observer, not by a defect in any of the organs of sense. *Legal use.*

**Imbecility**   An advanced decay or feebleness of the mind. It varies in degrees from mere eccentricity to almost total madness. *Legal use.*

**Immediate**   An immediate release from prison. *Prison use, 1934.*

**Immediate cause**   The final act in a chain of events or causes; that which directly produces the results or events without further intervention, not necessarily the same as the proximate cause. *Legal use.*

**Imminent danger**   One of the essential elements of a self-defense plea in a homicide case, this is a person's belief of impending peril, with no reasonable way of escape except to meet force with force. *Legal use.* Cf. **homicide**.

**Imminently dangerous article**   An object that is reasonably certain to put life or limb at risk. *Legal use.*

**Imminent peril**   A position of danger where death or bodily injury is reasonably certain. *Legal use.*

**Immunity, grant of.**   See **immunity from prosecution**.

**Immunity from prosecution**   A government promise not to prosecute a witness based on his testimony. Usually granted in cases where a witness has refused to testify on the grounds that such testimony might be self-incriminating. There are two types. Transactional immunity protects the witness from being prosecuted for the specific crime or crimes that his testimony concerns. Use immunity prohibits using the witness's testimony and its fruits against him but does not prohibit prosecution. The U.S. government switched from the former to the latter in 1970; a.k.a. **grant of immunity**. *Legal use.*

**Impeach**   To dispute, contradict, deny, disparage, malign, denounce, accuse, indict, charge, sue, challenge; to impeach a witness is to challenge his credibility. *Legal use.*

**Impeachment**   The bringing of criminal charges against a public officer before a quasi political court (e.g., a legislative body). *Legal use.*

**Impersonate**   To portray or assume the character of another. *General use.*

**Implicate**   To connect a person with an illegal act. *Legal use.*

**Implied consent**   A presumption that consent has been given based on certain signs or actions, or by lack of action or silence. *Legal use.*

**Impound**   To confine someone or place one in the custody of the law. *General use.*

**Impoundment**   Placement of a person in custody. *General use.*

**Imprison**   To confine a person, usually in a prison. *General use.*

**Imprisonment**   The act of confining a person. *Legal use.*

**Impulse.**   See **irresistible impulse rule**.

**Impulse crime**   An illegal act committed on the spur of the moment (e.g., shoplifting, mugging, stabbing). *General use.*

**Impunity**   Protection or exemption from penalty or punishment. *Legal use.*

**Imputed knowledge**   Knowledge attributed to a person because the facts at issue were accessible to him, and he had a duty to be aware of them. *Legal use.*

**Inadmissible**   That which cannot be received into evidence (e.g., hearsay testimony). *Legal use.*

**Inalienable**   That which is absolute and cannot be waived, taken away, bought, sold, or transferred; for example, in the United States, the right to life, liberty, and the pursuit of happiness. *Legal use.*

**In camera**   A Latin phrase which means "in private," usually used to refer to a courtroom not open to the public, or a conference held out of the courtroom, usually in the judge's chambers. *Legal use.*

**Incarceration**   Confinement in a prison. *Legal use.*

**Inchoate crimes.**   See **inchoate offenses**.

**Inchoate offenses**   Crimes that usually lead to another crime; for example, assault generally leads to battery, though assault is a crime by itself; a.k.a. **inchoate crimes**. *Legal use.*

**Incite**   To provoke to action; urge; arouse; encourage; instigate; set in motion. To move or persuade another to commit a crime. *General use.*

**Inciter** One who incites an action; an abettor. *Legal use.*

**Included offense** A lesser crime that is included in a greater offense; for example, assault and battery are included in every murder. *Legal use.*

**Incoercible** Impossible to control, dominate, or restrain. *General use.*

**Incog** Shortened form of incognito. *Underworld use.*

**Incognita.** See **incognito.**

**Incognito** Living with one's identity concealed or disguised; "incognita" applies to females only. *General use.*

**In cold blood** Without mercy or compassion, deliberately and with premeditation. *General use.* Cf. **cold blood**.

**Incommunicado** To be held in custody, accused of a crime, and not allowed to communicate with anyone other than those investigating the crime and those in charge of custody. *Legal use.*

**Incompetency** The lack of fitness, legal qualification, or ability to carry out the required duty. *Legal use.*

**Incompetency to stand trial** A ruling made when a defendant is found to be mentally ill to the point where he is unable to assist in his own defense and does not understand the charges against him. The trial is then suspended and the defendant is placed in a mental institution until he recovers. *Legal use.*

**Incompetent evidence** Defective evidence that does not meet the requirements of the established rules of evidence and is therefore ruled inadmissable; evidence that is defective or lacks originality. *Legal use.*

**Incompetent persons** Persons who have legally been declared not competent and are therefore not responsible for their criminal acts. *Legal use.*

**Incorrigible** Not capable of being corrected or changed, unreformable; applied to a juvenile means the juvenile cannot be controlled or managed by his parents or guardians. *Law enforcement and legal use.*

**Incriminate** 1. To subject oneself or another to criminal charges or the risk thereof. 2. To charge with a crime. *Legal use.*

**Incriminating admission** An acknowledgement of facts, which tend to establish guilt. *Legal use.*

**Incriminating circumstance** A fact or occurrence collateral to the commission of a crime, which tends to show that the crime has been committed or that a specific person committed it. *Legal use.*

**Incriminating evidence** Facts that tend to establish guilt, either by themselves or with other evidence. *Legal use.*

**Incrimination** The act of implicating oneself or another in a criminal charge. *Legal use.*

**Incriminatory** Tending to incriminate. *Legal use.*

**Incriminatory statement** Any statement that tends to establish guilt, either by itself or along with other evidence. *Legal use.*

**Inculpate** To accuse, or to involve one in crime or the guilt of crime. *Legal use.*

**Inculpatory** Type of testimony or other evidence, which tends to, or is intended to, establish guilt. *Legal use.*

**In delicto** Literally, at fault. *Legal use.*

**Indemnification for errors of justice** Compensation for those who have been wrongly convicted and imprisoned. *Legal use.*

**Indeterminate sentence** A prison sentence, authorized by statute, for which the court imposes the minimum and maximum length of the incarceration (e.g., three to five years). The actual date of release is determined by an administrative board, usually based on the inmate's conduct in prison. *Law enforcement use.* Cf. **disparity of sentences**.

**Index crimes** Crimes compiled by the FBI in its *Uniform Crime Report. Law enforcement use.*

**Indices** An alphabetical index listing every name mentioned in all FBI files. *Law enforcement use.*

**Indict** To charge with a crime. *Legal use.*

**Indictable** Type of action or deed that may lead to an indictment. *Legal use.*

**Indictment** A formal written statement charging a person with a criminal offense. The charge must then be proven at trial. *Legal use.*

**Indictor** A person who causes another to be indicted. The person indicted is sometimes referred to as the indictee. *Legal use.*

**Indigent defendant** A person charged with a crime who does not have the funds to hire a lawyer for his defense. In most cases the court appoints counsel to represent the defendant, based on the Sixth and Fourteenth Amendments to the U.S. Constitution. *U.S. legal use.*

**Indirect evidence** Evidence which does not prove the fact or facts in question, but from which inferences can be made and presumptions drawn to prove the hypothesis claimed. *Legal use.*

**Inducement**    The motive that leads to a crime, or the attraction that lures one toward a crime. *Legal use.*

**Infamy**    1. An evil reputation resulting from something blatantly malicious, wrong, or startling. 2. An evil or criminal act that is well-known and extreme in nature. *General use.*

**Infancy**    The status of a person who is under the age of legal majority. In common law children under fourteen are presumed to be without criminal capacity, but, if they are over seven, this presumption can be rebutted by the introduction of proof of malice or of the defendant's ability to distinguish right from wrong. *Legal use.*

**Inference**    1. A logical method of reasoning in which facts already proven or admitted are used to establish subsequent facts. 2. A reasonable deduction drawn from established facts. *Legal use.*

**Inform**    To provide another with information. *General use.*

**Informant**.    See **informer**.

**Information**    A formal accusation, without an indictment, alleging that a certain person has committed a specific crime, usually a misdemeanor. *Legal use.*

**Informer; informant**    A person who secretly passes information on criminal affairs to law enforcement officials, sometimes as a form of employment. *General use.* Cf. **narc**, **stool pigeon**, **squeal**.

**Informer's privilege**    The government's power to withhold the identity of a person who passes on information about criminal acts. *Legal use.*

**Infraction**    A violation, infringement, or breach of a duty or law or statute, punishable by a fine or other penalty but not by incarceration. *Legal use.*

**Infringe**    To intentionally encroach on another person's rights. *Legal use.*

**Infringement**    A violation of, or encroachment upon, a regulation, right, or privilege. *Legal use.*

**Initial appearance**    The first appearance in court by the defendant after his arrest, usually an arraignment or preliminary hearing. *Legal use.*

**Innocence**    Not guilty of a crime. *General use.*

**Innocent**    Not guilty. *General use.*

**Innocent agent**    One who, as the instrument of another, is involved in the commission of an unlawful act while being ignorant of the unlawful intention of the principle, and, through a defect of understanding or lack of knowledge, does not incur legal guilt. *Legal use.*

**Innocent bystander**    One who without knowledge or desire for involvement in a criminal act becomes part of that act, for example, a bank patron wrongly accused of collusion with robbers. *General use.*

**Inns of Court**    The council of education in London, which has sole privilege of bestowing the degree of barrister at law on law students; this degree is necessary to practice as counsel or an advocate in the superior courts. This association is comprised of collegiate-type houses, including the Inner Temple, the Middle Temple, Lincoln's Inn, and Gray's Inn. *U.K. legal use.*

**Inpo**    The technique of hiding. *Japanese underworld use.*

**In propria persona**    Translates to "in one's own proper person," and means to be without the aid of an attorney in a legal matter. *Legal use.*

**Inquest**    A legal inquiry, often by a jury, into a certain matter, for example, a coroner or medical examiner's inquiry into a certain death. *Legal use.*

**Inquiry**    The systematic investigation into a matter, usually one of interest to the public (e.g., an unexplained death). *General use.*

**Inquisition**    An inquest or inquiry usually led by a sheriff along with a jury he impanels for the investigation. *Legal use.*

**Inquisitive**    A judge or magistrate. *Obsolete underworld use, 1890s.*

**Inquisitor**    A person who investigates or inquires into a matter, especially one who is overly severe or malicious in his methods. *General use.*

**Insane**    Displaying insanity; psychotic or crazed behavior. *Legal and general use.*

**Insanity**    Any mental illness which prevents one from attaining the required mental capacity to be held responsible for one's actions. *Legal use.*

**Insanity, partial**    An unsound mental condition in someone, which always exists but is only occasionally apparent. *Legal use.*

**Insanity as a bar to execution**    A provision of the British Criminal Lunatics Act of 1884; it bars the execution of criminals condemned to die for their crimes if it is found that they were insane at the time of the crime or have since become insane. This includes cases where a plea of insanity was rejected by the jury. *Legal use.*

**Insanity as a bar to trial**    A rarely used provision of the British Criminal Lunatics Act of 1884; it says that in exceptional cases a defendant can be removed to a mental institution before trial. *Legal use.*

**Insanity defense**.    See **defense of insanity**.

**Insanity on arraignment**   A provision of the British Criminal Lunatics Act of 1800 says that a defendant who appears insane and unfit to plead at the time of arraignment may be declared so by the jury. The court may then order the accused to be detained in an institution. *Legal use.*

**Insider**   1. An accomplice inside a place where a crime is to be committed. *Underworld use, 1857.* 2. Someone who has inside information, part of a select group. *General use.*

**Insolvable**   Allowing or having no foreseeable solution (e.g., a baffling murder case). *General use.*

**Inspect**   To thoroughly look into or investigate a matter. *General use.*

**Inspection**   An evaluation of an FBI field office by senior agents, usually done annually. *Law enforcement use.*

**Inspector**   A high-ranking law enforcement official. *Law enforcement use.*

**Inspector's aide**   An FBI agent who serves as a junior member of the inspection staff. *Law enforcement use.*

**Instigate**   To initiate or incite, for example, provoke a riot or criminal act. *General use.*

**Instigator**   One who incites or provokes an action. *General use.*

**Institutionalize**   To place a person in the hands or care of an institution. *General use.*

**Instruction to the jury**.   See **jury instructions**.

**Insubstantial**   Having a lack of substance or material nature, for example, evidence that does not carry much weight. *General use.*

**Intake unit**   A government agency that screens juveniles received from the police or other agencies and recommends certain action by the juvenile court. A case may be closed or referred for treatment or supervision. *Law enforcement use.*

**Intelligence**   An agency or department of an organization involved in the gathering and dissemination of information (e.g., police intelligence). *General use.*

**Intelligence gathering**   Recording, collecting, analyzing, and disseminating information, usually for national security, military, or law enforcement use. *General use.*

**Intelligence investigation**   A law enforcement investigation where the immediate goal is not arrest or prosecution. *Law enforcement use.*

**Intensive care unit**   A locked correctional unit for juvenile offenders. *Law enforcement use.*

**Intent**   The desire to cause the consequences of an act, or the knowledge that those consequences will almost certainly follow. Not to be confused with motive, which leads a person to act or not act. Intent refers simply to the state of mind with which an act is done or not done. *Legal use.* Cf. **motive.**

**Intent, criminal**.   See **criminal intent**.

**Intent, general**   The intent to do what the law prohibits. It is not necessary to prove that the defendant intended the precise outcome of events precipitated by his actions if general intent can be proven. *Legal use.*

**Intent, specific**   The intent to perform the specific act prohibited by law (e.g., assault with intent to kill). *Legal use.*

**Intent to do serious bodily injury murder**   One is considered guilty of murder when he intends to cause serious or great bodily injury to another, but the result is death, even when the intention was only to cause harm and not death. *Legal use.* Cf. **depraved heart murder; murder**.

**Intent to kill**   An element of certain aggravated assault and battery cases that requires proof of the intent to kill as well as other elements of assault and battery. Other elements include assault with intent to rape, rob, commit mayhem or do great bodily injury. *Legal use.*

**Intent to kill murder**   Murder resulting from a premeditated or unpremeditated intention of killing another, whether the intended victim or someone else is killed. If a person shoots at someone intending to kill him but ends up killing another, the crime is still murder because there was an intention to commit such a crime. *Legal use.*

**Internal Affairs Division (IAD)**   The branch of a police department charged with ferreting out police corruption. *Police use.*

**Interrogate**   To ask questions systematically and formally. *General use.*

**Interrogation**   1. The act of formally and systematically questioning someone. *General use.* 2. The craft of compelling someone to reveal information that he is trying desperately to conceal. In the crudest form, this involves violence and torture. Historically, the Inquisition employed the rack, the Chinese their water torture; in modern times, electrodes are fixed to sensitive body areas. The KGB and Chinese intelligence for years adopted an interrogation that simply wore out the subject, keeping a person without sleep for days until his will was worn down and exhaustion forced the desired answers, a system termed "brainwashing." As in police work, intelligence interrogation teams often use the good man/bad man technique, where one interrogator is brutal and offensive, the other sympathetic and kind, until the subject turns in gratitude to the latter to tell all. When IRA terrorism was at its height in Northern Ireland, the British army placed hoods over suspects and made them lean against walls, supported only by their fingertips, while dinning into their ears a "white noise," a piercing, high-pitched screech. After several hours of this torture, subjects invariably told all. When released, the subjects bore no telltale signs of torture. (This kind of interrogation was discarded after the press described its use and a public outcry ensued.) Drugs and truth serums are also employed by interrogators, as well as hypnosis. The most sophisticated and effective police and intelligence interrogators are those who assemble an overwhelming amount of evidence and then patiently, systematically present this to the subject, probing until a weakness is found and then exploiting that weakness until the subject breaks and confesses. One of the most skillful MI5 interrogators was William Skardon (d. 1987), who induced Soviet agents Emil Klaus Fuchs (1911–1988) and Anthony Blunt (1907–1983) to admit their espionage. *Intelligence use.*

**Interrogator**   One who asks questions during an interrogation. *General use.*

**In the back room**   The execution chamber in a prison; a.k.a. **in back**; **in the back**. *Prison use, 1928.*

**In the clear**   1. Not implicated, responsible, or guilty. *General use, 1901.* 2. Out of prison with all time served. *Prison use.*

**Intoxication**   Diminished mental or physical faculty that results when alcohol or drugs are introduced into the body. Intoxication is only a defense to a crime if the condition was involuntarily produced. A crime committed while voluntarily intoxicated is not any less a crime than if committed sober. But if a specific intent or other state of mind is a required element to constitute a certain crime, intoxication may be taken into consideration in determining that aspect of the crime. *Legal use.* Cf. **habitual drunkenness.**

**Intrinsic fraud**   Fraud that occurs during the course of a trial (e.g., perjury) or the misrepresentation or concealment of evidence that applies to and affects

the determination of the issues brought up at trial. *Legal use.*

**Intrude**   To force oneself into or upon a situation without permission or invitation; to trespass. *General use.*

**Intruder**   Someone who enters another's property or land without permission of the rightful owner. *General use.* Cf. **trespass**.

**Invade**   To enter (e.g., a building) in order to steal. *General use.*

**Invader**   One who trespasses upon another's property with intent to steal. *General use.*

**Invasion**   Entrance (e.g., into a house) with the intention of stealing. *General use.*

**Inveigle**   1. To entice another by clever persuasion. 2. To take possession of something by means of cajolery or connivance. *General use.*

**Investigate**   To examine, observe, or study closely and meticulously, especially as part of an official inquiry. *General use.*

**Investigation**   The process of evidence gathering. *Legal use.*

**Investigative lead**   Information that directs an investigator to an additional source of information. *Law enforcement use.*

**Investigatory field stop**   The detention of a suspect by a police officer who determines whether the person should be arrested or released. *Police use.*

**Invisible crimes**   Crimes that for one reason or another are never recorded. *Law enforcement use.*

**Invitation**   A summons to appear in court. *Law enforcement use.*

**Involuntary act**   An act committed under force, duress, or coercion; one performed with constraint or without the will or knowledge that the act is being done, for example, an act committed while sleepwalking or in a hypnotic state. *Legal use.*

**Involuntary confession**   A confession obtained through threats or acts of violence, or by implied or outright promises, or by any means that might cause or influence a person to confess to a crime he did not commit. *Legal use.*

**Involuntary manslaughter**   The unlawful killing of another human being through criminal negligence or during the commission of an unlawful act, which is not grave enough to be considered a felony. *Legal use.*

**Iron maiden**   A medieval instrument of torture consisting of a coffin-like iron container shaped like a woman and lined with spikes to impale the victim when closed. *General use.*

**Irons**   Handcuffs and/or leg irons. *Underworld use.*

**Irrefutable**   Beyond refute or dispute— incontrovertible evidence. *General use.*

**Irresistible impulse rule**   This rule requires a verdict of not guilty in a criminal prosecution if it can be proven that the defendant was suffering from a mental disease or defect that kept him from controlling his actions. This holds true even if the defendant knew what he was doing and could distinguish between right and wrong. This legal point was emphasized in the 1959 Otto Preminger film, *Anatomy of a Murder. Legal use.*

**Isolation**   Solitary confinement; a.k.a. **iso**; **iso cell**; **izo**. *Prison use.*

**Jacking; jackin'**   A prison beating, usually with a club. *Prison use, 1934.*

**Jackleg**   Marked by a dishonest, degenerate, or disreputable nature. *General use.*

**Jackleg lawyer**   A dishonest, inferior, or unethical lawyer. *Underworld use.*

**Jail**   A building, more than a police lockup and less than a prison, used for the confinement of persons held in legal custody, usually those awaiting trial or those convicted of minor crimes. *General use.*

**Jailhouse lawyer**   An inmate who studies law and gives legal advice to other prisoners. *General use.*

**Jaw coves**   Attorneys. *Underworld use.*

**Jawer**   An unscrupulous lawyer. *U.S. underworld use, 1929.* Cf. **mouthpiece**.

**Jedburgh justice**   Justice by a lynch mob. Named after a Scottish town near the English border, where cattle rustlers and other suspected criminals were often hanged without benefit of trial; a.k.a. **Jeddart Justice**; **Jedwood Justice**; **Lydford Law**. *U.K. general use.*

**Jekyll and Hyde**   Someone possessing a dual personality, one side of which is good and the other evil, based on the character of the protagonist in the 1886 novel by Robert Louis Stevenson (1850–1894), *The Strange Case of Dr. Jekyll and Mr. Hyde. General use.*

**Jeopardy**   1. Risk, hazard, peril, or danger. 2. The threat or danger of conviction, punishment, and incarceration. *Legal use.* Cf. **double jeopardy**.

**Job**   *n.* 1. A criminal act, especially one planned in advance (e.g., a bank robbery). *Underworld use, 1722.* 2. A stolen car. *Underworld use, 1930.* 3. When someone is framed for a crime he did not commit. *U.S. underworld use, 1925. v.* 1. To burgle. *Underworld*

use, *1860.* 2. To perjure oneself; to convict an innocent person. *U.S. underworld use, 1903.*

**John; John**   1. Any law-abiding citizen. *Underworld use, 1914.* 2. A police officer; a.k.a. **John Law.** *Underworld use, 1935.*

**John Doe**   1. A name given to a perpetrator of a crime when that person's identity is unknown. 2. The name given to a dead body when the true identity is unknown. *Law enforcement use.*

**John Hancock**   Any signature. *U.S. general use, 1914.*

**Johnny; Johnnie**   A police officer or a prison guard. *Underworld use, 1930.*

**Johnny Law**   The police. *U.S. underworld use, 1921.*

**Joinder of defendants**   The practice of charging two or more defendants in the same indictment or information. *Legal use.*

**Joinder of offenses**   The practice of charging two or more offenses as separate counts on the same indictment. The offenses must be of similar character, based on the same transaction or act, or part of a common plan or scheme. *Legal use.*

**Joint offense**   A crime committed by two or more persons working together. *Legal use.*

**Joint trial**   One trial of two or more persons charged with the same or similar offenses. *Legal use.*

**Journey**   A prison sentence. *Prison use, 1920.*

**Journey's end**   The prison cells housing convicts sentenced to life terms, after the 1929 play of the same name by Robert Cedric Sherriff. *Prison use, 1930.*

**Judas; Judas**   A person who betrays someone toward whom he feigned friendship. *General use.*

**Judge**   1. A public officer either elected or appointed to preside over a court of law. *Legal use.* 2. An adept, well-respected criminal. *Obsolete 1900 underworld use.*

**Judge's rules**   Guidelines drafted by a panel of British judges, which state that any statement made by an accused person and tendered as evidence should be one that was voluntarily made after a caution has been issued by the officer doing the questioning. *Legal use.*

**Judge trial**   A bench trial presided over by a judge without the presence of a jury. *Legal use.*

**Judgment**   The final decision of a court, which sets forth the plea, the verdict, and any sentence; a.k.a. **judgment of conviction**. *Legal use.*

**Judicial hanging**   A court-ordered hanging. *Legal use.*

**Judicial officer**   1. A magistrate or judge. 2. A person exercising judicial power in a court of law. *Legal use.*

**Judiciary**   1. The legal court system. 2. The judges who preside in courts of law. *General use.*

**Juice**   Power or connections, usually of a political nature, used to accomplish set goals. *U.S. general use.*

**Jump bail**   To fail to appear in court after a bond has been posted guaranteeing that appearance; the bond is then forfeited. *Legal use.*

**Jungle**   1. A prison. *U.S. underworld use, 1904.* 2. An area rife with criminals and criminal activity. *U.S. underworld use, 1928.* 3. A depressed and lawless area of a city. *General use.*

**Jurimetrician**   A lawyer who uses scientific methods. *Legal use.*

**Jurimetrics**   The use of scientific methods to resolve legal matters. *Legal use.*

**Jurisdiction**   1. The right and power of a court to try a specific case. 2. The areas of authority of a court, either geographic or by the subject matter of a specific case. *Legal use.*

**Juris Doctor**   The degree of Doctor of Laws. *General use.*

**Jurisprudence**   The science or philosophy of law. *Legal use.*

**Jurist**   A person with a thorough knowledge of legal matters. *General use.*

**Juror**   A member of a jury. *Legal use.*

**Jury**   A group of citizens selected and sworn in to hear evidence and decide the truth of a certain legal matter. The jury probobably originated in England out of the inquest system, a device used by William the Conqueror, in which selected men in a community were placed under oath and questioned concerning taxes owed to the king. *Legal use.*

**Jury, grand.**   See **grand jury**.

**Jury, hung.**   See **hung jury**.

**Jury, petit.**   See **petit jury**.

**Jury, sequestration of.**   See **sequester**.

**Jury box**   The enclosed place in the courtroom, usually raised, where the jury sits during the course of the trial. *Legal use.*

**Jury challenge**   A request by either side in a trial to remove a prospective juror from the panel. There are typically two types of challenges. Those for cause—for knowledge of the case or bias—must satisfy the judge who makes the ruling on the challenged juror, and peremptory challenges, which in effect remove the juror without a stated reason. Unlike the challenges for cause, peremptory challenges are limited in number, with usually only a few allowed to each side during jury selection. *Legal use.*

**Jury fixer**   One who bribes a jury to bring in a specific verdict. *Legal use.*

**Jury instructions**   The statements or directions given by the judge to the jury before the jurors begin their deliberations, informing them of their duty and of principles of law applicable to the case. *Legal use.*

**Jury panel**   The group of citizens from which a jury is selected; a.k.a. **jury pool**. *Legal use.*

**Jury pool.**   See **jury panel**.

**Jury selection**   The process by which a jury is picked. This usually involves questioning by the judge and attorneys of both sides, who use challenges to remove potential jurors. *General use.*

**Jury trial**   A trial by jury, as opposed to one decided by a judge. The right to a trial by jury is guaranteed by the U.S. Constitution. *Legal use.*

**Jus gentium**   The laws that are accepted and enforced internationally. Latin for "law of nations." *Legal use.*

**Just cause of provocation**   The level of provocation that will constitute second-degree murder. The lesser charge of manslaughter would result when there is "lawful provocation." *Legal use.*

**Justice**   1. Administration and enforcement of just principles and regulations, especially by those determined to provide an impartial view of what is right or wrong; a.k.a. **substantive due process**. 2. A judge. *General use.*

**Justice model of corrections**   A proposal to shift the goals of correction from rehabilitation to uniformity. This, in theory, would be accomplished by abolishing indeterminate sentences and parole, and limiting the discretion of judges in sentencing by introducing uniform sentences for specific crime categories. *Prison use.* Cf. **disparity of sentences**.

**Justice of the peace**   A state magistrate whose duties include administering justice for minor offenses and committing cases to trial at higher courts. *General use.*

**Justifiable**   That which can be justified or defended. *General use.*

**Justifiable cause**   The well-founded belief in the existence of facts needed for prosecution is justifiable cause for prosecution. *Legal use.* Cf. **probable cause**.

**Justifiable homicide**   1. A killing in self-defense, where danger of death or serious bodily injury exists. 2. An execution ordered by the state. 3. The act of killing by an officer of the law in the prevention of a crime or unlawful escape. *Legal use.*

**Justification**   A lawful or just reason to act or not to act. It is an acceptable excuse for the action taken or not taken, and the ability to justify one's actions to a court by the use of supporting evidence. *Legal use.*

**Justinian code**   The code of laws that forms the basis for much of modern European law, named for the early Roman emperor Justinian I, who issued it. *Legal use.*

**Juvenile**   A person yet to reach the age of being treated as an adult for the purposes of criminal law. This age varies with jurisdiction. Under U.S. federal law, a person who has not yet reached the age of eighteen is a juvenile; a.k.a. **juve**; **juvie**. *Legal use.*

**Juvenile adjudication**   The final decision of a juvenile court. *Legal use.*

**Juvenile courts**   The courts that have jurisdiction over juvenile delinquents and dependent and neglected juveniles. *Legal use.*

**Juvenile delinquency**   Any criminal or antisocial acts committed by a youth who has not reached the legal age of adulthood. *Legal use.*

**Juvenile delinquent**   A person who has yet to reach the legal age of adulthood and who commits criminal or antisocial acts. *Law enforcement and legal use.*

**Juvenile-justice agency**   A governmental department handling the investigation, adjudication, confinement, care, and supervision of juveniles. *General use.*

**Juvenile officer**   A police officer whose duties include detecting, prosecuting, and caring for juvenile delinquents. *Law enforcement use.*

**Juvenile record**   The official records of a juvenile, including court proceedings and detention or referral records. *Legal use.*

**Kangaroo**   *n.* An unjust prison sentence. *U.S. underworld use, 1925.* *v.* 1. To convict an innocent person. *U.S. underworld use, 1919.* 2. To try someone at a kangaroo court. *Underworld use.*

**Kangaroo-court**   A small town court where the judge imposes exorbitant fines on tourists caught in the local speed trap; often the money is then split with the arresting officer. *U.S. general use.*

**Keeley cure**   A prison cell where alcoholics and drug addicts go through detoxification, named for Dr. Leslie E. Keeley (1852–1900), an American physician from Dwight, Illinois, who treated chronic alcoholism. *U.S. prison use, 1904.*

**Keystone cop**   A small-town or incompetent police officer, security guard, or private detective, taken from the Keystone Cops silent movies, which portray the police as the butt of many jokes. *Underworld use.*

**Kick**   *n.* 1. A charge made to the police. *U.S. underworld use, 1920.* 2. The third degree. *Police use.* *v.* 1. To end a drug habit, since drug withdrawal is often accompanied by involuntary twitching. *Drug addict use.* 2. To complain or object. *General use.*

**Kick a parole**   To violate the terms of one's parole. *Underworld use.*

**Kickback; kick back**   1. Part of the loot, profit, or pay that is illegally given to the police or other officials to avoid prosecution, or as a reward for a job or a contract. *General use.* 2. Stolen property that is returned for one reason or another, usually to avoid prosecution. *U.S. underworld use, 1930.* *v.* To relax while serving a prison sentence, and let the time pass and freedom or death move that much closer. *Prison use.*

**Kick loose**   1. To part with something valuable, usually under duress or as the result of a confidence trick. *Con artist use.* 2. To be released by police after surviving third-degree interrogation.

**Kick the bucket**   To commit suicide, originally by standing on an upside down bucket, placing a noose around the neck, and then kicking the bucket off to the side; the term has evolved to mean any death, even a natural one. *General use.*

**Kidnapper**   One who abducts human beings, usually to hold for ransom; originally those who abducted children from Africa and shipped them to America where they were sold as slaves. *Underworld use.*

**Kidnapping**   The criminal act of forcibly abducting another human. *General use, 1666.* Cf. **child snatching**, **ransom**.

**Kill**   *n.* A murder. *U.S. underworld use, 1934.* *v.* 1. To deprive a human or animal of life. *General use.* Cf. **accidental killing**; **homicide**; **manslaughter**; **murder**. 2. To fix or quash (e.g., an indictment). *U.S. underworld use, 1933.*

**Kill a rap**   To withdraw, or cause to be withdrawn, a criminal prosecution, often through bribery or influence. *Underworld use.*

**Killer**   One who kills. *General use.*

**Killing**   *n.* 1. The act of murder. 2. Large gambling winnings. *Gambling use.* *adj.* Able to bring about death. *General use.*

**Killing by misadventure**   The accidental killing of one human being by another while the killer is engaged in some lawful act, without criminal carelessness or reckless conduct. *Legal use.*

**King's Bench**   A division of the British superior courts system, so named because a king or queen, at one time, sat there in person. *U.K. general use.* Cf. **Queen's Bench.**

**King's College**   The King's Bench Prison in London. *Obsolete U.K. underworld use, 1796.*

**Kiss of death**   An act or event that brings about destruction or doom, from the biblical story of Judas's kiss. *General use.*

**Kleptomania**   An abnormal and often irresistible impulse to steal, usually without an economic motive or need. *Medical use.*

**Kleptomaniac**   A person who suffers from kleptomania. *Medical and law enforcement use.*

**Kleptophobia**   A person with an abnormal fear of stealing or of thieves. *General use.*

**Knight of the post**   False or manufactured evidence. *General use, 1580.*

**Knock-off**; **knock off**   *n.* A murder, robbery, arrest, raid, kidnapping, or the price paid for protection. *Underworld use, 1936. v.* 1. To murder, rob, arrest, raid, or kidnap. *Underworld use, 1914.* 2. To indulge in a brief amount of something or in something for a brief period of time (e.g., drugs, alcohol, or sleep). *General use.*

**Knowingly and willfully**   With conscious knowledge and decision. *Legal use.*

**Knowledge**   The state of understanding; comprehending; knowing. *Legal use.*

**Kosher**   Clean, guiltless, innocent, above reproach. *Underworld use, 1930.*

**L**   The law; any law enforcement agency or a representative of any law enforcement agency. *Underworld use.*

**Lab**   Short term for a scientific laboratory for the study of criminal evidence. *Police use.*

**Lab boys**   Police laboratory technicians. *Police use.*

**Lability**   A mental condition characterized by emotional instability. *Medical use.*

**Laboratory, mobile crime.**   See **mobile crime laboratory**.

**Lam**   *n.* 1. An escape from justice before trial. *Underworld use, 1914.* 2. A departure from a jurisdiction in which a crime has been committed in order to escape justice. *Underworld use. v.* 1. To run away and escape apprehension. *U.S. underworld use, 1921.* 2. To leave the scene of a crime, escape from prison, or jump bail. *U.S. underworld use, 1920.*

**Lamaster; lamester; lamister; lammister**   1. An individual who misses an assigned trial date and forfeits bail money; a fugitive; a person "on the lam." *Underworld use, 1904.* 2. A prison escapee. *Prison use.*

**Larcenous**   Resembling or having to do with larceny. *Legal use.*

**Larcenous intent**   The aim of depriving someone of his property. *Legal use.*

**Larceny**   The crime of taking another's personal property without consent and with the felonious intent of depriving the owner of the property. This crime is often statutorily divided into different degrees (e.g., grand or petty larceny), with penalties differing in severity. *Legal use.*

**Larceny, compound**   Theft from a person or a house; a.k.a. **larceny, mixed**. *Legal use.*

**Larceny, constructive**   Larceny in which felonious intent is inferred from the conduct of the accused even though the original taking of property did not appear felonious. *Legal use.*

**Larceny, grand**   Stealing property or merchandise valued at over $100, or at another amount established by local law. *Legal use.*

**Larceny, mixed.**   See **larceny, compound**.

**Larceny, petit**   Stealing property or merchandise valued at a total dollar amount that does not exceed $100 or another amount established by local law; a.k.a. **petty larceny**. *Legal use.*

**Larceny, simple**   Theft that does not entail violence in order to obtain the stolen property. *Legal use.*

**Larceny by bailee**   Theft committed by a person responsible for guarding a particular piece of property, who fraudulently transfers the ownership of that property to himself or to another person. *Legal use.*

**Larceny by fraud, deception, or trick**   Obtaining property from its owner by using fraudulent tactics. *Legal use.*

**Larceny from the person**   The physical theft of property from an individual without the use of violence. *Legal use.*

**Larceny of auto**   The theft of an automobile. *Legal use.* Cf. **auto theft**.

**Last mile**   The final walk to the death chamber of a convict sentenced to death. *U.S. underworld use.*

**Last waltz, the**   The final walk of a convict sentenced to death, usually to the gallows, guillotine, gas chamber, or electric chair. *U.S. underworld use, 1934.*

**Latent**   Potential, capable of being perceived with help (e.g., a latent fingerprint). *General use.*

**Latent fingerprint**   A fingerprint accidentally left at the scene of the crime but not visible unless treated in some way. *Law enforcement use.*

**Lateral pressure**   Handwriting that contains visible horizontal movements of the pen due to a specific type of pressure by a writer. *Handwriting analysis use.*

**Law**   1. The rules of conduct as defined by a legitimate authority (e.g., a legislature or court) that are binding on all individuals within that jurisdiction of authority. 2. An official act adopted by the legislature. 3. Unwritten customs, codes of conduct, or judicial decisions, referred to as common law. 4. A question of principle, as opposed to a question of fact. *Legal use.* 5. A criminal activity or profession. *Underworld use, 1552.* 6. The opportunity for a criminal to escape through a loophole in the justice system. 7. A representative of any law enforcement agency (e.g., a policeman, a prison guard). *U.S. underworld use, 1929.*

**Law-abiding**   Obedient to laws. *General use.*

**Lawbreaker**   A person who violates laws. *General use.*

**Law enforcement**   The profession of crime prevention, accomplished through the investigation of individual criminal cases and the apprehension of suspects by a member of a law enforcement agency. *General use.*

**Law enforcement agency**   The federal, state, or local association responsible for law enforcement within established jurisdictions. *General use.*

**Law enforcement officer**   An individual whose responsibility is to administer the rules and regulations established by a jurisdiction. *General use.*

**Lawful**   Within the law; not specifically forbidden by law. *General use.* Cf. **legal; legitimate**.

**Lawful age**   The legal age, established by jurisdictions, which denotes that an individual is no longer regarded as a minor. Once an individual reaches this age, usually eighteen, he is accountable for his own actions and may be tried in a court of law as an adult. *Legal use.*

**Lawful arrest**   Taking into custody a person suspected of a crime based on probable cause or using a valid arrest warrant issued by a court. Cf. **probable cause**; **search**. *Legal use.*

**Lawgiver**.   See **lawmaker**.

**Lawless**   Acting outside the boundaries of the rules established by a legitimate authority.

**Lawmaker**   A person who creates laws for a group of people; a legislator; a.k.a. **lawgiver**. *General use.*

**Lawman**   A person who enforces the laws of an area. *General use.*

**Lay low**   1. To hide from the law. 2. To curtail criminal activities for an unspecified amount of time. *Underworld use.*

**Leak**   *n.* 1. A disclosure of confidential information. *U.S. underworld use, 1873.* 2. A confidential way of obtaining something illegal. *U.S. underworld use, 1900s. v.* To tell a secret. *Underworld use, 1859.*

**Lean on; lean against**   1. To raid a criminal establishment. *Underworld use, 1949.* 2. To use or threaten violence against a person or members of that person's family in order to obtain information, suppress information, or extort money. *Underworld use.*

**Leech**   A police informant, someone considered a traitor by the underworld. *Gulf state area prison use.*

**Legal**   1. Pertaining to the law. 2. Permitted by law. *Legal use.* Cf. **lawful**.

**Legal age**   The age at which a person is said to be capable of possessing the full legal rights of an adult. *General use.*

**Legal beagle**   A clever attorney; a.k.a. **legal eagle**. *General use.*

**Legal impossibility**   A defense used when an individual's actions would not have violated the law if he had been able to complete them. *Legal use.*

**Legality**   1. Adherence to the law. 2. A technicality or item of the law. *General use.*

**Legal weapon**   A device that is legally permitted for use in self-defense. Legal weapons include aerosol sprays, kitchen knives, nail files, umbrellas, whistles, a scream, or threats with a hammer or hatchet. *General use.*

**Legitimate**   Lawful or abiding by and following the precepts of the law. *General use.*

**Lesser included offense**   A crime that necessarily occurs while committing a larger, more serious crime. A crime is considered a lesser included offense of another if proving the greater crime necessarily means establishing the elements of the lesser crime, plus at least one more element necessary to prove the greater offense. *Legal use.*

**Lethal chamber**   The room in a prison where condemned criminals are executed. *Prison use.*

**Level**   Honest or truthful. *Underworld use, 1931.*

**Level, on the**   Honest or truthful. *Underworld use, 1905.*

**Lex**   A collection or body of laws, either written or unwritten. *Legal use.*

*Lex loci delictus*   The law of the jurisdiction where a crime occurs. *Legal use.*

*Lex succurrit minoribus*   Literally, "the law assists minors." *Legal use.*

*Lex talionis*   The principle that the severity of the punishment for a crime should match the severity of the crime itself. *Legal use.*

**Liable**   Having responsibility or being obligated by law. *General use.*

**Libel**   The malicious publication of lasting defamation of another. *Legal use.* Cf. **slander.**

**Liberate**   1. To set free or at liberty. *General use.*

**Liberty**   The right of an individual to live in a society and to operate within the parameters of established rules and regulations, imposed in the interest of the community at large, without fear of restraint from extraneous forces. *General use.*

**Lidford law**   A type of lynch law that entails punishing individuals for a crime before legally trying them. *Underworld use.*

**Lie**   To tell an untruth in order to deliberately deceive. *General use.* Cf. **perjury.**

**Lie detector.**   See **polygraph.**

**Life**   A prison sentence requiring the offender to serve the remainder of his life in jail. Life sentences are usually defined by individual jurisdictions; a.k.a. **life bit.** *Legal use.* Cf. **life, habitual offender; life, natural; life, one to.**

**Life, five to.**   See **life, one to.**

**Life, habitual offender**   A life sentence, usually prescribed after several felony convictions with parole possible under most circumstances. *Legal use.*

**Life, natural**   A life sentence in which parole is not permitted. *Legal use.*

**Life, one to**   A life sentence that includes minimum and maximum limits of servitude. Most convicts who receive this sentence are paroled within a few years; a.k.a. **five to life.** *Legal use.*

**Life bit.**   See **life.**

**Lifeboat**   A pardon, a court-granted retrial, or the revocation of a death sentence. *Underworld use, 1918.*

**Life liner**   Amnesty or forgiveness. *Underworld use, 1924.*

**Life on the installment plan**   1. Excessive recidivism; repeated returns to prison as a result of successive parole violations. *Prison use.* 2. Recurring criminal violations. *General use.* 3. Indeterminate sentence with high maximum limits of incarceration. *Legal use.*

**Life or limb**   A phrase that is part of the protection guaranteed by the Fifth Amendment to the U.S. Constitution ensuring that an individual will not be tried more than once for the same offense. *Legal use.*

**Lifer**   1. A convict who has received or is serving a life sentence at a penal colony. *Underworld use, 1860.* 2. A convict serving any life sentence. *Underworld use, 1832.*

**Life sentence**   A criminal sentence committing a convicted felon to a prescribed punishment for the rest of his natural life.

**Light-headed**   Lacking full mental capacities; disoriented. *General use.*

**Lineup; line up**   *n.* The daily review of prisoners by law officers at police headquarters. *Police use. v.* 1. To stand in line for review by law officers. *Police use.* 2. To take a position in a police lineup. 3. To consider and execute a particular crime. *U.S. underworld use.*

**Lineup, police**   The law enforcement practice of placing individuals suspected of a particular crime in a viewing line to determine if the victim or a witness can identify an individual as the perpetrator of the crime. *Police use.*

**Lip**   A defense attorney. *U.S. underworld use, 1929.* Cf. **mouthpiece.**

**Litigant**   A party involved in a legal proceeding (e.g., the defendant). *Legal use.*

**Litigate**   To contest a dispute in a legal proceeding. *General use.*

**Logistics**   The component of a police operation that is concerned with the supply of equipment or facilities used during a law enforcement operation. *Law enforcement use.*

**Long arm of the law; long arm**   Any crime prevention bureau or a representative of any law enforcement agency. *Underworld use.*

**Loophole**   A means by which escape or evasion is possible, especially through an ambiguity in a law. *General use.*

**Loser**   Any person who has been convicted of a felony.

**Low profile**   Making oneself unrecognizable; being incognito. *General use.*

**Low-profile crime**   A violation of the law committed without an eyewitness. *Underworld use.* Cf. **high-profile crime.**

**Lucid interval**   A segment of time when a medically insane person regains sufficient mental control of his faculties that he is capable of performing a legal act without disqualification because of his illness. *Legal use.*

**Lunacy** A mental disorder; impaired faculties of the human mind; insanity. *Legal use.*

**Lunacy, commission of** A court order requiring an investigation to establish the alleged insanity of an individual. *Legal use.*

**Lunacy, inquest of.** See **lunacy, inquisition of.**

**Lunacy, inquisition of** A court-ordered examination to investigate the mental state of an individual. This often leads to the assignment of a guardian for the mentally ill person or commitment to an institution; a.k.a. **lunacy, inquest of.** *Legal use.*

**Lunatic** A deranged person suffering from psychosis.

**Lure** *n.* The enticement for the victim of a crime. *v.* To entice or attract another with a hint of gain or pleasure. *General use.*

**Lust murder** A homicide that often entails mutilation of sex organs. *Legal use.*

**Lynch** To execute by hanging without first providing the accused due process of law in a traditional judicial arena. Lynching was commonly practiced by residents of the southern United States to terrorize blacks. The practice was named after Captain William Lynch.

**Lynch law** So-called justice carried out by the illegal execution of a person accused of a crime and sentenced to death by individuals with no legal right to try criminal cases. *General use.*

**Lynch mob** A riotous and angry group of people that is bent on killing, usually by illegally hanging someone they feel is guilty of a crime or they otherwise oppose. *General use.*

**Magistrate** 1. A public official vested with executive, legislative, or judicial powers, such as a mayor or prefect. 2. A judge with limited authority, such as a justice of the peace or the presiding judge in a traffic court. *Legal use.* 3. A judicial officer who receives his appointment from a federal district court. *U.S. legal use.*

**Magistrate, police.** See **police magistrate.**

**Magistrate's courts** A court of limited jurisdiction generally confined to dealing with petty offenses or preliminary hearings. *Legal use.*

**Magna culpa** Any extreme negligence or great fault. *Legal use.*

**Magna culpa dolus est** Extreme negligence equals fraud; a.k.a. *magna negligentia culpa est. Legal use.*

**Magna negligentia culpa est.** See *magna culpa dolus est.*

**Maim** To mutilate or cripple. *General use.* Cf. **mayhem; mutilation.**

**Major case squad** The department in the Detective Bureau assigned to investigate serious or well-publicized crimes. *NYPD use.*

**Major classification** The method of recording and filing a suspect's fingerprints. *Police use.*

**Major crime** 1. A serious crime such as murder, rape, arson, and armed robbery. *Legal and police use.* 2. A crime for which the defendant is entitled to a jury trial. *Legal use.*

**Make a deal** To reach an agreement with a judge, a district attorney, or any other public official whereby immunity is granted in exchange for a guilty plea or information leading to the arrest or conviction of someone else. Many wrongly-convicted persons have been victimized through this generally corrupt practice. *Underworld use.*

**Malefactor** A person found guilty of a crime. *Legal use.* Cf. **convict.**

**Malfeasance** 1. Any unlawful act. *General use.* 2. Any unlawful conduct by a public servant; for example, wrongful conduct that affects, interrupts, or interferes with the performance of official duties. *Legal use.* Cf. **misfeasance; nonfeasance.**

**Malice** The state of mind accompanying the intentional commission of a wrongful act without justification or excuse. *Legal use.* Cf. **libel; slander.**

**Malice aforethought** The intent to carry out murder. In old English law, murder was subdivided into two categories: felonious homicide, whereby a person planned to kill someone with malice aforethought, and nonfelonious murder, or manslaughter. Malice aforethought does not necessarily imply personal ill will or hatred against the intended victim; a.k.a. **malice prepense.** *Legal use.* Cf. **premeditation.**

**Malice in fact** The desire or intent to injure someone; either express or actual malice. *Legal use.*

**Malice in law** Implied malice; presumed from acts committed without justification or excuse. *Legal use.*

**Malice prepense.** See **malice aforethought.**

**Malicious** Involving malice; regarding an act carried out wrongfully and without justification. *Legal use.* Cf. **willful.**

**Malicious abandonment** In criminal law, desertion of one's spouse without cause. *Legal use.*

**Malicious abuse of process** The subversion of the judicial process to obtain an outcome that the law does not intend. *Legal use.*

**Malicious accusation** An unjust charge based on a wrongful motive and lack of probable cause. *Legal use.*

**Malicious act**   An act committed with the intention to injure or damage without legal justification. *Legal use.*

**Malicious assault with a deadly weapon**   Aggravated assault using a gun, knife, or any other deadly weapon. *Legal use.* Cf. **aggravated assault**.

**Malicious damage**   1. The unlawful killing or wounding of an animal. 2. The destruction of another person's property, as outlined in the Malicious Damage Act of 1861. *U.K. legal use.*

**Malicious injury**   Harm willfully done to another because of malice toward him. *Legal use.*

**Malicious killing**   The intentional taking of someone's life without justification, and not within the sphere of voluntary manslaughter. *Legal use.*

**Malicious motive**   The desire to prosecute someone for reasons other than to bring him to justice. *Legal use.*

**Malicious prosecution**   1. A prosecution that has commenced with the knowledge that the charges cannot be sustained. *Legal use.* 2. A legal action brought before a court by a person who has had criminal proceedings brought against him for malicious reasons and without probable cause. *Legal use.*

**Malpractice**   Careless or willful mistreatment of a medical patient by a medical doctor or public health official. *Medical use.*

*Malum in se; mala in se*   A crime regarded as wrong by its very nature (e.g., murder or arson); from Latin for "wrong in itself." *Legal use.*

*Malum prohibition*   An act prohibited by law but not inherently immoral or evil; a.k.a. *mala prohibita*. *Legal use.*

**Mandamus**   A judicial writ issued to a corporation, its officers, or to an official or lower court, commanding a specific action or deed, which is part of the person or entity's duty or responsibility; used only in extraordinary or emergency situations; a.k.a. **writ of mandamus**. *Legal use.*

**Mandatory sentence**   The minimum length of a prison sentence for various crimes, enacted into law by state legislatures. *Legal use.*

**Manhunt**   A massive police search for an escaped fugitive or convict. *Police use.*

**Mania**   A mental disease characterized by hyperactivity and hallucinations. *Medical use.*

**Manic-depressive insanity**   A mental disorder in which the sufferer undergoes extreme mood swings, fluctuating between periods of joy and severe depression. *Medical use.*

**Manner of execution**   A legal requirement that law officers serve a search warrant in a carefully prescribed manner; for example, the warrant must be executed at certain times of the day and to individuals of legal age. *Legal use.*

**Manslaughter**   The unlawful killing of someone without malice, either express or implied. Voluntary or nonnegligent manslaughter is the intentional killing of someone with provocation, as in the case of someone who is accidentally killed in a quarrel. If, in the heat of passion or during temporary loss of self-control, the defendant was reasonably provoked to an act of violence, a charge of manslaughter rather than murder may be appropriate if the evidence suggests that someone else might have acted accordingly in similar circumstances (e.g., victims of adultery); a.k.a. **voluntary manslaughter**. *Legal use.* Cf. **involuntary manslaughter**; **negligent manslaughter**; **vehicular manslaughter**.

**Mark**   *n.* 1. An easy target for a thief or a con man. *Con artist use, 1742.* 2. A prison scapegoat. *Prison use, 1879.* 3. A place or person designated as the target of a thief or an assault. *Underworld use, 1890.* 4. The amount of money collected in a robbery. *Underworld use.* 5. A drug victim. *Drug addict use. v.* 1. To brand someone as an informer. *Underworld use.* 2. To target a person as a likely victim of a robbery or assault. *Underworld use, 1886.*

**Marking evidence**   Sorting, classifying, and tagging of evidence for police or later court use. *Police use.*

**Marshal**   1. A U.S. law enforcement officer appointed to each judicial district by presidential order. *Government use.* 2. A county law officer empowered to serve court orders. *Police and government use.* Cf. **provost marshal**; **sky marshal**; **United States marshal**.

**Martyr**   *n.* Someone who gives his life voluntarily for a principle, especially as a refusal to renounce his religion. *v.* 1. To put one to death for his or her religious or political beliefs or principles. 2. To torture or inflict great pain. *General use.*

**Mass murder**   The killing of three or more persons at the same time, usually within a twenty-four-hour period and usually in the same location or area, sometimes weeks. *General use.*

**Mass murderer**   One who kills more than two people. *General use.*

**Mastermind**   The "brains" of a criminal operation. *Underworld use.*

**Master of the Crown Office**   An officer of the Supreme Court of England who serves as the Queen's coroner and attorney in the criminal department of the Queen's Bench. *U.K. legal use.*

**Material.**   See **material witness.**

**Material fact**   An essential fact; one necessary to resolve issues. *Legal use.*

**Material witness**   The only person, or one of a few, capable of offering particular testimony at a trial. In selective criminal cases, the material witness may be placed in custody against his will at the government's insistence to make sure that he appears. *Legal use.*

**Matrons, jury of**   A special jury summoned to determine the legitimacy of a defendant's pregnancy claim when the defendant has received a death sentence. *Legal use.*

**Maturation**   The measurement of an individual's social maturity, and the degree to which that person takes direct responsibility for his actions. The Vineland Social Maturity Scale attempts to measure the detailed stages of a person's mental and emotional development. The analysis offered by proponents of the Vineland Scale provides prison officials with information to help determine an inmate's readiness for parole and his ability to assimilate back into society. *Sociological use.*

**Max**   The maximum prison sentence provided by law for any crime except crimes that call for capital punishment. *Legal use.* Cf. **maximum punishment.**

**Maximum custody**   1. An escape-proof setting, usually in a prison where it is all but impossible to scale the walls or hack through the bars using a tool. 2. A high-security prison with a large number of guards intent on maintaining a tight disciplinary regime. *Prison use.*

**Maximum punishment**   The most severe form of punishment for a specific crime established by law. *Legal use.* Cf. **cruel and unusual punishment.**

**Maximum sentence**   The affirmation of the upper limits of punishment for a crime, established by law. *Legal use.*

**Mayhem**   A violent crime in which the victim has been willfully and permanently maimed or crippled. Under current statutes, dismemberment of limbs and permanent disfigurement generally constitute an act of mayhem. *Legal use.* Cf. **mutilation.**

**McCarthyism**   A political attitude of the early 1950s in the United States marked by opposition to thoughts and beliefs held to be subversive, creating an air of panic and leading to widespread persecution based on indiscriminate and unsupported allegations. The term is named for the chief proponent of this movement, U.S. Senator Joseph Raymond McCarthy (1908–1957) of Wisconsin. This term has come to mean any collusive and malicious actions taken against an innocent person or persons and is often applied in cases involving wrongly convicted persons. *General use.*

**Mea culpa**   A formal admission of one's own guilt or blame. Literally, it means "through my fault." *General use.*

**Meagerness**   A handwriting style that lacks expansion. *Handwriting analysis use.*

**Measure**   1. To examine or size up a criminal closely. *Underworld use, 1859.* 2. To use the Bertillon prisoner identification method to check the bone sizes of a prisoner. *Prison use, 1880.*

**Mediate**   To bring an end to discordance between two parties. *General use.*

**Mediator**   One who acts as a go-between for two conflicting parties. *General use.*

**Medical examiner**   1. The public official responsible for investigating the sudden and mysterious deaths reported in the city and for conducting autopsies; a.k.a. **ME**. *Forensic use.* 2. A physician in the employ of insurance companies or other private agencies. *Medical use.*

**Medical model of corrections**   The classification and diagnosis procedure employed by correctional facilities to identify and treat the causes of criminal behavior. The medical model of corrections places the penal institution in a much broader context. It is not enough to provide custody for a convicted felon. The treatment phase attempts to correct the defect in personality that led to the criminal act. *Prison and sociological use.*

**Medium custody**   A prison or jail designed for inmates who do not pose a great threat to society. The relaxed standards permit a prisoner greater mobility and the opportunity to reform. *Prison use.*

**Megalomania**   A mental disorder in which the victim experiences delusions of grandeur, believing that he is a celebrated person from history or contemporary life, and that he is all-powerful and all-seeing. Cf. **schizophrenia.**

**Melancholia**   A state of severe depression. It is considered a mental disease when the patient experiences periods of hallucination and is a danger to himself and others. *Medical use.*

**Men of straw**   Professional witnesses and courtroom loungers known to attorneys by the presence of a straw in one of their shoes. When asked to do so, the "man of straw" will testify as a material witness to a crime whether he had witnessed the crime or not. *Obsolete U.S. and U.K. legal use.*

**Mens rea**   A guilty mind. The criminal state of mind or intent that accompanies a crime. The requisite state of mind varies depending on the particular crime. The model penal code classifies crime into four different states of mind, or mens rea: crimes that require intention, crimes that require knowledge of the nature of the crime, crimes of recklessness which require that the person realize the degree of risk his actions entail, and crimes of gross negligence. *Legal use.* Cf. **actus reus**; **malice**; **mental state**.

**Mental alienation**   Insanity. *Medical and legal use.*

**Mental capacity**   A person's psychological competence; one's understanding of the nature and consequences of an act about to be undertaken; a.k.a. **mental competence**. *Legal and medical use.*

**Mental competence**.   See **mental capacity**.

**Mental cruelty**   Abusive behavior or conduct of one spouse toward another which makes a harmonious marriage all but impossible. The act of mental cruelty is normally grounds for divorce, but it is defined differently in various states. *Legal use.*

**Mental defect**   1. Ignorance or lack of mental capability that renders one unfit to serve as a juror. 2. Lack of mental ability of an offender that is taken into consideration in the handling of some criminal cases in some states. *Legal use.*

**Mental deficiency**   A legal and scientific classification for individuals with arrested or incomplete social development. Once the mental deficiency has been established, the person will commonly fall into one of three categories: (1) the idiot, with a mental and social age below three, (2) the imbecile, or middle level, with a mental and social age between three and seven, (3) and the moron, the highest grade, with a mental age between eight and twelve and a social age of between ten and twenty. These three classifications are frequently predicated on the results of IQ (intelligence quotient) and SQ (social quotient) tests. *Medical and legal use.* Cf. **moron**.

**Mental disease**   1. A diseased or defective condition of the mind. *Medical use.* 2. A lack of fitness to be held responsible for crime in a court of law. *Legal use.* Cf. **insanity**.

**Mental mechanisms**   The functions and variety of activity that go on inside the mind. Seventeen stages of activity have been identified by psychiatrists, including identification, sublimation, repression, reaction formation, undoing, isolation, displacement, symbolization, condensation, conversion, rationalization, idealization, transference, projection, introjection, unconscious fantasy, and dreaming. *Sociological use.*

**Mental state**   The condition of a person's mind at the time a criminal act is committed. *Legal use.*

**Mental tests and measurements in criminology**   Various testing methods have been employed by social workers and criminologists over the years to analyze a criminal offender's psychological state. The traditional approach has been to test for intelligence using the Revised Stanford Binet Scale. Today various psychological tests that include verbal and written sections are administered, making it possible to better gauge human behavior. *Medical and sociological use.*

**Mercy**   A judge's discretion to waive punishment or curtail the sentence of an offender based on mitigating circumstances. *Legal use.*

**Merger**   The incorporation of the charge of a lesser offense committed during a major crime into a major charge; a.k.a. **merger of offenses**. *Legal use.*

**Merger of offenses**.   See **merger**.

**Microchemistry**   The clinical analysis of small chemical substances left behind at the scene of a crime. It is an essential tool of a police crime laboratory. *Police and forensic use.*

**Military court**   1. A court that hears cases involving military personnel. 2. A court subject to the Code of Military Justice. *Military use.*

**Military criminology**   The foundation of military law, by which persons found guilty of crimes against the armed forces are judged. The United States Articles of War establish three tribunals commonly known as courts-martial. (1) The summary court-martial can sentence an offender to a month of hard labor if he has committed a minor offense; (2) the special court-martial can pass a sentence of six months' confinement at hard labor; and (3) the general court-martial, consisting of five or more members, can impose the supreme penalty of death or, in less serious cases, dishonorable expulsion with forfeit of salary and pension. A less formal "fourth court," or "company court," is the authority vested in commanding officers to punish an offender without benefit of trial for petty offenses. This is called the disciplinary powers of commanding officers under the Article of War 104. The offending party in all cases is offered the choice of a court-martial or punishment by the commanding officer. Most will accept the judgment of the officer, as the limits of punishment are less severe. Sitting members of the general courts-martial are appointed by executive order of the president and the superintendent of West Point Military Academy. *Military and legal use.*

**Military execution**   Death by military firing squad. *Military use.*

**Military jurisdiction**   The legal authority of the military to oversee the personnel of the U.S. armed forces. The Constitution provides for three levels of military jurisdiction: one that is exercised in peace and war, one that is exercised during a time of war and outside U.S. boundaries, and one that is exercised during invasion or open rebellion within the country. In periods of chaos and internal strife, the third category of military jurisdiction may be employed. It is commonly known as martial law. *Military and legal use.*

**Military law**   A system of regulations, rules, and laws that guide the conduct of armed forces personnel but does not extend to civilians. *Military and legal use.*

**Military offenses**   Crimes against the armed forces committed by uniformed personnel (e.g., sleeping on duty, absent without leave, insubordination). *Military use.*

**Military police**   A division of the army that handles police and guard duties. *General use.*

**Military Review, Courts of**   A military review board within each branch of the armed forces for the purpose of considering court-martial decisions. *Military use.*

**Minatur innocentibus qui parcit nocentibus**   He who spares the guilty threatens the innocent. *Legal use.*

**Minimum custody**   A prison, work farm, or camp that offers an inmate the greatest degree of freedom. *Prison use.*

**Minimum sentence**   The least amount of time a convicted defendant will spend in jail before he is eligible for parole. *Legal use.*

**Minor**   A person who has not yet reached the legal age of competence, which varies from one jurisdiction to another. *Legal use.*

**Miranda rule**   The legal doctrine that requires law enforcement officials to advise arrested persons of certain rights before the officers are allowed to question them. These rights are: a warning that the arrested person has the right to remain silent; that any statements made by him could be used against him in a court of law; that he has the right to the presence of an attorney; and that if he cannot afford a lawyer, one will be appointed for him. This doctrine is a result of the 1966 *Miranda v. Arizona* decision handed down by the U.S. Supreme Court. See **Miranded.** *Legal use.*

**Miranded**   To have received the Miranda warning from a police officer. *Legal use.*

**Misbehavior**   1. Any unsuitable or unlawful behavior. *Legal use.* 2. Conduct unbecoming to participants in a judicial case, a judge, juror, lawyer, spectator, or witness. *Legal use.*

**Miscarriage of justice**   An outcome or decision that is substantially prejudicial to the rights of the defendant. A miscarriage of justice generally warrants a reversal when the court determines that in all probability, the appealing party would have won the case had it not been for the error. *Legal use.*

**Misconduct**   Any violation of an established law or rule. *Legal use.*

**Misconduct in office**   The willful and unlawful performance or nonperformance of duties by an elected or appointed official. *Legal and government use.*

**Miscreant**   Someone who has a criminal or vicious nature. *General use.*

**Misdeed**   An offense or wrongful act. *General use.*

**Misdemeanant**   A person who is guilty of a misdemeanor. *Legal use.*

**Misdemeanor**   An infraction of the law less serious than a felony, and usually punishable by a small fine or jail sentence of less than one year. In the U.S., a misdemeanor and a felony are usually defined by local statutes. Generally, the accused felon must always be present for his court hearing, while the misdemeanant may be tried in his absence. A convicted felon may not be allowed to hold public office or serve on a jury in some jurisdictions, while a person guilty of a misdemeanor may usually do so. *Legal use.* Cf. **felony**; **high crimes and misdemeanors**.

**Misdoubt**   To suspect a falsehood. *General use.*

**Mise-en-scène**   The scene of a crime. *General use.*

**Misfeasance**   The improper performance of an act that might otherwise be done in a legal manner. Cf. **malfeasance**; **nonfeasance**. *Legal use.*

**Misprision**   A word used for any crime that does not have a specific name. It has been used, for example, to describe maladministration of a public office or the concealment of information that should be revealed, or seditious or treasonous behavior against a sovereign government. *Legal use.* Cf. **malfeasance**.

**Misrepresent**   1. To give misleading representation, usually with intent to deceive. 2. To poorly represent, either deliberately or unintentionally. *General use.*

**Misrepresentation**   A false representation or distortion of the facts tending to mislead or deceive. *Legal use.*

**Mistaken identity**   An incorrect identification of an innocent person as the perpetrator of a crime, often involving the physical double of the real culprit. *Police use.*

**Mistrial**   A trial that has been terminated prior to the jury or judge returning a verdict because of an error of the judge, attorneys, jurors, or other parties, or other circumstances. The death of a juror, improper jury selection, or a prejudicial error that cannot be remedied during the deliberations are common reasons for declaring a mistrial. *Legal use.*

**Miswriting**   An error in writing not caused by poor spelling. *Handwriting analysis use.*

**Mitigating circumstances**   Facts that justify reducing a penalty or a charge but do not excuse the conduct of the accused, for example, reducing a charge of murder to manslaughter when the crime was committed in a sudden heat of passion evoked by sufficient legal provocation. *Legal use.*

**Mitigation of punishment**   The judge's decision to reduce a defendant's punishment because of family circumstances, past cooperation with the police or the court, no prior criminal record, etc. *Legal use.*

**Mittimus**   1. A court order that a judge issues to the jailer to commit a person to prison or to transfer records from one court to another. 2. The court transcript of a conviction and sentence certified by the court clerk. *Legal use.*

**Mobile crime laboratory**   A fully equipped police van used to collect evidence and take photographs at the scene of a crime. Some police units have come under severe criticism claiming that mobile crime experts have conducted shoddy examinations and collected "contaminated" evidence that result in the convictions of innocent persons or the exonerations of others most probably guilty; a.k.a. **mobile crime**. *Police use.*

**Modus of an indictment**   The portion of an indictment that spells out the way in which the crime was committed. *Legal use.*

**Modus operandi**   Method of operation, or the way in which a crime is carried out; a.k.a. **MO**. *Legal use.*

**Monitor**   1. To observe or watch carefully. *General use.* 2. To carry out a telephone wiretap done through a central clearinghouse. *Underworld use.*

**Monnicker; monicker; monocker; monacher**   A person's name or signature. *Underworld use, 1859.*

**Morgue**   A public storage facility where the bodies of deceased persons are maintained for purposes of identification. After a limited time, an unclaimed body is turned over to the sanitary department for disposal. *General use.*

**Moron**   Medical and legal classification for a person whose mental capacity does not exceed that of a twelve-year-old, or whose IQ is between 50 and 70. *Legal and medical use.* Cf. **mental deficiency**.

**Mortis causa**   By reason of death or in contemplation of death. *Legal use.*

**Motion**   A verbal or written request made by the defense or prosecuting attorney to the judge before, during, or after a trial, requesting that the judge rule on a particular issue or order a particular action. *Legal use.*

**Motion for a directed verdict**   A request to the court by the defense for an acquittal because the prosecution has failed to prove the defendant's guilt. In criminal cases, there may not be a directed verdict for conviction. *Legal use.*

**Motion for a judgment notwithstanding the verdict**   A motion put forth to the judge that he reverse the jury's decision because the evidence submitted could not sustain their verdict. *Legal use.*

**Motion for a new trial**   A motion for a judge to set aside a verdict and order a new trial because of an impropriety, unfairness, or legal error that took place during the proceedings. *Legal use.*

**Motion to suppress**   A formal request to eliminate from a criminal trial damaging evidence that has been secured through illegal means in violation of the U.S. Constitution's Fourth Amendment protection against search and seizure, the Fifth Amendment protection against self-incrimination, or the Sixth Amendment right to legal counsel. *Legal use.*

**Motive** The reason why a person carries out a particular act. It is generally not necessary to establish a motive to secure a conviction for a crime, but it is often desirable. *Legal and police use.* Cf. **intent**.

**Mouthpiece** 1. A criminal lawyer. *Underworld use, 1857.* 2. A police informant. *U.S. underworld use, 1900.*

**Mug book** A photograph album of known criminal offenders classified by offense, and shown to victims of a crime by the police or FBI for purposes of identification. *Police and underworld use.*

**Mugged** Having one's picture included in the rogues' gallery of a police station. *Police use, 1901.* Cf. **unmugged**.

**Mug room** The prisoner identification room in a police station. *Police use, 1934.*

**Mugshot** A frontal and side portrait of a criminal, usually taken at the time of arrest and maintained in a file in the police station. *Police and underworld use.*

**Multiple murder** The killing of a number of people over an extended period of time, usually one person at a time. *General use.* Cf. **serial killer**.

**Multiple murderer** One who kills a number of people over an extended time period, usually one person at a time. *General use.* Cf. **serial killer**.

**Multiple offender** A criminal who has been convicted of more than one offense. *Legal use.*

**Multiple offenses** The principle that a criminal act may violate two statutes. *Legal use.*

**Multiple sentences** Sentences that will be served consecutively by a defendant who has been judged guilty of more than one crime. *Legal use.*

**Municipal court** A court of law having jurisdiction over criminal matters that take place in the urban area in which the court is established. *General use.*

**Murder** *n.* The unlawful killing of another person with malice aforethought. *General use.* Cf. **assassination**; **felony murder**; **heat of passion**; **homicide; lust murder; manslaughter; willful murder.** *v.* 1. To kill another with malice aforethought. *Legal use.* 2. To stupidly ruin a well-planned crime through omission, carelessness, or haste. *Underworld use.*

**Murder, depraved heart.** See **depraved heart murder**.

**Murderee** The victim, or intended victim, of a murder. *Police use.*

**Murderer** The person committing the murder. *General use.*

**Murder in the first degree.** See **first-degree murder**.

**Murder in the second degree.** See **second-degree murder**.

**Murder one.** See **first-degree murder**.

**Mute, stand.** See **stand mute**.

**Mutilate** To sever or cripple a portion of the anatomy, or disfigure. *Legal use.* Cf. **maim**.

**Mutilation** The act of depriving a person of the use of his limbs, or disfiguring the body in some way. *Legal use.* Cf. **mayhem**.

**Mutineer** A person who rebels against authority, usually a superior. *General use.*

**Mutiny** *n.* A seditious rebellion against the legally constituted authority, usually against the military commander or the captain of a vessel. A party is guilty of the crime of mutiny when he and others refuse to carry out the orders of the superior officer. *Legal and military use.* Cf. **desertion**. *v.* To rise up and overthrow the existing order. *Legal and political use.*

**Mutual aid agreements** The agreement between various city and state police agencies to cooperate with each other during criminal investigations. *Police and law enforcement use.*

**Mythomania** An extraordinary penchant for exaggerating or telling falsehoods. *General use.*

**Narcotic drugs** Drugs regulated by federal and state laws that are classified in the following five groups: marijuana, opium and derivatives, coca plant substances, the meperdine group, and any synthetically derived drugs. *Drug addict and law enforcement use.*

**Narcotics** 1. A special branch of the Organized Crime Control Bureau in which agents wear plain clothes. *NYPD use.* 2. The police department division that handles any narcotics-related crime. *LAPD use.*

**Narcotism** Addiction to narcotics. *Drug addict use.*

**Necktie party** 1. A hanging without a trial. *U.S. underworld use, 1878.* 2. A hanging of properly convicted prisoners; a.k.a. **necktie sociable; necktie social.** *Prison use, twentieth century.*

**Necropsy** An examination of a dead body; an autopsy. *Medical and legal use.* Cf. **forensic medicine**.

**Negative sanction** Any punishment or threat of punishment. *Law enforcement use.*

**Negligence** Failure to exercise the degree of care that a reasonable person—one of ordinary prudence—would exercise in similar circumstances. *Legal use.* Cf. **high degree of negligence; negligence, gross; negligence, criminal.**

**Negligence, criminal**   Negligence involving a greater deviation from the level of care required for civil liability, justifying the imposition of criminal sanctions. Must be a greater degree of unreasonableness than is involved in negligence, for example, reckless disregard for the safety of others. *Legal use.*

**Negligence, gross**   Willful disregard for one's actions and the resulting consequences. *Legal use.*

**Negligent homicide**   A criminal offense by one whose negligence causes another's death, usually involving the negligent operation of a motor vehicle. *Legal use.*

**Negligent manslaughter**   A death that results from neglect of ordinary precautions without malicious intent; often a statutory crime. *Legal use.*

**Negotiated plea**   Plea bargaining in which the defendant agrees to plead guilty in exchange for the prosecutor's recommendation for a reduced sentence. *Legal use.*

**Newly discovered evidence**   Material evidence that is brought forth after a decision has been made concerning a case. *Legal use.*

**Night court**   A court of law in a large city that hears criminal cases at night, usually limited to summary dispositions or the granting of bail. *General use.*

**Nightstick**   A police officer's club. *Police use.*

**Noah's ark**   A police informant. *Australian and U.K. police use, twentieth century.*

**No contest**   See **nolo contendere**.

**No-knock law**   A law that allows police, with a warrant and under certain circumstances, to forcibly enter a building without announcing themselves prior to entry, usually when prior announcement would result in destruction of evidence or place undue risk on the police. *Law enforcement and legal use.*

**Nol-pros.**   See **nolle prosequi**.

**Nolle prosequi**   The prosecuting officer's statement on record that no further prosecution will be sought; a.k.a. **nol-pros**. *Legal use.*

**Nolo.**   See **nolo contendere**.

**Nolo contendere**   A plea in which the defendant states he does not contest the charges brought against him; literally, I will not contest it. Although it has the same effect as a guilty plea, it is not an admission of guilt and cannot be used against the defendant in a civil suit or in any trial to prove incorrigibility. In making this plea, the accused does not admit or deny the charges against him. The court has discretion to accept or reject this plea. *Legal use.*

**Nomology**   The study of law. *Legal use.*

**Nonappearance**   Failure to keep a court appearance. *Legal use.* Cf. **appearance**.

**Nonbailable**   A criminal offense so serious that bail cannot be set by the court. *Legal use.* Cf. **bailable offense**.

*Non capex doli*   Not able to understand the nature of the act or the crime for which the defendant is charged.

**Non compos mentis**   Insane or having qualities of insanity. *Legal use.*

*Non culpabilis*   Not guilty. *Legal use.*

**Nonfeasance**   The failure of a public official to perform the duties that are required of his office. *Legal use.* Cf. **malfeasance**; **misfeasance**; **mandamus**.

**Nonnegligent manslaughter**   To cause another's death accidentally. *Law enforcement use.*

**Non vult.**   See *non vult contendere*.

*Non vult contendere*   A variation of nolo contendere meaning literally, he will not contest it; a.k.a. **non vult**. *Legal use.*

**Nose**   n. 1. A police informant. *Underworld use, 1789.* 2. A prisoner who complains of mistreatment by fellow inmates. *Prison use, 1856.* 3. An investigator. *Underworld and police use, 1860.* 4. An informant to criminals about police activity. *Underworld and police use, 1910.* v. 1. To turn over evidence. *Underworld use, 1809.* 2. To discover a criminal's identity. *Obsolete 1920 police use.* 3. To observe and gather information. *Police use, 1877.* Cf. **chirp**; **crack**; **snitch**.

**Nose, turn**   To give information that the state can use as evidence. *Obsolete 1910 underworld use.*

**Nose out**   To detect by investigating. *General use.*

**Not guilty**   A decision by the judge or jury that the accused is innocent of the crime or that there is insufficient evidence to return a guilty verdict. *Legal use.*

**Not guilty by reason of insanity**   A verdict that the accused is innocent of the charges by virtue of being insane when the crime was committed; usually the jury is asked to determine whether the defendant is guilty or not before deciding the question of insanity. *Legal use.* (As stated under U.S. law, this verdict is misleading in that it suggests that the defendant, though insane, was not physically responsible for committing the criminal act; in England, a more appropriately titled verdict correctly places the physical responsibility upon the convicted defendant by reading. "Guilty, but insane.")

**Not guilty plea**    A formal answer by the defendant stating that he is innocent of the charges brought against him. *Legal use.*

**Notice of appeal**    Official notice of an intent to appeal presented to the other party in the case and filed with the appellate court. *Legal use.*

**Not proven**    A verdict returned by the jury in a Scottish criminal court which results in an acquittal. Other possible verdicts are "Guilty" or "Not Guilty." *Scottish legal use.* Cf. **Scottish verdict**.

**Nullen poena sine lege**    There will be no punishment without due legal process; literally, no punishment without law. *Legal use.*

**Nullify**    To declare void, especially in a legal sense. *Legal use.*

**Nullum crimen sine lege**    There can be no crime committed unless there is a law prohibiting such action; literally, no crime without law. *Legal use.*

**Oath**    A declaration of the truth or that one will tell the truth. *General use.*

**Oath purgatory**    A statement made by someone in an effort to clear himself of suspicions, charges, or contempt of court. *Legal use.*

**Obedientia est legis essentia**    A phrase meaning "for obedience is the essence of the law." *Legal use.*

**Objection**    Opposition to a procedure or evidence put forth by the other party during a trial. An objection made during open court will be useful if an appeal is to be made. *Legal use.*

**Obstruct**    To hinder or impede someone or something from happening. *General use.*

**Obstructing an officer**    Forcibly resisting a police officer from carrying out his duties. *Legal use.*

**Obstructing justice**    Inhibiting the way of lawful proceedings or hindering justice in any way, for example, getting in the way of police investigations, preventing subpoenas from being served or witnesses from testifying. *Legal use.* Cf. **withholding of evidence**.

**Obstructing process**    Purposefully preventing or attempting to prevent a legal process from taking place. *Legal use.*

**Obstruction**    Someone or something that prevents an act from being carried out (e.g., an obstruction of justice). *Legal use.*

**Offender**    1. A person who commits a crime. Most offenders are those guilty of misdemeanors or traffic violations. *Legal use.* 2. One convicted of a crime. *Law enforcement use.* Cf. **alleged offender**; **first offender**; **multiple offender**; **status offender**; **youthful offender**.

**Offense**    An act that breaks the law, usually a misdemeanor or felony violating public and private rights. *General use.* Cf. **bailable offense**; **capital offense**; **lesser included offense**; **merger**; **petty offense**; **status offense**.

**Offensive weapon**    An instrument used primarily for attacking someone with injurious intent (e.g., a dangerous weapon). *Legal use.*

**Officer**    One who is employed in an aspect of law enforcement. *General use.* Cf. **parole officer**; **peace officer**; **police community relations officer**; **police officer**; **probation officer**; **truant officer**.

**Officer of justice**    A person whose duty is to make sure the process of the courts is carried out (e.g., a bailiff). *General use.*

**Official act**    An authorized duty performed by a public officer in his official capacity. *Legal use.*

**Official misconduct**    Conduct by a public official that is unlawful in regard to the office he holds. The conduct may be an intentional act or a refusal to act. *Legal use.* Cf. **malfeasance**.

**Oil**    Money given to influence someone to be dishonest or falsely testify against an innocent person in a criminal case. *Underworld use, 1936.*

**Old Bailey**    The famous criminal court in London, which has jurisdiction over all crime in the city, surrounding counties, and at sea; a.k.a. **OB**. *General use.*

**Ombudsman**    A prison mediator who helps resolve conflicts that arise between prisoners and correction officials. This position is designed to see that the government does not abuse its authority in handling prisoners. In order to ensure impartiality, ideally, the prison ombudsman is not employed by a state corrections department. *Prison use.*

**Omission**    Failure to act as the law requires or commission of a crime by neglecting one's duties. *Legal use.* Cf. **negligence**.

**On the legit**    Leading a life free of crime. *Underworld use, 1925.*

**On the run**    Continually moving from one place to another to avoid arrest. *General use.*

**On the up and up**    Trustworthy. *Underworld use, 1924.*

**Operation Identification**    A system of identifying valuables in the home as a deterrent to crime, since items the owners can positively identify are more likely to be returned. *General use.*

**Opinion evidence or testimony**   Evidence presented not as personal knowledge of the facts, but as what the witness believes to be true, thinks, or infers regarding certain facts. *Legal use.*

**Opponent**   A person who opposes another. *General use.*

**Oppression**   Abuse of authority by a person in power. *Legal use.*

**Opprobrium**   Public disgrace brought about by wrongful actions or grossly vicious conduct. *General use.*

**Oral confession**   An admission of guilt by the defendant that may or may not be admissible in court. Generally the prosecution must prove the confession's admissibility by showing that it was given voluntarily, legal procedures were followed, and other factors. *Legal use.* Cf. **confession**; **Miranda rule**.

**Ordinance**   A statute, rule, or regulation enforced by a political unit smaller than a state (e.g., a county or city), where fines are imposed for disobedience. *Legal use.*

**Ordinary negligence**   Failure to use the care that a reasonably prudent person would exercise under similar circumstances. Though one is liable, it is not as serious as gross negligence. *Legal use.*

**Original jurisdiction**   A court's authority to hear a case when it first comes to trial, as contrasted with appellate jurisdiction, which refers to a court's power to hear a case after it has been decided in a lower court. *Legal use.*

**O-r release; OR**   A release on one's own recognizance, without posting bail or remaining imprisoned prior to the trial. *Law enforcement use.* Cf. **release on own recognizance**.

**Outlaw**   *n.* 1. A person who is placed outside the law's aid and protection. *U.K. legal use.* 2. A violator of the law, especially someone running from the law. *General use. v.* To declare an act illegal. *Legal use.*

**Overbreadth doctrine**   The requirement that a law be invalidated if it not only punishes criminal activity, but also prohibits or inhibits constitutionally protected activity (e.g., freedom of speech). *Legal use.*

**Overrecommend**   To recommend a greater punishment or sentence than would generally be imposed for a similar crime, in order to have the upper hand during future plea bargaining. *Police use.*

**Overrule**   1. To invalidate an earlier decision or judgment passed by the same or lower court within the same judicial system. 2. To deem insufficient or refuse to sustain an objection during a trial. *Legal use.* Cf. **reverse**; **vacate**.

**Overt act**   An action constituting more than mere speech or planning from which criminal intent may be inferred. Some statutes include this as an element in the crime of conspiracy. *Legal use.*

**Overt information**   Legally gathered information from published sources, which may or may not be reliable and is questionable in court. *Intelligence use.*

**Owe time**   1. Continued vulnerability to imprisonment while on parole. 2. Beginning one sentence before completing another. *Prison use.*

**Paid off**   To be bribed. *Underworld use.*

**Palm prints**   The impression made by a palm that has been inked or that was left on a smooth surface. *Legal use.*

**Paper time**   Additional time given to an inmate by a parole board because of pressure from newspapers. *Prison use.*

**Paper war**   A tactic to impede a trial, used by attorneys who try to barrage the opposition with such actions as motions and countersuits. *Legal use.*

**Parade**   A group of suspects viewed in a police lineup. *Underworld use, 1929.*

**Paralegal**   One who assists a lawyer by performing such tasks as assembling documents and summarizing depositions. *General use.*

**Paranoia**   A mental disease in which the patient functions normally, except that he erroneously thinks he is being persecuted or wronged. *Sociological use.*

**Pardon**   An action by a governing power such as a governor or the president that frees one from the punishment normally administered for a crime, reinstates all privileges, releases one from prison, and wipes the record clean. *Legal use.* Cf. **board of pardons**; **commutation**; **parole**; **probation**.

**Pardon attorney**   A Justice Department administrator who evaluates applications for federal pardons and recommends cases for presidential pardons. *Legal use.*

**Parole**   The conditional release of a prisoner from confinement before he has served his entire sentence. He is required to report to a parole officer, and if he breaks any conditions of parole, he will be sent back to prison. *Police use.* Cf. **bench parole**; **parole board**; **probation**.

**Parole agency**   An agency that supervises prisoners released on parole. *Police use.*

**Parole authority** An agency or officer with the power to release prisoners or revoke their privileges if they violate parole. *Police use.*

**Parole board** A group that has the power to release a prisoner on parole, set and modify conditions of a prisoner's parole, and revoke parole. *Prison use.*

**Parole contract** A legally enforceable agreement between a prisoner, the prison, and the parole board stating conditions that must be met for parole to be granted. Usually the contract includes a stipulation for good behavior and goals for education, training, or therapy. *Prison use.*

**Parolee** A prisoner released from prison with the stipulation that he remain under the supervision of a parole officer. *Police use.*

**Parole jitters** Anxiety while waiting for a meeting with or decision from a parole board; a.k.a. **parolitis**. *Prison use.*

**Parole officer** A law enforcement official assigned to investigate and oversee a parolee as he reenters society. The primary responsibility of the officer is to ensure that the ex-convict is meeting the conditions of his parole. *Legal use.*

**Parole time** The amount of a convict's sentence still remaining when he is released on parole. *Prison use.*

**Parole violation** A failure to comply with any requirement of parole; parole is usually revoked and the prisoner is sent back to prison. *Police use.*

**Parolitis.** See **parole jitters**.

**Parties to crime** Those who commit, help commit, or finance a crime. *Legal use.* Cf. **accessory**; **accomplice**; **principal**.

**Part I crimes** Major crimes in the FBI uniform crime reports: criminal homicide, robbery, rape, automobile theft, burglary, and aggravated assault. *Police use.* Cf. **Uniform Crime Report**.

**Part 30** A courtroom of the U.S. Supreme Court where defendants originally were arraigned; the name has since been applied to other rooms where arraignments now take place. *Legal use.*

**Part II crimes** Lesser crimes outlined in the FBI uniform crime reports. *Police use.*

**Passion** A flash of emotion such as hate, anger, or terror; the term is used in manslaughter cases to describe an action that is done without premeditation but in the heat of passion. *Legal use.* Cf. **heat of passion**.

**Passive infrared intrusion detector** A mechanism used by law enforcement officials to detect criminals such as smugglers and burglars. *Police use.*

**Pasty writing** Broad handwriting strokes that are made without noticeable pressure. *Handwriting analysis use.*

**Pathologist** A person proficient in the examination and study of changes in bodily fluids and tissue caused by disease or other factors, such as decomposition. *Forensic use.*

**Pathology** The science of diseases, their causes and symptoms. *Medical use.*

**Patrol beat** The area patrolled by one or more law enforcement officials; in almost all U.S. cities police patrols are conducted in police cars; the police officer walking a beat through a neighborhood is mostly a law enforcement ritual of the past. *General use.*

**Patrol car** A police car. *General use.*

**Patrol guide** A manual of the New York Police Department that outlines rules, regulations, duties, and forms for all ranks in all possible arrest situations. *NYPD use.*

**Patrolman** 1. A police officer who walks or drives a certain beat or area. *General use.* 2. Usually a police officer whose rank is private, below sergeants and lieutenants. *Police use.*

**Patrol wagon** A truck used by police to transport prisoners. *General use.*

**Payoff; pay off; pay-off** *n.* 1. A confession. *Underworld use.* 2. Revenge obtained by murder or informing the authorities about a crime. *Underworld use, 1930.* 3. A bribe, especially one given a police officer. *Underworld use, 1935.* *v.* 1. To bribe. *Underworld and prison use, 1933.* 2. To kill or harm for revenge. *Underworld use.* 3. To impose a penalty or inflict punishment on another. *General use.*

**Peace bond** A surety bond between the court and one who has threatened to break the peace. *Legal use.*

**Peace officer** An official entrusted with enforcing and keeping the peace; a police officer, corrections officer, court officer, patrolman, or guardian. *Legal use.*

**Peach** To inform; double-cross. *U.K. underworld use, 1857.*

*Peccavi* A confession; the term means "I have sinned." *General use.*

**Pedigree** A criminal record. *Underworld use, 1910.*

**Peel** *n.* 1. A police officer. *Obsolete 1890 U.K. underworld use. v.* To arrest. *Underworld use.*

**Peeler** A police officer, from Sir Robert Peel, head of the early-day London police force. *Obsolete U.K. underworld use.*

*Peine forte et dure* A form of medieval capital punishment, especially in France. The condemned was crushed to death by weights that were systematically and slowly added to a board strapped on top of the condemned person. Used only once on record in the United States, the 1692 execution of Giles Cory, who was wrongly convicted of witchcraft in the notorious trials at Salem, Mass. *Obsolete general use.*

**Pen** 1. A penitentiary, usually state or federal. *Prison use, 1884.* 2. A forger. *Underworld use, 1912.*

**Penal** Pertaining to punishment or a penalty. *Legal use.*

**Penal action** 1. Prosecution of criminals. 2. A punishment in criminal or civil cases. *Legal use.*

**Penal code** A system of laws dealing with crimes and their punishment. *Legal use.* Cf. **code of criminal procedure**.

**Penal institution** Any place, such as a prison or penitentiary, where convicted prisoners are confined. *Legal use.*

**Penal isolation** Solitary confinement for prisoners. *Police use.*

**Penalize** To administer a punishment upon. *General use.*

**Penal laws** Laws outlining specific criminal violations, punishments, and fines. *Legal use.*

**Penal servitude** In British criminal law, imprisonment with labor. *Legal use.*

**Penalty** A punishment for a violation of the law, including confinement or a fine. *Legal use.*

**Penetration** In criminal law concerning rape, the act of a male's sex organ entering the female's to any extent. *Legal use.*

**Penitentiary** A place where prisoners are legally confined after sentencing, sometimes with hard labor; a prison. *Legal and general use.* Cf. **prison; jail**.

**Penitentiary agent** A public defender; an attorney appointed by the court. *Prison use.*

**Penologist** A social scientist who studies correctional institutions and the effectiveness of punishment as a crime deterrent. *Police use.*

**Penology and corrections** The study of penal facilities: their management, offender rehabilitation, means of restitution for crime victims, the ramifications of crime, and effectiveness of punishment as crime prevention. *Prison use.*

**Percentage bull** A police officer who ignores or protects a criminal in return for a share of the stolen goods. *Prison use.*

**Perception** 1. Immediate knowledge gained through one's senses. *Handwriting analysis use.* 2. The result of observation. *General use.*

**Peremptory challenge**. See **challenge, peremptory**.

*Per fraudem* Literally, "by fraud." *Legal use.*

**Perjure** To lie or commit perjury. *Legal use.*

**Perjury** A crime of purposely giving false or misleading information when one is under oath, or supplying false information in another form such as an affidavit. *Legal use.*

**Perpetrate** To commit. *Legal use.*

**Perpetrator** One who commits a crime or directs a crime to be carried out. *Legal and police use.*

**Per se** By or in itself; inherently. *Legal use.*

**Persecute** To harass or torment. *Legal use.*

**Persecution** 1. The practice or act of harassing or inflicting harm upon another. 2. The condition of receiving such actions. *General use.*

**Personal recognizance** Release of someone who has been accused of a crime based on his promise to appear in court when required; used instead of a bail bond when the judge believes the accused will subsequently appear without having to post a surety bond or other security. *Legal use.*

**Personate** To take on another's identity in order to gain something illegally. *Legal use.*

**Petition** 1. A formal written request for judicial or governmental action. *General use.* 2. A document filed with a juvenile court requesting that a juvenile fall under the court's jurisdiction because of a crime he committed or that a juvenile be sent to a criminal court and tried as an adult. *Legal use.*

**Petition not sustained** A decision by a juvenile court that there is not adequate evidence for a juvenile to be found delinquent or dependent. *Legal use.*

**Petit jury** A trial jury as opposed to a grand jury. *Legal use.* Cf. **grand jury**.

**Petit larceny** Generally theft of goods or personal property whose value is under an amount set by law, usually under $100. Cf. **larceny**. *Legal use.*

**Petty** Small, usually minor offense. *Legal use.*

**Petty larceny**. See **petit larceny**.

**Petty offense** A crime for which the maximum punishment is usually a short jail term or a fine; procedurally, a crime for which trials involving a jury are not required; a.k.a. **minor offense**. *Legal use.*

**Petty theft**. See **petit larceny**.

**Phobia** A continuing illogical fear of something. *General use.*

**Photography**   Photography has become an important tool for police investigations. Photographs are taken of crime scenes to show the relationship of something being investigated to other fixed objects in the area. Infrared or ultraviolet photos can be used to detect forgeries. Sometimes photographs are enlarged to try to glean information not otherwise noticeable. Pictures are also taken of prisoners for identification. *Police use.*

**Photo surveillance**   Recording the movements of suspects by cameras. *Police use.*

**Phrenology**   A concept advanced as a science by American physician Charles Caldwell (1772–1853) in 1824, based on the works of Franz Joseph Gall (1758–1828) and Cristoph Spurzheim (1776–1832), which was widely accepted from 1850 to 1900. Phrenology was used to analyze psychological characteristics, including criminal tendencies, based on the theory that the mind can be divided into faculties and functions that are related to the shape of a suspect's skull, a science or identification process that has been generally discarded in the modern era. The physiological aspects of phrenology were pioneered by French criminologist Alphonse Bertillon (1853–1914), who limited the measuring of a suspect's or convicted criminal's physical characteristics to identification purposes only. *Sociological use.* Cf. **bertillonage**.

**Physical description**   A description of someone's physical features. *General use.*

**Physical evidence**   Concrete evidence, not testimony; a.k.a. **physical fact**. *Legal use.*

**Physical fact.**   See **physical evidence**.

**Physiognomy**   The discernment of criminal characteristics from facial features, an identification system similar to phrenology. *Sociological use.* Cf. **phrenology**.

**Picture gallery**   Files containing the pictures of known or wanted criminals. *Underworld use.*

**Piece of work**   1. A crime. *Underworld use.* 2. A contract murder. *Underworld use.*

**Piece one off**   To bribe. *Underworld use.*

**Pillory**   *n.* A wooden frame with holes for the hands and head; criminals were locked in the contraption and displayed for public ridicule; a.k.a. **stocks**. *Obsolete legal use. v.* To ridicule or humiliate. *General use.*

**Pin**   *n.* A police officer. *Underworld use, 1925. v.* 1. To arrest or catch. *Underworld use, 1859.* 2. To cause a conviction. *Prison use.*

**Pin a rap on**   1. To accuse and convict a criminal or an innocent person. 2. To place blame. *Underworld use.*

**Pipeline**   A direct route of information, for example, communications between law enforcement agencies with information concerning a case. *General use.*

**Plain**   A police officer wearing plainclothes. *Underworld and police use, 1925.*

**Plain arch**   A fingerprint pattern. *Legal use.*

**Plainclothesman**   A police officer dressed in civilian clothes. *Police use.*

**Plain error rule**   A doctrine allowing an obvious error in judicial proceedings to be corrected, even if no objection was made when the error occurred, because it affected substantial rights of the defendant. *Legal use.*

**Plaintiff**   The person in a legal proceeding who brings the suit forward; the complainant. *General use.*

**Plain view doctrine**   An exception to the general rule that there must be a valid search warrant for police to conduct a seizure; an officer may seize without a warrant objects in his plain view when he has the right to be in the position to have that view. *Legal use.*

**Plain whorl**   A fingerprint pattern. *Legal use.*

**Plant**   *n.* 1. A trap, a frame-up, a plan to deceive, or a person hired to trap another. *Underworld use, 1812.* 2. An isolation cell for prisoners or protective custody for prisoners. *Prison use, 1935.* 3. Arson investigators at a scene where an arsonist will probably strike, waiting to catch him with the evidence. *Arson investigation use.* 4. A plainclothes policeman, a narcotics agent, or an informer who has been placed where he can gather information about criminals. *Police use. v.* 1. To hide, conceal, or bury. *Underworld use, 1610.* 2. To plot against someone. *Underworld use, 1790.* 3. To select a person or place to be robbed. *Underworld use, 1839.* 4. To observe, guard, or spy. *Underworld use.* 5. To place in an isolation cell. *Prison use.* 6. To go to an isolated place, murder someone, and hide the body. *Underworld use.*

**Planting evidence**   To place incriminating evidence in hiding places where it can later be found and used against innocent persons in a criminal charge or criminal trial. *General use.*

**Plea**   1. A formal answer of guilty, not guilty, or nolo contendere to a charge or indictment. *Legal use.* 2. A guilty plea. *Underworld use.*

**Plea bargaining**   Negotiation between the defense lawyer and prosecution in which the defendant agrees to plead guilty to a lesser charge or to only one of several charges, usually in exchange for a lighter sentence; the agreement is subject to court approval. This procedure has come under severe criticism in recent years in that prosecutors have flagrantly allowed felons to plea-bargain sentences for capital offenses in exchange for testimony against others; in some states, plea bargaining has been prohibited. *Legal use.*

**Plead**   To state or file a pleading, to make a formal statement of guilt or innocence, or to argue a case in court. *Legal use.*

**Plead a five**.   See **plead the fifth**.

**Pleading**   A formal assertion or accusation of the charges that are being brought in a legal proceeding and the respective rejoinders and rebuttals put forth by the defendant and plaintiff in arguing the case. *Legal use.*

**Plead the fifth**   1. To refuse to take the witness stand to testify against oneself based on the Fifth Amendment to the U.S. Constitution; a.k.a. **plead a five**. *Legal use.* 2. To refuse to give one's opinion, reasoning, or an objection. *Underworld use.*

**Plea minor**   To plead guilty to a minor offense. *Legal use.* Cf. **guilty**.

**Plea of guilty**.   See **guilty plea**.

**Plea of not guilty**.   See **not guilty plea**.

**Plenary challenge**   An objection to all jurors on a panel. *Legal use.*

**Plenary confession**   A complete confession, which, if believed, constitutes decisive evidence against the person who confesses. *Legal use.*

**Plus peccat auctor quam actor**   The term means "the one who instigates a crime offends more than the person who carries it out." *Legal use.*

**Poison pen letter**   A letter written anonymously to threaten, reveal, or make obscene propositions; usually the information is false. *Underworld use.*

**Poisonous tree doctrine**   Any evidence the police obtain through exploitation of information gained by means of unlawful conduct; for example, an illegal search is generally inadmissible in a criminal prosecution. *Legal use.* Cf. **fruit of the poisonous tree**.

**Police**   *n.* An organization that works to keep a community safe and orderly. *v.* 1. To maintain order. 2. To patrol or guard. *General use.*

**Police action**   Military tactics used against such unlawful groups as pirates, guerrillas, and mobs. *Obsolete police use.*

**Police administration**.   See **police department**.

**Police agency**.   See **police department**.

**Police artist**   One who sketches the picture of a criminal from another's description. *Police use.*

**Police brutality**   The practice by some law enforcement officers of employing excessive force during the arrest of criminal suspects, or third-degree tactics during interrogations. *Legal use.*

**Police commissioner**   An appointed civilian officer who is responsible for controlling and disciplining the police department. *Police use.*

**Police community relations officer (PCRO)**   A police officer whose job is to organize and continue relations between the police and the community. *Police use.*

**Police corruption**   Dishonest use of police power for profit, favors, or revenge. *General use.*

**Police court**   In some states, a lesser court that has authority over minor infractions, traffic and city ordinance violations, some matters of the justice of the peace, and certain civil cases; may conduct preliminary hearings for those accused of more serious crimes. *Legal use.*

**Police criminalistics**   The process used to gather facts in crime detection; a.k.a. **police science**. *Police use.*

**Police department**   A government department of law enforcement officials whose responsibility is to keep public order and safety and to prevent and detect criminal offenders; a.k.a. **police administration**; **police agency**; **sheriff**; **state police**. *Legal use.*

**Police dog**   A dog, often a German shepherd, trained to protect people or property, sniff out smuggled items, track criminals, or control mobs. *Obsolete police use.*

**Policedom**   A police system. *Police use.*

**Police force**   A group of trained police officials responsible for keeping the public peace and safety and preventing and discovering crime. *Police and general use.*

**Police inspector**   A police officer of high rank, under a commissioner, superintendent, or chief of police, who has authority over other police officers. *Police use.*

**Police jury**   A governing body of Louisiana parishes; a Louisiana parish is similar to a county. *Legal use.*

**Police justice**.   See **police magistrate**.

**Police lineup**   A parade of suspects viewed by crime witnesses and victims. *Police use.*

**Police magistrate**   A police court judge who has authority over matters such as minor criminal infractions of the law and violations of police rules; a.k.a. **police justice**. *Legal use.*

**Policeman** A male police officer. *General use.*

**Policemanship** Character of a capable, competent police force. *Police use.*

**Police matron** A policewoman responsible for women or children kept in the police station. *Police use.*

**Police offense** A minor infraction that can be handled in the police court. *Police use.*

**Police officer** One who enforces city regulations and ordinances to keep the order and safety in a locale, usually a city rather than county officer. *Legal use.*

**Police power** The power of states, commonly delegated to local governments, to adopt laws and regulations to prevent crime and promote public safety, morals, and health; enables municipalities to establish police departments. Police power is conferred by the Tenth Amendment to the U.S. Constitution. *Legal use.*

**Police regulations** Laws passed to protect the public and keep the peace. *Police and legal use.*

**Police reporter** A journalist who regularly covers police happenings. *General use.*

**Police reserve officer** A volunteer in uniform who helps the regular staff. *Police use.*

**Police review board** A panel of citizens that investigates allegations of police misconduct. *Police use.*

**Police science.** See **police criminalistics**.

**Police state** A nation under the control of secret government police who suppress government dissenters. *General use.*

**Police station** The police headquarters for a particular jurisdiction. *General use.*

**Police sweep** A coordinated attempt to clean up a high crime area by making simultaneous arrests of pimps, drug pushers, thieves, pornography vendors, and vagrants. *Police use.*

**Policewoman** A female police officer. *General use.*

**Political crime** A crime against the government for a political purpose, such as sedition or treason. *Legal use.*

**Political offense** A crime that is part of a political agitation, an assault on political order, or a crime for political gain. *Legal use.*

**Polling the jury** Requiring that each juror state his verdict. *Legal use.*

**Polyg** An abbreviation for polygraph, polygrapher, polygraphy, and polygraphic. *Police use.*

**Polygraph** 1. A lie detector test or the machine used to administer the test. The device is electromechanical and registers blood pressure, respiration, and heart rate and electronically measures nervous reflexes to a series of questions. This is done by placing a pneumograph around the chest to monitor the subject's breathing and a rubber cuff around the upper arm to measure any drastic rise or fall in blood pressure and pulse rate. Electrodes are also placed on the subject's hands to record excessive sweating. Wires from these apparatus feed to a needle that marks a continuous roll of paper. If the needle records a steady pattern in response to questions asked, the subject is then deemed to be telling the truth. Any needle marks that are at wide variance with the norm indicate the subject is lying in response to certain questions. CIA traitor Aldridge Ames (b. 1941) was given regular polygraph tests and claimed he overcame anxiety by staying up all night and taking the test in a state of utter exhaustion and relaxation. Further, any involuntary body changes that occur while a person is being questioned are recorded and may indicate the person may be lying. In general, the test results cannot be used as evidence because of a judicial determination that polygraph machines allow for error; a.k.a. **lie detector**. *Legal use.* 2. The police department that administers and evaluates the results of a polygraph test. *LAPD use.* 3. The intelligence agency that administers and evaluates the result of a polygraph test. *Intelligence use.*

**Polyneuritic insanity** Insanity caused by multiple inflamed nerves, often resulting from tuberculosis or alcoholism; the condition is often characterized by delusions; also called Korsakoff's syndrome. *Sociological use.*

**Pontius Pilate** A judge. *Underworld use, 1934.*

**Possession** 1. A punishable offense for possessing certain items, including controlled substances, with the intention to distribute them, stolen goods, stolen mail, or a concealed weapon. 2. Control and dominion over property. *Legal use.*

**Postconviction remedies** The ways, on the state or federal level, a convicted prisoner can challenge constitutional violations after his conviction. *Legal use.*

**Post facto** Literally, after the fact. *Legal use.*

**Posthumous** After death. *Legal use.*

**Postmortem** After death, usually referring to legal procedures such as an autopsy to determine the cause of death. *Police and legal use.*

**Postmortem examination**   The examination of a corpse to determine the cause of death. *General use.*

**Post nointer**   1. One who can be hired to swear to anything. 2. Fake evidence. *Obsolete eighteenth-century U.K. underworld use.*

**Powder, take a**   To escape, to run from. *Prison and underworld use, 1939.*

**Pragmatists**   People who advocate short-term reforms within the penal system to make prisons more humane and effective. They believe rehabilitation, parole, and indeterminate sentences have failed. They favor reducing the size of prison populations, imprisoning only serious offenders, and instituting flat sentencing. *Prison use.*

**Precept**   The order of an authority or a public official. *Legal use.*

**Precinct**   A police district or division based on population and police hazards. *Police use.*

**Precipitant test**   A test used to determine whether blood is animal or human. *Police use.*

**Predicate felon**   An offender who has committed his second felony. *Legal use.*

**Prediction of criminal behavior**   Methods that have been developed to predict the likelihood of criminal behavior, juvenile delinquency, recidivism, response to treatment programs, and probability of successful parole. These methods have been developed by analyzing information such as type of offense, residence and work history, and criminal record. *Sociological use.*

**Predisposition report**   A report concerning a juvenile offender that is prepared by a probation agency to help a juvenile court decide what action should be taken; the report contains information about the offender's family, past record, and attitudes. The report is similar to a presentence report prepared for an adult criminal. *Legal use.*

**Prefect**   The chief magistrate or chief officer of the police. *General use.*

**Prejudge**   To make a decision prior to a hearing or before a complete examination. *General use.*

**Prejudice**   A preconceived bias or decision prior to judgment and without regard to justice. *Legal use.*

**Prejudicial**   Tending to promote preconceived or premature judgments. *General use.*

**Preliminary hearing**.   See **pretrial hearing**.

**Premeditate**   To plan or come to a decision beforehand. *General use.*

**Premeditated**   Planned, thought out beforehand. *Legal use.*

**Premeditated design**   In homicide, the intent to kill. *Legal use.*

**Premeditation**   Planning in advance. A decision to do something before it is done (e.g., murder). *Legal use.* Cf. **malice aforethought**; **willful**.

**Preparation**   Actions that are associated with getting ready to carry out a crime but are too vague to be considered crimes or attempted crimes. *Legal use.*

**Preponderance of the evidence**   Evidence that is more persuasive than opposing evidence; evidence demonstrating that the fact sought to be proved is more probable than not. While usually sufficient to win a civil case, it falls short of the proof of guilt—beyond a reasonable doubt—required in a criminal case. *Legal use.*

**Presence**   One's existence in a certain place at a specified time. *Legal use.*

**Presence of defendant**   The right of a defendant being tried for a felony to generally be present during all criminal proceedings. *Legal use.*

**Present**   *n.* The determination of a grand jury to report that a crime has been committed. *v.* To find or judicially determine. *Legal use.*

**Present danger**.   See **clear and present danger doctrine**.

**Presentence hearing**   A procedure prior to sentencing in which the judge may consider pertinent information before deciding on a sentence. *Legal use.*

**Presentence investigation**   An investigation of the pertinent history of a convicted defendant, usually completed by a probation officer or agency; the investigation is to aid the judge who passes a sentence. *Legal use.*

**Presentence report**   A report prepared by a probation officer or social worker that is based on the findings of the presentence investigation and is submitted to the sentencing judge. The report usually includes information about the convicted offender's education, employment, social background, medical history, residences, type of environment to which he will return, resources that could help him, the probation officer's opinion about the offender's motivation and ambition, complete criminal record, and recommendations. *Legal use.*

**Presentment**   A written accusation initiated by a grand jury, which in effect directs that an indictment be drawn. Cf. **indictment**. *Legal use.*

**Pressure**   A police investigation. *Underworld use, 1910.*

**Presumed intent**   The legal doctrine that one presumably intended the natural and probable consequences of his acts. Criminal intent, therefore, can be inferred from acts. The prosecution in criminal cases does not have to prove that the defendant meant to happen what did happen. *Legal use.*

**Presumption** A statutory or judicial rule of law in which a fact is assumed from another fact or group of facts unless it is rebutted. *Legal use.*

**Presumption of death** A belief that one is dead if he disappears for no apparent reason for a specified period, usually seven years. *Legal use.*

**Presumption of innocence** The U.S. legal doctrine that a defendant is innocent unless his guilt is proven beyond a reasonable doubt. *Legal use.*

**Presumptive sentence** A sentence based on local statutes that attach a specified penalty for an offense but allow the presiding judge the latitude to modify it according to extenuating circumstance.

**Pretend** To assert a falsehood or misrepresent. *General use.*

**Pretrial detention** Confinement in jail without bond or bail during the time between arrest and trial proceedings. *Legal use.*

**Pretrial hearing** The hearing at which a judge decides whether the accused should be held for trial; generally the prosecution must show that there is probable cause to believe that a crime has been committed and that the accused was the perpetrator; a.k.a. **preliminary hearing; probable cause hearing**. *Legal use.*

**Pretrial publicity** Press coverage or great public interest concerning a criminal case which may prevents the defendant from receiving a fair trial. *Legal use.*

**Pretrial release** Allowing an accused person being detained in jail to go free prior to and during his trial. *Legal use.*

**Prevaricate** To lie or speak evasively. *Legal use.*

**Prevarication** Deliberate misrepresentation of the truth. *Legal use.*

**Preventive detention** Confining a defendant awaiting trial without bail because of a high probability that he will commit another crime, which will endanger the community. *Legal use.* Cf. **commitment**.

**Preventive justice** A system of government measures for crime prevention requiring those who are highly likely to commit a crime in the future to give a pledge or security such as a peace bond, for good conduct. *Legal use.*

**Prima facie case** A case sufficient to prevail unless evidence refutes it. *Legal use.*

**Prima facie evidence** Evidence that is adequate by itself to establish a fact, and which will remain sufficient unless refuted. *Legal use.*

**Principal** One who commits a crime or is actually or constructively present during the commission of a crime. *Legal use.*

**Principal in the first degree** A person who engages in an act or omits to act in such a way that causes the criminal result. *Legal use.*

**Principal in the second degree** One who is actually or constructively present when a crime is committed and aids, advises, commands, or encourages the principal in the first degree. *Legal use.*

**Prior record** Any past criminal history involving court or correctional action against a person, which occurred before a current action. *Police and legal use.*

**Prior restraint** Government action through a judicial order to prevent the publication of materials deemed harmful to that government or to a court case; a.k.a. **censorship**.

**Prison** A public structure in which persons convicted of crimes are confined as punishment, or for other purposes in the course of the administration of justice. "Prison" and "penitentiary" usually refer to places for the imprisonment of those convicted of more serious crimes, as compared to jails or reformatories. *Legal use.* Cf. **jail**; **penitentiary**.

**Prisoner** One who is confined in a prison or jail as punishment for a crime. *Legal use.*

**Prisoner at the bar** A defendant who is being tried. *Legal use.*

**Prison sentence** A penalty for which a criminal is sent to a correctional facility for confinement. *Legal and general use.*

**Privacy, right of** The right of an individual to be left to himself, without unnecessary publicity and without unjustified governmental interference in his relationships, his family, or his activities. *Legal use.*

**Private detective** One who investigates a matter for a group or individual other than on behalf of the public. Private detectives are usually licensed by the state; a.k.a. **private investigator.** *General use.*

**Privilege against self-incrimination** The right guaranteed by the Fifth Amendment to the U.S. Constitution not to testify against oneself. A defendant may invoke this right if he is called to the witness stand against his wishes, but that is waived if he voluntarily takes the stand. *Legal use*. Cf. **immunity**.

**Privileged communications.** See **privileged relationship**.

**Privileged evidence** Protected information that generally does not have to be divulged, such as classified government information, an informant's name, some kinds of accident reports, or the proceedings of a grand jury. *Legal use*.

**Privileged relationship** The special relationship such as between husband and wife or lawyer and client, which the law sometimes protects by forbidding the forcing of one to take the stand to reveal communications from the other; a.k.a. **privileged communications**. *Legal use*. Cf. **attorney-client privilege**.

**Privilege from arrest** A privilege, temporary or permanent, that is granted to people such as foreign ministers or witnesses, exempting them from prosecution for some criminal charges. *Legal use*. Cf. **immunity from prosecution**.

**Privileges and immunities clauses** Clauses in the U.S. Constitution and amendments that prohibit states from curtailing privileges of U.S. citizens. They ensure that a citizen of one state may go to a second and be guaranteed the same privileges as the citizens of the second state. *Legal use*. Cf. **full faith and credit**.

**Probable cause** In a criminal case, reasonable grounds to believe that a person should be arrested or searched, or that property subject to search and seizure is at a certain location; a.k.a. **reasonable and probable cause**; **reasonable belief**; **reasonable cause**; **reasonable cause for an arrest**. *Legal use*.

**Probable cause hearing** A procedure in a criminal case in which a judge determines whether a complaint should be issued or the case sent to a grand jury. *Legal use*. Cf. **preliminary hearing**; **pretrial hearing**.

**Probation** A sentence allowing a convicted person to avoid confinement with the stipulation that he be supervised by a probation officer and that he maintain good conduct. If he violates the terms of his probation, he can be brought before a court. Prisoners were released on probation beginning in the mid-1800s. *Legal use*. Cf. **parole**.

**Probation agency** An agency that supervises prisoners released on parole and conducts investigations for predisposition and presentencing reports. *Police use*.

**Probationer** A convicted offender, who is placed on probation rather than imprisoned. *Police use*.

**Probation officer** One who supervises a convicted criminal released on probation and makes periodic reports to the court concerning the probationer and reports any probation violations. *Legal and police use*.

**Probation sentence** A court stipulation that a parolee must be under the supervision of a probation officer and meet certain behavioral requirements. *Police use*.

**Probation violation** Failure to meet any conditions of probation, which may result in the court revoking probation and sending the probationer back to prison. *Police use*.

**Probe** An exhaustive investigation. *General use*.

**Procedural due process** Safeguards in the U.S. Constitution guaranteeing that persons have a fair opportunity to be heard and that reasonable notice be given before being deprived of property, liberty, or life. *Legal use*.

**Procedural law** Laws or regulations that govern criminal prosecution methods. *Legal use*.

**Procedure, criminal.** See **criminal procedure**.

**Proceeding** An action or the conduct of business before a court of law. *Legal use*.

**Proclivity** A strong predisposition. *Legal use*.

**Professional criminal** 1. An expert criminal or prostitute. *Underworld use, 1931*. 2. An expert burglar; one who makes his living as a burglar. *Underworld use*.

**Professional privilege** Legal protection prohibiting the forced disclosure of communications between a lawyer and his client. *U.K. legal use*. Cf. **privileged relationship**.

**Professional secrecy** The body of law preventing the disclosure of information given to a doctor by a patient without the patient's permission. In some cases, the law requires that certain information be revealed, especially confessions of capital crimes to psychiatrists. *Legal use*.

**Prohibition** A law or an act that forbids something, such as the Eighteenth Amendment to the U.S. Constitution (in effect from January 16, 1919, to December 5, 1933), which forbade the making, selling, or conveying of alcoholic liquor, except for medical use. *Legal use*. This federal law is considered one of the most ill-fated laws on record. It gave rise to the bootleg gangs, enriching Prohibition gangsters with millions and literally funding the establishment of the American crime syndicate. 2. The period in

U.S. history when the Eighteenth Amendment was in effect. *General use.*

**Proof** The establishment of facts through evidence. *Legal use.*

**Proof, standard of** The description of how persuasive evidence must be to meet the burden of proof; the standard of proof in a criminal case is proof beyond a reasonable doubt. *Legal use.*

**Proscribe** 1. To make illegal or prohibit under law. 2. To name in public those condemned to die with their property forfeited to the state. *General use.*

**Proscription** A prohibition or restriction that is imposed. *General use.*

**Pro se** A defendant acting as his own attorney. *Legal use.* Cf. **in propria persona**.

**Prosecute** To begin, follow, and conclude legal action against the accused in a criminal case. *Legal use.*

**Prosecuting attorney** A government official who is elected or appointed to carry out criminal prosecutions on behalf of the public. *Legal use.*

**Prosecuting witness** 1. The victim of a crime who initiates the complaint and prosecution, and who testifies against the defendant. 2. More broadly, anyone who testifies as a witness for the prosecution. *Legal use.*

**Prosecution** 1. A criminal proceeding in which the guilt or innocence of an accused is decided through a legal process. *Legal use.* 2. The official or authority, who carries out the proceedings against the accused. *Legal use.*

**Prosecutor** A lawyer who prosecutes a criminal case on behalf of the government, including initiating and conducting the criminal prosecution; some prosecutor titles include U.S. attorney, attorney general, district attorney, commonwealth attorney, and state's attorney. *Legal use.*

**Prosecutorial** Characteristic of the prosecution or prosecutor in a legal proceeding. *General use.*

**Prosecutorial agency** A agency involved in criminal prosecution of suspects. *Police use.*

**Protective custody** The legal confinement of someone by law enforcement officers for his own safety, such as a witness whose life is threatened. *Legal use.*

**Provocation** An action by one person that incites anger or resentment in a second person, causing that second person to commit a crime against or connected with the first person. Provocation will generally not entirely excuse a defendant from the charge of homicide, but it may be justification for reducing a murder charge to manslaughter. *Legal use.*

**Provost court** A military court hearing minor criminal cases in unfriendly occupied territory. *General use.*

**Provost guard** A group of soldiers acting as police for the provost marshal. *General use.*

**Provost marshal** The head of a military police operation, which has authority to arrest, try, and punish those who have violated martial law. The position is similar to a chief of police. *Legal use.*

**Proximate cause** The primary action or lack of action that results in damage, injury, or an accident. *Legal use.*

**Psychiatry** A branch of medicine concerned with mental disorder, including its study, diagnosis, prevention, and treatment. *General use.*

**Psycho** A psychotic personality. *Underworld and general use.*

**Psychoanalysis** The method of treating psychotic behavior and other emotional or mental disorders developed by Sigmund Freud. Freud believed that all behavior is a result of the forces acting on the unconscious part of the human brain, and that personality disorders can be cured by exploring the unconscious through free association, interpretation of dreams, and resistance and transfer analysis. *Scientific use.*

**Psychodiagnosis** An examination of a patient's mental condition, determined by the results of psychological tests and past history. *Medical use.*

**Psychology** 1. The science concerned with ways to gauge, understand, and alter mental activities and behavior. *Scientific use.* 2. The emotional, mental, and behavioral traits of an individual. *General use.*

**Psychoneurosis** A behavioral or emotional disorder with no physical source or change, including mania, mania hallucinatoria, primary acute dementia, and melancholia. *Medical use.*

**Psychopath** One who suffers from a mental disorder in which he perceives reality but does not understand social or moral responsibility and commits crimes or is involved in bizarre behavior for instant gratification. The psychopath completely disregards the welfare of others and is unable to establish meaningful relationships with others. *Sociological use.*

**Psychopathic hospital** An insane asylum. *Sociological use.*

**Psychopathic personality**   Criminal character, especially a criminal psychopath. *Police use.*

**Psychopathology**   The study of mental abnormalities. *Sociological use.*

**Psychopharmacology**   The study of the psychological and social impact of drugs. *Sociological use.*

**Psychoquack**   An unqualified, uncertified psychiatrist or psychologist. *General use.*

**Psychosis**   A mental disorder in which an individual has difficulty sustaining relationships, shows no concern for social convention, has time and space distortions, experiences breaks with reality, and has extreme departures from normal thought and actions; more severe than a psychoneurosis. *Medical use.*

**Psychotherapy**   A treatment for nervous disorders, especially by conversation between patient and doctor; the doctor encourages and motivates the patient, and sometimes prescribes drugs. *Medical use.*

**Psychotic.**   See **psychotic personality**.

**Psychotic personality**   An individual who cannot function normally; he usually cannot reason well, has great mental and emotional swings, and may be dangerous to himself and others; a.k.a. **psycho**; **psychotic**. *Medical use.*

**Psycho ward**   A hospital ward for psychopaths. *Sociological use.*

**Public defender**   An attorney representing indigent defendants who cannot afford a lawyer's services. The lawyer generally either works for the government or is a private attorney appointed by the court. *Legal use.*

**Public defender's office**   A government agency that represents criminal defendants who cannot afford a lawyer. *Legal use.*

**Public investigations**   A thorough examination of possible mismanagement or corruption, made public, which often results in public interest and subsequent change. *General use.*

**Public offense**   An act or omission prohibited and punishable by law; characterizes crimes as opposed to civil infringements on private rights. *Legal use.*

**Public prosecutor**   An attorney working for the government whose job is to prosecute accused criminals. *Legal use.*

**Public servant**   An official or employee of the government. *General use.*

**Public trial**   A trial that is open to the general public. *Legal use.*

**Puerperal insanity**   A mental disorder in women during or just after the time when they give birth to a child, also called "eclampsia parturientium." *Medical use.*

**Pull off**   1. To successfully complete a plan, especially for a crime. 2. To cause a complainant or witness to be dismissed. *Prison use.* 3. To cause a rule violation report or pending warrant to be dropped. *Underworld use.*

**Punctuated writing**   A type of handwriting in which dots are made in strokes or curves. *Handwriting analysis use.*

**Punish**   To penalize or inflict a penalty upon someone who has committed a wrong. *General use.*

**Punishable**   Warranting or liable to punishment. *Legal use.*

**Punishment**   A penalty such as a fine, imprisonment, or suffering that is administered to an offender for committing a crime or offense. *Legal use.* Cf. **sentence.**

**Punishment, cruel and unusual.**   See **cruel and unusual punishment**.

**Punishment, cumulative**   Increasing an offender's punishment for additional convictions for the same crime. *Legal use.* Cf. **sentence**.

**Punishment, infamous**   Confinement in a prison, sometimes at hard labor. *Legal use.*

**Purgation**   A process of clearing oneself of suspected guilt. The accused declares his innocence under an oath, which is supported by the oaths of twelve others swearing they believe him; or the accused undergoes an ordeal such as trial by hot and cold water, fire, or hot irons; a.k.a. **purgatory oath**. *Obsolete legal use.*

**Purgatory oath.**   See **purgation**.

**Purge**   1. To remove any information from police records about earlier arrests. *Police use.* 2. To clear from a charge. *Legal use.*

**Pursue**   To give chase with the purpose of capturing, defeating, or killing. *General use.*

**Pursuit**   A chase, usually after a criminal suspect, in order to overtake and catch him. *Legal use.*

**Pursuit vehicle**   A police automobile being used to chase and catch suspects. *Police use.* Cf. **hot pursuit.**

**Put away**   1. To send to prison. *Underworld use, 1859.* 2. To inform to police authorities. *Underworld use, 1875.* 3. To be committed to an insane asylum or prison. *General use.*

**Put on the spot**   To lure a victim somewhere to be murdered. *Underworld use.*

**Put out**    1. To bribe or pay protection money. *Underworld use, 1933.* 2. To arrange, as in a contract. *Underworld use.* Cf. **contract.**

**Put the arm on**    1. To arrest or hold. 2. To hurt a victim by placing his head in a powerful arm lock. 3. To use coercion or intimidation. *Underworld use.*

**Put the finger on**    1. To inform on someone to police. *Underworld use, 1886.* 2. To choose a person or place to rob. *Underworld use.* 3. To arrest. *Underworld use, 1937.* 4. To recognize a criminal or identify a suspect in a police lineup. *Underworld use.*

**Put the frame on**    1. To cause one to be imprisoned. 2. To cause an innocent person to be convicted. 3. To convict a guilty person with improper procedure. *Prison use.*

**Put-up job**    1. A planned robbery. *Underworld use, 1812.* 2. A frame, a prearranged plan to get someone in trouble with the law. *Underworld use, 1952.*

**Pyromania**    A pathological obsession to set fires, often accompanied by sexual excitement. *Sociological use.*

**Pyromaniac**    One with an unnatural compulsion to set fires. *Sociological use.*

**Q & A session**    The question-and-answer session held between a suspect and the police during the first stage of interrogation. *Police use.*

**Quash**    1. To murder. *Obsolete 1918 underworld use.* 2. To overturn or declare void, especially an indictment. *Legal use.*

**Quasi judicial**    Characterized by a partly judicial nature, in that hearing and investigation of a particular matter are performed similarly to judicial review but without the power or authority of the judiciary. *General use.*

**Queen's Bench**    Term used to denote the court or counselors during the reign of a British queen. *U.K. legal use.* Cf. **King's Bench.**

*Qui parcit nocentibus, innocentes punit*    He who spares the guilty punishes the innocent. *Legal use.*

*Quo warranto.*    See **writ of** *quo warranto.*

**Rail**    To set a person up for a prison conviction. *Underworld use, 1925.*

**Railroad**    To send someone to prison without bringing him to trial, or to try to convict without genuine evidence of guilt. *Underworld use, 1877.*

**Rain check**    1. A prisoners lineup or parade. *Prison use, 1934.* 2. A sentence reduction, usually from a death sentence to a life term. *Prison use, 1920.* Cf. **lifeboat.** 3. A parole. *Prison use.*

**Rake-off**    1. A bribe given to police by gamblers. *Gambling use, 1880, and underworld use, 1920.* 2. A

bribe; illicit profit. *Underworld use.* 3. A portion or percentage of the profits taken, for example, a gambling operator's share of the winnings. *General use. v.* To collect a rake-off of money obtained illicitly. *Underworld use.*

**Rank**    *n.* 1. A surprising discovery. *Underworld use, 1922.* 2. A failed crime, especially one halted by an interruption; a foiling of plans. *Underworld use. v.* 1. To accidentally or purposely disturb or ruin the execution of a crime; to betray. *Underworld use.* 2. To deceive; to cheat. *General use, 1860.* 3. To bungle; to fail at. *U.S. underworld, 1924.* 4. To accidentally reveal a past crime, for example, by being recognized by witnesses. *Underworld use, 1928.* 5. To discover the commission of a crime or clues to a crime. 6. To have a suspect. *Underworld use, 1929.*

**Ransom**    1. Money or price paid or demanded in a kidnapping. *Legal use.* 2. A payment for forgiveness or pardon for a serious crime under old English law. *Obsolete U.K. legal use.* 3. In international law, money paid for the return of captured property from an enemy. *Legal use.*

**Rap**    1. A criminal complaint or charge. *U.S. underworld use, 1904, and police and media use, 1920s.* 2. A prison sentence or punishment. *Underworld use, 1925.* 3. A warning or hint. *U.S. underworld use, 1911. v.* 1. To lie under oath; to commit perjury. *Obsolete underworld use, 1732.* 2. To prosecute; to make a formal charge; to arrest. *U.S. underworld use, 1901.* 3. To sentence. *U.S. underworld use, 1920.* 4. To kill; to knock out. *Australian underworld use, 1850.* 5. To hit a person. *General use.* 6. To falsely accuse someone. *Underworld use.*

**Rape**    Forcible sexual intercourse with a person without his or her consent. *Legal use. v.* To plunder. *General use.* Cf. **carnal abuse; carnal knowledge; forcible rape; statutory rape.**

**Rape, forcible**    Criminal sexual intercourse with another by violence or threats of violence. *Legal use.*

**Rape without force or consent**    Sexual intercourse with a person of legal age of consent who is unconscious or whose judgment or self-control are impaired by mental defects or intoxicants such as drugs or alcohol. *Legal use.*

**Rapper**    1. A judge. *Obsolete twentieth-century underworld use.* 2. A plaintiff. 3. A prosecutor. *Obsolete underworld use, 1904.* 4. A criminal case in which the defendant confesses or fails to appeal in order to improve the police department's reputation. *Underworld use, 1920s.* 5. A crime for which the wrong person is punished. *Underworld use, 1940.* 6. The chief witness against a defendant. *Obsolete underworld use, 1928.*

**Rat** *n.* 1. An unethical person; a cheat; a betrayer. *U.S. general use, 1859.* 2. A sneaky police informant. A term primarily used in the United States. *Underworld use, 1902, and police use, 1920s.* 3. A thief. *Underworld use, 1918.* 4. A prison inmate who steals from another. *U.S. prison use, 1904.* 5. A police officer. *Australian underworld use, 1910. v.* 1. To squeal to police or prison officials. *Underworld use, 1910.* 2. To pilfer from a human corpse. *Australian underworld use, 1920.*

**Reach** *n.* A thief who steals from bank tills or vaults. *Underworld use, 1925. v.* 1. To bribe or persuade someone to obstruct justice; to corrupt, usually a law official. *Underworld use, 1906, and police and media use, twentieth century.* 2. To raise one's hands, as in a holdup. *Underworld use.* 3. To grab for a weapon. *Police and underworld use.*

**Read** To tell that a person is lying, for example, a suspect in a police investigation. *General use, twentieth century.*

**Reasonable and probable cause.** See **probable cause.**

**Reasonable belief.** See **probable cause.**

**Reasonable cause.** See **probable cause.**

**Reasonable cause for an arrest.** See **probable cause.**

**Reasonable doubt** The absence of a reasonable and moral certainty of guilt. Proof "beyond a reasonable doubt" does not mean beyond all possible doubt, which would exclude all circumstantial evidence and could never be attained in human affairs, but simply proof which precludes all reasonable hypotheses except the one that it tends to support. *Legal use.*

**Reasonable doubt, beyond a** The point at which a conviction can be reached; a judge or jury may not find a defendant guilty unless he is certain, except for the same doubt that a normal, reasonable person might have. *Legal use.*

**Reasonable force** 1. The scope of force that can be lawfully used by law enforcement officials in the execution of their duties. 2. The scope of force that can be lawfully used in self-defense. *Legal use.*

**Reasonable grounds.** See **probable cause.**

**Reasonable suspicion** The level of suspicion a police officer must possess to stop an individual in a public place; amounts to a reasonable belief that a criminal activity is being committed or is imminent. *Legal use.* Cf. **probable cause.**

**Rebuttable presumption** A belief assumed true unless refuted by evidence. *Legal use.*

**Rebuttal** The period during a trial in which evidence is presented to rebut or refute earlier evidence. *Legal use.*

**Rebuttal evidence** Evidence given to disprove or explain facts given as evidence by an opposing party. Also used to refute a prima facie case or a presumption of fact. *Legal use.* Cf. **prima facie case.**

**Recant** To renounce or withdraw publicly and formally, for example, to renounce a statement made against another. *General use.*

**Recidivism** Habitual antisocial behavior or criminal activity and imprisonment. Repeat offenders commonly receive strict sentences and therefore consistently make up a good percentage of the prison population. Exact numbers are difficult to determine because it is expensive and possibly a breach of civil rights to trace released prisoners. Also, penologists disagree on how to compare repeat serious offenders with released felons who are reimprisoned on lesser charges. *Penology use.*

**Recidivism statutes** Laws applying harsher sentences to convicted felons with previous felony convictions. *Legal use.*

**Recidivist** A habitual criminal. *Law enforcement use.*

**Reckless homicide** Unlawful homicide characterized by a deliberate lack of concern for the consequences of an action, resulting in a death; established by statutes, sometimes amounting to manslaughter. *Legal use.* Cf. **homicide.**

**Recklessness** Dangerous behavior marked by a wanton disregard concerning the life and safety of others, but without the intention of causing harm. *Legal use.*

**Recognizance** 1. An official obligation by which the accused may bind himself to make a prearranged court appearance. 2. An official obligation by which a convicted individual binds himself to refrain from specific acts or to keep the peace. Cf. **release on own recognizance.** 3. An obligation between a citizen and the British government. *Legal use.*

**Recommendation to mercy** A suggestion to a judge from a jury reaching a verdict of guilt to impose a lighter sentence than might otherwise be the case. The jury is not required to give reasons for the recommendation, and the judge does not remind the jury of this option to make certain that it is the jury's free choice. *U.K. legal use.*

**Recrimination**  A charge made by the accused against his accuser. *Legal use.*

**Recross-examination**  The questioning of a witness by a cross-examiner following a redirect questioning of the witness. *Legal use.*

**Redirect examination**  The questioning of a witness by the party that conducted the direct examination of the same person, after cross-examination by the other side. *Legal use.*

**Redress**  Satisfaction or reparation for a wrong or injury. *Legal use.*

**Reexamination**  The questioning of a witness after a cross-examination, concerning issues revealed in the cross-examination. *Legal use.*

**Reform**  To bring an end to something, usually a vice, by enforcing a different or better method, for example, a reform in the treatment of prison inmates. *General use.*

**Reformatory**  1. Any institution for young lawbreakers emphasizing the reformation of behavior or treatment for substance addiction. *General use.* 2. A school to which juvenile delinquents are sent by court order. *Legal use.*

**Reformatory school**  An institution where juvenile offenders are sent under English law by the court for offenses punishable by at least ten days' imprisonment. *General use.*

**Reformer**  One who seeks reform, especially in prison. *General use.*

**Reform school**  An institution intended to reform juvenile delinquents, but more likely to cause them to become hardened criminals as they learn criminal techniques from peers. *General use.*

**Refute**  To prove a falsehood by display of evidence or by arguments. *General use.*

**Rehabilitate**  To reform; to return to society. *General use.*

**Rehabilitation**  The reformation of a criminal so that he may return to society. *General use.*

**Release**  The liberation of a prisoner. *Legal use.* Cf. **bail**.

**Release from detention**  The authorized departure from detention of an adult or juvenile lawbreaker. *Prison use.*

**Release from prison**  Any legal exit from a federal or state confinement facility, including death and transfer to other jurisdictions, and all unconditional and conditional releases. *Prison use.*

**Release on bail**  The release of the accused by a judge before or during a trial, on condition that the accused will forfeit money or property for failing to return to court when ordered. *Legal use.*

**Release on own recognizance**  The liberation of an arrested person upon his nonmonetary promise to appear in court at a later date with no money laid out as a guarantee; a.k.a. **ROR**. *Legal use.* Cf. **OR release**.

**Release procedures**  Methods of releasing prisoners that are divided into two categories: unconditional and conditional. Unconditional release includes pardon, expiration of sentence, and commutation of sentence. Conditional release includes conditional pardon and parole. Probation is not included because it is initiated by court order and is not an administrative act. *Legal use.*

**Release to a third party**  The release of the accused by a judge on a promise by a third party to return the accused to court when ordered. *Legal use.*

**Remand**  *n.* 1. The sending of a prisoner back to court to attend or continue a hearing. 2. The sending of a prisoner back to confinement. *Legal use. v.* To send a prisoner into the custody of either the courts or the prison system. *Legal use.*

**Reparation**  Satisfaction given or amends made for a wrong committed. *General use.*

**Repeater**  1. One who is jailed or imprisoned at least twice in the same town. *Underworld use, 1895, and LAPD use.* 2. A professional criminal. *Underworld use, 1899.* 3. A second crime committed against the same person. *Underworld use.* 4. A recidivist. *Penology use.*

**Repeat offenders**  Criminals who are convicted more than once, especially for the same offense. More common for felons than for those convicted of misdemeanors, according to recent studies. *Law enforcement use.*

**Represent**  To act on behalf of or for another in a legal proceeding. *Legal use.*

**Reprieval**  A reprieve of punishment. *Obsolete general use.*

**Reprieve**  A temporary postponement of a criminal sentence or punishment, usually granted to a prisoner so that he can attempt to obtain a lighter sentence. *Legal use.* Cf. **Royal Prerogative of Mercy**.

**Repudiate**  To reject or refuse to acknowledge. *General use.*

**Restitution**  1. Statutory programs under which a lawbreaker must repay the victim or society with money or services as part of his punishment. Many juvenile criminals are paroled if they return stolen goods to their rightful owner or perform community work. 2. The return of stolen items or other valuable goods that were unlawfully obtained. *Legal use.*

**Restraining order** A preliminary court order that restricts a person while an injunction is deliberated. *Legal use.*

**Restraint** 1. Confinement. 2. A prohibition of action. *Legal use.* Cf. **imprisonment**; **kidnapping.**

**Restraint, unlawful** Confining another without legal authority. *Legal use.* Cf. **false imprisonment; kidnapping**.

**Retrial** A second trial concerning the same case. *General use.*

**Retribution** 1. A punishment for a crime. 2. Something given to compensate for a crime. *General and legal use.* Cf. **restitution**.

**Reverse** To overturn or declare void a judgment, sentence, or rule. *Legal use.*

**Revocation** 1. The administrative removal of a person from parole by a parole authority, such as a parole board. 2. A court order removing a person from probation or parole due to a violation by the parolee or probationer. *Legal use.*

**Revocation hearing** An administrative and/or court hearing concerning whether or not to change a person's parole or probation status. *Legal use.*

**Rib-up**; **rib up** *n.* 1. A setting-up of someone as a victim. 2. A frame-up. *Underworld use, 1924. v.* To arm oneself. *Underworld use, 1912.*

**Ride** *n.* 1. A trip to prison; a transfer from one prison to another. *Underworld use, 1925.* Cf. **take for a ride**. 2. The process by which a victim is driven out to a desolate area and killed. 3. A conviction and imprisonment on false charges or without due process. 4. Harassment, especially for a lengthy period. *Underworld use. v.* 1. To send someone to prison. *Underworld use, 1925.* 2. To harass. *Underworld use.*

**Ride one around the horn** To move a suspect from one city jail to another on the pretense of showing him to crime victims, but actually to prevent those who might bail him out from finding him. *U.S. underworld use and police use, 1927.*

**Ridge** 1. The marks or lines in a fingerprint. *Law enforcement use.*

**Rig** To unlawfully or unethically manipulate the end result of something, especially a trial or conviction or a sports event; to fix. *Underworld use, 1933.*

**Right and wrong test** A test of criminal responsibility whereby a sufferer of mental illness is relieved of criminal culpability. To successfully invoke this defense, the accused must not have known that the act he committed was wrong. *Legal use.*

**Right fall** An arrest based on strong evidence. *Underworld use.*

**Right mouthpiece** A corrupt lawyer whose clients are usually criminals. *Underworld use.*

**Rights of the defendant** The constitutional rights of the accused, including the right to an attorney, the right to a speedy public trial with a judge or jury, the right to confront the witnesses against oneself, and the right not to incriminate oneself. *Legal use.*

**Right to counsel** The constitutional right of defendants to be represented by an attorney. An attorney will be provided for defendants who are indigent. A 1972 Supreme Court decision, *Argensinger v. Hamlin*, expanded this right to persons accused of all crimes rather than just felonies. *Legal use.* Cf. **indigent defendant**.

**Right to know** The power to obtain criminal records, criminal investigative data, or intelligence reports granted to an agency or person by a court or legislative mandate. *Legal use.*

**Rigor mortis** Literally, the stiffening of death, referring to the stiffening which occurs in corpses, first appearing in the face and jaws, and gradually going down from the neck to the feet. An entire corpse stiffens in eight to twelve hours after death; within thirty hours, the stiffening process is complete. The upper half of the corpse gradually grows limp during the next three or four hours. The detection of these stages of rigor mortis is frequently used to estimate the time of death of a homicide victim. *Forensic and legal use.*

**Ringer** 1. A substitute; an impostor. *U.S. underworld use, 1904.* 2. An innocent look-alike person mistakenly identified as a criminal. *General use.*

**River, up the** 1. In prison. *Underworld use, 1910, and police and media use, twentieth century.* 2. Imprisoned at Sing Sing, up the Hudson River from New York City. *U.S. underworld use, 1891.*

**Robbery** The felonious theft of another's property, against his will, through the threat or use of violence. Robberies are usually categorized as simple or aggravated; the chief example of aggravated robbery is armed robbery, which involves the taking of property of another through the use or threat of the use of force while armed with a dangerous weapon; also sometimes classified as strong-arm robbery, which is theft by the use or threat of the use of force without an actual weapon. *Legal use.*

**Rose room**   A room used in police interrogations. *Underworld use, 1937.*

**Rough up**   To injure or beat someone, especially as a means of coercion. *Underworld use.*

**Royal prerogative of mercy**   A power executed by the sovereign to commute a death sentence to life imprisonment, if so advised by the Home Secretary (or secretary of state in Scotland). Both officeholders review every death sentence to check for grounds for a commutation by the sovereign. The reasons for the clemency are never disclosed. *U.K. legal use.*

**Rubber hose**   A short length of rubber hose, used to punish mobsters and prisoners or intimidate suspects into false confessions during third-degree interrogations; it leaves few if any marks on the victim. *Underworld use.*

**Rules of criminal procedure**   Federal rules promulgated by the U.S. Supreme Court pursuant to congressional authority governing the process of all criminal proceedings in the United States, including special proceedings before U.S. magistrates; many states have adopted similar rules. *legal use.*

**Rules of evidence**   Rules governing the admissibility of evidence in federal trials and before U.S. magistrates; many states have adopted similar rules. *U.S. legal use.*

**Run-out powder**   An escape; a quick departure. *Underworld use.* Cf. **powder, take a.**

**Salve**   To bribe a policeman with money or kind words. Cf. **grease.** *Underworld use, 1924.*

**Same offense**   The U.S. Constitution specifies that no one can be tried for the same crime twice. *Legal use.* Cf. **double jeopardy; jeopardy.**

**Sanction**   *n.* The part of a law that imposes a penalty or punishment for its violation. *v.* To reaffirm or support an action, or decision. *Legal use.*

**Sandbag**   1. To ambush a person from behind, then strike him over the head. *Underworld use.* 2. To entrap an innocent person in an effort to wrongly convict that person, or to provide false evidence in bringing about that wrongful conviction. *General use.*

**Sanity**   The emotional and psychological state of well-being in an individual. A sane person distinguishes between right and wrong and functions as a contributing member of society. *Legal, sociological, and medical use.* Cf. **insanity.**

**Sanity hearing**   A preliminary court hearing, usually held before the legal action commences, to determine an individual's competence to stand trial. Sanity hearings are also convened to decide if a person should be committed to a public or private institution. *Legal and medical use.*

**Schizophrenia**   A mental disorder in humans characterized by the slow withdrawal from reality and the complete disarray of the senses. *Sociological, medical, and legal use.*

*Scienter*   Literally, knowingly; in criminal law, the defendant's previous knowledge of an illegal act. *Legal use.* Cf. **mens rea.**

**Scientific intelligence**   Technical applications to espionage and counterespionage. These include a myriad of fields: biology in detecting subtle poisons; chemistry, which employs sensitive acids to examine documents (to make invisible writings apparent); electronics, which employs bugging devices and, for military intelligence, the use of radar, sonar, and direction-finding equipment; medicine, which employs the polygraph or truth serums and mind-altering drugs; photography, which has produced microfilm and the microdot to contain condensed messages; physics, which may involve laser beams. *Intelligence use.*

**Scientific investigation**   A division of the police department involved in the analysis of criminal evidence or items relating to the commission of a crime. *LAPD use.*

*Scire facias*   1. A legal writ based on a court matter already on record, which demands that the party whom the action is brought against demonstrate why the record should not be annulled, dismissed, or enforced. 2. A court proceeding begun by a writ of *scire facias.* *Legal use.*

**Scottish verdict.**   See **not proven.**

**Sealed verdict**   A verdict reached while the court is not in session, so the members are permitted to write their decision on a paper, which is placed in a sealed envelope. When court is reconvened, the verdict is read into the records. *Legal use.*

**Sealing of records**   A policy in some jurisdictions, which safeguards a defendant's privacy by having all his criminal records removed from the public domain. Persons seeking to examine a document would have to secure approval from the court or a designated official. This is usually done in cases involving underage offenders. *Legal use.*

**Search**   A thorough investigation of a person, his property, or other possessions to establish guilt or to determine if he has concealed some illegal contraband, or items that would relate to a specific criminal action for which he is charged. An unreasonable search and seizure is prohibited by the Fourth Amendment of the Constitution. This would refer to any police or government search conducted without a properly executed warrant. *Legal and law enforcement use.* Cf. **poisonous tree doctrine**; **probable cause**; **search warrant**; **seizure**; **unreasonable search and seizure**.

**Search incident to arrest**  The discretionary power granted to the police by the courts to search a suspect or the immediate area around him at the time of arrest. The police generally may search the suspect's person or areas within his immediate control—areas into which he might reach to grab a weapon or destroy evidence. If police want to search any other area at or after the time of arrest, a search warrant generally must be obtained. *Legal and law enforcement use.*

**Searching**  Thorough and comprehensive. *General use.*

**Search warrant**  An order issued by a judge authorizing a policeman, constable, sheriff, or special agent to search for and seize an individual or certain property, from a private residence, place of business, or other location. A search may not extend past the specific areas outlined in the warrant. The Fourth Amendment to the U.S. Constitution outlaws illegal searches and specifies that a warrant must be based on probable cause and supported by an oath and affirmation. *Legal and law enforcement use.* Cf. **exclusionary rule**; **exigent circumstances**; **frisk**; **probable cause**.

**Second-degree crime**  Less serious by its very nature, second-degree crime carries with it weaker penalties. Some local jurisdictions define various criminal acts in first, second, and third degrees. The punishment is commensurate with the act. *Legal use.*

**Second-degree murder**  Generally defined as the taking of a person's life with malice aforethought, but without the premeditation or deliberation found in first-degree murder. *Legal use.* Cf. **homicide**.

**Seizure**  The act of taking a person or his property into custody. The Fourth Amendment of the U.S. Constitution protects individuals from an unlawful seizure. *Government and legal use.* Cf. **search**.

**Selective enforcement**  The power vested in a district attorney or public prosecutor to decide which persons will be prosecuted and which go free. *Legal use.*

**Self-defense**  Protection of oneself, one's family, or one's property, from harm by others. The right to such protection can be a valid defense to a criminal prosecution. An individual who is attacked or whose property is threatened by another generally may defend himself using necessary force. The person acting in self-defense must not have incited the attacker, and there must be clear evidence of imminent peril to justify force. Criminal law makes an important distinction between the use of nondeadly force and deadly force. A victim may utilize deadly force, such as discharging a loaded gun, only when he believes that by not doing so he will perish at the hands of the attacker or suffer serious bodily injury. However, the law does not excuse the use of deadly force against an unarmed assailant, unless there were mitigating circumstances, for example, the presence of more than one attacker or the attacker's reputation for extreme violence. The victim may justifiably employ nondeadly force in situations where he is threatened with injury but not death. *Legal use.* Cf. **imminent danger**; **reasonable force**.

**Self-incriminating**  Characteristic of involving oneself with a crime. *General use.*

**Self-incrimination**  Offering testimony as a witness against oneself. The provisions of the Fifth Amendment to the U.S. Constitution guarantee that no one should be compelled to testify against himself in a criminal proceeding. The U.S. Supreme Court has long upheld that a suspect detained by the police has the constitutional right to remain silent, lest he incriminate himself in some way. A defendant cannot be forced to assist the government's case by testifying. *Legal and police use.* Cf. **confession**.

**Sell down the river**  To betray or abandon someone in the same manner that southern slave owners once sold human cargo. The slave trade was practiced in New Orleans and other ports of call along the Mississippi River. *U.S. underworld use.* Cf. **sold down the river**.

**Sellout; sell out**  *n.* A betrayal of a friend to the police in return for immunity from prosecution or a reduced charge. *U.S. underworld use, 1872. v.* To testify against or betray a friend to gain a special favor from the authorities. *Underworld use.*

**Send-up; send up**  *n.* The part an outsider plays in helping the courts secure a guilty verdict accompanied by a prison sentence. *Prison use. v.* To transport a prisoner to a penitentiary. *Underworld use, 1848.*

**Sentence** *n.* The penalty handed down to a defendant by the courts in consideration of a crime the party committed. *v.* To determine the specific punishment a defendant should receive. *Legal and underworld use, 1904.* Cf. **concurrent sentence; cumulative sentence; deferred sentence; determinate sentence; final sentence; fixed sentence; indeterminate sentence; life sentence; mandatory sentence; maximum sentence; minimum sentence; presumptive sentence; straight sentence; suspension of sentence.**

**Sentence, concurrent.** See **concurrent sentence.**

**Sentence, cumulative.** See **cumulative sentence.**

**Sentence in absentia** A sentence handed down when the defendant is not present. *Legal use.*

**Sentencing** A formal legal procedure requiring the guilty party to stand before the court and hear what his penalty will be. Usually the trial judge is charged with this responsibility, but in some local jurisdictions the task is performed by the jury or sentencing council. *Legal use.*

**Sentencing council** A panel of three or more judges who convene to determine the penalty to be handed down in a criminal case; an infrequent law practice. *Legal use.*

**Sequester** To isolate a jury so that it will not be subjected to, or influenced by, the media and popular opinion, especially during sensational criminal cases. *Legal use.*

**Serial killer** A murderer who follows a pattern in committing murder, usually killing one person at a time over an extended period of time, months, or even years, for profit, sexual pleasure, or more arcane reasons. *General use.*

**Serious crime** A classification of crime primarily used by the courts to distinguish which offenses will be tried by jury. Usually crimes that carry a penalty of more than six months' incarceration are considered serious. Anything calling for less than six months is a petty offense. *Legal use.*

**Serve** 1. To be tried, convicted, and sentenced. *Underworld use, 1811.* 2. To undergo a prison sentence. *Prison use, 1873.*

**Served with one's papers, be** To be classified by the police as a career criminal. *Police use, 1925.*

**Session** 1. The period during a single day when a court is hearing cases before it, from the opening statements to the adjournment. *Legal use.* 2. A British court of law. *U.K. legal use.*

**Set in** Having the protection of the law in advance of committing a crime. In some cases, the police may grant immunity for a thief to engage in petty larceny in return for his help in solving more serious crimes. *Underworld use, 1920.*

**Settled wrong** Committed to prison unjustly or when there is strong evidence that the conviction violated due process. *Underworld use.*

**Setup; set up** *n.* 1. A frame-up luring a crook or an innocent person directly into a police trap. 2. A detailed criminal plan. 3. A swindle in which the perpetrator of the crime and the claimant are in collusion to commit a crime. *Underworld use.* Cf. **plant.** *v.* 1. To lead a victim into a trap. 2. To stake out the site of a crime. *Underworld use.*

**Severance** Two defendants standing trial for the same offense, but separated by two pleas. *Legal use.*

**Sex crimes** Illegal acts of a sexual nature (e.g., rape, incest, child molestation, etc). *Legal and law enforcement use.*

**Sex criminal** An individual who perpetrates sexual offenses or crimes. An overtly psychopathic personality vents its hostile aggression through rape or violent sex. One who exhibits neurotic tendencies would manifest his aggressions in a more passive way (e.g., voyeurism). *Legal and law enforcement use.*

**Sexual assault** Any sexual act perpetrated against a person through coercion, the threat of violence, or without the express consent of the injured party. Most U.S. jurisdictions will classify sexual assaults according to the nature of the act and the age and sex of the victims. *Legal and police use.*

**Shade** To cover up an illegal act or withhold evidence. *Underworld and con artist use, 1925.*

**Shake a parole** 1. To escape a parole officer by means of bribery, intimidation, or extortion. *Underworld use.* 2. To end parole surveillance legally by following prison guidelines. *Prison use.*

**Shakedown; shake down** *n.* 1. A blackmail plot. *U.S. underworld use, 1933.* 2. A bribe payment made to a corrupt police official or politician. *Underworld use.* 3. Extortion money received because of the threat of violence or public exposure of some scandalous act. *U.S. underworld use.* 4. A general search made of prison cells by guards in search of weapons, drugs, or other contraband. *U.S. prison use.* *v.* 1. To receive payment from someone through blackmail or the threat of force. *U.S. underworld use, 1872.* 2. To rob a person of all his worldly belongings. *Underworld use, 1823.* 3. To thoroughly search a place, especially a prisoner's jail cell. *Underworld use, 1910.* 4. To bully or intimidate a person into submission. *Australian underworld use, 1920.*

**Shanghai**   1. To kidnap. The term originates from the eighteenth- and nineteenth-century practice of drugging seamen and impressing them into duty aboard vessels bound for the Orient. Though obsolete in the United States, it is still recognized as a crime under federal statutes. *Obsolete historical and underworld use.* 2. To illegally send an innocent person to prison on false evidence. *General use.*

**Sharp writing**   Lettering characterized by thin, angular strokes. *Handwriting analysis use.*

**Sheet**   1. The police blotter listing the day's arrest activity. *Police use.* 2. The career record of a criminal maintained by the local police. *U.S. prison use.* 3. A prison or hospital order confining a person to bed if he exhibits violent behavior. *Medical use.*

**Sheriff**   The chief law enforcement officer of a community responsible for the enforcement of local statutes, the maintenance of the county jail, assisting the criminal courts in his jurisdiction, summoning a jury, and executing legal writs. In other geographic areas, the office of sheriff may be limited by the existence of local police departments or legislation. The position may be either elective or appointed. *Law enforcement use.* Cf. **constable; marshal.**

**Shield law**   A ruling protecting journalists from having to disclose confidential sources. *Legal use.*

**Show trial**   A proceeding with a rigged verdict, generally accompanied by a public confession. *General use.*

**Shyster**   From the distorted name of an early-day New York criminal attorney named Scheuster, who practiced in the 1840s. Scheuster was a judge baiter who employed every trick and loophole in the law. His name was mispronounced "Shoister" and he so troubled Justice Osborne of the Essex Market Police Court that the judge made it a practice to rebuke other lawyers using Scheuster's tactics, admonishing them to "stop using Shoister practices," hence, shyster techniques. *General use.*

**Sidebar rules**   Under the terms of old English law, there were certain rules that could be granted by officers without a formal application being submitted by the barristers. They included the rule of pleading, which was a court order requiring that a defendant plead within a specified amount of time.

The sidebar was the area adjacent to the bench where these motions were presented. However, revisions in criminal and civil procedure have made the practice all but obsolete. *Obsolete U.K. legal use.* Present-day sidebar conferences are held briefly with a presiding judge to clarify procedures.

**Simple kidnapping**   The imprisonment of a person against his will without aggravating circumstances such as the demand of extortion money or ransom. *Legal use.*

**Simple robbery**   The theft of property by intimidation, coercion, or force, but without the use of a deadly weapon. *Legal use.*

**Sine die**   That which is indefinite. To many convicts it is their prison sentence. *Prison use.*

**Sing**   *n.* A stool pigeon. *U.S. underworld use.* *v.* 1. To squeal to the police or turn informer. *U.S. underworld use, 1930.* 2. To complain to the warden or a prison guard. *U.S. prison use.* 3. To confess one's guilt to the police or the warden. *U.S. underworld and prison use.*

**Skip**   To jump bail. *Underworld use, twentieth century.*

**Sky marshal**   An armed security guard assigned to prevent skyjackings or terrorist activities on board any airplane or within the operations of any airport by whatever means necessary. *Law enforcement use, twentieth century.*

**Slander**   To defame or impugn a person through the spoken word. *Legal use.* Cf. **libel**.

**Slip**   *n.* The announcement of the parole board that a prisoner is to be released or slipped away. *Prison use.* *v.* 1. To discreetly convey information to someone. *Underworld use, 1920.*

**Slug up**   An attempt to falsely pin the blame on someone else, a frame-up. *Australian underworld use, 1920.*

**Slurred writing**   Careless, often illegible writing. *Handwriting analysis use.*

**Smack**   *n.* 1. False testimony, a lie under oath. *Obsolete U.K. underworld use, 1760.* 2. A prison sentence. *U.S. prison use, 1925.* *v.* 1. To commit a defendant to prison upon conviction. *U.S. prison use, 1925.* 2. To swear to something that might not be true. *Obsolete U.K. underworld use, 1760.*

**Smacking**   Adept at perjury. *Obsolete underworld use, 1789.*

**Smear**   To destroy the reputation of a person through false statements or accusations. *Underworld and general use.*

**Smudging**   A term used by ballistics experts to describe the smoky soot found near the bullet wound on the skin. It cannot be found if the area near the wound was protected by clothing. *Forensic and police use.*

**Snake in the grass**   A stool pigeon who conceals his deed from his criminal associates or fellow prison inmates. *U.S. underworld and prison use.*

**Sneeze**   1. To seize and hold for questioning by the police. *Obsolete police and underworld use, 1914.* 2. To arrest. *Police use.* 3. To inform to the police. *Underworld use, 1925.* 4. To rob a victim. *Underworld use, 1925.* 5. To kidnap. *Obsolete 1931 underworld use.* 6. To forcibly interrogate a suspect, using the "third degree." *Underworld use, 1934.* 7. A general release from prison. *Prison use, 1935.*

**Sneeze down**   To coerce information from a drug addict by withholding the addictive narcotic from him until he agrees to provide authorities holding him in custody with the necessary information.

**Snide**   Deceitful, false, counterfeit. *General use.*

**Snitch**   *n.* 1. A criminal associate who betrays the gang's secrets to the police. *Underworld use, 1809.* 2. A prison inmate who informs to the warden. If he is detected, he will likely be killed. *Prison use. v.* 1. To nab a crook in the act of burglary. *Obsolete underworld use, 1718.* 2. To inform to the police. *Underworld use, 1781.*

**Sociopath**   A social misfit whose moral development is retarded to the point where he cannot distinguish between right and wrong. *Legal and medical use.*

**Sodomite**   An individual who practices unnatural intercourse with a person or an animal. *Legal use.*

**Sodomy**   Anal intercourse between two males, a man and woman, or between a man and an animal; sometimes defined to include oral sex; from the ancient city of Sodom. In many U.S. jurisdictions sodomy is illegal (rarely enforced) and is classified as an assault when it involves forcible oral or anal sexual acts. *Legal use.*

**Sold down the river**   Framed on a criminal charge and sent to prison. The term may have originated with the black slave trade as it was practiced in the river ports adjacent to the Mississippi River in the antebellum South. A slave would be sold at an auction and conveyed to a plantation by riverboat. *Underworld use, 1920s.* Cf. **sell down the river**.

**Solicit**   1. To coax or persuade a person to commit a felony crime, which is a crime in and of itself. *Legal use.* 2. To offer a bribe or special favor to induce someone to grant a consideration. *Legal use.* 3. To

accost someone with an offer of sexual favors in return for money. *Legal and law enforcement use.*

**Solicitation**   1. Propositioning, cajoling, or persuading a person to commit an illegal act; viewed as a crime whether the act was carried out or not. *U.K. and U.S. legal use.* 2. Offering money to a person in exchange for the individual's participation in a sexual act. *Legal use.*

**Solicitation of a bribe**   Inducing another person to offer a bribe to a third party. *Legal use.*

**Solicitor general**   The federal official who selects, prepares, and reviews cases that will be brought before the Supreme Court. The solicitor general is the government's legal counsel before the high court, supervising the legal briefs and arguing the important cases himself. *General use.*

**Solitary confinement**   The isolation of a prisoner from the general inmate population and contact with persons on the outside. The warden may allow an inmate in solitary confinement occasional interaction with his peers or complete isolation predicated on the theory that it will hasten his reform. *U.K. and U.S. prison use.*

**Solitary system**   The theory that a prisoner will reform if he is kept isolated from other inmates. During these long, lonely periods, the prisoner has time to contemplate his actions and reflect on the directions his life will take after his incarceration. *Prison and sociological use.*

**Somnambulism**   Walking while asleep. Physiologists have not been able to determine the cause of this peculiar condition. The U.S. courts have long maintained that a person who commits a crime while not fully coherent is not responsible for his actions. This is the automatism defense, and it encompasses somnambulism, epilepsy, and the state of mind brought on by a concussion or similar physical trauma. *Legal and medical use.*

**Special grand jury**   A grand jury assembled to review a specific case or several cases involving similar crimes. *Legal use.*

**Special jury**   A jury picked by the court from a list of jurors who are better educated or could understand more readily than others the facts and legalities of a complicated or serious felony case. *Legal use.*

**Specific intent**   More than general intent, specific intent is the required mental state that must be determined to have existed in order to convict an accused of certain crimes. For example, assault is a general intent crime whereas assault with intent to rape is a specific intent crime. *Legal use.*

**Specimen**  An item of physical evidence; a sample. *Legal use.*

**Speedy trial**  The Sixth Amendment to the U.S. Constitution guarantees every defendant the right to a prompt trial. The four major factors which are generally considered in determining if a delay was excessive or not include the actual time it took for the case to be heard, the government's reason for the delay, whether and how the defendant was informed of his right to a speedy trial, and the prejudice that might have resulted from a delay. *Legal use.*

**Speedy Trial Act**  An act of the U.S. Congress passed in 1974 specifying time limits for completing the major elements (e.g., indictment and arraignment) in federal criminal prosecutions. The judicial officer is required by law to schedule the case on the court calendar after consultation with the defendant and attorney for the government. *Legal use.*

**Spill**  1. To betray or ruin a person in some way. *Obsolete U.K. underworld use, 1818.* 2. To confess to the police or inform on a friend. *U.S. police and media use, 1914.* 3. To affect a release, usually from jail. *Underworld and police use, 1924.*

**Spill one's guts**  To reveal all of the information about a specific crime or crimes to the police; a.k.a. **spill the dirt**; **spit one's guts**.

**Spill the berries**  To provide a truthful account of an incident. *Underworld use.*

**Spill the dirt.**  See **spill one's guts**.

**Spill the works**  To confess to a deed or action. *Underworld use, 1929.*

**Split**  n. 1. A police stool pigeon. *Underworld use, 1812.* 2. The portion of the proceeds of a criminal endeavor given to a gang member. *Underworld use.* 3. A betrayal of one's friends to the police department. *U.K. underworld use, 1828.* 4. A police detective. *U.K. underworld use, 1890.* v. 1. To turn evidence in return for legal guarantees. *U.K. underworld use, 1795.* 2. To say too much to the wrong person. *U.S. underworld use, 1925.* 3. To divide up the spoils of a criminal operation equally among gang members. *Underworld use, 1925.*

**Split sentence**  A court decision to enforce one portion of a sentence and suspend the other, usually a fine and imprisonment; for example, the jail sentence may be suspended, but the fine collected. *Legal use.*

**Spot, be in a**  To be in a very difficult position, especially with the local police. *Underworld use, 1929.*

**Spouse abuse**  Sociologist's term for the crime of wife or husband beating. *Sociological use.*

**Spouter**  A criminal lawyer. *Underworld use.*

**Spring**  n. 1. A release from prison, legal or otherwise. *Prison use, 1901.* 2. A suspended prison sentence. 3. Release on bond. *Underworld use.* v. 1. To obtain an item through theft, deception, or fraud. *Obsolete U.S. underworld use, 1821.* 2. To find and tell where the stolen merchandise is hidden away. *Underworld use, 1846.* 3. To release a person from the clutches of the law (e.g., a prison break or general parole). *U.S prison use, 1886.* 4. To offer an official a bribe. *Underworld use.*

**Square a rap**  1. To agree to suspend a criminal complaint with the consent of the parties who brought the original complaint. *Underworld use.* 2. To bribe or otherwise compel a warden or prison guard to drop a formal charge about to be made. *Prison use.*

**Squarehead**  A reluctant thief; one unsure about the rightness or wrongness of his actions. *Underworld use, 1903.*

**Squash**  To quash (or suppress) a criminal indictment. *Law enforcement and underworld use.*

**Squeak**  n. 1. A thief who tells everything to the police immediately after being arrested. *Obsolete underworld use, 1797.* Cf. **spill one's guts**. 2. One who freely offers information to the police without coercion. *Underworld use, 1827.* 3. A close escape, from either the police or a serious criminal charge. *Underworld use, 1874.* 4. A police informant in general. *Police use, 1891.* 5. A person who files a complaint to the police. *U.S. underworld use.* v. To inform. *U.K. underworld use, 1698.*

**Squeal**  n. 1. An informant. *Underworld use, 1821.* 2. Information given to the police, usually in the form of a complaint. *U.S. underworld and police use, 1872.* v. 1. To give information to the police after an arrest. *U.S. underworld use, 1821.* 2. To inform a prison guard or the police about the movements of one's criminal associates. It is one of the most serious crimes by underworld standards. *U.S. underworld use.*

**Squealer**  One who snitches to the police. *U.K. and U.S. underworld use, 1864.*

**Squealer's mark**  A scar on the face inflicted as punishment for squealing to the police. *U.S. underworld use.*

**Squeezer**  1. The police. *U.S. underworld use, 1925.* 2. A police informant. 3. A cop who employs the "third degree" to force a confession. *Underworld use.*

**Stacked deck** A rigged or framed trial in which an innocent person is convicted. *General use.*

**Stand** To undergo severe hardship (e.g., the third degree in a police station). *Underworld use.*

**Standard form** A writing style with letters shaped as prescribed in standard school texts. *Handwriting analysis use.*

**Standard of proof** In criminal law, the burden or standard of proof rests with the prosecution in establishing the guilt of a defendant. This means that the evidence of guilt must be proved beyond a reasonable doubt. *Legal use.*

**Standup; stand up** *n.* 1. A lineup of suspects in the police identification room. *Police use, 1903.* 2. A quick search by police for guns or other concealed weapons. *Police use. v.* 1. To stick to an alibi or story under intense questioning by the police. *Underworld use.*

**Star Chamber** Any legal proceeding in which due process is lacking and the prevailing opinion is heavily slanted in favor of one party. In old English law, a Star Chamber was a special court convened to hear matters that a lower court could not handle, due to the legal manipulations and influence exerted by one party. Henry VIII and his successors used Star Chamber proceedings to punish those who challenged their authority. The device fell out of favor and is largely obsolete today. *Legal and historical use.* Cf. **kangaroo court.**

**Star class** An English prisoner classification including first-time inmates who face lengthy sentences. *U.K. prison use.*

**Stare decisis** The term means "let the decision stand." It is the long-standing policy of the Anglo-American courts to rely on established precedent as a basis for rendering a decision in a criminal or civil matter. Once a fundamental principle of the law has been established, the same rulings will generally apply in all future matters if the circumstances of the case are fundamentally the same. The rationale for this policy is that the judicial system and the public at large will benefit from the elements of stability and certainty in decisions. The dilemma arises when the precedent is found to be defective or incorrect. *Legal use.*

**Star power** The powers vested in the state and its law enforcement agency to carry out the statutes that will ensure the safety, health, and well-being of its citizens. This right is guaranteed to the individual states by the Tenth Amendment to the U.S. Constitution. *Legal use.* Cf. **police power**.

**State attorney general** The chief law enforcement officer of a state who advises the governor and other agencies about various legal matters. The attorney general represents the people of the state in all matters brought before the courts. The position is elective. *U.S. government use.*

**State chemist** The executioner who administers the gas chamber. *Prison use.*

**State electrician** The executioner who throws the switch of the electric chair. *Prison use.*

**State lawyer** Legal counsel assigned to the indigent or to individuals unable to secure their own lawyer; a.k.a. **state mouthpiece**. *Legal use.*

**State of mind** The reasons or motivation for a criminal's actions; the emotional background of the criminal. *Legal use.*

**State police** The policing agency of an individual state. It is charged with enforcing state law outside local municipalities, assisting various other law enforcement divisions during criminal investigations, and safeguarding public property. *U.S. law enforcement use.*

**State's attorney** The district attorney, prosecutor, or chief law enforcement officer for a state or county. This individual represents the people of the state in securing criminal indictments and prosecuting offenders in court. With few exceptions, the office is generally elective. *Law enforcement use.* Cf. **prosecutor**.

**State's evidence** The testimony given freely by a defendant against his criminal accomplices in return for immunity from prosecution or a reduced charge. In British law, it is known as King's or Queen's evidence. *Legal use.*

**Status crime** A classification of crime that does not involve a prohibited action or failure to act, but rather the personal condition or character of the offender (e.g., vagrancy). *Legal use.*

**Status offender** An underage offender who has been found by a juvenile court to have committed a status offense, for example, curfew violations and running away from home. *Legal use.* Cf. **youthful offender**.

**Status offense** A crime or mischievous act that is an offense when committed by a juvenile; it can be prosecuted only in juvenile court. *Legal use.*

**Statute** A law enacted by a legislature; crimes and punishments for such laws are commonly defined in state statutes. Cf. **common law**. *Legal and government use.*

**Statute, criminal** An act defining what constitutes a crime and the accompanying punishment. The legislature has amendatory power to revise criminal statutes. *Legal use.* Cf. **crime**; **criminal law**; **penal code**; **penal laws**.

**Statute, penal** A state or federal law that spells out a criminal offense and the degree of punishment that goes with it. *Legal use.* Cf. **crime**; **criminal law**; **penal code**; **penal laws**.

**Statute book** The entire body of legislative law pertaining to a particular jurisdiction, whether or not published as a whole. *Legal use.*

**Statute of limitations** A legislative enactment stating that once a certain period of time has elapsed following the commission of a crime no one may be prosecuted for that crime; varies for type of crime and jurisdiction. *Legal use.*

**Statutory crime** A crime defined by local statute. *Legal use.* Cf. **offense**.

**Statutory extortion** The unlawful procurement of money or something else of value as a consequence of a verbal threat, but not rising to the level of robbery. *Legal use.*

**Statutory offense.** See **statutory rape**.

**Statutory penalty** The punishment imposed on a statutory offender by the courts. *Legal use.*

**Statutory rape** 1. Sexual relations with a woman under the age of consent. In the United States, the age of legal consent varies from state to state, with eighteen being the usual age specified. Statutory rape is viewed as a criminal offense regardless of whether the individual gave her consent. The juvenile is viewed as incapable of making a decision of this nature because of her tender age and maturity level. 2. In some jurisdictions, sexual intercourse between a custodian and patient (e.g., in a mental hospital) or a custodian and prisoner; a.k.a. **statutory offense**. *Legal use.* Cf. **rape**; **without her consent**.

**Stay** A judicial order that interrupts or suspends a judicial proceeding, a prosecution, portions of a prosecution, or punishment of an offender. *Legal use.*

**Stay of execution** A court order that temporarily halts the planned execution of a criminal offender, usually pending further appeals. *Legal use.*

**Stiff** *n.* 1. A formal pardon from the governor. *U.S. prison use, 1859.* 2. A criminal's lie. *U.S. underworld use, 1891.* 3. A dead body, especially one in rigor mortis. *U.S. underworld use, 1859.* 4. Any kind of police search warrant. *U.S. underworld use, 1911.* 5.

The prison warden. *U.S. prison use, 1925.* 6. Any policeman. *U.S. underworld use, 1925.* *v.* 1. To pass a forged check or one with insufficient funds. *U.S. underworld use.* 2. To walk out of a commercial establishment without paying the bill. *General use.*

**Stiff rap** 1. An unusually harsh prison sentence. *Prison use.* 2. A criminal charge made against an innocent person. *Underworld use.*

**Stonewall** To hold up the progress of an investigation by supplying distorted testimony, innuendo, and irrelevant information. *Prison use.*

**Stool** Short for stool pigeon; one who regularly spies for the police. *U.S. underworld and police use, 1903.*

**Stool pigeon** 1. A prison inmate or petty criminal who volunteers information about his associates to the warden or the police in return for considerations. At one time pigeons were tied to wooden stools to decoy other pigeons, hence the term. *Prison use, 1904.* 2. A criminal spy in the employ of the police. *Police and underworld use.*

**Stop and frisk** The widely recognized right of a police officer to detain and search a person or his property if there is sufficient belief that the individual is about to or has committed some offense or is carrying a concealed weapon. The search is limited only to the person or the immediate area in question. *Legal use.* Cf. **arrest**; **detain**; **investigate**.

**Story** A falsehood or lie. *General use.*

**Straight sentence** A sentence that does not carry provisions for a minimum or maximum period of incarceration, but rather establishes a fixed term; a.k.a. **flat sentence**. *Legal use.*

**Strappado** An earlier form of torture or punishment in which the victim was hoisted up by a rope and then let fall the length of the rope. Used to obtain false confessions during the Spanish Inquisition. *General use.*

**Stretch** *n.* 1. A prison sentence of one year. *Police use, 1821.* 2. Any prison sentence. *Prison use, 1903.* *v.* 1. To hang from the gallows. *Obsolete twentieth-century prison use.* 2. To murder someone or render them unconscious. *Underworld use.*

**Strip frisk** A police search conducted on a suspect who has removed his clothes. *Police use. v.* To remove one's clothes so that the police can conduct a body search. *Police use.*

**Strong-arm** *n.* 1. A hired thug who employs violence to rob his victims. *Underworld use, 1907.* 2. A holdup man, prison guard, or any powerfully built individual who uses brute force to impose his will on others.

*Underworld use.* 3. A brutish criminal hired for the purpose of carrying out acts of violence for his employer. *U.S. underworld use, 1830.* 4. A criminal assault or robbery. *Underworld use. v.* 1. To bruise, intimidate, or coerce to effect result. *Underworld use, 1930.* 2. To rob someone at the point of a gun. *Underworld use, 1931. adj.* Violent or with armed force. *U.S. underworld use, 1901.*

**Stum**   To force a person to remain silent about a matter through coercion. *Underworld use, 1925.*

**Stylized writing**   Handwriting that conforms to a distinct style or school method. *Handwriting analysis use.*

**Suborn**   1. To induce a witness to commit perjury. 2. To inveigle a person to commit some illegal act, usually as a result of bribery. *Legal use.*

**Subornation**   *n.* The crime of inducing a person to commit an illegal act. *Legal use.*

**Subornation of perjury**   The illegal act of inducing a witness to swear a false oath and commit perjury on the stand. *Legal use.*

**Subpoena**   A court order, or writ from the grand jury, commanding a person to appear at a specified time to testify; a.k.a. **subpoena as *testificandum*.** *Legal use.*

**Subpoena as *testificandum*.**   See **subpoena**.

**Subpoena *duces tecum***   A written order directing a person who has certain relevant documents, books, papers, and material to deliver them to the grand jury or the court of local jurisdiction. *Legal use.*

**Substantial capacity**   Phrase comprising part of the Model Penal Code definition of legal insanity. It means that one is not responsible for his criminal conduct if, because of a mental disorder, he lacked substantial capacity to appreciate that his conduct was wrong or to conform his behavior to the law's requirements. *Legal use.*

**Substantive due process**   A guarantee of the U.S. Constitution that prohibits the federal government and state and local authorities from denying a person the right to life, liberty, or property without due process of law. *Legal use.* Cf. **justice**.

**Substantive evidence**   Evidence used to prove or disprove a fact in dispute as opposed to evidence given to discredit a witness or corroborate his testimony. *Legal use.*

**Substantive felony**   A felony that stands alone and does not rely on the conviction of another individual's crime. *Legal use.*

**Substantive offense**   A crime complete by itself; it does not depend on another crime. *Legal use.*

**Sucker one in**   To convince a person to do something, using deceit and false promises. *Con artist use.*

**Sudden heat of passion**   An enraged state of mind that provokes a person to kill another. The provocation must occur immediately prior to the crime and place, with the killer in an uncontrollable state. If the killing was done in the sudden heat of passion, the charge may be reduced from homicide to manslaughter. *Legal use.* Cf. **manslaughter**.

**Suicide**   The taking of one's own life. In England, suicide was a common law crime, and at one time was punishable by burial under a public highway with a wooden stake driven through the heart. The victim's worldly goods were forfeited to the Crown. Today in the United States, the forfeiture of property or similar penalties no longer exists. However, attempted suicide is considered a crime in some, but not all, jurisdictions. Rarely does an unsuccessful suicide attempt result in the imposition of a penalty as long as it did not involve others. A person who causes someone else to take his life as a result of a physical or mental act may face charges of murder or manslaughter. *Legal use.*

**Summation**   The summing up of a legal proceeding before a jury in which opposing counsel or the judge provides a recapitulation of evidence brought forth in the trial so that jurors have a clearer understanding before making their decision. *Legal use.*

**Summons**   A written order issued by a court commanding a defendant to appear at a specified time to answer criminal charges or supply answers to specific questions from the bench. *Legal use.*

**Superior court**   A court having general or extensive jurisdiction and, depending on the state, either an intermediate court between trial courts and the highest appellate court, or a trial court. *Legal use.*

**Suppression of evidence**   1. An order handed down by the presiding judge preventing the prosecution from introducing certain damaging evidence against a defendant because it was illegally obtained. 2. The offense of compounding a felony by refusing to testify or give evidence. *Legal use.*

**Supreme Court**   In the federal court system of the United States, and most of the individual states, the highest appellate court. It also functions as the court of last resort. *Legal and government use.* Cf. **court of appeals**.

**Supreme Court of the United States**   The highest court in the nation, with nine sitting justices appointed for life. The chief justice and the eight associate justices are appointed by the president and are subject to congressional review and approval. *Legal use.*

**Supreme penalty**   The penalty of death. *Legal use.*

**Surrender of criminals**   An official act that authorizes the transfer of a wanted criminal from one jurisdiction to the jurisdiction where the deed was allegedly committed. *Legal and government use.* Cf. **extradition.**

**Surveillance**   A police stakeout or close observation of a suspect, dwelling, or moving automobile. The technique can involve the use of electronic listening devices, wiretapping, or other devices within the limits of the law. *Law enforcement and government use.*

**Survivor syndrome**   The psychological complications experienced by the victim of a crime that normally set in during the immediate aftermath. Recurring nightmares, anxiety, guilt, and depression are common ailments reported by people who survive violent crimes; a.k.a. **legacy of terror**. *Medical and sociological use.*

**Suspect**   A person who is believed to be a participant or instigator of a crime, whether he is arrested or not. If there is sufficient evidence of probable cause, the police are legally empowered to make an arrest. *Police and legal use.* v. To think that a person might be guilty of an act. *U.K. and U.S. underworld use, twentieth century.*

**Suspended sentence**   The judge's decision to postpone pronouncing sentence or to suspend the execution of a sentence after it is pronounced. In the latter instance, the defendant is not obligated to serve the sentence imposed by the court. *Legal use.*

**Suspended stroke**   A down stroke of the pen that is not carried all the way to the writing base. *Handwriting analysis use.*

**Suspension of sentence**   Postponement of the sentencing of a defendant after conviction, or putting off the execution of a sentence after it has been pronounced. *Legal use.*

**Suspicion**   The belief, based on opinion or fact, that a person may be guilty of a certain offense, but conclusive proof is lacking. *Legal and police use.* Cf. **suspect**.

**Suspicious**   Arousing mistrust because of words, actions, or deeds. *Legal use.*

**Suspicious character**   An individual who is known to have committed illegal acts in the past or is strongly suspected of planning a crime. *Legal and police use.*

**Swear out**   To make a sworn accusation in securing an arrest warrant. *General use.*

**Sweat**   n. 1. A police attempt to extract a confession or relevant information out of a suspect or prisoner by means of the third degree. *Police use, twentieth century.* 2. Hard labor in prison. *Prison use.* 3. Excessive worry. *General use.* v. 1. To force a confession out of a suspect through coercion or implied threat. *U.S. police use, 1880.* 2. To be confined in a small, dank cell without benefit of light or fresh air. *Prison use.*

**Sweatbox**   1. A prison cell or police room where inmates are questioned at length by police officers before arraignment. *U.K. and U.S. police use, 1890.* 2. A narrow, 7 foot by 4 foot tin enclosure placed near the highway by prison officials. An unruly convict from the chain gang was placed inside and hung by his wrists as punishment. The heat from the sun made the enclosure a fiery inferno. When the prisoner was unconscious or weak from exhaustion, the guard removed him. *Obsolete southern U.S. prison use.*

**Sweat it out**   1. To attempt to break a drug dependency through complete and total abstinence. *Drug addict use, 1910.* 2. To administer the third degree to a prisoner. *Prison use.*

**Sweeten**   1. To swindle by means of flattery, false praise, and lavish attentions. *Obsolete con artist use, 1698.* 2. To offer a bribe to the prison warden or guard. *Prison use, 1890.* 3. To offer a suspect or a convicted felon a lenient sentence in exchange for testimony in a criminal case against another defendant. *General use.*

**Swindle**   n. Any confidence game or fraud. *General use.* v. From the German word *schwindlin*, meaning "to waver or fall." In modern usage, it means to obtain money, property, services, or goods through deception, fraud, or chicanery. *Con artist use.*

**Syphilitic insanity**   The advanced state of untreated syphilis in which the victim's mind is nearly gone. Crime czar Al Capone (1899–1947) died of this insanity-producing venereal disease; a.k.a. **metasyphilis; parasyphilis**. *Medical use.*

**T 1.**   A federal officer. *Underworld use, 1950s.*

**Table, under the**   Not officially recorded or reported, usually bribe money. *Underworld use, 1920.*

**Take a rap**   To accept full responsibility for a crime, especially to exonerate one's accomplices or an innocent person convicted of the crime; a.k.a. **take the rap**. *U.S. underworld use.*

**Take for a ride**   1. A trip to a prison. 2. To force or invite someone along on an automobile ride and then murder him, usually at some secluded spot. This term was first made popular in the 1928 part talkie film *Lights of New York.*

**Take over the hurdles**   To treat someone roughly; to administer the third degree. *Police and underworld use.*

**Take the knock**   1. To accept full responsibility for a crime, especially to exonerate others. Cf. **cop a plea**. 2. To allow oneself to be arrested without complaint or struggle. *U.S. underworld use.* Cf. **fall guy**.

**Take the lump**   To accept responsibility for a crime or to be framed for a crime. *Underworld use, 1920s.*

**Taken into custody**   Lawfully detained as a person or the care of some article, such as potential evidence. *Legal use.* Cf. **custodial interrogation**.

**Tamp up**   To beat, strike, or assault; to administer the third degree; a.k.a. **tamp up on**. *U.S. prison use, 1933.*

**Tamper**   1. To meddle or interfere with something, and by so doing to alter that thing, especially in a corrupt, perverted, or illegal way (e.g., tampering with criminal evidence or a jury). 2. To engage in deceitful negotiations (e.g., accepting a bribe). *General use.*

**Tampering with a jury.**   See **embracery**.

**Tangible evidence**   Evidence that can be seen or touched, in contrast to evidence that comes completely from testimony (e.g., a knife in a homicide trial). *Legal use.*

**Target witness**   The person whose testimony an investigating body is primarily seeking, often the person a government is seeking to indict. *Legal use.*

**Technical services**   The communications, laboratory, identification, record keeping, and other specialized branches of a law enforcement agency. *Law enforcement use.*

**Term**   A fixed or definite period of time, for example, a prison sentence or time that a court is in session. *General use.*

**Terrorize**   To fill with horror, terror, or anxiety; to attempt to coerce by threats or acts of violence. *Legal use.*

**Testify**   To swear under oath in court for the purpose of establishing a fact or corroborating evidence. *Legal use.*

**Testimony**   The sworn statements of witnesses in a legal proceeding. *Legal use.*

**Theft by false pretext**   Inducing someone to part with something of value by false statements or by the misrepresentation of facts. *Legal use.*

**Third degree**   A prolonged interrogation, usually with force or threats of force, in an attempt to elicit information or a confession from a prisoner; a.k.a. **third**. *General use.* Cf. **inquest**; **interrogation**; **Miranda rule**.

**Threat**   The communication of one's intention to injure the body or property of another. *Legal use.* Cf. **coercion**; **duress**; **extortion**.

**Three-time loser**   A criminal who has been convicted of a felony for the third time in a jurisdiction where such a conviction carries a mandatory life sentence. *Law enforcement use.*

**Throw one's guts**   To give much information, usually to the police, often under the third degree; a.k.a. **throw the guts**. *U.S. underworld use, 1927.* Cf. **spill one's guts**.

**Throw the book at**   To charge someone with the maximum crime or to sentence a defendant to the maximum term; to use the entire weight of the law against an offender. *U.S. underworld use, 1932.*

**Throw the book away**   1. To disregard the due process of law and convict a defendant on little or no evidence; to "throw the law book away." 2. To sentence to the maximum term. *Underworld use.*

**Thumbprint**   A distinctive mark left by a specific person, especially a criminal whose method of operation is well-known. *Law enforcement use.*

**Ticket**   An arrest warrant. *Police and underworld use.*

**T-man**   A federal law enforcement agent, especially a U.S. Treasury agent. *U.S. general use, 1938.*

**Toe the line**   To appear in a police identification lineup. *Underworld use, 1910.*

**Tort**   A wrong that is civil in nature and is usually not punishable criminally; the wronged party may be entitled to a monetary award. *Legal use.*

**Tough gaff**   Any hard ordeal, for example, a long term of imprisonment, the third degree, or any harsh punishment. *U.S. underworld use.*

**Toxicologist**   A scientist who studies poisons and the effects they produce. *General use.*

**Toxicology**   The study and science of poisons and their effects, and the treatment of poisoning. *General use.*

**Transactional analysis therapy**   A psychotherapy treatment program first introduced into prisons at the Marion, Illinois, federal penitentiary in 1968 by Martin Groder. The program adheres to principles developed by psychiatrist Eric Berne (1910–1970); human beings have three ego states: the adult, which is controlled by an objective mind; the child, which deals with experiences prior to reaching adolescence; and the parent, which lends itself to memories of parental praise and admonishment from childhood. These ego states interact with one another, and analysis may explain why people behave the way they do. This program is believed to help inmates communicate and interact with the society around them in a more positive way. *Sociological use.*

**Transcript**   The official document of a courtroom proceeding, including everything that was said on the record. *Legal use.*

**Transfer hearing**   A juvenile court proceeding to determine if a juvenile defendant should be tried in juvenile court or transferred to criminal court for trial as an adult. *Legal use.*

**Transportation**   The practice of sentencing prisoners to be sent overseas to a penal colony or offshore to an island prison. *General use.*

**Tremor**   The trembling of handwriting caused by an involuntary shaking of the hand or body. *Handwriting analysis use.*

**Trespass**   Entering the property of another without permission or lawful authority, or any illegal interference with a person's property or rights. *Legal use.* Cf. **intruder.**

**Trespass *ab initio***   A phrase used to describe a lawful or innocent entry that becomes a trespass from the beginning because the conduct after the lawful entry constitutes trespass by an abuse of privilege. *Legal use.*

**Trespasser**   One who commits the crime of trespass. *Legal use.* Cf. **intruder.**

**Trial**   A formal judicial examination to determine if the defendant is guilty of the crime as charged. It is the part of a judicial proceeding that comes after preliminary hearings and pleadings, which includes testimony and evidence, opening and closing arguments, and the verdict. *Legal use.* Cf. **abortive trial; examining trial; fair and impartial trial; mistrial; public trial; speedy trial.**

**Trial by jury**   A trial in which a duly sworn jury determines questions of fact and arrives at a verdict after deliberation and after receiving instructions from the judge, who determines questions of law. The right to a jury trial is guaranteed in Article 3 of the U.S. Constitution. *Legal use.*

**Trial court**   The first court to litigate a matter, the court of original jurisdiction, as opposed to an appellate court. *General use.*

**Trial lawyer**   An attorney who practices law mainly in cases before courts of original jurisdiction. *General use.*

**Tribunal**   The seat of justice, either of a single judge or of all the judges in a panel, or jurisdiction. Originally the elevated seat occupied by the praetor, a magistrate in ancient Rome. *Legal use.*

**Truant officer**   One who makes certain that people attend a compulsory activity, usually school. *General use.*

**True crimes**   According to some penologists, murder, rape, robbery, burglary, aggravated assault, and grand theft are the crimes to which law enforcement should give priority. *Law enforcement use.*

**True verdict**   The voluntary verdict of an impartial jury reached after careful deliberation and without coercion. *Legal use.*

**Trump up**   To invent or create with the intention of deception. *General use.*

**Turn copper**   To become a police informer, especially a member of the underworld. *Underworld use.*

**Turn down**   The denial of a request for parole. *U.S. prison use.*

**Turn oneself in**   To surrender to police. *U.S. underworld use.*

**Turn out**   1. To acquit a defendant and turn him out into the street; to release a prisoner. *Underworld use, 1899.* 2. To take full responsibility for a crime and, by doing so, to set an innocent person or an accomplice free. *U.S. underworld use.*

**Turn the hose on**   To beat a suspect usually at third-degree interrogation with a length of rubber hose, leaving no marks as evidence for a brutality complaint. *Police use.*

**Twenty-two fifty men**   Police informers. The term originated in New York City in the 1920s when it was believed that the police department paid men who were waiting to go on the police force $22.50 a week to act as aides or informers. *U.S. underworld use.*

**Two-bit mouthpiece**   An inexpensive criminal lawyer, especially one who is not even worth his small fee. He takes whatever fee he can get and then advises his client to plead guilty. In some jurisdictions, defendants are allowed to sign over their bond receipts directly to their attorneys. Once they have done this, the "two-bit mouthpiece" wants to guarantee that the case is soon concluded, whatever the verdict, so he can collect the bond deposited by the defendant; a.k.a. **two-bit shyster**. *U.S. underworld use*. Cf. **mouthpiece**.

**Ultimate penalty**   The death sentence or life imprisonment without parole. *Underworld use*.

**Unappealable**   That which cannot be appealed. *General use*.

**Unconscious**   Being unaware of one's own actions (e.g., due to sleepwalking). A person generally cannot be convicted of a criminal act if he was unconscious during its execution. *Legal use*. Cf. **automatism**.

**Under the influence of intoxicating liquor**   Legal term used in statutes and ordinances prohibiting the operation of a motor vehicle while inebriated. Blood alcohol tests are typically employed to determine the degree of intoxication. The standard for legal intoxication is determined by statute. *U.S. legal use*. Cf. **intoxication**.

**Under the light**   Being questioned by the police in the interrogation room, especially receiving the third degree. *U.S. underworld use*.

**Uniform Code of Military Justice**   The body of law that governs U.S. military personnel. *Legal use*. Cf. **military jurisdiction**.

*Uniform Crime Report*   The annual FBI report on criminal activity for the year. Part 1 of this report lists statistics for index crimes: auto theft, larceny, burglary, aggravated assault, robbery, forcible rape, and willful homicide. This yearly report is based on the gathering of information on federal offenses, as well as reports from all U.S. statewide police departments. The report, which is used by the FBI to convince Congress to continue and increase funding for the Bureau, is often incomplete, mostly due to the lack of cooperation from some municipal police departments. Where some municipal police departments suppress or minimize information on major offenses in their areas to avoid criticism for being ineffective, the FBI, at least under the direction of the dictatorial J. Edgar Hoover (1895–1972), has been criticized for inflating the number of major crimes each year in order to obtain approval for increased yearly budgets. *FBI use*.

**United States attorney; U.S. attorney**   A federal officeholder appointed to each of the sixty-four judicial districts by the president of the United States. U.S. attorneys prosecute all offenses against the country and represent the United States in all civil matters, criminal actions, and proceedings brought by litigants within their local jurisdiction. The U.S. attorney prosecutes for the collection of fines, forfeitures, and penalties resulting from violations of revenue laws. *U.S. legal use*. Cf. **prosecutor**.

**United States attorney general**   The cabinet officer appointed by the president to head the U.S. Department of Justice. *General use*.

**United States marshal**   A law enforcement officer appointed to each federal judicial district by the president of the United States; supervised by the U.S. attorney general of the Department of Justice. *Legal use*.

**United States Supreme Court**   The highest court of the land; this nine-justice body is the last resort for many doomed convicts. *Legal use*. Cf. **Supreme Court**.

**United States Treasury Department**   The department of the federal government responsible for tax collection and currency production. It is also charged with the prevention of smuggling and counterfeiting, the control of alcohol, tobacco, and firearms, and the protection of the president. *General use*.

**University training for the police profession**   It was not until the early 1900s that formalized training in police procedure became a requirement for all new police personnel. Courses in criminal and traffic law and prisoner identification were usually conducted in cramped station houses or small police academies. Today many universities offer specialized fields of study to better prepare law enforcement personnel. The objectives are threefold: to prepare a person for a career in law enforcement, to develop the necessary leadership qualities, and to promote the ideals of public service and professional standards. Students are taught the methods of criminal identification, police administration, patrol systems, records, traffic regulation, and dealing with the youthful offender. *Law enforcement use*.

**Unmugged**   A criminal who has never been listed on police records and whose photograph is not displayed on the mug board or in suspect books. *Underworld use, 1901*.

**Unreasonable search and seizure**   Any search or seizure made without a warrant or legal excuse or one executed with a warrant, but lacking probable cause; prohibited by the Fourth Amendment to the U.S. Constitution. *U.S. legal use*. Cf. **probable cause**; **search**.

**Unrelated offenses**  A defendant's prior record is generally not admissible by a prosecuting team attempting to demonstrate criminal character. In certain instances, unrelated crimes may be introduced for other purposes (e.g., to prove intent, motive, knowledge, or preparation of a plan). *Legal use.*

**Unusual punishment.**  See **cruel and unusual punishment**.

**Unwritten law**  The body of the law that, while not reflected in statutes, is nevertheless observed and administered in court (e.g., judicial precedents). *Legal use.*

**Up the river**  Sent to prison. A "trip up the river" refers to the train or boat ride a prisoner will take to Sing Sing prison, located forty miles north of Manhattan adjacent to the Hudson River. It was the title of several popular films released in 1930 and 1938. *U.S. underworld and media use, 1900s.*

**Utmost resistance**  Refers to the principle recognized in some jurisdictions that for a rape charge to be sustained, the victim must have offered utmost resistance—the most effort of which she is capable—to fend off the attacker. *Legal use*

**Vacate**  To make or render a legal decision or a record void. *Legal use.*

**Vehicular homicide**  A murder caused by the careless operation of a motor vehicle. State statutes vary concerning the elements of the crime but may encompass both negligence and intentional behavior. *Legal use.* Cf. **homicide**.

**Vehicular manslaughter**  Bringing about the death of another through the reckless operation of a motor vehicle. *Legal use.* Cf. **felonious homicide**; **involuntary manslaughter**; **manslaughter**.

**Vehicular weapon**  Any car, truck, motorcycle, or automotive vehicle used as an assault weapon by its driver. *Legal use.*

**Venire facias**  A judicial writ commanding the county sheriff to name a jury or list from which to choose a jury for the trial of an action that took place in his county. From the Latin phrase meaning "cause to come." *Legal use.*

**Venireman**  A prospective or current member of a jury. *Legal use.*

**Venue**  The proper locality in which a court having jurisdiction may hear and decide a case. Jurisdiction concerns a court's authority to decide a case, while venue concerns the geographic area where that authority may be exercised. A judge may order a change of venue if he believes that a community's citizens are predisposed to reach a certain verdict, for example, when there is substantial pretrial publicity of the crime. *Legal use.*

**Verdict**  Derived from *veredictum*, meaning a true declaration. It is the official decision made by a jury or judge concerning the defendant's guilt or innocence. In criminal cases, the verdict, which must be unanimous, is typically announced to the judge in an open court. *Legal use.* Cf. **directed verdict**; **general verdict**; **guilty verdict**; **not guilty**; **polling the jury**; **sealed verdict**; **true verdict**.

**Verdict, open**  A verdict by a coroner's jury stating that the jury does not know the cause of death or the parties who may have caused it. This may result in a criminal investigation. *Legal use.*

**Victim**  A person who has suffered direct harm from a criminal offender during the execution of a crime (e.g., murder or robbery). *General use.*

**Victimal**  Involving or being a victim, the opposite of criminal. *General use.*

**Victim assistance programs**  Various states have established programs to assist the victims of serious crime in their hour of need. This may include compensating the injured party for lost wages, medical expenses, or funeral arrangements. *Law enforcement use.*

**Victimization**  The condition of being a victim. *General use.*

**Victimize**  To defraud or cheat someone. *General use.*

**Victimless crime**  An illegal act in which the victim willingly participates (e.g., prostitution, gambling, or drug consumption). The rightness or wrongness of prosecuting certain victimless crimes such as prostitution remains a source of continuing debate among moralists and those involved in the legal profession. *Legal and police use.*

**Victimological**  Relating to a study of the criminal-victim relationship. *Sociological use.*

**Victimologist**  A professional who conducts research on the criminal-victim relationship; a scholar in this particular endeavor. *Sociological use.*

**Victimology**  The study of the relationship between criminals and victims, and the impact of crime on a society. It is the opposite of criminology. *Sociological use.*

**Victimous**  Relating to or being a victim. *Sociological use.*

**Vindicate** 1. To release from imprisonment. *Obsolete general use.* 2. To find one not guilty or free of blame. *General use.*

**Vindication** Found not guilty of committing a crime. *Legal use.*

**Violation** 1. Any action that breaches a law, official rule, or obligation. 2. Penal statutes frequently classify a violation as the ravishment or sexual abuse of another person. *Legal use.* 3. The crime of breaking a prison parole. *U.S. prison use.*

**Violator** A released prisoner who breaks a parole agreement. The offender is returned to prison. *U.S. underworld use.*

**Violence** 1. Physical force that injures, abuses, or damages. *General use.* 2. The unauthorized or unfounded use of force, frequently accompanied by fury, outrage, or strong emotion. *Legal use.*

**Violent** Characterized by physical force, especially extreme, sudden, unfounded, unauthorized, or furious force. *Legal use.*

**Violent crime** Crimes involving the excessive use of force (e.g., murder, aggravated assault, and rape). *Legal use.*

**Violent death** A sudden death caused by the violent actions of another; distinguished from a natural death, which is the deterioration of the vital organs due to disease or old age. *Legal use.*

**Violent offenses** Crimes involving the extreme use of physical force (e.g., murder). *Legal use.*

**Voiceprint** An aural representation of a person's voice created through spectrography. It is used primarily in criminal identification. *Law enforcement use.*å

**Voir dire** A preliminary examination used when objection is made to a witness or juror because of alleged bias, competency, or other disqualifying reasons. *Legal use.*

**Voluntary** A statement given freely by a criminal to a police officer. *U.K. police use.*

**Voluntary confession** An admission of guilt made by an individual who has not been coerced or otherwise improperly induced into an act of self-incrimination. *Legal use.* Cf. **confession; extrajudicial confession**.

*Voluntas in delictis, non exitus spectatur* Legal term meaning "in crimes, the will, and not the consequence, is looked to." *Legal use.*

**Vouch** To give corroborating evidence or verification. *Legal use.*

**Wade hearing** A pretrial hearing to determine the admissibility of eyewitness identification of a defendant. The U.S. Supreme Court mandated the Wade hearing in the 1967 *Wade v. U.S.* decision. *Legal use.*

**Waiver** 1. The intentional and voluntary relinquishment of a known right, privilege, or claim. 2. The abandonment or disposal of stolen property during escape from the scene of the crime. *Legal use.* Cf. **abandonment; forfeiture**.

**Waiver of immunity** A witness's renunciation prior to testifying or producing evidence of the constitutional right to not be forced to testify against himself in a criminal case. *Legal use.*

**Walk** To be acquitted of a criminal charge; to be released from prison. *Underworld use.*

**Warrant** 1. A court-issued document that allows a law enforcement officer to make an arrest, search specified premises, or take other actions specified in the warrant (e.g., seizure of property). *Legal use.* Cf. **arrest; arrest warrant; backing a warrant; bench warrant; blank warrant; death warrant; search warrant**. 2. A division in the Records and Identification Department of the Los Angeles Police Department in charge of tracking all warrants issued within the jurisdiction. *LAPD use.*

**Warrant, arrest.** See **arrest warrant**.

**Warren Court** The name given the U.S. Supreme Court when, beginning after the appointment of Chief Justice Earl Warren (1891–1974) in 1953, the high court adopted a liberal view of the Constitution. Many of the most controversial Supreme Court decisions were made during this era, which ended in 1969 with Warren's resignation. These cases included *Brown v. Board of Education*, which prohibited forced school segregation, *Gideon v. Wainwright*, which provided legal counsel to all defendants charged with a crime, and *Miranda v. Arizona*, which required that persons arrested be advised of their rights at the time of arrest. *Legal use.*

**Washout** 1. A sentence to life imprisonment without the possibility of parole. 2. A death sentence. *U.S. underworld use.*

**Weapon** Any device designed to defeat or injure an individual, whether used defensively or offensively. The laws concerning possession or ownership of weapons vary with jurisdictions. *Legal use.* Cf. **dangerous weapon; deadly weapon; offensive weapon**.

**Weeping and waiting** Awaiting the result of an appeal for retrial or criminal pardon while still incarcerated. *Prison use, 1931.*

**Weight of evidence** The tendency of the larger amount of credible evidence offered during a trial to support more strongly either the case by the prosecution or the defense; the preponderance of the evidence. *Legal use.* Cf. **preponderance of the evidence**.

**Wesensgehalt** A term (from German) referring to the amount and the severity of tension an individual is experiencing, as indicated through his handwriting. *Handwriting analysis use.*

**Wharton rule** A rule of criminal law which states that if two individuals have been charged with a crime that necessarily requires the participation of both persons (e.g., adultery), they cannot be charged with the additional offense of conspiracy to commit that crime. *Legal use.*

**Whistle, to blow the** 1. To inform on or testify against fellow criminals; to file a complaint against any individual or party suspected of violating established regulations. *U.S. underworld use.* 2. To inform prison officials of the actions of fellow inmates. *U.S. prison use.*

**Whistle-blower** An informer. *Underworld use.*

**Whistler** A person who divulges confidential information; an informant. *U.S. underworld use, 1925.*

**White-collar crime** Crimes committed by individuals and corporations during the course of their occupational activities, usually upper-class and upper-middle-class professionals, businesses, and corporations whose crimes are often nonviolent and may include theft of office supplies, fraud, embezzlement, antitrust violations, price fixing, insider trading, and the violation of antitrust laws. *Law enforcement use.*

**Whole cloth** Something that is entirely fabricated. *General use.*

**Whorls** Fingerprints. *Underworld use, 1925.*

**Will** 1. One's choice, desire, or inclination. 2. A legal document designed to dispose of or distribute the property of an individual after death. *Legal use.*

**Willful** Conscious, voluntary, or intentional. *Legal use.*

**Willfully** Intentionally. *General use.* Cf. **knowingly and willfully**.

**Willful murder** Intentionally killing another without excuse or mitigating circumstances. *Legal use.* Cf. **heat of passion**; **premeditation**.

**Willingly** Anything done voluntarily, without coercion or reluctance. *Legal use.*

**Wiretapping** 1. Attaching or installing illegal electronic devices in order to eavesdrop on another individual or party. *General use.* Cf. **eavesdropping, electronic**. 2. Intercepting telephone conversations or messages in the gathering of secret information. *Intelligence use.*

**Withholding of evidence** To suppress or destroy evidence with the knowledge that the evidence is wanted in a court proceeding or is sought by law enforcement officials may constitute an obstruction of justice. Cf. **obstructing justice**.

**Without her consent** A term used in many statutes regarding rape. The term means that sexual penetration during rape occurred against the will of the victim, and that the victim resisted the attack. *Legal use.* Cf. **statutory rape**.

**Witness** A person who makes a declaration or oath in a court of law, through testimony, deposition, or affidavit, explaining the actions that he has seen, heard, or observed or the perceptions that he may have drawn based on personal experience or examination of evidence. *v.* To observe an event. *Legal use.* Cf. **affidavit**; **competent witness**; **credible witness**; **deposition**; **expert witness**; **hostile witness**; **material witness**.

**Witness, adverse** A witness who gives evidence prejudicial to the examining party; one whose relationship to the examining party indicates that his testimony may be prejudiced against that party; a.k.a. **hostile witness**. *Legal use.*

**Witness, credible.** See **credible witness**.

**Witness, grand jury** An individual who provides testimony to a grand jury. *Legal use.*

**Witness, material** A witness in a criminal trial who provides important testimony that is integral to either the case for the defense or for the prosecution. Often the material witness is required to post bond for his appearance or is protected or confined by law enforcement agencies until he is able to testify. *Legal use.*

**Witness against himself** A provision of the U.S. Constitution's Fifth Amendment that prohibits an individual from being forced to testify against himself in order to prevent self-incrimination. *Legal use.* Cf. **self-incrimination**.

**Witness box** An enclosed area from where a witness gives testimony from during a courtroom trial. *U.K. general use.*

**Witness stand** The location in a courtroom from which witnesses or defendants give testimony during a trial. *General use.*

**Work for the state**   A practice among some defense attorneys of ignoring and neglecting the needs of their clients in favor of those of the local law enforcement agency or legal jurisdiction. *U.S. underworld use.*

**Workout**   1. A severe beating by law enforcement officers. *U.S. underworld use.* 2. A severe beating by prison guards or prison inmates. *Prison use.* To complete the entire length of the court-ordered prison sentence. *U.S. underworld use, 1931.*

**Work over**   1. To beat up a person. *Underworld use.* 2. To intimidate a suspect with questions; to give someone the third degree. *Underworld use, 1931.*

**Work release program**   A rehabilitative program that allows convicts to work at jobs outside of prison during the day but requires them to return for lockup at night. *Law enforcement use.*

**Wound**   An injury that results in bruising, breakage, or piercing of the skin. The legal definition of a wound varies from jurisdiction to jurisdiction. *Legal use. v.* To injure another individual. *General use.*

**Wrinkle**   A falsehood or lie. *Obsolete use, 1890.*

**Writ**   A court order requiring that a specific act be performed, or authorizing that an act be done. *Legal use.* Cf. **habeas corpus**; **mandamus**; **writ of assistance**.

**Writing base**   The horizontal line or plane, running parallel to the top and bottom margins of a page, at which the downward strokes of handwritten lower case letters end. *Handwriting analysis use.*

**Writ of assistance**   A search warrant frequently issued during the 1750s, which permitted the search and seizure of suspected contraband with disregard to individual rights. The use of these writs was discontinued in the 1760s due to the extreme pressure on U.S. colonial courts. *Legal use.*

**Writ of error**   An order issued by an appellate court to a lower court requiring the release of records on a particular case. The writ allows the appellate court to review the records of the case for error and to reverse, correct, or affirm the lower court's decision. *Legal use.*

**Writ of habeas corpus.**   See **habeas corpus**.

**Writ of mandamus.**   See mandamus.

**Writ of prohibition**   A writ ordering a court to cease the prosecution of a particular case or individual, or

requiring that a public official discontinue a specific action. Cannot be used to settle conflicts handled by ordinary proceedings or appeals and can only be used in cases of severe hardship or necessity. *Legal use.*

**Writ of protection**   A judicial writ requiring attendance in court, either as a party to the case or a juror, with the intention of guarding him from arrest as he appears in, arrives at, or leaves court. *Legal use.*

**Writ of *quo warranto***   A civil court writ sometimes used in criminal proceedings to challenge authority that is being unlawfully asserted. *Legal use.*

**Wrong bit**   A conviction and sentence for a crime of which one is innocent; an illegal conviction. *U.S. underworld use.*

**Wrong drop**   1. False arrest. *U.S. underworld use.* 2. Prison punishment for rule violations of which one is innocent. *U.S. convict use.*

**Wrong fall**   1. Arrest of an innocent person for a wrongful charge. *U.S. underworld use.* 2. Prison punishment for rule violations of which one is innocent. *U.S. convict's use.*

**Wrongful**   Anything that is reckless, unfair, or unjustified. *Legal use.*

**Wrongly accused**   An innocent person who is wrongly accused of committing a crime. *General use.*

**Wrongly convicted**   An innocent person who is convicted of a crime he did not commit. *General use.*

**Wrong rap**   An unwarranted, unjustified charge or conviction of an innocent individual. *U.S. underworld use.*

**Yank**   To arrest. *Obsolete U.S. underworld use, 1891.*

**Yarn**   A fabricated story (e.g., a phony alibi). *General use.*

**Yell copper**   To become a police informant. *U.S. underworld use, 1928.* Cf. **turn copper**.

**Yell murder**   To confess or inform on others emphatically and without reservation. *U.S. underworld use.*

**Yellow sheet**   A record containing all of a prisoner's or suspect's prior arrests. *NYPD use.*

**Youthful offender**   A person regarded in juvenile court as a delinquent rather than a criminal. The qualifying age varies from state to state; a.k.a. **YO** *Legal use.*

# Bibliography

**Note**: In addition to the author's own extensive interviews and correspondence, innumerable police and court records, and hundreds of newspapers and periodicals with thousands of articles dealing with wrongly convicted persons were consulted in researching this work, which are too numerous to cite here. What follows is a bibliography of published primary and secondary sources on the subject and related or relevant subjects where many of the major cases profiled in this work can be referenced. Early works dating back centuries cited herein were acquired through extracts and copies from numerous national archives. No Internet sources are cited as they are universally deemed by qualified and recognized authorities as unreliable and, for the most part, without credibility due to inherent and routine online electronic virus corruption, and human alteration, tampering, and intentional or unintentional misrepresentation, unless emanating from a recognized authority, which should nevertheless be directly and exclusively consulted and confirmed through actual print sources by the true researcher seeking authentic and dependable information.

*The Accused and The Accusers: The Speeches of the Eight Chicago Anarchists in Court*. Chicago: Socialistic, n.d.

Ackernecht, Erwin Heinz. *Franz Joseph Gall: Inventor of Phrenology*. Madison: University of Wisconsin Press, 1956.

Adam, H. Pearl. *Murder Most Mysterious*. London: Sampson, Low, 1932.

Adam, Hargrave Lee. *C.I.D.: Behind the Scenes at Scotland Yard*. London: Sampson, Low, 1931.

———. *Murder by Persons Unknown*. London: Collins, 1931.

———. *Murder Most Mysterious*. London: Sampson, Low, 1932.

———. *Woman and Crime*. London: T. W. Laurie, 1912.

Adam, W. H. Davenport. *Witch, Warlock, and Magician: Historical Sketches of Magic and Witchcraft in England and Scotland*. Farmington Hills, Mich.: Gale, 1973.

Adamic, Louis. *Dynamite: The Story of Class Violence in America*. New York: Viking, 1931.

Adams, Brooks. *Emancipation of Massachusetts: The Dream and the Reality*. Boston: Houghton Mifflin, 1919.

Adams, Cynthia. *Mysterious Case of Sir Arthur Conan Doyle*. Greensboro, N.C.: Morgan Reynolds, 1999.

Adams, Randall. *Adams V. Texas*. New York: St. Martin's, 1992.

Adams, Samuel Hopkins. *Incredible Era: The Life and Times of Warren Gamaliel Harding*. Boston: Houghton Mifflin, 1939.

Adams, W. S. *Edwardian Portraits*. London: Secker, 1957.

Adler, Friedrich. *The Witchcraft Trial in Moscow*. New York: Pioneer, 1937.

Ady, Thomas. *A Candle in the Dark*. London: T. Newberry, 1656.

———. *A Perfect Discovery of Witches*. London: H. Browne, 1661.

Ai Camp, Roderic. *Politics in Mexico: The Democratic Transformation*. New York: Oxford University Press, 2002.

Ainsworth, William Harrison. *The Lancashire Witches*. London: H. Colburn, 1849.

Akagi, Roy H. *The Town Proprietors of the New England Colonies: A Study of Their Development, Organization, Activities, and Controversies*. Philadelphia: University of Philadelphia Press, 1924.

Alexander, Henry A. *Some Facts About the Murder Notes in the Phagan Case.* Atlanta, Ga.: Author, n.d.

Allen, Frederick Lewis. *Only Yesterday: An Informal History of the Nineteen Twenties.* New York: Harper, 1931.

————. *Since Yesterday.* New York: Harper, 1940.

Almandos, Luis. *Bertillon et Vucetich.* La Plata, Argentina: n.p., 1928.

Altgeld, John Peter. *Live Questions.* New York: Humbold, 1890.

————. *Our Penal Machinery and Its Victims.* Chicago: Janson, McClurg, 1884.

Altick, Richard D. *Victorian Studies in Scarlet.* London: J. M. Dent, 1970.

Akrigg, G. P. V. *Letters of King James VI and I.* Berkeley: University of California Press, 1984.

Amir, Menachem. *Patterns in Forcible Rape.* Chicago: University of Chicago Press, 1971.

Amory, Cleveland, and Bradlee, F. *Cavalcade of the 1920's and 30's.* London: Bodley Head, 1961.

————. *The Proper Bostonians.* New York: Dutton, 1947.

Anderson, James M. *Daily Life During the Spanish Inquisition.* Westport, Conn.: Greenwood, 2002.

Andrews, C. M. *The Colonial Period of American History.* 4 vols. New Haven, Conn.: Yale University Press, 1934.

Ankarloo, Bengt, ed. *Witchcraft and Magic in Europe: The Period of the Witch Trials.* Philadelphia: University of Pennsylvania, 2002.

Ankarloo, Bengt, and Clark, Stuart, eds. *Witchcraft and Magic in Europe: The Eighteenth and Nineteenth Centuries.* Philadelphia: University of Pennsylvania Press, 1999.

Archer, Fred. *Killers in the Clear.* New York: W. H. Allen, 1971.

*Argument of William H. Seward in Defense of William Freeman, on His Trial for Murder at Auburn, July 21st and 22nd, 1846.* Auburn, N.Y.: H. Oliphant, 1846.

Armitage, G. *History of the Bow Street Runners.* London: Wishart, 1932.

Armstrong, Erma. *Improper Submission: Records of a Wrongful Conviction.* Dallas, Ore.: Tanglewood Hill, 2005.

Arnett, Alex Mathews. *The Populist Movement in Georgia.* New York: Columbia University Press, 1922.

Arnold, Reuben R. *The Trial of Leo Frank: Reuben R. Arnold's Address to the Court in His Behalf.* New York: Classic, 1915.

Asbury, Herbert. *The Barbary Coast: An Informal History of the San Francisco Underworld.* New York: Alfred A. Knopf, 1933.

————. *The Gangs of New York.* New York: Alfred A. Knopf, 1927.

————. *Gem of the Prairie: An Informal History of the Chicago Underworld.* New York: Alfred A. Knopf, 1940.

Astel, Ann W., and Wheeler, Bonnie, eds. *Joan of Arc and Spirituality.* New York: Palgrave Macmillan, 2003.

Astor, Gerald. *The Charge Is Rape.* New York: Playboy, 1974.

————. *The New York Cops.* New York: Scribner's, 1971.

Atholl, Justin. *Shadow of the Gallows.* London: John Long, 1954.

Avrich, Paul. *The Haymarket Tragedy.* Princeton, N.J.: Princeton University Press, 1984.

————. *Sacco and Vanzetti.* Princeton, N.J.: Princeton University Press, 1996.

Axenfeld, Alexandre. *Jean Wier et la sorcellerie.* Paris: Germer Bailliere, 1866.

Badel, Emile. *D'une sorciere qu'aultrefois on brusla dans Sainct-Nicholas.* Nancy: Berger-Levrault, 1891.

Baden, Michael, and Roach, Marion. *Dead Reckoning: The New Science of Catching Killers.* New York: Touchstone/Simon & Schuster, 2001.

Bailey, F. Lee. *Defending Business and White Collar Crimes: Federal and State.* Rochester, N.Y.: Lawyer's Co-operative, 1969.

————. *The Defense Never Rests.* New York: Signet, 1972.

————. *To Be a Trial Lawyer.* New York: Wiley, 1994.

Bailey, F. Lee, and Greenya, John. *For the Defense.* New York: Atheneum, 1975.

Bailey, F. Lee, and Rothblatt, Henry B. *Crimes of Violence, Rape, and Other Sex Crimes.* Rochester, N.Y.: Lawyers Co-Operative, 1973.

Bailey, Sarah Loring. *Historical Sketches of Andover.* Boston: Houghton Mifflin, 1880.

Balding, David J. *Weight-of-Evidence for Forensic DNA Profiles.* New York: Wiley, 2005.

Baldwin, H. W., and Stone, Shepard. *We Saw It Happen.* New York: Simon & Schuster, 1938.

Ballantine, William. *Some Experiences of a Barrister's Life.* London: Richard Bentley, 1822.

Barnard, Harry. *Eagle Forgotten: The Life of John Peter Altgeld.* Indianapolis: Bobbs-Merrill, 1938.

Barsham, Diana. *Sir Arthur Conan Doyle.* Burlington, Vt.: Ashgate, 2000.

Barstow, Anne Llewellyn. *Joan of Arc: Heretic, Mystic, Shaman.* Lewiston, N.Y.: Edwin Mellen, 1986.

_____. *Witchcraze: A New History of the European Witch Hunts.* Reprint. San Francisco: HarperCollins, 1995.

Barthel, Joan. *A Death in Canaan.* New York: Dutton, 1977.

Batt, John. *Stolen Innocence: A Mother's Fight for Justice.* London: Ebury Press/Random House, 2004.

Batten, Jack. *Mind over Murder: DNA and Other Forensic Adventures.* Toronto: McClelland & Stewart, 1997.

Baughman, Laurance. *Southern Rape Complex.* Atlanta, Ga.: Pendulum, 1966.

Beard, George M. *Psychology of the Salem Witchcraft Excitement of 1692.* New York: Putnam's, 1882.

Beaumont, John. *An Historical, Physiological, and Theological Treatise of Spirits, Apparitions, Witchcrafts, and Other Magical Practices.* London: D. Browne, 1705.

Beaune, Henri. *Les sorciers de Lyon.* Dijon: Rabutot, 1868.

Bechhofer, Robert. *Famous American Trials.* London: Jarrolds, 1947.

Beevers, John. *Saint Joan of Arc.* Rockford, Ill.: TAN, 1974.

Behringer, Wolfgang. *Witches and Witch-Hunts: A Global History.* Cambridge, U.K.: Polity, 2004.

Beigel, Hermann. *The Examination and Confession of Certain Witches at Chelmsford.* London: Philobiblon Society, 1864.

Belloc, Hilaire. *Charles I.* Reprint. Norfolk, Va.: I.H.S. Press, 2003.

_____. *Charles II: The Last Rally.* Reprint. Marshall, Mass.: Paul & Co., 2003.

_____. *Joan of Arc.* New York: Declan X. McMullen, 1929.

Bennett, Benjamin. *Genius for the Defense: Life of Harry Morris, K.C.* Cape Town, South Africa: Howard B. Timmins, 1959.

_____. *Why Did They Do It?* Cape Town, South Africa: Howard Timmins, 1953.

Bergen, Raquel Kennedy. *Issues in Intimate Violence.* Thousand Oaks, Calif.: Sage, 1998.

Bergeron, David Modre. *King James and Letters of Homoerotic Desire.* Iowa City: University of Iowa Press, 1999.

_____. *Royal Family, Royal Lovers: King James of England and Scotland.* Columbia: University of Missouri Press, 1991.

Bevan, Bryan. *King James VI of Scotland and I of England.* Baltimore: Rubicon, 1996.

Binz, Carl. *Doctor Johann Weyer.* Bonn, Germany: A. Marcus, 1885.

Birkenhead, Frederick E. *Famous Trials of History.* Reprint. Whitefish, Mont.: Kessinger, 2003.

Birmingham, George A. *Murder Most Foul!* London: Chatto & Windus, 1929.

Birnbaum, Pierre. *The Anti-Semitic Movement: A Tour of France in 1898.* New York: Hill & Wang, 2002.

Bishop, George. *Executions.* Los Angeles: Sherbourne, 1965.

_____. *Witness to Evil.* Los Angeles: Nash, 1971.

Bixley, William. *The Guilty and the Innocent: My Fifty Years at the Old Bailey.* London: Souvenir Press, 1957.

Black, George F. *A Calendar of Cases of Witchcraft in Scotland, 1510–1727.* New York: New York Public Library, 1938.

_____. *List of Works in the New York Public Library Relating to Witchcraft in Europe.* New York: New York Public Library, 1911.

_____. *List of Works in the New York Public Library Relating to Witchcraft in the United States.* New York: New York Public Library, 1908.

_____. *Some Unpublished Scottish Witchcraft Trials.* New York: New York Public Library, 1941.

Blaetz, Robin. *Visions of the Maid: Joan of Arc in American Film and Culture.* Charlottesville: University Press of Virginia, 2001.

Blakeney, T. S. *Sherlock Holmes: Fact or Fiction?* Morristown, N.J.: Baker Street Irregulars, 1954.

Blakeslee, Nate. *Tulia: Race, Cocaine, and Corruption in a Small Texas Town.* New York: Public Affairs, 2005.

Bleackley, Horace. *The Hangmen of England.* London: Chapman & Hall, 1929.

_____. *Ladies Fair & Frail: Sketches of the Demi-Monde During the Eighteenth Century.* London: Bodley Head, 1909.

_____. *Some Distinguished Victims of the Scaffold.* London: Kegan Paul, Trench, Trubner, 1905.

Block, Eugene B. *Lie Detectors.* New York: David McKay, 1977.

_____. *Science vs. Crime.* New York: Caroline House, 1980.

_____. *Voiceprinting.* New York: McKay, 1975.

_____. *The Wizard of Berkeley.* New York: Coward-McCann, 1958.

Block, Sharon. *Rape and Sexual Power in Early America.* Chapel Hill: University of North Carolina Press, 2006.

Boardman, Andrew. *A Defense of Phrenology.* London: Fowler & Wells, 1850.

Boas, Ralph P., and Boas, Louise. *Cotton Mather: Keeper of the Puritan Conscience.* Hamden, Conn.: Archon, 1964.

Bode, Janet. *Fighting Back: How to Cope with the Medical, Emotional, and Legal Consequences of Rape.* New York: Macmillan, 1978.

Booth, Martin. *The Doctor and the Detective: A Biography of Sir Arthur Conan Doyle.* New York: Thomas Dunne Books / St. Martin's, 2000.

Borchard, Edwin Montefiore. *Convicting the Innocent.* New Haven, Conn.: Yale University Press, 1932.

Boulton, Richard. *A Complete History of Magic.* London: E. Curll & W. Taylor, 1715.

Bourdrel, Philippe. *Histoire des juifs en France.* Paris: Albin Michel, 1974.

Bowen-Rowlands, Ernest. *In Court and Out of Court.* London: Hutchinson, 1925.

_____. *In the Light of the Law.* London: Grant Richards, 1931.

_____. *Seventy-Two Years at the Bar.* London: Macmillan, 1924.

Boyer, Paul S., and Nissenbaum, Stephan, eds. *Salem Possessed: The Social Origins of Witchcraft.* Cambridge, Mass.: Harvard University Press, 1974. Reprinted as *Salem-Village Witchcraft: A Documentary Record of Local Conflict in Colonial New England* in 1993 by the Northeastern University Press, Boston.

Boys, Reverend J. *The Case of Witchcraft at Coggeshall, Essex, 1699.* London: A. R. Smith, 1901.

Bradford, William. *An Enquiry How Far the Punishment of Death Is Necessary in Pennsylvania.* Philadelphia: T. Dobson, 1793.

_____. *History of Plymouth Plantation.* Boston: Houghton Mifflin, 1896.

_____. *Of Plymouth Plantation, 1620–1647.* New York: Alfred A. Knopf, 1952.

Bragge, Francis. *A Defense of the Proceedings Against Jane Wenham.* London: E. Curll, 1712.

_____. *A Full and Impartial Account of the Discovery of Sorcery and Witchcraft Practiced by Jane Wenham.* London: E. Curll, 1712.

_____. *Witchcraft Further Displayed.* London: E. Curll, 1712.

Brand, Christianna. *Heaven Knows Who.* New York: Scribner's, 1960.

Brandon, R., and Davies, C. *Wrongful Imprisonment.* London: George Allen & Unwin, 1973.

Bredin, Jean-Denis. *Affair: The Case of Alfred Dreyfus.* New York: George Braziller, 1987.

Breen, Timothy H. *The Character of the Good Ruler: A Study of Puritan Political Ideas in New England, 1630–1730.* New Haven, Conn.: Yale University Press, 1970.

Brennan, James F. *Reflection of the Dreyfus Affair in the European Press, 1897–1899.* New York: Peter Lang, 1998.

Brewton, William Wade. *The Life of Thomas E. Watson.* Atlanta, Ga.: Author, 1926.

Bridenbaugh, Carl. *Cities in the Wilderness: Urban Life in America, 1625–1742.* Reprint. New York: Capricorn, 1966.

Bridges, B. C. *Practical Fingerprinting.* New York: Funk & Wagnalls, 1942.

Bridges, B. C., and Boolsen, F. M. *Fifty-one Fingerprint Systems.* Privately printed, 1935.

Bridges, Yseult. *Two Studies in Crime.* London: Hutchinson, 1959.

Brien, Steve. *Azaria: The Trial of the Century.* Melbourne: Progress, 1984.

Brock, Alan. *A Casebook of Crime.* London: Watmoughs, 1948.

Brodie-Innes, John William. *Scottish Witchcraft Trials.* London: Chiswick, 1891.

Brome, Vincent. *Reverse Your Verdict.* London: Hamilton, 1971.

Brookes, Cannon J. R. *Murder in Fact and Fiction.* London: Hurst & Blackett, 1926.

Brooks, Polly Schroyer. *Beyond the Myth: The Story of Joan of Arc.* Boston: Houghton Mifflin, 1999.

Brooks, Van Wyck. *The Flowering of New England, 1815–1865.* New York: Random House, 1936.

_____. *New England: Indian Summer, 1865–1915.* New York: Dutton, 1940.

Brophy, John. *The Meaning of Murder.* London: Ronald Whiting & Wheaton, 1966.

Broun, Heywood. *Collected Edition of Heywood Broun.* New York: Harcourt, Brace, 1941.

_____. *It Seems to Me.* New York: Harcourt, Brace, 1935.

Brown, Joyce Ann. *Justice Denied.* Dallas: Mass, 1990.

Brown, Robert. *Demonology and Witchcraft.* London: J. F. Shaw, 1889.

Brown, Walter J. *J. J. Brown and Thomas E. Watson: Georgia Politics, 1912–1928.* Macon, Ga.: Mercer University Press, 1988.

Browne, Douglas G. *The Rise of Scotland Yard.* New York: Putnam's, 1956.

_____. *Sir Travers Humphreys.* London: Harrap, 1960.

Browne, Douglas G., and Brock, Alan. *Fingerprints: Fifty Years of Scientific Crime Detection*. New York: Dutton, 1954.

Browne, Douglas G., and Tullett, E. V. *The Scalpel of Scotland Yard: The Life of Sir Bernard Spilsbury*. New York: Dutton, 1952.

Browne, G. Lathom, and Stewart, C. G. *Trials for Murder by Poisoning*. London: Stevens, 1883.

Browne, Waldo Ralph. *Altgeld of Illinois: A Record of His Life and Work*. New York: B. W. Huebsch, 1924.

Brownmiller, Susan. *Against Our Will: Men, Women, and Rape*. New York: Simon & Schuster, 1975.

Bruce, Duncan. *The Scottish 100: Portraits of History's Most Influential Scots*. New York: Carroll & Graf, 2002.

Bryant, Arthur. *The England of Charles II*. North Stratford, N.H.: Ayer, 1977.

Bryson, John. *Evil Angels*. New York: Summit, 1987.

Buckleton, John S., Triggs, Christopher M., and Walsh, Simon J., eds. *Forensic DNA Evidence Interpretation*. Boca Raton, Fla.: CRC, 2004.

Budiansky, Stephen. *Her Majesty's Spymaster: Elizabeth I, Sir Francis Walsingham, and the Birth of Modern Espionage*. New York: Viking, 2005.

Bullard, Scott R., and Collins, Michael Leo. *Who's Who in Sherlock Holmes*. New York: Taplinger, 1980.

Burgess, Anne Wolbert, and Holmstrom, Lynda Lytle. *Rape: Victims of Crisis*. Bowie, Md.: Robert J. Brady, 1974.

Burgess, Anne Wolbert, and Holmstrom, Lynda Lytle, et al. *Sexual Assault of Children and Adolescents*. Lexington, Mass.: Lexington, 1975.

Burns, Michael. *Dreyfus Affair*. New York: St. Martin's, 1998.

_____. *Rural Society and French Politics*. Princeton, N.J.: Princeton University Press, 1984.

Burns, Robert E. *I Am a Fugitive from a Georgia Chain Gang*. New York: Vanguard, 1932.

Burr, George Lincoln, ed. *Narratives of Witchcraft Cases, 1648–1706*. New York: Barnes & Noble, 1959.

Burton, John Hill. *Narratives from Criminal Trials in Scotland*. New York: AMS Press, 1976.

Busch, Francis X. *Guilty or Not Guilty: An Account of the Trials of the Leo Frank Case, the D.C. Stephenson Case, the Samuel Insull Case, the Alger Hiss Case*. Indianapolis: Bobbs-Merrill, 1952.

_____. *Prisoners at the Bar*. Indianapolis: Bobbs-Merrill, 1952.

_____. *They Escaped the Hangman*. London: Arco, 1957.

Butler, Ivan. *Murderers' England*. London: Robert Hale, 1973.

Butler, John M. *Forensic DNA Typing*. San Diego: Academic, 2005.

Bye, Raymond T. *Capital Punishment in the United States*. Philadelphia: Committee on Philanthropic Labor of Philadelphia Yearly Meeting of Friends, 1919.

Caesar, Gene. *Incredible Detective: The Biography of William J. Burns*. Englewood Cliffs, N.J.: Prentice-Hall, 1968.

Cahm, Eric. *Dreyfus Affair in French Society and Politics*. Boston: Addison-Wesley, 1996.

Caldwell, Charles. *Elements of Phrenology: With a Preliminary Discourse in Vindication of the Science*. New York: A. G. Meriwether, 1927.

_____. *Phrenology Vindicated*. New York: J. Clark, 1835.

Calef, Robert. *More Wonders of the Invisible World*. London: N. Hillar & J. Collyer, 1700.

Calmeil, Louis Francois. *De la folie*. Paris: J. B. Baillire, 1845.

Campbell, John Gregorson. *Superstitions of the Highlands*. Glasgow: J. MacLehose, 1900.

_____. *Witchcraft and Second Sight in the Highlands and Islands of Scotland*. Glasgow: J. MacLehose, 1902.

Campbell, John H., and Denevi, Don, eds. *Profilers: Leading Investigators Take You Inside the Criminal Mind*. Amherst, N.Y.: Prometheus, 2004.

Canning, John. *50 True Tales of Terror*. New York: Bell, 1972.

Carr, Howie. *The Brothers Bulger: How They Terrorized and Corrupted Boston for a Quarter Century*. New York: Grand Central, 2006.

Carr, John Dickson. *The Life of Sir Arthur Conan Doyle*. New York: Harper, 1949.

Carter, Dan T. *Scottsboro: A Tragedy of the American South*. New York: Oxford University Press, 1969.

Carter, Hodding. *The Angry Scar*. New York: Doubleday, 1959.

Carter, Rubin. *The Sixteenth Round: From Number 1 Contender to #45472*. New York: Penguin (reprint), 1991.

*The Case of the Hertfordshire Witchcraft Considered*. London: J. Pemberton, 1712.

Cauzons, Thomas de. *Les Albigeois et l'Inquisition*. Paris: Bloud, 1908.

_____. *Histoire de l'Inquisition en France*. Paris: Bloud, 1909.

_____. *La Magie et la Sorcellerie en France*. Paris: Dourbon-am, 1910.

Chaffee, Zechariah. *The Mooney-Billings Report Suppressed by the Wickersham Commission.* New York: Gotham House, 1932.

Chaiton, Sam, and Swinton, Terry. *Lazarus and the Hurricane: The Freeing of Rubin "Hurricane" Carter.* Reprint. New York: St. Martin's, 2000.

Chalmers, Allan Knight. *They Shall Be Free.* Garden City, N.Y.: Doubleday, 1951.

Chalmers, David Mark. *Hooded Americanism: The First Century of the Ku Klux Klan, 1865–1965.* New York: Doubleday, 1965.

Chandler, Peleg W. *American Criminal Trials.* Boston: Little, Brown, 1841–1844.

Chapel, Charles Edward. *Fingerprinting.* New York: Coward-McCann, 1941.

Chaplin, J. P. *Rumor, Fear, and the Madness of Crowds.* New York: Ballantine, 1959.

Chaplin, Ralph. *Wobbly: The Rough-and-Tumble Story of an American Radical.* Chicago: University of Chicago Press, 1948.

Chapman, Guy. *The Dreyfus Case.* London: Rupert Hart-Davis, 1955.

Chappell, Duncan, et al., eds. *Forcible Rape: The Crime, the Victim, and the Criminal.* New York: Columbia University Press, 1977.

Chappell, Duncan, and Monahan, John, eds. *Violence and Criminal Justice.* Lexington, Mass.: Lexington/D.C. Heath, 1975.

Cherrill, Fred. *Cherrill of the Yard.* London: Popular Book Club, 1955.

———. *The Fingerprint System at Scotland Yard.* London: H. M. Stationery Office, 1954.

*The Chicago Anarchists and the Haymarket Massacre.* Chicago: Blakely, 1887.

Christiani, Leon. *St. Joan of Arc: Virgin Soldier.* Boston: Daughters of St. Paul, 1977.

Christianson, Scott. *Innocent: Inside Wrongful Conviction Cases.* New York: New York University Press, 2006.

Christie, John, ed. *Witchcraft in Kenmore (Perthshire), 1730–57: Extracts from Kirk Session Records.* Aberfeldy: D. Cameron, 1893.

Churchill, Winston Leonard. *Joan of Arc.* New York: Dodd, Mead, 1969.

Clark, Loremne. *Rape.* Toronto: Womens, 1977.

Clark, Stuart. *Thinking with Demons: The Idea of Witchcraft in Early Modern Europe.* New York: Oxford University Press, 1999.

Clawson, Patrick, and Rensselaer, W. Lee. *The Andean Cocaine Industry.* New York: Palgrave Macmillan, 1996.

Clegg, Eric. *Return Your Verdict.* Sydney: Angus & Robertson, 1965.

Coates, Tim, ed. *Sacco and Vanzetti: The FBI Files.* London: Tim Coates Books, 2002.

Cobb, Belton. *Trials and Errors: 11 Miscarriages of Justice.* London: W. H. Allen, 1962.

Cobban, Alfred. *History of Modern France, 1871–1962.* New York: Viking, 1965.

Cohen, Ellis A., with Shapiro, Milton J. *Dangerous Evidence.* New York: Berkley, 1995.

Cohn, Norman. *Europe's Inner Demons: The Demonization of Christians in Medieval Christendom.* Rev. ed. Chicago: University of Chicago Press, 2001.

Cole, Simon. *Suspect Identities: A History of Fingerprinting and Criminal Identification.* Cambridge, Mass.: Harvard University Press, 2002.

*A Collection of Rare and Curious Tracts on Witchcraft and the Second Sight.* Edinburgh: D. Webster, 1820.

Combe, George. *A System of Phrenology.* New York: Harper, 1858.

*A Condensed Report of the Trial of James Albert Trefethen, and William H. Smith for the Murder of Deltena J. Davis in the Superior Court of Massachusetts.* Boston: Wright & Potter, 1895.

Connell, Noreen, and Wilson, Cassandra, eds. *Rape: The First Sourcebook for Women.* New York: Plume, 1974.

Connelly, Mark Thomas. *The Response to Prostitution in the Progressive Era.* Chapel Hill: University of North Carolina Press, 1980.

Connery, Donald S., ed. *Convicting the Innocent: The Story of a Murder, a False Confession, and the Struggle to Free a "Wrong Man."* Upper Falls, Mass.: Brookline, 1996.

———. *Guilty Until Proven Innocent.* New York: Putnam's, 1977.

Connolly, C. P. *The Truth About the Frank Case.* New York: Vail-Ballou, 1915.

Connors, Edward. *Convicted by Juries, Exonerated by Science: Case Studies in the DNA Evidence to Establish Innocence After Trial.* Washington, D.C.: U.S. Department of Justice, Office of Justice Programs, National Institute of Justice, 1996.

Conrad, Earl. *Scottsboro Boy.* Garden City, N.Y.: Doubleday, 1950.

Conser, James. *Law Enforcement in the United States.* Sudbury, Mass.: Jones & Bartlett, 2005.

Conway, James, and Kalish, Bob. *Innocent Son: The True Story Behind the Peter Reilly Case by the Private Eye Who Helped Break It.* Avon, Mass.: Adams Media, 1994.

Cook, Kerry Max. *Chasing Justice: My Story of Freeing Myself After Two Decades on Death Row for a Crime I Didn't Commit*. New York: William Morrow, 2007.

Cooper, Courtney Riley. *Designs in Scarlet*. Boston: Little, Brown, 1939.

_____. *Here's to Crime*. Boston: Little, Brown, 1937.

_____. *Ten Thousand Public Enemies*. Boston: Little, Brown, 1935.

Cooper, Cynthia L. *Mockery of Justice: The True Story of the Sheppard Murder Case*. Boston: Northeastern University Press, 1995.

Cooper, Thomas. *The Mystery of Witchcraft*. London: N. Oakes, 1617.

Coote, A., and Gill, T. *The Rape Controversy*. London: NCCL, 1975.

Coote, Stephen. *Royal Survivor: The Life of Charles II*. New York: St. Martin's, 2000.

Cooter, Roger. *Phrenology in the British Isles: An Annotated Historical Bibliography and Index*. Lanham, Md.: Scarecrow, 1989.

_____. *Phrenology in Europe and America*. New York: Routledge, 2001.

Cortner, Richard. *A "Scottsboro" Case in Mississippi: The Supreme Court and Brown vs. Mississippi*. Jackson: University Press of Mississippi, 1986.

Costello, Peter. *The Real World of Sherlock Holmes: The True Crime Casebooks of Arthur Conan Doyle*. New York: Avalon, 1991.

Coston, Stephen A. *King James VI of Scotland, I of England Unjustly Accused*. St. Petersburg, Fla.: Konigswort, 1996.

Costopoulos, William C. *Principal Suspect*. Philadelphia: Camino, 1996.

Cotta, John. *The Trial of Witchcraft Showing the True and Right Method of Discovery*. London: Samuel Rand, 1616.

Cox, Don Richard. *Arthur Conan Doyle*. New York: Continuum, 1985.

Crenshaw, Files, and Miller, Kenneth A. *Scottsboro: The Firebrand of Communism*. Montgomery, Ala.: Brown, 1936.

Croft, J. Pauline. *King James*. New York: Palgrave Macmillan, 2002.

Crosskey, W. C. S. *The Single Fingerprint Identification System*. San Francisco: Privately printed, 1923.

Crow, W. B. *A History of Magic, Witchcraft, and Occultism*. London: Aquarian, 1968.

Crowther, M. A., and White, B. *On Soul and Conscience: The Medical Expert and Crime*. Aberdeen: Aberdeen University Press, 1998.

Culpin, Howard. *The Newgate Noose*. London: Frederick Muller, 1951.

Cummings, Homer. *Selected Papers*. New York: Scribner's, 1939.

Cummings, Homer, and McFarland, Carl. *Federal Justice: Chapters in the History of Justice in the Federal Executive*. New York: Da Capo, 1970.

Cummins, Harold, and Midlo, Charles. *Finger Prints, Palms, and Soles*. New York: Dover Publications, 1961.

Cuthbert, C. R. M. *Science and the Detection of Crime*. New York: Philosophical Library, 1958.

Cutler, Brian L. *Mistaken Identification: The Eyewitness, Psychology, and the Law*. New York: Cambridge University Press, 1995.

D'Alessandro, Frank M. *The Verdict of History on Sacco and Vanzetti*. New York: Jay Street, 1997.

Darrow, Clarence. *The Story of My Life*. New York: Scribner's, 1932.

_____. *Verdicts Out of Court*. Chicago: Quadrangle, 1963.

Daughen, Joseph R., and Binzen, Peter. *The Cop Who Would Be King: The Honorable Frank Rizzo*. Boston: Little, Brown, 1977.

David, Henry. *The History of the Haymarket Affair*. New York: Farrar & Rinehart, 1936.

Davies, John Dunn. *Phrenology: Fad and Science: A Nineteenth-Century American Crusade*. New Haven, Conn.: Yale University Press, 1955.

Davies, Nick. *White Lies: Rape, Murder & Justice Texas Style*. New York: Avon, 1993.

Davies, Owen, and De Blecourt, Willem, eds. *Beyond the Witch Trials: Witchcraft and Magic in Enlightened Europe*. Manchester, U.K.: Manchester University Press, 2004.

Davies, Reginald Trevor. *Four Centuries of Witch-Beliefs; with Special Reference to the Great Rebellion*. London: Methuen, 1947.

Davis, Kevin. *Defending the Damned: Inside Chicago's Cook County Public Defender's Office*. New York: Atria/Simon & Schuster, 2007.

_____. *The Wrong Man*. New York: Avon, 1996.

Deacon, Richard [Donald McCormick]. *The French Secret Service*. London: Grafton, 1990.

Dedmon, Emmett. *Fabulous Chicago*. New York: Random House, 1953.

De Givry, E. Grillot. *Illustrated Anthology of Sorcery, Magic, and Alchemy*. New York: Causeway, 1973.

_____. *Witchcraft, Magic & Alchemy*. Boston: Houghton Mifflin, 1931.

Delamater, Jerome A. *Representing Sacco and Vanzetti*. New York: Palgrave Macmillan, 2004.

De la Torre, Lillian. *Villainy Detected*. London: D. Appleton-Century, 1947.

Delcambre, Etienne. *Le concept de la sorcellerie dans le Duche de Lorraine*. Nancy: Socit d'Archologie Lorraine, 1948.

Delsohn, Gary. *The Prosecutors: A Year in the Life of a District Attorney's Office*. New York: Dutton, 2003.

Demaris, Ovid. *America the Violent*. New York: Cowles, 1970.

Demos, John Putnam. *Entertaining Satan: Witchcraft and the Culture of Early New England*. New York: Oxford University Press, 1982.

Dempewolf, Richard. *Famous Old New England Murders*. Brattleboro, Vt.: Stephen Daye, 1942.

Derfler, Leslie. *The Dreyfus Affair*. Westport, Conn.: Greenwood Press, 2002.

Derleth, August. *Wisconsin Murders*. Sauk City, Wis.: Mycroft & Moran, 1968.

DeSario, Jack P., and Mason, William D. *Dr. Sam Sheppard on Trial: Case Closed: The Prosecutors and the Marilyn Sheppard Murder*. Kent, Ohio: Kent State University Press, 2003.

Devries, Kelly. *Joan of Arc: A Military Leader*. Gloucestershire, U.K.: Sutton, 2002.

Dewes, Simon. *Doctors of Murder*. London: John Long, 1962.

Dickinson, Alice. *The Sacco and Vanzetti Case, 1920–27: Commonwealth of Massachusetts vs. Nicola Sacco and Bartolomeo Vanzetti*. Danbury, Conn.: Franklin Watts, 1972.

Diefenbach, Johann. *Der Hexenwahn vor und nach der Glaubensspaltung in Deutschland*. Mainz: F. Kirchheim, 1886.

_____. *Der Zauberglaube*. Mainz: F. Kirchheim, 1900.

Dilnot, George. *Rogues' March*. London: Geoffrey Bles, 1934.

Dinnerstein, Leonard. *The Leo Frank Case*. New York: Columbia University Press, 1968.

Dintzer, Lucien. *Nicholas Remy et son oeuvre demonologique*. Lyons: L'imprimerie de Lyon, 1936.

DiStefano, Christopher. *Anything You Say: The True Story of One Man's Ordeal with a Derailed Murder Investigation*. Dunmore, Pa.: Humboldt, 2006.

Doleman, James. *King James I and the Religious Culture of England*. Dover, N.H.: D. S. Brewer, 2000.

Dorr, Lisa Lindquist. *White Women, Rape, and the Power of Race in Virginia, 1900–1960*. Chapel Hill: University of North Carolina Press, 2003.

Dorsey, Hugh M. *Argument of Hugh M. Dorsey, Solicitor General, Atlanta Judicial Circuit, at the Trial of Leo M. Frank, Charged with the Murder of Mary Phagan*. Atlanta, Ga.: Johnson-Dallis, 1914.

Douglas, John, and Olshaker, Mark. *Mind Hunter: Inside the FBI's Elite Serial Crime Unit*. New York: Pocket Books, 1996.

Doyle, Adrian Conan. *The True Conan Doyle*. New York: Coward McCann, 1946.

Doyle, Sir Arthur Conan. *The Case of Oscar Slater*. London: Hodder & Stoughton, 1912.

_____. *The True Crime Files of Sir Arthur Conan Doyle*. New York: Berkley, 2003.

Doyle, James M. *True Witness: Cops, Courts, Science, and the Battle Against Misidentification*. New York: Palgrave Macmillan, 2005.

Drake, Samuel G. *Annals of Witchcraft in New England*. Boston: W. E. Woodward, 1866.

Dreyfus, Alfred. *Five Years of My Life: A Diary of Captain Alfred Dreyfus*. Reprint. Woodstock, N.Y.: Beekman, 1977.

Dreyfus, Mathieu. *L'Affaire telle que je l'ai vecue*. Paris: Grasset, 1978.

Dreyfus, Pierre, ed. *Capitaine Alfred Dreyfus: Souvenirs et correpondence*. Paris: Grasset, 1936.

Duby, Georges. *France in the Middle Ages, 987–1460: From Hugh Capet to Joan of Arc*. Oxford: Blackwell, 1993.

Duke, Thomas S. *Celebrated Criminal Cases of America*. San Francisco: James H. Barry, 1910.

Duke, Winifred, ed. *Six Trials*. London: Victor Gollancz, 1934.

Dunbar, Dorothy. *Blood in the Parlor*. New York: A. S. Barnes, 1964.

Dunn, Jane. *Elizabeth and Mary: Cousins, Rivals, Queens*. New York: Knopf, 2004.

Duples-Agier, H. *Registre criminel du Chatelet de Paris*. Paris: C. Lahure, 1861.

Eames, Hugh. *Sleuths, Inc.* Philadelphia: Lippincott, 1978.

Earley, Pete. *Circumstantial Evidence: Death, Life, and Justice in a Southern Town*. New York: Bantam, 1996.

Edds, Margaret. *An Expendable Man: The Near-Execution of Earl Washington, Jr.* New York: New York University Press, 2003.

Edwards, Alison. *Rape, Racism, and the White Woman's Movement*. Chicago: Sojourner Truth Organization, 1976.

Edwards, Owen Dudley. *The Quest for Sherlock Holmes: A Biographical Study of Arthur Conan Doyle*. Lanham, Md.: Rowman & Littlefield, 1983.

Eggers, Dave. *Surviving Justice: America's Wrongfully Convicted and Exonerated.* San Francisco: McSweeney's, 2005.

Ehrmann, Herbert B. *The Untried Case: The Sacco-Vanzetti Case and the Morelli Gang.* New York: Vanguard, 1933.

Elliott, J. H. *Imperial Spain.* New York: Penguin, 2002.

Elliott, Mabel A. *Conflicting Penal Theories in Statutory Criminal Law.* Chicago: University of Chicago Press, 1931.

———. *Coercion in Penal Treatment.* Ithaca, N.Y.: Pacifist Research Bureau, 1947.

Elliott, Robert G., and Beatty, Albert R. *Agent of Death: The Memoirs of an Executioner.* New York: Dutton, 1940.

Ellis, J. C. *Black Fame: Stories of Crime and Criminals.* London: Hutchinson, 1926.

Emery, Richard W. *Heresy and the Inquisition in Norbonne.* New York: Columbia University Press, 1941.

Endore, Guy. *The Sword of God: Jeanne d'Arc or Joan of Arc.* Belle Fourche, S.D.: Kessinger, 2003.

English, T. J. *Paddy Whacked: The Untold Story of the Irish-American Gangster.* New York: Regan, 2005.

Evans, Humphrey. *The Queen's Man: James Hepburn, Earl of Bothwell, and Duke of Orkney, 1536–1575.* London: Frewin, 1975.

Ewen, Cecil H. L'Estrange. *Some Witchcraft Criticism.* London: Published by author, 1938.

———. *The Trials of John Lowes, Clerk.* London: Published by author, 1937.

———. *Witchcraft and Demonianism.* London: Heath, Crouton, 1933.

———. *Witchcraft in the Norfolk Circuit.* London: Published by author, 1939.

———. *Witchcraft in the Star Chamber.* London: Published by author, 1939.

———. *Witch Hunting and Witch Trials.* New York: Dial, 1930.

Fabian, Robert. *Fabian of the Yard.* London: Naldrett, 1950.

———. *London After Dark.* London: Naldrett, 1954.

Farr, Finnis. *Chicago: A Personal History of America's Most American City.* New Rochelle, N.Y.: Arlington House, 1973.

Fast, Howard Melvin. *The Passion of Sacco and Vanzetti.* New York: Blue Heron, 1953.

Faulds, H. *Guide to Finger Print Identification.* Hanley: Wood, Mitchell, 1905.

———. *A Manual of Practical Dactylography.* London: Police Review, 1923.

Federal Bureau of Investigation. *Classification of Fingerprints.* Washington, D.C.: U.S. Government Printing Office, 1941.

———. *Crime in the United States.* Washington, D.C.: U.S. Government Printing Office, 1983.

———. *Handbook of Forensic Science.* Washington, D.C.: U.S. Government Printing Office, 1984.

———. *Uniform Crime Reports.* Washington, D.C.: U.S. Government Printing Office, n.d.

Feldman, Egal. *Dreyfus Affair and the American Conscience.* Detroit, Mich.: Wayne State University Press, 1981.

Felix, David. *Protest: Sacco-Vanzetti and the Intellectuals.* Bloomington: Indiana University Press, 1965.

Felt, Jeremy P. *Hostages of Fortune.* Ithaca, N.Y.: Cornell University Press, 1965.

Felt, Joseph B. *The Annals of Salem from Its First Settlement.* Salem, Mass.: W. & S. B. Ives, 1827.

Felt, Mark. *The FBI Pyramid.* New York: Putnam's, 1979.

Ferguson, Ian. *The Philosophy of Witchcraft.* London: Harrap, 1924.

Feuerlicht, Roberta Strauss. *Justice Crucified: The Story of Sacco and Vanzetti.* New York: McGraw-Hill, 1977.

Fischlin, Daniel, and Fortier, Mark, eds. *Royal Subjects: Essays on the Writings of James VI and I.* Detroit, Mich.: Wayne State University Press, 2002.

Fisher, David. *Hard Evidence: How Detectives Inside the FBI's SCI-Crime Lab Have Helped Solved America's Toughest Cases.* New York: Simon & Schuster, 1995.

Flinn, John. *A History of the Chicago Police.* Chicago: W. B. Conkey, 1887.

Forster, Joseph. *Studies in Black and Red.* London: Ward & Downey, 1896.

Forth, Christopher. *The Dreyfus Affair and the Crisis of French Manhood.* Baltimore: Johns Hopkins University Press, 2004.

Foucault, Maurice. *Les proces de sorcellerie dans l'ancienne France devant les jurisdictions seculieres.* Paris: Bonvalot-Jouve, 1907.

Fowler, Orson S., and Fowler, Lorenzo N. *Phrenology: A Practical Guide to Your Head.* Broomall, Pa.: Chelsea House, 1980.

Fowler, Samuel Page. *Salem Witchcraft.* Salem, Mass.: H. P. Ives & A. A. Smith, 1861.

Fradella, Sal. *Jack Johnson.* Boston: Branden, 1990.

Fraenkel, Osmond K. *The Sacco and Vanzetti Case.* New York: Alfred A. Knopf, 1931.

Fraioli, Deborah A. *Joan of Arc: The Early Debate.* Rochester, N.Y.: Boydell & Brewer, 2002.

France, Anatole. *The Life of Joan of Arc.* Amsterdam: Fredonia, 2004.

Frank, J., and Frank, B. *Not Guilty.* London: Victor Gollancz, 1957.

Frankfurter, Felix. *The Case of Sacco and Vanzetti.* Boston: Little, Brown & Little, 1927.

Frankfurter, Marion, and Gardner, Jackson, eds. *The Letters of Sacco and Vanzetti.* New York: Viking, 1928.

Fraser, Antonia. *Charles II: His Life and Times.* New York: Orion, 1993.

———. *King James VI of Scotland, I of England.* London: Weidenfeld & Nicolson, 1974.

———. *Mary Queen of Scots.* Reprint. New York: Delta, 1993.

Freeman, Lucy. *Ordeal of Stephen Dennison.* Englewood Cliffs, N.J.: Prentice-Hall, 1970.

Frey, Robert Seitz, and Frey, Nancy Thompson. *The Silent and the Damned: The Murder of Mary Phagan and the Lynching of Leo Frank.* New York: Cooper Square, 2002.

Frisbie, Thomas, and Garrett, Randy. *Victims of Justice Revisited: Completely Updated and Revised.* Evanston, Ill.: Northwestern University Press, 2005.

Fritz, Dennis. *Journey Toward Justice.* Santa Ana, Calif.: Seven Locks Press, 2006.

Frost, Richard H. *The Mooney Case.* Stanford, Calif.: Stanford University Press, 1968.

Furneaux, Rupert. *Courtroom USA–1.* Baltimore: Penguin, 1963.

———. *Courtroom USA–2.* Baltimore: Penguin, 1963.

———. *Famous Criminal Cases, Vols. I–VII.* London: Allan Wingate, 1959.

———. *The Medical Murderer.* London: Elek, 1957.

———. *The World's Most Intriguing True Mysteries.* New York: Arco, 1966.

Gager, Nancy, and Schurr, Cathleen. *Sexual Assault: Confronting Rape in America.* New York: Grosset & Dunlap, 1976.

Gagnon, John H., and Simon, William. *Sexual Conduct: The Social Sources of Human Sexuality.* Chicago: Aldine, 1973.

———. *Sexual Deviance.* New York: Harper & Row, 1967.

———. *The Sexual Scene.* Chicago: Aldine, 1970.

Galton, F. *Fingerprint Directories.* London: Macmillan, 1895.

———. *Finger Prints.* London: Macmillan, 1892.

———. *Hereditary Genius.* London: Macmillan, 1869.

———. *Inquiries into Human Faculty.* New York: Dent, 1906.

———. *Method of Indexing Finger-Marks.* London: Proc. Royal Society of London, 1891.

Garcon, Maurice, ed. *L'Affair Bernardy de Sigoyer.* Paris: Albin Michel, 1948.

———. *The Devil.* Translated by Stephen Haden Guest. New York: Dutton, 1930.

———. *Histoires curieuses.* Paris: A. Fayard, 1959.

Gardner, Erle Stanley. *The Court of Last Resort.* New York: W. Sloane, 1952.

Garinet, Jules. *Histoire de la magie en France.* Paris: Foulon et cie, 1818.

Gaskill, Malcolm. *Witchfinders: A Seventeenth-Century English Tragedy.* Cambridge, Mass.: Harvard University Press, 2005.

Gaule, John. *Select Cases of Conscience Touching Witches and Witchcraft.* London: W. Wilson, Richard Clutterbuck, 1646.

Gemmill, W. N. *Salem Witch Trials.* Chicago: A. C. McClurg, 1924.

Genge, N. E. *The Forensic Casebook.* New York: Ballantine, 2002.

Gentry, Curt. *Frame-Up: The Incredible Case of Tom Mooney and Warren Billings.* New York: Norton, 1967.

Gerber, Jane S. *Jews of Spain: A History of the Sephardic Experience.* New York: Free Press, 1994.

Geter, Lenell. *Overcome, Succeed, and Prosper.* Columbia, S.C.: Marzinza, 2001.

Giannelli, Paul, ed. *Achieving Justice: Freeing the Innocent, Convicting the Guilty.* Chicago: American Bar Association, 2006.

Gibbons, John. *Forensic Linguistics: An Introduction to Language in the Justice System.* London: Blackwell, 2003.

Gies, Frances. *Joan of Arc: The Legend and the Reality.* New York: HarperCollins, 1981.

Gifford, George. *A Dialogue Concerning Witches and Witchcrafts.* London: H. Milford, 1931.

———. *A Discourse of the Subtle Practices of Devils by Witches and Sorcerers.* London: Toby Cooke, 1587.

Ginger, Raymond. *Altgeld's America.* Chicago: Quadrangle, 1965.

Ginzburg, Carlo. *The Night Battles: Witchcraft and Agrarian Cults in the Sixteenth and Seventeenth Century.* Translated by John Tedeschi. Baltimore: Johns Hopkins University Press, 1992.

Gitlitz, David M., and Stavans, Ilan. *Secrecy and Deceit: The Religion of the Crypto Jews.* Albuquerque: University of New Mexico Press, 2002.

Giustino, David D. *Conquest of the Mind: Phrenology and Victorian Social Thought*. Lanham, Md.: Rowman & Littlefield, 1975.

Given, James. *Inquisition and Medieval Society: Power, Discipline, and Resistance in Languedoc*. Ithaca, N.Y.: Cornell University Press, 2001.

Glaister, John. *Final Diagnosis*. London: Hutchinson, 1964.

Glaister, John, and Rentoul, E. *Medical Jurisprudence and Toxicology*. London: Livingstone, 1953.

_____. *The Power of Poison*. New York: William Morrow, 1954.

Glaister, John, and Smith, S. A. *Recent Advances in Forensic Medicine*. London: Churchill, 1931.

Glazer, Nathan. *Twentieth Century Cause Célèbre: Sacco and Vanzetti, Alger Hiss, the Rosenbergs*. Chicago: Regnery, 1983.

Glueck, B. *Studies in Forensic Psychiatry*. London: Heinemann, 1916.

Golden, Harry L. *A Little Girl Is Dead*. New York: World, 1965.

Goldsmith, Gloria. *Rape*. Beverly Hills, Calif.: Wollstonecraft, 1974.

Goldstein, Alan M., and Weiner, Irving B. *Handbook of Psychology, Forensic Psychology*. New York: Wiley, 2003.

Goodman, Derick. *Crime of Passion*. New York: Greenberg, 1958.

_____. *Villainy Unlimited*. London: Elek, 1957.

Goodman, Jonathan. *The Killing of Julia Wallace*. New York: Scribner's, 1969.

_____. *Posts-Mortem: The Correspondence of Murder*. New York: St. Martin's, 1971.

Gordon, Mary. *Joan of Arc*. New York: Viking, 2000.

Gragg, Larry. *The Salem Witch Crisis*. Westport, Conn.: Praeger, 1992.

Greaves, Richard L. *Secrets of the Kingdom: British Radicals from the Popish Plot to the Revolution of 1688–1689*. Stanford, Calif.: Stanford University Press, 1992.

Green, James. *Death in the Haymarket: A Story of Chicago, the First Labor Movement, and the Bombing That Divided Gilded Age America*. New York: Pantheon, 2006.

Green, Samuel Abbot. *Groton in the Witchcraft Times*. Groton, Mass.: J. Wilson, 1883.

Greenwood, William. *Guilty or Not Guilty*. London: Hutchinson, 1931.

Gribble, Leonard. *Stories of Famous Modern Trials*. London: Barker, 1973.

Griffiths, Arthur. *Mysteries of Police and Crime*. Vols. I, II, III. London: Cassell, 1902.

Griffiths, Richard. *Use of Abuse: The Polemics of the Dreyfus Affair and Its Aftermath*. New York: Palgrave Macmillan, 1991.

Griffin, Susan. *Rape*. New York: Harper & Row, 1979.

Grimes, J. Stanley. *The Mysteries of the Head and the Heart Explained: Including an Improved System of Phrenology*. New York: H. A. Sumner, 1881.

Grimshaw, Allen A., ed. *Racial Violence in the United States*. Chicago: Aldine, 1969.

Grisham, John. *The Innocent Man: Murder and Injustice in a Small Town*. New York: Doubleday, 2006.

Gropp, Ignatz. *Collectio Scriptorum et Rerum Wirceburgensium*. Frankfurt: Weidmanniana, 1741–1750.

Groth, A. Nicholas. *Men Who Rape*. London: Plenum, 1980.

Gunther, John. *Taken at the Flood*. New York: Harper, 1960.

Guy, John A. *Queen of Scots: The True Story of Mary Stuart*. Boston: Houghton-Mifflin, 2004.

Haas, Carl. *Die Hexenprozesse: ein cultur-historischer Versuch, nebst Dokumenten*. Tübingen: H. Laupp'sche, 1865.

Hahn, E. *Mary, Queen of Scots*. New York: Random House, 1963.

Halasz, Nicholas. *Captain Dreyfus*. New York: Simon & Schuster, 1955.

Hale, Don. *Town Without Pity: The Fight to Clear Stephen Downing of the Bakewell Murder*. London: Century, 2002.

Hale, John. *A Modest Inquiry into the Nature of Witchcraft and How Persons Guilty of That Crime May Be Convicted*. Boston: B. Eliot, 1702.

_____. *Narratives of the Witchcraft Cases, 1648–1706*. New York: Barnes & Noble, 1959.

Hale, Leslie. *Hanged in Error*. London: Penguin, 1961.

Hall, Benjamin F. *The Trial of William Freeman for the Murder of John G. Van Nest*. Auburn, N.Y.: Derby, Miller, 1848.

Hall, David. *The Faithful Shepherd: A History of the Puritan Ministry in the Seventeenth Century*. Chapel Hill: University of North Carolina Press, 1972.

Hall, Trevor H. *The Late Mr. Sherlock Holmes and Other Literary Studies*. New York: St. Martin's, 1971.

Hamilton, Bernard. *The Medieval Inquisition*. New York: Holmes & Meier, 1982.

_____. *Sherlock Holmes and His Creator*. New York: St. Martin's, 1977.

Hammett, Brian R. *A Concise History of Mexico.* New York: Cambridge University Press, 1999.

Hankins, Leonard. *Nineteen Years Innocent.* New York: Exposition, 1956.

Hansen, Chadwick. *Witchcraft at Salem.* Reprint. New York: Braziller, 1985.

Hansen, Joseph. *Quellen und Untersuchungen zur Geschichte des Hexenwahns und der Hexenverfolgung im Mittelalter.* Bonn: C. Georgi, 1901.

_____. *Westdeutsche Zeitschrift für Geschichte und Kunst.* Trier: F. Lintz, 1882.

_____. *Zauberwahn, Inquisition, und Hexenprozess im Mittelalter.* Munich: R. Oldenbourg, 1900.

Hardwick, Michael. *Doctors on Trial.* London: Herbert Jenkins, 1961.

Hare, Robert D. *Without Conscience: The Disturbing World of the Psychopaths Among Us.* New York: Guilford, 1999.

Harris, Tim. *London Crowds in the Reign of Charles II: Propaganda and the Politics from the Restoration Until the Exclusion Crisis.* New York: Cambridge University Press, 1987.

Harrison, Carter H. *Growing Up with Chicago.* Indianapolis: Bobbs-Merrill, 1944.

_____. *Recollections of Life and Doings in Chicago.* Chicago: Normandie House, 1945.

_____. *Stormy Years.* Indianapolis: Bobbs-Merrill, 1935.

Harrison, George Bagshawe. *Elizabethan Journal, 1591–94.* New York: Cosmopolitan, 1929.

Harrison, Michael. *In the Footsteps of Sherlock Holmes.* London: Cassell, 1958.

_____. *The London of Sherlock Holmes.* New York: Drake, 1972.

_____. *The World of Sherlock Holmes.* New York: Drake, 1973.

Harwick, J. M. D. *The Sherlock Holmes Companion.* London: John Murray, 1962.

Haskins, George Lee. *Law and Authority in Early Massachusetts: A Study in Tradition and Design.* New York: Macmillan, 1960.

Haskins, James. *The Scottsboro Boys.* New York: Henry Holt, 1994.

Hastings, Macdonald. *The Other Mr. Churchill: A Lifetime of Shooting and Murder.* New York: Dodd, Mead, 1963.

Hauben, P. J., ed. *Spanish Inquisition.* New York: Wiley, 1969.

Hauber, Eberhard David. *Bibliotheca, Acta et Scripta Magica.* Lemgo, Germany: J. H. Meyer, 1738.

Hay, Malcolm V. *Jesuits and the Popish Plot.* Belle Fourche, S.D.: Kessinger, 2003.

Hays, Arthur Garfield. *Trial by Prejudice.* New York: Covici, Friede, 1933.

Hazelwood, Robert R., and Burgess, Ann Wolbert, eds. *Practical Aspects of Rape Investigation: A Multidisciplinary Approach.* Boca Raton, Fla.: CRC, 2001.

Hazelwood, Roy, and Michaud, Stephen G. *Dark Dreams: A Legendary FBI Profiler Examines Homicide and the Criminal Mind.* New York: St. Martin's, 2002.

Heaps, Willard A. *Riots U.S.A., 1765–1965.* New York: Seabury, 1966.

Hennen, Gerhard. *Ein Hexenprozess aus der Umgegend von Trier aus dem Jahre 1592.* St. Wendel, Germany: Published by author, 1887.

Henningsen, Gustav. *The Witches Advocate: Basque Witchcraft and the Spanish Inquisition, 1609–1614.* Reno: University of Nevada Press, 1980.

Henson, Allen L. *Confessions of a Criminal Lawyer.* New York: Vantage, 1959.

Heppenstall, Rayner. *Bluebeard and After: Three Decades of Murder in France.* London: Peter Owen, 1972.

_____. *French Crime in the Romantic Age.* London: Hamish Hamilton, 1970.

_____. *A Little Pattern of French Crime.* London: Hamish Hamilton, 1969.

_____. *The Sex War and Others.* London: Peter Owen, 1973.

Herzog, Wilhelm. *From Dreyfus to Petain.* New York: Creative Age, 1947.

Hibbard, Carolyn M. *Charles I and the Popish Plot.* Chapel Hill: University of North Carolina Press, 1983.

Hibbert, Christopher. *The Roots of Evil.* Boston: Little, Brown, 1963.

Hichins, Mark. *Oscar Wilde's Last Chance: The Dreyfus Connection.* Bishop Auckland, U.K.: Pentland, 1999.

Hickey, Eric W. *Sex Crimes and Paraphilia.* Upper Saddle River, N.J.: Prentice-Hall, 2005.

Hicks, John D. *The Populist Revolt.* Minneapolis: University of Minnesota Press, 1931.

Hicks, Seymour. *Not Guilty M'Lord.* London: Cassell, 1939.

Higham, Charles. *The Adventures of Conan Doyle: The Life of the Creator of Sherlock Holmes.* New York: Norton, 1976.

Higham, John. *Strangers in the Land: Patterns of American Nativism, 1860–1925.* New York: Atheneum, 1973.

Hilberman, Elaine. *The Rape Victim*. Washington, D.C.: American Psychiatric Association, 1976.

Hill, Frances. *A Delusion of Satan: The Full Story of the Salem Witch Trials*. Reprint. Cambridge, Mass.: Da Capo, 2002.

_____. *The Salem Witch Trials Reader*. Cambridge, Mass.: Da Capo, 2000.

Hine, Darlene Clark. *The Path to Equality: From the Scottsboro Case to the Breaking of Baseball's Color Barrier*. Broomall, Pa.: Chelsea House, 1995.

Hinton, Kerry. *The Trial of Sacco and Vanzetti: A Primary Source Account*. New York: Rosen, 2002.

Hirsch, James S. *Hurricane: The Miraculous Journey of Rubin Carter*. Boston: Mariner, 2000.

Hodge, Harry. *The Black Maria, or the Criminal's Omnibus*. London: Victor Gollancz, 1935.

_____. *Famous Trials*. Baltimore: Penguin, 1941.

Hoehling, Mary D. *The Real Sherlock Holmes*. New York: Julian Messner, 1965.

Hoffer, Peter Charles. *The Salem Witchcraft Trials: A Legal History*. Lawrence: University Press of Kansas, 1997.

Hoffmann, Charles, and Hoffmann, Tess. *Brotherly Love: Murder and the Politics of Prejudice in Nineteenth-Century Rhode Island*. Amherst: University of Massachusetts Press, 1998.

Hoffman, Frederick J. *The Twenties: American Writing in the Postwar Decade*. New York: Free Press, 1962.

Hoffman, Robert. *More Than a Trial: The Struggle of Captain Dreyfus*. New York: Free Press, 1980.

Hofstadter, Richard, and Wallace, Michael, eds. *American Violence: A Documentary History*. New York: Vintage, 1971.

Holbrook, Richard Melville. *Political Sabotage: The LAPD Experience: Attitudes Toward Understanding Police Use of Force*. Victoria, B.C.: Trafford, 2004.

Hole, Christina. *A Mirror of Witchcraft*. London: Chatto & Windus, 1957.

_____. *Witchcraft in England: Some Episodes in the History of English Witchcraft*. Lanham, Md.: Rowman & Littlefield, 1977.

Holmes, Colin. *Anti-Semitism in British Society, 1876–1939*. London: Edward Arnold, 1979.

Holmes, Ronald M., and Holmes, Stephen T. *Profiling Violent Crimes: An Investigative Tool*. Thousand Oaks, Calif.: Sage, 2002.

Holmes, Stephen T., and Holmes, Ronald M. *Sex Crimes: Patterns and Behavior*. Thousand Oaks, Calif.: Sage, 2001.

Holmes, Thomas James. *Cotton Mather*. Cambridge, Mass.: Harvard University Press, 1940.

_____. *Cotton Mather and His Writings on Witchcraft*. Chicago: University of Chicago Press, 1926.

Holroyd, James Edward. *Baker Street Byways: A Book About Sherlock Holmes*. London: George Allen & Unwin, 1959.

_____. *The Gaslight Murders*. London: George Allen & Unwin, 1960.

_____. *The Sheppard Murder Case*. New York: David McKay, 1961.

Holzer, Hans. *The Truth About Witchcraft*. New York: Doubleday, 1969.

Holzworth, John M. *The Fighting Governor: The Story of William Langer and the State of North Dakota*. New York: Pointer, 1938.

Homza, Lu Ann, ed. *The Spanish Inquisition, 1478–1614: An Anthology of Sources*. Indianapolis: Hackett, 2006.

Hopkins, Ernest Jerome. *Our Lawless Police*. New York: Viking, 1931.

_____. *What Happened in the Mooney Case?* New York: Brower, Warren & Putnam, 1932.

Horne, Gerald. *Powell v. Alabama: The Scottsboro Boys and American Justice*. Danbury, Conn.: Franklin Watts, 1997.

Horne, Jed. *Desire Street: A True Story of Death and Deliverance in New Orleans*. New York: Farrar, Straus & Giroux, 2005.

Horos, Carol. *Rape: The Private Crime, a Social Horror*. New Canaan, Conn.: Tobey, 1974.

Horst, Georg Conrad. *Daemonomagie, oder Geschichte des Glaubens an Zauberei und daemonische Wunder*. Frankfurt: Gebrüdern Wilmans, 1818.

Horswell, John, ed. *The Practice of Crime Scene Investigation*. Boca Raton, Fla.: CRC Press, 2004.

House, Jack. *Square Mile of Murder*. London: W. & R. Chambers, 1961.

Houts, Marshall. *Where Death Delights: The Story of Dr. Milton Helpern and Forensic Medicine*. New York: Dell, 1968.

Howe, Irving, and Coser, Lewis. *The American Communist Party: A Critical History*. New York: Praeger, 1962.

Hubert, René Riese. *The Dreyfus Affair and the French Novel*. Cambridge, Mass.: Harvard University Press, 1951.

Huff, C. Ronald, Rattner, Arye, and Sagarin, Edward. *Convicted But Innocent: Wrongful Conviction and Public Policy*. Thousand Oaks, Calif.: Sage, 2003.

Hughes, Pennethorne. *Witchcraft*. New York: Penguin, 1965.

Hugo, Victor. *Torquemada*. Lanham, Md.: Rowman & Littlefield, 1989.

Humes, Edward. *Mean Justice: A Town's Terror, A Prosecutor's Power, A Betrayal of Innocence*. New York: Pocket Books, 2003.

Humphreys, Sir Travers. *A Book of Trials*. London: William Heinemann, 1953.

_____. *Criminal Days*. London: Hodder & Stoughton, 1946.

Hunt, Henry T. *The Case of Thomas J. Mooney and Warren K. Billings*. New York: C. G. Burgoyne, 1929.

Hunt, Peter. *Oscar Slater: The Great Suspect*. London: Carroll & Nicholson 1951.

Hursch, Carolyn. *The Trouble with Rape*. Chicago: Nelson-Hall, 1977.

Hussey, Robert. *Murderer Scot-Free*. New York: Great Albion Books, 1972.

Hutton, Ronald. *Charles the Second, King of England, Scotland and Ireland*. Oxford: Clarendon, 2000.

Inbau, Fred, and Reid, J. E. *Criminal Interrogations and Confessions*. Baltimore: Williams & Wilkins, 1976.

_____. *Criminal Investigation and Criminal Law*. Radnor, Pa.: Chilton, 1972.

_____, ed. *Criminal Law for the Layman*. Radnor, Pa.: Chilton, 1978.

_____. *Criminal Law for the Police*. Radnor, Pa.: Chilton, 1969.

_____. *Evidence Law for the Police*. Radnor Pa.: Chilton, 1972.

Inbau, Fred, and Reid, J. E. *Lie Detection and Criminal Interrogation*. Baltimore: Williams & Wilkins, 1953.

_____. *Scientific Police Investigation*. Radnor, Pa.: Chilton, 1972.

Inciardi, James A. *Careers in Crime*. Chicago: Rand McNally College, 1975.

_____. *The Drugs-Crime Connection*. Beverly Hills, Calif.: Sage, 1981.

_____. *A History and Sociology of Organized Crime*. Ann Arbor: University of Michigan Microfilms, 1974.

_____. *Radical Criminology*. Beverly Hills, Calif.: Sage, 1980.

_____. *Reflections on Crime*. New York: Holt, Rinehart & Winston, 1979.

_____. *The War on Drugs: Heroin, Cocaine, Crime, and Public Policy*. Palo Alto, Calif.: Mayfield, 1986.

Inciardi, James A., and Chambers, Carl D., eds. *Drugs and the Criminal Justice System*. Beverly Hills, Calif.: Sage, 1974.

Innes, Brian. *The History of Torture*. New York: St. Martin's, 1998.

Irving, Henry Brodribb. *A Book of Remarkable Criminals*. New York: George H. Doran, 1918.

_____. *French Criminals of the Nineteenth Century*. London: William Heinemann, 1901.

Jackson, Brian. *The Black Flag: A Look at the Strange Case of Nicola Sacco and Bartolomeo Vanzetti*. New York: Routledge, 1981.

Jackson, Joseph Henry. *The Portable Murder Book*. New York: Viking, 1945.

Jackson, Kenneth Terry, ed. *The Ku Klux Klan in the City, 1915–1930*. New York: Oxford University Press, 1970.

Jacobs, Janet Liebman. *Hidden Heritage: The Legacy of the Crypto Jews*. Berkeley: University of California Press, 2002.

Jacobs, Sunny. *Stolen Time*. London: Doubleday, 2007.

James I. *Demonology*. Reprint. New York: Book Tree, 2002.

Jasinski, Jana L., and Williams, Linda Meyer. *Partner Violence*. Thousand Oaks, Calif.: Sage, 1998.

Jeans, James W., Sr. *Classics in the Courtroom: The Matter of Sacco and Vanzetti, An Ethical Dilemma*. Minneapolis: Professional Education Group, 1992.

Johnson, Calvin. *Exit to Freedom*. Athens: University of Georgia Press, 2005.

Johnson, Douglas. *France and the Dreyfus Affair*. London: Blandford, 1966.

Johnson, Francis. *Famous Assassinations*. Chicago: A. C. McClurg, 1903.

Johnson, L. F. *Famous Kentucky Tragedies and Trials*. Louisville, Ky.: Baldwin Law Books, 1916.

Johnson, Martin Phillip. *Dreyfus Affair: Honor and Politics in the Belle Epoque*. New York: Palgrave Macmillan, 1999.

Jolly, Karen Louise, Raudvere, Catharina, and Peters, Edward. *Witchcraft and Magic in Europe: The Middle Ages*. Philadelphia: University of Pennsylvania Press, 2002.

Jonas, George, and Amiel, Barbara. *By Persons Unknown*. Toronto: Macmillan, 1977.

Jones, James R. *The First Whigs: The Politics of the Exclusion Crisis, 1678–1683*. New York: Oxford University Press, 1961.

Jones, Richard Glyn, ed. *Unsolved Classic True Murder Cases*. New York: Peter Bedrick, 1987.

Jordan, J. Glenn. *The Unpublished Inside Story of the Famous Scottsboro Case*. Huntsville, Ala.: White, 1932.

Joughin, G. Louis, and Morgan, Edmund M. *The Legacy of Sacco and Vanzetti*. New York: Harcourt, Brace, 1948.

Joyce, Michael. *Edinburgh: The Golden Age*. London: Longman, Green, 1951.

Judson, Horace Freeland. *The Great Betrayal: Fraud in Science*. San Diego: Harcourt, 2004.

Junkin, Tim. *Bloodsworth: The True Story of the First Death Row Inmate Exonerated by DNA*. Chapel Hill, N.C.: Algonquin, 2004.

Kadane, Joseph B., and Schum, David A. *A Probalistic Analysis of the Sacco and Vanzetti Evidence*. New York: Wiley, 1996.

Kamen, Henry. *The Spanish Inquisition: A Historical Revision*. New Haven, Conn.: Yale University Press, 1999.

Kanieski, Colleen Kohler. *Please Pass the Roses*. Middleton, Wis.: Waubesa, 1995.

Karlsen, Carol F. *The Devil in the Shape of a Woman: Witchcraft in Colonial New England*. New York: Norton, 1998.

Karpis, Alvin, and Trent, Bill. *The Alvin Karpis Story*. New York: Coward McCann & Geoghegan, 1971.

Kedward, H. Roderick. *The Dreyfus Affair*. New York: Harper & Row, 1965.

Kennedy, John F. *Profiles in Courage*. New York: Harper, 1956.

Kennedy, Randall. *Race, Crime, and the Law*. New York: Vintage, 1998.

Kenyon, J. P. *The Popish Plot*. New York: Sterling, 2001.

Kerrigan, Michael. *The Instruments of Torture*. Guilford, Conn.: Lyons, 2001.

Kilgallen, Dorothy. *Murder One*. New York: Random House, 1967.

Kingston, Charles. *The Bench & The Dock*. London: Stanley Paul, 1925.

———. *Dramatic Days at the Old Bailey*. New York: Frederick A. Stokes, 1927.

———. *Enemies of Society*. London: Stanley Paul, 1927.

———. *Famous Judges and Famous Trials*. New York: Frederick A. Stokes, 1923.

———. *A Gallery of Rogues*. London: Stanley Paul, 1924.

———. *The Judges and the Judged*. London: John Lane, Bodley Head, 1926.

———. *Law-Breakers*. London: John Lane, Bodley Head, 1930.

———. *Remarkable Rogues: Some Notable Criminals of Europe and America*. New York: John Lane, 1921.

———. *Rogues and Adventuresses*. London: John Lane, Bodley Head, 1928.

Kinkley, Jeffrey. *Chinese Justice, the Fiction: Law and Literature in Modern China*. Stanford, Calif.: Stanford University Press, 2000.

Kishlansky, Mark. *A Monarchy Transformed: Britain, 1603–1714*. New York: Viking, 1996.

Kittredge, George Lyman. *Studies in the History of Religions Presented to Crawford Howell Toy*. New York: Macmillan, 1912.

———. *Witchcraft in Old and New England: The Most Strange and Admirable Discovery of the Three Witches of Warboys*. Cambridge, Mass.: Harvard University Press, 1929.

Klaits, Joseph. *Servants of Satan: The Age of the Witch Hunts*. Bloomington: Indiana University Press, 1987.

Klarman, Michael J. *From Jim Crow to Civil Rights: The Supreme Court and the Struggle for Racial Equality*. New York: Oxford University Press, 2004.

Kleeblatt, Norman L. *Dreyfus Affair: Art, Truth, and Justice*. Berkeley: University of California Press, 1987.

Kneeland, George J. *Commercialized Prostitution in New York City*. Reprint. Montclair, N.J.: Patterson Smith, 1969.

Knights, Mary, et al., eds. *Politics and Opinion in Crisis, 1678–1681*. New York: Cambridge University Press, 1994.

Kobilinsky, Lawrence, Liotti, Thomas F., and Oeser-Sweat, Jamel. *DNA Forensic and Legal Applications*. New York: Wiley, 2004.

Kobler, John. *Some Like It Gory*. New York: Dodd, Mead, 1940.

Konig, David Thomas. *Law and Society in Puritan Massachusetts, Essex County, 1629–1692*. Chapel Hill: University of North Carolina Press, 1979.

Konradi, Amanda. *Taking the Stand: Rape Survivors and Prosecution of Rapists*. Westport, Conn.: Praeger, 2007.

Kors, Alan Charles, and Peters, Edward, eds. *Witchcraft in Europe, 400–1700: A Documentary History*. Philadelphia: University of Pennsylvania Press, 2000.

Krauze, Enrique. *Mexico: Biography of Power: A History of Modern Mexico, 1810–1996*. New York: Perennial, 1998.

Kuebert, Hans. *Zauberwahn, die Greuel der Inquisition und Hexenprozesse*. Munich: Buchhandlung Nationalverein, 1913.

Kunstler, William M. *The Case for Courage*. New York: William Morrow, 1962.

Lace, William W. *Joan of Arc and the Hundred Years' War in World History*. Berkeley Heights, N.J.: Enslow, 2003.

LaGumina, Salvatore J., et al., eds. *The Italian-American Experience: An Encyclopedia*. New York: Garland, 2000.

Lambert, R. S. *When Justice Faltered*. London: Methuen, 1935.

Lamond, John. *Arthur Conan Doyle*. London: John Murray, 1931.

Lamothe-Langon, Etienne Leon de. *Histoire de l'Inquisition en France*. Paris: J. G. Dentu, 1829.

Lamson, David. *We Who Are About to Die*. New York: Scribner's, 1935.

Landsburg, Alan. *In Search of Magic and Witchcraft*. New York: Bantam, 1976.

Lane, Jane. *Titus Oates*. Westport, Conn.: Greenwood, 1971.

Lane, Mark. *Arcadia*. New York: Holt, Rinehart & Winston, 1970.

Larkin, Maurice. *Church and State After the Dreyfus Affair*. New York: Harper & Row, 1974.

Larson, J. A. *A Single Fingerprint System*. New York: D. Appleton, 1924.

Lawson, Deodat. *A Brief and True Narrative*. Boston: Benjamin Harris, 1692.

Lawson, Dorie McCullough. *Along Comes a Stranger*. New York: HarperCollins, 2007. A novel based on the story of fugitive James "Whitey" Bulger.

Lawson, John D., ed. *American State Trials*. 17 vols. St. Louis: Thomas, 1914–1937.

Lazer, David. *DNA and the Criminal Justice System: The Technology of Justice*. Cambridge, Mass.: MIT Press, 2004.

Lea, Henry Charles. *History of the Inquisition of the Middle Ages*. New York: Harper, 1887.

———. *History of the Inquisition in Spain*. New York: Macmillan, 1906.

———. *History of Sacerdotal Celibacy in the Christian Church*. Secaucus, N.J.: University Books, 1966.

———. *Inquisition of the Spanish Dependencies*. Belle Fourche, S.D.: Kessinger, 2003.

———. *Materials Toward a History of Witchcraft*. Philadelphia: University of Pennsylvania Press, 1939.

———. *Minor Historical Writings*. Philadelphia: University of Pennsylvania Press, 1942.

———. *Studies in Church History*. London: S. Low & Son, & Marston, 1869.

———. *Superstitions and Force*. Philadelphia: Published by author, 1866.

Le Bourdais, Isabel. *The Trial of Steven Truscott*. Toronto: McClelland & Stewart, 1966.

Lee, Henry C., and Tirnady, Frank. *Blood Evidence: How DNA Is Revolutionizing the Way We Solve Crimes*. New York: Perseus, 2003.

Lee, Henry C., with Labriola, Jerry. *Famous Crimes Revisited: From Sacco and Vanzetti to O. J. Simpson: Including the Lindbergh Kidnapping, Sam Sheppard, John F. Kennedy, Vincent Foster, and JonBenet Ramsey*. New York: Strong, 2001.

Lee, Henry C., with O'Neil, Thomas W. *Cracking Cases: The Science of Solving Crimes*. Amherst, N.Y.: Prometheus, 2002.

———. *Cracking More Cases: The Science of Solving Crimes*. Amherst, N.Y.: Prometheus, 2004.

Lee, Maurice, Jr. *Great Britain's Solomon: King James VI and I in His Three Kingdoms*. Champaign: University of Illinois Press, 1990.

Leek, Sybil. *Phrenology*. New York: Macmillan, 1970.

Lehr, Dick, and O'Neill, Gerard. *Black Mass: The True Story of an Unholy Alliance Between the FBI and the Irish Mob*. New York: Public Affairs, 2002.

Leibowitz, Robert. *The Defender: The Life and Career of Samuel S. Leibowitz*. Englewood Cliffs, N.J.: Prentice-Hall, 1981.

Leighton, Isabel, ed. *The Aspirin Age, 1919–1941*. New York: Simon & Schuster, 1949.

Leitschuh, Friederich. *Beiträge zur Geschichte des Hexenwesens in Franken*. Bamberg, Germany: C. Hübscher, 1883.

Lerner, L. Scott. *Affaire Dreyfus: Et l'emergence de la France moderne*. Ann Arbor, Mich.: Gale, 1997.

Levack, Brian. *The Witch-Hunt in Early Modern Europe*. New York: Longman, 2006.

Leveritt, Mara. *Devil's Knot: The True Story of the West Memphis Three*. New York: Atria/Simon & Schuster, 2003.

Levin, David. *What Happened in Salem?* New York: Harcourt, Brace, 1956.

Levine, Allan. *Scattered Among the Peoples: The Jewish Dispora in 12 Portraits*. New York: Overlook, 2003.

Levy, Daniel C., Bruhn, Kathleen, and Zabadua, Emilio. *Mexico: The Struggle for Democratic Development*. Berkeley: University of California Press, 2001.

Lewis, Anthony. *Gideon's Trumpet*. New York: Random House, 1964.

Lewis, David L. *Prisoners of Honor: The Dreyfus Affair*. New York: Morrow, 1973.

Lewis, James R. *The Encyclopedia of Cults, Sects, and New Religions*. Amherst, N.Y.: Prometheus, 1998.

Lewis, Jayne Elizabeth. *Mary Queen of Scots: Romance and Nation*: New York: Routledge, 1998.

_____. *The Trial of Mary Queen of Scots: A Brief History with Documents*. New York: Bedford/St. Martin's, 1998.

Lewis, Lloyd, and Smith, Henry Justin. *Chicago: The History of Its Reputation*. New York: Harcourt, Brace, 1929.

*Life and Confessions of Henry Wyatt*. Auburn, N.Y.: J. C. Merrell, 1846.

Limborch, Philip van. *Historia Inquisitionis*. Amsterdam: H. Westenium, 1692.

Lindemann, Albert S. *The Jew Accused: Dreyfus, Beilis, Frank, 1894–1915*. New York: Cambridge University Press, 1991.

Linton, E. Lynn. *Witch Stories*. London: Chatto & Windus, 1883.

Llorente, Juan Antonio. *Histoire critique de l'Inquisition d'Espagne*. Paris: Treuttel et Wurtz, 1817.

Lockridge, Kenneth A. *A New England Town, The First Hundred Years: Dedham, Massachusetts, 1636–1736*. New York: Norton, 1985.

Logan, Guy. *Great Murder Mysteries*. London: Stanley Paul, 1931.

_____. *Guilty or Not Guilty?* London: Stanley Paul, 1928.

Loftus, Elizabeth F. *Eyewitness Testimony*. Cambridge, Mass.: Harvard University Press, 1996.

Lowenherz, David H. *50 Greatest Love Letters of All Time*. New York: Crown, 2002.

Lowenthal, Max. *The Federal Bureau of Investigation*. New York: William Sloane, 1950.

Lucas, A. *Forensic Chemistry and Scientific Criminal Investigation*. New York: Longmans, Green, 1935.

Lucie-Smith, Edward. *Joan of Arc*. New York: Penguin, 2000.

Luhan, Mabel Dodge. *Intimate Memoirs*. 4 vols. New York: Harcourt, Brace, 1933.

Lum, Dyer D. *A Concise History of the Great Trial of the Chicago Anarchists in 1886*. Chicago: Socialistic, 1886.

Lustgarten, Edgar. *The Murder and the Trial*. New York: Scribner's, 1958.

_____. *Verdict in Dispute*. New York: Scribner's, 1950.

_____. *The Woman in the Case*. London: Andre Deutsch, 1955.

Lustig, Nora. *Mexico: The Remaking of an Economy*. Washington, D.C.: Brookings Institution Press, 1998.

Lum, Dyer D. *A Concise History of the Great Trial of the Chicago Anarchists in 1886*. Chicago: Socialistic, 1886.

Lyon, Kathryn. *Witch Hunt: A True Story of Social Hysteria and Abused Justice*. New York: Avon, 1998.

Lyons, Eugene. *Assignment in Utopia*. New York: Harcourt, Brace, 1937.

_____. *The Life and Death of Sacco and Vanzetti*. New York: International, 1927.

McDermott, M. J., and Hindelang, M. J. *Rape Victimization in 26 American Cities*. Washington, D.C.: U.S. Government Printing Office, 1979.

Macdonald, Michael Patrick. *All Souls: A Family Story from Southie*. New York: Ballantine, 2000.

McElwee, William Lloyd. *The Wisest Fool in Christiandom: The Reign of King James I and VI*. Reprint. Westport, Conn.: Greenwood, 1974.

McFall, J. E. W., ed. *Buchanan's Text-Book of Forensic Medicine and Toxicology*. London: Livingstone, 1925.

Macfarlane, A. D. J. *Witchcraft in Tudor and Stuart England*. New York: Harper & Row, 1970.

McGrady, Mike. *Crime Scientists*. Philadelphia: Lippincott, 1961.

Mackenzie, Edward J., and Karas, Phyllis. *Street Soldier: My Life as an Enforcer for Whitey Bulger and the Boston Irish Mob*. New York: Steerforth, 2004.

Mackey, Thomas C. *Red Lights Out: A Legal History of Prostitution, Disorderly Houses, and Vice Districts, 1870–1917*. New York: Garland, 1987.

Maclean, Fitzroy. *Highlanders: A History of the Scottish Clans*. New York: Penguin, 1995.

McLean, George N. *The Rise and Fall of Anarchy in America*. New York: Haskell House, 1973.

Macleod, John. *Dynasty: The Stuarts, 1560–1807*. New York: St. Martin's, 2001.

McCormick, Ken. *Sprung: The Release of Willie Calloway*. New York: St. Martin's, 1964.

McPhaul, John J. *Deadlines and Monkeyshines: The Fabled World of Chicago Journalism*. Englewood Cliffs, N.J.: Prentice-Hall, 1962.

MacRobert, A. E. *Mary Queen of Scots and the Casket Letters*. London: I. B. Tauris, 2002.

Madison, Lucy Foster. *Joan of Arc*. Poughkeepsie, N.Y.: Vivisphere Publishing, 2000.

Mairs, G. T. *Fingerprint Study Data*. New York: Delehanty Institute, 1938.

Maistre, Joseph M. *Letters on the Spanish Inquisition*. New York: Academic Resources, 1977.

Mannix, Daniel P. *The History of Torture*. New York: Dorset, 1986.

Marks, Jeannette. *Thirteen Days*. New York: A. & C. Boni, 1929.

Marsden, John Buxton. *History of the Early Puritans.* London: Hamilton, Adams, 1850.

Marshall, Alan, et al., eds. *Intelligence and Espionage in the Reign of Charles II, 1660–1685.* New York: Cambridge University Press, 2003.

Marshall, F. *A Brief History of Witchcraft with Especial Reference to the Witches of Northamptonshire.* Northampton, U.K.: J. Taylor, 1866.

Marten, Manuel Edward. *The Doctor Looks at Murder.* Garden City, N.Y.: Doubleday, Doran, 1937.

Martinez, Severiano. *Phrenology.* New York: Writer's Club Press, 2001.

Marvin, Abijah P. *Life & Times of Cotton Mather.* New York: Haskell House, 1972.

Marx, Jean. *L'Inquisition en Dauphine.* Paris: E. Champion, 1913.

Maschke, Karen. *The Legal Response to Violence Against Women.* New York: Routledge, 1997.

Massachusetts General Court. *Record of Public Hearing before Joint Committee on the Judiciary of Massachusetts Legislature on the Resolution . . . Recommending a Posthumous Pardon for Nichola Sacco and Bartolomeo Vanzetti.* Boston: Boston Committee for the Vindication of Sacco and Vanzetti, 1959.

Masters, Anthony. *The Devil's Dominion: The Complete Story of Hell and Satanism in the Modern World.* New York: Putnam's, 1978.

Masters, R. E. L., and Lea, Eduord. *Perverse Crimes in History.* New York: Julian, 1963.

Mather, Cotton. *Diary of Cotton Mather.* Reprint. Whitefish, Mont.: Kessinger, 2006.

_____. *On Witchcraft.* Reprint. Mineola, N.Y.: Dover, 2005.

_____. *Wonders of the Invisible World: Being an Account of the Trials of Several Witches Lately Executed in New England.* Reprint. Whitefish, Mont.: Kessinger, 2003.

Maule, Thomas. *New England's Persecutors Mauled with Their Own Weapons.* New York: William Bradford, 1697.

_____. *The Truth Held Forth and Maintained.* New York: William Bradford, 1695.

Maxwell-Stuart, P. G. *An Abundance of Witches: The Great Scottish Witch-Hunt.* Stroud, U.K.: Tempus, 2005.

Medea, Andrea, and Thompson, Kathleen. *Against Rape.* New York: Farrar, Straus & Giroux, 1974.

Meadows, Robert J. *Evil Minds: Understanding and Responding to Violent Predators.* Upper Saddle River, N.J.: Prentice-Hall, 2004.

Meili, Trisha. *I Am the Central Park Jogger: A Story of Hope and Possibility.* New York: Scribner's, 2004.

Mello, Michael A. *Dead Wrong: A Death Row Lawyer Speaks Out Against Capital Punishment.* Madison: University of Wisconsin Press, 1997.

_____. *The Wrong Man: A Story of Innocence on Death Row.* Minneapolis: University of Minnesota Press, 2001.

Melnick, Jeffrey. *Black-Jewish Relations on Trial: Leo Frank and Jim Conley in the New South.* Jackson: University Press of Mississippi, 2000.

Meltzer, Francois. *For Fear of the Fire: Joan of Arc and the Limits of Subjectivity.* Chicago: University of Chicago Press, 2001.

Melville, Lewis, and Hargreaves, Reginald. *Famous Duels and Assassinations.* New York: J. H. Sears, 1930.

Mencken, August. *By the Neck.* New York: Hastings House, 1942.

Mencken, H. L. *The Days of H. L. Mencken (Heathen Days: 1890–1936).* New York: Alfred A. Knopf, 1947.

Messick, Hank. *Syndicate in the Sun.* New York: Macmillan, 1968.

Messick, Hank, and Goldblatt, Burt. *Kidnapping.* New York: Dial, 1974.

Moenssens, Andre A. *Fingerprint Techniques.* Radnor, Pa.: Chilton, 1971.

Michelet, Jules. *Histoire de France.* 5 vols. Paris: Hetzel et cie, 1870.

_____. *Joan of Arc.* Translated by Albert Gurard. Ann Arbor: University of Michigan Press, 1957.

_____. *La Sorciere.* Paris: Librairie Marcel Didier, 1952.

_____. *Satanism and Witchcraft.* Translated by A. R. Allinson. New York: Citadel, 1930.

Middlekauff, Robert. *The Mathers: Three Generations of Puritan Intellectuals, 1596–1728.* New York: Oxford University Press, 1971.

Miller, John. *Popery and Politics in England, 1660–1688.* New York: Cambridge University Press, 1973.

_____. *The Restoration and the England of Charles II.* London: Longman, 1997.

Miller, Perry. *The New England Mind: From Colony to Province.* Cambridge, Mass.: Harvard University Press, 1954.

_____. *The New England Mind: The Seventeenth Century.* Cambridge, Mass.: Harvard University Press, 1953.

Miller, Perry, and Johnson, T. H. *The Puritans.* New York: American Book, 1938.

Mitchell, C. Ainsworth. *Science and the Criminal.* London: Pitman, 1911.

_____. *The Scientific Detective and the Expert Witness.* London: Heffer, 1931.

Mitchell, Edwin Valentine, ed. *The Newgate Calendar.* Garden City, N.Y.: Doubleday, 1926.

Moiseiwitsch, Maurice. *Five Famous Trials.* New York: New York Graphic Society, 1962.

Molinier, Charles. *L'Inquisition dans le midi de la France au xiii et au xiv siecle.* Paris: Sandoz & Fischbacher, 1880.

Monter, E. William, et al., eds. *Frontiers of Heresy: The Spanish Inquisition from the Basque Lands to Sicily.* New York: Cambridge University Press, 2003.

Montgomery, Robert H. *Sacco-Vanzetti: The Murder and the Myth.* New York: Devin-Adair, 1960.

Moore, James P. *Human Sacrifice.* Vancouver, B.C.: Blackberry, 2006.

Moorehead, Caroline. *Hostages to Fortune.* New York: Atheneum, 1980.

Morain, Alfred. *The Underground of Paris.* Reprint. New York: Blue Ribbon, 1931.

Morgan, John. *Prince of Crime.* New York: Stein & Day, 1985.

Morland, Nigel. *Background to Murder.* London: Werner Laurie, 1955.

———. *Pattern of Murder.* London: Elek, 1966.

———. *Science in Crime Detection.* London: Robert Hale, 1958.

Morris, Douglas G. *Justice Imperiled: The Anti-Nazi Lawyer Max Hirschberg in Weimar Germany.* Ann Arbor: University of Michigan Press, 2005.

Morris, Stephen D. *Corruption and Politics in Contemporary Mexico.* Tuscaloosa: University of Alabama Press, 1991.

Mudge, Zachariah Atwell. *Witch Hill: A History of Salem Witchcraft.* New York: Carlton & Lanahan, 1870.

Musmanno, Michael A. *After Twelve Years.* New York: Alfred A. Knopf, 1939.

———. *Verdict!* Garden City, N.Y.: Doubleday, 1958.

Nash, Jay Robert. *Almanac of World Crime.* New York: Doubleday, 1981.

———. *Among the Missing: An Anecdotal History of Missing Persons from the 1800s to the Present.* New York: Simon & Schuster, 1978.

———. *Bloodletters and Badmen: A Narrative Encyclopedia of American Criminals from the Pilgrims to the Present.* New York: M. Evans, 1973.

———. *Citizen Hoover: A Critical Study of the Life and Times of J. Edgar Hoover and His FBI.* Chicago: Nelson-Hall, 1972.

———. *Darkest Hours: A Narrative Encyclopedia of Worldwide Disasters from Ancient Times to the Present.* Chicago: Nelson-Hall, 1976.

———. *Dictionary of Crime.* New York: Paragon, 1992.

———. *Encyclopedia of Western Lawmen and Outlaws.* New York: Paragon, 1992.

———. *Encyclopedia of World Crime.* 8 vols., 1990–1999. Wilmette, Ill.: History, Inc., 1999.

———. *The Great Pictorial History of World Crime.* 2 vols. Wilmette, Ill.: History, Inc., 2004.

———. *Hustlers and Con Men: An Anecdotal History of the Confidence Man and His Games.* New York: M. Evans, 1976.

———. *The Innovators: Sixteen Portraits of the Famous and Infamous.* Chicago: Regnery Gateway, 1982.

———. *Jay Robert Nash's Crime Chronology: A Worldwide Record, 1900–1983.* New York: Facts on File, 1984.

———. *Look for the Woman: A Narrative Encyclopedia of Female Poisoners, Kidnappers, Thieves, Extortionists, Terrorists, Swindlers, and Spies from Elizabethan Times to the Present.* New York: M. Evans, 1981.

———. *The Motion Picture Guide.* 17 vols. Chicago: Cinebooks, 1985–1990.

———. *Murder, America: Homicide in the United States from the Revolution to the Present.* New York: Simon & Schuster, 1980.

———. *Murder Among the Mighty: Celebrity Slayings That Shocked America.* New York: Delacorte, 1983.

———. *Open Files: A Narrative Encyclopedia of the World's Greatest Unsolved Crimes.* New York: McGraw-Hill, 1983.

———. *People to See: An Anecdotal History of Chicago's Makers and Breakers.* Piscataway, N.J.: New Century, 1981.

———. *Spies: A Narrative Encyclopedia of Dirty Tricks and Double Dealing from Biblical Times to Today.* New York: M. Evans, 1997.

———. *Terrorism in the Twentieth Century: A Narrative Encyclopedia from the Anarchists Through the Weathermen to the Unabomber.* New York: M. Evans, 1998.

———. *World Encyclopedia of Organized Crime.* New York: Paragon, 1992.

———. *World Encyclopedia of Twentieth-Century Murder.* New York: Paragon, 1992

———. *Zanies: The World's Greatest Eccentrics.* Piscataway, N.J.: New Century, 1982.

Nash-Marshall, Siobhan. *Joan of Arc: A Spiritual Biography.* New York: Crossroad, 1999.

Naylor, M. J. *Four Sermons Preached at All Saints Church, Huntingdon, on the 25th Day of March 1792-3-4-5: The Inanity and Mischief of Vulgar Superstitions.* Cambridge, U.K.: J. Deighton & W. H. Lunn, 1795.

Neal, Daniel. *The History of the Puritans.* London: R. Hett, 1732.

Nee, Patrick. *A Criminal and an Irishman: The Inside Story of the Boston Mob–IRA Connection.* New York: Steerforth, 2006.

Neff, James. *The Wrong Man: The Final Verdict on the Dr. Sam Sheppard Murder Case.* New York: Random House, 2002.

Nelson, Jill, ed. *Police Brutality: An Anthology.* New York: Norton, 2001.

Netanyahu, B. *The Origins of the Inquisition in Fifteenth-Century Spain.* New York: New York Review of Books, 2001.

Neville, John F. *Twentieth-Century Cause Célèbre: Sacco, Vanzetti, and the Press.* Westport, Conn.: Praeger, 2004.

Nevins, Winfield Scott. *Witchcraft in Salem Village in 1692.* Boston: Lee & Shepard, 1892.

Newby, Richard. *Kill Now, Talk Forever: Debating Sacco and Vanzetti.* Bloomington, Ind.: Authorhouse, 2002.

Nickell, Joe, and Fischer, John F. *Crime Science: Methods of Forensic Detection.* Lexington: University Press of Kentucky, 1999.

Nixon, Edna. *Voltaire and the Calas Case.* London: Victor Gollancz, 1961.

Noble, John Wesley, and Averbuch, Bernard. *Never Plead Guilty: The Story of Jake Ehrlich.* New York: Farrar, Strauss, Cudahy, 1955.

Nolan, William A. *Communism Versus the Negro.* Chicago: Henry Regnery, 1951.

Nordon, Pierre. *Conan Doyle: A Biography.* New York: Holt, Rinehart & Winston, 1966.

Norris, Clarence, and Washington, Sybil D. *The Last of the Scottsboro Boys.* New York: Putnam's, 1979.

Norton, Mary Beth. *In the Devil's Snare: The Salem Witchcraft Crisis of 1692.* Reprint. New York: Vintage, 2003.

Notestein, W. *A History of English Witchcraft from 1558–1718.* Washington, D.C.: American Historical Association, 1911.

O'Brien, John Anthony. *The Inquisition: A Tragic Mistake.* New York: Macmillan, 1973.

O'Dell, Stackpole E. *Phrenology: Essays and Studies.* London: London Phrenological Institution, 1899.

O'Donnell, Bernard. *Great Thames Mysteries.* London: Harrap, 1965.

———. *The Old Bailey and Its Trials.* London: Clerke & Cockeran, 1950.

———. *Should Women Hang?* London: W. H. Allen, 1956.

———. *The Trials of Mr. Justice Avory.* London: Rich & Cowan, 1935.

———. *The World's Strangest Murders.* London: Frederick Muller, 1957.

Ogg, David. *England in the Reign of Charles II.* New York: Oxford University Press, 1984.

Oldridge, D. *The Witchcraft Reader.* New York: Routledge, 2001.

Ollard, Richard Lawrence. *The Image of the King: Charles I and Charles II.* New York: Phoenix, 2001.

Olsen, Jack. *Last Man Standing: The Tragedy and Triumph of Geronimo Pratt.* New York: Anchor, 2001.

———. *Predator: Rape, Madness & Injustice in Seattle.* New York: Delacorte, 1991.

O'Neill, Gerard, and Lehr, Dick. *The Underboss: The Rise and Fall of a Mafia Family.* New York: Public Affairs, 2002.

Oney, Steve. *And the Dead Shall Rise: The Murder of Mary Phagan and the Lynching of Leo Frank.* New York: Pantheon, 2003.

Oppenheimer, Andres. *Bordering on Chaos: Mexico's Roller-Coaster Journey Toward Prosperity.* New York: Little, Brown, 1996.

Paget, R. T., and Silverman, Sydney. *Hanged—And Innocent?* London: Victor Gollancz, 1953.

Paleologue, Georges Maurice. *An Intimate Journal of the Dreyfus Case.* Reprint. Westport, Conn.: Greenwood, 1975.

Palfrey, John Goodman. *History of New England During the Stewart Dynasty.* Boston: Little, Brown, 1897.

Paolantonio, S. A. *Frank Rizzo.* Philadelphia: Camino, 1994.

Pardue, Michael, and Pardue, Becky. *Freeing the Innocent: How We Did It.* Seattle: Justice Denied, 2001.

Park, W., and Doyle, Sir Arthur Conan. *The Truth About Oscar Slater: With the Prisoner's Own Story.* London: Psychic, 1927.

Parloff, Roger. *Triple Jeopardy: A Story of Law and Its Best—And Worst.* Boston: Little, Brown, 1996.

Parminter, Geoffrey de C. *Reasonable Doubt.* London: Arthur Baker, 1938.

Parrinder, Geoffrey. *Witchcraft: European and African.* Baltimore: Penguin, 1958.

Parry, Sir Edward Abbott. *The Drama of the Law.* New York: Scribner's, 1924.

Parry, Dr. Leonard. *Some Famous Medical Trials.* London: Churchill, 1927.

Pascal, Janet B. *Arthur Conan Doyle: Beyond Baker Street.* New York: Oxford University Press, 2000.

Pearce, Charles. *Unsolved Murder Mysteries.* New York: Stokes, 1924.

Pearson, Edmund. *Five Murders.* Garden City, N.Y.: Doubleday, Doran, 1928.

_____. *Instigation of the Devil.* New York: Scribner's, 1930.

_____. *Masterpieces at Murder.* Boston: Little, Brown, 1924.

_____. *More Studies in Murder.* New York: Smith & Haas, 1936.

_____. *Murder at Smutty Nose and Other Murders.* Garden City, N.Y.: Doubleday, 1927.

_____. *Studies in Murder.* New York: Macmillan, 1924.

Pekkanen, John. *Victims: An Account of Rape.* New York: Popular Library, 1976.

Pendergrast, Mark. *Victims of Memory: Sex Abuse Accusations and Shattered Lives.* Hinesburg, Vt.: Upper Access, 1996.

Perez, Joseph. *The Spanish Inquisition: A History.* Translated by Janet Lloyd. New Haven, Conn.: Yale University Press, 2006.

Perkins, William. *A Discourse of the Damned Art of Witchcraft.* Cambridge, U.K.: Thomas Pickering, 1608.

Perley, Sidney. *The History of Salem, Massachusetts.* Salem, Mass.: Published by author, 1924.

Pernoud, Regine. *Joan of Arc: By Herself and Her Witnesses.* Chelsea, Mich.: Scarborough House, 1994.

Perske, Robert. *Deadly Innocence?* New York: Abingdon, 1995.

Peters, Edward. *Heresy and Authority in Medieval Europe: Documents in Translation.* Philadelphia: University of Pennsylvania Press, 1980.

_____. *Inquisition.* Berkeley: University of California Press, 1989.

Pfeffer, Leo. *This Honorable Court.* Boston: Beacon, 1965.

Pfister, Christian. *Nicolas Remy et la sorcelliere en Lorraine a la fin du XVI siecle.* Paris: n.p., 1907.

Phillips, James Duncan. *Salem in the Seventeenth Century.* Boston: Houghton Mifflin, 1933.

Pierce-Baker, Charlotte. *Surviving the Silence: Black Women's Stories of Rape.* New York: Norton, 2000.

Pitts, John Linwood. *Witchcraft and Devil Lore in the Channel Islands.* Guernsey, Canada: Guille-Allès Library, 1886.

Plaidy, Jean. *The Lady in the Tower: The Wives of Henry VIII.* New York: Three Rivers / Crown, 2003.

_____. *Mary Queen of Scots: The Fair Devil of Scotland.* New York: Putnam's, 1975.

_____. *Spanish Inquisition.* Albuquerque, N.M.: Trans-Atlantic, 1978.

Plowden, Alison. *Two Queens in One Isle: The Deadly Relationship of Elizabeth I and Mary, Queen of Scots.* Gloucestershire, U.K.: Sutton, 1999.

Pollack, Jack Harrison. *Dr. Sam: An American Tragedy.* Chicago: Regnery, 1972.

Pollen, John Hungerford. *Mary Queen of Scots and the Babington Plot.* Edinburgh: University of Edinburgh, 1922.

Ponzinibio, Giovanni Francesco. *Subtilis et Utilis Tractatus de Lamiis.* N.p., n.d.

Porch, Douglas. *The French Secret Service: From the Dreyfus Affair to the Gulf War.* New York: Farrar, Straus & Giroux, 1995.

Potter, Arthur Gray. *I Can Go Home Again.* Chapel Hill: University of North Carolina Press, 1943.

Potter, John. *The Tangled Web.* Middleton, Wis.: Waubesa, 1993.

Potter, John Deane. *The Art of Hanging.* New York: A. S. Barnes, 1969.

_____. *Scotland Yard.* London: Burke, 1972.

Potts, Thomas. *The Trial of the Lancaster Witches.* London: P. Davies, 1929.

_____. *The Wonderful Discovery of the Witches in the County of Lancaster.* London: John Barnes, 1613.

Powers, Edwin. *Crime and Punishment in Early Massachusetts.* Boston: Beacon, 1966.

Powers, Richard Gid. *Secrecy and Power: The Life of J. Edgar Hoover.* New York: Free Press, 1987.

Pratt, Sister Antoinette Marie. *Attitude of the Catholic Church to Witchcraft.* Washington, D.C.: National Capital Press, 1915.

Prejean, Helen. *The Death of Innocents: An Eyewitness Account of Wrongful Executions.* New York: Vintage, 2006.

Protess, David, and Warden, Rob. *Gone in the Night: The Dowaliby Family's Encounter with Murder and the Law.* New York: Delacorte, 1993.

_____. *A Promise of Justice: The Eighteen-Year Fight to Save Four Innocent Men.* New York: Hyperion, 1998.

Purcell, Catherine, and Arrigo, Bruce A. *The Psychology of Lust Murder: Paraphilia, Sexual Killing, and Serial Homicide.* San Diego: Academic, 2006.

Purkiss, Diane. *At the Bottom of the Garden: A Dark History of Fairies, Hobgoblins, Nymphs, and Other Troublesome Things.* New York: New York University Press, 2001.

_____. *The English Civil War: Papists, Gentlewomen, Soldiers, and Witchfinders in the Birth of Modern Britain.* New York: Basic, 2006.

_____. *The Witch in History: Early Modern and Twentieth Century Representation.* New York: Routledge, 1996.

Putnam, Allen. *Witchcraft of New England Explained by Modern Spiritualism.* Boston: Colby & Rich, 1888.

Pyrek, Kelly. *Forensic Science Under Siege: The Challenges of Forensic Laboratories and the Medico-Legal Investigation System.* San Diego: Academic, 2007.

Raab, Selwyn. *Justice in the Back Room.* New York: World, 1967.

Rabinowitz, Dorothy. *No Crueler Tyrannies: Accusation, False Witness, and Other Terrors of Our Times.* New York: Free Press, 2004.

Raby, R. Cornelius. *Fifty Famous Trials.* Washington, D.C.: Washington Law Books, 1937.

Radelet, Michael L., Bedau, Hugo Adam, and Putnam, Constance E. *In Spite of Innocence: Erroneous Convictions in Capital Cases.* Boston: Northeastern University Press, 1994.

Ramsland, Katherine. *The Forensic Science of C.S.I.* New York: Berkley Boulevard Books, 2001.

_____. *The Science of Cold Case Files.* New York: Berkley Boulevard Books, 2004.

Radin, Edward D. *The Innocents.* New York: William Morrow, 1964.

Radzinowicz, Leon, and Wolfgang, Marvin E., eds. *Crime and Justice.* 3 vols. New York: Basic, 1971.

_____. *Crime and Society.* New York: Basics, 1977.

Radzinowicz, Leon, and Hood, Roger. *Criminology and the Administration of Criminal Justice.* London: Mansen Information, 1976.

Radzinowicz, Leon, and King, Joan. *The Growth of Crime.* New York: Basic Books, 1977.

_____. *A History of English Criminal Law and Its Administration from 1750.* 4 vols. London: Stevens, 1948–1968.

_____. *Ideology and Crime.* New York: Columbia University Press, 1966.

_____. *In Search of Criminology.* Cambridge, Mass.: Harvard University Press, 1962.

_____, and Turner, J. W. C., eds. *The Modern Approach to Criminal Law: English Studies in Criminal Science.* London: Macmillan, 1945.

_____, ed. *Sexual Offences.* London: Macmillan, 1957.

_____. *Sir James F. Stephens and His Contributions to the Development of Criminal Law.* London: B. Quaritch, 1957.

Ranalli, Ralph. *Deadly Alliance: The FBI's Secret Partnership with the Mob.* New York: Harper, 2001.

Randel, William Pierce. *The Ku Klux Klan: A Century of Infamy.* New York: Chilton, 1965.

Rascoe, Burton. *The Case of Leo Frank: A Factual Review of One of the Most Sensational Murder Cases in Court Annals.* Girard, Kan.: Haldeman-Julius, 1947.

Raviart, Georges. *Sorcières et possédées.* Lille: E. Raoust, 1936.

Rawlings, Helen. *The Spanish Inquisition.* Oxford: Blackwell, 2005.

Read, Conyers. *Mr. Secretary Walsingham and the Policy of Queen Elizabeth.* Cambridge, Mass.: Harvard University Press, 1925.

Reid, Ed. *Mafia.* New York: Random House, 1952.

Reinach, Joseph. *Histoire de l'affaire Dreyfus.* 7 vols. Paris: Fasquelle, 1901–1911.

Reis, Elizabeth. *Damned Women: Sinners and Witches in Puritan New England.* Ithaca, N.Y.: Cornell University Press, 1999.

Remy, Nicholas. *Demonolatry.* Secaucus, N.J.: University Books, 1947.

*Report on the Trial of Henry Wyatt.* Auburn, N.Y.: J. C. Derby, 1846.

Ressler, Robert K., and Schachtman, Thomas. *Whoever Fights Monsters: My Twenty Years Tracking Serial Killers for the FBI.* New York: St. Martin's, 1993.

Reppetto, Thomas A. *The Blue Parade.* New York: Free Press, 1978.

_____. *NYPD: A City and Its Police.* New York: Henry Holt, 2001.

Reynolds, Quentin R. *Courtroom: The Story of Samuel S. Leibowitz.* New York: Farrar, Straus & Cudahy, 1950.

_____. *Police Headquarters.* New York: Harper, 1955.

Rhodes, Henry Taylor-Fowkes. *Alphonse B. Bertillon.* New York: Abelard-Schumann 1956.

_____. *Clues and Crime.* London: John Murray, 1933.

_____. *The Criminals We Deserve.* London: Methuen, 1937.

_____. *In the Tracks of Crime.* London: Turnstile, 1952.

_____. *The Satanic Mass: A Sociological and Criminological Study.* London: Rider, 1954.

_____. *Science and the Police Officer.* London: Police Chronicle, 1934.

Rice, Craig. *45 Murderers.* New York: Simon & Schuster, 1952.

Richards, Jeffrey. *Sex, Dissidence, and Damnation: Minority Groups in the Middle Ages.* New York: Routledge, 1994.

Richey, Stephen W. *Joan of Arc: The Warrior Saint.* Westport, Conn.: Praeger, 2003.

Roach, Marilynne K. *The Salem Witch Trials: A Day-by-Day Chronicle of a Community Under Siege.* Philadelphia: Taylor, 2004.

Robbins, Russell Hope. *The Encyclopedia of Witchcraft and Demonology.* New York: Bonanza, 1981.

Roberts, C. E. B. *The New World of Crime: Famous American Trials.* London: Burrows, Eyre & Spottiswoode, 1933.

Roberts, Mary Louise, ed. *Disruptive Acts: The New Women in Fin-de-Siecle France.* Chicago: University of Chicago Press, 2002.

Roberts, Randy. *Papa Jack: Jack Johnson and the Era of White Hopes.* New York: Free Press, 1985.

Robertson, James R., Ross, A. M., and Burgoyne, L., eds. *DNA in Forensic Science.* Boca Raton, Fla.: CRC, 1990.

Robertson, Stephen. *Crimes Against Children: Sexual Violence and Legal Culture in New York City, 1880–1960.* Chapel Hill: University of North Carolina Press, 2005.

Robinson, Henry Morton. *Science Catches the Criminal.* Indianapolis: Bobbs-Merrill, 1935.

Rochester, Anna. *The Populist Movement in the United States.* New York: International, 1943.

Rodell, Marie F., ed. *Boston Murders.* New York: Duell, Sloan & Pearce, 1948.

———. *Charleston Murders.* New York: Duell, Sloan & Pearce, 1947.

———. *Chicago Murders.* New York: Duell, Sloan & Pearce, 1945.

———. *Cleveland Murders.* New York: Duell, Sloan & Pearce, 1947.

———. *Denver Murders.* New York: Duell, Sloan & Pearce, 1946.

———. *Detroit Murders.* New York: Duell, Sloan & Pearce, 1948.

———. *Los Angeles Murders.* New York: Duell, Sloan & Pearce, 1947.

———. *New York Murders.* New York: Duell, Sloan & Pearce, 1944.

———. *San Francisco Murders.* New York: Duell, Sloan & Pearce, 1947.

Roediger, David R., and Rosemont, Franklin. *Haymarket Scrapbook.* Chicago: Charles H. Kerr, 1986.

Roper, Lyndal. *Witch Craze: Terror and Fantasy in Baroque Germany.* New Haven, Conn.: Yale University Press, 2006.

Rosen, Barbara. *Witchcraft in England, 1558–1618.* Boston: University of Massachusetts Press, 1991.

Rosenfeld, Daniel. *The Fall of the Spanish Inquisition.* N. p., 2002.

Rosenthal, Bernard. *Salem Story: Reading the Witch Trials of 1692.* New York: Cambridge University Press, 1995.

Roth, Cecil. *Spanish Inquisition.* New York: Norton, 1996.

Roughead, William. *Classic Crimes.* London: Cassell, 1951.

———. *The Murderer's Companion.* New York: Readers Club, 1941.

———. *Trial of Oscar Slater: Notable British Trials.* Edinburgh: Hodge, 1910.

Rowan, David. *Famous American Crimes.* London: Frederick Muller, 1957.

———. *Famous European Crimes.* London: Frederick Muller, 1956.

Rowland, John. *Criminal Files.* London: Arco, 1957.

———. *More Criminal Files.* London: Arco, 1958.

———. *Murder by Persons Unknown.* London: Mellifont, 1941.

———. *Murder Mistaken.* London: J. Long, 1963.

———. *The Wallace Case.* London: Carroll & Nicholson, 1949.

Rowley, William, Dekker, Thomas, and Ford, John. *The Witch of Edmonton.* Manchester, U.K.: Manchester University Press, 1999.

Rudin, Norah, and Inman, Keith. *An Introduction to Forensic DNA Analysis.* Boca Raton, Fla.: CRC, 2001.

Russell, Donn, ed. *Best Murder Cases.* London: Faber & Faber, 1958.

Russell, Francis. *Sacco and Vanzetti: The Case Resolved.* New York: HarperCollins, 1986.

———. *Tragedy in Dedham.* New York: McGraw-Hill, 1962.

Russell, Guy. *Guilty or Not Guilty?* London: Hutchinson, 1931.

Russell, Jeffrey B. *A History of Witchcraft, Sorcerers, Heretics, and Pagans.* London: Thames & Hudson, 1982.

Sabatini, Rafael. *Torquemada and the Spanish Inquisition.* Belle Fourche, S.D.: Kessinger, 2003.

Sacco, Nicola, and Vanzetti, Bartolomeo. *The Letters of Sacco and Vanzetti.* New York: Penguin, 1997.

*The Sacco-Vanzetti Case: Transcript of the Record of the Trial.* New York: Henry Holt, 1928–1929.

Sackville-West, Vita. *Saint Joan of Arc.* New York: Doubleday, Doran, 1936.

Saferstein, R. *Criminalistics: An Introduction to Forensic Science.* Englewood Cliffs, N.J.: Prentice-Hall, 1977.

Salter, Anna C. *Predators: Pedophiles, Rapists, and Other Sex Offenders.* New York: Basic, 2004.

Samenow, Stanton. *Inside the Criminal Mind.* New York: Crown, 2004.

Samuels, Charles, and Samuels, Louise. *Night Fell on Georgia.* New York: Dell, 1956.

Sanders, Bruce. *Murder Behind the Bright Lights.* London: Herbert Jenkins, 1958.

_____. *Murder in Big Cities.* New York: Roy, 1962.

_____. *Murder in Lonely Places.* London: Jenkins, 1960.

Savino, John O., and Turvey, Brent E. *Rape Investigation Handbook.* San Diego: Academic, 2004.

Sayer, James Edward. *Clarence Darrow: Public Advocate.* Dayton, Ohio: Wright State University, 1978.

Sayers, Dorothy L. *Tales of Detection, Mystery, and Horror.* London: Gollancz, 1928.

Schaack, Michael J. *Anarchy and the Anarchists.* Chicago: F. J. Schulte, 1889.

Schaefer, Carol. *Mary Queen of Scots.* New York: Crossroads/Herder & Herder, 2002.

Seth, Ronald. *Witches and Their Craft.* New York: Taplinger, 1967.

Shea, John "Red." *Rat Bastards: The Life and Times of South Boston's Most Honorable Irish Mobster.* New York: William Morrow, 2006.

Scheck, Barry, Neufeld, Peter, and Dwyer, Jim. *Actual Innocence: Five Days to Execution, and Other Dispatches from the Wrongly Convicted.* New York: Doubleday, 2000.

_____. *Actual Innocence: When Justice Goes Wrong and How to Make It Right.* New York: NAL, 2003.

Schecter, A. *The Dreyfus Affair.* Boston: Houghton Mifflin, 1965.

Schlesinger, Louis B. *Sexual Murder: Catathymic and Compulsive Homicides.* Boca Raton, Fla.: CRC, 2003.

Schwartz-Noble, Loretta. *Engaged to Murder: The Inside Story of the Mainline Murders.* New York: Viking, 1987.

Schwickerath, Robert. *Attitude of the Jesuits in the Trials for Witchcraft.* Philadelphia: N.p., 1902.

Scott, Jonathan. *Algernon Sidney and the Restoration Crisis, 1677–1683.* New York: Cambridge University Press, 1991.

Scott, Reginald. *The Discoverie of Witchcraft.* Reprint. Mineola, N.Y.: Dover, 1989.

Scott, Sir Walter. *Letters on Demonology and Witchcraft.* New York: J. & J. Harper, 1830.

Seagle, William. *Acquitted of Murder.* Chicago: Henry Regnery, 1958.

Searles, Patricia, and Berger, Ronald J. *Rape and Society: Readings on the Problem of Sexual Assault.* Boulder, Colo.: Westview, 1995.

Sellers, Alvin V. *Classics of the Bar: Stories of the World's Greatest Legal Trials and Forensic Masterpieces.* Washington, D.C.: Washington Law Books, 1942.

Seltzer, Louis Benson. *The Years Were Good.* New York: World, 1956.

Sermoise, Pierre de. *Joan of Arc and Her Secret Missions.* London: R. Hale, 1973.

Seth, Ronald. *Witches and Their Craft.* New York: Taplinger, 1967.

Seymour, St. John Drelincourt. *Irish Witchcraft and Demonology.* Baltimore: Norman, Remington, 1682.

Sharpe, Charles Kirkpatrick. *Witchcraft in Scotland.* New York: Barnes & Noble, 1972.

Sharpe, James. *The Bewitching of Anne Gunter: A Horrible and True Story of Deception, Witchcraft, Murder, and the King of England.* New York: Routledge, 2000.

_____. *Instruments of Darkness: Witchcraft in Early Modern England.* Philadelphia: University of Pennsylvania Press, 1997.

Shears, Richard. *Mother on Trial: The Mysterious Death of an Outback Baby.* New York: St. Martin's, 1988.

Sheppard, Sam. *Endure and Conquer.* New York: World, 1966.

Sheppard, Stephen A. *My Brother's Keeper.* New York: McKay, 1964.

Sheridan, Leo W. *I Killed for the Law.* Mechanicsburg, Pa.: Stackpole Sons, 1938.

Shew, E. Spencer. *A Companion to Murder.* New York: Alfred A. Knopf, 1960.

_____. *A Second Companion to Murder.* New York: Knopf, 1961.

Shore, W. Teignmouth, ed. *Crime and Its Detection.* London: Gresham, 1931.

Silverman, Kenneth. *The Life and Times of Cotton Mather.* Norwalk, Conn.: Easton, 1989.

Simpson, Alan. *Puritanism in Old and New England.* Chicago: University of Chicago Press, 1955.

Simpson, Helen, ed. *The Anatomy of Murder.* New York: Macmillan, 1934.

Simpson, Keith. *Forensic Medicine.* London: Arnold, 1964.

_____. *Forty Years of Murder.* New York: Scribner's, 1979.

Sinclair, George. *Satan's Invisible World Discovered.* London: J. Bailey, 1915.

Singer, Charles Joseph, ed. *Studies in the History and Method of Science.* Oxford: Clarendon, 1917–1921.

Sinistrari, Ludovico Maria. *De Daemonialitate et Incubis et Succubis.* Translated by I. Liseaux. Paris: I. Liseaux, 1876.

_____. *Demoniality.* Translated by Montague Summers. London: Fortune, 1927.

Sizer, Nelson. *Forty Years in Phrenology.* London: Fowler & Wells, 1882.

_____. *Heads and Faces and How to Study Them: A Manual of Phrenology and Physiognomy for the People.* London: Fowler & Wells, 1885.

Skolnick, Jerome H., and Fyfe, James. *Above the Law: Police and Excessive Use of Force.* New York: Free Press, 1994.

Smith, E. W. *Baker Street and Beyond: A Sherlockian Gazetteer.* New York: Pamphlet House, 1940.

_____. *The Incunabular Sherlock Holmes.* New York: Morrison, 1957.

_____. *Profile by Gaslight: An Irregular Reader About the Private Life of Sherlock Holmes.* New York: Simon & Schuster, 1944.

Smith, Edward Henry. *Famous American Poison Mysteries.* New York: Dial, 1927.

_____. *Mysteries of the Missing.* New York: Dial, 1927.

_____. *You Can Escape.* New York: Macmillan, 1929.

Smith, Homer W. *Man and His Gods.* Boston: Little, Brown, 1952.

Smith, John Holland. *Joan of Arc.* London: Sidgwick & Jackson, 1973.

Smith, Sydney. *Mostly Murder.* London: Harrap, 1959.

Snell, Otto. *Hexenprozesse und Geistesstörung.* Munich: J. F. Lehmann, 1891.

Snyder, Louis, ed. *The Dreyfus Case: A Documentary History.* New Brunswick, N.J.: Rutgers University Press, 1973.

Snyder, Louis, and Morris, Richard B., eds. *They Saw It Happen.* Mechanicsburg, Pa.: Stackpole, 1951.

_____. *A Treasury of Great Reporting.* New York: Simon & Schuster, 1949.

Soldan, Wilhelm Gottlieb. *Geschichte der Hexenprozesse aus der Quellen dargestelt.* Munich: G. Muller, 1912.

Sommerville, Diane Miller. *Rape and Race in the Nineteenth-Century South.* Chapel Hill: University of North Carolina Press, 2004.

Sorensen, Lita. *The Scottsboro Boys.* New York: Rosen, 2003.

Southwell, Robert, et al. *Diaries of the Popish Plot, 1678–1685: Being the Diaries of Israel Tonge, Sir Robert Southwell, James Joyne, Edmund Warcup, and Thomas Dangerfield.* New York: Scholars Facsimiles & Reprint, 1999.

Spurzheim, Johann Christoph. *Phrenology, Or the Doctrines of the Mental Phenomena.* New York: Lippincott, 1908.

_____. *The Physiognomical System of Drs. Gall and Spurzheim: Founded on an Anatomical and Physiological Examination of the Nervous System in General.* London: Baldwin, Cradock & Joy, 1814.

Stanton, Mike. *The Prince of Providence: The Rise and Fall of Buddy Cianci, America's Most Notorious Mayor.* New York: Random House, 2004.

Starkey, Marion L. *The Devil in Massachusetts: A Modern Inquiry into the Salem Witch Trials.* New York: Anchor, 1969.

Stashower, Daniel. *Teller of Tales: The Life of Arthur Conan Doyle.* New York: Henry Holt, 2000.

Stavert, Geoffrey. *A Study in Southsea: The Unrevealed Life of Dr. Arthur Conan Doyle, The Creator of Sherlock Holmes.* Ripon, Calif.: Milestone, 1987.

Stearne, John. *A Confirmation and Discovery of Witchcraft.* London: W. Wilson, 1648.

Stephens, Edward. *A Collection of Modern Relations of Matter and Fact Concerning Witches and Witchcraft.* London: John Harris, 1693.

Stephens, Walter. *Demon Lovers: Witchcraft, Sex, and the Crisis of Belief.* Chicago: University of Chicago Press, 2003.

Stevens, C. L. McCluer. *From Clue to Dock.* London: Stanley Paul, 1927.

Stevens, George Washington. *The Tragedy of Dreyfus.* New York: Harper, 1899.

Stewart, Alan. *The Cradle King: A Life of James VI and I, The First Monarch of a United Great Britain.* New York: St. Martin's, 2003.

Stone, Irving. *Clarence Darrow for the Defense.* Garden City, N.Y.: Doubleday, 1941.

Stowers, Carlton. *Careless Whispers.* New York: St. Martin's, 2001.

Strickland, Alice. *Life of Mary Queen of Scots.* London: George Bell, 1907.

Sullivan, George. *Not Guilty.* New York: Scholastic, 1997.

Sullivan, Karen. *The Interrogation of Joan of Arc.* Minneapolis: University of Minnesota Press, 1999.

Summers, Montague. *An Examen of Witches.* London: J. Rodker, 1929.

_____. *The Geography of Witchcraft.* London: Routledge & Kegan Paul, 1927.

_____. *The History of Witchcraft and Demonology.* New Hyde Park, N.Y.: University Books, 1956.

_____. *The Malleus Maleficarum of Kramer and Sprenger.* Reprint. Mineola, N.Y.: Dover, 1971.

_____. *Popular History of Witchcraft.* New York: Dutton, 1937.

_____. *The Vampire in Europe.* New York: Dutton, 1929.

_____. *The Vampire: His Kith and Kin.* New York: Dutton, 1929.

_____. *The Werewolf.* New York: Dutton, 1934.

_____. *Witchcraft and Black Magic.* New York: Rider, 1934.

Surette, Ray. *Media, Crime, and Criminal Justice: Images, Realities, and Policies.* Belmont, Calif.: Wadsworth, 2006.

Sutherland, Sidney. *Ten Real Murder Mysteries.* New York: Putnam's, 1929.

Swain, John. *A History of Torture.* New York: Award, 1969.

Swisher, Carl Brent, ed. *Selected Papers of Homer Cummings.* New York: Scribner's, 1939.

Symons, Julian. *Conan Doyle: Portrait of an Artist.* New York: Warner, 1987.

Tallant, Robert. *Murder in New Orleans.* London: William Kimber, 1952.

_____. *Ready to Hang.* New York: Harper & Brothers, 1952.

Tanon, Celestin Louis. *Histoire des tribunaux de l'Inquisition en France.* Paris: L. Larose & Forcel, 1893.

Taylor, John Metcalfe. *The Witchcraft Delusion in Colonial Connecticut 1647–97.* New York: Grafton, 1908.

Tengler, Ulric. *Layenspiegel.* Strasbourg: H. Knoblouch den Jungen, 1530.

_____. *Der neu Layenspiegel.* Colophon, France: Gednuckt du Strass-burg, durch Johannem Knoblouch, 1527.

Terry, Karen. *Sexual Offenses and Offenders: Theory, Practice, and Policy.* Belmont, Calif.: Wadsworth, 2005.

Thomas, Marcel. *L'Affaire sans Dreyfus.* Paris: Fayard, 1961.

Thompson, C. J. S. *Poison Mysteries in History.* Philadelphia: Lippincott, 1932.

_____. *Poison Mysteries Unsolved.* London: Hutchinson, 1937.

_____. *Poisons and Poisoners.* London: Harold Shaylor, 1931.

Thomson, Sir Basil. *The Criminal.* London: Hodder & Stoughton, 1925.

_____. *Queer People.* London: Hodder & Stoughton, 1922.

_____. *The Scene Changes.* London: Collins, 1938.

_____. *The Story of Scotland Yard.* London: Grayson & Grayson, 1925.

Thornhill, Randy, and Palmer, Craig T. *A Natural History of Rape: Biological Bases of Sexual Coercion.* Cambridge, Mass.: MIT Press, 2001.

Thorwald, Jürgen. *The Century of the Detective.* New York: Harcourt, Brace & World, 1964.

_____. *Crime and Science: The New Frontier in Criminology.* Orlando, Fla.: Harcourt, Brace & World, 1967.

_____. *Dead Men Tell Tales.* London: Thames & Hudson, 1966.

_____. *The Marks of Cain.* London: Thames & Hudson, 1965.

_____. *Proof of Poison.* London: Thames & Hudson, 1966.

Tibballs, Geoff. *Legal Blunders.* London: Constable & Robinson, 2000.

Tidyman, Ernest. *Dummy.* Boston: Little, Brown, 1974.

Tierney, Kevin. *Darrow: A Biography.* New York: Crowell, 1979.

Timewell, James. *Is Stinie Morrison Innocent?* London: Published by author, 1914.

_____. *The Prison Life of Stinie Morrison.* London: Published by author, 1914.

Tindall, George B. *The Emergence of the New South, 1913–1945.* Baton Rouge: Louisiana State University Press, 1967.

_____. *South Carolina Negroes, 1877–1900.* Columbia: University of South Carolina Press, 1952.

Toledano, Ralph de. *J. Edgar Hoover: The Man in His Time.* New Rochelle, N.Y.: Arlington House, 1973.

Tomilson, Stephen. *Headmasters: Phrenology, Secular Education, and Nineteenth-Century Social Thought.* Tuscaloosa: University of Alabama Press, 2005.

Topp, Michael M. *The Sacco and Vanzetti Case: A Brief History with Documents.* New York: Bedford/St. Martin's, 2004.

Toughill, T. *Oscar Slater: The Mystery Solved.* Edinburgh: Canongate, 1993.

Touhy, Roger. *The Stolen Years.* Cleveland, Ohio: Pennington, 1959.

Trask, Willard R. *Joan of Arc: Self Portrait.* Mechanicsburg, Pa.: Stackpole, 1936.

Trent, Bill. *Who Killed Lynne Harper?* Maxville, Ontario: Optimum, 1979.

Trestrail, John Harris III. *Criminal Poisoning: Investigational Guide for Law Enforcement, Toxicologists, Forensic Scientists, and Attorneys.* Totowa, N.J.: Humana, 2000.

Trevelyan, G. M. *England Under the Stuarts.* New York: Routledge, 2002.

*Trial, Confession, and Execution of Isobel Insh, John Stewart, Margaret Barclay, and Isobel Crawford for Witchcraft.* Ardrossan, Scotland: Herald Office, 1855.

Truscott, Steven, with Trent, Bill. *The Steven Truscott Story.* New York: Simon & Schuster, 1971.

Turberville, Arthur Stanley. *Medieval Heresy and the Inquisition.* London: George Allen & Unwin, 1920.

Tuchman, Barbara W. *The Proud Tower.* New York: Macmillan, 1966.

Turner, R. F. *Forensic Science and Laboratory Techniques.* Springfield, Ill.: Charles C. Thomas, 1949.

Tuttle, William M., Jr. *Race Riot: Chicago in the Red Summer of 1919.* New York: Atheneum, 1970.

Twain, Mark [Samuel Clemens]. *Joan of Arc.* Reprint. Fort Collins, Colo.: Ignatius, 1989.

Upham, Charles W. *Salem Witchcraft and Cotton Mather: A Reply.* Reprint. Ann Arbor: University of Michigan Library, 2005.

Uschan, Michael. *The Scottsboro Case.* New York: World Almanac Library, 2004.

Uttal, William R. *The New Phrenology: The Limits of Localizing Cognitive Processes in the Brain.* Cambridge, Mass.: MIT Press, 2003.

Vacandard, Abbe Elphege. *L'Inquisition: A Critical and Historical Study of the Coercive Power of the Church.* Translated by Bertrand L. Conway. New York: Longmans, Green, 1926.

Van Dam, Carla. *Identifying Child Molesters: Preventing Child Sexual Abuse by Recognizing the Patterns of the Offenders.* Binghamton, N.Y.: Haworth, 2001.

———. *The Socially Skilled Child Molester: Differentiating the Guilty from the Falsely Accused.* Binghamton, N.Y.: Haworth, 2006.

Van Deusen, Glyndon G. *William Henry Seward.* New York: Oxford University Press, 1967.

Van Passen, Pierre. *Days of Our Years.* New York: Dial, 1940.

———. *To Number Our Days.* New York: Scribner's, 1964.

Van Winkle, Marshall. *Sixty Famous Cases.* 10 vols. New York: Ayers, 1956.

Van Wyhe, John. *Phrenology and the Origins of Victorian Scientific Naturalism.* Burlington, Vt.: Ashgate, 2004.

Vice Commission of Chicago. *The Social Evil in Chicago: A Study of Existing Conditions.* Chicago: American Vigilance Association, 1911.

Vidal, Jean Marie. *Bullaire de l'Inquisition française.* Paris: Librarie Letouzey et Ane, 1913.

Vigarello, Georges. *A History of Rape: Sexual Violence in France from the 16th to the 20th Century.* Cambridge, U.K.: Polity Press, 2000.

Villiers, Alan. *Posted Missing.* New York: Scribner's, 1956.

Villiers, Elizabeth. *Riddles of Crime.* London: Werner Laurie, 1928.

Vollen, Lola, and Eggers, Dave. *Surviving Justice: America's Wrongly Convicted and Exonerated.* San Francisco: McSweeney's Books, 2005.

Wagenknecht, Edward C., ed. *Joan of Arc: An Anthology of History and Literature.* New York: Creative Age, 1948.

Wagstaffe, John. *The Question of Witchcraft Debated.* London: Edward Millington, 1671.

Waite, Gary K. *Heresy, Magic, and Witchcraft in Early Modern Europe.* New York: Palgrave Macmillan, 2003.

Walker, Marcia J., and Brodsky, Stanley L., eds. *Sexual Assault: The Victim and the Rapist.* Lexington, Mass.: Heath, 1976.

Wall, W. J. *The DNA Detectives.* London: Robert Hale, 2005.

Wallace, Susan Helen. *Saint Joan of Arc: God's Soldier.* Boston: Pauline Books and Media, 2000.

Walls, H. J. *Forensic Science.* New York: Praeger, 1968.

———. *Scotland Yard Scientists: My Thirty Years in Forensic Science.* New York: Taplinger, 1973.

Walsh, William Thomas. *Characters of the Inquisition.* Rockford, Ill.: TAN, 1987.

Wambaugh, Joseph. *Echoes of Darkness.* New York: William Morrow, 1987.

Ward, Geoffrey C. *Unforgivable Blackness: The Rise and Fall of Jack Johnson.* New York: Vintage, 2006.

Ward, John. *The Animals Are Innocent: The Search for Julie's Killers.* North Pomfret, Vt.: Trafalgar Square, 1993.

Ward, Tony, et al. *Theories of Sexual Offending.* New York: Wiley, 2005.

Warner, Marina. *Joan of Arc: The Image of Female Heroism.* Berkeley: University of California Press, 1999.

Washburn, Emory. *Sketches of the Judicial History of Massachusetts.* Boston: Little, Brown, 1840.

Watson, James D. *DNA.* New York: Arrow, 2004.

Watson, Thomas E. *The Celebrated Case of the State of Georgia vs. Leo Frank: The Official Record in the Case of Leo Frank, A Jew Pervert*. Atlanta, Ga.: Jeffersonian, 1915. This hateful work by the anti-Semitic Watson, with its repulsive title, unintentionally exposes the deep racial hatred that brought about the railroading and lynching of the innocent Frank, a framing that was orchestrated by Watson, the leading political power of populist Georgia at the time. The "pervert," as this work blatantly reveals in Watson's grotesque and vicious text, was Watson himself.

Watters, Pat, and Gillers, Stephen. *Investigating the FBI*. New York: Doubleday, 1973.

Weber, Harold. *Paper Bullets: Print and Kingship Under Charles II*. Lexington: University Press of Kentucky, 1996.

Webster, David. *A Collection of Rare and Curious Tracts on Witchcraft and the Second Sight*. Edinburgh: D. Webster, 1820.

Webster, John. *The Displaying of Supposed Witchcraft*. London: J. M., 1677.

Weeden, William B. *Economic and Social History of New England*. New York: Hilary House, 1963.

Weeks, Kevin, and Karas, Phyllis. *Brutal: The Untold Story of My Life Inside Whitey Bulger's Irish Mob*. New York: Harper, 2007.

Weeks, Robert P., ed. *Commonwealth vs. Sacco and Vanzetti*. Englewood Cliffs, N.J.: Prentice-Hall, 1958.

Weinberg, Arthur, ed. *Attorney for the Damned*. New York: Simon & Schuster, 1957.

Weinberg, Arthur, and Weinberg, Lila. *Clarence Darrow*. New York: Putnam's, 1980.

———. *Verdicts Out of Court*. Chicago: Quadrangle, 1963.

Weiner, Irving B., and Hess, Allen K. *The Handbook of Forensic Psychology*. New York: Wiley, 2005.

Weir, Alison. *The Life of Elizabeth I*. New York: Ballantine, 1999.

———. *Mary, Queen of Scots and the Murder of Lord Darnely*. New York: Ballantine, 2003.

Weis, Frederick Lewis. *The Colonial Clergy and the Colonial Churches of New England*. Lancaster, Mass.: Publications of the Society of the Descendants of the Colonial Clergy, 1936.

Weiser, Brian. *Charles II and the Politics of Access*. Rochester, N.Y.: Boydell & Brewer, 2003.

Wells, Charlotte Fowler. *Some Account of the Life and Labors of Dr. Franz Joseph Gall, Founder of Phrenology*. London: Fowler & Wells, 1896.

Wendell, Barrett. *Cotton Mather: A Biography*. Northvale, N.J.: Marlboro, 1993.

Westervelt, Saundra D., and Humphrey, John A., eds. *Wrongly Convicted: Perspectives on Failed Justice*. New Brunswick, N.J.: Rutgers University Press, 2001.

Weyer, Johan. *De Lamiis*. Basel: Oporiana, 1564.

———. *De Praestigiis Daemonum*. Basel: I. Oporinum, 1564.

———. *Histoires*. Translated by Simon Goulart. Paris: A. Delahaye & Lecrosnier, 1885.

Wheeler, Bonnie, and Wood, Charles T., eds. *Fresh Verdicts on Joan of Arc*. New York: Garland, 1999.

Whitechapel, Simon. *Flesh Inferno: Atrocities of Torquemada and the Spanish Inquisition*. New York: Creation, 2003.

Whitehead, Don. *The F.B.I. Story*. New York: Random House, 1956.

Whitelaw, David. *Corpus Delicti*. London: Geoffrey Bles, 1936.

Whitlock, Brand. *Forty Years of It*. New York: D. Appleton, 1914.

Whittington-Egan, R. *The Oscar Slater Murder Story: New Light on a Classic Miscarriage of Justice*. Glasgow: Neil Wilson, 2001.

Wice, Paul B. *Rubin "Hurricane" Carter and the American Justice System*. New Brunswick, N.J.: Rutgers University Press, 2000.

Wickwar, John William. *Witchcraft and the Black Art*. New York: R. M. McBride, 1926.

Wiesner-Hanks, Merry E. *Witchcraft in Early Modern Europe*. Boston: Houghton Mifflin, 2006.

Willard, Samuel. *Some Miscellany Observations on Our Present Debates Respecting Witchcraft*. Philadelphia: William Bradford, 1692.

Williams, Charles. *Witchcraft*. London: Faber & Faber, 1941.

Williams, Howard. *Superstitions of Witchcraft*. London: Longman, Green, Longman, Roberts, Green, 1865.

Williams, Selma R. *Riding the Nightmare: Women and Witchcraft from the Old World to Colonial Salem*. Reprint. New York: Perennial, 1992.

Williamson, Hugh Ross. *Historical Whodunits*. New York: Macmillan, 1956.

Williamson, W. H. *Annals of Crime: Some Extraordinary Women*. London: George Routledge, 1930.

Willis, Deborah. *Malevolent Nurture: Witch-Hunting and Maternal Power in Earl Modern England*. Ithaca, N.Y.: Cornell University Press, 1995.

Willison, George Finlay. *Saints and Sinners*. New York: Reynal & Hitchcock, 1945.

Wilmot-Buxton, E. M. *The Story of Joan of Arc*. Mineola, N.Y.: Dover, 2004.

Wilson, Colin. *Witches*. New York: Crescent, 1981.

Wilson, Nelly. *Bernard-Lazare*. New York: Cambridge University Press, 1998.

Wilson, Stephen, et al., eds. *Ideology and Experience: Antisemitism in France at the Time of the Dreyfus Affair*. Cranbury, N.J.: Fairleigh Dickinson University Press, 1982.

Wilton, G. W. *Fingerprints: History, Law, and Romance*. London: William Hodge, 1938.

Windsor, William. *Phrenology: The Science of Character*. New York: Ferris-Windsor, 1921.

Winthrop, John. *The History of New England*. Boston: Little, Brown, 1853.

Wise, Stephen Samuel. *The Case of Leo Frank: A Last Appeal*. New York: Bloch, 1915.

*Witchcraft in Old and New England*. Cambridge, Mass.: Harvard University Press, 1929.

Wolfe, Burton H. *Pileup on Death Row*. Garden City, N.Y.: Doubleday, 1973.

*The Wonderful Discovery of the Witchcrafts of Margaret and Philip Flower*. London: G. Eld, I. Barnes, 1619.

Wood, John Maxwell. *Witchcraft and Superstitious Record in the Southwestern District of Scotland*. Dumfries: J. Maxwell, 1911.

Woodward, C. Vann. *Tom Watson: Agrarian Rebel*. New York: Macmillan, 1938.

Woodward, Ian. *The Werewolf Delusion*. New York: Paddington, 1979.

Woodward, W. Elliot. *Records of the Salem Witchcraft*. Roxbury, Mass.: Published by author, 1864.

Work, Clemens P. *Darkest Before Dawn: Sedition and Free Speech in the American West*. Albuquerque: University of New Mexico Press, 2005.

Wormald, Jenny. *Mary, Queen of Scots: Pride, Passion, and a Kingdom Lost*. London: I. B. Tauris, 2001.

Wyatt-Brown, Bertram. *Honor and Violence in the Old South*. New York: Oxford University Press, 1986.

Wyndham, Horace. *Consider Your Verdict*. London: W. H. Allen, 1946.

_____. *Crime on the Continent*. Boston: Little, Brown, 1928.

_____. *Dramas of the Law*. London: Hutchinson, 1936.

_____. *Famous Trials Re-told*. London: Hutchinson, 1925.

_____. *Feminine Frailty*. London: Ernest Benn, 1929.

Wyndham-Brown, W. F. *The Trial of Herbert Wallace*. London: Gollancz, 1933.

Yant, Martin. *Presumed Guilty: When Innocent People Are Wrongly Convicted*. Amherst, N.Y.: Prometheus, 1991.

Young, William. *Postmortem: New Evidence in the Case of Sacco and Vanzetti*. Amherst: University of Massachusetts Press, 1985.

Zelt, Johannes. *Proletarischer Interationalismus im Kamp um Sacco und Vanzetti*. East Berlin: Dietz Verlag, 1958.

Zilboorg, Gregory. *The Medical Man and the Witch During the Renaissance*. Baltimore: John Hopkins University Press, 1935.

Zola, Emile. *The Dreyfus Affair: J'Accuse and Other Writings*. New Haven, Conn.: Yale University Press, 1996.

Zonderman, Jon. *Beyond the Crime Lab: The New Science of Investigation*. New York: Wiley, 1999.

# Index

**Note**:  This is an annotated ready-reference index designed to aid general readers and researchers in law enforcement, criminal justice and related fields, who are seeking particular information on specific cases. The names of all wrongly convicted persons appear in boldface in A–Z entries, as well as entries for some wrongly accused but not convicted persons. (Any wrongful convictions indicated by boldface listings do not necessarily indicate actual innocence.) Following these boldfaced name entries, the country or city/state where the crime occurred, along with the year of conviction, and financial compensation given for some wrongful convictions appear in parenthesis. Locations and dates of homicides (or dates of fatal attacks that later resulted in death) for murder victims, as well as victims of other violent crimes, are also shown in parenthesis following those name entries. Locations for forensic experts, defense attorneys and officers of the court (judges, police officers, prosecutors) and other government officials appear in parenthesis following those name entries. All wrongful cases also appear under locations (country/state and or province/city or town) in alphabetical name order under those specific locations and additionally appear in alphabetical order by wrongful genre (coercion, false confessions, etc.) as further reference in defining collective and separate jurisdictions and the types of illegal or unreliable methods employed in achieving wrongful arrests and convictions. Some of the latter entries have multiple applications.

Gedney, Judge Major Bartholomew (Salem, Massachusetts witchcraft trials), 356

**Gell, Alan** (Aulander, North Carolina; 1995), 563

Genego, William (defense attorney), 541

General Registry Building (La Plata, Buenos Aires, Argentina), 165

Genetic Designs, Inc. (Greensboro, North Carolina), 283

GeneScreen (Dallas, Texas), 557

Genius for the Defense (book, Bennett), 92

Geoghan, William F. X. (Brooklyn, New York district attorney), 493

George V (England), 405–406

Georgeff, John (murder victim; Columbus, Ohio; June 12, 1973), 51

Georgia Bureau of Investigation, 212

Georgia Innocence Project (Atlanta, Georgia), 211, 212

Georgia Board of Pardons and Paroles, 329, 513

Georgia Prison Commission, 378

Georgia State University College of Law (Atlanta, Georgia), 212

Georgia Supreme Court, 39, 55, 518, 560–561

Geraghty, Thomas (director of Bluhm Legal Clinic, Northwestern University), 469

Gerardi, Bishop Juan Jose (murder victim; Guatemala City, Guatemala; April 26, 1998), 173, 348–349

Gerardi, Michael (murder victim; New Orleans, Louisiana; May 2, 1995), 447–448

Gerber, Dr. Samuel, 431, 432, 433, 434

Gerdes, Henry J., 119

**Gergel, William** (Jackson Heights/Queens, New York; 1987; not convicted), 147

German, Ernestine (murder victim; Fort Lauderdale, Florida; 1979), 516

Germond, Kate (Centurion Ministries), 512, 542

Gershon, Sim (Florida defense attorney), 579

Gertner, Judge Nancy (federal justice), 452

Gestapo, 85

**Geter, Lennell** (Balch Springs, Texas; 1982), 347

Geter Justice for All Foundation, 347

Giarratano, Joseph, 269

Gibbons, Barbara (murder victim; Canaan, Connecticut; September 28, 1973), 257–259

Gibbons, Bill, 123

Gibson, Sherry Lee (murder victim; Vincennes, Indiana; March 1, 1975), 256

Gifford, Gilbert, 301

**Giddens, Charles Ray** (Oklahoma; 1978), 515

**Gideon, Clarence Earl** (Bay Harbor, Florida; 1961), 502

Gideon's Trumpet (1980 made-for-TV film), 502

Gierke, Raymond (murder victim; Bear Rocks, Pennsylvania; 1977), 546

Giese, Petra (murder victim; Bruckhausen, Germany; April 23, 1962), 502–503

Gilbert, C. A., 142–143

Gilbert, Police Captain Daniel A. "Tubbo" (Chicago, Illinois), 408

Gilbert, Rev. W. A., 18

**Giles, James** (Towson, Maryland; 1961), 39–40

**Giles, James Curtis** (Dallas, Texas; 1983), 453–454

Giles, James Earl "Quack," 454

**Giles, John** (Towson, Maryland; 1961), 39–40

Giles Food Market (Baltimore, Maryland), 504

Gilley, Orville, 334

Gillis, Judge Joseph A. (Detroit, Michigan), 20

Gilmore, Governor James S. III (Virginia), 270

Gilmour, Addie, 66–67

Gilson, Matthew, 481

Ginsberg, Justice Ruth Bader (U.S. Supreme Court), 442

Giofreddi, John (Florida defense attorney), 555

**Girdler, Raymond** (Yavapai County, Arizona; 1982), 526

Gittleson, Judge Harry (Brooklyn, New York), 40

**Gladden, David** (Harrisburg, Pennsylvania; 1995), 563

**Gladish, Thomas** (Alburquerque, New Mexico; 1974), 507–508

Gladstone Commission of the Home Office (London, England), 312

Glaister, John, 10

Glancy Motel (Clinton, Oklahoma), 52–53

Glass, Robert (New Orleans, Louisiana defense attorney), 537

Glazier, Mike (North Carolina defense attorney), 525

Gleason, Judge John (Brooklyn, New York), 578

Gleason, Police Officer John V., Jr. (murder victim; Plainfield, New Jersey; July 16, 1967), 46

Glorious Revolution (1688), 304

Goddard, Dr. Calvin R., 151

Goddard, Richard, 479

Godfrey, Deputy Sheriff A. M. (Modoc, West Virginia), 166

Godfrey, Sir Edmund Berry (murder victim; London, England; October 17, 1678), 302–303

Godfrey, Mark, 117

Powers, Judson L. (assault victim; Washington, D.C.; September 20, 1922), 141

Prance, Miles, 302–303

**Pratt, Elmer "Geronimo"** (Los Angeles, California; 1972), 505–506

Pray, John (co-founder, Wisconsin Innocence Project), 279–280, 575

Prebish, Harry W. (defense attorney), 23

Preparedness Day Parade (San Francisco, California; July 22, 1916), 373, 374, 376

Presley, Elvis, 60

**Preston, James W**. (Los Angeles, California; 1924), 167

Preston, Sherman (serial rapist-killer), 525

Price, Victoria, 332–335

Prichard, Jeremy, 579

**Prince, Christopher** (Culpepper, Virginia; 1994), 109–110

Prince, Mary, 110

Princeton Theological Seminary (Princeton, New Jersey), 172

**Priscillian** (or Priscillia; Avila, Spain; 385 A.D.), 473

Pritchard, Gary O. (Chicago, Illinois defense attorney), 278

Pritico, John, 342

Proctor, Judge Benjamin (Eau Claire County, Wisconsin), 575

**Proctor, Elizabeth** (Salem, Massachusetts; 1692), 366, 367

**Proctor, Eric** (Springfield, Oregon; 1986; awarded $1 million compensation), 543

**Proctor, John** (Salem, Massachusetts; hanged August 19, 1692), 362, 363, 364, 367

Proctor, Mayme, 494

Professor Moriarty, 8

Protess, Professor David (Northwestern University), 41, 385, 435

**Proulx, Benoit** (Quebec, Canada; 1991; awarded $1.6 million compensation in 1997,

overturned; awarded $2.2 million compensation in 2001 without challenge), 435–436

**Provoo, John David** (Manhattan, New York; 1953), 501

Pruvot, Raymond, 499

Public Broadcasting System, 56

**Pudeator, Ann** (Salem, Massachusetts; hanged September 22, 1692), 365, 367

**Pugh, Earl Heywood** (Chicago, Illinois, 1936; awarded $51,000 compensation), 36–37, 89

Pugh, Judge James H., Jr. (Maryland), 39

Pulitzer Prize, 22, 521

Pullen, Judge J. F. (Sacramento, California), 490

Pulling, Maria (forensic scientist), 467

Pullman Company, 141

Purdy, William, 38

Purola, Robert (Ohio defense attorney), 52

**Purvis, John Gordon** (Fort Lauderdale, Florida; 1985), 535–536

Purvis, FBI Agent Melvin, 404

**Purvis, Will** (Marion County, Mississippi; 1893; awarded $5,000 compensation), 131–136

Putnam, Ann, 355, 357, 359, 361, 362, 363, 366–367

Putnam, John, 362

Putnam, Thomas, 361, 362

Pye, Constable Cecil (London, England), 37–38

**Pyle, Harry** (Kansas; 1935), 496

**Qin Yongmin** (Beijing, China; 1998), 571

Quality Finance (Johnston County, North Carolina), 572

Qualtrough, R. M., 71, 72

Queen, Diana, 551

Queens (New York) Legal Aid, 562

Queen's Head Alehouse (Kingston, England), 128

Quemeneur, Pierre, 330–331

Quesada, Rudy, 42

Quezada, Leoncio, 439

**Quick, Wesley** (Birmingham, Alabama; 1997), 389–390

**Quindt, David** (Sacramento, California; 1999; awarded $17,200 compensation), 573–574

Quinn, Michael (murder victim; Braddock, Pennsylvania; January 1, 1890), 415, 416

Quinn, Patrick J. (Chicago, Illinois assistant state's attorney), 338

Quinn, Patrick S., 118

Quinn, William (convicted killer), 145

Quintieri, Julia Musso (murder victim; Bronx, New York; September 15, 1929), 492

**Qvist, Soren** (Veilby, Denmark; 1880; executed), 399–400

Raab, Selwyn, 103

Rabil, Mark (North Carolina defense attorney), 214

Rabstein, Ruth (New Jersey defense attorney), 499

Race, Michael S. (New York private detective), 548–549, 558

Rackaukas, Tony (Orange, California deputy district attorney), 525–526

Rader, Judge Clifford (Ohio), 51

Ragen Colts (Chicago, Illinois gang), 343

Rahn, Gordon, 551

Raiford State Penitentiary (later Raiford or Union Correctional Facility; Florida), 340, 380, 578

Rainey, Judge (Georgia), 378

Rainey, David, 552–553

**Rainge, Willie** (Ford Heights, Illinois; 1979; awarded $36 million compensation along with three other defendants), 383–385

Raley, Jane (Illinois defense attorney), 84, 287

Ramadanovic, Michael, 82